Fodor's  South America

"When it comes to information on regional history, what to see and do, and shopping, these guides are exhaustive."

—*USAir Magazine*

"Usable, sophisticated restaurant coverage, with an emphasis on good value."

—Andy Birsh, *Gourmet Magazine* columnist

"Valuable because of their comprehensiveness."

—*Minneapolis Star-Tribune*

"Fodor's always delivers high quality...thoughtfully presented...thorough."

—*Houston Post*

"An excellent choice for those who want everything under one cover."

—*Washington Post*

Fodor's Travel Publications, Inc.
New York • Toronto • London • Sydney • Auckland

Fodor's South America

Editor: Chelsea S. Mauldin

Production Editor: Laura M. Kidder

Editorial Contributors: Rob Andrews, Tony Bianchi, Bob Blake, Lyndell Brookhouse-Gil, Matthew Doman, Philip Eade, Peter Hudson, Carla Hunt, Richard Jarvie, Krishna Kandeth, Nicolás Lynch, Sarah Lythe, Richard Neill, Jane Onstott, Parker Pascua, Chris Philipsborn, Tom Quinn, Lake Sagaris, Corinne Schmidt-Lynch, Mary Ellen Schultz, M. T. Schwartzman (Gold Guide editor), Ed Shaw, George Soules, Dinah Spritzer, Rik Turner, Phillip Withers Green.

Creative Director: Fabrizio La Rocca

Cartographer: David Lindroth

Cover Photograph: Gunter Ziesler/Peter Arnold

Text Design: Between the Covers

Copyright © 1995 by Fodor's Travel Publications, Inc.

Special Sales

Fodor's Travel Publications are available at special discounts for bulk purchases for sales promotions or premiums. Special editions, including personalized covers, excerpts of existing guides, and corporate imprints, can be created in large quantities for special needs. For more information, contact your local bookseller or write to Special Markets, Fodor's Travel Publications, 201 East 50th Street, New York, NY 10022. Inquiries from Canada should be directed to your local Canadian bookseller or sent to Random House of Canada, Ltd., Marketing Department, 1265 Aerowood Drive, Mississauga, Ontario L4W 1B9. Inquiries from the United Kingdom should be sent to Fodor's Travel Publications, 20 Vauxhall Bridge Road, London SW1V 2SA.

MANUFACTURED IN THE UNITED STATES OF AMERICA

10 9 8 7 6 5 4 3 2

CONTENTS

Contents

Maps

ON THE ROAD WITH FODOR'S

A GOOD TRAVEL GUIDE is like a wonderful traveling companion. It's charming, it's brimming with sound recommendations and solid ideas, it pulls no punches in describing lodging and dining establishments, and it's consistently full of fascinating facts that make you view what you've traveled to see in a rich new light. In the creation of *Fodor's South America*, we at Fodor's have gone to great lengths to provide you with the very best of all possible traveling companions—and to make your trip the best of all possible vacations.

About Our Writers

The information in these pages is due to the collaboration of a number of extraordinarily talented and well-traveled writers, including the following:

Tony Bianchi has worked in Europe and across the Americas as a correspondent for the Associated Press, Reuters, and the *London Times*. Since 1988 he has been the editor-in-chief of Venezuela's English-language newspaper, the *Daily Journal,* as well as a frequent contributor to several European and American publications. In 1990, Mr. Bianchi was the recipient of the Order of Andres Bello, Venezuela's highest artistic and literary award for services to journalism.

Lyndell Brookhouse-Gil's first trip to Uruguay was in the pursuit of her ethnomusicological interests—and to meet her in-laws. She holds a degree in ethnomusicology from the City University of New York and does freelance writing and design.

Richard Jarvie has lived and worked in South America for more than 15 years, and as a correspondent for the world's major international news agencies, he has witnessed far-reaching changes in the politics and economies of the region. His extensive travels through Argentina, Brazil, Paraguay, and Uruguay have left him with a profound respect for their people, customs, and culture.

Jane Onstott was primed for adventure travel in her late teens, when she wandered Honduras for six months after being stood up at the airport by an inattentive suitor. A stoic if inefficient traveler, she has since survived a near plunge into a gorge in the highlands of Mexico, knife-wielding robbers in Madrid, and a financial shipwreck on one of the more remote Galápagos islands. The last, happily, led to a position as Director of Communications and Information at the Darwin Research Station on Santa Cruz Island. Today, when she's not traversing mystical Guatemalan mountains or covering Ecuador and Mexico for various travel publications, Ms. Onstott makes her home in California.

We'd also like to thank John Benus at the Venezuelan Tourism Association; Joaquin Pradas at the Bolivian Tourist Information Office; and SAETA Airlines.

What's New

A New Design

If this is not the first Fodor's guide you've purchased, you'll immediately notice our new look. More readable and easier to use than ever? We think so—and we hope you do, too.

Travel Updates

Just before your trip, you may want to order a Fodor's Worldview Travel Update. From local publications all over South America, the lively, cosmopolitan editors at Worldview gather information on concerts, plays, opera, dance performances, gallery and museum shows, sports competitions, and other special events that coincide with your visit. See the order blank at the back of this book, call 800/799–9609, or fax 800/799–9619.

And in South America

As this guide went to press, there were a number of developments of interest to visitors. In **Argentina,** the new Inter-Continental Buenos Aires has opened; the luxury property caters to travelers with a "transit lounge," an area in which guests can shower, store their luggage, and use the hotel's recreational facilities before check-in or after checkout. Reservations are available through Inter-Continental's U.S. toll-free line. The newest tourist attraction in Buenos Aires is the Tren de la Costa. An abandoned railroad track was renovated and now carries trains 20 miles through the quiet suburb of Olivos to Tigre, a colorful port town where barges unload fruit, timber, and other produce from the north. Travelers are encouraged to stop at some of the tastefully redone stations along the 40-minute route, many of which now house restaurants, cafés, and shops. Trains leave every 15 minutes from Buenos Aires's Mitre station, which is reachable from the Retiro station downtown.

Visitors returning to **Brazil** after a few years' absence are certain to notice some of the consequences of the economic stabilization program initiated in 1994. The currency has changed names again—there are now 100 *centavos* in a *real*—and is being held by the government at a rate that makes one real worth slightly more than one U.S. dollar. Prices for North American visitors, therefore, have increased by 50% to 100%, and while pressure from Brazil's exporters is bound to deflate the overvalued real eventually, expect it to be later rather than sooner. Meanwhile, Brazilian authorities have woken up to tourism's potential as a moneymaker. Salvador, in particular, has made serious advances in the restoration of colonial structures downtown. A number of larger cities now have tourist police, but don't expect miracles—you should still refrain from wearing jewelry (especially anything gold) or expensive watches.

Recent years have seen the continued wane of terrorist activity in **Peru,** making the country safer for residents and visitors alike. Economic conditions have moved to the forefront, and although poverty remains a major problem, inflation seems to be coming under control and growth continues. The government's privatization program—which brokered the sale of the national airline, Aeroperú, and the Hotel de Turistas chain—has been receiving increased criticism, and it is possible that the pace will slow. (ENAFER, the national railroad company, and Córpac, the airports manager, are the major tourism-related assets still in state hands.) Competition among a number of start-up private airlines has been working to keep fares down, but the smaller carriers seem to be concentrating on more offbeat locations, many of which are of little interest to tourists.

How to Use This Guide

Organization

Up front is the **Gold Guide,** comprising two sections on gold paper that are full of information about both traveling within South America and traveling in general. Each section lists information in alphabetical order by topic. **Important Contacts A to Z** gives addresses and telephone numbers of organizations and companies that offer destination-related services, detailed information, or useful publications. This is also where you'll find information about how to get to South America from wherever you are. **Smart Travel Tips A to Z,** the Gold Guide's second section, gives specific tips on how to get the most out of traveling, as well as hints for having a (relatively) hassle-free trip to South America.

Chapter 1, **Destination: South America,** contains a historical introduction to the continent, plus several sections to help you enjoy the best South America has to offer: **What's Where** gives you short run-downs on what to expect in each country covered in this guide; **Pleasures & Pastimes** covers all the sights and activities that make South America such a rich and exciting vacation destination; and **Fodor's Choice** has our picks for the very best there is to do and see—from remarkable resorts and delicious dining to best buys and great art. Chapter 2, **Adventure and Learning Vacations,** has descriptions of exciting sports, outdoor, cruise, and cultural or scientific trips to South America, as well a list of the top U.S. companies that arrange South American adventure vacations and tips on how to pick the package that's best for you.

The **country chapters** that follow are arranged alphabetically. Each is broken into city and regional sections that have information on exploring, shopping, sports, dining, lodging, and arts and nightlife. At the back of each chapter is a section called **Essentials,** which gives you all the basics on getting around—from transportation and telephones to customs and currency.

Restaurant Criteria and Price Categories

Restaurants are chosen with a view to giving you the cream of the crop in each location and in each price range. Stars in the margin are used to denote highly recommended establishments. While neat, casual clothing is generally acceptable in all but the most swank South American restaurants, check the introductory remarks that precede big-city dining sections for more specific information on what's standard in a particular area. When an establishment prefers or requires that men wear a jacket or a jacket and tie (and, presumably, that female diners dress with equal formality), we make note at the bottom of the review. Reservations information is included only when necessary—when reservations are required, strongly recommended, or not available. In all restaurant price charts, costs are per person, excluding drinks, tip, and tax.

Hotel Criteria and Price Categories

In hotel price charts, rates are for a standard double room, excluding any sales or room taxes. Stars in the margin are used to denote highly recommended establishments. Unless we note otherwise, hotel rooms have a private bath. Be aware that you may incur charges when you use many hotel services and facilities. We tell you what facilities a hotel has to offer, but we don't always specify whether or not there's a charge, so when planning a vacation that entails a stay of several days, it's wise to ask what's included in the rate.

Addresses

The most common street terms are *calle* (street), *avenida* (avenue), and *bulevar* (boulevard); while the latter two terms are often abbreviated (as Av. and Bul.), calle is either spelled out or, in some countries, dropped entirely so the street is referred to by proper name only. Street numbering does not enjoy the wide popularity in South America that it has achieved elsewhere. In some listings in this guide, establishments have necessarily been identified by the street they're on and their nearest cross street—Calle Bolívar at Av. Valdivia, for example, or in the Spanish form, Calle Bolívar y Av. Valdivia. In extreme cases, where neither address nor cross street are available, you may find the notation "s/n," meaning "no street number."

Credit Cards

The following abbreviations are used: **AE,** American Express; **DC,** Diners Club; **MC,** MasterCard; and **V,** Visa. Discover is not accepted outside the United States.

Please Write to Us

Everyone who has contributed to *Fodor's South America* has worked hard to make the text accurate. All prices and opening times are based on information supplied to us at press time, and the publisher cannot accept responsibility for any errors that may have occurred. The passage of time will bring changes, so it's always a good idea to call ahead and confirm information when it matters—particularly if you're making a detour to visit specific sights or attractions. When making reservations at a hotel or inn, be sure to mention if you have a disability or are traveling with children, if you prefer a private bath or a certain type of bed, or if you have specific dietary needs or any other concerns.

Were the restaurants we recommended as described? Did our hotel picks exceed your expectations? Did you find a museum we recommended a waste of time? We would love your feedback, positive and negative. If you have complaints, we'll look into them and revise our entries when the facts warrant it. If you've happened upon a special place that we haven't included, we'll pass the information along to the writers so they can check it out. So please send us a letter or postcard—you can address it to South America Editor, Fodor's Travel Publications, 201 East 50th Street, New York, New York 10022. We'll look forward to hearing from you. In the meantime, have a wonderful trip!

Karen Cure
Editorial Director

South America

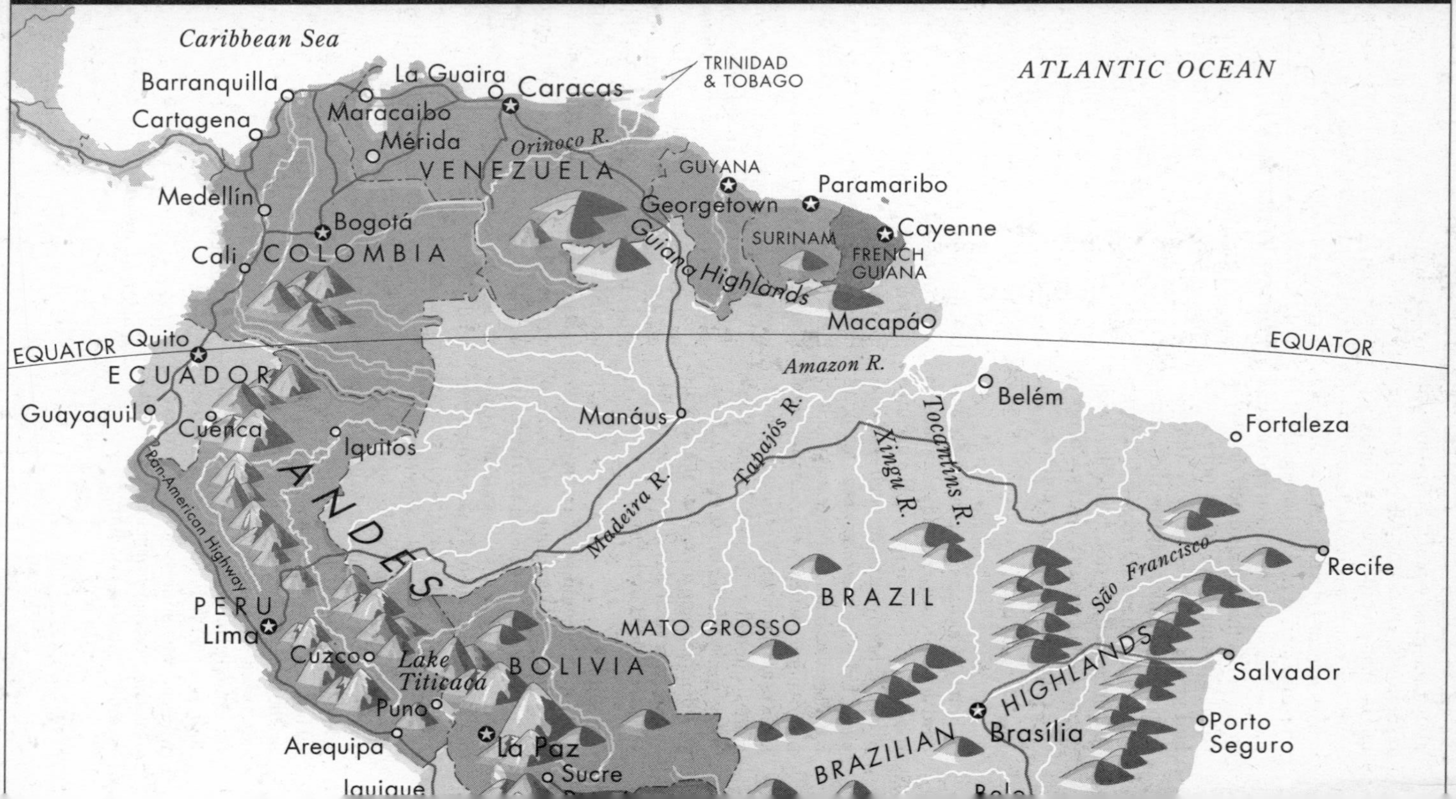

Rio de Janeiro

São Paulo

PARAGUAY

EL CHACO

Asunción

Iguazú Falls

Uruguay R.

Paraná R.

URUGUAY

Punta del Este

Montevideo

Río de la Plata

Rosario

Buenos Aires

Mar del Plata

ARGENTINA

N

1000 miles

1500 km

South Georgia (UK)

Stanley

Falkland Islands (UK)

PATAGONIA

ANDES

CHILE

PACIFIC OCEAN

San Félix (Chile)

Viña del Mar

Valparaíso

Santiago

Islas de Juan Fernandez (Chile)

Tierra del Fuego

Cape Horn

Punta Arenas

World Time Zones

Numbers below vertical bands relate each zone to Greenwich Mean Time (0 hrs.).
Local times frequently differ from these general indications,
as indicated by light-face numbers on map.

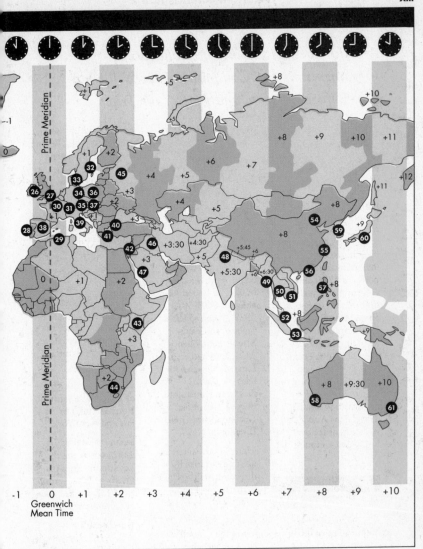

IMPORTANT CONTACTS A TO Z

*An Alphabetical Listing of Publications,
Organizations and Companies That Will Help
You Before, During, and After Your Trip*

No single travel resource can give you every detail about every topic that might interest or concern you at the various stages of your journey—when you're planning your trip, while you're on the road, and after you get back home. The following organizations, books, and brochures will supplement the information in *Fodor's South America*. For related information, including both basic tips on visiting South America and background information on many of the topics below, study Smart Travel Tips A to Z, the section that follows Important Contacts A to Z.

A

AIR TRAVEL

The major gateways to South America include Rio de Janeiro, Buenos Aires, Caracas, and Quito. New York, Miami, and Los Angeles are major gateways for flights to South America from the United States. Flying times from New York are: 9 hours to Rio, 10½ hours to Buenos Aires, 5 hours to Caracas. Flights from Miami are: 7 hours to Rio, 8½ hours to Buenos Aires, 3 hours to Caracas. Flights from Los Angeles are routed through Miami, so add five hours to the Miami

times given above. Flights originating in Houston fly to Bogotá in five hours and to Quito in six hours.

CARRIERS

Major U.S. carriers serving South America include **American Airlines** (☎ 800/433–7300), which flies to all countries covered in this book, and **United Airlines** (☎ 800/538–2929), flying to Rio de Janeiro, São Paulo, Montevideo, Buenos Aires, Santiago, and Lima. **Continental Airlines** (☎ 800/231–0856) flies from Houston to Bogotá, Colombia, and Guayaquil and Quito in Ecuador.

Many South American national airlines fly directly from the United States to their home countries.

Aces (☎ 800/846–2237) serves the Colombian cities of Medellín and Bogotá from Miami.

Aerolineas Argentinas (☎ 800/333–0276) flies to Buenos Aires from Los Angeles, Miami, and New York.

AeroPeru (☎ 800/777–7717) runs between Miami and Lima, Peru.

Avensa (☎ 800/872–3533) flies from Miami to Caracas, Maracaibo, and Porlamar, Venezuela.

Avianca (☎ 800/284–2622), a Colombian

carrier, provides service to Barranquilla, Bogotá, Cali, and Cartagena from Los Angeles, Miami, and New York.

Faucett (☎ 800/334–3356) flies from Miami to the Peruvian cities of Iquitos and Lima.

LAB (☎ 800/327–7407) operates between Miami and La Paz, Bolivia.

Ladeco (☎ 800/825–2332) has service to Santiago, Chile, from New York, Baltimore, and Miami.

LanChile (☎ 800/735–5526) flies to Santiago from Miami, Los Angeles, and New York.

Saeta (☎ 800/827–2382) serves the Ecuadoran cities of Quito and Guayaquil from Miami, Los Angeles, and New York.

Transbrasil (☎ 800/872–3153) has service from Miami and New York to Brasília, Belo Horizonte, São Paulo, Rio, and Salvador.

Varig (☎ 800/468–2744), Brazil's largest international carrier, has service to Rio de Janeiro and São Paulo from Chicago, Los Angeles, Miami, New York, and San Francisco; additionally, Varig serves Manaus, Recife, Fortaleza, and Salvador from Miami.

Vasp (☎ 800/732–8271) flies from Miami,

New York, and Los Angeles to São Paulo and Rio; and from Miami to Recife and Brasília.

Viasa (☎ 800/468–4272) a Venezuelan carrier, operates to Caracas, Maracaibo, and Porlamar from Houston, Miami, and New York.

Zuliana (☎ 800/223–8780) runs from Miami to Caracas, Venezuela.

COMPLAINTS

To register complaints about charter and scheduled airlines, contact the U.S. Department of Transportation's **Office of Consumer Affairs** (400 7th St. NW, Washington, DC 20590, ☎ 202/366–2220 or 800/322–7873).

CONSOLIDATORS

Established consolidators selling to the public include **BET World Travel** (841 Blossom Hill Rd., Suite 212-C, San Jose, CA 95123, ☎ 800/747–1476); **TFI Tours International** (34 W. 32nd St., New York, NY 10001, ☎ 212/736–1140 or 800/745–8000); and **UniTravel** (Box 12485, St. Louis, MO 63132, ☎ 314/569–0900 or 800/325–2222).

PUBLICATIONS

For general information about charter carriers, ask for the Office of Consumer Affairs' brochure **"Plane Talk: Public Charter Flights."** The Department of Transportation also publishes a 58-page booklet, **"Fly Rights"** (Consumer Information Center, Dept. 133-B, Pueblo, CO 81009; $1.75).

For other tips and hints, consult Consumers Union's monthly **"Consumer Reports Travel Letter"** (Box 53629, Boulder CO 80322, ☎ 800/234–1970; $39 a year); the newsletter **"Travel Smart"** (40 Beechdale Rd., Dobbs Ferry, NY 10522, ☎ 800/327–3633; $37 a year); *The Official Frequent Flyer Guidebook,* by Randy Petersen (4715-C Town Center Dr., Colorado Springs, CO 80916, ☎ 719/597–8899 or 800/487–8893; $14.99 plus $3 shipping); *Airfare Secrets Exposed,* by Sharon Tyler and Matthew Wonder (Universal Information Publishing; $16.95 plus $3.75 shipping from Sandcastle Publishing, Box 3070-A, South Pasadena, CA 91031, ☎ 213/255–3616 or 800/655–0053); and *202 Tips Even the Best Business Travelers May Not Know,* by Christopher McGinnis (Irwin Professional Publishing, Box 52927, Atlanta, GA 30355, ☎ 708/789–4000 or 800/634–3966; $10 plus $3 shipping).

B

BETTER BUSINESS BUREAU

For local contacts in the home town of a tour operator you may be considering, consult the **Council of Better Business Bureaus** (4200 Wilson Blvd., Arlington, VA 22203, ☎ 703/276–0100).

C

CAR RENTAL

Major car-rental companies represented in South America include **Alamo** (☎ 800/327–9633, 0800/272–2000 in the United Kingdom); **Avis** (☎ 800/331–1084, 800/879–2847 in Canada); **Budget** (☎ 800/527–0700, 0800/181–181 in the United Kingdom); **Hertz** (☎ 800/654–3001, 800/263–0600 in Canada, 0181/679–1799 in the United Kingdom); and **National** (sometimes known as Europcar InterRent outside North America; ☎ 800/227–3876, 0181/950–5050 in the United Kingdom).

CHILDREN AND TRAVEL

FLYING

Look into **"Flying With Baby"** (Third Street Press, Box 261250, Littleton, CO 80126, ☎ 303/595–5959; $5.95 plus $1 shipping), cowritten by a flight attendant. **"Kids and Teens in Flight,"** free from the U.S. Department of Transportation's Office of Consumer Affairs (400 7th St. NW, Washington, DC 20590, ☎ 202/366–2220 or 800/322–7873), offers tips for children flying alone. Every two years the February issue of *Family Travel Times* (*see* Know-How, *below*) details children's services on three dozen airlines.

KNOW-HOW

Family Travel Times, published 10 times a year by Travel With

Your Children (TWYCH, 45 W. 18th St., New York, NY 10011, ☎ 212/206–0688; annual subscription $55), covers destinations, types of vacations, and modes of travel. The **Family Travel Guides** catalogue (☎ 510/527–5849; $1) lists about 200 books and articles on family travel. **Traveling with Children—And Enjoying It,** by Arlene K. Butler (Globe Pequot Press, Box 833, 6 Business Park Rd., Old Saybrook, CT 06475, ☎ 203/395–0440, 800/243–0495, or 800/962–0973 in CT; $11.95 plus $3 shipping) helps plan your trip with children, from toddlers to teens. Also check **Take Your Baby and Go! A Guide for Traveling with Babies, Toddlers and Young Children,** by Sheri Andrews, Judy Bordeaux, and Vivian Vasquez (Bear Creek Publications, 2507 Minor Ave., Seattle, WA 98102, ☎ 206/322–7604 or 800/326–6566; $5.95 plus $1.50 shipping).

TOUR OPERATORS

If you and the kids are outdoorsy, look into nature and conservation tours offered by the following: **American Wilderness Experience** (Box 1486, Boulder, CO 80306, ☎ 303/444–2622 or 800/444–0099); **American Museum of Natural History** (79th St. and Central Park W, New York, NY 10024, ☎ 212/769–5700 or 800/462–8687); **Ecology Tours** (c/o the Audubon Center of the North

Woods, Box 530, Sandstone, MN 55072, ☎ 612/245–2648), which mix travel and nature study; and **Wildland Adventures** (3516 N.E. 155th St., Seattle, WA 98155, ☎ 206/365–0686 or 800/345–4453).

CRUISING

For information on cruise lines with itineraries that include South America, *see* Cruises *in* Chapter 2, Adventure and Learning Vacations. Also see our guide to all things cruise related, *Fodor's Cruises and Ports of Call* (available at bookstores or from Fodor's Travel Publications, ☎ 800/533–6478; $19).

CUSTOMS

U.S. CITIZENS

The **U.S. Customs Service** (Box 7407, Washington, DC 20044, ☎ 202/927–6724) can answer questions on duty-free limits and publishes a helpful brochure, **"Know Before You Go."** For information on registering foreign-made articles, call 202/927–0540.

CANADIAN CITIZENS

Contact **Revenue Canada** (2265 St. Laurent Blvd. S, Ottawa, Ontario, K1G 4K3, ☎ 613/993–0534) for a copy of the free brochure **"I Declare/ Je Déclare"** and for details on duties that exceed the standard duty-free limit.

BRITISH CITIZENS

HM Customs and Excise (Dorset House, Stamford St., London SE1 9NG, ☎ 0171/202–

4227) can answer questions about customs regulations in the U.K. and publishes **"A Guide for Travellers,"** detailing standard procedures and import rules.

D

FOR TRAVELERS WITH DISABILITIES

COMPLAINTS

To register complaints under the provisions of the Americans with Disabilities Act, contact the U.S. Department of Justice's **Public Access Section** (Box 66738, Washington, DC 20035, ☎ 202/514–0301, FAX 202/307–1198, TTY 202/514–0383).

ORGANIZATIONS

FOR TRAVELERS WITH HEARING IMPAIRMENTS➤ Contact the **American Academy of Otolaryngology** (1 Prince St., Alexandria, VA 22314, ☎ 703/836–4444, FAX 703/683–5100, TTY 703/519–1585).

FOR TRAVELERS WITH MOBILITY PROBLEMS➤ Contact the **Information Center for Individuals with Disabilities** (Fort Point Pl., 27–43 Wormwood St., Boston, MA 02210, ☎ 617/727–5540, 800/462–5015 in MA, TTY 617/345–9743); **Mobility International USA** (Box 10767, Eugene, OR 97440, ☎ and TTY 503/343–1284; FAX 503/343–6812), the U.S. branch of an international organization based in Belgium (*see below*) that has affiliates in 30 countries; **Moss-Rehab Hospital Travel Information Service** (1200 W. Tabor Rd.,

Philadelphia, PA 19141, ☎ 215/456–9603, TTY 215/456–9602); the **Society for the Advancement of Travel for the Handicapped** (347 5th Ave., Suite 610, New York, NY 10016, ☎ 212/447–7284, FAX 212/725–8253); the **Travel Industry and Disabled Exchange** (TIDE, 5435 Donna Ave., Tarzana, CA 91356, ☎ 818/344–3640, FAX 818/344–0078); and **Travelin' Talk** (Box 3534, Clarksville, TN 37043, ☎ 615/552–6670, FAX 615/552–1182).

FOR TRAVELERS WITH VISION IMPAIRMENTS➤ Contact the **American Council of the Blind** (1155 15th St. NW, Suite 720, Washington, DC 20005, ☎ 202/467–5081, FAX 202/467–5085) or the **American Foundation for the Blind** (15 W. 16th St., New York, NY 10011, ☎ 212/620–2000, TTY 212/620–2158).

In the United Kingdom, contact the **Royal Association for Disability and Rehabilitation** (RADAR, 12 City Forum, 250 City Rd., London EC1V 8AF, ☎ 0171/250–3222) or **Mobility International** (Rue de Manchester 25, B1070 Brussels, Belgium, ☎ 00–322–410–6297), an international clearinghouse of travel information for people with disabilities.

PUBLICATIONS

Several free publications are available from the U.S. Information Center (Box 100, Pueblo, CO 81009, ☎ 719/948–3334): **"New Horizons for the Air Traveler with a Disability"** (address to Dept. 355A), describing legally mandated changes; the pocket-size **"Fly Smart"** (Dept. 575B), good on flight safety; and the Airport Operators Council's worldwide **"Access Travel: Airports"** (Dept. 575A).

The 500-page **Travelin' Talk Directory** (☎ 615/552–6670; $35) lists people and organizations who help travelers with disabilities. For specialist travel agents worldwide, consult the **Directory of Travel Agencies for the Disabled** (Twin Peaks Press, Box 129, Vancouver, WA 98666, ☎ 206/694–2462 or 800/637–2256; $19.95 plus $2 shipping).

TRAVEL AGENCIES AND TOUR OPERATORS

The Americans with Disabilities Act requires that travel firms serve the needs of all travelers. However, some agencies and operators specialize in making group and individual arrangements for travelers with disabilities, among them **Access Adventures** (206 Chestnut Ridge Rd., Rochester, NY 14624, ☎ 716/889–9096), run by a former physical-rehab counselor. In addition, many of the operators and agencies listed below (see Tour Operators) can also arrange vacations for travelers with disabilities.

FOR TRAVELERS WITH MOBILITY IMPAIRMENTS➤ A number of operators specialize in working with travelers with mobility impairments: **Accessible Journeys** (35 W. Sellers Ave., Ridley Park, PA 19078, ☎ 610/521–0339 or 800/846–4537, FAX 610/521–6959) is a registered nursing service that arranges vacations; **Hinsdale Travel Service** (201 E. Ogden Ave., Suite 100, Hinsdale, IL 60521, ☎ 708/325–1335 or 800/303–5521) is a travel agency that will give you access to the services of wheelchair traveler Janice Perkins; and **Wheelchair Journeys** (16979 Redmond Way, Redmond, WA 98052, ☎ 206/885–2210) can handle arrangements worldwide.

FOR TRAVELERS WITH DEVELOPMENTAL DISABILITIES➤ Contact the nonprofit **New Directions** (5276 Hollister Ave., Suite 207, Santa Barbara, CA 93111, ☎ 805/967–2841) as well as the general-interest operations above.

Options include **Entertainment Travel Editions** (Box 1068, Trumbull, CT 06611, ☎ 800/445–4137; fee $25–$48, depending on destination); **Great American Traveler** (Box 27965, Salt Lake City, UT 84127, ☎ 800/548–2812; $49.95 annually); **Moment's Notice Discount Travel Club** (425 Madison Ave., New York, NY 10017, ☎ 212/486–0503; $25 annually, single or family); **Privilege Card** (3391 Peachtree Rd. NE, Suite 110, Atlanta, GA

30326, ☎ 404/262–0222 or 800/236-9732; $74.95 annually); **Travelers Advantage** (CUC Travel Service, 49 Music Sq. W, Nashville, TN 37203, ☎ 800/548–1116 or 800/648–4037; $49 annually, single or family); and **Worldwide Discount Travel Club** (1674 Meridian Ave., Miami Beach, FL 33139, ☎ 305/534–2082; $50 annually for family, $40 single).

E

ELECTRICITY

Send a SASE to the **Franzus Company** (Customer Service, Dept. B50, Murtha Industrial Park, Box 142, Beacon Falls, CT 06403, ☎ 203/723–6664) for a copy of their free brochure, "Foreign Electricity Is No Deep Dark Secret."

G

GAY AND LESBIAN TRAVEL

ORGANIZATIONS

The **International Gay Travel Association** (Box 4974, Key West, FL 33041, ☎ 800/448–8550), a consortium of 800 businesses, can supply names of travel agents and tour operators.

PUBLICATIONS

The premier international travel magazine for gays and lesbians is *Our World* (1104 N. Nova Rd., Suite 251, Daytona Beach, FL 32117, ☎ 904/441–5367; $35 for 10 issues). The 16-page monthly "Out & About" (☎ 212/645–

6922 or 800/929–2268; $49 for 10 issues), covers gay-friendly resorts, hotels, cruise lines, and airlines.

TOUR OPERATORS

Contact **Hanns Ebensten Travel** (513 Fleming St., Key West, FL 33040, ☎ 305/294–8174), one of the nation's oldest operators in the gay market, and **Toto Tours** (1326 W. Albion, Suite 3W, Chicago, IL 60626, ☎ 312/274–8686 or 800/565–1241), which has group tours worldwide.

TRAVEL AGENCIES

The largest agencies serving gay and lesbian travelers are **Advance Travel** (10700 Northwest Freeway, Suite 160, Houston, TX 77092, ☎ 713/682–2002 or 800/695–0880); **Islanders/Kennedy Travel** (183 W. 10th St., New York, NY 10014, ☎ 212/242–3222 or 800/988–1181); **Now Voyager** (4406 18th St., San Francisco, CA 94114, ☎ 415/626–1169 or 800/255–6951); and **Yellowbrick Road** (1500 W. Balmoral Ave., Chicago, IL 60640, ☎ 312/561–1800 or 800/642–2488). **Skylink Women's Travel** (746 Ashland Ave., Santa Monica, CA 90405, ☎ 310/452–0506 or 800/225-5759) works with lesbians.

H

HEALTH ISSUES

FINDING A DOCTOR

For members, the **International Association for Medical Assistance to Travellers**

(IAMAT, 417 Center St., Lewiston, NY 14092, ☎ 716/754–4883; 1287 St. Clair Ave., Toronto, Ontario, Canada M6E 1B8, ☎ 416/652–0137; membership free) publishes a worldwide directory of English-speaking physicians who meet IAMAT standards.

MEDICAL-ASSISTANCE COMPANIES

Contact **International SOS Assistance** (Box 11568, Philadelphia, PA 19116, ☎ 215/244–1500 or 800/523–8930; Box 466, Pl. Bonaventure, Montréal, Québec, Canada H5A 1C1, ☎ 514/874–7674 or 800/363–0263); **Medex Assistance Corporation** (Box 10623, Baltimore, MD 21285, ☎ 410/296–2530 or 800/573–2029); **Near Services** (Box 1339, Calumet City, IL 60409, ☎ 708/868–6700 or 800/654–6700); and **Travel Assistance International** (1133 15th St. NW, Suite 400, Washington, DC 20005, ☎ 202/331–1609 or 800/821–2828). Because these companies also sell death-and-dismemberment, trip-cancellation, and other insurance coverage, there is some overlap with the travel-insurance policies sold by the companies listed under Insurance, *below.*

PUBLICATIONS

The Safe Travel Book, by Peter Savage (Lexington Books, 866 3rd Ave., 22nd Floor, New York, NY 10022, ☎ 212/702–4771 or 800/223–23485, FAX 212/605–4872; $12.95), and

Traveler's Medical Resource, by William W. Forgey (ICS Books, Box 10767, Merrillville, IN 45410, ☎ 219/769–0585 or 800/541–7323; $19.95), are authoritative.

WARNINGS

The **National Centers for Disease Control** (Center for Preventive Services, Division of Quarantine, Traveler's Health Section, 1600 Clifton Rd., MSE03, Atlanta, GA 30333, automated hot line 404/332–4559) provides information on health risks abroad and vaccination requirements and recommendations.

I
INSURANCE

Travel insurance covering baggage, health, and trip cancellation or interruptions is available from **Access America** (Box 90315, Richmond, VA 23286, ☎ 804/285–3300 or 800/284–8300); **Carefree Travel Insurance** (Box 9366, 100 Garden City Plaza, Garden City, NY 11530, ☎ 516/294–0220 or 800/323–3149); **Near Services** (Box 1339, Calumet City, IL 60409, ☎ 708/868–6700 or 800/654–6700); **Tele-Trip** (Mutual of Omaha Plaza, Box 31716, Omaha, NE 68131, ☎ 800/228–9792); **Travel Insured International** (Box 280568, East Hartford, CT 06128-0568, ☎ 203/528–7663 or 800/243–3174); **Travel Guard International** (1145 Clark St., Stevens Point, WI 54481, ☎ 715/345–0505 or 800/826–1300); and **Wallach & Company** (107 W. Federal St., Box 480, Middleburg, VA 22117, ☎ 703/687–3166 or 800/237–6615).

IN THE U.K.

The **Association of British Insurers** (51 Gresham St., London EC2V 7HQ, ☎ 0171/600–3333; 30 Gordon St., Glasgow G1 3PU, ☎ 0141/226–3905; Scottish Provident Bldg., Donegall Sq. W, Belfast BT1 6JE, ☎ 01232/249176; and other locations) gives advice by phone and distributes a free publication, **"Holiday Insurance,"** which sets out typical policy provisions and costs.

M
MONEY MATTERS

ATMs

For specific foreign **Cirrus** locations, call 800/424–7787. For foreign Plus locations, consult the **Plus** directory at your local bank.

CURRENCY EXCHANGE

If your bank doesn't exchange currency, contact **Thomas Cook Currency Services** (41 E. 42nd St., New York, NY 10017 or 511 Madison Ave., New York, NY 10022, ☎ 212/757–6915 or 800/223–7373 for locations) or **Ruesch International** (☎ 800/424–2923 for locations).

WIRING FUNDS

Funds can be wired via **American Express MoneyGram℠** (☎ 800/926–9400 from the United States and Canada for locations and information) or **Western Union** (☎ 800/325–6000 for agent locations or to send using MasterCard or Visa, 800/321–2923 in Canada).

P
PASSPORTS AND VISAS

U.S. CITIZENS

For fees, documentation requirements, and other information, call the information line of the **Office of Passport Services** (☎ 202/647–0518).

CANADIAN CITIZENS

For fees, documentation requirements, and other information, call the Ministry of Foreign Affairs and International Trade's **Passport Office** (☎ 819/994–3500 or 800/567–6868).

BRITISH CITIZENS

For fees, documentation requirements, and to get an emergency passport, call the **London passport office** (☎ 0171/271–3000).

VISAS

The addresses of offices that issue visas are provided below only when a visa is required; *see* Passports and Visas *in* Smart Travel Tips A to Z, *below,* for more information.

Bolivia. Canadian citizens should obtain a tourist visa from the Consulate of Bolivia: 130 Albert St., Suite 504, Ottawa, Ontario K1P 5G4, ☎ 613/236–8237.

Brazil. Canadian citizens should obtain a tourist visa from any of the following consulates and embassies: 77 Bloor St. W, Suite 1109, Toronto, Ontario M5S 1M2, ☎ 416/922–2503; 2000 Mansfield St., Suite 1700, Montréal, Québec H3A 3A5, ☎ 514/499–0968; and 1140 W. Pender St., Suite 1300, Vancouver, British Columbia V6E 4G1, ☎ 604/687–4589.

Citizens of the United States should obtain a tourist visa from any of the following consulates and embassies: 20 Park Plaza, Suite 810, Boston, MA 02116, ☎ 617/542–4000; 401 N. Michigan Ave., Room 3050, Chicago, IL 60611, ☎ 312/464–0244; 1700 W. Loop S, Room 1450, Houston, TX 77027, ☎ 713/961–3063; 8484 Wilshire Blvd., Room 730, Beverly Hills, CA 90211, ☎ 213/651–5833; 2601 S. Bay Shore Dr., Room 800, Miami, FL 33131, ☎ 305/285–6200; 630 5th Ave., Room 2720, New York, NY 10111, ☎ 212/757–3080; 300 Montgomery St., Suite 1160, San Francisco, CA 94014, ☎ 415/981–8170; and 3009 White Haven St. NW, Washington, DC 20008, ☎ 202/745–2828.

Uruguay. Canadians should contact the Consulate of Uruguay: 130 Albert St., Suite 1905, Ottawa, Ont. K1P 5G4, ☎ 613/234–2937.

PHONE MATTERS

For local access numbers abroad, check under Telephones in the Essentials section at the

end of each country chapter or contact **AT&T** (☎ 800/874–4000), **MCI** (☎ 800/444–4444), or **Sprint** (☎ 800/793–1153).

PHOTO HELP

The **Kodak Information Center** (☎ 800/242–2424) answers consumer questions about film and photography. Fodor's also publishes the *Kodak Guide to Shooting Great Travel Pictures* (available at bookstores or from Fodor's Travel Publications, ☎ 800/533–6478; $16.50), which has hundreds of tips and photos on everything from how to shoot common travel subjects—markets, beaches, architectural details, and so on—to how to compensate for various light and weather conditions.

S

SENIOR CITIZENS

EDUCATIONAL TRAVEL

The nonprofit **Elderhostel** (75 Federal St., 3rd Floor, Boston, MA 02110, ☎ 617/426–7788), for people 60 and older, has offered inexpensive study programs since 1975. The nearly 2,000 courses cover everything from marine science to Greek myths to cowboy poetry. Fees for two- to three-week international trips—including room, board, and transportation from the United States—range from $1,800 to $4,500.

For people 50 and over and their children and grandchildren, **Interhostel** (University of New

Hampshire, 6 Garrison Ave., Durham, NH 03824, ☎ 603/862–1147 or 800/733–9753) runs 10-day summer programs involving lectures, field trips, and sightseeing. Most last two weeks and cost $2,125–$3,100, including airfare.

ORGANIZATIONS

Contact the **American Association of Retired Persons** (AARP, 601 E St. NW, Washington, DC 20049, ☎ 202/434–2277; $8 per person or couple annually). Its Purchase Privilege Program gets members discounts on lodging, car rentals, and sightseeing.

For other discounts on lodgings, car rentals, and other travel products, along with magazines and newsletters, contact the **National Council of Senior Citizens** (1331 F St. NW, Washington, DC 20004, ☎ 202/347–8800; membership $12 annually) and **Mature Outlook** (6001 N. Clark St., Chicago, IL 60660, ☎ 312/465–6466 or 800/336–6330; subscription $9.95 annually).

PUBLICATIONS

The 50+ Traveler's Guidebook: Where to Go, Where to Stay, What to Do, by Anita Williams and Merrimac Dillon (St. Martin's Press, 175 5th Ave., New York, NY 10010, ☎ 212/674–5151 or 800/288–2131; $12.95), offers many useful tips.

"The Mature Traveler" (Box 50820, Reno, NV 89513; $29.95), a monthly newsletter, covers travel deals.

STUDENTS

HOSTELING

Contact **Hostelling International–American Youth Hostels** (733 15th St. NW, Suite 840, Washington, DC 20005, ☏ 202/783–6161) in the United States; **Hostelling International–Canada** (205 Catherine St., Suite 400, Ottawa, Ontario K2P 1C3, ☏ 613/748–5638) in Canada; and the **Youth Hostel Association of England and Wales** (Trevelyan House, 8 St. Stephen's Hill, St. Albans, Hertfordshire AL1 2DY, ☏ 01727/855215 and 01727/845047) in the United Kingdom. Membership ($25 in the United States, C$26.75 in Canada, and £9 in the United Kingdom) gets you access to 5,000 hostels worldwide that charge $7–$20 nightly per person.

ID CARDS

To get discounts on transportation and admissions, get the **International Student Identity Card** (ISIC) if you're a bona fide student or the **International Youth Card** (IYC) if you're under 26. In the United States, the ISIC and IYC cards cost $16 each and include basic travel-accident and illness coverage, plus a toll-free travel hot line. Apply through the Council on International Educational Exchange (*see* Organizations, *below*). Cards are available for $15 each in Canada from **Travel Cuts** (187 College St., Toronto, Ontario M5T 1P7, ☏ 416/979–2406 or 800/667–2887) and in the United Kingdom for £5 each at student unions and student travel companies.

ORGANIZATIONS

A major contact is the **Council on International Educational Exchange** (CIEE, 205 E. 42nd St., 16th Floor, New York, NY 10017, ☏ 212/661–1450) with locations in Boston (729 Boylston St., Boston, MA 02116, ☏ 617/266–1926); Miami (9100 S. Dadeland Blvd., Miami, FL 33156, ☏ 305/670–9261); Los Angeles (1093 Broxton Ave., Los Angeles, CA 90024, ☏ 310/208–3551); 43 college towns nationwide; and the United Kingdom (28A Poland St., London W1V 3DB, ☏ 0171/437–7767). Twice a year, it publishes *Student Travels* magazine. The CIEE's Council Travel Service is the exclusive U.S. agent for several student-discount cards.

Campus Connections (325 Chestnut St., Suite 1101, Philadelphia, PA 19106, ☏ 215/625–8585 or 800/428–3235) specializes in discounted accommodations and airfares for students. The **Educational Travel Centre** (438 N. Frances St., Madison, WI 53703, ☏ 608/256–5551) offers rail passes and low-cost airline tickets, mostly for flights departing from Chicago. For air travel only contact **TMI Student Travel** (100 W. 33rd St., Suite 813, New York, NY 10001, ☏ 800/245–3672).

In Canada, also contact **Travel Cuts** (*see above*).

T

TOUR OPERATORS

Among the companies selling tours and packages to South America, the following have a proven reputation, are nationally known, and offer plenty of options.

GROUP TOURS

Super-deluxe escorted tours through South America are available from **Abercrombie & Kent** (1520 Kensington Rd., Oak Brook, IL 60521, ☏ 708/954–2944 or 800/323–7308) and **Travcoa** (Box 2630, Newport Beach, CA, 92658, ☏ 714/476–2800 or 800/992–2003). Another operator falling between deluxe and first class is **Globus** (5301 S. Federal Circle, Littleton, CO 80123, ☏ 303/797–2800 or 800/221–0090). In the first class and tourist range, contact **Collette Tours** (162 Middle St., Pawtucket, RI 02860, ☏ 401/728-3805 or 800/832–4656).

ORGANIZATIONS

The **National Tour Operators Association** (546 E. Main St., Lexington, KY 40508, ☏ 606/226–4444 or 800/682–8886) and the **United States Tour Operators Association** (USTOA, 211 E. 51st St., Suite 12B, New York, NY 10022, ☏ 212/750–7371) can provide lists of member operators and information on booking tours.

PACKAGES

Independent vacation packages are available from major tour operators and airlines. Contact **Avanti Destinations** (851 S.W. 6th Ave., Portland, OR 97204, ☎ 503/295–1100 or 800/422–5053); **4th Dimension Tours** (1150 N.W. 72nd Ave., Suite 250, Miami, FL 33126, ☎ 305/477–1525 or 800/343–0020); **Ladatco Tours** (2220 Coral Way, Miami, FL 33145; ☎ 305/854–8433 or 800/327–6162); **Marnella Tours** (33 Walt Whitman Rd., Huntington Station, NY 11746, ☎ 516/271–6969 or 800/937–6999); and **Sun Holidays** (26 6th St., Suite 603, Stamford, CT 06905, ☎ 203/323–1166 or 800/243–2057).

PUBLICATIONS

Consult the brochure **"Worldwide Tour & Vacation Package Finder"** from the National Tour Operators Association (*see above*) and the Better Business Bureau's **"Tips on Travel Packages"** (Publication No. 24-195; 4200 Wilson Blvd., Arlington, VA 22203; $2).

THEME TRIPS

For a complete listing of special-interest and learning vacations—as well as cruise ships that sail to South American cities, the Amazon, and Antarctica—*see* Chapter 2, Adventure and Learning Vacations.

TRAVEL AGENCIES

For names of reputable agencies in your area, contact the **American Society of Travel Agents** (1101 King St., Suite 200, Alexandria, VA 22314, ☎ 703/739–2782).

U

U.S. GOVERNMENT TRAVEL BRIEFINGS

The U.S. Department of State's Overseas Citizens Emergency Center (Room 4811, Washington, DC 20520; enclose SASE) issues **Consular Information Sheets,** which cover crime, security, political climate, and health risks, as well as embassy locations, entry requirements, currency regulations, and other routine matters. (Travel Warnings, which counsel travelers to avoid a country entirely, are issued in extreme cases.) For the latest information, stop in at any U.S. passport office, consulate, or embassy; call the interactive hot line (☎ 202/647–5225 or FAX 202/647-3000); or, with your PC's modem, tap into the Bureau of Consular Affairs' computer bulletin board (☎ 202/647–9225).

V

VISITOR INFO

Most South American countries offer very little basic travel information. Few countries have tourist offices overseas, and there are no special travel sections in most embassies and consulates (although some consulates will mail packets of brochures and the like). Often your best bets are the airlines that fly to each country and tour operators with programs to South America (*see* Air Travel *and* Tours Operators, *above*). At press time there were only five organizations in the United States offering South American tourist information:

Argentina National Tourist Council (12 W. 56th St., New York, NY 10019, ☎ 212/603– 0443; 5055 Wilshire Blvd., Los Angeles, CA 90036, ☎ 213/930–0681; or 2655 Le Jeune Rd., Miami, FL 33134, ☎ 305/442–1366).

Bolivian Tourist Information Office (97-45 Queens Blvd., Suite 600, Rego Park, NY 11374, ☎ 718/897–7956 or 800/205–4842, FAX 718/275–3943).

Brazilian Travel Service (2441 Janin Way, Solvang, CA 93463, ☎ 805/688–2441 or 800/544-5503, FAX 805/688–1021).

Uruguayan Tourism Office (1077 Ponce de Leon Blvd., Coral Gables, FL 33134, ☎ and FAX 305/443–7431).

Venezuelan Tourism Association (Box 3010, Sausalito, CA 94966, ☎ 415/331-0100, FAX 415/332-9197).

W

WEATHER

For current conditions and forecasts, plus the local time and helpful travel tips, call the **Weather Channel Connection** (☎ 900/932–8437; 95¢ per minute) from a Touch-Tone phone.

SMART TRAVEL TIPS A TO Z

Basic Information on Traveling in South America and Savvy Tips to Make Your Trip a Breeze

The more you travel, the more you know about how to make trips run like clockwork. To help make your travels hassle-free, Fodor's editors have rounded up dozens of tips from our contributors and travel experts all over the world, as well as basic information on visiting South America. For names of organizations to contact and publications that can give you more information, *see* Important Contacts A to Z, *above*.

A

AIR TRAVEL

If time is an issue, **always look for nonstop flights,** which require no change of plane and, unlike direct flights, make no stops. If possible, **avoid connecting flights,** which stop at least once and can involve a change of plane, although the flight number remains the same; if the first leg is late, the second waits.

ALOFT

International travel between the Americas is a bit less wearing than to Europe or the Orient because there is far less jet lag. New York, for instance, is in the same time zone as Lima and there is only a three-hour time difference between Lima and Los Angeles. If you have a choice between day or night flights—and those

to Rio de Janeiro and Buenos Aires always depart after dark—take the night plane if you sleep well while flying. Especially en route to the Andean countries, you will have lovely sunrises over the mountains. Southbound, the best views are usually out windows on the left side of the plane.

AIRLINE FOOD➤ If you hate airline food, **ask for special meals when booking.** These can be vegetarian, low cholesterol, or kosher, for example. Commonly prepared to order in smaller quantities than standard catered fare, they can be tastier.

JET LAG➤ To avoid this syndrome, which occurs when travel disrupts your body's natural cycles, try to maintain a normal routine. At night, **get some sleep.** By day, move about the cabin to **stretch your legs, eat light meals, and drink water—not alcohol.**

SMOKING➤ Smoking is banned on all flights within the United States of less than six hours' duration and on all Canadian flights; the ban also applies to domestic segments of international flights aboard U.S. and foreign carriers. On U.S. carriers flying to South America and other destinations abroad, a seat in a no-smoking section must be pro-

vided for every passenger who requests one, and the section must be enlarged to accommodate such passengers if necessary as long as they have complied with the airline's deadline for check-in and seat assignment. If smoking bothers you, request a seat far from the smoking section.

Foreign airlines are exempt from these rules but do provide no-smoking sections; some nations have banned smoking on all domestic flights, and others may ban smoking on some flights. Talks continue on the feasibility of broadening no-smoking policies.

CUTTING COSTS

The Sunday travel section of most newspapers is a good source of deals.

CONSOLIDATORS➤ Consolidators buy tickets at reduced rates from scheduled airlines and sell them at prices below the lowest fare available from the airlines directly—usually without advance restrictions. Sometimes you can even get your money back if you need to return the ticket. Carefully read the fine print detailing penalties for changes and cancellations. If you doubt the reliability of a consolidator, **confirm your reservation with the airline.**

THE GOLD GUIDE / SMART TRAVEL TIPS

MAJOR AIRLINES➤ The least-expensive airfares from the major airlines are priced for round-trip travel and are subject to restrictions. You must usually **book in advance and buy the ticket within 24 hours** to get cheaper fares, and you may have to **stay over a Saturday night.** The lowest fare is subject to availability, and only a small percentage of the plane's total seats are sold at that price. It's good to **call a number of airlines,** and **when you are quoted a good price, book it on the spot**—the same fare on the same flight may not be available the next day. Airlines generally allow you to change your return date for a $25 to $50 fee, but most low-fare tickets are nonrefundable. However, if you don't use your ticket, you can apply its cost toward the purchase price of a new one, again for a small charge.

WITHIN SOUTH AMERICA

Because distances are great between and within countries and there is little long-distance transportation overland; most visitors travel from point to point within South America by plane.

Special air-travel passes are available in the United States for travel within Argentina, Bolivia, Brazil, Chile, Colombia, Peru, and Venezuela.(*See* Getting Around *in* the country Essentials section of individual chapters for details).

Always reconfirm your flights, even if you have a ticket and a reservation; departure times and days of operation may have changed and your reservations may be canceled. Moreover, on many routes all over the continent, every flight operates full—usually of passengers with a great deal of baggage to process before departure. So always arrive at the airport well in advance of takeoff to allow for the lengthy check-in. When leaving any country, you'll need to show your passport and pay often sizable departure taxes, either in the local currency or in dollars.

AIRPORT TRANSPORTATION

Bus service is not available to and from many South American airports. Taxi fares, however, are very reasonable; if you are concerned about your city destination not being understood, write it down on a piece of paper and present it to the taxi driver.

B

BUS TRAVEL

Bus service varies from country to country. Brazil, Chile, and Venezuela have relatively good service. Main routes are served by air-conditioned buses, some with toilets and movies. In Ecuador and Peru, badly built and/or washed-out roads can make for interminable delays—but the views are spectacular.

However, bus service is generally reliable. And since buses are the primary means of transportation for most South Americans, traveling by bus gives you a chance to get to know the people. It also lets you see their homelands: Buses go almost anywhere there's a road, to all corners of most countries. Without doubt, the low cost of bus travel is its greatest advantage; its greatest drawback is the time you must allow, not only to cover the distances involved but also to allow for breakdowns and delays due to faulty equipment.

When traveling by bus, it is best to **bring your own food and beverages,** although food stops are usually made en route. Travel lightly, dress comfortably, and **keep a close watch on your luggage and belongings.**

Tickets are sold at city bus terminals. Note that in larger cities there may be different terminals for buses to different destinations. Arrive early to get a ticket, and **expect to pay cash.** On holidays such as Christmas, Easter, or national independence days, buy your ticket as far in advance as possible and arrive at the station extra early.

C

CAMERAS, CAMCORDERS, AND COMPUTERS

LAPTOPS

Before you depart, **check your portable**

computer's battery, because you may be asked at security to turn on the computer to prove that it is what it appears to be. At the airport, you may prefer to **request a manual inspection,** although security X-rays do not harm hard-disk or floppy-disk storage. Also, **register your foreign-made laptop with U.S. Customs.** If your laptop is U.S.-made, call the consulate of the country you ll be visiting to find out whether or not it should be registered with local customs upon arrival. You may want to **find out about repair facilities at your destination** in case you need them.

PHOTOGRAPHY

FILM➤ If your camera is new or if you haven t used it for a while, **shoot and develop a few rolls of film** before you leave. Always **store film in a cool, dry place** never in the car s glove compartment or on the shelf under the rear window.

Every pass through an X-ray machine increases film s chance of clouding, particularly if it s a fast film (with ISO 400 or higher). To protect it, carry it in a clear plastic bag and **ask for hand inspection at security.** Such requests are virtually always honored at U.S. airports, and usually are accommodated abroad. Don t depend on a lead-lined bag to protect film in checked luggage the airline may increase the radiation to see what s inside.

EQUIPMENT AND CONDITIONS➤ The higher the altitude, the greater the proportion of ultraviolet rays in light. Light meters do not read these rays and consequently, except for close-ups or full-frame portraits where the reading is taken directly off the subject, photos may be overexposed. If you ll be visiting the Andes, **get a skylight (81B or 81C) or polarizing filter to minimize haze and light problems.** These filters may also help with the glare caused by white adobe buildings, sandy beaches, and so on. Jungle trips pose other problems. **Keep your equipment in resealable plastic bags to protect it from damp, and bring high-speed film to compensate for low light under the tree canopy.** To avoid the blurriness caused by hand shake, **buy a mini tripod** they re available in sizes as small as 6 inches. **Get a small beanbag to support your camera on uneven surfaces.**

VIDEO

Before your trip, **test your camcorder, invest in a skylight filter to protect the lens, and charge the batteries.** (Airport security personnel may ask you to turn on the camcorder to prove that it s what it appears to be.) The batteries of most newer camcorders can be recharged with a universal or worldwide AC adapter charger (or multivoltage converter), usable whether the voltage is 110 or 220.

All that s needed is the appropriate plug.

Videotape is not damaged by X-rays, but it may be harmed by the magnetic field of a walk-through metal detector, so **ask that videotapes be hand-checked.** Note that many South American countries use the same National Television System Committee (NTSC) video standard used by the United States, but Bolivia, Brazil, Paraguay, Uruguay, and the Falkland Islands use PAL technology. Blank tapes bought in South America can be used for NTSC camcorder taping, but they are pricey. Some U.S. audiovisual shops convert foreign tapes to U.S. standards; contact an electronics dealer to find the nearest.

CHILDREN AND TRAVEL

South Americans love children, and having yours along may prove to be your special ticket to meeting local people. Children are welcomed in hotels and in restaurants, especially on weekends, when South American families go out for lunch in droves.

Older children will adjust better if you let them join in on planning and if you find time to scout your library for picture books, storybooks, and maps about places you will be going. Try to explain the concept of foreign language; some kids, who may have just learned to talk, are thrown when they cannot understand strangers and strangers cannot understand them. For children of reading age, be sure to bring their books from home; locally, literature for kids in English is hard to find. Make sure that health precautions, such as what to drink and eat, are applied to the whole family. Children should have had all their inoculations before leaving home. Not cramming too much in a day will keep the whole family healthier while on the road.

BABY-SITTING

For recommended local sitters, **check with your hotel desk.** In top establishments, the management will probably have a list of them—though you can't count on their speaking fluent English.

DRIVING

If you are renting a car, **arrange for a car seat when you reserve.** Sometimes they're free.

FLYING

Always **ask about discounted children's fares.** On international flights, the fare for infants under age two not occupying a seat is generally either free or 10% of the accompanying adult's fare; children ages two through 11 usually pay half to two-thirds of the adult fare. Some routes are considered neither international nor domestic and have still other rules.

BAGGAGE➤ In general, the adult baggage allowance applies for children paying half or more of the adult fare.

Before departure, **ask about carry-on allowances,** if you are traveling with an infant. In general, those paying 10% of the adult fare are allowed one carry-on bag, not to exceed 70 pounds or 45 inches (length + width + height) and a collapsible stroller; you may be allowed less if the flight is full.

SAFETY SEATS➤ According to the Federal Aviation Administration (FAA), it's good to **use safety seats aloft.** Airline policy varies. U.S. carriers allow FAA-approved models, but airlines usually require that you buy a ticket, even if your child would otherwise ride free, because the seats must be strapped into regular passenger seats. Foreign carriers may not allow infant seats, may charge the child's rather than the infant's fare for their use, or may require you to hold your baby during takeoff and landing, thus defeating the seat's purpose.

FACILITIES➤ When making your reservation, **ask for children's meals or freestanding bassinets** if you need them; the latter are available only to those with seats at the bulkhead, where there's enough legroom. If you don't need a bassinet, **think twice before requesting bulkhead seats**—the only storage for in-flight necessities is in the inconveniently distant overhead bins.

LODGING

Most hotels allow children under a certain age to stay in their parents' room at no extra charge, while others charge them as extra adults; be sure to **ask about the cutoff age.** In South America, you can sometimes arrange special family rates when you take two rooms. You may want to try for hotels with pools or health-club facilities, which children usually enjoy. If your children are younger, hotels with cafeteria-style restaurants will probably work better than those with only formal dining rooms and room service.

CRUISES

For travel tips on booking a cruise to South America, *see* Cruises *in* Chapter 2, Adventure and Learning Vacations.

CUSTOMS
AND DUTIES

For information on customs in South America, *see* Customs *in* the Essentials section at the end of each chapter.

IN THE U.S.

You may bring home $400 worth of foreign goods duty-free if you've been out of the country for at least 48 hours and haven't already used the $400 exemption, or any part of it, in the past 30 days.

Travelers 21 or older may bring back 1 liter of alcohol duty-free, provided the beverage laws of the state through which you reenter the United States allow it. In addition, 100 non-Cuban cigars and 200 cigarettes are allowed, regardless of your age. Antiques and works of art more than 100 years old are duty-free.

Duty-free, travelers may mail packages valued at up to $200 to themselves and up to $100 to others, with a limit of one parcel per addressee per day (and no alcohol or tobacco products or perfume valued at more than $5); outside, identify the package as being for personal use or an unsolicited gift, specifying the contents and their retail value. Mailed items do not count as part of your exemption.

IN CANADA

Once per calendar year, when you've been out of Canada for at least seven days, you may bring in C$300 worth of goods duty-free. If you've been away less than seven days but more than 48 hours, the duty-free exemption drops to C$100 but can be claimed any number of times (as can a C$20 duty-free exemption for absences of 24 hours or more). You cannot combine the yearly and 48-hour exemptions, use the C$300 exemption only partially (to save the balance for a later trip), or pool exemptions with family members. Goods claimed under the C$300 exemption may follow you by mail; those claimed under the lesser exemptions must accompany you.

Alcohol and tobacco products may be included in the yearly and 48-hour exemptions but not in the 24-hour exemption. If you meet the age requirements of

the province through which you reenter Canada, you may bring in, duty-free, 1.14 liters (40 imperial ounces) of wine or liquor *or* 24 12-ounce cans or bottles of beer or ale. If you are 16 or older, you may bring in, duty-free, 200 cigarettes, 50 cigars or cigarillos, and 400 tobacco sticks or 400 grams of manufactured tobacco. Alcohol and tobacco must accompany you on your return.

An unlimited number of gifts valued up to C$60 each may be mailed to Canada duty-free. These do not count as part of your exemption. Label the package "Unsolicited Gift— Value under $60." Alcohol and tobacco are excluded.

IN THE U.K.

From countries outside the European Union, including those of South America, you may import duty-free 200 cigarettes, 100 cigarillos, 50 cigars or 250 grams of tobacco; 1 liter of spirits or 2 liters of fortified or sparkling wine; 2 liters of still table wine; 60 milliliters of perfume; 250 milliliters of toilet water; plus £136 worth of other goods, including gifts and souvenirs.

D
FOR TRAVELERS
WITH DISABILITIES

Although international chain hotels in large cities have some suitable rooms for travelers with disabilities and it is easy to hire private cars and drivers for

excursions, South America is not very well equipped to handle travelers with disabilities. There are few ramps and curb cuts, and it takes effort and planning to negotiate cobbled city streets, get around museums and other buildings, and explore the countryside. City centers such as Rio de Janeiro, Buenos Aires, Santiago, and Caracas are the most comfortable to visit, and cruising is convenient, since cruises make it easier to cover distances and give you the option of making many special excursions. Cruises to areas such as the Galápagos Islands, Antarctica, and the Amazon are not recommended.

When discussing accessibility with an operator or reservationist, **ask hard questions.** Are there any stairs, inside *or* out? Are there grab bars next to the toilet *and* in the shower/tub? How wide is the doorway to the room? To the bathroom? For the most extensive facilities, meeting the latest legal specifications, **opt for newer facilities,** which more often have been designed with access in mind. Older properties or ships must usually be retrofitted and may offer more limited facilities as a result. Be sure to **discuss your needs before booking.**

DISCOUNT CLUBS

Travel clubs offer members unsold space on airplanes, cruise ships, and package tours at as much as 50% below regular prices. Membership may include a regular bulletin or access to a toll-free hot line giving details of available trips departing from three or four days to several months in the future. Most also offer 50% discounts off hotel rack rates. Before booking with a club, **make sure the hotel or other supplier isn't offering a better deal.**

DRIVING

Road conditions vary from country to country. But where the highways are paved, they are manageable. Some common-sense rules of the road: Plan your daily driving distance conservatively. Don't drive after dark. Ask before you leave about gasoline stations. Obey speed limits (given in kilometers per hour) and traffic regulations. And above all, if you get a traffic ticket, don't argue—and plan to spend longer than you want on getting it settled.

H

HEALTH CONCERNS

Travelers staying on the main tourist routes will have few worries. However, you may need various shots or pills for some areas, particularly in the Amazon regions and for long periods of traveling in the interior. For short stays, they probably won't be necessary.

ALTITUDE SICKNESS

Soroche, or altitude sickness, which results in shortness of breath and headaches, may be a problem when you visit Andean countries. To remedy any discomfort, walk slowly, eat lightly, and drink plenty of liquids (but avoid alcoholic beverages). If you have high blood pressure and a history of heart trouble, check with your doctor before planning to travel to such heights as those at Cuzco in Peru and La Paz in Bolivia, both above 11,000 feet.

DIVERS' ALERT

Scuba divers take note: **Do not fly within 24 hours of scuba diving.** Neophyte divers should have a complete physical exam before undertaking a dive. If you have travel insurance that covers evacuations, **make sure your policy applies to scuba-related injuries,** as not all companies provide this coverage.

FOOD AND WATER

Keeping healthy is key to enjoying South America. Hotels take pride in their drinking water, and longtime expatriate residents drink water in many major cities with no problem. However, if you've got just two weeks, you won't want to waste a minute of it in your hotel room. To be absolutely safe, be scrupulously careful about what you eat and drink all the way through your trip, on as well as off the beaten path.

In South America, the major health risk is posed by the contamination of drinking water, fresh fruit, and vegetables by fecal matter, which causes the intestinal ailment known in South America as *la tourista,* and elsewhere as Montezuma's Revenge or traveler's diarrhea. To prevent it, **watch what you eat.** Stay away from ice, uncooked food, and unpasteurized milk and milk products, and **drink only water that has been bottled or boiled** for at least 20 minutes. Mild cases may respond to Imodium (known generically as loperamide) or Pepto-Bismol (which is not as strong), both of which can be purchased over the counter; paregoric, another antidiarrheal agent, generally does not require a doctor's prescription in South America. Drink plenty of purified water or tea—chamomile is a good folk remedy for diarrhea. In severe cases, rehydrate yourself with a salt-sugar solution (½ tsp. salt and 4 tbsp. sugar per quart/liter of water).

SHOTS AND MEDICATIONS

According to the Centers for Disease Control (CDC) there is a limited risk of cholera, malaria, hepatitis B, dengue, chagas, and yellow fever. While a few of these you could catch anywhere, most are restricted to jungle areas. If you plan to visit remote regions or stay for more than six weeks, **check with the CDC's International Travelers Hot Line.** In areas with malaria and dengue, which are both carried by mosquitoes, take mosquito nets, wear clothing that covers the body, apply repellent containing DEET, and use a spray against flying insects in living and sleeping areas. The hot line recommends chloroquine (analen) as an antimalarial agent; no vaccine exists against dengue.

Children traveling to South America should have current inoculations against measles, mumps, rubella, and polio.

INSURANCE

Travel insurance can protect your investment, replace your luggage and its contents, or provide for medical coverage should you fall ill during your trip. Most tour operators, travel agents, and insurance agents sell specialized health-and-accident, flight, trip-cancellation, and luggage insurance as well as comprehensive policies with some or all of these features. Before you make any purchase, **review your existing health and homeowner policies** to find out whether they cover expenses incurred while traveling.

BAGGAGE

Airline liability for your baggage is limited by the terms of your ticket (see Packing for South America, below). Insurance for losses exceeding the terms of your airline ticket can be bought directly from the airline at check-in for about $10 per $1,000 of coverage;

note that it excludes a rather extensive list of items, shown on your airline ticket.

FLIGHT

You should **think twice before buying flight insurance.** Often purchased as a last-minute impulse at the airport, it pays a lump sum when a plane crashes, either to a beneficiary if the insured dies or sometimes to a surviving passenger who loses eyesight or a limb. Supplementing the airlines' coverage described in the limits-of-liability paragraphs on your ticket, it's expensive and basically unnecessary. Charging an airline ticket to a major credit card often automatically entitles you to coverage and may also embrace travel by bus, train, and ship.

HEALTH

If your own health insurance policy does not cover you outside the United States, **consider buying supplemental medical coverage.** It can provide from $1,000 to $150,000 worth of medical and/or dental expenses incurred as a result of an accident or illness during a trip. These policies also may include a personal-accident, or death-and-dismemberment, provision, which pays a lump sum ranging from $15,000 to $500,000 to your beneficiaries if you die or to you if you lose one or more limbs or your eyesight, and a medical-assistance provision, which may either reimburse you for the cost of referrals,

evacuation, or repatriation and other services, or may automatically enroll you as a member of a particular medical-assistance company. (See Health Issues in Important Contacts A to Z, above.)

FOR BRITISH TRAVELERS➤ You can buy an annual travel-insurance policy valid for most vacations during the year in which it's purchased. If you go this route, make sure it covers you if you have a preexisting medical condition or are pregnant.

TRIP

Without insurance, you will lose all or most of your money if you must cancel your trip due to illness or any other reason. Especially if your airline ticket, cruise, or package tour is nonrefundable and cannot be changed, it's essential that you **buy trip-cancellation-and-interruption insurance.** When considering how much coverage you need, look for a policy that will cover the cost of your trip plus the nondiscounted price of a one-way airline ticket should you need to return home early. Read the fine print carefully, especially sections defining "family member" and "preexisting medical conditions." Also **consider default or bankruptcy insurance,** which protects you against a supplier's failure to deliver. However, such policies often do not cover default by a travel agency, tour operator, airline, or cruise line if you bought

THE GOLD GUIDE / SMART TRAVEL TIPS

your tour and the coverage directly from the firm in question.

M

MEDICAL ASSISTANCE

No one plans to get sick while traveling, but it happens, so **consider signing up with a medical assistance company.** These outfits provide referrals, emergency evacuation or repatriation, 24-hour telephone hot lines for medical consultation, dispatch of medical personnel, relay of medical records, cash for emergencies, and other personal and legal assistance.

MONEY AND EXPENSES

ATMs

Cirrus, Plus, and many other networks connecting automated-teller machines operate internationally, but ATMs are fewer and farther between than in the United States and Canada. Chances are that you can **use your bank card at ATMs** to withdraw money from an account and get cash advances on a credit-card account if your card has been programmed with a personal identification number, or PIN. Before leaving home, **check in on frequency limits** for withdrawals and cash advances. Also **ask whether your card's PIN must be reprogrammed** for use in South America. Four digits are commonly used overseas. Note that Discover is accepted only in the United States.

On cash advances you are charged interest from the day you receive the money from ATMs as well as from tellers. Although transaction fees for ATM withdrawals abroad may be higher than fees for withdrawals at home, Cirrus and Plus exchange rates are excellent because they are based on wholesale rates only offered by major banks.

EXCHANGING CURRENCY

When you make a purchase in South America, you get a better exchange rate when you pay in traveler's checks than when you offer cash. On simple currency exchange, rates are better at banks but not significantly so—and there are lines. Take a few pesos less at a hotel, and save yourself some time. Plan ahead, however, since it is often hard to change large amounts of money at hotels on weekends, even in capital cities. If you're heading for rural areas, you will probably not be able to change currency at all, so don't leave the city without adequate amounts of local currency, in small denominations.

Since the dollar rarely loses strength against South American currencies, pay for costly items overseas, and use your credit card whenever possible—you'll come out ahead, whether the exchange rate at which your purchase is calculated is the one in effect the day the vendor's bank abroad processes the

charge, or the one prevailing on the day the charge company's service center processes it at home.

To avoid lines at airport exchange booths, **get a small amount of currency before you leave home.** Thomas Cook Currency Services is your best source of currency by mail, though it may occasionally not be able to supply what you need for some countries.

SAFETY

To safeguard your money, **lock traveler's checks and cash in a hotel safe,** except for what you need to carry each day. Funds that you do carry are best tucked into a money belt or carried in the inside pockets of your clothing. Always **remain alert for pickpockets.**

TRAVELER'S CHECKS

Whether or not to buy traveler's checks depends on where you are headed; **take cash to rural areas and small towns, traveler's checks to cities.** The most widely recognized are American Express, Citicorp, Thomas Cook, and Visa, which are sold by major commercial banks for 1% to 3% of the checks' face value—it pays to **shop around.** American Automobile Association (AAA) members can **get American Express checks with no surcharge at AAA offices.** Both American Express and Thomas Cook issue checks that can be countersigned and used by you or your traveling companion. **Carry your traveler's**

checks in small denomi-
nations. Particularly if
you are visiting several
countries, this will allow
you to change just the
amount you need (and
avoid being left with a
difficult-to-reconvert
surplus). Moreover,
hotels—the most conve-
nient place to change
money—often do not
have large amounts of
currency on hand.
Record the numbers of
the checks, cross them
off as you spend them,
and keep this informa-
tion separate from your
checks.

WIRING MONEY

You don't have to be a
cardholder to send or
receive funds through
MoneyGram℠ from
American Express. Just
go to a MoneyGram℠
agent, located in Ameri-
can Express Travel
Offices. Pay up to
$1,000 with cash or a
credit card, anything
over that in cash. The
money can be picked up
within 10 minutes (it
may take longer in
Paraguay) in the form
of U.S.-dollar traveler's
checks or local currency
at the nearest Money-
Gram℠ agent, or,
abroad, the nearest
American Express
Travel Office. There's
no limit, and the recipi-
ent need only present
photo identification.
The cost runs from 3%
to 10%, depending on
the amount sent, the
destination, and how
you pay.

P
**PACKAGES
AND TOURS**

A package or tour to
South America can

make your vacation less
expensive and more
convenient. Firms that
sell tours and packages
purchase airline seats,
hotel rooms, and rental
cars in bulk and pass
some of the savings on
to you. In addition, the
best operators have
local representatives to
help you out at your
destination.

A GOOD DEAL?

The more your package
or tour includes, the
better you can predict
the ultimate cost of your
vacation. Make sure
you know exactly what
is included, and beware
of hidden costs. Are
taxes, tips, and service
charges included?
Transfers and baggage
handling? Entertain-
ment and excursions?
These can add up.

Most packages and
tours are rated deluxe,
first-class superior, first
class, tourist, and
budget. The key differ-
ence is usually accom-
modations. Remember,
tourist class in the
United States might be
a comfortable chain
hotel, while in South
America you might
share a bath and do
without hot water. If
the package or tour
you are considering is
priced lower than in
your wildest dreams,
be skeptical. Also,
make sure your travel
agent knows the hotels
and other services. Ask
about location, room
size, beds, and whether
it has a pool, room
service, or programs
for children, if you care
about these. Has your
agent been there or
sent others you can
contact?

BUYER BEWARE

Each year consumers
are stranded or lose
their money when
operators go out of
business—even very
large ones with excel-
lent reputations. If you
can't afford a loss, take
the time to check out
the operator—find out
how long the company
has been in business,
and ask several agents
about its reputation.
Next, don't book unless
the firm has a con-
sumer-protection pro-
gram. Members of the
United States Tour
Operators Association
and the National Tour
Association are required
to set aside funds exclu-
sively to cover your
payments and travel
arrangements in case of
default. Nonmember
operators may instead
carry insurance; look
for the details in the
operator's brochure—
and the name of an
underwriter with a solid
reputation. Note: When
it comes to tour opera-
tors, don't trust escrow
accounts. Although
there are laws govern-
ing those of charter-
flight operators, no
governmental body
prevents tour operators
from raiding the till.

Next, contact your local
Better Business Bureau
and the attorney gen-
eral's office in both
your own state and the
operator's; have any
complaints been filed?
Last, pay with a major
credit card. Then you
can cancel payment,
provided that you can
document your com-
plaint. Always consider
trip-cancellation insur-
ance (see Insurance,
above).

THE GOLD GUIDE / SMART TRAVEL TIPS

BIG VS. SMALL

An operator that handles several hundred thousand travelers annually can use its purchasing power to give you a good price. Its high volume may also indicate financial stability. But some small companies provide more personalized service; because they tend to specialize, they may also be experts on an area.

SINGLE TRAVELERS

Prices are usually quoted per person, based on two sharing a room. If traveling solo, you may be required to pay the full double-occupancy rate. Some operators eliminate this surcharge if you agree to be matched up with a roommate of the same sex, even if one is not found by departure time.

USING AN AGENT

Travel agents are an excellent resource. In fact, large operators accept bookings only through travel agents. But it's good to **collect brochures from several agencies,** because some agents' suggestions may be skewed by promotional relationships with tour and package firms that reward them for volume sales. If you have a special interest, **find an agent with expertise in that area;** the American Society of Travel Agents can give you leads in the United States. (Don't rely solely on your agent, though; agents may be unaware of small niche operators, and some special-interest travel companies only sell direct.)

PACKING FOR SOUTH AMERICA

If you're doing business in South America, you will need the same business attire you would wear in U.S. and European cities: for men, suits and ties, and for women, suits for day wear and cocktail dresses or other suitable dinner clothes.

For sightseeing and leisure, casual clothing and good walking shoes are both desirable and appropriate, and most cities do not require very formal clothes, even for evenings. For beach vacations in the tropical countries, you'll need lightweight sportswear, a bathing suit, a sun hat, and sunscreen. Travel in tropical rain forest areas will require long-sleeve shirts, long pants, socks, sneakers, a hat, a light waterproof jacket, a bathing suit, and insect repellent. In the Andean countries, dress conservatively—no short shorts or halters. If you're visiting Patagonian areas in the south or high altitudes, bring a light jacket and sweater, or plan to acquire one of the hand-knit sweaters or ponchos crowding the marketplaces.

If there is a general rule for dressing in South America, it's this: Dress more conservatively in countries on the west coast than those on the east. Colombia is conservative, Venezuela is not. Argentineans are very clothes conscious, but don't demand high-style fashion of you.

Bring an extra pair of eyeglasses or contact lenses in your carry-on luggage; sunglasses are also essential. If you have a health problem, **pack enough medication** to last the trip or have your doctor write a prescription using the drug's generic name, because brand names vary from country to country (you'll then need a prescription from a doctor in the country you're visiting). In case your bags go astray, **don't put prescription drugs or valuables in luggage to be checked.** To avoid problems with customs officials, carry medications in original packaging. Also don't forget the addresses of offices that handle refunds of lost traveler's checks.

Other useful items include a screw-top water bottle that you can fill with bottled water from your hotel room, a money pouch, a travel flashlight and extra batteries, a Swiss Army knife with an attached bottle opener, a medical kit, binoculars, and a pocket calculator to help with currency conversions. Take more film than you ever thought you would use and extra batteries for your camera. If you are traveling with children, take books and games—they're hard to find in English in South America.

ELECTRICITY

To use your U.S.-purchased electric-powered equipment, **bring a converter and an adapter.** The electrical current in Argentina, Chile, Paraguay, Peru, Uruguay, and parts of Brazil is 220 volts, 50 cycles alternating current (AC); many wall outlets in South America take Continental-type plugs, with two round prongs.

If your appliances are dual voltage, you'll need only an adapter. Hotels sometimes have 110-volt outlets for low-wattage appliances marked "For Shavers Only" near the sink; don't use them for high-wattage appliances like blow-dryers. If your laptop computer is older, carry a converter; new laptops operate equally well on 110 and 220 volts, so you need only an adapter.

LUGGAGE

Free airline baggage allowances depend on the airline, the route, and the class of your ticket; ask in advance. In general, on domestic flights and on international flights between the United States and foreign destinations, you are entitled to check two bags—neither exceeding 62 inches, or 158 centimeters (length + width + height), or weighing more than 70 pounds (32 kilograms). A third piece may be brought aboard; its total dimensions are generally limited to less than 45 inches (114 centimeters), so it will fit easily under the seat in front of you or in the overhead compartment. In the United States, the FAA gives airlines broad latitude to limit carry-on allowances

and tailor them to different aircraft and operational conditions. Charges for excess, oversize, or overweight pieces vary.

If you are flying between two foreign destinations, note that baggage allowances may be determined not by piece but by weight—generally 88 pounds (40 kilograms) in first class, 66 pounds (30 kilograms) in business class, and 44 pounds (20 kilograms) in economy. If your flight between two cities abroad *connects* with your transatlantic or transpacific flight, the piece method still applies.

SAFEGUARDING YOUR LUGGAGE➤ Before leaving home, **itemize your bags' contents** and their worth, and label them with your name, address, and phone number. (If you use your home address, cover it so that potential thieves can't see it.) Inside your bag, **pack a copy of your itinerary.** At check-in, **make sure that your bag is correctly tagged** with the airport's three-letter destination code. If your bags arrive damaged or not at all, file a written report with the airline before leaving the airport.

PASSPORTS AND VISAS

If you don't already have one, **get a passport.** While traveling, **keep one photocopy of the data page** separate from your wallet and leave another copy with someone at home. If

you lose your passport, promptly call the nearest embassy or consulate, and the local police; having the data page can speed replacement.

PASSPORTS

U.S. CITIZENS➤ All U.S. citizens, even infants, need a valid passport to enter South American countries. New and renewal application forms are available at any of the 13 U.S. Passport Agency offices and at some post offices and courthouses. Passports are usually mailed within four weeks; allow five weeks or more in spring and summer. Adult passports remain valid for 10 years from the date of issue.

CANADIAN CITIZENS➤ You need a valid passport to enter South American countries. Application forms are available at 28 regional passport offices as well as post offices and travel agencies. Whether for a first or a subsequent passport, you must apply in person. Children under 16 may be included on a parent's passport but must have their own to travel alone. Passports are valid for five years and are usually mailed within two to three weeks of application.

BRITISH CITIZENS➤ Citizens of the United Kingdom need a valid passport to enter South American countries. Applications for new and renewal passports are available from main post offices as well as at the passport offices, located in Belfast,

Glasgow, Liverpool, London, Newport, and Peterborough. You may apply in person at all passport offices, or by mail to all except the London office. Children under 16 may travel on an accompanying parent's passport. All passports are valid for 10 years. Allow a month for processing.

VISAS

Argentina. U.S., Canadian, and British citizens do not need a visa for visits of up to 90 days.

Bolivia. U.S. and British citizens need only a valid passport for stays of up to 30 days. Canadian citizens additionally require a tourist visa, available for C$20 from the Consulate of Bolivia.

Brazil. British citizens need only a valid passport, but U.S. and Canadian visitors are required to obtain a tourist visa, valid for 90 days from its date of issuance, before arriving in Brazil. Apply either in person or through the mail to the nearest Brazilian consulate or embassy in the United States or in Canada. Submit a current passport (which must be valid for at least six months beyond your departure date), a photocopy of a round-trip ticket, and a 2-by-2-inch passport photograph with your application. For U.S. visitors, there's a $10 fee when applying by proxy or by mail, no charge in person; Canadians pay C$64 in person, C$80 by proxy or by mail.

Chile. Travelers with U.S., Canadian, or British passports do not require special visas. As you approach Santiago by plane, you'll receive a tourist card valid for 90 days. Don't lose it. You will face considerable difficulties if you cannot produce your original card upon departure.

Colombia. U.S., British, and Canadian citizens need only a valid passport to enter Colombia for up to 90 days; tourist visas are not required.

Ecuador. Only a valid passport is required for U.S., British, and Canadian citizens for stays of up to 90 days.

Paraguay. Visitors who hold U.S., Canadian, and European passports do not need visas to enter Paraguay.

Peru. Visitors from the United States, Canada, and the United Kingdom require only a valid passport and return ticket to be issued a 60-day visa at their point of entry into Peru.

Uruguay. U.S. and British citizens need only a valid passport for stays of up to 90 days in Uruguay. Canadian citizens further require a tourist visa (C$37.50), available from the Consulate of Uruguay.

Venezuela. U.S., British, and Canadian citizens who fly directly to Venezuela are issued 90-day tourist visas, free of charge, immediately upon arrival. If you arrive by car or bus, you may end up paying $3–$5 at the Venezuelan border. For additional information, contact the Consulate of Venezuela.

PERSONAL SECURITY AND COMFORT

Generally, most places in South America are no more dangerous than major cities in North America or the United Kingdom. By day, urban areas and the countryside should be quite safe, although it is always wise to use common sense and follow local advice on such decisions as whether or not it is safe to walk at night and where. At all times, **keep documents, money, and credit cards hidden in a waist or leg pouch or in zip pockets.** Don't carry valuables swinging from your shoulder or hanging around your neck. Passports and tickets are best left in hotel safes, when available. Wear the simplest of timepieces and **do not wear any jewelry you are not willing to lose**—stories of travelers having chains and even earrings yanked off of them are not uncommon. Keep cameras in a secure camera bag, preferably one with a chain or wire embedded in the strap.

R

RAIL TRAVEL

In most South American countries, trains do not play an important role in the transportation system. Still, there are high points. One country to see at least in part by rail is Paraguay, where some lines are operated with steam locomotives dating from the 19th century. In Peru, take the three-hour run to Machu Picchu from Cuzco and the all-day ride from Cuzco to Puno on Lake Titicaca. In Ecuador, a worthwhile trip is the dawn-to-dusk run through the Andes down the Avenue of the Volcanoes between Quito and Riobamba. Chile has a good rail system that runs south from the capital through the Lake District; take the overnight trip from Santiago to Puerto Montt. Argentina's rail system, in the process of being sold to private industry, was built by the British. The most popular routes are all from Buenos Aires—the all-day or all-night ride to Bariloche is recommended. The latter two countries have sleeping and dining cars, the other few facilities at all.

Ticket prices are low. Usually there are two classes of travel. Plan to **buy your train tickets three days ahead,** two weeks in summer months, and **arrive at the station well before departure time.** There are no rail passes except in Argentina (whose passes are difficult to obtain in the United States), and there is no way of reserving seats before you leave home.

Renting cars is not common among South American travelers. In cities, driving is chaotic; in the countryside, the usually rough roads and language differences are discouraging; and wherever you go, the cost of renting is steep. However, many seasoned travelers like to drive in South America, and certain areas are most enjoyable when explored on your own in a car: in Venezuela, Margarita Island and the mountains Merida; in Chile, the central valley around Santiago, its nearby ski areas and the Lake District; in Brazil, the beach areas of Buzios and the Costa Verde (near Rio) and the nearby Belo Horizonte region; in Peru, Ica and the Nazca plain on the new road from Lima.

Consider hiring a car and driver through your hotel concierge, or make a deal with a taxi driver you like for some extended sightseeing at a longer-term rate. You will have to pay cash—but you'll often spend less than you would have for a rental car.

CUTTING COSTS

For South America, you can't cut costs by booking before you leave home, as you can for other destinations outside the United States. Fly-drive packages are not sold in the United States, and only a few are available in Canada. Your best bet at getting a better rate is to rent on arrival, particularly from the smaller companies. (Reserve ahead only if you plan to rent during a holiday period, when vehicles may be in short supply.)

To get the best deal, **book through a travel agent and shop around.** When pricing cars, **ask where the rental lot is located.** Some off-airport locations offer lower rates—even though their lots are only minutes away from the terminal via complimentary shuttle. You may also want to **price local car-rental companies,** whose rates may be lower still, although service and maintenance standards may not be up to those of a national firm. Also **ask your travel agent about a company's customer-service record.** How has it responded to late plane arrivals and vehicle mishaps? Are there often lines at the rental counter, and, if you're traveling during a holiday period, does a confirmed reservation guarantee you a car?

Always **find out what equipment is standard** at your destination before specifying what you want. To save money, **do without automatic transmission or air-conditioning** if they're optional—in tropical locales, however, cool air may be worth a few extra bucks.

In South America, international operations will give you more help than local firms if you have a breakdown—though you should still give the car a once-over to check the headlights, jack, and the tires (including the spare) to make sure they're in working condition.

INSURANCE

When you drive a rented car, you are generally responsible for any damage or personal injury that you cause as well as damage to the vehicle. Before you rent, **see what coverage you already have** by means of your personal auto-insurance policy and credit cards. For about $14 a day, rental companies sell insurance, known as a collision damage waiver (CDW), that eliminates your liability for damage to the car; it's always optional and should never be automatically added to your bill.

REQUIREMENTS

In South America your own driver's license is acceptable. An International Driver's Permit, available from the American or Canadian Automobile Association, is a good idea. Minimum driving ages vary from country to country.

SURCHARGES

Before picking up the car in one city and leaving it in another, **ask about drop-off charges or one-way service fees,** which can be substantial. Because of the distances involved in South America, one-way rentals are pricey and not available between countries (except between Chile and Argentina). Note, too, that some rental agencies charge extra if you return the car before the time specified on your contract. To avoid a hefty refueling fee, **fill the tank just before you turn in the car.**

S

SENIOR-CITIZEN DISCOUNTS

Because South America is so interesting and varied, there is no reason that active, well-traveled senior citizens should not visit, whether on an independent (but prebooked) vacation, an escorted tour, or an adventure vacation. Before you leave home, however, determine what medical services your health insurance will cover outside the United States; note that Medicare does not provide for payment of hospital and medical services outside the United States. If you need additional travel insurance, buy it (*see above*).

The continent is full of good hotels and competent ground operators who will meet your flights and organize your sightseeing. To qualify for age-related discounts, **mention your senior-citizen status up front** when booking hotel reservations, not when checking out, and before you're seated in restaurants, not when paying your bill. Note that discounts may be limited to certain menus, days, or hours. When renting a car, **ask about promotional car-rental discounts**—they can net lower costs than your senior-citizen discount.

STUDENTS ON THE ROAD

To save money, **look into deals available through student-oriented travel agencies.** To qualify, you'll need to have a student ID card. Members of international student groups also are eligible. *See* Students *in* Important Contacts A to Z, *above.*

T

TELEPHONES

LONG DISTANCE

The long-distance services of AT&T, MCI, and Sprint make calling home relatively convenient and let you avoid hotel surcharges. Local access codes are listed under Telephones in the Essentials section of each country chapter.

W

WHEN TO GO

There is no single best time to go. Two factors should guide your travel planning: the climate in a particular country and an event or activity that interests you.

CLIMATE

Because of the great variety of latitudes, altitudes, and climatic zones on the continent, you will encounter many different kinds of weather in any given month. The highland areas of the Andes Mountains—which run north to south down the west coast of South America from Colombia through Ecuador, Peru, Bolivia, and Argentina—are at their most accessible and most comfortable in the dry season, May–October. July–September is the time to ski in Chile and Argentina or to cruise south to Antarctica.

An entirely different climate reigns in the Amazon Basin, whose tropical and subtropical rain forests spread in a broad west–east band from the headwaters in Ecuador and Peru across the northern third of Brazil. May–September, the Andes' dry season, is the nonrainy season here—that is, it's simply less rainy than at any other time. Contrary to what you may expect, you may prefer the rainy season for an Amazon River trip; the waters are higher then, and boats can venture farther upriver into the tributaries.

Certain ocean regions—the Atlantic coast from Brazil all the way down to the famous resort of Punta del Este in Uruguay, as well as the Caribbean shore of Venezuela—are at their hottest and most crowded during North America's winter, December–March. The sea moderates temperatures in most of South America's cities year-round, even as far south as Buenos Aires. The Pacific coast is bordered mostly by a strip of desert, whose climate is always hospitable. Southern Chile is fjord country, perfect for cruising from November through April.

Weather-wise, May is probably the best month to visit South America. From then through June you can expect both good weather and off-season prices. These months, as well as September and October, are also relatively uncrowded.

THE GOLD GUIDE / SMART TRAVEL TIPS

1 Destination: South America

REDISCOVERING SOUTH AMERICA

NEARLY 500 YEARS AFTER Columbus stumbled across South America, tourists from the north are finally exploring the diverse delights of their neighboring continent. Once considered too far away for shorter trips (indeed, Moscow is closer to New York than Buenos Aires), the jet age has brought South America's bustling cities and dramatic landscapes within easy reach. Increasing numbers of restless vacationers are now exchanging commuter trains, computer screens, and drab high-rise offices for the fascinating contrasts that await them the moment they arrive in South America.

In many cosmopolitan cities, smartly dressed socialites brush shoulders with women clad in traditional costumes that have changed little since the Spanish Conquest. Centuries-old colonial churches with dazzling Baroque facades stand in the shadow of sleek skyscrapers. In rural areas, shiny new Volvos and BMWs share dusty streets with lumbering oxcarts and men on horseback. Dry gives way to wet as the rainy season begins suddenly, and cold becomes hot within minutes of leaving the highlands for a coastal destination.

Such diversity means that there is, literally, something, somewhere, for everyone, on any budget, to see and do in South America. Indeed, any number of appetites can be satisfied on the same vacation. History buffs, for example, can spend the afternoon touring the summer palace of Brazilian Emperor Dom Pedro II in the mountains just north of Rio after a splendid morning of sunbathing on the beach at Ipanema. Admirers of superb horsemanship, on the other hand, might choose to pass the day at one of Buenos Aires's year-round racetracks, followed by an excellent Argentine wine at dinner and a night of tango in La Boca, the city's picturesque waterfront district.

For everyone from bird-watchers to beach bums, South America is the perfect destination, but often those who enjoy it the most do not fit into any category. They are the dreamers, the escapists, the lovers of the unusual, the ones who go with great expectations and few prejudices.

A Short History: From Pizarro to Pinochet

CHRISTOPHER COLUMBUS did not actually set foot on the continent until his third voyage in 1498, when he reached the mouth of the Orinoco River in what is now Venezuela. Both Spain and Portugal were eager to develop overseas empires at that time, so it did not take long for them to send others to explore and colonize this new territory. In 1531, Francisco Pizarro sailed south from Panama with some 180 men and 27 horses. He landed in Peru, and by 1533 he had conquered the entire Inca empire, doing in South America what Cortés had done more easily in Mexico. One of Pizarro's officers, Pedro de Valdivia, conquered northern Chile and founded Santiago in 1541, giving Spain control of the west coast of the continent from Panama to central Chile.

The Portuguese, meanwhile, were busy on the east coast laying claim to Brazil. Unlike the situation in the rest of South America, however, the colonization of Brazil was gradual and relatively peaceful. While Spanish conquistadors were seeking the gold of legendary El Dorado, wood was the first natural resource exploited by the Portuguese. Then came sugar, which gave rise to vast plantations along the coast—and to the importation of millions of African slaves to do the backbreaking labor. Afterward came gold and diamonds, opening up the first land in the interior. Coffee followed, and with it the appearance of planters on the red earth of southeastern Brazil.

Many Spaniards and Portuguese came to South America intending to make a quick fortune and return to Europe as soon as possible. Their expeditions, however, often included farmers and craftsmen who wished to begin life anew in the Americas. What these settlers encountered instead was an oppressive feudal system that evolved apace with such glittering colonial cities as Lima, Quito, and Ouro Prêto. For three centuries South American colonists labored under European rule, but between 1808 and 1823 the New World empires built by Spain and Portugal began to crumble—often due to political and economic factors similar to those that had precipitated the revolution in Britain's 13 North American colonies.

Although each country had its own revolutionary heroes, two men stand out as leaders in South America's struggle for independence. The first is Venezuelan general Simón Bolívar, a man of tremendous vision, whose courageous battles freed Bolivia, Colombia, Ecuador, Peru, and Venezuela. The second is José de San Martín, the Argentine general who helped win independence for Chile and Peru. Brazil won its independence from Portugal in 1822 without bloodshed and changed from colony to monarchy to republic fairly easily.

Inspired by the American and French revolutions, eager patriots in the Southern Hemisphere established republican forms of government. Unfortunately, as much as they may have been ready for independence in theory, in practice the newly sovereign nations had little preparation for self-government. Most of the early republics lacked the broad popular base necessary to enforce their fragile constitutions. A disheartening number of civil wars, coups d'état, and upheavals have shaken South America's nations since they gained independence. Down through the centuries since Pizarro, the real power in the Southern Hemisphere has always been vested in its charismatic leaders, rather than in well-intentioned but weak legislatures. Things do change, however, and recent elections have brought democratic rule (albeit fragile in some cases) to the entire region.

WHAT'S WHERE

The profusion of countries and cities might make selecting one destination—or even two or three—seem impossible. The truth is, however, that the Andes split the continent rather conveniently into two very distinct regions, so making sense of the whole thing is only half as hard. (There are actually three ranges of mountains that make up the great, jagged spine of South America, varying between 200 and 400 miles in width and averaging some 13,000 feet in height.)

No other part of the world can compare with the spectacular landscape west of this monumental chain of mountains. Here, nature is at its finest, from the highlands of Ecuador, Peru, and Bolivia to the headwaters of the mighty Amazon to the gemlike lakes of southern Chile. As if inspired by all the splendor, human artists, too, left marvelous pre-Columbian and colonial treasures for fascinated tourists to behold. But the larger part of the continent lies east of the Andes, and its marvels are no less alluring. Some of the world's largest and most exciting cities are found here—Rio de Janeiro, São Paulo, and Buenos Aires—along with incomparable natural wonders.

Argentina

Romantic notions of handsome gauchos and seductive tango dancers have given Argentina a mystique, but these images tell only half the story. Walk along Buenos Aires's classy Calle Florida, sit down to tea in an elegant *confitería,* or attend an opera at the world famous Teatro Colón, and you'll soon see that Porteños, as residents of Buenos Aires are called, are as educated, sophisticated, and urbane as anyone on earth. Their cosmopolitan city never sleeps—or so it seems. Dinner is often eaten at midnight, and the streets are still full of people when you leave the restaurant at 2 AM. Some 45 theaters, 200 movie houses, 150 parks, and an untold number of museums and galleries provide pastimes for a population in perpetual motion.

Away from the capital city's constant commotion, the pace is slower, the people more open, and the culture easier to appreciate. This is the continent's second-largest country, and the scenery—

ranging from the snowy heights of the Andes in the west to the flat grassy pampas along the Atlantic coast—is spectacular. Don't leave Argentina without visiting Patagonia, where you'll find the lake resort of Bariloche and the Península Valdés, where thousands of enormous seals bask on pebbled beaches. North of Buenos Aires are the stunning Iguazú Falls—in all, some 300 separate waterfalls that thunder over a 2½-mile-wide precipice on the border of Brazil, Argentina, and Paraguay. Myriad rainbows large and small dance in clouds of mist, and thousands of glittering, jewel-tone butterflies chase one another about like playful puppies, alighting affectionately on passersby.

Bolivia

Visitors are often giddy upon arrival in La Paz, perhaps with relief at having landed safely at the world's highest commercial airport, which is perched just above the world's highest capital city. (More likely it's due to *soroche,* a dizziness caused by the lack of oxygen at 13,000 feet; a pleasant coca-leaf tea or a tiny pill purchased at any pharmacy usually banishes the sensation.) Even after you are steady on your feet, Bolivia has tangible otherworldliness that deepens its appeal.

Not to be missed are the ruins of Tiahuanaco (Tiwanacu), a 50-mile ride from La Paz across the barren yet amazingly beautiful altiplano, the high plateau more than 600 miles long and 60 miles wide between two ranges of the Andes. Although the ruins are shrouded in mystery, some researchers believe Tiahuanaco was the cradle of American man some 7,000 years ago. As if to make up for having no access to the Pacific, Bolivia boasts Lake Titicaca, the highest navigable lake in the world. Upon this huge inland sea—100 miles long and as much as 50 miles wide—modern speedboats dart by traditional gondola-shape boats made of *totora* reeds. Crossing the deep-blue lake on a whirring hydrofoil is certainly an unforgettable way to reach the shores of neighboring Peru.

Brazil

Bigger than the continental United States, Portuguese-speaking Brazil is the fifth-largest country in the world and has an oversized vitality and sensuality to match. Although the nation's raw energy may not be visible to the naked eye, its effects can be seen everywhere—in highways, dams, industrial complexes, and even in the capital city of Brasília, which was constructed from scratch in the wilderness in an effort to promote development of the nation's vast interior.

To most North Americans, however, Brazil is Rio de Janeiro, famous for its spectacular bay-side setting, fabulous beaches, skimpy string bikinis, and riotous Carnival celebration. But Brazil goes far beyond its beaches and hedonistic pleasures. It is a fast-pace world of skyscrapers, stock markets, and agribusiness carried out in megalopolises like São Paulo and Belo Horizonte. Baroque art beautifies the colonial cities of the state of Minas Gerais. A unique Afro-Brazilian culture thrives in the tropical environs of Salvador, capital of the state of Bahia. And there is the amazing Amazon, the name given to both the legendary 4,000-mile-long river and the 750,000,000-acre expanse of trackless jungle, menacing wildlife, and merciless heat through which the river flows. Nowhere is that picture more accurate than in Manaus, a river city of some 1 million inhabitants that sprang up 1,200 miles from the Atlantic during the rubber boom of the 19th century. The city pulsates again today with commercial activity, and serves as a convenient point of departure for trips into the backwaters of Amazonia.

Chile

Chile, like Argentina, immediately strikes the visitor as very cosmopolitan. This 2,650-mile-long ribbon of a country averages only 110 miles in width. From north to south it cuts across five distinct ranges of soil and climate, producing a variety of exceptional scenic attractions. In the arid north is the Atacama Desert, so dry that in some areas no rain has ever been recorded. Next come the copper mines and rich nitrate deposits, followed by the fertile central valley where Santiago, the capital city, is located. The beautiful lake and forest region is below that, with outstanding fishing and skiing. Finally, in the extreme south lies cold, forbidding, windswept Tierra del Fuego.

Known for its award-winning wines and excellent seafood, Chile is also justly famous for the resort city of Viña del Mar, with its wide, white, sandy beaches and year-round casino overlooking the Pacific Ocean. Jet-set skiers from the United States and Europe often prefer the championship slopes at Portillo and Valle Nevado, outside Santiago, and Las Lenas, in Argentina, where they can schuss during summer months when snows melt in the Northern Hemisphere. Huge, mysterious *moai* statues await tourists looking for a different type of adventure on Chile's Easter Island, the world's most remote inhabited isle.

Colombia

Sometimes called "the corner of South America," Colombia is the only South American country to have beaches on both Pacific and Caribbean coasts. As in Ecuador, Colombia's major cities are at different altitudes, creating very different customs and ways of life. In Bogotá, the capital, at 8,700 feet, there is a formality reminiscent of Spain—not just in the conduct of business and social amenities but also in the Spanish that is spoken, which is said to be the purest in all of Latin America. The atmosphere grows progressively more relaxed and informal, however, as one descends 2,000 feet to Medellín, known as "the orchid capital of the world," and another 1,500 feet to Cali, the heart of the coffee country, and then finally to Cartagena at sea level, where there is a strong Afro-Caribbean influence shared with neighboring Venezuela. The music, cuisine, costumes, dialects, and attitudes reflect each region, creating a true potpourri that is much of the charm of Colombia.

Ecuador

A patchwork of highland and jungle, this tiny nation claims many of the hemisphere's most impressive volcanoes. A living quilt of terraced plots in a thousand shades of green covers the lower slopes of the cloud-capped peaks, where corn grows twice as tall as the sturdy peasant farmers who till the fertile soil. Quito, the nation's capital, lies at the foot of mighty Mt. Pichincha. The city has some of the best examples of Spanish colonial architecture found anywhere in South America, with the winding cobblestone streets, red-tile roofs, and ornately decorated churches typical of many towns in Spain. Just 15 miles outside the city, visitors enjoy having their picture taken as they straddle the equator at a monument indicating the dividing line between the Northern and Southern hemispheres.

Ecuador's exquisite handicrafts rival its natural beauty, and they are found in wondrous profusion in towns throughout the highlands. Cuenca, a beautifully preserved colonial city, offers both architectural charm and one of the country's best markets. The coastal region and its bustling port city of Guayaquil also have much to offer, and the most memorable way to get there from Quito is by rail. When in operation, the train maneuvers—on narrow-gauge tracks—up and down mountain passes via a series of switchbacks to the steamy lowlands. Guayaquil also serves as a departure point for planes and ships to the enchanting Galápagos Islands, home of the remarkable wildlife that sparked Darwin's theories of evolution.

Paraguay

Visitors to this largely undiscovered and unspoiled land enter a world where time and tradition have stood still for generations. Although this means that Paraguay may be short on extravagant facilities, it is long on the charm and authenticity missing in many other parts of South America.

Some would say Asuncíon is a provincial capital, and its pleasures are indeed simple ones—a stroll through the Botanical Gardens, a leisurely lunch at an outdoor café, or an afternoon of shopping for *ñandutí*, the country's uniquely beautiful and intricate spiderweb lace. The real Paraguay, however, is found in the countryside, where motorcycles and portable radios are just now starting to compete with oxcarts and traditional *polca* music in the hearts and minds of the rural people. The country's original inhabitants were the Guaraní, and high rates of intermarriage between European settlers and the indigenous peoples have led to a degree of cultural blending unknown elsewhere. Mission ruins near Encarnacíon are another impressive reminder of the Guaraní legacy. It was here that Jesuit priests converted the native population and organized a unique communal society. Several of the lovely missions, abandoned when the Jesuits were expelled in 1767, are currently being restored under the auspices of international organizations.

Peru

Nowhere else in South America is there such a wealth of history. Cuzco, once the capital of the Inca empire, is Peru's leading tourist attraction and one of the most interesting cities in the hemisphere. Although the Spaniards tried to superimpose their culture on the conquered Inca, they succeeded only in penetrating the surface. Symbolically, when the 1950 earthquake struck, it felled much of the Monastery of Santo Domingo, which had been built over the ruins of the sacred Temple of the Sun. The inner Inca walls that were revealed withstood the devastating quake.

The three-hour trip by rail from Cuzco to Machu Picchu, while exhilarating, does little to prepare you for the marvels of this fantastic hideaway. Thought by many to have been the last refuge of the Incas, it was never discovered by the Spaniards. The maze of temples, houses, terraces, and stairways lay abandoned in lofty solitude until Hiram Bingham, later a U.S. senator, stumbled upon the forgotten city in 1911. Today, along with Iguazú Falls, Machu Picchu is considered by many to be one of South America's greatest wonder's.

If the gems of Peru's Inca past are locked away on the altiplano, then its capital, Lima, is the safekeeper of its colonial treasures. Perhaps no other city in the Americas enjoyed such power and prestige during the height of the colonial era. For an entirely different side of Peru, you should also visit Iquitos, where the sounds of the Amazon jungle are ever present. Once a difficult place to visit, efficient air service has now made this region as accessible as the highlands.

Uruguay

Gently rolling hills and grasslands are the hallmarks of Uruguay, one of the smallest countries in South America. Ninety percent of the land is used for grazing, and Uruguayans are justifiably proud of their fine beef cattle. A visit to an *estancia*, one of the country's giant ranches, is an excellent way to experience both the scenery and people—well-educated yet unpretentious, industrious yet relaxed, they are the most remarkable aspect of Uruguay for many travelers. Another culture exists along the coasts. The country's beaches are among the best in the southern part of South America; without even leaving Montevideo, Uruguay's gracious capital, visitors can sample more than a half a dozen. Surely the most fashionable beach, however, is 85 miles to the east at Punta del Este, a haven for well-heeled vacationers from many foreign countries, especially nearby Argentina. Often called the Riviera of South America, this famous resort is also a popular site for international conferences and movie festivals.

Venezuela

Just a few hours from the east coast of the United States, the sophisticated metropolis of Caracas sprawls east–west along a narrow 9-mile valley, reminding many of Los Angeles. Like that city, it has horrible traffic jams as well as world-class art galleries, hotels, restaurants, and nightlife. Drawn by Caracas's high standard of living, waves of immigrants from other Latin American countries (as well as Venezuela's own rural poor) make the city more cosmopolitan every day.

But there are many attractions outside the city for those who prefer more peaceful pleasures. Mérida, for instance, in the snowcapped Andes to the west, is a picturesque colonial city of tiled roofs that also boasts the world's highest and longest cable car ride. In four stages, the *teleférico* rises to the summit of nearby Pico Espejo, a spectacular one-hour ascent. For those who fancy sunbathing, picture-postcard beaches stretch along the 1,730-mile coastal ribbon from Maracaibo to Cumaná. Margarita Island, just offshore in the Caribbean, has the added attraction of free-port shopping. The Gran Sabana, a tropical highland in Bolívar State, draws many visitors as well. It is here that Angel Falls drops 3,212 feet down the face of Auyán-tepuí Mountain, making it the world's highest waterfall. Camping trips upriver to the foot of the falls from the town of Canaima are very popular with adventuresome tourists.

PLEASURES AND PASTIMES

Archaeology

The mysteries of ancient ruins such as the silent, windswept stones and temples at Tiahuanaco, near La Paz in Bolivia, and majestic remains of Inca civilizations never fail to tantalize amateur and professional archaeologists alike. Peru alone has a wealth of pre-Columbian sites that would take weeks, if not months or years, to fully explore. Almost everything in the country is worth seeing, but the especially exceptional sights include Machu Picchu, Tipóm's agricultural terracing, the fortresses of Pisac and Ollantaytambo, and the Coricancha. If you have more time, visit the Nazca lines, gigantic, mysterious "drawings" in the desert; the Chimú city of Chán Chán, outside Trujillo; and the Moche tomb of the warrior priest at Sipán. In Colombia, you can visit la Ciudad Perdida (The Lost City), near Cartagena on the Caribbean Coast, and the mammoth, mysterious megaliths of San Agustín, near Cali. In Ecuador, there are Inca and pre-Inca ruins at Ingapirca, two hours beyond Cuenca.

Dining: The Flavors of South America

Culinary partisans may argue over whether exotic Afro-Brazilian concoctions, delicious Peruvian and Chilean seafood dishes, or sinfully succulent Argentine and Uruguayan meats should claim the title of South American's most delicious regional foods, but for most visitors the entire continent is a diner's delight.

ARGENTINA➤ To sample the best of Argentina's famed meats, try a mixed grill of blood sausage, short ribs, and internal and external organs at an *asado* or have a tender, 3-inch-thick steak grilled over charcoal at a *parrilla*. Favorite snacks include a *Milanesa*, a breaded meat or chicken cutlet, and empanadas, savories of pastry filled with cheese, corn, or meat. *Dulce de leche*, a thick, caramel-color cream of boiled-down milk with sugar and vanilla, is used as a topping or filling.

BOLIVIA➤ Try *timpu*, an Andean lamb stew, or a *salteña*, a slightly sweet pastry filled with eggs, olives, and chopped meat.

Chicha is a drink made from corn mash that's chewed, spat out, and left to ferment.

BRAZIL➤ *Feijoada* is the national dish, a mélange of stewed pork served over white rice, with collard greens, orange slices, and fried manioc on the side. In Minas Gerais, try *frango ao molho pardo*, broiled chicken served in a sauce of its own blood; for dessert, have the romantically named *Romeu e Julieta*, a slice of fresh Minas cheese spread with guava jelly. Noteworthy Bahian specialties include *muqueca* (the seafood catch of the day cooked in a clay pot with coconut milk, lemon, palm oil, dried shrimp, chili, tomato, and spices) and *acarajé* (a spicy deep-fried bean cake filled with crunchy dried shrimp, red pepper, and vinaigrette sauce); wash them down with chilled, refreshing *água de coco* (coconut milk). For a beverage with more kick, try *caipirinha*, a drink made with *cachaça* (sugarcane liquor), lime, and sugar.

CHILE➤ *Mariscal* (raw shellfish soup) and *machas* (razor clams) *à la parmesana* show Chile's famous seafood to good advantage, but *gazuela* (a hearty vegetable soup with a piece of meat or poultry) and *humitas* (ground corn seasoned and steamed in its own husk) are equally tasty. For dessert, try *vaina*, sweet sherry whipped with egg white and topped with a dash of cinnamon. Chile's wines are getting international attention; try a cabernet sauvignon from the Maipo Valley or a chardonnay from the Casablanca Valley.

COLOMBIA➤ In Bogotá, sample *ajiaco*, a stew made from three types of potato, chicken, corn, fresh cream, and avocado. *Sancocho de sábalo* (grilled fish with coconut milk, potatoes, plantains, and yucca) is a Caribbean coast specialty.

ECUADOR➤ Delicious Ecuadoran treats include *llapingachos*, mashed cheese and potato pancakes, from the Andes, and *humitas*, corn tamales usually washed down with black coffee.

PARAGUAY➤ Smoked *suribí*, a fish resembling a catfish, and grilled *dorado*, a salmonlike fish are among the tastiest of Paraguay's freshwater catches.

PERU➤ Peru's most famous dish is *cebiche*, raw fish (usually sea bass or flounder) served in a marinade of lime juice, chili, and garlic. Grilled *paiche* and other Amazon River fish, served with *chonta*, a spaghetti-shape vegetable from the tree-tops, is another taste sensation. The national drink is the pisco sour, made of lemon, egg white, sugar, crushed ice, and a liquor similar to tequila.

VENEZUELA➤ If you visit around Christmas, try *hallaca,* a holiday specialty made of chicken, corn, olives, and pork wrapped in banana leaves.

Festivals

Whatever the weather, it is fun to be in many countries—particularly Brazil and the Caribbean countries—during **Carnival,** the week before Ash Wednesday, which usually falls in February. In strongly Catholic South America, dozens of **saints days** are marked by processions and other festivities; **Holy Week,** the week of Easter, and **Corpus Christi,** eight Sundays later, are particularly important. In the Andean countries, the time between harvest and the next planting—that is, from June to November—sees many of the best **folkloric festivals,** usually village events. *See* Festivals and Seasonal Events, *below,* for more information on specific festivals of note.

Dates vary from year to year and can be difficult to obtain, so your best bet for catching one of these interesting events is to ask a tour specialist what's being held while you'll be visiting. (*Also see* National Holidays, *under* Opening and Closing Times *in* each country's Essentials section, for dates.) When planning your trip, keep in mind that airline and hotel reservations are more difficult to get during South America's high seasons, particularly around Easter, Christmas, and July school breaks.

Music

Pleasures abound for music lovers, whether they prefer a saucy samba in São Paulo, a lively *cumbia* in Bogotá, or the melancholy sound of Andean panpipes in Quito and La Paz.

Natural Wonders

Lovers of the outdoors will find some of Mother Nature's most splendid works in the continent's diverse topography and myriad climates. Volcanoes, some still active, run the length of the Andes; at their feet lie everything from the desolate, windswept desert and dunes of Peru's Paracas National Reserve to the turquoise lakes and burbling hot springs of Chile's Lake District.

The 30,000-year-old Perito Moreno Glacier broods in Argentina's Glacier National Park, while towering spires of ice slide off the San Rafael Glacier, south of Puerto Montt in Chile. A mighty roar fills the air as the raging waters of Iguazú Falls—higher and wider than Niagara—plunge over basalt cliffs where Argentina, Paraguay, and Brazil come together. Angel Falls, the world's highest waterfall, plummets nearly two-thirds of a mile down a cliff in a corner of Venezuela so remote that it was unknown to the world until 1937. From January to May, the Amazon Delta north of the Brazilian city of Macapá is the site of the spectacular *pororoca*—a violent convergence of the flooding Araguari River and the inward tide of the Atlantic that tosses up 15-foot waves and fills the air with a profound thundering sound. Farther upstream, near Manaus, the black waters of the Rio Negro and brown waters of the Rio Solimões flow side by side for more than 10 miles before swirling together to become the Amazon.

Photography

Few vacation spots provide better subjects for photographers (or other artists, for that matter), whether they specialize in landscapes, cityscapes, wildlife, or people. It is hard to imagine colors more brilliant, light more intense, or textures more complex than those that meet the eye at every glance. The perfectly shaped cones of Ecuador's volcanoes, the colonial splendor of Lima's churches, the riot of fishing skiffs plying Reloncavi Sound in southern Chile, and the masterpieces of modern architecture in Brasília all beg to be captured on film or canvas. Only that way will friends back home ever believe skies could be so blue, clouds so white, or mountains so majestic.

Shopping

Savvy shoppers can spend all day at chic boutiques brimming with good buys in Brazilian gemstones, Argentine leather, or Uruguayan furs. At the same time, handicraft lovers will marvel at the Paraguayan lace, Peruvian textiles, or fine Panama hats (from Ecuador, no less) sold in bustling *mercados,* the New World's answer to the chaotic bazaar. *See* Fodor's Choice, *below,* for our picks of the best markets and crafts in each country.

Sports and Beaches

The thrills of white-water rafting in the jungles of Peru, deep-sea fishing off the coast of Venezuela, and downhill skiing in the Argentine and Chilean Andes lure sports enthusiasts grown tired of Aspen and Vail, while the pristine mountain fastness of the Chilean lake district beckons to hikers and mountain climbers. Sun worshipers, those most dedicated of hedonists, can mingle with some of the world's most beautiful people on glittering beaches in posh Punta del Este, Viña del Mar, or Margarita Island. *See* Chapter 2, Adventure and Learning Vacations, for more information on sports vacations; *also see* How to Have an Adventure *in* Fodor's Choice, *below,* for our picks of the best adventure trips.

Wildlife

Nowhere in the world is there such a diversity of species and environments as in South America. Come nose to nose with sea lions and giant tortoises in the Galápagos Islands. Spot the pterodactyl-like hoatzin in Ecuador's Amazon jungle canopy. In Argentina, see whales and elephant seals frolic at Península Valdés and attend the annual gathering of the Magellanic penguin clan on the beaches at Punta Tombo. From September to March, giant sea turtles emerge from the ocean at night to lay their eggs on the beach at Brazil's Praia do Forte. Flamingos, llama-like guanacos, and foxes inhabit Chile's Torres del Paine National Park.

FODOR'S CHOICE

Where to Stay

Argentina

★ **Alvear Palace Hotel, Buenos Aires.** Conceived as a luxury apartment building in 1932, this hotel in the fashionable Recoleta district is close to the museums and good restaurants. $$$$

★ **Internacional Cataratas de Iguazú, Iguazú National Park.** Guests at this five-star hotel can have breakfast or a drink on spacious balconies that overlook the stunning falls, which are also directly visible from half the rooms. $$$–$$$$

Bolivia

★ **Hotel Real Audiencia, Sucre.** Set in a converted colonial mansion, the Real Audiencia combines period looks with modern fixtures and amenities. $$$

★ **Residential Rosario, La Paz.** A popular option with budget-conscious tourists, the Rosario has all the hallmarks of a devoted traveler's hotel. $

Brazil

★ **Quinta Pitanga, Salvador.** This country inn on the island of Itaparica is a favorite among filmmakers, jet-setters, and others who wish to escape from the "real" world. $$$$

★ **Sheraton Rio Hotel & Towers, Rio de Janeiro.** Built so that it dominates Vidigal Beach, between Ipanema and São Conrado, this is the only hotel in Rio that is directly on the beach. $$$$

★ **Tropical, Manaus.** The only major resort in the Amazon has verdant gardens all around and a privileged location overlooking the Rio Negro. $$$$

★ **Grande Hotel Ca D'Oro, São Paulo.** This Old World–style hotel near downtown boasts bar-side fireplaces, lots of wood and Persian rugs, classic European room decor, ultrapersonalized service, and one of the city's best restaurants. $$$

★ **Solar da Ponte, Tiradentes.** Long included among Brazil's finest small hotels, the Solar has the spirit of a house in the country, complete with sprawling lawns and gardens. $$$

★ **Ouro Verde, Rio de Janeiro.** One of only a handful of Rio hotels aimed at the "discriminating traveler," the Ouro Verde is famed for its efficient, personalized service. $$

★ **Taperapuan Praia Hotel, Porto Seguro.** This establishment's two-story thatched bungalows outside of town are perfect for families. $$

Chile

★ **Hotel Kennedy, Santiago.** Small details, such as telephones in all the bathrooms and excellent business services, show the care that has gone into providing amenities at this glass tower hotel. $$$$

★ **Hotel Salzburg, Frutillar.** All of the Salzburg's traditionally designed wooden cabins command excellent views of the lake; the staff can organize fishing trips, and the restaurant offers some of the best smoked salmon in the Lake District. *$$*

Colombia

★ **Caribe, Cartagena.** The oldest hotel on the Bocagrande Peninsula retains its relaxed, colonial mood; giant rubber trees shade the large pool, and only a narrow lane separates the property from the beach. *$$*

★ **Las Terrazas, Bogotá.** There's an almost rustic charm about this small hotel, which is built into a hillside overlooking the city—a location that guarantees that the scrupulously clean rooms have good views of downtown. *$$*

Ecuador

★ **Hotel Sebastián, Quito.** This attractive, modern, eight-story hotel is ideally situated in the busy Mariscal district, near shops and restaurants. *$$$*

★ **Hacienda Cusín, Lago San Pablo, Imbabura Province.** Built in 1602, this quiet hacienda—draped in a thick carpet of flowers and foliage—is a working farm as well as an inn. *$$*

★ **Hotel La Casona, Quito.** The most charming hotel in Quito's Old City is a lovely, restored, colonial-style house near the Sucre Theater. *$*

Paraguay

★ **Hotel Casino Yacht y Golf Club Paraguayo, Asunción.** One of South America's finest hotels, this resort is set on a riverbank in a 200-acre development; recreational options include water sports, fishing, golf, tennis, and squash. *$$$$*

★ **Centu Cué, Villa Florida.** A group of bungalows scattered along the bank of the Tebicuary River comprise this isolated lodge, an ideal spot from which to fish in one of South America's most beautiful rivers. *$$*

Peru

★ **Machu Picchu Pueblo Hotel, Aguas Calientes.** In this semitropical garden paradise, the stone bungalows have cathedral ceilings, exposed beams, flagstone floors, and cartwheel headboards, creating an atmosphere of rustic elegance. *$$$$*

★ **Hotel El Olívar, Lima.** Amid the greenery of San Isidro's olive grove, this new hotel has a glistening lobby full of plants and deep-green tile floors. *$$$*

★ **Hotel Mossone, Ica.** Set in a century-old mansion, the Mossone has an interior garden patio and dining on a veranda that overlooks the Huacachina lagoon. *$$$*

★ **Hotel Alhambra III, Sacred Valley of the Incas.** The colonial-style guest rooms at this 300-year-old former convent have balconies that overlook the gardens or the terraced hillsides. *$$*

★ **Hostal Miramar Ischia, Lima.** Set on a quiet street on a cliff above the ocean, this discreet hotel offers stunning views, floors of Spanish tile and parquet, and meals cooked by the Italian-Peruvian owners. *$$*

Uruguay

★ **Hostería del Lago, Montevideo.** This white-stucco, Spanish-colonial hotel has a relaxed atmosphere, a private lakefront beach, and a friendly multilingual staff. *$$$$*

★ **La Posta del Cangrejo, Punta del Este.** Mediterranean styling and an informal approach to luxury complement the impeccably decorated guest rooms here; the staff is warm, accommodating, and justifiably proud of their hotel. *$$$$*

Venezuela

★ **Eurobuilding, Caracas.** Business travelers are especially fond of this luxurious high-rise hotel, where glass-enclosed elevators run from the lobby, the site of numerous concerts and nightlife activities, to spacious rooms with good views of Mt. Avila. *$$$$*

★ **Festival Flamingo Beach Hotel, Margarita Island.** The stylish rooms at this first-class, six-story complex just north of the beach have views of the sea and, in many instances, the island itself. *$$$*

★ **Hotel Los Bordones, Cumaná.** This modern four-star hotel, Cumaná's best address, has a vast swimming pool and—best of all—a nearly secluded beach just a pebble's throw away. *$$$*

★ **Savoy, Caracas.** At this Sabana Grande budget hotel, service and style are not sacrificed. *$*

Museums and Works of Art

Bolivia

★ The Museo National del Arte in La Paz.

★ Sucre's Museo Antropológico Charcas.

★ Pre-Columbian gold and silver masks at the Museo Pedro Domingo in La Paz.

Brazil

★ *Balangandás*, oversize chains of silver tropical fruits once worn around the waist by slave women, at Museu Carlos Costa Pinto in Salvador.

★ Candomblé deity costumes and Hector Carybé's inlaid wooden panels in the Museu Afro-Brasileiro in Salvador.

★ Aleijadinho's life-size soapstone sculptures of the Old Testament prophets in Bom Jesus do Matosinho church, Congonhas do Campo, Minas Gerais.

★ Corcovado Mountain's 100-foot-tall statue of Cristo Redentor, with outstretched arms embracing Rio de Janeiro.

Chile

★ The huge carved-stone heads known as maoi, some more than 60 feet tall, scattered across Easter Island.

★ Santiago's Pre-Columbian Museum, for extraordinary artwork by Latin America's indigenous peoples.

Colombia

★ The gem-encrusted Tulua and Lechuga processional crosses at the Museo de Arte Religioso in Bogotá.

★ Bogotá's phenomenal Museo de Oro, with the world's largest collection of pre-Columbian gold artifacts.

Ecuador

★ The magnificently sculpted facade of La Compañía de Jesús church in Quito.

Paraguay

★ The carved-wood statue of St. Paul, with Indian faces at his feet, in the Museo de San Ignacio in San Ignacio.

Peru

★ Inca ceramics and mummies in the Museo de Historia Regional and the Pulpit of San Blas, both in Cuzco.

★ Chancay woven goods in the Museo Amano in Lima.

★ Chavín obelisks and Paracas weavings in the Museo Nacional de Antropología y Arqueología in Lima.

★ Gold treasures and the yellow-feather poncho in the Museo de Oro in Lima.

★ The *Venus de Frías* at the Brüning Museum in Lambayeque.

★ Paracas weavings and Nazca ceramic sculptures in the Museo Regional in Ica.

Uruguay

★ Montevideo's Museo del Gaucho y la Moneda, with displays on coins and on gaucho life.

Venezuela

★ Museo de Bellas Artes in Caracas.

★ The gilded baroque altar of Caracas's Catedral Metropolitano.

Great Markets and Crafts

Argentina

★ The San Telmo district in Buenos Aires hosts a fabulous Sunday flea market.

Bolivia

★ On Calle Sagarnaga, a thousand voices clamor for everything from llama fetuses to coca leaves to colorful alpaca sweaters.

Brazil

★ Belem's daily Ver-o-Peso market is stocked with everything from Amazon fish and good-luck charms to aphrodisiacs and medicinal roots and herbs.

★ Salvador's daily Mercado Modelo crafts market peddles local foodstuffs, lace, fossils, gemstones, African-print clothing, and regional musical instruments.

Chile

★ Hats, sweaters, lamps, antiques, and wicker work are sold at the daily Crafts Village, Pueblo de la Dominica, in Santiago.

Colombia

★ Blankets, ponchos, and crafts are available at the Pasaje Rivas market in Bogotá.

★ Rough emeralds are cut and polished at Sterling Joyeros in Bogotá.

Ecuador

★ Finely woven toquilla hats are available from the Ortega Brothers' factory in Cuenca.

★ Inca *tupus* (brooches) and other pre-Columbian–style jewelry are sold at the Saturday market in Otavalo.

Paraguay

★ Ao P'oí Raity in Asunción has excellent ñandutí lacework and *ao p'oí* embroidery.

★ Paraguayan harps and guitars are made and sold in Luque, outside Asunción.

Peru

★ In the Cuzco area, Pisac's Sunday market is the place for Andean demon masks and weavings.

★ Get religious crafts and handmade alpaca and llama woolens at the Indian Market in Lima.

★ Everything you could want or need for your favorite *brujería* (witch) and *curandero* (magical healer) is on hand at the market in Chiclayo on the North Coast.

Uruguay

★ The Tristan Narvaja market is Montevideo's premier Sunday attraction.

Venezuela

★ Caracas's Plaza Morelos has mountainous displays of trinkets, ponchos, and jewelry, as well as delicious grilled meats.

★ The Sunday market on the Plaza Las Heroínas in Mérida has an excellent selection of goods.

How to Have an Adventure

Bolivia

★ Hike Bolivia's rugged Cordillera Real mountain range.

★ Drive through the misty Chapare jungle between Santa Cruz and Cochabamba.

★ Descend into the dank, sweaty bowels of a Cerro Rico silver mine in Potosí.

Brazil

★ Sleep in a hammock under the stars aboard a double-decker commercial boat on the Amazon River.

Chile

★ Go white-water rafting in the rivers around Pucon.

★ Journey on horseback into the canyon from San Alfonso.

Ecuador

★ Cruise the Galápagos Islands aboard a motorized, double-masted Brigantine sailboat.

Paraguay

★ Fish for the salmonlike dorado from a launch on the Tebicuary River, whose banks are home to monkeys, capybaras, and the occasional alligator.

Peru

★ Fly over the Nazca lines.

Venezuela

★ Trek on the Llanos in search of jaguars and exotic birds

★ Ride the world's highest cable car in Mérida.

★ Fly over Angel Falls.

FESTIVALS AND SEASONAL EVENTS

ARGENTINA➤ **Vendimia,** the wine harvest in Mendoza, happens during the first week of March.

BOLIVIA➤ The **Festival of the Virgin of Candalaria (Candlemas)** takes place in Copacabana on Lake Titicaca early in February. All Bolivia celebrates **Carnival,** a weeklong binge that includes street dance and music performances, parades, and merrymaking. However, the ultimate expression of this centuries-old tradition of music and dance is the carnival held in the mining town of Oruro. Brass bands and troupes of dancers from all over the country converge on Oruro, and the highly charged and wildly costumed performers parade their way through the streets of the town for more than 10 kilometers (6 miles). Their outlandish masks and outfits are what makes this event so intriguing; every costume has a history and tradition behind it, as do the songs and dances performed. Eventually the whole procession ends at the mouth of the oldest mine, and here—at dawn and amidst the throng of exhausted dancers—an offering of coca leaves and alcohol is made to the spirit of the mine. The following night, the Dance of the Lucifers takes place at the same mine, with all the dancers carrying lighted torches; misunderstood as devil worship, the ceremony seeks to ward off the daily dangers the miners face underground and asks the spirit of the mine to be benevolent in the year ahead. In the week following Carnival, the village of Tarabuco near Sucre celebrates **Pujilay,** one of South America's most colorful festivals, honoring the 1816 victory by local Indians over the Spanish. **Good Friday** celebrations—featuring candlelit religious processions by masked suppliants—are particularly lively in La Paz and Copacabana.

BRAZIL➤ In Salvador, the **Festival of Iemanjá** is held on the second Sunday of February. The devotees of Brazil's African religious cult Candomblé begin singing the praises of the goddess of the sea at the crack of dawn along the city's beaches. **Carnival** is the biggest party of the year, featuring dancing and singing in the streets, Brazilians donning wild costumes, splashy floats in parades carrying samba dancers and musicians, and posh balls. Although Rio's version attracts the most tourists, Carnival is also spectacular in Bahia (especially in Salvador) and the northeastern cities of Recife and Olinda. The **Formula One Grand Prix** is held during March in São Paulo. **Holy Week** is celebrated in Ouro Prêto, in the state of Minas Gerais. Residents of this historic city gather the night before Easter Sunday along the route of the Easter religious procession and decorate the street with flowers and colored sawdust. Using these elements, they design intricate patterns as well as portraits of Christ and the saints. The result is an immense multicolored carpet over which the procession passes on Easter morning. Tourists gather on the city's streets the night before to watch and to help prepare this "magic carpet". April 21 is **Tiradentes Day,** a national holiday in honor of the father of the 18th-century Brazilian independence movement, Joaquim José da Silva Xavier, known as Tiradentes (tooth puller) because he was a dentist. On this date, Tiradentes was executed for treason by the Portuguese crown in the city of Ouro Prêto. The city itself celebrates the date over a four-day period, April 18–21, with civic ceremonies.

COLOMBIA➤ **Carnival** season is particularly festive in Cartagena and Barranquilla. **Holy Week** processions fill in the colonial towns of Popayán and Mompós.

ECUADOR➤ **Galápagos Days,** celebrating the islands' statehood, is held February 12–18 and features parades and all-out revelry throughout the inhabited islands. During **Carnival,** Ecuadorans douse one another (and tourists!) with buckets of water, water balloons, and squirt guns. Carnival motivates festivities in Cotopaxi Province—local dances and fairs are held in Saquisilí, Pujilí, Latacunga, and Salcedo.

PARAGUAY➤ The town of Itá celebrates the **Day of San Blas** (Feb. 3), the patron saint of Paraguay, with folk dancing, popular music, and horse racing.

PERU➤ In Puno, **Candlemas** starts on February 2 and lasts a week; parades and traditional dances are held. Nearby Acora holds a traditional dance festival the same week. **Carnival** is celebrated throughout Peru. In Lima and many other cities, the party has degenerated into a water fight—people throw buckets of water and water balloons—but Carnival in Cajamarca and Puno remains a colorful affair, with parades and dancing in the streets. Early March sees the **Vendimia Festival** in Ica, a celebration of the region's vineyards, with wine tastings and dances. On **Good Friday** there's a procession in Puno, while on **Easter Monday** a Cuzco procession honors the Lord of the Earthquakes.

URUGUAY➤ An annual citywide celebration of **Carnival** overtakes Montevideo with parades, dancing in the streets, and general all-hours revelry. **Semana Criolla,** celebrated the week before Easter Sunday at the Prado and Parque Roosevelt in Carrasco (a suburb of Montevideo), provides an excellent opportunity to observe traditional gaucho activities.

VENEZUELA➤ During **Carnival** the entire country goes on a Mardi Gras–like binge; in Caracas, nearly everyone vacates the city and heads for the beach. The German-colonized town of Colonia Tovar hosts a **Chamber Music Festival** in March. Of Venezuela's important cultural events,

the most famous is Caracas's biannual **International Theater Festival,** held every even-numbered year in April.

MAY–JULY

ARGENTINA➤ The northern city of Salta celebrates **Semana Salta** (Salta Week), a gaucho festival of note, in June. The gauchos are in their full cowboy regalia, barbecue perfumes the air, and hooves pound in furious displays of horsemanship. Buenos Aires hosts a major **livestock exhibition** in July—great to see since the Argentines take their cows seriously.

BOLIVIA➤ **Festivals of the Cross** take place around Lake Titicaca in early May. **Gran Poder,** celebrated in La Paz in late May or early June, features thousands of dancers performing "La Diablada," the Dance of the Devils. During the **Fiesta De San Juan,** held on June 24 in La Paz and other Andean cities, hundreds of fires and fireworks are lit at dusk to mark the passing of midwinter and to fend off the cold.

BRAZIL➤ **Festas Juninas** is a cycle of celebrations throughout the month honoring various saints. The festivals are particularly noteworthy in Paratí, in the state of Rio de Janeiro, and in several interior regions of the northeast such as Campina Grande in the state of Paraíba. **Bumba-Meu-Boi,** a festival held in São Luís (in the state of Maranho) and other cattle-raising areas, celebrates the religious legend of a slave who kills his master's ox

and must resurrect it or be put to death himself. The festivities, which begin June 24 and continue well into July, include street processions and dancing. The **Amazon Folklore Festival** takes place in Manaus.

COLOMBIA➤ The **flower festival** is held in Medellín in late May or early June. The **Folklore Festival** is held in Ibagué, usually the last week in June.

ECUADOR➤ **Corpus Christi** is observed in many mountain towns with fireworks, bands, and dances, while the **Feast of St. John** enlivens highland towns around Otavalo, particularly Oton, on June 24.

PERU➤ **Festivals of the Cross** take place around Lake Titicaca in early May. In celebration of **Corpus Christi,** statues of saints from all of Cuzco's churches are taken in procession to the cathedral. The **Festival of Inti Raymi** (Inca Sun Festival) takes place outside Cuzco on June 24; the Incas' winter solstice is commemorated with music, dancing, and a special procession. **St. Peter and St. Paul Day,** also called Pope's Day, is celebrated in honor of the pope.

AUG.–OCT.

BOLIVIA➤ The **Festival of the Black Virgin,** one of several such pilgrimages to this locally favored saint, takes place in Copacabana August 5–8.

BRAZIL➤ In every even-numbered year, São Paulo hosts its **Biennial Art Exposition,** the largest art show in Latin America; it begins in September and lasts several months. In

Blumenau, Santa Catarina, southern Brazil's large German colony holds a monthlong beer festival called **Oktoberfest.** Not only is October 12 the official day (celebrated all over the country and particularly in Aparecida, in the state of São Paulo) of Brazil's patron saint, **Nossa Senhora de Aparecida,** but it's also **Children's Day.**

CHILE➤ On national day in September, **Fiestas Patrias** take place all over the country, but there's extra fun around Rancagua, with hard-fought rodeo competitions.

ECUADOR➤ Otavaleños give thanks to Mother Earth for her bounty during the **Festival of Yamor,** celebrated the first two weeks in September. In Latacunga, September 24 is the **Fiesta de la Mamá Negra,** honoring Our Lady of Mercy with lively processions and dancers in disguise.

PERU➤ On August 30, **St. Rosa of Lima Day** is celebrated in the capital, and a parade is held in Arequipa for the **Day of the Campesino.** During Trujillo's **Spring Festival** in October, dancing, parades, and exhibitions of the stunning Peruvian *caballo de paso* dressage horses welcome spring. In late October, **Our Lord of the Miracles** is celebrated with processions in many cities, but the biggest celebration is in Lima; throughout October devotees wear purple. The **bullfight season** is on in the capital's ring.

URUGUAY➤ Montevideo holds an annual **cattle fair** in August.

NOV.–JAN.

ARGENTINA➤ December 8 is the **Festival of Our Lady of Lujan,** patron saint of the republic. The **National Folklore Festival,** which features costumes, dancing, and rodeos, runs for two weeks in Cosquin (province of Cordoba), starting on January 15.

BOLIVIA➤ All Saints' and All Souls' days, also called the **Days of the Dead,** are marked all around Lake Titicaca on November 1 and 2. The **Alicitas Fair** takes place in La Paz for two weeks beginning January 24. Vendors citywide sell miniature replicas of everything from household items, clothing, and shoes to houses and trucks; local belief holds that whatever miniatures you buy and bring home will come to you, full size, during the coming year.

BRAZIL➤ In November, Ouro Prêto's **Aleijadinho Week** honors the great 18th-century sculptor, whose work adorns many of the city's churches. **New Year's Eve** (Ano Novo) is celebrated all night on Copacabana Beach in Rio de Janeiro. Ritual music pulses as the priestesses of Brazil's African religious cult light candles and set up small shrines to Iemanjá, goddess of the sea. Dressed all in white, they set afloat boats carrying candles, white lilies, perfume, and other gifts; if the waves take a boat out to sea, the sender's wishes for the year will come true. On the first Sunday of January, Salvador's **Festival of the Boa Viagem,** the Good Lord Jesus of the Seafarers, is held for four days, with samba music,

capoeira, and feasts of Bahian food. The highlight is a procession of hundreds of small vessels led by a decorated galley to the end of Boa Viagem beach. Also in Salvador, on the third Sunday of January, is the **Feast of Bonfim.** Bahian women dressed in traditional white hoop skirts and tunics clean the steps of the Basilica of Bonfim with perfumed water; these festivities honor Oxala, a god of an Afro-Brazilian sect, and are celebrated jointly by Candomblé priestesses and the local Catholic clergy.

CHILE➤ The **Feast of the Virgin of Andacollo,** patron saint of miners, is honored on December 8th in this northern town near La Serena. In Santiago during the second week of December is the **International Artisans' Fair.** The **Festival Foclorico** (Folklore Festival) is held in Santiago during the fourth week of January.

COLOMBIA➤ In early November, Cartagena's **Reinado** features beauty contests and a full week of merrymaking. Cali holds its popular **feria** from December 25– January 1.

ECUADOR➤ Quito's **Las Fiestas de Quito** is vigorously celebrated December 1–6 with bullfights, exhibitions, and outdoor concerts.

PARAGUAY➤ On December 8, **Immaculate Conception,** the town of Caacupé attracts large numbers of pilgrims who worship the statue of the Virgin, which is paraded through the streets; this is followed by folk dancing and music.

PERU➤ Throughout Peru, people carry food, drink, and flowers to the local cemetery on **All Saints' and All Souls' Days** (Nov. 1–2). November 4–5, **Puno Days,** commemorate the legendary emergence of Manco Capac and Mama Ocllo, founders of the Inca empire, from Lake Titicaca. The highlight is a stupendous procession with masked dancers. In early January, dancing and parades for the **Festival of the Magi** take place in Puno, Cuzco, and nearby Ollantaytambo. During the last week of January, artists perform the most spectacular and seductive of the coastal Creole dances at the **National Festival and Competition of La Marinera** in Trujillo.

VENEZUELA➤ El Hatillo hosts an annual **music festival** with classical and pop performances.

2 Adventure and Learning Vacations

How to pick the trip of a lifetime—you could cruise the Amazon, scale Pichinicha, wander the ancient streets of Machu Picchu, sail the Galápagos—and book it all before you leave home.

By Kurt Kutay
and Jenny
Keller

Updated by
Dinah Spritzer

SOUTH AMERICA OFFERS a host of vacation possibilities beyond the usual tourist agenda of hotels and museums: Traverse the jungles and waterways of the Amazon Basin, explore the lost city of Machu Picchu, or join a first-time expedition to remote wetlands or archaeological sites—you might meet tribal peoples or view wildlife that only a handful of other intrepid travelers have ever encountered before. Despite the inherent difficulties of venturing into South America's hinterlands, such special-interest vacations as treks in the Andes and cruises up the Amazon have become more available, thanks to the development of facilities in remote areas and an increase in tour services that cater to the fit and adventurous. The safety record of established tour operators is excellent, although travel to remote areas is subject to delays, inconveniences, and risks—but then few visits to South America go entirely as planned!

If you want more information about programs to a specific destination than what's listed below, contact the country's tourist office or the **South American Explorers Club** (126 Indian Creek Rd., Ithaca, NY 14850, ☎ 607/277–0488, ℻ 607/277–6122).

Choosing Your Vacation

Hundreds of U.S. travel companies sell adventure and special-interest vacations to South America. There are several factors you should keep in mind when deciding which company and which package will best meet your traveling needs:

- **How strenuous a vacation do you want?** Adventure vacations are commonly split into "soft" and "hard" adventures. A hard adventure is physically demanding; previous travel experience in developing countries is recommended but usually not required. Although you won't necessarily need technical skills or athletic abilities, trips including mountaineering or rafting may require pre-trip training; a doctor's approval may be needed as well. A soft adventure emphasizes the destination itself, rather than the means of travel. A day's activity might include easy rafting or hiking, but you can usually count on a hot shower and warm bed at night. A little honesty goes a long way—make sure you know your own comfort needs and level of physical fitness before signing on to climb a glacier or navigate wild rapids.

- **Where is your tour operator based and how comprehensive is its operation?** Find out whether your travel firm has both an office in the United States and a base in South America or whether it hires another company to provide you with services on-site. Companies with a South American infrastructure often have superior expertise, access to the best guides, and lower costs since you aren't paying for an intermediary's markup. Due to their greater buying power, larger companies can sometimes offer better prices and more frequent departures.

- **How untrodden is your itinerary?** Many of the tours and itineraries detailed below may sound exotic, but since dozens of companies can charter the same riverboat or rent the same lodge, you may have plenty of company on your trip. The most authentic adventures book small groups into less touristed lodges, trekking camps, and vessels in regions where the wildlife and the locals are not accustomed to the clicking of cameras.

For more helpful hints on selecting a travel company, *see* Packages and Tours *in* Smart Travel Tips A to Z *in* The Gold Guide.

Tour Operators

Below are the addresses of the adventure and special-interest tour operators mentioned in this chapter, all of whom have representatives in the United States. The operators included in this chapter were chosen on the basis of their reputation for quality, the originality of their itineraries, the number of programs they offer, and the frequency with which they depart.

Abercrombie & Kent, 1520 Kensington Rd., Oak Brook, IL 60521, ☎ 708/954–2944 or 800/323–7308, FAX 708/954–3324.

Above the Clouds Trekking, Box 398, Worcester, MA 06102, ☎ 508/799–4499 or 800/233–4499, FAX 508/797–4779.

Adventure Associates, 13150 Coit Rd., Suite 110, Dallas, TX 75240, ☎ 214/907–0414 or 800/527–2500, FAX 214/783–1286.

Adventure Center, 1311 63rd St., Suite 200, Emeryville, CA 94608, ☎ 510/654–1879 or 800/227–8747, FAX 510/654–4200.

Adventures On Skis, 815 North Rd., Westfield, MA 01085, ☎ 413/568–2855 or 800/628–9655, FAX 413/562–3621.

Amazon Tours and Cruises, 8700 W. Flagler, Suite 190, Miami, FL 33174, ☎ 305/227–2266 or 800/423–2791, FAX 305/227–1880.

American Alpine Institute, 1515 12th St., Bellingham, WA 98225, ☎ 206/671–1505, FAX 360/734–8890.

American Wilderness Experience, Box 1486, Boulder, CO 80306, ☎ 800/444–0099, FAX 303/444–3999.

Backroads, 1516 5th St., Suite L101, Berkeley, CA 94710-1740, ☎ 510/527–1555 or 800/462–2848, FAX 510/527–1444.

Biological Journeys, 1696 Ocean Dr., McKinleyville, CA 95521, ☎ 707/839–0178 or 800/548–7555, FAX 707/839–4656.

Brazil Nuts, 79 Sanford St., Fairfield, CT 06430, ☎ 203/259–7900 or 800/553–9959, FAX 203/259–3177.

Butterfield & Robinson, 70 Bond St., Suite 300, Toronto, Ontario, Canada M5B 1X3, ☎ 416/864–1354 or 800/268–8415, FAX 416/864–0541.

Classical Cruises, 132 E. 70th St., New York, NY 10021, ☎ 212/794–3200 or 800/252–7745, FAX 212/249–6896.

Close-Up Expeditions, 1031 Ardmore Ave., Oakland, CA 94610, ☎ 510/465–8955 or 800/995–8482, FAX 510/465–1237.

Country Walkers, Box 180, Waterbury, VT 05676-0180, ☎ 802/244–1387, FAX 802/244–5661.

Cutting Loose Expeditions, Box 447, Winter Park, FL 32790-0447, ☎ 407/629–4700, FAX 407/644–9944.

Earthquest Adventures, Box 1614, Flagstaff, AZ 86002, ☎ 602/779–2585, FAX 602/773–9783.

Earthwatch, 680 Mount Auburn St., Box 403GB, Watertown, MA 02272, ☎ 800/776–0188, FAX 617/926–8532.

Encounter Overland, a London-based company represented in the United States by **Adventure Center,** *above*).

Environs, 1 Environs Park, Helena, AL 35080, ☎ 205/428–1700 or 800/633–4734, FAX 205/428–1714.

Far Horizons, Box 91900, Albuquerque, NM 87199-1900, ☎ 505/343–9400 or 800/552–4575, FAX 505/343–8076.

Field Guides, Inc., Box 160723, Austin, TX 78716, ☎ 512/327–4953, FAX 512/327–9231.

Fishing International, Box 2132, Santa Rosa, CA 95405, ☎ 707/539–3366 or 800/950–4242, FAX 707/539–1320.

FITS Equestrian, 685 Lateen Rd., Solvang, CA 93463, ☎ 805/688–9494 or 800/666–3487, FAX 805/688–2943.

Focus Tours, 14821 Hillside La., Burnsville, MN 55306, ☎ and 𝐅𝐀𝐗 612/ 892–7830.

4th Dimension Tours, 1150 N.W. 72nd Ave., Suite 250, Miami, FL 33126, ☎ 305/477–1525 or 800/343–0020, 𝐅𝐀𝐗 305/477–0731.

Frontiers, Box 959, 100 Logan Rd., Wexford, PA 15090, ☎ 412/935– 1577 or 800/245–1950, 𝐅𝐀𝐗 412/935–5388.

Galápagos Network, 7200 Corporate Dr., Suite 309, Miami, FL 33126, ☎ 305/592–2294 or 800/633–7972, 𝐅𝐀𝐗 305/592–6394.

Grand Circle Travel, 347 Congress St., Boston, MA 02210, ☎ 800/866– 0826, 𝐅𝐀𝐗 617/346–6120.

Hanns Ebensten Travel, 513 Fleming St., Key West, FL 33040, ☎ 305/ 294–8174.

Himalayan Travel, 112 Prospect St., Stamford, CT 06901, ☎ 203/359– 3711 or 800/225–2380, 𝐅𝐀𝐗 203/359–3669.

Inca Floats, 1311 63rd St., Emeryville, CA 94608, ☎ 510/420–1550, 𝐅𝐀𝐗 510/420–0947.

Joseph Van Os Photo Safaris, Box 655, Vashon Island, WA 98070, ☎ 206/463–5383, 𝐅𝐀𝐗 206/463–5484.

Lost World Adventures, 1189 Autumn Ridge Dr., Marietta, GA 30066, ☎ 404/971–8586 or 800/999–0558, 𝐅𝐀𝐗 404/977–3095.

Marine Expeditions, 13 Hazelton Ave., Toronto, Ontario, Canada M5R 2E1, ☎ 416/964–9069 or 800/263–9147, 𝐅𝐀𝐗 416/964–2366.

Mountain Travel-Sobek, 6420 Fairmount Ave., El Cerrito, CA 94530, ☎ 510/527–8100 or 800/227–2384, 𝐅𝐀𝐗 510/525–7710.

Myths and Mountains, 976 Tee Court, Incline Village, NV 89451, ☎ 702/832–5454 or 800/670–6984, 𝐅𝐀𝐗 702/832–4454.

Nature Expeditions International, Box 11496, Eugene, OR 97440, ☎ 503/484–6529 or 800/869–0639, 𝐅𝐀𝐗 503/484–6531.

Naturequest, 934 Acapulco St., Laguna Beach, CA 92561, ☎ 714/499– 9561 or 800/369–3033, 𝐅𝐀𝐗 714/499–0812.

Oceanic Society Expeditions, Fort Mason Center, Bldg. E, San Francisco, CA 94123, ☎ 415/441–1106 or 800/326–7491, 𝐅𝐀𝐗 415/474–3395.

Overseas Adventure Travel, 349 Broadway, Cambridge, MA 02139, ☎ 617/876–0533 or 800/221–0814, 𝐅𝐀𝐗 617/876–0455.

Quark Expeditions, 980 Post Rd., Darien, CT 06820, ☎ 203/656–0499 or 800/356–5699, 𝐅𝐀𝐗 203/655–6623.

River Odysseys Worldwide, Box 579, Coeur d'Alene, ID 83816, ☎ 208/ 765–0841 or 800/451–6034, 𝐅𝐀𝐗 208/667–6506.

Rod and Reel Adventures, 3507 Tully Rd., Modesto, CA 95356, ☎ 209/524–7775 or 800/356–6982, 𝐅𝐀𝐗 209/524–1220.

Safaricentre, 3201 N. Sepulveda Blvd., Manhattan Beach, CA 90266, ☎ 213/546–4411 or 800/223–6046, 𝐅𝐀𝐗 310/546–4411.

Sea & Sea Travel, 60 Francisco St., Suite 205, San Francisco, CA 94133, ☎ 415/434–3400 or 800/348–9778, 𝐅𝐀𝐗 415/434–3408.

Ski Vacation Planners, 2200 Fletcher Ave., Fort Lee, NJ 07024, ☎ 201/ 346–9125 or 800/822–6754, 𝐅𝐀𝐗 201/346–0511.

Society Expeditions, 2001 Western Ave., Suite 710, Seattle, WA 98121, ☎ 206/728–9400 or 800/548–8669, 𝐅𝐀𝐗 206/728–2301.

Southwind Adventures, Box 621057, Littleton, CO 80162, ☎ 303/972– 0701 or 800/377–9463, 𝐅𝐀𝐗 303/972–0708.

Special Expeditions, 720 5th Ave., New York, NY 10019, ☎ 212/765– 7740 or 800/762–0003, 𝐅𝐀𝐗 212/265–3770.

Tara Tours, 6595 N.W. 36th St., Suite 306A, Miami Springs, FL 33166, ☎ 305/871–1246 or 800/327–0080, 𝐅𝐀𝐗 305/871–0417.

Tumbaco-Quasar Nautica, 7855 N.W. 12th St., Suite 115, Miami, FL 33172, ☎ 800/247–2925, 𝐅𝐀𝐗 305/592–7060.

Tours International, 14855 Memorial Dr., Suite 811, Houston, TX 77079, ☎ and FAX 713/589–0870 or ☎ 800/247–7965.

Travcoa, 4000 MacArthur Blvd., Suite 650, Newport Beach, CA 92660, ☎ 714/644–1004 or 800/992–2003, in CA 800/992–2004; FAX 714/476–2538.

Tropical Adventures Travel, 111 2nd Ave. N, Seattle, WA 98109, ☎ 206/441–3483 or 800/247–3483, FAX 206/441–5431.

Turtle Tours, Box 1147, Dept. FG, Carefree, AZ 85377, ☎ 602/488–3688, FAX 602/488–3406.

University Research Expeditions Program, University of California, Berkeley, CA 94720, ☎ 510/642–6586, FAX 510/642–6791.

Venezuela Connection, 975 Osos St., San Luis Obispo, CA 93401, ☎ 805/543–8823 or 800/345–7422, FAX 805/543–3636.

Victor Emanuel Nature Tours, Box 33008, Austin, TX 78764, ☎ 512/328–5221 or 800/328–8368, FAX 512/328–2919.

Wilderness Travel, 801 Allston Way, Berkeley, CA 94710, ☎ 510/548–0420 or 800/247–6700, FAX 510/548–0347.

Wildland Adventures, 3516 N.E. 155th St., Seattle, WA 98155, ☎ 206/365–0686 or 800/345–4453, FAX 206/363–6615.

Wings, Inc., Box 31930, Tucson, AZ 85751, ☎ and FAX 602/749–1967.

Woodstar Tours, Inc., 908 S. Massachusetts Ave., De Land, FL 32724, ☎ 904/736–0327.

Zegrahm Expeditions, 1414 Dexter Ave. N, No. 327, Seattle, WA 98109, ☎ 206/285–4000 or 800/628–8747, FAX 206/285–5037.

SPORTS

Bicycling

Argentina and Chile

Season: January–February.
Location: The Lake District of northern Patagonia.
Cost: $2,555 for 11 days of inn-to-inn mountain biking.
Tour Operator: Backroads.

This excursion follows a moderately challenging route around the blue lakes and green valleys of the Lake District, a region comprising glacier-clad peaks in southern Argentina and foothills of volcanos in Chile. Highlights include biking up the slope of the Osorno Volcano, pedaling through the "Region of Seven Lakes," and staying at inns that are both comfortable and full of character.

Ecuador

Season: July–December.
Location: Northern highlands.
Cost: $1,795 for nine days of mountain biking with stays at hotels and country inns.
Tour Operator: Southwind Adventures.

This journey through the rolling hills of the north, past volcanos and glaciers, is suitable for both novice and experienced cyclists. The region is dotted with small colonial-style villages and ecological reserves where the best of the country's flora and fauna can be spotted. Biking is on rarely traversed roads at elevations ranging from 9,000 to 11,000 feet. The route takes travelers through the valleys at the foot of the Cayambe and Imbabura volcanos and onto the Intag Reserve, with a final stop at the festive weekly market in the town of Otavalo.

Peru
Season: April–October.
Location: Andes Mountains outside of Cuzco.
Cost: $1,875 for 11 days of mountain biking with inn stays and three nights of camping.
Tour Operator: Southwind Adventures.

Mountain bikers get the chance to connect with the traditional culture of Quechua hamlets in the land of the Incas. After visiting Chincheros, a five-day bike journey takes cyclists over Mojonpatapampa Pass to Tres Cruces for a mountain view of the Amazon Basin. Several small communities are visited before crossing the Huachuqasa Pass and descending into Sacred Valley. After visiting the Pisac ruins, cyclists board a train to Machu Picchu and spend two days exploring its mysteries.

Fishing

Argentina and Chile
Season: December–April.
Locations: Tierra del Fuego; Patagonia.
Cost: From $2,500 for five full days of fishing.
Tour Operators: Cutting Loose Expeditions, Fishing International, Frontiers, Rod and Reel Adventures.

For anglers, Argentina is the Southern Hemisphere's Alaska, offering world-class brown- and rainbow-trout fishing in clear streams. Frontiers offers Argentine angling in three regions: San Martín de los Andes, Esquel, and Tierra del Fuego. Fishing International, Frontiers, Cutting Loose Expeditions, and Rod and Reel Adventures conduct expeditions to Chile's Patagonian waters, where wild browns and rainbows are found in greater numbers and in significantly larger sizes than in the United States. Group size is limited to six or eight.

Brazil
Season: September–March.
Location: Amazon Basin.
Cost: From $2,650 for 6½ days of fishing.
Tour Operator: Frontiers.

This underfished region provides a wealth of peacock bass for the intrepid angler. Floatplanes whisk you to remote areas outside Manaus where mobile camps allow expeditions to adapt to the Amazon's ever-changing fishing conditions. Frontiers claims that you'll average 15 to 70 catches per day with at least two peacock bass weighing more than 10 pounds. Accommodations are tents with complete facilities.

Venezuela
Season: Year-round.
Locations: Throughout Venezuela.
Cost: $1,400–$2,600 for seven nights; shorter trips are available.
Tour Operators: Cutting Loose Expeditions, Frontiers, Rod and Reel Adventures.

In recent years Venezuela has gained a reputation for world-class bone-fishing at El Gran Roque Island. Guri Lake has also established itself as the world's premier place for peacock bass, and Río Chico offers options for tarpon and snook. Rod and Reel Adventures coordinates angling holidays to all these destinations. Cutting Loose Expeditions has offshore sportfishing trips out of Caracas as well as a Gran Roque package. Frontiers books travelers into the Manaka Jungle Lodge at

the meeting of the Orinoco and Ventauri rivers, where peacock bass
is the main attraction.

Horseback Riding

Argentina
Season: April–October.
Locations: Traslasierra region near La Paz in northern Patagonia;
Neuquén Province.
Cost: From $705 for seven days to $1,300 for 10 days.
Tour Operators: FITS Equestrian, Safaricentre.

Few countries in the world have a greater equestrian tradition than Argentina. FITS gives riders a taste of Argentina's gaucho culture in the
Sierra foothills at a working cattle ranch, Estancio Corralito. Three nights
are spent camping along remote mountain trails—prime opportunities
to spot some of the region's more than 100 bird species. FITS's Patagonia trip allows for even more wildlife encounters. Safaricentre lets you
ride in the Andes along the Chilean border with three nights on a ranch
and four nights of camping. Volcano climbing and meetings with Andean nomads are trip highlights.

Peru
Season: May–September.
Locations: Cuzco and Cordillera Vilcanota.
Cost: From $1,550 for 12 days.
Tour Operators: American Wilderness Experience, Wildland Adventures.

Both operators offer treks through some of the wildest country in the
world—past cascading waterfalls; over 15,000-foot passes; and among
remote, ancient Inca ruins. Horses carry expedition gear, and participants can hike with light day packs or ride.

Mountaineering

Argentina
Season: October–April.
Locations: Aconcagua Mountain; Patagonia; Andean Highlands.
Cost: Aconcagua, from $2,495 for 18 days; Patagonia, $2,060 for 14
days; Andean Highlands, from $1,950 for 16 days.
Tour Operators: Above the Clouds Trekking, American Alpine Institute, Mountain Travel-Sobek, Southwind Adventures.

About 2,500 feet higher than Alaska's Mt. McKinley, Argentina's Mt.
Aconcagua is the highest peak in the Western Hemisphere. When
climbed by the Polish Glacier on its eastern face—the route taken by
the American Alpine Institute, Mountain Travel-Sobek, and Southwind
Adventures—the ascent provides high-quality ice climbing. Climbs
range from grueling scrambles to severe technical challenges, making
this a strenuous, high-altitude ascent suitable for experienced mountaineers only; a slightly easier "standard route" is also an option. In
Patagonia, the American Alpine Institute offers a 14-day expedition
to Fitzroy Peak in February and to Torres del Paine in February and
March. Above the Clouds Trekking has Patagonia departures from December through February, as well as weeklong treks to the puna—Andean high plains—near the Bolivian border.

Bolivia
Season: April–September.
Locations: Lake Titicaca and the Bolivian altiplano; Cordillera Real range.
Cost: From $950 for eight days to $3,140 for 23 days.

Tour Operators: American Alpine Institute, Mountain Travel-Sobek, Southwind Adventures.

Though the 100-mile-long Cordillera Real of Bolivia boasts some of the continent's finest and most varied alpine climbing, it is probably the least-known and least-scaled range among comparable mountain groups; 22 19,000-foot or higher peaks make this Bolivia's largest glacier complex. American Alpine Institute has a series of climbing programs here, ranging from subalpine day hikes to advanced climbs for experienced mountaineers only. Climbers are required to acclimatize for at least seven days in La Paz and Tiahuanaco before participating in the institute's most strenuous programs, ideally spending the majority of their time between 10,000 and 12,000 feet. To round out their offerings, AAI sponsors a short expedition to the summit of 21,201-foot-high Nevado Illimani, the highest peak in Bolivia's Cordillera Real. Southwind Adventures's 11-day climb, designed for beginner to intermediate climbers, features a warm-up trek through Condoriri National Park followed by an ascension to the 19,975-foot summit of the Cordillera Real's Huayana Potosí. Mountain Travel-Sobek also treks through Condoriri before climbing to the summit of Nevado Illimani.

Ecuador

Season: November–February.
Location: Cordillera Real range (Galápagos extension available).
Cost: From $2,190 for 15-day Cotopaxi climb; from $1,490 for 10-day Antisana climb. Galápagos costs vary with boat and length of trip.
Tour Operators: American Alpine Institute, Mountain Travel-Sobek, and Southwind Adventures.

The American Alpine Institute runs 15-day programs to three of the Andes' finest peaks: 19,348-foot Cotopaxi (the world's highest active volcano), 19,107-foot Cayambe, and 20,703-foot Chimborazo, the highest peak in the Cordillera Real. These itineraries can also be followed by a seven-day motor-launch exploration of the Galápagos Islands. Groups are kept small, either three to five climbers with one guide or six to 10 climbers with two guides. Mountain Travel-Sobek also takes intermediate-level climbers up the slopes of Cotopaxi. While not technically demanding, snow and altitude make basic mountaineering skills a must for these Ecuadorian climbs.

Peru

Season: May–August.
Locations: Cordillera Blanca; Cordillera Vilcanota.
Cost: From $2,450 for 20-day Cordillera Blanca climb; from $2,590 for 16-day Vilcanota climb.
Tour Operators: American Alpine Institute, Mountain Travel-Sobek, Overseas Adventure Travel.

The Cordillera Blanca and the Cordillera Vilcanota, mountain ranges in Southern Peru, offer plenty of mountaineering excitement. Intermediate climbers seeking a high-altitude ice-and-snow-climbing experience will be satisfied with a trek up the Cordillera Blanca's Nevado Huascarán, the highest peak in Peru. The American Alpine Institute and Mountain Travel-Sobek take you to the summit at 22,334 feet. Severe storms are common at this altitude. The American Alpine Institute also climbs the Cordillera Blanca's beautiful Alpamayo from its base camp in the Santa Cruz Valley. Another option is trekking through the Vilcanota Range to Nevado Ausangate, a sacred Inca summit. Overseas Adventure Travel does the Inca trek at a more moderate level with excursions to Machu Picchu and rafting on the Río Vilcanota.

Skiing

Perhaps one of the greatest advantages to skiing in South America is that when everyone else back home is soaking up the sun, you can get in your season of summer downhill. Argentina's Las Lenas and the Chilean Andes are home to the continent's premier ski resorts, as popular for their animated nightlife as for their dramatic terrain.

Argentina and Chile
Season: June–September.
Locations: Las Leñas, Argentina; Valle Nevado and Portillo, Chile.
Cost: From $1,760 for quad occupancy in Portillo to $3,540, double, in Valle Nevado. Programs include seven hotel nights, round-trip airfare between New York and Buenos Aires or Santiago, a ski pass, lift tickets, and meals.
Tour Operators: Adventures on Skis, Ski Vacation Planners, Tours International.

In the heart of the Chilean Andes, Valle Nevado has 22,000 acres of skiable mountain served by nine lifts. Dining and nightlife are an integral part of the experience. The three main hotels range from luxury to rustic. Near the base of Mt. Aconcagua, the highest mountain in the Western Hemisphere, is the Portillo resort, with views across the waters of the lovely Laguna del Inca. There's one main hotel with rates for a variety of budgets. Portillo and Valle Nevado are not like Vail, Colorado, where ski facilities are only one attraction in a full-fledged community; these resorts exist without a community in sight. Accommodations at Valle Nevado are neater and spiffier; Portillo has become slightly run-down in recent years.

Argentina boasts the legendary Bariloche, an alpine-type resort town on the shores of Lake Nahuel Huapí. The ski mountain, Cerro Catedral, is 12 miles from town. It has 32 lifts with 50 runs on 5,000 acres. Skiing tends to be superb on the higher slopes and often slushy on the beginner slopes. This so-called "Little Switzerland of Argentina" has coffeehouses, nightclubs, expensive restaurants, and a casino. Hotels range from deluxe to moderate. For 35 miles of downhill trails and a vertical drop of 4,000 feet, try the expert slopes of Las Leñas, where several Olympic ski teams train. The resort is quite remote and has three main hotels—deluxe and first class—as well as apartments. There's a disco and restaurants serving traditional Argentine grilled meats.

Packages are available to Las Lenas, Valle Nevado, and Portillo from Adventures on Skis and Ski Vacation Planners, which also sells packages to Bariloche. Tours International visits historical sites in the Andes before spending seven nights in Portillo or Valle Nevado.

Snorkeling, Diving, and Sailing

Ecuador and Venezuela
Season: Year-round.
Locations: The Galápagos; Los Roques National Park.
Cost: From $2,095 for a seven-day Galápagos dive; from $595 for a three-day yacht cruise around Los Roques.
Tour Operators: Adventure Associates, 4th Dimension Tours, Galápagos Network, Inca Floats, Mountain Travel-Sobek, Southwind Adventures, Sea & Sea Travel, Tara Tours, Tropical Adventures Travel, Venezuela Connection.

Formed by a series of volcanic eruptions, the Galápagos Islands were the testing ground for Darwin's theory of evolution. Wildlife here developed without any influence from the outside world, resulting in an array of shockingly colorful and rare flora and fauna on both dry ground and under water. There are 20 dive sites among the 11 islands. Sea & Sea Travel has sent divers to the Galápagos for nearly 20 years. The company charters a 66-foot cabin cruiser, *Mistral,* with capacity for 10 divers. Cruises depart from San Cristóbal Island every Tuesday. The 10- or 14-night cruise includes the central and northern islands, where you can expect encounters with hammerhead and whale sharks, eels, rays, and many other unusual species. Divers average three dives per day in relatively cold waters. Tropical Adventures Travel has a seven-day live-aboard dive that typically includes sightings of barracuda, sea horses, marine iguanas, and mantas. Adventure Associates has charters available on several yachts for divers and snorkelers.

Companies such as 4th Dimension Tours, Mountain Travel-Sobek, Southwind Adventures, Tara Tours, and Inca Floats offer sails on 10- to 90-passenger yachts. Highlights include exploration of the remote western islands of Isabela and Fernandina, a horseback ride up Sierra Negra Volcano, and kayaking among penguins, sea turtles, and sea lions.

Another popular area for diving and snorkeling is Los Roques National Park, a collection of hundreds of small islands 113 miles north of Caracas. Venezuela Connections charters the two-cabin, 42-foot-long *Golden Lion* yacht for three-day diving and snorkeling cruises around the park.

Trekking

At the height of the Inca empire, the Andes were crisscrossed by a vast network of roads. They followed valleys and traced impossible pathways through narrow, precipitous terrain. Remnants of Inca trails and footpaths used by today's indigenous peoples of the Andes lead adventurous hikers to ancient ruins, spectacular mountain peaks, jungle highlands, and small local communities. Trekking usually refers to an organized tour led by experienced local guides and cooks who provide food, equipment, and camp services. Some companies offer more expensive treks with stays at inns and small hotels. Treks are graded according to difficulty in terms of their distance, terrain, and elevation. Porters or pack animals usually carry gear, leaving trekkers the freedom to hike with only a lightweight day pack. Some firms, however, have you carry your own gear, so check before picking your tour.

Argentina and Chile

Season: November–March.
Locations: Southern Andes (Patagonia and the Lake District); Tierra del Fuego; Atacama Desert; Easter Island.
Cost: From $1,835 for a 12-day trek to $3,195 for a 25-day trek.
Tour Operators: Above the Clouds Trekking, Adventure Center, Backroads, Butterfield & Robinson, Country Walkers, Earthquest Adventures, Mountain Travel-Sobek, Southwind Adventures, Wildland Adventures, Wilderness Travel.

Local mountaineering clubs and well-established national parks in both countries are responsible for the excellent trails, campsites, and shelters used by trekkers in Patagonia and the Lake District. Southern Argentina and Chile may be the most trekked region in South America: Long daylight hours, lasting until 11 PM, add to the attraction of trekking here. The best treks focus on a magnificent area of the southern Andes that is generally referred to as Patagonia in Argentina and as the Lake District in Chile. Earthquest, Mountain Travel-Sobek, and Southwind Adventures operate Patagonia treks ranging from 17 to 23 days, including a challenging climb up Grey Glacier in Torres del Paine. The precipitous walls of glacier-carved peaks in this national park jut a near-vertical 6,000 to 8,000 feet above rolling grasslands, wild chasms, and deep azure lakes. Wildland Adventures has a "Patagonian Wildlands Safari" that combines a series of short treks in Glacier National Park, Torres del Paine, and the Fitzroy Peak. Its Tierra del Fuego sail trek, dubbed "the southernmost trek in the world," follows the south Atlantic coast of Tierra del Fuego to Cape Horn. Backroads's 11-day northern Patagonia trek journeys north from Puerto Montt to Ensenada, Mt. Tonodor (the highest peak in the region), and Bariloche (the alpine playland of Argentina).

Above the Clouds Trekking, Adventure Center, and Wilderness Travel have easy Patagonia hiking trips that also take in Torres del Paine and Fitzroy national parks, the latter famous for its jagged spires and glacier park. For those wishing to stop and smell the roses, Butterfield & Robinson's 12-day walking tour takes in Torres Del Paine and the mysterious carved stone figures of Easter Island, while Wilderness Travel's 18-day natural history adventure pairs Easter Island with the Ayacara and Alerce forests in the southern Andes of Chile. Walkers can also relax on Country Walkers's nine-day meander just south of Puerto Montt and on the Ayacara Peninsula, home to dolphins, penguins, and albatross.

Bolivia
Season: April–September.
Location: Cordillera Real.
Cost: From $100 per day.
Tour Operators: Mountain Travel-Sobek, Wildland Adventures.

La Paz, the highest capital city in the world, is the base for trekking in Bolivia and the place to acclimatize before heading to even higher ground. A recommended highland-trekking itinerary combines a two-day trek over a pre-Inca road—the Takesi—with a three-day, high-elevation trek over two 16,500-foot passes to lakes and glaciers in the heart of the Cordillera Real mountain range. The trip, outfitted locally by Magri Turismo, can be booked through Wildland Adventures. Llamas and herders are used instead of pack horses. Mountain Travel-Sobek visits the pre-Inca ruins of Tiahuanaco, then travels to Lake Titicaca. Treks are outside of La Paz in the Takesi region and in the vicinity of the 18,630-foot-high Condoriri range.

Ecuador
Season: Year-round.
Locations: Central Valley; western and eastern Cordillera ranges; Amazon rain forest along the Río Aguarico; Machalilla National Park in the Andean Highlands on the Pacific coast.
Cost: From $478 for six days in Machalilla National Park to $2,855 for a 14-day trek through the Amazon.
Tour Operators: Adventure Associates, Encounter Overland, Mountain Travel-Sobek, Southwind Adventures, Wilderness Travel, Wildland Adventures.

The Andes cross Ecuador from north to south in two ranges. Between them lies the fertile Central Valley, along what German explorer Alexander von Humboldt called the "Avenue of the Volcanoes" because the valley is edged by one of the largest concentrations of volcanoes in the world. Spectacular trekking routes, such as the Antisana Highlands trek offered by Wildland Adventures and Southwind Adventures, lead to high-elevation and glacier-clad volcanic peaks and descend to the tropical highlands of the Amazon Basin. Other treks, such as those sold by Encounter Overland, combine short hikes in the Andean foothills with visits to rural villages and little-known Indian markets, where visitors can mingle with a variety of ethnic groups. Adventure Associates departs from Quito or Guayaquil for a hotel/camping trek through a cloud forest in Machalilla National Park and cruise to Plata Island, with its blue-foot boobies, albatross, and sea lions. Mountain Travel-Sobek explores the Mindo-Nambilla Protected Forest on the slopes of Pichincha Volcano near Quito, and Cuyabeno Reserve in the Amazon Basin. Or opt for another Amazon trek through Cotopaxi National Park. A more extensive Amazon trek along Rio Aguarico in the Cuyabeno and the Emerald Forest is one of the best itineraries available from Wilderness Travel.

Peru
Season: April–October.
Locations: Cordillera Blanca; Cordillera Vilcanota; Cordillera Vilcabamba.
Cost: From $300 for a four-day trek to $1,500 for a two-week itinerary.
Tour Operators: American Wilderness Experience, Encounter Overland, Mountain Travel-Sobek, Overseas Adventure Travel, Southwind Adventures, Wilderness Travel, Wildland Adventures.

The Inca Trail—from the ancient Inca capital Cuzco to the lost city of Machu Picchu, an archeological mecca—rivals Patagonia as South America's most popular trekking route. The diverse scenery, indigenous communities, Inca lore, and challenging yet safe climb are behind the region's appeal. The area has attracted trekkers from all over the world ever since Yale archaeologist Hiram Bingham discovered Machu Picchu in 1911. The 45-kilometer (28-mile) Inca Trail in the Cordillera Vilcabamba affords adventurous trekkers the opportunity to reach Machu Picchu as the Incas did, by hiking along the royal road built more than 500 years ago. This route passes through rare examples of cloud forest over a 14,000-foot pass, before descending into subtropical vegetation. Independent trekkers can book in the United States or join with others by booking directly with local trekking outfitters in Cuzco.

American Wilderness Experience, Wilderness Travel, and Mountain Travel-Sobek offer the greatest diversity of trekking programs in Peru. Tours run by American Wilderness Experience include horseback riding, rafting on the Urubamba River, and mountain biking, with an optional extension to Manu National Park in the Amazon. Southwind Adventures organizes a Salcantay Mountain trek in the Vilcabamba range in conjunction with the Inca Trail. Overseas Adventure Travel includes a rafting trip on the Río Vilcanota in its Sacred Valley trek. Encounter Overland combines the Inca Trail with Bolivia's Lake Titicaca.

Venezuela
Season: October–May.
Locations: Auyán-tepuí in the Gran Sabana; Sierra Nevada.
Cost: From $1,865 for 11 days to $2,875 for 17 days.
Tour Operators: Southwind Adventures, Himalayan Travel.

Conan Doyle's Lost World can be found in the Gran Sabana, with its more than 100 flat-top mountains soaring above tropical forests. The mountain summits have their origins in some of the oldest rock formations on earth. Two of the region's premiere attractions are Mt. Roraima, at the edge of Canaima Park, and the spectacular Angel Falls. Southwind Adventures lets you choose from a Lost World trek to the base of Mt. Roraima and a chartered flight to the falls or, for more experienced hikers, a trek through Sierra Nevada National Park, the northernmost extension of the Andes. Himalayan Travel's "Lost World" trek takes travelers by foot to the top of the Gran Sabana's largest plateau, Auyán-tepuí, and then continues by canoe to Angel Falls.

White-Water Rafting and Kayaking

Alternately exhilarating and relaxing, white-water rafting and kayaking provide a pace and perspective all their own. You don't have to be an expert paddler to enjoy a river adventure, but you should know how to swim. Rivers are rated from Class I to Class V according to how difficult they are to navigate, and South America has some of the wildest commercially rafted rivers in the world. Generally speaking, Class I to III rapids are rolling to rollicking and suitable for beginners. Many Class IV and V (potentially dangerous) rapids are strictly for the experienced.

Brazil
Season: June–October.
Location: Lake Mariana in the Pantanal.
Cost: From $2,395 for 14 days.
Tour Operator: Mountain Travel-Sobek.

Explore this vast wetland complex by kayak. Expect a constant show of wildlife in *vivieros,* nest areas with colorful wading birds by the thousands. Camp on sandy beaches, swim, and go fishing. A charter flight to Iguazú Falls with day hikes is also included.

Chile
Season: December–March.
Locations: Bío-Bío River, Class IV; Tierra del Fuego.
Cost: From $2,095 for 14 days, round-trip from Santiago.
Tour Operators: Mountain Travel-Sobek, Southwind Adventures, Wilderness Travel, Wildland Adventures.

Since the first descent of Bío-Bío, undertaken by Mountain Travel-Sobek in 1978, the river's reputation for white-water action has become known to rafters around the world. At the headwaters the gradient is gentle, as the river ripples through soft, rolling countryside. This changes abruptly, however, as metamorphic and granitic gorges pinch the river channel to create challenging and complex white-water sections. In 10 days on the river with Mountain Travel-Sobek or Southwind Adventures you ride nearly 100 rapids, but there are also opportunities to enjoy the scenery and hot springs along the way, fish for trout, lounge on soft beaches, and interact with the people who live along the river—farmers, cowboys, and native peoples. Mountain Travel-Sobek offers the option of adding on a hike up the 10,300-foot-high Callaqui Volcano.

Wilderness Travel and Wildland Adventures spend nine days kayaking in Tierra del Fuego, crossing the Straits of Magellan and making contact with the region's penguins, dolphins, and albatross. Explore narrow fjords and view enormous glaciers, waterfalls, and mountains.

Ecuador
Season: November–April for rafting; May–August, November for riverboating.
Locations: Quijos River, Class III, IV, and V; Toachi River, Class III; Upano River, Class II and IV.
Cost: From $45 for one day; from $180 for two days/one night (one day spent rafting); from $1,480 for 10 days aboard a riverboat.

Tour Operators: River Odysseys Worldwide.

River Odysseys Worldwide runs thrill-a-minute oar-power rafting trips in the Ecuadorian rain forest along 70 miles of the Upano River in the isolated province of Morona-Santiago. Also available are day trips from Quito on the Río Blanco.

Venezuela
Season: Year-round.
Locations: Orinoco and Caroní rivers, Classes IV and V.
Cost: From $1,490 for seven days.
Tour Operator: Lost World Adventures.

Orinoco's Ature Rapids in Amazonas Territory and the Caroní River's Nekuima Canyon in the Guayana Highlands give even experienced river rafters a memorable roller-coaster ride on giant frothy waves. Lost World Adventures's skilled river guides lead seven-day rafting expeditions along these formidable rivers. The cost includes four days of rafting, lodge and camp accommodations, meals, guide services, and equipment.

THE OUTDOORS

Amazon Jungle Camping and Lodges

Because the Amazon River provides easy and natural access to the jungle, it is a great starting point for Amazon-jungle camping and lodge excursions. Transportation is usually provided by thatch-roof motorboats, riverboats (*see* River Cruises, *below*), speedboats, and canoes. Passengers can expect to sleep on board in no-frills cabins, in hammocks, at improvised campsites in the jungle, at rustic lodges, or on sleeping mats in *tambos* (thatch-roof shelters with raised flooring). These expeditions can be tremendously rewarding for adventurers who want to see the deep rain forest and its inhabitants at close range, but participants need to be prepared for a rough-and-ready existence in the jungle, miles from the nearest village.

Brazil
Season: March to December.
Location: Top of the Rio Negro.
Cost: From $1,195 for eight days to $1,595 for 11 days.
Tour Operators: Naturequest, Southwind Adventures.

Traveling by wooden riverboat up the Rio Negro, the main Amazon tributary flowing from Manaus, you'll see waterfalls, visit Cabaclo villages, hike through the forest, and witness the famed Meeting of the Waters where the Negro and Amazon flow side by side without mixing. Spend nights in riverboat hammocks, hotels, and lodges.

Bolivia
Season: April–November.
Location: Isiboro-Secure National Park, near the Mamoré River in southern Amazonia.
Cost: From $1,395 for 10 days.
Tour Operator: Southwind Adventures.

Isiboro consists of nearly 3 million acres, from Andean highlands to tropical rain forest, making it one of South America's most important reserves. Your challenging expedition by riverboat and motorized canoes takes you to the park's most remote areas, where you might encounter tapirs, anteaters, sloths, ocelots, caimans, and even jaguars. Nights are spent camping or at rustic guest houses.

Ecuador
Season: May–August.
Locations: Amazon Basin; the highlands.
Cost: From $1,990 for nine days to $2,595 for 14 days, round-trip from Quito.
Tour Operators: Adventure Associates, 4th Dimension Tours, Overseas Adventure Travel, Tara Tours, Wilderness Travel, Wildland Adventures.

Wilderness Travel's 14-day expedition takes you deep into the forest to meet the Cofan Indians. Less demanding is a seven-day "Amazon Trek" along the Río Napo with the renowned La Selva Lodge as your base. Explore pristine jungle—sometimes on foot, sometimes in dugout canoes—and be greeted most nights by a prepitched camp and hot food. Departures are from Quito. La Selva's "Amazon Light Brigade" takes you from Quito to Coca and, over the next six days, to various camp-sites along the Challuacocha River. Accommodations are luxurious and the food delicious. La Selva is booked by Tara Tours, 4th Dimensions, and Wildland Adventures. Another moderate Amazon adventure is the lodge-based exploration of Cuyabeno Reserve by Overseas Adventure Travel; motorized canoe trips reveal huge orchids, iridescent blue morpho butterflies, macaws, toucans, and the South American alligator. A similar program with more trekking is available from Adventure Associates.

Peru
Season: June–August.
Locations: Manu National Park; Iquitos and Environs.
Cost: From $1,125 for 12 days to $2,450 for 17 days.
Tour Operators: Amazon Tours and Cruises, American Wilderness Experience, Environs, Grand Circle Travel, Southwind Adventures.

Located in Peru's Amazon Basin, Manu National Park is the most undisturbed, biologically rich region on the continent. Protected by unnavigable rivers, impenetrable forests, and the towering Andes, this remote region is now accessible to small groups; several tour operators offer Manu as a separate itinerary or in combination with mountain trekking in the highlands. Accommodations include tent camps and jungle lodges. If you prefer a more comfortable setting, the Amazon Camp, operated by Amazon Tours and Cruises, comprises 42 screened rooms constructed entirely of native material (thatch roofs and solid-bamboo siding), each with private facilities but no electricity. Southwind Adventures, Environs, and Grand Circle package Manu with a stay at the top-notch Explorama Lodge at the Amazon Center for Environmental Education and Research. The center is famous for its elevated canopy walkway, which allows observers to study jungle ecology from 120 feet above the forest floor.

Bird-Watching Tours

Argentina
Season: October–December.
Locations: Chaco; La Pampa; Patagonia.
Cost: From $2,495 to $5,775 for 17–21 days, and $4,695 for 32 days.
Tour Operators: Field Guides, Inc., Focus Tours, Woodstar Tours.

Ponds, marshes, and grasslands in the northern Argentine region of Chaco are the natural habitats of immense numbers of birds, including greater rheas, waterfowl, swans, red shovelers, and a host of others. On the Patagonian coast, most tours explore both the renowned Península Valdés and Punta Tombo, home to a colony of some 1 million Magellanic penguins. Tours include the grasslands around Río Grande, the forests of the far south at Ushuaia, and the shores of the Beagle Channel. With each company you can expect comfortable, quaint accommodations with world-class ornithologists and naturalists as your guides.

Brazil

Season: Year-round.
Locations: Pantanal; Itatiaia National Park; Amazon Basin.
Cost: From $1,000 for 6 days to $4,500 for 20 days.
Tour Operators: Field Guides, Inc., Turtle Tours, Victor Emanuel Nature Tours, Wings, Inc.

In southeastern Brazil, bird habitats range from coastal rain forest and wet pampas to cloud forest and plateau grassland. Such breathtaking birds as the red-billed curassow, bare-throated bellbird, and banded cotinga have their last stronghold here. Midway between Rio de Janeiro and São Paulo, in a beautiful national park of the same name, is Brazil's second-highest peak, Mount Itatiaia. A family-run inn here invites longer stays for extensive birding in the area. Many companies offer tours through these regions and through Brazil's Pantanal, a vast area of seasonally flooded grassland considered by some naturalists to be the most stunning spectacle of the Americas.

Ecuador

Season: Year-round.
Locations: Quito; Mt. Pichincha; Río Napo; Amazon; Galápagos Islands.
Cost: From $1,995 for two weeks to $4,745 for four weeks.
Tour Operators: Field Guides, Inc., Woodstar Tours, Inc.

Ecuador's bird habitats include the steaming Amazonian rain forests in the east, the lush temperate and subtropical forests on the slopes of the Andes, and the paramo grasses and marshes above the timberline. Each region is home to its own variety of birds—hummingbirds, the gigantic Andean condor, bush tyrants, and brush finches in higher elevations and the zigzag heron, harpy eagle, and Salvin's and nocturnal curassows in the jungle.

Venezuela

Season: December–February.
Location: The Llanos.
Cost: From $2,850 for 16 days.
Tour Operators: Field Guides, Inc., Victor Emanuel Nature Tours, Woodstar Tours, Inc.

Birds are especially abundant in Venezuela's vast expanse of savanna known as the Llanos. Among those you may see are seven species of ibis, herons, the primitive-looking hoatzin, and many raptors. Even yellow-knob curassows and the elegant sunbittern are easy to spot, as are scarlet macaws, noisy thorn birds, and a host of smaller birds.

Natural History

Many adventure vacations provide you with an insight into the importance and fragility of South America's ecological treasures. The itineraries mentioned below, however, focus on a specific aspect of the ecosystem or on a region not typically explored by other intrepid travelers. The physical adventure becomes secondary to the learning experience.

Argentina and Chile

Season: October–February.
Locations: Península Valdés; Iguazú Falls; Patagonia; Tierra del Fuego; Falkland Islands.

Cost: $3,295 for 19 days to $3,875 for 23 days with stays in lodges and hotels; for Falklands, from $5,590, including flight from the United States.
Tour Operators: Oceanic Society Expeditions, Southwind Adventures, Wilderness Travel.

Argentina offers a vast array of natural history experiences, from the tropical forests surrounding Iguazú Falls to the Antarctic environment of Tierra del Fuego, and from the Andes Mountains to the Patagonian steppe. Nature vacations combine day hikes in Tierra del Fuego National Park and in Chile's Torres del Paine with visits to the Península Valdés and the tropical rain forests around Iguazú Falls.

Oceanic Society Expeditions, which specializes in marine natural history trips, offers an in-depth, 18-day trip to the Falkland Islands, which boast some of the most ruggedly spectacular wilderness on the South American continent and an abundance of interesting wildlife. Flying inter-island in the Falklands, stops include visits to Macaroni, rockhopper, Magellanic, and gentoo penguin colonies, as well as huge seabird colonies. The December trip also includes a visit to the 4,000-foot granite towers in Torres del Paine National Park, a reserve for hundreds of graceful guanacos (cousins to the llama and alpaca).

Brazil
Season: Year-round.
Locations: Pantanal; Atlantic coast.
Cost: From $100 per day.
Tour Operators: Brazil Nuts, Focus Tours, Southwind Adventures.

The Pantanal, the world's largest wetlands, lies in the center of South America. Unlike the dense rain forests of the Amazon, this marshy grassland makes an ideal place for wildlife observation; during the rainy season (October through March) flooding forces animals to congregate in high areas. Backcountry travelers in the Pantanal will see a spectacle of colorful tropical birds, caimans (reptiles similar to alligators), anteaters, capybaras (large rodents), and possibly tracks of the elusive jaguar. Focus Tours specializes in the Pantanal and provides qualified naturalist guides who are sensitive to the environment. Their services are available only to preformed groups. Southwind Adventures can take you on a camping or lodge-based tour in the Pantanal and the Atlantic rain forest. Brazil Nuts has the widest range of lodge-based Pantanal safaris.

Ecuador
Season: Year-round.
Locations: Amazon; Andes; Galápagos.
Cost: From $900 to $3,000.
Tour Operators: Adventure Associates, Galápagos Network, Inca Floats, Southwind Adventures, Wilderness Travel, Wildland Adventures.

Enjoy a slow-pace nature hike through the highlands of the Cotacachi-Cayapas Reserve, search for brilliantly colored birds in the Pasochoa Forest, and study Ecuador's richest concentration of Amazonian mammals—including nine species of monkeys—in Cuyabeno Reserve or La Selva Rain Forest Reserve. Each operator can combine a mainland itinerary with a small-ship cruise to the barren, volcanic Galápagos Archipelago, habitat for some of the world's most bizarre animals and plants. Two-thirds of the resident birds and most reptiles at this showcase of evolution are found nowhere else in the world. Since the wildlife in Galápagos National Park never developed a fear of humans, you can approach the animals for close-up photography and observation.

One- and two-week itineraries begin in Baltra or San Cristóbal. To protect the Galápagos's rare flora, fauna, and aquatic life, Ecuador has banned all large cruise ships from sailing in the area. Approved ships range from 90-passenger vessels to small yachts with a capacity of 12 or fewer. Sailing in the Galápagos is the trip of a lifetime for most nature lovers: An advance deposit (six months to a year) should be made for the best boats, dates, and guides.

Venezuela

Season: November–March.
Locations: The Llanos; Guayana Highlands; Los Roques Archipelago; Orinoco River basin.
Cost: From $1,500 to $3,000 for a 15-day tour.
Tour Operators: Lost World Adventures, Mountain Travel-Sobek, Safaricentre, Southwind Adventures.

Some tours penetrate the largely uninhabited Guayana Highlands of Bolívar state, a region of mountainous tablelands, luxuriant rain forests, raging rivers, and spectacular waterfalls, including Angel Falls, the world's highest waterfall. Lost World Adventures offers one of the better treks in Venezuela, the "Auyán-tepuí Natural History Trek to the Guayana Highlands," a challenging ascent through the cloud forests to the top of a gigantic sandstone massif, or *tepuís,* one of many that dominate this bizarre landscape. Southwind Adventures navigates an open, motorized canoe on the Caura River to Pará Falls, while Mountain Travel-Sobek pairs a Llanos expedition with two days of snorkeling at Los Roques National Park.

Overland Safaris

There is no faster way to immerse yourself in a number of cultures and landscapes than by an overland trip in special vehicles designed to cross the toughest desert, jungle, and mountain areas. On such an adventure you journey far from the beaten path to explore a South America seldom seen by the average tourist. Camping is the most common way to spend the night, though you may prefer to stay in lodges, inns, and hotels occasionally. You'll be expected to help with pitching tents, cooking, and—if necessary—pulling the vehicle out of a ditch in more remote spots. A camaraderie evolves on these long-distance trips that often sparks long-term friendships. Flexibility and adaptability are key.

Season: Year-round.
Locations: Throughout South America.
Cost: From $35–$50 per day for 3- to 13-week itineraries.
Tour Operators: Adventure Center, Safaricentre.

Adventure Center specializes in cross-continental overland trips, covering as much of South America's culture, history, and geography as possible in one extended adventure tour. Complete itineraries run from one to three or more months, but can be broken into two- to four-week sections. Destinations range from Ecuador to the Patagonia region of Argentina, encompassing also the highlights in Peru, Bolivia, Chile, and Paraguay. You travel through high peaks, steaming jungles, endangered rain forests, flat grasslands, and barren desert. You visit lost kingdoms and bustling modern cities and meet with gauchos, indigenous Amazonians, and highland peoples. Safaricentre operates shorter, but still well-rounded, three-week overland adventures along the Inca Real in Peru; two-week Jeep safaris in Venezuela; and three-week trips to Argentina, Bolivia, and Chile.

Photo Safaris

The tours listed below are all led by professional photographers who will enhance your trip with instruction and valuable hands-on tips.

Argentina
Season: December.
Location: Falkland Islands by way of Santiago, Chile.
Cost: From $3,636 for 20 days.
Tour Operator: Joseph Van Os Photo Safaris.

Travel by Land Rover to photograph king penguin colonies at Gypsy Cove and York Bay. More penguins await you at the remote Volunteer Point. In Stanley, photographic points of interest include the 1892 Christ Church Cathedral and the hull of the *Charles Cooper*, the last surviving example of a north Atlantic packet ship. On the isolated Sea Lion Island, the focus is on elephant seals, sea lions, and possibly killer whales. Pebble Island boasts black-neck swans and silvery grebe, while Saunders Island is known by photographers for its 24,000 black-brow albatross. The trip is timed to capture the hatching of albatross chicks on film.

Ecuador
Season: Year-round.
Locations: Galápagos.
Cost: From $650 for four days nights to $1,355 for eight days.
Tour Operators: Galápagos Network, Inca Floats, Tumbaco-Quasar Nautica.

The Galápagos Archipelago is a paradise for wildlife photographers: There are frigate birds and blue-foot boobies, prehistoric iguanas, sea lions, fur seals, and 500-pound tortoises that seem to be suspended in time. Exceptionally rewarding for photographers is the rare opportunity to approach many of these animals closely, since they have remarkably little fear of people. Choose from comfortable accommodations aboard the 90-passenger *Galápagos Explorer* to no-frills six-passenger yacht charters. Cruises depart Wednesday and Saturday from San Cristóbal Island in the Galápagos. Island excursions are led by an expert photographer and a local naturalist guide.

Venezuela
Season: December–January.
Locations: The Llanos; Andes Mountains.
Cost: $3,500 for 14 days.
Tour Operator: Close-Up Expeditions.

Angel Falls, the colorful colonial villages of the Mérida region, and the 300 birds species of the Llanos are the highlights of this cross-country photographic safari. The Llanos wetlands are known to attract Maguari and jabiru storks, roseate spoonbills, and scarlet macaws. You can take a break from snapping photos and fish for piranha. Several nights are also spent at a jungle lodge on the shores of the Orinoco River and on Margarita Island.

CRUISES

Ocean Cruises

Season: December–March.
Locations: The most common cruise itineraries to South America, sometimes known as "Caribazon" sailings, combine Caribbean ports

of call with a navigation of the Amazon River. The grandest of all is a circumnavigation of South America, which takes in all the major ports in about 50 days. You can sign on for the whole cruise, or sail on single or multiple segments of the whole trip. The most popular ports are Caracas, Belém, Fortaleza, Salvador, Rio de Janeiro, Montevideo, Puerto Madryn, Cape Horn, Tierra del Fuego, and Puerto Montt. Many expedition ships headed for Antarctica (*see below*) depart from ports in Chile or Argentina. At press time, it was not possible to sail on a foreign cruise ship to the Galápagos Islands; these vessels have been banned by the Ecuadoran government for at least three years. You can, however, sail aboard one of several local vessels, although their on-board appointments are not up to the standards of the major cruise lines. *See* The Galápagos Islands *in* Chapter 8, Ecuador.

Cost: From $400, not including airfare, for a small cabin on a three-day cruise to tens of thousands of dollars for a suite on a circumnavigation of the continent.

Cruise Lines: For an ocean-and-Amazon cruise, contact Abercrombie & Kent (☎ 800/323–7308), Crystal Cruises (☎ 800/446–6620), Cunard Line (☎ 800/528–6273), Princess Cruises (☎ 310/553–1770), Royal Cruise Line (415/956–7200), Seabourn Cruise Line (415/391–7444), Special Expeditions (212/265–0003), or Sun Line (800/872–6400). For a cruise circling South America, contact Cunard Royal Viking (☎ 800/458–9000), Regency Cruises (☎ 212/972–4499), or Special Expeditions (*see above*). For other South America cruises, contact Radisson Seven Seas Cruises (☎ 800/333–3333) or Silversea Cruises (305/522-4477). You can also sail on a passenger-freighter from Ivaran Lines (☎ 800/451–1639).

Cruising is an all-inclusive way to book travel to South America if you're not interested in a land-based tour. To get the best deal, consult a cruise-only travel agency. For more information on itineraries and cruise lines that sail in South American waters, see *Fodor's Cruises and Ports of Call*.

River Cruises

Spanning 4,200 miles, the Amazon is the largest river in the world. From its source in southern Peru, the river encompasses western Brazil, eastern Peru and Ecuador, southern Colombia, and northern Bolivia. The Amazon and its more than 1,000 tributaries nourish the last great wooded wilderness of its kind on earth, a natural laboratory with more than half the world's species of birds and thousands of species of mammals and plants. The waterways also provide a vast liquid freeway used by vessels of all sizes and classes to bring travelers into the heart of the South American continent. Amazon-by-boat options range from a luxury cruise expedition with all the amenities to a low-budget adventure in native dugout canoes. Moderately priced riverboat cruises, with private or shared cabins and the basic comforts, are also quite popular.

Brazil
Season: Year-round.
Locations: Belém; Manaus; Rio Negro; upper Amazon.
Cost: From $390 for two nights.
Tour Operators: Amazon Tours and Cruises, Brazil Nuts, 4th Dimension Tours, Nature Expeditions International, Tara Tours, Southwind Adventures, Special Expeditions.

Southwind Adventures, 4th Dimension Tours, and Brazil Nuts sail up the Rio Negro from Manaus, Brazil, on a 20-passenger riverboat; nature hikes in Januauario Ecological Reserve and bird-watching at the Anavilhanas Reserve come with the cruise. Nature Expeditions, Tara Tours, Amazon Tours and Cruises, and many other companies charter the slightly better appointed 44-passenger *Río Amazonas* for trips from Tabatinga to Iquitos, Peru, with stays at the Explorama Lodge on the Río Napo. Yacht expeditions and canoe trips through the *igapo* (a black-water flooded forest) are also available. For luxury expedition cruising, Special Expeditions has a longer trip on the upper Amazon and Rio Negro from Manaus to Iquitos. Its ship, the M. S. *Polaris,* accommodates as many as 80 passengers.

Chile

Season: October–February.
Locations: Santiago; Tierra del Fuego.
Cost: From $700 to $3,000, depending on season and cabin class.
Tour Operator: 4th Dimension Tours.

Tiny fishing villages on remote waters are featured in a nine-day cruise through the glacier-studded fjords near Puerto Montt. Another option is a 10-day journey around South America's southernmost tip aboard the 100-passenger *Terra Australis*. The vessel provides all the comforts of an adventure cruise ship; onboard meals include such regional specialties as king crab, oysters, Argentine beef, and Chilean wines.

Peru

Season: Year-round.
Locations: Iquitos to Leticia; Pacaya-Samiria National Reserve.
Cost: From $495 for a four-day cruise to $2,795 for a 15-day cruise.
Tour Operators: Amazon Tours and Cruises, Environs, 4th Dimension Tours, Grand Circle Travel, Tara Tours, Tours International.

Amazon Tours and Cruises, 4th Dimension Tours, Tara Tours, and Tours International offers four-day downriver cruises from Iquitos to the town of Leticia, just over the Colombian border, aboard the *Río Amazonas;* four-day upriver cruises operate in reverse. The vessel has 20 air-conditioned cabins with private facilities and six non-air-conditioned cabins with shared facilities. Three-day cruises between Iquitos, Peru, and Leticia aboard the *Arca* (a smaller ship of similar design) are also available. Grand Circle Travel and Environs cruise the upper Amazon, Ucayali, and Marañón rivers on the 16-passenger air-conditioned *Esmerelda*. At Monkey Lake, there are chances to view rare primates including red uakari, saki, woolly monkeys, and saddleback tamarins. Machu Picchu extensions are offered on most cruises.

Antarctica Cruises

Season: November–February.
Locations: Most cruises depart from Ushaia in Tierra del Fuego, Argentina, while a few ships visit the Antarctic Peninsula en route from New Zealand or Australia.
Cost: $7,490 to $12,000 for 22 days; shorter cruises are available.
Tour Operators: Abercrombie & Kent, Biological Journeys, Classical Cruises, Society Expeditions, Marine Expeditions, Mountain Travel-Sobek, Quark Expeditions, Tours International, Travcoa, Zegrahm Expeditions.

Departing from Ushuaia, the world's southernmost town, you'll sail for two days through the Drake Passage to reach the Great White Continent. Accompanied by naturalists and Antarctic experts, you'll travel ashore from your expedition vessel in small groups to islands with thousands of penguins, nesting seabirds, and stunning icebergs. The best cruises visit research stations on the Antarctic Peninsula, where you'll learn about how dozens of nations work to protect Antarctica, especially from tourist groups! Several expedition cruise ships with ice-hardened hulls, such as Abercrombie & Kent's luxurious *Explorer,* Classical Cruises's *Bali Sea Dancer,* and Society Expedition's *World Discoverer* venture here, as do smaller (38- to 78-passenger) and less-swanky Russian polar-research ships that have been refitted for cruise passengers. Only two ships, the *Kapitan Dramitsyn* and the *Kapitan Khlebnikov,* chartered by Zegrahm Expeditions, Tours International, and Quark Expeditions, are icebreakers and can take you to the islands of the Weddell Sea to view emperor penguins. The ships also have helicopters for island landings where docking would be impossible. Some itineraries combine Antarctica with the Falkland, South Orkney, and South Georgia islands.

LEARNING VACATIONS

Cultural Tours

Many travelers to South America are captivated by the archaeological heritage preserved here in religious sites, fortresses, terraces, and tombs. Others seek the living legacy of cultural expression found in local art and handicrafts. Still others are drawn to experience the cultures of South America's rapidly vanishing indigenous tribes. Embedded in the fabric of so-called primitive societies are centuries-old secrets for living harmoniously with nature.

Bolivia

Season: October–August.
Locations: Andes; Potosí; Lake Titicaca; Tupiza.
Cost: From $1,095 for nine days to $2,250 for 17 days.
Tour Operator: Myths and Mountains.

The "Crafts and the Country" trip visits artisans in their homes and workshops. A highlight is the fiesta of San Bartolome in Potosí, where travelers participate in folk dancing and country celebrations. If archaeology compels you, try "Archeology of the Ancients," a tour that explores the fossilized remains of the Tiahuanaco civilizations, which arose 2,700 years before the Incas. For hikers, there's a journey through the snow-covered passes of the Cordillera Apolombamba to discover the medical secrets of the Kallaways, the medicine men of South America.

Chile and Easter Island

Season: February.
Locations: Santiago; Easter Island.
Cost: From $447 for four days (Easter Island, land transportation only) to $4,000 for 19 days (Chile and Easter Island, land transportation only).
Tour Operators: Far Horizons, Hanns Ebensten Travel, Nature Expeditions International, Tours International.

Despite its remote location in the Pacific Ocean, 2,300 miles west of Chile, windswept Easter Island continues to draw hundreds of visitors each year to its unique open-air archaeological museum. Nearly 1,000 stone statues, or *moai,* stand gazing with brooding eyes over the island's gently rolling hills, and hundreds of perplexing petroglyphs stand out from the statues' rock surfaces. Far Horizons's 12- or 19-day cultural discovery tour, led by archaeologist Dr. Georgia Lee, offers in-depth exploration of the island. Hanns Ebensten, who led one of the first tour groups to Easter Island some 25 years ago, offers a specialized 10-day tour during the Easter holiday, including five days on the island and three in Santiago. Nature Expeditions International has offered trips to Easter Island since its inception and now offers one of the most comprehensive explorations available, lasting anywhere from 5 to 14 days. Tours International is one of the few companies operating a four-night itinerary.

Ecuador

Season: April–September.
Locations: Throughout Ecuador including the Andes and the Amazon.
Cost: From $1,850 for 11 days; jungle trip to Jivaro Indians from $2,575 for 16 days.
Tour Operators: Myths and Mountains, Southwind Adventures, Turtle Tours, Wildland Adventures.

Myths and Mountains specializes in revealing the secrets of age-old Ecuadorian traditions, from the medicinal practices of healing shamans to the crafts of the Canari, Salasca, and Otavalo peoples. Traveling by private vehicle from Quito to Cuenca with Wildland Adventures, you will visit several remote markets and handicraft centers and explore significant archaeological ruins, including Ingapirca, the main Inca ruin in Ecuador. Between treks, accommodations are in hacienda-style inns near small towns; while trekking, large three-person tents are used. Turtle Tours and Southwind Adventures take visitors by small plane, foot, and canoe into the heart of the jungle to live among the Jivaro Indians for six days. You can join your hosts in fishing, jungle treks to thermal waterfalls, and canoe trips to neighboring villages. Monthly departures (except March and April) include hotels, meals, and guides.

Peru

Season: May–October; Sipan, year-round.
Locations: Cuzco; Pitumarca; Chincheros; San Blas; Urubamba; Lima; Sipan.
Cost: $1,200 for 10 days to $2,500 for 16 days.
Tour Operators: American Wilderness Experience, Earthquest, Environs, 4th Dimension Tours, Hanns Ebensten Travel, Wilderness Travel.

In Sipan archaeologists unearthed a sealed, pre-Inca tomb in 1988 to find treasures of pure gold: ornate headdresses and masks, exquisite jewelry, and intricately sculpted figures. This priceless trove is on permanent display at the Bruning Museum in Sipan. It is also featured on a 10-day archaeological tour sponsored by 4th Dimension Tours, with departures from Lima. With Hanns Ebensten Travel, American Wilderness Experience, Environs, and Wilderness Travel, travelers explore ancient Inca sites rarely visited in the remote Vilcabamba.

Venezuela

Season: Year-round.
Location: Amazonian rain forest.
Cost: $1,300 for 6 days and 5 nights to $3,450 for 15 days, including round-trip flights from Caracas.
Tour Operators: Lost World Adventures, Turtle Tours.

Previously available only to a select few explorers, anthropologists, and missionaries, the Lost World Adventures tour is still limited (six to a group) to those with serious ecological and anthropological interests. Conditions in these remote locations are extremely primitive: Participants sleep in hammocks hung in rustic dwellings and eat local fish and game. Wilderness experience and a high degree of cultural sensitivity are required. Similarly, Turtle Tours takes you on a riverboat down the

Orinoco River and its tributaries to live in the forest with the Yano Mano Indians. You'll spend eight days camping and sleeping in Indian thatch-roof huts. Your hosts will teach you the finer points of fishing and hunting. The Yano Mano are rarely visited by outsiders so their cultural traditions are intact. Three nights are spent at a ranch in the Llanos.

Scientific Research Trips

Whether your interests lie in helping to preserve the earth's dwindling resources, working on projects that will improve the lives of people in developing nations, or searching for clues to the past at archaeological sites, joining a research-expedition team contributes labor and money to the research. No prior research experience is necessary to join these trips. Instead, organizations look for people who are interested in learning, want to be part of a team, and have the flexibility and sense of humor needed to meet the challenges of a research expedition. Some programs are tax-deductible.

Brazil
Season: Year-round (one two-week trip offered each month).
Location: Ilha do Cardoso tropical rain forest, near São Paulo.
Cost: From $1,545, including lodging and meals.
Tour Operator: Earthwatch.

One of the last remnants of an Atlantic coastal rain forest lies near the city of São Paulo, on Ilha do Cardoso, an island state park. In 1976 a research center was established, and it is from this base that Earthwatch teams work in shifts around the clock to assess the island's animals and plants. The work is essential for understanding how this severely threatened habitat works and how to save what is left of it in other parts of Brazil. Teams search for caiman nests and observe the animals' behavior; record the local habitat; map streams, swamps, and other topographic features; photograph animals and habitats; and enter the data into computers. Lodging is in research station houses and dorms, which have electricity, water, and flush toilets.

Ecuador
Season: July–August.
Locations: Napo Province; Maquipucuna Reserve.
Cost: From $1,395 for two weeks, departing from Quito.
Tour Operator: University Research Expeditions Program.

University Research Expeditions Program (UREP) has a 15-year history of sending research teams of University of California scientists, teachers, students, and others to investigate issues of human and environmental concern throughout the world. Current projects in South America include two environmental-studies programs in Ecuador, with workshops in the field and forest for U.S. and Ecuadorian scientists and educators. On the "People of the Rain Forest: Conservation Their Way," expedition participants gather information to assist an indigenous Quechua community and a small-scale, nonintrusive ecotourism program that emphasizes traditional knowledge and resource use. Sensitivity to other cultures, the ability to speak Spanish, and wilderness experience are helpful. Accommodations are rustic.

Peru
Season: April–October.
Locations: Amazon Basin; Inca Trail.
Cost: From $1,950 for 8-day trip, $2,890 for a 15-day trip (includes airfare from Miami) for Amazon Dolphin Project; from $1,395 for an 11-day Inca Trail Preservation Trek.

Tour Operators: Oceanic Society Expeditions, Wildland Adventures.

Oceanic Society Expeditions, the travel affiliate of the conservation organization Friends of the Earth, has scheduled research trips in March, June, and July to study the *botos,* the largest river dolphin, native to the Amazon Basin. Participants in the Amazon Dolphin Project are to collect data to use in developing a long-term study focusing on the dolphins' movement patterns, social organization, and behavior in relationship to their environment. No special skills, other than knowing how to swim, are required. Headquarters is a 76-foot motor vessel with double-occupancy cabins.

Another conservation project in Peru is the Inca Trail Preservation Trek, cosponsored by Wildland Adventures, The Earth Preservation Fund, and local Peruvian conservation organizations. The trek offers participants the opportunity to help preserve the natural and cultural heritage of Machu Picchu National Park.

3 Argentina

Cosmopolitan Buenos Aires boasts hundreds of theaters and movie houses, dozens of parks, and myriad restaurants—all providing diversion for a population in perpetual motion. Away from the capital city's constant commotion, the pace is slower, the people are more open, and the scenery— ranging from the snowy heights of the Andes to the grassy pampas along the Atlantic coast to the thundering flow of Iguazú Falls—is spectacular.

By Ed Shaw

Updated by
Rick Jarvie

MOST TRAVELERS THINK they've stumbled on a long-lost European country when they get to Argentina. Most Argentines, too, are convinced they are more European than South American. A quick look at the people walking down the avenues of any Argentine city confirms the impression. There are more Italian surnames than Spanish and the largest colony of Yugoslavians outside of their fractured homeland. There are millions of descendants of Jewish immigrants from Eastern Europe, and communities of British, French, and German families enjoy cultural and financial clout far beyond their insignificant numbers.

But in spite of the symbiosis with Europe, the country has had a chaotic past, politically and economically. No one can thrive on inflation—and survive hyperinflation—like an Argentine can. Traditionally, a long-term bank note deposit has been measured in hours. The pitfalls of Argentine politics were not inappropriately characterized in the musical *Evita*: "Truth is stranger than fiction" is a maxim confirmed by the musical-chairs–like process that has placed both civilians and soldiers in the country's precarious presidency. But President Carlos Saúl Menem's massive privatization program—sell-offs that include the national railways and Argentina's telephone system—has gone a long way to get the economy back on track and attract outside investment.

Argentina is a me-first society that considers government a thorn in its side and whose citizens avoid paying taxes with the finesse of bullfighters. As a community, it's totally chaotic, but as individuals, Argentines are generous and delightful, full of life, and eager to explain the intricacies of their complex society. They are also nonstop philosophers, anxious to justify their often enviable existence. Friendship is a time-consuming priority, and family connections are strong—children leave the nest, but not the neighborhood. Argentines work longer hours than New Yorkers—just not so efficiently—and rival Madrileños at dining until dawn.

Geographically, Argentina more closely resembles the United States than Europe. Its vast territory stretches more than 5,000 kilometers (3,000 miles) from north to south and encompasses everything from snow-covered mountains to subtropical jungle. In the north, in the sultry province of Misiones, nature is raucous and rampant; here the spectacular Iguazú Falls flow amid foliage that is rain forest–thick. In the pampas, or plains, of central Argentina, the countryside recalls the American West: Gauchos herd the cattle that provide Argentina with the beef it consumes in massive quantities. In the west, the Andean backbone Argentina shares with Chile attracts climbers to Mt. Aconcagua, the Southern Hemisphere's highest peak, and draws skiers to Bariloche and other resorts. Patagonia, in the south, is like no other place on earth. Monumental glaciers tumble into mountain lakes, depositing icebergs like meringue on floating island. Penguins troop along beaches like invading forces, whales hang out with several yards of their tails emerging from the sea, and at the tip of Patagonia, South America slips into Beagle Channel in Tierra del Fuego.

BUENOS AIRES

Buenos Aires is a sprawling megalopolis that rises from the Río Plata and stretches more than 194 square kilometers (75 square miles) to

Argentina

Tartagal
JUJUY
San Salvador
Bermejo
Rivadavia
EL RAY NATIONAL PARK
Salta
SALTA
CATAMARCA
Pirámide El Triunfo
FORMOSA
Formosa
CHACO
PARAGUAY
Asunción
IGUAZA FALLS NATIONAL PARK
MISIONES
San Miguel de Tucumán
S. Fdo. del Valle de Catamarca
Santiago del Estero
SANTIAGO DEL ESTERO
Resistencia
Corrientes
CORRIENTES
Posadas
BRAZIL
LA RIOJA
Salinas Ambargasta
Salinas Grandes
SANTA FE
SAN JUAN
Córdoba
Laguna Chiquita
Monte Caseros
ENTRE RIOS
San Juan
Dolores
Santa Fe
Paraná
URUGUAY
Mendoza
Rosario
CORDOBA
San Luis
Mercedes
Rufino
Montevideo
Santiago
MENDOZA
CHILE
SAN LUIS
La Plata
Río de la Plata
Bahía Samborombón
San Rafael
Fortuna
General Pico
BUENOS AIRES
Dolores
Cabo San Antonio
Santa Rosa
Azulo
LA PAMPA
La Escondida
Puelches
Bahía Blanca
Tandil
Mar del Plata
NEUQUÉN
Neuquén
Cipolletti
Punta Alta
Necochea
Negro
La Margarita
Bahía San Blas
NAHUEL HUAPI NATIONAL PARK
RÍO NEGRO
Ingeniero Jacobacci
Viedma
Bariloche
Golfo San Matías
Puerto Madryn
Península Valdés
Esquel
Las Plumas
Trelew
Rawson
Isla de los Pájaros
CHUBUT
Cabo Raso
Malaspina
Punta Tombo
Comodora Rivadavia
Golfo San Jorge
Desca de PETRIFIED FOREST NATIONAL PARK
Cabo Blanco
Bahia Laura
Las Horquetas
SANTA CRUZ
Puerto Santa Cruz
Lake Argentino
Calafate
Bahía Grande
FALKLAND ISLANDS
Perito Moreno Glacier
Río Gallegos
Stanley
Strait of Magellan
San Sebastián
TIERRA DEL FUEGO
PARQUE NACIONAL TIERRA DEL FUEGO
ISLA GRANDE DE TIERRA DEL FUEGO
Ushaia
Canal del Beagle
Isla de los Estados
Cape Horn

PACIFIC OCEAN

ATLANTIC OCEAN

N

0   200 miles
0   300 km

the surrounding pampas, the famed and fertile Argentine plains. Block after block of tidy, high-rise apartment buildings interspersed with 19th-century houses continue as far as the eye can see. Dozens of suburban neighborhoods, each with its own particular character and well-groomed parks, surround the downtown area.

Unlike most South American cities, whose architectural styles reveal a strong Spanish colonial influence, Buenos Aires looks more like Paris, with wide boulevards lined with palatial mansions. It was built up into its present form at the turn of the century, when Argentine exports created a wealthy merchant class, and homes in the French classical style became a must among the elite. The city brings Paris to mind in other ways as well: Flowers are sold at colorful corner kiosks, the smell of freshly baked bread fills the air around well-stocked bakeries, and cafés appear on every block.

Porteños—as Buenos Aires residents are called, because many of them originally arrived by boat from Europe and started out in the city's port area, called La Boca—enjoy philosophical discussions and support a larger population of psychoanalysts per capita than any other city in the world. The city's women continue to care how they look, and with the men's flashing stares or piquant compliments, they receive ample recognition for their efforts.

Buenos Aires has no Eiffel Tower, no internationally renowned museum, no must-see sights that clearly identify it as a world-class city. Rather, it provides a series of small interactions—sunlight streaking through the trees, a block or two of great window-shopping, a flirtatious glance, a heartfelt chat, a juicy steak—that combine to create an accessible and vibrant urban experience.

Visitor Information

The national office of tourism is called **Secretaria de Turismo de la Nación** (Av. Santa Fe 883, ☎ 1/312–5611 or 1/312–5621); the office runs a **telephone information service** (☎ 1/312–2232 or 1/312–5550) for tourists. Information kiosks run by the city, located along Calle Florida, have English-speaking personnel and city maps, but few brochures. Occasionally a copy of the useful guides *Where* or *Buenos Aires Today* can be found at downtown newsstands, but they are published sporadically and are hard to find.

Arriving and Departing

By Plane

Buenos Aires is served by **American Airlines, United Airlines, Aerolíneas Argentinas, Ecuatoriana, LanChile,** and **Varig** from the United States; by **Canadian Airlines, Aerolíneas Argentinas,** and **Varig** from Canada; and by **Aerolíneas Argentinas** and **British Airways** from the United Kingdom. Most international flights land at **Ezeiza Airport,** 34 kilometers (21 miles) and 45 minutes from downtown. Flights within Argentina depart from **Aeroparque Jorge Newbury,** which is a 15-minute cab ride from downtown.

BETWEEN THE AIRPORT AND DOWNTOWN
Bus ($10) or taxi limousine ($47) tickets can be purchased from the well-marked transportation counter in the airport. **Manuel Tienda León** (Santa Fe 709, ☎ 1/383–4454) provides 24-hour airport bus service to all downtown hotels. For the return trip, Tienda León provides frequent van service to the airport from its office in front of the Obelisk. Regular taxi service from the airport to downtown costs about $35.

Buenos Aires

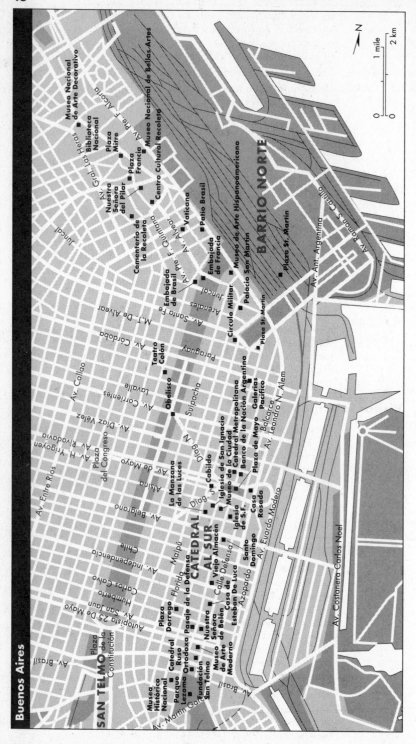

N

1 mile
2 km
0
0

SAN TELMO

CATEDRAL AL SUR

BARRIO NORTE

Museo Nacional de Arte Decorativo
Biblioteca Nacional
Museo Nacional de Bellas Artes
Av. Gral. Las Heras
Plaza Mitre
Av. Pres. F. Alcorta
Plaza Francia
Museo Nacional de Bellas Artes
Nuestra Señora del Pilar
Centro Cultural Recoleta
Cementerio de la Recoleta
Vaticana
Patio Brasil
Av. Pres. Quintana
Embajada de Brasil
Av. Pres. Alvear
Av. Alvear
Embajada de Francia
Museo de Arte Hispanoamericana
Arenales
Juncal
Palacio San Martín
M.T. De Alvear
Círculo Militar
Plaza St. Martín
Av. Santa Fe
Av. Ant. Argentina
Plaza St. Martín
Av. Ramón S. Castillo
Juncal
Av. Córdoba
Teatro Colón
Paraguay
Av. Callao
Obelisco
Lavalle
Av. Corrientes
Suipacha
Av. Díaz Vélez
N
Av. H. Yrigoyen
Av. Rivadavia
Diag.
Galerías Pacífico
Plaza del Congreso
Av. de Mayo
La Manzana de las Luces
Iglesia de San Ignacio
Museo de la Ciudad
Catedral Metropolitana
Banco de la Nación Argentina
Av. Leandro N. Alem
Alsina
Diag.
Cabildo
Plaza de Mayo
Balcarce
Av. Entre Ríos
Av. Belgrano
Iglesia de S.F.
Casa Rosada
Chile
Av. Independencia
Maipú
Santo Domingo
Av. Euardo Madero
Plaza Dorrego
Pasaje de la Defensa
Nuestra Señora
Museo de Arte de Belén
Casa de Esteban De Luca
Azopardo
Florida
Calle Defensa
Autopista 25 De Mayo
Av. San Juan
Humberto
Carlos Calvo
Museo Histórico Nacional
Parque Lezama
Catedral Ruso
Ortodoxa
Fundación San Telmo
Av. Brasil
Plaza de la Constitución
Av. Brasil
Av. Martín García
Av. Costanera Carlos Noel

By Train

At press time (winter 1995) **Ferrocarriles Argentinos** (Argentine Railways) was being privatized and, for the moment, international train service has been discontinued. The city is served by six commuter rail lines: **Línea Sarmiento** (Estación Once, Bartolomé Mitre 2815, ☎ 1/870041), **Línea Mitre** (Estación Retiro, Av. Ramos Mejía 1398, ☎ 1/311–4355), **Línea Belgrano** (Estación Retiro, Av. Ramos Mejía 1430, ☎ 1/311–1444), **Línea Roca** (Estación Constitución, Av. Brasil 1138, ☎ 1/953–9214), **Línea San Martín** (Estación Retiro, Av. Ramos Mejía 1552, ☎ 1/311–8704), and **Línea Urquiza** (Estación Lacroze, Av. Federico Lacroze 4181, ☎ 1/553–9214).

By Car

Paved highways run from Buenos Aires to the Chilean, Bolivian, Paraguayan, and Brazilian borders.

By Bus

Most long-distance and international buses arrive at and depart from the **Estación Terminal de Omnibus** (Av. Ramos Mejía 1680, ☎ 1/315–3404 or 1/315–3405). There are numerous types of service, from standard to deluxe, with videos, meals, rest rooms, and sleeper seats.

By Hydrofoil and Ferry

Hydrofoils and ferries cross the Río de la Plata between Buenos Aires and Uruguay several times a day. Hydrofoils are run by **Aliscafos** (downtown: Calle Lavalle 607, ☎ 1/311–6160, 1/311–1346, or 1/311–7501; in the port: Darsena Norte, Av. Madero at Av. Córdoba, ☎ 1/311–134) and **Buquebus** (downtown: Av. Córdoba 867, ☎ 1/313–4444; in the port: Av. Pédro de Mendoza 20, ☎ 1/361–9186, 1/361–9232, or 1/361–9190). Ferries are operated by **Ferrylíneas** (downtown: Calle Florida 780, ☎ 1/394–8421; in the port: Darsena Sur, Ribera Este, ☎ 1/361–3140). **Buquebus** also runs hovercraft and ferry service between Montevideo, the Uruguayan capital, and Buenos Aires.

Getting Around Buenos Aires

By Car

Porteños drive with verve and independence. For the rest of us, it's a guaranteed thrill learning how to negotiate along tremendously broad boulevards where traffic lanes are only a state of mind. A more convenient and comfortable option is to have your travel agent or hotel arrange for a car with a chauffeur, especially for a day's tour of the suburbs or nearby pampas. An approximate price is $15 per hour, but add an additional charge per kilometer if you drive outside the city limits. Small firms offering this service are **Novas Tour** (Balcarce 914, ☎ 1/361–8929), **Remises Universal** (Corrientes 2565, 11th Floor, Office 344, ☎ 1/951–6900, 1/952–1888, or 1/953–7951), and **Remises Plaza de Mayo** (Azopardo 523, ☎ 1/343–4735).

PARKING

Parking has been privatized in Buenos Aires, so ticket-happy entrepreneurs are busy putting yellow metal hobbles on the front wheels of cars that stand too long at a meter, and tow trucks haul violators off to a nearby parking lot. Fines start at $75. There are a few public underground parking garages and numerous private garages. They start at $2–$3 for the first hour.

By Bus or Metro

There is no central terminal for urban buses, or *colectivos;* the routes are marked on blue signs at their stops. Buenos Aires's subway system is excellent; it is the oldest in South America, dating from 1913, and many of the stations are decorated with original artwork showing historic scenes of the city or murals by contemporary artists. Tokens cost about 45¢ and can be used throughout the system. The subway closes between 1 and 4 AM.

By Taxi

In the central downtown area, fares are about $2–$4; out to the Palermo–Recoleta, about $7. It is never difficult to hail a taxi in Buenos Aires, although you might want to call a private taxi service in the predawn hours (☎ 1/972–4991 or 1/552–2939).

By Train

Commuter trains serve the northern suburbs, leaving from Retiro, the central station across from the British Clock Tower, in front of the Sheraton Hotel. The fare for an *ida y vuelta* (round-trip) ticket to Tigre on the delta is only $1.30, and you can stop at San Isidro and other fancy suburbs on the route without charge.

Tour Operators

Bus Tours

Buenos Aires Tours (Calle Lavalle 1444, ☎ 1/374–6655, 1/402390, or 1/402381) offers an extensive bus tour of the city.

Walking Tours

Visitors who understand Spanish can take advantage of the free guided walking tours offered by the **Municipalidad** (City Hall, Sarmiento 1551, 5th Floor, ☎ 1/476–3612). The schedule varies each month; details are available from the information booths (*see* Visitor Information, *above*).

Tours to Other Parts of Buenos Aires Province

The pampas start at the edge of Buenos Aires, and a convenient way to experience gaucho life would be to join the full-day program offered Wednesday and Sunday at the **Estancia Susana** (Susana Ranch); book through City Service Travel Agency (Calle Florida 890, ☎ 1/312–8416). Outings to this Thoroughbred ranch include lunch with folk music entertainment and fine displays of the horses and gauchos. **La Cinacina** (in Buenos Aires, Bartolomé Mitre 734–10B, ☎ 1/342–1986 during office hours; at other times, call La Cinacina restaurant, ☎ 1/326–2773) runs a Tuesday and Friday tour that provides a closer look at today's pampa traditions as well as the life of the gauchos.

Exploring Buenos Aires

Buenos Aires spreads from south to north along the shores of the Río de la Plata (River Plate). La Boca (the mouth, in this case, of a small, filthy river) is the most picturesque neighborhood, now run-down and shabby but colorful, with brightly painted pressed-tin houses. North of La Boca, San Telmo, a seedy sort of Greenwich Village, is the area to go to to trace the city's origins in layers of 19th-century masonry buildings covered with interesting decorative details, good and bad tango bars, and tempting and tawdry antiques shops. The city grew north from there in leaps and bounds: Wide avenues, parks, and skyscrapers spill over into seemingly endless residential areas. The city's early 20th-century commercial center was established in a neighborhood known as Catedral al Sur, just south of the Plaza de Mayo, but as residential areas continued to grow northward, the city's center sprang up to around Plaza San Martín, finally establishing itself in Barrio Norte in the 1920s. The Barrio Norte maintains its elegant charm, although many prominent families have moved to the northern suburbs and now commute to their offices or to the theater.

San Telmo

San Telmo is halfway between midtown Buenos Aires and the south end of the city, a setting similar to that of Manhattan's SoHo district. Along with its neighbor to the south, La Boca, San Telmo is a self-proclaimed republic whose folkloric traditions are preserved by a bevy of self-appointed authorities. San Telmo's main attraction is the Sunday flea market, which offers junk at outrageous prices and people-watching at its most intense. On weekdays the dozens of antiques shops are easier to browse.

Plaza Dorrego, at the corner of Calles Defensa and Humberto Primo, is the focal point of San Telmo. On weekdays it provides a peaceful haven for chess-player pensioners, with outdoor tables shaded by the plaza's stately old trees. On Sunday from 10 to 5 the plaza is alive with the bustling San Telmo Antiques Fair, a magnet for both Porteño and tourist. A young couple dances frenzied tangos on one corner to the music of a tape recorder; veteran tango musicians play violin and a *bandoneon*—the local version of the accordion—nearby. A look up at the buildings that surround the plaza provides a sampling of all the architectural styles—leftover Spanish colonial, French classical, and lots of ornately decorated masonry done by Italian craftsmen—that have gained a significant presence in the city over the past century.

Marking the southern edge of San Telmo are the gardens of **Parque Lezama,** with its enormous magnolia, palm, cedar, and elm trees planted on the sloping hillside and winding paths that lead down to the river. The land fell into the hands of an English family in the 1840s, who sold it to George Ridgely Horne, an American businessman, who in turn sold it in 1858 to Gregorio Lezama, an entrepreneur who decorated the gardens of his luxurious estate with life-size statues and enormous urns. At the end of the last century, Lezama's widow donated the property to the city, and it has since become a popular spot for family picnics on weekends.

The Lezama homestead became the **Museo Histórico Nacional** (National Historical Museum). The official history of Argentina is on display in the stately if decaying old mansion, covering the country's past from the 16th century to the beginning of this century. Most prominently displayed are the memorabilia dedicated to General José de San Martín and his campaigns during the War of Independence in 1810. The jewel that shouldn't be missed is the collection of paintings by **Cándido López,** a forceful forebear of contemporary primitive painting. López, who lost an arm in the Paraguayan War of the 1870s, which Paraguay fought against Argentina and Brazil, learned to paint with his left hand and produced an exciting series of war scenes on a scale that would have captivated Cecil B. DeMille. *Calle Defensa 1550,* ☎ *1/304–1182.* ☛ *Entry fee.* ⊙ *Tues.–Fri. 3–6, Sun. 3:30–7.*

Overlooking the park, visible above the trees that line Avenida Brasil, the onion-shape domes of the small **Catedral Ruso Ortodoxo** (Russian Orthodox Cathedral) emerge. The sky-blue-dome church was hastily built in the late-1910s by the eclectic Danish architect Alejandro Cristophersen for the congregation of Russians who had settled in the city. The property, strangely, still belongs to Russia.

Continuing north from the park along **Calle Defensa,** with its neighborhood shops and tenement apartments, San Telmo offers its most distinctive flavor, that of a down-at-the-heels dowager. Halfway between what was once the colonial city and Riachuelo, the port where immigrants flocked at the end of the last century, San Telmo has changed its facades to adapt to the circumstances of the moment. Now it is a magnet for antiques shops. In the past 20 years, real-estate operators and decorators have converted the formerly derelict old houses, with large courtyards draped with ivy and wisteria, into shops, art galleries, restaurants, and bars.

Heading north, Calle Defensa leads to many of the city's important art spaces. The **Fundación del Rotary Club** (Rotary Club Foundation), which took over the former San Telmo Foundation, is housed in an example of what post-Colonial houses, with their enclosed courtyards adorned with flowering shrubs, were like. The foundation offers stimulating monthly shows by contemporary Argentine and international artists, and concerts. *Calle Defensa 1344,* ☎ *1/361–5485.* ☛ *Entry fee.* ☉ *Weekdays after 4, all day Sat.; closed in summer.*

An old cigarette factory on Calle Defensa with a classical brick facade recently became the new site of the **Museo de Arte Moderno** (Museum of Modern Art), which shows temporary exhibitions of the work of local painters and sculptors. Renovations are still underway and only part of the building is open. *Calle Defensa 1344,* ☎ *1/361–3953.* ☛ *Entry fee.* ☉ *Tues.–Sun. 4–8.*

The **antiques shop district** begins at the corner of Calle Defensa and Avenida San Juan. Old family homes have been converted into shops, or a series of them, like **Pasaje de la Defensa** (Defensa Alley), the elaborate Italianate house of the Ezeiza family, built in the 1850s, that was turned into a tenement for immigrants at the turn of the century and now houses several dozen antiques shops.

Close to the corner of the Plaza Dorrego, on Calle Humberto Primo, stands **Nuestra Señora de Belén** (Our Lady of Belén), also known as the Parroquia de San Pedro González Telmo (San González Telmo Parish). The church was abandoned halfway through its construction by the Jesuits in 1767, when the order was expelled from Argentina, and was not completed until 1858. The cloisters and the domed chapel to the left, designed by Father Andrés Blanqui in 1738, are the only visible remnants of the original construction. *Calle Humberto Primo 340,* ☎ *1/361–1168.* ☛ *Free.* ☉ *Daily 4:30–7.*

The Jesuits also built the adjoining cloister, which later became a hospice and then a prison for women. It is now the **Museo Penitenciario** (Penitentiary Museum), a modest museum with a few amusing mementos of early 20th-century prison life. Behind the museum's large courtyard is the **Capilla de Nuestra Señora del Carmen,** a chapel that dates from the Jesuit period. *Calle Humberto Primo 378,* ☎ *1/361–5803.* ☛ *Entry fee.* ☉ *Weekdays 10–noon, 2–5; Sun. 10–noon, 1–5.*

A few relics of the colonial period still stand on **Calle Carlos Calvo,** just off Calle Defensa. **La Casa de Esteban De Luca,** an old home turned into a restaurant, is a prime example of what a simple city dwelling looked like in the late 1700s. A glimpse at **Pasaje Giuffra,** a short alley running toward the river, offers a more complete panorama of what the city looked like two centuries ago. At Calle Defensa, just south of Avenida Independencia, the old **Cine Cecil,** once the neighborhood cinema, has been turned into a rambling antiques market similar to those on Portobello Road in London.

The **Viejo Almacén,** on Avenida Independencia, once a popular tourist nightspot that featured tango shows, is another of the few remaining examples of colonial architecture. Originally an old store, as its name indicates, the building became the English Hospital in the 1830s.

Catedral al Sur

Calle Chile, a street that was originally a stream, once separated Buenos Aires's first residential community from the more rural southern suburbs. A little bridge along Calle Defensa once linked the two neighborhoods. Here the district known as Catedral al Sur (South of the Cathedral) starts and extends to the Plaza de Mayo, half a dozen blocks to the north. Once a warehouse area with easy access to the port, this district is now the city's tourist tango center, with dozens of small clubs offering lively evening entertainment.

Santo Domingo, one of the city's oldest churches, dates from the 1750s. Its austere exterior has been maintained as it was originally. The church is dedicated to Our Lady of the Rosary, in whose chapel four banners captured in 1806 from fleeing British troops—after their unsuccessful attempt to invade the then-Spanish colony—are on display, as well as two flags taken from the Spanish armies during the War of Independence. On one of the bell towers, bullet craters—testimony of the battle with British soldiers—are reminders of the conflict. The remains of General Manuel Belgrano, a hero of the War of Independence, rest in the atrium in an imposing marble coffin guarded by marble angels. *Calle Defensa 422,* ☎ *1/331–1668.* ☞ *Free.* ☉ *Daily 4:30–7.*

Farther along Calle Defensa, at the corner of Calle Alsina, climb the steep stairs to the **Museo de la Ciudad** (Municipal Museum), which displays whimsical and probing temporary exhibitions about many aspects of domestic and public life in Buenos Aires in times gone by. The Farmacia La Estrella (La Estrella Pharmacy), a quaint survivor from the 19th century, is on the ground floor of the building. *Calle Alsina 412,* ☎ *1/331–9855 or 1/343–2123.* ☞ *Entry fee.* ☉ *Weekdays 11–7, Sun. 3–7; closed Sat.*

The **Iglesia de San Francisco,** and the smaller **Capilla San Roque** to its left, are just across Calle Defensa. This remodeled church was originally built in 1754. Its Bavarian baroque facade was added in 1911, and the interior was lavishly refurbished after the church was looted and burned in 1955 in the turmoil just before Peron's government fell. *Calle Defensa at Calle Alsina.* ☞ *Free.* ☉ *Daily 4:30–7.*

La Manzana de las Luces (the Block of Bright Lights), at the corner of Calles Alsina and Perú, is the name that was given to the cultural institutions that were housed in various large buildings built here in the early 19th century. Before that the block belonged to the Jesuits until they were expelled from the Spanish colonies in 1767. The bulky, neoclassical building on the site where the old San Ignacio School stood is the **Colegio Nacional,** the leading public high school.

Next to the school stands what is probably Buenos Aires's oldest church. **San Ignacio** was started in 1713 and is the only church from that era to have a Baroque facade. Behind the church, a neoclassical facade dating from 1863 hides the old colonial building that headquartered the administrators of the Jesuits' vast land holdings in northeast Argentina and Paraguay. In 1780 the city's first Facultad de Medicina (Medical School) was established here. In the early 19th century, the Universidad de Buenos Aires (the University of Buenos Aires) was here. The tunnels underneath the building, which crisscrossed the colonial town and were used by the military or by smugglers, depending on which version you believe, can still be visited. *Calle Perú 272,* ☎ *1/342–6973.* ☛ *Entry fee. Tours on weekends at 3:30 and 5.*

A short walk along Diagonal Sur (also called Avenida Roque Saenz Peña), one of two wide avenues bisecting the access streets, leads to the **Plaza de Mayo,** the city's most historic plaza, named after the Revolution of May in 1810. This two-block-long plaza has been the stage for many important events in local history, including the uprising against Spain on May 25, 1810. The tradition of staging both celebrations and protests in this central plaza continues to this day. It is here that the Madres de la Plaza de Mayo (Mothers of Plaza de Mayo), the mothers of young people who vanished during the military government's reign from 1976 to 1983, hold their Thursday afternoon marches, which attracted international attention in the late 1970s. The present layout dates from 1912, when the obelisk known as the **Piramide de Mayo** was placed in the center. The pyramid was erected in 1811 to celebrate the first anniversary of the Revolution of May. A bronze equestrian statue of General Manuel Belgrano at the east end of the plaza was made in 1873. Looking west at the far end of Avenida de Mayo, the tall dome of the home of Argentina's parliament, the **Congreso,** on the Plaza del Congreso, is often framed against spectacular sunsets. The dozen blocks of Avenida de Mayo, built at the turn of the century in the manner of Parisian boulevards, offer many sidewalk cafés. A look at the architecture along the avenue, with whimsical towers and imposing facades, is worth the risk of tripping on the often uneven or broken sidewalk.

At the eastern end of the square, the Casa de Gobierno (Presidential Office Building), better known as the **Casa Rosada,** dominates the view toward the river. The first-floor balcony on the northern wing of this pale-pink palace is used by the country's leaders to harangue the enormous crowds that gather below. In the back, at the basement level, the thick ground-floor brick walls of the Taylor Customs House (named for the builder), the old customs house dating from the 1850s, have been partially uncovered after being buried for half a century when the Plaza Colón was built. The site can be visited from the outside or as part of a visit to the adjoining **Museo de la Casa Rosada,** a museum that features anecdotal presidential memorabilia. *Calle Hipólito Yrigoyen 211,* ☎ *1/342–0421; for guided tours,* ☎ *1/342–0421.* ☛ *Free.* ☉ *Sun.–Tues. and Thurs.–Fri.*

The **Cabildo,** directly in front of the Casa Rosada on the Plaza de Mayo, is considered one of Argentina's national shrines. Here is where patriotic citizens gathered in May 1810 to vote against Spanish rule. The original building dates from 1725. *Calle Bolivar 65,* ☎ *1/343–1782.* ☛ *Entry fee.* ☉ *Thurs.–Sun. 2–6.*

Across Avenida Rivadavia, adding a conservative tone to the plaza's profile, is the **Banco de la Nación Argentina,** the state bank, designed in 1940 in monumental neoclassical style by architect Alejandro Bustillo, who designed most of the city's government buildings in the 1930s and 1940s. On the next block, the **Catedral Metropolitana** hardly looks like a Latin American church. The neoclassical facade of the city's cathedral was initiated in 1822, but the building predates the facade by a century. The remains of General José de San Martín, known as the Argentine Liberator in the War of Independence against Spain, are buried here in a marble mausoleum carved by the French sculptor Carrière Belleuse. The tomb is permanently guarded by soldiers of the Grenadier Regiment, a troop created and trained by San Martín in 1811.

At the intersection of Diagonal Norte (also called Avenida Roque Saenz Peña), Avenida Corrientes and the Avenida 9 de Julio stands the **Obelisco,** the enormous, pointed 221½-foot-tall tower that is one of the city's most prominent landmarks. It was built in 1936 as part of a major public works program.

Calle Florida, a pedestrians-only shopping street, runs from Diagonal Norte to the Plaza San Martín. The closer you get to the San Martín Plaza, the better the offerings. Once the shopping was Buenos Aires's best, but no longer. Now the crowd is composed of businesspeople and secretaries scurrying to work and those who prey on unsuspecting passersby, trying to lure them into nearby shops.

Calle Lavalle, another pedestrian street, intersects Calle Florida a block north of Avenida Corrientes. Corrientes and Lavalle between Florida and Avenida 9 de Julio house cinemas and theaters. Lavalle, being narrower, becomes a solid sea of flesh when the street's dozen cinemas simultaneously change their clientele. On weekends these few blocks are packed until 3 AM, when the last moviegoers are finishing their post-show pizza.

The **Teatro Colón,** the world-famous opera house and lyric theater, has hosted the likes of María Callas, Arturo Toscanini, Igor Stravinsky, and Enrico Caruso. The Italian-style building with French decoration is the result of a joint effort by several successive turn-of-the-century architects. With only 3,500 seats, many of which are held by season-ticket holders, the lines stretch around the block when an international celebrity is starring. A fascinating guided tour of the theater and museum provides a glimpse at the building's inner workshops, which are like medieval cities in which the guilds busily ply their trades. The international season runs from April to November. *Ticket office: Calle Cerrito 618, ☎ 1/355–4146, ext. 230. Tours by appointment only, Mon.–Sat. hourly 10–4.*

The former headquarters of the Buenos Aires–Pacific Railway, a building designed during Buenos Aires's turn-of-the-century golden age after Milan's Gallerie Vittorio Emanuele, was refurbished in 1992 into a glossy, multilevel California-style shopping mall called **Galerías Pacífico.** In an earlier renovation a large central dome was added, and five leading Argentine artists were commissioned to paint murals.

Plaza San Martín

Once a field in a muddy suburb, **Plaza San Martín** gradually evolved at the northern end of the city next to the steep riverbanks. Originally populated by vagrants and marginal members of a rough-and-tumble colonial society, the area eventually became the site of some of the most sumptuous town houses in Buenos Aires. The imposing bronze equestrian monument to General José de San Martín, built in 1862 by French artist Louis Daumas, dominates the park. French landscape architect Charles Thays designed the park in the 19th century with a mix of traditional local and exotic imported trees that continue to add to the stately feel of the neighborhood.

On the southern side of the plaza, the **Edificio Kavanagh,** a soaring apartment tower built in the 1930s in the then-popular Rationalist style, rises in all its glory. It is still one of the few truly handsome apartment buildings in the city. Next to it, local financier Ernesto Tornquist commissioned German architect Alfred Zucker in 1908 to build the **Plaza Hotel,** a building which—like its namesake in New York City—still maintains its glow.

The city's most active art gallery, **Galería Ruth Benzacar** (Calle Florida 1000, ☎ 1/313–8480), is down a flight of stairs just where Florida ends in front of the Plaza San Martín. If you want a stimulating overview of contemporary Argentine art, ask to see the vast stock of paintings in the basement. The gallery itself is well designed and offers monthly shows of significant modern Argentine artists.

The **Círculo Militar,** a monument to the nobler historic pursuits of the Argentine armed forces, was built in 1902 in the heavily ornamental French style of the period as the Paz family residence by French architect Louis Sortais. The **Museo Nacional de Armas** in the basement is packed with military memorabilia. *Calle Maipú 1092,* ☎ *1/311–0729, ext. 130.* ☛ *Free.* ☉ *Tues.–Fri. 3–7, Sat. 9–1; closed Sun.*

Across Avenida Marcelo T. de Alvear from the Círculo, behind the sixth-floor windows of the corner apartment (Maipú 994) are the rooms where Jorge Luis Borges lived and wrote many of his poems and short stories.

The **Palacio San Martín,** which was once the residence of the Anchorena family, has been the Ministry of Foreign Affairs since 1936. The ornate building, designed in 1909 by Alejandro Cristophersen in the grandiose French neoclassical style, is an example of the turn-of-the-century opulence in Buenos Aires that rivaled that of Manhattan.

Barrio Norte

Barrio Norte, a residential and shopping district just north of the Plaza San Martín, is a wonderful walking area, packed with boutiques and cafés, handsome old homes, clubs, and plazas. Here many of the city's most distinguished—and wealthy—citizens live, some in palatial splendor. The not-as-affluent live in one-room boxes built in the '60s, when ceilings were reduced to less than 7 feet. It's basically a residential neighborhood, so at night the streets are quiet and uncrowded. In the morning, the only people to be seen early are hordes of uniformed kids scurrying off to school and *porteros* (janitors) hosing down the sidewalk in front of their buildings; Buenos Aires is a city of late risers.

Barrio Norte boasts one of the city's few winding streets, **Arroyo,** which has become a magnet for boutiques, galleries, and antiques shops. The **Museo de Arte Hispanoamericano Isaac Fernández Blanco** (Museum of Hispano-American Art) was built as the residence of the architect Martín Noel, who designed it in the late 18th century in an eclectic post-Spanish style. The overgrown, almost junglelike garden provides an awesome background for outdoor theatrical performances mounted here in summer. The museum has an extensive collection of colonial silver, wood carvings, and paintings, which give a hint of the wealth and quality of craftsmanship in colonial South America. *Calle Suipacha 142,* ☎ *1/327–0183, 1/327–9268, or 1/476–3981.* ☛ *Entry fee.* ☉ *Tues–Sun. 2–6.*

The **Plaza Carlos Pellegrini** is surrounded by a cluster of important buildings, also formerly residences of the country's large landowning families. The **Embajada de Brasil** (Arroyo 1142) has a stately neoclassical facade, but it holds an even better treasure inside: A series of murals by Spanish artist **José Luis Sert** cover the walls and ceilings.

The **Embajada de Francia,** once the home of the Ortiz Basualdo family, was designed in the early 20th century by French architect Phillipe Pater; it is so monumental that the city decided to loop the continuation of Avenida 9 de Julio around the back of it. Across the street the **Atucha** family home and the **Jockey Club** are two more examples of neoclassical French architecture. A French Renaissance house, the

Alzaga Unzué residence, built in the late 19th century, was saved from demolition by a group of local conservationists. The Park Hyatt Hotel rises from what was the property's garden, and the old home has been converted into suites.

Patio Bullrich, on Calle Posadas, is the most exclusive shopping center in town. The multilevel mall was once the headquarters for the Bullrich family auction house, Buenos Aires's most renowned auctioneers. The basement held hundreds of head of cattle during auctions and the upper floors were dedicated to selling paintings, furniture, and antiques, including portraits of the livestock and their owners. If you look carefully at the walls on the upper level, you'll see stucco heads of steers emerging in relief. The auction business now functions next door under the name of **Posadas** (Calle Posadas 1227, ☎ 1/327–2025); its exhibits, furnishings and artwork from many important local estates offer a penetrating look at how Argentines traditionally decorate their homes.

The five-block-long **Avenida Alvear** is a condensed version of New York's Park Avenue. At the beginning of the century it became the exclusive site for mansions in the French grand hôtel tradition. The **Vatican** has its local headquarters, the Papal See, near the corner of Calle Libertad, and the property stretches downhill to Calle Posadas, giving the papal ambassador one of the finest gardens and views in the city. On the other side of Avenida Callao are the best jewelers and the fanciest boutiques in town, along with the spectacular **Alvear Palace Hotel,** whose roof garden and lobby are famous gathering places; the lobby, set out with tables, is a great spot to stop for a cup of tea or a drink.

The **Recoleta,** at the far end of Avenida Alvear, was once notorious as a neighborhood where no one wanted to live because it bordered a cemetery. About 20 years ago a few brave restaurateurs decided to take advantage of the low rents. Now the two blocks next to the cemetery form the most fashionable dining area in the city. Several years ago part of the area was closed to traffic and street-side cafés spread into the street. Here people-watching is a highly developed art practiced predominantly by the perennially tanned and trim. This is a sight not to be missed on a sunny spring day. The **Centro Cultural Recoleta** (Recoleta Cultural Center) attracts tens of thousands of visitors on weekends to its art shows and concerts. *Calle R. M. Ortiz 1750,* ☎ *1/804–0878 or 1/806–3456.* ☛ *Free.* ☉ *Tues.–Sat. after 2, all day Sun.*

The first buildings at the Recoleta date from the early 18th century, when Franciscan monks were given the land by the Spanish crown to develop. The friars built **Nuestra Señora del Pilar,** a rambling church and cloister complex that is a fine example of early colonial Baroque. The principal altar is made of engraved silver from Peru. Today the church is a popular place for weddings, and you can sometimes see the elegantly dressed guests mingling with the craftsmen who hold a weekend fair on the slopes of the adjoining park.

The **Cementerio de la Recoleta** (Recoleta Cemetery), next to the church, contains the elaborate mausoleums of a *Who's Who* of Argentine history: presidents, political leaders, soldiers, authors, ranchers. The embalmed body of Eva Duarte de Peron rests here in the Duarte family tomb, and there is a handsome statue of Luis Angel Firpo, the world heavyweight boxing champion known as the "Bull of the Pampas." To see the highlights, proceed from the entrance along the main avenue until you reach the central crossing, then turn right and continue counterclockwise through the back pathways.

The **Museo Nacional de Bellas Artes** (National Museum of Fine Arts), Buenos Aires's only major art museum, is housed in a building that was once the city's waterworks. The collection includes several major Impressionist paintings and an overview of 19th- and 20th-century Argentine art, the highlight of which is a room dedicated to the Paraguayan war scenes painted by a soldier, Cándido López, whose paintings are also in the National Historical Museum (*see above*). A new wing offers a challenging selection of contemporary Argentine art. *Av. del Libertador 1473,* ☎ *1/803–0802 for a tour.* ☛ *Entry fee.* ☉ *Tues.–Sun.*

At the center of **Plaza Francia,** between Avenida Pueyrredon, Avenida del Libertador, and Calle Luis Agote, is a large outdoor group of statuary donated by the French government for the centennial. A large equestrian statue of General Bartolomé Mitre, a former president, dominates **Plaza Mitre,** on Avenida del Libertador between Calles Luis Agote and Aguero. The site, which was once at the edge of the river, provides a perspective on the surrounding parks.

It took three decades to build the **Biblioteca Nacional** (National Library), which finally was inaugurated in 1991. The eccentric modern building was the result of an international design competition won by Argentine architects Clorindo Testa and Francisco Bullrich. *Calle Aguero 2502,* ☎ *1/806–6155.* ☛ *Free.* ☉ *Mon.–Sat.*

The **Museo Nacional de Arte Decorativo** (National Museum of Decorative Arts), housed in a magnificent French classical landmark building, has a fascinating collection, mostly donated by the country's leading families. The **Museo de Arte Oriental** is also housed here on a "permanent" temporary basis. *Av. del Libertador 1902,* ☎ *1/801–8248.* ☛ *Entry fee.* ☉ *Wed.–Fri.*

Parks and Gardens

Plaza Italia, a busy place in the Palermo district, is bordered by three important sites: the **Jardín Zoológico** (zoo; Republica de la India 2900, ☎ 1/806–7415 or 1/806–7418), the **Jardín Botánico** (botanical gardens; Av. Santa Fe 3817, ☎ 1/831–2951 or 1/832–1601), and the **Sociedad Rural Argentina** (livestock fairgrounds; Av. Las Heras 4051, ☎ 1/774–1702), which often have exhibitions of interest to children. **Palermo Park,** which extends north parallel to the river, just beyond the zoo, is vast, with lakes, walking trails, and places to eat or have coffee. It is solid humanity on weekends, with cars parked on the grass and flying soccer balls everywhere.

Shopping

Shopping Districts
Calle Florida, the downtown shopping street, is a good place to look first and establish a quality standard by which you can gauge so-called bargains in factory outlets. Downtown **Avenida Santa Fe** is designed for browsing, along with the streets and avenues in the **Recoleta** neighborhood. Sensational Art Deco items can occasionally be found at **San Telmo's** antiques shops.

Specialty Shops
FUR
Furs are gorgeous and great bargains in Argentina, at times costing half the price of a coat of the same quality in the United States. The stubtailed nutria, a cousin of the beaver, is native to Argentine rivers and lakes. Its long outer hair is waterproof and a bit harsh to the touch, but the short fur underneath is as soft as velvet. Plucked nutria, there-

fore, is more costly. Fox from Tierra del Fuego is a reddish color, while the Magellanic fox is a more silky, beigy gray. **Dennis Furs** (Calle Florida 989, ☎ 1/311–8920) is one of the leading fur dealers. Look also at the excellent selection at **Charles Calfun** (Calle Florida 918, ☎ 1/311–1147).

JEWELRY

Precious and semiprecious stones are priced similarly all over Latin America. What varies is the price and quality of the workmanship. Argentina has benefited from the expertise of French, German, and Italian jewelers who brought with them a sophisticated sense of design. **H. Stern** (Sheraton, Plaza, Hyatt, and Alvear Palace hotels) is a good place to begin looking at what Argentine designers do with Brazilian stones. One semiprecious stone—known as the Rose of the Inca, or *rodocrosita*—is native only to Argentina; stones range from pink to red, with some of them as red as rubies. Sculptures of birds in flight from **Cousino** (Paraguay 631, 3rd Floor, Suite A, ☎ 1/312–2336, and the Sheraton Hotel) are exhibited in the National Museum of Decorative Arts. **Guthman** (Viamonte 597, ☎ 1/312–2471) has an acclaimed selection of jewelry. **Santarelli** (Calle Florida 688, ☎ 1/393–8152) is another top jeweler.

LEATHER

Argentina's reputation for fine leathers is occasionally well deserved, and you can find cowhide, kidskin, pigskin, sheepskin, lizard, snake, or porcupine. A seasoned buyer can choose from a rainbow of pastels and vivid colors, rough suedes and others that are soft as baby's skin.

In clothing, styles range from conservative to hip; women can find everything from bikinis to evening gowns. **Casa López** (M. T. de Alvear 640 and other locations, ☎ 1/311–3044) has generations of experience in dealing with travelers. **Lofty** (M. T. de Alvear 519, ☎ 1/311–1424) features reversible coats with smooth suede on one side and shiny leather on the other. **Jota IJ Cueros** (Pasaje Tres Sargentos 439, ☎ 1/311–0826) specializes in sewing any style or color to your measurements within a few hours.

For men's loafers, **Guido** (Calle Florida 704, ☎ 1/802–6340) is Argentina's favorite. For men's shoes that look great and last forever, try **López Taibo** (Av. Corrientes 350, ☎ 1/311–2132). Shoes, boots, and saddles can be found at **Rossi y Caruso** (Av. Santa Fe 1601, ☎ 1/811–1538), a London-style shop that offers the best in riding equipment as well as handbags and clothing; King Juan Carlos of Spain and many other celebrities are clients here. Polo equipment and saddles can be found at **H. Merlo** (Calle Juncal 743, ☎ 1/327–6116). **La Martina** (Calle Paraguay 661, ☎ 1/311–5963) also carries furnishings for the discriminating equestrian.

For briefcases, try **Pullman** (Calle Florida 985, ☎ 1/311–0799), which features the latest yuppie-lawyer styles as well as lightweight leather bags for carry-on luggage.

SHEEPSKIN AND WOOL KNITWEAR

Argentina has traditionally been the world's largest exporter of wool. One legitimate factory outlet for sweaters that is located downtown is **IKS** (Calle Paraguay 472, ☎ 1/311–4452). **Silvia y Mario** (Calle M. T. de Alvear 550, ☎ 1/311–4107), another downtown outlet, stocks a huge selection of cashmere and very elegant, two-piece knit dresses. Sheepskin jackets at the **Ciudad de Cuero** (Calle Florida 940) would make the Marlboro man leap off his mount to purchase a winter's supply; **Jota U Cueros** (Pasaje Tres Sargentos 439, ☎ 1/311–0826) can provide quickly made-to-order sheepskin clothing in stunning combinations of gray, black, and brown.

Shopping Centers

For many years the city's most luxurious shopping arcade was the galleried **Patio Bullrich** (Av. del Libertador 750) near the Park Hyatt, but it has recently been eclipsed in popularity by **Alto Palermo** (corner of Av. Santa Fe and Av. Colonel Diaz; take the D subway line to Bulnes) and **Paseo Alcorta** (Calle Salguero 3212, Palermo Chico), which opened in 1992 and has a gigantic Carrefour hypermarket. The most recent addition is **Galerías Pacífico** (Calle Florida 755). This spectacular mall—the only one downtown—is decorated with murals by several of Argentina's most important artists and has an eating area with first-rate people-watching.

Sports

Chess

Pursuing a hobby, especially one with such a universal language as chess, is a good way to meet Argentines. It is played in the basement lounge of the **Richmond** (Calle Florida 468, ☎ 1/322–1341), where you can also play billiards; upstairs at the **Confitería Ideal** (Calle Suipacha 384, ☎ 1/294–1081); and at **Café Tortoni** (Av. de Mayo 825, ☎ 1/342–4328), where dice shooters are also welcome. The newest spot for chess is in the mansion wing of the **Park Hyatt Buenos Aires** (*see* Lodging, *below*), where you can also find an elegant game of billiards.

Golf

The city has a public golf course 10 minutes from downtown: **Cancha Municipal de Golf** (Calles Tornquist and Olleros, Palermo, ☎ 1/772–7576). For practicing, try **Costa Salguero Golf Center** (Av. Costanera and Calle Salguero, ☎ 1/805–1216), a driving range with the city's best view of the river. For more information, call the **Asociación Argentina de Golf** (Argentine Golf Association, Av. Corrientes 538, ☎ 1/394–2743).

Horse Racing

Historians consider the strong Thoroughbreds from Argentina one of the factors that favored the British in the South African Boer War. Argentines on spending binges brought, and occasionally still bring, the best stock in the world home to breed, and swift Argentine horses are prized throughout the world. Although the past 40 years of rough economic times have handicapped the Thoroughbred industry, Argentine horses still win their share of stakes races in North America and Europe. There are two main tracks in Buenos Aires; check the English-language *Buenos Aires Herald* for schedules. Generally, races take place on Wednesday and weekends at **Hipódromo de San Isidro** (Av. Márquez 504, ☎ 1/743–4010) in the historic suburb of San Isidro. Closer to downtown is the dirt track at the traditional **Hipódromo Argentino** (Av. del Libertador 4499, Palermo, ☎ 1/772–6022).

Paddle Tennis

The city has hundreds of courts; call for a reservation at one of the following: Calle Ayacucho 1669, ☎ 1/801–3848; Calle Necochea 854, ☎ 1/361–7277; Calle Salguero 3450, ☎ 1/802–2619; or Calle Río Bamba 515, ☎ 1/373–2573.

Polo

Argentine polo has been compared to a performance of Moscow's Bolshoi Ballet in its heyday—a strenuous display of stunning athletic showmanship. At the Canchas Nacionales in Buenos Aires, sold-out crowds of 20,000 cheer on national heroes such as Gonzalo Pieres, a 10-goaler ranked tops in the world. For match information, contact the **Asociación Argentina de Polo** (H. Yrigoyen 636, 1st Floor, ☏ 1/343–0972). Seasons run March–May and September–December. The best teams compete in the World Championships in November, and the world polo set gathers in Buenos Aires to celebrate.

Soccer

Soccer matches are played year-round. Passions run high when Boca Juniors from the fanatic community of La Boca take on their arch-rivals, River Plate, at the **Estadio Boca.** To see another side of Argentine passion, go to a game. Try to find an Argentine to show you the ropes. Sitting among tens of thousands of roaring fans can be a disconcerting experience, especially if you get swept off your perch in the bleachers as a human wave slides five rows back and forth to cheer a goal.

Squash

Try the centrally located **Olimpia Cancilería** (Calle Esmeralda 1042, ☏ 1/313–7375), which also offers racquetball; **Posadas Squash Club** (Calle Posadas 1265, 7th Floor, ☏ 1/327–0548); or the **Tribunales Squash Courts** (Calle Montevideo 550, ☏ 1/373–8358).

Tennis

Professional tennis is played at the **Buenos Aires Lawn Tennis Club** (Av. Olleros 1510, ☏ 1/772–9227). Guillermo Vilas, José Luis Clerc, and Gabriela Sabatini are products of local clubs.

There are public tennis courts at the **Buenos Aires Lawn Tennis Club** (Av. Olleros 1510, ☏ 1/772–9227), **Parque Norte** (Calles Cantilo and Guiraldes, Costanera Norte, ☏ 1/784–9653), and **Parque Jose Hernandez** (Av. Valentin Alsina 1270, Palermo, ☏ 1/782–0936). Arrangements can be made through the executive offices at the **Sheraton** (San Martín 1225, ☏ 1/311–6331) to play on the hotel's courts.

Other Sports

Boxing and wrestling matches are held in **Luna Park** (Calle Bouchard 465, ☏ 1/311–1990 or 1/312–2538), an indoor arena; cricket at the suburban **Hurlingham Club** (Av. J. A. Roca 1411, ☏ 1/665–0401) and other Anglo-Argentine enclaves. Check the *Herald*.

Dining

Dining out is one of the Argentines' favorite pastimes, and a very time-consuming diversion, with three-course dinners lasting two or three hours. No one can linger over an espresso longer than an Argentine—and no waiter would consider rushing a client through his conversation—but then Argentine waiters enjoy the sport of conversation as much as the customers. One consequence is that the restaurant ambience, whether elegant or casual, is a delightful combination of gusto and languidness. Reservation times for second sittings tend to be elastic, as it is impossible to calculate how long any table may stay and chat.

Except in the hottest months of summer (December–February), Argentines dress up to go out; particular dress codes are noted in reviews. In general, reservations are not necessary, except in the fanciest establishments and on weekends. Most restaurants serve dinner from around 8:30 PM to 2 AM or later, and several are closed for vacation in January and February, when many transfer their staff to branches at the beaches. For price ratings, *see* Dining *in* Argentina Essentials, *below.*

Argentine

$$$ **La Cabaña.** Catering to an international crowd, this classic, elegant steak
★ house specializes in steaks, but also offers a wide selection of interna-
tional cuisine. Two stuffed steers greet guests at the front door; the for-
mal dining room within is done in dark paneling, and the tables are
spaced so that you don't feel squeezed in. A baby beef (a gigantic steak
from a young steer) and omelet surprise (baked Alaska) make a meal
you'll never forget. ✗ *Av. Entre Ríos 436,* ☎ *1/381–2373. Reserva-
tions advised. AE, DC, MC, V.*

$$$ **La Herradura.** This suburban parrilla features meats prepared over char-
coal embers. Favorites include grilled lamb and suckling pig, plus a wide
range of imaginative salads. ✗ *Calle Dardo Rocha 1260, San Isidro,*
☎ *1/798–5962. Weekend reservations required. AE, DC, MC, V.*

$$ **A Los Amigos.** Steaks, ribs, and innards of various sorts are the fare at
this eatery at the edge of the Río de la Plata. Both outdoor and indoor
dining areas offer panoramic views. ✗ *Av. Rafael Obligado/Costan-
era Norte,* ☎ *1/782–9140. Reservations advised. AE, DC, MC, V.*

$$ **Dora.** This is the basic Argentine eatery at its best; the place to go for
★ your first Argentine steak, if you like your steak thick and juicy. Walls
and ceiling are hung with hams and wine bottles. The portions are generous and the quality of the food excellent. Perhaps the only restaurant in Argentina with a line at the door, it can be noisy when full, but
it is well worth experiencing. Try to arrive early—by 12:30 for lunch
and 8:30 for dinner. ✗ *Av. Leandro N. Alem 1016,* ☎ *1/311–2891.
No reservations. No credit cards. Closed Sun.*

$$ **Happening.** This restaurant on the Costanera Norte stands out among
the many eateries strung along the river beyond the city airport. Com-
peting with the water view are good service and good food—broiled
or grilled beef, pork, or fish—that goes beyond the area's usual steak-
and-potato meals. Porteños gather here in hordes on weekends. ✗ *Calle
Costanera Norte,* ☎ *1/782–8207. AE, DC, MC, V.*

$$ **Happening II.** Under the same management as the riverside Happening (*above*), this restaurant in Recoleta is all urban elegance, with a
glass roof and plants. Here, too, grilled beef, pork, and fish are the specialties; especially recommended is grilled *chernia*, a tasty fish from the
south Atlantic. ✗ *Calle Guido 1931,* ☎ *1/805–2633. Reservations advised. AE, DC, MC, V.*

$$ **La Caballeriza.** This grill occupies what was once a renowned racing
stable and a courtyard shaded by grapevines. Excellent grilled steaks
are the specialty. The ambience, the young, enthusiastic staff, and the
fine preparation and presentation combine to make the journey to the
northern suburbs well worth the effort. Take the Mitre line train from
Estación de Retiro to the Acassuso station in Martinez; the restaurant
is a 5–10-minute taxi ride from the station. ✗ *Calle Dardo Rocha 1740,
Martinez,* ☎ *1/793–6085. Reservations required. No credit cards.*

$$ **La Mosca Blanca.** You shouldn't let the name—The White Fly—or the
crazy location put you off. Be prepared for super-huge menus, an
amusingly eclectic clientele, and gigantic portions; you can split a plate
with your dinner partner. Try a *Milanesa rellena* (a cutlet topped with
ham, cheese, and tomato) or other typical Argentine food at its tastiest—your reward for being adventurous enough to attempt to find this
place. It is on the access road between the Belgrano and San Martín
railway stations in Retiro. ✗ *Turn at Av. Ramos Mejía 1430, across
from the Sheraton hotel,* ☎ *1/313–4890. Weekend reservations required.
AE, DC, MC, V. Closed Sun.*

$$ **Las Nazarenas.** This popular parrilla is across the street from the Sher-
aton in a two-story, Spanish colonial–style building with wrought-iron
sconces and potted ferns. A popular lunch stop for Argentine busi-

nessmen, it features grilled steaks and brochettes. For an appetizer, try sliced *matambre* (a stuffed roll of flank steak) or thick slices of grilled provolone cheese sprinkled with oregano. ✗ *Calle Reconquista 1132,* ☎ *1/312–5559. Reservations advised. AE, DC, MC, V.*

$$ **La Tranquera.** This is one of the few *asado*, or grilled meat, restaurants that serves *chivito* (kid)—and it's grilled to finger-licking perfection. You can also order parrilladas with the works: tripe, sweetbreads, kidneys, and specialties from the south. Banks of coals and sizzling meat on spits flank the entrance pavilion. Icy pitchers of *clericot* (white-wine sangria) are a cooling choice on summer nights. ✗ *Av. Figueroa Alcorta 6464,* ☎ *1/784–6119. Reservations advised. AE, DC, MC, V.*

$$ **Parrilla Rosa.** What is currently the city's trendiest grill on a corner in Villa Freud, the neighborhood where the city's analysts practice, serves well-prepared brochettes, *Lomo a la mostaza* (beef fillet with mustard sauce), and steaks. The plain decor is the backdrop for lots of people talking as fast as they can. ✗ *Calle Uriburu 1488,* ☎ *1/806–7720. Reservations advised. AE, MC, V. No lunch.*

$$ **Río Alba.** This eatery serves up juicy, lean pork served with lemon slices and shoestring potatoes and an excellent variety of plates from the grill, such as tuna steak. The decor is basic Argentine, with lots of stacked wine bottles, hanging hams, and sports-related memorabilia. Its location near the U.S. Embassy makes it a favorite of the American expatriate crowd, among others. It's noisy when packed. ✗ *Calle Cerviño 4499,* ☎ *1/773–9508. Weekend reservations required. AE, DC, MC, V.*

$ **El Ceibal.** The food here is from the northwest part of the country that borders Bolivia and Chile, with Spanish-Inca dishes, such as *carbonada* (a beef stew) and *locro* (a rich, savory soup made with potatoes and corn). ✗ *Av. Las Heras 2379,* ☎ *1/803–5522. No credit cards. Closed Mon.*

$ **El Palacio de la Papa Frita.** A family restaurant with good steaks and an endless general menu, this restaurant is an institution, packed at lunch and dinner, catering to the movie crowd. ✗ *Calle Lavalle 735,* ☎ *1/393–5849. AE, DC, MC, V.*

$ **La Querencia.** The classic gaucho fare in this tidy little hole-in-the-wall restaurant includes various types of empanadas and tamales, plus rich local soups and stews. ✗ *Two locations: Calle Esmeralda 1392 and Calle Junín 1304,* ☎ *1/822–4644. Reservations advised. No credit cards.*

British

$$$ **Alexander.** It's a bit on the shabby side, but the food outclasses the environment. The rare rack of lamb melts in the mouth and is a classic choice for the city's anglophiles, especially at lunch. Dinner is less crowded. ✗ *Calle San Martín 774,* ☎ *1/311–2878. Jacket and tie. AE, DC, MC, V. Closed Sun.*

$$$ **Down Town Matías.** Tucked behind the Plaza Hotel on the ground floor of a modern high-rise, this establishment serves such typical English fare as lamb stew and kidney pie in a chummy, publike atmosphere. ✗ *Calle San Martín 979,* ☎ *1/312–9844. Reservations required. AE, DC, MC, V. Lunch only, pub closes at 10 PM; closed Sun.*

$$$ **London Grill.** Tasty roast beef and Yorkshire pudding, chicken pie, and steak-and-kidney pie are all served in a clublike atmosphere with paneling that has the proper patina. ✗ *Calle Reconquista 455,* ☎ *1/311–2223. Reservations advised. AE, DC, MC, V. Lunch only.*

Chinese

$$ **Cantina China.** Probably the best-known and oldest Asian restaurant in town, the Cantina has been a favorite for years. The chicken with almonds and the seafood plates are good choices. The decor is pure

Hong Kong: gold and red with an eclectic selection of paintings. ✕ *Calle Maipú 967,* ☎ *1/312–7391. AE, DC, MC, V.*

$$ **Chinatown.** In a city not noted for its Chinese cuisine, Chinatown stands out. It's in Belgrano near the train station, with the traditional red-and-black pagoda-style decor. ✕ *Av. Juramento 1656,* ☎ *1/786–3456. AE, DC, V.*

French

$$$ **Au Bec Fin.** Delectable prawn mousse and a tartly sweet plum *bavaroise*
★ (creamy liqueur-flavored drink) are the culinary stars in this baronial town house, the perfect site for a splurge or a romantic occasion. Trout stuffed with shrimp and a beef fillet with cheddar-and-mushroom sauce are two other delicious choices. ✕ *Calle Vicente López 1825,* ☎ *1/801–6894. Reservations required. AE, DC, MC, V. Closed Sun.*

$$$ **Catalinas.** Chef Ramiro Pardo gives a personal touch to a basically French
★ menu in which seafood and game stand out. Decorated in the fashion of a countryside auberge, this restaurant offers unforgettable meals. Lobster tail on country-fresh eggs with caviar and cream, and *pejerrey* (a small freshwater fish) stuffed with king-crab mousse are not to be missed. The dining room is packed wall-to-wall with businessmen at lunch, but it draws a more varied crowd at night. Several fixed-price menus make this gourmet's delight easier on the pocket. ✕ *Calle Reconquista 875,* ☎ *1/313–0182. Reservations required. AE, DC, MC, V. Closed Sat. and Sun. lunch.*

$$$ **Hippopotamus.** This trendy, ultramodern dining room attached to a high-tech nightclub serves such light but satisfying dishes as pink salmon baked in foil with an herb sauce. The view of the Recoleta Park at lunchtime is delightful. Dinner is frequented by an elegant international crowd. ✕ *Calle R. M. Ortiz 1787,* ☎ *1/318–3000 or 1/313–7403. Reservations required. AE, DC, MC, V. Closed Sun.–Mon.*

$$$ **La Cave de Valais.** This small, cozy restaurant is one of the few places in town to try venison. There's a fixed-price menu. Or have a fondue or raclette, a Swiss melted-cheese dish. ✕ *Calle Zapiola 1779,* ☎ *1/551–4435. Reservations required. AE, DC. Closed lunch and Sun.*

$$$ **La Mansion.** With its turn-of-the-century French decor, this fine restaurant in the mansion wing of the Park Hyatt hotel is one of the most exclusive dining experiences in Buenos Aires. Try the appetizer of smoked salmon with dill-cream sauce, or the pheasant with port wine sauce as a main course. Afternoon tea is served weekdays 4–7. ✕ *Calle Posadas 1086,* ☎ *1/326–3610. Reservations required. Jacket required. AE, DC, MC, V. Closed Sat. lunch and Sun.*

$$$ **La Pergola.** This restaurant in the Hotel Libertador Kempinski offers a classic French menu that is rated very highly by local connoisseurs for savor and service. Crepes *aux champignons* (with mushrooms) are among the lighter options; pastas and grilled steaks are also available. ✕ *Calle Maipú and Av. Córdoba,* ☎ *1/322–2110, 1/322–2186, or 1/322–2288. Reservations required. AE, DC, MC, V.*

$$$ **Lola.** With a full house day and night, this is the obligatory place to be
★ seen on the city's restaurant circuit. A terrine of duck and truffles prepared in cognac, and chicken stuffed with ham, cheese, and mushrooms are good ways to test the usually brilliant chef. ✕ *Calle R. M. Ortiz 1805,* ☎ *1/804–3410. Reservations required. AE, DC, MC, V.*

International

$$$ **Blab.** A varied menu of international favorites such as stuffed veal cutlets and tender fresh sole is offered at this intimately decorated basement hideaway. An upbeat luncheon spot, it's a favorite of the bankers and politicians who work nearby. ✗ *Calle Florida 325, ☎ 1/394–2873. Reservations required. AE, DC, MC, V. Lunch only.*

$$$ **Clark's.** Sophisticated California-style food is served in an elegant, dark-wood paneled setting, with an outdoor garden for summer dining. Traditionally Clark's is one of the city's most popular spots; the chefs are ambitious and innovative but sometimes fall short. ✗ *Calle R. M. Ortiz 1777, ☎ 1/801–9502. Reservations required. AE, DC, MC, V.*

$$$ **Clark's II.** Carlos Dumas kept the paneling of this former menswear
★ store, added a few trophy heads, and installed what is perhaps the city's handsomest restaurant. Don't miss lomo Clark's, a whole beef fillet wrapped in a crisp crust. ✗ *Calle Sarmiento 645, ☎ 1/325–1960. Lunch reservations advised. AE, DC, MC, V. Closed weekends.*

$$$ **El Repecho de San Telmo.** This restaurant is tucked into a small 1807 house on a plaza in the San Telmo historic district. The luxurious dining room has a colonial atmosphere, with Spanish arches, white linen tablecloths, sterling silver utensils on the tables, and waiters in tuxedos. Elaborate meat dishes such as baby beef on creamed watercress and glazed sweet potatoes are served. ✗ *Calle Carlos Calvo 242, ☎ 1/362–5473. Reservations required. AE, DC, MC, V. Closed lunch and Sun.*

$$$ **Gato Dumas.** The focus here is on Continental fare with an emphasis on naturally grown vegetables and herbs lovingly tended and harvested by the restaurant's rather eccentric owner, Carlos "The Cat" Dumas. A recent specialty was "Black Spaghetti Surrounded by the Cosmos." ✗ *Calle R. M. Ortiz 1745, ☎ 1/804–5828. Reservations required. AE, DC, MC, V.*

$$$ **Harper's.** A popular luncheon and dinner spot serves an upscale, yuppie crowd. It's a place to see a revealing cross section of locals and to enjoy a tender steak or a good plate of pasta. *Cordero del Diablo* (a tangy lamb dish) is a traditional favorite. Paintings by local artists hang on the walls. ✗ *Calle R. M. Ortiz 1763, ☎ 1/801–7140. Reservations advised. AE, MC, V.*

$$$ **Patagonia.** Young chef Francis Mallman has a new spot—a small, rustic, and homey establishment where he serves such specialties as sirloin with potatoes Patagonia (prepared with cream and herbs), and tenderloin with hash browns. Mallman never disappoints his faithful clientele, so reservations are at a premium. ✗ *Calle Salguero 3118, ☎ 1/806–0608. Reservations required. AE. Closed Sun.*

$$$ **Pedemonte.** The traditional businessman's lunch at this establishment is a three-course, fixed-price meal well worth trying. The menu is extensive and the plates are well prepared, especially the *pascualina de alcauciles* (artichoke pie) and the pepper steak. ✗ *Av. de Mayo 676, ☎ 1/331–7179. Reservations required. AE, DC, MC, V. Closed Sat.; no Sun. dinner.*

$$$ **Plaza Hotel Grill.** This traditional gathering place for top executives
★ and politicians offers a Continental menu and wine list that are up to the Plaza's high standards. Specialties include sole meunière, rabbit stewed in red wine, and a chestnut mousse. ✗ *Calle Florida 1005, ☎ 1/318–3000 or 1/313–7403. Reservations required. Jacket required. AE, DC, MC, V.*

$$$ **Puerto Marisko.** Fresh seafood is served in a cluttered nautical atmosphere, with fish trophies and thick ropes hanging on the walls. Fried rings of squid are a favorite starter; follow with the fresh catch of the day, flown in from Mar del Plata. Simply prepared grilled fish, prawns, and scallops are specialties. ✗ *Calle Demaria 4658, ☎ 1/773–9051. AE, DC, MC, V. Closed lunch.*

$$$ **Tomo Uno.** Ada Cocaro has been serving up the best food in Buenos
★ Aires for more than a decade and recently left her comfortable old town

house for the more central Hotel Panamericano. Try either lamb with herbs, garnished with Spanish potatoes and green salad, or trout cooked in light butter with lemon sauce and roasted almonds. ✕ *Calle Carlos Pellegrini 525,* ☎ *1/393–6017. Reservations required. AE, DC, MC, V. Closed Sun.; no lunch Mon.*

$$$ Veracruz. This old-fashioned restaurant, which caters to a mature crowd, is representative of what dining in Buenos Aires has always been about. Carefully prepared Spanish-style seafood dishes are served by staid, seasoned waiters. Try a jam-packed *cazuela* (seafood stew with clams, shrimp, octopus, scallops, and lobster) or lobster Veracruz. ✕ *Uruguay 538,* ☎ *1/371–1413. Reservations advised. Jacket required. DC. Closed Sun. and Feb.*

$$ Club Vasco Francés. This old-fashioned racquet club with a vast dining room, recently spruced up, is one of the few places in Buenos Aires to get frogs' legs. Seafood is flown in from Spain for a homesick Basque clientele. ✕ *Calle Moreno 1370,* ☎ *1/382–0244. Reservations advised. AE, V. Closed Sun.*

$$ Elevage. The dining room of this restaurant in the Elevage Hotel displays a decorator's idea of British clubbiness, with a giant chandelier, fox-hunt tapestries, dark wood furniture, and lots of mirrors, but the meals can be excellent. Try chicken with tarragon sauce or *lenguado* (sole) with Roquefort sauce. ✕ *Calle Maipú 960,* ☎ *1/313–2082. Reservations advised. AE, DC, MC, V.*

$$ Friday's. Although the decor is uninspired, this small, intimate restaurant is an ideal place for a quiet tête-à-tête. Brochettes of prawns and mushrooms or tenderloin scallops with martini sauce are specialties worth a try. ✕ *Calle San Martín 961,* ☎ *1/311–5433. Reservations advised. AE, MC. Closed Sun.*

$$ La Vendeta. Despite a change of name—this restaurant was formerly called Il Barbetto—the cuisine is unchanged in this small, cozy establishment. Try the *malfatti* (chicken with polenta). ✕ *Calle Posadas 1387,* ☎ *1/812–8306. Reservations advised. AE, DC, MC, V. Closed Sun. and Jan. 1–Feb. 15.*

$$ Ligure. This longtime favorite of diplomats and other frequent visitors
★   to Argentina offers French cuisine adapted to Argentine tastes, including unusual dishes like thistles au gratin, as well as more standard steak au poivre (with brandy sauce and pepper); the dessert pancakes are a must. The service is exemplary, not surprising because the waiters have part ownership of the restaurant. ✕ *Calle Juncal 855,* ☎ *1/394–8226. AE, DC, MC, V.*

$$ Mora X. Large and airy, this restaurant is a pleasant mix of modern architecture and decor typical of Recoleta eateries. Profiteroles with raspberry sauce make a fine finish to a delightful meal of grilled sirloin with cheddar sauce and mushrooms, or sole with lemon sauce. The handsome wooden bar and potted plants contrast with the stark postmodern architecture. ✕ *Calle Vicente López 2152,* ☎ *1/803–0261. Reservations required. AE, DC, MC, V. Closed Sun.*

$$ Munich Recoleta. This jam-packed gathering spot has been a favorite
★   for almost 40 years. The basic fare is great steak, creamed spinach, and shoestring fried potatoes. Arrive early if you don't want to wait. ✕ *Calle R. M. Ortiz 1879,* ☎ *1/804–3981. No reservations. No credit cards.*

$$ Zum Edelweiss. This classic restaurant starts to swing after midnight, when the nearby after-theater crowd, actors included, comes to dine. The fare is German and the people-watching superb. Goulash, sauerkraut and sausages, and steak tartare are all well prepared. ✕ *Calle Libertad 431,* ☎ *1/382–3351. Reservations advised. AE, DC, MC, V.*

$ Brizzi. Trout mousse with a fresh salad, and sweetbreads prepared in sherry with yams are two good choices at this simple restaurant, which also offers a good brunch. ✗ *Calle Lavalle 445, ☎ 1/393–5364. AE, MC, V. No dinner.*

$ Sabot. In this no-frills, good-value spot, standard international fare such as steak au poivre with green peas and cream are favorites among a lunchtime banker clientele. ✗ *Calle 25 de Mayo 756, ☎ 1/313–6587. Reservations advised. No credit cards. Closed lunch Sat. and Sun.*

Italian

$$$ Círcolo Italiano. This elegant restaurant in the Barrio Norte, housed in a turn-of-the-century French mansion with high ceilings and spacious rooms, caters to the city's influential Italian community. Its varied menu offers more than just excellent pasta. Meat and fish plates are also well prepared. ✗ *Calle Libertad 1264, ☎ 1/811–1767. Reservations required. Jacket and tie. AE, DC, MC, V. Closed Sun.*

$$$ Clo-Clo. An Italian restaurant with a river view, Clo-Clo is a new addition to the waterfront. *Trucha Capri* (trout in a cream sauce with prawns) is a good way to start. ✗ *Calles Costanera Norte and La Pampa, ☎ 1/788–0487. Reservations advised. AE, DC, MC, V.*

$$ A'Nonna Immacolata. Amusingly, the walls of this Italian-American restaurant along the Costanera Norte are papered with out-of-circulation 1,000-peso notes. The tablecloths are pink to complement the pale orange bills. Homemade pastas, saltimbocca *à la Romana* (sautéed veal with ham, sage, and white wine), and such seafood dishes as lobster pescatore and linguine with clams are the specialties. ✗ *Av. Rafael Obligado, ☎ 1/782–1757. Reservations advised. AE, DC, MC, V.*

$$ Pizza Cero. Crisp crust and frothy mozzarella make the pizzas quite memorable at this eatery on a quiet street corner. There are tables on the sidewalk and a sparkling dining room is bathed in greenery—an upscale setting for the city's most "in" pizza parlor. ✗ *Calle Cerviño 3701, ☎ 1/803–3449. AE, DC, MC, V. No lunch.*

$$ Robertino. Glorious northern Italian delectables like *cassunzei* (pasta with beets, ricotta, and egg) and fillet of veal are served in a rustic but elegant dining room in an old house. Little pots, plates, and jars hang here and there as in an old-fashioned restaurant in Tuscany. ✗ *Calle Vicente López 2158, ☎ 1/803–1460. Reservations advised. AE, DC, MC, V. No lunch Mon.–Sat.*

$ Broccolino. Pizza and pasta dishes are served efficiently on red-checker
★ tablecloths. Families crowd the place for dinner on Sunday, the traditional maid's night off. It also bustles with tourists and nearby office workers. ✗ *Calle Esmeralda 776, ☎ 1/322–7652. No credit cards.*

Japanese

$$$ Kitayama. Here, tourists mix with the city's Japanese population, who come to enjoy the well-prepared sushi, tempura, and seafood, and to browse through the restaurant's collection of Japanese comic books. Japanese-style private dining rooms for six or more are available (with plastic backrests for less flexible patrons). ✗ *Calle Mexico 1965, ☎ 1/941–8960. Reservations advised. AE, DC, MC. Closed Sun.*

$$$ Yuki. Sashimi, yakitori, and other favorites are attractively presented in this restaurant, which caters to visitors from Japan. Private dining rooms are available. ✗ *Calle Venezuela 2145, ☎ 1/942–5853. Reservations advised. No credit cards. Closed lunch, Sun., and Dec. 15–Jan. 15.*

$$ Midori. This sushi bar in the Caesar Park hotel serves Japanese dishes in a typically Tokyo atmosphere: brightly lit, modern, clean, and crisp. Try the teppanyaki dishes—prime cuts of meat, fish, and seafood grilled right at your table. ✗ *Calle Posadas 1232,* ☎ *1/814–5150. Reservations required. AE, DC, MC, V. Closed Mon.*

Middle Eastern

$$ Asociación Cultural Armenia. Ex-generals and future presidents can be found enjoying extraordinary Armenian fare alongside the moguls of the city's powerful Armenian community in this rather institutional-looking club. The hummus, tabbouleh, and stuffed eggplant are authentic and well prepared. ✗ *Calle Armenia 1366,* ☎ *1/771–0016. Jacket required. Weekend reservations advised. AE, DC, V. Closed Mon.; no lunch Tues.–Sat.; no dinner Sun.*

$$ Colbeh Melahat. This cozy, delightful spot is Buenos Aires's only authentic Iranian restaurant—and well worth a journey out to the suburbs. Try *fesendjan* (duck with a grenadine sauce) or the Pakistani dishes. ✗ *Av. del Libertador 13041, Martinez,* ☎ *1/793–3955. Weekend reservations required. Jacket and tie. AE, DC, MC, V. Closed Sun; no lunch.*

Spanish

$$ Club Español. A down-at-the-heels club with a once-aristocratic dining hall, this restaurant serves earthy Spanish fare including varied fish dishes. Octopus *à la Gallega* (in Galician paprika sauce) is well prepared. The restaurant is busy at lunchtime but quieter for dinner. ✗ *Calle Bernardo de Irigoyen 180,* ☎ *1/334–4876. Reservations required on Sat. AE, DC, MC, V. Closed Sun.*

$$ Hispano. In a scene straight out of Madrid circa 1950, several dining rooms are filled with garrulous Galicians devouring Serrano ham and gigantic platters of paella accompanied by bottles of crisp Chablis. Rustic and bordering on chaotic at rush hour, this is the place to savor the still-predominant Spanish presence along the Avenida de Mayo in downtown Buenos Aires. ✗ *Av. Rivadavia 1199,* ☎ *1/382–7534. Reservations advised. No credit cards.*

$$ Mayorazgo. Spanish fare—with an emphasis on seafood—is cooked with fresh ingredients, natural flavors, and the spirit of the Iberian peninsula. Grilled squid comes tender and tasty. ✗ *Calle Uspállata 701,* ☎ *1/362–3121. Weekend reservations required. DC, MC, V. Closed Sat. lunch, Sun., and Jan.*

$$ Taberna Baska. Old World decor combined with efficient service is offered in this busy, no-nonsense restaurant with dark wood paneling. A Basque clientele is drawn by such well-prepared dishes as *chiripones en su tinta* (a variety of squid in ink). ✗ *Calle Chile 980,* ☎ *1/334–0903. Weekend reservations required. AE, DC, MC, V. Closed Mon. and Jan.*

Vegetarian

$ Yin-Yang. A comfortable spot, Yin-Yang caters to the health-conscious with a well-balanced menu of tasty plates of brown rice, fresh vegetables, and vegetable tarts. Nonfat pastry is a specialty. ✗ *Calle Paraguay 858,* ☎ *1/311–7798. DC, V. Closed Sun; no dinner.*

Cafés

Cafés with good locations are always busy, from the first espresso before breakfast to the last one long after dinner. Some people talk, others write, many just look at the handsome array of passersby. Some cafés offer a wider fare and are called *confiterías*. They serve open-face fillet sandwiches, grilled ham and cheese, and "triples" (three-decker clubs filled with ham, cheese, tomatoes, olives, eggs, and onion). Sandwiches can be made on *media lunas* (croissants); and salads and desserts are also available. There are about 400 cafés in midtown Buenos Aires; the average bill comes to around $10 with a small bottle of wine.

Confitería del Molino. Politicians have been gathering to argue here since the nearby Congress Building was inaugurated in 1906. ✕ *Corner Av. Rivadavia 1801,* ☎ *1/952–6016.*

Florida Garden. Customers line up elbow to elbow along the 20-foot bar to sip espresso and cappuccino, and drink hot chocolate—the smoothest, richest drink in the city. ✕ *Calle Florida 889, near the Plaza San Martín, no* ☎.

Gran Cafe Tortoni. This is the oldest confitería in town, dating from 1858, and it is as popular now as it was then. Its interior is grand, with elaborate, two-story-high, tin ceilings and the faded air of a glorious past. ✕ *Near Plaza de Mayo at Av. de Mayo 829,* ☎ *1/342–4328.*

Ideal. This downtown Buenos Aires landmark is a turn-of-the-century tearoom with a loyal following. There is a piano player, and high teas are excellent. ✕ *Calle Suipacha 384, near the corner of Av. Corrientes,* ☎ *1/294–1081.*

Lodging

One of the great pleasures of Buenos Aires is the variety of fine hotels. Several of the more expensive ones were built for the 1978 World Cup soccer matches, while others opened at the turn of the century. All listed here are in the city center. For price ratings, *see* Lodging *in* Argentina Essentials, *below.*

$$$$ **Alvear Palace.** Conceived as a luxury apartment building in 1932, the
★ building was converted to a hotel in 1991. Guest rooms are soothingly decorated in burgundy and deep blues, with large windows. The roof garden has a spectacular view of the city and the river. The location in the fashionable Recoleta section makes this hotel convenient to the museums and good restaurants. 🏨 *Av. Alvear 1891,* ☎ *1/804–4031,* 🖷 *1/804–0034; U.S.* ☎ *800/448–8355. 200 rooms, 80 suites. Restaurant, coffee shop, lobby lounge, piano bar, tea shop, indoor pool, health club, business services, meeting rooms. AE, DC, MC, V.*

$$$$ **Caesar Park.** Located opposite Patio Bullrich, this Westin-operated hotel is near the Recoleta and Plaza San Martín. Upper floors have a panoramic view of the river. The lavish, spacious rooms have tasteful fabrics, period furniture, marble bathrooms, and good light. Guests have access to a nearby 18-hole golf course. 🏨 *Calle Posadas 1232,* ☎ *1/814–5150,* 🖷 *1/814–5191; U.S.* ☎ *800/228-3000. 167 rooms, 6 suites. 3 restaurants, 2 bars, in-room modem lines, room service, indoor pool, beauty salon, massage, sauna, exercise room, business services, meeting rooms. AE, DC, MC, V.*

$$$$ **Claridge.** This stylishly appointed hotel sports a British elegance in its public rooms, which has wood paneling and high ceilings, and an Anglo-Argentine clientele to match. Guest rooms are decorated in shades of blue, with dark wood furnishings with bronze fittings. It has a good location near the financial district. 🏨 *Calle Tucumán 535,* ☎ *1/314–7700,* 🖷 *1/314–8022; U.S.* ☎ *800/223–5652. 155 rooms, 6 suites. Restaurant, bar, room service, pool, massage, sauna, exercise room, business services, meeting rooms. AE, DC, MC, V.*

$$$$ **Crown Plaza Panamericano.** A newish, 18-floor building has been tastefully disguised as a conservative, classic hotel, with an emphasis on good service and spotlessness. A room at the top guarantees a good night's sleep and a view over the Obelisk and the Colón Theater. 🏨 *Calle Carlos Pellegrini 525,* ☎ *1/348–5000,* 🖷 *1/348–5250; U.S.* ☎

800/448–8355. *204 rooms, 6 suites. 2 restaurants, 2 bars, room service, indoor pool, sauna, exercise room. AE, DC, MC, V.*

$$$$ **Libertador Kempinski.** Its central location in a modern 22-story building just a few blocks from the banking district makes this hotel headquarters for many businesspeople. The huge marble-floor lobby area has a bar, and the pastel-shaded deluxe rooms have walk-in closets, marble baths, and mahogany furniture. ☎ *Av. Córdoba 680,* ☎ *1/322–2288,* FAX *1/322–9703; U.S.* ☎ *800/426–3135. 203 rooms, 15 suites. Restaurant, bar, coffee shop, room service, indoor-outdoor pool, massage, sauna, exercise room, concierge, meeting rooms, travel services. AE, DC, MC, V.*

$$$$ **Marriott Plaza Hotel.** The city's most gracious hotel is across from the
★ towering old trees of Plaza San Martín. Some rooms have great bay windows overlooking the park. Crystal chandeliers and deep red Persian carpets decorate the public rooms. The president of Argentina entertains visiting statespeople here. ☎ *Calle Florida 1005,* ☎ *1/318–3000,* FAX *1/318–3008; U.S.* ☎ *800/228–9290. 320 rooms, 10 suites. 2 restaurants, bar, café, room service, pool, health club, business services. AE, DC, MC, V.*

$$$$ **Park Hyatt Buenos Aires.** Argentina's first Hyatt has a strategic location at the end of Avenida 9 de Julio on the fringe of the Recoleta district. In addition to the 12-story building that houses the crisp, comfortable guest rooms and executive suites, it occupies a redecorated turn-of-the-century French town house where sumptuous suites and a gourmet restaurant cater to VIP visitors. ☎ *Calle Posadas 1086,* ☎ *1/326–1234,* FAX *1/326–3736; U.S.* ☎ *800/233–1234. 166 rooms, 50 suites. Restaurant, 2 bars, coffee shop, pool, exercise room, business services, meeting rooms. AE, DC, MC, V.*

$$$$ **Sheraton Buenos Aires Hotel and Towers.** As the headquarters of Sheraton's South American division, this hotel at the bottom of Plaza San Martín has a broad range of facilities. The institutionally decorated guest rooms have views of either the River Plate or the British Clock Tower and park. It is popular with American businesspeople and tour groups. ☎ *Calle San Martín 1225,* ☎ *1/318–9000,* FAX *1/318–9346; U.S.* ☎ *800/325–3535. 603 rooms, 29 suites. 3 restaurants, 4 bars, coffee shop, pool, sauna, 2 tennis courts, exercise room, business services, car rental. AE, DC, MC, V.*

$$$ **Bisonte Hotel.** Located on a popular shopping street in the center of the city, the Bisonte has a sunny two-story lobby and a coffee shop overlooking a small park. Rooms are small and decor is on the stiff side. ☎ *Calle Paraguay 1207,* ☎ *1/394–8041,* FAX *1/393–9086. 87 rooms. Coffee shop, business services. AE, DC, MC, V.*

$$$ **Bisonte Palace Hotel.** Sister hotel to the Bisonte, this more brightly lit version is centrally located. Because it's on a busy corner, rooms higher up are better bets for peace and quiet. Decor is standard—modern and comfortable, and guests are well attended. ☎ *Calle M. T. de Alvear 902,* ☎ *1/394–8041, 1/394–8129, 1/394–8154,* FAX *1/393–0986. 65 rooms. Coffee shop. AE, DC, MC, V.*

$$$ **Buenos Aires Bauen Hotel.** With its theater, auditorium, and active entertainment program, the Bauen is a beehive of activity. It is near the intersection of two noisy avenues lined with lively restaurants and cafés, cinemas, and theaters, so avoid lower floors if you're sensitive to noise. ☎ *Av. Callao 360,* ☎ *1/476–1400,* FAX *1/476-0315; U.S.* ☎ *800/448–8355. 226 rooms, 28 suites. Restaurant, 2 bars, coffee shop, refrigerators, room service, indoor pool, barbershop, beauty salon, nightclub, convention center. AE, DC, MC, V.*

$$$ **Carsson.** A long mirrored corridor leads to the lobby, which is far from the sound and fury of downtown traffic, in this centrally located sleeper. An English atmosphere pervades; rooms have been redone in staid stripes of green and deep red, with Louis XIV–style furniture. ⊞ *Calle Viamonte 650,* ☎ *1/322–3551,* FAX *1/322–3551. 108 rooms, 9 suites. AE, DC, MC, V.*

$$$ **City.** This dowager of the downtown hotels is the last one to resist renovation. With its hand-operated elevators, enormous lobby, and period paintings, it's definitely a nostalgia trip. Rooms are large and in various stages of redecoration, with plastic-covered furniture and foam paneling on doors. Not for the fussy, but a good choice for the price-conscious who want to be on the San Telmo side of town. ⊞ *Calle Bolivar 160,* ☎ *1/342–6490,* FAX *1/342–6490. 400 rooms, 80 suites. AE, DC, MC, V.*

$$$ **De las Américas.** In this hotel just off the best shopping stretch of Avenida Sante Fe, the sunken lobby is drearily decorated, but the rooms are comfortable and larger than one expects in a 10-year-old property. The clientele consists mainly of South American tour groups and visitors from the provinces, but solitary visitors who want to be in a basically residential area will also feel at home. ⊞ *Calle Libertad 1020,* ☎ *1/393–3432,* FAX *1/393–0418. 150 rooms, 15 suites. Coffee shop. AE, DC, MC, V.*

$$$ **El Conquistador.** This hotel, well situated near Plaza San Martín, is popular with Argentine businessmen. There is a cheerful restaurant for breakfast or a snack, and the wood paneling in the public rooms lends a cozy touch. Large windows, flowered bedspreads, and light pink carpets brighten the recently redecorated guest rooms. ⊞ *Calle Suipacha 948,* ☎ *1/313–3012,* FAX *1/313–3012. 130 rooms, 14 suites. Restaurant, piano bar, massage, sauna. AE, DC, MC, V.*

$$$ **Hotel Salles.** This quiet, centrally located establishment is the only family-oriented hotel in the heart of the theater district. Rooms are adequate, the decor businesslike and neutral; personal service is a focus. ⊞ *Calle Cerrito 208,* ☎ *1/382–3962,* FAX *1/382–0754. 90 rooms, 5 suites. Coffee shop. AE, DC, MC, V.*

$$$ **Lancaster.** The countess who decorated this handsome hotel made
★ good use of her family heirlooms. Old family portraits, museum-quality landscapes, and a 200-year-old clock grace the lobby, where elegant porteños come regularly for tea or drinks. Rooms have antique mahogany furniture and views of the port. ⊞ *Av. Córdoba 405,* ☎ *1/312–4061,* FAX *1/311–3021. 88 rooms, 16 suites. Restaurant, bar. AE, DC, MC, V.*

$$$ **Plaza Francia.** This is the best located small hotel in town. The guest rooms—large and French in feel—have great views overlooking La Plaza Francia park. It's also near the Recoleta and the museums. If traffic noise bothers you, sacrifice the view for a quiet inside room. ⊞ *Calle Pasaje E. Schiaffino 2189,* ☎ *and* FAX *1/804–9631. 36 rooms, 14 suites. AE, DC, MC, V.*

$$$ **Posta Carretas.** Although tucked right in the heart of the city, this mod-
★ ern and very comfortable property has the atmosphere of an auberge. Some of the brightly decorated rooms have hot tubs. Wood paneling abounds, creating a coziness that contrasts with the bustle outside. ⊞ *Calle Esmeralda 726,* ☎ *1/322–8534,* FAX *1/313–6017. 40 rooms, 11 suites. AE, DC, MC, V.*

$$$ **Regente Palace.** The small but pleasant rooms are decorated with black wood furniture, and bedspreads and curtains in beiges and rose. The location is convenient, near Plaza San Martín on a block with several new cafés and trendy shops. American breakfast is served in the

restaurant. ☎ *Calle Suipacha 964,* ☎ *1/313–6628,* FAX *313–7460. 150 rooms, 6 suites. Restaurant, snack bar. AE, DC, MC, V.*

$$ Crillon. Superbly located across from Plaza St. Martín, the Crillon was
★ built in the classic French style in 1948 and remodeled in 1992. Front rooms have beautiful views and are large and luminous. The lobby is statesmanly and sedate, which may explain why this establishment appeals to provincial governors and the well-to-do from the interior. ☎ *Av. Santa Fe 796,* ☎ *1/312–8181,* FAX *1/312–9955. 96 rooms, 12 suites. Restaurant, bar, dance club, meeting room. AE, DC, MC, V.*

$$ Gran Hotel Colón. Near the Obelisk, on the busy Avenida 9 de Julio, the Colón has suites with private patios, but normal rooms are shoe-box small. Everything is shiny and modern. Airport buses leave from next door. ☎ *Carlos Pellegrini 507,* ☎ *1/325–1017,* FAX *1/325–4567. 192 rooms, 10 suites. Snack bar, indoor pool, beauty salon, sauna. AE, DC, MC, V.*

$$ Gran Hotel Dora. A cozy lobby with a small bar greets guests. The atmosphere is old-fashioned and the rooms are comfortably elegant, with their Louis XVI–style decor. The Dora caters to Europeans and to Argentines who want a Continental atmosphere. ☎ *Calle Maipú 963,* ☎ *1/312–7391,* FAX *1/313–8134. 100 rooms. Bar, snack bar, meeting rooms. AE, DC, MC, V.*

$$ Principado. Built for the World Cup soccer matches in 1978, this hotel has reception areas with large windows and lots of light, and a two-tier Spanish colonial–style lobby with leather couches. The highlight is the friendly coffee shop. Rooms are modest but comfortable. ☎ *Paraguay 481,* ☎ *1/313–3022,* FAX *1/313–3952. 88 rooms. Coffee shop. AE, DC, MC, V.*

$ Gran Hotel Orly. On the river side of Calle Florida, the Orly caters to Brazilian tourists and visitors from the interior who are on a budget. Though the entrance is impressive, the comfortable rooms are small and rather plain. ☎ *Calle Paraguay 474,* ☎ *1/312–5344,* FAX *1/312–5344. 168 rooms, 8 suites. Bar, coffee shop. AE, DC, MC, V.*

$ Hotel Deauville. The Deauville, in the most elegant part of town, is aging gracefully, as is most of its provincial clientele. The dining room is family-oriented, and the guest rooms are fairly large, with ample drawer and closet space. For the budget-conscious traveler who wants to be away from tourists, this is one of the best choices. ☎ *Calle Talcahuano 1253,* ☎ *1/811–3629,* FAX *1/812–1560. 60 rooms, 4 suites. Restaurant. AE, DC, MC, V.*

$ Rochester. Get an inside room at this 20-year-old hotel, which is on a busy street that's convenient to movies and shops. The lobby is simple and rooms are basic. ☎ *Calle Esmeralda 542,* ☎ *1/326–2079 or 1/326–5838,* FAX *1/322–4689. 155 rooms, 20 suites. Breakfast room, room service. AE, DC, MC, V.*

The Arts

Partial listings of entertainment and cultural events in English appear in the daily edition of the English-language *Buenos Aires Herald.*

Dance

BALLET AND MODERN

The **National Ballet Company** is headquartered at the Colón (*see* Opera, *below*) but gives open-air performances in Palermo Park in summer. Don't miss the world-class contemporary dance company that performs several times a year at the **Teatro San Martín** (Av. Corrientes 1532, ☎ 1/374–8611 or 1/331–7553).

TANGO

Argentine tango, that sensual dance and soulful song, is philosophizing and passion set to music. Haunting Andean pipe music from Salta–Jujuy in the north combines with flirtatious handkerchief dancing in the sentimental *zambas*. A typical tango performance in a nightclub includes a serious singer, a passionate, woeful singer, a virtuoso bandoneon star flashing his fingers across double sets of accordionlike buttons, and finally, the peacocklike performances of tango dancers. To watch the drama unfold, Argentines and tourists sit together in tango clubs, sipping drinks and listening to seasoned singers wade their way through the emotion-packed lyrics. Clubs can be sampled on nightclub tours of the city, available through hotels, but an easier way to slip into the feeling of tango is to attend a folkloric show, which costs about $40, including two drinks.

Currently the best folkloric performance is at **Casa Blanca** (Calle Balcarce 668, ☎ 1/334–5010), President Menem's favorite spot. **Café Homero** (Calle J. A. Cabrera 4946, ☎ 1/733–1979) is a good place to start one's initiation into the rites of the tango. Highly polished **Michelangelo** (Calle Balcarce 433, ☎ 1/334–4321 or 1/334–4322) combines folkloric, tango, and international music in its dinner show in a striking, remodeled old warehouse. Another way to delve deeper into the music is to visit **La Casa de Carlos Gardel** (Jean Jaures 735, ☎ 1/962–4265), open only at night, where there are audiovisual displays, a tango show, and a museum of the life of tango's most famed figure. Gardel, known for his dark, Tyrone Power looks, died in a plane crash in 1935 at the age of 40. Some claim that Gardel's 1,200 recordings continue to outsell all others in Argentina. Once you have settled into the mood of tango, head for San Telmo and try **Bar Sur** (Calle Estados Unidos 299, ☎ 1/362–6086) or any of a number of spots that have more spontaneous outbursts of tango at lower cost.

Film

International first-run films, the often powerful films of Argentine directors, and Italian comedies can be found at the more than 50 theaters in the downtown area alone. Most of these are along two parallel streets, Avenida Corrientes and Calle Lavalle. The *Herald* has daily listings. The names of the films are generally given in Spanish, but English-language films are shown undubbed, with Spanish subtitles.

Music

The season of the **National Symphony,** headquartered in the Colón Theater, runs from April to November (Calle Cerrito 618, ☎ 1/396–5414).

Opera

By any standard of comparison, the **Colón Theater** (Calle Cerrito 618, ☎ 1/382–0554, 1/382–0584, or 1/382–3306) is one of the world's finest opera houses. Tiered like a wedding cake, the gilt and red-velvet auditorium has unsurpassed acoustics. An ever-changing stream of imported talent bolsters the well-regarded local company. The opera season runs from April to November.

Theater

Some 40 theaters are open almost constantly, ranging from those presenting Argentine dramatic works or translations of foreign plays to *revista* (revue) theaters with comics who strike out at local political mishaps, and chorus lines notable for the brevity of the costumes and the dimensions of their wearers. Publicly supported dance, mime, puppet shows, and theater are performed on the three stages of the municipal theater complex, **Teatro San Martín** (Av. Corrientes 1532, ☎ 1/374–

8611 or 1/331–7553). An entertainment center worth a visit is **La Plaza** (Av. Corrientes 1660, ☎ 1/372–6079), an open-air mall with a small outdoor amphitheater and two theaters, along with shops and small restaurants with tables under the trees.

Nightlife

It is good to begin with a basic understanding of the Argentine idea of nightlife. A date at 7 PM is considered an afternoon coffee break. Theater performances start at 9 or 9:30, the last movie after midnight, and nightclubs don't begin filling up until 2 AM. Tango begins after midnight and never seems to stop. Porteños never go early to discos—no one you'd want to be seen with goes before 2 AM.

Dance Clubs

Tango is meant to be danced more than watched, and Buenos Aires has many exciting dance halls. Most don't open until 11 PM, and many open only one night a week, so the tango crowd circulates from place to place, from night to night. Most tango joints have no telephones, and opening days and times listed below regularly change. To get ready for your evening out, you can call **Antonio Todaro** (Estudio Superior de Arte, Av. Belgrano 2259, ☎ 1/952–1109); considered the best tango teacher in town, he offers formal tango instruction in his studio weekdays 11 AM–9 PM.

Akarense (Calle Donado 1355, at Av. Los Incas; Fri. 11 PM–3 AM) draws the best dancers to its beautiful hall, where pure tango music from the 1920s to the 1960s is featured. The very special **Sin Rumbo** (Av. Constituyentes 6000, at Calle Tamborini; Sat. 11 PM–3 AM) attracts old dancers of the *milonga* (a samba-like dance that predates the tango) and features music from the '20s and '40s. **Salón Helénico** (Av. Scalabrini Ortiz 1331; Fri. and Sun. 11 PM–3 AM, preceded by tango lessons from 8 to 11) recalls larger dance halls from the '30s, with a melancholy atmosphere and bucolic Greek landscapes on the walls. The very large **Social Rivadavia** (Av. Rivadavia 6400, at Boyaca; Fri.–Sun. 11 PM–3 AM) has two dance floors, many milonga dancers, and music mainly from the '40s, but with a lot of tropical music and jazz as well. **Regine's** (Av. Río Bamba 416; Wed. 11 PM–3 AM) is a small place reminiscent of Fellini's *Satyricon*. **Viejo Correo** (Av. Diaz Velez 4820; Mon., Thurs., Sat. 11 PM–3 AM) has a more sophisticated atmosphere than most of the other tango spots. **La Galería del Tango Argentino** (Av. Boedo 722; Fri., Sat., and Sun. 11 PM–3 AM) has competitions and shows and draws both older milonga dancers and young dancers; tango *fantasía,* a fancy version that allows dancers to show off their abilities, is more popular here than in the other halls.

For international dancing that sometimes includes a tango as well, **Atalaya** on the 23rd floor of the Sheraton (☎ 1/311–6331) has an orchestra, a view of the city, and the elegant spirit to draw full crowds on weekends. **Africa** in the Alvear Palace Hotel (Av. Alvear 1885, ☎ 1/807–2760) is a disco that appeals to the 25–45 crowd. The popular **Hippopotamus** (Calle R. M. Ortiz 1787, ☎ 1/802–0500) in the Recoleta appeals to middle-age dancers and a younger crowd, both affluent. A new arrival is **Coyote** (Av. Casares at corner of Viaducto Ferrocarril San Martin, ☎ 1/806–3533 or 1/806–3556), a Santa Fe–style nightspot built in converted railway arches, which draws a young crowd with its live salsa band and frozen margaritas; the restaurant, which opens at 8:30, serves rather bland Tex-Mex dishes.

Jazz Clubs

Jazz in Buenos Aires is treated seriously by audiences and played enthusiastically by musicians. In San Telmo, for local and foreign groups, try **Gazelle Jazz Club** (Calle Estados Unidos 465, ☏ 1/361–4685) or **Balcon de La Plaza** (Calle Humberto Primo 461, ☏ 1/362–1144). **Café Tortoni** (Av. de Mayo 825, ☏ 1/342–4328) has jazz on weekends, and **Patio Bullrich** (Av. del Libertador 750, no ☏) frequently has jazz concerts in the evening. For a combination of jazz and traditional *mate* (herbal tea) drinking, try **Oliverio Mate Bar** (Calle Paraná 328, ☏ 1/542–1537).

Excursion from Buenos Aires

Tigre

A 30-kilometer (18-mile) drive through the shady riverside suburbs of Buenos Aires takes you to the river port town of Tigre, the embarkation point for boats that ply the vast delta of the Paraná River. Most North Americans skip this day trip, but it's worth trying, especially when the weather is warm: The boat ride is pure nostalgia and a favorite local weekend escape. Of the several sightseeing possibilities, all involving boats, the most comfortable option is to tour aboard a large catamaran. In addition, the small motor launches that deliver groceries and mail and take children to school and workers to their jobs will drop you off at the island of your choice along the delta's tentaclelike canals. The boats travel past colorfully painted houses built on stilts to survive floods.

Getting There

Cities Service Travel Agency (Calle Florida 890, ☏ 1/312–8416) runs guided tours from downtown. If you prefer to go on your own, catch a Mitre commuter line train, departing every 15 minutes from Retiro Station (Av. Ramos Mejía 1398, ☏ 1/312–6597). Four-hour catamaran cruises around the delta, offered by **Cruceros Catamarán** (Estación Tigre, ☏ 1/731–0261 or 1/731–0262; $10 per person), depart daily from a canal dock parallel to Tigre Station at noon and 4 PM; an inexpensive lunch or snack is available on board.

IGUAZÚ FALLS

Iguazú Falls (called the Cataratas de Iguazú in Argentina, but spelled Iguaçú in Brazil and Iguassu in Paraguay) is one of the wildest wonders of the world, with nature on the rampage in a show of sound and fury that cannot be duplicated anywhere. The grandeur of this Cinemascope sheet of white water cascading in constant cymbal-banging cacophony makes Niagara and Victoria Falls seem sedate by comparison. Set at a bend in the Iguazú River at the border of Argentina and Brazil, it consists of some 275 separate waterfalls—in the rainy season as many as 350—that send their white cascades plunging 250 feet onto the rocks below. Dense, lush jungle surrounds the falls: Here the tropical sun and the omnipresent moisture set the jungle growing at a pace that produces a towering pine tree in two decades instead of the seven it takes, say, in Scandinavia. By the falls and along the roadside, rainbows and butterflies are set off against vast walls of red earth, which is so ubiquitous that eventually even peso bills long in circulation in the area turn red from the stuff.

Allow at least two full days to see this magnificent sight, and be sure to see it from both the Brazilian and Argentine sides. The Brazilians are blessed with the best panoramic view, an awesome vantage that suffers only from the sound of the gnatlike helicopters that erupt out of the lawn of the Hotel das Cataratas right in front of the falls. (Unfortunately, most of the indigenous macaws and toucans have abandoned the area to escape the whine of the helicopters' engines.) The Argentine side offers the better close-up experience of the falls, with excellent hiking paths, catwalks that approach the falls, a sandy beach to relax on, and places to bathe in the froth of the Iguazú River, where you can swim right up to a cascade and feel its power. If tropical heat and humidity hamper your style, plan to visit between April and October. Be aware, however, that the river can be so high in April and May that access to certain catwalks is impossible. Whatever time of year you visit, be sure to bring rain gear (or buy it from vendors along the trails on the Brazilian side), because some of the catwalks take you right through the cascades and leave you thoroughly drenched.

Visitor Information

In Buenos Aires

Contact the **Administración de Parques Nacionales** (National Park Administration, Av. Santa Fe 690, ☎ 1/311–1943) or the **Casa de Misiones** (House of Misiones, Av. Santa Fe 989, ☎ 1/393–1812).

At the Falls

For information and guides, contact **Centro de Visitantes** (visitors center; at the falls, ☎ 0757/20180; open daily 8–6); *see* Exploring, *below,* for more details. The **Oficina de Turismo** (Av. Victoria Aguirre 396, ☎ 0757/20800) for the international zone of Iguazú is in the town of Puerto Iguazú, as is the **Intendencia del Parque** (☎ 0757/20382; open weekdays 7–1), the local park administrative offices.

Arriving and Departing

By Plane

Argentina and Brazil each have an international airport at Iguazú. The Argentine airport is 16 kilometers (10 miles) from the town of Puerto Iguazú, Argentina; **Aerolíneas Argentinas** (Av. Aguirre, Puerto Iguazú, ☎ 0757/20849) and **Austral** (Av. Aguirre 429, ☎ 0757/20144) fly to and from Buenos Aires in an hour and a half. An occasional Aerolíneas flight goes on to São Paulo and Rio de Janeiro. The Brazilian airport is 11 kilometers (7 miles) from Foz do Iguaçu and 17 kilometers (10½ miles) from the national park. The Brazilian airlines **Varig** and **Cruzeiro** (☎ 0455/741424), **Vasp** (☎ 0455/742999), and **Transbrasil** (☎ 0455/742029) have offices in Foz do Iguaçu and offer connecting flights all over Brazil. **Líneas Aéreas Paraguayas** flies between the airport on the Brazilian side and Asunción, Paraguay.

FROM THE AIRPORT TO THE FALLS

Asociación de Taxis (Av. Córdoba 370, ☎ 0757/20973) provides taxi service to both sides of the park. The Hotel Internacional Cataratas and the visitor center at the national park are 8 kilometers (5 miles) from the Argentine airport.

By Train

At press time (winter 1995), the Argentine railroads were being privatized and the **Urquiza Line** from Buenos Aires to Posadas was no longer running. If it is revived, the overnight train ride, through Entre Ríos and Corrientes, will be a low-cost alternative to flying.

By Car

Iguazú is a two-day, 1,290-kilometer (800-mile) drive from Buenos Aires on national highways 12 and 14. The roads are paved, but often empty, and cross vast stretches of farmland. Much of the area is dedicated to rice, so the fields at the sides of the road are often covered with herons, ducks, and storks; there's even an occasional flamingo. There are a number of picturesque towns in which you can spend the night along the Paraná River and inland, among them San Nicolás, Rosário, Santa Fe, Goya, Corrientes, Posadas, and El Dorado.

By Bus

Buses are a comfortable way to see the often bird-filled lagoons that at times seem to swallow the highway. The trip from Buenos Aires takes 21 hours; **Expreso Singer** (Perito Moreno 150, ☎ 0757/21560; Buenos Aires ☎ 1/315–2653) provides regular service, leaving from the **Central Terminal** in Buenos Aires. Organized tours to Iguazú by bus are available at most Buenos Aires travel agencies.

Getting Around Iguazú Falls

The falls should be seen from both sides of the Iguazú River, which means that you must establish headquarters on one side of the Argentine–Brazilian border and take a taxi or one of the regularly scheduled buses across the International Bridge to the national park on the other side. (United States, British, and Canadian citizens need a visa to visit Brazil, which is easy and quick to get at the border after crossing the bridge.) At each park, well-marked trails provide access to the best views of the falls; the view from the Brazilian side is accessible to people with mobility problems. If you are staying in the Argentine town of Puerto Iguazú, there is an hourly bus service back and forth to the Argentine side of the park; the 16-kilometer (10-mile) trip takes half an hour. Taxis are available in Puerto Iguazú, at the visitor center, and at the Hotel Internacional Cataratas (*see* Brazilian Side: Dining and Lodging, *below*).

Tour Operators

Jungle tours and photo safaris are conducted by the Puerto Iguazú–based **Güembé Tours** (Av. Victoria Aguirre 481, ☎ 0757/20413 or 0757/20510). When you book, ask for a wildlife list. Take binoculars to see distant birds, and a tape recorder if you want to remember their songs. Butterflies, parrots, woodpeckers, hummingbirds, lizards, inch-long ants, and spectacular spiders are usually spotted, along with toucans, the biggest stars of the skies around Iguazú. Park ranger Daniel Somay offers personalized Jeep tours through his **Explorador Expediciones** (☎ 0757/20338) in Puerto Iguazú.

Exploring Iguazú Falls

The best way to immerse yourself—figuratively and literally—in the falls is to wander the many access paths. These paths are a combination of bridges, ramps, stone staircases, and wooden catwalks set in a forest of ferns, begonias, orchids, and tropical trees. The catwalks over the water put you right in the middle of the action, so be ready to get doused by the rising spray. When the river floods, many of the installations have to be replaced; the floods of 1983 swept away many of the walkways. The last major rebuilding program was undertaken when the Hollywood movie *The Mission,* starring Robert De Niro and Jeremy Irons, was filmed here.

Because the falls themselves are mostly on the Argentine side, there is more to see and do there. The **Centro de Visitantes** (☎ 0757/20180), in what was the park's original hotel, makes a good first stop. Useful maps are posted on the walls, and friendly, multilingual rangers are happy to help you understand the layout of the park. The rangers also preside over a small zoo and museum that have local fauna and exhibits related to the area's history. In an adjoining room, slide shows on Argentina's national park program are offered. On the night of a full moon, rangers lead groups from the visitor center for a night walk through the upper trails when the moon is high. The sensation of walking through the subtropical forest at night is eerie and exciting and shouldn't be missed. The roar of the falls drowns out the sounds of the jungle and what was all bright green, red, and blue in the daytime takes on luminous hues of phosphorescent whites. Check at the visitor center for details.

There is a snack bar in the visitor center that has tables on the lawn, and a restaurant, **El Fortín**—across from the parking lot—where Paraguayans come to sing and play their soulful melodies, and then sell their traditional instruments. Most tourists are Argentines, and it is a colorful spot for a good steak or a sandwich.

Lower Circuit

The **Circuito Inferior** (the Lower Circuit) is a loop trail that leads to the brink of several falls. To get to the trail, follow the well-marked path from the Hotel Internacional and then the main path leading from the visitor center. After a five-minute walk down an access road, you'll see signs for the circuit, indicating which sights are in each direction. Protected promontories, rimmed with wooden or metal fences, offer close-ups of the wonderful view. At times the falls rise above you, framed by primeval forest.

The approximately 1-kilometer-long (half-mile-long) Lower Circuit leads to the edge of the **Río Iguazú** (Iguazú River)—with the Hotel das Cataratas and the noisy helicopter launching pad almost directly above on the opposite bank, a mile downstream from where the falls take their first magnificent leap. On this route you cross the small, peripheral **Salto Alvar Núñez,** falls named for the Spanish conquistador Alvar Núñez Cabeza de Vaca, who accidentally stumbled onto the spectacle in the 16th century; the **Peñon de Bella Vista** (Rock of the Beautiful View); and the **Salto Lanusse** (Lanusse Falls), the falls farthest from the Devil's Throat. These preliminaries get you warmed up for the main event. In the distance on the right, **Salto Dos** and **Salto Tres Mosqueteros** (Two and Three Musketeers Falls) fall obliquely, offering a head-on view to those on the Brazilian side. Wear your bathing suit on this route, and take a dip in the calm pools at the trail's edge.

Halfway along this circuit you get a panoramic peek at what is to come. Through the foliage you can see the gigantic curtain of water in the distance. The trail leads along the lower side of the **Brazo San Martín,** a branch of the river that makes a wide loop to the south. This tributary pushes to get back to the river's main course, opening up dozens of minor and a few major waterfalls along a face of rock that measures almost a mile. On the back side of the circuit—that is, where the trail loops around and starts heading back to your starting point—the **Salto Ramiréz** (Ramirez Falls), the **Salto Chico** (Small Falls), and the **Salto Dos Hermanos** (Two Brothers Falls) appear directly before you, opposite the bridge. This section of your circuit, about a half-mile long, offers the most exciting panoramic view of the Devil's Throat, the **Salto**

Bossetti (Bossetti Falls), and Salto Dos Hermanos. Two or three hours are needed to appreciate all the views along the circuit.

At the vantage point opposite the Bossetti Falls, a trail leads along the edge of the river to a small pier, where sturdy little boats will take you across a branch of the river to **Isla San Martín** (San Martín Island). The service operates all day, except when the river is too high. On the island, a steep climb up a rustic 160-step stairway leads to a circular trail that opens out onto three spectacular panoramas of the **San Martín Falls,** the Devil's Throat, and the **Ventana Falls** (Window Falls). If you want to just sit and watch 1,300 cubic yards of water splash below you every second, this is the place to do it. From the southernmost point you see **Salto Escondido** (Hidden Falls), and from the easternmost point, the panorama is breathtaking. The falls on the Brazilian side come into view: **Salto Santa María, Salto Floriano,** and **Salto Deodoro.** Few people make the effort to cross the river to San Martín Island and do this climb, so you can often enjoy the show in solitary splendor. The island has a small beach near the point where the boats land; frustrated sunbathers stretch out on its sands to dry out from the mist and warm up after losing sun under the thick tropical greenery.

Upper Circuit

The **Circuito Superior** (Upper Circuit)—not a circuit at all but a path about 2,300 feet long—borders the ridge on the south side of the river, along the top of the falls. The trail leads across the rapid waters of the **Brazo San Martín,** a branch of the river, as far as the **Cresta de los Saltos,** providing great views of **Dos Hermanos, Bossetti, Chico, Ramirez,** and **San Martín** falls. You can also see San Martín Island and the Brazilian side.

The Devil's Throat

The most renowned cataract, evocatively named **Garganta del Diablo** (Devil's Throat), is 492 feet wide and 2,460 feet long. To stand at the brink and watch the river fall off into space is an awesome sight, especially when accompanied by the sound of nature at its most outrageous.

The best viewing point is a short walk from **Puerto Canoas,** a settlement 4 kilometers (2½ miles) up the river from the visitor center. Puerto Canoas has a campsite nearby (on the banks of the Nandú River), a restaurant, and a bar. Many prefer to walk along the road that borders the river and then take the quarter-mile catwalk across the river to the top of the gorge. The hourly bus from Puerto Iguazú to the national park ends its route at Puerto Canoas, and taxis are available at the visitor center.

A Jungle Hike

Mix your outings to the different panoramic points overlooking the falls with a hike in the jungle. The **Centro de Investigaciones Ecológicas Subtropicales** (Center for Subtropical Ecological Investigation; information from the visitor center, ☎ 0757/20180) is a five-minute walk from the visitor center on the road to Puerto Iguazú. The center maintains the **Sendero Macuco** (Macuco Trail), which extends 4 kilometers (2½ miles) into the jungle, ending at the **Arrechea Falls,** farther downriver from the main falls. The trail is very carefully marked and descriptive signs in Spanish explain the jungle's flora and fauna. The closest you'll get to a wild animal is likely to be a paw print in the dirt, though you may be lucky enough to glimpse a monkey. The foliage is dense, so the most common surprises are the jungle sounds that seem to emerge out of nowhere. You can turn back at any point, or continue on to the refreshing view of the river and the Arrechea Falls. The best time for hearing animal calls and for avoiding the heat is either early in the morning or just before sunset. The battalions of butterflies, also best seen in the early morning or late afternoon, can be marvelous, and the intricate glistening cobwebs that crisscross the trail are a treat in the dawn light.

The Jungle by Car

A 29-kilometer (18-mile) circuit especially for vehicles gives a more complete overview of the jungle. Macaws, parrots, and toucans rest in the tree branches, and brightly colored butterflies flit across the road. The birds and animals come out in numbers at sunrise and sunset, and conceivably you could catch sight of a fleeing feline. Poachers from Brazil ford the river above the falls and come to hunt the little wildlife that is left in Argentina's national park. There are not enough rangers to provide adequate protection. A Jeep can be hired through the visitor center to undertake this simple safari, which takes two or three hours, depending on what there is to look at.

Brazilian Side

The Brazilian national park, one of the few worthy of the name in Brazil, covers 1,550 square kilometers (600 square miles) of rain forest. The central attraction is the incredible panoramic view of the falls, which can be seen starting at the Hotel das Cataratas (*see* Dining and Lodging, *below*). Well-groomed pathways lead from the terrace of the hotel directly down to the edge of the cliff overlooking the falls, and steps take you to the river itself, where a catwalk penetrates the flow. Vendors sell plastic rainwear on the trail. A path then leads to the head of the falls, where you can take an elevator ride back up for a small fee (open daily year-round).

Just a little farther along, you can brave one of the boat rides that venture over the Devil's Throat. These rides feature a local variation on the old jalopy sport, "chicken": The driver turns off the boat's motor and drifts downstream toward the gorge, awaiting the panic-stricken response of his passengers. No boats have ever gone over the edge—yet.

The astonishing panorama extends all along the path that leads from the hotel to the observation tower by the **Floriano Falls** and finally to the **Santa María Falls.** The path that follows the river's edge on the Brazilian side is about 2 kilometers (1 mile) long, and the paved roadway running parallel to it leading to and from the hotel can be easily negotiated with a wheelchair.

If you want another perspective, **Helisul Taxi Aero** operates an obnoxiously noisy helicopter ride, which does, nonetheless, offer impressive aerial views. The seven-minute ride starts in front of the Hotel das Cataratas. ☎ 0455/741786. *Cost: $50 adults, $25 children under 10.* ☉ *Apr.–Oct., daily 9–5; Nov.–Mar., daily 9–7.*

Dining and Lodging

Argentine Side

$$$–$$$$ **Internacional Cataratas de Iguazú.** Half the rooms in this five-star hotel
★   have direct views of the falls, so be sure to ask for a view when you make a reservation. Floor-to-ceiling windows let the inspiring scene into the lobby, restaurants, and bars, and even the pool has a view. The large lobby combines antique colonial and concrete-slab modern furniture. Guests can have breakfast or a drink on spacious balconies. The handsomely decorated main restaurant serves a memorable trout maitre d'hôtel (stuffed trout wrapped in pastry). At sunset and at dawn, an occasional parrot or toucan crosses in front of the view of the roaring waters. ⊞ *Parque Nacional Iguazú,* ☎ *0757/20295 or 0757/20311;*

U.S. ☎ *800/448–8355. 180 rooms. 2 restaurants, 3 bars, pool, 2 tennis courts. AE, DC, MC, V.*

$$$ **Hotel Esturion.** This hotel in Puerto Iguazú isn't right on the falls, but it has gardens and a sweeping view of the river. ⊞ *Av. Fronteras 650, Puerto Iguazú,* ☎ *0757/20020 or 0575/210161,* 𝖥𝖠𝖷 *0757/20414; U.S.* ☎ *800/338–2288. 114 rooms, 4 suites, 4 apartments. Restaurant, coffee shop, pool, sauna, 2 tennis courts, exercise room, nightclub. AE, DC, MC, V.*

Brazilian Side

$$$ **Bourbon.** This large, comfortable hotel is in Foz do Iguaçú, the nearest town to the park on the Brazilian side. ⊞ *Rodovía das Cataratas, km 2½,* ☎ *0455/231313; U.S.* ☎ *800/544–5503. 310 rooms, 11 suites. 3 restaurants, 2 bars, coffee shop, pool, sauna, 2 tennis courts, health club, shops. AE, DC, MC, V.*

$$$ **Das Cataratas.** This handsome old building surrounded by galleries and
★ gardens provides the more traditional comforts—large rooms, terraces, hammocks—of a colonial-style hotel. The restaurant serves a smorgasbord-style dinner featuring *feijoada,* the Brazilian national dish based on rice, black beans, and pork, with a variety of tasty side dishes. ⊞ *Rodovía das Cataratas,* ☎ *0455/232266,* 𝖥𝖠𝖷 *0455/232266; in São Paulo,* ☎ *011/829–5477. 110 rooms. 2 restaurants, bar, coffee shop, pool, 2 tennis courts, shops. AE, DC, MC, V.*

PATAGONIA

Patagonia, the vast territory that covers the southern half of Argentina and Chile, is a state of mind that has possessed travelers and writers since the first sailing ships touched its gale-swept shores centuries ago. Brilliantly publicized by Charles Darwin after his cruises on the *Beagle* in the 1840s, by Reverend Lucas Bridges at the turn of the century in his inspiring *Uttermost Part of the Earth,* and brought back to a human scale by British writer Bruce Chatwin's more recent *In Patagonia,* the region—like the Amazon—attracts polemic attention. Briefly an empire under the aegis of an ambitious Frenchman—even today there is an office in Paris dedicated to recovering the empire—Patagonia is too vast and complex to get to know in a single visit.

It's a land for romantic adventurers whose idea of a good time includes an ample dose of physical discomfort and unexpected challenges. You can't rent a camper and circle this vast territory in a week. Tackling Patagonia means hit-and-run plane trips into desolate, windswept airports. (It was here that Antoine de Saint-Exupéry got his start as a commercial pilot, struggling to keep his tiny aircraft and its brave passengers from blowing off the runway before takeoff.) Comfortable accommodations are available near the four major visited areas: Bariloche, the Atlantic coast around Península Valdés, Perito Moreno Glacier National Park, and Tierra del Fuego. Getting from one place to the other, however, is still a time- and energy-consuming struggle involving dawn flights, poor connections, and unpredictable weather conditions that stymie the best-laid plans. In addition, tourists are often seen as a cash crop to be fleeced, like the sheep whose wool used to be the region's major money producer. Given these conditions, it's recommended that you arrange your Patagonian adventure in advance; vacations ranging from skiing packages to bird-watching tours are available from numerous operators (*see* Chapter 2, Adventure and Learning Vacations, for details).

Bariloche and the Lake Region

Bariloche and the nearby lake district, for many years the queen bee of Argentine winter sports, has the best-developed tourism infrastructure, so it is the easiest place to start a tour of Patagonia. There's nowhere in South America comparable to this enclave of idyllic scenery reminiscent of Switzerland, Scandinavia, and the Rockies. Often called "Brazil-oche" because so many Brazilians flood in to enjoy the snow, Bariloche mixes Teutonic architecture with Italian levity.

Arriving and Departing

By Plane

The town of Bariloche is the gateway to the Andean lake region. **Aerolíneas Argentinas** and **Austral** fly daily from Buenos Aires to Bariloche. **LADE** and **CATA** are less expensive but have fewer flights. The 1,935-kilometer (1,200-mile) trip takes two hours. There are several flights a week between Bariloche and Trelew and Esquel.

By Train

Train service at press time (winter 1995) had been suspended pending the outcome of the privatization program. If reinstated, this 30- to 40-hour trip is a great way to experience the vastness of Argentina's plains.

By Car

Driving to Bariloche from Buenos Aires is a long haul. Half the trip is over a rocky, rippling dirt road. The local roads in the lake region are dusty but passable.

By Bus

Chevallier (Calle Moreno 107, ☎ 0944/23090; in Buenos Aires, ☎ 1/314–0111 or 1/314–5555) and **La Estrella** (Calle Palacios 246, ☎ 0944/22140; in Buenos Aires, ☎ 1/313–7231) run comfortable and reliable overnight buses to Bariloche; the trip takes 22 hours.

Exploring

The area around Bariloche is postcard-pretty: forests of evergreens; snow-capped peaks as a constant backdrop; large lakes of deep, deep blue, transparent green, or luminous gray; alpine architecture with updated postmodern details; and spring wildflowers galore. A show as impressive as the fall change of seasons in New England happens here in April, when the southern beech turns outrageous tones of yellow, red, and orange. Nature keeps tourists' cameras snapping away at the scenery.

It's a region that offers plenty for everyone: *Town and Country* magazine billed it "The Last Great Place" for its appeal to European and American jet-setters who spend a season here riding, fishing, or hunting and build beautiful homes here. The less well-heeled traveler can enjoy the same scenery and sports at one of the many inns dotted around the region. European aristocrats without their own homes have a fabulous small hotel, **El Casco** (Casilla de Correo 436, Bariloche, Neuquen, ☎ 0944/61032 or 0944/61068; $$$$), where they stay while visiting the game preserves or private trout streams tucked away in indescribably beautiful foothills. If you enjoy nature in small doses, stay in town, and you'll feel the impact of consumerism at its normal touristic clip. If you can take a stronger diet of the great outdoors, then settle into one of the area's many inns. Most are at the edge of a lake and offer access to all the region's activities and sports. Downtown Bariloche is swamped in July, and in January and February, but the countryside is calm enough even then that it doesn't feel crowded.

Travel agents can provide details for all the excursions listed below. There are dozens of small hotels and inns in strategically scenic spots, rivers for rafting, hills to be hiked, and campgrounds (ask at the **Automovil Club Argentino,** Av. 12 de Octubre 785, Bariloche, ☎ 0944/23000). This is vacationland, whether as a winter wonderland or a summer haven from the heat.

Bariloche

Bariloche is on the northeastern shore of **Lake Nahuel Huapi** and is blessed with a fabulous view of the Andes across the blue waters. Much of the area around Bariloche is part of the **Parque Nacional Nahuel Huapi,** which in itself offers no services to tourists. To find out what is available, go to the **Municipal Tourist Office** in the unexpectedly Germanic-looking **Centro Cívico** on the plaza (Civic Center; ☎ 0944/22775, 0944/26416, or 0944/26499). The **Club Andino** (20 de Febrero 30, ☎ 0944/24351 or 0944/22266; open Mon.–Thurs. 4–10) provides information on trail conditions, refuges, and mountain climbing. There is the small **Museo de la Patagonia** (Patagonia Museum) in the Civic Center; it offers an overview of the region's now-scarce wildlife. Hand-knit woolen sweaters, jams made with local berries, and locally made chocolate—items that make up 99% of what tourists take home—can be bought within a short walk of the Civic Center.

Excursions in the Lake District

SMALL CIRCUIT

The most popular driving tour out of Bariloche is a three-hour excursion south along the lake, up into the foothills of the **Cerro Catedral** (Mt. Cathedral), whose slopes were groomed for Argentina's first ski resort earlier in the century. The chairlift ride up the side of the gentle 7,000-foot mountain from the parking area at the base provides a bird's-eye panorama of lakes, peaks, and plains, mixed in a kaleidoscope of bright colors. The **Hotel Catedral,** just above the point where the cable car takes off, is a favorite of upscale winter-sports lovers and a good spot for a meal or tea for day-trippers. Drive back down the mountain to the lake's edge and continue east along its coast. You are now on what is called the **Circuito Chico** (Small Circuit), a 57-kilometer (35-mile), half-day tourist trail that follows the lake to the **Península San Pedro,** which juts out several miles into the lake and is the site of many spectacular homes. The more adventurous can take an unmarked dirt road off to the left before getting back to the lake; it leads to the rustic village of **Colonia Suiza,** a good spot for tea or lunch. Follow the road through the village and bear south, skirting **Lago Moreno** and **Laguna El Trebol.** Soon you'll come out on the **Península Llao Llao** behind the **Hotel Llao Llao,** a monumental hotel recently reopened after being closed for more than a decade. Don't worry about getting lost on the unmarked roads: They all wind around and get you back to where you started. And there is an Austrian- or German-run inn or restaurant at every bend where you can ask directions over hot chocolate and strudel.

LARGE CIRCUIT

The **Circuito Grande** (Large Circuit) is a more ambitious tour, covering 242 kilometers (150 miles) of lakes and forests, with many spots to stop and enjoy views of lakes and mountains. It's an all-day trip along mostly dirt roads. It first takes in the **Valle Encantado** (Enchanted Valley), with its wall of strange rock formations, called, for example, the Finger of God, the Siamese Twins, and the Express Train, along the valley of the **Limay River.** The road then bears west along the **Traful River,** reaching a large lake of the same name and later **Lago Correntoso** and the village of **Villa La Angostura.** By then you'll be ready for a typical Bariloche tea or a cup of hot chocolate; luckily, confiterías abound in La Angostura. The excursion ends at the edge of Nahuel Huapí Lake. The Large Circuit is particularly lovely in spring and fall; during the fishing season, you can stop along the way and try your luck in any of the lakes.

SEVEN LAKE CIRCUIT

The **Circuito de los Siete Lagos** (Seven Lake Circuit) takes you along 403 kilometers (250 miles) of fairly deserted, mostly dirt roads through a twisting, turning chain of seven lakes: **Correntoso, Espejo** (Mirror), **Traful, Villarino, Falkner, Hermoso** (Beautiful), and **Meliquina.** If you drive on to **San Martín de los Andes,** at the end of **Lake Lácar,** for lunch, you can visit the area's second city, a paradise for fishermen in summer and a center for skiers in winter.

VICTORIA ISLAND

Another day trip is to **Isla Victoria** (Victoria Island), the home of the **Parque Nacional Los Arrayanes** (Arrayanes National Park). Walt Disney himself was inspired by the *arrayanes,* native trees with a cinnamon-color bark and dark green foliage, for his film *Bambi,* according to local lore. In any case, on the boat ride across the Nahuel Huapí, you'll pass the spot where Dwight D. and Mamie Eisenhower caught the largest trout of their lives. The day trip includes an institutional lunch at the Victoria Island Inn. Spend as much time as you can walking about the park: The arrayanes create a mysterious, surreal atmosphere.

Sports and the Outdoors

Fishing

Driving out of Bariloche to the north, past the airport, takes you to some of South America's great fishing streams. Trout fanatics flock here from all over the world during the season (November 15–April 15). The bar and dining room at the handsome, large old **Hotel Correntoso** (Ruta 231, km 3, Villa Correntoso, ☎ 0944/94361) near Villa La Angostura is the place to go to swap stories and discover where the rainbows are biting. When your neighbor mentions his recent 12-pounder, he may not be exaggerating. The Argentine record for a trout—weighing in at 35 pounds!—was a brown caught in the waters of the Nahuel Huapí in 1952. Boats are available, but the tried-and-true method is to hike the banks in search of that perfect pool along the **Chimehuin,** the **Limay,** or the **Correntoso** itself, where a legendary trophy has been seen lurking for years. An easy-to-get license allows you to catch brown trout, rainbow trout, perch, brook trout, and *salar sebago* (landlocked) salmon. Driving a bit farther gets you to another favorite fishing center, **Junín de los Andes,** a picturesque town. Here the **Malleo River** and the **Currhué, Huechulaufquen, Paimún,** and **Lácar** lakes are where you'll find the real pros. Although many a fisherman releases his trophy, most hotels and inns will grill or bake your catch of the day for dinner.

Skiing

With about 80 kilometers (50 miles) of skiable terrain, Bariloche is the largest ski resort in Argentina. It is also the oldest: The cable car has been carrying skiers up Cerro Catedral since the 1950s. The resort is popular with Brazilians who have never seen snow. Although rain often washes snow from the base by mid-August, Bariloche's four bowls are superb through September. Bariloche has eight chairlifts, three

T-bars, seven Pomas, and a cable car. Bariloche ski packages, which include a six-day pass, seven nights in Bariloche, breakfast, and transportation to the slopes, run $500–$900 per person, depending on the accommodations you choose. The **Latin America Reservation Center** (Box 1435, Dundee, FL 33838, ☎ 800/327–3573) offers reasonable rates on a range of hotels, or ask **Aerolíneas Argentinas** (U.S. ☎ 800/333–0276) for names of U.S. agencies that offer ski packages.

The Atlantic Coast

The coast along the Patagonian province of Chubut is a mainland Galápagos, the second most important concentration of visible marine wildlife in South America. Few sights match the annual gathering of the Magellanic penguin clan. At least a million of the elegant creatures come back to roost every August on the stark beaches at Punta Tombo, south of Trelew, the main gateway to the region.

Península Valdés, north of Trelew near the town of Puerto Madryn, is another haven for hard-core nature lovers. Right-whale watching is a less predictable activity than penguin spotting, but worth the chance to feel the spray of a jet of water launched from a whale's spout an arm's length away. Birds, seals, sea elephants, and sea lions round out the menu of natural marvels at this aquatic wonderland.

Visitor Information

The **Tourist Office of Chubut Province** (☎ 0965/20121) has stands in Trelew at the bus terminal at Calles Lewis Jones and Urquiza. In Puerto Madryn the tourist office is at Avenida Roca 201 (☎ 0965/73029).

Arriving and Departing

By Plane
Aerolíneas Argentinas and **Austral** fly daily to the town of Trelew from Buenos Aires. The airlines provide bus service from the airport to the town of Puerto Madryn; the 50-minute trip costs less than $10. There are also occasional flights to Trelew from Río Gallegos.

By Bus
Donotto (☎ 0965/32434) and **La Puntual** (☎ 0965/33748) offer regular bus service between Buenos Aires and both Trelew and Puerto Madryn.

Tour Operators

Once you get to Argentina, tours to all of the areas mentioned below can be set up through **Nievemar Tours** (Italia 20, Trelew, ☎ 0965/34114 or 0965/35646). Remember that the best time to go is in October or November—the local tourists haven't started to migrate yet. (*See* Natural History *and* Birding-Watching Tours *in* Chapter 2, Adventure and Learning Vacations, for details on U.S.-based packages.)

Exploring

The best time to catch the migrant maritime population at home and without visitors—and in various stages of the rites of reproduction—is in October and November (in December, when vacations start, the area becomes crowded with families and school excursions). During the warm summer months from December to March, wildlife-watching can be complemented with swimming, diving, and deep-sea fishing.

Trelew and the Welsh Towns

While the action is on the coast, a day tour to the nearby Welsh communities is another option. In 1865, a group of Welsh nationalists settled the valley of the Chubut River to establish a community where they could keep their customs intact. Now the towns of Gaiman, Trevelin, and Esquel still reflect their culture. While the settlers' descendants all now speak Spanish and have intermarried, they have maintained their traditions, including the recipes for their delicious cakes, which are features of their teas. Trelew (pop. 52,000) is the largest town in the community, and it is here that most travelers stay—busing or driving out to the wildlife colonies, which are all within a couple of hours' drive along good roads.

Wildlife Excursions

PENGUINS

Most tourists go straight to **Punta Tombo** (120 kilometers/75 miles south of Trelew) after checking into their hotel in Trelew. Try to visit between August and April, because the Magellanic penguin clan breaks up and heads north to the warmer waters from May through July. In August, future parents spring-clean the burrows they've left for the winter. In September they are rapt in the rites of romantic courtship. In October—the mating season—they pair off with their permanent partner (penguin relationships last for years). In November the eggs are laid and both parents share the task of incubating them and then finding tasty tidbits of fresh fish for the newly born, who appear late in the month. In summer, the babies are protected and raised amid great spurts of activity. In February, the adults molt, which means they cannot go to sea to fish. This is a sad time, with multitudes of scraggly penguins moping about the beach like frustrated bathers grounded by a shark warning. Once the feathers grow back, the entire family heads north.

WHALES

Rivaling the penguins are the whales, which are to be found north of Trelew near Puerto Madryn, in the gulfs on both sides of the **Península Valdés.** With the whales, too, timing is everything: The southern right whale—the right got its name because it was the "right" whale for commercial purposes, so persistently sought by the whalers of yore—comes to the Argentine coast at the end of winter to mate. A year later, at the same time and place, the mothers return to give birth between August and October. The whales, which weigh more than 30 tons and measure up to 40 feet in length, thrive on krill, the abundant and nutritious shrimplike crustaceans, collecting them like lawn mowers by cruising the surface of the sea with their mouths wide open. The tourist may get to see them leap, which they do for no apparent reason. At other times, they hang out for up to a quarter of an hour with several yards of their tails sticking up out of the water. When it isn't being chased by an aggressive killer whale, the right whale can be found basking in the waters of three bays, the **Golfo San José,** the **Caleta Valdés,** and the **Golfo Nuevo.** At Puerto Pirámides, boats and scuba-diving equipment can be rented, and tour organizers advertise "Close Encounters with Right Whales," with a money-back guarantee if you don't get within a hundred yards of one. Whale-watching tours are conducted on six-passenger catamarans moving slowly through the waters; the whales often come close enough to touch! Two- to three-hour tours cost $20 per person and can be arranged through your hotel.

SEALS AND SEABIRDS

Another great sea sight is the southern elephant seal, which has established its northernmost mainland colony at Península Valdés. If you climb down the cliffs near the lighthouse at **Punta Delgada** in the **Reserva Faunística de Punta Norte,** you can visit an *elefantería,* a colony of elephant seals (your hotel can arrange transportation). They, too, appear in late winter to set up homes for the summer. Their mating rites are colorful and noisy. Males weigh up to 4 tons and thrive on a good fight, which can be an awesome spectacle. A colony of fur seals, called a *lobería,* can be found at Punta Norte at the northern tip of the peninsula.

The **Isla de los Pájaros,** about 37 kilometers (22 miles) from Puerto Madryn, is home to an infinite number of seabirds, such as cormorants, herons, flamingos, and gulls.

Perito Moreno Glacier National Park

The Perito Moreno Glacier, in the southern Andes near the border with Chile, is one of the world's greatest natural monuments. A sight as awesome as Iguazú Falls, it's a solid translucent mass of ice that is always on the move. Soon after the discovery of the Perito Moreno Glacier late in the last century, scientists crossed the Patagonian desert to hike up into the Andean foothills to study this icy wonder of the world. Each year around 20,000 travelers, half of them from the Northern Hemisphere, follow in their footsteps to gaze upon the 1.5 million acres of ice, water, mountains, and virgin forest that make up Parque Nacional Los Glaciares (Glacier National Park), nature's number-one ice show.

Getting to the glacier can be an arduous exercise. If you go by land from Río Gallegos, the nearest (250 kilometers/150 miles) sizable town, the trip can take up to five hours across desolate plains filled with more sheep than you can count in a lifetime of sleepless nights, but the journey is occasionally enlivened by a sighting of *ñandu* (rhea), herds of the elegant llama-like guanaco, silver-gray foxes, and fleet-footed hares. The solitude of Patagonia pervades the landscape, and the traveler is swept along with the never-flagging wind. But the memory of the effort involved in the drive vanishes instantly when the glacier comes into view near Calafate, a frontier town that slows down in winter, when inclement weather makes visiting the national park more difficult.

Visits to the glacier are basically by tour and rather brief, considering the time and energy it takes to get there. As space on glacier tours is limited, reservations must be made in advance. Any travel agent can do the booking in Buenos Aires if it hasn't been arranged before the trip. Although this is a one-sight attraction, there are two ways to see the glaciers, and it's worth two days to see the spectacle both from land and from the water.

Visitor Information

You can find an **Oficina de Turismo** in Calafate (Coronel Rosales 25, ☎ 0902/91090) and in Río Gallegos (☎ 0966/22702).

Arriving and Departing

By Plane

Aerolíneas Argentinas and **Austral** fly from Buenos Aires to Río Gallegos. In summer **LADE,** the Air Force transport line, flies small planes from Río Gallegos to Calafate, the jumping-off point for tours to the glacier, a 50-minute flight.

By Car

Localiza (Sarmiento 237, ☎ 0966/24417), **Riestra Rent-a-car** (Av. San Martín 1504, ☎ 0966/21321), and other car rental agencies operate in Río Gallegos; rates are high by U.S. standards.

By Bus

Interlagos (Fragano 35, Oficina 5, ☎ 0966/22466) runs regular bus service between Río Gallegos and Calafate. The bus leaves from the airport in Río Gallegos. In summer a bus runs from Puerto Natales, Chile, to Calafate.

Exploring

The View from the Water

Take the boat that goes across the northern branch of **Lago Argentino** (Lake Argentina) to as close to the **Glaciar Upsala** (Upsala Glacier) as it dares to get, dodging icebergs along the way. Off to the side, the **Onelli Glacier** also tumbles its blocks of ice into the lake below. This trip takes 11 hours, with a two-hour lunch break at a lodge on the banks of the lake. The expedition starts with a half-hour bus ride along the side of Lago Argentino to the pier at **Puerto Bandera,** at the confluence of the lake's north and south basins. There a comfortable, enclosed motorboat carries up to 120 passengers through 15,000-year-old Lake Argentina—which has a milky, emulsive appearance—and between the multitoned icebergs. The seven glaciers that feed the chilly lake melt, filling it with minerals ground to fine powder by the glacier's moraine—an accumulation of boulders, stones, and other debris swept along in its path. At one time the ice of the glacier measured 3,000 feet high; now it has shrunk considerably, and the melted ice covers almost 2,590 square kilometers (1,000 square miles). After a 2½-hour cruise, the boat crisscrosses in front of the Upsala Glacier while everyone takes their fill of pictures. Then the boat docks alongside **Onelli Bay** for a bracing lunch. After lunch, passengers walk as far as they can inland, past baby icebergs fallen from the **Agassiz, Boladas, Heim,** and **Onelli glaciers,** which fill **Onelli Lake,** a small body of water that looks like an aquatic sculpture garden. Icebergs of all sizes and shapes compete for your attention, and each inspires all sorts of associations. The side of the lake is overflowing with ferns and *lenga* trees, a scraggly variety native to the region. If you are lucky, you can observe condors soaring overhead, flying from perch to perch in the towering peaks to the west. If you miss your condor here, the captain will probably point one out on the ride homeward.

The View from Land

Save the best for day two. A two-hour drive from Río Gallegos by bus gets you to the wooden gate of **Parque Nacional Los Glaciares** (Glacier National Park), and a few bends farther down the road, one of the sights of a lifetime zaps into view. You get out of the bus at the tip of **Península de Magallanes** and walk 50 yards to the guardrails, where you look across the **Canal de los Témpanos** (Iceberg Channel) at an astounding 3.2-kilometer-wide (2-mile-wide) wall of ice that partially disintegrates before your eyes, producing the thundering sound of crackling and splashing ice, turned up to rock-concert volume. Declared a World Heritage Site by UNESCO, the **Perito Moreno Glacier** is a 30,000-year-old elongated ice cube shaded in tones of white and a deep blue hue that is caused by compression, which squeezes the oxygen out of the ice. The Perito Moreno is a river in solid form creeping down out of the Andean Cordillera like a snake in a polar-bear fur coat. To the left of the glacier, the **Brazo Rico** (Rico Branch) of the lake is divided from the main body of the lake by accumulated icebergs; once every four or five years the weight of the accumulated water is so great that it breaks through with a crash that can be heard back in Calafate, 48 kilometers (30 miles) away. No one can predict the exact time of the next crash.

After an hour's stop, the tour bus heads back to town. Most travelers bring a prepackaged picnic lunch, which your hotel can provide, to munch while waiting for the next crash. Ideally, one should visit the glacier by car and go early or late, to savor the sight before or after the tour buses have moved on. Should the lake be too rough on the day you plan your boat trip, you can try shore fishing for trout from the side of the road (your hotel can get you tackle and steer you to the best spots) or drive up into the mountains near Fitzroy. A brief walk onto the edge of the glacier can be arranged at local travel agencies, as can fishing outings with guides.

Dining and Lodging

Within sight of the glacier, an hour's drive from Calafate, is a small but elegant auberge, **Los Notros** (reserve from Buenos Aires: Arenales 1457, 7th Floor, 1061 Buenos Aires, ☎ 1/812–2166, ℻ 1/814–0317). In Calafate the choice spot is **Hotel Kau-yatun** (Estancia 25 de Mayo, ☎ 0902/91059), a former ranch redone in deluxe comfort. Both places offer mouthwatering, country-fresh meals.

Tierra del Fuego

Tierra del Fuego, an island at the southern tip of Argentina, is the capital of Everyman's imaginary Patagonia. Yet its allure is based more on its mythic past than on reality. Darwin's Indians are long gone, and the capital town—Ushuaia, located at 55 degrees latitude south—can be called picturesque at best. It resembles an oversize mining camp awaiting the next strike. But what makes the place special is the light: At sundown, it casts the landscape in a subdued, sensual tone; everything feels closer, softer, more human in dimension despite the vastness of the setting. You can also catch record-size seagoing brown trout and put your toe in the Beagle Channel, as Magellan must have done so long ago. Perhaps the greatest lure is that the traveler setting foot in Ushuaia gets to add a notch to his own personal record book: It is the southernmost city on the globe, just a proverbial stone's throw from Antarctica.

Visitor Information

Zagier & Urruty (C. C. 94 Sucursal 19B, 1419 Buenos Aires, ☎ 1/572–1050, ℻ 1/572–5766) publishes a guide to Tierra del Fuego with an excellent map as well as an English-language adventure guide to all of Patagonia, both of which can be found in some bookstores in Buenos Aires. In Ushuaia, tourism information on Tierra del Fuego can be obtained at the **Hotel Albatros** (Av. Maipú 505, ☎ and ℻ 0901/23340).

Arriving and Departing

By Plane

Aerolíneas Argentinas has regular flights to Ushuaia, the capital of the newly created province of Tierra del Fuego. **LADE** flies from Calafate and Río Gallegos and other southern towns to Río Grande, Tierra del Fuego's largest city. Aerolíneas's twice-weekly transpolar flight from Buenos Aires to Auckland and Sydney stops in Río Gallegos for fuel: A traveler from the other side of the world can stop over and visit Tierra del Fuego. Note: Cruises to Antarctica and the Malvinas (Falkland Islands) rarely stop at Ushuaia nowadays; they call instead at Punta Arenas in Chile.

Tour Operators

Local travel agencies offer specialized tours and adventure trips (*see* Chapter 2, Adventure and Learning Vacations, for U.S.–based operators). Fishing, trekking, hunting, mountain climbing, horseback expeditions, and sailing trips that head south toward Antarctica are all available.

Adventure Tours
Kilak Expeditions (Kuanip 67, Ushuaia, ☎ 0901/22234), **Caminante** (Deloqui 368, Ushuaia, ☎ 0901/23689), and **Tiempo Libre** (Av. San Martín 154, Ushuaia, ☎ 0901/21917) offer a wide variety of adventurous treks through the Parque Nacional Tierra del Fuego.

Orientation Tours
Gador Viajes (Tucumán 941, 1049 Buenos Aires, ☎ 1/322–6344 or 1/322–9806) offers carefully prepared and managed tours of the area, with connecting trips to Lago Argentino, Trelew, and Bariloche. **Tolkeyén** (12 de Octubre 150, Ushuaia, ☎ 0901/22637) and **Rumbo Sur** (Av. San Martín 342, Ushuaia, ☎ 0901/21139) offer bus tours that give an overview of the national park.

Sailing Tours
Sailing out to sea usually means contact with wide-eyed seals, sea elephants, and sea lions sunning on the rocks, plus gigantic albatross who fly in from Dunedin, New Zealand. To charter a sailboat, contact **Velero Croix St. Paul** (Julio Brunet, Club Nautico, Gob. Fernández Valdéz 290, Ushuaia, ☎ 0901/23159).

Exploring

When you stand on the banks of the **Canal del Beagle** (Beagle Channel) near Ushuaia, the spirit of the farthest corner of the world takes hold. The light is magical, the air exhilarating. The snowcapped mountains of Chile reflect the illumination of the setting sun back onto a stream rolling into the channel, as nearby peaks echo their image—on a windless day—in the still waters. Ushuaia itself looks like a mining town between booms. Wooden huts, precariously mounted on upright tree trunks, ready for speedy displacement to a different site, look like entrants in a contest for most original log cabin. An occasional brightly painted structure gives the chaotic urban landscape a touch of much-needed color. Town planning has never been a strong point in Ushuaia; instead, irregular rows of homes sprout with the haphazardness of mushrooms in a moist field. While staying in Ushuaia, try tidbits of *corderito* (baby lamb) right off the spit, the tasty mainstay of Patagonian cuisine, as well as *centolla*, the large crab trapped off the town's shores, and gigantic *mejillones* (mussels), often 5 inches long.

Above the city, the last mountains of the Andean Cordillera rise, and just south and west of Ushuaia they finally vanish into the often-stormy sea. Snow dots the peaks with white well into summer. Nature is the principal attraction here, with trekking, fishing, horseback riding, and sailing among the most rewarding activities. In winter, when most international tourists stay home to enjoy their own summer, the adventurous have the place to themselves for cross-country skiing and snowmobiling across the powdery dunes (*see* Sports and the Outdoors, *below*).

Between **Parque Nacional Tierra del Fuego** (information: Av. San Martín 395, ☏ 0901/21315) and **Estancia Harberton,** the area's oldest ranch, most visitors spend at least three days exploring Tierra del Fuego. Visits to both sites are generally arranged through tour operators (*see above*). Options for seeing the park, tucked up against the Chilean border 19 kilometers (12 miles) from town, range from bus tours to more adventurous excursions—horseback trips; camping trips to **Lake Kami** or **Fagnano;** or treks led by seasoned mountaineers that include hiking through forests and peat bogs with the snowcapped Andes as a constant backdrop, then canoeing across Lapataia Bay.

Estancia Harberton (Harberton Ranch) consists of 50,000 acres of coastal marshland and wooded hillsides. The property was a late-19th-century gift from the Argentine government to Reverend Thomas Bridges, officially considered the "Father of Tierra del Fuego." Today the ranch is managed by Bridges's great-grandson, Thomas Goodall, and his American wife, Natalie, a scientist who has cooperated with the National Geographic Society on conservation projects; most visitors come in organized tours, but they welcome the stray tourist who stumbles onto their spread. They serve up a solid and tasty tea in their home, the oldest building on the island.

Sports and the Outdoors

Skiing

Ushuaia is the cross-country skiing center of South America, thanks to enthusiastic Club Andino members who took to the sport in the 1980s and made the forested hills of a high valley about 20 minutes from town a favorite destination for traveling skiers. From **Hosteria Tierra Major** and **Hosteria Los Cotorras,** two small inns, trails lead out through evergreen boxwoods and past beaver huts. Skis, poles, and boots can be rented in town, as can windskis, snowmobiles, and Sno-Cats. For downhill skiers, the club has bulldozed a couple of short, flat runs directly above Ushuaia.

ARGENTINA ESSENTIALS

Customs and Duties

If you come directly to Buenos Aires by air or ship, you will find that customs officials usually wave you through without any inspection. Also, the international airports have introduced a customs system for those with "nothing to declare," which has streamlined the arrival process. Foreign bus passengers usually have their suitcases opened, as do all other passengers.

Personal clothing and effects are admitted free of duty, provided they have been used, as are personal jewelry and professional equipment, including portable computers. Travel agents or airlines can make advance arrangements for hunting equipment. Fishing gear presents no problems. Up to 2 liters of alcoholic beverages, 400 cigarettes, and 50 cigars are admitted duty-free.

Dining

Specialties

ENTRÉES

Beef, or *bife,* as they say in Argentine Spanish, is still the staple of the country's diet. Once a major export, cattle traditionally have outnumbered people two to one in Argentina. Gauchos spent their lifetimes in the saddle eating exclusively the range-fed native cattle they raised. Some 50 million cattle—Angus, Hereford, and a dozen other breeds—thrive on the pampa grasses, which are so nutritious that there is no need for grain supplements.

Nothing can duplicate the indescribable flavor of a lean, tender, 3-inch-thick steak grilled over coals of a log from the *quebracho* tree, an ax-breaking hardwood from the Chaco. Many different cuts of a steer are grilled on the parrilla (grill) at an asado, as a barbecue is called here. Steaks can be accompanied by *picante* (hot) sauce, although Argentines traditionally prefer theirs straight. (Picante does not burn like Mexican chiles or Indian curries.) If you ask for *chimichurri,* chefs will serve a picante sauce prepared with garlic, olive oil, vinegar, and cilantro. Bife *de chorizo* is a basic strip sirloin, but three times the size; bife *de lomo* can be a 3-inch-high fillet. Often a half portion is more than enough. *Jugoso* means rare, but Argentines like their meat well-done, so it is hard to get a *parrillero* to prepare a steak so that it is red when sliced.

Adventurous meat eaters will want to have their steak served sizzling on a miniature grill, the parrillada, whose hot coals keep the cuts warm at the table. The mixed grill includes blood sausage, short ribs, and various internal and external organs like intestines and udder. A typical beef hors d'oeuvre consists of thin slices of matambre, made by laying out boiled eggs, chunks of ham, and hearts of palm on flank steak, rolling it into a loaf, soaking it in a marinade, and baking it. Beef is also traditionally served in the form of a breaded cutlet, called a *Milanesa,* wrapped in ham and cheese and sometimes served with a tomato sauce. The simple version is referred to as a Milanesa, while the kind with ham, cheese, and sauce is a Milanesa *Napolitana.* Hamburgers are usually served at home or at fast-food emporiums; Argentines don't have the knack for making great burgers. Stick to steaks.

ETHNIC CUISINE

Italian cuisines, particularly those of Naples and Sicily, are found throughout Argentina. Buenos Aires has the most concentrated immigrant influence, with Jewish delicatessens, British restaurants (especially good for high tea), and French, German, Irish, Cantonese, and Middle Eastern cuisines, to name a few. Corderito *al asador* (lamb asado), centolla, and hot potato salads are popular in Ushuaia, while in the Trelew–Puerto Madryn area, the favorites are Welsh high teas with seven varieties of rich cakes, and local fish—trucha, sea salmon, corvina, and calamari.

DESSERTS

Most Argentine desserts are made with one principal ingredient: *dulce de leche,* a sticky sweet made of milk boiled with sugar, a pinch of soda, and a few drops of vanilla. The thick, brownish cream is spread on breakfast toast, baked in cakes, meringues, and tarts, and is often eaten alone by the spoonful. Mixed with bits of chocolate, it is a favorite flavor in Argentine ice cream shops. Most Argentines travel with several pots of it when they go abroad.

WINES

Given the high consumption of beef rather than fish, Argentines understandably drink *vino tinto* (red wine). For those who prefer *vino blanco* (white wine), try vintages from Mendoza and from lesser known wineries farther north: La Rioja and Salta. Here the Torrontés grape thrives. The Torrontés varietal produces a dry white with an overwhelming, unforgettable bouquet that has been a consistent prizewinner in recent competitions in Germany and France.

A popular summer cooler is clericot, a white version of sangria, made with strawberries, peaches, oranges, or whatever fruits are in season or appeal to a particular bartender. Sangria is also available in many restaurants.

Mealtimes
Breakfast is usually served until 10; lunch runs from 12:30 to 2:30; dinner is from 9 to midnight. Several restaurants in Buenos Aires and other large cities stay open all night, catering to the after-theater crowd.

Dress
Jacket and tie are suggested for evening dining at more formal restaurants in the top price category, but casual chic or informal dress is accepted in most restaurants.

RATINGS
Prices quoted here are per person and include a first course, a main course, and a dessert, without wine or tip.

CATEGORY	COST
$$$	over $25
$$	$15–$25
$	under $15

Embassies and Consulates

United States
Embassy: Calle Colombia 4300, Buenos Aires, ☏ 1/774–2282.

Canada
Embassy: Calle Suipacha 1111, Buenos Aires, ☏ 1/312–9081.

United Kingdom
Embassy: Calle Luis Agote 2412, Buenos Aires, ☏ 1/803–7070.

Getting Around

By Plane
All medium-size and large cities in Argentina are served by the jets of **Austral** (☏ 1/325–0505) and **Aerolineas Argentinas** (☏ 1/393–5122, U.S. ☏ 800/333–0276), which also flies the international routes. Aerolíneas was privatized in late 1990 and purchased by a consortium composed of the Spanish airline Iberia, the Argentine government, and local investors. **CATA** (☏ 1/775–6800), another private service, offers a limited number of flights at competitive rates, particularly in summer. Small remote towns in the south are visited regularly by **LADE** (☏ 1/361–7071), whose commuter-size airplanes are operated by the Argentine Air Force. Again, frequencies are greatly reduced in the winter.

Like the United States and Canada, Argentina has large, sparsely inhabited areas to cross, so many travelers find themselves taking several internal flights. The **Visit Argentina** pass is designed for them: Four coupons cost $450; each additional coupon is $120 up to a maximum of eight; all must be used within 30 days of the first flight, and you cannot stop twice in any city except to connect. The passes can be purchased only outside the country and only through Aerolíneas Argentinas, upon the presentation of an international ticket. Seats are usually available on domestic flights, even in high season, except at holiday peaks. Keep in mind that Buenos Aires's domestic and international airports are 61 kilometers (38 miles) apart.

By Train

At the moment the railway system is being privatized and most long-distance and overnight service has been suspended. Trains to Buenos Aires's suburbs run frequently, as do trains to Mar del Plata and Rosario. Up-to-date information can be obtained from **Argentine Railways** (Maipú 88, ☎ 1/331–3280).

By Car

The **Automovil Club Argentino** (ACA, Av. del Libertador 1850, ☎ 1/802–6061 or 1/802–0522) operates gas stations, motels, and campgrounds, and provides tow trucks and a large team of motorized mechanics for unexpected breakdowns and subsequent repairs.

The club, which has several hundred thousand active members, also offers detailed maps and experts (some of whom speak English) to help plan your route. For drivers who rent a car and want to see the country, ACA provides gas coupons and can make accommodation arrangements according to a series of standard itineraries. Automobile Association of America (AAA) members can use the consulting services without charge, with proof of membership.

ROAD CONDITIONS

Superhighways do not exist in Argentina. Most roads are not divided and are not in good condition. Highways have also been privatized, so there are now more roads, even old ones, on which the driver must pay tolls. Night driving can be hazardous, as cattle often get onto the roads and trucks seldom have all their lights working.

RULES OF THE ROAD

Give everyone else on the road priority in Buenos Aires, especially aggressive colectivos and taxi drivers who think they're race-car drivers. Seat belts are required by law but are not often used. Turning left on avenues is prohibited unless there is a traffic-light arrow showing that this is permitted. Traffic lights, however, are not always observed. Proceed with care. In towns and cities, a 40 kilometers-per-hour (25 miles-per-hour) speed limit applies on streets, and a 60-kph limit is in effect on avenues; on expressways the limit is 120 kph (75 mph), and on other roads and highways out of town it's 80 kph (50 mph). At press time (winter 1995), the government was considering raising the limits on out-of-town highways and on expressways to 120 and 130 kph (75 and 80 mph), respectively.

RENTALS

All cities and most remote areas that attract tourists have rental-car agencies. When these companies have branches in other towns, arrangements can be made for a one-way drop off. **Avis** (Calle Cerrito 1122, ☎ 1/326–5542), **Hertz** (Pasaje Ricardo Rojas 451, ☎ 1/312–1317), **National** (Calle Esmeralda 1084, ☎ 1/312–4318), and **Localiza** (Calle Paraguay 1122, ☎ 1/375–1644) offices in Buenos Aires can make reservations in other locations; provincial government tourist offices also have information on car-rental agencies in their areas. Car rental is expensive by U.S. standards—$95 per day for a medium-size car, $475–$600 weekly. Ask about special rates; generally a better price can be negotiated.

GASOLINE

Argentina produces and markets its own gasoline. It is sold by the liter in regular and premium octanes. At press time (winter 1995), a U.S. gallon cost the equivalent of $2.80 for premium and $2.45 for regular.

By Bus

Frequent and dependable bus service links Buenos Aires with all the provinces of the country and with neighboring countries. Luxurious buses of a kind unknown in the United States, with sleeper seats similar to first-class airline seats, travel to the most remote destinations; more spartan buses cover the same routes at lower fares. Long-distance buses leave from the central terminal at the port end of **Retiro** (Av. Ramos Mejía 1680, ☎ 1/315–3404 or 1/315–3405), one of the city's central train stations. There are dozens of competing bus companies that cover the country like a cobweb.

By Boat

There is no internal boat travel in Argentina. Cruise ships stop in Tierra del Fuego, and hydrofoils and ferries connect Buenos Aires with nearby Uruguay (*see* Arriving and Departing *in* Buenos Aires, *above*).

Language

Argentines speak Spanish. English replaced French as the country's second language in the 1960s. Just about every high school graduate has a working knowledge of English, and most shops have English-speaking personnel. Because many Argentines are of Italian descent, Italian is understood by many Porteños (residents of Buenos Aires).

Lodging

While Argentina has very few world-class deluxe hotels, it offers many more excellent tourist-class hotels than most countries both north and south of the equator.

Hotels

Amenities in most hotels are above average, with private baths, 24-hour room service, heating and air-conditioning, cable TV, dry cleaning, and restaurants.

Albergues Transitorios

Albergues transitorios, or temporary lodgings, is the euphemistic name for drive-in hotels, which generally are used for romantic trysts; those that are legitimate motels can be found through the **Automovil Club Argentino's** nationwide network. These motels are inexpensive and more than adequate, costing $35–$45 a night. Make reservations through the ACA (Av. del Libertador 1850, ☎ 1/805–6061 or 1/802–0522).

Youth Hostels

The Buenos Aires branch of the **Youth Hostel Association** (Av. Brasil 675, ☎ 1/362–9133) is open 24 hours a day, seven days a week; it provides details on hostels throughout the country.

Camping

Campsites can be found in popular tourist destinations, including some of the beach areas. Usually they have running water, electricity, and bathroom facilities with toilets and showers. The **Automovil Club Argentino** (*see* Getting Around: By Car, *above*) can provide a list of campgrounds nationwide. Provincial tourist offices in Buenos Aires have lists of campgrounds in their regions. Some have telephones so that you can make reservations.

RATINGS

Prices are for two people in a double room and include all taxes.

CATEGORY	COST
$$$$	over $120
$$$	$70–$120
$$	$50–$70
$	$30–$50

Mail

Postal Rates and Delivery

When delivery is normal and there are no strikes or postal vacations, a letter takes 7–15 days to get from Buenos Aires to the United States; 10–15 days to the United Kingdom. An international airmail letter costs 70¢. Put postcards in envelopes and they will arrive more quickly.

Receiving Mail

Visitors can receive mail at the **Correo Central** (Central Post Office, Sarmiento 151, 1st Floor, ☎ 1/312–1048). Letters should be addressed to Lista/Poste Restante, Correo Central, 1000 Buenos Aires, Argentina. American Express cardholders can have mail sent to the company's Buenos Aires office: c/o American Express, Arenales 707, 1061 Buenos Aires, Argentina, ☎ 1/312–0900 or 1/312–1661.

Money and Expenses

Currency

In March 1991, as part of the government's program to stabilize the economy, Argentina's currency was pegged to the dollar. As a result, the Argentine peso (which replaced the austral) is on a one-to-one parity with the U.S. dollar. In the past, dramatic value swings occurred during periods of hyperinflation. In fact, in a bleak, short-lived moment, a cup of coffee cost twice as much in local currency after dinner as it did for breakfast. Nevertheless, economic stability has gradually occurred in the last few years, and the currency appears to be considerably more stable as well.

Changing Money

At press time (winter 1995), the exchange rate was one peso to the U.S. dollar, 0.75 pesos to the Canadian dollar, and 1.55 pesos to the pound sterling. Dollars are the most flexible form of exchange in Argentina, so residents of other countries should change their currencies to dollars before their journey. Be sure the bills are not torn or dirty; bills in poor condition won't be accepted. You can change money at your hotel, at banks, or at *casas de cambio* (money changers), which offer small competitive variations on rates. Some display rates for all major currencies.

Forms of Payment

The long period of price stability has also meant a boom in the acceptance of credit cards. American Express, Diners Club, MasterCard, and Visa are the most commonly accepted, although there are often good discounts to be found for using U.S. dollar bills. Larger stores in downtown areas catering to foreign visitors will often accept payment by a personal check drawn on a major U.S. bank, or traveler's checks. Smaller shops and restaurants are leery of traveler's checks.

What It Will Cost

For decades, Argentina has had one of the most volatile economies in the world, a boom–bust seesaw driven by inflation that sometimes rose several percentage points in a day. At press time (winter 1995), inflation had been tamed, and indications that the trend would continue were plentiful, making it more likely that costs can be predicted with some degree of accuracy. Argentina is no longer inexpensive, although bargains can be discovered by those accustomed to New York and London prices. The most sumptuous dinners, particularly in French restaurants, can run as high as $100 per person with wine and tip. But a thick slab of rare, wood-grilled sirloin with salad, potatoes, a house wine, and an espresso will cost $20 at steak houses in Buenos Aires, less in the hinterlands.

Order only national liquors in the bars or you'll pay a tremendous import premium. Shops get $75–$100 for a bottle of the all-time Latin American favorite, Chivas Regal. Simply ask for *"whiskey nacional por favor"* or *"vodka nacional."*

SAMPLE PRICES
A cup of coffee in a café, $1.50; a bottle of soda, $2.50. Taxi ride in central Buenos Aires, $2–$5. About $40 for a tango show with a couple of drinks; $80–$100 for a double room in a moderately priced, well-situated hotel, including taxes.

Opening and Closing Times

Banking hours are 10–3. Shops in Buenos Aires are open weekdays 9–7 or 8, Saturdays 9–1. In the city's suburbs—with the exception of the large malls such as Unicenter and Shopping Soleil—and most places outside the capital, shops close for a siesta break from approximately 12:30 to 3:30 or 4, when they open again until 7:30 PM. Post offices are open weekdays 8–6, Saturdays 8–1. There is 24-hour telephone and telex service at Avenida Corrientes 707.

National Holidays

New Year's Day (Jan. 1); Maundy Thursday (April 4, 1996; March 27, 1997), an optional holiday when some offices close; Good Friday (April 5, 1996; March 28, 1997); Labor Day (May 1); Anniversary of the 1810 Revolution (May 25); Malvinas Day (June 10); Flag Day (June 20); Independence Day (July 9); Anniversary of San Martín's Death (Aug. 17); Columbus Day (Oct. 12); Immaculate Conception (Dec. 8); and Christmas (Dec. 25).

Precautions

Health

Drinking tap water and eating uncooked greens is safe in Buenos Aires. There are several hundred cases of cholera registered in the northern part of Argentina each year, mostly in the indigenous communities near the Bolivian border; your best protection is to avoid raw seafood. Overeating and overdrinking, constant temptations, may cause health problems that cannot be blamed on Argentine fare.

Safety

Women are safer in Buenos Aires than in any other major city in the world. Don't over- or under-dress, or flash jewelry in the streets. Just act like you know what you are doing, and you should have no problems.

Shopping

The appeal of shopping in Argentina depends on the exchange rate of the moment. When the dollar is strong, Buenos Aires is a great place to buy clothing, leather goods, and furs, all of which are available in top designs with fine materials and good workmanship. When the peso is strong, as it has been in recent years, paintings, engravings, and wine are possible options. In any case, just looking at the displays—of Tierra del Fuego fox in the latest Yves St. Laurent styles, butter-soft leathers, evening gowns with snakeskin appliqués, French designer suits for men, cashmere sweaters, loafers and high boots, briefcases and bags—can be a window-shopper's delight. Look for *liquidaciones* (sales) signs in the window. Argentine shops have fixed prices but often give discounts for cash.

Telephones

Local and Long-Distance Calls

For information dial 110, and for the time, 113. Pay phones can be found on the streets, in public buildings, offices, airports, and other transportation terminals, and in pharmacies, bars, and restaurants. They operate on tokens called *fichas* or on cards, both of which can be bought at newsstands, kiosks, and in many bars and restaurants. One ficha or card unit buys two or three minutes of time, depending on whether you are calling at prime time (8 AM–8 PM) or otherwise.

Using a phone anywhere in the country can be a frustrating experience. Despite the recent privatization of ENTEL, the formerly government-run telephone monopoly, service in the city is still erratic. Phone numbers are being changed, and a common phone greeting is *equivocado* (e-kee-voh-*ca*-do), meaning wrong number. Argentines, accustomed to living with the frustrating infrastructure, are uncomfortable doing business by phone. The fax is now replacing the phone as the easiest form of speedy in-city communications. Often the best bet is to get operator assistance or have the operator at your hotel help put through calls. Using phones in post offices is another good option.

International Calls

International calls can be made from telephone company offices around Buenos Aires and from private companies with street-front offices. Most hotels have direct-dial international lines in the rooms. **Telefónica de Argentina** (Av. Corrientes 707 at the corner of Maipú, ☎ 0800–30112) offers 24-hour international service.

For an international operator, dial 000. For information about international calls, dial 953–8000. AT&T, MCI, and Sprint have direct-calling programs that allow you to call collect or charge calls from abroad to your calling card. To reach **AT&T,** dial 011–800–200–1111 (this number may not work from pay phones). For **MCI,** dial 001–800–333–1111. To reach **Sprint,** dial 001–800–777–1111.

Tipping

Add 10–15% in bars and restaurants; 10% is enough if the bill runs high. Argentines round off a taxi fare, but there is no need to tip cab drivers, although a few of the cabbies who hang around hotels popular with North Americans seem to expect it. Hotel porters should be tipped at least $1. Give doormen about 50¢ and beauty- and barbershop personnel about 5%.

When to Go

If you can handle the heat, Buenos Aires can be wonderful in summer, which peaks in January. At this time, the traditional vacation period, Argentines are crowding inland resorts and beaches, but Buenos Aires has no traffic, and there is always a seat at shows and restaurants. Avoid visiting popular resort areas in January and February and in July, when they become overcrowded again due to school holidays.

The best time to visit Iguazú Falls is August–October, when temperatures are lower and the spring coloring is at its brightest. Rain falls all year, dropping about 205 centimeters (80 inches) annually. Summer temperatures (January–February) usually range in the high 90s to low 100s (35°C–40°C). Winter temperatures (June–August) drop considerably.

Resort towns such as Bariloche and San Martín de los Andes stay open all year. Summer temperatures can get up into the high 70s (about 25°C), but most of the year, the range is from the 30s to the 60s (0°C–20°C).

The Patagonia coast is on the infamous latitude that sailors call the "Roaring Forties," with southern seas that batter Patagonia throughout the year. Thirty-mph winds are common, and 100-mph gales are not unusual. Summer daytime temperatures reach the low 80s (about 28°C), but can drop suddenly to the 50s (10°C–15°C). Winters hover near the freezing mark.

Most travelers visit Tierra del Fuego in the summer, when temperatures range from the 40s to the 60s (5°C–20°C). Fragments of glaciers cave into southern lakes with a rumble throughout the thaw from October to the end of April, which is the best time to enjoy the show.

Climate

From the northern subtropical jungles to the southern glaciers, Argentina's climate encompasses it all. Temperatures, though, are generally slightly milder than they are in equivalent latitudes in the Northern Hemisphere, because of weather systems blowing off of both the Atlantic and the Pacific.

The following are the average daily maximum and minimum temperatures for Buenos Aires.

Jan.	85F	29C	May	64F	18C	Sept.	64F	18C
	63	17		47	8		46	8
Feb.	83F	28C	June	57F	14C	Oct.	69F	21C
	41	5		63	17		50	10
Mar.	79F	26C	July	57F	14C	Nov.	76F	24C
	60	16		42	6		56	13
Apr.	72F	22C	Aug.	60F	16C	Dec.	82F	28C
	53	12		43	6		61	16

The following are the average daily maximum and minimum temperatures for Bariloche.

Jan.	70F	21C	May	50F	10C	Sept.	50F	10C
	46	6		36	2		34	1
Feb.	70F	21C	June	45F	7C	Oct.	52F	11C
	46	8		34	1		37	3
Mar.	64F	18C	July	43F	6C	Nov.	61F	16C
	43	6		32	0		41	5
Apr.	57F	14C	Aug.	46F	8C	Dec.	64F	18C
	39	4		32	0		45	7

4 Bolivia

Bolivia has a tangible otherworldliness that stays with the visitor long after a trip is over, an impression—created by high peaks, impenetrable lakes, mysterious ruins, thin air, and a stately population—that only deepens its appeal.

LANDLOCKED AND SOFT-SPOKEN, Bolivia is perhaps the least discovered—and certainly the least talked about—country in South America. But anonymity has a few distinct advantages. Despite being larger than Texas and California combined, Bolivia has fewer inhabitants than New York City. And with most of its 6.8 million people concentrated in a handful of urban centers such as La Paz, Santa Cruz, Cochabamba, and Sucre, there's little to detract from Bolivia's sometimes brooding, sometimes austere, but always captivating landscapes.

By Chris
Philipsborn and
Sarah Lythe

Updated by
Phillip Withers
Green

Bolivia contains every type of geologically classified land—from tropical lowlands to parched desert to rugged Andean plains. Although generally considered an Andean nation, nearly two-thirds of the country sweats it out in the steamy Amazon basin, remote, overlooked, and as inhospitable as it is soul-stirring. On Bolivia's wildest frontier, indigenous tribes live as they have for centuries, unimpressed, it seems, by the displays of modern civilization. (In the departments of Beni and Santa Cruz, near the border of Brazil, tribes have been known to attack riverbank villages with bows and arrows.)

Beyond these tropical lowlands, just west of Cochabamba and Santa Cruz, the Andes rise sharply to form the backbone of South America's Pacific coast. This two-prong mountain range shelters between its eastern and western peaks a rambling high-altitude plain. Known as the *altiplano*, this bleak, treeless plateau, about 85 miles wide and 520 miles long, claims 30% of Bolivia's landmass and supports more than half the country's population. For centuries, the Aymara Indians have clung to the hostile land, harvesting small crops of potatoes and beans, or fishing the deep-blue waters of Lake Titicaca, the world's highest navigable lake, which forms Bolivia's western border with Peru.

Perched on the edge of the altiplano is La Paz, the capital, overlooking the barren plateau at an altitude of 11,811 feet. If you fly into La Paz's 13,000-foot-high El Alto airstrip, the plateau breaks without warning and reveals below a deep jagged valley covered with adobe and brick homes clinging to the hillsides. At dusk, as the sun settles on the bare flatlands surrounding La Paz, a reddish glow envelops the city's greatest landmark, the 21,000-foot Mt. Illimani—a breathtaking backdrop to the world's highest capital.

From its earliest days, Bolivia's fortunes have risen and fallen with its mineral wealth. Centuries ago it was the Inca and Aymara who dug deep for precious silver. In the 17th century, Spain's colonization of South America was fueled largely by the vast amounts of silver hidden deep in the bowels of Cerro Rico, the "Rich Hill" that towers over Potosí, in Southern Bolivia. Cerro Rico's rich lode, first discovered in 1545, quickly brought conquerors, colonists, and prospectors to what was at the time the greatest mining operation in the New World. During the 17th and 18th centuries, Potosí, the most populous city in the Americas, was transformed with grand colonial mansions, stately baroque churches, and thick-walled fortresses. For the Spanish, *"vale un Potosí"* ("worth a Potosí") became a favorite description for untold wealth.

As the silver mines in Cerro Rico were exhausted, modern Bolivia began to take shape. Spanish aristocrats fled north to Sucre, Cochabamba, and La Paz, leaving Bolivia's eastern and northern extremes to Aymara Indians and the Quechua-speaking Inca. Today, Bolivia remains equally

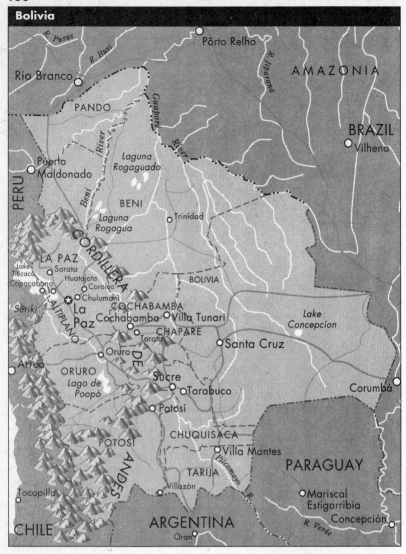

divided between the Old and New World: more than 50% of its people are direct descendants of the Aymara and Inca, while the other half are a mix of mestizo and *criollo*, people of Spanish ancestry born in the Americas.

Centuries of Spanish conquest have left their mark on Bolivia, particularly in the cities of Sucre and Potosí, where ebullient baroque cathedrals crowd both cities' narrow streets. But modern Bolivia remains a land of Indian farmers, ranchers, and artisans. On the windswept Andean plateau, you will still see Indian weavers toting their red-cheek children and crafts to weekly markets. By the time the sun has risen, the brightly dressed Aymara are in place, ready to offer a wide variety of textiles and ponchos, not to mention vegetables, fruits, live pigs, and medicinal herbs.

LA PAZ

One of the most often-heard comments made by visitors to the world's highest capital city is, "Why here?" La Paz, set in a lunarlike landscape of great—if rather stark—beauty, nestles in a bowl-shape valley that ranges in altitude from 11,811 to 9,951 feet. The high elevation forces even the locals to walk slowly, and the pace of life here seems more gentle than in other South American capitals.

Though you may have to struggle to get used to La Paz's rarefied air, you'll find certain advantages to the altitude and climate. There are none of the bugs, or mosquitoes, or stifling humidity that you encounter at lower altitudes. There is no smog; the air, though thin, is crystal clear, and the colors of the sky and landscape can be magically vibrant. (If you still find yourself suffering from the altitude, locals recommend a cup of piping hot *mate de coca*, an herbal tea made from coca leaves and sweetened with sugar.)

Nearly half of the city's 1.5 million residents live in the deep jagged valleys encircling La Paz, in adobe and brick homes that cling to the hillside. In downtown La Paz, the feeling is more cosmopolitan: Buses and taxis, business people and Aymara Indians crowd the city's cobblestone streets. During the lunchtime ritual, when many Paceños, as La Paz residents are called, head home for lunch and a nap, the capital miraculously clears itself of people. As the sun fades, the streets of La Paz once again fill with merchants and gawkers, and with well-heeled Paceños headed for one of the city's many bars, restaurants, or nightclubs.

La Paz is a compact city, with the main sites gathered in and around the city center. Yet while there are some excellent museums and interesting buildings, the bulk of the downtown area is burdened with undistinguished high-rises. The real allure of La Paz is its small side streets, its vibrant outdoor markets, where you can buy everything from food to computers, and its stunning natural setting under the shadow of Mount Illimani's triple-peaked and snowcapped crown.

Visitor Information

Oficina de Turismo (Edificio Mariscal Ballivián, 18th Floor, Calle Mercado, ☎ 02/367463 or 02/367464, FAX 02/374630).

Arriving and Departing

By Plane

All international and domestic flights to La Paz arrive at **El Alto** airport (☎ 02/810122), situated high above the city on the altiplano plain, 12 kilometers (7 miles) from downtown. From El Alto, the state-run airline, **Lloyd Aereo Boliviano** (LAB), and **Aerosur** fly regularly to Sucre, Santa Cruz, and Cochabamba. At the airport all departing passengers must pay a tax at the booth marked IMPUESTOS ($20 for international passengers, less than $3 for domestic passengers).

Some La Paz hotels run their own shuttle buses to and from the airport; check with the hotel when you make your reservation. Taxis are the only real alternative. The current going rate for the 30- to 45-minute journey is around 35 bolivianos ($7.50), but be sure to fix a price with the driver before getting in.

By Train

La Paz is served by a single railway station, the **Estación Central de Ferrocarriles** (Plaza Kennedy, ☎ 02/373069); a cab to downtown costs

La Paz

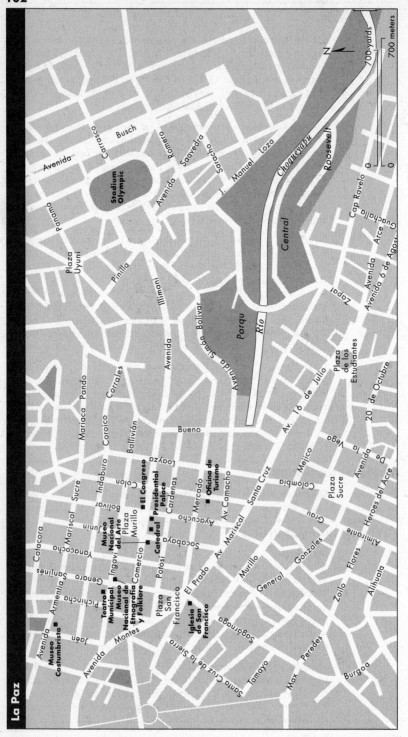

Museo
Costumbrista

Avenida

Museo
Municipal

Teatro
Municipal

Museo
Nacional de
Etnografía
y Folklore

Museo
Nacional
del Arte

Catedral

Presidential
Palace

El Congreso

Oficina de
Turismo

Iglesia
de San
Francisco

Plaza
San
Francisco

El Prado

Plaza
Murillo

Jaén

Montes

Avenida

Sucre

Indaburo

Colón

Bolívar

Murillo

Comercio

Potosí

Socabaya

Cárdenas

Mercado

Ayacucho

Av. Camacho

Av. Mariscal Santa Cruz

Santa Cruz de la Sierra

Sagárnaga

Murillo

General

Gonzales

Grau

Colombia

Melico

Plaza
Sucre

Plaza
de los
Estudiantes

Av. 16 de Julio

Bueno

Loayza

Ballivián

Coroico

Corrales

Mariaca   Pando

Calacoto

Mariscal

Genaro Sanjinés

Pichincha

Armenia

Junín

Yanacocha

Ingaví

Catacora

Avenida

Plaza
Uyuni

Panamá

Carrasco

Busch

Avenida

Romero

Saavedra

Saracho

J. Manuel Loza

Avenida

Illimani

Pinilla

Avenida

Avenida Simón Bolívar

Parqu

Río

Choqueyapu

Central

Roosevelt

Cap Ravelo

Guachalla

Arce

Avenida 6 de Agos.

Zoilo

Plaza
de los
Estudiantes

20 de Octubre

Avenida

De la Vega

Héroes del Acre

Almirante

Flores

Zoilo

Alihuata

Burgoa

Max   Paredes

Tamayo

N

700 yards

700 meters

0

0

less than $1. The only rail destinations from La Paz are Sucre, Potosí, Villazón, a handful of towns along the Argentine frontier, and Arica on the coast of Chile.

By Bus

All buses to La Paz arrive at the **Terminal de Buses** (Av. Péru, ☎ 02/367274), which is not quite centrally located but still only a $1 taxi ride from downtown. You can travel almost anywhere in Bolivia from here, though you should reserve your seat at least a day in advance for the numbingly long rides to Sucre, Potosí, and Santa Cruz. Contact **Flota Copacabana** (☎ 02/362803), **Trans Copacabana** (☎ 02/322888), or **Expreso Mopar** (☎ 02/377443), all of which have agents at the Terminal de Buses.

Getting Around La Paz

By Car

In La Paz you can rent standard and four-wheel-drive vehicles from **IMBEX** (Av. Montes 522, ☎ 02/379884) or **National Car Rental** (Calle Mexico 1554, ☎ and FAX 02/376581).

By Bus

La Paz is served by a comprehensive network of yellow *colectivos* (buses), which run daily from 6:30 AM to 10 PM. There is a flat fare of roughly 17¢ per person in the city center, payable to the driver upon entry. Slightly more expensive are *micros*, 12-seat minivans that travel the same bus routes, only more quickly. Micros and colectivos are short on comfort and sometimes rather crowded, but are safe for tourists and stop everywhere.

By Taxi and Trufi

Shared taxis, easily identifiable from the taxi sign lodged in the windshield, are cheap and plentiful; expect to pay less than 50¢ for trips within the city center. Newer-looking radio taxis, identified by the illuminated sign perched on the roof, are not shared and cost more— around $1–$2 depending on the length of your journey.

If you are simply going down a main street, take a *trufi*, a taxi with two white or green flags fixed to its front bumper and a sign in the window indicating which main areas it serves. The fare varies from between 20¢ and 40¢, depending on your destination, a fare even cheaper than a shared taxi. Be prepared to share a four-seat car with up to six occupants, plus small children.

Tour Operators

The following companies offer guided, English-language walking tours of La Paz for $10–$15 per person: **Diana Tours** (Calle Sagarnaga 328, ☎ 02/375374), **Seul Tours** (Av. Mariscal Santa Cruz 1032, ☎ 02/365144 or 02/371261), and **Tourismo Balsa** (Av. 16 de Julio 1650, ☎ 02/357817).

Exploring La Paz

Crossing the downtown area is the busy tree-lined thoroughfare, called **El Prado** for half its length, after which it becomes **Avenida Mariscal Santa Cruz.** Downhill and away from the city center, the Prado splits into two major one-way streets, Avenida 6 de Agosto and Avenida Arce, leading to the residential areas of San Jorge and Sopocachi, where most of La Paz's best bars and restaurants are located.

Downtown La Paz

At the heart of downtown is broad **Plaza San Francisco,** where Indian sellers hawk all sorts of handicrafts as well as more prosaic goods such as cassette tapes, watches, and electrical items. Numerous shoe-shine boys also ply their trade with persistence; a shine should cost you less than 15¢. Flanking the plaza is the impressive **Iglesia de San Francisco** (San Francisco Church), built in 1549 and considered one of the finest examples of Spanish colonial architecture in South America. The carved facade is adorned with birds of prey, ghoulish masks, pinecones, and parrots, a combination of Spanish and Indian motifs created by local artisans who borrowed heavily from the Baroque style of 16th- and 17th-century Spain. Indian weddings can sometimes be seen spilling out onto the plaza on Saturdays. A warren of handicraft stalls line the church wall; most days you'll find colorful weavings and handmade Bolivian musical instruments such as the *quena, zampoña tarka,* and *charango.*

Adjacent to the church lies the extremely steep **Calle Sagarnaga,** dotted with crafts shops and street vendors selling more weavings, jewelry, carvings, clothing, and colonial-style (mainly reproduction) silverware. The street is also lined with inexpensive pensions and hotels, as well as the famous peña Naira.

Continue along Calle Sagarnaga and turn right at **Calle Max Paredes.** In this area you will find whole streets filled with peddlers hawking traditional shawls, hats, and clothing. A number of stalls offer traditional Indian cures used by modern-day *callawayas,* the medicine men who attended the ancient Inca courts, not to mention dried llama fetuses and other ingredients used by many Bolivians in ceremonies to bless new dwellings or offices. Tucked away in alleys and courtyards are *tambos,* where oranges, bananas, and coca leaves are sold. The latter are chewed by farmers and miners (and tourists) to ward off hunger and the effects of altitude.

Back at the Plaza San Francisco, walk down Avenida Mariscal Santa Cruz and take a left at Calle Ayacucho. Keep walking uphill until you reach **Plaza Murillo** and La Paz's principal **Catedral** (Cathedral), built in 1835 in a severe neoclassical style, with a sober facade and imposing bronze doors. *Plaza Murillo.* ☛ *Free.* ☉ *Tues.–Thurs.*

Adjacent to the cathedral is the **Presidential Palace** (closed to the public), which was guarded by tanks and machine-gun-toting soldiers until 1982, when the constitutional government was restored following a coup in 1979. In front of the palace is a statue of former President Gualberto Villarroel. In 1946 a mob attacked the palace, forcibly brought Villarroel to the square, and then hanged him from a lamppost; a nearby statue commemorates the event. Diagonally across from the palace is Bolivia's congress building, **El Congreso,** which has a visitor's gallery. *Plaza Murillo.* ☛ *Free.* ☉ *Weekdays.*

The **Museo Nacional del Arte** (National Museum of Art) is housed in a stunning baroque mansion commissioned by a Spanish noble in 1775. The carved facade and high walls keep the noise of Calle Comercio, a busy shopping street, at bay. Inside, a broad courtyard opens onto three stories of painting and sculpture. The first floor is devoted to contemporary Bolivian and foreign artists; the second, to the master of Andean colonial art, Melchor Perez Holguin, and his disciples; and the third, to a permanent collection of Bolivian artists. *Plaza Murillo (at Calle Comercio),* ☎ *02/371177.* ☛ *Charged.* ☉ *Mon.–Sat.*

From Plaza Murillo continue on Calle Comercio and turn right up Calle Genaro Sanjines. Just ahead is the **Teatro Municipal** (Municipal Theater, Calle Ingavi, ☎ 02/375275), a handsome building both inside and out, as a result of extensive restoration completed in April 1994. The theater regularly stages traditional dance and music, as well as classical music performances and opera.

A few doors down, the **Museo Nacional de Etnografía y Folklore** (National Ethnographic and Folklore Museum), housed in an ornate 18th-century building, exhibits feathers, masks, and weavings. It also has permanent displays on the Ayoreos Indians, who live in the Amazon region, and the Chipayas Indians, who come from the surrounding altiplano. *Calle Ingavi 916,* ☎ *02/358559.* ☛ *Charged.* ⊘ *Weekdays.*

Calle Jaén, one of the city's few remaining colonial streets, houses four excellent museums: The **Museo Costumbrista** (Calle Jaén at Calle Sucre, ☎ 02/378478), dedicated to the political and cultural history of La Paz; the **Museo de Metales Preciosos** (Museum of Precious Metals, Calle Jaén 777, ☎ 02/371470), with an extensive collection of pre-Columbian gold and silver artifacts, in addition to Inca and pre-Inca ceramics; the **Museo Pedro Domingo Murillo** (Calle Jaén 79, ☎ 02/375273), with exhibits of masks, herbal medicines, and weavings housed in a restored colonial mansion; and the **Museo de Litoral** (Seashore Museum, Calle Jaén 789, ☎ 02/371222), a repository for artifacts connected with the 1867 War of the Pacific, when Bolivia lost its Pacific ports to Chile. ☛ *Joint ticket for all 4 museums sold at Museo Costumbrista.* ⊘ *Tues.–Thurs. 9:30–noon, 2:30–6; weekends 10–12:30.*

The city's main avenue, **El Prado,** is a colorful blur of trees, flowers, and monuments. The street is often clogged with pedestrians and vendors, especially on weekends, and many of La Paz's luxury hotels are found here, rising high above the old colonial-style homes with their elaborate latticework and balustrades. Continue south down El Prado until it turns into Avenida 6 de Agosto, turn right after two blocks onto the Calle Fernando Guachalla, past a number of chic bars and restaurants. Three blocks up is **Avenida Ecuador,** the heart of the Sopocachi district and, where it intersects Calle Fernando Guachalla, is the site of the vast indoor Sopocachi market, worth seeing for its colorful displays of fresh produce and flowers. Vegetarians should avoid the meat stalls, which display such delicacies as freshly cut beef tongue and cow udders.

From the market, go up to **Avenida Ecuador** and turn left, take a taxi, or walk along Ecuador (which becomes a small side street) until you reach beautiful little **Montículo Park.** Served by a small church, it has breathtaking views of 21,000-foot Mount Illimani, especially fine during a blazing altiplano sunset. Continue along the main road, Calle Victor Sanjinez, and you will soon reach **Plaza España,** a pleasant residential square.

The Lower Suburbs

The **Muela del Diablo** (Devil's Molar) is a tooth-shape rock perched on the edge of a small farming village on the outskirts of La Paz. Take a taxi or trufi to Los Rosales and walk uphill until you reach the cemetery, then follow the path uphill all the way. You will soon see the unmistakable outline of the Muela. There are several trails you can follow; one of them encircling the rock itself and offering spectacular views of La Paz and the surrounding countryside. Keep an eye peeled for condors, which can often be seen soaring overhead.

Eucalyptus-lined **El Parque Mallasa** (Mallasa Park) has been partly appropriated by the city zoo, which moved from the center of La Paz in

1994. Still, the park remains a fragrant escape for picnicking Paceños on sunny weekends. Take a taxi for less than $3 from downtown and, at the front entrance, turn left, keep walking until you reach the edge of a precipice with its stunning views of the river valley below and of the Devil's Molar opposite. ☛ *Free.* ☉ *Sunrise–sunset.*

Shopping

In La Paz you'll find everything from roughly made silver plates to sophisticated jewelry, from woven-rope sandals to intricately designed sweaters made of the softest alpaca and angora wools. Prices are reasonable by North American standards, although good quality, as always, does not come cheaply.

Shopping Districts
Calle Sagarnaga is a good place to begin. The small streets leading off to the right and left harbor a variety of crafts shops, while Calle Murillo, first on the left as you walk up the hill, is devoted entirely to cheap furniture. The extensive black-market area on **Avenida Buenos Aires,** still farther up the hill, is crammed with every sort of craft and contraband; some of the peasant women selling computers seem to know more about their wares than your average computer nerd. The police don't seem to mind the blossoming black market, but as always, buyer beware—for instance, a lot of the electronic goods are 110 volts, not the 220 common in North America.

For traditional Aymara embroidered shawls, try the market area around **Calle Santa Cruz de la Sierra** and **Calle Max Paredes.** Prices start at $15 and peak at more than $200 for vicuña (a cousin of the llama and the smallest member of the camel family) wool shawls. *Polleras,* the traditional skirts worn by local Indians, are priced between $50 and $100; distinctive bowler hats sell for up to $150. Also browse the craft shops just past the entrance to Iglesia de San Francisco; some sell high-quality masks and weavings.

Specialty Shops
For alpaca sweaters, the rule is: You get what you pay for. Many vendors will claim their sweaters are made from baby alpaca or—even more unlikely—vicuña wool. Try to visit one of the better stores mentioned below to get an idea of what real quality feels like before going bargain-hunting. High-quality hand-knit designs go for around $100, though you may cheer yourself with the fact that they can sell for three or more times that amount at home. A wide range of sweaters and cardigans can be found at **Casa Fisher** (Handal Center, Av. Mariscal Santa Cruz), **Fotrama** (Calle Colombia), and **Edificio Hoy** (Av. 6 de Agosto at Calle Guachalla). On Calle Sagarnaga, **Toshy Export** and **Artesanias Sorata** have a selection of hand-knit sweaters and cardigans with ethnic designs. Just before Toshy there is an arcade with a good selection of medium-price alpaca sweaters. For one-stop shopping, the basement of the **Radisson Plaza Hotel** (Avenida Arce), refurbished in 1994, has a wide range of top-quality boutiques selling the whole gamut of artisanal products. Given the location there are no bargains to be had, but the quality of materials and designs is first-class.

Shopping Centers
Two of the three main shopping malls in the city center are on Calle Potosí near Calle Ayacucho; the better one is the glass-pyramid–capped **Shopping Norte,** which has a variety of small restaurants serving good-value *almuerzos* (set lunches) on the top floor. The third, known as the **Handal Center,** is on Avenida Mariscal Santa Cruz, just down from

Plaza San Francisco. Each shopping center carries a wide selection of jeans, T-shirts, shoes, and sports equipment.

Sports

Soccer

Bolivians would be lost without their weekly soccer fix; even the poorest, most remote villages have their own playing field, which, as it's usually on the only flat piece of ground in town, often does double duty as a grazing ground for sheep and cows. La Paz itself has two teams: Bolivar and The Strongest. Both strut their stuff in the **Hernando Siles** stadium (Plaza de los Monolitos, ☎ 02/357342), in the Miraflores district.

Volleyball

Three major teams—San Antonio, Litoral, and Universidad—compete regularly in the **Coliseo Julio Borelli** (Calle Mexico, ☎ 02/320224), in the San Pedro District.

Dining

La Paz restaurants have become increasingly cosmopolitan of late, with cuisines ranging from Italian, German, Swiss, and French to Chinese and Japanese. Traditional Bolivian food is widely available, and despite the country's landlocked status, seafood restaurants are starting to become more plentiful. Avenida Arce, Plaza Abaroa, and the residential Sopocachi district probably have the widest selection of restaurants in La Paz, while Calle Sagarnaga generally harbors the least expensive. Mid-morning is the time when Paceños eat *salteña*, a hearty beef, olive, hard-boiled egg, potato, and pea stew wrapped in a crisp, slightly sweet dough, available from stands throughout the city for less than 50¢. For price ranges, *see* Dining *in* Bolivia Essentials, *below.*

Bolivian

$$$$ **Utama.** Situated on the penthouse floor of the Hotel Plaza, this rooftop restaurant is a must for its panoramic views of the city and surrounding mountains. There is a well-stocked salad bar, and the grilled entrées—generally steak and chicken accompanied with rice and beans—are passable. ✗ *Hotel Plaza, El Prado,* ☎ *02/378311. Reservations advised. AE, MC, V.*

$$ **El Refugio.** Pepper steak and Lake Titicaca trout are favorites at this small, quiet restaurant on the Plaza Abaroa, a short walk from El Prado and the university. In season, indulge yourself with strawberries and cream for dessert. ✗ *Av. 20 de Octubre 2453,* ☎ *02/355651. MC, V. No lunch Sat.; closed Sun.*

Café

$$ **Café La Paz.** This quaint old café, opposite the main post office, is a popular hangout with many La Paz politicians, journalists, and expatriates. It used to be the haunt of Nazi war criminal Klaus Barbie, until he was expelled from Bolivia in 1983. Lunch at the café is overpriced, but stop in for potent espresso and cappuccino, *café helados* (ice-cream coffee), and elaborate pastries, including the very best *empanada de manzana* (apple pie). ✗ *Calle Ayacucho at Av. Camacho, no* ☎. *No credit cards.*

Chinese

$$$ **Chifa Emy.** As long as you remember where you are—Bolivia, that is—you shouldn't be too disappointed with the Chinese dishes at Chifa Emy, a popular meeting place for well-heeled Paceños. The atmosphere is lively, no doubt fueled in part by the selection of interesting cocktails. An English-language menu will help guide you through the maze of chow meins, sweet and sours, and seafood dishes. ✕ *Calle Cordero 257,* ☎ *02/323725. AE, MC, V.*

German and Swiss

$$$$ La Suisse/El Gourmet. Two restaurants in one, La Suisse is a small, very comfortable eatery with a range of Swiss and German dishes; try the veal cooked with cream and mushrooms and served with lightly fried *rösti* (hash-brown–type) potatoes. The more formal El Gourmet, located upstairs and open only for dinner, is better known for its meat and cheese fondues. ✕ *Av. Arce 2164,* ☎ *02/353150. Reservations advised. AE, MC, V. Closed Sun.*

International

$$$ Quebecois. Top quality French-Canadian food, as well as Bolivian and international dishes, are served at this richly decorated new arrival to the La Paz dining scene. Subdued lighting, an open fire, and classical music make it a romantic place to have a tête-à-tête. ✕ *Av. 20 de Octubre, no* ☎. *MC, V. Closed Sun.*

$$ Pig & Whistle. A short walk south from the University is this slightly
★ difficult to find replica of a turn-of-the-century British pub. The rustic beams, fireplace, and wood-paneled interior make it a genteel place to relax after a day of sightseeing; throw in the English-speaking owners, an unparalleled selection of whiskeys, and imported and home-grown beers and you'll see why this bar-cum-restaurant becomes many travelers' home away from home. Stop by in the afternoon for good-value almuerzos, or come back in the evening when some of Bolivia's only authentic Indian and Southeast Asian cooking is served. Low-key live music, performed at the end of the week, ranges from light classical through bossa nova to jazz. ✕ *Calle Goitia 155, off Av. Arce, no* ☎. *No credit cards. Closed Sun.*

$$ Restaurant de la Paz. Near the Pig & Whistle is this cozy spot with low ceilings. Pick from among moderately priced Bolivian and international dishes. ✕ *Calle Goitia, no* ☎. *No credit cards. Closed Sun.*

Italian

$$$ Pronto. This small but inviting basement restaurant, decorated with
★ modern artwork and artistic flair, is one of the few places in La Paz that serves really good fresh pasta: The ravioli, tortellini, and tagliatelli are prepared fresh daily and smothered in a variety of tomato, garlic, and basil sauces. The hors d'oeuvres, however, can be disappointing. ✕ *Pasaje Jauregi 2248, off Calle Guachalla,* ☎ *02/355869. Reservations advised. AE, MC, V. No lunch.*

$ Pizzeria Morello. At Morello, possibly the best pizzeria in La Paz, you can order what's hot from the oven or design your own pizza from the voluminous list of toppings. The dining area is cramped and characterless, which may be why many Paceños use Morello's takeout and delivery services. ✕ *Av. Arce 2132,* ☎ *02/372973. No credit cards. Closed Sat.; no lunch Sun.*

Lodging

La Paz has a limited number of hotel rooms, and hotels at either end of the price spectrum are sometimes booked solid during holidays and festivals. Make reservations in advance whenever possible. There are inexpensive pensions and small hotels on Calle Sagarnaga, but what you save in price may not adequately compensate for the lack of facilities and cleanliness. For price ranges, *see* Lodging *in* Bolivia Essentials, *below.*

$$$$ **Hotel Plaza.** Although downgraded to four stars on the reopening of the Radisson, this hotel is centrally located on El Prado and commands fine views of the city center and the surrounding countryside, especially from the rooftop restaurant and bar. The rooms are comfortable if without much character, and you can opt for an executive room or a suite as well as standard digs. Ask for quarters facing Mt. Illimani; not only are the views better, but street noise is less noticeable. ☎ *Av. 16 de Julio 378–300,* ☎ *02/378311,* FAX *02/343391; U.S.* ☎ *800/442–2955. 175 rooms, 10 suites. 2 restaurants, 2 bars, indoor pool, sauna, business services. AE, MC, V.*

$$$$ **Hotel Presidente.** One of the more modern but stylistically dated of La Paz's luxury hotels, the Presidente is a short walk from Plaza San Francisco and the downtown sights. The rooms are plain but comfortable; most face the street, but at least on the upper floors, noise is not a problem. The restaurant does inexpensive but nevertheless excellent buffet lunches. The top-floor dance club gives stunning views of the city. ☎ *Calle Potosí 920,* ☎ *02/367193,* FAX *02/354013. 101 rooms, 18 suites. 2 restaurants, 2 bars, indoor pool, sauna, exercise room, casino, dance club. AE, MC, V.*

$$$$ **Radisson Plaza Hotel.** At press time (winter 1995), this eight-floor former Sheraton—touted as the largest hotel in Bolivia—had been acquired by the Radisson chain and totally refurbished. ☎ *Av. Arce 2177,* ☎ *02/316161,* FAX *02/316302; U.S.* ☎ *800/777–7800. 239 rooms, 7 suites. 2 restaurants, bar, café, indoor pool, hot tub, massage, sauna, exercise room, business services, meeting rooms. AE, MC, V.*

$$$ **Hotel Gloria.** If you don't mind sacrificing a few creature comforts— many rooms do not have phones or televisions, and there's nothing even remotely like a sports or recreation facility—you will appreciate the Gloria's rooftop restaurant and its location, one block from the central San Francisco church. ☎ *Calle Potosí,* ☎ *02/370010,* FAX *02/370123. 79 rooms. Restaurant, bar. AE, MC, V.*

$$$ **Hotel Sucre Palace.** The suites are fairly charming at this centrally located hotel on the Prado. A redecoration in early 1995 improved the standard rooms and the public spaces, but they're still somewhat gloomy. ☎ *Av. 16 de Julio 1636,* ☎ *02/363323,* FAX *02/392052. 137 rooms, 4 suites. Restaurant, bar. AE, MC, V.*

$$ **El Dorado.** This is a functional but popular mid-size hotel in the city center just opposite the university. Rooms that face the street tend to be noisy, as do those near the elevator shaft. ☎ *Av. Villazón,* ☎ *02/ 363355 or 02/363403,* FAX *02/391438. 50 rooms, 2 suites. Restaurant, bar, cafeteria. AE, MC, V.*

$$ **Hotel Max Inn.** The location is perhaps not all it could be (the San Pedro Jail is adjacent), but the recently built Max Inn offers comfortable quarters, and the prices are reasonable. The Plaza San Pedro itself is lively and quite pleasant. ☎ *Plaza San Pedro,* ☎ *02/374391,* FAX *02/341720. 50 rooms, 5 suites. Restaurant. MC, V.*

$ **Hostal República.** The República is a good choice for travelers on a budget. The comfortable rooms are reasonably priced, and a number overlook a small, quiet garden. Some rooms share a communal bathroom. ☎ *Calle Comercio 1455,* ☎ *02/357966. 35 rooms. Restaurant. No credit cards.*

$ **Residential Rosario.** A popular option with budget-conscious tourists, ★ the Rosario has all the hallmarks of a traveler's hotel, including, in the lobby, a useful bulletin board and a travel agency that arranges tours in Bolivia and to Machu Picchu in Peru. ☎ *Calle Illampu 704,* ☎ *02/ 326531,* FAX *02/375532. 40 rooms. Restaurant, travel services. No credit cards.*

The Arts

The tourist office (*see* Visitor Information, *above*) can fill you in on local festivals and special events. For concert and cinema listings pick up a copy of *Ultima Hora* or *La Razón,* two Spanish-language daily newspapers, and the English-language *Bolivian Times,* which comes out weekly on Friday.

Film

The **Cinemateca Boliviana** (Calle Pichincha at Calle Indabura, ☎ 02/325346), an art theater, regularly screens foreign and even a few Bolivian films.

Galleries

The **Galleria Emusa** (Av. 16 de Julio 1607), centrally located on El Prado, hosts rotating exhibits of Bolivian sculpture and art. **Arte Unico** (Av. Arce 2895) mounts varied exhibits.

Theater and Music

The **Teatro Municipal** (Calle Genaro Sanjines, ☎ 02/375275) stages folk events and traditional music and dance concerts.

Nightlife

Bars

Calle Belisario Salinas boasts the city's largest selection of bars, which fill up around 10:30 PM. Along the avenue, look for **Panyco,** owned by a Frenchman who knows how to attract trendy Paceños with off-beat decorations and live music. Up the street and more popular with professional Bolivians, **Caras y Caretas** often features live bands. Exactly opposite is the **Café Montmartre,** a popular singles hangout with live music on weekends and delicious crepes for the hungry. Away from Calle Belisario Salinas, the intimate **Matheus** (Calle Guachalla at Av. 6 de Agosto) has a well-stocked bar and the occasional live band. The **Andromeda** (Av. Arce at Aspiazu) hosts live music as well. (*Also see* **Pig & Whistle** *in* Dining, *above*). **Forum** (Calle Victor Sanjines 2908, ☎ 02/325762) is a large club two blocks from the Plaza España mainly frequented by the under-thirty set. The **Hotel Plaza** and **Hotel Presidente** (*see* Lodging, *above*) have rooftop bars worth a visit if only for the stunning views.

Nightclubs

El Loro en Su Salsa (Calle Rosendo Gutierrez at 6 de Agosto, ☎ 02/342787) is a popular, lively salsa club. Trendy **Socavón** (Calle 20 de Octubre, near Calle Guachalla, ☎ 02/353998) draws crowds of younger Paceños and foreigners with live dance music most nights. **New Tokio** (Av. 6 de Agosto, ☎ 323654), a smaller venue, attracts slightly more mature boppers.

Peñas

Peñas are nightclubs that showcase Bolivian folkloric music and dance. The energetic live performances are popular with tourists and Paceños alike and usually include dinner in the price—from $8 to $20 per person. Popular peñas are **Casa del Corregidor** (Calle Murillo 1040, ☎ 02/363633), **Peña Naira** (Calle Sagarnaga 161, ☎ 02/325736), and **Los Escudos** (Av. Mariscal Santa Cruz, Edificio Club de la Paz, ☎ 02/322028).

Excursions from La Paz

Tiahuanaco

Tiahuanaco is Bolivia's most important archaeological site. Unfortunately, much of the site has never been fully excavated, and there is little to see apart from the Gate of the Sun, an imposing stone fixture that is thought to be a solar calendar built by a civilization that mysteriously surfaced around 600 BC only to disappear around AD 1200. The gate is part of an elaborate observatory and courtyard that contain monoliths and a subterranean temple. Although the site lacks the splendor of Peru's Machu Picchu, it does provide a glimpse into the ancestry of the Aymara, the last people to be conquered by the Inca before the Spanish came. The descendants of the Aymara still farm the ingeniously constructed terraces built nearby by their ancestors.

Getting There

Tiahuanaco is 80 kilometers (50 miles) west of La Paz and 32 kilometers (20 miles) east of Lake Titicaca. There are no guides available at the site, so book in advance with a travel agency in La Paz; try **Diana Tours** (Calle Sagarnaga 328, ☎ 02/375374); **Tourismo Balsa** (Av. 16 de Julio 1650, ☎ 02/357817); **Seul Tours** (Av. Mariscal Santa Cruz 1032, ☎ 02/365144 or 02/371261); or **Plaza Tours** (Hotel Plaza, Av. 16 de Julio 1650, ☎ 02/378311).

Los Yungas

Within easy reach of La Paz, Los Yungas (literally "The Valleys") is a semitropical paradise where the snow-covered Andes tower above waterfalls and valleys carpeted with lush vegetation. The drive to the Yungas is an experience in itself: Dropping in altitude by some 9,840 feet in just under 80 kilometers (50 miles), the poorly maintained, mostly single-lane highway is one of the most scenic and hair-raising in South America—the views certainly make up for any discomfort.

Your first glimpse of small, picturesque **Coroico** is unforgettable, particularly after three hours of tortuous hairpin bends. Set in steep, undulating hills overrun with citrus and banana trees, coffee plants, and coca bushes, Coroico is a resort town for Paceños, who flock from the capital on weekends. You can rent horses from Dany and Patricio of **Ranch Beni,** signposted near the hospital, for around $5 per hour. You can also bargain for jewelry and crafts at one of the shops huddled around the main square. A 30-minute walk from Coroico on the road to Caranavi, **El Viejo Molino** (☎ 0811/6004 or 02/361076 for reservations) is the best hotel for miles. You can linger over a plate of grilled steak in the excellent restaurant, or ponder intense valley views from the balcony of your clean, spacious bedroom (from $50 per night). The most popular restaurant in town is **La Casa** (Calle Kennedy, no ☎), which specializes in meat and cheese fondues for about $6 per person. La Casa also has a handful of clean, simple rooms priced at less than $5 per night.

Chulumani, in the southern Yungas, is surrounded by waterfalls and sprawling ranch properties and offers an authentic glimpse of traditional life in the Andes. Although a bit larger than Coroico, Chulumani is not really geared for tourists: Its busy market offers local produce rather than crafts, and the only hotel, the **San Bartolomé** (☎ 0811/6114), a 30-minute walk downhill from the main square, is rustic at best (though it does have a pool and restaurant).

Getting There

Tours of Coroico and Los Yungas cost $70–$80 per person per day, including lunch. Try the La Paz–based **Seul Tours** (Av. Mariscal Santa Cruz 1032, ☎ 02/365144 or 02/371261); **Plaza Tours** (Hotel Plaza, Av. 16 de Julio 1650, ☎ 02/378311); or **Turismo Balsa** (Av. 16 de Julio 1650, ☎ 02/357817). From La Paz, the private bus companies **Veloz del Norte** (Av. de las Americas 283, ☎ 02/311753) and **Transporte 20 de Octobre** (Calle Yanacachi 1434, ☎ 02/317391) also make the three- to four-hour trek to Coroico ($8) and Chulumani ($8). If you're planning to drive yourself, get a four-wheel-drive vehicle. Remember that cars traveling downhill have the right of way, and that when traveling on the mountain passes of Los Yungas, people drive on the left-hand side of the road when passing heavy trucks.

LAKE TITICACA

Lake Titicaca, which at an altitude of 12,506 feet is the world's highest navigable lake, is in fact two bodies of water joined at the narrow Strait of Tiquina. The smaller section of the lake—freshwater Lago Huiñaymarca—is the easiest to reach from La Paz; for a sight of the larger section—brackish Lago Chucuito—you need to include Copacabana on your itinerary. Either way, the lakes' still waters reflect an equal measure of high-altitude sun and cloudless blue sky, in addition to the palette of browns injected by the sunbaked hills encircling Lake Titicaca.

Beyond the bumpy profile of islands with names like Suriki, Sun, and Moon, each with a smattering of Inca ruins in varying states of decay, the horizon-wide panorama encompasses fishing vessels and tourist launches headed for port. On the lakeshore, the scene may include local Aymara Indians who have come to tend a crop of potatoes and beans or to fish for trout from their small wooden boats.

At its largest point, Lake Titicaca measures 200 kilometers by 60 kilometers (124 miles by 37 miles). On a clear day you can see Peru, which borders the lake to the west and can be reached overland or by boat from the Bolivian port of Copacabana. Most visitors, however, are content to remain on the eastern shore, in the Bolivian villages of Puerto Perez or Huatajata, from where you can arrange boat treks to the island of Suriki. Tour operators in La Paz cover Lake Titicaca (and occasionally the islands) in a long but rewarding day. Yet with the wide selection of hotels and restaurants in the area, adventure-minded travelers should consider renting a four-wheel-drive vehicle in La Paz and striking out on their own.

Arriving and Departing

By Car

From La Paz, take El Alto Highway northwest. After the tollbooths, follow signs for Batallas, Río Seco, Huatajata, and Tiquina. The road is paved between La Paz and Tiquina, and barring heavy traffic it takes less than two hours to drive. Be very careful about leaving your car unattended, particularly in Copacabana.

By Bus

Minibuses run regularly from the gates of the Old Cemetery in La Paz to destinations along the lakeshore, including Batallas, Huatajata, and Tiquina. One-way prices to Huatajata are about $1. Private buses collect passengers from their hotel at 8 AM and charge roughly $10 round-trip to Copacabana (4 hours), $15 to Sorata (6 hours); in La Paz, contact

Combi Tours (Calle Illampu 735, ☎ 02/375378), **Diana Tours** (Calle Sagarnaga 328, ☎ 02/340356 or 02/375374), or **Turibus** (Calle Illampu, Residencia Rosario, ☎ 02/325348).

By Taxi

Taxis waiting outside La Paz's Hotel El Dorado will take you to Puerto Perez or Huatajata and back for about $50 (up to four people). The fare to Copacabana is roughly $100.

By Boat

There is no direct boat service between Peru and Bolivia, but you can travel by bus and catamaran or by bus and hydrofoil between La Paz and the Peruvian port of Puno, with brief stops in Copacabana. Purchase tickets for the four- to five-hour trek in La Paz from **Diana Tours** (Calle Saranaga 328, ☎ 02/340356 or 02/375374), or in Puno from **Transturin** (Jíron Libertad 176, ☎ 054/35–2771).

Tour Operators

Travel agencies and the large hotels in La Paz arrange guided treks around the lake, sometimes in conjunction with a short boat tour and overnight stay, for $50–$80 per person. Contact: **Crillon Tours** (Av. Camacho 1223, ☎ 02/350363), **Diana Tours** (Calle Sagarnaga 328, ☎ 02/340356 or 02/375374), **Plaza Tours** (Hotel Plaza, Av. 16 de Julio 1650, ☎ 02/378311), or **Turismo Balsa** (Av. 16 de Julio 1650, ☎ 02/357819 or 02/357817).

Exploring Lake Titicaca

Puerto Perez

Just one hour from La Paz, after trekking across the barren landscape of the altiplano, you can see the smaller section of Lake Titicaca glistening in the distance. Take a left off the main road at Batallas—a forgettable outcrop of ramshackle houses—and, 15 minutes farther down a dusty dirt road, you'll come to the village of Puerto Perez (72 kilometers [42 miles] from La Paz). Nestled on the banks of Lake Titicaca, Puerto Perez, like most lakeshore villages, is barely developed: Houses are made of brick and adobe, and farm animals graze in fields nearby. An advantage to staying in Puerto Perez is location: It's one of the few villages with easy access to long, rambling walks through the small farming villages flanking Lago Huiñaymarca. From Puerto Perez's lazy main square, there are also inspiring views of Titicaca's placid waters at dusk.

Huatajata

Back on the main road, continuing north, it's a 40-minute drive to lakeside Huatajata, a popular weekend escape for Paceños and a regular stop on the guided-tour circuit. Huatajata, endowed with a handful of hotels, makes a practical base for exploring the area, but it lacks lakefront walking paths; for picnics try the tree-lined waterfront at **Chúa,** the next village beyond Huatajata.

Suriki

The hotels in Puerto Perez and Huatajata organize frequent trips to Suriki, a small, hilly island visible from the shore. In 1970, when Norwegian explorer Thor Heyerdahl wanted to sail from Morocco to South America in a reed-and-wood boat, to prove that South American cultures could have made contact with Europe long before the age of Columbus, he commissioned local craftsmen on Suriki to build his vessel, the *Ra II*. (In 1947, Heyerdahl sailed from Peru to Polynesia in the balsa wood *Kon-Tiki* to test his theory that the first Polynesians came from South America.) Although the *Ra II* is on display in Oslo, Norway, several of the original builders maintain a souvenir shop and **museum** close to the main pier; Paulino Esteban, the curator, accepts small donations for entry to the museum, which is littered with newspaper clippings, photos, and diagrams of the *Ra II*. There are no hotels or restaurants on Suriki, so pack a picnic lunch and set out on one of the dirt roads that crisscross the island; at some point, they all seem to skirt the shore, offering good views of the lake. If you do not wish to join a guided tour of Suriki, fishermen in Huatajata will take you over for a small, negotiable fee.

Copacabana

From Huatajata, the road continues to Tiquina, where you can see the handful of tiny patrol boats that make up Bolivia's navy (Bolivia was left landlocked after Chile seized 160 miles of coast in 1879). In Tiquina, vehicles are loaded precariously onto rafts and taken across the Strait of Tiquina to San Pedro. From unmemorable San Pedro it's a 90-minute drive to Copacabana, a pleasant, almost laid-back town fronting Lago Chucuito from the shelter of a protected bay. Copacabana is the main stopping point for those headed to Peru, and it provides easy access to the lake and surrounding countryside, as well as to the islands of the Sun and Moon.

During Holy Week, throngs of young Paceños walk to Copacabana from the capital to pay homage to the miracle-working Black Virgin of Copacabana; the candlelight procession on Good Friday is especially spectacular. In town, the highlights of the **Catedral,** built between 1610 and 1619, are the majestic gilded altar and the striking sculpture of the Black Virgin carved by the Inca Tito Yupanqui in 1592. The town boasts its own replica of Calvary to the east, while a small stony hill just to the west is worth ascending to see the remains of an Inca observatory: Once a year—at 8 AM on June 21, the winter solstice in the southern hemisphere—the sun's rays shine through a hole in a rock and are projected onto the **Horca del Inca,** a carved slab of stone laid horizontally between two pillars.

Isla del Sol and Isla de la Luna

The nearest Bolivia gets to the Mediterranean, Isla del Sol (Island of the Sun) has beautiful coves with white sandy beaches and lies just a few miles off the coast from Copacabana in the serene upper lake, Lago Chucuito. The island sees relatively few tourists and is the perfect place to savor the splendor of Lake Titicaca, particularly if you have time to get away from the main landing point and cross the island on foot—a four- to five-hour proposition. There are a number of beautiful walks along the island's shore: dirt paths crisscross the terraced terrain, leading to secluded coves and the dilapidated remains of Inca structures. According to ancient myths, Isla del Sol is the cradle of Inca civilization, and the birthplace of the mighty sun itself. Take a look at the Inca ruins known as the **Palacio de Pilkokaina** and, in the northwest corner of the island, a strange rock formation where Inca legend has it the sun and moon were born. There are two small guest houses on Isla del Sol, and you can also arrange to stay overnight with locals for less than $5.

Isla de la Luna (Island of the Moon) or Koati, smaller and more difficult to reach than the Isla del Sol, contains the ruins of an Inca temple and observatory known as the **Palacio de Iñak Uyu.** Boatmen anchored at Copacabana's beach will take you to either island for $20–

$80 depending on how long you want to remain ashore and whether you travel by sail or motor.

Sorata

Roughly 45 kilometers (28 miles) north from Huatajata via the villages of Huarina and Warisata, Sorata lies in a lush mid-altitude valley—nearly 8,200 feet above sea level—at the foot of **Mt. Illampu** (21,277 feet). A lively Sunday market is held in Sorata's tree-lined square, though most visitors are drawn by various hiking opportunities: either up snowcapped Mt. Illampu, recommended only for experienced hikers, or along the **Camino del Oro** (Trail of Gold), an arduous weeklong trek through lush tropical valleys to where gold-mining cooperatives still ply their dangerous trade. For information about these and other hikes, contact Plaza Tours or Diana Tours (*see* Tour Operators, *above*).

Dining and Lodging

Throughout the region, reservations are recommended for the Easter festivals and on weekends, when many Paceños migrate to the area. For price ranges, *see* Dining *and* Lodging *in* Bolivia Essentials, *below*.

Copacabana

DINING

$ **Restaurant Puerta del Sol.** The specialties at this locally popular and sometimes boisterous eatery, located next to the Hotel Playa Azul, are fresh trout and *pejerrey*, a Lake Titicaca whitefish. ✕ *Av. 6 de Agosto, no* ☎. *No credit cards.*

DINING AND LODGING

$$ **Hotel Playa Azul.** Recent renovations have given the Playa Azul a cozy
★ dining room romantically lit with gas fires. The comfortable, simple bedrooms, most of which overlook a courtyard, are equipped with private bathrooms. ☎ *Av. 6 de Agosto,* ☎ *08/622227 or 02/320068. 35 rooms. Restaurant. MC, V.*

$ **Hotel Ambassador.** The best that can be said of this clean but basic hotel is that some rooms have private toilets and that it does have atmosphere. The adjacent restaurant serves typical Bolivian dishes—mostly chicken and steak accompanied by rice and beans—and fresh trout when it's available. ☎ *Plaza Sucre,* ☎ *02/343110 for reservations. 45 rooms, some with bath. Restaurant. No credit cards.*

Huatajata

DINING AND LODGING

$$$$ **Hotel Inca Utama.** This well-maintained hotel has tremendous, romance-inspiring views over the lake, perhaps best appreciated after a drink in the lounge or dinner in the simple, traditional Bolivian restaurant. The small rooms are comfortable enough but lack character. The hotel also arranges excursions to the islands. ☎ *Reservations: Crillon Tours,* ☎ *02/350363. 44 rooms. Restaurant, bar. AE, V.*

$$$ **Hotel Lake Titicaca.** Coming from La Paz, you'll see this well-equipped but slightly dated complex on the lakeshore a few kilometers before Huatajata. The sweeping views of the lake almost justify the inflated prices. ☎ *Reservations:* ☎ *02/374877. 24 rooms. Restaurant, bar, sauna, racquetball, boating, recreation room. AE, MC, V.*

Puerto Perez

DINING AND LODGING

$$$ **Hotel las Balsas.** Perched on the lakeshore, Las Balsas occupies a cor-
★ ner of the main square and is within reach of walking trails to nearby farming villages. The owner, Swiss-born Jean-Jacques Valloton, maintains a respectable on-site restaurant and can arrange visits to Suriki

Island. ⚀ *Main square,* ☎ *02/357817 for reservations. 16 rooms, 2 suites. Restaurant, bar. MC.*

Sorata

DINING AND LODGING

$$ **Hotel Prefectural.** Accommodations here are simple at best, and what lures most visitors are the traditional Bolivian restaurant, the outdoor garden, and the lovely views across the valley. Coming from La Paz, the hotel is on the main highway less than a kilometer from Sorata's central square. ⚀ *Reservations: SERVITUR, Edificio Naira, Calle Potosí, La Paz,* ☎ *02/350559. Restaurant. No credit cards.*

CENTRAL BOLIVIA

Central Bolivia stretches from Cochabamba, nestled in the eastern foothills of the Andes, to the lowland city of Santa Cruz, perched on the edge of the Amazon Basin. Climates range from mild and sunny in Cochabamba to hot and humid in Santa Cruz, with heavy rainfall throughout the region between October and March.

Both Cochabamba and Santa Cruz have a good selection of tourist facilities, including hotels ranging from colonial style to ultramodern. Yet the real attraction is not so much the cities themselves—both are large urban centers, after all—but rather the surrounding landscape. Santa Cruz, easy to reach by plane, gives a strong sense of Bolivia's tropical lowlands; Cochabamba, the so-called "City of Eternal Spring," balances rugged mountain scenery with fertile valley vegetation.

The highlight, however, may be a quick trek through the Chapare, where most of the coca used for illegal cocaine production is grown. Traveling by car or bus through the Chapare region—in other words, traveling between Cochabamba and Santa Cruz—is an unforgettable experience: The road snakes its way through bare, arid highlands before dropping into a vast expanse of cloud and tropical rain forests shrouded in mist. There are few tourist centers in the area, but those who make it to the village of Villa Tunari may find themselves wishing to linger a while.

Arriving and Departing

By Plane

LAB and AeroSur fly daily from La Paz and Sucre to Cochabamba's **Aeropuerto Jorge Wilsterman** (☎ 04/221635) and Santa Cruz's **Aeropuerto Viru-Viru** (☎ 03/44411), a 16-kilometer (10-mile) taxi ride ($6.50) from downtown. Cochabamba's airport is a 10-kilometer (6-mile) taxi trek ($4) from downtown.

By Car

It takes nearly five hours to drive between La Paz and Cochabamba, even though the road is fully paved all the way. From La Paz drive in the direction of Oruro until you reach the village of Caracollo, some 190 kilometers (118 miles) south from La Paz and one of the few villages en route with a gas pump. Beyond Caracollo is a poorly signposted, left-hand turn for Cochabamba. The drive between Cochabamba and Santa Cruz takes 10 hours on the Nuevo Camino (New Road) and is recommended only for four-wheel-drive vehicles. You can break the trip into almost equal parts by staying overnight at Villa Tunari in the Chapare.

In Cochabamba you can rent a car for around $40 per day from **Barrons Rent-a-Car** (Calle Sucre E. 0727, ☏ 04/222774 or 04/223819) or **National Car Rental** (Calle Nataniel Aguirre S. 0685, ☏ 04/226911 or 02/376581). In Santa Cruz contact **IMBEX** (Calle Monseñor Peña 320, ☏ 03/533603), **Barrons** (Av. Cristobal de Mendoza 286, ☏ 03/333886 or 03/338823), or **AB Rent-a-Car** (Av. Alemana, Segunda Anillo, ☏ 03/420160, FAX 03/423412).

By Bus

Depending on breakdowns and the state of the road, it takes about seven hours to travel by bus between La Paz and Cochabamba; roughly 20 hours between La Paz and Santa Cruz. One-way tickets for either trek cost between $10 and $15. **Flota Copacabana** (☏ 02/362803) buses leave La Paz terminal at 9 and 9:30 AM for both cities. **Trans Copacabana** (☏ 02/322888) buses depart La Paz at 8:30 AM, 1:30 PM, and 10 PM. To avoid standing in the aisle for 20 hours, book tickets at least one day in advance.

Cochabamba

Visitor Information

Oficina de Turismo (Plaza 14 de Septiembre, ☏ 04/223364); **Fremen Travel** (Calle Tumusla 0245, ☏ 04/247126).

Exploring

Cochabamba, set in a lush grassy valley at an altitude of 8,430 feet, is the third-largest city in Bolivia, with a population of more than 320,000. Although it is more compact than sprawling Santa Cruz, Cochabamba's sights are scattered between the apartment-lined Río Rocha (Rocha River) and, a dull 25-minute walk to the southwest, **Plaza 14 de Septiembre,** the city's tree-lined and colorful heart. Flanking the square, the **Catedral** (☛ Free), started in 1701 and completed in 1735, stands sentinel over the old men and street vendors who sometimes congregate in the plaza at dusk.

One block southeast from the square stands the **Temple of San Francisco,** a colonial masterpiece built in 1581 but thoroughly recast in 1782 and again in 1926. Still, it boasts elaborately carved wooden galleries and a striking gold-leaf altar. *Calle 25 de Mayo, no ☏. ☛ Free.*

Cochabamba's excellent **Museo Arqueológico** (Museum of Archaeology) is one of the more comprehensive and interesting museums outside of La Paz; on display are pre-Columbian pottery, silver and gold work, and strikingly patterned, handwoven Indian textiles. Hour-long, English-language tours can be arranged for a small fee. *Calle 25 de Mayo 145, no ☏. ☛ Charged. ☾ Mon.–Sat.*

Plaza Colón, at the eastern foot of Calle 25 de Mayo, marks the start of **El Prado** (sometimes called Avenida Ballivián), a shop- and bar-lined avenue that stretches north to the Río Rocha. Cross the river and hail a taxi for the five-minute trip to **Centro Portales.** This elegant mansion was completed in 1927 after 10 years of building by Simón Patino, a local tin baron who amassed one of the world's largest private fortunes. The mansion now houses a cultural center, which sponsors the occasional art exhibition, but the extensive grounds and gardens are the real reason to visit. *Av. Potosí 1450, no ☏. ☛ Free. ☾ Weekdays.*

To get a good view of Cochabamba, take a taxi from the city center to **Cerro Coronilla** (Coronilla Hill, also called San Sebastián Hill), on the city's outskirts, with sweeping views of surrounding hillside farms. At the top there's a monument honoring the women and children who died during Bolivia's protracted War of Independence, which ended in 1825.

Tarata, a tiny, well-preserved colonial village 25 kilometers (15 miles) southeast of Cochabamba, hosts a busy open-air market on Thursdays. Tarata is known throughout Bolivia for its chorizo sausage, which you can buy in bulk—along with other handicrafts—on the village's flower-filled main square. For fine views of Tarata, consider the 15-minute uphill walk to **Iglesia San Pedro** (San Pedro Church). Although the nearby **Convento de San Francisco** (San Francisco Monastery) is currently being restored, as are many of the finer old buildings around the town, a visit is highly recommended. In Cochabamba, buses for Tarata depart from Avenida Barrientos, at the corner of Avenida 6 de Agosto. Alternatively, Fremen Travel (*see* Visitor Information, *above*) offers weekly tours of Tarata and the nearby village of Hayculi, famous for its pottery and ceramics.

Shopping

Cochabamba is well known for its high-quality alpaca sweaters and knitwear, but don't expect prices to be much lower than in La Paz. Some of the better-quality (and more expensive) knitwear shops include **Asarti** (Calle Roche 375), **Casa Fisher** (Calle Ramorán Rivero 0204), **Fotrama** (Av. Heroínas), and **Amerindia** (Av. San Martín 6064). The local market, **La Cancha,** held Wednesday and Saturday on Avenida Aroma, is a good place to browse for less expensive crafts.

Dining

For price-category definitions, *see* Dining *in* Bolivia Essentials, *below.*

$$$ Guadalquivir. Parrots in cages and a small but beautifully laid-out garden create the mood at this popular outdoor eating venue; its shady trees means it's a pleasant place to eat lunch, too. Dishes are a mix of traditional and more international stock-in-trade. ✗ *Cala Cala district, no ☎. AE, MC, V.*

$$ Casa de Campo. Informal and lively, the Casa de Campo features traditional Bolivian specialties—mostly grilled meats and a perfectly fiery *picante mixto* (grilled chicken and beef tongue)—served on a shaded outdoor patio. ✗ *Av. Aniceto Padilla, ☎ 042/43937. No credit cards.*

$$ Chifa Lai Lai. All Chinese restaurants in Bolivia are called Chifa. This one has excellent food, cheap wines, and the kind of service usually found only in much more expensive places. Try the Ecuadoran shrimp dishes. ✗ *Av. Anicetto Padilla 729, no ☎. MC, V.*

$$ Rodizio Buffalo. This Argentine-style eatery offers not only an excellent salad bar and all the meat you can eat, but also great views of the city. ✗ *Calle Oquendo in the Torres Sofer, no ☎. AE, V.*

$ The Cantonata. Come to this high-quality spot for pizza and pasta at very reasonable prices. ✗ *Calle España at Mayor Rocha, no ☎. No credit cards.*

Lodging

For price-category definitions, *see* Lodging *in* Bolivia Essentials, *below.*

$$$$ Hotel Portales. Cochabamba's most luxurious address has lush gardens, numerous recreation facilities, and extremely well-equipped rooms with air-conditioning, TVs, and phones. Plan on a short taxi ride to reach the center of town. ⌑ *Av. Panda 1271, ☎ 042/48507, FAX 042/*

42071. *98 rooms, 8 suites. 2 restaurants, piano bar, 2 pools, beauty salon, exercise room. AE, MC, V.*

$$$ **Gran Hotel Cochabamba.** Much at the Gran Hotel highlights its lush courtyard, where you are likely to hear soothing bird song in the evening; in fact, most of the hotel's simple but comfortable rooms—all with TV and phone—overlook the plant-filled courtyard. The adjoining Restaurant Carillon serves an excellent *pique macho* as well as *surubí*, a delicious Amazon River fish with white flesh and few bones. ☎ *Plaza Ubaldo Anze,* ☎ *042/43300 or 042/82551,* FAX *042/82558. 43 rooms, 5 suites. Restaurant, bar, pool, tennis court. AE, V.*

$$ **Hotel Aranjuez.** A short walk from the city center brings you to this intimate, elegant hotel, noted for its lovely terraces and gardens. Aranjuez's well-equipped rooms are spacious and comfortable. A live jazz band plays in the lobby bar most weekends. ☎ *Av. Buenos Aires E. 0563,* ☎ *042/41935 or 042/80076,* FAX *042/40158. 30 rooms, 3 suites, most with bath. Restaurant, bar, minibars, pool. AE, MC, V.*

$ **Hotel Uni.** Budget-minded travelers will appreciate the Uni's central location, one block from the main square, and its simple, clean rooms, all of which have a phone and a TV. ☎ *Calle Baptista S. 9111,* ☎ *042/ 22444. 50 rooms. Restaurant, bar. AE, MC, V.*

The Chapare

Traveling between Cochabamba and Santa Cruz on the Nuevo Camino, you're in a section of Bolivia known as the **Chapare,** a sparsely populated region of low-lying mountains and thickening jungle. The few communities that survive here tend to earn a living through the harvesting of coca, the raw ingredient used in the production of cocaine. Locals assume that all light-skinned people are connected with the U.S. Drug Enforcement Agency. But once it's recognized that you are only passing through, people tend to be friendly. The village of **Villa Tunari** (*see* Dining and Lodging, *below*) is well equipped to deal with overnight visitors.

Dining and Lodging

For price-category definitions, *see* Dining *and* Lodging *in* Bolivia Essentials, *below.*

Villa Tunari

$ **El Puente.** The secluded El Puente is situated in thick forest a few kilometers outside Villa Tunari, at the end of a rough, pebble-strewn path accessed from the Nuevo Camino. Trails cut into the undergrowth lead to a nearby river with clear, swimmable pools. The scattered cabins do not have hot water, but considering the outside temperature, this is not a serious drawback. Reservations are recommended and should be made through Fremen Travel in La Paz (Plaza Abaroa, Calle Pedro Salazar, ☎ 02/327073). The on-site restaurant serves hearty, simple food. ☎ *Off Nuevo Camino, no* ☎. *12 cabins. Restaurant. AE, MC, V.*

$ **Hotel las Palmas.** Despite the roadside setting, the centrally located Las Palmas offers a range of modern comforts, including private showers and toilets. The hotel restaurant features a menu of grilled chicken and pique macho, as well as some forest game and river fish. ☎ *Nuevo Camino,* ☎ *0411/4103. 10 rooms, 4 cabins. Restaurant, pool. No credit cards.*

Santa Cruz

Visitor Information

Oficina de Turismo (Immigration Ministry Building, Av. Irala, ☎ 03/348644); **Tajibos Tours** (Tajibos Hotel, Av. San Martín 455, ☎ 03/429046); **Umpex Travel** (Calle René Moreno 226, ☎ 03/336001).

Exploring

Santa Cruz is a lively lowland city whose sprawling industrial districts are connected by a series of *anillos*, or ring roads. Twenty years ago, oxen pulled carts through the mud streets of Santa Cruz; today, well-dressed business people dodge taxis and street sellers as they maneuver between modern downtown office buildings—a sure sign that Santa Cruz and its more than 600,000 inhabitants have been dramatically transformed in recent years. Apart from its main plaza, Santa Cruz has little to offer in terms of sites, museums, or architecture. After a brief downtown tour, consider hiring a taxi to explore the handful of nearby farming villages, many of which host small produce and livestock markets on a regular basis. The going rate is less than $4 per hour. Also note: Carry your passport at all times in Santa Cruz. The police have a bad reputation and may harass or even fine you for not carrying your documentation.

Santa Cruz has grown up around **Plaza 24 de Septiembre,** its busy main square, lined with modern shops—of the souvenir, clothing, and travel variety—and a few sober architectural relics from the colonial era. The colonnaded streets feeding the plaza are lined with food stands and slightly run-down electronic and curio shops that are still fun to browse.

More attention-grabbing is the **Basílica Menor de San Lorenzo,** built between 1845 and 1915 on the ruins of a 17th-century cathedral. Inside the imposing but architecturally uninspired church, the **Museo Catedralicio** (Cathedral Museum) exhibits colonial-era religious objects, paintings, and sculptures. *Plaza 24 de Septiembre.* ☛ *Free.* ☉ *Tues., Thurs., and Sun.*

The adjacent **Casa de la Cultura** hosts art exhibitions, recitals, and concerts, in addition to a permanent exhibit of local Indian crafts. *Plaza 24 de Septiembre, no* ☎. ☛ *Free.* ☉ *Daily 9–noon, 3–6.*

At the **Zoologico Municipal** (City Zoo), considered one of the finest in South America, you'll see llamas and alpacas, flamingos, owls, snakes, bears, and a good collection of native species that includes jaguars, tapirs, and toucans. The animals are well cared for and displayed in settings that approach natural. Taxis will take you from the main square to the zoo for less than $5. *3ero Anillo Interno at Av. Banzer, no* ☎. ☛ *Charged.* ☉ *Daily 9–7.*

A popular day trip from Santa Cruz is **Lomas de Arena,** a large freshwater lake surrounded by mammoth sand dunes. The white sand dunes provide the perfect desert backdrop for swimming and sunbathing, while the juxtaposition of barren desert and lowland Andean scenery, besides giving off a vaguely surreal quality, entices visitors to take long walks and hikes. Umpex Travel (*see* Visitor Information, *above*) arranges excursions from Santa Cruz to Lomas de Arena that include visits to the colonial village of El Palmar. Umpex also organizes treks to the far-flung Jesuit Missions of the Chiquitania, beautifully carved Baroque wooden chapels deep in the rain forests, many of which have been restored to their former glory.

Shopping

Crafts stands and shops are scattered around the main square. The goods they sell are more typical of La Paz than of the lowlands, and don't expect any real bargains. That said, **Artecampo** (Calle Monseñor Salvatierra 407) is an outstanding cooperative crafts shop with a good selection of handmade hammocks and crewelwork cushion covers made from locally grown cotton, mobiles, ceramics, and intricate hand-painted woodwork. **Areka Bambú** (Calle Murillo 334) offers fine ceramics and macramé in addition to handwoven baskets. The main city market, **Mercado los Pozos,** held at Calle Quijarro at the corner of Avenida 6 de Agosto, features mounds of fresh local produce. **Mercado Siète Calles** is also worth a look, especially if you want to buy clothes or cheap cotton materials.

Dining and Lodging

Hotel restaurants are your best dining bet here. For price-category definitions, *see* Dining *and* Lodging *in* Bolivia Essentials, *below.*

$$$ **Gran Hotel Santa Cruz.** The rooms—and even the suites—are on the small side, but all accommodations at the family-owned Santa Cruz feature full air-conditioning and cable television, and rooms overlooking the pool have small private balconies. ☎ *Calle Pari 59,* ☎ *03/348811,* FAX *03/324194. 22 rooms, 12 suites, most with bath. Restaurant, 2 bars, cafeteria, pool. AE, MC, V.*

$$$ **La Quinta.** This ideal family hotel is only 10 minutes by taxi from the city center, although the service and food do not justify its four-star rating. Two-story self-contained chalets—arranged around three courtyards, each with its own small pool—house the guest accommodations, which have kitchens, a dining/living area, and up to four bedrooms. Rooms are noisily air-conditioned and most have balconies. ☎ *Barrio Urbari, Calle Arumá,* ☎ *03/522244,* FAX *03/522667. 31 rooms, 2 suites, most with bath. Restaurant, bar, 3 pools. AE, MC, V.*

$ **Hotel Colonial.** It's hard to believe that the ancient-looking air conditioners and televisions at this budget hotel actually work, but they do. Even more surprising are the private shower and toilet facilities. The adjoining restaurant is open for breakfast and snacks only. ☎ *Calle Buenos Aires 57,* ☎ *03/327316. 21 rooms. Restaurant. AE, MC, V.*

POTOSÍ

Modern Potosí is one of Bolivia's poorest cities: The lack of road links and a depressed mining industry have taken their toll on the city and its 110,000 inhabitants. Still, Potosí retains a great deal of historic flavor, with its narrow cobblestone streets and elaborate though largely neglected colonial architecture. Towering above Potosí, Cerro Rico is the "rich hill" that has provided most of Bolivia's mineral wealth and is now depicted on the national flag. In the 17th century, Cerro Rico also fueled Spain's conquest of the South American continent. Despite some very sobering facts—among them, that the average life span of a miner is just 45 years—a visit to Potosí would not be complete without a trip down a working cooperative mine.

Visitor Information

Oficina de Turismo (Cámara de Minería, 2nd Floor, Calle Quijarro, ☎ 06/225288); **Transamazonas** (Calle Quijarro 12, ☎ 06/227175); **Koala Tours** (Calle Oruro 136, ☎ 06/224708).

Arriving and Departing

By Train

Trains leave La Paz every Tuesday and Saturday at 6 PM for Potosí's **Estación Ferrocarriles** (Av. Sevilla, ☎ 06/231001); the journey takes 12–14 hours and costs about $10 each way.

By Car

From La Paz, take the main highway south to Oruro and look for signs for Potosí (12 hours) near the village of Machacamarca. The road is paved from the capital to Oruro; after that, expect dirt and many pot-holes.

By Bus

Buses leave La Paz daily at 6:30 PM and 8 PM for Potosí; the 15-hour trek costs less than $15. Buses for Santa Cruz and Cochabamba also depart from Potosí's **Terminal de Buses** (Av. Universitaria, ☎ 06/225422).

Exploring Potosí

At the heart of Potosí lies the **Plaza 10 de Noviembre,** bordered by an imposing baroque **Catedral** open only on Sunday morning. More intriguing is the nearby **Casa de Monedas,** a massive block-long mint once used to forge coins with silver mined from the depths of Cerro Rico, around which Potosí is built. Opened in 1572 and then rebuilt in 1753, the stone-and-brick mint contains a wide range of colonial treasures—from the 8-foot-high wheels used to produce silver ingots to galleries lined with Spanish and South American coins. Also on display are colonial statuary, furniture, and paintings, including works by Bolivia's celebrated 20th-century painter Cecilio Guzmán de Rojas. Admission is by guided tour only (at 9 and 1:30), and wandering is definitely not allowed. English-speaking guides are available for a small fee. *Plaza 10 de Noviembre,* ☎ *06/222777.* ☛ *Charged.* ☉ *Mon.–Sat.*

Many of Potosí's churches have erratic opening times. It is important to check with the tourist office for current schedules, or to arrange special visits to the **Iglesia San Agustín** (Calle Bolívar), the **Iglesia San Martín** (Calle Hoyos), and the **Iglesia Jerusalén** (Plaza del Estudiante). Potosí's most spectacular church is the **Iglesia San Lorenzo** (Calle Bustillos), which offers some of the finest examples of baroque carvings in South America: an elaborate combination of mythical figures and indigenous designs carved in high relief on the stone facade.

The **Convento y Museo Santa Teresa** (Convent and Museum of Saint Theresa), three blocks below the main plaza, displays a strange mix of religious artifacts. In one room there are sharp iron instruments once used to inflict pain on penitent nuns, as well as a blouse embroidered with wire mesh and prongs meant to prick the flesh. Other rooms contain works by renowned colonial painters such as Melchor Pérez Holguín. *Calle Chicas,* ☎ *06/223847.* ☛ *Charged.* ☉ *Weekdays.*

Five thousand tunnels wend their way through the distorted mound of **Cerro Rico,** the "rich hill" of silver that helped to fill Spain's imperial coffers until the reserves were exhausted during the early 19th century. Today tin is the primary extract, though on the barren mountainside, independent miners still sift for silver in the remnants of ancient excavations. If you are accustomed to the altitude and not affected by confined spaces, consider a tour through one of the active cooperative mines. Along with hundreds of local miners, you will descend into the dark and humid tunnels where it's common to work almost naked because of the intense heat. Conditions are shocking in these noisy, muddy shafts, and tours are not recommended for anyone with a weak stomach. Be sure to wear the dirtiest clothes you have. Koala Tours and Transamazonas (*see* Visitor Information, *above*) organize excursions into Cerro Rico, as do the independent, English-speaking guides Raul Braulio (☎ 06/225304) and Marco Alarcón (☎ 06/226432 or 06/227677).

Potosí is surrounded by natural lagoons that are fed by hot thermal springs. Koala Tours and Transamazonas (*see* Visitor Information, *above*) arrange trips to two such lagoons, **La Laguna del Inca** and **Kari Kari,** and they can advise you regarding which of the seething pools are safe for bathing (some have strong currents and literally boiling-hot water).

Shopping

Despite Potosí's rich mineral wealth, do not expect bargains on hand-crafted silver jewelry. However, brass and low-grade silver jewelry and silver coins can be found at an outdoor market between Calle Oruro and Calle Bustillos. Another market on Calle Bolívar features fresh tropical fruits and produce, while one on the corner of Calle Sucre and Calle Modesto Omiste, four blocks from San Lorenzo Church, has locally produced crafts.

Dining

By no stretch of the imagination can Potosí be called a gourmet's delight: The choice of restaurants in this industrial mining town is severely limited. For price-category definitions, *see* Dining *in* Bolivia Essentials, *below.*

$$ El Mesón. With its international menu and central location opposite the cathedral, El Mesón bills itself as Potosí's most exclusive restaurant. But beyond the linen napkins and tablecloths, you'll find walls in need of paint and a rather characterless, very quiet dining room. The menu includes traditional Potosí and international dishes, so if the lure of offal is wearing thin, consider the lasagna. ✕ *Plaza 10 de Noviembre, no ☎. No credit cards.*

$$ Sky Room. You'll have a fine view of central Potosí from this third floor, rooftop restaurant. The menu features traditional Potosí dishes such as *pichanga,* a mixture of intestines and offal served with salad. Less adventurous diners may want to try a grilled chicken entrée. ✕ *Edificio Matilde, 3rd Floor, Calle Bolívar 701, ☎ 062/26345. No credit cards.*

$ Cherry's. At this delightful coffee shop you can sip mugs of coffee or ★ mate de coca while pondering the delicious selection of cakes and strudels. ✕ *Calle Padilla 8, no ☎. No credit cards.*

Lodging

Hotels in high-altitude Potosí are rarely heated, encouraging the use of thermals or pajamas on cold nights. For price-category definitions, *see* Lodging *in* Bolivia Essentials, *below.*

$$ Hostal Colonial. This whitewashed and stone-flagged, vaguely colonial-looking low rise is just two blocks from the main square. Many of the well-equipped but undistinguished rooms overlook the hotel's two airy courtyards; all have a TV and a phone. Breakfast—there is no lunch or dinner service—is brought to your bedside or served in the dining room. ☎ *Calle Hoyos 8, ☎ 062/24265, FAX 062/27146. 20 rooms. Dining room. MC, V.*

$$ **Hotel Claudia.** More practical than refined, the newly built Claudia matches well-equipped rooms—all have phone and TV—with other features rarely found in Potosí: an on-site restaurant, bar, and terrace. Breakfast is included in the room price. ⌦ *Av. El Maestro 322,* ☎ *062/ 22242,* 🅵🅰🆇 *062/24005. 22 rooms. Restaurant, bar. No credit cards.*

$ **Hostal Carlos V.** Budget-minded travelers will appreciate this basic but clean hotel near the main square. The bare, undecorated rooms share communal showers and toilets. Breakfast is served on the enclosed balcony. ⌦ *Calle Linares 42,* ☎ *062/25121. 12 rooms, none with bath. No credit cards.*

SUCRE

Sucre, founded in 1540 by the Spaniard Pedro de Anzurez, manages to sustain a population of more than 100,000 without feeling too urban. In fact, La Ciudad Blanca (The White City)—so called because the town's houses are whitewashed every year by government edict—is a pleasant throwback to the colonial era with its many churches and grand mansions. At an altitude of only 9,022 feet, Sucre is further blessed with a mild climate and offers some relief from the thin atmosphere of La Paz and Potosí. Sucre is also Bolivia's official capital and the seat of the Supreme Court: In 1776, Spain crowned Sucre capital of its eastern Andean territories, and in 1825 it was named capital of the newly created Republic of Bolivia. All government offices have since relocated to La Paz, Bolivia's de facto capital, but Sucre's tone remains upbeat due to its University of San Xavier, founded in 1624. On balmy evenings, students pack Sucre's trendy downtown cafés and bars.

Visitor Information

Oficina de Turismo (Calle Potosí 102, ☎ 06/425983); **Fremen Travel** (Plaza 25 de Mayo 4, ☎ 06/430351); **SurAndes** (Calle Nicolás Ortiz 6, ☎ 06/421983).

Arriving and Departing

By Plane
Lloyd Aereo Boliviano (LAB, Av. Camacho 1460, La Paz, ☎ 02/371020; U.S. ☎ 800/327–3098) flies regularly from La Paz to Sucre ($51).

By Train
Trains leave La Paz every Tuesday and Saturday at 6 PM for Sucre's centrally located **Estación Ferrocarriles** (Plaza 25 de Mayo, ☎ 06/421205); the journey takes 12–14 hours and costs around $10 each way.

By Car
From La Paz, take the main highway south to Oruro and look for signs for Sucre (18 hours) near the village of Machacamarca. The road is paved from the capital only to Oruro; be prepared for rough going after that.

By Bus
Buses leave La Paz daily at 6:30 PM and 8 PM for Sucre (via Potosí); the 19-hour trek costs less than $15. To reserve space on the five-hour ride between Sucre and Potosí, contact **Transmin** (☎ 06/421328) or **Andesbus** (☎ 06/424251). The former leaves Sucre at 7 AM from Calle Loa 639, the latter at 7 AM from Calle Bolívar 621. Buses for Santa Cruz and Cochabamba also depart from Sucre's **Terminal de Buses** (Calle Ostria Gutiérrez, ☎ 06/422029).

Exploring Sucre

In Sucre's city center, throngs of ice-cream vendors and shoe-shine boys fill the tree-lined **Plaza 25 de Mayo,** the city's social fulcrum. Waiting taxis can take you on brief city tours for less than $5 per hour, but there's little in Sucre that's not within walking distance of the main plaza. The baroque **Catedral Metropolitana,** one of three impressive monuments flanking the square, is famous for its priceless statue of the Virgin of Guadalupe, garbed in diamonds, gold, emeralds, and pearls donated during the 17th century by residents with secure mining fortunes. Next door, the **Museo de la Iglesia** (Cathedral Museum; ☛ Free; closed Mon.) displays colonial paintings, volumes of parchment, and religious statuary. Also on the plaza, **Casa de la Libertad** (☛ Free; closed weekends) is where Bolivia's Declaration of Independence was signed in 1825. Fittingly, the small museum now displays historical documents and artifacts related to Bolivia's turbulent struggle for independence.

Two blocks from the square, the mammoth 17th-century **El Templo de San Felipe Neri** (Church and Monastery of San Felipe Neri) testifies to the wealth once enjoyed by the Roman Catholic Church in Bolivia. From the church's domed roof and towers you can enjoy the grand panorama of Sucre's spire-entangled skyline. The nearby Universidad de Tourismo (Calle Nicolás Ortiz 182) arranges guided tours of the church and monastery. *Calle Nicolás Ortiz 182, no* ☏. ☛ *Charged.* ◷ *Daily 4–6.*

From the main plaza, Calle Calvo leads past the Church of Santo Domingo to the **Museo y Convento de Santa Clara** (Museum and Convent of Santa Clara), founded in 1639, which houses a magnificently hand-painted organ dating from the 17th century along with devotional paintings and colonial statuary. Also on display are works by colonial painter Melchor Pérez Holguín and his Italian mentor, Bernardo Bitti. Visit the chapel where the sisters who died here have been buried under a special floor equipped with numerous doors that can be opened for the curious. *Calle Calvo 212, no* ☏. ☛ *Charged.* ◷ *Weekdays 10–11, 5–7; Sat. 10–11:30.*

Don't leave Sucre without visiting the impressive **Caserón de la Capellenía,** with its exhibit of modern Indian weavings. The adjacent ASUR gift shop sells a range of locally produced weavings; future plans include traditional music available on cassettes and compact disc. *Calle San Alberto 413 (near Calle Potosí),* ☏ *06/423841.* ☛ *Free.* ◷ *Mon.–Sat.*

Beyond the textile museum, Calle San Alberto curves and joins Calle Polanco, at the end of which is **Plaza Pedro Anzures,** a beautiful residential square set atop the less-than-towering Churuquella Mountain. Still, there are good views of Sucre's tiled roofs and whitewashed homes as well as of the ragged mountains and farmland that fade into the horizon. On one corner of the square, the **Museo y Convento de la Recoleta** (Museum and Convent of the Retreat), founded in 1601 by Franciscan monks, displays colonial religious works in a setting of serene courtyards and gardens. Equally noteworthy is the restored chapel and its intricately carved choir seats. *Plaza Pedro Anzures, no* ☏. ☛ *Charged.* ◷ *Weekdays 9–11, 3–5.*

The most popular exhibit at the **Museo Antropológico Charcas** (also called the Museo Universitario) are mummified bodies discovered in the 1960s (museum curators believe the centuries-old mummies were entombed as human sacrifices). More tame are the galleries of colonial painting and textiles. *Calle Bolívar 698,* ☏ *06/423455.* ☛ *Charged.* ◷ *Weekdays 9–noon, 2–6; Sat. 9–noon.*

The faded wonder **La Glorieta** (The Summerhouse) lies 6 kilometers (4 miles) southwest of Sucre on the road to Potosí. Built at the end of the 19th century by wealthy industrialist Don Francisco Argandoña, La Glorieta featured Venetian-style canals and expansive gardens crowned by an exotic residential palace built in a combination of Moorish, Spanish, and French styles. Today, the house and gardens, though still impressive, are in ruins, mainly due to a long period of occupation by the army. You may still have to show your passport to one of the army cadets from the adjacent military base. The taxi ride from town costs less than $2 per person. ☛ *Free.* ☉ *Weekdays 9–noon, 2–6; Sat. 9–noon.*

Tarabuco, 80 kilometers (50 miles) east from Sucre along a rough and dusty road, is best seen on Sunday during its colorful crafts and produce market. Mingle with local Indians in traditional dress, and browse the stalls for handcrafted weavings and ponchos, musical instruments, and *chuspas* (bags for carrying coca leaves and money). In early March, Tarabuco hosts one of South America's liveliest traditional festivals, the **Pujilay,** celebrating the March 12, 1816, victory by local Indians over the Spanish. Buses leave year-round for Tarabuco from Calle Calvo in Sucre. Round-trip tickets cost less than $3.

Shopping

The ASUR gift shop at the **Caserón de Capellanía** (Calle San Alberto) has a good selection of local weavings, and the cooperative ensures that the majority of profits go directly to the weavers rather than middlemen. For a spot of local color, the market at Calle Ravelo and Calles Junín features produce and household items.

Dining

Sucre has a good range of restaurants and cafés, though many are closed at lunchtime. The local cuisine is distinctly spicy: If you do not appreciate a little fire with your meal, avoid dishes prefaced with the word *ají* or *picante*. For price-category definitions, *see* Dining *in* Bolivia Essentials, *below*.

$$$ **El Huerto.** Vegetarians can indulge in all sorts of pastas and meat-free lasagnas at El Huerto, located near the municipal park, while adventurous carnivores should try a traditional Bolivian entrée such as picante *de lengua* (beef tongue). The open-air patio is a fine place to linger over a long meal. ✗ *Ladislao Cabrera 86,* ☎ *06/421538. No credit cards.*

$$ **Arco Iris.** Cheese and meat fondues draw crowds to the Swiss-owned Arco Iris. Chocolate lovers may have difficulty waiting until dessert to tackle the decadent chocolate mousse. ✗ *Calle Nicolás Ortiz 42,* ☎ *06/422902. No credit cards.*

$ **Alliance Française la Taberna.** The traditional French menu at La Taberna includes hard-to-find delicacies such as coq au vin, ratatouille, and dessert crepes. Seating is available indoors or on the outside courtyard, where you must be prepared to deal with wandering street vendors pushing their crafts. ✗ *Calle Aniceto Arce 35, no* ☎. *No credit cards.*

$ **Bibliocafé.** The dinner menu—mostly pastas and grilled meats—may be small, but most people come instead for post-dinner coffee and dessert. Crepes stuffed with banana and smothered in chocolate sauce are a divine option. ✗ *Calle Nicolás Ortiz 30, no* ☎. *No credit cards. No lunch.*

Lodging

Hotels in Sucre maintain reasonably high standards, though you may experience the occasional shortage of electricity and water. For price-category definitions, *see* Lodging *in* Bolivia Essentials, *below.*

$$$ Hostal Sucre. The colonial-style Sucre, just two blocks from the main square, is built around two inner courtyards, keeping noise to a pleasant minimum. An on-site restaurant serves light meals and snacks. ☎ *Calle Bustillo 113,* ☎ *and* FAX *06/421411. 30 rooms. Restaurant. MC, V.*

$$$ Hotel Municipal. You can expect typically comfortable and clean—if not also characterless—rooms at this modern mid-rise near the municipal pool. The main plaza with its bars and restaurants is only 10 minutes by foot, or enjoy traditional Bolivian meals in the lobby restaurant. ☎ *Av. Venezuela 1052,* ☎ *064/21216 or 06/425508,* FAX *06/424826. 39 rooms. Restaurant, bar. AE, MC, V.*

$$$ Hotel Real Audiencia. The newly renovated Real Audiencia combines period looks—it's set in a converted colonial mansion—with modern fixtures and styling. The spacious rooms feature an above-average range of amenities. From the hotel restaurant there are good views over the city. ☎ *Calle Potosí 142,* ☎ *06/430823,* FAX *06/432809. 22 rooms. Restaurant, bar. V.*

BOLIVIA ESSENTIALS

Customs and Duties

On Arrival

Bags are usually checked on arrival at La Paz's El Alto airport. Visitors are allowed to import 400 cigarettes and three bottles of wine or 2 liter bottles of spirits. There is no limit on the amount of foreign currency you can bring in to the country. For certain electronic goods—video cameras and personal computers, for example—you should carry your receipt or proof of purchase unless the items show obvious signs of wear. Passengers flying internationally from Santa Cruz are often asked to produce a yellow-fever certificate; have yours handy, or you may be required to get an injection before being allowed to leave. Do not attempt to import or export contraband drugs of any kind—penalties are severe.

On Departure

At the airport all passengers must pay a departure tax—$20 for international flights, under $3 for domestic flights—at an easily identifiable booth marked IMPUESTOS.

Dining

Lunch, the main meal of the day in highland Bolivia, often means a set, four-course menu. The only choice you may have is between entrées, so once you sit down, simply relax and wait for your meal to arrive, course by course. Many people find it hard to digest large evening meals at high altitude, so dinner tends to be light and informal. To ease your transition, many restaurants offer English-language menus, but local cuisine still figures highly on most menus as Bolivians are extremely fond of their own cuisine and are still a little suspicious about novelty. In major cities such as La Paz, Santa Cruz, Sucre, and Cochabamba restaurants run the gamut from elegant international to basic hole-in-the-wall. In rural areas your choice is largely limited to basic Bolivian cooking in simple surroundings.

Specialties

Traditional Bolivian cuisine is very regional. In the highlands, where carbohydrates are the dietary mainstay, look for *chuño* and *tunta*, two kinds of freeze-dried potatoes that are soaked overnight and boiled, then used to accompany main dishes. Other traditional highland dishes are *timpu* (lamb stew), *conecho cuis* (roast guinea pig), and *asado de llama* (llama steak). A ubiquitous traditional dish is pique macho, beef grilled with hot peppers, chopped tomatoes and onions, and often served with fried potatoes and gravy, or *sajta de pollo,* a kind of chicken stew made with peppers and onions. Surubí, a popular Amazon River fish, is delicious grilled or baked. Bolivians satisfy a mid-morning hunger pang with a salteña, a slightly sweetened pastry, filled with meat (beef or chicken), diced vegetables, olives and egg in a rich gravy. Vegetarians will have a hard time of it because meat, usually grilled, figures prominently in the Bolivian diet. However, a new wave of specialist vegetarian restaurants have started to appear, prompted, one suspects, by a steady growth in tourist numbers.

Each major city still has its own brewery, generally founded by Germans, and with that heritage and the superb mountain water, beer quality is very good. Bolivian or Chilean wines are also widely available; try the Concepción range of wines from Tarija to see just how far Bolivia's wine industry has come in recent years. *Singani,* a refined grape alcohol or eau-de-vie, is the national liquor. Traditional cocktails include the potent *pisco sour,* made from singani and lime juice, or the slightly-easier-to-get-along-with *chuflay* with singani and lemonade. *Chicha* is a grain alcohol made from chewing maize, spitting out the resulting mash, adding water, and allowing the mixture to brew; the sweet and rather cloudy result is mainly drunk in the lowland valleys in and around Cochabamba.

Mealtimes

Lunch is usually served from noon to 2; dinner between 7 and 10.

Dress

Informal dress is acceptable in all restaurants.

Ratings

Prices are per person for a four-course meal, not including alcohol and gratuities. A tip of 5–10% is expected unless the service is really dismal. Also note that some establishments add a cover charge to your bill—from 10¢ to $2 per person—whether you eat a full meal or simply stop for a cup of coffee.

CATEGORY	LA PAZ	OTHER AREAS
$$$$	over $15	over $5
$$$	$10–$15	$3–$5
$$	$5–$10	$1–$3
$	under $5	under $1

Embassies and Consulates

United States

Embassy: Banco del Peru building, Calle Mercado at Colón, La Paz, ☎ 02/350251. Consulate: Av. Potosi 1265, La Paz, ☎ 02/320494.

Canada

Consulate: Av. 20 de Octubre 2475, Plaza Avaroa, La Paz, 02/375224.

United Kingdom

Embassy: Av. Acre, 2732–2754, Casilla 694, La Paz, ☎ 02/357424.

Getting Around

By Plane

The state-run airline, **Lloyd Aereo Boliviano** (LAB, Av. Camacho 1460, La Paz, ☎ 02/371020; U.S. ☎ 800/327–3098), flies regularly from La Paz to Sucre ($51), Santa Cruz ($82), Cochabamba ($38), Trinidad ($52), and Tarija ($80); round-trip fares are about 60% more than the cost of a one-way ticket. **AeroSur** (Av. Camacho, La Paz, ☎ 02/371822), a private airline, tends to complement Lloyd schedules and also serves a number of smaller destinations. Most domestic flights are heavily booked, so try to reconfirm your reservation and arrive at the airport at least an hour in advance lest your seat be given to a standby passenger.

By Train

Train timetables in Bolivia are generally works of fiction, and even express trains tend to move at a snail's pace. However, first-class carriages offer a relatively high standard of service and comfort—though even in first class crowds can be a problem. Overnight *ferrobus* trains, such as the one to the coast of Chile or the Argentine border, have reclining seats. When you purchase a ticket, you will be issued a meal voucher that can be exchanged in the dining car for a set-menu meal.

The Bolivian rail network is being updated and expanded; the privatization process was expected to be completed by 1996. At press time (winter 1995), train services were limited to La Paz, Sucre, Potosí, and Villazón (on the Argentine border). Trains also join Santa Cruz with Puerto Suarez, on the Brazilian border. One-way tickets between La Paz and Potosí cost $15; between La Paz and Sucre, $20.

By Car

ROAD CONDITIONS

Bolivia's paved road network is very limited. Away from urban centers there are only two decent roads in the entire country, those that link the city of La Paz to Oruro and to Cochabamba. Elsewhere, you'll be constantly jolted by dirt tracks littered with potholes. During the rainy season, prepare for impassable roads and lots of mud. In rural areas you will see few private cars, and even fewer roadside facilities. Parking is a problem in larger cities, and cars left out at night can face the morning bereft of wheels and mirrors. Bolivia's drinking-and-driving laws are rarely enforced, so exercise caution when driving at night or on small mountain roads.

RENTALS

Renting can be an expensive business in Bolivia, particularly because you really need a four-wheel-drive vehicle. The going rate for a four-by-four is $300–$700 per week, including 700 free kilometers (435 free miles), depending on whether you hire a small Suzuki four-wheel-drive vehicle or a top-of-the-line Toyota or Mitsubishi. Compact cars cost $150–$250 per week, a fee that also includes 700 free kilometers (435 miles).

EMERGENCY ASSISTANCE

There is no national roadside automobile service, though Bolivians will often stop and offer help in the case of a breakdown.

GASOLINE

The national oil company, **YPFB,** maintains service stations on most major roads. Station opening times vary, though a number are open 24 hours. Away from the main roads, *gasolina* (gasoline) signs alert you to private homes where fuel is sold (make sure they filter the gasoline for impurities when they fill your tank). Unleaded gasoline is still a novelty in Bolivia.

By Bus

A variety of private bus companies connect Bolivia's major cities—two of the best are Mopar and Copacabana. Because of the often poor state of road surfaces, bus journeys do not always make sense for travelers with limited time: The La Paz–Santa Cruz trip, for example, can take more than 24 hours. Crowds can be a problem on some routes; but if you can get a seat, it's likely to be fairly comfortable. Between La Paz and Santa Cruz expect to pay $30 one-way; between La Paz and Cochabamba, $5; between La Paz and the Yungas, around $3.

By Boat

Bolivia is landlocked, so the only international arrivals are from the Peruvian port of Puno, on Lake Titicaca. The rest of Bolivia is crisscrossed by navigable rivers served by supply ships, which often accept passengers for a small, negotiable fee.

Language

Spanish is the main language in the cities and lowlands, and travelers find Bolivian Spanish to be one of the easiest on the continent to understand. Quechua and Aymara are the commonest languages spoken by the highland peoples, who may or may not also understand Spanish. Hotel staff usually have some knowledge of English, French, or German.

Lodging

The Bolivian tourist board rates hotels on an escalating one- to five-star basis. Apart from the Radisson in La Paz, there are no international chain hotels in Bolivia, which is not necessarily a bad thing because even the most expensive resorts are often family-run affairs. Some hotels have two pricing systems—one for Bolivians and one for foreigners. Still, even if you fall into the latter category, good, clean rooms can be found for $25 or less, particularly away from the cities. Do not be afraid to ask to see the room in advance—it's common practice in Bolivia.

Ratings

Prices are for two people in a double room.

CATEGORY	LA PAZ & SANTA CRUZ	OTHER AREAS
$$$$	over $100	over $40
$$$	$50–$100	$25–$40
$$	$25–$50	$10–$25
$	under $25	under $10

Mail

Most cities and towns have at least one post office, and these are generally open weekdays 8–7:30, Saturday 9–6, and Sunday 9–noon.

Postal Rates

International airmail costs 60¢ (about 40¢ for international postcards) and generally arrives in Europe or the United States within 5–10 days.

Receiving Mail

Mail can be sent care of Poste Restante, Correo Central, to the city of your choice. You will need a passport to retrieve your mail from the central post office.

Money and Expenses

Currency

The unit of currency is the boliviano (Bs), which can be divided into 100 centavos. Bolivianos come in bills of Bs 2, Bs 5, Bs 10, Bs 20, Bs 50, Bs 100, and Bs 200. Coins come in denominations of 10, 20, and 50 centavos and 1 and 2 bolivianos. At press time (winter 1995), the exchange rate was Bs 4.73 to the U.S. dollar and Bs 7.6 to the pound sterling.

Changing Money

Money changers, who can be found on the main streets of most cities, offer competitive rates and are usually reliable. Traveler's checks are not usually accepted in banks, though they can be changed, at slightly inferior rates, in *casas de cambio*.

Forms of Payment

Credit cards are accepted in many hotels and restaurants, but never in small villages or outside major urban centers. U.S. dollars (but not British pounds) are widely accepted, though the notes must be in perfect condition with no torn edges.

What It Will Cost

Because the boliviano is a relatively stable currency, Bolivia remains one of the least expensive countries in South America for travelers. A basic meal at a basic restaurant should cost no more than $5, and even at the most elegant of restaurants you can eat well for less than $15. Moderate hotels cost $30–$50 for a double room, often including breakfast. The most expensive luxury hotels are more pricey, at $120–$150 per night for a double.

TAXES

Throughout Bolivia, a 13% value-added tax (IVA) is added to hotel and restaurant bills and to most store-bought purchases.

SAMPLE PRICES

Cup of coffee or mate de coca, 20¢–60¢; bottle of soda, 50¢–$1; bottle of beer, 75¢–$2; crosstown taxi ride in a communal taxi 40¢, in a personal or radio taxi $1–$2.

Opening and Closing Times

Banks are open weekdays 9–11:30 and 2:30–5. **Museums** are generally open Tuesday–Friday 9–noon and 3–7. **Shops** close for lunch between 12:30 and 3, after which they open again until 8 or so. Many shops are also closed Saturday afternoon and Sunday.

National Holidays

New Year's Day (Jan. 1); Shrove Tuesday and the preceding Monday (1996: Feb. 19–20; 1997: Feb. 10–11); Good Friday (1996: Apr. 5; 1997: Mar. 28); Labor Day (May 1); Corpus Christi (1996: June 6; 1997: May 27); Independence Day (Aug. 6); All Saints' Day (Nov. 2); Christmas (Dec. 25).

There are a number of local carnivals and feast days when shops may be closed; check with local tourist offices for more details.

Precautions

Health

The cholera epidemic that swept through Peru in the early '90s and spilled over into Bolivia has now burnt itself out. However, both cholera and typhoid are endemic to the region, and new incidences of both diseases are at a low but persistent level. Although tap water is considered generally safe in the larger cities, it is preferable to boil it first; cautious travelers stick with bottled water, which is safe if not always appetizing. It's also advisable to avoid all fruit juices made with unboiled water, raw vegetables, raw fish, and washed salads. Food on the street should generally be avoided, unless you see it being thoroughly cooked.

If you're headed for the Amazon region, lay in a supply of antimalarial medicine and be sure that you have an up-to-date yellow-fever vaccination certificate with you. Because of the altitude in La Paz, upon arrival you may suffer from *sorojchi* (altitude sickness); most people who fly directly to La Paz do. Avoid alcohol and strenuous exercise at first, and get plenty of sleep. If your symptoms persist, consult a doctor, especially if you have a history of high blood pressure. Locals recommend several cups of mate de coca, an herbal (and completely legal) tea made from coca leaves; it helps to stimulate your kidneys, the organs responsible for assisting your adjustment to altitude.

Safety

Compared with its neighbors, Bolivia is an island of peace and tranquility. The civilian government remains strong, bolstered by a stable economy and a controlled rate of inflation. As far as crime goes, you are more likely to be chased by bad-tempered llamas than muggers. However, in such larger cities as La Paz, Cochabamba, Sucre, and Santa Cruz, petty theft—from pickpocketing to bag slashing—is on the rise. Avoid displays of money and be aware of your surroundings at all times, especially on busy plazas and in markets, or if you travel in crowded city buses.

Shopping

Bolivia has a wealth of traditional crafts ranging from weavings and knitwear to gold and silver jewelry. Crafts shops are usually grouped together (in La Paz, for instance, most can be found on Calle Sagarnaga). However, it is always worth looking for cooperative crafts shops outside the capital. These sell traditional textiles made in rural areas, especially in the departments of Chuquisaca and Potosí. The traditional shawls, hats, and skirts worn by highland women are sold in local markets and certain shopping districts in La Paz, but shopkeepers sometimes refuse to sell traditional garments to foreigners. In La Paz, there are black-market sellers hawking electronic and other goods smuggled in from Southeast Asia and the United States through Chile or Peru.

Owing to the low level of tourism experienced by Bolivia in the past, tourist-oriented goods tend to be realistically priced, and although bargaining is expected, many sellers will only drop their prices by small amounts, typically 5% to 10%.

Telephones

Local Calls

Pay phones use 40-centavo tokens, usually sold by people sitting right next to the phone booth. Many street vendors also have telephones available for local calls and charge between 50–70 centavos a call; look for

TELÉFONO signs. Local calls can also be made from the local telephone cooperative offices; there is at least one in every major town—in La Paz, try COTEL, in Santa Cruz, COTAS.

Long-Distance and International Calls

Long-distance and International calls can be made from ENTEL offices, found in all towns and cities. Collect and direct-dial calls can be made from ENTEL offices or by calling 35–67–00, which connects you with a Bolivian international operator who will ask for the city and number you wish to reach, then, up to 20 minutes later, call you back after the connection has been made. The least expensive way to make international calls is through an **MCI** operator, who can be reached by dialing 0800–2222. To reach **AT&T,** dial 0800–1112. To reach **Sprint,** dial 0800–3333.

Tipping

Taxi drivers do not expect tips unless you hire them for the day, in which case a $5–$10 tip is appropriate. Waiters expect a 10% gratuity. Airport porters expect $1 per trolley they handle.

When to Go

Bolivia has every climate and terrain imaginable, and temperatures are determined largely by altitude. The rainy season runs from November to March and is typified by heavy downpours that, particularly in the lowlands, make many roads virtually impassable. In the highlands, though it may rain only for an hour or two, the rainy season brings dark and cloudy skies that cast a gloom over the high-altitude landscape. If you plan to travel by bus or car, come in the dry season, between April and October. No matter when you come, there are still relatively few visitors and no real tourist season as such in Bolivia.

Climate

Climate varies significantly between the highlands and lowlands: In high-altitude La Paz and around Lake Titicaca, the weather can get very chilly, particularly at night, while in the lowland city of Santa Cruz and the central Chapare, the climate is tropical—in other words, hot and humid. Cochabamba, known as the "City of Eternal Spring," enjoys a Mediterranean climate year-round.

The following are the average monthly maximum and minimum temperatures for La Paz.

Jan.	64F	18C	May	66F	19C	Sept.	62F	17C
	43	6		35	2		38	3
Feb.	64F	18C	June	60F	16C	Oct.	65F	18C
	43	6		36	2		40	4
Mar.	64F	18C	July	61F	16C	Nov.	67F	20C
	43	6		34	1		42	6
Apr.	66F	19C	Aug.	62F	17C	Dec.	64F	18C
	40	4		35	2		43	6

5 Brazil

Brazil covers more than half of South America and has a raw energy and diversity to match its size. Although hedonistic Rio and tropical Salvador may grab the lion's share of attention, Brazil is also businesslike São Paulo and booming Manaus. The trackless jungle of the Amazon is one of the most spectacular wild corners of the earth, but human hands have also created splendors here, from the gilded Baroque churches of Minas Gerais to the planned city of Brasília.

Updated by
Rik Turner

NOWHERE IN SOUTH AMERICA is the catchphrase "land of contrasts" more appropriate than in Brazil. From one end to the other of this continent-size nation, you will go from tropical rain forest to urban jungle, from primitive native culture to modern high-rises, from distressing poverty to embarrassing wealth.

The two extremes of national life are summed up in the frantic hedonism of Rio de Janeiro and the primeval beauty of the Amazon rain forest. Beaches, sun, and fun are the obvious calling cards of Rio, still South America's premier beach resort, although suffering from growing pains. Even as crowded as it is with cars and people, Rio remains one of the world's most seductive cities, uniting the raw beauty of granite monoliths and jungle-covered mountains with white sand and blue water.

At the other extreme is the country's vast northern region, occupying 42% of the national landmass and dominated by the Amazon forest, home to 20% of the world's freshwater reserves and responsible for more than 30% of the earth's oxygen. Although gold prospectors and farmers have been making rapid inroads into the forest over the past decade, most of the destructive development in their wake has occurred on the southern and western edges, leaving the bulk of the forest relatively untouched. For travelers, the adventure remains—eased today by comfortable accommodations and pleasant river cruises. From Manaus and Belém, the two gateway cities to the region, Amazon tours spread out along the great river and its tributaries, reaching into the jungle itself.

With the largest continuous coastline of any nation in the Americas at 7,700 kilometers (4,600 miles), Brazil boasts a seemingly infinite variety of beaches. Styles range from the urban setting of Rio's Copacabana and Ipanema to isolated, unspoiled treasures along the northeastern coast. Brazil's Portuguese colonizers chose to concentrate on the coastal region, avoiding the inland areas with rare exceptions—a preference that has dictated national life to this day. In the 1960s, the government moved the capital from Rio to inland Brasília in an effort to overcome the "beach complex," but three decades later, the majority of the population remains concentrated along a narrow coastal strip.

To understand Brazil, it is necessary to always keep in mind the awesome size of this country, the fifth largest in the world. It is larger than the continental United States, four times the size of Mexico, and more than twice as large as India. Occupying most of the eastern half of South America, it borders on all of the other nations of the continent, with the exception of Chile and Ecuador. Its population of 146 million is equal to that of the continent's other nations combined, making Brazil truly the colossus of South America.

Brazil's population stands out as one of the most heterogeneous in the world, a melting pot of races and cultures that rivals that of the United States. Beginning with its Portuguese colonizers, Brazil has attracted waves of immigrants from throughout the globe, including the forced immigration of black slaves from Africa. The result is the ethnic mix of modern-day Brazil—Italian and German communities in the south, a prosperous Japanese colony in the state of São Paulo, a thriving Afro-Brazilian culture in Bahia and the northeast, the remnants of Indian cultures in the Amazon region. But what is most striking in Brazil's population are its colors, produced by centuries of intermarriage. Brazil-

Brazil

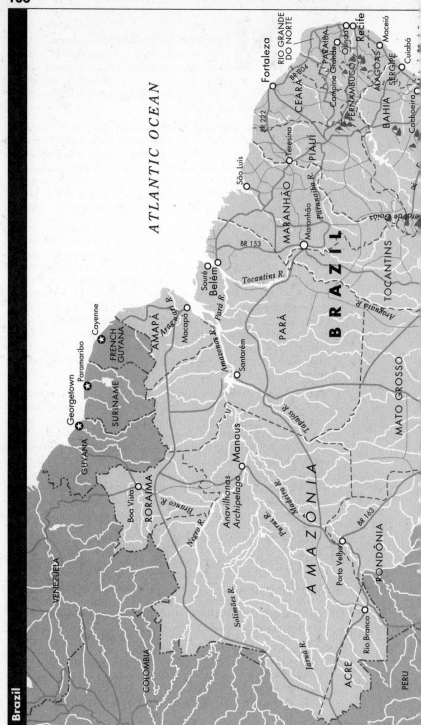

ATLANTIC OCEAN

Recife
Maceió
Cuiabá
Olinda
Campina Grande
RIO GRANDE DO NORTE
PARAÍBA
PERNAMBUCO
ALAGOAS
SERGIPE
BAHIA
Cachoeira
BR 304
Fortaleza
CEARÁ
BR 222
Teresina
PIAUÍ
Parnaíba R.
São Luís
Parnaíba R.
MARANHÃO
BR 153
Maranhão
B R A Z I L
erol de Goiás
Souré
Belém
Pará R.
Tocantins R.
TOCANTINS
PARÁ
Araguaia R.
Cayenne
FRENCH GUYANA
Paramaribo
Macapá
AMAPÁ
Araguari R.
Amazonas R.
Santarém
MATO GROSSO
Georgetown
SURINAME
Tapajós R.
GUYANA
Manaus
Anavilhanas Archipelago
A M A Z Ô N I A
VENEZUELA
Boa Vista
RORAIMA
Branco R.
Negro R.
Purus R.
Madeira R.
BR 163
Porto Velho
RONDÔNIA
COLOMBIA
Solimões R.
Juruá R.
Rio Branco
ACRE
PERU

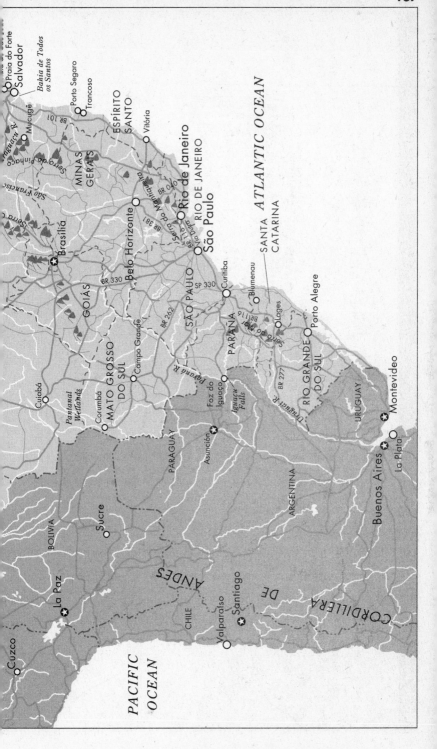

Praia do Forte
Salvador
*Bahia de Todos
os Santos*
Porto Seguro
Trancoso
Mucugê
BR 101
ESPÍRITO
SANTO
Vitória
Jequitinhonha R.
Serra do Espinhaço
MINAS
GERAIS
São Francisco R.
Rio de Janeiro
RIO DE JANEIRO
BR 040
Serra da Mantiqueira
São Paulo
BR 381
Brasília
Belo Horizonte
BR 116
Serra do Mar
ATLANTIC OCEAN
SANTA
CATARINA
BR 330
GOIÁS
SP 330
Curitiba
Blumenau
BR 262
SÃO PAULO
Campo Grande
Paraná R.
PARANÁ
Lages
Serra do Mar
BR 116
Porto Alegre
Cuiabá
*Pantanal
Wetlands*
Corumbá
MATO GROSSO
DO SUL
Foz do
Iguaçu
*Iguaçu
Falls*
RIO GRANDE
DO SUL
BR 277
Uruguai R.
URUGUAY
Montevideo
Asunción
PARAGUAY
ARGENTINA
Buenos Aires
La Plata
Sucre
BOLIVIA
La Paz
ANDES
Santiago
DE
Valparaíso
CHILE
CORDILLERA
Cuzco
*PACIFIC
OCEAN*

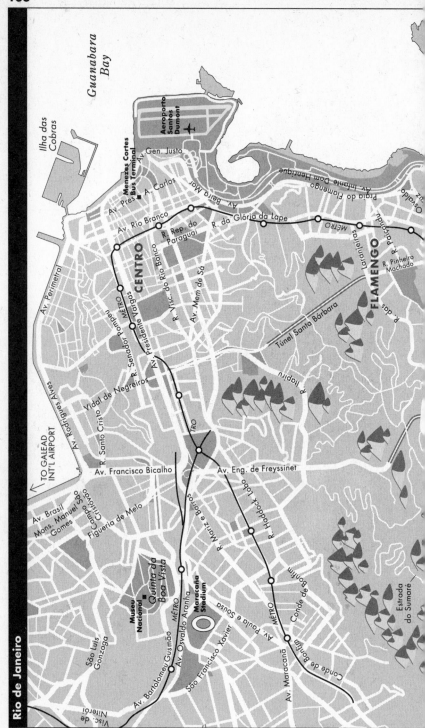

Guanabara
Bay

Ilha das
Cobras

Aeroporto
Santos
Dumont

Gen. Justo

Menezes Cortes
Bus Terminal

Av. Pres. A. Carlos

Av. Rio Branco

Av. Beira Mar

Av. Infante Dom Henrique

Praia do Flamengo

Oswaldo

R. da Glória da Lape

R. Rep. do
Paraguai

CENTRO

MÉTRO

Av. Visc. do Rio Branco

Av. Mem de Sá

MÉTRO

Laranjeiras

FLAMENGO

R. Pinheiro
Machado

R. Senador Pompeu

Av. Presidente Vargas

Túnel Santa Bárbara

R. Santo Cristo

Vidal de Negreiros

Av. Perimetral

Av. Rodrigues Alves

TO GALEAD
INT'L AIRPORT

Av. Brasil
Mons. Manuel São
Gomes

Campo São
Cristóvão

Figueira de Melo

Av. Francisco Bicalho

Av. Eng. de Freyssinet

TRO

R. Itapiru

R. Haddock Lobo

R. Mariz e Barros

Museu
Nacional

Quinta da
Boa Vista

Maracaña
Stadium

São Luís
Gonzaga

Av. Bartolomeu Gusmão

MÉTRO

Av. Osvaldo Aranha

São Francisco Xavier

Av. Paula e Sousa

MÉTRO

Conde de Bonfim

Estrada
do Sumaré

Visc. de
Niterói

Av. Maracanã

Conde de

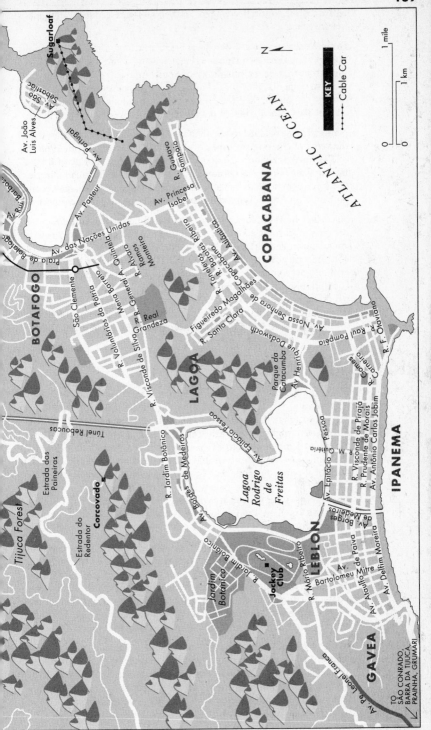

Sugarloaf

Av. João Luis Alves

Av. São Sebastião

Av. Rui Barbosa

Av. Pasteur

Av. Portugal

Praia de Botafogo

Av. das Nações Unidas

BOTAFOGO

São Clemente

R. Voluntários da Pátria

R. Mena Barreto

R. Visconde de Silva

R. General A. Quintela

R. Álvaro Ramos

R. Real Grandeza

Av. Pasteur

Av. Princesa Isabel

R. Gustavo Sampaio

R. Toneleiros

R. Barata Ribeiro

Av. Copacabana

Av. Atlântica

COPACABANA

ATLANTIC OCEAN

N

KEY

••••• Cable Car

0 _____ 1 mile
0 _____ 1 km

Figueiredo Magalhães

R. Santa Clara

Av. Nossa Senhora de Copacabana

Av. Henrique Dodsworth

Parque da Catacumba

Av. Raul Pompéia

Gomes Carneiro

R. F. Otaviano

LAGOA

Av. Epitácio Pessoa

Túnel Rebouças

Estrada das Paineiras

Estrada do Redentor

Corcovado

R. Jardim Botânico

Av. Borges de Medeiros

R. M. Guiteria

Av. Epitácio Pessoa

R. Visconde de Piraja

R. Prudente de Morais

Av. Antônio Carlos Jobim

IPANEMA

Lagoa Rodrigo de Freitas

Av. Borges de Medeiros

LEBLON

Tijuca Forest

Jardim Botânico

R. Jardim Botânico

Jockey Club

R. Mário Ribeiro

Av. Bartolomeu Mitre

Av. Ataulfo de Paiva

Av. Delfim Moreira

GÁVEA

Av. Pe. Leonel Franca

TO SÃO CONRADO, BARRA DA TIJUCA, PRAINHA, GRUMARI

ians are white, black, brown, red, and yellow—and seemingly all shades in between.

Despite their apparent differences, Brazil's various ethnic and cultural groups are united by a common language and a cultural heritage distinct from that of the remainder of South America. As Brazilians are quick to point out, they speak Portuguese, not Spanish, and unlike most of their neighbors, they were never a Spanish colony. This distinction, and the size of their country, is a source of immense pride to Brazilians.

National pride reached its zenith in the 1970s, when Brazil appeared on the verge of entering the ranks of the developed world. From 1968 to 1980, Brazil's economy expanded by an average annual rate of 8.9%. During these boom years, known as the period of the Brazilian miracle, the nation completed its industrialization and emerged as the largest economy in Latin America and the world's 10th largest economic power.

Since then, however, the country's march to superpower status has been derailed by chronic economic instability marked by stagnant growth and uncontrolled inflation. Although the military relinquished control of the federal government in 1985 after 21 years in power, the first two civilian governments were compromised by economic problems and corruption scandals, culminating in the impeachment of President Fernando Collor de Mello in 1992. Today, Brazil's political leaders are attempting to restore the public's faith in the nation's still young democracy while attacking the sizable economic and social problems left over from previous governments.

RIO DE JANEIRO

When you first arrive in Rio de Janeiro, think of the journey from airport to hotel as a brief spell of purgatory, minor dues to be paid for entry into what harried Americans will consider heaven. If you've traveled overnight, your tongue can be thick and your eyes bleary, and the initial sights that welcome you—mostly gray, nondescript industrial buildings—are unpromising. But by the time you reach Avenida Atlântica, flanked on one side by white beach and azure sea, and on the other by the pleasure-palace hotels that stand as testimony to the city's eternal lure, your heart will leap with expectation. Now you're truly in Rio, where the wicked angels and shimmering devils known as Cariocas dwell.

The word "carioca" comes from the country's earliest European history, when it meant "white man's house" and was used to describe a Portuguese trading station. Today the word defines more than birthplace, race, or residence: It represents an ethos of pride, sensuality, and a passionate dedication to life. Much of the Carioca verve comes from the sheer physical splendor of the city: seemingly endless beaches, sculpted promontories, and the ocean stretching to infinity.

While in Rio, prepare to have your senses engaged and your inhibitions untied. You'll be seduced by a host of images: the joyous bustle of vendors at Sunday's Hippie Fair; the tipsy babble of a sidewalk café as latecomers sip their last glass of wine under the stars; the blanket of luminescent lights beneath Sugarloaf. Borrow the Carioca spirit for your stay; you may find yourself reluctant to give it back.

Visitor Information

The Rio de Janeiro city tourism department, **Riotur** (021/297–7117), is at Rua da Assembléia 10, downtown, near Praça XV Square. In addition, Riotur has information booths at the Sugarloaf cable car station (Av. Pasteur 520, Urca, open 8–8), Marinha da Glória (Atêrro do Flamengo, Glória, ☎ 021/205–6447, open 8–5), and the Rodoviária Novo Rio (the main bus depot at Av. Francisco Bicalho 1, São Cristóvão, ☎ 021/291–5151, open 6 AM–midnight).

The Rio de Janeiro state tourism board, **Turisrio,** is also downtown at Rua da Assembléia 10, 7th and 8th Floors. For information call 021/531–1922 weekdays 9–6.

Brazil's national tourism board, **Embratur,** is headquartered in Rio near the Túnel Rebouças (inconveniently far from beach neighborhoods and hotels) at Rua Mariz e Barros 13, Praça da Bandeira, ☎ 021/273–2212.

Arriving and Departing

By Plane

AIRPORTS

All international flights, and most domestic flights, arrive and depart from the **Galeão International Airport.** The airport is approximately 45 minutes from the beach area where most of Rio's hotels are located and is served by most major airlines. The **Santos Dumont Airport,** just outside downtown Rio, serves the Rio–São Paulo air shuttle and a few air-taxi firms. Santos Dumont is 20 minutes from the beaches and walking distance from downtown.

FROM THE AIRPORTS INTO TOWN

Exiting Galeão can be confusing. Taxi drivers will assault you, but to be safe, stick to either the special airport taxis or to buses. Air-conditioned buses park curbside outside customs; for about $4 they will take you to the beaches where the majority of Rio's hotels are located. The trip takes about an hour, and drivers follow the beachfront drives, stopping at all hotels. If you are going to a hotel inland from the beach the driver will stop at the nearest corner (but remember, you'll have to handle your own luggage). Buses leave from the airport every half hour from 5:20 AM to 11 PM. Buses to the airport leave from the Hotel Nacional in São Conrado every half hour from 6:30 AM to 11 PM; pickup times at other hotels vary, so ask the concierge or at the front desk where you're staying.

Special airport taxis are operated by two firms, **Transcoopass** (☎ 021/270–4888) and **Cootramo** (☎ 021/270–1442), both of which have booths in the arrival area of the airport. Fares to all parts of Rio are posted at the booths, and you pay in advance in the range of $20–$30. Also trustworthy are the white radio taxis parked in the same area, which charge on the average 20% less than the special airport cabs. Avoid all yellow taxis.

If you come to Rio from São Paulo via the air shuttle, you land at Rio's downtown Santos Dumont Airport. Here the same transportation options exist as at the international airport. Again, stick to the special buses, the airport taxis, or the radio cabs, and avoid the yellow city cabs.

By Car

Before taking the wheel into your own hands, be aware that driving in Brazil is only for the brave. Travelers arriving by car from São Paulo and Brasília will enter Avenida Brasil, which connects directly with the downtown area's beachside drive, Avenida Infante Dom Henrique, known popularly as the Atêrro. This expressway runs along Rio's Guanabara Bay and passes through the Copacabana Tunnel. On the far side of the tunnel is the beach neighborhood of Copacabana, site of most of Rio's hotels. The beachside street here is called Avenida Atlântica, and it continues into the neighborhoods of Ipanema and Leblon along Avenidas Antônio Carlos Jobim (Ipanema) and Delfim Moreira (Leblon). For travelers arriving at Galeão Airport, take the Airport Expressway, known in Portuguese as the Linha Vermelha, to the beach area. This expressway takes you through two tunnels and into the Lagoa neighborhood. Exit on Avenida Epitácio Pessoa, the winding street that circles the lagoon. To reach Copacabana, exit again at Avenida Henrique Dodsworth (known popularly as the Corte do Cantagalo). For Ipanema and Leblon, there are several exits beginning with Rua Maria Quitéria.

Some distances: Rio–São Paulo, 429 kilometers (266 miles); Rio–Brasília, 1,150 kilometers (714 miles); Rio–Belém, 3,250 kilometers (2,018 miles).

By Bus

Regular, generally good bus service is available to and from Rio. Long-distance buses leave from the **Rodoviária Novo Rio station** (Avenida Francisco Bicalho 1, São Cristóvão, ☎ 021/291–5151), near the port area. Any local bus marked RODOVIÁRIA will take you to the bus station. Tickets can be purchased at the depot or, for some destinations, from a travel agent. Buses also leave from the more conveniently located **Menezes Cortes terminal** (Rua São José 35, Centro, ☎ 021/242–5414), near Praça XV downtown.

Getting Around Rio de Janeiro

Getting around in Rio can be a colossal headache, especially during the hot summer months. The infamous Carioca traffic jam, which can occur at any time of day, leaves exasperated motorists pounding their car horns in the midst of 90° heat. Parking is another major problem. Rio has few parking garages, which results in drivers leaving their vehicles anywhere they will fit, including sidewalks.

By Car

Driving in Rio is not recommended. The Carioca flair for driving is usually enough to leave most tourists shaking in their shoes. In addition, there are the traffic jams and the endless confusion of the city's streets, not all of which have street signs. If you wish to have an automobile without the headache of having to drive it, hire a car and driver. The firm **Transcoopass** (☎ 021/270–4888) will supply both for $70 for three hours.

By Bus

Local buses in Rio are inexpensive and will take you anywhere you want to go, but for tourists there are definite liabilities. The principal one is the threat of being robbed. You enter a Rio bus at the rear and exit at the front, paying in the middle when you pass through a turnstile. Thieves often pick your pocket or grab your wallet while you fumble to pay the man at the turnstile; then they either keep a low profile and stay behind you (exiting soon after you pass through the turnstile) or they push their way through the turnstile before you do, signal the bus to stop, and get off before you even sit down. To avoid being robbed, have your fare in your hand when you go to the turnstile and use coins (most fares are in the range of 40¢). Keep a low profile—don't wave your money around or shout to your friends in English, making yourself a target. Also, should you be victimized, never react. Many of these thieves are armed.

Most hotels recommend that their guests avoid city buses, with two exceptions: the safer *frescão* and *jardineira* bus lines. The air-conditioned frescão buses provide transportation between the beaches, downtown, and Rio's two airports. The standard fare is about $4. These vehicles, which look like highway buses, stop at regular bus stops but also may be flagged down wherever you see them. Also recommended are the jardineira buses, open-sided vehicles that follow the beach drive from Copacabana to São Conrado, and also take passengers to the Barra da Tijuca neighborhood. Fares are about 40¢, and white posts along the street mark jardineira bus stops. These buses, which look like old-fashioned streetcars, were introduced specifically for tourists and have become a major hit. They offer excellent views of the scenery and drive slowly along the beach avenue, a welcome relief to anyone who has ridden the regular city buses, whose drivers are considered the city's most reckless.

By Subway

Rio's metrô system operates Monday through Saturday 6 AM to 11 PM. Unfortunately, it is not yet finished. The part that is completed, though, offers the fastest and most comfortable transportation in the city. In the stations and in each car are maps showing the subway stops.

A single metrô ticket costs 37¢, a double costs 66¢. Combination metrô-bus tickets allow you to ride special buses to and from the Botafogo station: The M-21 runs to Leblon via Jardim Botânico and Jóquei, while the M-22 goes to Leblon by way of Túnel Velho, Copacabana, and Ipanema.

By Taxi

Taxis are plentiful in Rio and are the most convenient mode of transportation available to tourists. Dealing with cab drivers, however, is not always a pleasant experience. Few of them speak English, and most will attempt to increase the fare for tourists. Taxis are required to post a chart noting the current fares on the inside of the left rear window. The driver may try to tell you that the chart is out of date. Don't believe it. Also, beware of the meter itself. When the driver resets the meter he raises a flag, which will have either the number one or two on it (for digital meters the numbers one and two appear in red). Number two means 20% more but can only be used in certain circumstances: between 10 PM and 6 AM, on Sundays and holidays, during the month of December, in the neighborhoods of São Conrado and Barra da Tijuca, or when climbing steep hills. In most cases, it should be on number one. Cabbies also like to tell tourists that the number two means double the fare. Not true.

To avoid hassle, ask your hotel to call a radio cab or use one of the taxis that routinely serve hotel guests. Radio cabs charge 30% more but are honest, reliable, and usually air-conditioned. Other cabs working with the hotels will also charge more, normally a fixed fee explained before you leave.

Tour Operators

Boat Tours

Boat tours are available to nearby islands. The tropical-islands tours depart from the fishing village of Itacuruçá, about 90 minutes by car from Rio. Brazilian schooners, *saveiros*, are used, and the daylong trips include lunch and time for swimming at some of the beautiful deserted beaches on the 36 islands of Sepetiba Bay. The trips are offered by Rio-based operators; the two best are run by **Itacuruçá Turismo** (☎ 021/259–2599) and **Gray Line** (Rio Sheraton Hotel, Avenida Niemeyer 121, Vidigal, ☎ 021/274–7146). The cost is about $36 and includes ground transportation to Itacuruçá.

Bus Tours

Gray Line (☏ 021/274–7146) excels in transportation and in tour guides. Their guides are superb and will speak your language. The tours available include the following: Sugarloaf and the city (4 hours, $30); Corcovado and the Tijuca Forest (4 hours, $20); Rio by night (6 hours, $50); helicopter tour (30 minutes, $75); Petrópolis (6 hours, $20).

Personal and Special-Interest Tours

Personal English-speaking guides are not common in Rio. **Marlin Tours** (☏ 021/255–4433), which caters to English-speaking tourists, and **Rio Custom Tours** (☏ 021/274–3217) are the best options.

Peter O'Neill, a respected travel agent and longtime member of Rio's foreign community, organizes tailor-made tours for groups. He specializes in trips for nature lovers, and has arranged visits to Rio's Tijuca Forest, the Amazon, the mineral spas in Minas Gerais, and the historic towns of Paratí and Salvador. You can reach him through Marlin Tours.

Carlos Roquette (☏ 021/322–4872), a Brazilian history professor, conducts, in English and French, historical tours of Rio's neighborhoods; he also offers tours focusing on antiques shopping, eating out, and the city's nightlife. Similar services are provided by **Luis Lemos** (☏ 021/286–5614) for about $20 an hour.

Precautions

Better safe than sorry should be your motto while in Rio. Although not every tourist in Rio is a crime victim, petty theft is an always-present threat, so take precautions. If you are victimized, the police emergency number is 190. Multilingual operators should be on duty.

Most crimes involving tourists occur in public areas where there are large numbers of people, particularly on beaches, crowded sidewalks, and city buses. Pickpockets, usually children, work in groups. One will distract their victim while another grabs a wallet, bag, or camera. Be particularly wary of children who suddenly thrust themselves in front of you and ask for money or offer to shine your shoes. Another member of the gang may strike from behind, grab your valuables and disappear into the crowd. Do not pursue or attempt to stop one of these robbers—many of them are armed and can be dangerous. Leave valuables in your hotel room or safe. Don't be ostentatious in your dress, and don't wear expensive jewelry or watches. Keep cameras out of sight in bags.

Don't walk alone at night on the beach. Be aware of Rio's hillside shantytowns, which in some cases are close to hotels and tourist attractions; don't walk in front of them. If at all possible don't take city buses except for the air-conditioned frescão buses or the open-sided jardineiras. In particular avoid the Santa Teresa streetcar and the 553 bus around the Inter-Continental and Nacional hotels. Also, don't get involved with drugs. Penalties in Brazil for possession of drugs are severe, and dealers are the worst of the worst.

Exploring Rio de Janeiro

Nearly all of Rio's attractions are found in the affluent Zona Sul, the neighborhoods on or near the beach. It is here that hotels, restaurants, shops, and nightlife are concentrated.

During the day, Rio life focuses on the beaches, the most active of which remains Copacabana. To sense the Carioca spirit, spend a day on Copacabana Beach and the sidewalk cafés that populate its beachfront drive, Avenida Atlântica. Ipanema beach life is more restrained and cliquish, and thus harder for outsiders to penetrate; also, there are only three beachside bars in the entire length of Ipanema and its western extension, Leblon. The more distant southern beaches, beginning with São Conrado and extending past the Barra to Grumari, are rich in natural beauty and increasingly isolated.

Although Rio is more than 400 years old, it is in every respect a modern city. Most of the city's historic structures have fallen victim to the wrecking ball, leaving only a handful that can be visited by tourists. What's left is found in and around the downtown area in churches and other buildings scattered about the city center. Organized tours, both walking and in sightseeing buses, are highly recommended. The scattered nature of these sites, plus the sometimes undesirable nature of their surroundings, makes individual sightseeing problematic at best. If you are not on an organized tour, the best approach to visiting the historic sights is to take the subway.

Admission to most of Rio's museums, churches, and other sites is free. If there is a fee, it is usually 5¢ or 10¢ or less.

Historic Rio

A half block from the Catete subway station is the **Catete Palace,** the former official residence of Brazil's presidents and today the **Museu da República** (Museum of the Republic). This elegant granite-and-marble 19th-century building became the presidential residence after the 1889 military coup that overthrew the monarchy and installed the Republic of Brazil. All of Brazil's presidents lived in the palace until 1954, when then-president Getúlio Vargas committed suicide in his palace bedroom. Today its three floors house presidential memorabilia, including period furniture and paintings, from the proclamation of the Republic in 1889 to the end of Brazil's latest military regime in 1985. *Rua do Catete 153,* ☎ *021/225–4302.* ☛ *Entry fee.* ☉ *Tues.–Fri.*

One subway stop north of Catete is the Glória station and the nearby **Nossa Senhora da Glória do Outeiro** church. This elegant 1720 church, with its bell tower and carved ceiling, is a prime example of colonial Brazilian Baroque architecture. It stands sentinel-like atop an *outeiro* (a small hill) with an unobstructed view of the downtown area. Each year on August 15, the church's saint's day, Glória comes into her full glory, shining in the night sky with a crown of white lights. *Praça da Glória 135,* ☎ *021/225–0735.* ☉ *Weekday afternoons and weekend mornings.*

Directly across the freeway from the Glória church is the Glória Marina, and at the northern edge of the marina is the imposing **Monumento aos Pracinhas** (Monument to the Brazilian Dead of World War II), two soaring columns flanking the tomb of an unknown soldier. A small museum relates the country's war effort. ☛ *Free.* ☉ *Tues.–Sun. 10–5.*

Cinelândia is a downtown landmark marked by a conglomeration of movie theaters and a large open space that has become Rio's version of London's Hyde Park. Political debates and speeches are continuous here with rival groups sometimes coming to blows. On the outer edge of Cinelândia is the **Teatro Municipal** (Municipal Theater, Praça Floriano 210, ☎ 021/210–2463), a scaled-down version of the Paris Opera House. The theater is at the beginning of **Avenida Rio Branco,** the main thoroughfare of downtown. Modeled after the Champs-Elysées, Rio Branco was constructed in 1905 with 115 classical buildings. Time and progress, however, have eliminated all but 10 of those original structures, the most impressive of which is the theater and the downstairs **Café do Teatro,** one of the city's most unusual restaurants (*see* Dining,

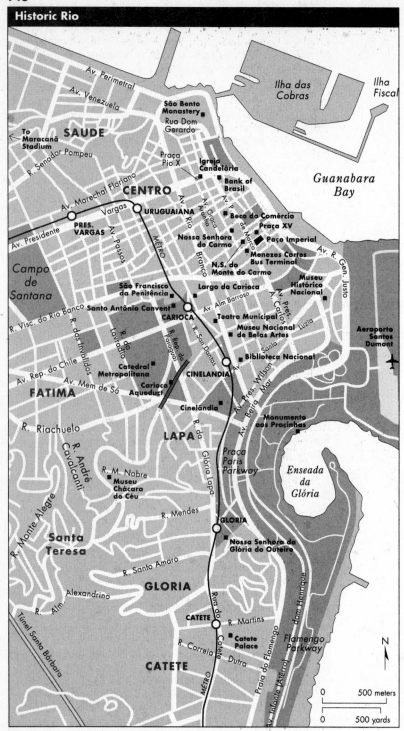

Av. Perimetral

Av. Venezuela

São Bento
Monastery
Rua Dom
Gerardo

To
Maracanã
Stadium

SAUDE

R. Senador Pompeu

Praça
Pio X

Igreja
Candelária

Bank of
Brasil

Beco do Comércio

Praça XV

Paço Imperial

CENTRO

Av. Marechal Floriano

URUGUAIANA

Vargas

PRES.
VARGAS

Av. Presidente

Nossa Senhora
do Carmo

Menezes Cortes
Bus Terminal

N.S. do
Monte do Carmo

Campo
de
Santana

São Francisco
da Penitência

Largo da Carioca

Museu
Histórico
Nacional

Santo Antônio Convent

R. Visc. do Rio Banco

CARIOCA

Av. Alm. Barroso

Teatro Municipal

Museu Nacional
de Belas Artes

Aeroporto
Santos
Dumont

R. dos Invalidos

Catedral
Metropolitana

Biblioteca Nacional

Av. Rep. do Chile

Av. Mem. de Sá

Carioca
Aqueduct

CINELANDIA

FATIMA

R. Riachuelo

Cinelândia

LAPA

Monumento
aos Pracinhas

R. André Cavalcanti

R. M. Nobre

Museu
Chácara
do Céu

Praça
Paris
Parkway

Enseada
da
Glória

R. Monte Alegre

Santa
Teresa

R. Mendes

GLORIA

Nossa Senhora da
Glória do Outeiro

R. Santo Amaro

GLORIA

Alexandrino

R. Alm.

Túnel Santa Bárbara

CATETE

R. Martins

Catete
Palace

Flamengo
Parkway

R. Correia Dutra

CATETE

Ilha das
Cobras

Ilha
Fiscal

Guanabara
Bay

N

| 0 | | 500 meters |
| 0 | | 500 yards |

below). Two blocks south of the theater is the Victorian **Biblioteca Nacional** (National Library, Av. Rio Branco 219, ☎ 021/220–3040).

Next to the library is the French neoclassical **Museu Nacional de Belas Artes** (Museum of Fine Arts). The museum houses works by Brazil's leading 19th- and 20th-century artists, including canvases by the country's best-known modernist, Cândido Portinari. *Av. Rio Branco 199,* ☎ *021/240–0160.* ☛ *Free.* ☉ *Tues.–Fri. and weekend afternoons.*

Five blocks down Avenida Rio Branco and one block west is the **Largo da Carioca,** a large public square. Atop a low hill overlooking the Largo is the **Santo Antônio Convent** (Largo da Carioca, ☎ 021/262–0129). The convent was completed in 1780, but parts of its construction date from 1608, making it the oldest surviving structure in Rio. Its Baroque interior contains priceless colonial art, including wood carvings and wall paintings. Next door, the **São Francisco da Penitência** church (Largo da Carioca 5, ☎ 021/262–0197; closed for renovations) dates from 1739 and is famed for its wood sculptures and the rich gold leaf that covers its interior.

Continuing down Avenida República do Chile are two other Rio landmarks, the **Catedral Metropolitana** (Av. Rep. do Chile 245, ☎ 021/240–2869) and the city's 18th-century aqueduct. The cathedral resembles an American space capsule from the early 1960s, the period when the building was designed and construction began. The **Carioca Aqueduct** (known to Brazilians as the **Arcos da Lapa**) is an imposing structure of 36 colossal stone arches built in 1723 to carry water from the hillside neighborhood of Santa Teresa to the downtown area. In 1896 the city transportation company took over the then-abandoned aqueduct and converted it to a viaduct, laying trolley tracks across its length. Since then, Rio's distinctive trolley cars (called *bondes* because they were financed by foreign bonds) have carried passengers between Santa Teresa and downtown. Rio's soaring crime rate has made this particular diversion virtually off-limits for tourists. The open-sided, slow-moving cars invite purse snatchers; take a taxi to Santa Teresa.

Santa Teresa, with its cobblestone streets, is Rio's most delightfully eccentric neighborhood. Gabled Victorian mansions are intermingled with alpine chalets and more prosaic dwellings, often hanging at unbelievable angles from the flower-encrusted hillside. Santa Teresa's special flavor has attracted artists and intellectuals to its eclectic slopes. Their hangout is the **Bar do Arnaudo** (Rua Almirante Alexandrino 316-B, ☎ 021/252–7246), a nondescript bar and restaurant whose main appeal is as a neighborhood listening post.

One of Santa Teresa's most popular attractions is the **Museu Chácara do Céu,** an outstanding modern-art collection left by one of Rio's greatest patrons of the arts, Raymundo de Castro Maya. Included are originals by such 20th-century masters as Picasso, Braque, Dalí, Degas, Matisse, Modigliani, and Monet. It also contains works by Brazil's leading modernists, such as Portinari, Volpi, and Di Cavalcanti. The grounds of the museum offer Santa Teresa's finest views of the bay and downtown with the aqueduct in the foreground. *Rua Murtinho Nobre 345,* ☎ *021/224–8981.* ☛ *Free.* ☉ *Tues.–Sun.*

At the beginning of Avenida Presidente Vargas, closest to the bay, stands the solid form of the **Igreja Candelária** (Candelária Church). The classic symmetry of Candelária's white dome and bell towers casts an unexpected air of sanity over the chaos of downtown traffic. Construction on the church began in 1775, and while it was formally dedicated by the emperor in 1811, work on the dome was not completed until 1877. *Praça Pio X,* ☎ *021/233–2324.* ☛ *Free.* ☉ *Week-days and weekend mornings.*

Facing the entrance of Candelária is the former headquarters of the **Bank of Brazil,** a six-story building constructed in 1888, which has been renovated and converted into a cultural center where art exhibits are held. *Rua Primeiro de Março 66,* ☎ *021/216–0237.*

Five blocks north along the bay is the **São Bento Monastery.** Its ornate interior with gold-leaf-covered wood carvings is extraordinarily rich and beautiful, and getting to it is half the fun. The monastery is on a slight elevation that can only be reached by an elevator from a store at Rua Dom Gerardo No. 40. The monastery and grounds are one flight up. The view of Guanabara Bay from here is one of the most peaceful in Rio. *Rua Dom Gerardo 68,* ☎ *021/291–7122.* ☛ *Free.* ☉ *Daily 7:30–11:30, 2:30–6:30.*

South of Candelária is **Praça XV,** the site of a number of historic buildings, including the former imperial palace. This square, known during colonial days as Largo do Paço, was the center of the imperial government that ruled Brazil for most of the 19th century. Its modern name is from the date of the declaration of the Republic of Brazil, November 15, 1889.

The dominating structure in the square is the **Paço Imperial,** one of Rio's few restored colonial buildings. This two-story structure is notable for its thick stone walls and entranceway, and its courtyard paved with huge stone slabs. The Paço was built in 1743, and for the next 60 years it was the headquarters for Brazil's viceroys, appointed by the Portuguese court in Lisbon. When King João VI arrived, he converted it into his royal palace. With Brazil's declaration of independence and the founding of the Empire of Brazil, the Paço became the imperial seat and was home to emperors Pedro I and II. After the monarchy was overthrown, the palace became Rio's central post office. Restoration work in the 1980s transformed it into a cultural center and concert hall. *Praça XV 48,* ☎ *021/232–8333.* ☛ *Free.* ☉ *Tues.–Sun.*

Facing Praça XV, across Avenida Primeiro de Março, are two 18th-century churches. The larger of the two, **Nossa Senhora do Carmo** (☎ 021/242–7766), was built in 1761 to serve as Rio's first metropolitan cathedral. Both of Brazil's emperors were crowned here. Next door is the smaller **Nossa Senhora do Monte do Carmo** (☎ 021/242–4828), circa 1770, noted for its Baroque facade.

Behind Avenida Primeiro de Março is a network of narrow streets and alleys highlighted by the **Beco do Comércio,** a pedestrian street flanked by restored 18th-century buildings and homes, now converted to offices. The best known is the **Telles de Menezes** building (Praça XV 34) whose famous arch, the **Arco dos Telles,** links this fascinating street with Praça XV. A popular stop here for lunch or drinks is the **English Bar** (Beco do Comércio 11, ☎ 021/221–6901), where you can partake of Old World cuisine in a New World setting.

A few blocks south of Praça XV is the **Museu Histórico Nacional** (National History Museum), an intriguing collection of colonial buildings. The museum's archive includes rare documents and colonial artifacts. Much of this, however, is shut away in sections undergoing "renovations," a euphemism for a dearth of funding to prepare and maintain exhibits. In 1988 the museum unveiled the first of what is planned to be a series of modular showcases dividing Brazil's history into distinct periods. The first section, called "Brazil as a Colony," is now on permanent display. *Praça Marechal Ancora,* ☎ *021/220–5829.* ☛ *Free.* ☯ *Tues.–Sun.*

Guanabara Bay

The vast 147-square-mile Guanabara Bay is where the first Portuguese explorers anchored their ships in 1500. Guanabara is an Indian name meaning "arm of the sea," and it was along the banks of this bay that the city of Rio de Janeiro de São Sebastião took shape and grew. It's said that the city received its full name from these early Portuguese explorers, who believed that they were on a river when they made their historic landfall—a landfall that occurred on St. Sebastian's day, in January. Virtually the only remaining evidence of the bay's historical importance are two small forts that guard its narrow entrance, Santa Cruz (17th century) and the São João (19th century).

Once the playground of Rio's wealthy, the bay-side beaches are no longer fit for bathing, and tourists should avoid them. The principal attraction of the bay is the view it offers of Rio, best seen on day cruises. Cruises also provide a chance to cool off from the oppressive summer heat of the city. Boat trips are available at both ends of the fare scale. Inexpensive ferries and only slightly more expensive hydrofoils toil and scoot across the bay at regular intervals. If you are traveling in a group, you may be interested in renting a saveiro with a crew for a day's outing. For information on boat rentals call the **Glória Marina** (☎ 021/205–6447 or 021/285–2247).

There are 84 islands in the bay, the largest of which is **Paqueta,** once the site of holiday homes for Rio's upper class. Today Paqueta's main attraction is its slow pace of life. Cars are banned from the island, so transport is by bicycle or horse-drawn buggy (a buggy trip around the island costs $3). You can make the trip in 90 minutes by ferry or in 15 minutes by hydrofoil. Both depart from the **Estação dos Barcos** at Praça XV, downtown. *Ferries (*☎ *021/231–0396) run daily 5:30 AM–11 PM. Tickets: $2 each way. Hydrofoils (*☎ *021/231–0339) operate weekdays 10–4, weekends 8–5. Tickets: $6 each way.*

For Cariocas, the only reason to visit **Niterói** across the bay is to admire the view of Rio. The best views are from Niterói's bay-side beaches, beginning with **Icarai** and continuing on to **Jurujuba.** Beyond Jurujuba on the coastal highway is the **Santa Cruz Fort** (☎ 021/711–0166 or 021/711–0462), the time-honored guardian of the entrance to Guanabara Bay. In its three centuries, the well-preserved fort has also served as a military prison. Its most famous prisoner was 19th-century Italian revolutionary Giuseppe Garibaldi, who learned the art of guerrilla warfare while fighting with a separatist movement in the south of Brazil. The galleries, dungeons, and courtyards of this sprawling fort are fascinating to explore, but access is difficult because the fort is still controlled by the military. Organized sightseeing tours are the best option.

Sugarloaf

With the cable car ride to the top and the unsurpassed views on all sides, the trip to Sugarloaf is not to be missed. This soaring 1,300-foot granite block standing at the mouth of Guanabara Bay was originally called *pau-nd-acugua* by the Indians, meaning "high, pointed peak." To the Portuguese the Indian phrase was similar to their *pão de açucar,* or "sugarloaf," and the rock's shape reminded them of the mold used to refine sugar into the conical form known as a sugarloaf. Italian-made bubble cars holding 75 passengers each move up the mountain in two stages, the first stopping at the **Morro da Urca,** a smaller mountain (705 feet high) in front of Sugarloaf, and the second continuing on to the summit, each stage taking three minutes.

The viewpoints on Urca Mountain and Sugarloaf offer unobstructed vistas of most of the city below. Sunsets are awe inspiring, and at night the lights below are an unforgettable sight. Urca Mountain is also home to an international restaurant called **Sugarloaf** (☎ 021/541–3737).

During high season, from January to March, long lines often form for the cable car trip. For the remainder of the year, the wait is seldom more than 30 minutes. *Cable cars: Praia Vermelho. Tickets: about $7.50. Run 8 AM–10 PM daily.*

Close to Sugarloaf in the Botafogo neighborhood is the **Casa Rui Barbosa,** the former home, now turned museum, of one of Brazil's most important 19th-century statesmen and politicians. This pink mansion houses memorabilia of Barbosa's life, including an extensive library, which is often consulted by scholars from Brazil and abroad. *Rua São Clemente 134,* ☎ *021/286–1297.* ☛ *Entry fee.* ☉ *Tues.–Sun.*

Corcovado

An eternal argument among Brazilians and tourists is which view is better, that from Sugarloaf or that from its "rival," Corcovado. Corcovado Mountain has two advantages: At 2,300 feet it is nearly twice as high as Sugarloaf and offers an excellent view of Sugarloaf itself. Whichever you favor, don't leave Rio without making the trip up to the top of Corcovado, where the powerful image of Christ with arms outstretched crowns the summit.

The sheer 1,000-foot granite face of Corcovado (the name means "hunchback" in Portuguese and refers to the mountain's shape) has always been a difficult undertaking for climbers. A railroad was constructed in 1885, later joined by a road. It was not until 1921, the centennial of Brazil's independence from Portugal, that someone had the idea of placing a statue on top. The project was handed over to a team of French artisans headed by sculptor Paul Landowski. The idea was to build a statue of Christ with his arms apart as if he were embracing the city. It took 10 years, but finally on October 12, 1931, the **Cristo Redentor** (Christ the Redeemer) statue was inaugurated. The figure stands 100 feet tall atop a 20-foot pedestal and weighs 700 tons. A 1981 cleanup of the statue and the installation of a powerful lighting system have enhanced the forceful presence of this unique image, visible night and day from most of the city's neighborhoods.

There are two ways of reaching the top of Corcovado, either by a cogwheel train or by the winding road that climbs the mountain. The train is the more interesting of the two, providing a close look at the thick mountain vegetation during the steep, 2.3-mile ascent, which lasts about 20 minutes. The train is comfortable and the view spectacular, but as at all tourist attractions, keep your eyes on your valuables when entering and leaving the cars. If you wish to go up by the road, you will need either to rent a car, hire a taxi, or go with a sightseeing tour. Of these, a tour is the safest choice, assuring you of the best price (around $25) and an English-speaking guide.

Should you go by train, there will probably be at least a 30-minute wait at the **Cosme Velho train station.** Trains leave every 30 minutes, daily 8:30–6. Late-afternoon trains are the most popular; on weekends be prepared for a long wait. *Train station: Rua Cosme Velho 513,* ☎ *021/ 285–2533. Nominal fee.*

Whether you arrive by train, bus, or car, there is a formidable climb up long, steep staircases to reach the summit, where the statue and viewpoints are located (there are no elevators or ramps for wheelchairs). Once you have reached the top, all of Rio stretches out before you. The best time to visit, lines permitting, is the late afternoon shortly before sunset.

The Beach Neighborhoods

Rio is home to 23 beaches, an almost continuous 45-mile stretch of white sand. You can't fit them all into one day, but try to leave time to explore the city's different beaches and their neighborhoods during your visit. (*Also see* Beaches, *below.*)

FLAMENGO AND BOTAFOGO

These two bay-side beaches were once the city's prime location for bathing. Pollution and population shifts have changed that, and today the two are no longer recommended for sunbathing or strolling.

During the years Rio served as Brazil's capital, Botafogo was the site of Rio's glittering embassy row. The embassies are gone now, transferred to Brasília, but the mansions that housed them remain scattered along Botafogo's tree-lined streets. The neighborhood also contains many of Rio's better small restaurants. Try the boisterous **Café Pacifico** (Rua Visconde de Silva 14), Rio's only Mexican restaurant. Among the neighborhood's more interesting streets, lined with the mansions built in Botafogo's heyday, are **Mariana, Sorocaba, Matriz,** and **Visconde de Silva.**

COPACABANA

Maddening traffic, unbearable noise, packed apartment blocks, and one of the world's most famous beaches—this is Copacabana, a Manhattan with bikinis. The privileged live on beachfront **Avenida Atlântica,** famed for its wide mosaic sidewalks, hotels, bars, and cafés. A walk along the classic 2-mile crescent curve of the beach is a must. On Copacabana you see the essence of Rio beach life, a cradle-to-grave lifestyle that begins with toddlers accompanying their parents to the water and ends with graying seniors walking hand in hand along the beach sidewalk. Two blocks from the beach and running parallel to it is **Avenida Nossa Senhora de Copacabana,** the neighborhood's main commercial street, whose sidewalks are always crowded with the colorful characters that give Copacabana its special flavor.

Stop in for a drink at one of Avenida Atlântica's outdoor cafés. The draft beer is cold and cheap, and the view of Copacabana beach life is unmatched. Try **Lucas** (Av. Atlântica 3744, ☎ 021/247–1606); **Rio-Jerez** (Av. Atlântica 3806, ☎ 021/267–5644); or **Terraço Atlântico** (Av. Atlântica 3432, ☎ 021/521–1296).

IPANEMA

Today, Ipanema, nearby **Leblon,** and the blocks surrounding the nearby **Rodrigo de Freitas Lagoon** comprise Rio's money belt. For a close-up look at the city's most posh apartment buildings, stroll down beachfront **Avenida Antônio Carlos Jobim** and its extension **Delfim Moreira,** or take a drive around the lagoon on **Avenida Epitácio Pessoa.** The tree-lined streets between Ipanema Beach and the lagoon are among the most peaceful and attractive of the city. For sophistication, stroll down the **Rua Garcia D'Avila,** where most of Ipanema's boutiques are clustered. Other "in" addresses of Rio's trendiest neighborhoods are **Praça da Paz, Rua Vinicius de Morais, Farme de Amoedo,** and **Anibal Mendonça.**

On the beachfront, the lone watering hole in Leblon is the **Caneco 70** (Av. Delfim Moreira 1026, ☎ 021/294–1180), a good stop for a beer or cooling orange juice. The upstairs tables have the best view of the beach action, while the downstairs tables have the closest view of Rio's promenading beautiful people.

Have you ever wondered if there really *was* a girl from Ipanema? The song was inspired by schoolgirl Heloisa Pinheiro, who caught the fancy of songwriter Tom Jobim and his pal lyricist Vinicius de Morais as she walked home from school past the two bohemians sitting in their favorite bar. The two then penned one of the century's top pop classics. That was in 1962, and today the bar has been renamed **Garota de Ipanema** and is one of Ipanema's most "in" addresses for drinks and conversation. *Rua Vinicius de Morais 49-A,* ☎ *021/267–8787.*

SÃO CONRADO AND THE SOUTHERN BEACHES

For a wonderful outing, take a cab from Ipanema to the fishing village of **Pedra da Guaratiba,** 45 minutes west. The drive starts out by climbing **Avenida Niemeyer** at the end of Ipanema where the imposing **Dois Irmãos Mountain** stands. The road hugs the rugged cliffs with spectacular sea views on the left before snaking down to sea level again in São Conrado, a natural amphitheater surrounded by forested mountains and the ocean.

São Conrado is a mostly residential neighborhood divided, starkly, between high- and low-income families. Wealthy Cariocas live on the valley floor in plush condominiums, while the high ground has been largely taken over by Rio's largest shantytown, **Rocinha,** which "houses" more than 80,000 people. Called *favelas,* these hillside slums are present throughout the South Zone of Rio and are the result of the city's chronic housing problem coupled with the unwillingness of many of the city's poor to live in distant working-class neighborhoods. Most of these makeshift dwellings have electricity, and in some cases there is running water, but there is no sewage system and the slums are subject to flooding and landslides when the summer rains come. The favelas are crime centers, and tourists should consider them off-limits.

São Conrado is also home to less disturbing sights. Hang gliders float overhead preparing to land on the beach—part of the São Conrado beach experience is the occasional shout of a hang glider making an unscheduled landing near your towel—while in the middle of the small valley is the exclusive Gávea Golf and Country Club. The far end of São Conrado is marked by the towering presence of **Gávea Mountain,** a huge flattop granite block. Next to it is **Pedra Bonita,** the mountain from which the gliders depart.

Continuing along the coast, the road becomes an elevated viaduct hanging half over the water, with views of the ocean on the left and sheer mountain cliffs on the right, where sumptuous homes hang at precarious angles. Emerging from a tunnel you enter **Barra da Tijuca,** Rio's suburbia. Condominium complexes are springing up along the beach, while inland the city's largest shopping centers and supermarkets have made the Barra their home. Drive along the beachfront avenue, **Sernambetiba.** At the end is a massive rock that marks the **Recreio dos Bandeirantes,** a small cove popular for bathing.

From here the road again climbs, following the undulating coastline to the small surfers' beach **Prainha,** and beyond that to the crown jewel of Rio's beaches, **Grumari.** From Grumari, a potholed road climbs almost straight up through the thick forest, finally emerging at the top of a hill overlooking the vast **Guaratiba flatlands.** Down the hill is the fishing village of **Pedra da Guaratiba,** site of some of Rio's finest, albeit rustic, seafood restaurants, including **Quatro Sete Meia** (*see* Dining, *below*).

Parks and Gardens

The **Flamengo Parkway,** known popularly as the **Atêrro,** or "Landfill," flanks the bay beginning in the Flamengo Beach neighborhood and ending in Glória. It was built through landfill and lovingly designed by Brazil's master landscape architect Roberto Burle Marx. Long paths used for jogging, walking, and bicycling wind through the park, and there are also public tennis and basketball courts and playgrounds for children. On weekends the freeway that runs alongside the park is closed to traffic, and the entire area becomes one enormous public park.

Quinta da Boa Vista is home to the **Jardim Zoológico,** Rio's zoo, and to the **Museu Nacional** (National Museum), Brazil's natural history museum. The landscaped parks, pools, and marble statues on the grounds are entrancing. The museum, a former imperial palace dating from 1803, features exhibits on Brazil's past and its flora, fauna, and minerals; the zoo presents animals from Brazil's wilds in recreations of their natural habitats. *Metro: San Cristóvão. Museum* ☎ *021/264–8262, zoo* ☎ *021/254–2024.* ☛ *Entry fee.* ☉ *Tues.–Sun.*

Surrounding Corcovado Mountain is a dense, beautiful tropical forest called the **Tijuca Forest.** The forest was once part of a private estate belonging to a Brazilian nobleman and is studded with exotic trees, thick jungle vines, and a delightful waterfall, the **Cascatinha de Taunay.** About 200 yards beyond the waterfall is the small but distinctive **Mayrink Chapel,** with an altar painting by Brazil's most famous 20th-century artist, Cândido Portinari. Many of Rio's most breathtaking viewpoints are along the 60 miles of narrow, winding roads that pass through this national park. The most famous are the **Dona Marta Viewpoint,** on the way up Corcovado; the **Emperor's Table,** supposedly the site where Brazil's last emperor, Pedro II, took his court for picnic lunches; and the **Chinese View,** farther down the road.

The **Jardim Botânico** (Botanical Garden) is one of Rio's most striking natural attractions. The 340-acre garden contains more than 5,000 species of tropical and subtropical plants and trees, including 900 varieties of palm tree. The garden was created by Portuguese King João VI in 1808, during his exile in Brazil. In 1842 the garden gained its most impressive adornment, the **Avenue of the Royal Palms,** an 800-yard-long double row of 134 soaring royal palms that graces the edge of the garden next to **Rua Jardim Botânico.** The garden makes for a marvelous afternoon stroll—especially on a hot day, when the temperature here is usually a good 10° cooler than it is on the street. *Rua Jardim Botânico 1008,* ☎ *021/294–6012.* ☛ *Free.* ☉ *Weekdays.*

The pleasant, statue-filled **Parque da Catacumba** is off the western edge of Avenida Epitácio Pessoa, the road that circles the Rodrigo de Freitas Lagoon. The lagoon is also surrounded by a jogging path and has several tennis courts.

Shopping

Rio de Janeiro is one of South America's premier shopping cities. Shoppers can stroll down city streets lined with fashionable boutiques, wander through modern, air-conditioned malls, or barter with the vendors at street markets and fairs.

Shopping Districts

Ipanema is the most fashionable shopping district in Rio, with a seemingly endless array of exclusive boutiques. Cool summer clothing in natural fibers, appropriate for the climate, is the top item here. Many of Ipanema's shops are concentrated in arcades, the majority of which are along Rua Visconde de Pirajá. Try **Forum de Ipanema** at No. 351 near the Praça da Paz square; **Quartier de Ipanema** at No. 414; the upscale **Galeria 444** at No. 444; and **Vitrine de Ipanema** at No. 580.

Although **Copacabana** has lost some of its former glamour, attractive shops still line Avenida Nossa Senhora de Copacabana and the side streets. Here you'll find a number of souvenir shops, bookstores, and branches of some of Rio's better stores, although for top-of-the-market jewelers, head for Avenida Atlântica.

Specialty Shops

ART

For collectors as well as tourists looking for distinctive gifts, Brazilian art has great appeal. The following galleries can be counted on to contain a worthwhile, representative sampling.

Bonino is the most traditional, best known, and most visited of Rio's art galleries. It has been around for some 30 years and is very active, with a high turnover of shows. *Rua Barata Ribeiro 578, Copacabana,* ☎ *021/294–7810.*

Contorno is a more eclectic gallery, but the art it displays is certainly Brazilian. *Shopping Center da Gávea, Rua Marquês de São Vicente 52, Gávea,* ☎ *021/274–3832.*

Galeria de Arte Jean-Jacques specializes in paintings by Brazilian primitive artists. *Rua Figueiredo Magalhães 219, Sobreloja 201, within walking distance of Sugarloaf cable car station,* ☎ *021/236–1397.*

The **Rio Design Center** contains several galleries, including Borghese, Beco da Arte, Montesanti, Museum, and Way. *Av. Ataulfo de Paiva 270, Leblon,* ☎ *021/274–7893.*

BEACHWEAR

Bum Bum, with three stores (Rua Vinicius de Morais 130, ☎ 021/521–1229; and in the Rio Sul and Barra Shopping malls), is the market leader in beachwear.

Cantão (Rio Sul, ☎ 021/542–4848) has a good selection of bikinis in various colors and styles.

CLOTHING

Aspargus (Rua Maria Quitéria 59B, Ipanema, ☎ 021/287–3994) is known for its classic and knit fashions for women.

Bee (Rua Visconde de Pirajá 483, Ipanema, ☎ 021/239–4941; Barra Shopping mall, ☎ 021/325–7181), offers original, casual designs for men, women, and children.

C&A (Av. Nossa Senhora de Copacabana 749, Copacabana, ☎ 021/325–0179), a giant department store, sells apparel for men, women, and children, including accessories, shoes, and a sporting line.

Dijon (Rua Garcia D'Avila 110, Ipanema, ☎ 021/297–8849; Rua Barata Ribeiro 496-A, ☎ 021/255–0239; and Av. Nossa Senhora da Copacabana 680, Copacabana, ☎ 021/235–0260) carries handsome, quality men's clothing.

Krishna (Rio Sul, ☎ 021/542–2443) specializes in classic, feminine dresses and separates, many in linen and silk.

Mesbla (Rua do Passeio 42/56, downtown, ☎ 021/534–7720), Rio's largest department-store chain, focuses on mostly casual fashions for men, women, and children. But it also has a wide selection of toys, records, cosmetics, musical instruments, and sporting goods.

Mr. Wonderful (Rua Visconde de Pirajá 503A, Ipanema, ☎ 021/274–6898) has trendy, but quality, men's fashions.

Richard's (Rua Maria Quitéria 95, Ipanema, ☎ 021/227–8649, and in Barra Shopping, ☎ 021/325–8158) specializes in classic and elegant casual clothes for men.

Spy & Great (Barra Shopping, ☎ 021/325–5294) is known for its casual women's clothing.

JEWELRY

Brazil is one of the world's largest producers of gold and the largest supplier of colored gemstones, with important deposits of aquamarines, amethysts, diamonds, emeralds, rubellites, topazes, and tourmalines. Besides H. Stern and Amsterdam-Sauer, other reliable jewelers are Roditi, Masson, M. Rosenmann, Maximino, Natan, Sidi, Moreno, Gregory and Sheehan, and Ernani G. Walter.

At the **H. Stern** world headquarters (Rua Visconde de Pirajá 490, Ipanema, ☎ 021/259–7442), you can see exhibits of rare gemstones and take a free tour demonstrating how raw stones are transformed into sparkling jewels.

Amsterdam-Sauer (☎ 021/259–8495) is the other top name in jewelry in Rio; its large outlet is next door to H. Stern.

LEATHER GOODS

Brazil's thriving leather industry means that prices are lower than what most visitors are used to at home. Shoes in larger sizes can be hard to find, but having a pair custom made is quite economical.

Birello (☎ 021/295–1898) carries both men's and women's dress shoes.

Bottega Veneta (Shopping Center da Gávea, ☎ 021/274–8248) has fine women's shoes and bags.

Dá no Pé (☎ 021/255–2538) has shoe prices you can't beat on stock ends of export models.

Formosinho (Avenida Nossa Senhora de Copacabana 582, ☎ 021/287–8998), sells men's and women's shoes at low, wholesale prices; three other stores are along Rua Visconde de Pirajá.

Frankie Amaury (Shopping Center da Gávea, ☎ 021/294–8895) is the first name in leather clothing in Rio.

Germon's (Rio Sul, ☎ 021/541–1995) carries high-quality, dressy women's shoes.

Mariazinha (Praça Nossa Senhora da Paztel, ☎ 021/541–6695), in the Forum de Ipanema arcade, carries fashionable footwear.

Nazaré (Shopping Center da Gávea, ☎ 021/294–9849) has bags and fine women's shoes.

Pucci (Rua Visconde de Pirajá 371, ☎ 021/247–7370), in Ipanema, sells a large variety of exclusive and casual women's shoes and bags.

Rotstein (Rua Visconde de Pirajá 371, ☎ 021/267–2412) carries one of Ipanema's best selections of bags and women's shoes.

Sagaró (Rio Sul, ☎ 021/287–3729) has an excellent selection of dressy women's footwear.

Santa Marinella (Rio Sul, ☎ 021/275–9346) specializes in handbags for women.

Soft Shoes (☎ 021/247–1828), at the Forum de Ipanema arcade on Praça Nossa Senhora da Paz, has a fashionable section of shoes.

Victor Hugo (Rio Sul, ☎ 021/275–3388) carries women's handbags.

Markets

Known in Rio as the **Hippie Fair,** the colorful handicraft street fair held every Sunday from 9 AM to 6 PM on Ipanema's Praça General Osório is popular among foreign visitors. Paintings and wood carvings, leather bags, sandals and clothing, batik fashions, jewelry, hand-printed T-shirts, rag dolls, knickknacks, and even furniture are on sale. Be aware, however, that finely crafted items are mixed in with basic junk. One noisy, popular booth sells samba percussion instruments.

In the evenings along the median of **Avenida Atlântica,** artisans spread out their wares. Here you will find paintings, carvings, handicrafts, sequined dresses, and hammocks from the northeast. On Saturday there is an **open-air antiques fair** during daylight hours on Praça Marechal Ancora, downtown near Praça XV. Here you can purchase china and silver sets, old watches, Oriental rugs, chandeliers, rare books, all types of paintings and art objects, and even old records. The fair moves out to the Casa Shopping Center in Barra da Tijuca on Sunday.

The **Feira Nordestino (Northeastern Fair),** held every Sunday morning at the Campo de São Cristóvão from 6 AM to 1 PM, is a social event for northeasterners living in Rio, who gather to hear their own distinctive music, eat regional foods, and buy tools and cheap clothing. The crowded, noisy market offers a glimpse of a side of Brazil not often seen by tourists.

Shopping Centers

Rio's shopping malls are modern and attractive, based on the American model. Hours are generally from 9 or 10 AM to 10 PM, Monday through Saturday.

Barra Shopping (Av. das Américas 4666, ☎ 021/431–2161) is the largest and most complete of Rio's malls. Although it is in Barra da Tijuca, shoppers from all over town head for this large complex.

Rio Sul (Av. Lauro Müller 116, ☎ 021/295–1332) in Botafogo has the city's best boutiques and traditional clothing stores represented in its more than 400 shops.

São Conrado Fashion Mall (Auto-Estrada Lagoa-Barra, ☎ 021/322–0300) sells many fashionable clothes; because the mall is within walking distance of the nearby hotels, it has unfortunately attracted the attention of petty thieves.

Shopping Center Cassino Atlântico (Av. Nossa Senhora de Copacabana, 1417, ☎ 021/247–8709), adjoining the Rio Palace hotel, has a selection of antiques stores, art galleries, and souvenir shops.

Shopping Center da Gávea (Rua Marquês de São Vicente 52, ☎ 021/274–9896) in Gávea has a mixture of fashionable clothing stores as well as many leather goods stores, and top art galleries, of which the best are Ana Maria Niemeyer, Beco da Arte, Borghese, Bronze, Paulo Klabin, Saramenha, and Toulouse.

Sports

Horse Racing

Races are held year-round at Rio's **Jockey Club** (Praça Santos Dumont 31, Gávea, ☎ 021/274–0055) beginning Monday and Thursday at 7 PM and weekends at noon. The big event of the year, the **Brazilian Derby,** is held the first Sunday of August.

Soccer

Rio, like the rest of Brazil, is soccer mad. The top three teams are **Flamengo** (currently the best and most popular), **Fluminense,** and **Vasco da Gama.** Play between any of these three is soccer at its finest.

Even if the game doesn't turn you on, the 180,000-seat **Maracanã Stadium** (Rua Prof. Eurico Rabelo, Gate 18, ☎ 021/264–9962) is impressive, and the crowd itself is half the spectacle. During the season the top game each week is played on Sunday starting at around 5 PM. The easiest way to see a game is through a guided tour. Admission to the grandstand is only about 50¢, but you may not enjoy rubbing shoulders with the huge crowds and sitting on a hard concrete slab; reserved seats are around $2 and far more comfortable.

Beaches

The following is a list of Rio's primary beaches. All are public and all, except Prainha and Grumari (the most westward), are served by buses and taxis. There are no public rest rooms or changing rooms, although you may use the rest rooms at nearby restaurants and cafés. Despite increased security (especially near the major hotels), theft is still a big problem on Rio's beaches. Don't bring any valuables with you, and try not to leave your towel or beach chair unattended.

Barra da Tijuca

Rio's longest beach is the 18-kilometer (11-mile) Barra da Tijuca. Water pollution is not a problem here, and for most of its length, the Barra beach escapes the crowds that flock to Copacabana, Ipanema, and São Conrado. The exception is the first 6 kilometers (4 miles) of the beach, where the construction of apartment buildings has been concentrated. The waves here tend to be strong, so swim with caution. Entrepreneurs have begun renting surfboards and Windsurfers on the beach.

Copacabana

You can swim here, although pollution levels are not always perfect and there is a strong undertow. Lifeguard stations are found once every kilometer along the beaches. At the Sugarloaf end of Copacabana is **Leme,** really no more than a natural extension of Copacabana. Here a rock formation extends into the water, forming a quiet cove less crowded than the rest of the beach and good for bathing. Avoid the opposite end near the Copacabana Fort, where an ever-present stench will extinguish forever your romantic notions of Copacabana.

Grumari

What preserves this spectacular beach, the most beautiful and unspoiled of Rio, is precisely the fact that it has not yet been "discovered." Located 30 minutes from Ipanema on a road that hugs the coastline, Grumari, like Prainha, can be reached only by car. Grumari doesn't have the amenities of the other beaches—only two unimpressive snack bars—but it does have a glorious beach and quiet cove backed by low hills covered with tropical vegetation.

Ipanema

The most chic of Rio's beaches, Ipanema and its extension, **Leblon** (the two are divided by a canal), are favored by affluent Cariocas. Pollution levels on Leblon Beach in recent years have reached the point where bathing has occasionally been prohibited. Swimmers should also be aware that there is an undertow here. **Arpoador,** the Copacabana end of Ipanema, is good for surfing, as is the end of Leblon, next to Dois Irmãos Mountain.

Prainha

The length of two football fields, this vest-pocket beach is a favorite for surfers who take charge of it on the weekends. The swimming here is good, but keep alert for flying surfboards!

Recreio dos Bandeirantes

Located at the far end of the Barra beach is the Recreio, a half-mile stretch of sand anchored by a huge rock, which creates a small protected cove. Its quiet, secluded nature makes it popular with Carioca families. The calm, pollution-free water, with no waves or currents, is good for bathing, but don't try to swim around the rock—it's bigger than it looks.

São Conrado

São Conrado lies in a natural amphitheater surrounded on three sides by forested mountains including the imposing Gávea Mountain. Unfortunately, São Conrado is also home to Rio's largest favela, and sewage from the slum runs freely into the ocean at the end closest to Ipanema. Bathers should stay on the far end, near the hang-glider landing point.

Dining

The most popular Brazilian restaurants among visitors are the *churrascarias,* or steak houses, especially those serving meat *rodízio*-style. Rodízio in effect means "going around," and waiters circulate nonstop carrying skewers laden with charbroiled hunks of beef, pork, and chicken, which is sliced at each table. For a set price you get all the meat and side dishes you can eat. The traditional weekend lunch, *feijoada* (black beans cooked with dried meats), is offered by most hotel restaurants every Saturday.

Lunch is typically a full meal, as dinner is usually eaten late. If you arrive for dinner at 7, you may be the only diner in the restaurant. Popular restaurants will still be seating customers after midnight on weekends; the normal closing hour is 2 AM. Many restaurants are closed on Monday. Dress in Rio's eateries is almost always casual; when there is an exception to this rule, it is noted in the reviews below.

Many restaurants offer a special fixed-price menu, but in all instances an à la carte menu is also available. Every restaurant includes a cover charge for the bread and other appetizers placed on the table, and a 10% service charge is added to the final bill. It is customary to leave an additional 5% tip. For price-category definitions, *see* Dining *in* Brazil Essentials, *below.*

Brazilian

\$\$\$ **Club Gourmet.** Owner and master chef José Hugo Celidonio has created a unique cuisine (as yet unnamed) that includes the basics of Brazilian cooking but employs European (especially French) techniques. Try the honey-glazed duck breast served with an almond and prune *farofa* (manioc flour toasted in butter or olive oil). A favorite dessert is the passion fruit crepes. Guests choose one item from each of four courses, paying a set price for the meal. ✕ *Rua General Polidoro 186, Botafogo,* ☎ *021/295–1097. Reservations required. No credit cards. No lunch Sat. or dinner Sun.*

\$ **Casa de Feijoada.** Tourists anxious to sample Brazil's national dish, feijoada, no longer need to wait until Saturday. Saturday comes seven days a week at this relaxed Ipanema restaurant, and feijoada is always on the menu. Diners may also choose from other traditional Brazilian meals. ✕ *Rua Prudente de Morais 10, Ipanema,* ☎ *021/267–4994. No reservations. AE, DC, MC, V.*

\$ **Moenda.** For Brazilian food, you can do no better than this time-hon★ ored eatery in the Hotel Trocadero. Here, while you enjoy the view of the Copacabana beachfront, waitresses in white turbans and long flowing dresses serve meals from Bahia. The emphasis is on seafood served with spicy sauces prepared with tomatoes, peanuts, and okra. Popular dishes are *vatapá* (farofa, oil, pepper, meat and fish), *moquecas* (fish or mussels simmered in oil and pepper), *camarão a baiana* (shrimp cooked in tomatoes and coconut oil, similar to shrimp Creole), and *caruru* (a shrimp-and-okra gumbo cooked in palm oil). ✕ *Av. Atlântica 2064 (Hotel Trocadero), Copacabana,* ☎ *021/257–1834. Reservations advised. AE, DC, MC, V.*

British

$ **The Lord Jim.** This is a Carioca version of a London pub, right down
★ to the red phone box at the front door. Steak-and-kidney pie, Yorkshire pudding, fish-and-chips, and appetizing curries await those who climb up a cast-iron spiral staircase to the pub's upper two floors. The cuisine is as determinedly British as the decor, although a few asides for Americans include barbecued ribs and T-bone steaks. A special attraction is the afternoon tea, served from 4 to 6:45. ✕ *Rua Paul Redfern 63, Ipanema,* ☎ *021/259–3047. Reservations required for afternoon tea. No credit cards.*

Cafés

$ **Barril 1800.** Snacks and cold draft beer are the most popular items at this beachside café, an Ipanema landmark and one of only three bars along the entire length of the Ipanema–Leblon beach. The menu ranges from hamburgers and french fries to seafood (try shrimp rolled inside balls of mozzarella) and steaks of prodigious size. ✕ *Av. Antônio Carlos Jobim 110, Ipanema,* ☎ *021/287–0085. No reservations. DC, MC.*

$ **Colombo.** At the turn of the century, this was Rio's preeminent café, home to afternoon teas for high-society senhoras and a center of political intrigue and gossip. Food here clearly loses out to ambience. The meals are adequate, although on the heavy side; portions will usually serve two. Stop in for a pastry and coffee and absorb the atmosphere and history. ✕ *Rua Gonçalves Dias 32, Centro,* ☎ *021/232–2300. No reservations. No credit cards. No dinner; closed Sun.*

Churrascarias

$$$ **Rodeio.** In this popular traditional churrascaria, dishes are served à la carte rather than as an all-you-can-eat meal. As you enter the restaurant you pass by the grill, where succulent meats sizzle over charcoal. The decor is slightly rustic, with wine bottles lining the wood-paneled walls. ✕ *Av. Alvorada 2150, Barra da Tijuca,* ☎ *021/325–6166. Reservations advised. AE, DC, MC.*

$$ **Baby Beef Paes Mendonça.** This traditional churrascaria occupies a top spot among the city's steak houses. Its huge rooms, seating a total of 600, are packed seven nights a week, an impressive testimony to the quality of the charbroiled beef, pork, and chicken served here. Portions are equally impressive. ✕ *Av. das Américas 1510, Barra da Tijuca,* ☎ *021/494–2187. Reservations advised. AE, DC, MC, V.*

$$ **Porcão.** The quintessential churrascaria, rodízio-style, Porcão (literally
★ "big pig") is everything that its name implies. Waiters fly up and down between rows of wooden tables wielding giant skewers laden with sizzling barbecued beef, pork, and chicken. This steak house captures the good humor of a slightly primitive form of eating. ✕ *Two locations: Rua Barão da Torre 218, Ipanema,* ☎ *021/521–0999; and Av. Armando Lombardi 591, Barra da Tijuca,* ☎ *021/493–3355. No reservations. AE, DC, MC, V.*

French

$$$$ **Le Pré Catelan.** Le Pré Catelan has a menu divided between the mod-
★ ern and the traditional, and is a must stop for aficionados of gracious French dining. A menu *confiance* (the chef's choice) will guide you

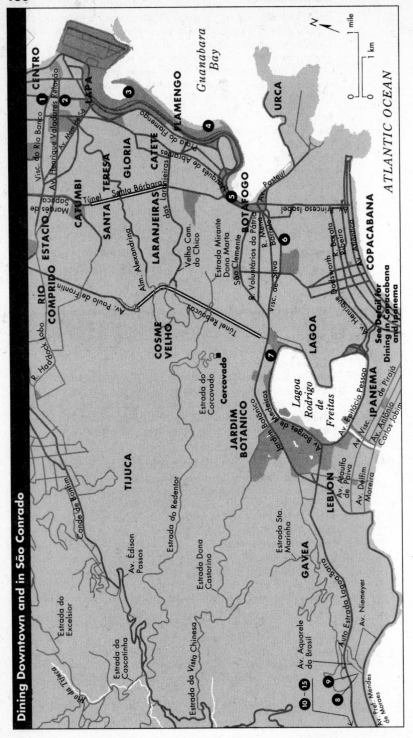

160

Dining Downtown and in São Conrado

CENTRO

LAPA

FLAMENGO

Guanabara Bay

URCA

ATLANTIC OCEAN

N

1 mile

1 km

Visc. do Rio Branco

Av. Henrique Valadares Retardão

Av. Mem de Sá

CATUMBI

SANTA TERESA

GLORIA

CATETE

LARANJEIRAS

Marquês de Abrantes

Praia do Flamengo

das Laranjeiras

Túnel Santa Bárbara

Mardas de Sapeçá

BOTAFOGO

Av. Pasteur

Av. Princesa Isabel

COPACABANA

RIO COMPRIDO

ESTACIO

Alm. Alexandrina

Velho Cam. do Chico

Estrada Mirante Dona Marta

São Clemente

R. Voluntários da Pátria

R. Mena Barreto

Av. Atlântica

R. Bogota

R. Ribeiro

Bolsworth

Av. Henrique

Av. Paulo de Frontin

R. Hadock Lobo

COSME VELHO

Túnel Rebouças

Corcovado

Estrada do Corcovado

JARDIM BOTANICO

LAGOA

Visc. de Silva

See Detail for Dining in Copacabana and Ipanema

IPANEMA

Av. Epitácio Pessoa

Av. Visc. de Pirajá

Av. Antônio Carlos Jobim

TIJUCA

Conde de Bonfim

Av. Édison Passos

Estrada do Redentor

Estrada Dona Castorina

Jardim Botânico

Av. Borges de Medeiros

Lagoa Rodrigo de Freitas

LEBLON

Av. Ataulfo de Paiva

Av. Delfim Moreira

Estrada do Excelsior

Estrada da Cascatinha

Estrada da Vista Chinesa

Estrada Sta. Marinha

GAVEA

Av. Aquarele do Brasil

Av. Niemeyer

Auto Estrada Lagoa

Copacabana

Rio do Tijuca

Av. Pref. Mendes de Moraes

1 2 3 4 5 6 7 8 9 10 – 15

Dining in Copacabana and Ipanema

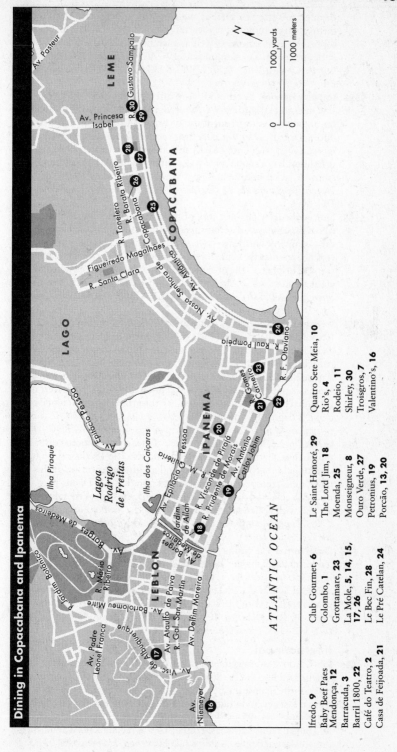

LEME

COPACABANA

IPANEMA

LEBLON

LAGO

Lagoa Rodrigo de Freitas

ATLANTIC OCEAN

Av. Pasteur

Av. Princesa Isabel

R. Gustavo Sampaio

R. Tonelero

R. Barata Ribeiro

Av. N. Sra. de Copacabana

Figueiredo Magalhães

R. Santa Clara

Av. Nosso Senhora de

Av. Atlântica

R. Raul Pompéia

R. F. Otaviano

R. Gomes Carneiro

Av. Antônio Carlos Jobim

R. Prudente de Morais

R. Visconde de Piratá

Av. Epitácio Pessoa

Av. Borges de Medeiros

Jardim de Alláh

Av. Henrique Dumont

Ilha Piraquê

Ilha dos Caiçaras

Av. Epitácio Pessoa

Borges de Medeiros

R. Mário Ribeiro

R. Jardim Botânico

Av. Padre Leonel Franca

Av. Bartolomeu Mitre

Av. Visc. de Albuquerque

Av. Ataulfo de Paiva

R. Gal. San Martin

Av. Delfim Moreira

Av. Niemeyer

N

0   1000 yards
0   1000 meters

Ifredo, **9**
Baby Beef Paes
Mendonça, **12**
Barracuda, **3**
Barril 1800, **22**
Café do Teatro, **2**
Casa de Feijoada, **21**

Club Gourmet, **6**
Colombo, **1**
Grottamare, **23**
La Mole, **5, 14, 15, 17, 26**
Le Bec Fin, **28**
Le Pré Catelan, **24**

Le Saint Honoré, **29**
The Lord Jim, **18**
Moenda, **25**
Monseigneur, **8**
Ouro Verde, **27**
Petronius, **19**
Porcão, **13, 20**

Quatro Sete Meia, **10**
Rio's, **4**
Rodeio, **11**
Shirley, **30**
Troisgros, **7**
Valentino's, **16**

through two starters, sherbet, main course, and dessert. Although the menu changes monthly, it is certain to contain succulent meat dishes topped by light sauces, as well as such house classics as quail stuffed with apricots in a cinnamon sauce. ✗ *Av. Atlântica 4240 (Rio Palace hotel), Copacabana,* ☎ *021/521–3232. Reservations advised. AE, DC, MC, V. No lunch.*

$$$$ Le Saint Honoré. Le Saint Honoré offers diners excellent French cui-
★ sine and an extraordinary view of Copacabana Beach. The accent is on originality, with frequent use of Brazilian fruits and herbs to produce such gems as *les pièces du boucher marquées sauces gamay et béarnaise,* a fillet with both béarnaise and red-wine sauces. For lunch the restaurant has a special prix-fixe menu, one of Rio's great dining bargains. A jacket and tie are advised. ✗ *Av. Atlântica 1020 (Meridien Hotel), Copacabana,* ☎ *021/275–9922. Reservations required. AE, DC, MC, V.*

$$$$ Monseigneur. A pleasing mix of modern and traditional French cui-
★ sine is the calling card of this superb restaurant. The decor here matches the elegance of the meals—two striking lighted columns of translucent crystal dominate the center of the restaurant. Try the rabbit terrine with tropical raspberry jelly or the sautéed slices of salmon on a bed of vegetables and sorrel. ✗ *Av. Prefeito Mendes de Morais 222 (Inter-Continental Hotel), São Conrado,* ☎ *021/322–2200. Reservations required. AE, DC, MC, V. No lunch.*

$$$$ Troisgros. Considered by many to be Rio's finest restaurant, Troisgros has suffered slightly from the exit of its founder, distinguished French chef Claude Troisgros. The menu is famed for nouvelle cuisine relying entirely on Brazilian ingredients. Every dish, whether a crab or lobster flan or chicken, fish, or duck prepared with exotic Brazilian herbs and sauces, is pure pleasure, always exceptionally light. The dessert menu is headed by passion fruit mousse, a Troisgros classic that alone could make a trip to Rio memorable. ✗ *Rua Custódio Serrão 62, Jardim Botânico,* ☎ *021/226–4542. Reservations required. AE, DC.*

$$$ Le Bec Fin. Le Bec Fin has maintained a menu of traditional dishes not unlike those with which it opened its doors in 1948. If you're a fan of traditional French cuisine, you'll find all of your favorites at this intimate, nine-table restaurant—steak au poivre, steak Diane, plus a few house specialties, like fresh fish stuffed with smoked salmon and topped with hollandaise sauce. ✗ *Av. Nossa Senhora de Copacabana 178, Copacabana,* ☎ *021/542–4097. Reservations required. AE, DC, MC, V. No lunch.*

$$$ Ouro Verde. The cuisine here is primarily French. The ample and var-
★ ied menu has remained largely unchanged for two decades. The decor is traditional and elegant, with soft, green hues, exquisite table settings, and Old World chandeliers. Recommended is the *filet Muscovite,* a chateaubriand with a caviar and vodka sauce that is set ablaze at your table. ✗ *Av. Atlântica 4240 (Ouro Verde Hotel), Copacabana,* ☎ *021/542–1887. Reservations advised. AE, DC, MC, V.*

International

$$$ Rio's. Above-average international cuisine and an unbeatable view of Guanabara Bay and the Sugarloaf are a winning combination here. Located flush against the bay, this is one of the few places in town with a great vista even on rainy days. At night, the view by starlight is one of the most romantic in Rio. The menu has both seafood and meat dishes, and famed flambé desserts. Formal dress is recommended at lunch, but unnecessary at dinner. ✗ *Parque do Flamengo, Flamengo,* ☎ *021/551–1131. Reservations required. AE, DC, MC, V.*

$$ **Café do Teatro.** The international food, while palatable, is an afterthought at this extraordinary restaurant, which has easily the most unusual decor in Rio. Taking center stage is the Assyrian motif, replete with columns and wall mosaics that look like something out of a Cecil B. DeMille epic. The bar resembles a sarcophagus, and two sphinxes flank the sunken dining area. Even if you have no interest in eating here, stop by for a drink and a look at this spectacle, in the basement of the Teatro Municipal. ✗ *Av. Rio Branco, Centro,* ☎ *021/262–4164. Reservations advised. AE, DC, MC, V. No dinner; closed weekends.*

Italian

$$$$ **Valentino's.** The emphasis here is on dishes mixing seafood and pasta
★ with succulent cheese sauces. Among the dishes that have earned enthusiastic praise are *nido di fettuccine con ostriche fresche al burro di salivia* (fettuccine with fresh oysters and sage butter) and lobster tail in a truffle cream sauce. Romantic piano music, subdued lighting, and Valentino's luxurious appointments all spell sophistication and a memorable dining experience. A jacket and tie are advised. ✗ *Av. Niemeyer 121 (Rio Sheraton Hotel), Vidigal,* ☎ *021/274–1122. Reservations required. AE, DC, MC, V. No lunch.*

$$$ **Alfredo.** In this Rio franchise of the famed Roman eatery, the main-
★ stay is the pasta that made the original Alfredo world famous—fettuccine Alfredo. An ample cold buffet of antipasto can start off your meal, which may include traditional pastas served with a variety of sauces. The restaurant is in the Inter-Continental Hotel with a view of the pool area. ✗ *Av. Prefeito Mendes de Morais 222 (Inter-Continental Hotel), São Conrado,* ☎ *021/322–2200. Reservations advised. AE, DC, MC, V.*

$ **La Mole.** This popular chain of low-cost Italian restaurants is a good
★ bet for that day when you are not interested in spending a great deal of money for lunch or dinner. Yet for low prices (less than $8 for a filet mignon), the food is surprisingly good and servings are hearty. Pasta is the main item, and lasagna, fettuccine, and gnocchi dishes are all tasty. ✗ *Five locations: Rua Dias Ferreira 147, Leblon,* ☎ *021/294–0699; Av. Nossa Senhora de Copacabana 552, Copacabana,* ☎ *021/235–3366; Praia de Botafogo 228, Botafogo,* ☎ *021/551–9499; Av. Armando Lombardi 175, Barra da Tijuca,* ☎ *021/399–0625; Barra Shopping, Barra da Tijuca,* ☎ *021/325–5271. No reservations. No credit cards.*

Seafood

$$$ **Petronius.** Although it overlooks the action-packed beachfront of
★ Ipanema, the mood is one of quiet elegance. For sheer indulgence order the imperial seafood platter—a meal for two with lobster, shrimp, shellfish, and three types of fish fillets, all grilled and served with herb butter. ✗ *Av. Antônio Carlos Jobim 460 (Caesar Park Hotel), Ipanema,* ☎ *021/287–3122. Reservations advised. AE, DC, MC, V. No lunch.*

$$$ **Quatro Sete Meia.** Internationally renowned, this restaurant is one hour
★ by car from Copacabana, at the end of a highway that offers stunning views of the coastline. Simplicity is the soul of the village and the restaurant, whose name in Portuguese is its street number. There are only 11 tables—five indoors and six in the garden at water's edge. The menu carries seven delicious options, divided between shrimp and fish dishes, from moquecas to grilled seafood to curries. ✗ *Rua Barros de Alarcão 476, Pedra da Guaratiba,* ☎ *021/395–2716. Reservations required. No credit cards. Closed Mon.–Tues.; no dinner Wed.–Thurs.*

$$ **Barracuda.** Hidden away inside the Glória Marina, this intimate seafood restaurant is an excellent choice for a quiet dinner away from the rush of Copacabana and Ipanema. At lunchtime it is usually crowded with downtown executives, probably eating the restaurant's famed grilled jumbo shrimp served on a skewer. ✗ *Marina da Glória, Glória,* ☎ *021/ 265–4641. Lunch reservations required. AE, DC, MC, V.*

$$ **Grottamare.** This seafood establishment is popular with tourists, who make up the majority of its customers during high season. The lobster, shrimp, and octopus are excellent, but the house specialty is fish baked with rosemary and other herbs, olive oil, tomatoes, and potatoes. Grottamare's own fishermen venture out daily to bring in the day's catch. ✗ *Rua Gomes Carneiro 132, Ipanema,* ☎ *021/287–1596. Reservations required after 9 PM. AE, DC, MC, V. No lunch weekdays.*

$$ **Shirley.** Spanish seafood casseroles and soups are the draw at this traditional Copacabana restaurant. Try the *zarzuela,* a seafood soup, or *cazuela,* a fish fillet served with white wine sauce. Don't be turned off by the simple decor—nothing more than a few paintings hung on wood-paneled walls: The food is terrific. There is usually a line, so step up to the bar while you wait. ✗ *Rua Gustavo Sampaio 610, Leme,* ☎ *021/275–1398. No reservations. No credit cards.*

Lodging

Rio's largest concentration of hotels is in Copacabana and Ipanema. Copacabana hotels are close to the action, but the noise level in Copacabana must be the highest in the world, and few hotels in the neighborhood escape it. Ipanema is better in this respect, but hotels in São Conrado and Barra da Tijuca are the quietest, although somewhat removed from the center of things. There are at present no downtown hotels worth recommending; those that exist are aging relics that most visitors will want to avoid. For business travelers there are a handful of hotels in the near-downtown neighborhoods of Glória and Flamengo, but most businesspeople will choose to travel to a beachfront hotel, several of which offer executive services.

Rio has many "motels," but be warned that they are not aimed at tourists. They attract couples looking for romance and privacy, and usually rent by the hour.

Room rates given in this guide are for high season (approximately December to April), although the days just prior to and during Carnival can see rates double, or even triple, according to what the traffic will bear. Remember that if you are traveling during Carnival or other peak periods it is important to make reservations as far in advance as possible.

Expect to pay a premium for a room with a view: Rooms overlooking either the beach or Rio's distinctive mountain backdrop will cost an average of $25 more per night. All hotels include breakfast in the room rate, although the quality ranges from a full buffet to a hard roll with butter. Rates are calculated at the official exchange rate. For price-category definitions, *see* Lodging *in* Brazil Essentials, *below.*

$$$$ **Caesar Park.** Since its opening in 1978, this beachfront hotel has established itself as a favorite of business travelers, celebrities, and heads
★ of state, who appreciate its impeccable service. The lobby reflects the hushed elegance of the hotel with its marble walls, thick carpeting, and rosewood furnishings topped by fresh flowers. The rooms are decorated in soft tones of rose, beige, blue, and gray. To assist business guests, the hotel provides secretarial services, as well as fax machines and microcomputers for use in guest rooms. The Caesar Park boasts Rio's finest Japanese restaurant, the Mariko, and an acclaimed Saturday feijoada. ⌂ *Av. Antônio Carlos Jobim 460, Ipanema, 22420,* ☎ *021/287–3122,* ⒻⒶⓍ *021/247–7975; U.S.* ☎ *800/228–3000. 184 rooms, 37 suites. 3 restau-*

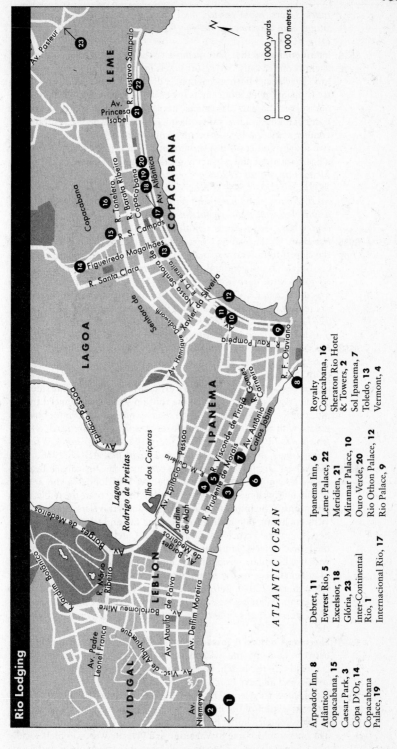

rants, 3 bars, room service, pool, massage, sauna, health club, baby-sitting, laundry service, concierge, business services, meeting rooms. AE, DC, MC, V.

$$$$ **Inter-Continental Rio.** This member of the respected Inter-Continental
★ chain is one of only two resort hotels in the city. It is in the São Conrado Beach neighborhood right next door to the Gávea Golf and Country Club. Standing alone on its own slice of beachfront, the hotel gives one a pleasant feeling of isolation. Attractions include one of Rio's smartest cocktail lounges, a lively discotheque, the Monseigneur restaurant (*see* Dining, *above*), a business center, convention facilities, and access to two nearby golf courses. Every room has an original tapestry done by a Brazilian artist and a balcony overlooking the ocean. ⊞ *Av. Prefeito Mendes de Morais 222, São Conrado, 22600, ☎ 021/322–2200, FAX 021/322–5500; U.S. ☎ 800/327–0200. 483 rooms and suites. 5 restaurants, 2 bars, piano bar, room service, 3 pools, sauna, 3 tennis courts, health club, dance club, nightclub, shops, business services, convention center, travel services, car rental. AE, DC, MC, V.*

$$$$ **Meridien.** Of the leading Copacabana hotels, the 37-story Meridien is
★ the closest to downtown, making it a favorite among business travelers. Service is efficient and the rooms are tastefully decorated in pastel tones with dark wood furniture. The hotel features a complete executive center, a VIP room for its business guests, and Le Saint Honoré restaurant (*see* Dining, *above*). ⊞ *Av. Atlântica 1020, Copacabana, 22012, ☎ 021/275–9922, FAX 021/541–6447. 443 rooms, 53 suites. 3 restaurants, bar, pool, sauna, business services. AE, DC, MC, V.*

$$$$ **Rio Othon Palace.** The flagship of the Othon chain, Brazil's largest hotel group, this 30-story hotel is a Copacabana landmark. The high point, literally, of the hotel is its rooftop pool-bar and sundeck, offering the best view of Copacabana's distinctive black-and-white sidewalk mosaic. At night the magic of the rooftop setting is enhanced by live music at the Skylab Bar. The hotel reserves one entire floor for business guests, with access to the executive services. ⊞ *Av. Atlântica 3264, Copacabana, 22070, ☎ 021/521–5522. 554 rooms, 30 suites. 2 restaurants, 2 bars, pool, sauna, health club, nightclub. AE, DC, MC, V.*

$$$$ **Rio Palace.** This is recognized as the best hotel on Copacabana Beach—
★ a case in studied elegance, from the marbled lobby to the antique Brazilian furnishings and colonial artwork that decorate the public areas and rooms. The Imperial Club offers business travelers a range of services, including bilingual secretaries and fax and telex machines. The hotel has a fine French restaurant, Le Pré Catelan (*see* Dining, *above*), the Horse's Neck piano bar, and the Palace Club, a private nightclub with live Brazilian music. The building's *H*-shape gives all rooms views of either the sea or the mountains—or both. ⊞ *Av. Atlântica 4240, Copacabana, 22070, ☎ 021/521–3232, FAX 021/247–3582. 418 rooms and suites. 2 restaurants, 2 bars, tea shop, 2 indoor pools, sauna, exercise room, shops, nightclub, business services, convention center. AE, DC, MC, V.*

$$$$ **Sheraton Rio Hotel & Towers.** Built so that it dominates Vidigal Beach,
★ between Ipanema and São Conrado, this is the only hotel in Rio that is directly on the beach. Guest rooms are decorated in soft, soothing colors, and all have beach views. Four floors (97 rooms) are reserved for business travelers, who receive special treatment. Called the Towers, this section of the hotel has its own check-in, a private lounge, a business center, a buffet breakfast, and around-the-clock butler service. The Sheraton is home to Valentino's, a favorite with Rio high society (*see* Dining, *above*), and to the lively beat of Brazilian music at the One Twenty One Lounge. ⊞ *Av. Niemeyer 121, Vidigal, 22450, ☎ 021/274–1122, FAX 021/239–5643; U.S. ☎ 800/325–3535. 561 rooms, 22*

suites. 4 restaurants, 2 bars, 3 pools, sauna, 3 tennis courts, exercise room, shops, nightclub, business services, meeting rooms, travel services, car rental. AE, DC, MC, V.

$$$ **Copacabana Palace.** At one time this hotel was better known than Copacabana Beach itself. Built in 1923, Copacabana Palace was the first luxury hotel in South America, and it held this singular distinction for the next 30 years. In 1990 the hotel was purchased by the British Orient-Express group and has now undergone the first stage in a $40 million renovation. The Copa, as it is known to Cariocas, retains the timeless grace marked by high ceilings, large public areas, and long, wide corridors. The hotel's ice-cream–cake facade has been restored, and the sizable, individually decorated guest rooms still have such luxurious touches as inlaid Brazilian agate and mahogany. Rio's largest hotel pool has been redesigned, and in-room computer facilities, an executive floor, and a rooftop tennis court have been added. 🖼 *Av. Atlântica 1702, Copacabana, 22021,* ☎ *021/255–7070,* 🖹 *021/235–7330; U.S.* ☎ *800/237–1236. 122 rooms, 102 suites. 2 restaurants, 2 bars, in-room modem lines, pool, sauna, tennis court, theater. AE, DC, MC, V.*

$$$ **Everest Rio.** Offering impeccable service and one of Rio's finest rooftop
★ views (a postcard shot of Corcovado and the lagoon), this hotel is a favorite with those who know the ins and outs of Rio's hotels. Back rooms offer sea views, and front rooms above the 14th floor look out on Corcovado and the lagoon. A block away from Ipanema Beach, the hotel is in the heart of the neighborhood's premier shopping and dining area. 🖼 *Rua Prudente de Morais 1117, Ipanema, 22420,* ☎ *021/ 287–8282,* 🖹 *021/521–3198. 159 rooms, 11 suites. Restaurant, bar, pool. AE, DC, MC, V.*

$$$ **Internacional Rio.** The red frame of Rio's newest beachfront hotel, the Internacional, has quickly become a Copacabana landmark. Swiss-owned and aimed at business travelers, the hotel offers a rarity for Copacabana—all rooms have balconies with sea views. 🖼 *Av. Atlântica 1500, Copacabana, 22010,* ☎ *021/295–2323. 117 rooms, 12 suites. Restaurant, 2 bars, pool, sauna, business services. AE, DC, MC, V.*

$$$ **Leme Palace.** Large rooms and a quiet beachfront location have made
★ Leme Palace the hotel of choice with frequent Rio visitors. Built in 1964, it was partially remodeled in 1987 and 1988 but still retains its original subdued, conservative air. 🖼 *Av. Atlântica 656, Leme, 22010,* ☎ *021/275–8080. 168 rooms, 26 suites. Restaurant, bar. AE, DC, MC, V.*

$$$ **Miramar Palace.** One of Rio's veteran hotels, the Miramar is a satis-
★ fying mix of the old and the new. The beachfront hotel's rooms are among the largest in Rio, and the public areas are dominated by classic touches, from the Carrara marble floor of the lobby to the spectacular glass chandeliers that light the two restaurants. The hotel's 16th-floor bar is notable for its unobstructed view of the entire sweep of Copacabana; after 6 PM live Brazilian music adds a special touch of romance to the view. 🖼 *Av. Atlântica 3668, Copacabana, 22010,* ☎ *021/287–6348. 133 rooms, 11 suites. Restaurant, 2 bars, coffee shop, tea shop. AE, DC, MC, V.*

$$ **Copa D'Or.** The newest and largest nonbeachfront hotel in Rio, the Copa D'Or has quickly established an excellent reputation for service and amenities. Businesspeople are well served, because of the hotel's location on a thoroughfare to downtown. For beachgoers, the hotel provides free transportation to Copacabana Beach, four blocks away. 🖼 *Rua Figueiredo Magalhães 875, Copacabana, 22060,* ☎ *021/235–6610,* 🖹 *021/235–6664. 195 rooms, 20 suites. Restaurant, 2 bars, pool, sauna, convention center. AE, DC, MC, V.*

$$ **Debret.** This former apartment building scores points for combining a beachfront location with moderate prices. The decor pays tribute to Brazil's colonial past: In the lobby there are baroque statues and prints depicting colonial scenes, and in the rooms there is dark, heavy wood furniture. The hotel has a loyal following among diplomats and businesspeople. ⌂ *Av. Atlântica 3564, Copacabana, 22041,* ☎ *021/521–3332,* ℻ *021/521–0899. 90 rooms, 10 suites. Restaurant, bar. AE, DC, MC, V.*

$$ **Excelsior.** More than any of its contemporaries, this 1950s hotel has retained its original style and flavor. The result is a Copacabana beachfront hotel with surprising touches of refinement, such as a marble lobby with leather-upholstered sofas, and closets paneled in rich jacarandá (Brazilian redwood). ⌂ *Av. Atlântica 1800, Copacabana, 22000,* ☎ *021/257–1950. 175 rooms, 13 suites. Restaurant, bar. AE, DC, MC, V.*

$$ **Glória.** The grande dame of Rio's hotels, this classic was built in 1922. Frequent renovations and convenience for business travelers (it's a five-minute taxi ride from downtown) have helped it retain its popularity. The hotel responded well to its transition to catering to businesspeople, and it provides ample convention and meeting facilities. Its major liability is its distance from the beaches, which forces guests to rely on taxis for transportation. ⌂ *Rua do Russel 632, Glória, 22210,* ☎ *021/205–7272,* ℻ *021/245-1660. 600 rooms, 33 suites. 4 restaurants, 3 bars, 2 pools, sauna, exercise room, meeting rooms. AE, DC, MC, V.*

$$ **Ouro Verde.** One of only a handful of Rio hotels aimed at the "dis-
★ criminating traveler," this has been a preferred lodging for visiting businesspeople for three decades. The hotel is famed for its efficient, personalized service. Tasteful Brazilian colonial decor and dark wood furniture are right in step with the hotel's emphasis on quality and graciousness. All front rooms face the beach, and back rooms from the 6th to 12th floors have a view of Corcovado. A lively alfresco bar plus one of Rio's finest restaurants, the namesake Ouro Verde (*see* Dining, *above*), attract patrons into the morning hours. ⌂ *Av. Atlântica 1456, Copacabana, 22041,* ☎ *021/542–1887,* ℻ *021/542–4597. 61 rooms, 5 suites. Restaurant, bar, library. AE, DC, MC, V.*

$$ **Royalty Copacabana.** Opened in 1987, this hotel's moderate price has made it one of the best bargains in Rio, and it has caught the attention of travelers who want to escape the hectic pace of the beachfront Avenida Atlântica. The hotel's location, three blocks from the beach, is convenient for beachgoers yet removed enough to satisfy those looking for peace and quiet—a rarity in Copacabana. The back rooms from the third floor up are the quietest, and all have mountain views; front rooms have sea views. ⌂ *Rua Tonelero 154, Copacabana, 22030,* ☎ *021/235–5699. 130 rooms, 13 suites. Restaurant, bar, pool, sauna, exercise room. AE, DC, MC, V.*

$$ **Sol Ipanema.** Another of Rio's crop of tall, slender hotels, this one anchors the eastern end of Ipanema Beach. Guest rooms have motel-style beige carpets and drapes and light-color furniture. The front rooms have panoramic views of the beachfront, while the back rooms, from the eighth floor up, have views of the lagoon and Corcovado. ⌂ *Av. Antônio Carlos Jobim 320, Ipanema, 22420,* ☎ *021/267–0095,* ℻ *021/247–1685. 66 rooms, 12 suites. Restaurant, bar, pool. AE, DC, MC, V.*

$ **Arpoador Inn.** This pocket-size hotel occupies one of Rio's more priv-
★ ileged locations, a stretch of beach known as Arpoador at the Copacabana end of Ipanema. Here surfers ride the waves and pedestrians rule the roadway—a traffic-free street that gives the hotel's guests direct access to the beach. Simple but comfortable, the hotel is reasonably priced considering the location. At sunset the view from the rocks

that mark the end of the beach is considered one of the most beautiful in Rio. Both sights are visible from the hotel's back rooms. Avoid the front rooms, which face a noisy street. ⊡ *Rua Francisco Otaviano 177, Ipanema, 22080, ☎ 021/247–6090. 46 rooms, 2 suites. Restaurant, bar. AE, DC, MC, V.*

$ Atlântico Copacabana. One of Rio's newer hotels, this was built in 1986. The large lobby with its marble walls, red carpeting, black leather furniture, and mirrors will look modern to some, pretentious to others. Guest rooms are slightly larger than the average for Rio hotels. The Atlântico is four blocks from the beach in a residential area. ⊡ *Rua Sigueira Campos 90, Copacabana, 20000, ☎ 021/257–1880. 97 rooms, 18 suites. Restaurant, 3 bars, pool, sauna. AE, DC, MC, V.*

$ ★ Ipanema Inn. This small, no-frills hotel was built for tourists who want to stay in Ipanema but have no interest in paying the high prices of a beachfront hotel. To that end, it has been a complete success. Just a half block from the beach, it is convenient not only for sun and water worshipers but also for those seeking to explore Ipanema's varied nightlife. ⊡ *Rua Maria Quitéria 27, Ipanema, 22410, ☎ 021/287–6092. 56 rooms. Bar. AE, DC, MC, V.*

$ Toledo. This unpretentious hotel goes the extra mile to make the best of what it has. There are few amenities, but service is friendly and efficient. Its main plus is its location on a quiet back street of Copacabana, one block from the beach. The back rooms from the 9th to the 14th floors have sea views. ⊡ *Rua Domingos Ferreira 71, Copacabana, 22050, ☎ 021/257–1990. 87 rooms, 8 suites. Bar, coffee shop. DC, MC, V.*

$ Vermont. Newly renovated, this hotel is clean, reliable, and just two blocks from the beach—a good choice for budget travelers. The hotel's only drawback is its location on the main street of Ipanema, which means incessant noise during the day, although it tends to quiet down at night after the shops close. ⊡ *Rua Visconde de Pirajá 254, Ipanema, 22410, ☎ 021/521–0057, FAX 021/267–7046. 54 rooms. Bar. AE, DC, MC, V.*

The Arts

There are many performing arts options in Rio, including theater, music, dance, and film. The city's main venue is the renovated **Teatro Municipal.** Dance, opera, and theater events are scheduled year-round, although the season officially runs from April to December. For current listings for this and other venues, pick up a copy of the bilingual *Este Mês no Rio/This Month in Rio* or similar publications available at most hotels. Also check the entertainment sections of the Portuguese-language newspapers *Jornal do Brasil* and *O Globo* (which are generally easy to understand even for those who don't speak Portuguese).

Tickets are inexpensive by international standards and may be purchased at the theater or concert hall box offices. Dress is informal but upscale at most cultural events in Rio, and the conservative upper crust still likes to dress up for the Teatro Municipal. No matter what you wear, though, remember not to wear valuable jewelry and to carry minimal cash.

Dance

In addition to the Teatro Municipal's own ballet company and the international ballet festival held in the theater during April and May, dance in Rio takes many other forms. Check local listings under *Dança* for information on these venues.

Casa Laura Alvim (Av. Antônio Carlos Jobim 176, Ipanema, ☎ 021/247–6946); **Teatro João Caetano** (Praça Tiradentes, Centro, ☎ 021/221–0305); **Teatro Municipal** (Praça Floriano, Centro, ☎ 021/294–4411); **Teatro Na-**

cional (Hotel Nacional, Av. Niemeyer 769, São Conrado, ☎ 021/322–1000); **Teatro Nelson Rodrigues** (Av. Chile 230, Centro, ☎ 021/262–0942); **Teatro Villa Lobos** (Av. Princesa Isabel 440, Leme, ☎ 021/275–6695).

Film

Original-language films are screened in small *cineclubes*, or state-of-the-art movie theaters. Cinelândia, the area where many of Rio's theaters are concentrated, is dangerous at night. The following are the most comfortable first-run movie theaters; check local listings under "Cinema" for current programs. All movies are shown in their original language with Portuguese subtitles.

Art Casa Shopping I, II, & III (Casa Shopping, Barra da Tijuca, ☎ 021/325–0746); **Art Fashion Mall I, II, III, & IV** (São Conrado Fashion Mall, São Conrado, ☎ 021/322–1258); **Barra I, II, & III** (Barra Shopping, Barra da Tijuca, ☎ 021/325–6487); **Condor Copacabana** (Rua Figueiredo Magalhães 286, Copacabana, ☎ 021/255–2610); **Largo do Machado I & II** (Largo do Machado 29, Flamengo, ☎ 021/205–6842); **Mêtro Boavista** (Rua do Passeio 62, Centro, ☎ 021/240–1291); **Ricamar** (Av. Nossa Senhora de Copacabana 360, Copacabana, ☎ 021/237–9932); **Roxy** (Av. Nossa Senhora de Copacabana 945, Copacabana, ☎ 021/236–6245); **São Luiz I & II** (Rua do Catete 307, Catete, ☎ 021/285–2296); **Veneza** (Av. Pasteur 184, Botafogo, ☎ 021/295–8349).

Music

While the proliferation of Brazilian popular music (known in Portuguese as *música popular brasileira,* or MPB) may overshadow música *erudita* (classical music) in the city, Rio has a number of orchestras. The Orquestra Sinfônica Brasileira and the Orquestra do Teatro Municipal are the most prominent. The following are the most patronized, most reliable places to hear classical music in Rio. For current information check the "Música Erudita" listings in local periodicals.

Sala Cecilia Meireles (Largo da Lapa 47, Centro, ☎ 021/232–4779) is a center for classical music.

Teatro Dulcina (Rua Alcindo Guanabara 17, Centro, ☎ 021/240–4879) is a small theater that features classical opera and concerts.

Teatro João Caetano (Praça Tiradentes, Centro, ☎ 021/221–0305) offers nightly variety shows featuring comedy, music, and dance.

Teatro Municipal (Praça Floriano, Centro, ☎ 021/210–2463) presents a variety of arts—ballet, concerts, and theater, to name a few.

Teatro Paço Imperial (Praça XV, Centro, ☎ 021/232–7762), like the Teatro Municipal, features a varied schedule of theatrical, musical, and dance performances.

Opera

The **Teatro Municipal's** (Praça Floriano, Centro, ☎ 021/210–2463) opera company puts on superb productions and often attracts international divas as guest artists. Also try the **Teatro João Caetano** (Praça Tiradentes, Centro, ☎ 021/221–0305), and check listings under *"Ópera"* in local periodicals.

Theater

The following theaters are among the most active in the city, but there are dozens more, so check local listings under *"Teatro"* for current programs.

Casa Laura Alvim (Av. Antônio Carlos Jobim 176, Ipanema, ☎ 021/247–6946); **Teatro Cândido Mendes** (Rua Joana Angélica 63, Ipanema, ☎ 021/267–7098); **Teatro Copacabana Palace** (Av. Nossa Senhora de Copacabana 327, Copacabana, ☎ 021/257–0881); **Teatro Ipanema** (Rua Prudente de Morais 824, Ipanema, ☎ 021/247–9794); **Teatro João Caetano** (Praça Tiradentes, Centro, ☎ 021/221–0305); **Teatro Municipal** (Praça Floriano, Centro, ☎ 021/210–2463); **Teatro Villa Lobos** (Av. Princesa Isabel 440, Leme, ☎ 021/275–6695).

Nightlife

Apart from Rio's beaches, the city's biggest year-round draw for natives and visitors alike is its nightlife. Options range from samba shows shamelessly aimed at the tourist, to sultry dance halls called *forrós*, which originated in Brazil's northeast during World War II when American GIs stationed at refueling stops opened up their clubs "for all." Musically, you'll find nightspots featuring the sounds of big band, rock, and everything in between. One of the happiest mediums is MPB, the generic term for current Brazilian sounds ranging from pop to jazz. Nightlife establishments often keep unusual schedules. Always call ahead to make sure they are open.

Bars and Lounges

These establishments often charge a nominal cover in the form of either a drink minimum or music charge, and, as opposed to nightclubs, usually admit single patrons with no fuss. Don't overlook the hotel bars and lounges, which are often as popular with locals as they are with hotel guests.

Banana Café (Rua Barão da Torre 368, Ipanema, ☎ 021/521–1047) is one of the city's most popular bar-restaurants. Owner Ricardo Amaral is an international socialite and draws a chic crowd to this laid-back nightspot.

Biblo's Bar (Av. Epitácio Pessoa 1484, Lagoa, ☎ 021/521–2645), with its magnificent nighttime views of Corcovado, houses a discotheque and is attached to the French restaurant Rive Gauche. The biggest draw is its piano bar, which offers a program of jazz and MPB in an intimate candlelit setting.

Chico's Bar (Av. Epitácio Pessoa 1560, Lagoa, ☎ 021/287–3514) is owned by Rio nightspot entrepreneur Chico Recarey. Both the bar and the adjoining restaurant, Castelo da Lagoa, are big with affluent Cariocas, both singles and couples.

Jazzmania (Av. Rainha Elizabeth 769, Ipanema, ☎ 021/227–2447) is Rio's number one jazz club and the only place in town that offers jazz exclusively.

La Tour (Rua Santa Luzia 651, Centro, ☎ 021/240–5493), a revolving eatery set atop a downtown office building, offers a grand view of the downtown historic area, the bay, and virtually all of the city's leading landmarks. The food is always bad, so step up to the bar and sip a drink while the restaurant revolves.

Le Rond-Point (Av. Atlântica 1020, Copacabana, ☎ 021/275–9922), with its red leather banquettes just off the lobby of the Meridien hotel, gets a mixed crowd to listen to *le jazz hot*, Brazilian-style.

Mistura Fina (Av. Borges de Medeiros 3207, Lagoa, ☎ 021/266–5844), also houses a restaurant and an outdoor café. A guitarist or pianist is featured until 10 PM, when a livelier band takes over until 2 AM.

One Twenty One Lounge (Sheraton Rio Hotel, Av. Niemeyer 121, Vidigal, ☎ 021/274–1122) is among the most pleasant of the city's hotel lounges.

People (Av. Bartolomeu Mitre 370, Leblon, ☎ 021/294–0547) has a musical-instrument decor and is the most popular place in the city for listening to MPB and meeting people.

Skylab Bar (Av. Atlântica 3264, Copacabana, ☎ 021/521–5522), true to its name, occupies the top floor of the Rio Othon Palace hotel, with views of the ocean and hills on either side.

Cabaret

Variety is the byword of the cabaret scene in Rio, which provides visual and sensual stimulation to suit all tastes.

Frank's (Av. Princesa Isabel 185, Copacabana, ☎ 021/275–9398) is one of the most established of many dark little clubs devoted to burlesque, striptease, and sex shows along Avenida Princesa Isabel near the Meridien hotel.

Oba-Oba (Rua Humaitá 110, Botafogo, ☎ 021/286–9848) is a private-house-turned-club where Oswaldo Sargentelli, known locally as Mr. Samba, emcees one of Rio's two remaining grand-scale samba shows.

Plataforma I (Rua Adalberto Ferreira 32, Leblon, ☎ 021/274–4022) holds the older and more spectacular of Rio's two samba shows, with elaborate costumes and a greater variety of Brazilian musical numbers. Each night's performance begins at 10.

Choperias

Besides discos, plain but pleasant bars called *choperias* attract an unattached crowd. An ice-cold *chope,* or Brazilian draft beer, is the order of the day.

Alberico's (Av. Antônio Carlos Jobim 236, Ipanema, ☎ 021/267–3793) is packed on weekends, especially the tables facing Ipanema Beach.

Barril 1800 (Av. Antônio Carlos Jobim 110, Ipanema, ☎ 021/287–0085) is an unpretentious and popular beachfront place to meet before an evening at the nearby club Jazzmania (*see above*).

Garota de Ipanema (Rua Vinicius de Morais 39, Ipanema, ☎ 021/267–5757) is where Vinicius de Morais, author of "The Girl from Ipanema," used to sit and longingly watch the song's heroine head for the beach.

The Lord Jim Pub (Rua Paul Redfern 63, Ipanema, ☎ 021/259–3047), attracts a lively crowd of English speakers. Chope is served in beer mugs and if drinks turn to dinner there is a full menu of pub-style specialties (*see* Dining, *above*).

Lucas (Av. Atlântica 3744, Copacabana, ☎ 021/247–1606), ranks as Copacabana's most popular beachfront gathering spot. Draft beer has been served here for more than 40 years.

Dance Clubs

In addition to discos, there are a number of places in Rio that offer Brazilian rhythms for dancing to live music. Samba clubs specialize in the beat of the country's best-known dance. *Gafieiras* are old-fashioned ballroom dance halls, usually patronized by an equally old-fashioned clientele. *Forrós* are much funkier and feature the rhythms of Brazil's northeast.

Asa Branca (Av. Mem de Sá 17, Lapa, ☎ 021/252–4428) is Chico Recarey's large and glamorous nightclub, where the decor combines modern, geometric designs with old-fashioned fixtures. Big bands and popular Brazilian musicians keep the crowd moving until the wee hours.

Sôbre as Ondas (Av. Atlântica 3432, Copacabana, ☎ 021/521–1296) overlooks Copacabana Beach. Here you can dance to live music, usually MPB or samba, and dine at the Terraço Atlântico restaurant downstairs.

Vogue (Rua Cupertino Durão 173, Leblon, ☎ 021/274–4145), in addition to dancing, has a busy bar-restaurant-karaoke club that keeps its chic young patrons busy.

Danceterias

Rio's *danceterias* (discos) offer flashing lights, loud music, and exclusive memberships. Staying at one of Rio's better hotels guarantees admission to the most selective places; ask the concierge to call ahead for you. Otherwise, try to arrange to go with a member.

Biblo's Bar (Av. Epitácio Pessoa 1484, Lagoa, ☎ 021/521–2645) is one of Rio's most active places for live music and disco dancing; it is especially popular with singles.

Caligula (Rua Prudente de Morais 129, Ipanema, ☎ 021/287–1369) is decorated in the glamorous decadence of the late Roman Empire, with both live and taped music providing the entertainment.

Help (Av. Atlântica 3432, Copacabana, ☎ 021/521–1296) is Rio's largest and noisiest disco. It attracts a huge, mixed crowd of tourists, single men, and single women, many looking to offer some "help" of their own, for a price.

Hippopotamus (Rua Barão da Torre 354, Ipanema, ☎ 021/247–0351) is the most exclusive and expensive of Rio's discos, requiring membership (available to guests of the better hotels) and a stiff cover (about $30 per person) to get in. The disco is often closed for private parties, so be sure to call.

Zoom (Largo de São Conrado 20, São Conrado, ☎ 021/322–4179) is a glitzy mecca for reggae, rock, and café music. Its elaborate light show, six bars, and casual atmosphere attract a young crowd, usually couples.

Nightclubs

The following nightclubs serve food, but because their main attraction is usually music, it's best to eat elsewhere earlier if you're looking for serious dining. Remember that many clubs have a policy of admitting couples only; singles should have their hotel check to make sure they'll be admitted.

Canecão (Av. Venceslau Braz 215, Botafogo, ☎ 021/295–3044) is the city's largest nightclub. It can seat nearly 2,500 people at the tiny tables in its cavernous space, making it the logical place for some of the biggest names on the international music scene to hold their concerts.

Circo Voador (Arcos da Lapa, Lapa, ☎ 021/220–1496) presents top MPB artists in a circus-tent setting, and after the concert you can stay and dance. There is limited seating, so be sure to reserve in advance or you may wind up sitting on the dance floor.

Scala (Av. Afrânio de Melo Franco 292, Leblon, ☎ 021/239–4448) is Chico Recarey's flagship nightclub, whose "gringo show" offerings include well-known Brazilian musicians.

SÃO PAULO

Crowded buses grind through the streets spouting black smoke, endless stands of skyscrapers block the horizon, and the din of traffic and construction deafens the ear. But native Paulistanos love this megalopolis of 17 million, though during Brazil's postwar industrialization it grew too fast for urban planners to keep up with. São Paulo now sprawls across 7,951 square kilometers (3,070 square miles), 1,502 square kilometers (580 square miles) of which make up the city proper.

The draw is the dynamism of the immigrants who have been coming since the start of the century, from Italy, Portugal, Spain, Germany, and Japan, as well as from other regions of Brazil, to put their talents and energy to work here. That energy has turned São Paulo from a sleepy Jesuit mission post into the financial hub of Latin America. The city is now home to the developing world's largest industrial park and the capital of an eponymous Brazilian state that accounts for half of the country's $450 billion GNP. And as crime and pollution have increasingly beset Rio de Janeiro, São Paulo has aggressively moved in to take over that city's role as Brazil's cultural center.

Ultimately, the immigrants, their offspring, their varied lifestyles, and the overall fast-pace urban culture they have generated are the focus of the visitor's interest. Even as the smog reddens the eyes, there is much to learn here about a city committed to making dreams come true.

Visitor Information

The **Secretaria de Esportes e Turismo do Estado de São Paulo,** or SEST (Praça Antônio Prado 9, ☎ 011/239–5822; open weekdays 9–5:30) provides maps and information about attractions in the city and excursions in the rest of the state of São Paulo. SEST also has booths at Guarulhos–Cumbica airport, in the arrivals terminal (☎ 011/945–2380; open daily 9 AM–10 PM).

The city-operated **Anhembi Turismo e Eventos da Cidade de São Paulo** (Anhembi Convention Center, Avenida Olavo Fontoura, 1209, ☎ 011/267–0702; open weekdays 9–6) has four branch locations, all open daily 9–6: on the Praça da República, facing Rua Sete de Abril (☎ 011/231–2922); Avenida São Luís in front of the Praça Dom José Gaspar (☎ 011/257–3422); Avenida Paulista, across from the Museu de Arte de São Paulo (☎ 011/231–2922); and in front of the Shopping Iguatemi, on Avenida Brigadeiro Faria Lima (☎ 011/211–1277). New branches were expected to be open by press time (winter 1995).

The **Delegacia de Turismo,** or tourist police, has offices at Avenida São Luís 115 (☎ 011/254–3561 or 011/214–0209) and Rua XV de Novembro 347, mezzanine (☎ 011/37–8332 or 011/37–5642). Both are open weekdays 8–8.

The small, red, English-language *Pocket Guide/The Best of São Paulo,* which lists addresses and telephone numbers of museums, theaters, restaurants, art galleries, shops, and other places of interest to visitors, is sold at newsstands and bookstores.

Arriving and Departing

By Plane

São Paulo's international airport, **Cumbica** (☎ 011/945–2111), also known as **Guarulhos,** is the industrial suburb of Guarulhos, 30 kilometers (19 miles) and a 45-minute drive from downtown. All international flights land here, as well as domestic flights of the large airlines. The airlines using Cumbica are American, United, Varig, Vasp, Canadian, British Airways, Transbrasil, and charter flights by Tower Airlines and World Airlines. The smaller **Congonhas Airport** (☎ 011/536–3555, ext. 195) serves the smaller regional airlines and the **Ponte Aérea,** the Rio–São Paulo shuttle. Congonhas is 14 kilometers (9 miles) from the city center, about a 15-minute drive, but the city's unpredictable traffic can double this time. In the winter, both airports are sometimes fogged in during the early morning, and flights are rerouted to the **Viracopos Airport** (☎ 0192/47–0909), in the city of Campinas; airlines transfer passengers by bus (an hour's ride) to their original destination in São Paulo.

FROM THE AIRPORTS INTO TOWN

EMTU executivo buses (☎ 011/945–2505), fancy green-stripe vehicles, shuttle between Cumbica and Congonhas, and also link the international airport with the Tietê bus terminal and the downtown Praça da República. The bus to São Paulo costs about $5.50 and runs every half hour to an hour from around 6 AM to 11 PM or midnight, depending on the departure point. Municipal buses, with "CMTC" painted on the sides, stop at the airport and go downtown by various routes, such as via Avenida Paulista to the Praça da Sé and Tietê bus station. The sleek blue and white, air-conditioned **Guarucoop radio taxis** (☎ 011/940–7070) will convey you from Cumbica to downtown for around $40; regular, or *comum,* taxis, charge the same amount from this airport. The radio taxi fare from Congonhas to downtown is around $18, and around $12 in a regular taxi. **Fleet Car Shuttle** (counter at Cumbica Airport's arrivals Terminal 1, ☎ 011/945–3030; open daily 6 AM–midnight) serves groups of up to 10 people in a van, stopping at only one destination of choice. For one downtown stop, for example, the company charges a flat rate of about $70 per van load.

By Train

A private company called **Trem de Prata** (☎ 011/825–7022) runs a thrice-weekly overnight train service between São Paulo and Rio de Janeiro that has all the trappings of a journey on the Orient Express. The train leaves Monday, Wednesday, and Friday from a private terminal (R. Capitão Mor Gonçalo Monteiro 6) near the Estação Barra Funda. A single one-way ticket costs around $160, and a suite for two costs $320.

Most travel to the interior of the state is done by bus or automobile. The principal train station is the **Estação da Luz** (Praça da Luz 1, ☎ 011/991–3062), near São Paulo's liveliest and cheapest shopping district, 25 de Março; trains run from here to small towns in the interior and to some metropolitan suburbs. The west zone's **Estação Barra Funda** (Av. Marquês de São Vicente, ☎ 011/66–1677) serves towns in the western part of the state. The **Estação Júlio Prestes** (Praça Júlio Prestes 148, ☎ 011/223–7211), in the downtown Campos Eliseos neighborhood, operates trains to the southeast and some suburban trains; and the **Estação Roosevelt** (Praça Agente Cícero, ☎ 011/292–5417) serves the suburbs only.

By Car

The main highway linking São Paulo and Rio de Janeiro is the Via Dutra (BR 116 North). The modern Rodoviária dos Trabalhdores (SP 70) charges small tolls, runs parallel to the Dutra for about a quarter of the trip beginning at São Paulo, and is an excellent alternative route, but the rest of the trip must be done on the obsolete, dangerous Dutra, which is traveled largely by trucks; the entire trip takes five hours. If you have time, consider taking the much longer, spectacular coastal corniche, the Rio–Santos Highway (SP 55 and BR 101). The trip can be easily made in two days, with a midway stopover at the Portuguese colonial city of Paratí in the state of Rio de Janeiro.

Other main highways are the Castelo Branco (SP 280), which links the southwestern part of the state to the city; the Via Anhanguera (SP 330), which originates in the state's rich northern agricultural region, passing through the university town of Campinas; SP 310, which also runs from the farming heartland; BR 116 South, which comes up from Curitiba; plus the Via Anchieta (SP 150) and the Rodovia Imigrantes (SP 160), parallel roads that run to the coast, each operating one way on weekends and holidays.

By Bus

There are four bus stations (information for all stations: ☎ 011/235–0322) in São Paulo. The main station, serving all Brazilian state capitals, other important cities, and Paraguay, Argentina, Uruguay, and Chile, is the **Tietê Terminal** (Av. Cruzeiro do Sul), in the north zone, on the Marginal Tietê Beltway. Service to Rio is every half hour on the half hour. The others are the **Bresser Terminal** (Rua do Hipódromo), in the east zone district of Brás, with service to the south of Minas Gerais state and Belo Horizonte; **Jabaquara Terminal** (Rua Jequitibas) in the south zone near Congonhas airport, with buses to and from coastal towns; and the **Barra Funda Terminal** (Rua Mário de Andrade 664), in the west zone near the Latin America Memorial. All stations have or are close to metrô stops.

Getting Around São Paulo

Your choice of transportation will depend largely on the weather and the level of air pollution during your stay. In winter, taxi and metrô are the best ways to see the sights while avoiding rain and/or the dirty air caused by thermal inversions. In summer, walking is fine for downtown sights and for shopping in the Jardins district, as long as you carry an umbrella for the inevitable heavy but short-lived rains. Details on the bus and subway systems can be found in a book of street maps, the *Guia São Paulo,* available at newsstands and bookstores. Driving is not recommended in São Paulo because of inadequate roadways and traffic control, antiquated vehicles that often break down, and the generally poor level of driving; plus the city's 4.5 million vehicles frequently clog main arteries.

By Bus

Ample bus service (CMTC information ☎ 133) complements the metrô, but regular buses (white with a red horizontal stripe on the sides) are overcrowded at rush hour and when it rains. Bus stops are clearly marked, but routes are spelled out only on the buses themselves. The fare is about 60¢. For bus numbers and names, routes, and schedules for CMTC buses, purchase the *Guia São Paulo Ruas,* published by *Quatro Rodas* magazine. Passengers enter at the front and exit the back, after paying the fare to the *cobradòr* seated on a platform at the back of the bus. Often the cobrador has no change, and gives out *vale transporte* slips, or bus fare vouchers, instead. The green and gray **CMTC executivo** buses (☎ 158), whose numbers all end in the letter *E,* are more spacious and cost around $2, paid on entry to the driver. There are also many *clandestino* (unlicensed, privately run buses) traversing the city; most of them are quite battered, and some are painted to look like the CMTC buses. They charge the same fares as the CMTC.

Metrô

Safe, quick, comfortable, and clean, the metrô, or subway (☎ 011/284–8877), is by far the best means of transportation, but unfortunately it leaves out a large portion of the city's southern districts. There are three lines: the blue North–South, the orange East–West, and the new green Vila Prudente–Vila Madalena line, which runs under Avenida Paulista to the Clínicas Hospital. The blue and orange lines run daily 5 AM–midnight and cross at the downtown Praça da Sé. The third line runs daily 6 AM–8:30 PM. Magnetic tickets are sold for around 80¢ in the metrô stations, with a discount for round-trips; they are inserted into a turnstile at the platform entrance and returned only if there is unused mileage. Transfers within the subway system are free, and for bus–subway trips (one bus only), a *bilhete integração* can be purchased on buses or at subway ticket windows for $1.50, with a round-trip discount. Multiples of 10 tickets can also be purchased at a discount. Ticket sellers do not have to make change for large bills. Maps of the metrô system are available from the Departamento de Marketing Institucional (Avenida Paulista 1842, 19th Floor, ☎ 011/283–4933).

By Taxi

Owner-driven taxis are the best maintained, and these unbattered vehicles are the ones to look for among São Paulo's gray-blue comum fleet to avoid breakdowns and trips that never emerge from second gear. Fares are calculated from the number of UTs (units) shown on the meter, using a chart pasted in the back window. Each UT is about 60¢, and each ride begins with four UTs already on the meter; additional UTs are accumulated with each kilometer (half mile), and also while the cab is not in motion, on the basis of 27 clicks of one-second duration. Radio taxis are very reliable and quick. **Radio Taxi São Paulo** (☎ 011/ 251–1733) is the most popular and accepts credit cards.

Tour Operators

Driving Tours

At press time (winter 1995), the municipal tourism board, Anhembi Turismo e Eventos da Cidade de São Paulo, was planning to bring back 12 different half-day bus tours it had operated on Sundays in previous years. For more information, call 011/267–2122, ext. 640, or 011/267–0702.

Local travel agencies with downtown offices, such as **Gol Tour Viagens e Turismo** (Av. São Luís 187, Basement, Shop No. 12, ☎ 011/256–2388) and **Opcional Tour and Guide Viagens e Turismo** (Av. Ipiranga 345, 14th Floor, Office 1401, ☎ 011/259–1007), offer a variety of guided automobile tours for small groups, and are willing to create tours to meet specific interests. Typical tours are a half-day city tour costing about $40 a person (group rate); a visit to the zoo and the Simba Safari, where jungle animals can be seen from the safety of a car, for $45–$50 a person; a São Paulo night tour that includes a samba show, dinner, and drinks, for around $100 a person; and, for $80–$90, daylong excursions to the Guarujá beach resort, a coffee farm, an ecological farm preserve, or the Portuguese colonial city of Embu, site of a Sunday arts and crafts fair (*see* Excursions from São Paulo, *below*).

Walking Tours

There are no regularly scheduled guided walking tours offered in São Paulo, but you can design your own with the aid of information provided by SEST or Anhembi booths around the city (*see* Visitor Information, *above*). You can hire a bilingual guide through a travel agency or hotel concierge to accompany you for about $15 an hour (minimum of four hours). The best areas to explore on foot are the Japanese neighborhood of Liberdade, the Italo-Portuguese Bexiga-Bela Vista quarter, the pedestrian-only streets of the old financial district, downtown (with great attention to security), and for shopping, the boutique-packed, hilly Jardins neighborhood.

Precautions

Security is a concern in São Paulo, much as it would be in any large city. The local tourist police caution travelers to be alert and watch belongings carefully at all times, especially at tourist attractions. Wearing shorts, expensive running shoes, or flashy accessories will bring unwanted attention, they add. Be aware of a local scam in which one

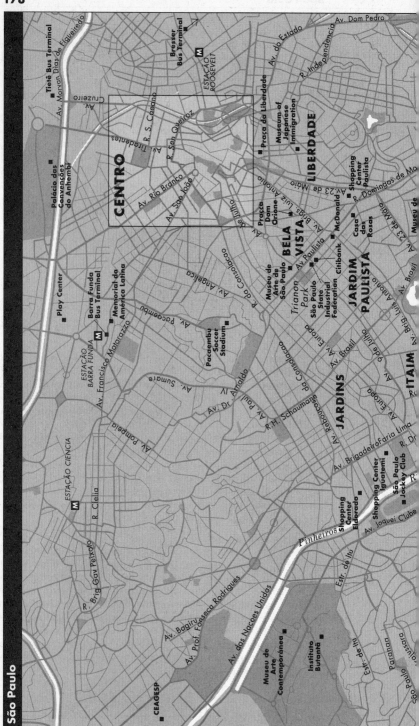

CENTRO

Tietê Bus Terminal
Bresser Bus Terminal
ESTAÇÃO ROOSEVELT
Av. Dom Pedro
Av. do Estado
R. Independencia
Av. Morvan Dias de Figueiredo
Av. Cruzeiro
R. S. Caetano
Av. Tiradentes
R. Sen Queiroz
Praça da Liberdade
Museum of Japanese Immigration
LIBERDADE
Palácio das Convenções do Anhembi
Av. Rio Branco
Av. São João
Av. 9 de Julho
Av. 23 de Maio
Shopping Center Paulista
R. Domingas de Ma
Play Center
Barra Funda Bus Terminal
Memorial da América Latina
Praça Dom Orione
Av. Brig. Luiz Antonio
Av. Paulista
McDonald
Casa das Rosas
Museu de
ESTAÇÃO BARRA FUNDA
Av. Francisco Matarazzo
Av. Pacaembu
Museu de Arte de São Paulo
BELA VISTA
Trianon Park
São Paulo State Industrial Federation
Citibank
JARDIM PAULISTA
Av. 23 de Maio
Av. Brasil
Av. Brig. Luiz Antonio
Av. Sumaré
Pacaembu Soccer Stadium
R. do Consolação
Av. Angélica
Av. Europa
ITAIM
ESTAÇÃO CIÊNCIA
Av. Pompéia
Av. Sumaré
Av. Paul IV
Av. Dr. Arnaldo
R.H. Schaumann
Rebouças
Av. do Consolação
Av. Brasil
JARDINS
Av. Europa
Av. 9 de Julho
R. Clélia
R. Brig. Gav Teixoto
Av. Brigadeiro Faria Lima
Shopping Center Iguatemi
São Paulo Jockey Club
R. Dr
Shopping Center Eldorado
Av. Joquei Clube
Pinheiros
Estr. de Itu
Av. Bagtry
Av. Prof. Fonseca Rodrigues
Av. das Nações Unidas
Museu de Arte Contemporânea
Instituto Butantã
CEAGESP
Estr. de Itu

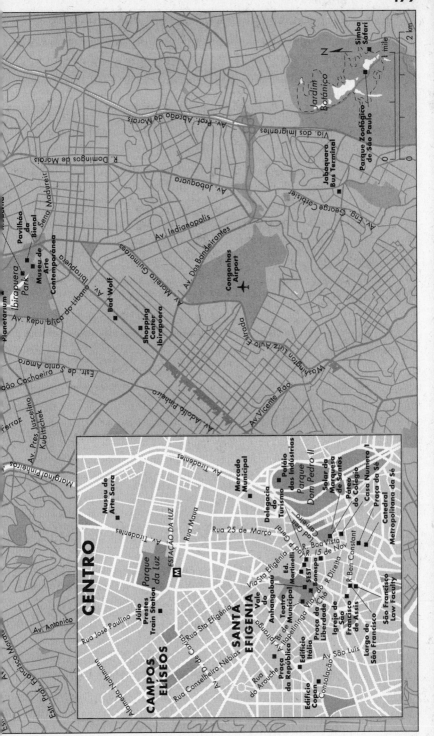

2 km

1 mile

0

N

Simba
Safari

Jardim
Botânico

Parque Zoológico
de São Paulo

Via dos Imigrantes

Jabaquara
Bus Terminal

Av. Jabaquara

Av. Eng. George Corbisier

Av. Prof. Abrão de Morais

R. Domingos de Morais

Av. Indianópolis

Av. Das Bandeirantes

Congonhas
Airport

Washington Luiz Auto Estrada

Av. Vicente Rao

Av. Adolfo Pinheiro

Estr. de Santo Amaro

Av. República do Líbano

Bad Wolf

Shopping
Center
Ibirapuera

Av. Morelto Guimarães

Av. Ibirapuera

Senai Madureira

Pavilhão
da
Bienal

Museu de
Arte
Contemporânea

Ibirapuera
Park

Planetarium

João Cachoeira

Av. Pres. Juscelino
Kubitschek

Ferraz

Marginal Pinheiros

Av. Antônico

Av. Francisco Morato

Estr. Prof. Francisco Prol

Alameda Nothmann

CENTRO

**CAMPOS
ELÍSEOS**

**SANTA
EFIGÊNIA**

Museu de
Arte Sacra

Parque
da Luz

ESTAÇÃO DA LUZ

M

Júlio
Prestes
Train Station

Rua José Paulino

Rua Sta Efigênia

Av. Duque de Caxias

Av. Rio Branco

Av. Ipiranga

Rua Conselheiro Nébias

Rua
do Arouche

Av. Sto António Nébias

Edifício
Copan

Edifício
Itália

Consolação

Praça
da República

Teatro
Municipal

Vale
do
Anhangabaú

Praça
Ramos

Av. São Luís

Largo de
São Francisco

Igreja de
São
Francisco
de Assis

Praça
Liberdade

Via Sta Efigênia

Ed.
Martinelli

SEST

Via do Gonesp

Viad de Cha

R. 15 de Nov

R. Boa Vista

R. Direita

R. Ben Constant

São Francisco
Law Faculty

Av. Tiradentes

Rua Mauá

Rua 25 de Março

Mercado
Municipal

Delegacia
do
Turismo

Rua do Carmo

Parque
Dom
Pedro II

Palácio
das Indústrias

Solar da
Marquesa
de Santos

Pátio
do Colégio

Casa Número 1

Praça da Sé

Catedral
Metropolitana da Sé

man throws a dark liquid on a tourist's back and another offers to help clean up while the first *really* cleans up!

Exploring São Paulo

The city's enormous energy has dispersed over time, as its sources have changed and developed. The largely pedestrian-only hilltop and valley area centering on the downtown **Vale do Anhangabaú** was where São Paulo's first inhabitants, Jesuit missionaries and treasure-hunting pioneers, lived. Later it became a financial and cultural center, and it is still home to the stock exchange and many banks. Decadent from the mid-1970s to the start of this decade, the district is now the focus of a municipal bid to revitalize the downtown. The **Bela Vista** and **Bexiga** neighborhoods, which abut downtown, house most of the city's theaters and bars. As coffee became the focus of Paulista wealth in the late 19th century, many families built whimsical-looking mansions on the ridge-top **Avenida Paulista,** homes that, beginning in the post–World War II industrial boom, gave way to skyscraper bank headquarters. Many of the city's best hotels are also near this avenue. The next growth spurt came in the 1970s, when real estate firms, advertising agencies, fancy restaurants, and other companies went west and literally downhill to a former swamp, to take up residence in the tall buildings of **Avenida Brigadeiro Faria Lima,** near the stylish homes of the **Jardins** neighborhood and the Iguatemi Shopping Center (Brazil's first mall), just off the banks of the **Pinheiros River.** Large-scale construction of many corporate headquarters continues just south of this area, between the **Marginal Pinheiros Beltway** and the **Avenida Engenheiro Luís Carlos Berrini,** not far from the luxurious Shopping Center Morumbi, with many high-income apartment buildings going up just across the river from this district.

Downtown

If you are willing to brave what many Paulistanos believe is the most dangerous part of the city (*see* Precautions, *above*), this is the place to start, devoting at least a half day to the area, on foot and by subway. Begin by taking in the overpowering view of the world's third-largest city from its highest building, the **Edifício Itália.** To do so, you'll have to patronize the bar or dining room of the **Terraço Itália** restaurant (Av. Ipiranga 344, ☎ 011/257–6566) on its 41st floor; the restaurant is expensive and not one of the city's best. Afternoon tea or a drink is the quickest, least expensive option; tea is served 3–5:30, and the bar opens at 6 PM.

A few doors up to the left is the **Edifício Copan,** the serpentine apartment and office building designed by renowned Brazilian architect Oscar Niemeyer. Walk back down Avenida Ipiranga, cross Avenida São Luís, and cross Ipiranga itself to the **Praça da República,** the large central square where a huge fair with arts and crafts, food, and semiprecious stones is held every Sunday, sometimes with live music. Some artisans display their work here all week long, so it's worth a peek anytime.

Now cross back over Ipiranga and walk down the pedestrian-only **Rua Barão de Itapetininga,** packed during the week with dawdling messenger boys, street vendors and entertainers, and men bearing sandwich boards advertising jobs. The neo-baroque **Teatro Municipal,** inspired by the Opéra de Paris and built between 1903 and 1911 with Art Nouveau elements, lies at the end of this street on the **Praça Ramos de Azevedo,** facing the **Mappin** department store, once the purlieu of high-class ladies who purchased only European imports. Unfortunately, the theater's fully restored auditorium, full of gold leaf, moss-green velvet, marble, and mirrors, is only open to those attending cultural events (*see* The Arts, *below*), but it is sometimes possible to walk in for a quick view of the vestibule.

Now cross the square eastward to walk over the Art Deco **Viaduto do Chá,** into the heart of São Paulo. *Chá* means tea, and the bridge is so named because tea was once grown in the **Vale do Anhangabaú** it crosses. Keeping pace with the city's haphazard development, the Anhangabaú later became a city park, then a noisy and dirty thoroughfare, and in 1992, with the completion of two vehicular-traffic tunnels, was turned back into breathable people space. Frequented by office workers, the area is also the site of outdoor concerts and large political rallies. Stopping for a moment on the viaduct, look north at the crowded **Viaduto Santa Ifigênia,** whose metal structure was imported from Belgium at the start of this century.

Turn right onto Rua Líbero Badaró at the end of the Viaduto do Chá. This street leads into the Largo São Francisco, home to the São Francisco Law Faculty, one of Brazil's first educational institutions, founded in 1824. Nearby is the Baroque **Igreja de São Francisco de Assis** (St. Francis of Assisi Church). The church actually consists of two churches by the same name, one run by Catholic clergy, and one by lay brothers. One of the city's best-preserved Portuguese colonial buildings, the complex was built from 1647 to 1790. *Largo São Francisco 133,* ☎ *011/606–0081.* ☛ *Free.* ☺ *Lay brothers' church closed weekdays 11:30–1, weekends after 10 AM.*

A short walk from here up Rua Benjamin Constant is the **Praça da Sé,** the city's most central spot. The huge, busy square, under which the city's two major metrô lines cross, is where migrants from Brazil's poor northeast region often go to enjoy their typical music and to sell and buy products from that region, such as medicinal herbs, sold in sacks spread out on the ground. It is also the central hangout for São Paulo's street children and the focus of periodic (and controversial) police sweeps to get them off the street. The square and most of the historic area and financial district to its north have been set aside for pedestrians, official vehicles, and public transportation only.

The square is also the location of the **Catedral Metropolitana da Sé,** the Metropolitan Holy See Cathedral, a fairly ugly neo-Gothic structure with a crypt, completed in 1954. *Praça da Sé,* ☎ *011/607–6832.* ☛ *Free.* ☺ *Thurs.–Sun. afternoons.*

Moving north out of the square on the Rua Roberto Simonsen, you will come across **Casa Numero 1,** at Rua Roberto Simonsen 136B, sole intact survivor of a wave of European-style chalets that swept São Paulo in the 1880s and now home of the city archives, open only for historical research.

Next door is the **Solar da Marquesa de Santos,** the only late-18th-century residence remaining in the city. From 1834 to 1867, this home belonged to the Marchioness of Santos, the mistress of Emperor Pedro II and a hostess to much of Brazilian aristocracy of her day. *Rua Roberto Simonsen 136A,* ☎ *011/606–2218.* ☛ *Free.* ☺ *Tues.–Sun.*

A little farther up the street and around the corner to the right is the **Pátio do Colégio,** a complex of white-walled buildings on the site of the first Jesuit mission in the city, founded by Father José de Anchieta in 1554 to convert the local Indians. The complex houses a museum, the **Casa de Anchieta,** that displays rustic Portuguese colonial furniture, a model of the early city, and a piece of the mud and wattle wall from the original mission; and a chapel, the **Capela de Anchieta.** *Museum:* ☎ *011/239–5722.* ☛ *Entry fee.* ⊙ *Tues.–Sun. afternoons. Chapel:* ☎ *011/605–6899.* ☛ *Free.* ⊙ *Sun. afternoon and weekdays.*

Now walk north down Rua Boa Vista and take a left onto Rua Direita, then the first right onto Rua 15 de Novembro. No. 275, on the left, houses **BOVESPA,** the São Paulo Stock Exchange, Brazil's busiest and a hub for the new foreign investment attracted here by the government's efforts to privatize state-owned companies. Those who leave an ID with the guard at the front desk can go up to the mezzanine gallery to watch the hurly-burly; computer terminals in the observation gallery carry the latest stock quotes, as well as general information in various languages. BOVESPA offers personalized tours in English to representatives of foreign investment institutions, but these must be set up in advance; direct requests to the Superintendência Executiva de Desenvolvimento, FAX 011/239–4981. *Rua 15 de Novembro 275,* ☎ *011/ 233–2000, ext. 516.* ☛ *Free.* ⊙ *Weekdays except lunchtime.*

Near the end of Rua 15 de Novembro, at Rua João Brícola 24, stands the 36-floor **Banespa Building** (☎ 011/259–7722), built in 1947 and modeled after New York's Empire State Building. If you couldn't fit tea or drinks at the top of the Edifício Itália into your downtown walking tour (*see above*), here's a second, no-frills chance for a panoramic look at the city. A radio traffic reporter squints through the smog every morning from this tower. To the north, you will note the whimsy of the penthouse residence on the 30-floor **Edifício Martinelli** (Rua Líbero Badaró 504, ☎ 011/605–1664), the city's first skyscraper, built in 1929 by Italian immigrant-turned-count Giuseppe Martinelli. This rooftop is open weekdays 10:30–4 to visitors by permission of the building administrator, located on the ground floor. Just leave a photo ID at the front desk and ride the elevator to the 34th floor, then walk up two more flights.

If you're up for a last thrill from this megalopolis that draws buyers, sellers, watchers, and doers from all over the continent, top off your downtown walking tour with a foray into the crush of the crowds on the **Ladeira General Carneiro, Rua 25 de Março,** and the **Ladeira Porto Geral.** *Ladeira* means incline, and from the first one listed here you will get a quick view of the **Palácio das Indústrias** (Industrial Palace), an eclectic-style convention and exhibition center with two red towers built in 1924 and, in 1993, reinaugurated as São Paulo's **city hall.** Ladeira Porto Geral, named for a port on the Tamanduateí River now shrunk into the confines of a concrete canal, is the street of Carnival costume shops; you'll find sequins, towering feather headdresses, and masks galore year-round. Finally, Rua 25 de Março, precinct of the city's Lebanese population, is a wholesale and retail shopping district stuffed with textiles, clothing, carpets, toys, birthday party materials— you name it. Not far to the north of this area is the **Mercado Municipal** (Municipal Market), fruit of São Paulo's coffee wealth, built in 1933 and still functioning, with beautiful stained-glass windows depicting harvest and cattle-raising activities.

Campo Elíseos

A short metrô ride from the central downtown area to the Santa Cecília stop brings you to a district that until recently was a virtual slum, studded with decrepit relics of the era when coffee was king and the railroads were the route to its rule. Now the Campos Elíseos neighborhood, adjacent to both the Júlio Prestes and Luz railroad stations, is undergoing slow but sure renovation.

The governor's seat was originally at **Palácio Campos Elíseos,** but in 1965, the official residence moved to a new mansion in Morumbi. Built between 1896 and 1899 in a combination of Italian Renaissance and French Baroque Revival styles, the Palácio has become a rather elegant state secretariat of science, technology, and economic development. With an eye toward the area's rebirth, the secretariat now holds art exhibitions in the palace. *Av. Rio Branco 1269,* ☎ *011/220–0033.* ☛ *Free.* ☾ *Wed.–Sun. afternoons.*

The district also has several restored turn-of-the-century mansions, along streets that are amazingly still tree-lined (and in some cases named after the affluent families who once lived here), such as **Alameda Nothmann** and **Rua Conselheiro Nébias.** Nearby is the **Júlio Prestes train station,** built between 1926 and 1937, with its two huge stained-glass windows depicting the role of train travel in the Brazilian economy. At press time (winter 1995), the station was under restoration, with completion scheduled for some time in 1995. And just around the corner from that station is another, the **Estação da Luz,** inaugurated in 1901 and built of iron and red brick shipped mostly from England. To the west of the station is **Rua José Paulino,** once a redoubt of Jewish Brazilians in the textiles business, now given over to Koreans who have continued in the neighborhood tradition.

Paulista

In the 1960s, São Paulo builders began directing their energies toward a wide ridge-top avenue about five minutes from downtown and lined with the eclectic, turn-of-the-century mansions of the coffee barons. Avenida Paulista quickly became the showplace of São Paulo, and perhaps even Brazil's most important street, with its myriad bank headquarters and other business institutions. An imposing, long, straight shot, the avenue has also increasingly lent itself to protest marches, which often finish down in the Anhangabaú. The avenue is also part of the annual St. Sylvester footrace, which takes place on New Year's Eve.

As historic preservation came late to São Paulo, only a handful of the old mansions remain; one of them, totally restored, now houses a McDonald's, at No. 709. Another, the Casa das Rosas (No. 35), has been preserved for its historic value, and now houses art exhibitions.

Avenida Paulista's other attractions include the Tenente Siqueira Campos Park, better known as the **Trianon Park** (Rua Peixoto Gomide 949; ☛ Free), a rare remaining patch of the Atlantic forest that once lined most of eastern Brazil; the **Museu de Arte de São Paulo,** known as **MASP** (*see* Museums, *below*), at No. 1578; the sloping grilled facade of the **São Paulo State Industrial Federation** (FIESP), one of the country's most important business groups, at No. 1313; and the postmodern **Citibank** headquarters, at No. 1111, whose pink-marble and blue-glass facade spills down to the street in a curve like a waterfall.

Little Tokyo

At the beginning of the century, a group of Japanese immigrants arrived to work as contract farm laborers in the state of São Paulo. In the next five decades, more than a quarter of a million of their countrymen followed, forming the largest Japanese colony outside Japan. Distinguished today by a large number of college graduates and successful businesspeople, professionals, and politicians, the colony made important contributions to Brazilian agriculture and the seafood industry. The Liberdade neighborhood, which is south of Praça da Sé behind the cathedral, and whose entrance is marked by a series of red porticoes, is home for many first-, second-, and third-generation

Japanese-Brazilians. Here, clustered around Avenida Liberdade, you will find shops selling everything from imported bubble gum with miniature robots in the box, to Kabuki face paint. It's also the setting for some of the city's finest sushi bars and Japanese restaurants, plus a growing number of Korean and Chinese dining spots.

On Sunday morning the **Praça Liberdade,** by the Liberdade metrô station, hosts a sprawling Asian food and crafts fair, where the free and easy Brazilian ethnic mix is in plain view; you'll see, for example, black Brazilians dressed in colorful kimonos hawking grilled shrimp on a stick. Liberdade also hosts several ethnic celebrations, such as the April Hanamatsuri, commemorating Buddha's birth, and the July Feast of Stars.

Just a 10-minute walk from the Liberdade metrô station, you will find the intriguing **Museum of Japanese Immigration,** with two floors of exhibits about the immigrants' culture and farm life and their contributions to Brazilian horticulture, such as the persimmon, azalea, and tangerine. *Rua São Joaquim 381,* ☎ *011/279–5465.* ☛ *Entry fee.* ⊘ *Tues.–Sun. afternoons.*

Museums

A city that has long been on the go, São Paulo has allocated relatively little space or funds for the arts. Its museums do house some treasures, but because they often operate on a shoestring, they can be disappointing for those expecting exhibits on a par with the world's leading institutions.

Fundação Maria Luiza e Oscar Americano. This private wooded estate is an especially pleasant place to spend an afternoon. The collection includes Portuguese colonial, imperial, and modern furniture, sacred art, silver, porcelain, engravings, personal objects of the Brazilian royal family, paintings, tapestries, and sculpture. The foundation holds Sunday concerts, and afternoon tea is served until 6. *Av. Morumbi 3700,* ☎ *011/842–0077.* ☛ *Entry fee.* ⊘ *Tues.–Fri. afternoons, weekends.*

Instituto Butantã. In 1888, a Brazilian scientist, with the aid of the São Paulo state government, turned a farmhouse into a center for the production of snake serum. Today, the Instituto Butantã is the largest snake farm in South America, with a collection of more than 70,000 snakes, spiders, scorpions, and lizards. The institute extracts venom and processes it into serum available to victims of poisonous bites throughout Latin America. Unfortunately, the institute has suffered from underfunding and is somewhat run-down. Far behind modern museum technology, exhibits are not as accessible to children as they could be. *Av. Vital Brasil 1500,* ☎ *011/813–7222.* ☛ *Entry fee.* ⊘ *Tues.–Sun.*

Memorial da América Latina. In addition to displaying a permanent exhibition of Latin American handicrafts, the Memorial da América Latina, a new state-run complex designed by Oscar Niemeyer, holds a series of Latin American art shows throughout the year. *Rua Mário de Andrade 644,* ☎ *011/823–9611.* ☛ *Free.* ⊘ *Tues.–Sun.*

Museu de Arte Contemporânea. Located on the campus of the University of São Paulo, the Museu de Arte Contemporânea (Museum of Contemporary Art) consists of the main building and an annex. Together they contain almost 5,000 works by foreign and Brazilian artists, including Modigliani, Picasso, Chagall, Matisse, Miró, Di Cavalcanti, Anita Malfatti, João Câmara, and Wesley Duke Lee. *Main building: Rua da Reitoria 109,* ☎ *011/211–3467.* ☛ *Free.* ⊘ *Tues.–Sun. Annex: Rua da Reitoria 160.* ☛ *Free.* ⊘ *Tues.–Sun.*

Museu de Arte Moderna. Designed by Oscar Niemeyer, the Museu de Arte Moderna (Museum of Modern Art) houses 2,600 paintings, sculptures, works on paper, and objects centering on the Brazilian modernist movement, which began in the 1920s. The museum often holds shows of up-and-coming local artists. *Ibirapuera Park,* ☎ *011/549–9688.* ☛ *Entry Fee.* ☉ *Tues.–Fri. afternoons, weekends.*

Museu de Arte de São Paulo (MASP). A striking low rise elevated on two massive concrete pillars 256 feet apart, the Museu de Arte de São Paulo (MASP) is the city's premier fine-arts museum. The highlights are a few dazzling, world-famous works by Bosch, Rembrandt, Poussin, Van Gogh, Renoir, and Degas, suspended from the ceiling in glass "sandwiches." The huge open area underneath the building is often used for cultural events, and is the scene of a Sunday antiques fair (*see* Shopping, *below*). *Av. Paulista 1578,* ☎ *011/251–5644.* ☛ *Entry fee.* ☉ *Tues.–Sun. afternoons.*

Parks and Gardens

Ibirapuera Park. Only 15 minutes by taxi from downtown, Ibirapuera Park is São Paulo's answer to New York's Central Park, although it's slightly less than half the size and gets infinitely more crowded on sunny weekends. The park's 395 acres contain jogging and bicycle paths, a lake, and rolling lawns, as well as 10 exhibition halls. The **Japanese Pavilion** is an exact replica of the Katura Imperial Palace in Kyoto, Japan. The internationally renowned São Paulo Biennial Art Show is held here, in the **Pereira Pavilion,** in even-numbered years (*see* The Arts, *below*). In addition to being the setting for several museums (*see* Museums, *above*) and many fairs and other special events, the park is also home to São Paulo's **planetarium,** extremely popular among Paulistanos; there are special shows for children over 7 on weekends 4–6, and for children aged 5–10 Sunday at 10:30. *Ibirapuera Park, Av. Pedro Álvares Cabral, s/n. Planetarium:* ☎ *011/575–5206.* ☛ *Entry fee.* ☉ *Weekday afternoons, weekends.*

Parque Zoológico de São Paulo. Among the world's 10 best zoos, the sprawling Parque Zoológico de São Paulo is a must, even if you don't have children in tow as an excuse for a visit. Its 200 acres include a lake with small islands where monkeys live in houses on stilts, plus more than 2,000 animal species, many of which are endangered. The animals are housed not in cages but in large open areas separated from visitors by ditches. The simian, reptile, and bird sections are especially good. *Av. Miguel Stéfano 4241,* ☎ *011/276–0811.* ☛ *Entry fee.* ☉ *Daily.*

Jardim Botánico. Next door to the zoo are the botanical gardens, an immense nursery of about 3,000 plants belonging to more than 340 native species. There is also a hothouse of Atlantic forest species, an orchid house, and a collection of aquatic plants. *Av. Miguel Stéfano 3031/3687,* ☎ *011/584–6300.* ☛ *Entry fee.* ☉ *Wed.–Sun.*

Shopping

People come from all over Brazil and even from neighboring countries to shop in São Paulo, where boutiques and shopping malls help shoppers forget the city's lack of beauty and the extreme poverty of many of its residents. São Paulo street shops are open weekdays from about 9 to 6:30, closing Saturday around 1. A few are open on Sunday—for a list of these shops and their Sunday hours, call 011/210–4000 or 011/813–3311. Shopping malls open weekdays 10–10 and Saturday 9 AM–10 PM; they open Sundays preceding gift-giving holidays.

Shopping Districts

The **Jardins** neighborhood, centering on **Rua Augusta** (a cross street of Avenida Paulista) and **Rua Oscar Freire,** is the most traditional and chic shopping area. Double-parked Mercedes-Benzes, BMWs, and Mitsubishis point the way to the city's fanciest clothing and leather goods boutiques, jewelers, gift shops, antiques stores, art galleries, restaurants, bars, and beauty salons. Most of the same boutiques can be found at upscale shopping malls. **Downtown,** the **Rua do Arouche** is noted especially for leather goods. The area surrounding **Rua João Cachoeira,** in the **Itaim** neighborhood, has evolved from a neighborhood of small clothing factories into a wholesale and retail clothing sales district. Nearby is **Rua Dr. Mário Ferraz,** stuffed with elegant clothing, gift, and home decoration stores.

Specialty Shops

ANTIQUES

Most of the stall owners at the Sunday Museu de Arte de São Paulo antiques fair also have shops, and they hand out their business cards so you can browse throughout the week at your leisure. There are many stores specializing in high-price European antiques in the Jardins, on and around Rua da Consolaçao. A slew of lower-price antique-furniture stores line Rua Cardeal Arcoverde in Pinheiros, and there are also some shops selling smaller items on Rua Tabapuã, in Itaim.

Arte e Companhia (Rua Oscar Freire 146, ☎ 011/641574) is a group of three dealers selling local, Latin American, and European antiques, such as lamps, silver, and decorative birds.

Patrimônio (Alameda Ministro Rocha Azevedo 1068, ☎ 011/641750) has Brazilian antiques at reasonable prices, as well as some Indian artifacts and modern furnishings crafted from iron.

Paulo Vasconcelos (Alameda Gabriel Monteiro da Silva 1881, ☎ 011/852–2444) sells 18th- and 19th-century Brazilian furniture, plus folk art.

Renato Magalhães Gouvêa Escritório de Arte (Av. Europa 68, ☎ 011/853–2569) offers a potpourri of antiques and modern furnishings and art, both European and Brazilian.

ART

Camargo Vilaça (Rua Fradique Coutinho 1500, ☎ 011/210–7390) specializes in up-and-coming Brazilian artists.

Galería Jacques Ardies (Rua do Livramento 221, ☎ 011/884–2916) is a must if naïf art is your thing.

Galería São Paulo (Rua Estados Unidos 1456, ☎ 011/852–8855) is a leader in contemporary, mainstream art.

Mônica Filgueiras de Almeida (Rua Haddock Lobo 1568, ☎ 011/282–5292) is a trendsetting mainstream gallery.

CLOTHING

Much of Brazil's best women's designer clothing can be found in Jardins's boutiques and shopping-mall branch stores, such as **Maria Bonita** (Rua Oscar Freire 702, ☎ 011/852–6433; also at Shopping Center Iguatemi), **Reinaldo Lourenço** (Rua Bela Cintra 2173, ☎ 011/853–8150), and **G** (Rua Oscar Freire 978, ☎ 011/852–3346; also at Shopping Center Iguatemi). **Huis Clos** (Rua Dr. Mário Ferraz 538, ☎ 011/820–2396) is another top store, in the Itaim neighborhood. Another option for those who, like some Brazilian first ladies, enjoy personalized attention and privacy, are the "closed" (no storefront) designer-label boutiques of the **Vila Nova Conceição** neighborhood, such as **Daslu** (Rua Domingos Leme 284, ☎ 011/822–7461), **Claudete e Deca** (Rua Brás Cardoso 201, ☎ 011/532–1855), and **Bebé** (Rua Lourenço de Almeida 811, ☎ 011/531–0190).

Although men's clothing generally doesn't meet European or U.S. standards, the best sportswear is found under a trendy Rio de Janeiro label, **Richard's** (Alameda Franca 1185, ☎ 011/282–5399; also at Shopping Center Iguatemi), at stores of the same name. At the **Vila Romana factory store** (Via Anhanguera, km 17.5, ☎ 011/706–2211, open Sun.), a 40-minute car ride from downtown, you can't beat the prices for suits, blazers, jeans, and even some women's wear such as silk blouses. For children's outfits, try **Giovanna Baby** (Shopping Center Iguatemi, ☎ 011/814–8463).

GEMS AND JEWELRY

Aside from the mainstream **Natan, H. Stern,** and **Amsterdam Sauer** stores in the shopping malls, there are many smaller, innovative (and sometimes cheaper) jewelry designers.

Antônio Bernardo (Rua Bela Cintra 2063, ☎ 011/883–5034) does exclusive modern and classical designs that use only precious stones. **Bella Golzer** (Rua Bela Cintra 1833, ☎ 011/853–8094) has creative costume jewelry. **Christina Kursell** (☎ 011/492–3673) will visit you with her collection of Brazilian stones set mostly in gold; her artisans can inexpensively copy any piece from a photograph. The work usually takes two or three days. **Francesca Romana** (Rua Carlos Steinenn 50, ☎ 011/884–4691) crafts inexpensive but great-looking Italian-style pieces out of gold-plated metal and Brazilian semiprecious stones. **Sérgio Penteado** (Rua Moacir Piza 84, ☎ 011/851–0487) is an architect who has a penchant for silver and gold jewelry with whimsical moving parts and Brazilian stones. **Serpui Marie** (Alameda Lorena 1742, Casa 1, ☎ 011/280–1677) specializes in interesting costume pieces.

HANDICRAFTS

Arte Nativa Aplicada (Rua Dr. Mário Ferraz 351, ☎ 011/829–6511) carries upscale handiwork inspired by abstract local motifs. **Art Índia** (Rua Augusta 1371, Store No. 119, ☎ 011/283–2102), which is government-run, has Indian tribal work from across Brazil. **Casa do Amazônas** (Galeria Metropôle, Av. São Luís 187, Store No. 14, ☎ 011/258–9727) sells a wide selection of products from the Amazon. **Dentelles** (Rua Augusta 2483, ☎ 011/853–9566) carries embroidered home furnishings.

HOUSEWARES

Pewter is a specialty here, made from tin mined in Minas Gerais. The place to buy stunning reproductions of 17th- and 18th-century pewter goblets, dishes, and other shipboard wares is the **John Somers** store (Shopping Center Morumbi, ☎ 011/612945).

LEATHER GOODS

Santa Marinella sells gorgeous Italian-style shoes and bags (Shopping Center Iguatemi, ☎ 011/814–2481). For a more modern look, try **Franziska Hübener** (Shopping Center Iguatemi, ☎ 011/814–3575). There are also many leather shops in the Jardins area.

Markets

CEAGESP, an agricultural clearinghouse where the Pinheiros and Tietê beltways and rivers meet, houses a **flower market** selling both dried and fresh varieties at wholesale prices. It's open to the public Tuesday and Friday 6 AM–noon. A **fruit and vegetable market** there is closed mornings except for Saturday. CEAGESP's restaurant (Av. Dr. Gastão Vidigal 1946, ☎ 011/260–3366), with its famed onion soup, is a favorite pit stop for wintertime all-night revelers. In addition, almost every neighborhood has a weekly outdoor food market (days are listed in local newspapers) featuring loudmouthed hawkers, exotic scents, and piles of colorful fruit, vegetables, herbs, fish, dried meats, and chicken.

The city's best **arts and crafts fair,** featuring gemstones, embroidery, leather goods, toys, clothing, paintings, musical instruments, and jewelry, takes place Sunday morning at the downtown Praça da República; many booths move over to the nearby Praça da Liberdade neighborhood in the afternoon, joining Japanese-style ceramics, wooden sandals, cooking utensils, food, and bonsai trees.

On Sunday the open space under the Museu de Arte de São Paulo shelters the city's best **antiques fair** (Av. Paulista 1578, ☎ 011/251–5644), competing with a similar fair on Sunday afternoon in the Shopping Center Iguatemi's parking lot (Av. Brigadeiro Faria Lima 1191, ☎ 011/816–6116). There is also a **flea market** on Sunday at the Praça Dom Orione, in the Italian Bela Vista neighborhood.

Shopping Centers
São Paulo has seen a crush of malls since 1980, largely in response to safety considerations. As in the United States, a "mall culture" has come into being, but ubiquitous security guards are quick to snuff out any teenage (or other) misbehavior.

Shopping Center Iguatemi (Av. Brigadeiro Faria Lima 1191, ☎ 011/210–1333), the city's oldest and most sophisticated mall, has a recent addition, replete with the latest in fashion and fast food. A movie theater often shows U.S.-made films in English with Portuguese subtitles.
Shopping Center Morumbi (Av. Roque Petroni Jr. 1089, ☎ 011/553–2444), just to the south in the city's fastest-growing area, is a top competitor to Iguatemi. It houses about the same boutiques, record stores, bookstores, and restaurants, plus a movie theater and department stores at either end.

Sports

Auto Racing
São Paulo hosts the Formula One race every March, bringing this city of 4.5 million cars to heights of spontaneous combustion, especially when a Brazilian driver wins. For ticket information contact the **Confederação Brasileira de Automobilismo** (Rua da Glória 290, 8th Floor, Rio de Janeiro, RJ 20241–180, ☎ 021/221–4895, FAX 021/242–4494).

Basketball
The clubs are amateur and privately sponsored; many of their players have made a name at the Olympics. For information on venues and schedules, contact the **Federação Paulista de Basquete** (☎ 011/251–1466). The best women's team is Ponte Preta; the best men's club is All Star de Franca.

Horse Racing
Thoroughbred races are held at the **São Paulo Jockey Club** (Av. Lineu de Paulo Machado, ☎ 011/016–4011) weeknights 7:30–11:30 except Tuesday, and weekends 2–6. Card-carrying members of other jockey clubs gain entry to the best seats and the club's elegant restaurant.

Soccer
Brazil's only professional sport, this is also São Paulo's favorite. Each of the city's five clubs (São Paulo, Palmeiras, Portuguesa, Corinthians, and Juventus) has its own stadium, but the major ones are São Paulo's **Morumbi** (Praça Roberto Gomes Pedrosa, ☎ 011/842–3377) and the

municipally run **Pacaembu** (Praça Charles Miller, ☎ 011/256–9111). Covered seats offer the best protection against rowdy spectators.

Tennis

International tournaments are held in the region sporadically. For information, contact the **Paulista Tennis Federation** (☎ 011/549–7955).

Volleyball

These clubs are amateur and privately sponsored, and some players have gained world renown. The best clubs are the women's São Caetano and Vila São José clubs, and the men's União Suzano Pirelli and Banespa. For information, contact the **Federação Paulista de Voleibol** (☎ 011/887–2833).

Beaches

São Paulo rests on an elevated plateau only 64.5 kilometers (40 miles) from the coastline, so a quick getaway from smog and gray buildings to warmer weather and blue ocean is just a matter of facing traffic on the parallel Imigrantes (BR 160) or Anchieta (BR 150) highways, each of which becomes one way on weekends and holidays. Buses run down to the coast from the Jabaquara terminal near the Congonhas Airport, and there are once-daily trains to the Santos port from the Estação da Luz.

Just after the Cubatão industrial park, once known as "Death Valley" because of its pollution (which has lessened in the last decade), comes the port of **Santos;** once a fashionable seaside area, it turned seedy long ago but is trying to clean up its beaches. To the north, by ferry or roadway, is **Guarujá,** a very popular resort where the summer social scene pretty much drowns out the crash and roar of the waves. Guarujá has numerous hotels, restaurants, nightclubs, bars, and good beach facilities. The cleanest and best beaches, however, are farther north, past Bertioga, about 2½ hours from São Paulo by car (longer by bus or on holidays or hot summer weekends), where the mountains hug numerous small sandy coves, such as **Juquey, Barra do Sahy,** and **Maresias.** Some of these beaches are untouched, but many are sadly succumbing to the inevitable condominium encroachment. Still, on weekdays when school is in session, the region is gloriously deserted. Farther north still lies the huge, pristine island of **Ilha Bela,** where many Paulistanos brave terrorist mosquitoes to commune with nature and Neptune.

Dining

This is the focus of social life in São Paulo, centering on the Jardins district; there are, however, a great variety of ever-changing eateries in other parts of the city. The latest food trend—besides fast food—is Italy's *nuova cucina.* The city's immigrant groups are extremely well represented, with many German, Lebanese, Japanese, Spanish, Italian, and Portuguese restaurants, plus top-quality French and Indian spots. There are uncountable churrascarias, a favorite among Paulistanos; some of the best ones are up and down Rua Haddock Lobo, in the Jardins district. As in other Brazilian cities, many restaurants serve feijoada— the national rice, beans, and pork dish—on Wednesday and Saturday; top restaurants do it up in fancy buffet style, with each type of pork meat presented separately. Lebanese immigrants have contributed a wonderful sandwich to the city's menu, the *beirute,* a Middle Eastern version of a submarine sandwich, served hot in toasted Syrian bread and sprinkled with oregano.

Restaurants in São Paulo frequently change their credit card policies, sometimes adding a surcharge for their use or not accepting them at all. No restaurant requires jacket and tie, but those in the $$ to $$$$ categories expect patrons to look tidy and elegant (no shorts or muddy or torn jeans). *Veja São Paulo*, inserted in the newsweekly *Veja*, is an excellent source of restaurant listings, especially new establishments.

For price-category definitions, *see* Dining *in* Brazil Essentials, *below*.

Brazilian

$$$ Bolinha. This is the place to have feijoada, served daily for the last 47 years. It's fun to nip a preprandial *caipirinha*, an icy lime-and-liquor beverage, at one of the sidewalk tables while you take in the crowded Saturday street scene—almost every other store nearby is an imported-car dealership, and new car owners seem to adore driving back and forth. ✕ *Av. Cidade Jardin 53*, ☎ *011/852–9526. AE, DC, MC, V.*

$$$ Esplanada Grill. A beautiful-people hangout (especially at the bar), this is one of three top churrascarias on the same street. The thin-sliced *picanha* steak (similar to rump steak) is excellent and great with the house salad (prepared with hearts of palm and shredded, fried potatoes), onion rings, and creamed spinach. The restaurant's rendition of the traditional *pão de queijo* (hot cheese-bread balls) is just right. ✕ *Rua Haddock Lobo 1682*, ☎ *011/881–3199. Reservations advised. V.*

$$ Yellow Giraffe. The fashionable atmosphere here—clean Italian modern decor, beautiful people eyeing one another, and valet parking—lends refinement to the lowly beirute, São Paulo's answer to the hero sandwich. Other great eats include grilled chicken and mashed sweet potatoes, "garnished" with a breaded, deep-fried whole banana. ✕ *Rua Amauri 356*, ☎ *011/853–2438. No credit cards.*

$ ★   Frevo. Paulistanos of all ilks and ages flock to this Jardins luncheonette near the U.S. Consulate for its beirute sandwiches, draft beer, and fruit juices in flavors like *acerola* (Antilles cherry), passion fruit, and papaya. ✕ *Rua Oscar Freire 603*, ☎ *011/282–3434. No credit cards.*

French

$$$$ ★   Freddy. You'll leave behind the grunge and noise of São Paulo's streets when you walk through the doors of this long-lived eatery with the feel of an upscale Parisian bistro. Try the house duck with Madeira sauce and apple puree, pheasant with herb sauce, hearty cassoulet (a casserole of white beans, lamb, preserved duck, and garlic sausage), or the fish quenelles. ✕ *Praça Don Gastão Liberal Pinto 111*, ☎ *011/ 829–0977. Reservations advised. AE, DC, MC, V.*

$$$$ Laurent. Famous for his alchemy of Brazilian ingredients with French nouvelle cuisine, chef Laurent Suaudeau recently relocated this Rio de Janeiro restaurant to a São Paulo apartment hotel, where the decor is modern with classical French touches, such as 18th- and 19th-century art reproductions. Specialties include broccoli crepes with cashew curry, and codfish tart rolled in spinach leaves, with basil, tomato, and soya. ✕ *Alameda Jaú 1606*, ☎ *011/853–5573. Reservations advised. AE, DC. Closed Sun.; no lunch Sat.*

$$$ ★   La Casserole. Located downtown facing a little flower market, this charming bistro has been around for generations. Surrounded by cozy wood-paneled walls decorated with eclectic posters, you can dine on such delights as *gigot d'agneau aux soissons* (roast leg of lamb in its own juices, served with white beans) and cherry strudel. ✕ *Largo do Arouche 346*, ☎ *011/220–6283. Reservations advised. AE, DC, MC, V. Closed Mon.; no lunch Sat.*

Indian

$$$$ **Govinda.** Authentic Indian cuisine is served in a spacious skylit dining room in a former aluminum factory, where ceiling fans whir in summer and three fireplaces plus assorted coal stoves roar in winter; additional heat comes from the chili (you can specify your chili tolerance). The house curry, a subtle blend of 16 spices, seasons dishes such as the clay-oven-baked tandoori chicken, lamb curry in yogurt, and curried filet mignon with apples and mushrooms. Live sitar music is played Friday and Saturday. ✗ *Rua Princesa Isabel 379,* ☎ *011/531–0269. Reservations advised. AE, DC, MC. No dinner Sun.*

International

$$$ **Alfama dos Marinheiros.** This Portuguese restaurant serves Continental cuisine, amid blue Portuguese tiles, paintings of famous personages from the old country, and upstairs, candlelight. But the real stand-outs here are the 20 codfish dishes; the most popular is codfish *Vila Real,* baked with olive oil, potatoes, tomatoes, and onions. ✗ *Rua Pamplona 1285,* ☎ *011/884–9203. DC, MC.*

$$$ **La Tambouille.** A favorite among advertising executives and their clients, this Italo-French restaurant with a partly enclosed garden is a place to be seen. The food is also worth a visit, with delightful seafood lasagna, filet mignon stuffed with Parma ham and *funghi secchi* (dried mushrooms), and *marron-glacé* (sugared chestnut) crepes with ice cream. ✗ *Av. Nove de Julho 5925,* ☎ *011/883–6276. Reservations advised. AE, V.*

$$$ **Paddock.** A traditional spot for relaxed business lunches, this restaurant in two locations is equally professional with its Continental cuisine. Try lamb with mint sauce or the poached haddock. ✗ *Av. São Luís 258,* ☎ *011/257–4768; Av. Brigadeiro Faria Lima 1541, Store No. 109,* ☎ *011/814–3582. Reservations advised. AE, DC, MC, V. Closed Sun.*

$$ ★ **Brahma.** Located downtown at an intersection made famous by a popular Brazilian song, this longtime favorite offers a menu which includes both Brazilian and Continental dishes, with specialties such as chicken pie, roast duck with red cabbage, and apple strudel. ✗ *Av. São João 677,* ☎ *011/223–6720. AE, DC, MC, V. Closed Sun.*

$ **Ritz.** The fare is basic but the look is artsy at this Jardins eatery, which is popular with the gay community at night. Go for the chicken pie, penne *Mediteránneo* (with buffalo mozzarella, black olives, fresh tomatoes, and basil), and hot apple pie with ice cream. ✗ *Alameda Franca 1088,* ☎ *011/280–6808. No credit cards.*

Italian

$$$$ ★ **Ca' D'Oro.** In the hotel of the same name (*see* Lodging, *below*), this is a longtime northern Italian favorite among Brazilian bigwigs, many of whom have their own regular tables in the Old World–style chandeliered dining room. Quail, osso buco, and veal and raisin ravioli are winners, but the most famous specialty is the Piedmontese *gran bollito misto,* a variety of steamed meats and vegetables accompanied by three sauces and served from a wheeled cart. ✗ *Rua Augusta 129,* ☎ *011/256–8011. Reservations advised. AE, DC, MC, V.*

$$$$ **Fasano.** Both the decor and the northern Italian cuisine here are impressive: The former boasts marble, mahogany, and a skylight; the latter, innovative salmon in a yogurt and rosemary sauce and risotto with arugula pesto and giant shrimp. The traditional tiramisù makes a great finish. ✗ *Rua Haddock Lobo 1644,* ☎ *011/852–4000. Reservations advised. AE, DC, MC, V. No lunch Sat., no dinner Sun.*

$$$$ **La Vecchia Cucina.** Chef Sergio Arno changed the face of the city's Italian restaurants with his nuova cucina, exemplified by such dishes as frog risotto, duck ravioli with watercress sauce, and apple crepes. Well-to-

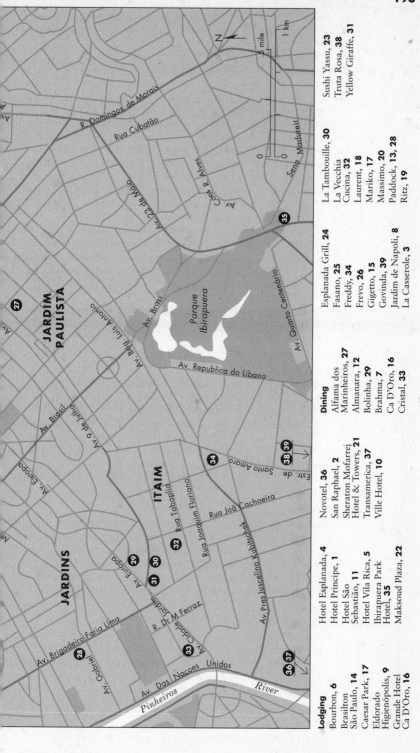

JARDIM
PAULISTA

JARDINS

ITAIM

Parque
Ibirapuera

Av. Republica do Libano

Av. Brasil

Av. Brig. Luis Antonio

Av. 23 de Maio

R. Domingos de Morais

Rua Cubatão

Av. 9 de Julho

Av. Europa

Av. Brasil

Rua Tabapuã

Rua Joaquim Floriano

Rua João Cachoeira

Estr. de Santo Amaro

Av. Pres. Juscelino Kubitschek

Av. Brigadeiro Faria Lima

Av. Europa

Av. Cidade Jardim

R. Dr. M. Ferraz

Av. Gabriel

Av. Das Nacoes Unidos

Pinheiros River

Av. Quarto Centenário

Cons. R. Alves

Sena Madureit

N

5 mile
1 km
0
0

Lodging
Bourbon, **6**
Brasilton
São Paulo, **14**
Caesar Park, **17**
Eldorado
Higienópolis, **9**
Grande Hotel
Ca D'Oro, **16**
Hotel Esplanada, **4**
Hotel Principe, **1**
Hotel São
Sebastião, **11**
Hotel Vila Rica, **5**
Ibirapuera Park
Hotel, **35**
Maksoud Plaza, **22**
Novotel, **36**
San Raphael, **2**
Sheraton Mofarrej
Hotel & Towers, **21**
Transamerica, **37**
Ville Hotel, **10**

Dining
Alfama dos
Marinheiros, **27**
Almanara, **12**
Bolinha, **29**
Brahma, **7**
Ca D'Oro, **16**
Cristal, **33**
Esplanada Grill, **24**
Fasano, **25**
Freddy, **34**
Frevo, **26**
Gigetto, **15**
Govinda, **39**
Jardim de Napoli, **8**
La Casserole, **3**
La Tambouille, **30**
La Vecchia
Cucina, **32**
Laurent, **18**
Mariko, **17**
Massimo, **20**
Paddock, **13, 28**
Ritz, **19**
Sushi Yassu, **23**
Truta Rosa, **38**
Yellow Giraffe, **31**

do patrons feast either in the ocher-color dining room decorated with Italian engravings and huge sprays of fresh flowers or in the glassed-in garden gazebo. ✗ *Rua Pedroso Alvarenga 1088,* ☏ *011/282–5222. Reservations advised. AE, DC. Closed Sun. No lunch Sat.*

$$$$ **Massimo.** Just off Avenida Paulista, this is the city's prime spot for heavy-weight lunchtime deal-making over such refined Italian pleasures as leg of lamb with leeks or gnocchi with shrimp, tomato, and pesto sauce. Owner Massimo Ferrari, a tubby man in shirtsleeves and suspenders, keeps the best tables on standby for the nation's VIPs. ✗ *Alameda Santos 1826,* ☏ *011/284–0311. Reservations advised. No credit cards.*

$$ **Jardim de Napoli.** This neighborhood restaurant is so good it draws
★ outsiders. No matter where you've come from, you'll have to wait patiently in line to feast on meatballs stuffed with mozzarella cheese in Parmesan sauce, linguine with mushrooms and cream sauce, and other Italian specialties. ✗ *Rua Dr. Martinico Prado 463,* ☏ *011/66–3022. No credit cards. Closed Mon.*

$ **Cristal.** This Jardins pizzeria with ovens in an atrium and modern art on the walls serves the thin-crust variety to upper-crust families and singles. Toppings on the personal pizzas include *portuguesa,* with ham, onion, hard-boiled egg, cheese, and olives; and *marguerita,* with cheese, basil, and tomatoes. ✗ *Rua Professor Artur Ramos 551,* ☏ *011/816–6227. No reservations. V.*

$ **Gigetto.** This often-packed cantina stays open late for the after-theater
★ crowd—spectators and performers both. Try the tender deep-fried squid or the cappelletti pasta in cream sauce with peas, ham, and mushrooms. ✗ *Rua Avanhandava 63,* ☏ *011/256–9804. AE, DC, MC, V.*

Japanese

$$$ **Mariko.** Perched atop the Japanese-owned Caesar Park hotel (*see* Lodg-
★ ing, *below*), this restaurant caters to demanding Japanese business executives and boasts a view of the city. Everything from sushi to tempura is top quality; the grilled whole anchovy is superb. ✗ *Rua Augusta 1508,* ☏ *011/253–6622. Reservations advised. AE, DC, MC, V. Closed Mon.*

$$ **Sushi Yassu.** At one of the best Japanese restaurants in Liberdade (Little Tokyo), you'll dine on sushi, sashimi, tempura, yakisoba, or grilled fish, made with the freshest ingredients. ✗ *Rua Tomás Gonzaga 98,* ☏ *011/279–6622. AE. Closed Mon.*

Lebanese

$ **Almanara.** Part of a chain of Lebanese semi-fast-food outlets that began at this downtown location, Almanara is perfect for a quick lunch of hummus, tabbouleh, grilled chicken, and rice. There is also a full-blown restaurant on the premises serving Lebanese specialties rodízio-style (you get a taste of everything until you can ingest no more). ✗ *Rua Dr. Basílio da Gama 70,* ☏ *011/257–7580. AE, DC, MC, V.*

Seafood

$$ **Truta Rosa.** Homegrown trout, prepared in an endless variety of ways, is making this small new restaurant with a huge fish-shape window a hit. You'll cross a metal bridge over a small lagoon to reach the dining room, where sashimi and quenelles are reeling in the customers. ✗ *Av. Vereador José Diniz 318,* ☏ *011/247–8629. Reservations advised. AE. MC. Closed Mon. No dinner Sun.*

Lodging

São Paulo's hotels are almost exclusively geared to the business traveler, both homegrown and foreign. For this reason, most hotels are in and around downtown and the Avenida Paulista area, with a few new ones springing up near the up-and-coming Marginal Pinheiros neighborhoods. Because of the size of the city and its frequent traffic jams, your choice should depend a great deal on the activities you plan to undertake.

Less-expensive hotels are mostly found right in the city center, which can be dangerous for tourists, especially at night (the Largo do Arouche area, however, is fairly safe and quiet at night, and there are many good hotels there). For longer stays, the city offers many apart-hotels, which usually have small in-room kitchenettes but also house a fairly good restaurant at street level. The **Grande Hotel Ca' D'Oro** (*see below*), a top European-style hotel, caters to families who are moving to or leaving São Paulo, offering no fewer than 60 suites. Two youth hostels charge about $8 a night; contact the **Associação Paulista de Albergues da Juventude** (Rua Jandaia 154, São Paulo, 01320–040, ☎ 011/605–3077).

Many hotels offer discounts of 20%–40% for cash payment or weekend stays, and all include breakfast in the room rate. São Paulo hosts many international conferences, training courses, and business meetings, and these fill hotels, so it is wise to make reservations well ahead of your arrival. For price-category definitions, *see* Lodging *in* Brazil Essentials, *below*.

$$$$ **Caesar Park.** Halfway between downtown and Avenida Paulista and
★ appointed with myriad mirrors, granite floors, and Chinese rugs, this hotel caters to demanding business travelers, especially Japanese executives. Rooms are done in beige or blue, with mahogany furniture and reproductions of 19th-century Brazilian genre scenes by French artist Jean-Baptiste Debret; some of the city's best sushi can be had at the top-floor restaurant, Mariko (*see* Dining, *above*). ☎ *Rua Augusta 1508, ☎ 011/253–6622, toll-free in Brazil ☎ 0800/111164, FAX 011/288–6146; U.S. ☎ 800/228–3000. 158 rooms, 19 suites. 3 restaurants, pub, room service, pool, beauty salon, sauna, massage, health club, business services, meeting rooms. AE, DC, MC, V.*

$$$$ **Maksoud Plaza.** Ronald Reagan *almost* stayed overnight here on a 1982
★ presidential visit, but the Secret Service thought the soaring atrium lobby, with its panoramic elevators, fountains, greenery, artwork, and shops, presented too much of a security risk! The staff provides highly professional service, the hotel's six restaurants are very good, and the in-house theater and Maksoud 150 nightclub offer some of the city's best entertainment. ☎ *Alameda Campinas 1250, ☎ 011/251–2233, FAX 011/253–4544. 420 rooms. 6 restaurants, 3 bars, indoor pool, health club, nightclub, theater, business services. AE, DC, MC, V.*

$$$$ **Sheraton Mofarrej Hotel & Towers.** Located just behind Avenida Paulista, next to the Trianon Park, this hotel features a subdued lobby done in glass, with dark granite floors, plants, a bar, and an art gallery. Guest rooms are decorated in brown, ocher, and orange tones, and four floors boast butler service plus other extras; rooms on the west side overlook the park. ☎ *Alameda Santos 1437, ☎ 011/284–5544, FAX 011/289–8670; U.S. ☎ 800/325–3535. 2 restaurants, 2 bars, indoor pool, outdoor pool, business services. AE, DC, MC, V.*

$$$$ **Transamerica.** Located directly across the Pinheiros River from the Centro Empresarial office complex, where many U.S. companies are housed, this hotel is a highly comfortable and convenient choice. The skylit lobby is decorated with granite, marble, Persian carpets, palm trees, leather sofas, and oversize modern paintings; the spacious rooms have no special charm, but their pastel colors, wood furnishings, and beige carpeting create a relaxing ambience for the business traveler. ☎ *Av. das Nações Unidas 18591, ☎ 011/523–4511, toll-free in Brazil ☎ 0800–126060, FAX 011/548–8884. 211 rooms. Restaurant, 2 bars, pool, 9-*

hole golf course, 5 tennis courts, exercise room, jogging, squash, business services. AE, DC, MC, V.

$$$ Brasilton São Paulo. The smaller of two Hiltons in downtown São Paulo, this one attracts many foreign musicians who perform in the concert halls nearby. There's a cozy bar with a good lunch buffet in the understated lobby, which is decorated with travertine marble floors and wood paneling. Rooms are done in blue, maroon, and brown with wood details, and bathrooms have granite sinks. ☎ *Rua Martins Fontes 330,* ☎ *011/258–5811,* FAX *011/258–5812; U.S.* ☎ *800/445–8667. 250 rooms. 3 restaurants, bar, pool, sauna. AE, DC, MC, V.*

$$$ Eldorado Higienópolis. Set in one of the city's oldest residential neighborhoods, only a five-minute taxi ride from downtown, this hotel has a large pool and a lobby dressed in travertine marble with a pink granite floor. The green-carpeted rooms have print bedspreads, beige walls, and wooden furniture; the noise level is lowest in the back rooms or in the front above the fifth floor. ☎ *Rua Marquês de Itu 836,* ☎ *011/ 222–3422,* FAX *011/222–7194. 155 rooms. 2 restaurants, bar, pool. AE, DC, MC, V.*

$$$ Grande Hotel Ca' D'Oro. Owned and run by a Northern Italian fam-
★ ily for more than 40 years, this Old World–style hotel near downtown boasts bar-side fireplaces, lots of wood and Persian carpeting, a great variety of room decor (all along classic European lines), ultrapersonalized service, and one of the city's best restaurants (*see* Dining, *above*). All these amenities attract Brazilian bigwigs, expatriate families arriving and departing São Paulo, and travelers who have been returning for decades. ☎ *Rua Augusta 129,* ☎ *011/256–8011,* FAX *011/231–0359. 290 rooms. 2 restaurants, bar, indoor pool, outdoor pool, sauna, exercise room. AE, DC, MC, V.*

$$$ Novotel. This French-chain hotel is a bit run-down but is undergoing gradual renovation. One of the few accommodations in the Morumbi neighborhood (and less expensive than the nearby Transamerica), Novotel has rooms that sport stucco walls and a basic brown decor; the lobby is somewhat dark, with maroon leather armchairs and matching carpeting, but it gives onto a pleasant patio and pool area. ☎ *Rua Ministro Nelson Hungria 450,* ☎ *011/844–6211,* FAX *011/844– 5262. 190 rooms. Restaurant, bar, pool. AE, DC, MC, V.*

$$ Bourbon. Both guests and furnishings are well cared for in this small
★ hotel near the Largo do Arouche, one of the few downtown districts that has retained the city's erstwhile charm. A brass-accented basement bar features live piano music; the lobby has upholstered print sofas, an abstract handcrafted black and white wall hanging, and granite flooring, while the rooms are decorated in beige and blue, with marvelously large and sunlit bathrooms. ☎ *Av. Vieira de Carvalho 99,* ☎ *011/223– 2244,* FAX *011/221–4076. 122 rooms. Restaurant, bar, sauna. AE, DC, MC, V.*

$$ Hotel Vila Rica. Also in the Largo do Arouche vicinity, this hotel is smaller, less grand, and less expensive than the Bourbon. The lobby and guest rooms are decorated in Brazilian colonial style, with details in carved wood and stone; back rooms are less noisy. ☎ *Av. Vieira de Carvalho 167,* ☎ *and* FAX *011/220–7111. 60 rooms. Restaurant, bar. AE, DC, MC, V.*

$$ Ibirapuera Park Hotel. A short cab ride from Congonhas Airport, this hotel, which has excellent sports facilities and is five minutes from Ibirapuera Park, is an ideal choice for visitors addicted to exercise. The rooms and lobby are unpretentious, done in shades of brown, with lots of granite, wood, and leather. ☎ *Rua Sena Madureira 1355,* ☎ *011/ 572–0111,* FAX *011/572–3499. 79 rooms. Restaurant, bar, pool, sauna, 2 tennis courts, exercise room. AE, DC, MC, V.*

$$ San Raphael. Right on the charming Largo do Arouche, with its flower market, great restaurants, and cafés, this hotel has a tastefully decorated lobby, with lots of oil paintings and watercolors. Rooms have small balconies, with furnishings in beige leather, Formica, marble, and tiles. 🖃 *Largo do Arouche 150,* ☎ *011/220–6633,* 𝔽𝔸𝕏 *011/221– 3202. 219 rooms. Restaurant, bar. AE, DC, MC, V.*

$$ ★ Ville Hotel. Located in the lively Higienópolis neighborhood of apartment buildings, bars, and bookstores abutting Mackenzie University, this hotel costs about $70 a night. The small lobby features a black and pink granite floor, recessed lighting, and black leather sofas; rooms are done in pastel colors with brown carpeting. 🖃 *Rua Dona Veridiana 643,* ☎ *and* 𝔽𝔸𝕏 *011/255–1216. 54 rooms. Restaurant, pool, sauna, exercise room. AE, DC, MC, V.*

$ Hotel Esplanada. It's old and worse for wear, but it's clean and in a safe neighborhood. Next door are a great bakery and a movie theater. Many business travelers on a budget stay at this downtown hotel, which costs only about $20 a night, breakfast included. 🖃 *Largo do Arouche 414,* ☎ *011/220–5711. 52 rooms. No credit cards.*

$ Hotel Principe. This is a simple, clean hotel with attentive staff, near the central Praça da República. The decor is somewhat helter-skelter, with a mosaic stone floor in the lobby, old wallpaper and modern tile decorations in the corridors, and orange and brown room furnishings. 🖃 *Av. São João 1072,* ☎ *011/221–8155,* 𝔽𝔸𝕏 *011/222–6079. 84 rooms. Restaurant, bar. AE, DC, MC, V.*

$ ★ Hotel São Sebastião. This rock-bottom option, popular among European backpackers, costs only $16 a night without a bathroom, $22 with a bathroom. Room rates include breakfast. The plain but tasteful accommodations, reminiscent of a Continental pension, are housed in the oldest building on a central, pedestrian-only street, which means it's quiet at night. 🖃 *Rua Sete de Abril 364,* ☎ *011/257–4988 or 011/255–1594. 50 rooms. No credit cards.*

The Arts

São Paulo presents a growing challenge to Rio de Janeiro's traditional position as the country's cultural center. The world's top orchestras, opera and dance companies, and other troupes always include the city in their South American tours, often performing for vast open-air audiences in Ibirapuera Park during their stays. In the realm of contemporary arts expression, São Paulo boasts a world-class dance company, the **Ballet Stagium** (☎ 011/852–3451), and a contemporary music ensemble, **Grupo Novo Horizante** (☎ 011/256–9766), neither of which have permanent homes.

Sunday-to-Sunday listings of cultural events appear in the **Veja São Paulo** insert of the newsweekly **Veja.** The arts sections of the dailies **Folha de São Paulo** and **O Estado de São Paulo** also carry arts listings and reviews.

Festivals

The city hosts several arts festivals, the most significant being the internationally renowned biennial art exhibition known as the **São Paulo Biennial,** held every even year from mid-October to mid-December in Ibirapuera Park. For more information contact the Fundação Bienal (Parque Ibirapuera, Portão 3, 04098-900, ☎ 011/572–7722, 𝔽𝔸𝕏 011/ 549–0230).

Other festivals include the **Carlton Dance Festival,** held annually in June and July, and the annual three-day **Free Jazz Festival** in August, both organized by Dueto Produções e Publicidade Ltda. (attn: Monique Gardenberg, Rua Lauro Müller 116, Sala 4203, Rio de Janeiro, RJ 22290-160; ☎ 021/542–3938 or 021/541–3743). An international film festival, **Mostra Internacional de Cinema** (Alameda Lorena 937, cj. 303, 01424-001, ☎ 011/883–5137 or 011/64–5819), is held in October.

Although it often rains in São Paulo just prior to Lent, the city's colorful **Carnival** celebration, centering on a dancing parade, is a viable alternative for those unable to travel to Rio de Janeiro or Salvador. The samba schools (groups that participate in the parade) rehearse throughout the year Wednesday–Friday evenings and Sunday, and hold samba parties on Saturday night. For more information, call **Anhembi** (☎ 011/267–0702).

Film

It is wise to call ahead for confirmation because theaters often change their programming without notice. Only foreign children's movies are dubbed; the rest carry subtitles with the original dialogue intact. European and other non-American foreign films are shown mostly at the **Belas Artes** movie theater complex (Rua da Consolação 2423, ☎ 011/258–4092 or 011/259–6341). The **Museu da Imagem e do Som** (Museum of Image and Sound) hosts special free film festivals (Av. Europa 158, ☎ 011/852–9197).

Music

CLASSICAL AND OPERA

Local orchestras include the São Paulo State Symphony and the Municipal Symphony Orchestra, both of which are suffering the debilitating effects of inadequate funding. A local cultural organization, the **Mozarteum Brasileira Associação Cultural** (Av. Brigadeiro Faria Lima 1664, 10th Floor, ☎ 011/815–6377), sponsors a lively April–October season of classical music concerts at the Teatro Municipal, including performances by visiting musicians.

Most of São Paulo's serious music, ballet, and opera are performed in the intimate gilt and moss-green-velvet surroundings of the turn-of-the-century **Teatro Municipal** (Praça Ramos de Azevedo s/n, ☎ 011/223–3022).

The **Teatro da Cultura Artística** (Rua Nestor Pestana 196, ☎ 011/258–3616), with its fine acoustics, also hosts classical-music performances.

Chamber music is performed at the new **Sala São Paulo Luiz** (Av. Juscelino Kubitschek 1830, ☎ 011/827–4556).

CONTEMPORARY

Popular, jazz, and rock concerts are held at the locations below, as well as at top discotheques and clubs (*see* Nightlife, *below*).

Olympia (Rua Clélia 1517, ☎ 011/252–6255) has a deluxe club atmosphere.

The Palace (Av. dos Jamaris 213, ☎ 011/531–4900) is a fully carpeted venue.

Sesc-Pompéia (Rua Clélia 93, ☎ 011/864–8544) is housed in a converted, exposed-brick factory.

Teatro Hall (Rua Rui Barbosa 672, ☎ 011/284–0290) is newly renovated.

FREE CONCERTS

Free city-sponsored concerts often attract large crowds to public spaces such as the open area under the **Museu de Arte de São Paulo** and the new pedestrian-only **Anhangabaú Valley** area. Visiting international orchestras often are invited to play for Sunday morning concertgoers in **Ibirapuera Park;** local musicians also frequently perform there. Free state-sponsored concerts take place at the **Memorial da América Latina** (Rua Mário de Andrade 644, ☎ 011/823–9611; closed Mon. except during concerts).

Theater

São Paulo's theater district in the bohemian Bela Vista neighborhood, also known as Bexiga, boasts dozens of theaters dedicated mostly to plays, especially comedies, in Portuguese. The São Paulo Hilton, Transamerica, Maksoud, and Holiday Inn Crowne Plaza hotels have in-house theaters featuring plays and musical events; the one at the Holiday Inn is a venue for "fringe" performances. In addition to these and the theater district per se, other top venues are listed below.

SESC Anchieta (Rua Dr. Vila Nova 245, ☎ 011/256–2322) is known for dance and classical theater with a contemporary twist.

Teatro Artur Rubinstein (Rua Hungria 1000, ☎ 011/814–4433) at the Hebraica Club has plays and concerts.

Teatro da Cultura Artística (Rua Nestor Pestana 196, ☎ 011/258–3616) hosts dance, musicals, and plays.

Teatro Faculdade Armando Álvares Penteado (FAAP) theater (Rua Alagoas 903, ☎ 011/824–0233) shows old movies and puts on concerts and plays.

The Catholic University's **Tuca** (Rua Monte Alegre 1024, ☎ 011/65–0111) puts on counterculture concerts and theater.

BOX OFFICES

Tickets are sold at the various theater box offices and are also available at special booths in the **Shopping Center Morumbi** (Av. Roque Petroni Jr. 1098, Top Floor, no ☎; ☉ Weekdays 10–8, Sat. 10–6); **Shopping Center Ibirapuera** (Av. Ibirapuera 3103, Top Floor, ☎ 011/61–0194; ☉ Weekdays 10–8, Sat. 10–6); and **Shopping Center Iguatemi** (Av. Brigadeiro Faria Lima 1191, Top Floor, ☎ 011/212–7623; ☉ Weekdays 10–10, Sat. 10–4). Some theaters will deliver tickets for a surcharge, as will **Lucas Shows** (☎ 011/858–5783). Half-price tickets are available for students only, except during sporadic promotional events.

Nightlife

Sunday-to-Sunday listings of entertainment events appear in the *Veja São Paulo* insert of the newsweekly *Veja.* The monthly booklet *"São Paulo Este Mes,"* distributed in hotels and for sale at some newsstands, has current nightlife listings.

Brazilian Clubs

Popularly known as MPB (Música Popular Brasileira) clubs, these venues book quiet, largely acoustic instrumental and vocal music in the style of Milton Nascimento, Chico Buarque, and Gilberto Gil, with an emphasis on the samba and bossa nova.

Bar da Virada (Rua Simão Álvares 575, ☎ 011/210–0635) is a traditional address for samba and popular music from the 1960s.

Café Paris (Rua Waldemar Ferreira 55, ☎ 011/813–5158) is known for its bossa nova and other Brazilian pop music.

Café Soçaite (Rua Treze de Maio 46, ☎ 011/259–6562) is one of the most popular spots for Brazilian popular music, especially with singles, playing all kinds of local sounds.

Dance Clubs

Caipirasso (Av. Marquês de São Vicente 319, ☎ 011/67–2328) rounds up crowds with Brazilian country music and a mechanical bull.

Columbia (Rua Estados Unidos 1570, ☎ 011/282–8086 and 011/64–3380), in the Jardins, is one of the city's hottest clubs, attuned to the latest fads and fashions; the best night to go is Tuesday.

Palladium (Eldorado Shopping Center, Av. Rebouças 3970, ☎ 011/813–9045) offers a little of everything, including samba, rock, *axé* (Bahian music with a fast-pace rhythm), boleros, and popular Brazilian music.

Resumo da Ópera (Eldorado Shopping Center, Av. Rebouças 3970, ☎ 011/211–2411), sister club of a Rio spot of the same name, is a wild place for the young set, with quick-change-artist DJs, a slide down to the dance floor, and decor inspired by the musical *Phantom of the Opera*.

Sra. Kravitz (Rua Fortunato 34, ☎ 011/220–6220), named after the Mrs. Kravitz character in the TV sitcom *Bewitched*, attracts an eclectic crowd, including transvestites and yuppies.

Star Dust (Rua Franz Schubert 135, ☎ 011/210–5283) is just one in a row of clubs on the same street specializing in flashbacks for the over-40 crowd.

The bohemian **Teatro Vento Forte** (Rua Brigadeiro Haroldo Veloso 150, ☎ 011/820–3095), housed in a shed that's a children's drama school by day, does Brazilian music every which way, Saturday only, bringing in college students and soap opera stars.

Victoria Pub (Alameda Lorena 1604, ☎ 011/881–3822), not far from Columbia, is dedicated to classic rock.

Gay Clubs

Gents Theater House (Avenida Ibirapuera 1911, ☎ 011/572–8227), frequented by men of all ages, is one of the best discos for Saturday-night dancing. There are three bars, a stage for shows, and a big screen with music videos.

Nostromundo (Rua da Consolação 2554, ☎ 011/257–4481), one of the oldest gay discos in São Paulo, features transvestite shows and a wild "anything goes" atmosphere.

Jazz Clubs

The Blue Note (Av. São Gabriel 558, ☎ 011/884–9356) is a venue for traditional jazz and blues.

Café Piu Piu (Rua Treze de Maio 134, ☎ 011/258–8066), in the bohemian Bexiga district, is best known for jazz, but also hosts groups that play rock, bossa nova, and the tango.

Sanja Jazz Bar (Rua Frei Caneca 304, ☎ 011/255–2942) is an old town house in Bexiga dedicated to live jazz.

Singles' Clubs

At **Clyde's** (Rua da Mata 70, ☎ 011/883–0300), *correio elegante* (or elegant mail, notes delivered from table to table by messenger) is the latest way to make a match; there's also a bar, a restaurant, and live music.

Supremo (Rua Oscar Freire 950, ☎ 011/881–2250) is a lively, beautiful-people corner bar in the Jardins.

Zeibar's Paulista (Av. Paulista 2678, ☎ 011/257–1019 and 011/256–0040), another home of the "elegant mail" scene, has live music.

Women's Entertainment

Clube das Mulheres (Rua Padre João Manuel 199, ☎ 011/851–1070; shows Tues. and Thurs. only) features spicy striptease acts by male dancers, who, in the best belly dancer tradition, expect cash donations from the audience.

Excursions from São Paulo

Embu

Only 27 kilometers (17 miles) southwest of the city, this is a Portuguese colonial town of whitewashed houses, old churches, a museum and an apiary, wood-carvers' studios, and antiques shops. A huge handicrafts fair is held here every Saturday and Sunday, the latter day being the best for shopping. Sightseeing information is available at the municipal tourism board, the **Secretaria do Turismo** (Largo 21 de Abril 139, Embu, ☎ 011/494–5333).

Getting There
To make the half-hour drive, take Avenida Professor Francisco Morato to the Rodovia Régis Bittencourt, then follow the signs for Embu. The **Soamin** bus company (☎ 011/495–2520) has service to Embu every half hour, with buses departing from several locations around the city.

Itu

This Portuguese colonial town 90 kilometers (55 miles) northwest of São Paulo is famous for its 18th-century churches (Igreja do Bom Jesus and Nossa Senhora da Candelária), loads of antiques stores, and a tendency to exaggerate; after a television comedian from Itu made his career in the 1960s with a routine about how things in his town were bigger than anywhere else, the local chamber of commerce decided to capitalize on the idea and built an oversize traffic light and pay phone. The gimmick still pays off at local stores, where giant hats, pencils, and other gargantuan items are sold. Tourist information is available at the **Secretaria de Cultura** (Rua Paula Souza 664, Itu, ☎ 011/299–8974).

Getting There
To make the 50-minute drive to Itu, take the Rodovia Castello Branco to SP 312 (Rodovia do Açucar) west, which runs right through town. The **Viação Vale do Tietê** bus company (☎ 011/299–8974) has buses to Itu every hour from the Tietê bus station.

MINAS GERAIS: BELO HORIZONTE AND THE HISTORIC CITIES

Brazil's mountainous central region is dominated by the state of Minas Gerais, a name (meaning "general mines") inspired by the area's great mineral wealth. In the 18th century, vast precious-metal reserves provoked a gold rush that for a time made Minas Gerais, particularly Ouro Prêto, the de facto capital of the Portuguese colony. The legacy of that period of gold, diamond, and semiprecious stone trading is preserved in the so-called historic cities scattered throughout the mountains.

Exploration of Minas Gerais began in the 17th century, when bands of adventurers from the coastal areas came in search of Indian slaves and gold. Near the town of Vila Rica, the explorers found a black stone that was later verified to be gold (the black coloring came from the iron oxide in the soil of Minas). Vila Rica thus came to be called Ouro Prêto (black gold), and at the beginning of the 18th century, Brazil's first gold rush began. The population of the region quickly mushroomed. Along with the wealth seekers came Jesuit priests, and by the middle of the century the colonial cities of Minas were gleaming with new churches built in the Baroque style of Europe.

With the possible exception of Salvador, there is no better preserved example of colonial Brazil than in the mountains of Minas Gerais. Unlike Bahia, however, Minas was blessed with the presence of an artistic genius: The mulatto son of a Portuguese architect and a former slave, his given name was Antônio Francisco Lisboa, and he was born in 1738 in what is today Ouro Prêto, then called Vila Rica. Nicknamed O Aleijadinho, "the little cripple," he was left deformed as an adult by an illness that has been variously described as leprosy or syphilis, but is generally assumed to have been arthritis. Working in cedarwood and soapstone, O Aleijadinho carved the passion of his religious beliefs in sculptures that grace churches throughout the region.

Disabled as he was, with the use of his hands hindered, Aleijadinho could not have chosen a more demanding profession than that of sculptor. Yet little does one perceive in the delicately expressive features of his figures the pain and effort in their creation; legend has it that in the advanced stages of his disease, the artist had to strap his hammer and chisel to his wrists with leather thongs so he could work. Beginning in the 1760s and continuing practically until his death in 1814, Aleijadinho traveled back and forth between the cities and towns of Minas, sculpting and overseeing the construction of the region's churches, in the process leaving for posterity an artistic heritage unmatched anywhere in Brazil.

By the end of the 18th century, the gold began to run out, and Ouro Prêto's population and importance decreased. The Baroque period itself came to an end at the start of the 19th century, when the Portuguese royal family, in flight from the conquering army of Napoléon Bonaparte, arrived in Brazil, bringing with them architects and sculptors who had different ideas and artistic styles.

Today, Minas Gerais is Brazil's second most industrialized state, after São Paulo. The iron that darkened the gold of Ouro Prêto is today an important source of income for Minas, which has evolved into one of the world's leading producers of iron ore. The steel industry followed, and today the capital, Belo Horizonte, is home to a Fiat auto production plant and other large industrial facilities. Minas is also a major coffee producer. The state, however, has paid a price for its development: The once heavily wooded mountains of Minas are now for the most part stripped bare. For visitors, though, the principal attractions remain—magnificent Baroque churches that contain prized sculptural masterpieces, and cities whose hilly cobblestone streets lined with whitewashed buildings retain the atmosphere of 18th-century towns.

Getting Around Minas Gerais

Belo Horizonte is the gateway to Minas Gerais and the hub for visiting the state's colonial cities. Well-maintained roads link Belo Horizonte with all the historic cities, which may be reached only by car or bus. For information on buses, call 031/201–8111 in Belo Horizonte or 031/862–1603 in Ouro Prêto.

Shopping

Regional arts and crafts are sold throughout Minas. Hand-carved wood and soapstone figures and objects, such as crucifixes and ashtrays, are sold by street vendors in all the historic cities. Other typical handicrafts include pottery and tapestries, in particular the hand-woven *arraiol* tapestries for which the area around Diamantina is famous.

Dining

Dining options are admittedly limited in the historic cities, but you will find several excellent restaurants offering typical Minas Gerais food

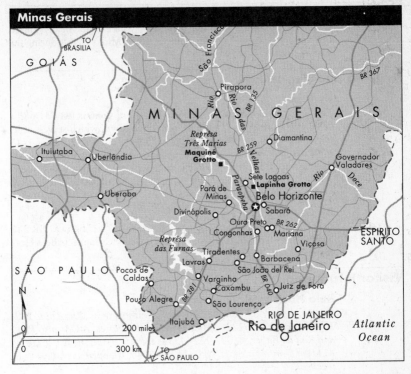

in Ouro Prêto, Tiradentes, São João del Rei, and Diamantina. The mainstay of Mineiro cuisine is *tutu,* a tasty mash of black beans, bacon, and manioc meal served with meat dishes. Another bracing favorite is *feijão tropeiro,* a combination of brown beans, bacon, and manioc meal. Among meat dishes, pork is the most common, in particular the famed *lingüiça* (Minas pork sausage) and *lombo* (pork tenderloin). The most typical chicken dish is *frango ao molho pardo,* broiled chicken served in a sauce made with its own blood. The region's wonderful, very mild, white cheese is known throughout Brazil simply as *queijo do Minas* (cheese from Minas).

Lodging

Accommodations vary dramatically in the colonial cities, although in general, hotels tend to be small and unpretentious. In recent years a number of small, intimate hotels that capture the colonial spirit of the area have been built; all of these are in Ouro Prêto and Tiradentes. Some of the cities—including Congonhas, Mariana, and Sabará—have virtually no accommodations. Visitors to the former two can comfortably stay in Ouro Prêto, while the latter town is most easily visited from Belo Horizonte.

Belo Horizonte and Sabará

Brazil's third-largest city, with a population of almost 2.4 million, Belo Horizonte is the capital of Minas Gerais, a state as renowned for its conservative traditions as for its gold, gemstones, and iron ore. Tradition is all-important in Minas: In terms of family values and politics, Mineiros are considered the most conservative of Brazilians. For visitors, Belo Horizonte is primarily a jumping-off point for trips to the surrounding region, as the town itself offers little of historic value.

(It is, in fact, relatively young, having been founded in 1897.) Half an hour east of Belo Horizonte is Sabará, where fantastically gilded churches drive home the enormous wealth of Minas Gerais during the gold rush days.

Arriving and Departing

By Plane

The city has two airports, **Tancredo Neves,** or **Confins** (☎ 031/689–2700), 39 kilometers (24 miles) from downtown, which serves international flights, and **Pampulha** (☎ 031/441–2000), 9 kilometers (5 miles) from downtown, which serves domestic airlines, primarily shuttle flights from Rio and São Paulo. Between them the two airports connect Belo Horizonte with every major city in Brazil. Varig, Transbrasil, and Vasp airlines fly to both airports.

By Car or Bus

Highway BR 040 connects Belo Horizonte with Rio; Highway BR 381 links the city with São Paulo. Frequent bus service connects Belo Horizonte to both cities.

Visitor Information

Belo Horizonte

Belotur, the city tourism authority, has four locations. *Rua Tupis 149, 10th Floor,* ☎ *031/222–5500; Mercado das Flores, Av. Afonso Pena and Rua da Bahia,* ☎ *031/222–4336; at the bus station,* ☎ *031/201–8111; at Confins airport,* ☎ *031/689–2140. All open weekdays 8–8, weekends 8–4.*

Turminas, the Minas Gerais state tourism authority, can supply information on the historic cities and other attractions in the state. *Av. Bias Fortes 50,* ☎ *031/212–2134.* ⊙ *Weekdays 12:30–6:30.*

Exploring

Belo Horizonte

The **Parque Municipal** is in the heart of the business district and close to several hotels. With its tree-lined walks, small lakes, and rustic bridges, the well-maintained park is an example of the passion for orderliness that is a characteristic of Mineiros. This same trait has helped make Belo Horizonte one of the cleanest and safest of Brazil's leading cities. Within the park is the **Palácio das Artes** (Palace of the Arts, Av. Afonso Pena 1537, ☎ 031/237–7333; ☛ Free), a cultural center containing a library, art gallery, theater, and the **Centro de Artesenato Mineiro,** with examples of contemporary Minas Gerais handicrafts, including works of soapstone and wood, Minas pottery, and tapestries, all for sale.

Ironically, though tourists come to Belo to visit the nearby historic region, one of the principal attractions of the city is the Pampulha neighborhood, famed for its examples of modern Brazilian architecture. Foremost among these is the **Chapel of São Francisco,** completed in 1943 and considered one of the most important works of Brazil's famed architect Oscar Niemeyer. Inside the small but distinctive chapel with its undulating roof, a Niemeyer signature, are frescoes painted by one of Brazil's most important 20th-century painters, Cândido Portinari. The Cubist works depict St. Francis and the Stations of the Cross. To reach the chapel, take a taxi or a bus that goes north on Avenida Presidente Antônio Carlos. The chapel is on the edge of an artificial lake a half hour from downtown. *Av. Otacílio Negrão de Lima, km 12,* ☎ *031/441–2628.* ☛ *Free.*

Sabará

Just east of Belo Horizonte, 19 kilometers (12 miles) away on Highway BR 383, about a half-hour ride from the town center, is the city of Sabará. In this former colonial town, today a sprawling suburb of 90,000, historic buildings are scattered about, requiring tourists either to join a tour or drive. The interiors of the Baroque churches of Sabará are rich in gold leaf paneling. In the main square, Praça Melo Viana, sits the unfinished **Senhora do Rosário dos Pretos** (1767), built, like its counterpart in Ouro Prêto, by former slaves. In Sabará, however, they ran out of gold before the project could be completed.

The ornate **Nossa Senhora da Conceição** was completed in 1710. The simple exterior of this small church gives no indication as to the wealth inside, typified by its luxurious gold altar. *Praça Getúlio Vargas,* ☎ *031/671–1724.* ☛ *Entry fee.* ☾ *Wed.–Sun. and Tues. afternoon.*

Even more impressive, however, is the interior of the narrow **Nossa Senhora de Ó church,** another explosion of gold leaf; it dates from 1720. Both churches contain paintings with Asian themes that are said to have been executed by 23 Chinese artists brought from the Portuguese colony of Macao, on the coast of China. *Largo do Ó, no* ☎. ☛ *Entry fee.* ☾ *Wed.–Sun. and Tues. afternoon.*

Examples of Aleijadinho's work can be found in the nearby church of **Nossa Senhora do Carmo,** where he designed the pulpits, choir loft, and doorway. This is one of several Minas churches on which Aleijadinho and the painter Manuel da Costa Ataíde, a contemporary of Aleijadinho and a brilliant artist in his own right, collaborated. *Rua do Carmo,* ☎ *031/671–152.* ☛ *Entry fee.* ☾ *Tues.–Sun. afternoons.*

Shopping

Gemstones

Gems are the obvious focus in an area still famous for its mines. The state is particularly well-known for the quality of its topazes. Gemstones should be purchased only from reputable dealers. In Belo Horizonte, try the **Gem Center** (Av. Afonso Pena 1901, 5th Floor, ☎ 031/222–8189); **Hans Stern** (Trevo Nova Lima Shopping Center, BR 040, Belvedere Ioja 105-106, ☎ 031/286–1568); **Amsterdam Sauer** (in the Othon Palace Hotel, Av. Afonso Pena 1050, ☎ 031/273–3844); or **Manoel Bernardes** (Trevo Nova Lima Shopping Center, BR 040, Nivel BL, Ioja 29-30, ☎ 031/286–2492; Rua Espírito Santo 835, 3rd Floor, ☎ 031/201–3822).

Handicrafts

Belo Horizonte's **Centro de Artesenato Mineiro** (Av. Afonso Pena 1537, ☎ 031/201–8900), in the Palace of the Arts, offers a wide range of regional crafts. A large **outdoor crafts market** is held on Thursday evening and Sunday morning in Praça da Liberdade.

Sports and the Outdoors

Soccer

Mineirão Stadium (Av. Antônio Abrão Carão 1001, Pampulha, ☎ 031/441–6133) in Belo Horizonte is the third-largest stadium in Brazil and the home field for the city's two professional soccer teams, Atletico Mineiro and Cruzeiro.

Spelunking

For amateur spelunkers, the mountains of Minas Gerais are replete with caves to be explored. The largest and most popular cavern is the **Maquiné Grotto** (☎ 031/931–1313; ☛ Entry fee), 113 kilometers, or 70 miles, northwest of Belo Horizonte near the town of Cordisburgo, where six large chambers are open to visitors but must be seen as part of a guided tour. The **Lapinha Grotto** (no ☎; ☛ Entry fee) is closer to Belo, only 48 kilometers (30 miles) away, near the city of Lagoa Santa and 12 kilometers (7 miles) from Confins Airport on the road leading from the airport; it also must be seen with a guided tour.

Dining and Lodging

As Sabará is best visited as a day trip, all the establishments listed below are in Belo Horizonte. For price-category definitions, *see* Dining *and* Lodging *in* Brazil Essentials, *below*.

Dining

$$$$ Casa do Baile. Considered the best restaurant in the stylish Pampulha
★ neighborhood, the emphasis here is on international cuisine, but there is also a healthy selection of regional cuisine. An excellent view of Pampulha Lake and live music contribute to the romantic atmosphere. ✕ *Av. Octacílio Negrão de Lima 751,* ☎ *031/443–3486. Reservations advised. AE, DC, MC, V. Closed Sat.*

$$$$ L'Apogee. This self-described French restaurant actually has a wide-ranging menu that even includes Italian cuisine. Meat and fish dishes and some pasta dishes are served. ✕ *Rua Antônio de Albuquerque 729,* ☎ *031/227–5133. Reservations required. No credit cards. Closed Sun.–Tues.*

$$$ Chez Dadette. Although most of Belo's better restaurants specialize in
★ traditional Minas Gerais cuisine, this establishment in the Santo Agostinho neighborhood, near downtown, is a delightful exception to the rule. The cooking is classic French, with such specialties as steak au poivre, and the quality surprisingly high for what Paulistanos and Cariocas consider to be "the provinces." ✕ *Rua Coelho de Souza 70,* ☎ *031/275–1400. AE, DC, MC, V. Closed Sun.*

$$ Brock's Steak House. At this restaurant in the Mangabeiras neighborhood, a wide variety of cuts of beef and pork are offered in a colonial-style dining room with blue Portuguese tiles on the walls. Customers may choose from 20 types of potato dishes, ranging from baked to soufflé, and nine kinds of sauces, including béarnaise and mustard. ✕ *Av. Afonso Pena 4276,* ☎ *031/223–7686. AE, DC, MC, V.*

$$ Casa dos Contos. The menu at this gathering place for local journalists, artists, and intellectuals is unpretentious and varied, ranging from fish and pasta to traditional Minas cuisine. In keeping with its bohemian clientele, Casa dos Contos serves well past midnight. ✕ *Rua Rio Grande do Norte 1065,* ☎ *031/222–1070. AE, DC, MC, V.*

$ Chico Mineiro. Dining Minas Gerais–style means ample portions of hearty
★ dishes such as tutu *à mineira,* the local equivalent of meat and potatoes. Nowhere is it better prepared than at this traditional restaurant in the Savassi neighborhood, home to Belo's liveliest nightspots. ✕ *Rua Alagoas 626,* ☎ *031/261–3237. AE, DC, MC, V.*

$ Dona Lucinha II. Traditional Minas dishes are offered in this cafeteria-style eatery in the Savassi neighborhood, a prime example of a recent fad for "self-service" among Minas restaurants. ✕ *Rua Sergipe 811,* ☎ *031/261–5930. AE, DC, MC, V.*

Lodging

$$$ **Brasilton Contagem.** This modern, motel-style hotel in the Contagem
★ industrial district belongs to the Hilton chain and is popular among
business travelers. Guest rooms face a central courtyard with a pool
and tropical gardens, creating an atmosphere of total relaxation. ☎
Hwy. BR 381, km 3.65, ☎ *031/396–1100,* ℻ *031/396–1144. 144
rooms. Restaurant, bar, pool. AE, DC, MC, V.*

$$$ **Othon Palace.** The acknowledged top downtown hotel, the Othon is
reliable but undistinguished and in need of renovation. The hotel over-
looks the trees and lakes of the downtown Parque Municipal. ☎ *Av.
Afonso Pena 1050,* ☎ *031/273–3844,* ℻ *031/212–2318. 302 rooms.
Restaurant, bar, pool. AE, DC, MC, V.*

$$$ **Real Palace.** Recently renovated, this downtown hotel close to the Mu-
★ nicipal Park has ample, comfortable rooms decorated in pastel colors,
with views of the park and the distant mountains. ☎ *Rua Espírito Santo
901,* ☎ *031/213–1211,* ℻ *031/273–2643. 256 rooms. Restaurant,
bar, pool. AE, DC, MC, V.*

$$ **Terminal Center Hotel.** This new downtown hotel is next door to the
★ bus station that serves the historic cities. Spacious rooms and efficient
service make this an excellent value. ☎ *Av. Amazônas 1445,* ☎ *031/
291–0022,* ℻ *031/275–3955. 120 rooms. Restaurant, bar, pool,
travel services. AE, DC, MC, V.*

$$ **Wembley Palace.** This traditional, aging, high-rise downtown hotel of-
fers clean rooms, reliable service, and a central location. ☎ *Rua Es-
pírito Santo 201,* ☎ *031/201–6966,* ℻ *031/224–9946. 105 rooms.
Restaurant, bar. AE, DC, MC, V.*

$ **Amazônas.** This downtown hotel is clean, simply furnished, and rea-
sonably priced. There's an excellent restaurant on the 11th floor. ☎
Av. Amazônas 120, ☎ *031/201–4644,* ℻ *031/202–4236. 76 rooms.
Restaurant, bar. AE, DC, MC, V.*

$ **Palmeiras da Liberdade.** This new, comfortable, and inexpensive hotel
is in the chic Savassi neighborhood. ☎ *Rua Sergipe 893,* ☎ *and* ℻
031/261–7422. 62 rooms. Restaurant, bar. AE, DC, MC, V.

The Arts and Nightlife

The center of cultural life in Belo Horizonte is the downtown **Palácio
das Artes** (Rua Afonso Pena 1537, ☎ 031/201–8900), where ballet
companies and symphony orchestras sporadically perform. The box
office is only open when performances are coming up.

Mineiros are conservative by nature, and nightlife is extremely limited.
The action in Belo Horizonte is concentrated in the Savassi neighbor-
hood, where there are many outdoor bars as well as a handful of clubs
with live Brazilian music. One popular nightspot is **Era Uma Vez um
Chalezinho** (Rua Paraíba 1455, ☎ 031/221–2170), where you can dip
into an excellent fondue while listening to live music. Another tradi-
tional bar is the **Cervejaria Brasil** (Rua Aimorés 78, ☎ 031/225–1099),
Belo's late-night hangout for artists and intellectuals. For homesick
cowboys, there is nothing better than **Pau e Pedra** (Av. Getúlio Vargas
489, ☎ 031/223–5669), Belo's only country-and-western bar.

Ouro Prêto, Mariana, and Congonhas

The best place to see Aleijadinho's artistry is Ouro Prêto, the former
gold rush capital. Now a lively university town, it has been preserved
as a national monument and a World Heritage site. The surrounding
mountains, the geometric rows of whitewashed buildings, the red-tile
roofs that climb the hillsides, the morning mist and evening fog that

drift over the city all give Ouro Prêto a strongly evocative air, as if at any moment it could be transported back two centuries.

The true treasures of Ouro Prêto, however, are its 13 colonial churches, representing the supreme achievement of Mineiro Baroque architecture. Typically, the Minas Baroque style is marked by elaborately carved doorways with strongly curving lines. Most distinctive, though, are the interiors, richly painted and decorated lavishly with cedarwood and soapstone sculptures. In many of the churches, the interior style is unabashedly rococo, with an often ostentatious use of gold leaf, a by-product of the gold boom that brought wealth to this region.

Nearby are Mariana and Congonhas, both of which are home to not only prime examples of Aleijadinho's work, but also to that of his brilliant contemporary, the painter Manuel da Costa Ataíde.

Visitor Information

Mariana

Associação de Guias. Praça Tancredo Neves, ☎ 031/557–1122. ⊘ Weekdays 8–5.

Ouro Prêto

The **Associação de Guias,** formed by the city's professional tour guides, can provide general information on the city. The association's well-informed and courteous guides also conduct walking tours of the historic area. Tours are available in English and typically last six to seven hours. Be prepared for some stiff hiking up and down Ouro Prêto's numerous hills. *Praça Tiradentes 41, ☎ 031/551–2655. ⊘ Weekdays 8–6, weekends 8–5.*

Exploring

Ouro Prêto

Located 97 kilometers (60 miles) southeast of Belo Horizonte (south on Highway BR 040 and then east on BR 356), at an elevation of 3,200 feet, Ouro Prêto is a city of narrow cobblestone streets and alleys built on a series of steep hills. In its heyday, Ouro Prêto was not simply a city of gold and churches. It was also one of the most progressive cities in Brazil and the birthplace of the colony's first stirrings of independence. A movement called the Inconfidência Mineira was organized to overthrow the Portuguese rulers and establish an independent Brazilian republic. It was to have been led by a resident of Ouro Prêto, Joaquim José da Silva Xavier, a dentist known as Tiradentes, or "tooth puller." But the Minas rebellion never got off the ground. In 1789, word of Tiradentes's intentions reached the capital of Rio de Janeiro and the leader of the rebels was hanged and quartered, and his followers were either imprisoned or exiled.

Artifacts of this turbulent era, such as clothing, toys, slaves' manacles, firearms, books, and gravestones, as well as works by Aleijadinho and Ataíde, can be seen at the **Museu da Inconfidência,** housed in a former 18th-century prison in Praça Tiradentes, in the city center. *Praça Tiradentes 139, ☎ 031/551–1121. ☛ Entry fee. ⊘ Tues.–Sun. after noon.*

The **Casa dos Contos,** the colonial coinage house, contains the foundry used to mint the coins of the gold-rush period plus examples of the coins and period furniture. *Rua São José 12, ☎ 031/551–1444. ☛ Entry fee. ⊘ Daily after 1.*

The former opera house, built between 1746 and 1769, is now the **Teatro Municipal.** The theater still presents shows and plays, thus making it the oldest municipal theater still in operation in Latin America. There is no regular schedule for performances, however; check with the Associação de Guias to see if a play is being performed. *Rua Brigadeiro Mosqueira.* ☛ *Entry fee.* ☼ *Daily after noon.*

The **Museu da Mineralogia e das Pedras,** housed opposite the Museu da Inconfidência in the former governor's palace, contains an excellent collection of precious gems, gold, and crystals. *Praça Tiradentes 20, no* ☏. ☛ *Entry fee.* ☼ *Weekdays after noon, weekends after 1.*

Most visitors to Ouro Prêto come not to visit the city's museums, however, but to see its justly famed churches, all of which are within walking distance of one another and are relatively close to the central square, Praça Tiradentes.

Two blocks east of Praça Tiradentes is the distinctive twin-tower **Igreja São Francisco de Assis,** Aleijadinho's masterpiece, which was completed in 1810. In addition to designing the church, Aleijadinho was responsible for the wood and soapstone sculptures on the portal, high altar and side altars, pulpits, and cross arch. The panel on the nave ceiling representing the Virgin's glorification was painted by Ataíde. Cherubic faces, garlands of tropical fruits, and allegorical characters are carved into the main altar, and are still covered with their original paint. *Largo de Coimbra, no* ☏. ☛ *Entry fee.* ☼ *Tues.–Sun. 8–11:30, 1–5.*

Three blocks south is the **Igreja da Nossa Senhora das Mercêse Perdões,** built from 1740 to 1773. The church contains etchings done by Aleijadinho as studies for his sculptures. *Rua das Mercês,* ☏ *031/ 551–3282.* ☛ *Entry fee.* ☼ *Tues.–Sun.*

Three blocks east is the **Igreja da Nossa Senhora da Conceição,** a lavishly gilded church completed in 1760 that contains the tomb of Aleijadinho as well as a museum dedicated to the artist. *Praça Antônio Dias,* ☏ *031/551–3282.* ☛ *Entry fee.* ☼ *Tues.–Sun. 8–11:30, 1–5.*

The **Igreja Nossa Senhora do Carmo,** on the west side of the Praça Tiradentes, contains major works by Aleijadinho and Ataíde. The church was originally designed by Aleijadinho's father, himself an architect, but was later modified by the son, who added more Baroque elements, including characteristic soapstone sculptures of angels above the entrance. The church was completed in 1776. ☏ *031/551–1209.* ☛ *Entry fee.* ☼ *Tues.–Sun. 8–11:30, 1–5.*

Next door to the church is the **Museu de Arte Sacra do Carmo,** a museum dedicated to religious art, with wood carvings of saints by Aleijadinho and other 18th-century art. *Rua Brigadeiro Mosqueiro,* ☏ *031/ 551–4736.* ☛ *Entry fee.* ☼ *Tues.–Sun. 8–11, 1–5.*

Three blocks west of Carmo is the **Nossa Senhora do Pilar** church, built in 1733 and the most richly decorated of Ouro Prêto's churches; it's said that 400 pounds of gold leaf was used to cover the interior. *Praça Mons. Castilho Barbosa,* ☏ *031/551–1209.* ☛ *Entry fee.* ☼ *Tues.–Sun. 1–5.*

One of the smaller but more intriguing churches is the domed **Igreja Nossa Senhora do Rosário dos Pretos** (1785), built by slaves, some of whom bought their freedom with the gold they found in Ouro Prêto. According to legend, the interior of the church is bare because the slaves ran out of gold after erecting the Baroque building. *Largo do Rosário,* ☏ *031/551–1209.* ☛ *Entry fee.* ☼ *Tues.–Sun. 1–5.*

Other prominent churches are the 1771 **Nossa Senhora das Mercês e Misericórdia** (Rua Padre Rolim, ☏ *031/551–1209;* ☛ Entry fee; open Fri.–Sun. 1–5), containing soapstone sculptures by Aleijadinho; the 1785

Basílica do Senhor Bom Jesus de Matosinhos (Rua Alvarenga, 1½ km [1 mi] from Tiradentes, ☎ 031/551–1209; ☛ Entry fee; open Tues.–Sun. 1–5), the most distant of the churches, which at press time (winter 1995) was closed for restoration; and the 1745 **Igreja de Santa Efigênia** (Id. de Santa Efigênia, ☎ 031/551–3282; ☛ Entry fee; open Tues.–Sun. 8–noon), containing cedar sculptures by Francisco Xavier de Brito, Aleijadinho's teacher.

Mariana

Eleven kilometers (7 miles) east of Ouro Prêto along Highway BR 365 is the colonial mining city of Mariana; on the road from Ouro Prêto to Mariana is the **Minas de Passagem** (☎ 031/557–1340; ☛ Entry fee), a former gold mine that can be visited on a guided tour.

The oldest city in Minas Gerais (founded in 1696) is also the birthplace of Aleijadinho's favorite painter, Ataíde. Mariana, like Ouro Prêto, has preserved much of the appearance of an 18th-century gold-mining town. Its three principal churches all showcase examples of the art of Ataíde, who intertwined sensual romanticism with religious themes. The faces of Ataíde's saints and other figures often have mulatto features, reflecting the composition of the area's population at the time.

The **Catedral Basílica da Sé,** completed in 1760, contains paintings by Ataíde, although it is probably better known for its 1701 German organ, transported by mule from Rio de Janeiro in 1720. *Praça Cláudio Manoel,* ☎ *031/557–1237.* ☛ *Entry fee.* ☉ *Tues.–Sun.*

Behind the cathedral is the **Museu de Arte Sacra,** which claims to have the largest collection of Baroque painting and sculpture in the state, including wood and soapstone works of Aleijadinho and paintings of Ataíde. *Rua Frei Durão 49,* ☎ *031/557–1237.* ☛ *Entry fee.* ☉ *Tues.–Sun. noon–1 and Mon.*

Nearby is the 1793 **São Francisco de Assis church,** featuring soapstone pulpits and altars by Aleijadinho. The church's most impressive works, however, are ceiling panels in the sacristy that were painted by Ataíde; they depict, in somber tones, the life and death of St. Francis. Considered by many to be the artist's masterpiece, the wooden panels have unfortunately been damaged by termites and water. *Praça Minas Gerais, no* ☎. ☛ *Entry fee.*

Next door is the **Nossa Senhora do Carmo church,** with works by Ataíde, which at press time (winter 1995) was closed for restoration work. The artist is buried at the rear of the church. *Praça Minas Gerais,* ☎ *031/ 557–1635.*

Congonhas do Campo

To see Aleijadinho's crowning effort, head east to the small gold-rush town of Congonhas do Campo, some 50 kilometers (31 miles) away. Dominating Congonhas is the hilltop pilgrimage church of **Bom Jesus do Matosinho,** built in 1757, the focus of great processions during Holy Week and the major reason for coming here. At the entrance to the churchyard, you'll see the Aleijadinho's 12 life-size Old Testament prophets carved in soapstone, a towering achievement and one of the greatest works of art anywhere of the Baroque period. Every facial expression seems marked with the sculptor's own pain during his final years. Leading up to the church on the sloping hillside are six chapels, each containing a scene representing a Station of the Cross. Each of the 66 figures in this remarkable procession was carved in cedar by Aleijadinho and painted by Ataíde. *Praça da Basílica,* ☎ *031/731–1590.* ☛ *Entry fee.* ☉ *Tues.–Sun.*

Shopping

Gemstones

Reputable gem dealers in Ouro Prêto include **Amsterdam Sauer** (Praça
Tiradentes 69, ☎ 031/551–3383) and **Manoel Bernardes** (Rua Conde
de Bobadela 48, ☎ 031/551–2487).

Handicrafts

In Ouro Prêto, an **outdoor fair** is held daily in the Largo do Coimbra,
and there are stores around the central Praça Tiradentes and along nearby
streets where gemstones and soapstone carvings are sold.

Sports and the Outdoors

Trekking

The best source of information about hiking in the region is the **Associação de Guias** (Praça Tiradentes 41, ☎ 031/551–2655) in Ouro Prêto.
The association also organizes hiking tours and rents sports equipment.

Dining and Lodging

Some families in Ouro Prêto rent rooms in their homes, although usually only during Carnival and Easter, when the city's hotel rooms fill
up. For a list of rooms to rent, contact the **Associação de Guias de Turismo** (Praça Tiradentes 41, ☎ 031/551–2655). The association also
provides information on areas where camping is permitted. Tourist facilities in Mariana and Congonhas are limited; all of the following restaurants and hotels are in Ouro Prêto. For details and price-category
definitions, *see* Dining *and* Lodging *in* Brazil Essentials, *below.*

Dining

$$ **Casa Grande.** This colonial-style restaurant in Praça Tiradentes pro-
★ vides a view of the 18th-century buildings that line the square. Among
the regional dishes served are *lombo com tutu à mineira* (pork tenderloin
served with beans, cabbage, and hard-boiled egg), frango ao molho
pardo, and, for dessert, *dôce de leite com queijo* (fresh white cheese
with caramelized milk). ✗ *Praça Tiradentes 84,* ☎ *031/551–2976. No
credit cards.*

$–$$ **Casa do Ouvidor.** This walk-up over a jewelry store in the heart of the
★ historic district has garnered several awards for regional dishes such
as tutu à mineira and lingüiça. It's a favorite stop for tours, but don't
be discouraged—it's worth going here at odd hours. ✗ *Rua Conde de
Bobadela 42,* ☎ *031/551–2141. No credit cards.*

$ **Taverna do Chafariz.** Regional cuisine is served cafeteria-style in this
informal eatery near the colonial coinage house. ✗ *Rua São José 167,*
☎ *031/551–2828. No credit cards.*

Lodging

$$$$ **Pousada do Mondego.** This converted house dating from 1747 and fur-
★ nished with period antiques is next door to the church of São Francisco de Assis. In addition to the colonial ambience, the small and intimate
pousada (inn) provides highly personalized and professional service.
Reservations are a must. 🏨 *Largo de Coimbra 38,* ☎ *031/551–2040,
Rio reservations* ☎ *021/287–3122, ext. 601,* FAX *031/551–3094. 23
rooms. Restaurant, bar, travel services. AE, DC, MC, V.*

$$$ **Estrada das Minas Gerais.** Spacious yet cozy rooms and delightful chalets
with fireplaces are the calling cards of this roadside hotel at the en-
trance to Ouro Prêto on the highway from Belo Horizonte. Be sure to
book ahead. 🏨 *Rodovia dos Inconfidentes, km 87,* ☎ *031/551–2122,*
FAX *031/551-2709. 30 rooms, 12 chalets. Pool. AE, DC, MC, V.*

$$ **Grande Hotel.** Immense by Ouro Prêto standards—35 rooms—it's the city's largest hotel. It's also the premier modernist structure in town—a curving two-story building on concrete pillars—designed by world-acclaimed architect Oscar Niemeyer, but cultural purists consider it an eyesore. ☎ *Rua Senador Rocha Lagoa 164, ☎ and* ﬀ *031/551–1488. 35 rooms. Restaurant, bar. AE, DC, MC, V.*

$ **Colonial.** This is a good example of the small, no-frills inns that can be found in most of the historic cities. What you'll get is a very basic, clean room for a low price. ☎ *Rua Camilo Veloso 26, ☎ 031/551–3133,* ﬀ *031/551-3361. 18 rooms. No credit cards.*

Tiradentes and São João del Rei

Visitor Information

São João del Rei
Terminal Turístico. Praça Dr. Antônio Viegas, ☎ 032/371–3522. ✆ Weekdays 7–noon and 1–5.

Tiradentes
Secretária de Turismo. Rua Resende Costa 71, ☎ 032/355–1212. ✆ Weekdays 8–5, weekends 12–5.

Getting Around

By Train
A restored 19th-century train makes the 13-kilometer (8-mile), 30-minute journey between the cities of Tiradentes and São João del Rei. The train operates only Friday through Sunday and on holidays. It departs São João del Rei (☎ 032/371–2888) at 10 AM and 2:15 PM; it leaves from the Tiradentes station (Praça da Estação, ☎ 032/355–1269) at 1 and 5.

Exploring

Tiradentes
Continuing south on Highway BR 040, then west on BR 265 for a total of 129 kilometers (80 miles), brings you to Tiradentes, the birthplace of the eponymous martyr (the town was formerly called São José del Rei). Tiradentes can also be reached from Rio by BR 040, a 388-kilometer (230-mile) trip. Life in this tiny village—nine streets with eight churches!—moves slowly, and one can easily believe that time here has stopped in the 18th century. This quality has recently attracted wealthy residents of Rio, São Paulo, and Belo Horizonte, who have sparked a local real estate boom by buying up 18th-century properties as weekend getaways.

Besides the excellent selection of handicrafts—some 20 shops line Rua Direita in the town center—the charming town's principal attraction is the **Igreja de Santo Antônio,** built in 1710 and containing some of the best-preserved gilded carvings—of saints, cherubs, and biblical scenes—in the historic cities. The church's soapstone frontispiece was sculpted by Aleijadinho, and the church also boasts a sundial created by the artist. *Rua da Câmara, no ☎.* ☛ *Entry fee.*

São João del Rei
Continue 13 kilometers (8 miles) southwest to São João del Rei, the second largest of the historic cities, with a population of 80,000. On weekends the trip from Tiradentes can be made aboard a restored 19th-century train (*see* Getting Around, *above*). Although far more modern in appearance than the other colonial cities, São João has preserved

three superb Baroque churches. The three are within walking distance of one another in the downtown area, close to the train station.

The Victorian train station is a treat in itself, containing a **railway museum and roundhouse** with a collection of locomotives dating from the 19th century. *Av. Hermílio Alves 366,* ☎ *032/371–2888.* ☛ *Entry fee.* ☉ *Tues.–Sun., except 11:30–1.*

The church of **Nossa Senhora do Carmo** (Largo do Carmo, no ☎; ☛ Entry fee), built in 1734, was designed by Aleijadinho, and its interior contains several sculptures by the master. The **Catedral Nossa Senhora do Pilar** (Rua Getúlio Vargas, ☎ 032/371–2568; ☛ Entry fee), constructed in 1721, is known for its seven richly decorated altars. One of Aleijadinho's most brilliant designs, the twin-towered church of **São Francisco de Assis** (Praça Frei Orlando, ☎ 032/371–3966; ☛ Entry fee; closed daily noon–1:30) is notable for its elegant symmetry. The church also contains two of his sculptures, including the crucifix on the altar, in which rubies represent the blood of Christ.

Dining

For price-category definitions, *see* Dining *in* Brazil Essentials, *below.*

São João del Rei

$$ Cantina do Italo. One of the few restaurants in the region that serve nonregional cuisine, this Italian cantina, with the requisite chianti bottles hanging from the walls, offers a generous range of pasta dishes. ✗ *Rua Min. Gabriel Passos 317,* ☎ *032/371–2862. DC, MC, V.*

$$ Rex. This downtown restaurant is one of the city's best options for regional cooking. Specialties include pork tenderloin accompanied by either tutu or feijão tropeiro. ✗ *Rua Artur Benardes 137,* ☎ *032/371–1449. No credit cards.*

Tiradentes

$$ Casa dos Cantos. One of the region's more unusual eateries, this
★   Tiradentes restaurant has two tables and three fixed meals—fish broiled in an herb sauce, chicken curry, and roast beef. All three are excellent, but the main reason for the line at the door is dessert—mint mousse covered with chocolate sauce. ✗ *Rua da Cadeia 37, no* ☎. *No credit cards.*

$–$$ Canto do Chafariz. This center of regional cuisine is rated tops for its tutu. ✗ *Largo do Chafariz 37,* ☎ *032/355–1377. No reservations. No credit cards. Closed Mon.*

$–$$ Estalagem. Another Tiradentes favorite, the Estalagem draws raves for
★   its feijão tropeiro. ✗ *Rua Min. Gabriel Passos 280,* ☎ *032/355– 1144. No credit cards. Closed Mon.*

Lodging

For price-category definitions, *see* Lodging *in* Brazil Essentials, *below.*

São João del Rei

$$ Porto Real. This small hotel on the city's main street is a good option if you want to stay in São João del Rei and make day trips to the nearby mountain towns. 🏨 *Av. Eduardo Magalhães 254,* ☎ *and* FAX *032/371– 1201. 30 rooms. Restaurant, bar, pool. AE, DC, MC, V.*

Tiradentes

$$$ Solar da Ponte. Long included among Brazil's finest small hotels, the
★   Solar has the spirit of a house in the country, complete with sprawling lawns and gardens. In every respect, from the design of the comfortable beds to the choice of ceramic tableware, the hotel is a faithful

example of regional style. The breakfast and afternoon tea, included in the room rate, are special treats. ✉ *Praça das Mercês,* ☎ *032/355–1255, Rio reservations* ☎ *021/287–3122 ext. 601,* FAX *032/355–1201. 12 rooms. Bar, pool, sauna. No credit cards.*

$$ **Pousada Richard Rothe.** This inn, named after a German antiques
★ dealer who used to live in the town, is in the historic center of Tiradentes. It is extravagantly decorated with antiques such as Louis XV armchairs in the living area and French tapestries on the walls of the guest rooms. Children under 12 will not be warmly welcomed. ✉ *Rua Pedro Toledo 124,* ☎ *032/355–1333. 6 rooms. MC.*

Diamantina

Seeing the lone historic city north of Belo Horizonte (290 kilometers/180 miles away) requires an overnight trip. Diamantina took its name from the diamonds that were extracted in great quantities from its soil in the 18th century. Perhaps because of its remote setting in the barren mountains close to the semiarid Sertão area, Diamantina is considered the best-preserved colonial town in Minas, although its churches lack the grandeur of those in some of the other towns. Its white-walled homes and churches stand in pristine contrast to the iron red of the surrounding mountains. As in the other historic cities of Minas, the principal attraction in Diamantina is the simple pleasure of walking along the clean-swept cobblestone streets surrounded by colonial houses—note the covered overhanging roofs with their elaborate brackets.

Visitor Information

Casa da Cultura. Praça Antônio Eulálio 53, ☎ 038/931–2137. ☺ Weekdays 7–noon and 1–6.

Exploring

The city was the home of two legendary figures of the colonial period: diamond merchant João Fernandes and his slave mistress Xica da Silva, today a popular figure in Brazilian folklore. According to legend, Xica had never seen the ocean, so her lover built her an artificial lake and then added a boat. You can visit the **home of Xica da Silva** (Praça Lobo Mesquita 266; no ☎), whose highlights are its colonial furniture and Xica's private chapel. On the same square is the **Igreja Nossa Senhora do Carmo** (Rua do Carmo; no ☎), built in 1751 as a gift from Fernandes to his mistress. Supposedly Xica ordered that the bell tower be built onto the back of the building so that the ringing would not disturb her. Both may be seen only by guided tour; contact the Casa da Cultura (*see* Visitor Information, *above*).

The **Museu do Diamante** (Rua Direta 14, ☎ 038/931–1382; ☛ Free; open Tues.–Sat. before noon, Sun. after noon), the city's diamond museum, is housed in a 1789 building and displays equipment used in the colonial-period diamond mines. A few blocks away is the **birthplace of Juscelino Kubitschek** (Rua São Francisco 241, no ☎; ☛ Free; open Tues.–Fri. before noon, weekends after noon, and Mon.), one of Brazil's most important 20th-century presidents and the man who built Brasília. On Rua da Glória, a covered wooden footbridge connects the second stories of two buildings that once served as the headquarters of the colonial governors.

At night, Diamantina enjoys a special distinction. The city is famed as Brazil's center of serenading, although the art form has never had the popularity in Brazil that it enjoys in the rest of Latin America. Still, on weekend nights and often during the week, the city's romantics gather in a downtown alley known as **Beco do Mota,** the former red-light district and now home to several popular bars frequented by students and young professionals. Strolling guitar players also gather on Rua Direita and Rua Quitanda.

Sports and the Outdoors

Trekking

The two most popular wilderness areas for hiking are the mountainous area just south of Diamantina, famed for its waterfalls, and the **Serra do Cipó National Park** (96 kilometers, or 60 miles, northeast of Belo Horizonte on BR 367), with waterfalls, lakes, and two canyons. At both areas, facilities are poor and the park rangers are not very helpful. Thus, unless you have been there before and know your way around, you should hire a guide or visit the areas as part of an organized tour.

Dining and Lodging

For price-category definitions, *see* Dining *and* Lodging *in* Brazil Essentials, *below.*

$–$$ **Cantina do Marinho.** This well-respected restaurant specializes in Mineiro cuisine. Favorites are pork steak with tutu and pork tenderloin with feijão tropeiro. ✗ *Beco do Mota 27,* ☎ *038/931–1686. No credit cards.*

$–$$ **Tijuco.** Virtually the only lodging option in Diamantina, this small inn is in the heart of the historic center of the city. 🏨 *Rua Macau do Meio 211,* ☎ *038/931–1022. 26 rooms. Restaurant, bar. AE, DC, MC, V.*

BAHIA: SALVADOR

Misery and mystery live side by side in Brazil's first capital, founded in 1549 to protect the nascent Portuguese colony against Dutch invaders. Built on a bluff, Salvador, capital of the state of Bahia, overlooks the astonishing Bahia de Todos os Santos (All Saints' Bay), one of the world's widest, covering 1,036 square kilometers (400 square miles). The Portuguese court moved the capital to Rio de Janeiro in 1763, and ever since, Salvador's strategic and shipping importance—and its great wealth, originally deriving from sugar and tobacco—have been in decline, giving rise to widespread poverty and crime. Happily, however, the city's decadence has also preserved the music, art, dance, religions, cuisine, folkways, and festivals of the thousands of African slaves settled there by the Portuguese.

It is this legacy that captivates visitors to Salvador, where at least 70% of the 2.5 million population is black. African rhythms roll forth everywhere, from buses and construction sites to the giant drums of musicians such as the Olodum percussion group, which has recorded with Paul Simon. The scents of coriander, coconut, and palm oil waft around corners that also play afternoon host to white-turbaned women cooking and selling deep-fried spicy shrimp and bean cakes. Baroque church interiors covered with gold leaf hark back to the riches of the Portuguese colonial era, when slaves masked their religious beliefs under a thin veneer of Catholicism. And partly thanks to modern-day church acceptance of those beliefs, Salvador has become the fount of Candomblé, a religion based on personal dialogue with the *orixás,* a family of African deities closely linked to nature.

The influence of Salvador's African heritage on Brazilian music has turned this city into one of the most stirring places in the world to spend Carnival, the bacchanalian last fling that precedes Lent (and only one of more than 20 marvelous processions and festivals punctuating the local calendar). As Bahia's distinctive *axé* music has gained popularity around the country, the city has begun to compete with Rio de Janeiro's more traditional celebration. Salvador's Carnival means dancing night after night in the street to the ear-splitting, bone-rattling music of bands perched atop special sound trucks. It means watching the parades of outlandish Carnival associations, such as the Filhos de Gandhi, or Sons of Gandhi (founded by striking stevedores in 1949), men dressed in white tunics and turbans that are the relics of ancient Muslim conversions in Africa. This movable feast formally lasts a week in February or March but begins in spirit at New Year's and continues even into Lent in small towns outside Salvador, with street festivals called *micaretas*.

Bahia is the largest state in Brazil's poor Northeast. Although the inland areas suffer periodically from severe drought, the coast, including Salvador, has a healthier economic outlook, being the country's most popular travel destination. The state government spent $10 million in 1993 to restore Salvador's historic district, while private investors have focused on developing southern Bahia's pristine beaches.

Brazil's economic problems have also led to a constant scarcity of resources needed to provide top-quality travel services. Travelers ideally should speak at least some Spanish if they know no Portuguese and be prepared for delays and mix-ups; Bahians pride themselves on a laid-back approach to life.

Visitor Information

The main office of the state tourist board, **Bahiatursa,** is far from tourist attractions, but there are five other conveniently located branches.

Airport: *Aeroporto Internacional 2 de Julho s/n,* ☎ *071/204–1244.* ☉ *Daily 8:30–10.*

Bus station: *Av. Antônio Carlos Magalhães s/n, Terminal Rodoviário,* ☎ *071/358–0871.*

Downtown historic center: *Terreiro de Jesus s/n,* ☎ *071/321–0388.* ☉ *Daily 8–6.*

Main: *Centro de Convenções, Jardim Armação s/n, 41750–270,* ☎ *071/ 370–8400.* ☉ *Weekdays 7–7.*

Mercado Modelo crafts market: *Praça Visconde de Cairú s/n,* ☎ *071/ 241–0240.* ☉ *Daily 8–6.*

Upper City: *Porto da Barra s/n,* ☎ *071/247–3195.* ☉ *Daily 8–6.*

Emtursa, the municipal tourist board, has two offices. *Largo do Pelourinho 12,* ☎ *071/243–6555 or 071/243–5738; open weekdays 8–6. Travessa da Ajuda 2, 2nd Floor,* ☎ *071/321–4346 or 071/321–9307; open weekdays 8–6.*

Dial 131 for **Disque Turismo,** a phone hot line offering spotty multilingual information on special events and tourist attractions. The *Bahia Tourist Guide* is available in bookstores and at newsstands, and Bahiatursa periodically publishes a leaflet with updated basic tourist information, available at hotel reception desks.

Arriving and Departing

By Plane
The **2 de Julho Airport** (☎ 071/204–1010), 37 kilometers (23 miles) outside the city, has scheduled flights by the Brazilian airlines Varig, Vasp, and Transbrasil. The only international carriers serving the airport are Lufthansa, Trans Europa, and Aeroflot.

Avoid taking comum taxis at the airport, as drivers often jack up the fare by refusing or "forgetting" to turn on the meter. Prepaid *cooperativa* (co-op) taxis, white with a broad blue stripe, are preferred, and cost $30–$45 for the 20- to 30-minute drive downtown. The *ônibus executivo*, an air-conditioned bus, runs daily from 6 AM to 9 PM at no set intervals, costs about $1.10 and takes about an hour to reach downtown, stopping at hotels along the way. Drivers don't speak English, but will stop at a specific hotel if shown a written address. Several companies operate these buses, the largest being **Transportes Ondina** (Av. Vasco da Gama 347, ☎ 071/245–6366). The municipal **Circular** bus line, operated by both Transportes Ondina and **Transportes Rio Vermelho** (Av. Dorival Caymmi 18270, ☎ 071/377–2587), costs about a quarter and runs along the beaches to downtown, ending up at São Joaquim, where ferries depart for Itaparica Island.

By Car
Coming from Rio de Janeiro, Salvador can be approached by two highways, BR 101 and BR 116. Drivers on BR 101 should leave the highway at the city of Santo Antônio/Nazaré and follow the signs for Itaparica, 61 kilometers (38 miles) away. At Itaparica, either take the 45-minute ferryboat ride to Salvador, or continue on until BR 101 connects with BR 324. Heading north on BR 116, exit at the city of Feira de Santana, 107 kilometers (67 miles) from Salvador, for BR 324, which approaches the city from the north. Follow the signs marked IGUATEMI/CENTRO for downtown and nearby destinations. Coming from Brasília, take BR 20 north, BR 242 east, then from Ponte Paraguaçu take BR 116 north to the city of Feira de Santana, where you can pick up BR 324 south into Salvador.

By Bus
Terminal Rodoviário (Av. Antônio Carlos Magalhães, Iguatemi, ☎ 071/358–6633).

Getting Around Salvador

The Baroque churches, museums, Portuguese colonial houses, and narrow, cobbled streets are best seen on foot with a Bahiatursa-accredited personal guide (*see* Tour Operators, *below*). To get around the rest of the city, use inexpensive comum taxis. To get from the Upper to the Lower City, or vice versa, it's fun to travel in the room-size Lacerda Elevator (*see* Exploring Salvador, *below*), or the more utilitarian funicular railway that runs from behind the cathedral down to the city's commercial district.

By Car
Because of a lack of parking, rental cars are impractical for sightseeing in the Upper City (although the government plans to build more parking areas), but are handy for visiting outlying beaches and some far-flung attractions.

By Bus
Buses are crowded, dirty, and dangerous, but service most of the city and cost a pittance (50¢ for adults and nothing for children who can

squeeze under the turnstile). The fancier **executivo** buses ($1.20 for adults, free for children under five) serve tourist areas more completely but have been subject to a spate of robberies. The glass-sided green, yellow, and orange **jardineira** bus (marked "Praça da Sé"), running from the downtown Praça da Sé to the Stella Mares beach, along the beachfront **Orla Maritima** series of avenues, is fine for getting to the beach. (Note that some hotels also provide this service.)

By Taxi

Comum taxis (white with a red and blue stripe) can be hailed on the street or called by phone (Ligue Taxi, ☎ 071/358–0733). Both these and the more expensive and usually air-conditioned **especial taxis,** which can be called by telephone (Coometas, ☎ 071/244–4500; Contas, ☎ 071/245–6311), line up in front of the top hotels. They charge on the basis of a unit registered on the meter that must be converted into Brazilian currency using a chart posted in the window. Tipping isn't expected. If you bargain, a comum taxi can be hired for the day for as little as $50.

By Boat

Itaparica and the other harbor islands can be reached by taking a ferry or a launch, by hiring a motorized schooner, or by joining a harbor schooner excursion, all departing from the docks behind the Mercado Modelo.

Tour Operators

Boat Tours

The same tour agencies that organize orientation tours (*see below*) also offer full-day harbor excursions on motorized schooners. For $50, you get hotel pickup and drop-off, a 90-minute stop at the beach and drinks and appetizers on one of the 38 islands in All Saints' Bay, plus a stop for lunch (included in the price) on the largest island, Itaparica.

Orientation Tours

Group tours provide some initial orientation, but are fairly cursory, with guides often speaking minimal English; these larger groups are also targeted by hordes of street vendors at almost every stop of the way. Several travel agencies offer half-day minibus orientation tours with hotel pickup and drop-off for about $20–$25. Agencies also offer "By Night" packages, which include dinner and an Afro-Brazilian music and dance show, for $40–$45, and daylong harbor tours on motorized schooners, costing $30–$35 (*see* Boat Tours, *above*). A private beach tour including the Lagôa de Abaeté can be arranged as well, with a car and guide provided for about $30 a head (minimum 2 people). Reservations for all tours can be made through your hotel.

The leading agencies offering these tours are **L.R. Turismo** (Av. Otávio Mangabeira 2365, ☎ 071/248–3333); **Crismota Turismo** (in Salvador Praia Hotel, Av. Presidente Vargas 2338, ☎ 071/247–9888); **Globe Turismo** (Rua Dra. Praguer Fróes 97, ☎ 071/245–9611); and **Lilás Viagens e Turismo Ltda.** (Av. Tancredo Neves 274, Bloco B, Centro Empresarial Iguatemi II, ☎ 071/358–7133 or 071/358–9254). Crismota Turismo also offers 15-minute helicopter fly-overs costing $85 per person with a four-passenger minimum.

Private Guides

Bahiatursa guides, hired through your hotel, a travel agency, or a Bahiatursa kiosk, carry credentials you can ask to check. For about $80 per couple per day (or $80 per single or $120 for a small group), the guide will provide a car, hotel pickup, and lunch; his presence also enhances security. Beware of guides who pick up tourists at church entrances and overcharge for telling tall tales.

Walking Tours

The most complete and personalized English-language walking tours are offered by **Tatu Tours** (Ed. Victoria Center, Sala 1108, Av. Centenário No. 2883, ☎ and FAX 071/237–7562), which also operates special-interest tours and excursions to locations outside Salvador (*see* Excursions from Salvador, *below*).

Precautions

Bahia's extreme poverty and growing tourism dollars together have made security a major travel consideration. Leave valuables at home. The Salvador tourist police suggest that travelers not change dollars with strangers on the street and that they photocopy passports, leaving originals at the hotel. However, even hotel safes and rooms may not be totally secure. Saturday afternoon and Sunday are the days with the least police presence in historic areas.

The office of the **Delegacia de Proteção do Turista** (☎ 071/320–4103), the tourist police, is down the steps at the back of the Belvedere at the Praça da Sé. This office deals as best it can with tourist-related crime after the fact, on a shoestring budget; there are also military police foot patrols wearing armbands identifying them as **polícia turística** officers, who speak rudimentary second languages.

Exploring Salvador

Salvador sprang up on a cliff overlooking All Saints' Bay, and today occupies a triangle sided by the bay and the ocean, coming to a point at the **Farol da Barra** (Barra lighthouse). The original city is called the **Cidade Histórica** (Historic City), the site of the oldest government, ecclesiastical, and residential buildings, dating as far back as the 16th century. Over the years, the city spread down the cliff, and in the space between the drop off and the bay, a commercial district grew up; today this area is also the site of the fully enclosed handicrafts market, the Mercado Modelo, and the port, from which harbor excursions depart. Sleepy **Itaparica Island,** the largest of the harbor's 38 islands, is across the water. The city also grew sideways; to the northwest around the bay lies the **Itapagipe Peninsula,** site of the Nossa Senhora do Bomfin church and the Mont Serrat Fort, as well as the city's outdoor fruit and vegetable market, factories, and poorer neighborhoods. The beaches and better residential neighborhoods and hotels begin close to the Barra lighthouse and north of it on the ocean side. Up on the cliff, south toward the mouth of the bay from the historic city, there are numerous old mansions, churches, and some hotels; the city's main shopping street, **Avenida Sete de Setembro;** and the **Campo Grande,** the square where Carnival begins. To the east lies a series of hills and valleys crowded with many poor districts, beyond which lie the better oceanside neighborhoods. The tree-lined Avenida Sete de Setembro continues south through the **Vitória** neighborhood and down past the Iate Club (Yacht Club) to the **Barra** neighborhood, a mix of beach, yuppie bars, good cheap restaurants, low-life cafés, and moderately priced hotels. Here the city comes to a point at the Barra lighthouse before running up east and north again on the oceanside leg of the triangle. The next beaches, **Ondina** and **Rio Vermelho,** are home to Salvador's most expensive resort hotels; the latter neighborhood is quite bohemian, with some of the city's best bars and music. Going north along the so-called **Orla Marítima** (a series of connecting avenues running along the coast), there are many restaurants, the cleanest beaches, and, at the city's northernmost point, the mysterious **Lagôa de Abaeté,** a deep, black, freshwater lagoon.

Upper City

The **Terreiro de Jesus,** a large square with three churches and a small handicrafts fair, opens the way to exotic, historic Salvador. Where nobles once strolled under imperial palm trees, protected by their slaves, visitors will see men practicing *capoeira,* a stylized, dancelike foot-fight with African origins, to the thwang of the *berimbau,* a rudimentary but mesmerizing bow-shape musical instrument.

Walk east down the Ladeira do Cruzeiro de São Francisco to enter the most famous of the city's 176 churches, the 18th-century Baroque **Igreja de São Francisco** (Church of St. Francis), and its still-active monastery. Listen for the sound of African drums in the square outside as you appreciate the ceiling painted in 1774 by José Joaquim da Rocha, a mulatto who founded Brazil's first art school. The ornately carved cedar and rosewood interior virtually writhes with images of mermaids, acanthus leaves, and caryatids—all bathed in shimmering gold leaf. Guides will tell you that there is as much as a ton of gold here, but restoration experts say there is actually much less, as the leaf used is just a step up from a powder. A super Sunday morning alternative to crowded beaches is mass here (9–11, 11–11:45); stay until the end, when the electric lights go off, to catch the wondrous subtlety of gold leaf under natural light. On Tuesday at 6:30 PM there is a blessing of the church, followed by an open street rehearsal by the Afro-Brazilian Olodum percussion group. *Praça Padre Anchieta,* ☎ *071/243–2367.* ☛ *Free.* ⊙ *Mon.–Sat. 8–12, 2–5; Sun. 8–12.*

Next door is the **Igreja da Ordem Terceira de São Francisco** (Church of the Third Order of St. Francis), whose 18th-century Spanish plateresque sandstone facade—carved to resemble Spanish silver altars made by beating the metal into wooden molds—is unique in all Brazil. The facade was hidden for decades under a thick coat of plaster, until, the story goes, a drunk electrician went wild with a hammer in the 1930s. *Praça Anchieta s/n,* ☎ *071/242–7046.* ☛ *Free.* ⊙ *Same hrs as main church.*

Walk back up toward the Terreiro de Jesus, past the coffin shops. At the top left corner where the Terreiro begins is **Simon** jewelers, whose obliging owners will allow you the use of their bathroom and give you a free glass of cold water or a cup of coffee. This is one of Salvador's top jewelry manufacturers, with a window onto the room where goldsmiths work. *Rua Ignácio Accioli,* ☎ *071/242–521. Closed Sun. afternoon.*

Moving into the square itself, turn right and see the **Igreja São Domingos de Gusmão da Ordem Terceira** (Church of the Third Order of St. Dominick), which was begun in 1723. The lay clergy of this Baroque church were restoring it at press time (winter 1995), hoping to open a museum in a side chapel to display their fascinating collection of carved processional saints and other sacred objects. Such sculptures often had hollow interiors used to smuggle gold into Portugal to avoid government taxes. You will see Asian features and details in the church decoration, evidence of long-ago connections with Portugal's Asian colonies of Goa and Macao. Upstairs are two impressive rooms with carved wooden furniture used for the lay brothers' meetings and receptions. *Terreiro de Jesus,* ☎ *071/242–4185.* ☛ *Free.* ⊙ *Mon.–Sat., except noon–2.*

Directly at the other end of the Terreiro is the 17th-century **Catedral Basílica,** where an Asian influence also is seen: Note the intricate ivory and tortoise shell inlay from Goa on the Japiassu family altar, third on the right as you enter; the Asian facial features and clothing of the figures in the transept altars; and the 16th-century tiles from Macao in the sacristy. A Jesuit who lived in China painted the ceiling over the cathedral entrance. *Terreiro de Jesus,* ☎ *071/321–4573.* ☛ *Free.* ☉ *Tues.–Sat. 8–11, 3–6; Sun. 5–6:30.*

Also on the square, just to the left of the cathedral, is a building that housed Brazil's first medical school, today home of the **Museu Afro-Brasileiro.** This rich collection of African costumes, masks, musical instruments, tools, and statues plumbs much that drives contemporary Bahian culture. Don't miss the stunning series of wooden panels—inlaid with silver, gold, shells, copper, and brass—by the Argentine-born artist Hector Carybé. The museum also sells literature on African culture. *Terreiro de Jesus,* ☎ *071/321–0383.* ☛ *Entry fee.* ☉ *Weekdays 9–5.*

Turning left as you exit the museum, go left again onto Rua Alfredo de Brito, once a high-class address, later a slum, and recently restored to pastel cleanliness. On the right you'll find the **Casa Santa Barbara** (☎ 071/244–0458; closed Sat. afternoon and Sun.), selling Bahian clothing and lacework of top quality, albeit at prices slightly higher than elsewhere. A bit farther down the street on the left is a garden on the grounds of the former medical school, featuring a cacau tree, native to Brazil and southern Bahia's top source of income. Walk a bit more to No. 20, on the left, housing several shops, the Hotel Pelourinho, and the site of a house where Bahian writer Jorge Amado, author of *Dona Flor and Her Two Husbands,* lived and wrote in his student days. Cut through the shopping gallery to a courtyard and up some stairs to the left for a panoramic view of the city shoreline and the bay, and you'll understand why the Portuguese felt so well protected here. Downstairs is a café. Rua Alfredo de Brito leads into the famed triangular **Largo do Pelourinho** (little pillory), named for the pillory where slaves were punished, now the setting for one of the largest groupings of Brazilian colonial architecture.

Down to the right stands the Baroque **Igreja de Nossa Senhora do Rosário dos Pretos,** built by and for slaves between 1704 and 1796. Guides tend to skip over this church, but it's worth a look at the side altars, to see statues of some of the few black saints of the Catholic church. Each has a fascinating story. A fellow at the entrance organizes groups to watch Candomblé ceremonies (*see* Off the Beaten Track, *below*). *Ladeira do Pelourinho s/n,* ☎ *071/312–6280.* ☛ *Free.* ☉ *Weekends 8–2, weekdays 8–5.*

Walk up the hill past ancient pastel-color houses growing beards of ferns on cornices, and African handicrafts shops and art galleries to the **Igreja e Museu do Convento do Carmo.** The 17th-century church is famous for its restored French organ and carved cedar figure of Christ, the latter kept in the sacristy. Studded with tiny Indian rubies to represent blood, the figure was once carried through the streets in a silver-handled litter during Holy Week, but is now too fragile to be removed. The monastery, which was occupied by the Dutch when they invaded in 1624, features a small church built in 1580 and a chapel with blue Portuguese tiles that recount the story of the Jesuit order. *Largo do Carmo s/n,* ☎ *071/242–2042.* ☛ *Free. Church:* ☉ *Daily for mass only, 7 AM, but accessible from museum. Museum:* ☉ *Mon.–Sat. 8–noon, 2–6; Sun. 8–noon.*

Mercado Modelo

Besides walking or taking a taxi, you can travel between the Upper City (Cidade Altá) and Lower City (Cidade Baixa) aboard the popular **Lacerda Elevator,** which costs about 2¢ and covers 236 feet in a minute. The elevator runs between the Praça Municipal in the Upper City and Praça Visconde de Cairú and the Mercado Modelo, Salvador's main handicrafts market. Built in 1872, the elevator ran on steam until its 1930 restoration. Bahians joke that the elevator is the only way to "go up" in life.

Exiting the elevator at the Lower City, cross the Praça Visconde de Cairú to get to the market building. Outside, you'll hear the nasal-voiced *repentistas*, regional folksingers who make up songs on the spot. Notice the blue Portuguese tiles on a building with Gothic-style windows, once a sort of chamber of commerce, now a supermarket. The Mercado Modelo (closed Sun. afternoon) may not be the cheapest place to buy handicrafts—and you do have to bargain—but it must be experienced. This enclosed market assaults the senses, with its *cachaça* (Brazilian firewater made from sugarcane), cashew nuts, pepper sauces, cigars, the dried shrimp that are an integral part of Bahian cooking, manioc flour, leather goods, hammocks, lace goods, musical instruments, African sculptures, fossils, and gems. Be sure to visit **Didara** (upstairs, stalls 9–10) for striking African print clothing by Goya, a local designer. The upper floor also has a restaurant with a gorgeous view of the bay. Be prepared for extraordinarily persistent salesmen in and around the building. At the rear of the market outside, boys practice capoeira and sell monkeys; the harbor excursion boats are moored across the way.

Itapagipe Peninsula

A 20-minute taxi ride from the market, around the bay to the northwest, brings you to the Itapagipe Peninsula and the **Igreja de Nosso Senhor do Bonfim,** Salvador's most important church. A procession of women dressed in petticoat-puffed Empire-waist white dresses, turbans, and ritual necklaces comes here the Thursday before the third Sunday in January to wash the steps with holy flower water. Built in the 1750s, the simple church is filled with *ex-votos*—wax, wooden, and plaster replicas of body parts—objects of devoted prayer and believed to be capable of miraculous cures. Many figures in Catholicism have a counterpart deity in Candomblé; Nosso Senhor do Bonfim's is Oxalá, the father of all the gods and goddesses. Thus the seemingly bizarre mixture of figurines found in the shops opposite the church: St. George and the Dragon, devils, Indians, monks, sailors, warriors plus ex-votos that include house keys and Volkswagen Beetles for the devotees of consumerism. *Praça do Senhor do Bonfim, Alto do Bonfim, Itapagipe,* ☎ *071/312–0196.* ☛ *Free. Closed Tues.–Sun. noon–2:30 and Mon.*

Here or in the square facing the church you will be accosted by someone selling a printed ribbon, willing to tie it around your wrist with three knots (and sell 20 more to take home to friends), each good for one wish if you wear the ribbon until it falls off and throw it into the ocean. Each color stands for a paired Catholic saint and Candomblé deity.

A five-minute drive from the church is the dazzling white **Mont Serrat Fort,** built in 1500 and named for the shrine of the Black Virgin at Montserrat, near Barcelona. Still used by the Brazilian military, the fort is not open to the public. There is a church by the same name nearby, rarely open, with a renowned carving of St. Peter.

Elsewhere

Housed in a former Carmelite monastery near the Upper City, the **Museu de Arte Sacra** (Sacred Art Museum) and its adjoining **Igreja de Santa Teresa** (Church of St. Teresa) are two of the city's best-cared-for repositories of religious objects. An in-house restoration team has worked miracles that bring alive Bahia's 1549–1763 golden age as Brazil's capital city and main colonial port. See the silver altar in the church, moved there from the demolished Sé church, and the blue-and-yellow-tiled sacristy replete with a bay view. *Rua do Sodré 276,* ☎ *071/243–6310.* ☛ *Entry fee.* ◎ *Weekdays 1–6.*

Up the cliff from the Sacred Art Museum, in the Vitória district, is the **Museu Carlos Costa Pinto,** fruit of one wealthy couple's fascination with art and antiques and a rare example of private support for the arts in Brazil. Among the museum's 3,000 objects fashioned around the world over the last three centuries is Costa Pinto's collection of oversize gold and silver jewelry worn by favored slave women. Here are some prime examples of the *balangandã,* a chain of large silver tropical fruits worn by slave women around the waist, said alternately to be good-luck charms or symbols of the owner's wish for freedom. The balangandã usually includes a *figa,* a closed fist with thumb sticking out the top, supposedly used among slaves as an invitation to sex and at the very least a fertility symbol. (The figa is also used as a symbol of good luck: Brazilians say *"tomara figa"* much as English speakers say "keep your fingers crossed.") Many jewelry and crafts stores sell replicas of these charms. *Av. 7 de Setembro 2490,* ☎ *071/247–6081.* ☛ *Entry fee.* ◎ *Wed.–Mon. 2:30–6:30.*

Just off the Avenida 7 de Setembro, a five-minute taxi ride south from the historic Upper City, lies the **Largo da Piedade,** worth a visit for a look at some very impressive, well-hidden residents: the yard-long chameleon lizards that inhabit the square's flame trees! Not far away is **Praça Campo Grande** (also known as Praça 2 de Julho), where the crowd first gathers for the Carnival procession to **Praça Castro Alves,** the square named for the abolitionist and Bahia's foremost 19th-century poet (said to have had 54 wives, he died of tuberculosis at age 24), where more than a million people cram in to dance to those bands perched atop special sound trucks.

A mid-16th-century waterfront mill set between the Upper and Lower Cities houses the **Museu de Arte Moderna da Bahia** (Bahian Museum of Modern Art), with its permanent collection of artwork by some of Brazil's top modern painters, including Cândido Portinari, Alfredo Volpi, Siron Franco, and Hector Carybé. The museum building is part of a complex that includes the **Solar do Unhão,** a former sugar mill/residential complex dating from the 18th century. The slave quarters is now a restaurant where Salvador's best Afro-Brazilian dinner show takes place (*see* The Arts and Nightlife, *below*). *Avenida Contorno s/n,* ☎ *071/243–6174. Museum:* ☛ *Free.* ◎ *Tues.–Sun. 1:30–5.*

Off the Beaten Track: Candomblé Ceremonies

Salvadorans are willing and eager to share their African practices and rituals with visitors. You can make an appointment to see the three types of ritual listed below through hotels or tour agencies.

Capoeira exhibitions: Take a taxi to a capoeira practice, and have the driver wait while you watch this hypnotic African sport-cum-dance accompanied by the sounds of the berimbau. Exhibitions take place Tuesday, Thursday, and Saturday night at 7 at the 17th-century **Forte**

Santo Antônio Além do Carmo, just a bit north of the Carmo museum and monastery, in the Upper City, a 5- to 10-minute taxi ride from downtown. There are two schools practicing here; the more traditional is the **Grupo de Capoeira Angola,** run upstairs by Mestre (Master) Morães. Weekday nights are classes; the real show happens on Saturday. The schools charge no admission but accept donations.

Shell readings: A *pãe de santo* or *mãe de santo* (Candomblé priest or priestess) can perform a reading of the *búzios* for you; the small brown shells are thrown like jacks into a circle of beads—the pattern they form tells about your life. Don't select your mãe de santo through an advertisement or sign, as many shell-readers who advertize are best not at fortune-telling but at saying "one hundred dollars" in every language under the sun. One of the most authentic is Mãe Edina (☎ 071/241–8154; cost approximately $10). Make an appointment yourself, or contact Tatu Tours (*see* Walking Tours *in* Tour Operators, *above*) to provide a car and interpreter for the 10-minute ride from downtown.

Temple ceremonies: The Candomblé temple ceremony, in which believers sacrifice animals and become possessed by the gods, is performed nightly except during Lent. Candomblé temples, usually in poor neighborhoods at the city's edge, do not allow photographs or video or sound recordings. Visitors should not wear black (white is preferable) or revealing clothing. The ceremony is long and repetitive, there is no airconditioning and sometimes not even chairs; men and women are separated.

Shopping

Art
For paintings, especially *art naïf,* visit the many galleries in the Upper City in and around the **Largo do Pelourinho.** Top local artists (many of whom use only first names or nicknames) include Totonho, Calixto, Raimundo Santos, Joailton, Nadinho, Nonato, Maria Adair, Carybé, Mário Cravo, and Jota Cunha.

Handicrafts
In addition to the overwhelming variety and quantity of goods at the **Mercado Modelo** (*see* Exploring, *above*), Salvador has several state-run handicrafts stores, with lower prices and smaller selections. One of the best is the **Instituto Mauá** (Praça Azevedo Fernandes 2, ☎ 071/235–5440; closed weekend afternoons). **Artesanato Fieb-Sesi** (Rua Borges dos Reis 9, ☎ 071/245–3543; closed weekend afternoons) also carries woven and lace goods, musical instruments, sandals, and pottery.

Shopping Centers
Two big shopping malls boast Brazil's top boutiques, cinemas, and restaurants. **Shopping Center Iguatemi** (Av. Antônio Carlos Magalhães 148) is the older and more traditional of the two, located near the bus station. **Shopping Barra,** in the Barra neighborhood back from the beach (Av. Centenário 2992), is newer and glitzier. The top hotels provide free transportation to it. Both the Iguatemi and Barra malls have boutiques selling locally manufactured clothing as well as franchise outlets or branch stores of Rio, São Paulo, and Minas retailers. The city's most traditional shopping area for a variety of everyday goods, with lower prices than in the malls, is **Avenida Sete de Setembro.**

Sports

Soccer

Bahia (☏ 071/230–4227) and **Vitória** (☏ 071/231–1055) are the two best local teams, and they play year-round (except at Christmastime) Wednesday night and Sunday at 5 PM at the **Estádio da Fonte Nova** (Av. Vale do Nazaré, Dique do Tororó, ☏ 071/243–3322 ext. 237), formally known as the Estádio Governador Otávio Mangabeira. Tickets are sold at the stadium one day in advance. Avoid sitting behind the goals, where the roughhousing is worst. The best seats are in the *arquibancada superior* (high bleachers).

Beaches

Beaches are wall-to-wall people on the weekends, but if you don't mind a crowd it's fun to soak up both sun and beach culture, which includes sand sports, firewater drinks, spicy seafood snacks (don't miss the *acarajé,* a deep-fried bean cake with dried shrimp and sauce) at beachside kiosks, live music, and the briefest of swimwear.

At most local beaches the food and drink kiosks provide chairs and umbrellas free of charge; you pay only for what you consume. Some also offer rudimentary bathroom, changing, and shower facilities free of charge for patrons. Aside from these, there are no functioning bathrooms on the beaches, but some have public showers that run on one-minute tokens costing less than 25¢. Do not sit directly on the sand, as it's likely to have fungi that cause skin diseases. And don't leave belongings unattended.

The jardineira bus stops at all the beaches along the coast, from downtown north as far as the Stella Maris beach. A more comfortable ônibus executivo (marked "Roteiro das Praias") runs from Praça da Sé to Flamengo beach, stopping at all the same stops. As a rule, the farther away from the port, the better the beach.

Barra do Jacuípe

A river runs down to the ocean at this long, wide, pristine beach lined with coconut palms, about 40 kilometers (25 miles) north of Salvador. There are beachfront snack bars and, if you like it so much you decide to stay overnight, you can check in at an inn beside the surf. The Santa Maria/Catuense bus company (☏ 071/359–3474) operates six buses (marked "Praia do Forte") daily that stop at this beach.

Guarajuba

With palm trees and calm waters banked by a reef, this is the nicest beach of them all, though it's 60 kilometers (38 miles) north of Salvador. The bus to Barra do Jacuípe (*see above*) continues on to Guarajuba. There are snack kiosks, fishing boats, surfing, dune buggies, and even a children's playground.

Itapuã

Frequented by artist types who live nearby, this beach is the farthest away along the city beachfront and polluted at some points, but one of the best for atmosphere. At around K and J streets, there are food kiosks, music bars, and amusement park rides, too. The beach is served by the executivo and jardineira buses, which leave from Praça da Sé.

Jaguaribe

This is the "in crowd" hangout, frequented by singles on Saturday and good for surfing, windsurfing, and sailing. There are the ubiquitous snack bars, of course. The executivo and jardineira buses stop at Jaguaribe.

Piatã

Leaving the more built-up areas of the city behind, the first truly safe (healthwise) beach is the wide oceanside Piatã (20 km, or 9 mi, north of downtown), whose calm waters and golden sand attract many families with children.

Porto da Barra and Farol da Barra

Some Salvadorans, especially singles, swear by the urban beaches Porto da Barra and Farol da Barra, which boast a colorful fauna including workers who live nearby and tourists staying at neighboring hotels. Petty thievery is a problem here. There are no bathrooms or kiosks, but you can rent a beach chair for about $1. The corner of Porto da Barra closest to the Grande Hotel da Barra is a gay hangout. Toward the other end, around the corner from the lighthouse, lie the hotel districts of **Ondina** and **Rio Vermelho,** where the beaches intermittently suffer pollution problems.

Stella Maris

The Stella Maris beach (28 km, or 13 mi, from downtown) is popular with surfers, but it's most famous for its kiosks, especially the Padang Padang, with beach dancing on weekends, and Kajila, with its delicious appetizers and live music in the evenings.

Dining

Seafood is the thing in Bahia, in great variety and quantity, prepared either Bahian style or using more traditional Continental recipes. A happy mix of African and local ingredients has come down the centuries from the hands and hearts of slave women, and then maids, working in Bahian kitchens.

The basic raw materials are coconut milk, lemon, coriander, tomato, *dendê* (palm oil), onions, dried shrimp, salt, and hot chili peppers. The ubiquitous *muqueca,* which has all these ingredients plus the seafood catch of the day, is cooked quickly in individual portions (though big enough for two) in a clay pot over a high flame. Other main dishes include vatapá, a fish pudding made of bread, ginger, peanuts, cashews, and olive oil; caruru, okra mashed with ginger, dried shrimp, and palm oil; *ximxim de galinha,* chicken with peanuts and coconut; and *efo,* a bitter chicorylike vegetable cooked with dried shrimp. Most restaurants serve hot pepper sauce on the side, as well as farofa, seasoned manioc meal that does a delicious job of soaking up sauces. Palm oil is high in cholesterol and hard to digest; you can order these dishes without it. And if you've had enough of Bahian food, most restaurants are happy to prepare a simpler fish or shrimp dish even if it's not on the menu.

Batida, a strong drink made from cachaça (sugarcane liquor) and fruit juice, prepares the way for Bahia's spicy, heavy food, which also goes well with beer or white wine. Bahian desserts are very sweet, providing relieving contrast with the spicy food they follow. They are usually made from some combination of sugar, coconut, fruit, eggs, or milk. *Cocada* is shredded coconut caked with sugar; *quindim* is a little tart made from egg yolks and coconut; *doce de banana* (or any other fruit) is banana cooked in sugar; ambrosia is a lumpy milk and sugar pudding.

You can easily find restaurants serving Bahian specialties in Barra, a yuppie neighborhood full of bars and sidewalk cafés. There are also many good spots in bohemian Rio Vermelho, near the Meridien hotel, and a slew of newer places along the beachfront drive beginning around Jardim de Alah. At press time (winter 1995), many new restaurants were opening up in and around the restored Pelourinho area in the Upper City. It is wise to order meat only in churrascarias, avoiding it in seafood places.

For price-category definitions, *see* Dining *in* Brazil Essentials, *below*. Some restaurants give discounts for cash.

$$$$ **Chez Bernard.** Discerning *soteropolitanos* (the pompous but nonetheless correct term for natives of the city) say this is undoubtedly the best, as well as one of the oldest, French restaurants in town. Although there are no particular specialties, everything is worth trying. ✕ *Gamboa de Cima 11,* ☎ *071/321-9402. Reservations advised Fri.–Sat. in summer (Dec.–Feb.). AE, V. Closed Sun.*

$$$ **Bargaço.** Typical Bahian food is served in this oversize, brightly lit shed, a 20-minute drive along the beach from downtown, once a must in Salvador that now caters mostly to tour groups. Starters such as *pata de caranguejo* (vinegared crab claw) are hearty and plentiful, but they may do more than take the edge off your appetite for the requisite *muqueca de camarão* (of shrimp) or muqueca *de siri mole* (soft-shell crab); try the cocada *baiana* (sugar-caked coconut) for dessert, if you have room. ✕ *Rua P, Lote 1819, Quadra 43, Jardim Armação, Boca do Rio,* ☎ *071/231–5141 or 071/231–3900. Reservations advised in high season. AE.*

$$$ **Casa da Gamboa.** A longtime favorite of Bahian writer Jorge Amado, ★ this small Portuguese colonial house close to downtown boasts excellent Bahian cooking and, from some of its 14 tables, a stirring view of All Saints' Bay. *Casquinha de siri* (breaded crab in the shell) comes as a complimentary starter; then try the muqueca *de ouro,* a Bahian bouillabaisse, or the *peixe com risoto de ostras* (grilled fish with oyster risotto), followed by the very good traditional desserts. ✕ *Rua Newton Prado 51, Gamboa de Cima,* ☎ *071/321–3393. Reservations required. No credit cards. Closed Sun.*

$$$ **Phelippe Camarão.** Named for a shipwreck off the Brazilian coast and decorated with nautical treasures, this dining spot draws many local advertising executives, journalists, and artists just for its outstanding lemon pie. Its lovely outdoor terrace with view is the perfect place to top off a day at the beach, over such tropicalized Continental fare as *núvola de caranguejo* (crab pudding); a house salad of vegetables, fruit, and shrimp; or the chateaubriand, served with noodles and vegetables. ✕ *Rua Alexandre Gusmão 104, Rio Vermelho,* ☎ *071/237–4404 or 071/235–1596. Reservations required. AE, MC.*

$$ **Baby Beef Martinez.** Those seeking a break from Bahian cooking will welcome top-quality beef served attentively in comfortable air-conditioned surroundings. While the chateaubriand comes with Argentine-style puffed potatoes, the *bisteca* (steak) Martinez is served with garlic sauce and rice with minced meat; feijoada is on the menu Wednesday and Saturday. ✕ *Ondina Apart Hotel, Av. Oceania 2400,* ☎ *071/203–8314. AE, DC, MC, V.*

$$ **Frutos do Mar.** This plain, traditional seafood spot in the hopping Barra neighborhood is a favorite among cash-conscious locals for its shrimp muquecas and *ensopados* (catch-of-the-day stews resembling bouillabaisse), which come with a typical, sweet-flavored bean called *feijão de leite.* ✕ *Rua Marquês de Leão 415, Barra,* ☎ *071/245–6479 or 071/254–6322. AE, DC, MC, V.*

$$ **Iate Clube da Bahia.** From your captain's chair in this informal air-conditioned yacht club restaurant, set on the cliff between Barra and the Vitória neighborhood, you get a spectacular view of boats bobbing in the bay and honest Continental and Bahian cooking, such as double gratinéed fish and muquecas. ✕ *Av. 7 de Setembro 3252, Barra,* ☎

071/336–9011. Weekend reservations advised. AE, DC, MC, V. Closed Mon.

$$ Iemanjá. Probably the best value for regional cooking, here's a place with a bubbly, underwater atmosphere, replete with aquamarine sea-goddess murals and aquariums. The service is somewhat slow and there's no air-conditioning, but most patrons don't seem to mind, concentrating instead on plowing through mountainous portions of muqueca or ensopado. ✗ *Av. Otávio Mangabeira 929,* ☎ *071/231–5770. No credit cards.*

$$ Quinta Pitanga. This restaurant, part of an inn (*see* Lodging, *below*)
★ set in a fruit grove, is a must even though a meal means a ferry ride over the bay to the island of Itaparica. The trip is made more than worthwhile by the ever-evolving menu, the Magical Realism–inspired paintings and decor, and the personalized attention of American owner-artist Jimmy Valkus and partner-chef Jacinto Batista. Favorite dishes, sometimes served buffet style, are chili-style feijoada, baked stuffed fish, stir-fried soft-shell crab, and curried chicken with peanuts presented in a pineapple half; sweet finishes include a torte of *pitanga* (a berrylike fruit) and passion fruit mousse. ✗ *No street address, Itaparica,* ☎ *071/831–1554. Reservations required. No credit cards. Owner stops seating for dinner between 8 and 10.*

$ Arroz de Hauçá. Two unemployed brothers convinced their family's 70-year-old cook to go public, and turned their plant-filled house into a restaurant. The restaurant, in turn, put the home-cooked dish it's named for on the map of Bahian cuisine. This hefty plate of rice, in coconut milk and covered with a sauce of shrimp paste and onions, has a circle of fried jerked beef and onions in the middle. And while the *arroz de hauçá* is the star here, you can also find the usual Bahian specialties on the menu. The management doesn't frown on sharing dishes. ✗ *Rua Sabino Silva 598, Jardim Apipema,* ☎ *071/247–3508. Weekend reservations advised. AE, MC, DC, V.*

$ Extudo. Young professionals and singles jam-pack this bar and restaurant near Le Meridien hotel just about every night. Bahian and international dishes include *camarão comodoro,* shrimp and prunes gratinéed in a creamy tomato sauce; Finnegan's, steak with black pepper sauce; and *frango flambado,* flambéed chicken. ✗ *Rua Lídio Mesquita 4, Rio Vermelho,* ☎ *071/237–4669. No credit cards. Closed Mon.*

$ Galletu's. This simple whitewashed veranda overlooking the main drag in Barra puts a grill of cooked food right on the table, with piping, succulent meat, sausage, or chicken served with potato salad and fried polenta. Cars race by, and across the street, waves crash against the sand as the evening gears up in this neighborhood full of nighttime fun. ✗ *Av. Oceanica 693, Barra,* ☎ *071/245–5391. AE, DC, MC, V.*

Lodging

No hotel combines a great beach setting with convenience to historic areas, so you will have to decide which has greater priority. There are few hotels in the **Upper City** historic district overlooking the bay, but this may change as its renaissance takes root. Going south into the Vitória neighborhood along **Avenida 7 de Setembro,** there are many inexpensive hotels, convenient both to the Barra area beaches and to historic sights. Just around the corner from the bay is the yuppie Barra neighborhood, with many less expensive hotels, and cafés, bars, restaurants, and clubs within walking distance. The city's resort hotel district lies farther north, somewhat isolated from the rest of the city, a 10-minute taxi ride from downtown and historic areas, on and around the Ondina and Rio Vermelho beaches (*see* Beaches, *above*). If you decide to stay outside the city itself, consider Praia do Forte, where, aside from the Praia do Forte Resort Hotel (*see below*), there are many smaller hotels and inns to choose from.

Because of Brazil's shaky economic situation, even the best hotels are a bit run-down, with most of the rest downright shabby. As the government awards stars according to local criteria, many guests are surprised to find that a Salvador five-star property is far below U.S. or European standards.

At peak season (December–March and the month of July), especially during Carnival, the rates are higher and reservations must be made months in advance. Many hotels give discounts of up to 30% for cash payment. All rates include Continental breakfast. For price-category definitions, *see* Lodging *in* Brazil Essentials, *below.*

$$$$ **Bahia Othon.** A short drive from most historic sights, nightlife, restaurants, and in-town beaches, this busy modern business and tourist hotel offers an ocean view from all rooms, whose ceramic-tile floors and wood furniture are a bit worn. Top local entertainers often perform at the hotel's outdoor park, and during the high season, the staff organizes poolside activities, plus trips to better beaches. ⌕ *Av. Presidente Vargas 2456,* ☎ *071/247–1044 or toll-free 800–4877,* FAX *071/245–4877. 300 rooms, 25 suites. Restaurant, bar, coffee shop, pool, sauna, health club, dance club, concierge floor. AE, DC, MC, V.*

$$$$ **Hotel Sofitel Salvador.** Located just beyond the city's northern perimeter, this resort and convention hotel near good beaches is a world unto itself, decorated with local art and oversize, old-fashioned farm implements. The green-and-blue–accented rooms all have a view of the spacious grounds and the ocean beyond. Amenities include a gallery, on-site boutiques, crafts demonstrations, and free minibus service to downtown. ⌕ *Rua da Pasárgada s/n, Farol de Itapuãn,* ☎ *071/374–9611,* FAX *071/374–6946; U.S.* ☎ *800/763–4835. 194 rooms, 9 suites. 2 restaurants, bar, 2 pools, beauty salon, massage, 9-hole golf course, 3 tennis courts, boating. AE, DC, MC, V.*

$$$$ **Praia do Forte Resort Hotel.** A 90-minute drive north of Salvador, this
★ beachfront complex is not only a complete resort but is also right next door to the Tamar sea turtle preservation project and an artsy fishing village (*see* Excursions from Salvador, *below*). Public areas are decorated in deluxe Robinson Crusoe style, using natural materials, while rooms are like hideaways, with verandas, hammocks, and ceiling fans. Activities include kayaking, sailing, and bird-watching. Room rates include breakfast and dinner. ⌕ *Rua do Farol s/n, Praia do Forte, Mata de São João,* ☎ *071/876–1111,* FAX *071/876–1112. 132 rooms, 4 suites. 2 restaurants, 3 bars, 4 pools, 2 tennis courts, health club, snorkeling, windsurfing, boating, dance club, children's programs. AE, DC, MC, V.*

$$$$ **Quinta Pitanga.** This boarding school and Catholic retreat turned
★ country inn on the island of Itaparica is a favorite among filmmakers and other jet-setters looking to escape the "real" world. It's owned— and decorated in Magic Realist style—by American artist Jimmy Valkus, who along with partner-chef Jacinto Batista has developed a superb menu for the inn's restaurant (*see* Dining, *above*); all meals are included in the price of lodging, as is free transportation to the mainland. Children under 12 are not welcome. ⌕ *No street address, Itaparica,* ☎ *and* FAX *071/831–1554. 7 rooms, 6 with bath. Restaurant, massage, beach. No credit cards.*

$$$$ **Tropical Hotel da Bahia.** Owned by Varig Airlines and often included in package deals, this centrally located hotel is a bit tattered, but quite practical for those whose priority is Salvador's history and culture, not beachcombing (although there is a free beach shuttle). Some rooms overlook the square where Carnival begins; the Concha Acústica do Teatro Castro Alves, site of many big musical shows, is within walking distance, and performers there often stay at the hotel. ☎ *Praça Dois de Julho 2, Campo Grande,* ☎ *071/321–9922 or 071/321–3699,* 𝔽𝔸𝕏 *071/321–9725. 282 rooms, 10 suites. Restaurant, bar, coffee shop, 2 pools, massage, sauna, dance club. AE, DC, MC, V.*

$$$ Ondina Apart-Hotel Residência. In the resort hotel district a short drive from the sights, nightlife, and restaurants, this recently opened apartment-hotel complex on the beach has simple, modern furniture and kitchenettes. Many businesspeople and families opt for this hotel when they are staying in Salvador for an extended period. ☎ *Av. Presidente Vargas 2400, Ondina,* ☎ *071/203–8000,* 𝔽𝔸𝕏 *071/247–9434. 100 suites. Restaurant, bar, coffee shop, 2 pools, 2 tennis courts, health club, dance club. AE, DC, MC, V.*

$$$ Praiamar. Practically across the street from the best downtown beaches, this hotel could use a renovation, and its furniture is mismatched, but it functions efficiently, has a big pool, and is close to a bus stop for lines going almost everywhere. ☎ *Av. Sete de Setembro 3577, Porto da Barra,* ☎ *071/247–7011,* 𝔽𝔸𝕏 *071/247–7973. 170 rooms, 10 suites. Restaurant, bar, pool. AE, DC, MC, V.*

$$ Grande Hotel da Barra. This older hotel with a 1980 addition, located by the best downtown beaches and convenient to the historic center, has comfortable, well-maintained rooms with such decorative touches as pink-and-green-flower bedspreads, latticework screens, and lots of wood carvings. The front rooms sport verandas, and guest rooms in the "new" section have ocean views; all rooms have a VCR. ☎ *Av. Sete de Setembro 3564, Porto da Barra,* ☎ *071/336–6011,* 𝔽𝔸𝕏 *071/247–6223. 112 rooms, 5 suites. Restaurant, bar, pool, beauty salon, sauna. AE, DC, MC, V.*

$$ Hotel Bahia do Sol. This hotel's low rates and prime location, close to museums and historic sights, may make up for its battered wooden furniture. Front rooms have a partial ocean view, but those in the back are less noisy. ☎ *Av. Sete de Setembro 2009, Vitória,* ☎ *071/336–7211,* 𝔽𝔸𝕏 *071/336–7776. 86 rooms, 4 suites. Restaurant, bar. AE, DC, MC, V.*

$ Hotel Bella Barra. Owned by a Chinese family with a restaurant next door, this hotel is right in the middle of one of the city's liveliest districts, both night and day. The rooms and furniture are rickety, but plain and clean, with less noise in side rooms and an ocean view from the front quarters. ☎ *Rua Afonso Celso 439, Barra,* ☎ *071/237–8401,* 𝔽𝔸𝕏 *071/235–2313. 21 rooms. AE, DC, MC, V.*

$ Hotel Vila Romana. Located on a quiet street minutes from the beach and not far from many upscale bars and cafés, this Bahian version of a Roman palazzo that has seen better days is favored by many Italian visitors, who don't seem to mind the rudimentary plumbing. Try for one of the back rooms, which are better ventilated. ☎ *Rua Prof. Leme de Brito 14, Barra,* ☎ *071/336–6522,* 𝔽𝔸𝕏 *071/247–6748. 46 rooms, 3 suites. Restaurant, bar, pool. AE, DC, MC, V.*

The Arts

Considered by many artists as a laboratory for the creation of new rhythms and dance steps, Salvador has a lively performing arts scene. Some of the most electric local performers are Daniela Mercury, Gerónimo, Chiclete com Banana, Roberto Mendes, and Margareth Menezes.

Carnival Rehearsals

Afro-Brazilian percussion groups begin "rehearsing"—actually, these are creative jam sessions that are worth visiting anytime—for Carnival around midyear. Olodum, Salvador's most innovative percussion group, has its own venue, the **Casa do Olodum** (Rua Gregório de Matos 22, Pelourinho, ☎ 071/321–5010); see the events calendar published by Bahiatursa or local newspapers for performance schedules and locations of others, such as the more traditional black drumming group Ilê Aiyé, or Araketu.

Festivals

Festin Bahia is a three-day international music festival held every August or September, featuring foreign and local performers; past participants have included Maxi Priest, Youssou N'Dour, China Head, Carlinhos Brown, Pepeu Gomes, and Olodum. Many of the events, most of which take place at the Centro de Convenções in Jardim Armação, are free, but those that do require tickets cost $8. Tickets go on sale a month before the festival begins and are available through a U.S. travel agency representing **DL Turismo** (Rua Dra. Praguer Froes 102, Barra, Salvador, 40130–020); write DL Turismo for details.

Music, Theater, and Dance Venues

Casa do Comércio offers music and some theater (Av. Tancredo Neves 1109, ☎ 071/371–8700). All kinds of music are heard at **Concha Acústica do Teatro Castro Alves** (Ladeira da Fonte s/n, ☎ 071/247–6414), a band shell. New musicians can be discovered at **Teatro ACBEU** (Av. 7 de Setembro 1883, ☎ 071/247–4395 and 071/336–4411), where both contemporary and classics are represented in music, dance, and theater performed by both Brazilian and international talent. **Teatro Castro Alves** (Ladeira da Fonte s/n, ☎ 071/247–6414) is a top venue for theater, music, and dance. Small theater groups perform at the German-Brazilian Cultural Institute's **Teatro ICBA** (Av. 7 de Setembro 1809, ☎ 071/237–0120), which also screens German films. You can see theatrical, ballet, and musical performances at the **Teatro Iemanjá** (Jardim Armacão s/n, Centro de Convenções). Theater and music are performed at **Teatro Maria Bethânia** (Largo da Mariquita, ☎ 071/247–6419).

Nightlife

The after-hours scene is changing in Salvador as the historic district makes a comeback, with new bars and nightspots expected to open there. Activity centers on the neighborhoods of Barra and Rio Vermelho, catering to yuppies and bohemian types, respectively, and both areas are quite near to most hotels.

Bars

Some of the most popular bars in Barra are **Berro D'Agua** (Rua Barão de Sergi 27, no ☎), with a relaxed atmosphere, attracting a more intellectual set; and **Tiffany's** (Rua Barão de Sergi 37, ☎ 071/247–4025) and **Le Privê** (Av. Sete de Setembro 3554, no ☎), both catering to yuppie sophisticates. In Rio Vermelho the top spots are **Extudo** (Rua Lídio Mesquita 4, ☎ 071/237–4669; *see* Dining, *above*), **Opus 65** (Rua do Meio 65, ☎ 071/248–0185), and **Off the Wall** (Rua da Paciência 30, ☎ 071/235–0385). The watering holes in the Upper City's historic district include the somewhat grungy but well-located **Cantina da Lua** (Terreiro de Jesus 2, ☎ 071/321–0331) and the tranquil **Casa do Benin** (Rua Padre Agostinho 17, ☎ 071/321–6835), with an indoor waterfall and also a restaurant.

Dinner Shows

Many visitors enjoy the Afro-Brazilian dinner shows at the **Solar do Unhão** (Av. do Contorno s/n, ☎ 071/321–5588; Mon.–Sat. at 8 PM), and the **Moenda** (Jardim Armação, Rua P, Quadra 28, Lote 21, ☎ 071/231–7915 or 071/230–6786; daily at 8 PM). Both serve buffets that are best foregone in favor of an early dinner elsewhere or ordering from the à la carte menu.

Nightclubs

Two top members-only nightclubs catering to older, moneyed couples who like to dance are in hotels and are open to hotel guests: **Le Zodiac,** at the Hotel Le Meridien (Rua Fonte do Boi 216, ☎ 071/248–8011), and the **Hippopotamus,** at the Bahia Othon (Av. Presidente Vargas 2456, ☎ 071/247–1044). Another upper-class favorite is **Bual'Amour** (Rua do Corsário s/n, ☎ 071/231–9775). **Mobi Dick** (Av. Presidente Vargas 3719, ☎ 071/235–1596) draws a younger, dating crowd.

Excursions from Salvador

Cachoeira

This riverside Portuguese colonial town 121 kilometers (70 miles) west of Salvador is the site of some of Brazil's most authentic Afro-Brazilian rituals and festivals. Every August 14–16, the **Irmandade da Boa Morte** (Sisterhood of the Good Death, once a slave women's secret society) holds a half-Candomblé, half-Catholic festival honoring the spirits of the dead, featuring a solemn procession and a spinning samba street dance. Other special events in Cachoeira include a feast marking the town's anniversary (March 13), and the typical St. John's feast (June 23–24) commemorating the harvest season, with children dressing up as hillbillies.

However, an excursion to Cachoeira is worthwhile any time of the year. You can walk through the colorful country market, see architecture preserved from an age when Cachoeira shipped tons of tobacco and sugar downriver to Salvador, and visit the sisterhood's small museum (Largo D'Ajuda s/n, ☎ 075/725–1343 [private phone of Dona Anália, one of the sisters]; ☛ Voluntary; open weekdays 10–1, 3–5) and meet these elderly but energetic women.

Getting There

The Camurujipe bus company has hourly service from Salvador's bus terminal, Terminal Rodoviário, from 5:30 AM to 7 PM. You can also get there by a combination of boat and bus: A boat leaving weekdays at 2:30 PM from the **Terminal Marítimo** (behind the Mercado Modelo, Av. França s/n, ☎ 071/243–0741) to Maragojipe takes three hours; you then board a bus (Via Azul and Camurujipe companies) for the bumpy half-hour ride to Cachoeira. If you're going by car, drive north out of Salvador on BR 324 for about 55 kilometers (34 miles), then west on BR 420 through the town of Santo Amaro. The trip takes 1½ hours. **Tatu Tours** (*see* Walking Tours *in* Tour Operators, *above*) offers a two-day trip that includes a ferry ride upriver, and tours of a cigar factory, cacau farm, and manioc flour mill.

Lodging

You can stay overnight or have lunch at a 17th-century former Carmelite monastery, **Pousada Convento do Carmo** (Praça da Aclamação s/n, ☎ 075/725–1716).

Itaparica

Originally settled because of its ample supply of fresh water, Brazil's largest maritime island doesn't boast notable beaches, but there are some very good restaurants (*see* Dining, *above*), set in quiet shady cobbled streets lined with pastel-color colonial homes. The Club Méditerranée is also here, open only to guests. As the complete schooner tour can be tiresome, one super option is to take it one way, get off at Itaparica, skip the cattle-call lunch, take a taxi to a good restaurant, enjoy a postprandial afternoon stroll, and ride the ferry back to Salvador.

Getting There

Although harbor tours stop here for lunch (*see* Tour Operators, *above*), you may want to make a more leisurely visit to this bucolic retreat, taking a launch or the ferry from the docks behind the Mercado Modelo. Launches cost about $1 and leave every 45 minutes from 7 AM to 6 PM from **Terminal Turístico Marítimo** (Av. França s/n, ☎ 071/243–0741). The ferry takes passengers and cars and leaves every half hour between 6 AM and 10:30 PM from the **Terminal Ferry-Boat** (Terminal Marítimo, Av. Oscar Ponte 1051, São Joaquim, ☎ 071/321–7100). The fare is around $1 for passengers, $6–8 for cars, and takes 45 minutes to cross the bay. Reservations are accepted for small cars.

Lagoa de Abaeté

This mystical freshwater lagoon lies inland from Itapuã Beach, at the end of the string of beaches stretching north from Salvador, about a half-hour drive from downtown. Set in lush greenery, its black depths provide a startling contrast with the fine white sand of its shores. No one knows the source of these waters, where Bahian women wash their clothes every morning. The state government is building a small shopping mall to house the crafts kiosks that have long lined the lagoon; it is hoped that the commercialism won't spoil the atmosphere.

Getting There

City buses going to the lagoon leave from Campo Grande or Estação da Lapa and cost less than 50¢. If you are driving, take the Orla Marítima beach drive north out of the city until Itapuã. At the Largo da Sereia (a square with a mermaid statue), follow signs for the lagoon. Tour operators include the lagoon on their beach tours, which cost about $25.

Praia do Forte

For those seeking a little R and R, this beach resort and ecological preserve 70 kilometers (44 miles) north of Salvador might well be a destination in itself, functioning as a base for day visits to Salvador (*see* Lodging, *above*). This is the site of the **Projeto Tamar,** an ecological project set up to protect the giant sea turtles that emerge at night from September to March to lay their eggs along Brazil's northeastern coastline. Other attractions are the 1,500-acre **Reserva Sapiranga,** which preserves a remnant of the forest that once lined most of the Brazilian coast until Portuguese colonization, with a great diversity of flora and fauna (including monkey families that eat from visitors' hands); the ruins of the Portuguese Garcia D'Avila family's **stone castle and chapel,** dating from 1600; a **fishing village** full of great snack bars and restaurants; the **Pojuca River falls and rapids;** and the **Timeantube Lake,** with more than 50 bird species.

Getting There

Santa Mana Catuense (☎ 071/359–3474) has hourly bus service from Salvador's main bus terminal starting at 7:30 AM, with the last bus returning to the city at 5:30 PM; tickets cost around $3. By car, take the Estrada do Côco north and follow signs for Praia do Forte; there is a short stretch of unpaved road at the end.

Tour Operator

Odara Turismo is the main tour operator at Praia do Forte, but has gotten pricey of late. It offers half- and full-day Jeep tours for $110–$150, with hotel pickup in Salvador. *In Praia do Forte Resort Hotel, Av. do Farol s/n, Mata de São João. Mailing address: Visconde do Rosário 114, Sobreloja 103, Comércio, Salvador, Bahia, 40015.* ☎ 071/876–1080, FAX 071/876–1018.

BAHIA: PORTO SEGURO AND ENVIRONS

The entire southern coastal area of Bahia has much to offer, including the Abrolhos archipelago marine preserve and the cacau capital of Ilhéus, where Bahian writer Jorge Amado was born and where he set one of his most famous novels, *Gabriela, Clove and Cinnamon*. The hub of this region, however, is quickly becoming Porto Seguro, which means "safe port" in Portuguese.

Here, 713 kilometers (442 miles) south of Salvador, is where Portuguese explorer Pedro Álvares Cabral in the year 1500 discovered Brazil and named it after the *pau Brasil* (brazilwood) that is native to the region. Almost 500 years later, as Bahia's transportation infrastructure improves and Rio de Janeiro's appeal dims, modern-day travelers are rediscovering Porto Seguro, with its stunning beaches, exciting nightlife, outstanding restaurants, and timeless fishing villages.

Besides miles of clear water, coral reefs, and coconut palms, the region offers a bewitching mix of sophistication and simplicity. Europeans and Brazilians from other parts of the country have abandoned the big-city rat race to move here, bringing with them such cosmopolitan delights as sushi and Polynesian-style sportswear. But even as they and others help to improve the tourism infrastructure, much of the region remains lost in time. Fishing communities, home to artists and hippies, are connected by dirt roads, and center on tiny 17th-century churches and main squares where donkeys are tied to shade trees and chickens peck the dust. The Pataxó Indian tribe of about 3,000 also lives here, moving back and forth among the towns to sell their simple handicrafts.

Visitor Information

Portur has information on hotels, restaurants, beaches, excursions, shopping, car rentals, foreign exchange, and campgrounds for Porto Seguro and nearby towns. *Praça Antônio Carlos Magalhães s/n, Porto Seguro, Bahia,* ☎ 073/288–2126. ☉ *Weekdays 8–noon and 2–6.*

Bahiatursa, in Salvador, also can provide information about the region. *Centro de Convenções, Jardim Armação s/n, Salvador, Bahia 41750–270,* ☎ 071/370–8400.

Arriving and Departing

By Plane

At press time (winter 1995), only two carriers were flying directly into the Porto Seguro Airport: **Rio Sul** (☎ 073/288–2327), with daily flights from São Paulo and Rio de Janeiro; and **Nordeste** (☎ 073/288–1888), which flies weekdays from Salvador. **Tam** runs charter weekend flights from São Paulo; reservations must be made through the Turnac travel agency (Rua Barão de Itapetininga 93, 10th Floor, São Paulo, ☎ 011/231–2044) in São Paulo.

By Car

From either north or south, take BR 101 to Eunápolis, which is linked to Porto Seguro by BR 367.

By Bus

The **São Geraldo bus company** (Porto Seguro: ☎ 073/288–1198; São Paulo: 011/290–8344; Rio: 021/263–7618) serves Porto Seguro from São Paulo and Rio de Janeiro; **Águia Branca** (Porto Seguro: ☎ 073/288–1039; Salvador: 071/358–4704, 071/358–1153, or 071/358–4973) also connects with Salvador. Local bus service is provided by **Espresso Brasileiro** (☎ 073/288–1048). There are two lines, one from Porto Seguro to Cabrália and back, and one that only goes as far as Taperapuan and back to Porto Seguro.

Getting Around

The attractions in this area are spread apart, so it's advisable to rent a car (Localiza National, Av. dos Navegantes 580, ☎ 073/288–2662). Alternatively, you can hire a taxi (Chametaxi, ☎ 073/288–2046; ask for Marco, who speaks some English and charges about $50 for a full day for four people, or $20 for a three-hour orientation tour) or take a bus or boat tour (Grou Turismo, Av. 22 de Abril 1077, ☎ 073/288–2714; either costs just over $10 a person). Public buses do run down Porto Seguro's main drag, but they're not convenient for late nights out.

Exploring Porto Seguro and Environs

Porto Seguro

Perched on a bluff overlooking Praia do Cruzeiro, the tiny **Upper City** (Ciudade Alta) is composed of the ruins of a 16th-century Jesuit school, some small pastel-color colonial houses, and several simple churches washed in the blinding sun mirrored on the sea below. To the left of the Igreja da Matriz (Mother Church), facing the cross erected in 1503 to mark Portugal's possession of Brazil, is the **former jail and city hall**, now the offices of the local tourism board, Portur (*see* Visitor Information, *above*).

Bounded by Avenidas Getúlio Vargas, 22 de Abril, and dos Navegantes, the **Lower City** (Ciudade Baixa) is full of hotels, inns, shops, cafés, and restaurants, a great place for strolling day or night. Aptly named for the firewater drinks you can buy there at night, the **Passarela do Álcool** (Alcohol Way), an oceanside promenade (*see* Nightlife, *below*) right around the corner from a nightly handicrafts fair also has booths selling fruit. Brazil's first or second mass—no one is quite sure—was said in 1500 at **Coroa Vermelha** beach, a 15-minute drive north of town. The Pataxó Indians sell their handicrafts at booths surrounding a giant cross marking the spot.

Santa Cruz de Cabrália

Ten minutes' drive farther north is the fishing town of Santa Cruz de Cabrália, with its own 17th-century historic area and a reef-protected beach. **Coroa Alta,** a coral atoll full of natural pools at low tide, lies 4 kilometers (2½ miles) off the coast at Cabrália, and can only be reached by boat. Excursions are easily arranged through hotel reception desks or local travel agencies.

Arraial d'Ajuda

Arraial means pilgrim campsite, and this town, an eight-minute ferry ride across the Buranhém River from Porto Seguro, centers on one that is now a main square of grass and dirt, populated by burros, goats, and chickens. Pilgrims are still drawn by the town's **miraculous spring,** now housed in a tiny chapel. Sophisticated restaurants, boutiques, and cafés turn up on the side streets, while a walk on **Broadway** reveals simple outdoor cafés and restaurants. The blue and white **Igreja Nossa Senhora d'Ajuda** (Our Lady of Help Church), built by Jesuits in 1549, has an ocean view in the back.

Trancoso

Trancoso, a fishing town that became a hippie hideout in the 1970s, lies 20 kilometers (13 miles) south down a dirt road. On the way, stop 5 kilometers (3 miles) outside of Trancoso at the **Mirante de Taipe** to see the majestic purple clay cliffs above **Lagoa Azul** (Blue Lagoon). There is a road down to Taipe beach; the lagoon lies a kilometer (half-mile) walk north, where bathers spread the soothing white clay on their skin. Up a short trail and back from the beach is a grove with a waterfall (dry when rainfall has been low). Trancoso has its own beaches (one for nude bathing) and a huge arraial, bordered by hotels, inns, galleries, bars, and the Igreja de São João (St. John's Church), a country church built in 1580; ask for the key to it at Silvana & Cia., a café on the campsite.

Shopping

Porto Seguro

The nightly *feira hippie* (hippie fair) in Porto Seguro's Lower City showcases a variety of handicrafts, including Pataxó Indian artifacts, at low prices. At stall No. 22, Vera de Moura sells stunning tropical-color batik prints of parrots, flowers, and fruit. For local fashion, there is also the **Mini-Shopping** mall (Av. dos Navegantes 69, no ☎) of boutiques, selling mostly T-shirts and souvenirs. For every imaginable kind of locally produced cachaça, complete with bawdy labels in Portuguese, try **Cachaçaria Colonia Brasil II** (Av. Getúlio Vargas 528, no ☎).

Arraial d'Ajuda

The **Beco das Cores** minimall (Rua Assis Chateaubriand, altura No. 60, no ☎), open till midnight, has 10 stores that sell sportswear and resort wear (even Polynesian imports!), and a food court featuring a range of fast-food outlets.

Sports and Beaches

Porto Segurans have invented a unique, all-around beach entertainment center, a must-see even if you'd rather be alone with the coral and the coconuts. Called *barracas* (kiosks), as they are elsewhere in Bahia, these are different. They offer not only restaurants, snack bars, ice-cream stands, and boutiques, but inflatable boat rides, live music shows, even bank branches, nude sunbathing areas set away from the restaurant and bar crowds, and dance lessons. There are chairs on the sand, or chairs and shaded tables on a wooden platform, where you can sit for free and pay only for what you consume. They usually serve fried snacks and seafood, plus regional dishes (enough for two), soft drinks, alcoholic beverages, and fruit juices. Thousands cram into these places at Carnival time. The two hottest locales are at Taperapuan beach, a 15-minute drive north from town: **Barramares** (BR 367, km 70.02, ☎ 073/288–2980) and **Virasol** (BR 367, km 69, no ☎).

Equipment for snorkeling, windsurfing, and canoeing can be rented from the **Club Mistral** (in Hotel Porto Bello, BR 367, km 6.5, Praia de Itaperapuã, ☎ 073/288–2320). **Porto Mar Nautica** (Rua 2 de Julho 178, ☎ 073/288–2606) rents diving equipment and organizes diving trips with experienced instructors to the coral reefs.

Other, less crowded, clean beaches can be found up and down the entire 89 kilometers (56 miles) of coastline (except right in town), especially from Mucugê to Trancoso.

Dining and Lodging

The region's beaches, shopping, nightlife, historic sights, and fishing villages are spread over a wide area. If you're into the social scene, day or night, stay in Porto Seguro itself. Taperapuan beach is best if you want to hang out on the beach, while the Lower City in Porto Seguro itself is where the action is at night. If you prefer wide empty spaces and artsy sophistication, stay across the Buranhém River, in Arraial d'Ajuda or Trancoso, linked to Porto Seguro by ferry service.

For price-category definitions, *see* Dining *and* Lodging *in* Brazil Essentials, *below.*

Arraial d'Ajuda

DINING

$$ **Baghdad Café.** The French, Vietnamese, and typical Bahian cooking
★ here makes the most of the local seafood, served at 14 tables on a wood and thatch beach deck. ✕ *Estrada d'Ajuda s/n, 250 meters from the ferry landing,* ☎ *073/875–1247. Reservations advised in high season. No credit cards. Closed Mon.*

$$ **Bistro Mucugê.** In this tiny tropical bistro in the Mucugê Hotel Village
★ (*see* Lodging, *below*), recorded jazz music accompanies such imaginative fare as seafood in a béchamel sauce with Brazilian *catupiry* cheese, whipped up by Cícero, who doubles as the house architect. ✕ *Sítio Mucugê, Arraial d'Ajuda,* ☎ *073/875–1238 or 073/875–1212. Reservations required. No credit cards.*

$$ **Restaurante Rosa dos Ventos.** Continental recipes with an emphasis on Austrian desserts, a surprising treat in this locale, are the fare at this seven-table restaurant, which also features recorded classical music and candlelight at night. ✕ *Alameda dos Flamboyans s/n,* ☎ *073/875–1271. Reservations advised in high season. No credit cards.*

$ **La Vie en Rose.** Off the main square, this rustic spot has its own wood-burning pizza oven, and also serves French food, with unexpected delights such as profiteroles for dessert. ✕ *Praça São Brás s/n, no* ☎. *V. Closed Sun.*

LODGING

$$$$ **Hotel Paradise.** Although it's the fanciest hotel in the region, located just beyond the ferry landing, it could use a bit of redecorating in the lobby. Still, the guest rooms, which face the river or the ocean, are fine, done in wood and polished granite, with tile floors, big bathroom mirrors, and verandas. ☎ *Ponta do Apaga Fogo,* ☎ *073/875–1010,* FAX *073/875–1016. 168 rooms, 4 suites. Restaurant, bar, pool, sauna, 2 tennis courts, basketball, beach, kayaking. AE, MC, V.*

$$ Hotel Pousada das Brisas. A honeymooner's paradise, this inn amid
★ breeze-rustled palm fronds affords breathtaking hilltop views of the
ocean. Bungalows are rustic, with brick walls, a small veranda, and
mosquito netting hanging from the ceiling over the beds. Jeep tours
can also be arranged. ⚏ *No street address,* ☎ *073/875–1033,* ☏ *073/
875–1147. 10 bungalows, 4 duplex suites. Bar, coffee shop, pool. No
credit cards.*

$$ Mucugê Hotel Village. Robert De Niro has hidden away in one of these
★ beachside bungalows of brick, wood, and tile, camouflaged by Atlantic
forest vegetation covering 100 hectares. An in-house travel agency arranges excursions and boat, motorcycle, and dune buggy rentals, and
nearby tennis courts are available to guests. ⚏ *Sítio Mucugê, Arraial
d'Ajuda,* ☎ *and* ☏ *073/875–1238 or 073/875–1212 and 073/875–
1875. 8 3-person bungalows, 2 larger bungalows. 2 restaurants, pizze-
ria, pool, sauna, horseback riding. AE, DC, MC, V (30% surcharge
with credit card).*

$$ Pousada Berro D'Agua. This beachfront inn has thatch-roof bunga-
lows, woodblock-frame beds, and wooden ceilings; some rooms are
air-conditioned. ⚏ *Estrada d'Ajuda, km 1,* ☎ *and* ☏ *073/875–1073.
15 rooms, 4 duplex suites. Restaurant, pool, beach. No credit cards.*

$ Pousada Araçaipe. These bungalows are quite simple, in brick and wood,
with hammocks and Indian print fabric adorning the walls for an ex-
otic, tentlike look, and rudimentary bathrooms. ⚏ *Estrada d'Ajuda,
km 17,* ☎ *073/875–1028. 5 bungalows. Beach, boating, kayaking. No
credit cards.*

Porto Seguro
DINING

$$ Bar e Restaurante do Japonês. This sushi bar above a grocery store serves
both Japanese (cooked and raw) and Chinese specialties, plus break-
fast. ✕ *Praça dos Pataxós 38,* ☎ *073/288–2592. AE, DC, MC, V.*

$$ Restaurante Grelhados. Under a bamboo roof, shrimp, fish, and meat
★ come to your table already cooked; food stays hot on wrought-iron
grills. The concept is simple, the results delicious. ✕ *Av. 22 de Abril
212,* ☎ *073/288–1177. No credit cards.*

$$ Terra Brasilis. After their textile business burned down in São Paulo,
the Korean owners turned to cooking. They've met with great success,
serving up Korean, Japanese, Chinese, and Bahian fare, with an emphasis on seafood. Specialties include *lagosta tropical* (lobster with fruit);
and lighter (less palm oil) moquecas. ✕ *Av. Portugal 258,* ☎ *073/288–
1607. V.*

$ Corais do Porto. This restaurant with a beachside deck serves Italian
and Bahian food, everything from snacks to full dinners. Arrive hungry—most dishes are big enough for two. ✕ *Praia de Taperapuan, km
69,* ☎ *073/288–2859. No credit cards.*

$ Sambuca. Locals flock to this authentic Roman-style pizzeria. Try the
caprichosa pizza with mozzarella cheese, hearts of palm, ham, and mushrooms. ✕ *Praça dos Pataxós 216,* ☎ *073/288–2366. No credit cards.*

LODGING

$$$$ Porto Bello Praia Hotel. This efficiently run hotel across from Taperapuan beach is decorated with lots of wicker, ceramics, plants, and woven
rugs, with blue slate floors and candy-stripe bed linens in the guest rooms.
It offers a great Brazilian country-style breakfast, with eggs, fruit,
cheese, cereals, etc. ⚏ *BR Mar 367, km 68.5,* ☎ *073/288–2329,* ☏
*073/288–2911. 51 rooms, 1 suite. Restaurant, 2 bars, 2 pools, sauna,
health club, soccer, video games. AE, DC, MC, V (lodging only; surcharge).*

$$$$ **Porto Seguro Praia Hotel.** Owned by the town's mayor (a big-time cacau farmer), this large hotel (spread out over 50,000 square meters) with a country-club atmosphere is frequented by bus tour groups and is right across the street from Taperapuan beach. ☎ *BR 367, km 65,* ☎ *073/ 288–2321,* FAX *073/288–2069. 120 rooms, 6 suites. Restaurant, bar, 2 pools, tennis court, sauna, health club. AE, DC, MC, V.*

$$ **Hotel Adriático.** This comfortable, homey in-town hotel sports an
★ atrium pool with batik wall hangings and bamboo furniture. Each guest room, with its high, sloping ceiling, blue slate floors, and clean white linens, has its own private veranda. ☎ *Av. 22 de Abril 1075,* ☎ *073/ 288–1188. 37 rooms, 2 suites. Pool, sauna. AE, DC, MC, V.*

$$ **Pousada Aconchêgo.** It's easy to forget that this inn is downtown, with its garden of coconut palms and caged parrots. The bungalow guest rooms have hammocks and handwoven bedspreads. ☎ *Av. 22 de Abril 435,* ☎ *073/288–2522,* FAX *073/288–2207. 15 bungalows. Coffee shop, pool, sauna. AE, DC, MC, V.*

$$ **Taperapuan Praia Hotel.** These two-story thatched bungalows 5
★ kilometers (2 miles) from town are perfect for families. All have hammocks, lace curtains, and porches; the front ones offer an ocean view. ☎ *BR 367, km 67.6,* ☎ *073/288–2449,* FAX *073/288–2597. 8 bungalows, 4 duplex suites. Restaurant, pool, exercise room, volleyball, kayaking. V.*

Santa Cruz de Cabrália
LODGING

$$$ **Bahia Cabrália Hotel.** This is one of the few hotels in the area with its own beach—and it has a natural-reef pool. The Bahia Cabrália boasts lobby art by local wood sculptor Antônio Carlos Portela de Carvalho and spacious guest rooms. ☎ *Rua Sidrack de Carvalho 141,* ☎ *and* FAX *073/282–1176 or 073/282–1145. 78 rooms, 6 suites. Restaurant, bar, 2 pools, 2 saunas, health club, volleyball. AE, DC, MC, V (surcharge).*

Trancoso
DINING AND LODGING

$$ **Pousada e Restaurante Capim Santo.** The bungalow units here have loft beds, two doors for cross-ventilation, and ceiling fans. Originally specializing in health food, the restaurant ($$$, closed Sun.) has expanded its menu from whole (unpolished) rice and fish to include such varied fare as lobster mousse, Argentine beef, and homemade ice cream, served both outside and inside at picnic tables. ☎ *Praça São João s/n,* ☎ *and* FAX *073/868–1122. 9 bungalows. No credit cards.*

LODGING

$$ **Hotel da Praça.** Set in a garden, these bungalows have brick floors, tile roofs, and a veranda where you can hang a hammock and relax. ☎ *Arraial de Trancoso,* ☎ *and* FAX *073/868–1177. 8 bungalows, 3 suites. No credit cards.*

$ **Pousada Hibisco.** The edges are literally smoother in these rustic ocherwall bungalows, as the Argentine owner is a carpenter and made all the furniture himself. The rooms are about 400 yards from the beach. ☎ *Rua Bom Jesus s/n, Ladeira de Trancoso (mailing address: Caixa Postal 133, Porto Seguro 45820),* ☎ *073/868–1129. 8 bungalows. Volleyball. No credit cards.*

Nightlife

Evening entertainment—dining, drinking, and dancing—centers on Arraial d'Ajuda and Porto Seguro's Lower City, where the sensual *lambada* dance was born. **Broadway** is the main drag in the former; in the latter, it's the **Passarela do Álcool,** with its myriad square wooden tables set outside and booths overflowing with fruit.

The Passarela is a great place to stoke up (try a *guaraxaxá,* a deadly mixture of energizing guaraná powder and cachaça) for the **Boca da Barra** (Praia do Cruzeiro, no ☎), a thatch-roof, barnlike structure open to the beach on one side, where every night people of all ages, colors, shapes, and sizes dance the lambada, sometimes till dawn. Periodically, the best dancers lead line dances, teach steps, and give out prizes. Classes are held between 5:30 and 9, with dancing thereafter. Entrance is free except for the bleacher area, where the cover charge is about 50¢.

THE AMAZON

For both outsiders and inhabitants of the Amazon, there is a mystical attraction to this legendary region and its two great constants, the river and the jungle. A flight over the jungle is an unforgettable experience; the jungle seems to go on forever, an endless green carpet sliced by the curving contours of the area's 1,000 rivers and broken only occasionally by a clearing.

From the sky, it is easy to believe that the Brazilian Amazon is the largest tropical rain forest in the world, larger than all of Western Europe and accounting for 60% of the nation's total territory—and yet it is inhabited by only 16 million people, less than the population of metropolitan New York. The rain forest is also home to more than 35,000 plant species, a number that is constantly being upgraded.

The region's life centers on its rivers, the largest and most important of which is the Amazon itself, the second-longest river in the world at 6,290 kilometers (3,900 miles). Of the Amazon's hundreds of tributaries, 17 are more than 1,600 kilometers (1,000 miles) long. It is along these rivers that Amazon society has developed. Although in recent years there has been an increasing urbanization of the region, 45% of its residents still live in rural areas, many of them in frontier settlements along the riverbanks.

Whatever class of boat you take, a trip along the Amazon River or one of its principal tributaries—especially the 1,700 kilometer (1,020-mile) journey between the region's two major cities, Belém and Manaus— is unmatched anywhere in the world. In some spots the Amazon is so wide that neither bank is visible, giving the impression of traversing an inland sea. At night, the only light that can be seen is that of the moon and stars, reinforcing the sense of being in one of the world's greatest wilderness areas.

By day, each sighting is an adventure in itself: people fishing from canoes, wooden huts on the banks of the river, small river settlements, frontier homesteads, and extraordinary flora, with trees ranging from 50–150 feet high. (Spotting wildlife on the banks of the rivers, however, is a rare occurrence. The density of the vegetation makes such sightings, with the exception of birds, extremely difficult.) More direct contact with the river's inhabitants, both human and animal, occurs on the narrower waterways that you can tour on day trips, which typically include a visit to the home of a river dweller.

The vast size of the Amazon region has always been its principal source of security. In the past decade, however, civilization has been gnawing away at the edges of this great forest. Settlers from Brazil's festering urban centers have been pouring into the western Amazon, slashing and burning the forest and setting up small homesteads. At the same time, major gold discoveries throughout the southern Amazon have lured thousands of prospectors into the region. In the southeastern Amazon, a series of major development projects are underway, most of them designed to exploit the region's untapped mineral wealth, including the world's richest iron ore deposits.

All of this activity in one of the world's most ecologically sensitive regions has attracted the ire of conservationists, who view plans to develop the Amazon as a threat to humanity. Thus far, however, the Brazilian government has adopted the view that the fate of the region is a purely domestic matter and has rejected outside pressures to curtail development.

Getting Around the Amazon

By Plane
There are daily flights between Manaus, Belém, and Santarém.

By Bus
Land transportation in the Amazon is mostly limited to the area south of the Amazon River. There are highways linking southern and southeastern Brazil with Belém and another major Amazon city, Porto Velho. The most famous of these is the Belém–Brasília Highway, the 2,118-kilometer (1,300-mile) stretch of roadway made famous by the movie *Bye Bye Brazil*. The 45-hour jaunt through the center of the country is hot (buses are not air-conditioned) and dusty, and road maintenance is poor. The road is subject to frequent closings due to mud slides and washouts. Bus companies plying this route on a daily basis are **Transbrasiliana** (☎ 061/233–7572) and **Rapido Marajó** (☎ 061/233–7572); the bus station in Belém is about 15 minutes from downtown (Praça do Operário, ☎ 091/228–0500).

From Belém it is also possible to travel by bus to Santarém via the city of Marabá, south of Belém. The trip, however, is not recommended because of the poor state of the roads, some of which are remnants of the Transamazon Highway, a classic Amazon boondoggle built in the 1970s in an attempt to provide an east–west link running south of the Amazon River. Today most of the highway has been reclaimed by rain forest. In theory, the bus trip to Santarém, with a stopover in Marabá, takes 50 hours, but because of such common problems as blowouts and rainstorms, it can last three to four days. There are no highways connecting either Belém or Santarém with Manaus. From Manaus, the only land connection south is Highway BR 319, which runs 900 kilometers (540 miles) southwest of Porto Velho. The highway, however, is closed more often than it is open, and there is no bus traffic at present.

By Boat
A growing number of oceangoing cruise ships now make calls at Belém, continuing upriver to Manaus. The most important cruise lines stopping at the two cities are **Marquest, Ocean Cruise Lines, Princess, Seabourn, Special Expeditions,** and **Sun Line. Crystal Cruises** goes to Belém but not to Manaus.

Many visitors to the region prefer to experience firsthand the Amazon's primary mode of transportation, the river-going boat. Such boats travel throughout the region, on all of the Amazon's leading tributaries, connecting Belém with Manaus and numerous river towns in between, which tend to be austere in their accommodations. Although the region encompasses hundreds of navigable rivers, local commerce—and boats specifically designed for tourists—follow a few well-beaten paths, mainly the Amazon, Negro, Solimões, Madeira, Pará, and Tapajós rivers.

TOURIST BOATS

First-time visitors to the Amazon can gain a sensation of river life in a few hours on a "tourist boat" on the Negro River in Manaus, the Pará in Belém, or the Tapajós and Amazon in Santarém (halfway between Belém and Manaus). Longer tourist boat trips on the Negro departing from Manaus—which last three to five days, or even longer if you choose to take a customized private expedition—have become increasingly popular in recent years because they explore the upper reaches of the Negro, where the river is narrower and river life is easier to observe. These boats do not travel at top speed and sail close to the banks to allow a better look at the jungle. Tourist boats are more comfortable than standard riverboats, with an open upper deck that permits the best vantage points for observing the river and forest, and meals are included in the fare. The better tours have an expert on the region on board, usually an ecologist or a botanist, who is fluent in English. Passengers can either sleep out on deck in hammocks they must purchase themselves (don't worry about mosquitos; the humic acid in the Negro River serves as a natural insect repellent) or in cabins, which usually have air-conditioning or a fan. While the cabins may seem like a more attractive option, keep in mind that one of the jungle's primary attractions is its night sounds. With air-conditioning you may sleep better, but you will miss part of the show.

STANDARD RIVERBOATS

The major trips, however, are reserved for commercial boats on the Amazon and Madeira rivers and are recommended only if you have the time and the willingness to rough it. The most exciting of these is a cruise on the mighty Amazon itself, between Belém and Manaus with a stop in Santarém. The voyage lasts between four and seven days, depending on the direction of sail and the type of vessel. The level of comfort on different kinds of boats can vary dramatically.

Those for whom comfort takes a back seat to adventure may want to consider a trip aboard a standard double-decker boat that carries both freight and passengers. (Keep in mind, however, that while romantic in appearance, these aging boats have shown themselves in recent years to be increasingly unreliable—major accidents have occurred on the average of once every two years.) Usually only one kind of accommodation is available, and the ships tend to be overcrowded. Conditions are primitive: Passengers sleep out on deck in hammocks, and the sanitary conditions are the worst imaginable. Food is served, but the quality is deplorable. Experienced Brazilian travelers bring their own food and bottled water on board, together with gas-powered stoves, plates, cups, and cutlery; fresh fruit may be purchased at the various stops along the way.

Although some of the riverboats have first-class cabins in addition to the third-class hammock space, those that do usually have very few of them. In some cases it is necessary to bribe the captain to get one. The cabins are seldom air-conditioned. Fares can vary widely, but hammock space generally costs between $75 and $120 for a trip between Belém and Manaus; a cabin averages about $250.

BOAT OPERATORS

Several private companies operate riverboats along the region's extensive river system. Among those offering service between Belém and Manaus are **Antônio Rocha** (Travessa Almirante Vandercopa 561, Belém,

☎ 091/224–3969) and **Alves é Rodrigues** (Eco de Curro 73, Sala 2, Belém, ☎ 091/225–1691), both of which operate boats that have first-class (cabins) as well as third-class (hammock) accommodations. In 1993 the government-owned **Enasa** line suspended their operations. A luxury catamaran service operated by Enasa between Manaus and Belém, run by a private tour operator, **Sandpiper Turismo** (Av. Rio Branco 277, Gr. 1601, Rio de Janeiro, ☎ 021/262–2892) costs $650 per person for a double cabin.

For Amazon riverboat schedules and information about individual boats and their facilities, contact the **Paratur** office in **Belém** (Praça Kennedy, ☎ 091/223–6198) and **Emamtur,** the Amazon Tourism Authority, in **Manaus** (Av. Tarumã 379, ☎ 092/234–5503).

Belém

Belém is a fast-growing river port of 1.2 million on the southern bank of the Amazon River 145 kilometers (90 miles) from the sea. Like the upriver city of Manaus, Belém has ridden the Amazon booms and busts, at times bursting with energy and opulence, then slumping into relative obscurity. Founded in 1616 as a trading center and defense against European invaders, the city had its first taste of prosperity with the Amazon rubber boom at the start of this century. Wood and mining operations have since provided the impetus for the city's growth.

Visitor Information

Paratur (☎ 091/224–9633 or 091/223–2130, open weekdays 8–6, Sat. 8–noon), the tourist authority for the state of Pará, has an office in Belém at Praça Kennedy on the waterfront.

Arriving and Departing

Varig operates weekly flights from Miami to Belém's **International Airport Val de Cans** (☎ 091/257–0522), 11 kilometers (6 miles) from downtown. There are daily flights on the major domestic carriers to the airport from Rio, São Paulo, and Brasília as well as daily flights from Belém to Manaus and Santarém.

Tour Operator

River excursions, which range from trips of a few hours to half- and all-day tours and often include jungle stops, depart daily from the port area as well as from the docks of the Novotel Hotel (Av. Eng. Azarias Neto 17). One of the better operators is **Ciatur** (☎ 091/223–0787), which offers half-day trips and a short hike through the jungle. Half- and full-day tours include meals.

Exploring

In the past 10 years, Belém has enjoyed a rapid expansion, pushed in large part by major development projects in the surrounding area, including the construction of the Tucurui hydroelectric dam, the second-largest in Brazil, and the development of the Carajás iron-ore mining region. All of this is evident in the architecture of the increasingly cosmopolitan city, where modern high-rises are gradually replacing the colonial structures. Still surviving are several distinctive turn-of-the-century buildings, located along the downtown tree-lined streets and around the Praça Frei Caetano Brandão, an area known as the **Old City.**

Here you will find the **Catedral da Sé** (Praça Frei Caetano Brandão, ☎ 091/223–2362; ☛ Free; closed Tues.–Sun. before 1 PM and Mon.), completed in 1771, known for its Carrara marble interior. On the other side of the square, with an excellent view of the Pará River (a tributary of the Amazon), is the city's fort, **Forte do Castelo,** constructed in 1878 and today housing a restaurant whose tables are set out on a part of the ramparts (*see* Dining, *below*).

Other venerable buildings in the Old City are the 17th-century **Nossa Senhora das Mercés Igreja** (Largo das Mercés, ☎ 091/224–2402; ☛ free; closed Tues.–Sun. before 11 AM and Mon.), the city's oldest church, and the **Nossa Senhora do Carmo Igreja** (Praça do Carmo, ☎ 091/241–1100; ☛ Free), built between 1626 and 1766.

In the port area next door to the fort is one of Belém's primary attractions, the daily market known as **Ver-o-Peso** (literally, "see the weight," a colonial-era sales pitch). The market is a hypnotic confusion of colors and voices, with vendors hawking regional fruits, "miracle" roots from the jungle, alligator teeth, and good-luck charms for the body and soul. There are jars filled with animal eyes, tails, and even heads, plus an endless variety of herbs, each with its own legendary power. A regional oddity are the sex organs of the river dolphin, supposedly unmatched cures for romantic problems. Here you will get a close-up look at the fish of the Amazon, including the pirarucu, the river's most colorful species; the *mero,* which can weigh more than 91 kilos (200 pounds); and the silver-scale *piratema.*

In the Nazaré neighborhood, east of the Old City, is the **Basílica de Nazaré,** built in 1908 and financed with the wealth of the rubber boom. The basilica's ornate interior is replete with Carrara marble and gold. On the second Sunday in October, a religious procession carries a replica of the basilica's image of the Virgin to the cathedral. Known as the **Cirio,** it is one of the Amazon's most impressive public festivals, attracting hundreds of thousands of worshipers. *Praça Justo Chermont,* ☎ *091/241–3402.* ☛ *Free.* ◔ *Daily, except for Sun. morning.*

Close to the basilica is the **Praça da República,** dominated by the municipal theater, the **Teatro da Paz.** The neoclassical-style theater, completed in 1874, is the third oldest in Brazil. ☎ *091/224–7355.* ☛ *Entry fee.* ◔ *Weekdays, except noon–2.*

Belém is home to one of Brazil's most unusual museums, the **Museu Emílio Goeldi.** The museum contains an extensive collection of Indian artifacts, including samples of the distinctive and beautiful pottery of the Marajó Indians, known as *marajoara.* Attached to the museum complex is a small zoo with native animals and a jungle park, an area of virgin rain forest containing reflection pools with giant Victoria Régia water lilies. *Av. Magalhães Barata 376,* ☎ *091/249–1233.* ☛ *Entry fee.* ◔ *Weekends and Tues.–Thurs. 9–noon, 2–5; Fri. 9–noon.*

Shopping

Belém's main shopping area is **Avenida Presidente Vargas,** which runs along one side of Praça da República. Here you will find numerous shops selling regional crafts, such as **Artinida** (Av. Presidente Vargas 762, Loja 6, ☎ 091/223–6248), which specializes in Indian handicrafts. **Paratur** (Praça Kennedy, ☎ 091/224–9633) operates a handicrafts center. In all of these shops you will find examples of the region's two unique styles of pottery: **marajoara,** distinguished by its intricate, hand-painted geometrical designs, and **tapajônica,** marked by well-defined human and animal figures. In addition, Belém's shops sell various handmade objects of wood, straw, and leather. Indian crafts include straw wrist-bands and headdresses decorated with parrot feathers.

Beaches

A string of 18 beaches lined with hotels, bars, and restaurants is along the Pará River's **Mosqueiro Island,** a one-hour drive from Belém. Several of the beaches—Farol, Grande, Chapé, Virado, São Francisco, and Baía do Sol—have spectacular views of the island's jungle, just a stone's throw away. Closer to the city are the beaches on the island of **Oureiro,** linked to the mainland by ferry.

Dining

In general, dining in the Amazon is as different as everything else in the region. Besides water buffalo steak, you will have the opportunity to try armadillo, wild Amazon duck, piranha, and other river fish with such exotic Indian names as *tucunaré,* pirarucu, *tambaquí, curimatá, jaraquí,* and *pacú.* Although it's against the law, alligator and turtle are also found on menus. Watch out for the *pimenta-de-cheiro,* a local hot pepper whose potency can burn your fingers. For dessert, try some of the region's tropical fruits, such as *cupuaçu, graviola, taperebá, pupunha, biribá, bacabá, abio,* and *açaí.* Belém's Cerpa beer is excellent, mild, and tasty. For price-category definitions, *see* Dining *in* Brazil Essentials, *below.*

$$$ O Teatro. This restaurant in the Hilton International Belém (*see* Lodging, *below*) offers an excellent sampling of Amazon cuisine in a small and intimate setting. River fish prepared with regional herbs and sauces is the specialty. ✕ *Av. Presidente Vargas 882,* ☏ *091/223–6500. AE, DC, MC, V.*

$$ Círculo Militar. The combination of good regional food and excellent
★ location—on the ramparts of Forte do Castelo, overlooking the river—makes this the city's most appealing restaurant for visitors. Try the *filhote salgado,* sautéed river fish in a spicy coconut milk sauce. ✕ *Praça Frei Caetano Brandão,* ☏ *091/223–4374. AE, DC, MC, V.*

$$ Lá em Casa. This downtown restaurant is famous for Amazon specialties, including the premier dish of Belém, *pato no tucupi,* duck in a yellow herb sauce made from the juice of the manioc root and served with kale. ✕ *Av. Governador José Malcher 247,* ☏ *091/223–1212. AE, DC, MC, V.*

$$ Miako. This rooftop Japanese restaurant close to the Hilton offers a wide variety of fish and meat dishes. At night a refreshing breeze blows off the river, making for comfortable outdoor dining. ✕ *Rua 1 de Março 76,* ☏ *091/223–4485. AE, DC, MC, V.*

Lodging

Belém is quickly emerging as the business and financial center of the Amazon region, and the city's better hotels are geared toward business travelers. For price-category definitions, *see* Lodging *in* Brazil Essentials, *below.*

$$$ Hilton International Belém. Easily the top hotel in Belém, the Hilton of-
★ fers reliability and comfort and is especially popular among business travelers, with an excellent location in the downtown commercial center, close to the Old City. ⌧ *Av. Presidente Vargas 882, Praça da República,* ☏ *091/223–6500,* 𝖥𝖠𝖷 *091/225–2942; U.S.* ☏ *800/445–8667. 361 rooms. 2 restaurants, 2 bars, pool, sauna. AE, DC, MC, V.*

$$ **Equatorial Palace.** Generally considered to be the city's number-two hotel in terms of amenities and quality of service, the Equatorial is near downtown in the Nazaré neighborhood, within walking distance of the Old City and the port area. ☒ *Av. Braz de Aguiar 612,* ☎ *091/241– 2000,* F̄Ā̄X̄ *091/223–5222. 211 rooms. Restaurant, bar, pool. AE, DC, MC, V.*

$ **Vanja.** This downtown hotel is a favorite of backpackers and other bargain hunters. The rooms are clean and comfortable and an outstanding value for the money. ☒ *Tr. Benjamin Constant 1164,* ☎ *091/ 222–6688 or 091/222–6709. 154 rooms. Restaurant, bar, pool. AE, DC, MC, V.*

Elsewhere in the Amazon Delta

Accessible from Belém are two of the Amazon Delta's most interesting sights: Ilha do Marajó, one of the world's largest river islands, has an unspoiled landscape interrupted only by huge herds of buffalo— visitors can even arrange to stay at buffalo farms. Macapá is the departure point for seeing the *pororoca,* the spectacular coming together of the flooding Araguari River and the incoming Atlantic tide.

Ilha do Marajó

Arriving and Departing

Ilha do Marajó can be reached from Belém by boat (a five-hour trip) or plane (30 minutes). If you travel by boat, however, you will have to spend at least one night on the island before returning. The flight from Belém offers an incomparable view of the meeting of the waters of the Amazon and Tocantins rivers with the ocean. Boats (☎ 091/223– 3011) leave from Belém to Souré, the island's main city, on Wednesday and Friday at 8 PM and Saturday at 2 PM, with return trips leaving Thursday at 5 PM and Sunday at 5 PM and midnight. **Taba** (☎ 091/241– 1770) has flights to Souré departing from Belém's international airport on Monday, Wednesday, and Friday.

Tour Operators

Tour operators conducting trips to the island from Belém include **Gran Pará** (Hilton International Belém, Av. Presidente Vargas 882, ☎ 091/ 224–2111), **Lisotur** (Av. Braz de Aguiar 612, ☎ 091/241–2000), and **Mururé** (Av. Presidente Vargas 132, ☎ 091/241–0891).

Exploring

The island of Marajó, which has an area larger than Denmark, claims to be the largest river island in the world. The island is famed for its vast herds of water buffalo and its unspoiled natural environment. Sparsely populated, Ilha do Marajó is one of the few accessible sites in the Amazon that give a true feeling of isolation from the civilized world. In addition to abundant wildlife, the island also possesses excellent beaches.

Many tourists opt to visit the island as part of a tour from Belém, by far the easiest way, because there are very few buses or taxis. A typical tour includes a visit to a buffalo ranch, canoeing on inland waterways, and demonstrations of a local dance, the *carimbo,* performed to music combining African and Indian rhythms. Some tours stay overnight at a ranch, also featuring four-wheel-drive trips into the backlands, horseback riding, and bird-watching. (*See* Tour Operators, *above.*)

Dining and Lodging

While on the island, sample the distinctive local cuisine, with such delicacies as water buffalo steak and desserts made with water buffalo milk. For an unusual but memorable lodging experience on Marajó, visitors should seek out one of several buffalo ranches that offer accommodations. You do not need to be part of a tour to stay at these ranches. The top ranches, accessible only by plane, are **Fazenda Bom Jardim** (☎ 091/224–3233, FAX 091/241–5531) and **Fazenda Jilva** (☎ 091/225–3728), both of which charge $1,100 for two people for a three-day, two-night stay including meals. In a more moderate price range are **Fazenda Marçal** (☎ 091/223–3177) and **Fazenda Carmo Camará** (☎ 091/223–5330).

For price-category definitions, *see* Dining *and* Lodging *in* Brazil Essentials, *below.*

$–$$ **Pousada Marajoara.** Visitors to Ilha do Marajó who wish to stay the night have few options. Located on the river in the island's main city, Souré, this lodging is the best choice, with clean rooms that are air-conditioned, always an important consideration in the Amazon region. The restaurant, the top choice on the island, specializes in grilled water buffalo steak. ☒ *Quarta Rua, Souré,* ☎ *091/741–1287. 14 rooms. Restaurant, bar. No credit cards.*

Macapá

Visitor Information

For tourist information on Amapá, contact the state tourism authority in downtown Macapá, **Coordenaria Estadual de Indústria, Comércio e Turismo** (Rua Raimundo Alvarce da Costa 18, ☎ 096/223–4135).

Arriving and Departing

The city is 40 minutes' flying time from Belém (there are scheduled flights on Varig and Vasp airlines). Boats also link the two cities, but service is irregular. Usually there is a boat at least once a week in each direction; the trip takes one to two days, depending on the boat. For information, call the **Capitania dos Portos** (Av. FAB 427, ☎ 096/222–0415).

Getting Around

The mouth of the Araguari can be reached by boat, although the round-trip excursion takes 15 hours. It is also possible to arrange flights to the site of the pororoca. For information on river and air transportation, call the **Martinica Tourism Agency** (☎ 096/222–3569).

Exploring

To the north of Ilha do Marajó is the state of Amapá and its capital, Macapá, which sits on the northern channel of the Amazon delta. The city, one of only five in the world that lies directly on the equator, has a population of 150,000 and is beginning to shed its frontier image. Like Belém, Macapá was an Amazon outpost built by the Portuguese to develop the region and protect Brazil from her European enemies. The fort constructed for this end, **Fortaleza de São José de Macapá** (Av. Amazônas, next to Novotel Macapá, no ☎; ☛ Free) was the largest in Brazil. Completed in 1764, the fort was built of stones brought from Portugal as ship ballast. Its well-preserved ruins are today one of Macapá's top attractions. There is also a recently opened regional handicrafts center, the **Núcleo Artesenal** (Av. Eng. Azarias Noto, ☎ 096/222–2313).

The main lure here, however, is nature, in the form of the **pororoca,** an extraordinary phenomenon that occurs daily from January to May, when the Amazon delta is in flood stage and the incoming ocean tide crashes against the outflowing waters of the Araguari River 200 kilometers (120 miles) north of Macapá. The violent meeting produces churning waters and waves that reach 15 feet in height. And for nearly an hour before the final clashing of the waters, the air is filled with what sounds like a continuous crack of thunder, gradually building in intensity until, at the end, the rushing ocean waves sweep into the forest along the riverbanks.

Dining

For price-category definitions, *see* Dining *in* Brazil Essentials, *below.*

$$ **O Boscão.** This downtown eatery is considered the city's best choice for river fish. ✕ *Rua Hamilton Silva 997, no ☎. No credit cards.*

Lodging

For price-category definitions, *see* Lodging *in* Brazil Essentials, *below.*

$$ **Novotel.** The newest and best hotel in Macapá, the Novotel is downtown on the riverfront. Although the decor is undistinguished, the hotel is immaculate, and all the guest rooms are air-conditioned. ⊡ *Av. Eng. Azarias Neto 17, ☎ 096/223–1144, ℻ 096/223–1115. 76 rooms. Restaurant, bar, pool, tennis court. AE, DC, MC, V.*

$ **Amapaense Palace.** This Amazon veteran offers no frills but is clean and has air-conditioning (although you should check first to make sure yours is working). ⊡ *Av. Tiradentes, ☎ 096/222–3366. 44 rooms. No credit cards.*

Santarém

Founded in 1661, Santarém has weathered all the various booms of the region—first wood, then rubber, and today mineral wealth have been the lures for thousands of would-be magnates hoping to carve their fortunes out of the jungle. Today this laid-back port of 242,000, rich in history and legend, is a traditional stopping point for Amazon boats.

Visitor Information

The closest tourist information office is in Belém. The leading travel agencies in Santarém are **Amazônia** (☎ 091/522–3325), **Lago Verde** (☎ 091/522–1645), and **Tapan** (☎ 091/522–1946).

Arriving and Departing

As the city is halfway between Belém and Manaus, a riverboat trip from Belém usually lasts two days, while trips to Manaus can run from two to five days, depending on the vessel.

Exploring

Many of Santarém's would-be colonizers have left behind decaying monuments to their frustrated dreams. The most noteworthy of these is **Fordlândia,** an Amazon boondoggle envisioned by Henry Ford, who in a period of 20 years starting in 1927, poured $80 million into a vast rubber plantation to supply him with the raw material for the tires of his cars. The scheme, however, failed, primarily due to the workers succumbing to malaria and yellow fever and to Ford's eventual loss of enthusiasm for the enormous undertaking. Today, the rusted remains of trucks and electric generators together with abandoned American-style bungalows can be seen in the jungle some 40 miles outside the city.

The principal attraction of Santarém, however, is the river. The city is on the Tapajós River about 3.2 kilometers (2 miles) from its confluence with the Amazon. Local tour operators such as Amazônia and Lago Verde offer two standard all-day river cruises on specially outfitted boats. One trip takes passengers to the rivers' meeting point, continuing on the Amazon to **Pouso das Garças,** a beautiful region of small rivers, lakes, and forest marked by the presence of hundreds of snow-white egrets. Another boat trip follows the Tapajós to **Alter do Chão,** a picturesque Amazon village in an *enseada* (inlet) of Lago Verde and renowned for its white, sandy beaches.

Dining

For price-category definitions, *see* Dining *in* Brazil Essentials, *below.*

$$ Tropical. This restaurant of the Hotel Tropical Santarém (*see* Lodging, *below*) is known for the high quality of its fish dishes, in particular pirarucu *tropical* and *caldeirada,* a type of fish stew. ✕ *Av. Mendonça Furtado 4120,* ☎ *091/522–1533. AE, DC, MC, V.*

$–$$ Storil. This establishment near the Santarém Palace Hotel offers excellent river fish dinners, including filet of pirarucu, and tucunaré prepared in a corn sauce. ✕ *Rua Turiano Meira 115,* ☎ *091/522–3159. No credit cards.*

Lodging

For price-category definitions, *see* Lodging *in* Brazil Essentials, *below.*

$$ Tropical Hotel Santarém. This riverfront hotel, the city's top accom-
★ modation, offers river tours that depart from the hotel's docks. Although not as deluxe as its upriver sister hotel, the Tropical Manaus, the Santarém version is still one of the region's finer hotels, with sprawling grounds and comfortable rooms, all with river views. River tours can also be arranged here. ⌕ *Av. Mendonça Furtado 4120,* ☎ *091/522–1533,* ℻ *091/522–2631. 122 rooms. Restaurant, bar, pool, river tours. AE, DC, MC, V.*

$ Santarém Palace. Compared with the Tropical, the city's other hotels come out decidedly on the short end. The best among this rather nondescript grouping is this traditional downtown hotel. ⌕ *Av. Rui Barbosa 726,* ☎ *091/522–5285. 47 rooms. Restaurant. No credit cards.*

Manaus

Manaus is an urban oasis in the midst of the rain forest, a sprawling, hilly city of more than 1 million built on the banks of the Negro River in the densest part of the jungle. The capital of the state of Amazônas, the city has long flirted with prosperity, first at the turn of the century, when for 25 years the Amazon rubber boom turned Manaus into the rubber capital of the world, supplying 90% of the globe's rubber. The immense wealth that resulted was monopolized by a handful of Amazon rubber barons, never numbering more than 100, who lived in Manaus and dominated the region like feudal lords.

Visitor Information

The Amazon Tourism Authority, **Emamtur** (Av. Tarumã 379, ☎ 092/234–5503) is open weekdays 7:30–6. Emamtur operates information desks at the airport (☎ 092/621–1210; open 24 hours a day) and at the Canto da Cultura (near Opera House, corner of Av. Eduardo Ribeiro and José Clemente, ☎ 092/232–1646; open weekdays 8–6, Sat. 8–1). It also has a 24-hour telephone service, Disk-Tur (☎ 092/232–1646).

Arriving and Departing

The **International Airport Eduardo Gomes** (Av. Santos Dumont, ☎ 092/621–1210) in Manaus, 17 kilometers (10 miles) from downtown, is served by Varig flights from Miami and Los Angeles. There are daily flights on the major domestic carriers to the airports from Rio, São Paulo, and Brasília, as well as daily flights from Manaus to Belém and Santarém.

Exploring

The rubber boom ended abruptly in the 1920s with the appearance of competition from Malaysia, but the vestiges of this opulent era still remain in Manaus. Foremost among these is the city's symbol, the Opera House, **Teatro Amazônas,** which was completed in 1896 after 15 years of labor. This grandiose theater was restored to its former splendor in 1990, when a major renovation, the third in its history, was completed. The Italian Renaissance–style interior provides a clear idea of the wealth and ostentation that marked the Amazon rubber boom: marble doorways from Italy, wrought-iron banisters from England, crystal chandeliers from France, and striking panels of French tiles and Italian frescoes depicting Amazon legends. One-hour tours are conducted daily between 10 and 5. *Praça São Sebastião,* ☎ 092/622–2420. ☛ *Entry fee.* ☉ *Tues.–Sun.*

Another classic rubber-era structure is the yellow **Alfândega,** the Customs House, built by the British in 1902 of Scottish bricks imported as ship ballast and erected alongside the floating dock that was built at the same time to accommodate the annual 40-foot rise and fall of the river. The Customs House is now the home of the regional office of the Brazilian tax department and is not open to the public. Also in the port area is the 1882 municipal market building, the **Mercado Adolfo Lisboa,** a wrought-iron copy of the market (destroyed) in Les Halles in Paris; the ironwork is said to have been designed in Paris by Gustave Eiffel. Vendors at the market sell Amazon food products and handicrafts.

The city's newest attraction is the **Museu de Ciências Naturais de Amazônia,** a natural history museum of the region that displays collections of insects, butterflies, and Amazon river fish in large tanks. The museum is on the outskirts of the city in the suburb of Aleixo. *Cachoeira Grande,* ☎ 092/644–2799. ☛ *Free.* ☉ *Tues.–Sun.*

Easily the best museum in the Amazon region is the **Museu do Índio** (Indian Museum), which displays handicrafts, weapons, ceramics, ritual masks, and clothing of the tribes of the upper Amazon. *Rua Duque de Caxias 356, Manaus,* ☎ 092/234–1422. ☛ *Entry fee.* ☉ *Weekdays 8–11:30, 2–5; Sat. 8–11:30.*

Manaus has a zoo, the **Mini-Zoo do CIGS,** run by the Brazilian army's jungle survival training school; some 300 animals native to the Amazon can be seen. *Estrada de Ponta Negra 750,* ☎ 092/625–2044. ☛ *Entry fee.* ☉ *Tues.–Sun. 8–5.*

Located a half-hour boat ride from the Tropical Hotel along the Tarumã bayou is the **Tarumã Ecological Park,** containing a monkey jungle, waterfalls, and a large collection of Amazon birds. The park offers half- and full-day tours ($30 and $60 respectively) with professional guides. ☎ *092/234–0939.* ☞ *Entry fee.*

Shopping

Although Manaus is a free-trade zone, visitors who are not from South America will find little of interest in the dozens of shops scattered throughout the downtown district, most of which offer duty-free electronics imports at prices higher than in their countries of origin. Regional crafts include straw baskets, hats, and other articles; fantastical necklaces and headpieces made from iridescent bird feathers; and jewelry made of seeds. These and other handicrafts are sold at the shop at the **Museu do Índio** (Rua Duque de Caxias 356, ☎ 092/234–1422); the **Mercado Adolfo Lisboa; Artíndia** (Praça Adalberto Vale 2, ☎ 092/ 232–4890); and the **Artesanal Centro,** or Handicraft Center (Rua Recife 1999, ☎ 092/236–1241).

Sports and the Outdoors

Beaches

Manaus's popular **Ponta Negra** beach, known to locals as the Copacabana of the Amazon, is a sandy stretch along the river. Don't worry about piranhas; there is no danger here.

Fishing

Most river trips of two days or longer include some fishing, usually for piranha; equipment is supplied by the boat operators. For more extensive fishing expeditions, contact **Amazon Explorers** (☎ 092/232– 3052), **Anavilhanas** (☎ 092/671–1411, ℻ 092/671–3888), or the **Tropical Hotel** (☎ 092/238–5757).

Dining

River fish is the obvious specialty here, and which is the city's best fish restaurant is hotly debated. There is no clear winner, and factors such as the quality of the view often tip the balance. Other than fish, the city's restaurants offer few specialties, and the quality of food in general ranges from average to poor. For price-category definitions, *see* Dining *in* Brazil Essentials, *below.*

$$$$ **Tarumã.** Always a reliable choice for good regional cuisine, this restau-
★ rant in the Tropical Hotel (*see* Lodging, *below*) has a varied menu of international fare in addition to serving the traditional river fish. The hotel is a 20-minute taxi ride from downtown, but the ride is pleasant, with good views of the river. ✗ *Estrada da Ponta Negra,* ☎ *092/ 658–5000. Reservations advised. AE, DC, MC, V. No lunch.*

$$$ **La Barca.** One of Manaus's most popular eateries, this fish restaurant
★ is noted for its huge variety of preparations, such as pirarucu, a stew of shrimp, river fish, and vegetables in a tomato and manioc broth. Meals are accompanied by live music. ✗ *Rua Recife 684,* ☎ *092/236– 8544. AE, MC, V.*

$$ **Panorama.** Fish servings are large here, although their preparation tends to be slightly unimaginative, with an over-reliance on tomato and onion sauces. Devoted patrons, though, swear by the restaurant, mainly because of its excellent view of the Rio Negro. ✗ *Boulevard Rio Negro 199,* ☎ *092/624–4626. AE, DC, MC, V.*

$ **Caçarola.** Simple and unpretentious, this fish restaurant has won a large following in recent years for its creative cuisine, a rarity in Manaus, where most restaurants tend to use the same sauces and preparation.

You will have to take a taxi to reach the restaurant, but the effort is worthwhile. ✗ *Av. Maués 188-A,* ☎ *092/233–3021. No credit cards.*

Lodging

The recent surge of international interest in ecological tourism to the area, plus the city's free-trade zone, has created a soaring demand for hotel rooms, the supply of which remains woefully inadequate. This problem is especially acute at the so-called jungle lodges, the hotels that are the most sought after by international travelers (*see* Jungle Lodges, *below*). For price-category definitions, *see* Lodging *in* Brazil Essentials, *below.*

Hotels

$$$$ **Tropical.** This, the only major resort in the Amazon, is considered to
★ be the region's best hotel. The sprawling complex is 20 kilometers (12 miles) from downtown and has a privileged location overlooking the Negro River and verdant gardens all around. Besides an on-site zoo, it also has its own dock from which excursions depart daily. You can book rooms here through Varig Airlines. ☎ *Praia de Ponta Negra,* ☎ *092/238–5757,* 𝖥𝖠𝖷 *092/238–5221. 606 rooms. 2 restaurants, bar, 2 pools, sauna, 2 tennis courts, dance club. AE, DC, MC, V.*

$$$ **Amazônas.** Located in the center of Manaus, the Amazônas is the city's oldest and most traditional hotel, frequented by many tour groups. The hotel, however, is showing its age, and you may not enjoy musty corridors in the middle of the Amazon. ☎ *Praça Adalberto Valle,* ☎ *092/ 622–2233,* 𝖥𝖠𝖷 *092/622–2064. 182 rooms. Restaurant, bar, pool. AE, DC, MC, V.*

$$ **Lord.** Another downtown hotel in the heart of the free-trade zone, this hotel is better preserved than the Amazônas and less expensive. The staff is particularly helpful and efficient. ☎ *Rua Marcílio Dias 217,* ☎ *092/622–2844,* 𝖥𝖠𝖷 *092/622–2776. 102 rooms. Restaurant, bar. AE, DC, MC, V.*

$ **Sombra Palace.** Like several small downtown hotels that have been built in the last 15 years, this establishment, Manaus's newest hotel, is aimed primarily at Brazilian tourists visiting Manaus to shop in the free-trade zone. ☎ *Av. 7 de Setembro 1325,* ☎ *092/234–8777,* 𝖥𝖠𝖷 *092/234–3395. 43 rooms. Restaurant. AE, DC, MC, V.*

Jungle Lodges

In recent years, the demand for "authentic" Amazon experiences has resulted in the construction of several jungle lodges, actually small hotels within the rain forest. These lodges, all in the $$$ or $$$$ price categories, typically offer jungle treks, alligator "hunts" (*see* Excursions from Manaus, *below*), canoe trips, fishing, and swimming plus the obvious attraction of staying amid the jungle. Many of the lodges are near the Negro River. Accommodations are limited, so if you wish to stay at one of these lodges, you must make reservations well in advance.

$$$$ **Ariaú Jungle Tower** is the most renowned of the jungle lodges. This
★ remarkable compound, which is three hours by boat from Manaus on the Ariaú River near the Anavilhanas Archipelago, is made up of three four-story wooden towers with thatched roofs, supported on stilts and linked by catwalks. Its most popular accommodation, especially sought after by honeymooners, is the Tarzan House, a tree house lodged 100 feet off the ground amid the treetops. As with most jungle lodges, the primitive surroundings are not repeated in the interiors, where electric generators and indoor plumbing ensure basic comforts. The complex also contains a 130-foot-high observation tower and its own helipad. Various jungle and river excursions can be arranged. ☎ *Mail-*

ing address: Rua Silva Ramos 20, Centro, Manaus 69010-180, ☎
092/234–7308, FAX *092/233–5615. 92 rooms. Restaurant, bar, pool,
dock. AE, DC, MC, V.*

Other excellent lodges include:

Acajatuba Jungle Lodge is four hours by boat from Manaus. *Mailing
address: Rua Dr. Alminio 36, Centro, Manaus, 69005-200,* ☎ *and* FAX
092/233–7642.
Amazon Lodge is three hours by boat from Manaus. *Mailing address:
Rua Leonardo Melcher 734, Centro, Manaus, 69010-170,* ☎ *092/622–
4144,* FAX *092/622–1420.*
Lago Salvador Lodge is a 40-minute boat ride from Manaus. *Mailing
address: Estrada da Ponta Negra s/n, Centro, Manaus 69037-060,* ☎
092/658–5000, FAX *092/238–5221.*
Pousada das Guanavenas, on the Urubu River, is six hours from Manaus by car and boat. *Mailing address: Av. Constantino Nery 2486, Bairro
Flores, Manaus 69050-002,* ☎ *092/656–3656,* FAX *092/656–1500.*

Excursions from Manaus: Into the Jungle

River and jungle tours from Manaus vary from a few hours to several
days. The most common is a tourist boat trip, lasting six–eight hours,
to the point just east of the city where the Negro and Solimões rivers
join to form the Amazon. Here, about 15 kilometers (9 miles) from
Manaus, you can see the black waters of the Negro flowing beside the
muddy brown Solimões for 18 kilometers (11 miles) without mixing
before merging into one as the Amazon River. All of these "Meeting
of the Waters" tours include side trips, usually motorboat rides through
narrow Amazon streams or bayous, providing a close-up view of the
remarkable Amazon vegetation. (These motorboat trips cannot be
made during the low-water season, October to January.) Many of
these tours also stop at the **Parque Ecológico do Janaury,** where you
can see a number of Amazon birds, and within it the **Lago de Janaury,**
a lake filled with giant Victoria Régia water lilies.

Overnight boat trips that bring you into contact with the rain forest
are also popular excursions from Manaus. A typical excursion of this
sort follows the Negro River, exploring flooded woodlands and narrow waterways and stopping for a hike on a jungle trail. At night, guides
take you by canoe on an alligator "hunt." The guides shine flashlights
into the eyes of the alligators, momentarily transfixing them, after which
they are grabbed and held for photographs and then released.

Similar tours of up to five days are offered, as well as customized private expeditions. The longer trips have become increasingly popular
because they explore the upper reaches of the Negro, where the river
is narrower and therefore life along the banks is easier to observe. These
trips usually make stops at river settlements, with visits to the homes
of typical Amazon families. They also offer jungle treks, bathing at river
beaches, and piranha fishing, and invariably enter the **Anavilhanas.** The
world's largest freshwater archipelago, it contains some 350 islands
with exuberant Amazon flora. Because of the dense vegetation, however, do not expect to spot much wildlife other than birds and, in the
narrow channels or onshore, monkeys.

Tour Operators

Among the operators that offer the above tours are **Amazon Explorers** (Rua Nhamunda 21, Praça da Afilhadora, ☎ 092/232–3511,
092/232–3319, or 092/232–3433), **Anavilhanas** (Rua Coração de

Jesus 11, ☎ 092/671–1411), and **Fontur** (in Tropical Hotel, Estrada da Ponte Negra s/n, ☎ 092/568–5000). Tours leave from the downtown harbor area.

BRASÍLIA

Completed in 1960 in an astonishing three years' time, Brasília is one of the world's unique cities. The Brazilian government, headed by President Juscelino Kubitschek, who was looking to develop the isolated interior of the country, chose an all-star Brazilian design team: urban planner Lúcio Costa, landscape architect Burle Marx, and architect Oscar Niemeyer. Commonly described as a monument to the future, to its many critics, however, Brasília is a city trapped in a 1950s vision of the future, a brave new world that is overly functional, cold, impersonal, and lost in the middle of Brazil.

Conceived as a unified design, the city embodies some of the major trends of post–World War II design. Whether you view this homage to the glass box as the International Style at its purest and most refined, or at its most banal and monotonous, Brasília is a rare reflection of a single moment in the history of architecture.

In recent years, however, this image has begun to change as the city has acquired a certain sense of maturity. Although it remains an urban island in the heart of Brazil's hinterlands, Brasília is a far more hospitable setting for working and raising families than Brazil's coastal cities. The preponderance of well-paid (by Brazilian standards) civil servants has given Brasília the highest standard of living of any Brazilian city, and while crime problems are beginning to appear, the city is considerably safer than the nation's other urban centers. Traffic also flows smoothly in the city, which was built for the car, with ample freeways. Because space was abundant, large areas were reserved for parks and public squares. Homes and apartments also tend to devote large spaces to gardens and lawns. As a result, Brasília has more green space per inhabitant than any other city in Brazil.

Brasília's principal problems today originate in the surrounding suburbs, once home to the construction workers who were brought in from other states to build the capital. In contrast to the orderly efficiency of the city proper, these so-called satellite cities have developed into urban jungles similar to São Paulo and Rio and are growing at a far faster rate than the capital. Today Brasília itself accounts for only 22% of the total population of the federal district, with the other 78% living in the impoverished cities.

Most visitors find that half a day is more than enough to see the high points of the city. The best option is to take a three-hour city tour or hire a taxi. The distances between sights are great, so walking is not practical except in the area around the Congress building.

Because we recommend that you make a day trip to the city, we do not include dining and lodging information in the section that follows.

Visitor Information

Tourist information is available from the city's official tourism authority, **Detur.** *Setor de Divulgação Sul, Centro de Convenções, 3rd Floor, SDC Eixo Monumental,* ☎ *061/321–3318.* ☉ *Weekdays 1–7.*

Arriving and Departing

Brazil's capital, Brasília, is 726 kilometers (450 miles) northwest of Belo Horizonte and 960 kilometers (595 miles) from Rio, in the middle of a plateau that dominates the central region of Brazil.

By Plane

The city can be reached by air from all of Brazil's major cities. **Brasília International Airport,** 12 kilometers (7 miles) from downtown, is served by all of Brazil's domestic carriers as well as international flights of **Varig** airlines.

By Car

Highway 040 connects the city with Rio and Belo Horizonte; Highway 050 connects it with São Paulo. Get a recent, reliable road map before attempting to drive from Salvador.

By Bus

Bus service is available from all of Brazil's major cities. Daily service links the capital with Rio, São Paulo, Belo Horizonte, and Salvador. **Real** (☎ 061/361–4555) provides service between the city and São Paulo, a 14-hour ride. **Itapermirim** (☎ 061/233–7766) provides service from Belo Horizonte (11 hours) and Rio de Janeiro (17 hours); **Paraíso** (☎ 061/233–7656) serves Brasília from Salvador (24 hours).

Tour Operators

A tour of the city's architectural attractions is a must in Brasília. For the most part, the government buildings and monuments still preserve a daring, futuristic air even now, more than three decades after they were designed. You will quickly discover, however, that the buildings are essentially works of sculpture, marked by impressive exterior forms and generally unimpressive and often deteriorating interiors.

Recommended travel agencies that offer city tours include **Bradesco** (at the airport, ☎ 061/225–1511), **Power** (in the Hotel Nacional, Loja 48, ☎ 061/322–6699), and **Buriti** (CLS 402, Bloco A, Lojas 27/33, ☎ 061/225–2686).

Exploring Brasília

The highway from the airport passes beside the residential buildings of this planned city. The six-story, glass-encased buildings are set at right angles to one another in so-called **super blocks,** designed to be complete living units containing, in addition to apartments, shopping areas, supermarkets, schools, and playgrounds. Although at first criticized as artificial living environments, the super blocks have withstood the test of time. Today the residents praise them for their orderliness, especially when compared to the urban chaos of Rio and São Paulo.

To understand the layout of Brasília, head for the **Torre de Televisão Diversão Cultural,** or Television Tower (Eixo Monumental Oeste, no ☎; ☛ Free; closed daily after 8 PM). From its observation deck you can easily see Costa's master plan: a residential arc bisected by the **Eixo Monumental** (Monumental Axis), with the government buildings clustered east of the arc along the 8-kilometer-long (5-mile-long) axis. Farther east is a lake, **Lago do Paranoá,** that echoes the curve of the arc.

It was in the creation of the government ensemble, a five-minute drive from the Television Tower, that Niemeyer concentrated his major efforts in Brasília. The long, symmetrical mall, the **Esplanada dos Ministérios,** is flanked by 16 identical glass-sheathed rectangular high-rises split into two parallel rows separated by a grassy promenade. The **Cat-edral Metropolitano Nossa Senhora Aparecida** (Esplanada dos Min-istérios s/n, Eixo Monumental, ☎ 061/224–4073; ☛ Free) on the south side takes its inspiration from Jesus's crown of thorns. The high-rises, which are not unlike a series of dominoes, terminate in a cluster of major buildings on the triangular **Praça dos Tres Poderes** (Plaza of the Three Powers).

On the north side of the plaza is the **Palácio da Justiça** (☎ 061/312–7000; ☛ Free; closed to public weekdays 11:30–5 and weekends), a low concrete box sheathed in marble and surrounded by a phalanx of soaring white marble columns and arches. Facing it across the wide plaza is the presidential palace, the **Palácio do Planalto** (☎ 061/311–1241), another slab of a building, with curved abstract columns and glass walls; note the abstract figures of *The Warriors,* a sculpture by Bruno Giorgi, nearby. (The building is closed to visitors, but the chang-ing of the palace guard can be seen Tuesday at 8:30 and Friday at 5:30.)

The apex of the mall is the highly photogenic symbol of the city, the **Congressional complex** (Chamber of Deputies: ☎ 061/311–5107; Senate: 061/311–4141; ☛ Free; closed weekends and Jan. and July), a low, horizontal platform flanked by a shallow dome (the Senate chamber), a saucerlike inverted dome (the Chamber of Deputies), and 25-story twin glass-wrapped towers.

Niemeyer's masterpiece here, however, is generally considered to be the **Palácio dos Arcos** (the Foreign Ministry building, or Itamarity), on the south side of the plaza, which seems to float, suspended by its el-egant concrete arches above a surrounding reflecting pool. Unlike his other creations, all faced with marble, this building is exposed concrete, a square pavilion set within a frame of landscaped pools. The interior is exceptionally opulent, a luxurious mix of polished marble, mirrors, deep carpets, tapestries, and fine furniture. The plaza also contains the **Museu Histórico de Brasília** (☛ Entry fee; closed Sat.–Mon.), com-memorating the founding of the city, famed for the oversize bust of the city's founder, ex-president Juscelino Kubitschek, that protrudes from its walls.

East of the plaza is the center of Brasília's social life, the manmade **Para-noá Lake.** Since its construction, the lake has become landlocked Brasília's answer to Rio's Copacabana beach. Private social clubs, for-eign embassies, and the residences of the city's power brokers, in-cluding ministers and other high government officials, line the winding contour of the lake. On the east side of the lake is the **Palácio da Alvo-rada,** official residence of the president, although only two of Brazil's last six presidents have lived there. The simple, boxlike form is enhanced by a screen of decorative, tapering columns. The building is not open to the public.

Excursions from Brasília

According to legend, a 19th-century Catholic priest had a vision that one day on the central plateau of Brazil a city on a lake would rise and become the promised land. Since its inception, mystics have consid-ered Brasília the city envisioned by the priest, winning it the sobriquet "Capital of the Third Millennium" and turning it into one of Latin America's leading centers of spiritualism and religious cults.

The most unusual cult is the **Valley of the Dawn,** a commune of some 3,000 persons located 50 kilometers (30 miles) south of the city, where every Sunday followers dressed in long flowing robes gather in an outdoor arena containing oversize statues, ponds, fountains, and astro-logical symbols—easily one of Brazil's more unusual sights. The ritu-als (held at noon, 2:30, and 6:30; ☛ Entry fee) are open to the public.

Another popular mystical site is the pyramid-shape temple of the **Legião da Boa Vontade** (beside the Television Tower, SGAS 915, Lote 75-76; ☛ Free; open 24 hours a day), a nondenominational medita-tion center. The temple is famous for its "energy," which supposedly is transmitted to worshipers, who lift their hands toward the top of the pyramid.

Both of these sites, as well as others in the city and surrounding area, are included in the so-called **"mystical tours"** offered by several travel agencies in the area. These tours are by far the best way to visit the sites, which are widely scattered.

BRAZIL ESSENTIALS

Customs and Duties

Former strict import controls have been substantially liberalized as part of the Brazilian government's efforts to open the nation's economy to foreign competition. In addition to personal items, visitors are now per-mitted to bring in duty free up to $500 worth of gifts purchased abroad. An additional $500 worth of gifts, including alcoholic bever-ages, may be purchased at the airport duty-free shops.

Dining

You may be visiting Brazil, but you would hardly know it from the restaurants. Most of the finer restaurants in Rio and São Paulo are ei-ther French or Italian. In addition, there is excellent Portuguese, Chi-nese, Japanese, Arab, Hungarian, and Spanish cuisine to be sampled. Traditional Brazilian food may be hard to come by, but when it is found, it can make for a delicious dining experience. A typical, low-cost Brazilian meal consists of beans, rice, french fries, and beef, chicken, or fish. Brazilians are not fond of vegetables, and salads must be or-dered separately. Visitors will quickly discover that eating is a national passion, and they are often shocked by the huge portions. The num-ber of eateries is staggering: Restaurants of all sizes and categories, snack bars, and more recently, fast-food outlets line downtown streets and fight for space in shopping malls.

Specialties

Many Brazilian dishes are adaptations of Portuguese specialties. Fish stews called caldeiradas and beef stews called *cozidos* (a wide variety of vegetables boiled with different cuts of beef and pork) are popular, as is *bacalhau,* salt cod cooked in sauces or grilled. Dried salted meats form the basis for many dishes from the interior and northeast of Brazil, and pork is used heavily in dishes from Minas Gerais. The na-tional dish of Brazil is feijoada, traditionally served on Saturday at lunch. Originally a slave dish, feijoada now consists of black beans, sausage, beef, and pork. It is always served with rice, finely shredded kale, or-ange slices, and farofa, manioc flour that has been fried with onion and egg.

The cuisine of Bahia is often equated with Brazilian food as a whole, although it is actually best eaten in Salvador, where it originates. Muqueca is composed of many kinds of shellfish cooked quickly in a sauce of dendê (palm) oil, coconut milk, onions, tomatoes, and coriander.

Dried shrimp, coconut milk, and cashews are the basic ingredients of vatapá, a fish and shrimp stew cooked with peanuts and dendê oil, and *xinxim de galinha,* a vatapá-like chicken stew that uses lime juice instead of coconut milk.

From Brazil's southeast comes *churrasco*, meats marinated and grilled or roasted over charcoal. Restaurants specializing in steaks are called churrascarias, which serve either à la carte or rodízio (all you can eat) style.

You will find Brazilian desserts sweeter than you are used to. Desserts are referred to as *doces* (sweets) and are sold in street shops and restaurants. Many doces are direct descendants of the egg-based custards and puddings of Portugal and France.

Coffee is served black and strong with sugar in demitasse cups and is called *cafezinho*. Coffee is taken with milk—called *café com leite*—only at breakfast. Bottled mineral water is sold in two forms: with and without bubbles (*com gas* and *sem gas,* respectively).

The national drink is the caipirinha, made of crushed lime, sugar, and *pinga* or cachaça, strong liquor made from sugarcane. When whipped with crushed ice and fruit juices, the pinga becomes a batida, which sometimes contains condensed milk. Brazil's best bottled beer is Cerpa, sold at most restaurants. In general, though, Brazilians prefer tap beer, called chope, which is sold by all bars and some restaurants.

Mealtimes
Lunch and dinner typically are eaten later than in the United States. Lunch in a restaurant usually starts at around 1 and often lasts until 3. Dinner is always eaten after 8, in many cases not until 10.

Dress
Informality is the rule of thumb. Only at the top restaurants do Brazilians dress up, and men seldom wear jackets and ties.

Ratings
Prices are for one person and do not include alcoholic beverages and tips, but do include the *couvert* or *coberto,* an appetizer course that includes bread, butter, and, depending on the restaurant, cheese or pâté, olives, quail eggs, and sausage.

CATEGORY	RIO, SÃO PAULO	OTHER AREAS
$$$$	over $30	over $25
$$$	$20–$30	$15–$25
$$	$10–$20	$8–$15
$	under $10	under $8

Embassies and Consulates

United States
EMBASSY
Brasília: Av. das Nações, QD 801 lote 3, ☎ 061/321–7272.

CONSULATES
Rio de Janeiro: Av. Presidente Wilson 147, ☎ 021/292–7117. São Paulo: Rua Padre João Manoel 933, ☎ 011/881–6511.

Canada
EMBASSY
Brasília: Av. das Nações, Q 803 lote 16, ☎ 061/321–2171.

CONSULATES

Rio de Janeiro: Rua Lauro Müller 116, Room 1104, ☎ 021/542–7593.
São Paulo: Av. Paulista 1106, 1st Floor, ☎ 011/285–5099.

United Kingdom

EMBASSY

Brasília: Av. das Nações, QD 801 lote 8, ☎ 061/225–2710.

CONSULATES

Rio de Janeiro: Praia do Flamengo 284, 2nd Floor, ☎ 021/552–1422.
São Paulo: Av. Paulista 1938, 17th Floor, ☎ 011/287–7722.

Getting Around

By Plane

There is regular jet service between all of the country's major cities and a steadily growing number of medium-size cities. Flights can be long, lasting several hours on trips to the Amazon with stops en route. Planes tend to fill up on the weekends, so book in advance if you plan to fly anywhere on a Friday, especially to or from Brasília or Manaus.

Three major commercial airlines handle most of the domestic air traffic in Brazil: **Varig** (in Rio: ☎ 021/217–4591; in New York: ☎ 212/459–0210; in Toronto: ☎ 416/926–7500; in London: ☎ 0171/629–9408), **Vasp** (in Rio: ☎ 021/292–2080; in Los Angeles: ☎ 213/243–9207 or 310/364–0160), and **Transbrasil** (in Rio: ☎ 021/521–0300; in New York: ☎ 212/944–7374).

The most widely used service is the Rio–São Paulo shuttle, the **Ponte Aérea,** which has departures every hour from 6 AM until 10:30 PM (every half hour during morning and early evening rush hours). Other shuttle services now link the cities of São Paulo, Belo Horizonte, and Brasília. The south of Brazil is served by **Rio Sul** (☎ 021/263–2797), a regional airline that connects Rio and São Paulo with the principal cities of the southern states of Paraná and Rio Grande do Sul. **Nordeste** (☎ 071/233–7880) is a small regional airline with flights connecting Salvador with Porto Seguro, in the state of Bahia, and Vitória, capital of the neighboring state of Espírito Santo.

Prices are high by American standards, and there are no promotional fares. Brazilian airlines offer discounts of 30% for a 30-day advance purchase. Senior citizens over 60 have a right to a 30% discount. **Transbrasil** offers a 50% discount for its midnight flights linking Rio with São Paulo, Brasília, and Salvador.

If you are planning to do a good deal of flying in Brazil, consider purchasing the **Brazil Air Pass,** which is sold only outside the country and is offered by Varig, Transbrasil, and Vasp. This $440 pass permits five flights within Brazil for 21 days. All major destinations are served, including São Paulo, Manaus, Brasília, Belém, Recife, and Búzios.

By Train

Brazil has an outdated and insufficient rail network, the smallest of any of the world's large nations. The basic problem of Brazil's railroads is historical. Railroad construction was almost entirely overlooked during the early years of the country's development. Only in the 1930s were lines built along the coast, linking the large port cities mainly in the southeast. Inland regions, however, were largely forgotten in the initial transportation scheme. Brazil today has only some 30,000 kilometers (18,000 miles) of functioning rail lines, less than one-tenth the size of the United States's network and 20% smaller than that of Argentina, a country one-third the size of Brazil.

The failure to construct new lines, however, is only part of the problem. Nationwide, aging trains and tracks are rapidly deteriorating. Only 6,000 kilometers (3,600 miles) of the existing tracks were constructed since 1930.

Because of these continuing problems, passenger train service is spotty at best. The government-owned Federal Railway System, the only national rail network, no longer operates passenger trains between any of Brazil's leading cities. A subsidiary of the federal network, the Brazilian Urban Train Company (CBTU), is responsible for the nation's commuter trains. These trains, which are for the most part in terrible condition, carry the poor residents of the outskirts of Brazil's urban centers to work.

In Dec. 1994 a private company began operating a luxury overnight rail service between Rio de Janeiro and São Paulo three times a week (*see* Arriving and Departing *in* São Paulo, *above*).

By Car
ROAD CONDITIONS
Brazil's economic woes of the past 10 years have meant there has been little money left over for highway maintenance. This fact is particularly alarming when you consider that Brazil's network of federal highways was largely built between 1964 and 1976, with maintenance nearly nonexistent in the 1980s. The National Highway Department estimates that 50% of the nation's federal highways, which constitute 70% of Brazil's total road system, are in a dangerous state of disrepair, and each year an additional 3,000 kilometers (1,800 miles) fall into this category.

The evidence of this is everywhere. Potholes, lack of signalization, and inadequate shoulders are the most obvious of the precarious driving conditions on the federal roads. Landslides after heavy rains have become increasingly frequent, often shutting down entire stretches of key highways. The greatest danger, though, is the combination of decaying roads and increasing traffic, which has produced an explosion in deadly highway accidents. Brazilian drivers also tend to be reckless and pay little attention to the speed limit or the most basic rules of safe driving. The worst offenders are bus and truck drivers. For these reasons, you should avoid driving on Brazilian highways, but if you do drive, do so with the utmost caution.

RULES OF THE ROAD
Brazilians drive on the right-hand side of the road, and in general, traffic laws are the same as in the United States. The use of seat belts is mandatory. The national speed limit is 80 kph (48 mph) but is seldom observed or enforced. U.S. driver's licenses are accepted in Brazil in theory, but police, particularly highway police, have been known to invent violations in order to shake down drivers for bribes. It is therefore recommended to have an international driver's license, which is seldom challenged.

EMERGENCY ASSISTANCE
The **Automobile Club of Brazil** (Automóvel Club do Brasil; Rua do Passeio 90, Rio de Janeiro, RJ, ☎ 021/297–4455) provides emergency assistance to motorists in cities and on highways throughout the country. The club services members of foreign automobile clubs, but will not provide assistance to nonmembers.

GASOLINE

Gasoline in Brazil costs around 65¢ a liter ($2.40 a gallon). Unleaded gasoline is called *especial* and carries the same price. Brazil also has an extensive fleet of ethanol-powered cars. Ethanol fuel is sold at all gas stations, and costs 50¢ a liter ($1.90 a gallon). Although ethanol fuel is less expensive, alcohol cars get lower gas mileage, so they have no advantage over gasoline-power automobiles. Gas stations are plentiful both within cities and on major highways, and many are open 24 hours a day.

PARKING

Finding a parking space in most of Brazil's leading cities is a major task. This is particularly true in Rio, São Paulo, Belo Horizonte, and Salvador. The situation is somewhat better in Brasília. The best option is to find a parking garage and leave your car with the attendant. Should you find a parking space on the street, you will probably have to pay a parking fee. Because of Brazil's rampant inflation, which made the use of coins virtually impossible, there are no parking meters. There is instead a system involving parking coupons, which are purchased either from uniformed street parking attendants or at newspaper stands. Each coupon is good for two hours. No-parking zones are marked by a capital letter E that is crossed out. The E stands for *estacionamento,* which means parking. These zones are more often than not filled with cars, which are rarely bothered by the police.

By Bus

The nation's bus network is extensive and highly efficient, compensating for the lack of trains and the high cost of air travel. Every major city in the country can be reached by bus, and most of the small- to medium-size cities are also linked to the network. Buses are for the most part modern and comfortable, and the companies have excellent on-time records. On the well-traveled routes, service is frequent and inexpensive. Between Rio and São Paulo (6½–7 hours), for example, a bus departs every half hour, costing about $12 (a night sleeper costs about $24). The sleeper is basically a regular bus with fewer seats, permitting more space for each passenger to stretch out. The seats also recline more, and these buses are air-conditioned, the only ones today that guarantee this luxury (regular buses that are labeled air-conditioned often are not).

Trips to the north, northeast, and central Brazil tend to be long and tiring. The steady deterioration of the highways in recent years has also led to an increase in accidents involving buses. This is a recurring problem that is unlikely to be resolved in the short term. Lengthy bus trips anywhere in Brazil will inevitably involve travel over bad highways, an unfortunate fact of life in Brazil today.

There has been a recent spurt of robberies aboard buses traveling between Rio and São Paulo. In these cases, a member of the gang travels on board as a passenger, later pulling out a gun and forcing the driver to stop while his cohorts arrive in a car and rob the passengers.

Brazil's leading bus company is **Itapemirim** (Av. Brasil 12417, Rio de Janeiro), with countrywide operations. Tickets may be purchased only at the bus station (each city has one bus station). You cannot make reservations by phone, but you can buy a ticket at the station before the date you are traveling. This is a necessity when traveling the weekend of Carnival, over Easter, or during the holiday season at the end of the year.

By Boat

Some international cruise lines stop at Brazilian ports during world-wide or South American cruises. The most popular port of call is Rio during Carnival. International cruises also stop regularly at Santos, the port of the state of São Paulo, and Salvador. Some international liners include cruises along the Amazon River in their itineraries. These cruises and ports of calls, however, vary from year to year.

Check with your travel agent or contact one of the following cruise lines, which stop regularly at Brazilian ports: **Royal Viking Lines** (95 Merrick Way, Coral Gables, FL 33134, ☎ 305/447–9660), **Sun Line** (1 Rockefeller Plaza, Suite 315, New York, NY 10020, ☎ 212/397–6400), and **Cunard** (555 Fifth Ave., New York, NY 10017-2453, ☎ 800/221–4770).

Within Brazil, passenger traffic on inland waterways is limited to the Amazon region, where riverboats are the principal mode of transportation for inhabitants of the area (*see* Arriving and Departing by Boat *in* The Amazon, *above*).

Language

The language in Brazil is Portuguese, not Spanish. Although the two languages are distinct, common origins mean that many words are similar, and fluent speakers of Spanish will be able to make themselves understood. English is widely spoken among educated Brazilians and representatives of the tourist trade. In all hotels, someone on the staff will speak English, and in the better hotels, most of the staff will be at least able to answer basic questions. In restaurants, waiters will probably have only a smattering of English but maître d's will be able to speak well. Travel agencies and tour operators all employ bilingual staff. Taxi drivers, however, will rarely speak any English, and shop vendors outside of fashionable malls in large cities usually know very little. In such cities as Rio, São Paulo, Brasília, and Salvador, tourists have little difficulty in finding someone who speaks English to help them. The smaller the location, the further off the beaten track, the greater the difficulty of finding English-speaking Brazilians.

Lodging

Top prices are not always indicators of deluxe hotels in Brazil. The best hotels are in Rio and São Paulo, where the five-star rating given by the government tourism authority Embratur is usually reliable, although there is a tendency to elevate four-star hotels to the top rating for reasons that are not always clear. In general, the Embratur system merely takes into consideration the amenities offered by a hotel without evaluating such vital intangibles as the quality of service. Below four stars, the quality of hotels drops dramatically. Also, the quality of hotels, even the top rated, tends to fall in areas outside of Rio and São Paulo.

Although personal inspection of the premises is impossible if you are making reservations from afar, checking out the room in an inexpensive or moderate hotel before you take it is particularly important in Brazil. Reservations at expensive and deluxe establishments should be made well in advance, particularly if you're planning a trip during high season or special events. For Carnival, unless you are traveling with a tour, reservations in the best hotels must be made at least a year ahead. Unlike those in the United States, motels in Brazil do not have free parking, and are rented out for the hour, afternoon, or overnight. Though they are frequented by couples having assignations, these establishments are completely legitimate.

Ratings
Prices are for a double room and include all taxes.

CATEGORY	RIO, SÃO PAULO	OTHER AREAS
$$$$	over $200	over $100
$$$	$120–$200	$70–$100
$$	$70–$120	$30–$70
$	under $70	under $30

Mail

Post offices are called *correios,* and branches are marked by the name and a logo that looks somewhat like two interlocked fingers; most are open weekdays 8–5 and Saturday until noon. Mailboxes are small yellow boxes, marked CORREIOS, that sit atop metal pedestals on street corners.

Postal codes recently were converted from five to eight digits throughout Brazil. At press time (winter 1995), postal authorities were still delivering mail addressed with the old, five-digit codes.

Postal Rates
An airmail letter from Brazil to the United States and most parts of Europe, including the United Kingdom, costs approximately $1. Aerograms and postcards cost the same. Airmail takes at least five days to reach the United States from Brazil. Brazil has both national and international express mail service, the price of which varies according to the weight of the package and the destination. International express mail companies operating out of Brazil include Federal Express and DHL. Objects of value—especially currency, checks, or credit cards—should never be sent through the mail.

Receiving Mail
Mail can be addressed to "poste restante" and sent to any major post office. The address must include the code for that particular branch. American Express will hold mail for its cardholders.

Money Matters

Currency
In July 1994, Brazil underwent a currency reform with the replacement of the cruzeiro real (CR$) with a new currency, the real (R$; plural: reais). The reform was made necessary by chronic high inflation, which had rendered previous currencies increasingly worthless. The new currency's bills and coins completely replaced its predecessor's, so don't accept any money denominated in cruzeiros or cruzeiros reais.

There are 100 cents (centavos) to each real. The lowest value of the new currency system is one cent. There are notes worth one, five, 10, 50, and 100 reais (R$1, R$5, R$10, R$50, and R100), together with coins worth one, five, 10, 25, and 50 centavos, as well as one real.

Changing Money
At press time (winter 1995), Brazil had three different exchange rates, all floating and thus subject to daily variation: the tourism rate, called *câmbio turismo* (this is lower for traveler's checks and credit cards than for cash and personal checks); the official exchange rate (*comercial*), used only for government and business transactions; and the *paralelo* (parallel), or black market, rate. The official rate was slightly higher than the tourism rate, and the parallel rate was higher still. The three rates are published daily in local newspapers on the front page or in the financial section (look under the column labeled "Compra"), but

refer to the previous day's rate (with no change over the weekend) and often are not exactly the same as those used in actual transactions. Some big cities also have special phone numbers you can call to find out the day's exchange rates. As a tourist, the rate you will most often get is the tourism exchange rate, used by hotels and credit card companies. Brazil's exchange rate system is by no means set in stone and may change in response to the latest economic conditions.

For an average day in a Brazilian city, a good strategy is to convert up to $100 into reais before leaving your hotel, more if you are planning on a big meal. This provides sufficient cash for most of the day's expenses, such as taxis and small purchases and snacks, and saves the trouble of haggling over the exchange rate with taxi drivers and restaurant managers, who often try to take advantage of tourists.

Forms of Payment

Traveler's checks (well-known names are best), dollars in cash, credit cards, and, more rarely, personal checks (in dollars) are all accepted in Brazil, albeit at slightly varying exchange rates. You would do well to take your money in some of each of these forms.

Traveler's checks are safest, of course, especially given the dangers you may face in big cities and in the poorer parts of the country, where poverty often drives crime against tourists. These can easily be exchanged at the tourism rate for reais at hotels, banks, officially authorized *casas de câmbio* (exchange houses), travel agencies, and shops in shopping malls or those catering to tourists (many smaller tradesmen are at a total loss when faced with traveler's checks or even cash dollars). The rate for traveler's checks is lower than that for cash, and hotels often change them at a rate that is lower than that available at banks or casas de câmbio. You will need your passport to change dollars at the tourist rate.

During Brazil's hyperinflationary period of the early '90s, cash dollars were viewed as desirable hard currency because the local currency lost value on a daily basis. As of press time (winter 1995), however, the real was holding its strength against the dollar, and stores, waiters, and taxi drivers had become reluctant to accept greenbacks.

In Brazil's largest cities and leading tourist centers, top restaurants, hotels, and shops accept major international credit cards. Off the beaten track, however, tourists will have great difficulty in finding establishments that accept them. Credit cards can be used to pay hotel bills, but ask first if there is a discount for cash. You should try to bargain hard for a cash-on-the-barrel discount, then pay in local currency. Most gas stations in Brazil do not take credit cards.

Personal checks are a good last resort for luxury items (such as jewelry) or when an unexpected expense is incurred. Some hotels will accept personal checks from guests. These are usually exchanged on presentation of a passport, at the cash tourism or parallel rate, and only if the vendor has access to a U.S. bank account (which is increasingly common).

What It Will Cost

The mid-1994 anti-inflation program that accompanied the currency change resulted in a strong real against the dollar, and in general terms, the country became more expensive. Brazil is far from the bargain destination it once was. Prices in Brazil's largest cities, though, are still below prices for the same goods and services in comparable cities in the United States, Europe, and Asia. Top hotels in Rio and São Paulo go for more than $200 a night, but quality restaurants are surprisingly moderate, seldom more than $30 a person. Quality declines, often sharply, with lower prices. Outside of Brazil's two largest cities, prices for food and lodging tend to drop significantly, although Brasília is an exception to this rule. Fast-food outlets are now arriving in Brazil, led by the American McDonald's and Pizza Hut, with prices at roughly the same level as in the United States. Taxis, city buses, subways, and long-distance buses are all inexpensive. Plane fares, however, are definitely not: The round-trip airfare from Rio to São Paulo is $325, for example, and the fare from São Paulo to Manaus is $790 round-trip.

SAMPLE PRICES
A cup of coffee in São Paulo is 50¢; bottle of beer or glass of draft, $1.20; soft drink, 90¢; fresh fruit drink, $1.50; hamburger, $1.20-$3; 3-mile taxi ride, $5.

Opening and Closing Times

Banks
Banks are open weekdays 10–4:30. Nearly all the nation's major banks have automated teller machines scattered throughout the country.

Museums and Churches
Churches are typically open throughout the day, but museum hours vary considerably. Be sure to check in advance.

Shops
Stores generally open at 9 and close at 6:30 during the week and at 1 PM on Saturday. Shopping malls are open 10 AM to 10 PM weekdays and until 6 PM on Saturday. All stores are closed on Sunday, although newsstands and convenience stores that stay open on Sunday are beginning to appear in Rio and São Paulo. The business day generally begins at 9 and ends at 6, although punctuality is not a Brazilian trait. Stores and offices may open later and frequently stay open until the last customer leaves.

National Holidays
New Year's Day (Jan. 1); Epiphany (Jan. 6); Carnival, the week preceding Ash Wednesday (1996: Feb. 21; 1997: Feb. 12); Good Friday (1996: Apr. 5; 1997: Mar. 28); Easter (1996: Apr. 7; 1997: Mar. 30); Tiradentes Day (Apr. 21); Labor Day (May 1); Corpus Christi (1996: June 6; 1997: May 27); Independence Day (Sept. 7); Our Lady of Aparecida Day (Oct. 12); All Souls' Day (Nov. 2); Declaration of the Republic Day (Nov. 15); Christmas (Dec. 25).

Precautions

Health
No vaccinations are required to enter Brazil. In 1992, the Amazon region and the northeast coast were hit by an outbreak of cholera that had spread to Brazil from Peru. The disease has since reached Rio and São Paulo, but as of early 1995, the total number of recorded cases throughout Brazil was 50,000 out of the nation's total population of 146 million. Nearly all of the known cases of cholera have occurred either in rural areas or urban slums where sanitary conditions are precarious. There is no effective vaccine for cholera, a disease marked by severe diarrhea and that is contracted primarily through contact with contaminated water or food. The chances of a tourist coming down with cholera are extremely limited, but to be safe, observe the following precautions:

Do not drink water anywhere unless it is bottled mineral water. Do not drink beverages with ice made from tap water. Make sure that the fresh fruit you eat is peeled and that seafood (particularly in cold seafood salads) and vegetables are thoroughly cooked. Avoid all food and beverages from street vendors. To be safe, you should avoid fruits and vegetables unless you are certain they have been properly cleaned or cooked. For further information on cholera, contact the U.S. Department of Health and Human Services, Centers for Disease Control, ☏ 404/332–4559.

Malaria exists in regions of the Amazon, but these are isolated areas far from the routes frequented by tourists. Experienced and reliable travel operators who run Amazon trips say they have never advised tourists to concern themselves with malaria.

Safety

The rapid urbanization of Brazil over the past two decades has brought with it a growing crime problem that has been aggravated by the country's economic difficulties, in particular the most recent recession. In Rio, São Paulo, Salvador, Manaus, Belém, and major cities along the northeastern coast, tourists should take precautions to protect themselves from petty crime. Smaller cities tend to be safer, and Brasília and Belo Horizonte do not have the high crime rates of the nation's other large cities.

Most crimes involving tourists occur in public areas where there are large numbers of people, such as the beaches, crowded sidewalks, or on buses. In these settings, pickpockets, usually young children, work in groups. One or more will try to distract the victim while another grabs a wallet, bag, camera, or other target. Be particularly wary of children who suddenly thrust themselves in front of you to ask for money or to offer to shine your shoes. In such moments, it is easy for another member of the gang to strike from behind, grab whatever valuable is available, and take off to disappear in the crowd. Do not under any circumstances pursue or attempt to stop one of these robbers. Many of them are armed and although often quite young, they can be dangerous. Tourists, because they are considered easy victims, are unfortunately the primary targets of petty thieves.

Although women are gradually assuming a more important role in the nation's job force, the macho complex is still a strong force in Brazilian culture. Brazilian women rarely travel alone, especially young women. In Rio, São Paulo, and Brasília, the sight of women alone at night in restaurants or bars is more common today than in the past, but even in these cities it is liable to attract attention. In the rest of the country, women alone, depending on the time and setting, run the risk of being considered prostitutes.

Shopping

Department stores do exist, but they generally lack the glitz of their U.S. counterparts; well-to-do Brazilians prefer the personal attention they get in smaller stores. Price and quality vary dramatically, according to the country's ever-fluctuating economy. Most stores either tack on a hefty surcharge for credit cards or give discounts for cash. Prices in department stores are fixed, but in smaller shops and boutiques there is usually some room for discussion. Shops in areas that cater to tourists invariably charge more. At outdoor antiques and art fairs, crafts markets, and food markets, bargaining is a way of life. If you wish to try your hand at haggling over prices, the Portuguese phrase for too expensive is *"Está muito caro."*

Telephones

Local and Long-Distance Calls

All parts of Brazil are serviced by Embratel, the national telephone company. Public phones are everywhere and are called *orelhões* (big ears). These are yellow with the blue phone company logo for local calls, or solid blue for calls between cities (*interurbana*). To use the public phones, you must buy tokens, called *fichas*, at newspaper stands or phone company stations. Local fichas, which are good for three minutes, cost the equivalent of 8¢; long-distance tokens cost about 30¢ and last 18 seconds. It is wise to buy several at a time so that you can insert them in advance and avoid getting cut off. A three-minute call from Rio to São Paulo requires 10 long-distance tokens. Unused fichas are returned when you hang up. Rates double during peak hours (9 AM–noon and 2–6 PM). The lowest rates are available after 11 PM.

Although the public phones are visible on every street corner, vandalism is on the increase in Rio and São Paulo. As a result, you may have to try several of the phones before you find one that is working. Commercial establishments do not usually have public phones, although a bar, restaurant, or drugstore will probably allow you to use their private phone if you are a customer. Otherwise, you may be refused or be required to pay to use the phone. Phone company stations are found at airports, many bus stations, and in downtown neighborhoods of large cities. At these you can pay in cash after making the call. International credit cards are not accepted.

For local directory assistance, dial 102. For directory assistance in another Brazilian city, dial the area code of that city plus 121.

International Calls

International calls from Brazil are extremely expensive, double the international rates in the United States. Hotels also add a surcharge, increasing this cost. For international phone calls with the assistance of the operator, dial 000111. For international information, dial 000333. To dial direct, dial 00 plus the country code, the area code of the city you are calling, and then the number. Collect international calls can be made from any public phone either by dialing 107 and then asking for any international operator, or by dialing 000107 from a blue public phone.

To pay American long-distance rates and deal with American operators, AT&T, MCI, and Sprint cardholders can dial direct to a U.S. operator from any phone in Brazil. To reach an AT&T operator, dial 000–8010. For MCI, call 000–8012. For Sprint, dial 000–8016.

Tipping

At restaurants that levy a 10% service charge, it is customary to give the waiter a 5% tip in addition to the service charge included on the check. If there is no service charge, leave a 15% tip.

In deluxe hotels, tip porters 50¢ per bag, chambermaids 50¢ per day, $1 for room and valet service. Tips for doormen and concierge vary and depend primarily on the services provided. A good tip would be $10 or higher, average $5. For moderate and inexpensive hotels, tips tend to be minimal. At this level, salaries are so low that virtually anything is well received. If a taxi driver helps you with your luggage, a per bag charge of about 35¢ is levied in addition to the fare. In general, tip taxi drivers 10% of the fare.

At the barber shop or beauty parlor, a 10%–20% tip is expected. If a service station attendant does anything beyond filling up the gas tank, leave him a small tip of a nickel or dime. Tipping in bars and cafés follows the rules of restaurants, although at outdoor bars Brazilians rarely leave a tip if they have had no more than a soft drink or beer. In general, tip washroom attendants and shoe-shine boys about one-third what you would tip at home. At airports and at train and bus stations, tip the last porter who puts your bags into the cab (50¢ a bag at airports, 25¢ a bag at bus and train stations). In large cities you will often be accosted on the street by children looking for handouts; 25¢ is an average "tip."

When to Go

Throughout Brazil the high tourism season runs from November to April, although there are festivals, special events, and sporting attractions year-round. Carnival, the year's principal festival, occurs during the four days preceding Ash Wednesday, which usually falls in February but can occur in March. For top hotels in Rio and Salvador, the two leading Carnival cities, you must make reservations a year in advance. Hotel rates go up on the average 20% for Carnival, and you should also expect to pay more for taxis, up to double regular fares. Besides crowded hotels, you will find the downtown streets in Salvador packed with revelers during Carnival. In Rio, street Carnival is more sedate, but spontaneous groups of dancers parade across streets in the city's south zone on a regular basis.

Not as well known outside of Brazil but equally impressive is Rio's New Year's Eve celebration. More than a million people gather around the crescent curve of Copacabana beach for a massive fireworks display. In the hours preceding midnight, the beach is alive with the throbbing of drums as followers of Brazil's African religious cult Umbanba conduct ceremonies to honor the sea goddess Iemanjá. At the stroke of midnight, the white-clad faithful rush to the water's edge and throw in their offerings to the goddess, culminating in a unique spectacle. As with Carnival, Rio's better hotels usually fill up for New Year's Eve, especially those overlooking Copacabana beach. To ensure a room, book at least six months in advance.

Seasons below the Equator are the reverse of the north—summer in Brazil runs from December to March and winter from June to September. The rainy season in Brazil occurs during the summer months, but this is rarely a nuisance. Showers can be torrential but usually last no more than an hour or two, after which the sun reappears. The only area of the country with a pronounced rainy season is the Amazon. In this region, the rainy season runs from November to May and is marked by heavy downpours that usually occur twice a day.

Prices in beach resorts invariably are higher during the high season (Brazilian summer). If you are looking for a bargain, stick to the off-season (from May to October). In Rio and at beach resorts along the coast, especially in the northeast, these months offer the added attraction of relief from the often oppressive summer heat, although in Rio the temperature can drop to uncomfortable levels for swimming in June through August.

Climate

Rio de Janeiro is on the Tropic of Capricorn, and its climate is just that—tropical. Summers are hot and humid, with temperatures rising as high as 105°F (40°C), although the average ranges between 84–95°F (29–35°C). In winter, temperatures stay in the 70s (20s C), occasionally dipping into the 60s (15–20°C). The same pattern holds true for all of the Brazilian coastline north of Rio, although in general temperatures are slightly higher year-round in Salvador and the coastal cities of the northeast. In the Amazon region where the equator crosses the country, temperatures in the high 80s to the 90s (30s C) are common throughout the year. São Paulo, the inland state of Minas Gerais, and Brasília, because of their higher altitude, are substantially cooler than Rio. These regions tend to have more of a change of seasons, although nowhere in Brazil, with the exception of the south, are there four distinct seasons. In the south, in São Paulo and Belo Horizonte, winter temperatures can fall to the low 40s (5–8°C). In the southern states of Santa Catarina and Rio Grande do Sul, snowfalls occur in the winter, although it is seldom more than a dusting.

The following are the average daily maximum and minimum temperatures for Rio de Janeiro.

Jan.	84F	29C	May	77F	25C	Sept.	75F	24C
	69	21		66	19		66	19
Feb.	85F	29C	June	76F	24C	Oct.	77F	25C
	73	23		64	18		63	17
Mar.	83F	28C	July	75F	24C	Nov.	79F	26C
	72	22		64	18		68	20
Apr.	80F	27C	Aug.	76F	24C	Dec.	82F	28C
	69	21		64	18		71	22

The following are the average daily maximum and minimum temperatures for Salvador.

Jan.	87F	31C	May	80F	27C	Sept.	78F	26C
	76	24		70	21		69	21
Feb.	88F	31C	June	80F	27C	Oct.	80F	27C
	76	24		67	19		69	21
Mar.	87F	31C	July	78F	26C	Nov.	83F	28C
	77	25		66	19		72	22
Apr.	84F	29C	Aug.	80F	27C	Dec.	86F	30C
	73	23		67	19		77	25

6 Chile

Bounded by the sea on one side and the sharp spine of the Andes on the other, Chile makes up in spirit what it lacks in width. The proximity of active volcanoes and crumbling glaciers only increases the lush pleasures of award-winning vineyards, excellent ski slopes, and such beachside resorts as Viña del Mar.

By Lake
Sagaris

Updated by
Richard Neill

I **LIVE NOW IN A COUNTRY** as soft / as the autumnal flesh of grapes," begins "Country," a poem by the Chilean poet and Nobel prizewinner Pablo Neruda. With his odes to artichokes, birds, hope, Valparaíso, fish soup, socks, and September, he sang Chile into being and taught us to inhale its sharp salt air or the dry winy bouquet of its Andean peaks before we hold them to our lips and drink them down.

Chile is as luminous and pungent, as rustic and urban, as any of Neruda's poems about it. It combines the world's driest desert, a pie slice of Antarctica, the "navel of the universe" (Easter Island), Robinson Crusoe's former haunts, a sophisticated urban landscape, and a temperate southern jungle—all in one slim extension of land squeezed between the Pacific Ocean and the Andes, with a vast and varied human geography to match. In some places the 200-mile territorial limit is wider than the country itself, making Chile as much ocean as earth.

From 1973 to 1990, Chile was virtually synonymous with the name of General Augusto Pinochet, who, with U.S. support, led a coup against the elected socialist government in September 1973. His regime's reputation for human-rights violations and violent social conflict discouraged many visitors, but the advent of a civilian, elected government in March 1990 brought improvements. Today the country enjoys considerable social harmony and the most advanced economy in South America.

The first traveler to reach Chile barely gave it a glance: Hernando de Magallanes left his name and little else behind when he journeyed up the southwestern coast in 1520. Later, Pedro de Valdivia traveled south along the Camino del Inca (Incas' Road) with a motley assortment of adventurers and a sole woman, his lover, Inés de Suárez; they founded Santiago in 1541.

For the next 300 years, Chile's original inhabitants, especially the southern Mapuche, successfully defended a sizable territory and their way of life against Spanish encroachment. Chilean independence from Spain, after a war that lasted from 1810 to 1818, marked the beginning of the end of the Mapuche's independence. Their last great rebellion failed in 1881, and soon after, Chilean governments started shipping in German, Swiss, and other European colonists to fill their "empty" lands.

Today's Chileans are a mixture of European and indigenous gene pools, with the lightest hair, skin, and eyes to be found at the top of a hierarchically organized society. Native peoples include about half a million Mapuche living in the region around Temuco; the Aymara, who live in Chile's difficult north, in the world's driest desert; and the Polynesians, who still form the majority of the population of Rapa Nui (Easter Island).

SANTIAGO

A curious mixture of modern skyscrapers, 19th-century European architecture, and Spanish colonial adobe bungalows, Santiago's architecture reflects the fact that the city is really a universe composed of multiple worlds. The population is more than 5 million; nevertheless, residents are always likely to bump into an acquaintance along the city center's overcrowded streets and bustling walkways, since they're concentrated in a small area around the Ahumada and Huérfanos pedes-

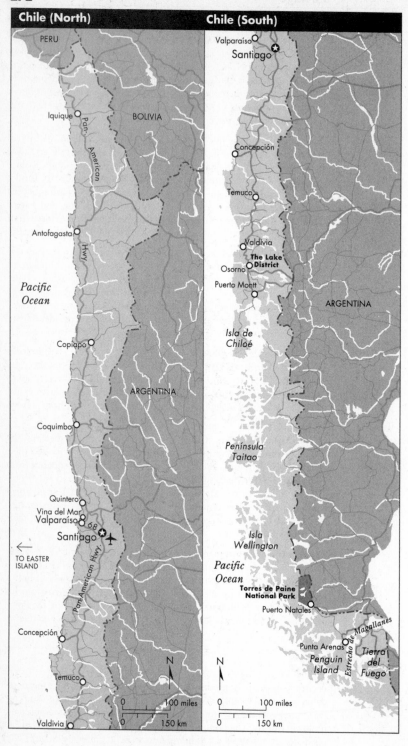

PERU

Iquique

BOLIVIA

Pan-American

Antofagasta

Hwy

*Pacific
Ocean*

Copiapo

ARGENTINA

Coquimbo

Quintero

Vina del Mar
Valparaíso
68
Santiago

←

TO EASTER
ISLAND

Pan-American Hwy

Concepción

Temuco

Valdivia

N

0   100 miles
0   150 km

Valparaíso
Santiago

Concepción

Temuco

Valdivia
**The Lake
District**
Osorno
Puerto Montt

*Isla de
Chiloé*

ARGENTINA

*Península
Taitao*

*Isla
Wellington*

*Pacific
Ocean*
**Torres de Paine
National Park**
Puerto Natales

Punta Arenas
*Penguin
Island*

Estrecho de Magallanes

*Tierra
del
Fuego*

N

0   100 miles
0   150 km

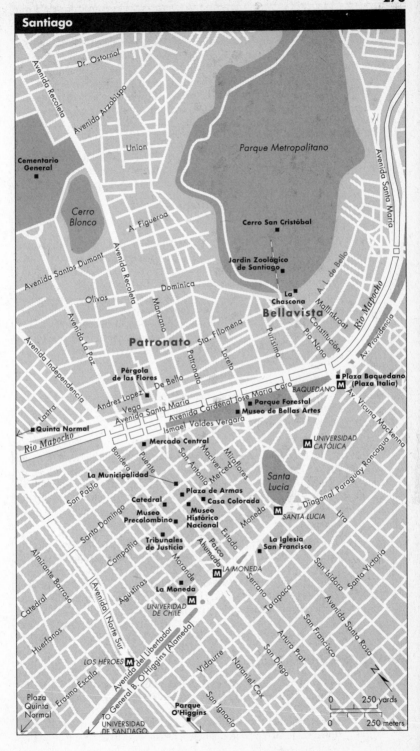

Santiago

Dr. Ostornol

Avenida Recoleta

Avenida Arzobispo

Union

Parque Metropolitano

Cementario
General

Cerro
Blonco

Avenida Santos Dumont

A. Figueroa

Avenida Recoleta

Cerro San Cristóbal

Avenida La Paz

Olivos

Dominica

Jardin Zoológico
de Santiago

Avenida Santa Maria

Avenida Independencia

Marzano

La
Chascona

Bellavista

Av. I. de Bello

A. I. de Bello

Mallinkroat

Rio Mapocho

Av. Providencia

Patronato

Sta. Filomena

Constitución

Pio Nono

Purisima

Loreto

Patronato

De Bello

Lastra

**Pérgola
de las Flores**

Andres Lopez

Vega

Avenida Santa Maria

Avenida Cardenal Jose Maria Caro

**Plaza Baquedano
(Plaza Italia)**

BAQUEDANO

Av. Vicuna Mackenna

Parque Forestal

Museo de Bellas Artes

Quinta Normal

Rio Mapocho

Ismael Valdes Vergara

**UNIVERSIDAD
CATÓLICA**

Bandera

Puente

San Antonio

Mercado Central

Mackver

Miraflores

Merced

Santa
Lucia

Diagonal Paraguay Rancagua

La Municipalidad

San Pablo

San Pablo

Santo Domingo

Catedral

**Museo
Precolombino**

Plaza de Armas

Casa Colorada

**Museo
Histórico
Nacional**

Estado

Moneda

SANTA LUCIA

Lira

Almirante Barroso

Compañia

**Tribunales
de Justicia**

Morande

Pasco

Ahumada

**La Iglesia
San Francisco**

San Isidoro

Santa Victoria

Catedral

Agustinas

La Moneda

LA MONEDA

Estado

Serrano

Tarapaca

San Francisco

Avenida Santa Rosa

Huerfonos

**UNIVERDAD
DE CHILE**

Avenida Norte Sur

La Moneda

Avenida del Libertador

LOS HÉROES

Avenida del Libertador (Alameda)

Avenida General B. O'Higgins (Alameda)

Vidaurre

Arturo Prat

San Diego

Erasmo Escala

Plaza
Quinta
Normal

Natatiel Cox

San Ignacio

**Parque
O'Higgins**

TO
UNIVERSIDAD
DE SANTIAGO

N

0   250 yards

0   250 meters

trian malls. The Paseo Ahumada stretches northward from the Alameda (Avenida Libertador Bernardo O'Higgins) to the Plaza de Armas and is bisected about halfway along by Paseo Huérfanos. Modern stores and banks in skyscrapers and 19th-century buildings stretch out for blocks around the Plaza de Armas, which is full of colorful gardens and fountains. The parks, the food, and a more relaxed attitude toward time exercise a magnetic attraction on visitors, as do dancing and nightlife, which begins at 10 PM and goes on most of the night.

Visitor Information

SERNATUR (Providencia 1550, Santiago, ☎ 562/236–1416, FAX 562/236–1417), the national tourist service, is on Providencia Street between the metro stops Manuel Montt and Pedro de Valdivia.

Arriving and Departing

By Plane

Chile's new international airport terminal is about 30 minutes' drive west of Santiago, alongside the rather dilapidated old terminal which now services domestic flights. The former is an efficient and beautifully designed metal-and-glass structure that contains far better facilities than its predecessor. You can get from the airport to Santiago by taxi for less than $18, via **Buses Tour Express** (☎ 2/671–7380) for $2, or in a **Navett** (☎ 2/695–6868) minibus, which will deliver you to any address within the city center. You can rent a car in the airport from **Avis** (☎ 2/601–9966), **Budget** (☎ 2/601–9421), or **Hertz** (☎ 2/601–9262). There is no subway connection.

By Train

The train station is **Estación Central** (Central Station) on Alameda (Av. Bernardo O'Higgins) at Exposición Street. It has its own metro stop of the same name.

By Car

If you're coming into Santiago from the north, you'll probably arrive via the Pan-American Highway, also called Highway 5; from Viña or Valparaíso, Highway 68; from the south, the Pan-American Highway South, still Highway 5; from the Andes (Argentina) Highway 57. Route 78 brings you into Santiago from San Antonio and other coastal towns.

By Bus

The **Terminal Norte** (Amunátegui 920, ☎ 2/671–2141) handles northern and northeastern (coastal) service. **Terminal Santiago** (Av. Libertador Bernardo O'Higgins 3848, ☎ 2/779–1385) handles southern and coastal traffic. **Terminal Los Héroes** (Roberto Pretot 21, ☎ 2/696–9076, 2/696–9080, or 2/696–9082) handles some northern and southern traffic. **Terminal Alameda** (Av. Libertador Bernardo O'Higgins 3750, ☎ 2/776–3690) handles some coastal and southern traffic. (*See* Chile Essentials, *below*, for phone numbers of individual lines.)

Getting Around Santiago

Much of Santiago is best explored on foot; use the metro and an occasional taxi to manage larger distances. However, a combination of the metro and taxis is probably the quickest, most comfortable, and most economical way to get around. The metro is best for reaching downtown, or anywhere along its east–west axis. You'll probably want the rented car or taxi to get to the *barrio alto* (upper-class neighborhoods) or take a general tour of the city. Most individual taxi drivers are willing to be hired for the day; to increase your bargaining power, head for the taxi stand at Huérfanos and MacIver streets in the heart of downtown, where you can talk to more than one driver. You can catch buses to the Maipo Canyon, about an hour's drive south of the city, in the Parque Bernardo O'Higgins.

By Car

Drivers in Santiago don't respect traffic signs, lights, or lines on the road, and rush hour means wall-to-wall cars lined up along major and minor thoroughfares. However, a rented car or taxi is still your best bet for an overview of the city or for enjoying short drives into the surrounding countryside. Between May and August, roads, underpasses, and parks flood whenever it rains, and they can become very dangerous, especially for drivers who don't know their way around. Avoid driving if it has been raining for several hours.

By Bus

Buses have improved but are still fast, reckless, and unreliable; bus drivers almost invariably say they go where you want to go, whether they do or not. Bus fare is usually 120 pesos–130 pesos (about 30¢), paid upon boarding, and drivers can usually change up to a 1,000-peso bill.

By Metro

Santiago's metro is modern, comfortable, cheap, and safe; make it the backbone of your explorations. Every station has a clear map of the north–south (the secondary route) and east–west (the main route) lines, with adjoining roads. The Universidad de Chile stop on the east–west line is the main station for the city center; the Escuela Militar is the upper-class end of the city; and Pudahuel is the poorer, less developed area. Buy tickets in the glass booths at the stations; a *boleto valor* (value ticket)—good for up to 10 journeys and valid on both metro lines—is cheapest at about $3.50. Main line tickets can be used on the secondary lines as well, but the cheaper, north–south tickets can't be used on the main line.

By Taxi

Taxi drivers aren't as honest as they used to be, but taxis, especially when combined with the metro for large distances, are a reasonable alternative for most transportation needs. You can flag one down on most streets; the average ride costs around $10 (more for designated airport taxis). Radio-dispatched cabs—call **Alfa** (☎ 2/773–7228 or 2/773–7634) or **Andes Pacífico** (☎ 2/225–3064 or 2/204–0104)—are slightly more expensive but will pick you up at your door.

Tour Operators

Adventure Tours

Altué Expediciones (Encomenderos 83, ☎ 2/232–1103, FAX 2/233–6799) offers adventure trips such as rafting on wild rivers and hiking to the mouths of volcanoes.

Orientation Tours

SERNATUR maintains a register of experienced individual tour guides who, for a half-day fee (around $35 per group), will take you on a personalized tour of Santiago and the surrounding area. These guides can greatly enrich visits to Santiago's less documented museums, for example, by providing background knowledge that is not generally available to the public.

Other operators include **Turismo Cocha** (El Bosque Norte 0430, ☎ 2/232–1488, FAX 2/233–4956) and **Chilean Travel Services** (Antonio Dellet 77, Office 101, ☎ 2/251–0400, FAX 2/251–0423), who handle tours of both Santiago and the rest of Chile. A smaller agency offering individualized tours, both guided and group, is the reliable and imaginative **Rigtur** (Ahumada 312, Office 606, ☎ 2/698–5766 or 2/698–7535, ℻ 2/797–9668).

Winery Tours

Chile Wine Tours (☎ 2/821–4224, ℻ 2/821–1962) runs half-day, full-day, and weeklong tours of Chile's vineyards and wineries. Short tours are based on some of the oldest wineries such as Viña Cousiño Macul and Viña Santa Rita, whose beautiful old family houses and private gardens are close to the capital. Longer tours will take you to some of the newer boutique wineries to the south and to the home of Chile's best white wines, the Casablanca Valley. Customized tours can also be arranged.

Exploring Santiago

Santiaguinos orient themselves along an east–west axis, with the Cordillera (the Andes mountain range) to the east and the coastal mountains to the west. Santiago itself nestles in the valley between them and is cut approximately in half north–south by the Mapocho River. The Avenida Libertador Bernardo O'Higgins, better known as the Alameda, is laid out over what was once the southern arm of the Mapocho River, from east to west. In Plaza Baquedano, also known as Plaza Italia, the Alameda becomes Providencia, an upscale shopping district; farther east and northward it's called Apoquindo; and yet farther along it turns into Las Condes and is the address of some of the city's fanciest houses.

The city center nestles just to the south of the Mapocho, radiating out on a grid pattern from the central square known as the Plaza de Armas (Weapons Square). The Central Market is on the river's south side, about three blocks north of the plaza; the Vega, a cheaper, more colorful version of the market, is across the river. The General Cemetery is about five minutes' drive north from the Vega, and the Bellavista area—full of restaurants, theaters, and art galleries—is about five minutes' drive east of the Vega. The Parque O'Higgins is about 20 minutes' drive south of downtown, or about 10 minutes via the north–south metro line.

Downtown

If you really want to get to know Santiago, start at the city's heart, the central **Plaza de Armas,** between Estado, Catedral, and Compañía streets and four blocks north of the Universidad de Chile metro station. Flanked by **La Municipalidad** (City Hall), the **Museo Histórico Nacional** (National History Museum), **la Catedral,** and a motley assortment of commercial arcades, the square is a genuine center for activities, top among them loafing and people-watching. Its distinctive fountains and gardens, constantly being replanted, reveal Chileans' pride of place. Here you will view a cross section of Chileans, many of whom speak a few words of English: the *pelusas* (street children); the photographers, with their old-fashioned box cameras, who make a living taking people's pictures; the street vendors who hawk toys, candies, and the latest peculiar knickknack; and the elderly and unemployed who sun themselves on the benches.

The **National History Museum,** on the square, is remarkable mostly for the quality of a recent restoration performed on the building itself, which dates from 1804. As a source of information about Chilean history it's extremely poor. For example, it marks 300 years of native resistance to Spanish and Chilean invasions with a pen-and-ink sketch titled "La

Pacificación de la Araucanía" ("The Pacification of the Araucanian Territories"), and it reduces most major historical events to the uniform worn by such-and-such a general or the bed that X slept in every night. *Plaza de Armas,* ☎ *2/638–1411.* ☛ *Entry fee; free Sun. mornings. Closed Mon.*

Just south of the square and a block east on Merced Street you'll find the **Casa Colorada** (Reddish House), a red-washed, colonial-style building that now houses the modest but informative Santiago Museum, an excellent place to learn some of Santiago's and Chile's long history—if you can read Spanish. *Merced 860,* ☎ *2/633–0723.* ☛ *Entry fee. Closed Mon.*

If you plan to visit only one museum in Santiago, it should be the **Museo Precolombino** (Pre-Columbian Museum), about three blocks west of the Plaza de Armas, in the city center. It contains a well-endowed collection of artifacts of Central and South America's indigenous peoples housed in a beautifully restored colonial building that once served as the Royal Customs House. The permanent collection includes textiles and ceramics from what is now Mexico southward, including Chile. As in most Chilean museums, there isn't a lot of information with the displays, so you might want to call upon a local guide who has expertise in the museum's area (*see* Tour Operators, *above*). *361 Bandera,* ☎ *2/695–3851.* ☛ *Entry fee. Closed Mon.*

Just across the street from the Pre-Columbian Museum are Chile's lordly **Tribunales de Justicia** (Tribunals of Justice), the site of many a human-rights demonstration during the military government and still today. If you continue southward on Bandera Street for three blocks, then follow Moneda Street westward one block, you'll find yourself at **La Moneda** (literally, "the coin," so-called because the structure was originally built as the national mint), designed by the Italian architect Joaquín Toesca in 1799. The traditional Spanish colonial–style palace complex, with offices and galleries built around spacious cement courtyards (one planted with orange trees), has housed Chilean presidents since the 19th century but was bombed during the 1973 military coup and then restored and occupied by General Pinochet.

Around the Market

The Central Market area, three blocks north of the Plaza de Armas, offers a smelly, colorful, intriguing glimpse of everyday life in Santiago. The **Mercado Central** (Central Market) itself was prefabricated in England and erected in Chile between 1868 and 1872. It has the lofty wrought-iron ceiling of a Victorian train station and soars above a matchless selection of Chilean fruits and vegetables, along with many rare delicacies that can be purchased only in this market, including exotic mushrooms and piñones, Chile's giant pine nuts from the monkey puzzle tree.

The *pescadería* (fish market), just to the east in an adjoining building, provides a complete introduction to Chile's varied and marvelous sea creatures. Depending on the season, you might see the delicate beak of *picorocos,* the world's only edible barnacle; the orange stars of sea urchins in their prickly shells; or shadowy pails full of succulent bull-frogs. You can find a cheap, filling meal at most of the stands along the south end of the whole market. You can expect to be served a clandestine glass of wine with your meal if you ask, although most stands don't have a liquor license.

Santiago's green and grassy **Parque Forestal** (Forest Park) starts near the market and runs parallel to the Mapocho River for several blocks.

A stroll under banana and other imported and Chilean trees takes you past a children's play area to the park's pointed tip, distinguished by the Wagnerian-scale **Fuente Alemana** (German Fountain) in Plaza Baquedano.

Along the way you'll pass the **Museo de Bellos Artes** (Fine Arts Museum), with paintings, drawings, and sculpture by 16th- to 20th-century Chilean and European artists. Closed during the time of the military regime but reopened in 1990, the museum has worked hard to reach international standards of quality. *Calles José Miguel de la Barra and Loreto,* ☏ *2/633–0655.* ☛ *Entry fee. Closed Sun. afternoon.*

Across the river from the central market, you'll find the **Pérgola de las Flores** (Trellis of Flowers), the source of the complex wreaths and flower arrangements made mostly for visitors to the two cemeteries in the area. Right next door is the **Vega,** a low-ceilinged collection of stands where many Santiaguinos buy their fruits and vegetables and where the vendors joke congenially with their customers and each other.

Patronato and Bellavista

Just across Recoleta Avenue, east of the Vega, is Santiago's **Patronato** area, with bargains on clothes, sheets, and towels. Once the exclusive preserve of Chileans of Arab origin, this traditional textile neighborhood is now home to more and more Korean-owned shops. If you continue eastward along Antonia López de Bello, you'll pass the storefront shops in old Arab-style mansions built by families who made their fortune in textiles, and you'll eventually reach the trendy **Bellavista** neighborhood, where the streets are lined with acacia trees, small cafés, and one-story adobe homes painted in pinks, aquamarines, and blues.

The heart of Bellavista is at Pío Nono and Antonia López de Bello streets; one of its main attractions is the **Parque Metropolitano** (Metropolitan Park), at the north end of Pío Nono Street, which covers the entirety of Santiago's highest hill, **Cerro San Cristóbal** (St. Christopher Hill; ☏ 2/777–6666 for park administration). If you turn left at Pío Nono Street and walk two blocks northward along a paved road, then up a steep but well-cleared path, you'll reach the entrance to the hill. You can walk up (it's a steep but enjoyable one-hour climb) or take the funicular or an open bus to the summit, which is crowned by a huge white statue of the Virgin Mary and a fabulous view of the entire city. If you're going up to watch the sunset, avoid walking back down alone since the area is not well patrolled and muggings are frequent. Halfway up the hill is the **Jardín Zoológico de Santiago** (Santiago Zoo), a good place to see examples of many Chilean species, some nearly extinct, that you might not otherwise encounter. Be careful: Some of the cages aren't properly protected, and the animals can bite.

At the foot of the hill, just a block east along Constitución and then left on Fernando Márquez de la Plata Street, you'll find the house Pablo Neruda designed, **La Chascona** (Woman with Tousled Hair, named for Mathilde Urratia, the lover with whom he lived his final years). Visits, by appointment only, allow you to step into the extraordinary mind of the poet who has been called an "organic architect": winding this way and that around the hillside is a path through the garden, leading to a library stuffed with books, a bedroom in a tower, and a secret passageway—all filled with the collections of butterflies, books, seashells, bowsprits, wine glasses, and other odd objects that inspired Neruda's poetry. *Fernando Márquez de la Plata 192,* ☏ *2/777–8741.* ☛ *Entry fee. Closed Sun.–Mon.*

Parks, Gardens, and Cemeteries

It may be unusual as far as tourist attractions go, but the **Cementerio General,** Santiago's general cemetery, at the end of Avenida la Paz, a short taxi ride northwest from the Cerro San Cristóbal or downtown, is a fine source of insights into traditional Chilean society. You pass through the lofty stone arches of the main entrance and find yourself among marble mausoleums, the squat mansions belonging to Chile's wealthy families. The cemetery has well-maintained gardens, neat roads and walkways, stained-glass windows, and religious icons. The 8- or 10-story "niches" farther along—literally concrete shelves housing thousands of coffins—resemble middle-class apartment buildings; their inhabitants lie here until the "rent" runs out and they're evicted.

On the south side of the city is the large **Parque Bernardo O'Higgins,** at the southern line subway stop by the same name. The park, named for Chile's national liberator, who led rebel troops to victory against the Spanish, thus creating an independent Chile in 1818, has an open area, complete with paved marching grounds for military parades, swimming pools, and lots of space to fly kites. Street vendors sell kites and string outside the park year-round; high winds make September and early October the prime kite-flying season.

To the north of the city center is another park, the **Quinta Normal,** founded in 1830 to reproduce foreign plant species. It's a popular place for a stroll or picnic and has a small pond, and rowboats that can be rented. The park also contains the **Museo Nacional de Historia Natural** (National Natural History Museum), with displays on Chilean animal life, and the **Museo de Ciencia, Tecnología, Ferroviario e Infantil** (Museum of Science and Technology, Railway Museum, and Children's Museum). The Children's Museum caters primarily to prearranged tours by groups of local schoolchildren. The main entrance to the park is at Avenida Matucana, near Agustinas. *Natural History Museum,* ☎ *2/681–4095; Science and Technology and Railway Museum,* ☎ *2/681–6022; Children's Museum,* ☎ *2/681–8800.* ☛ *Entry fee at all. Closed Mon.*

Shopping

Specialty Shop
<u>WINE</u>
If you want to take home some Chilean wine, you can choose from almost the entire export range at **The Wine House** (Av. El Bosque Norte 0500, ☎ 2/232–7257).

Markets
The **Pueblo de los Artesanos** is a crafts "village" with a wonderful display of cockatoos, exotic chickens, and other live birds. It's a nice place to visit, especially on weekends when traveling musicians and performers add live entertainment to an already interesting mix of handicrafts and antiques. *Los Graneros del Alba, Av. Apoquindo 8600, beside the Church los Domínicos. Closed Mon.*

There's a **permanent crafts fair** in Bellavista in the evenings, in the Domingo Gómez Park near the Law School on Pío Nono, just across the river from Plaza Baquedano. More vendors gather on weekends to display their handicrafts. For other spots to buy handcrafted articles, check with SERNATUR to learn where local crafts fairs are currently operating.

Shopping Centers

Santiago now has plenty of places where an A to Z of brand names sits under the same roof. **Alto Las Condes Shopping Center** (Av. Presidente Kennedy 9001) contains the aptly named Jumbo supermarket, where the staff wears roller skates to restock the aisles. It has a wide range of Chilean export wines. **Falabella** (Nueva de Lyon 064, ☎ 2/233–7171) offers anything from perfume to plates, all within the glide of an escalator and all under the soothing influence of elevator music. **Almacenes París** (Av. 11 de Setiembre 2221, ☎ 2/233–5045) provides perfume to plates to those who can't be bothered to walk across the street to Falabella. **Parque Arauco** (Av. Kennedy 5413, ☎ 2/242–0600) is a typical North American–style mall, with an eclectic mix of department and boutique stores. There's even a McDonald's for those who have acute bouts of homesickness.

Sports

Horse Racing

Horse racing is popular at every level of society. There are two large hippodromes in Santiago, the **Club Hípico** (Blanco Encalada 2540, ☎ 2/683–6535), with racing weekend and Wednesday afternoons, and the **Hipódromo Chile** (Hipódromo Chile 1715, ☎ 2/736–9276), where post times tend to be earlier.

Skiing

While the Northern Hemisphere swelters, it's Chile's peak snow season, and three ski resorts operate a mere 45 minutes from Santiago. For more details, *see* Andean Ski Resorts *in* Excursions from Santiago, *below*.

Soccer

Chile's most popular and most absorbing spectator sport is soccer, but a close second is watching the endless battles and bickering that go on among owners, players, and trainers whenever things aren't going well. The venue is the **Estadio Nacional** (Av. Grecia 2001, ☎ 2/238–8102); the season is March through December; and matches are on weekends and some Wednesdays.

Dining

In the past five years, restaurants have blossomed in Santiago, particularly in the Bellavista neighborhood. Many specialize in "international cuisine," a term that can mean just about anything, from lasagna to sushi to fiery Szechuan beef. Ethnic restaurants in general are not necessarily very good: Chile hasn't had the kind of immigration that has produced the excellent Chinese and other restaurants in Peru and other neighboring countries. In addition to good Chilean restaurants, however, there are several restaurants that serve above-average Italian, Argentine, Spanish, and Peruvian fare. Prices vary enough between dishes that, depending on what you order, your meal may move the restaurant up or down a category. Beware: Most restaurants are closed on Sunday. For details and price-category definitions, *see* Dining *in* Chile Essentials, *below*.

Chilean/International

$$$ **Balthazar.** Nouvelle cuisine with a Chilean twist is served in this care-
★   fully restored old adobe stable. In the center of the small dining room, a rough-hewn wooden trestle table groans with a buffet of exquisite, inventive salads and hors d'oeuvres that borrow from Indonesian, Japanese, Chinese, Arab, and other cuisines. The scallops and stuffed

trout with olive sauce are spectacular. ✗ *Av. las Condes 10690,* ☎ *2/215–1090. Reservations advised. AE, DC, MC, V. Closed Sun.*

$$$ **Metro.** Worth visiting just for the interior design, this former nightclub has a boat suspended above the bar, aquariums, and cattle skins on the walls. It's actually two restaurants in one—the upper-level sushi bar could compete with any Japanese establishment, while below you can dine on anything from Asian-inspired dishes to the best burgers and ribs in town. Both dining areas offer great people-watching along with the food. ✗ *Av. las Condes 10690,* ☎ *2/217–3130. AE, DC, MC, V.*

$$ **Torres.** Fronting on Alameda, this claims to be the oldest surviving restaurant in the downtown area. The huge shiny wooden bar, old fans, and light fixtures take you back to the era of President Barros, the teens of the 20th century. As well as specializing in classic Chilean dishes, it offers excellent sandwiches, making it a perfect lunch spot. On Thursday through Saturday nights, tangos and boleros are performed. ✗ *Av. Libertador Bernardo O'Higgins 1570,* ☎ *2/698–6220. AE, MC, V. Closed Sun.*

$ ★ **Don Peyo.** For first-rate Chilean food at reasonable prices, Don Peyo's is hard to beat. The hand-kneaded country bread, hot sauce, and garlic and avocado spreads in themselves warrant a visit, but the beef dishes, especially the *plateada,* a Chilean version of roast beef, are what put this restaurant on the map. A mixed group of working- and middle-class Chileans enjoy a night out here amid the rustic decor and woven straw chairs. ✗ *Av. Grecia 448 and Lo Encalada 465, Nuñoa,* ☎ *2/274–0764. Weekend reservations advised or arrive early (around 8 PM). DC, MC, V. Closed Sun.*

$ ★ **El Venezia.** Long before the Bellavista neighborhood became fashionable, there was the Venezia, a tacky, bare-bones restaurant where TV stars and publicists rub elbows with the people of the street. The beer is icy, the waiters are simpatico, and the food is abundant and well prepared. There's no fish on Monday, but the *congrío frito* (fried conger eel, really a fish), available the rest of the week, is delicious, as are the *costillar de chancho* (pork ribs), the filet mignon, and the roast or stewed chicken. ✗ *Pío Nono 200,* ☎ *2/737–0900. AE, DC, MC, V.*

French

$ **Les Assassins.** The immediate impression on entering this neighborhood institution is of a rather somber bistro with an odd jumble of fittings and fixtures. However, the atmosphere and service is friendly and the Provence-influenced food is first-rate. The steak au poivre (with brandy and pepper) and crêpes suzette would make even a Frenchman's eyes water. If you want to practice your Spanish, there's always a line of talkative locals in the cozy ground-floor bar. ✗ *Merced 297–B,* ☎ *2/638–4280. Reservations advised. MC, V. Closed Sun.*

Indian

$$$ **TajMahal.** Adorned with colored silks and characteristic handicrafts, this restaurant offers a spicy change from the often bland Chilean cuisine. The curries aren't as fiery as you'd expect, but the flavors of the traditional Tandoori cooking are as authentic as you'll find this far from India. ✗ *Av. Isadora Goyenechea 3215,* ☎ *2/232–3606. AE, DC, MC, V.*

Italian

$$$ **Valerio.** A simply designed interior gives the feel of eating in someone's home—a sensation that's borne out by the fresh pasta, all of which is made on the premises. Don Valerio, the Italian owner, even imports ingredients such as dried mushrooms direct from Italy, and he's usually on hand to guide you around such classic dishes as risotto *al* *funghi* (with mushrooms) and black pasta with shrimp. ✘ *Coronel Pereira 139,* ☎ *2/208–6953. AE, DC, MC.*

Mexican

$$ Santa Fe. Brightly decorated in blues, pinks, and ochers, this Tex-Mex restaurant is always full. If you're over six feet, you'll feel cramped, but it's worth squeezing in for the fajitas (with seafood or meat fillings), frozen margaritas, and authentic guacamoles. Don't come if you want a quiet, romantic dinner, as it's always noisy; there is, however, a quieter brunch on Sunday morning. ✘ *Av. las Condes 10690,* ☎ *2/ 215–1091. Reservations advised. AE, DC, MC, V.*

Peruvian

$$ Cocoa. Although it's probably the smallest restaurant in Santiago, what this spot lacks in size, it makes up for in delicious Peruvian cuisine. The *pisco* sours (lemon, egg white, sugar, and pisco—a Chilean liquor, similar to tequila) and ceviche (seafood marinated in lemon juice, wine, and seasonings) are the best in town; other choices change regularly and are simply read out by the owner. The desserts are all homemade, and the cheesecakes and *suspiro limeño* (a rich meringue-topped lemon dish) are now being supplied to other nearby establishments. ✘ *José Victorino Lastarria 297,* ☎ *2/632–1272. Reservations advised. AE, MC, V. Closed Sun.*

Seafood

$$ Aquí Está Coco. The best fish and shellfish in Santiago are served up
★ in comfortable surroundings decorated with a nautical theme; the walls are covered with flotsam and jetsam from Chilean beaches. Ask your waiter what's best each day. This is a good place to try Chile's famous *machas* (similar to razor clams but unique to Chile), here served *à la parmesana,* or *corvina* (corbina, a kind of whiting), one of Chile's tastiest fish, offered with a choice of various butters and sauces. ✘ *La Concepción 236, Providencia,* ☎ *2/205–5985 or 2/251–5751. Weekend reservations required. AE, DC, MC, V. Closed Sun.*

$ Donde Augosto. Situated inside the bustling Central Market, Donde Augosto offers the best values on seafood in town. If you don't mind informal service and the odd tear in the tablecloths, you can dine on delicious *erizos* (bright orange sea-urchin's eggs), *locos* (giant sea snails), or ceviche. Placido Domingo eats here on every visit to Chile. If you can't get a table, try one of the many stalls in the fish market; it may not look as if it's the most hygienic place you've ever eaten in, but the seafood is the freshest in Santiago. ✘ *Mercado Central,* ☎ *2/672– 2829. No reservations. MC, V.*

Spanish

$$ La Esquina al Jerez. This noisy establishment with hams hanging from
★ the rafters specializes in food from the *madre patria* (mother country), as many Chileans refer to Spain. The mixed shellfish hors d'oeuvres are tasty and a bit on the hot side. If you want to try *callos* (beef stomach lining boiled and then sautéed in oil with chorizo, red pepper, garlic, and red wine), a Spanish delicacy, this is the place to do it. The filet mignon, seasoned with mountain herbs similar to sage and thyme, is a delight for the less daring. ✘ *Mallinkrodt 102, Barrio Bellavista,* ☎ *2/735– 4122. Weekend reservations required. AE, DC, MC, V. Closed Sun.*

Thai

$$$ Anakena. The best of the Hyatt's two excellent restaurants, this bright,
★ spacious Thai establishment serves some of the finest spicy food in Santiago. It also offers a unique way of ordering your food: As if in a market, you choose which piece of fish or meat you want and then tell the

chef whether you want it cooked in the traditional wok or on the grill.
✕ *Hyatt Regency, Av. Presidente Kennedy 4601, Las Condes,*
☎ *2/218–1234. AE, DC, MC, V.*

Vegetarian

$ **El Huerto.** Situated in the heart of Providencia, this vegetarian restaurant and café has become a hangout for young, trendy Santiaguinos. The natural foods it offers are made with a wide range of fresh vegetables, tofu, and dairy products. Simple dishes like stir-fried veggies with saffron rice and pancakes stuffed with asparagus and mushrooms are full of flavor, but it is the soups and freshly squeezed juices that score highest. Besides lunch and dinner, afternoon tea is also served. ✕ *Orrego Luco 54,* ☎ *2/233–2690. AE, DC, MC, V.*

Lodging

In Santiago, accommodations range from five-star international hotels to comfortable, inexpensive *residenciales*, the Chilean equivalent of bed-and-breakfasts. The city is slowly overcoming a chronic shortage of rooms, but it's still wise to reserve well in advance, especially for the peak seasons (Jan.–Feb. and July–Aug.). For details and price-category definitions, *see* Lodging *in* Chile Essentials, *below.*

$$$$ **Carrera.** Recent renovations have maintained the traditional atmosphere of Santiago's oldest hotel yet have added up-to-date amenities, including many for businesspeople. An executive floor offers butler service and a private bar. The flavor is distinctly English, with chintz bedspreads, hunting prints, and floral upholstery on the comfortable armchairs. Try for a room on the plaza; interior rooms tend to be dark. 🏨 *Teatinos 180, behind the Moneda,* ☎ *2/698–2011,* 🖷 *2/672–1083. 325 rooms, 30 suites. 2 restaurants, bar, kitchenettes, in-room VCRs, pool, health club, business services, meeting rooms. AE, DC, MC, V.*

$$$$ **Hotel Kennedy.** Opened in late 1994, this tall glass structure has
★ emerged confidently from the shadow of the nearby Hyatt. Small details such as telephones in all the bathrooms and beautiful vases on top of the wardrobes show the care that has gone into providing amenities. Bilingual secretarial services and an elegant boardroom are among the pluses available for visiting executives. The Aquarium restaurant has a first-rate French chef, five-star international cuisine, and a cellar of excellent Chilean export wines. 🏨 *Av. Kennedy 4570,* ☎ *2/219–4000,* 🖷 *2/218–2188. 133 rooms, 10 suites. Restaurant, bar, pool, beauty salon, exercise room, business services, travel services. AE, DC, MC, V.*

$$$$ **Hyatt Regency.** Far from downtown in the wealthy residential area known as Las Condes, the Hyatt Regency compensates by offering its own transportation services, air that's slightly less smoggy, and first-class accommodations. The building is an architectural wonder, with rooms curving around a 24-story central shaft completely lined with windows; each room has an excellent view and many have terraces. The four-story executive suites have private dining and games areas. The health club is large, and its windows overlook a kidney-shape pool complete with waterfall. 🏨 *Av. Kennedy 4601, Las Condes,* ☎ *2/218–1234,* 🖷 *2/218–2513. 310 rooms, 10 suites with hot tubs. 2 restaurants, bar, tea shop, in-room VCRs, pool, health club, baby-sitting, business services. AE, DC, MC, V.*

$$$$ **Plaza San Francisco Kempinski.** One of Santiago's newer offerings, this
★ executive-oriented hotel has cozy rooms with large beds, custom antique-style furniture, and marble-trimmed bathrooms. The restaurant,

with its heavy wooden trim, richly colored wallpapers, and bronze lamps, has a slightly nautical feeling. Artwork is modern and sophisticated, a tribute to the owners' private collection, and there's an art gallery in the basement. ⊞ *Alameda (Av. Bernardo O'Higgins) 816,* ☎ *2/639–3832,* FAX *2/639–7826. 160 rooms, 20 suites. Restaurant, bar, in-room modem lines, in-room VCRs, indoor pool, health club, business services. AE, DC, MC, V.*

$$$ Hotel Torremayor. Another recent addition to Providencia's list of top-rate accommodations, this Mediterranean-style hotel is now affiliated with the Best Western group in the United States. It has a light, airy feel—all rooms have large windows and are decorated in bright pastel colors. The staff makes an effort to recognize every guest, which, added to the attractive character of the building, makes for a hotel with more personality than the big chains. ⊞ *Av. Ricardo Lyon 322,* ☎ *2/234–2000,* FAX *2/234–3779. 80 rooms, 2 suites. Restaurant, bar, exercise room, business services, meeting rooms. AE, DC, MC, V.*

$$$ Santiago Park Plaza. Receptionists sitting behind individual mahogany desks, elegant English-style furniture, and deep burgundy and cream decorations set the mood in this self-proclaimed "classic European-style" hotel. The refined atmosphere extends to the adjoining Park Lane restaurant, whose new chef has added an Asian twist to international and Chilean cuisine. The glass-roof terrace area on the top floor offers great views of the city and is a wonderful place for afternoon tea. ⊞ *Av. Ricardo Lyon 207,* ☎ *2/233–6363,* FAX *2/233–6668. 104 rooms, 6 suites. Restaurant, bar, indoor pool, sauna, exercise room, business services. AE, DC, MC, V.*

$$ ★ Acacias of Vitacura. The rooms are modest, with thick gray carpets, textured wallpaper, and printed bedspreads in quiet colors, but the owner's eclectic collection of old carriages and Asian handicrafts gives this hotel personality, as does its extraordinary location in the midst of a lush garden and towering eucalyptus and acacia trees, some more than 100 years old; outdoor concerts are occasionally offered in the woods. The hotel is quite a distance from the city center (about 30 minutes by bus), in the wealthy shopping and residential area of Vitacura, in the northwest section of Santiago. ⊞ *El Manantial 1781,* ☎ *2/211–8601,* FAX *2/212–7858. 36 rooms, 3 suites. Dining room, pool. AE, DC, MC, V.*

$$ Foresta. This seven-story hotel just across the street from Santa Lucía Hill, on the edge of Santiago's city center, feels like an elegant old home. Guest rooms have flowered wallpaper and antique furnishings, accented by bronze and marble. Rooms on the upper floors overlooking the hill are best. The building was remodeled in 1993 and includes a rooftop restaurant and bar and, at street level, a popular piano bar. ⊞ *Victoria Subercaseaux 353,* ☎ *and* FAX *2/639–6261. 35 rooms, 4 with hot tubs; 8 suites. Restaurant, bar, piano bar. AE, DC, MC, V.*

$$ Hotel Bonaparte. Designed in the style of a small French château, this charming hotel on the quieter part of the tree-lined Avenida Ricardo Lyon deserves more than its three-star rating. The lightest rooms are on the top floor, but all are tastefully decorated and have big bathrooms. On the ground floor there's a small restaurant and a cozy lounge with a bar to one side. ⊞ *Av. Ricardo Lyon 1229,* ☎ *2/223–8554,* FAX *2/204–8907. 25 rooms, 2 suites. Restaurant, bar. AE, DC, MC, V.*

$ Apart-Hotel Marqués del Forestal. An excellent alternative for families or groups, the Marqués offers small apartments for four people for less than $80. Rooms are furnished simply in pinks and browns, with sofa beds and double beds and kitchenettes. It's near the Central Market area and overlooks the Forest Park. ⊞ *Ismael Valdés Vergara*

740, ☎ 2/633–3462, FAX 2/639–4157. *14 apartments with shower. Bar, kitchenettes. AE, DC, MC, V.*

$ **Hotel Principado.** Rooms at this hotel a block from Plaza Baquedano overlook a busy street but are generally not noisy; some have rounded corners and leafy views and all have kitchenettes. Amenities include a common lounge area and direct dial phones. ☎ *Arturo Burhle 015 (off Vicuña Mackenna),* ☎ 2/635–3879, FAX 2/222–6065. *24 rooms. AE, DC, MC, V.*

$ **Residencial Londres.** This older-style house in the picturesque Londres/París neighborhood is across the road from the city center and just behind the San Francisco Church. Rooms are bare-bones but comfortable, and the hosts are friendly and helpful to visitors. ☎ *Londres 54,* ☎ 2/638–2215. *25 rooms. No credit cards.*

The Arts

Music

Good Chilean music is hard to find these days, but the **Teatro Municipal** (San Antonio at Agustinas, ☎ 2/633–2549), Santiago's 19th-century theater, presents excellent classical concerts and ballet by national and international groups throughout the March–December season.

Theater

Provided you understand Spanish, you can enjoy Chilean theater, which is among the best in Latin America. Long respected ICTUS performs in the **Teatro la Comedia** (Merced 349, ☎ 2/639–1523). **Teatro la Feria** (Crucero Exeter 0250, ☎ 2/737–7371) mounts Chilean versions of English comedies. **El Conventillo** (Bellavista 173, ☎ 2/777–4164) produces a mixed offering of Latin American humor and drama.

Nightlife

After years of curfews during the military government, Santiago is slowly developing an active nightlife, with good food, music, theater, dancing, and comedy as the main activities.

Comedy

If you understand Spanish, look out for Chile's best, most intelligent humorist, **Coco Legrand,** who has his own theater (Providencia 1176, ☎ 2/235–1822).

Dancing

Dancing is best at *salsotecas*, which play music that combines the sensuous, cheerful rhythms of such Latin American performers as Rubén Blades and Juan Luís Guerra with the catchy, socially critical lyrics of salsa. Discotheques are divided between the cheap (which play Nirvana and the Stone Temple Pilots to under-age Chileans) and the expensive (where designer-clad yuppies don't mind remortgaging their Las Condes flats to buy a beer).

Broadway (Km 22, Ruta 68, Parcela 2A, ☎ 2/601–9969), with a capacity of up to 2,000 people, must be the biggest discotheque in Chile; it's about a 30-minute drive out of Santiago, but the sheer size and great atmosphere are worth the effort.

The Loft (Bombero Nuñez 159, ☎ 2/737–1716) is aimed at hard-core dancers who appreciate the water that's sprayed from the ceiling to help keep temperatures down—not the place to be wearing your favorite leather pants, though.

The Oz (Chucre Mansur 6, ☎ 2/737–7066), the best of the expensive spots, plays a good mix of techno, hip-hop, and jazz-funk; a huge stairway leads down from the upper bar to a wide dance area, so if you want to make a show of yourself, this is the place to do it.

Late-Night Dining

There are good after-hours restaurants throughout most of the city, particularly in Bellavista, Providencia, and Las Condes. **La Candela** (Purísima 129) offers Chilean folk music hosted by Charo Cofré, with homemade empanadas and other Chilean delicacies. A block away on Purísima, near Antonia López de Bello, is the **Café Libro** (Book Café), always packed with young people.

Excursions from Santiago

Santiago offers many interesting excursions, most of which can be taken by bus. The most diversified is a visit to the Cajón del Maipo, or Maipo Canyon, deep in the Andes, an outing that can include a soak in a natural hot spring, visits to interesting mountain villages where low adobe houses line the road, and a drive through the stark but majestic landscape. If you're a snow-sports enthusiast and visit during the winter months, the Andes hold other opportunities—three major ski resorts less than an hour from the city.

Andean Ski Resorts

Between June and October, as the winter smog shrouds Santiago, the majestic Andes become both a clean-air refuge and home to some of the Southern Hemisphere's best winter-sports facilities. Most of Chile's ski resorts are in the high Cordillera close to the capital, and with the top elevations at the majority of ski areas extending to 11,000 feet, you can expect long runs and deep, dry snow. Most of the recent investment has gone into the higher-altitude Valle Nevado, where snowboarding, heli-skiing, and para-gliding are also available to those with enough money and nerves. Despite millions of dollars being invested over the last two years, however, the Chilean ski industry is still very underdeveloped, with frustratingly slow lifts and often far from luxurious facilities. The majority of the accommodations is either apartments or apart-hotels, and it's essential to book early. It is also not uncommon for the road up to the resorts (which still has no safety barriers) to be closed, even after the lightest of snowfalls.

The Resorts

Peak season is July–August; during this time you can expect to pay around $60 a day for a ski pass covering the three main resorts, all of which are interconnected.

Farellones–Colorado. This 7,300-foot area has nine lifts. *Centro de Ski, Av. Apoquindo 4900, Local 47–48,* ☎ *2/246–3344,* 🖷 *2/220–7738.*

La Parva. The snow is skiable as early as May at this 8,000-foot spot. *Av. las Condes 12,233,* ☎ *2/217–3737,* 🖷 *2/217–3250.*

Valle Nevado. This ski area has 25 runs and 8 lifts. *Gestrudis Echeñique 441,* ☎ *2/206–0027,* 🖷 *2/208–0695.*

Getting There

It takes about two hours to reach the resorts above, which lie 30–35 miles from Santiago.

BY CAR

If you intend to drive, make sure you have either a four-wheel-drive vehicle or snow chains. There's a police checkpoint before the road starts to climb up into the Andes, and they will not let you pass if you don't have chains with you. In any case, be warned—the road is narrow, dangerous, and full of Chileans who think they're Alain Prost.

Get onto Avenida Presidente Kennedy or Avenida las Condes and drive east toward the Andes. Follow the signs for Farellones. The three resorts are well signposted once you get into the mountains.

BY BUS

Skitotal runs a bus service that leaves from their office at 8:45; a round-trip ticket is $13. You can also hire a minibus that holds up to 12 people for $125. The helpful staff at Skitotal can also organize everything from ski lessons and accommodations to equipment rental. You can buy most items from their shop, which doubles as the office. *Av. Apoquindo 4900, Local 39,* ☎ *and* ℻ *2/246–0156.*

Maipo Canyon

The landscape of the Maipo Canyon is so diverse that you can spend an hour, an afternoon, or several days on this excursion. A narrow road winds its way up into the Andes mountain range along the route of the Maipo River, which supplies most of Santiago's drinking water. As you drive along the river, you'll see massive mountains of sedimentary rock, heaved up and thrown sideways, as if ready for a geology lesson. On a sunny day, colors are subtle but glowing, ranging from oranges and reds to ochers, buffs, beiges, and elusive greens and browns. Small mountain villages lie along the road. At the far end of the canyon, if you reach it, you'll find yourself in an austere moonscape of blue and gray rocks, where hot springs spill from the earth and the mountains display shades of violet and purple.

Any of the small towns you pass is worth a visit. Most have small cafés offering basic Chilean meals at reasonable prices; groceries are available, but you're better off buying lunch supplies in Santiago. Near the village of **El Manzano** is a picnic area where you can barbecue a good piece of *asado* (beef) and spend the day enjoying the sun and fresh air. The canyon's main town, **San José de Maipo,** an hour's journey from the Pueblito bus terminal in Santiago's Parque O'Higgins, is another nice place to stop for refreshment, stretch your legs, and generally get a sense of small-town mountain life.

Five kilometers (3 miles) farther along is **San Alfonso,** a small but extraordinary village where the traditional landowning family went hippie, producing fantastic houses that look as if they've been stolen from a fairy tale. One of their creations, the **Cascada de las Animas** (Waterfall of the Spirits; Orrego Luco Norte 054, 20 piso, Providencia, Santiago, ☎ 2/232–7214, ℻ 2/232–7214) is off to the right of the highway, straddling the Maipo River. It has a circular outdoor swimming pool, a jealously protected wildland park, and lovely cabins that can be rented at reasonable prices; you must, however, book well ahead in the busy season. The family also organizes daily and overnight trips on horseback high up into the Andes. The guides are excellent. At the **Hostería los Ciervos** (Av. Argentina 711, San Alfonso; no ☎), you can have a filling lunch—of hot Chilean dishes like pork and pot roast or of such typical summer foods as *porotos granados* (a thick bean, corn, and squash soup), or *pastel de choclo* (corn and chicken mixture)—and spend a satisfying afternoon strolling around the area; there are nine simple guest rooms, plus a small outdoor pool for guests.

About 15 minutes farther up the road is the abandoned mining town of **El Volcán,** where you can visit the old abandoned copper mine shafts, and peer into the decaying, cramped miners' quarters.

If you really want to make a day of it, don't settle for the temptations of the low-level mountain villages: Instead, push on up the canyon, past San Alfonso and El Volcán, and take the gravel road into the mountains. The landscape becomes harsher and more majestic as green slopes give way to drier and barer mountain cliffs. Here you'll see layer on layer of sedimentary rock, packed with fossils from the time when this whole area was under the ocean. There are hot springs at **Baños Morales,** but if you're driving and have the time, take the right fork onward and upward to **Lo Valdés,** stopping for refreshment or a filling lunch or tea at the **Refugio Alemán** (☎ 2/850–1773); it's well worth staying the night here (one night's spartan accommodations and three meals cost just over $50, but you're really paying for the location). The refugio will organize transport to the **Baños de Colina** hot springs. It's an 11-kilometer (7-mile) ride along a difficult road through an impressive, rocky moonscape of mauves, grays, and steely blues, but these huge natural bowls, scooped out of the mountain edge and overflowing with hot water, are well worth the trip. Here you can slip into a bathing suit (in your car—there are no changing rooms) and choose the pool that has the temperature most to your liking. Let your body float gently in the mineral-rich waters, and enjoy the view down the valley as your fellow soakers give one another medical advice, trade salt and lemons to suck on, and chat about the medicinal properties of these waters.

On your way back to Santiago, the Café Vienés in **Guayacán,** clearly visible from the highway, is a good place to stop for a strong espresso or cappuccino and delicious pastries or kuchen.

Getting There

You may rent a car, hire a taxi for the day (about $60), or simply take one of the buses that travel daily from the **Parque O'Higgins** up into the canyon as far as its main town, **San José de Maipo,** or beyond. A car gives you maximum flexibility, but driving along the narrow mountain road can be demanding, especially if there's a lot of traffic.

BY CAR

From Plaza Baquedano, turn south on Ramón Carnícer (one block east of Vicuña MacKenna) to Grecia, and left (east) on Grecia to Avenida José Alessandri; turn right and continue southward to the Rotonda Departamental, a large traffic circle. There you can take Camino Las Vizcachas, following it south into the canyon as far as you choose to go.

BY BUS

Bus service to Maipo Canyon is cheap (around $4 for a round-trip ticket to Refugio Alamán) and frequent. Only the 7:30 AM bus, however, goes all the way up to Baños Morales and the Refugio, approximately a 1½-hour trip. Take the Santiago metro southern line to the Parque O'Higgins stop, turn left on leaving the station, and enter the park through the main gates. This area, with adobe restaurants and museums, is called the Pueblito, and it is where you catch the bus. Within half an hour you'll have started the climb through the canyon; sit on the right side of the bus for a good view of the river.

VALPARAÍSO AND VIÑA DEL MAR

Twin cities could hardly be more different than these two are, side by side on Chile's Pacific coast, just over an hour and a half's drive from Santiago. Valparaíso (population 3 million) is a working port complete with naval installations, sailors' bars, and bordellos as well as the winding, hilly streets and colorful houses that have made it a classic setting for travel posters. Viña del Mar (literally, "the Sea's Vineyard") with a population of 400,000, is an international showcase, with beautifully kept gardens, expensive hotels, stylish restaurants, and a luxury casino. There is cheap, regular bus service between the two. If you want to lie on the beach, arrange to stay overnight in Viña. It's lively, crowded, fashionable, and somewhat expensive, with plenty of nightlife in its central cafés. But if you want to watch the workings of a busy international port, check out Valparaíso; there are plenty of good walks, most of which converge upon Plaza Victoria.

Visitor Information

SERNATUR (Av. Valparaíso 507, Office 305, Viña del Mar, ☎ 032/882285, FAX 032/684117).

Arriving and Departing

By Car

Route 68 runs westward from Santiago to Valparaíso and Viña.

By Bus

There's excellent, continual bus service between Santiago and Valparaíso/Viña. Take the metro to the Universidad de Santiago station, south side exit, and check out the **Terminal Alameda** (Av. Libertador Bernardo O'Higgins 3724) or the main **Terminal Santiago** (Av. Libertador Bernardo O'Higgins 3848, ☎ 2/779–1385) just a block westward for regular service.

Tour Operators

Contact **Chilean Travel Services** (Agustinas 1291, 5th Floor, Office F, ☎ 2/696–7820 or 2/696–7193, FAX 2/251–0423) or **Turismo Cocha** (Agustinas 1173, ☎ 2/698–3341, FAX 2/233–4956) in Santiago, or **Trans Tourcargo** (Diego Portales 325, ☎ 032/664459, FAX 032/621707) in Viña del Mar.

Exploring Valparaíso and Viña del Mar

Valparaíso

The most pleasant way to see ships loading and unloading their cargo at the port is to take an hour-long motorboat tour around the harbor from the **Muelle Prat** (Prat Dock) in Valparaíso, which costs about $4. The dock, which has permanent crafts kiosks, is between the historic buildings of the Dirección Nacional de Aduana (National Customs House) and the Estación Puerto del Ferrocarril (Port Railway Station).

Five miles west of the dock in Valparaíso is the 19th-century customs building; next to it is the **Ascensor Artillería,** a cable car that will pull you uphill to the **Paseo 21 de Mayo,** a wide cliff's-edge balcony, surrounded by well-tended gardens and tall, old trees, from which you can survey the port and a goodly portion of Valparaíso. Here you are in the **Cerro Playa Ancha** (Wide Beach Hill), one of Valparaíso's nicest neighborhoods. Near the top of the cable car is a large neoclassical mansion that until recently housed the Naval School and still belongs to the navy. Avid picture takers should be careful, because much of Valparaíso Harbor is considered part of the naval base, and photography is prohibited. In this same building is the **Museo Naval y Marítimo** (Naval and Maritime Museum), which offers historical information on the port and displays of the ships and forts that once defended it. *Subida Astillera,* ☎ *032/281845.* ☛ *Entry fee. Closed Mon.*

Take the cable car back down the hill, then head down the first street on your right, Bustamante Street. Here, in Valparaíso's oldest neighborhood, you'll see the **Plaza y Iglesia de la Matriz** (Plaza and Church of la Matriz), built in 1842, which contains a 17th-century carving of Jesus on the cross donated by the king and queen of Spain.

If you'd like to see a sampling of the sort of wall murals that have made several Latin American artists famous, head down Bustamante Street to **Plaza Victoria** (Victory Square) to visit Valparaíso's **Museo a Cielo Abierto** (Open-Air Museum). Start from the Plaza Victoria and follow along Molina Street to Aldunate Street, then right one block to Huito, toward the hill, where there's a long, long stairway and the first of 17 murals painted by Chile's most important painters. As the name suggests, the exposition takes the form of colorful murals painted on the walls that line the many stairs, walkways, and streets leading up and down Valparaíso's crowded hillsides. An easier route is to take the **Ascensor Espíritu Santo** (Holy Spirit Elevator; ☛ Entry fee, ⊙ daily 7 AM–11 PM), from Calle Aldunate, near the bottom of the hill, up and then walk down through the museum.

You can have an excellent breakfast, light lunch, or delicious afternoon tea at the Vitamin Service, one of the few spots in Valparaíso that serves fresh-squeezed orange juice, along with hot espresso, just half a block from **Plaza Victoria** along Pedro Montt Street.

Viña del Mar

Viña del Mar's **Central Square,** with majestic palms and the possibility of a short tour in a horse-drawn buggy ($5 for a 15-minute tour), is worth a visit. A stroll through the adjoining shopping areas will take you through glittering stores and all kinds of cafés and ice cream parlors.

Viña has one of Chile's best botanical gardens, the **Quinta Vergara,** which includes its own palace, **Museo de Bellas Artes** (Fine Arts Museum), a fine arts school, and a large, open-air theater famous for an international music festival held every February. *Park ⊙ daily 7:30– 6 and until 8 Jan.–Feb. Fine Arts Museum: Errazuriz 563,* ☎ *032/ 680618.* ☛ *Entry fee. Closed Mon.*

Shopping

The **Feria Internacional de Artesanía** (International Crafts Fair) sets up in the Quinta Vergara from mid-January through early February. Outdoor stalls feature weaving, leather crafts, jewelry, paintings, ceramics, and toys. For more information, contact the Viña del Mar Tourist Office (☎ 032/883154).

Sports and the Outdoors

Golf can be played at the **Granadillas Country Club** (☎ 032/689527). Ship owners and operators at the Prat Dock in Valparaíso rent out their boats or take passengers on ocean excursions. **Empresa de San Juan** (Golfo de Corcovado 580, Canal Beagle, Viña del Mar, ☎ 032/852937) and **Lobo de Mar** in the nearby town of Quintero (Arturo Prat 2070,

Quintero, ☎ 032/931040) offer skin diving, scuba diving, boat trips, and fishing for tuna, corvina, sea bass, and conger eel.

Beaches

Follow Viña's Avenida Pedro Montt until you reach a large, solar-powered clock, consisting of continually replanted flowers and two large working hands. Just across from the clock you'll find **Playa Los Marineros** (Los Marineros Beach). This is followed by a long stretch of coastline belonging to the navy (off-limits to the public) that ends at **Playa Las Salinas** (Las Salinas Beach), a sheltered area packed with sun-loving crowds in summer. Quieter seaside areas lie to the north: **Concón**, 8 kilometers (5 miles) up the coast; **Quintero**, 18 kilometers (11 miles); **Maitencillo**, 65 kilometers (40 miles); and **Papeete**, 88 kilometers (55 miles).

Pollution is a problem around Viña and up the coast, in addition to strong currents, undertow, and sudden, large waves. A red flag indicates you should definitely not swim at a specific beach, although you'll probably see people in the water anyway. The Humboldt Current, which flows northward up the coast of Chile, brings cold water to almost all the country's beaches. If you plan to windsurf or surf, you'll need a wet suit.

Dining

For price-category definitions, *see* Dining *in* Chile Essentials, *below.*

Valparaíso

$$ **Bar Inglés.** The "English Bar" has the longest bar in Chile and incorporates Dutch lamps and American oak furnishings as part of its effort to imitate an English country pub. The specialty is international cooking, particularly hot and cold soups, beef, and shellfish baked with cheese, sautéed with garlic, or dipped in mayonnaise; also try such imaginative vegetable dishes as an artichoke, mushroom, and asparagus combination. ✗ *Cochrane 851,* ☎ *032/214625. Reservations advised, particularly for lunch. No credit cards. Closed Sun. and holidays.*

$$ **Bote Salvavidas.** This restaurant at the end of Prat Dock in Valparaíso
★ offers the best view of the harbor and, naturally, specializes in seafood. Greek-style fish dishes, such as fillet of tuna wrapped around fresh sage then wrapped in a thin slice of ham and sautéed, are among the popular specialties that are served in the simple plant-filled dining room. ✗ *Muelle Prat,* ☎ *032/251477. Weekend reservations advised. AE.*

$$ **Cafe Turri.** Set among other large mansion houses on the Concepción hill, this 19th-century property commands one of the best views of Valparaíso and offers some of the finest seafood. The corvina in almond sauce alone is worth driving to the coast for, and the *tortilla de erizos* (Spanish-style omelet filled with local sea urchin) is far tastier than it sounds. ✗ *Templeman 147, Paseo Gervasoni,* ☎ *032/252091. AE, MC.*

Viña del Mar

$$$ **Cap Ducal.** This ship-shaped restaurant rises out of the sea and affords
★ excellent views of the shore and the horizon. The creative kitchen specializes in European-style cooking as well as its own inventions, including a popular eel stew and grilled fish in a spicy herb sauce. ✗ *Av. Marina 51,* ☎ *032/626655. Weekend reservations advised. AE, MC, V.*

$$$ **La Fontana.** Inside the Viña del Mar Casino, this elegant Italian restaurant is decorated with views of Venice and the characteristic bougainvilleas of Viña. It offers a complete fish and shellfish menu, but it's the

pasta and risotto dishes that have built its reputation. After a plate of fettucine with fresh salmon and caviar, you'll feel ready to gamble the night away. ✗ *San Martín 199,* ☏ *032/689200. Reservations advised. AE, DC, MC, V.*

Lodging

For price-category definitions, *see* Lodging *in* Chile Essentials, *below.*

Viña del Mar

$$$ Hotel Miramar. This 40-year-old fixture is Viña's only five-star hotel. It's right on the sea's edge, with a gorgeous terrace restaurant from which you can devour your food and the horizon to your heart's content— the view is also available from most of the public rooms and some guest rooms. The rooms are decorated in pastels and floral patterns and are hung with landscape paintings, some by Chilean artists. ▣ *Av. Marina, Caleta Abarca,* ☏ *032/626677, 2/671–3165 in Santiago,* FAX *032/ 665220. 120 rooms, 12 suites. 2 restaurants, 2 bars, pool, sauna, exercise room. AE, DC, MC, V.*

$$$ Hotel O'Higgins. Dominating one side of the main square in Viña del Mar, this grand seaside hotel was built in 1935 and has huge rooms with high ceilings. Many parts of the hotel are in need of renovation, but if you don't mind the occasional faded curtain and worn carpet, it offers ample space, charm, and traditional service. ▣ *Plaza Vergara,* ☏ *032/882016,* FAX *032/883537. 262 rooms, 12 suites. Restaurant, bar, pool, dance club, business services. AE, DC, MC, V.*

$$ Apart-Hotel Sahara. Each room in this comfortable small hotel has thick, dark carpeting and cream-color walls, and each opens onto its own small, semiprivate garden. ▣ *Alberto Blest Gana 397,* ☏ *032/685161. 14 rooms. No credit cards.*

The Arts and Nightlife

Viña's artistic activities and nightlife vary considerably according to the season, with the most glittering attractions concentrated in the summer months, January and February. Check the newspapers (including Santiago's) for listings.

The **Casino** (Av. San Martín 199, Viña del Mar, ☏ 032/689200) has a restaurant, dancing, a cabaret, and, of course, games of the roulette and blackjack sort. It's open nightly until the wee hours; formal dress is required in the game rooms.

Cocodrilo (Av. Vorgono 13101, Viña del Mar, ☏ 032/831158), a miniature castle perched on the cliff between Viña and Reñaca, is always packed on the weekends and often stays open until 8 AM; thick stone walls, a catacomb-like dance floor, and bartenders who mix Chile's best *caipirinahs*—Brazil's national drink, made with lime, ice, sugar, and *cachaça* (Brazilian rum)—make it a unique and atmospheric night out.

THE LAKE DISTRICT

If you've never flirted with a volcano, Chile's Lake District is the place to start. As you travel along roads bordered by grazing cattle or through dense forests of eucalyptus and pine, the broad, snowcapped shoulders of volcanoes emerge, then mysteriously disappear, then materialize again, peeping through trees or towering over lake-lined valleys. The sometimes difficult journey along narrow mountain roads that wind through breathtaking passes is almost inevitably rewarded by a clear mountain lake—vibrant and blue—and often there are hot springs in which tired travelers can soak stiff muscles.

Your best route is to start in Temuco and work your way south through the Valdivia–Seven Lakes area to Lake Llanquihue and Puerto Montt, a journey of about 340 kilometers (212 miles). You'll find information about these destinations following the general Lake District information immediately below.

Unlike in Chile's fertile Central Valley region between Santiago and Temuco, weather can be a major factor in your seeing and enjoying the Lake District. The summer (December–early March) offers the most likelihood of sunshine, although if you're prepared for rain, a few showers probably won't bother you.

Arriving and Departing

BY PLANE

LanChile and Ladeco have flights from Santiago to—and between—the main cities within the Lake District, including **Temuco** (LanChile ☎ 045/211339, Ladeco ☎ 045/214325); **Valdivia** (LanChile ☎ 063/213042, Ladeco, ☎ 063/213392); and **Puerto Montt** (LanChile ☎ 065/253141, Ladeco, ☎ 065/252090). (Also, *see* Getting Around *in* Chile Essentials, *below.*)

BY TRAIN

Chile's **State Railway Company** (Santiago ☎ 2/689–5401, 2/632–2802, or 2/228–2983; Temuco ☎ 045/233522; Valdivia ☎ 063/214978; Puerto Montt ☎ 065/254908) has frequent service southward from Santiago, usually several times a day, particularly in the peak period during the summer. The journey to Temuco, at the northern limit of the Lake District, takes about 11½ hours; to Puerto Montt, at the southernmost end of the line, is a 20-hour trip. If you prefer to rent a vehicle in Santiago, you can use the auto-train service from there to Temuco or Puerto Montt, but it's probably cheaper to rent a car in Temuco or Puerto Montt. (Also, *see* Getting Around *in* Chile Essentials, *below.*)

BY CAR

While it's useful to rent a car once you've reached the Lake District, it will be easier on your nerves if you skip driving down on the Pan-American Highway, and fly or take the train to your first Lake District destination.

Getting Around the Lake District

BY CAR

You'll see a lot more of the Lake District if you have a vehicle. Rental-car companies such as Hertz and Avis will allow you to hire a car in Temuco and return it to any of their other offices in the south, so you can even avoid the inconvenience of retracing your steps.

Once you're this far south, driving is much easier because there's far less traffic, even on the Pan-American Highway. However, many of the mountain roads you must follow are gravel at best, so a four-wheel-drive vehicle is ideal; if you don't feel comfortable driving one, most new cars will serve just as well, at least on the main routes.

Rentals are available through **Automóvil Club** (Puerto Montt ☎ 065/254776, Temuco ☎ 045/213949), **Autovald** (Puerto Montt ☎ 065/256355), **Avis** (Temuco ☎ 045/211515), **First** (Temuco ☎ 045/233890, Valdivia ☎ 063/215973), **Hertz** (Temuco ☎ 045/235385, Valdivia ☎ 063/218316), and **Turismo Safari Tehuel'che** (Puerto Montt ☎ 065/250412), as well as a few local travel agencies; several of the latter include a return service.

The Lake District

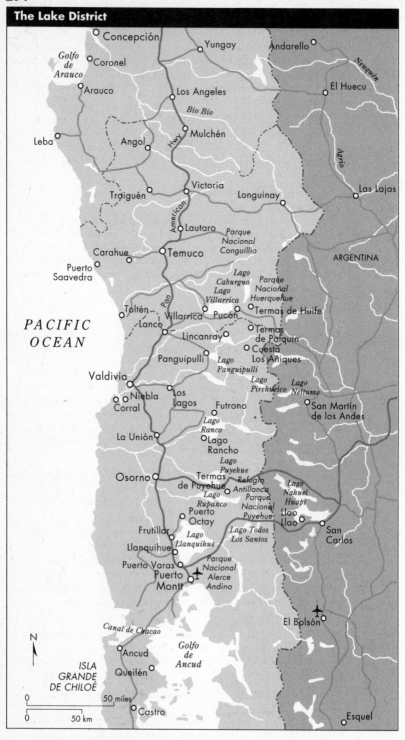

Concepción
Yungay
Andarello
Golfo de Arauco
Coronel
El Huecu
Arauco
Los Angeles
Neuquén
Leba
Bío Bío
Angol
Mulchén
Hwy
Traiguén
Victoria
Longuinay
Las Lajas
Agrio
American
Lautaro
Parque Nacional Conguillio
Carahue
Temuco
ARGENTINA
Puerto Saavedra
Lago Caburgua
Lago Villarrica
Parque Nacional Huerquehue
Toltén
Pon
Villarrica
Pucón
Termas de Huife
Lanco
Lincanray
Termas de Palquin
Panguipulli
Cuesta Los Añiques
Lago Panguipulli
PACIFIC OCEAN
Valdivia
Lago Pirehueico
Lago Nettume
Niebla
Los Lagos
Futrono
San Martin de los Andes
Corral
Lago Ranco
La Unión
Lago Rancho
Lago Puyehue
Osorno
Termas de Puyehue
Refugio Antillanca
Lago Nahuel Huapi
Parque Nacional Puyehue
Lago Rupanco
Llao Llao
Puerto Octay
San Carlos
Frutillar
Lago Todos Los Santos
Llanquihue
Lago Llanquihue
Puerto Varas
Parque Nacional Alerce Andino
Puerto Montt
El Bolsón
Canal de Chacao
N
Ancud
Golfo de Ancud
ISLA GRANDE DE CHILOÉ
Queilén
0   50 miles
0   50 km
Castro
Esquel

BY BUS

There are two levels of service within the region: regular intercity buses provided by companies based primarily in Santiago, and local buses that bump between Lake District cities and the small towns that adjoin them; both services are reasonably priced. Three of the most reliable companies are **Buses Pullman del Sur** (☎ 2/696–9797), **Varmontt** (☎ 2/232–1116), and **Fenix** (☎ 2/776–3253); all numbers are for Santiago.

In Temuco, there's no central bus terminal, but several companies are close together along Vicuña MacKenna: **Cruz del Sur** (Vicuña MacKenna 671, ☎ 045/210701) and **Buses JAC** (Vicuña MacKenna 798, ☎ 045/210313). Both Puerto Montt and Valdivia have their own bus terminals, where most bus companies' offices are concentrated. Valdivia's bus terminal is on Anfión Muñoz 360 (☎ 063/212212). Puerto Montt's is on Avenida Diego Portales (no ☎); each bus line has its own phone number, listed in the local phone book's Yellow Pages.

Sports and the Outdoors

BEACHES AND WATER SPORTS

The entire Lake District is full of beaches offering every kind of water sport and comfort imaginable, except perhaps solitude. **Licanray** and **Lake Villarrica** offer the most in the way of waterskiing, motorboat rental, and more sophisticated water sports. **Lake Tinquilco** in Huerquehue National Park is quieter and more isolated. You can rent a rowboat and tow a fishing line through the depths. The beaches along **Lake Panguipulli** are clean and comfortable. There is some current concern about possible pollution of Lake Villarrica, but nearby **Lake Caburgua** remains crystalline and is slightly warmer for swimming, thanks to volcanic activity in the surrounding region.

For ocean beaches, Puerto Montt and the coast west of Valdivia are the best choices. Puerto Montt's main beach is 3 kilometers (2 miles) east of town along the shoreline, in the village of **Pelluco,** which offers several restaurants specializing in seafood and a scenic lookout point. If your idea of a good beach is something a little more peaceful and solitary, head west past Angelmó on the road to Chinquihmó, and choose from beaches at camping sites at El Ciervo (☎ 065/255271), 1 kilometer (½ mile) west of Puerto Montt; Paredes (☎ 065/258394), 6 kilometers (3½ miles) west; and Chinquihue (no ☎), 10 kilometers (6 miles) west. Be careful: In recent years, many beaches have been polluted owing to developing industry in the region.

FISHING

Trout (brown, rainbow, steelhead, and sea), salmon (ketta, coho, chinook, salar, sakura, and king), perch, and smelt are among the popular sport fish in Chile; many areas within the Lake District were first developed as fishing resorts. However, the restocking programs were suspended and good fishing is now harder to find. To fish the rivers and lakes of Chile, you must get a permit from the National Fisheries Service, known as **SERNAP** (San Antonio 427, Office 801, Santiago, ☎ 2/632–4765, FAX 2/632–1918). The permit is personal and valid throughout Chile; if you're fishing on private property and the landowner is nearby, be sure to get his or her permission. SERNAP is a good source of information on what's biting and where; also check with local tourist offices. **SERNATUR** publishes a brochure in English called "Lakes and Fishing," and it provides location-specific details of the fishing rules, creel limits, and the like. **APSA** travel agency (Matías Cousiño 82, Office 1104, ☎ 2/632–7215, FAX 2/696–6319) specializes in fishing trips in Chilean Patagonia. For further information on fishing tours, *see* Chapter 2, Adventure and Learning Vacations.

HOT SPRINGS

Hot springs are common in the Lake District, and spa resorts have sprung up to accommodate visitors looking for a relaxing—or purportedly medicinal—soak. (For additional listings, *see* Dining and Lodging *in the Seven Lakes Region, below.*)

Termas de Puyehue. These hot springs are part of a resort center ($$$) in Puyehue National Park that offers skiing, indoor thermal baths, meeting facilities, horseback riding, and sportfishing. To reach the springs, head west out of Osorno, which is halfway between Valdivia and Puerto Montt. ☎ *Termas de Puyehue Hotel, on Lake Puyehue, ☎ 064/232157; Santiago ☎ 2/231–3417. 120 rooms. Restaurant, 2 tennis courts, travel services. MC, V.*

Termas de Liquiñe. The hot springs are the main attraction here, but you can also rent a cabin ($$) for the night. ☎ *Casilla 202, Liquiñe, ☎ 063/311060. 13 cabins, all with spring-fed thermal bath. No credit cards.*

TREKKING

Southern Chile has several of the country's most beautiful national parks, including **Conguillío,** near Melipeuco, and **Villarrica,** near the town of Villarrica, and **Huerquehue,** near Pucón. All provide sites for camping, as well as well-marked hiking trails of differing degrees of difficulty. All also provide necessary information at their ranger stations, but not all have telephones. Contact the national forestry service, **CONAF** (☎ 045/236312), which administers the parks, or **SERNATUR** in Santiago (☎ 2/236–1417) or in the town nearest the park.

RVs are virtually nonexistent in Chile. Camping equipment is available from major department stores, but it's not cheap; you're better off bringing your own. To rent camping equipment, contact **Aire Libre** (☎ 2/233–3100) and **Industrias Jesus Yarur y Hijo** (☎ 2/672–3696) in Santiago.

Temuco

Visitor Information

SERNATUR (Bulnes 586, Temuco, ☎ 045/211969).

Exploring

The starting point for this tour of the Lake District lies 675 kilometers (405 miles) south of Santiago. In addition to its claim as the fastest growing city in Chile, Temuco is home to a large population of Mapuche, one of Latin America's most long-lived groups of native peoples. Many Mapuche sell their products in Temuco, and the **Mercado Municipal** (in the square bounded by Bulnes, Portales, Aldunate, and Rodríguez) is one of the best places to find traditional Mapuche woolen ponchos, pullovers, and blankets.

The **Museo Araucano** (Araucanian Museum) covers some aspects of Mapuche history, along with a general history of the area. Although much official rhetoric tries to reduce the colonization of this area to a process called the "Pacificación de la Araucanía" ("The Pacification of the Araucanian Territories"), which took place in the 1880s, in reality the Mapuche successfully fought off the Spanish and defended a huge tract of territory for the better part of three centuries before finally facing defeat in the shape of the Chilean army, fresh from war with Peru and Bolivia. A smaller museum over the library in Villarrica has a number of fascinating relics on display, but with little explanation. *Av. Alemania 084,* ☎ *045/212208.* ☞ *Entry fee. Closed Mon. in winter.*

If you have time and a car, the **Parque Nacional Conguillío** is an unforgettable experience. In the shadow of the active Volcán Llaima (which erupted as recently as 1994), the park is home to thousands of araucaria pines, often known as monkey puzzle trees. Heavy snow can cut off the area in winter, and November to March is the best time to visit. To get to the park, take the Pan-American Highway north out of Temuco as far as Lautero, then head 54 kilometers east to the town of Curacautin, from where the park is well signposted. **CONAF** (Av. Bilbao 931, Temuco, ☎ 045/238900) provides maps and information, and in summer, organizes hikes to the Sierra Nevada. The only accommodation available close to the park is **Cabañas y Camping Conguillío** (Temuco office, ☎ 045/220254).

Dining

Establishments come and go frequently in this region, and many close up after the peak summer and winter seasons. A stroll through the towns should reveal other dining choices. For price ranges, *see* Dining *in* Chile Essentials, *below.*

$$$ **La Estancia.** This restaurant offers good southern beef in the form of
★ steaks, roasts, and barbecues in a traditional country atmosphere. Cured hams hang from the ceiling, and the walls are decorated with reindeer heads. ✕ *Rudecindo Ortega 02340-A Interior, Temuco,* ☎ *045/220287. Weekend reservations advised. MC, V. Closed Sun. dinner.*

$$ **Café 2001.** For a thick, filling sandwich and an espresso or cappuccino made from freshly ground beans, topped off with a freshly baked kuchen, this is the place to stop in Villarrica. Pull up around a table up front, or slip into one of the quieter booths by the fireplace in the back. The sandwich known as the "Lomito Completo," with a slice of pork, avocado, sauerkraut, tomato, and mayonnaise, is one of the best in the south. ✕ *Camilio Henríquez 379, Villarrica,* ☎ *045/441241. MC, V.*

$$ **Grill de la Piscina Municipal.** In summer, this spot at the municipal swimming pool is an excellent place to stop for lunch, especially if you're traveling with children. You can savor a good meal and the pleasant view while they enjoy the water. ✕ *Municipal Pool, Av. Estadio 01080, Temuco,* ☎ *045/240649. No credit cards. Closed Apr.–Nov. 14.*

$ **Club Alemán.** Temuco's German club is open to the public year-round. The spacious restaurant overlooks a lush Valdivian garden; the green walls feature murals of German landscapes and folk figures. In summer there are tables outside. Specialties include roast pork, lemon-marinated *tártaros* (minced beef on toast), goulash, and meatballs. ✕ *Senador Estzbañez 772, Temuco,* ☎ *045/240034. No reservations. No credit cards. Closed Jan. 1.*

$ **Temuco Market.** In the central market around the produce stalls are small stands and kitchens offering such typical Chilean meals as *gazuelas* (soup that includes a piece of meat—beef, pork, chicken, or turkey—usually with bone), fried fish, winter fish soup, and other seasonal fare such as empanadas and pastel de choclo. ✕ *Manuel Rodríguez 960, Temuco.*

Lodging

For price ranges, *see* Lodging *in* Chile Essentials, *below.*

$$$ **Gran Hotel Pucón.** Leveled by fire and then rebuilt a few years ago, this imposing building sprawls along one end of the Lake Villarrica, providing access to the beach and a good view of the lake. ☎ *Clemente Holtzapfel 190, Pucón, ☎ and* FAX *045/441001; in Santiago, ☎ 2/232– 6008,* FAX *2/233–4367. 135 rooms with bath, 10 with shower. Dining room, bar, pool, 4 saunas, 2 tennis courts, exercise room. AE, DC, MC, V.*

$$$ **Hotel Nueva la Frontera.** This elegant modern hotel on Temuco's central square has rooms that are comfortable, light, and airy, especially if you can arrange for one with a view of the plaza. ☎ *Bulnes 726, Temuco, ☎ 045/210718; in Santiago, ☎ 2/232–6008,* FAX *2/233– 4367. 65 rooms. Restaurant, bar, pool, sauna, meeting rooms. AE, DC, MC, V.*

$$ **Hotel Gudenschwager.** Once a fishing lodge, this attractive three-story building, covered with the wooden shakes typical of southern Chile, has a view of a corner of the lake and a comfortable country atmosphere. ☎ *Pedro de Valdivia 12, Pucón, ☎ and* FAX *045/441156. 30 rooms, most with bath. Restaurant. MC, V. Closed Apr.–Aug.*

$ **Hospedaje.** Miguel Castro and Nelly Epul offer comfortable B&B-style accommodations in their home in Villarrica. Breakfast features freshly baked bread and homemade jams. ☎ *General Korner 442, Villarrica, ☎ 045/411235. 4 rooms with shared bath. No credit cards.*

The Seven Lakes Region

East of the Pan-American Highway between Temuco and Valdivia is one of the loveliest, least spoiled areas of the southern Andes. Towering volcanoes shoot off wisps of vapor during the day and glow orange through the clear nights; roses and natural hot springs flourish in rural and wild settings. The ideal way to travel here is by car, spending the night in a local hot-springs resort or camping out. Wherever you sleep, step out at night to enjoy the southern sky, full of stars and constellations unfamiliar to those who live north of the equator.

Exploring

Pucón and Villarrica

Both of these towns on the southern shore of Lake Villarrica are small, rural supply centers most of the year, but during the summer holiday and winter skiing seasons they become trendy resorts crowded with wealthy, fashionable Chileans who come to enjoy their luxurious vacation homes, stroll along the main strips, and flock to the major nightspots. While neither town has sights per se, two stunning national parks lie nearby.

Villarrica National Park, between Villarrica and Pucón, offers skiing, good hiking, hot springs—and a volcano. You don't need to have any climbing experience to reach the 9,350-foot summit of Volcán Villarrica, but a guide is essential. Travel agencies such as **Expediciones Trancura** (O'Higgins 261, Pucón, ☎ 045/441959) will lease equipment and guides for less than $40 per person. It's an easy uphill walk to the snow line, and then crampons and ice axes are needed. Your reward for the five-hour climb is a rare view of an active crater, which continues to release clouds of sulphur and miniexplosions of lava, and superb views of the nearby inactive volcanoes, Quetrupillán and Lanín.

Unless you're an expert driver with a four-wheel-drive vehicle, **Huerquehue National Park** is accessible only during the summer. However, it's well worth a visit for the two-hour hike from the ranger station near the entrance. You head up into the high Andes through groves of araucaria pine to three startling lagoons with panoramic views of the whole area, including the distant Villarrica Volcano. Contact SERNATUR in Temuco (*see above*), CONAF (☎ 045/236312), or the rangers in the parks themselves for trail information.

Panguipulli
Gardeners will appreciate this pleasant hamlet on the shores of eponymous Lake Panguipulli. While it's a pleasant place to stop for lunch and swim on the beach, it's most noteworthy in spring and summer, when roads, houses, public squares, and private gardens seem to stagger under a display of roses of all sizes, scents, and colors.

Licanray
This resort town on Lake Calafquén has modern hotels and hostels, supermarkets, dance halls, restaurants, and some of the best beaches in the southern lakes. You can rent rowboats and sailboats along the shore.

Sports and the Outdoors

Pucón is the major departure point for adventure sports in the region, and there's plenty to choose from: river rafting, skiing, trekking, horseback riding, fishing, and biking. On the mellower side, the region's volcanic activity has given rise to a number of hot springs; for more information, *see* Spas *in* Dining and Lodging, *below.*

Bicycling
Dozens of shops along the main road in Pucón offer mountain-bike rentals during the summer.

Trekking
Both Huerquehue and Villarrica parks have well-marked hiking trails that zigzag past open fields and massive Chilean oak trees, with views of lakes and volcanoes occasionally appearing as you walk uphill. Try the visitor centers in the parks or SERNATUR in Temuco (*see* Visitor Information, *above*) or CONAF (☎ 045/236312) for more information.

White-Water Rafting
Pucón is the center for rafting expeditions in the Lake District. **Altué Expediciones** has a Santiago office (Encomenderos 83, ☎ 2/232–1103). Other small companies offer similar services during the summer season in Pucón. They usually set up shop along the main street, complete with photographic displays and other information on prices and services.

Skiing
The popular Villarrica-Pucón ski area is in Villarrica National Park, in the lap of the Villarrica Volcano. Villarrica is one of the best-equipped ski areas in southern Chile, with 15 runs, three rope tows, and three double-chair tows. Between June and September you can contact the **Centro de Esqui** (☎ 045/441176) in Pucón for ski information.

Dining and Lodging

Spas
$$$ **Termas de Huife** offers thermal baths and two hot pools made of natural stones beside an icy mountain stream. For an additional fee, you can enjoy an individual bath, massage, or both. The resort includes a small hotel with luxury apartments. Just past the spa, there's a country house where for a modest fee you can relax in hot pools in a more natural setting. ✉ *Casilla 18, Pucón,* ☎ *045/441222. 20 cabins. Restaurant, bar. No credit cards.*

$$ Termas de Palguín hot springs are near the Villarrica National Park, amid *mañio, tepa,* and other native trees, on the property of a comfortable hotel of the same name. You can stay overnight or simply enjoy afternoon tea after a pleasant stroll and a hot bath in the pools. ✉ *Casilla 1-D, Pucón,* ☎ *045/441968. 10 cabins. Restaurant. No credit cards.*

Campgrounds

The **Volcán Villarrica–Sector Rucapillán** camping area is in the lap of the Villarrica Volcano in the midst of a wood of *coigüe,* Chile's massive red oaks. For more information, contact SERNATUR in Temuco (☎ 045/211969). **La Playa** (3 km, or 2 mi, from Licanray on the road to Coñaripe, no ☎) offers grassy sites with cold showers near the Lake District's main resort and has an attractive, quiet beach.

Valdivia

Visitor Information

SERNATUR (Prat 555, Valdivia, ☎ 063/213596).

Exploring

One of Chile's oldest and most beautiful cities gracefully combines an architecture of wooden houses covered with shakes with the Germanic style brought by the well-to-do German settlers who colonized the area in the late 1800s. Situated between two rivers and near the coast, the town offers fine evening walks along the waterfront and restaurants that serve fresh fish and seafood and tasty kuchen. The region has many cattle ranches and farms, and native communities make a hardscrabble subsistence on the less fertile grounds. Valdivia is also an excellent base for day trips throughout the area or a good starting point for a journey northeast into the Andes.

For a historic overview of the region, start with a visit to the **Museo Histórico de Valdivia,** on the campus of the Austral University. The museum's valuable collection focuses on the German immigrants and the city's colonial period, during which it was settled by the Spanish, burned by the Mapuche, and invaded by Dutch corsairs. *Isla Teja,* ☎ *063/212872.* ☛ *Entry fee. Closed Mon. in winter.*

The **Botanic Gardens,** also on the university campus, is a fine place to walk, whatever the weather, although it's particularly enjoyable in spring and summer. *Isla Teja,* ☎ *063/216964.* ☛ *Free.*

Several companies in Valdivia offer boat rides along the rivers, among them **Lancha Ainlebu** (☎ 063/215889), **Motonave Calle Calle** (☎ 063/212464), and **Motonave Neptuno** (☎ 063/215889). Most of the companies are on Avenida Prat along the Calle Calle River. There are regular launches from the Puerto Fluvial (close to the SERNATUR office at Prat 555) to the 17th-century Spanish forts at Fuerte de Corral, Fuerte Castillo de Armagos, and Isla Mancera. Check boats for life jackets and an inflatable raft; there have been some serious boating accidents.

Beaches

The ocean beaches, 43 kilometers (27 miles) from Valdivia, make a good day trip from the city. The road is paved as far as **Niebla;** from there drive along ocean cliffs toward **Los Molinos** beach or **San Ignacio** beach or past the villages of Loncollén and Calfuco to the village and beach of **Curiñanco.**

Dining

For price ranges, *see* Dining *in* Chile Essentials, *below.*

$$$ **Camino de Luna Restaurant.** This unusual restaurant floats in the river,
★ near the Pedro de Valdivia bridge in Valdivia. It specializes in beef and
seafood; the congrío *calle calle* (conger eel served with a cheese-and-
tomato sauce) is particularly good. Most tables are by the windows
and offer views of the river, Teja Island, and Valdivia. ✗ *Costanera
s/n, Valdivia,* ☎ *063/213788. Reservations advised Jan.–Feb. AE, DC,
MC, V.*

$$$ **Castillo de Alba.** This large, comfortable restaurant in the Hotel Villa
de Río offers a fine view of the Calle Calle River. Specialties include
venison marinated in wine with a ham and mushroom sauce and duck
in a sauce made with local berries. ✗ *Av. España 1025, Valdivia,* ☎
063/216292. AE, DC, MC, V.

$$ **Café Haussmann.** Valdivia was the center of German and Swiss im-
★ migration at the turn of the century, and this is one place to enjoy the
fruits of that exchange: excellent *crudos* (steak tartare) and German-
style sandwiches, with delicious kuchen for dessert. ✗ *Libertador
Bernardo O'Higgins 394, Valdivia,* ☎ *063/213878. No credit cards.*

$$ **Centro Español.** For Spanish cooking, this is the best place in Valdivia.
Try the paella, a filling dish that blends chicken, pork, shellfish, and
saffron rice. ✗ *Camilo Henríquez 436, Valdivia,* ☎ *063/213540.
Weekend reservations advised. AE, DC, MC, V. Closed weekends
Apr.–Oct.*

$ **Café Paula.** This is part of a chain that is famous for ice cream and
pastries, but in Valdivia the café also offers sandwiches and full meals.
✗ *Vicente Pérez 633, Valdivia,* ☎ *063/212328. DC, MC, V.*

Lodging

For price ranges, *see* Lodging *in* Chile Essentials, *above.*

Hotels

$$$ **Hotel Pedro de Valdivia.** This hotel, a four-star-rated property with SER-
★ NATUR, is large, old, and elegant, with a pleasant view of the green
gardens of Valdivia. Access to golf and tennis clubs is available. 🏨
Carampagne 190, Valdivia, ☎ *and* 🖷 *063/212931, in Santiago,*
☎ *2/695–1151. 77 rooms. Restaurant, bar, pool, meeting rooms. AE,
DC, MC, V.*

$$ **Hotel Isla Teja.** This hotel on Teja Island (in the middle of Valdivia between three rivers), very near Austral University and its famous botan-
ical gardens, has the air of a university dorm. Rooms are comfortable
and modern. 🏨 *Las Encinas 220, Valdivia,* ☎ *063/215014,* 🖷
063/214911. 96 rooms, 32 with bath. Restaurant. AE, DC, MC, V.

Campgrounds

Most of the camping around Valdivia is along the rivers and is relatively expensive. **Isla Teja** (Los Cipreses, Valdivia, ☎ 063/213584) on
Teja Island, with an attractive view of the river, has campsites with electricity and hot showers.

Lake Llanquihue

Three charming small towns ring the western shore of Lake Llanquihue, which lies just east of the Pan-American Highway down into Puerto
Montt. As they are not richly endowed with visitor facilities, you may
want to stop by on your way to Puerto Montt, which lies just south.

Puerto Octay, the northernmost town, has a spectacular view of the Osorno and Calbuco volcanoes. The small **Museo El Colono** (Independencia 591; ☛ Free) displays farm machinery and other mementos of the town's turn-of-the century settlers.

Halfway down the western edge of the lake lies the small colonial town of **Frutillar** (actually two joined hamlets, Frutillar Alto and Frutillar Bajo), with its perfectly preserved German architecture. You can take a step back into the past by visiting the **Museo de la Colonización Alemana** (Museum of German Colonization; no ☎; ☛ Entry fee), which is a short walk up Arturo Prat from the lake. Besides displays of the 19th-century agricultural and household implements, there are full-scale reconstructions of buildings—a smithy and barn, among others—used by the original German settlers. Each January and February, the town hosts the **Semanas Musicales de Frutillar** (☎ 2/222–5116), a excellent series of classical concerts in an idyllic outdoor setting.

Puerto Varas, south of Frutillar, offers a comfortable hotel with reasonably priced cabins, a restaurant, and a full view of the Osorno Volcano. It's also known for its stunning rose arbors, which are in full bloom from December to March. A small **casino** in the Gran Hotel de Puerto Varas, open year-round, offers late-night bingo games that are popular with locals and tourists.

Dining and Lodging

$$ Gran Hotel de Puerto Varas. The building, constructed in the 1930s, is said to be the first summer home erected in southern Chile. Rooms are unremarkable, but many have views of the Osorno Volcano. Windows also line the walls of the restaurant, where you can dine on salmon fished fresh from the lake. ⊞ *Klenner 351, Puerto Varas,* ☎ *065/232282. 100 rooms. Restaurant, bar, casino. MC, V.*

$$ Hotel Salzburg. This mini-village is composed of traditionally designed wooden cabins, all commanding excellent views of the lake. The staff will help organize fishing trips, and the restaurant offers some of the best smoked salmon in the area. ⊞ *Costanera Norte, Frutillar Bajo,* ☎ *065/421589. 5 cabins. Restaurant, sauna, mountain bikes, travel services. No credit cards.*

Puerto Montt

For most of Chile's history, Puerto Montt has been the end of the line, whether you were traveling by railway, dirt road, or highway. Now the Austral Highway carries on southward, but for most intents and purposes, Puerto Montt remains the last significant outpost of civilization, a small provincial city that is the hub of local fishing, textile, and tourist activity. Today the town consists of low clapboard and wooden houses perched on hills above the ocean, with four- to six-story office buildings and stores, most built earlier this century. If it's a warm, sunny day, head east along the shoreline to **Pelluco** or one of the other beaches. If you're more interested in getting to know the area generally, drive along the shoreline through the city for a good view of the surrounding hillsides and the relatively protected stretch of ocean where the city is located.

Visitor Information

SERNATUR (Edificio Intendencia, 2nd Floor, Puerto Montt, ☎ 065/ 254580).

Tour Operators

Around Puerto Montt

You can arrange a boat ride through the Port Authority in Angelmó or by talking directly with the owner or captain of one of the boats. **Montonave Maité,** based in Calbuco (Av. los Héroes, ☎ 0659/588; closed Apr.–Aug.), offers excursions along the channel around Angelmó (two hours) or all the way to the small port and fishing village of Calbuco (three hours). You can spend the day, then return by the same boat or take a bus back along the main road to Puerto Montt for a different view.

To the San Rafael Glacier

If you have a limited amount of time, and want to experience the power and beauty of Chilean Patagonia, a cruise down the coast south of Puerto Montt will give you a unique perspective of the rugged coastline, fjords, and glaciers. **Turismo Skorpios** (Angelmó 1660, Puerto Montt, ☎ 065/252952, FAX 065/258315; Augusto Leguia Norte 118, Las Condes, Santiago, ☎ 2/231–1030, FAX 2/232–2269) runs a six-day cruise that visits the historic city of Castro on Chiloé, remote villages in the Guaitecas and Chonos archipelagoes, and 200-foot-high ice spires at the San Rafael Glacier. High-season prices (Dec.–Feb.) vary from $1,000 for a single cabin to $2,720 for a honeymoon suite.

Exploring

City Center

The **Museo Juan Pablo II** (Juan Pablo II Regional Museum), just east of the bus terminal, has a good collection of crafts and relics from one of Chile's strongest regional cultures, that of the Archipelago of Chiloé. Historical photos give a sense of the area's slow and often difficult growth and the impact of the 1960 earthquake, which virtually destroyed the port. *On the Costandera (Coast Road) by bus terminal, no ☎. ✔ Entry fee.*

Angelmó

A few kilometers west of downtown along the Coast Road is Puerto Montt's fishing cove, the **Caleta Angelmó.** From here you can get a good view of Tenglo Island, which protects a busy port serving small fishing boats, large ferries, and cruisers carrying travelers and cargo southward through the straits and fjords that form much of Chile's shoreline. On weekdays you'll notice the water traffic from many of the outlying islands—small launches and fishing boats that arrive early in the morning and leave in the afternoon. The **fish market** in Angelmó offers one of the most varied selections of seafood in all of Chile (*see* Dining, *below*).

An excellent selection of handicrafts sold at the best prices in Chile can be found in Angelmó's **Feria Artesanal** (Crafts Fair). Baskets, Chilote ponchos, mythical Chilote figures woven from different kinds of grasses and straws, and warm sweaters of raw, hand-spun, and hand-dyed wool are all offered. Most of the people selling here are intermediaries, and many of the styles have been adapted to buyers' tastes, but if you look carefully you'll also see the less commercial, more authentic offerings. Dickering over prices is expected. *On the Coast Road near Angelmó Fishing Cove.*

Dining

For price ranges, see Dining *in* Chile Essentials, *below*.

$$ **Café Central.** This old-style café in the heart of Puerto Montt has been
★ remodeled but retains the spirit of the 1920s and 1930s. It's a good
place for a filling afternoon tea, with its menu of creamy coffees, ice
cream, sandwiches, and pastries. ✗ *Rancagua 117, Puerto Montt,* ☎
065/254721. No credit cards.

$–$$ **Angelmó Market.** A wide selection of small and medium-size kitchens
offer *mariscal* (raw shellfish soup) and *caldillo* (hot soup), as well as
machas, *ostiones* (scallops), and *almejas* (clams) à la parmesana. There
are tables and counters for each kitchen at this enclosed market. ✗
*At Angelmó Fishing Cove, about 7 km (4.3 mi) west of Puerto Montt
along the Coast Road. No credit cards.*

$–$$ **Cafe Restaurant Vicorella.** This two-story café provides a warm, com-
fortable refuge and an inexpensive hot meal when the weather proves
unfriendly. You can order a steak and mashed potatoes, or try one of
the daily specials. ✗ *Av. Antonio Varas 515, Puerto Montt,* ☎
065/253759. No credit cards. Closed Sun.

Lodging

For price ranges, *see* Lodging *in* Chile Essentials, *below.*

Hotels

$$–$$$ **Viento Sur.** One of Puerto Montt's newer establishments, Viento Sur
sits on its hill like a castle, giving a majestic view of the city and the
sea. Rooms are comfortably furnished with generous use of native
Chilean woods; suites have hot tubs. ▦ *Ejército 200, Puerto Montt,*
☎ *065/258700,* ℻ *065/258700. 21 rooms with bath, 6 with shower;
2 suites. Sauna, exercise room. AE, MC, V.*

$$ **Hotel O'Grimm.** This three-year-old, four-story hotel in the center of
Puerto Montt offers rooms in pastel grays, roses, greens, and golds.
▦ *Guillermo Gallardo 211, Puerto Montt,* ☎ *065/252845,* ℻ *065/
258600. 27 rooms, 1 suite. AE, DC, MC, V.*

$$ **Hotel Puerto Montt.** This hotel, formerly called Residencial los Chilcos,
is known for its attentive service and comfortable family atmosphere.
Guest rooms are decorated in cheerful yellows and creams. ▦ *St.
Teresa 665, Puerto Montt,* ☎ *and* ℻ *065/257410. 1 room with bath,
14 with shower. No credit cards.*

$ **Don Luis Gran Hotel.** The rooms are comfortable, clean, and modern,
and there's a small salon for breakfast, which is included in the rate.
▦ *Urmeneta and Quillota, Puerto Montt,* ☎ *and* ℻ *065/259001. 12
rooms with bath, 48 with shower. AE, DC, MC, V.*

Campgrounds

Campgrounds around Puerto Montt all charge around $10 per vehi-
cle per night, but offer various comfort levels and views. **Chinquihue**
(on the Coast Road, 7 km, or 4 mi, west of Angelmó Fishing Cove, ☎
065/255498) has a restaurant, bathrooms, showers, and attractive
views of the beach. **El Ciervo** (on the Coast Road, 1 km, or ½ mi, west
of Angelmó, ☎ 065/255271) offers 20 sites with electrical hookups,
general lighting, hot showers, and boat rental. **Los Alamos** (on the Coast
Road, 11 km, or 6 mi, west of Angelmó, ☎ 065/254067) has fine views
of the Reloncaví Strait and Tenglo Island and offers electricity, roofed
sites, general lighting, water, bathrooms, hot showers, a dock and
launching area, a play area and sports field, and boat rentals. **Paredes**
(on the Coast Road, 6 km, or 3½ mi, west of Angelmó, ☎ 065/258394)
is short on shade but has a pretty beach, hot showers, a soccer field,
and a playground.

PUNTA ARENAS

The saying that "history is written by the conquerors" is never more true than in Punta Arenas, where the main streets and even the cemetery bear the names of the Yugoslav, Portuguese, and English settlers who colonized the area. They founded the enormous sheep ranches for which the region became famous and exploited the gold during a short-lived rush at the turn of the century. They also contributed to the genocide of the region's indigenous people through policies such as the hiring of headhunters who were paid a pound sterling for every ear and testicle they brought in. Of six native groups, only one woman survived.

Punta Arenas is 3,141 kilometers (1,960 miles) from Santiago and light-years away in attitude, too. It's the main city in a region with a fascinating history peopled by some of the world's most unusual indigenous groups and rapacious settlers from around the globe—daring explorers and pirates. Today's residents share this extraordinary natural landscape with flamingos, the llamalike guanacos, and other wildlife.

Punta Arenas looks like it's about to be swept into the Strait of Magellan, and on a windy day it feels that way, too. The houses are mostly made of sheets of tin with colorful tin roofs, best appreciated when seen from above. Although the general view of the city may not be particularly attractive, look for details: the pink-and-white house on a corner, the bay window full of plants, a garden overflowing with flowers.

In general, tourist services in the entire region are expensive, although you'll find exceptions. If you make the effort to come south, bring extra funds so you can really travel and enjoy some of the once-in-a-lifetime experiences that the region offers: a journey by car or bus through Patagonia to the Torres del Paine National Park; a boat trip north from Puerto Natales, the closest supply center to the park, to the glaciers; an excursion by car and boat to Penguin Island, in the Strait of Magellan; and day trips to historic sites. You'll probably want to spend a day or so visiting Punta Arenas itself, particularly the museums, which offer valuable background information on this extraordinary area. Tour offices conduct excursions to the old Fort Bulnes and Hunger Port region south of the city, where the original settlers attempted to establish a foothold in this windswept region. Punta Arenas is also South America's major jumping-off point for cruises and flights to Antarctica (*see* Chapter 2, Adventure and Learning Vacations).

Visitor Information

SERNATUR (Waldo Seguel 689, Punta Arenas, ☎ and FAX 061/241–1330).

Arriving and Departing

By Plane

Both **LanChile** and **Ladeco** have regular flights; if you don't have a Visit Chile pass (*see* Getting Around *in* Chile Essentials, *below*), try for a reduced fare seat. These must be booked at least two to three months in advance, especially if you plan to travel during the peak season in January and February, when the weather in Punta Arenas is at its best. Your best bet is to use a travel agency such as **Rigtur** (Ahumada 312, Office 606, in Santiago, ☎ 2/698–5766 or 2/698–7535, FAX 2/797–9668), since travel agents can work the occasional miracle of getting cheaper seats at the last minute.

By Car

It's an exhausting four- or five-day drive to Punta Arenas from Santiago. The prettiest route is via the Pan-American Highway south as far as Osorno, then eastward through the mountains via Paso Puyehue to Bariloche, Argentina. From there drive south through the Argentine National Parks (Nahuel Huapi, Los Alerces) to the town of Comodoro Rivadavia (1,200 km, or 750 mi, from Osorno) on Argentina's Atlantic coast. At Comodoro Rivadavia, drive south to Río Gallegos (1,916 km, or 1,200 mi, from Osorno) and on to Punta Arenas. Some sections of the route are unpaved. Punta Arenas is about 2,230 km (1,400 mi) from Osorno.

By Bus

Only **Turibus** (☎ 2/779–1377) runs the 36-hour route between Santiago and Punta Arenas, departing from the Terminal Santiago (Av. Libertador Bernardo O'Higgins 3848, ☎ 2/779–1385).

By Boat

Navimag (El Bosque Norte 0440, Santiago, ☎ 2/203–5030, FAX 2/203–5025) offers luxury cruises from Puerto Montt down Chile's west coast as far as the Strait of Magellan.

Getting Around Punta Arenas

Punta Arenas is a small, walkable city, with most of its main attractions concentrated around the central square. Tourist agencies and even cafés offer day trips to Penguin Island and Fort Bulnes, and there is regular bus service to Puerto Natales and the Torres del Paine National Park, so you can get to most places whether you've got a vehicle or not. To really explore the surrounding region, however, you may find a car worth the expense.

Exploring Punta Arenas

The best place to start a walking tour of Punta Arenas is from the central square, where you'll see the famous statue of a Selk'nam Indian whose toe you must touch if you want to return. Climb Calle Fagnano about four blocks to reach the **Mirador Cerro La Cruz** (Hill of the Cross Lookout). From there you have a truly breathtaking view of the city's colorful roofs, orderly streets, and the Strait of Magellan. From there walk back one block to Avenida España and turn left, walking six blocks through a primarily residential area to reach Avenida Colón, which has a narrow park running down the middle of the street. You can follow Colón all the way down to the oceanfront and enjoy a windy, invigorating walk along the edge of the strait westward, back toward the city and the port. If your tastes run toward a more urban experience, follow Bories or 21 de Mayo back along store- and restaurant-lined streets toward the city center.

From the central square, take Calle 21 de Mayo to Avenida Bulnes, where you'll find the best museum in the region, **Museo Salesiano de Mayorino Borgatello** (Mayorino Borgatello Museum, commonly referred to as the Salesianos), operated by the Salesian religious order, which came to Punta Arenas in the 19th century, ostensibly to bring God to the native people and help them integrate into Chilean society. The adventurous Italian clergy, most of whom spoke no Spanish, proved to be daring explorers; they traveled throughout the region, collecting artifacts as well as native survivors, who were "relocated" to a camp on Dawson Island, across the Magellan Strait, where they died by the hundreds. (The island was used as a prison camp by the military government after the 1973 coup.) The museum contains an extraordinary collection of everything from skulls and native crafts to stuffed animals (some with sensational birth defects, such as a two-headed lamb). *Av. Bulnes 398, ☎ 061/241096.* ☞ *Entry fee. Closed Mon.*

If you're interested in how Punta Arenas's European settlers lived, visit the **Museo Regional** (Regional Museum) in the central square; it's housed in what was once the mansion of the powerful Braun-Menéndez family. From the Mayorino Borgatello Museum, walk two or three blocks toward the water until you reach Hernando de Magallanes. With its lavish, marble-floored salons restored and filled with plush European-style furnishings, it provides an intriguing view of a wealthy provincial family's pretensions at the beginning of this century. The wall separating the main bedroom from the men-only games room carries two telling paintings: on the games room side, where women were never allowed, is a painting of a sexy young woman in a low-cut dress; on the bedroom side, an oil painting extols the virtues of the Virgin Mary. *Hernando de Magallanes 949, ☎ 061/244216.* ☞ *Donations accepted. Closed Mon.*

The **Club de la Unión** (Union Club), also in the central square, is in the former mansion of Sara Braun, the wealthy, powerful resident who also donated the main gate to the **cemetery** (Av. Bulnes and Calle Angamos) on the condition that she be the only person ever to use it! The city accepted, so when visitors enter the cemetery, it is through a side gate rather than the main entrance, which has not been opened since Braun's funeral. Huge yew trees carved into giant humps edge the cemetery paths; the niches lined with photographs of the dead citizens of Punta Arenas are particularly intriguing.

Dining

The limitations of dining in a small provincial city are compensated for in Punta Arenas by the delights of fresh seafood, especially salmon, crab, and scallops, along with the local staple, lamb, whose flavor is slightly stronger than in other regions in Chile. Watch out for warnings of red tide, which makes shellfish toxic, but health authorities are strict about monitoring toxin levels, so you're unlikely to have problems. For price-category definitions, *see* Dining *in* Chile Essentials, *below.*

$$$ Los Navegantes. This restaurant in the Hotel los Navegantes (*see* Lodging, *below*) serves delicious grilled salmon and roast lamb, with shellfish appetizers, in a simple but comfortable dining room with a bright garden at one end. ✗ *José Menéndez 647, ☎ 061/244677. Reservations advised. AE, DC, MC, V.*

$$ Café Garogha. This tea room and bar offers cable television, good espresso, fresh pastries, moderately priced sandwiches, and more expensive salmon and crab dinners. The proprietors also offer tours to Penguin Island and Fort Bulnes. ✗ *Bories 817, ☎ 061/241782. No reservations. DC, MC, V.*

$ Carioca. The decor is simple, with paneling of rough-hewn logs and
★ tables and chairs imprinted with Coca-Cola logos, but the sandwiches are unbeatable, especially the "Carioca" itself, a hamburger with cheese, bacon, tomato, avocado, egg, and green beans for less than $4. This place is popular with students and pensioners, who sit nursing a beer through hours of conversation. ✗ *Calles José Menéndez and Chiloé, no ☎. No reservations. DC, MC, V.*

$ El Rinconcito. Given its location across from the rail yards down by the port, this hole in the wall with a six-stool counter is for the adventurous, but the fresh raw shellfish soup, served with green and white onions, *ají* (chilies), oil, wine, and lemon, doesn't get any better, or any cheaper. ✕ *Take Independencia (it turns into Brasilera) until it ends near the port, and turn right on Costanera until you pass a doorway in the wall on the right. No reservations. No credit cards.*

Lodging

Hotels are springing up throughout Punta Arenas, so you may want to either wander around a bit before you choose or simply book into one place the first night and then move. For price-category definitions, *see* Lodging *in* Chile Essentials, *below.*

$$$ **Cabo de Hornos.** The Cabo de Hornos, Punta Arenas's only five-star hotel, occupies a massive eight-story building along the central square. It has seen better days: Lobby decor dates back to the '60s, and its carpets are stained. The saunas have been turned into meeting rooms, and the guest rooms, decorated in beige and browns, are clean and comfortable but nothing special. End rooms on upper floors have spectacular views of the Strait of Magellan; others overlook the square. ☎ *Plaza Muñoz Gamero 1025, ☎ and ᴲᴬˣ 061/242134. 103 rooms, 10 suites. Restaurant, bar, tea shop. AE, DC, MC, V.*

$$$ **José Nogueira.** The management of Punta Arenas's newest hotel is look-
★ ing for a five-star designation, and it probably deserves one. The place is delightfully comfortable and beautifully designed: Public rooms are decorated with richly textured striped wallpaper, pillars of polished wood, marble floors, and lots of bronze details. Guest rooms are on the small side, but they have high ceilings, thick carpets, antique-style wood furniture, and ceramic-tile bathrooms. The suites have hot tubs. ☎ *Bories 959, ☎ 061/248840, ᴲᴬˣ 061/248832. 23 rooms, 2 suites. Restaurant, bar. AE, DC, MC, V.*

$$ **Hotel los Navegantes.** This comfortable, unpretentious hotel has an excellent restaurant and spacious double rooms with gray-and-pink carpets and colorful paisley bedspreads; cable TV has been installed. The price includes a substantial, American-style breakfast and transportation from the airport. ☎ *José Menéndez 647, ☎ 061/244677, ᴲᴬˣ 061/247545. 52 rooms, 4 suites. Restaurant, minibars. AE, DC, MC, V.*

$ **Hostal Carpa Manzano.** This new and comfortable establishment is dec-
★ orated in warm pastel colors, with wicker furniture and low poster beds. It's centrally located and has a friendly, helpful proprietor. ☎ *Lautaro Navarro 336, ☎ 061/242296, ᴲᴬˣ 061/248864. 10 rooms. DC, MC, V.*

$ **Hostal de la Avenida.** The rooms of this comfortable, homey residen-
★ cial all overlook a garden that is lovingly tended by its owner, a local of Yugoslav origin. ☎ *Av. Colón 534, ☎ 061/247532. 6 rooms with showers only. Snack bar. No credit cards.*

$ **Hotel Condor de Plata.** The idiosyncratic decor includes scale models and photographs of old-fashioned airplanes that once traveled to the Magellan region. Rooms are small, carpeted, and colored in neutral browns and beiges; cable TV is available. ☎ *Av. Colón 556, ☎ 061/247987, ᴲᴬˣ 061/241149. 14 rooms. Cafeteria. DC, MC, V.*

Excursions from Punta Arenas

Penguin Island

Penguin Island, a half-day drive from Punta Arenas followed by a boat trip, provides an extraordinary opportunity for visitors to see penguins in their natural habitat. The island is a reserve where the birds are free to reproduce and raise their young with full protection from hunters.

Trips to the island usually last all day, and are offered by Café Garogha (*see* Dining, *above*), **Turismo Comapa** (Independencia 840, Punta Arenas, ☎ 061/224256, ℻ 061/225804), and **Traveltur Turismo** (in Punta Arenas, ☎ and ℻ 061/211107).

Torres del Paine National Park

A trip to **Torres del Paine National Park** offers a once-in-a-lifetime opportunity to view nature at its finest: The spectacular towering mountains that give the park its name are surrounded by sparkling turquoise lakes, some touched by the icy-blue sculptures of icebergs and glaciers. You'll see much of the typical wildlife of the region, including foxes, flamingos, guanacos, a woolly, graceful version of the llama, and *ñandús* (Chilean ostriches), along with a wide variety of birds, wild flowers, and berries.

Plan to spend an extra day in **Puerto Natales,** the largest town near the park, and take the daylong boat ride to view glaciers on the *21 de Mayo Cutter* (Eberhard 560, Puerto Natales, ☎ and ℻ 061/411978; $38). Arrange a bag or box lunch and take warm clothes. The trip takes you through canals lined with sheer rock walls, past a cormorant nesting area and a seal colony, and on to the glaciers, one of which you can visit on foot. On your way back to port, you can sip on a pisco or whiskey chilled with glacier ice.

Getting There
The best way to visit the park, which is 400 kilometers (250 miles) from Punta Arenas along a road that is gravel for the last 145 kilometers (90 miles), is to rent a car. **Buses Fernández** (☎ and ℻ 061/242313) and **Bus Sur** (Baquedano 534, Puerto Natales, ☎ and ℻ 061/411325) run a daily bus service between Punta Arenas and Puerto Natales; be sure to book and arrive early or you may not get on. **Turismo Michay** (Baquedano 388, Puerto Natales, ☎ 061/411149) and **Bus Sur** have daily bus service from Puerto Natales to the park.

Tour Operators
Arka Patagonia (☎ 061/241504) and **Andes Patagónicos Expeditions** (Blanco Encalada 226, Puerto Natales, ☎ 061/411594) offer one-day package tours to the park, which may or may not include transportation from Punta Arenas to Puerto Natales, the main town on the way to Torres del Paine. These tours are thorough but exhausting. You might want to spend the extra money and stay overnight, then catch the next day's tour back to Puerto Natales. Arka also organizes adventure tours and scientific expeditions.

Dining and Lodging
PUERTO NATALES
Puerto Natales is bursting with hotels; among the newer offerings are the **Hotel Glaciares** (Eberhard 104, ☎ and ℻ 061/411452) and the **Lady Florence Dixie** (Bulnes 659, ☎ 061/411158, ℻ 061/411943), a welcoming inexpensive hotel that has peach-color rooms with TV and telephones and breakfast included. If you stop overnight, try **Don Alvarito's** restaurant (Blanco Encalada 915, ☎ 061/411187) for carefully prepared scallops and filet mignon in simple, tasty sauces.

AT THE PARK
If you don't want to camp, stay in the **Hostería Pehoe** (☎ 061/241373, ℻ 061/248052; closed May–mid-Sept.). Its somewhat cramped rooms are rather expensive at $95 a night, but all have great views and the service is marvelous. Book well in advance. An even more deluxe alternative is the recently built eco-hotel **Explora** (Reservations: Américo

Vespucio Sur 80, 5th Floor, Santiago, ☎ 2/228–8081, ⅓ 2/228–4655), which is on the southeast corner of Lago Pehoé and offers spectacular vistas of the park's famous granite towers. As the name suggests, the focus of this hotel is on exploring the local environment, and bookings must be for a minimum of four days (sufficient time for you to become acquainted with nature). The interior is Scandinavian in style, with local woods used for ceilings, floors, and furniture. No expense has been spared, with bed linen from Barcelona, china from England, and wicker furniture from Chimbarongo. Every day, the hotel offers five different types of exploration, depending on the weather conditions and guests' requirements. Prices start at just under $2,000 for a six-night stay; this includes transportation to and from Punta Arenas, all meals, and daily excursions with bilingual guides. The owners are developing a similar project at San Pedro de Atacama, in the heart of the Atacama Desert.

EASTER ISLAND

Arriving and Departing

The only way to reach Easter Island, which lies 3,700 kilometers (2,300 miles) west of Chile, is by plane. The airport is a few minutes southwest of the island's only town, Hanga Roa. Service is via **LanChile** (☎ 2/632–3211 in Santiago, 800/735–5526 in the United States). Round-trip fare from Santiago is about $850; if you buy a Visit Chile pass before leaving home (*see* Getting Around *in* Chile Essentials, *below*), you can include a visit to Easter Island at a more moderate price.

Getting Around Easter Island

If you want to make reservations for any of the below from Santiago, dial 123122 and then give the operator the last three digits of the Easter Island number; for Viajes Kia Koe, for example, it would be 282. Alternatively, Entel has a special fax number for all reservations on the island (⅓ 562/690–2674).

Rental Transportation
You can rent a Jeep from **Gas,** the local gas station a few doors down from Hotel Hotu Matua (Av. Pont, ☎ 2/23242), from **Viajes Kia Koe** (Policarpo, ☎ 2/23282), or from **Hertz** (Av. Constanera 1469, ☎ 2/236–1323 in Santiago); count on spending about $75 per day for a jeep. Boats are available for rental in the *caleta* (fishing village) near Hanga Roa. You can rent a horse to explore the island, without guides, for less than $20 a day near the **Hotu Matua Hotel** (Av. Point, ☎ 2/635–3275).

Tour Operators
Orongo Easter Island Hotel (Policarpo, ☎ 2/23294) offers very informative full-day ($20 per person) and half-day ($10) tours of the island. You can also arrange for a skin-diving tour in the caleta near Hanga Roa.

Exploring Easter Island

Rapa Nui, known to most as Easter Island, is one of the world's most persistent mysteries, only 130 square kilometers (50 square miles) in size, with a mixed European-Chilean-Polynesian population that recalls its own history in a series of often contradictory stories. The landscape itself, formed by the action of a now-dormant volcano, is characterized by the idyllic palm-lined beaches of golden sand and low rocky mountains typical of most South Pacific islands. One small town on the southwest tip of this inverted triangle, Hanga Roa, houses the island's 2,500 permanent residents, and rough dirt roads trace the footsteps of the ancient and modern peoples who have used, and often abused, their island home. Huge stone statues known as *moai* are scattered all over the island, attesting to the skills of the craftspeople who carved, moved, and erected these imposing creatures, some more than 57 feet tall. Count on spending at least 1½–2 days here; you'll need 4–5 days to see the entire island without feeling rushed.

Conflicting theories battle to explain how Easter Island was first settled. Anthropologist Thor Heyerdahl argued that similarities between customs in parts of Peru and Easter Island indicate that native peoples from the South American mainland first settled the island. However, the dominant theory is that the island was first occupied by a thriving Polynesian culture that at its height had a population of 15,000 and developed a sophisticated system of beliefs expressed by the island's massive stone moai. Archaeologists believe the island's population experienced a crisis toward the end of the 16th century, possibly due to overpopulation, and after a lengthy period of violent conflicts, a new culture developed.

In 1870 a ship raced westward and claimed the island for Chile, before France could do so, and in 1888 Easter Island formally became part of Chile. Until 1952 the owners of a private sheep ranch ran the island as their own, shutting inhabitants up in the main town of Hanga Roa. Today the main activities of the town's 2,500 inhabitants, 75% of whom are of native origin, include servicing a growing tourism industry and conducting scientific excavations and studies, along with more traditional pursuits such as agriculture, fishing, and handicrafts produced in the form of wood carvings of ancient figures, necklaces, and other pieces worked in shells and coral.

In the town of **Hanga Roa** itself, it's well worth visiting the **church,** where traditional Catholic figures are rendered by island carvers with surprising results. The noon service on Sunday is usually in the island's indigenous language, and the songs have a distinctly Polynesian rhythm and flavor. There's also a modest **museum** that has shells, carvings, and other interesting pieces on view just outside town near the **Tahai** archaeological site, which is on the coast. A pleasant half-day walk along the dirt road to Tahai will take you through a coastal landscape dotted with buried and broken moai; you'll pass the **plaza** that once served as a ceremonial meeting place, near which religious and social leaders built their boat-shape residences, or *hare paenga* (meaning "the foundations of one who remains visible").

Take a day trip to **Orongo,** the small village to the south of Hanga Roa that has been re-created by Chile's National Parks division to provide insight into the mysteries of a culture that left 150 carvings behind on cliffs. Nearby is the **Rano Kau Volcano,** a ceremonial crater a mile wide that is decorated with characteristic petroglyphs. Bring solid, comfortable walking shoes appropriate for stony roads and some climbing, along with a light rain jacket and a flashlight for exploring caves. It's also worth driving across to the northeast shore of the island for a day at Anakena Beach, where natural caves that you can explore on your own once sheltered the island's earliest residents.

CHILE ESSENTIALS

Customs and Duties

On Arrival

You may bring into Chile up to 400 cigarettes, 400 grams of tobacco, 50 cigars, two open bottles of perfume, 2 liters of alcoholic beverages, and gifts. On arrival, you will be given a flimsy, minute piece of paper that is your three-month tourist visa. This has to be handed in when you leave; because getting a new one involves waiting in many lines and a lot of bureaucracy, put it somewhere safe.

On Departure

Visitors, although seldom questioned, are prohibited by regulation from leaving with handicrafts and souvenirs worth more than $500 total. You will be charged a $12.50 airport tax upon departure.

Dining

Santiago has the widest selection of restaurants and prices, but many of the local spots can provide meals as carefully prepared and as delicious. Several of the larger hotels in isolated cities or resorts have good chefs. There is no system of government classification of restaurants, although in theory they're all subject to the same standards. Your own eyes and nose are your best guides. *Fuente de soda* (soda fountain) is the most common classification for Chilean restaurants and, while they may be a good place for a soft drink, a cup of tea, or a light breakfast, you should be cautious about eating much else, because the hygiene may not be the best.

Specialties

Pisco sours are a refreshing start to an evening meal, as is the more gentle *vaina* (sherry or some other sweet wine, whipped with egg white and topped with a dash of cinnamon). Chilean food is simple, focusing on a main meat, fish, or shellfish dish, preceded by a salad and followed by a sweet desert. The food is seldom spicy, but watch for the delicious but hot red sauce ají, and *pebre,* a sauce made of fresh parsley, fresh coriander, onions, and sometimes tomatoes, using ají as a base.

Many simple country dishes are among the best offerings of Chilean cuisine. Gazuela, a superb soup that includes a piece of meat (beef, pork, chicken, or turkey, usually with bone), varied vegetables, and a thick, rich broth, is a full meal in itself. If your stomach's been rough, a rich chicken gazuela is just the thing. In the summer, *porotos granodos*, a thick bean, corn, and squash soup, is the rage with Chileans, as are *humitas,* ground corn seasoned and steamed in its own husk, and pastel de choclo, a corn pastry roll that usually contains minced beef, a piece of chicken, and seasonings. An *ensalada chilena* of tomatoes and onions is delicious if well prepared (the onions must be soaked in brine beforehand to reduce their acid flavor). Empanadas are the Chilean answer to hamburgers, but as with hamburgers, it's hard to find a good one.

Raw shellfish is a health hazard, but cooked with cheese or white wine, lemon, and fresh coriander, it's an excellent doorway to Chilean cuisine. Chile enjoys a variety of fine fish: the conger eel, corvina, and other species are all worth tasting, as is the humble *merluza* (hake), which makes a delicious, cheap lunch; the *centolla* crab, caught off the coast of Patagonia; and machas clams, similar to razor clams but unique to Chile.

Pork is another Chilean specialty, especially in *arrollados* (a stuffed pork roll encased in pork rind), *costillares* (ribs, often covered in ají), *lomo* (roast pork loin), and *pernil* (the whole leg, so make sure you're hungry).

Some Spanish-inspired dishes like *guatitas* (intestines) send Chileans into states of culinary bliss, as does blood sausage, *chunchules* (a spicy stew of beef or pork intestines), and other odds and ends of edible beasts. If you order a *parillada* (a barbecue at your table), check on the cuts being served so as to avoid those that are too peculiar for your taste.

CHILEAN WINE

The Chilean wine export boom of the last six years should mean that many readers of this guide will be familiar with the excellent value and high quality of Chilean wines. Unfortunately, within Chile, it's almost impossible to find wines of export quality, because the Chileans themselves prefer the old traditional style of wine. Prepare to taste oxidized white whites and reds that have sat for far too long in old beech barrels, and don't expect any assistance in the struggle to find the best of a bad bunch—there is only one professional sommelier in the whole of Santiago!

There is absolutely no wine culture within Chile, so while Santiago now offers a wide range of international cuisines, there is no corresponding display of wine styles to match. You'll barely notice the difference between wine lists around the capital, and if you manage to find a foreign wine, keep it to yourself. All that said, there are some inexpensive gems out there that you won't be able to find in your local wine shop back home.

As an aperitif or if you're celebrating, try either the Valdivieso or Mumm sparkling wine. The latter is made by the Chilean arm of the famous French champagne house, using grapes from the Casablanca Valley. As a rule, it is safer to go for red rather than white wine, and the best of the former include Canepa Novisimo (a big, weighty Cabernet Sauvignon), Santa Carolina Special Reserve Cabernet Sauvignon (full-bodied with intense rich black currant fruit), Santa Monica Merlot (a soft red, full of cassis and cherries), and Errazuriz Merlot (from one of the most reliable wineries in Chile). With whites, stick to Chardonnay rather than Sauvignon Blanc, since the latter will invariably be made from the inferior Sauvignonasse grape.

Wine fanciers may want to coordinate their trip with one of two food-and-wine fairs that are run annually in Santiago. **ExpoGourmand** (☎ 2/204–7766, FAX 2/223–2307), organized by the magazine *Gourmand,* is a gastronomic feast of wine tastings, cooking demonstrations, and stalls displaying local cuisines. The event runs over four days, during the third week of August. In November, the Chilean wine industry shows off the fruits of its hard labor at the annual **Feria del Vino;** information can be obtained from the Wine Export Association (☎ 2/234–2503, FAX 2/231–1706).

Mealtimes

Chileans usually eat a light breakfast, a hot and hefty lunch, afternoon tea, and a late dinner. Many households settle for a filling *once* (pronounced ON-say), an afternoon tea with bread, cheese, ham, and pastries, and skip the late dinner.

Ratings

Prices are per person and include a first course, main course, and dessert, but not wine. Fixed-price menus are uncommon, but some restaurants use them.

CATEGORY	COST
$$$	$25–$35
$$	$15–$25
$	under $15

Embassies and Consulates

United States
Embassy: 1343 Augustinas, 5th Floor, Santiago, ☎ 2/671–0133.

Canada
Embassy: Ahumada 11, Santiago, ☎ 2/696–2256.

United Kingdom
Embassy: Av. El Bosque Norte 0125, Santiago, ☎ 2/ 231–3737.

Getting Around

By Plane

Flying around Chile is fast and comfortable. Excellent-value air-travel packages are available, but only for purchase outside Chile. Both of Chile's main airlines, **Ladeco** (in North America ☎ 800/825–2332; in Chile ☎ 2/639–5053, FAX 2/639–7277) and **LanChile** (in North America ☎ 800/735–5526; in Chile, ☎ 2/632–3211, FAX 2/632–9334) offer Visit Chile passes. These passes, which are valid for up to 21 days, allow you to fly to cities *either* north or south of Santiago for around $300 ($1,080 if you include Easter Island) or to cities north *and* south of the capital for $550 ($1,290 including Easter Island). The advantage of flying is that you avoid the dangers of the Chilean highway; the disadvantage is that you miss the landscape. You can compensate for this by renting a car and exploring locally.

By Train

Good train service is a thing of the past in Chile; the only real advantage of trains now is that they allow travelers to avoid the Pan-American Highway. Accommodations include sleeper cars, salón, economy, and, for some destinations, first and second classes. There are daily departures from Santiago for most places in southern Chile, but be prepared for a painfully slow journey (Santiago–Puerto Montt takes 20 hours), with frequent delays. There is no northbound service from Santiago. Reservations are recommended; make them at the train station itself (☎ 2/689–5401), in the city center (☎ 2/632–2802), or in the Escuela Militar metro station (☎ 2/228–2983).

You can take advantage of an excellent train service that carries you and your vehicle between Santiago and southern Chile. Round-trip prices from Santiago to Temuco are $247 to transport your car, plus $183 for a private cabin for two or $88 for two coach seats. The respective round-trip prices to Puerto Montt are $292, $207, and $112. The trip must be booked well in advance, particularly if you intend to travel during the peak season; tickets must be paid for when you make a reservation (☎ 2/689–5401).

By Car

Your own driver's license and an International Driving Permit make it legal for you to drive, but your stay in Chile will probably be more pleasant if you avoid using a car or if you use one with great prudence.

ROAD CONDITIONS
Roads are hopelessly overcrowded, especially in Santiago, and parking is a problem in most major cities. The main national thoroughfare is the *Panamericana*, the Pan-American Highway, which begins on the Chile–Peru border and extends south through Santiago and on to Puerto Montt and beyond.

RULES OF THE ROAD
Chilean drivers are wild and reckless and tend to make up the rules as they go along. Foreign insurance may cover the basic costs of an accident, but if you're in an accident that kills or cripples someone, you can be sued, and a Chilean court may award damages far beyond your ability to pay. Local insurance is provided by rental car agencies. Speed limits are usually 100 kph (62 mph) on highways and 50 kph (31 mph) in cities, with the Pan-American being well monitored by police speed traps. Should you be stopped, never attempt to bribe the carabineros.

EMERGENCY ASSISTANCE
The Automóvil Club de Chile (Av. Vitacura 8620, ☎ 2/212–5702, FAX 2/211–9208) offers low-cost road service and towing in and around the main cities to members of the Automobile Association of America (AAA).

GASOLINE
Gasoline prices range from 45¢ per liter for 84 octane to 48¢ per liter for 93 and unleaded and 36¢ per liter for diesel. Prices increase the farther you travel from Santiago. There are plenty of gas stations on main routes, but they're more sparsely spread on the northern half of the Chilean Pan-American. If you plan on crossing the Atacama Desert, make sure your car is topped up with fuel and water.

By Bus
Bus travel in Chile is relatively cheap and safe, provided you use one of the better lines. Luxury bus travel between cities costs about one-third the plane fare and is more comfortable, with wide, reclining seats with footrests, drinks, music, movies, and meals or snacks. Intercity bus service is a comfortable, safe, and reasonably priced alternative for getting around Chile. The most luxurious and expensive service offered by most bus companies is known as *salón cama*.

Fenix (☎ 2/776–3253, FAX 2/779–1149) and **Varmontt** (☎ 2/232–1116 or 2/231–3505, FAX 2/555–8372) offer both luxury and regular service to many points between Santiago and Puerto Montt, as well as farther south. **Tramaca** (☎ 2/776–4110, FAX 2/776–3684) runs a widespread service to the north. You can often negotiate a cheaper fare with roaming vendors during a stroll through the relevant bus terminal. Most individual bus companies are difficult to phone; your best bet is to check schedules and purchase tickets personally. Buses can fill quickly on holiday weekends and over Christmas and Easter, so plan accordingly.

TERMINALS FOR TRAVEL SOUTH
Terminal Alameda (Av. Libertador Bernardo O'Higgins 3724) handles traffic for Pullman del Sur (☎ 2/776–2426) and Tur Bus (☎ 2/776–3133) buses. **Terminal los Héroes** (Roberto Pretot 21, ☎ 2/696–9087) handles Cruz del Sur (☎ 2/696–9324); and **Terminal Santiago** (Av. Libertador Bernardo O'Higgins 3848, ☎ 2/779–1385) handles another 20 or so bus companies. **Varmontt** has its own premises (Av. 11 de Setiembre 2212, Local 111, ☎ 2/231–3505).

TERMINALS FOR TRAVEL NORTH
Terminal de Buses Norte (Amuntegui 920, ☎ 2/671–2141) handles 16 bus companies; **Terminal los Héroes** (Roberto Pretot 21, ☎ 2/696–9250) handles Flota Barrios (☎ 2/699–0230); and **Terminal Torres de Tajamar** (Av. Providencia 1072) handles three other lines.

Language

Chile's official language is Spanish, and you'd be wise to learn at least a few words and carry a good phrase book. Many taxi drivers and hotel and restaurant reception staff speak English, as do many store salespeople. But you'll miss some of the best parts of Chile if you go only where English is spoken.

Lodging

Santiago is slowly getting over a shortage of high-quality hotels, with new ones opening throughout the city. Smaller towns and cities usually have at least one large hotel that serves as a local landmark. But don't forget the residenciales, especially if you're trying to stretch your budget. These accommodations are either modest, no-frills hotels or private homes, usually with a separate bathroom and a Continental-style breakfast. "Apart-Hotels" provide apartments by the day or week.

Hotel prices sometimes include the 18% VAT and sometimes don't. If you pay in cash or traveler's checks in U.S. dollars and if the hotel has an "export billing number," you do not have to pay it. Prices are generally lower in the off-season (in Santiago, January and February, when tourism is at its height in most other regions). Showers are common; full tubs are not.

Ratings

Prices are for double rooms and include all taxes.

CATEGORY	COST
$$$$	over $200
$$$	$125–$200
$$	$75–$125
$	under $75

Mail

Postal Rates

Postage on regular letters and postcards to Canada and the United States costs about 50¢. The postage to Britain is about 64¢. The postal system is efficient and, on average, letters take 4–5 days to reach the United States or Europe.

Money and Expenses

Currency

Exchange rates fluctuate constantly, so check your local newspaper for the most current information; at press time (winter 1995) there were approximately 275 Chilean pesos to the Canadian dollar, 400 pesos to the U.S. dollar, and 625 pesos to the pound sterling. Chilean coins come in units of 1, 10, 50, and 100 pesos; bills are issued in 500, 1,000, 5,000, and 10,000 pesos.

Changing Money

Besides banks, many travel agencies will change money at competitive rates and most don't charge commission on traveler's checks.

Costs

Chile is more expensive than most visitors expect, but less costly than most North American or European regions. Inflation has been low, around 8% in 1994, but the peso has been strengthening against the U.S. dollar, making Chile more expensive for North American visitors. There are plenty of less expensive alternatives to the top international hotels. In most small towns, dozens of residents provide B&B–type accommodations in their homes at quite reasonable rates. Prices do drop off substantially as soon as you move out of Santiago, but you'll find yourself paying for luxuries in more isolated areas, such as in and around Punta Arenas.

TAXES

There's an 18% value-added tax (VAT, called IVA here) added to the cost of most goods and services in Chile; often you won't notice because it's included in the price quoted. When it's not, the seller gives you the price, plus IVA. At many hotels you may receive an exemption from the IVA if you pay in American dollars or traveler's checks; some also offer this service if you use an American Express credit card.

SAMPLE PRICES

A cup of coffee in a restaurant usually costs about $1, espresso usually less than $1.50. Coffee fanatics beware: The brew served is invariably instant. Ask for espresso, cappuccino, or *cortado* if you want "real" coffee. A *barros luco,* a steak or a ham-and-cheese sandwich, will cost about $3. Add a cold draft beer for less than $2.

Opening and Closing Times

Banks

Banking hours are weekdays 9–2, with no exceptions.

Museums

Most museums are closed on Monday, as are theaters and many restaurants. Otherwise, museum hours tend to coincide with shopping hours.

Shops

Stores generally are open weekdays 10–7 and on Saturday until 2. In small towns, stores close for lunch between about 1 and 3 or 4.

National Holidays

New Year's Day (Jan. 1); Good Friday (1996: Apr. 5; 1997: Mar. 28); Labor Day (May 1); Day of Naval Glories (May 21); Corpus Christi (1996: June 6; 1997: May 27); Feast of St. Peter and St. Paul (June 29); Anniversary of Coup (Sept. 11); Independence Celebrations (Sept. 18–19); Discovery of the Americas (Oct. 12); Day of the Dead (Nov. 1); Immaculate Conception (Dec. 8); Christmas (Dec. 25).

Many shops and services are open as normal on these days, but transportation is always heavily booked up on and around the holidays.

Precautions

Health

From a health standpoint, Chile is one of the safer countries in which to travel. The cholera epidemic that swept the continent in the early 1990s has been effectively controlled here. Restaurants are not allowed to serve raw salads and seafood, which represent the prime sources of the bacteria that produce not only cholera but also typhoid fever, hepatitis, and gastroenteritis in general. Avoid raw vegetables unless you know they've been thoroughly washed and disinfected. Be wary of strawberries and other unpeeled ground fruits and vegetables for the same reason, because many farm fields are irrigated with barely treated sewage. When purchasing ice cream, pastries, and other sweet items, buy in locales with proper refrigeration. Avoid luncheon meats, except good-quality ham, because these are a prime source of bacterial infections, especially in summer. Almost all drinking water receives proper treatment and is unlikely to produce health problems. Mineral water is good and comes in carbonated and noncarbonated incarnations, but you'll probably do all right with tap water.

Should you need medical aid, the best facilities tend to be in the private hospitals in Santiago; two of the best are **Clinica Alemana** (Av. Vitacura 5951, ☎ 2/212–9700) and **Clinica Vitacura** (Av. Presidente Kennedy 3210, ☎ 2/228–9043).

Safety

Santiago's city center and most areas frequented by tourists are generally pretty safe, provided you dress down, don't wear flashy jewelry, and don't ever handle money in public. It's a good idea to keep your money in a pocket rather than a wallet, which is easier to steal. On buses and in crowded areas, hold purses or handbags close to the body; thieves use knives to slice the bottom of a bag and catch the contents as they fall out. In Santiago, areas to be particularly cautious include Bellavista, where recent increases in car theft have affected restaurant trade; pedestrian walkways such as Paseo Huérfanos in the downtown district; and around Santa Lucia at night. The poor residential areas of Santiago, known as *poblaciones,* which ring most neighborhoods and commercial centers, have an interesting history and informed, opinionated people, but you need a knowledgeable guide to visit them safely. Chilean men are more subtle in their machismo than men in other South American countries, but it's still a strong aspect of the culture, and foreign women are considered fair game. Men are apt to misinterpret a casual, informal attitude and take advantage.

Shopping

Chile is one of only two countries in the world that produces lapis lazuli, so it's worth checking out the workshops and stores along Bellavista Avenue in Santiago. Handicrafts include warm sweaters that are hand-dyed, spun, and knitted in southern Chile (it's cheaper to purchase them there) and ponchos, whose designs vary according to the region; the best ones are by the Mapuche artisans in and around Temuco and by the Chilote women on the islands of Chiloé, off the coast from Puerto Montt. Thick wool blankets are woven in Chiloé but are heavy to carry, as are the figures of reddish clay from Pomaire and the famous black clay of Quinchamalí, available at most crafts fairs. Santiago artisans are increasingly sophisticated, and you can find earrings, rings, and necklaces to please virtually every taste. Several towns specialize in wicker, particularly Chimbarongo (about an hour's drive from Santiago) and Chiloé, where baskets and woven effigies of that island's mythical figures abound.

Telephones

Local Calls

There are two kinds of phones for local calls. The large yellow phones require a 50-peso piece; you then dial in the usual way and will have three minutes to complete your call before a tone warns you to insert another 50 pesos or be cut off. The large metallic phones are called "intelligent," which means you can insert varying amounts of money and make several calls in succession, provided you don't hang up in between: there's a special button to push that cuts off one call and starts another. The intelligent phone also includes English-language instructions. Most city areas have standing phone booths, but phones are also found at restaurants and even newsstands. You may have to wait several seconds after picking up the receiver before a steady humming sound signals that you may dial. After dialing, you'll hear a characteristic beep-beep repeatedly as your call goes through; then there's a pause, followed by a long tone signaling that the other phone is ringing. A busy sound is similar but repeats itself with no pause in between.

Long-Distance and International Calls

In 1994 a multicarrier phone system was introduced in Chile, a development that has led to radical reductions in prices of long-distance calls. To dial an international number directly from a private phone, you first dial the number of the carrier you want to use (**Entel,** dial 123; **CTC,** dial 188; **Chilesat,** dial 171; **Bellsouth,** dial 181), then dial 0, followed by the country code, the area or city code, and the phone number. Price differences among the carriers are small.

For long-distance operator service, you must still choose one of the carrier codes before dialing. The national long-distance operator number is 122 or 123 and the international operator is 183. The latter is a bilingual service. AT&T, MCI, and Sprint have direct-calling programs. To reach **AT&T,** dial 123–00–0311; service may not available from pay phones. For **MCI,** dial 188–00, wait for the tone, then dial 0316. For **Sprint,** dial 181–00–0317.

Reduced rates to most places apply after 6 PM and on Sunday and holidays. Most hotels charge extra for long-distance calls made from your room. You may find it less expensive to use a phone center; they are centrally located in all major towns and cities.

Tipping

The usual tip in restaurants is 10%, more if you really liked the service. City taxi drivers don't usually expect a tip, because most own their cabs. If you hire a taxi to take you around a city, you should consider a good tip.

When to Go

Chile's seasons are the reverse of North America's—that is, June–August is Chile's winter. Tourism peaks during the hot summer months of January and February, except in Santiago, which tends to empty as most Santiaguinos head for the coast. Though prices are at their highest, it's worth braving the summer heat if you're interested in lying on the beach or enjoying the many concerts, folklore festivals, and outdoor theater performances offered during this period.

If you're heading for the Lake District or Patagonia and want good weather without the crowds, the shoulder seasons of December and March are the months to come; those planning to visit the Atacama Desert should arrive in late spring, preferably in November, when temperatures are bearable and air clarity is at its peak. In spring Santiago blooms, and the fragrance of the flowers will distract even the most avid workaholic. A second tourist season occurs in the Chilean winter, as skiers flock to Chile's mountaintops for some of the world's best skiing, available at the height of northern summers. Winter smog is a good reason to stay away from Santiago during July and August, unless you're coming for a ski holiday and won't be spending much time in the city.

Climate

Chile's climate is agreeable and, given the country's enormous length, varied. The north enjoys the extremes of desert weather, with hot, dry days and freezing nights, except on the coast, where the ocean moderates, providing a mild climate year-round. Santiago has hot summers, cool springs and falls, and very gray, smoggy winters. Farther south, in the Lake District, you should be prepared for hot days, cold nights, and rainstorms. And even farther south, in Punta Arenas, summer temperatures are seldom higher than 20°C (68°F), and you'll contend with snow and icy winds in winter.

The following are the average daily maximum and minimum temperatures for Santiago.

Jan.	85F	29C	May	65F	18C	Sept.	66F	19C
	53	12		41	5		42	6
Feb.	84F	29C	June	58F	14C	Oct.	72F	22C
	52	11		37	3		45	7
Mar.	80F	27C	July	59F	15C	Nov.	78F	26C
	49	9		37	3		48	9
Apr.	74F	23C	Aug.	62F	17C	Dec.	83F	28C
	54	7		39	4		51	11

The following are the average daily maximum and minimum temperatures for Punta Arenas.

Jan.	58F	14C	May	45F	7C	Sept.	46F	8C
	45	7		35	2		35	2
Feb.	58F	14C	June	41F	5C	Oct.	51F	11C
	44	7		33	1		38	3
Mar.	54F	12C	July	40F	4C	Nov.	54F	12C
	41	5		31	0		40	4
Apr.	50F	10C	Aug.	42F	6C	Dec.	57F	14C
	39	4		33	1		43	6

7 Colombia

Scattered from the peaks of the Andes to the foothills, Colombia's cities have nurtured customs and ways of life as disparate as their elevations—from the Old World formality of high Bogotá to the Caribbean charm of sea-level Cartagena—creating a potpourri of music, cuisine, costumes, dialects, and attitudes that is much of the nation's charm.

By Tom Quinn
and Philip
Eade

Updated by
Krishna
Kandeth

COLOMBIA, LAND OF EMERALDS and coffee, is blessed with more than its fair share of natural splendors. It faces two oceans, the Atlantic and the Pacific, and its fertile soils and varied climates are home to more plant and animal species than almost anywhere else on the planet. In Colombia, it's possible to jump on a plane and, less than an hour later, find yourself awed by a different dramatic landscape—be it the cobblestone streets of a weathered colonial port, the stalls of a crowded market where Indian sellers still speak the tongues of the ancient Chibcha and Inca, or a cluster of snow-covered volcanoes rising sharply from the steamy coastal plain.

Bogotá, Colombia's sprawling capital, stands on a vast plateau in the eastern Andes, commanding views over an olio of farms, suburban apartments, and shantytown ghettoes. Poverty and drug-related violence are facts of life in Bogotá, but there are sides to this city of 6 million rarely covered in the international press: elegant shopping streets, grand high-rise office towers, and chic La Zona Rosa nightclubs where young and stylish Bogotaños gather to watch the sunrise. Bogotá's other surprise is La Candeleria, the colonial old city, with its narrow streets and thick-walled mansions.

The western half of Colombia, traversed by the central ridge of the Andes, the Cordillera Central, is where the majority of the country's 33 million people live. As you begin your ascent of the mighty Andes, subtropical valleys give way to rigid, fern-carpeted mountains where ever-present mists are brightened only by the votive candles placed by truck drivers in roadside shrines. Heading west from Bogotá, you pass quiet Indian villages hugging the hillsides before reaching Medellín, home to the notorious Medellín drug cartel. Despite its reputation, Medellín is safe and strikingly beautiful, surrounded by velvety green hills and miles of lush farmland. Continuing south, the Pan-American Highway meanders through dramatic mountain landscapes before making its descent into Cali and colonial Popayán, famous across the continent for its Holy Week festival.

If you feel like lounging in the sun, Colombia has some of the best beaches on the continent. In particular, the resort islands of San Andrés and Providencia, separated from the mainland by more than 400 miles of Pacific Ocean, are where Colombians escape to sunbathe, swim, and shop in the shadow of palm trees and thatched waterfront bars. Back on the mainland, Cartagena, widely revered as the most striking colonial city in South America, makes an excellent base for forays along the Caribbean Coast.

Before the arrival of the Spanish, Colombia was sparsely inhabited by indigenous Indian tribes. In the high basins of the Andes, the most powerful of these tribes was the Chibcha, whose master goldsmiths may have sparked the El Dorado myth with their exquisite creations and their tradition of anointing a chief each year by rolling him in gold dust. The Chibchas had given up this custom long before the first Europeans landed on Colombian shores, but the legend lingered and drove a host of New World adventurers in search of gilded cities paved with gold.

The Spanish settled parts of Panama as early as 1510. But it was not until Rodrigo de Bastidas founded the Colombian port of Santa Marta, in 1525, that a permanent settlement was established. Explorers like Gonzalo Jiménez de Quesada were soon driving deep inland, plundering and pillaging as they went. Quesada reached Bogotá in 1535 and, after

Colombia

Caribbean Sea

0 _____ 200 miles
0 _____ 300 km

N

← SAN ANDRÉS AND
PROVINDENCIA ISLANDS

GUAJIRA

Riohacha

Sta. Marta
Barranquilla   PARQUE
                                TAYRONA
Cartagena   La Ciudad Perdida
Islas del   El Rodadero
Rosario   CESAR
           MAGDALENA
           SUCRE   Lago
                                       de
                         Mompós   Maracaibo
         Magangué

PANAMA   CORDOBA   VENEZUELA

Gulf
of   ANTIOQUIA   NORTE DE
Panama   SANTANDER
                  BOLIVAR
                                              Bucaramanga
Pan   ARAUCA
American   Medellin   SANTANADER
Hwy.   Orinoco R.
        RISARALDA   BOYACA
PACIFIC   CALDAS   Tunja   CASANARE
OCEAN   CHOCO   CUNDINAMARCA   VICHADA
        QUINDIO   Bogotá
                            Meta R.
Buenaventura   TOLIMA   Villavicencio
            Buga   COLOMBIA
        VALLE Palmira   Guaviare R.
           Cali   GUANINIA
        CAUCA   HUILA   META
Popayan   Silvia   GUAVIARE
                     San Agustin
NARIÑO   VAUPES
Ipiales   CAQUETA
         PUTUMAYO

        Quito   Caquetá R.
ECUADOR   AMAZONAS
                                        BRAZIL
                Napo R.
        PERU   Amazon
                River

Caracas

Pacific Ocean
Cauca R.
Magdalena R.
CORDILLERA CENTRAL

quickly dispatching the local Chibcha Indians, decided he had found a striking location for his Spanish settlement.

Despite their near extinction, Colombia's Indian cultures have left a lasting mark on the country. The extraordinary carved stones at San Agustín, in southwestern Colombia, speak of Indian empires once rich in gold, emeralds, and the technological skills necessary to erect massive temples to long-forgotten gods. In the Andes and on the coastal plains, you'll find modern descendants of these lost tribes living a simple, traditional life that hasn't changed all that much since Columbus presumptuously claimed Colombia in the name of King Ferdinand of Spain.

BOGOTÁ

Santa Fé de Bogotá, as it is officially named, is a city of many faces—a city of ostentatious wealth and shocking poverty, and the home of a people as heterogenous as the country itself. On the one hand there is ultramodern Bogotá, a city of futuristic glass towers and elegant shopping centers. Then there is historic Bogotá, a rich assemblage of colonial mansions grandly conceived by the Spanish and built by Indian slaves with plundered gold. Finally, there is Bogotá the metropolis that never sleeps, a city of nearly six million people that has grown twenty-fold in the past 50 years. This immense urban sprawl suffers the typical growing pains of a modern South American city, and a few uniquely its own: a collapsed transport system, chronic air pollution, squalid shantytowns, and a scurrilous drug trade responsible for the recent spate of political bombings.

Spanish conquistadors built their chain of cities in South America in magnificent locations, and Bogotá, which stands on a high plane in the eastern Andes, is no exception. During his disastrous search for the legendary El Dorado, Gonzalo Jiménez de Quesada, the Spanish explorer on whom Cervantes reputedly modelled Don Quixote, was struck by the area's natural splendor and its potential for colonization. Though it is a mere 1,288 kilometers (800 miles) from the equator, Bogotá's 8,500-foot altitude lends it a refreshing, bracing climate. Jiménez de Quesada failed to find the elusive City of Gold, but he did discover one of South America's most advanced pre-Columbian peoples, the Chibcha. Despite their great skills as goldsmiths, the Chibcha were no match for the Spaniards: On August 6, 1538, Quesada christened his new conquest Santa Fé de Bogotá, in honor of the razed Chibcha village of Bacatá.

Bogotá rapidly established itself as an important administrative center and during 1740 was crowned the capital of New Granada, an area comprising modern Colombia, Venezuela, Panama, and Ecuador. Because of the city's status, grand civic and religious buildings began to spring up, often with the hand-carved ceilings and sculpted doorways that were the hallmark of New Granada architecture. Nevertheless, by 1900 Bogotá was still only a city of 100,000. It was not until the 1940s that rapid industrialization and the consequent peasant migration spurred Bogotá's exponential growth.

Visitor Information

Corporacion Nacional de Turismo (El Dorado airport, ☎ 1/413–8292).

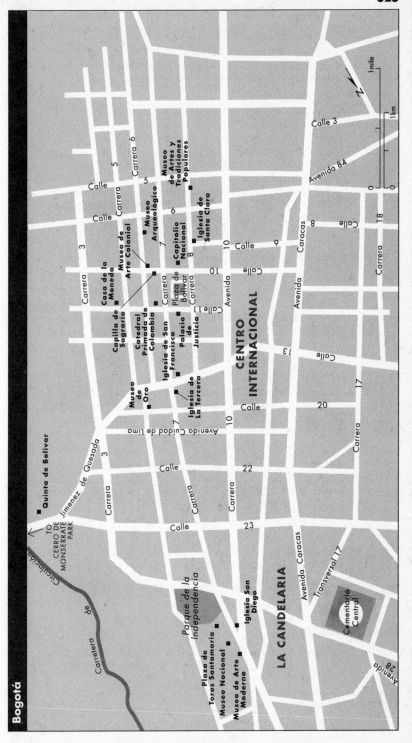

Bogotá

Calle 3

Avenida 84

1 mile

1 km

Carrera 6

Carrera 5

5

Calle 5

Museo de Artes y Tradiciones Populares

Calle

Museo Arqueológico

Iglesia de Santa Clara

Calle

6

Carrera 3

Museo de Arte Colonial

Capitolio Nacional

Calle 10

18

Caracas

8

Calle

Carrera

Carrera

Casa de la Moneda

7

8

Calle 10

Calle 9

Capilla de Sagraria

Carrera

Plaza de Bolívar

Avenida

Avenida

Carrera

CENTRO INTERNACIONAL

Catedral Primada de Colombia

Carrera

Calle 11

13

Calle

Palacio de Justicia

Iglesia de San Francisco

17

Museo de Oro

Iglesia de La Tercera

Calle

20

Avenida Ciudad de Lima

7

Calle 10

Carrera

Quinta de Bolívar

3

Calle

22

Jiménez de Quesada

Carrera

Carrera

Carrera

TO CERRO DE MONSERRATE PARK

Calle

23

Avenida Caracas

Circulación

Parque de la Independencia

Transversal 17

LA CANDELARIA

de

Carretera

Plaza de Toros Santamaría

Iglesia San Diego

Cementerio Central

Museo Nacional

Avenida 28

Museo de Arte Moderno

Arriving and Departing

By Plane
Aeropuerto El Dorado, a 20-minute taxi ride from downtown Bogotá, is served by some foreign and all major domestic carriers, including **Avianca, Intercontinental de Aviación, Aces,** and **AIRES.**

By Bus
The new **Terminal de Transportes** (Calle 33B No. 69–13, ☎ 1/295–1100) is served by all major bus companies. To reach the station, catch any bus traveling Carrera 13 with a sign marked TERMINAL, or take a taxi from downtown for less than $4. Dependable carriers for coastal destinations include **Copetrán** (Calle 33B No. 69–13, ☎ 1/263–2102) and **Omega** (Carrera 17 No. 15–71, ☎ 1/341–4056 or 1/341–8618). For Medellín and the interior regions contact **Flota Magdalena** (Calle 33B No. 69–35, office 225, ☎ 1/295–0651), **Flota La Macarena** (☎ 1/295–0539 or 1/295–1602), or **Expreso Bolivariano** (☎ 1/295–1200), all of which have agents at the Terminal de Transportes.

Getting Around Bogotá

By Car
The main international car-rental companies in Bogotá are **Avis** (El Dorado airport, ☎ 1/413–9500, ext. 2147; Av. 15 No. 101–45, ☎ 1/610–4810), **Hertz** (El Dorado airport, ☎ 1/413–9302; Av. 15 No. 107–24, ☎ 1/214–4228 or 1/214–9745), or **National** (Calle 100 No. 14–46, ☎ 1/612–5635 or 1/620–0055).

By Bus
Buses, mainly noisy, ancient, and driven at top speed, are divided into two categories: *busetas,* which cost 250 pesos per ride, and the larger and more comfortable *ejecutivos,* which cost 380 pesos per ride. Buses 7, 13, and 15 cross the city from north to south along *carreras* (roads) of the same numbers; *calles* (streets) in Bogotá run east–west.

By Taxi
Taxis are required by law to have meters—make sure they are used. The minimum charge is 700 pesos, plus 10 pesos per 260 feet. Fares increase by 30% after dark; a list of surcharges should be displayed. Taxis with bilingual drivers can be hired by the hour or for a full day at the Hotel Tequendama (*see* Lodging, *below*).

By Colectivo
Colectivo service, a cross between a taxi and a bus, is operated by surprisingly modern minibuses that, because of their size, are often able to get through traffic jams better than buses. Colectivos, which travel the same routes as buses, cost the same as ejecutivos but are a good deal more cramped.

Tour Operators
The **Tierra Mar y Aire** travel agency offers bus tours of the city, both by day and by night, for about $25 per person. *Carrera 7 No. 35–20,* ☎ *1/288–2088 or 1/288–1888. Closed Mon.*

Exploring Bogotá
Bogotá's oldest neighborhood, the Candelaria district, at the foot of Monserrate Peak, is packed with colonial churches and museums. To the north is the seedy downtown area, which nevertheless has a handful of fairly decent bars and restaurants. Farther uptown and marked

by towering office buildings is the Centro Internacional, the financial heart of the city. This modern development, built largely in the 1970s and now showing its age, is fringed by the Parque de la Independencia, a welcome area of green in Bogotá's urban landscape. The city becomes much smarter after Calle 72 (Av. Chile), and 10 blocks later you come to the leafy Zona Rosa, a popular boutique- and tavern-filled district.

La Candelaria

La Candelaria is where you will find the city's largest concentration of colonial mansions and churches. **La Plaza del Chorro del Quevedo,** an attractive little square surrounded by low whitewashed colonial buildings, is where Quesada and his soldiers celebrated the founding of Bogotá on August 6, 1538. In the center of the square stands a small fountain that recalls the "Chorro del Quevedo," the mythical brook where the conquistadors quenched their thirst and that today has been prosaically confined to subterranean drainage pipes.

From here it is only a short walk to **Plaza de Bolívar,** the most important historical point in the city. It was here that the formal founding of Bogotá took place in the presence of Spanish potentates. Dominating the square is the graceful **Catedral Primada de Colombia** (Cathedral of the Primate of Colombia), with its elegant French Baroque facade built from locally mined sandstone. Begun in 1565, it was not completed until nearly three centuries later due to a series of misfortunes—including the disastrous earthquake of 1785. The large windows give the immense interior a light and airy feel, even on one of Bogotá's many gray days. The ornate altar with gold leaf over heavily carved wood contrasts with the lack of ornamentation elsewhere. In one of the side chapels lies Quesada's tomb. ☛ *Free.* ⊙ *Mon.–Sat.*

Next door to the cathedral is one of the most important examples of religious architecture in Colombia, the late-17th-century **Capilla del Sagrario.** The exquisite canopied altar, a smaller version of that found at St. Peter's in Rome, would be reason enough for a visit. But the chapel also houses a splendid collection of paintings, including works by the Taller de Figueroa and Gregorio Vasquez. ☛ *Free.* ⊙ *Weekdays.*

At the square's southern end is the grand 19th-century **Capitolio Nacional,** where the national Congress sits. Behind this is the **Palacio de Nariño,** the Colombian "White House," rebuilt in 1949 following its destruction during a popular uprising in the capital. Each day at 5 PM the guard is changed with great pomp and ceremony. On the palace's northern side is the **Palacio de Justicia,** being rebuilt following its taking by guerrillas in November 1985.

Just around the corner look for the **Luis Angel Arango Cultural Center.** Of its several museums, the most interesting is the **Museo de Arte Religioso,** with rotating displays of colonial church art. Don't miss its two spectacular gold processional crosses, the Tunja and the Lechuga; the latter is encrusted with 1,600 emeralds. *Calle 11 No. 4–14,* ☎ *1/247–7200.* ☛ *Free.* ⊙ *Weekdays.*

The **Casa de la Moneda,** Colombia's former national mint, has a vast collection of coins; novelties include coins whose gold content was secretly reduced by the king of Spain, some made by revolutionaries from empty cartridges, and some made for use exclusively in Colombia's former leper colonies. At press time (winter 1995), the mint was temporarily closed for repair work. *Calle 11 No. 4–16,* ☎ *1/243–7200.* ☛ *Free.*

The **Museo Arqueológico** (Museum of Archaeology) occupies a magnificent mansion that once belonged to the Marquís of San Jorge, a colonial viceroy famous for his cruelty; on display today is a large collection of pre-Columbian ceramics. *Carrera 6 No. 7–43,* ☎ *1/282–0940.* ☛ *Entry fee.* ☉ *Tues.–Sun.*

The **Museo de Artes y Tradiciones Populares** (Museum of Art and Crafts) is housed in a former Augustinian cloister that dates back to 1583, making it one of the oldest surviving buildings in Bogotá. This is a good place to see a range of contemporary crafts made by Indian artisans from across the country. There is also a crafts shop and a good restaurant specializing in traditional Andes cooking. *Carrera 8 No. 7–21,* ☎ *1/284–5319 or 1/342–1266.* ☛ *Entry fee.* ☉ *Tues.–Sat.*

The simple, unadorned facade of the 17th-century **Iglesia de Santa Clara** gives no hint of the dazzling frescoes and wall reliefs—the work of nuns who were once cloistered here—that bathe the interior walls. Also inside is a small museum with paintings and sculpture by various 17th-century artists. *Carrera 8 No. 8–91,* ☎ *1/341–1009.* ☛ *Free. To arrange English-language tours, call 1/341–6017 or 1/284–1373.* ☉ *Weekday mornings.*

Between Plaza de Bolívar and the encroaching mountains, a network of narrow streets contains Bogotá's finest colonial mansions—thickwalled, refined, and austere, with heavily carved doorways, tiled roofs, and wide eaves. A good example south of the plaza is the **Museo de Arte Colonial** (Museum of Colonial Art), housed in a grand 17th-century Andalusian-style mansion. On display inside is a substantial collection of colonial art, including paintings by Vasquez and Figueroa, plus 17th- and 18th-century furniture and precious metalwork. *Carrera 6 No. 9–77,* ☎ *1/284–1373.* ☛ *Entry fee.* ☉ *Tues.–Sun.*

North of the plaza on Carrera 7 are two equally imposing colonial monuments. The first you'll encounter is the 16th-century **Iglesia de San Francisco** (Av. Jiménez at Carrera 7), famous for its fabulous Mudéjar interior, carved with intricate linear designs borrowed from the Islamic tradition. Also note the huge gilded altar, shaped like an amphitheater with shell-top niches. A short walk away is the equally elaborate **Iglesia de La Tercera** (Carrera 7 at Calle 16). The natural mahogany carvings on the altar, lauded as the most beautiful in Bogotá, are said to have so used up artist Pablo Caballero's artistic capacities that he died a madman.

Bogotá's phenomenal **Museo de Oro** (Gold Museum) contains the most comprehensive collection of pre-Columbian gold artifacts anywhere in the world. The collection consists of more than 36,000 pieces (by weight alone worth $200 million) culled over the centuries—often by force—from indigenous pre-Columbian cultures, including the Muisca, Nariño, Calima, and Sinú. Don't make the mistake of thinking of these treasures as primitive—they represent virtually all the techniques of modern gold making. Most of the gold—as well as one of the largest uncut emeralds in the world—is stored in a strong room on the top floor. Tours in English are given daily at 10:15 AM and 12:15 PM. *Calle 16 No. 5–41,* ☎ *1/342–1111 ext. 4545.* ☛ *Entry fee.* ☉ *Tues.–Sat.*

Centro Internacional

The **Iglesia San Diego,** a simple double-nave church built by Franciscan monks at the beginning of the 17th century, once stood on a quiet hacienda on the outskirts of colonial Bogotá; today trees and pastureland have been replaced with the towering offices of Bogotá's "little Manhattan," the Centro Internacional. Nonetheless, the church houses a very beautiful statue of the Virgin of the Fields, with a crown made of intricate filigree work in gold and silver. *Carrera 7 No. 26–37,* ☎ *1/341–2476.* ☛ *Free.* ☽ *Sun.–Fri.*

Nestled at the foot of Cerro de Monserrate (*see* Excursions from Bogotá, *below*) is **Quinta de Bolívar,** the charming rustic country house where Simón Bolívar, the Creole general who drove the Spanish from the northern half of the continent, passed the last years of his life with his mistress, Mañuela Saenz. Built in 1800, it was donated to Bolívar in 1820 in gratitude for his services to the fledgling republic. The house has a distinct Spanish flavor and is set in a lovely garden. *Calle 20 No. 3–23,* ☎ *1/284–6819.* ☛ *Entry fee.* ☽ *Tues.–Sun.*

Plaza de Toros Santamaría is Bogotá's bullring, designed by the Spaniard Lazcano in traditional Andalusian style. The best time to visit is in the morning, when you often can see young matadors polishing their skills. The main season only runs January through February, but small fights with local *toreros* (bullfighters) are held throughout the year. On the grounds, the **Museo Taurino** has exhibits devoted to bullfighting. *Carrera 7 at Calle 26.* ☛ *Free.* ☽ *Mon.–Sat. mornings.*

The **Museo de Arte Moderno** (Museum of Modern Art), housed in a beautifully designed building whose large windows give it a marvelous sense of spaciousness, has a strong permanent collection of contemporary Colombian art as well as rotating exhibitions of national and international artists. The museum bookshop stocks a wide range of (rather pricey) English-language titles on Colombian and international painters. *Calle 24 No. 6–00,* ☎ *1/286–0466.* ☛ *Entry fee.* ☽ *Tues.–Sun.*

The striking **Museo Nacional** (National Museum), designed by English architect Thomas Reed, housed a prison until its conversion in 1946; some parts of the museum, particularly the narrow galleries on the top floor, still have a sinister feel. On display is a mixed bag of pre-Columbian to contemporary art. The highlight is probably the third-floor collection of works by well-known 19th- and 20th-century Colombian artists—including Enrique Grau, Alejandro Obregón, Fernando Botero, and Andrés Santamaría, among others. *Carrera 7 No. 28–66,* ☎ *1/334–8366.* ☛ *Entry fee.* ☽ *Tues.–Sun.*

Shopping

Bogotá's shops and markets stock all types of leather and pure wool goods appropriate for life on the high plains. Handwoven *ruanas* (ponchos) are particularly popular; the oil in the wool makes them almost impervious to rain. Colombian artisans also have a way with straw: *Toquilla,* a tough native fiber, is used to make a dizzying variety of hats, shoes, handbags, and even umbrellas.

Specialty Shops
ANTIQUES
Antiques shops are found mainly in the districts of Chapinero and Chicó, in the north of the city; one of the best is **Medina's** (Carrera 7 at Calle 50). On Plaza de Bolívar, **Cancino Sisters** (Calle 63 No. 9–54, ☎ 1/249–8056) is a good place not just for Colombian antiques but also for pieces originally brought from Europe by aristocratic Colombian families. Another good bet is **Jaime Botero's** (Calle 10 No. 2–57), housed in the 17th-century La Toma de Agua building.

CLOTHING

There is a good selection of fashionable but relatively expensive clothing at boutiques in the Zona Rosa, roughly between Calles 81 and 84 and Carreras 11 and 15.

EMERALDS

Seventy percent of the world's emerald supply is mined in Colombia, but unless you know how to spot a fake you should buy only from reputable dealers, who provide certificates of authenticity. **Kawai** (Carrera 9 No. 99–02–P8, ☎ 1/618–3070) and **W. K. Bronkie** (Carrera 9A No. 99–02, office 1203, ☎ 1/211–4621) are well known. **H. Stern** (Tequendama Hotel, Carrera 7 No. 32–16, ☎ 1/232–9874) sells gold and gems. **Sterling Joyeros** (Calle 11 No. 68B–43, ☎ 1/262–6700) offers factory tours that give you a chance to see stones being cut, polished, and mounted.

HANDICRAFTS

In the cloister of Las Aquas, **Artesanías de Colombia** (Carrera 3 No. 18–60, ☎ 1/286–1766) stocks an excellent variety of high-quality handmade crafts—from straw umbrellas to handwoven ponchos. Also try **El Cacique** (Carrera 7 No. 3–40). The shop at the **Museo de Artes y Tradiciones Populares** (Carrera 8 No. 7–21, ☎ 1/342–1266) carries various handicrafts.

POTTERY

Pre-Columbian pottery can be found in several shops in the Centro Internacional; try **Precolombianos San Diego** (Carrera 10 No. 27–51, int. 167) or **Galeria Cano** (Carrera 13 No. 27–98, int. 1–19).

Markets

In the warren of stalls at the **Pasaje Rivas** market (Carrera 10 at Calle 10) look for bargain-priced ponchos, blankets, leather ware, and crafts. The **Mercado de Pulgas,** which sprawls northward along Carrera 3 from Calle 19, is a good place for bargain hunting on Sunday. Consider taking a taxi from downtown, and don't linger long after dark: The surrounding neighborhood has an unsavory reputation.

Shopping Center

The massive **Unicentro Shopping Center** (Av. 15 No. 123–30, ☎ 1/213–8800) in Bogotá's affluent northern quarter is one of the largest in South America and has a vast selection of crafts and specialty shops.

Sports

Bullfighting

Bullfights are held every weekend in January and February and at least once a month the rest of the year at the **Plaza de Santamaría,** near Parque de la Independencia.

Soccer

Soccer or *futbol* matches are held on most Sundays at 3:45 PM and Wednesdays at 8 PM at the **Estadio Municipal** (Municipal Stadium), near the Hipódromo del Techo; and at the **El Campín** stadium. Tickets can be bought from Cigarrería Bucana (Calle 18 No. 5–92). There is no need to book in advance except when there's a match between the two most popular local teams—Santa Fé and Millionarios.

Dining

The Bogotá yellow pages list more than 1,000 restaurants, and the best offer first-class service and outstanding Colombian cuisine. Bogotá's most traditional recipes aim to fill the belly and ward off the cold. Probably the most common dish on local menus is *ajiaco,* a thick soup with chicken and several types of potato, garnished with fresh coriander, capers, and sour cream. Another popular soup is *puchero,* with chicken, pork, beef, potato, yucca, cabbage, corn, and plantain, accompanied by rice and avocado. Bogotáños like to start the day off with chocolate *santafereño,* a steaming cup of chocolate accompanied by a slab of cheese—you are meant to melt the cheese in the chocolate.

Bogotáños have lunch between noon and 2. Restaurants open for dinner around 7, and the more expensive ones stay open until after midnight. For price categories, *see* Dining *in* Colombia Essentials, *below.*

Colombian

$$$ **Carbón de Palo.** This is Bogotá's premier grilled meat restaurant and
★ a favorite meeting place of senior politicians and plutocrats. Huge cooked-to-order beefsteaks (chicken or pork if you prefer) and excellent salads are served up with great aplomb in a delightful indoor patio full of hanging plants. On weekends, musicians serenade guests with traditional Colombian rancheros country music. ✕ *Av. 19 No. 106–12,* ☎ *1/214–0450. Reservations advised. AE, MC, V.*

$$ **Andrés Carne de Res.** This is a popular restaurant among Bogotáños who enjoy hearty Colombian fare in a rural, relaxed setting. The atmosphere is bohemian, with fittings ranging from auto parts (the ashtrays) to valuable Vasquez statues. Try a succulent steak or braised chicken accompanied by potatoes, fried yucca, and *patacon* (fried plantain). ✕ *Carrera 18 No. 109A–20, on road to Chia,* ☎ *1/214–4480. Reservations advised. AE, MC, V.*

French

$$$$ **Casa Medina.** Chef Ernest Reuter prepares outstanding French cuisine
★ that's unrivaled anywhere in Colombia. Try the medallions of trout bathed in fennel and onion or the excellent *coquilles St. Jacques* (scallops) with asparagus. Each of the elegant dining rooms evokes a different European country, strewn as they are with antique heirlooms brought over from the Old World by aristocratic Bogotáño families. ✕ *Carrera 7 No. 69A–22,* ☎ *1/217–0288,* 𝔽𝔸𝕏 *1/212–6668. Reservations advised. AE, MC, V.*

International

$$ **Crepes and Waffles.** Smartly dressed waiters rush to serve you a tasty selection of stuffed pancakes and waffles. With its wide variety of ice creams and its junior menu, this eatery is also a good place for families. ✕ *Carrera 11 No. 85–79,* ☎ *1/610–5298. AE, MC, V.*

$ **Intermezzo.** Based in a fine old brick home in the distinguished Chap-
★ inero neighborhood, Intermezzo has a graceful dining room and a pleasant adjoining sun room that's perfect for relaxed lunches. Chef and co-owner Luis Alberto Gonzalez has traveled the world picking up culinary cues from the French, Germans, Swiss, Italians, and North Americans. The cooking is essentially "nouveau," heavy on the vegetables, light on the oils. Particularly worthwhile is the *Schnecken mit Krauterbutter,* imported snails prepared in a delicate herb-butter sauce. ✕ *Calle 69 No. 10–85,* ☎ *1/248–9845. No credit cards.*

Italian

$ **El Patio.** None of the cutlery or plates match and the small dining room is a little cramped, but that simply adds to the charm of this eccentric Italian restaurant in the bohemian La Macarena neighborhood, a couple of blocks up from the bullring. Try one of the masterful salads, or the veal Parmesan. ✕ *Carrera 4A No. 27–86,* ☎ *1/282–6141. No credit cards. Closed Sun.*

Mexican

$$$ Harry's Cantina. This stylish restaurant and bar, in the heart of the glitzy Zona Rosa, is definitely the "in" place to eat and drink in Bogotá. Glitterati come here as much to see and be seen as for any other reason, although Harry's selection of Mexican food is wide—and the enchiladas and tacos are particularly good. Don't miss the potent *feijoa* margarita, made with tequila and fresh Colombian fruit. ✗ *Carrera 12A No. 83–11,* ☎ *1/257–4053. Reservations advised. AE, MC, V.*

Seafood

$$$$ La Fragata. With its slowly revolving dining room, this is probably the most striking of the capital's Fragata ("frigate") chain restaurants. And believe it or not, the dimly lit and dark oak wood interior successfully conveys the atmosphere of a 19th-century sailing ship. The lobster, crab, red snapper, and locally caught rainbow trout are satisfying but slightly overshadowed by the service and presentation. ✗ *Calle 100 No. 8A–55, 12th Floor,* ☎ *1/222–8806. Reservations advised. AE, MC, V. Closed Sun.*

Lodging

The standard of accommodation in Bogotá is quite high: Private bathrooms are standard features, and all but the very cheapest hotels have hot water. Bogotá's better hotels are in the leafy, very wealthy northern districts—undoubtedly one of the most pleasant parts of the city and also the safest (there are security guards quite literally on every corner). If you want to soak up the color of the bustling downtown area, look into the handful of picturesque places to stay in the historic La Candelaria neighborhood. No matter where you stay, avoid walking unescorted at night. For price categories, *see* Lodging *in* Colombia Essentials, *below.*

$$$$ Bogotá Royal. Besides offering spacious rooms with good views, cable TV, and excellent room service, the Royal is strategically located in Bogotá's World Trade Center on the tree-lined Avenida 100, a short taxi ride from both the airport and downtown. ☎ *Av. 100 No. 8A–01,* ☎ *1/218–9810,* FAX *1/218–3362. 144 rooms. Restaurant, 3 bars, sauna, exercise room. AE, MC, V.*

$$$$ Hotel Charleston. Just east of downtown is the very elegant and well-maintained Charleston, one of the few hotels in Bogotá where spacious suite accommodations are not exorbitantly priced. Plan on a short taxi ride to downtown sites. ☎ *Carrera 13, No. 85–46,* ☎ *1/218–0605,* FAX *1/236–7981. 30 rooms. Restaurant, bar. AE, MC, V.*

$$$$ Hotel Tequendama. This is one of Bogotá's oldest and most refined lux-
★ ury hotels, boasting a gym and casino as well as an impressive complex of boutiques and shops on the ground floor. Its central location—just five minutes by taxi from the Centro Internacional—makes it a popular choice with business travelers. Its large rooms lack real character but have impressive views of the city. ☎ *Carrera 10 No. 26–21,* ☎ *1/ 286–1111,* FAX *1/282–2860. 800 rooms. 2 restaurants, 2 bars, room service, beauty salon, sauna, exercise room, casino. AE, MC, V.*

$$$ Los Urapanes. At this intimate hotel in the heart of Zona Rosa, guests stay in modestly sized but luxurious suites with full room service and a minibar. The adjoining restaurant is popular for its exquisitely presented Colombian and international cuisine. ☎ *Carrera 13 No. 83–19,* ☎ *1/218–1188,* FAX *1/218–9294. 32 rooms. Restaurant, bar, minibars, room service. AE, MC, V.*

$$ El Presidente. You'll find the friendly El Presidente in a quiet, residential quarter just north of downtown; you'll need a taxi to reach La Candeleria and the bars and restaurants in Zona Rosa. Most suites and doubles have private bathrooms. ⊞ *Calle 23 No. 9–45,* ☎ *1/284–1100,* ℻ *1/284–5766. 160 rooms, some with bath. Restaurant, bar. MC, V.*

$$ ★ **Las Terrazas.** Despite its downtown location, this small hotel has an almost rustic charm about it, partly because it is built into the hillside overlooking the city. The scrupulously clean rooms come in various sizes and have good views of downtown. A respectable adjoining restaurant serves Bogotá specialties as well as standard international fare. ⊞ *Calle 54A No. 3–12,* ☎ *1/255–6834. 33 rooms. Restaurant, room service. MC, V.*

$ **Hosteria de la Candelaria.** This small, friendly hotel occupies a 1920s mansion in the heart of the historic Candelaria district. The comfortably sized rooms are strewn with colonial antiques—the owners also run a small antiques business, so if anything takes your fancy you may be able to strike a deal. ⊞ *Calle 9 No. 3–11,* ☎ *1/342–1727,* ℻ *1/282–3420. 14 rooms. Restaurant. No credit cards.*

The Arts

Bogotá's reputation for random violence and muggings has not put a damper on its ebullient nighttime scene, which often lasts well beyond sunrise. People start the evening at the cinema or theater and continue on to one of many restaurants or bars (*see* Nightlife, *below*).

Theaters

Bogotá has a lively and well developed theater scene, though you must understand Spanish to appreciate it. Among the better-known theaters are **Teatro Popular de Bogotá** (Carrera 5 No. 14–71, ☎ 1/242–8406) and **Teatro la Candelaria** (Calle 12 No. 2–59, ☎ 1/281–4814), which earned itself international fame for its recent production of the play *Guadalupe Años Sin Cuenta,* about Colombia's bloody political turmoil in the 1950s. **Teatro Nacional** (Calle 71 No. 10–25, ☎ 1/211–9119) puts on musicals and popular comedies.

Nightlife

Bogotá's two main partying areas are the Zona Rosa, between Calles 81 and 84 and Carreras 11 and 15, and La Calera in the affluent northern part of the city, shortly before it becomes almost entirely residential. Downtown at the intersection of Carrera 5 and Calle 27 there's also a handful of popular salsa bars. Zona Rosa and La Calera are full of security guards and quite safe. Less so is the lively, bohemian downtown district, La Macarena, though you still should not have any problem if you travel by taxi and don't wander alone and aimlessly.

BARS AND NIGHTCLUBS

Bogotá's top nightspot is **Bahia** (Via La Calera km 4, ☎ 1/610–0208), a large and beautifully designed club spread over two floors. The view of Bogotá stretching away to the horizon from Calera Hill is reason enough for the trip. **Coconuts** (Calle 82 No. 12–50, ☎ 1/257–2006) is really a restaurant in nightclub clothing, though the huge patio that overlooks the street is a popular spot for drinks and chitchat. **Charlotte's** (Calle 82 No. 12–51, ☎ 1/257–3508) is a popular Zona Rosa nightclub, complete with an outdoor dance floor and blazing log fires to keep you warm.

Excursions from Bogotá

Cerro de Monserrate

You can get a good overview of the city from the top of **Monserrate Peak,** which looms menacingly over the downtown area. Although dense smog often obscures the skyline, the view of chaotic Bogotá stretching to the horizon is still breathtaking. The panorama extends from the Río Bogotá to the colonial city, whose red Spanish tiles make it easy to spot.

Getting There

A *teleférico* (cable car) runs from Monserrate Station near Quinta de Bolivia to the top of the peak weekdays 9–6 and Sundays 6–6. The only other alternative is making the hour-long walk up the winding footpath that parallels the cable car route; however, as weekday robberies are all too common, attempt this only on Sunday when the path is busy.

Tunja

Tunja, the capital of Boyacá province, was founded in 1539 by Captain Gonzalo Suárez Rendón. Although modern Tunja is infested with industry and shantytowns, the historic center retains some of its original colonial character, with its stately churches and pre-Republic mansions. Of the latter you can tour **Casa del Fundador Suárez Rendón** (Plaza Bolívar), with a small museum devoted to Tunja's founder, and **Casa de Don Juan de Vargas** (Calle 20 near Carrera 8, closed Mon.), which exhibits colonial artwork and paintings. Don Juan was a scribe and his large library of art books was probably the inspiration for much of the imagery of the ceiling frescoes.

Getting There

Tunja lies 137 kilometers (85 miles) northeast of Bogotá on the road to Cúcuta, near the Venezuelan border. Buses depart regularly from Bogotá's Terminal de Transporte, and the three- to four-hour bus ride costs less than $4 each way.

WESTERN COLOMBIA: MEDELLÍN AND CALI

West of Bogotá the Pan-American Highway drops sharply into the stifling heat of the Tierras Calientes, or hot lands, of the Magdalena Valley. Continuing southwest along the highway, the landscape becomes rigid and mountainous as you approach the central ridge of the Andes, the Cordillera Central. The whole area is wonderfully fertile; the province of Antioquia, in particular, lies like a gigantic garden around its capital, Medellín. This sprawling though somewhat isolated city is lodged in a narrow valley and encircled by lush and thickly wooded hills—hardly what you would expect from Colombia's second-largest and perhaps most notorious city in terms of its industrial heritage and modern drug trade.

The fertile Valle de Cauca (Cauca Valley), dominated by its young and lively capital, Cali, is the center of Colombian agriculture, though colonial architecture and Indian markets are what draw the bulk of visitors to the region. Farther south, the Pan-American Highway climbs toward the colonial village of Popayán and, even farther south, on to the Ecuadorian border. Western Colombia, and the southwest in particular, is a treasure house of indigenous culture; with just a little effort—and a sense of adventure—you can visit the enigmatic carved stones of San Agustín and primitive Guambiano and Paez Indian villages near Popayán.

Medellín

Medellín, the capital of Antioquia Province, stands neck and neck with Cali as Colombia's second-largest city, with a population of more than 2 million; it is also the country's main industrial beehive. But don't expect a sooty city full of smoking chimneys. Medellín is set in a lush sylvan valley at an altitude of 4,880 feet, and the deep-green mountains that rise sharply all around provide an attractive backdrop to the glass-and-concrete towers of its elegant financial district.

A dynamic industrial and commercial center, Medellíín is lauded as Latin America's "Convention Center." It has three respected universities and a large student population, not to mention a sober hardworking middle class. It is also home to the notorious Medellín cocaine cartel. Though the security forces have dealt important blows to the drug mafia, it is no less violent or unpredictable. Visitors are unlikely to have any problems, but you should be cautious about wandering around Medellín after dark and stick to central areas of the city.

Visitor Information

Oficina de Turismo (Calle 57 No. 45–129, ☎ 4/254–0800). **Turantioquia** (Carrera 48 No. 58–11, ☎ 4/254–3864) stocks maps and organizes a nighttime bus tour of the city on Friday.

Arriving and Departing

By Plane
Medellín's **Jose Maria Córdoba** airport, 38 kilometers (24 miles) southeast of the city, is served by **Avianca, Aces,** and **Sam.** The flight from Bogotá takes 30 minutes and costs $100; the flight from Cali lasts one hour and costs $80. Between the airport and downtown Medellín expect to pay $12 for a taxi, $3 for a colectivo bus.

By Car
A paved, two-lane highway opened just a few years ago, connecting Bogotá and Medellín via Manizales and Honda. The 560-kilometer (347-mile) journey takes about nine hours and passes through some beautiful cattle country in the Magdalena Valley. Although this is one of Colombia's major cocaine routes, the road is generally well patrolled and safe, and there are police controls around Honda. Watch out for landslides in wet weather, and expect detours and potholes on the Medellín–Honda leg.

By Bus
Medellín's long-distance bus station, **Terminal de Transporte Mariano Ospina Pérez,** is 3 kilometers (2 miles) northwest of the city center and has a cafeteria and information desk. Plan on a nine- to 12-hour trek between Bogotá and Medellín.

Exploring

Downtown
The best views of Medellín are from the top of **Cerro Nutibara** (Nutibara Hill), a smallish peak overlooking downtown, best reached by taxi (less than $3) from anywhere in the city center. At the very top is **Pueblito**

Paisa, a reconstructed traditional Antioquian village complete with a church, town hall, barbershop, school, and village store. Surrounding the pueblito is the **Parque de las Esculturas,** a maze of paths dotted with modern and traditional sculptures by Colombian and other Latin American artists. There is also an open-air theater, used mainly for rock concerts on Saturday night.

At the heart of downtown Medellín lies **Parque Bolívar,** a surprisingly generous open space for such a central area of the city. In the evenings, the park is popular with young people, who congregate on the steps of the Romantic-style **Catedral de Villanueva,** whose ornate coffee-color facade dominates the park and is one of Medellín's most striking buildings. Designed by Frenchman Charles Carré and begun in 1875, it is the largest cathedral in South America and the third-largest brick building in the world. ☛ *Free.* ☽ *Tues.–Sun.*

Three blocks south of Parque Bolívar lies the elegant **Parque Berrío.** Be sure to look for the huge female torso by Colombia's most famous sculptor, Fernando Botero, which stands to the left of the Banco de la Republica building. On the other side of the bank stands a bronze fountain and a marble monument dedicated to Atanasio Girardot, an 18th-century freedom fighter who helped gain Colombia its independence.

Just two blocks from the park you can admire the fine 18th-century facade of the **Ermita de la Veracruz.** The cool interior of the church, while a little disappointing, is nonetheless a pleasant place to escape from Medellín's noisy streets. *Calle 52 No. 52–18.* ☛ *Free.*

In the old mint building opposite the main post office is the **Museo de Antioquia,** which contains the world's largest collection of paintings and sculptures by Fernando Botero and other well-known Colombian artists. *Carrera 52A No. 51A–29,* ☎ *4/251–3636.* ☛ *Entry fee.* ☽ *Tues.–Sun.*

Around Town

The **Museo El Castillo,** in the nearby suburb of El Poblado, is considered the most elegant palace in Medellín. This 1930s gothic-style structure, whose beautiful French-style gardens comprise sweeping lawns and exuberant flower gardens, was once the home of one of Medellín's most powerful families. Their original belongings are on display along with furniture and art collected from around the world. *Calle 9 Sur No. 32–269,* ☎ *4/268–6040.* ☛ *Entry fee.* ☽ *9–noon, 2–5.*

For a gastronomic tour of Antioquia, come to Medellín's **Parque de las Delicias** (Delicacies Park) on the first Saturday of each month, when a wealth of small stalls do a brisk business in everything from *obleas* (thin jam-filled waffles) to *lechona* (roast stuffed pork). *Carrera 73 and Av. 39D.*

The **Jardín Botánico Joaquín Antonio Uribe,** in the suburbs 10 minutes north of Parque Bolívar by taxi, has more than 500 native plant species, an aviary with strikingly colored tropical birds, and a massive greenhouse teeming with orchids. *Carrera 52 No. 73–298,* ☎ *4/233–7025.* ☛ *Entry fee.* ☽ *Daily 9–5.*

Santa Fé de Antioquia

Eighty kilometers (50 miles) northwest of the city is the historic town of **Santa Fé de Antioquia,** founded in 1541 and the former capital of the region. The town is a colonial masterpiece with an extremely well-preserved downtown district brimming with cobbled streets and old whitewashed houses. It's also well known for its *orfebrería* (gold work). Visit the workshops clustered on Carrera 10 between the cathedral and the Bogotá River. There are daily buses from Medellín's Terminal de Transporte, or take a taxi (up to four people) for about $50.

Shopping

Medellín's **Centro Commercial San Diego** shopping mall (Calle 12 No. 30–5), near the Inter-Continental Hotel, offers a good selection of crafts, jewelry, and clothing shops. Both **El Arhuaco** (Calle 56A No. 49–80) and **La Piel** (Calle 53 No. 49–131) stock a wide range of high-quality Antioquian crafts. However, the most comprehensive selection of handmade Antioquian crafts is available at an **open-air crafts market** held on the first Saturday of each month at the Parque Bolívar.

Dining

Traditional Antioquian cooking means hearty peasant fare—plenty of meat, beans, rice, and potatoes. But Medellín is full of high-quality restaurants where you'll find a wide range of foreign as well as traditional Colombian cuisines. For price ranges, *see* Dining *in* Colombia Essentials, *below.*

$$$ Las Cuatro Estaciones. Medellín's most popular restaurant balances first-rate food and service with decor that might easily be mistaken for tacky. Choose one of four thematic dining rooms—one is decorated in a Colombian style, others in European, Asian, and Spanish styles—or simply close your eyes and concentrate on the meal at hand. The house specialty is seafood, and the paella regularly draws crowds of devoted locals. ✕ *Calle 17 No. 43–79, El Poblado,* ☎ *4/266–7120. AE, MC, V.*

$ La Aguacatala. Housed in a colonial-style mansion in the leafy hills of the exclusive El Poblado district, this charming roadside tavern offers a good selection of local dishes, including excellent chicken and fríjoles served by staff dressed in traditional Antioquian peasant garb. ✕ *Carrera 43A No. 8–24, El Poblado,* ☎ *3/114–4830. MC, V.*

Lodging

Medellín's better hotels are in the wealthy El Poblado district to the east of the city center. Downtown, and just a stone's throw away from most of the city's monuments, there are some quite respectable places to stay—but you should avoid walking around here late at night. For price ranges, *see* Lodging *in* Colombia Essentials, *below.*

$$$$ Hotel Nutibara. The Nutibara is not laid out on such a grand scale as the Inter-Continental (*below*), but nevertheless it is a luxurious and well-maintained complex, housed in a stylish 1930s-era building replete with a casino and heated indoor pool. Although the Nutibara is conveniently situated in the heart of downtown and is only a short taxi ride from Medellín's restaurants and bars, the immediate surrounding area is not particularly safe at night and should be avoided. ☎ *Calle 52A No. 50–46, Medellín,* ☎ *4/511–5111,* FAX *4/231–3713. 90 rooms. Restaurant, bar, café, indoor pool, hot tub, casino, dance club. AE, MC, V.*

$$$$ Inter-Continental. This spacious modern hotel just outside Medellín has spectacular views of the city. The services are what you would expect from an international chain, with several good restaurants, a disco and casino, as well as a large outdoor swimming pool. The hotel is about 20 minutes by taxi ($6) from the city center and 35 minutes from the airport. ☎ *Variante Las Palmas,* ☎ *4/266–0680,* FAX *4/266–1548; U.S.* ☎ *800/327–0200. 294 rooms. 3 restaurants, bar, café, pool, massage,* *sauna, putting green, 2 tennis courts, basketball, exercise room, Ping-Pong, volleyball, casino, dance club, baby-sitting. AE, MC, V.*

$$$ **Veracruz.** With many of the facilities of the five-star internationals, the Veracruz is nevertheless a good deal less expensive. Rooms in the newly built "diplomatic" wing are slightly more expensive than in the older part of the hotel and a little more spacious and luxurious. There is a small pool on the 11th floor with a panoramic view over the city. The Veracruz's restaurant is one of the best in Medellín. ☎ *Carrera 50 No. 54–18, Medellín,* ☎ *4/511–5511,* FAX *4/231–0542. 60 rooms. Restaurant, bar, café, indoor pool, sauna, Turkish bath. AE, MC, V.*

$$ **Ambassador.** In an uninspiring 1970s tower block, the four-star Ambassador is a good example of how Medellín's poor reputation has kept lodging prices in check. All rooms have a private bathroom and cable TV, and the hotel facilities are excellent even by international standards. The lobby restaurant also has a first-rate reputation. ☎ *Carrera 50 No. 54–50, Medellín,* ☎ *4/511–5311,* FAX *4/231–5312. 134 rooms. Restaurant, bar, pool, beauty salon, sauna, Turkish bath, travel agency. AE, MC, V.*

$ **Mariscal Robledo.** Housed in a lovely colonial-style mansion in the heart of Santa Fé de Antioquia's old quarter, this roomy hotel has a beautiful pool on a quiet patio surrounded by trees. Breakfast and lunch are included in the room rate. ☎ *Santa Fé de Antioquia,* ☎ *4/826–1111. 35 rooms, some with bath. Bar, pool. MC, V.*

Cali and Valle de Cauca

Cali is the economic center of Valle Province, responsible for a hefty portion of the country's sugar, coffee, and maize exports. Cali itself lies at the southern end of Cauca Valley at an elevation of more than 3,000 feet, contributing to the city's springlike temperatures and the lush tropical vegetation that encroaches upon its shantytown outskirts. Despite vertiginous expansion in the 20th century (the city has grown fourfold in the past 40 years), Cali is better planned than most Colombian industrial centers. Cali has few historical monuments, but its tree-lined avenues and lazy open-air cafés attract small throngs of foreigners, particularly during the Christmas–New Year feria, when the city unapologetically devotes itself to merrymaking.

Visitor Information

Corporacion Regional de Turismo del Valle de Cauca (Av. 4N No. 4N–10, Cali, ☎ 3/667–5612 or 3/660–5000).

Arriving and Departing

By Plane

Most domestic carriers offer regular connections between Bogotá and Cali's **Aeropuerto Alfonso Bonilla Aragón** (☎ 94/442–2624), 20 kilometers (12 miles) northeast of the city. The only international carrier based in Cali, **Avianca,** has daily flights to New York, Miami, and Panama. Taxis from the airport to the city cost about $10; minibuses that connect the airport and bus terminal depart every 10 minutes and cost $1.

By Car

Although fully paved, the highway between Bogotá and Cali is in poor condition. The 680-kilometer (422-mile) journey takes around 10 hours, and, being one of Colombia's major routes, is relatively safe. South of Armenia the Cali road joins with the Pan-American Highway and climbs the spectacular Quíndio Pass (10,990 feet) before diverging west toward the coast at Palmira.

By Bus

Cali's bus terminal is at Calle 30n No. 2a–29. It's a 10- to 13-hour trip between Bogotá and Cali, and 11–13 hours between Cali and Medellín.

Exploring

Cali

At the heart of Cali is the quiet **Plaza de Caicedo,** guarded by rows of tall palms and a statue of Joaquín Caicedo y Cuero, an 18th-century freedom fighter who liberated Cali from the Spanish. The plaza is skirted by the neoclassical **Catedral** (☛ Free; open Tues.–Sun.), with its massive limestone walls, marble columns, and brilliantly gilded main altar. Across from the cathedral is the Republican-period **Palacio Municipal** (City Hall), with minutely carved doors set within equally ornate arches. A first-floor **museum** has a small exhibition of 300 years of sugar growing and processing, for which Cali and Valle de Cauca are famous. *Plaza de Caicedo.* ☛ *Entry fee.* ☉ *Tues.–Sun.*

One block beyond is the 18th-century church and monastery of **San Francisco** (☛ Free), a post-colonial redbrick structure that's undistinguished except for its domed bell tower, which is lavished with dazzling multicolored mosaics. A few doors down, the **Torre Mudéjar** (Moorish Tower), a curious brick bell tower that looks like an Islamic temple, is considered one of the finest examples of Spanish-Moorish art in South America. *Carrera 6 at Calle 10.* ☛ *Free.* ☉ *Tues.–Sun.*

A short walk away is Cali's oldest church, **La Merced,** built in 1680 on the site where the city's founders celebrated their first mass in 1536. The adjoining convent houses two museums: the **Museo de Arte Colonial,** featuring the country's most complete collection of Vazquez y Ceballos religious paintings, and the **Museo Arqueológico,** which displays pre-Columbian pottery and a scale-model reproduction of Cali and its aboriginal inhabitants. *Carrera 4 at Calle 7.* ☛ *Entry fee.* ☉ *Tues.–Sat.*

Avenida Colombia runs mostly parallel to the languid Río Cali and is lined with colossal palm trees and flower-filled parks. Looming over the avenue is the imposing **Iglesia de la Ermita,** a striking white-and-red neo-Gothic creation, built between 1930 and 1948. Its rococo towers have been locally dubbed *"la torta matrimonial"* for their resemblance to tiered wedding cakes. *Av. Colombia at Calle 13.* ☛ *Free.* ☉ *Only for mass.*

There are spectacular views from the stubby range of mountains overlooking Cali. A popular scenic overlook is **Alto de los Cristales** (1,421 meters/4,660 feet), atop which is a monumental statue of Christ visible from miles around. You can take Bus 3 to Bellavista and then scramble uphill to the top, or take a taxi from downtown for around $5.

Valle de Cauca

CAÑASGORDAS

At Cañasgordas, a colonial hacienda set in the countryside an hour's drive from Cali, relics of Cali's last royal sheriff are preserved. Visitors can still see the high canopied beds reached by ladders and an intriguing Moorish system of rainwater canals that supplies both water and a primitive form of air-conditioning. Cañasgordas was also the set-

ting for *El Alférez Real,* a film by Eustaquio Palacios. *Via Tulua.* ☛
Entry fee. ☉ *Tues.–Sun.*

PALMIRA

In this beautifully preserved Colonial village 42 kilometers (26 miles)
northwest of Cali, you can hire a horse-drawn carriage for a tour of
the town's compact center. Palmira is dominated by the soaring 279-
foot-tall tower of its 17th-century **cathedral.** On Palmira's outskirts
look for the 18th-century **Hacienda de la Concepción,** one of the most
beautiful country houses in Valle Province, built by a sugar baron who
had an eye for colonial furnishings and rich detailing. Spanish-language
tours are given every hour or so. *Via Palmira.* ☛ *Entry fee.* ☉ *Tues.–Sun.*

BUGA

Because of its status as a national monument, Buga, 50 kilometers (31
miles) beyond Palmira, is chockablock with preserved 17th- and 18th-
century buildings. Of particular note are the **Iglesia de San Francisco,**
the **Catedral de San Pedro,** and the **Basilica del Señor de los Milagros,**
all within four blocks of Buga's peaceful main square.

POPAYÁN

Founded in 1537 by Sebastian de Belalcázar, Popayán quickly became
an important administrative center of the Viceroyalty of New Granada
because of its position on the Cartagena–Quito gold route. Testimony
to that importance are the town's many colonial buildings. A catas-
trophic earthquake on Good Friday, 1983, left the town nearly in
ruins, but since then Popayán and its colonial treasures have been
painstakingly rebuilt. In fact, the best way to appreciate this historic
town is on foot, wandering its narrow streets or lingering in a plaza
outside one of its lavish, embellished churches. The most popular time
to visit is during Holy Week, when penitents parade the cramped
streets by candlelight, shouldering heavy platforms crowned with
freakish statues and religious icons.

SILVIA

Fifty kilometers (31 miles) northeast of Popayán, the village of Silvia,
really an isolated cluster of adobe houses, is home to the Gaumbiano,
a proud people who have managed to preserve many of their centuries-
old ancestral customs, among them a love for black bowler hats and
bright purple skirts, an ensemble worn by both women and men. The
best day to visit is Tuesday, market day, when the central square is
crammed with local products such as corn, Andean tubers, and heavy
wool ponchos.

PURACÉ NATIONAL PARK

Dedicated hikers will want to visit Puracé National Park, 60 kilometers (37 miles) east of Popayán and spread over one of Colombia's most
spectacular mountain regions. The park ranges in altitude from 8,202
feet to almost 15,748 feet and is the source of Colombia's largest
rivers—the Magdalena, Cauca, and Caqueta. The park also nurtures
an extraordinary variety of wildlife that includes the Andean condor,
the rare spectacled bear, the puma, and the tapir.

SAN AGUSTÍN

At San Agustín, nearly 50 kilometers (31 miles) southeast and a four-
hour drive from Popayán, mysterious, heroic-size statues are strewn
across what must once have been the sacred grounds of a forgotten
empire. These stubby gray stone statues look more like the megaliths
of Chile's Easter Island than anything else you'll find in Colombia—
hence the surrounding mystery. Some archaeologists have linked these
larger-than-life stone figures to the Maya, but it's likely they are the

work of a pre-Columbian tribe that was decimated by disease and simply vanished shortly after the arrival of Europeans on the continent.

The closest airport to San Agustín is in the village of **Pitalito** (☎ 88/360909), where you can rent a car ($30–$50) or taxi ($25 for the day) to take you to the site. The nearby Los Balcones hotel rents horses and guides for daytime treks through San Agustín. Ask your guide to detour to El Estrecho, a tight deep gorge through which the Río Magdalena rushes, crashing against the huge boulders that clog the chute.

Shopping

The region's handicrafts reflect the different races who conquered and colonized southwestern Colombia. Descendants of the black slaves brought to work on sugarcane plantations still hand-carve elaborate bowls and cutlery from Pacific Forest wood, while a Spanish influence is seen in the fine embroidered blouses and dresses offered in street markets. The indigenous Guambiano from Silvia are better known for their handwoven ponchos and *chumbes,* long multicolored woolen strips used for belts.

In Cali try the narrow streets surrounding the main square, where you'll find a decent selection of crafts shops. One of Cali's best handicrafts shops is **Artesanías Pancandé** (Av. 6AN No. 17AN–53, ☎ 2/668–6373). In Popayán there's a cluster of handicrafts stores near Ermita church, three blocks below the main square.

Dining

For price ranges, *see* Dining *in* Colombia Essentials, *below.*

Cali

$$$ **Cali Viejo.** This old stately manor is in the hills high above Cali, and the shady veranda makes a pleasant spot to sample some typical Cali dishes. Try *sancocho de gallina,* a local version of chicken soup; and Cali tamales, hand-rolled corn dough filled with pork and vegetables and wrapped in a banana leaf. ✗ *Casona Vieja del Bosque Municipal,* ☎ 2/882–3152. MC, V.

$$ **El Simonetta.** A stone's throw from the Hotel Inter-Continental, this stylish and airy restaurant, decorated in elegant shades of red and white, serves what many consider to be the finest Italian cuisine in Cali. The tagliatelle is superb, and there is a reasonable range of Italian wines from which to choose. ✗ *Diagonal 27 No. 27–117,* ☎ 2/381–8701. MC, V.

Lodging

For price ranges, *see* Lodging *in* Colombia Essentials, *below.*

Cali

$$$$ **Inter-Continental.** The main lobby is grand and sprawling, which simply highlights the deficiencies of the rather small and plain rooms. Still, the Inter-Continental is endowed with excellent facilities—including poolside and rooftop restaurants—and is probably Cali's most luxurious offering. It is also the social center of the city: When national and international artists come to Cali they invariably stay and perform here. ☷ *Av. Colombia No. 2–72,* ☎ 2/882–3222, ℻ 2/882–2567. *375 rooms, most with bath. 2 restaurants, bar, room service, pool, hot tub, sauna, 2 tennis courts. AE, MC, V.*

$$$ **Don Jaime.** This intimate 30-room hotel provides more personalized attention than its larger corporate rivals without sacrificing any of the com-

petition's luxuries, such as cable TV and air-conditioning. A popular feature is Don Jaime's pleasant café which overlooks the elegant Avenida 6. The hotel restaurant, too, is among the best in Cali. ☎ *Av. 6 No. 15N–25,* ☎ *2/667–2828 or 2/667–8287,* FAX *2/668–7098. 30 rooms, most with bath. Restaurant, bar, café, room service. MC, V.*

$$$ Hotel Dann. In an attractive residential quarter near the banks of the Río Cali, this luxury hotel offers excellent secretarial services for business travelers, and large air-conditioned rooms—each with a good view of the city—equipped with TVs and minibars. On balmy days cool off in the hotel's vast swimming pool. ☎ *Av. Colombia 1-40,* ☎ *2/882-3230,* FAX *2/883-0129. 90 rooms, most with bath. Restaurant, bar, minibars, pool, laundry service, business services. MC, V.*

Popayán

$$ Hotel Monasterio. Housed in a renovated 17th-century convent in downtown Popayán, the Monasterio is well kept and stylish, with high ceilings and colonial-style furnishings. The plumbing works best on the first two floors, which face a central courtyard. The on-site restaurant and bar are popular gathering spots during Holy Week, when reservations are imperative. ☎ *Calle 4 (between Carreras 9 and 10),* ☎ *28/243491 or 28/242191. 48 rooms. Restaurant, bar, pool. MC, V.*

San Agustín

$$ Hotel Osoguaico. If you want to sleep near the ruins at San Agustín, or if you simply crave a hearty lunch or dinner, keep an eye out for this basic hotel a few kilometers from the entrance to the archaeological site. Horseback riding and guided tours of the ruins are available. The rooms themselves are very simple but clean. ☎ *Via San Agustín,* ☎ *88/373069. 32 rooms. Restaurant. MC.*

THE CARIBBEAN COAST

A world away and lost to another time, it seems, is Colombia's sultry Caribbean Coast, a self-contained region linked to Bogotá and the interior only by the national flag, the milky Magdalena River, and a couple of snaking highways. The local *costeño* people project an air of gaiety unheard of in the capital, driven by Cuban funk and the accordion-heavy *vallenato* music, a regional specialty. Remarkably, perhaps, despite the strength-sapping heat and persistent Carnival-like atmosphere, the Caribbean Coast has nurtured Colombia's best-known writers and artists, including novelist Gabriel García Márques and painter Alejandro Obregón.

The appeal of the region lies in its diversity. Toward the western end of the 1,600-kilometer (992-mile) Caribbean shoreline, the city of Cartagena ranks as the most striking colonial relic in South America. And just offshore, the delicate Rosario Islands are ideal for snorkeling and diving. Heading east by car or bus, you pass the city of Barranquilla and mangrove-encircled lagoons before reaching the dramatic, snowcapped Sierra Nevada mountains, whose rain-forested slopes harbor the mysterious Ciudad Perdida—the Lost City—and magnificent Parque Tayrona, one of Colombia's finest national parks. The nearby port of Santa Marta is where drug traffickers discreetly load cocaine aboard U.S.-bound banana boats; it goes without saying that inquisitiveness in this feral, fascinating city is extremely unwise. The resort islands of San Andrés and Providencia lie 645 kilometers (400 miles) northwest off the coast, though frequent air service and San Andrés's duty-free status mean neither island has been overlooked by tourists. Despite its somewhat remote location, San Andrés, in particular, is where

Colombians and a few foreigners gather to dive and snorkel in between bouts of sunbathing and shopping.

Plan for a decent chunk of time in Cartagena, which is a convenient base for excursions to the enchanting colonial river port of Mompós. Santa Marta is a good base from which to explore Parque Tayrona's stunning tropical coastline. Treks to Ciudad Perdida (the Lost City) also set out from Santa Marta. Barranquilla deserves a visit only during its Ash Wednesday carnival.

Cartagena

With its barrel-tile rooftops and wooden balconies, modern Cartagena often looks more Spanish than Spain, but the feeling is tropical, Creole, and altogether more exotic. When founded in 1533 by Pedro de Heredia, Cartagena was the only port on mainland South America. Gold and silver, mined in the interior and looted from Indians, passed through here on the way to Spain, making Cartagena an obvious target for pirates. The most destructive of these was Sir Francis Drake, who in 1586 torched 200 houses, destroyed the cathedral, and made off to England with more than 100,000 gold ducats. Cartagena's magnificent walls and countless fortresses grew in response to these raids, helping to protect the most important African slave market in the New World (the Spaniards forbade Indian slavery).

Visitor Information

Oficina de Turismo (Rafael Nuñez Airport, ☎ 5/664–7015 or 5/664–8078); **Casa del Marqués Valdehoyos** (Calle de la Factoría No. 36–57, ☎ 5/364–7015).

Arriving and Departing

By Plane
There are daily flights between Bogotá and Cartagena's **Rafael Nuñez** international airport (☎ 5/666–1308 or 5/666–0134), 3 kilometers (2 miles) east of downtown. Carriers include **Avianca, Aces,** and **Intercontinental** (Cartagena ☎ 5/666–2995).

By Car
Traveling from Bogotá and the interior of Colombia is laborious but manageable; the drive between Bogotá and Cartegena, for example, takes 20 hours on the Pan-American Highway. Panama is inaccessible from the Caribbean Coast.

By Bus
Expresso Brasilia (Cartagena ☎ 5/666–1692) regularly connects Bogotá with Cartagena (24 hours). **La Costeña** (Cartagena ☎ 53/664058) departs every 20 minutes or so between 6 AM and 4 PM on the five-hour trip between Cartagena and Santa Marta.

Tour Operators

Tesoro Tours (Av. San Martín No. 6–129, Bocagrande, ☎ 5/665–4713) arranges city tours for $10 per person. Tours to the coral-encircled Islas del Rosario depart daily at 8 AM from the Muelle de los Pegasos and return by 4 PM; book through **Raphael Pérez** (☎ 5/660–4214), **Media Maranja** (☎ 5/666–4606), or **Caliente Tours** (☎ 5/665–5346).

Exploring

The ocher-painted **Casa de Marqués Valdehoyos,** although scantily furnished, exudes a powerful whiff of well-to-do colonial life (the sturdy mansion and its shady courtyards were built with the marqués's slave-trade fortune). Also note that the tourist office inside provides useful maps. *Calle Factoría No. 36–57,* ☎ *5/664–7015.* ☛ *Free.* ☉ *Daily 8–noon, 2–6.*

Walk two blocks south to **Plaza Santo Domingo.** The eponymous church looming over the plaza is the city's oldest; begun in 1539, it has a simple whitewashed interior, bare limestone pillars, memorial floor slabs, a raised choir, and an adjacent cloistered seminary. Local lore tells how the bell tower's twisted profile is the work of the Devil, who, dispirited at having failed to destroy it, threw himself into the plaza's well. The Dalmania Café alongside the seminary is a good spot for breakfast or a cooling *jugo* (fruit juice). ☛ *Free.*

Continue straight for one block, past pricey antiques stores, and turn left down Calle Inquisición to **Plaza Bolívar.** To your left stands the whitewashed **Palacio de la Inquisición** (Palace of the Inquisition) with its baroque limestone doorway. In their heyday, the repressive arbiters of political and spiritual orthodoxy who were headquartered in this building had jurisdiction over Colombia, Ecuador, Venezuela, Central America, and the Caribbean. The ground-floor rooms contain implements of torture—racks and thumbscrews, to name but a few—and architectonic models of bygone Cartagena. *Plaza Bolívar.* ☛ *Entry fee.* ☉ *Daily 8–11:30, 2–5.*

Directly opposite is the **Museo del Oro y Arqueologíca** (Gold and Archaeological Museum), which houses an interesting assortment of gold ornaments and pottery culled from the Zinús, an indigenous tribe who lived in the region 2,000 years ago. ☛ *Entry fee.* ☉ *Weekdays.*

Two blocks south lies the 17th-century convent of **San Pedro Claver,** named after a Spanish monk who devotedly ministered to black slaves until his death here in 1654 (in 1888 he became the New World's first saint). You can visit Pedro Claver's dim, cell-like bedroom and the infirmary where he died from Parkinson's disease. His body rests in a glass coffin beneath the altar of the adjoining church. ☛ *Entry fee.* ☉ *Daily 9–6.*

Five minutes by taxi or 15 on foot from the center rises the impregnable **Castillo de San Felipe de Barajas.** Designed by Antonio de Arévalo in 1639, the fort's steep-angled redbrick and concrete battlements were so arranged that, were part of the castle to fall into the wrong hands—which it never did—defenders in one part of the fort could fire on invaders in the other. A lengthy series of tunnels, minimally lit today to allow for spooky exploration, still connects vital points of the fort. ☛ *Entry fee.* ☉ *Tues.–Sun.*

For a spectacular view of Cartagena, take a cab up to **Cerro de la Popa,** a 500-foot hill crowned by the **Convento de Nuestra Señora de la Candelaria,** a monastery founded in 1608 and fortified two centuries later. *Cerro de la Popa.* ☛ *Entry fee.*

Finally, one late afternoon, find your way to **Plaza Fernandez de Madrid,** a garden square that marks the beginning of the old city's **Barrio San Diego.** The streets of this seldom-visited yet enchanting barrio are lined with squat colonial mansions that are brightly painted in white, ocher, and electric blue. Cascades of geraniums flow over balconies and open doorways reveal hidden, luxuriant courtyards. Zigzagging right then left toward the sea, you arrive at the **Bóvedas,** an arcaded row of 18th-century strong rooms, now occupied by crafts shops that have Cartagena's best selection of handicrafts and hats, hammocks and leather. Then, as the setting sun reddens the Caribbean, take a stroll along the nearby city walls.

Sports and the Outdoors

Beaches

Cartagena's tourist-oriented beaches are on the **Bocagrande** peninsula, although they are becoming ever narrower as the none-too-clear sea washes away the brownish sand. Still, the beaches are plied by vendors of *gaseosas,* ice cream, and sunglasses while vallenato musicians stroll tirelessly along the strand. For peace and quiet, white sand, and palm trees, your best bet is **Playa Blanca,** reached by boat from Cartagena's Muelle del Pescadores.

Fishing

The **Club de Pesca** in Manga (Calle 24 at Cra. 17, ☎ 5/660–4593) will take you sportfishing for marlin and sailfish for about $75 per person.

Snorkeling and Diving

The **Caribe Dive Shop** (☎ 5/665–0813) at the Caribe Hotel (*see* Lodging, *below*) organizes snorkeling treks to the Islas del Rosario archipelago and diving trips to underwater wrecks. The dive shop also organizes introductory dives for beginners. A number of travel agencies also arrange tours of the reef-ringed islands (*see* Tour Operators, *above*).

Dining

Seafood is the regional specialty, as is *arroz con coco* (rice cooked in coconut milk) and sancocho. Jugos are an excellent companion to *carimañolas* (stuffed yucca), *butifarras* (small meatballs), *arepas de huevo* (egg-filled pancakes), and, February through April, *huevos de iguana* (iguana eggs), which are threaded together like rosaries. For price ranges, *see* Dining *in* Colombia Essentials, *below.*

$$$ ★ **Classic de Andrei.** Swirling iron grilles, white classical columns, and patterned hardwood decorate this popular upmarket restaurant. The setting—vaguely belle epoque—is well suited to the top-notch Mediterranean cuisine; try the *trucha corcega* (trout with prosciutto, tomatoes, and tarragon) or, a unique offering, an order of sushi. ✕ *Calle de Las Damas at Calle Ricaurte,* ☎ *5/664–0284. Reservations advised. AE, DC, MC, V. Closed Sat. lunch and Sun.*

$$$ **Club de Pesca.** Time slips gently by in this 18th-century fortress that overlooks the adjacent marina. Diners linger on a terrace shaded by a giant rubber tree, treated to delicate specialties such as lemon-and-soy snapper garnished with tahini and mint. ✕ *Fuerte de San Sebastián del Pastelillo, Manga,* ☎ *5/6640594. AE, DC, MC, V.*

$$–$$$ **Paco's.** Heavy beams, rough terra-cotta walls, chunky wooden benches, and weekend tunes from an aging Cuban band are the hallmarks of this downtown eatery, a favorite with journalists and politicians. Drop by for a drink and tapas, or try the more substantial langostinos *a la sifú* (fried in batter). ✕ *Plaza Santo Domingo,* ☎ *5/664–4294. Dinner reservations advised. AE, DC, MC, V.*

$$ **El Ancora Café.** With his tables spilling across the lively harborside sidewalk, Frederico Bega serves costeño recipes against an interior backdrop of designer peeling plaster. Go for the langostinos *en salsa de tamarindo y coco* (in tamarind and coconut sauce). Live Cuban music daily competes with neighboring vallenato bands. ✕ *Calle del Arsenal 9A–47,* ☎ *5/664–8236. Reservations advised. AE, DC, MC, V.*

Lodging

Hotel reservations should be made well in advance for Holy Week and throughout June and December, when prices are typically inflated by 15%. For price ranges, *see* Lodging *in* Colombia Essentials, *below.*

Cartagena

$$$$ **Hilton.** Every room in this blandly modern Y-shape block at the far tip of El Laguito has a sea-facing balcony, but the best overlook the pool. Leafy gardens lead directly onto a beach lined with palms, magnolias, and thatched oyster bars. Children under 12 stay free. ▣ *Av. Almirante Brión,* ☎ *5/665–0666,* ℻ *5/665–2211; U.S.* ☎ *800/445–8667. 289 rooms, 5 suites. Restaurant, bar, pool, massage, sauna, tennis court, exercise room. AE, DC, MC, V.*

$$ **Caribe.** The oldest hotel on the Bocagrande peninsula has retained its
★ colonial mood despite expansion of the original structure. The pastel bedrooms in the refurbished old building have heaps more charm than those in the modern wings, though no rooms have balconies. Giant rubber trees shade a large pool at the rear, while out front only a narrow lane separates the hotel from the beach. ▣ *Cra. 1a No. 2–87, Bocagrande,* ☎ *5/665–0155,* ℻ *5/665–3707. 372 rooms. Restaurant, 2 bars, pool, massage, sauna, tennis court, exercise room. AE, DC, MC, V.*

$$ **Casa Grande.** An original Bocagrande beachfront house, now dwarfed by surrounding skyscrapers, Casa Grande takes first prize for intimacy. The rooms vary in style and price—those off the back garden have fans attached to their sloping wooden ceilings and are a good value; but choose for yourself on arrival. ▣ *Cra. 1 No. 9–128,* ☎ *53/653943,* ℻ *53/656806. 26 rooms. Restaurant, bar. AE, DC, MC, V.*

$ **Hostal Santo Domingo.** Well located in the walled city and close to the sea and sights, this colonial minimansion contains simple whitewashed rooms with fans, very basic bathrooms, and windows overlooking a leafy courtyard. ▣ *Calle Santo Domingo No. 33–46,* ☎ *53/642268. 10 rooms. No credit cards.*

Islas del Rosario

$$$$ **La Isleta.** This is a unique lodging and living experience that you can have all to yourself: a private tropical island with wooden houses scattered across two rustic and wooded hectares. The caretakers will cook for you, but bring any luxuries with you. Transportation is available to the island, which sleeps 20 or so; the price is about $100 per day for the entire facility. ▣ *Contact María Trujillo at ACT, Calle 71 No. 13–86, office 201, Bogotá,* ☎ *1/211–2338,* ℻ *1/211–9623; or the Hernandez family, Calle 74A No. 4–23, Bogotá,* ☎ *1/310–4986. AE, DC, MC, V.*

Excursions from Cartagena

Mompós

Founded in 1537 on the eastern branch of the Magdalena river, Mompós was a key trading link between the Caribbean and the interior for more than two centuries. However, in the 18th century the direction of the Magdalena's flow shifted toward the western branch, leaving Mompós stranded on what has become an unnavigable channel. Although the commercial vibrancy of the town quickly dissipated, its fine colonial architecture remains: Mompós's parallel streets, curved so as to thwart cannonball volleys, are lined with squat mansions guarded by intricate iron grilles, and several fine churches.

Simón Bolívar once stayed in Mompós at the **Casa Bolivariana.** The town's impression on the liberator was obviously profound for he reputedly said: "While to Caracas I owe my life, to Mompós I owe my glory." The house contains several of the liberator's effects and a collection of pre-Columbian gold. *Calle Media.* ☛ *Entry fee.* ⊘ *Mon.–Sat.*

One block farther is the **Casa de Cultura** (Calle Media, no ☎; ☛ Entry fee; ⊘ Weekdays), with its small Mompós history museum. Continue three blocks and turn left to find the **Iglesia de Santa Bárbara,** the most interesting of the town's various churches because of its Moorish bell tower. Mompós is also noted for its handworked gold-filigree jewelry, probably the finest to be found anywhere in Colombia.

Getting There
Expresso Brasilia (Cartagena, ☎ 5/666–1692; Santa Marta, ☎ 54/208612) has air-conditioned buses that travel six times daily between Cartagena and Magangué. From Magangué you can catch a *chalupa* (river launch) to Mompós. The boat trip takes two–three hours; the last launch leaves at 4 PM.

Dining and Lodging
$ **Hostal Doña Manuela.** The airy colonial-style rooms in this beautiful old *casona* (house) lead off a wide veranda that overlooks a patio and pool—indispensable features due to the sweltering summertime heat. ⌖ *Calle Real del Medio No. 17–41,* ☎ *528/55620. 28 rooms. Restaurant, bar, pool. DC, MC, V.*

Barranquilla

The Caribbean Coast's largest industrial center, set at the mouth of the muddy Río Magdalena, is also Colombia's fourth-largest city, home to the country's largest soccer stadium, the Metropolitana, and to its most modern—and hideous—cathedral. There's no doubt about it: Barranquilla is a bizarre mix of well-to-do grid development in the west and filthy, seedy urban sprawl elsewhere. The only time really worth visiting is during the four days leading up to Ash Wednesday, when its dusty streets are overcome by flower-covered floats, costumed dancers, and crazed drunks swilling *aguardiente* (firewater).

Getting There
Bus service between Cartagena and Santa Marta run by **La Costeña** (Cartagena ☎ 53/664058) has stops in Barranquilla.

Dining and Lodging
$$$$ **El Prado.** The chessboard-tile lobby complements the carpeted and taste-
★ fully furnished bedrooms at this elegant colonial-style hotel. Along with such sports facilities as clay tennis courts, El Prado is justly revered for its Principe Eduardo restaurant, which offers a variety of international dishes. ⌖ *Cra. 54 No. 70–10,* ☎ *58/450111,* FAX *58/451500. 280 rooms. Restaurant, 2 bars, hot tub, massage, sauna, 2 tennis courts, exercise room. AE, DC, MC, V.*

$$ **Majestic.** Refurbished in 1993, the Majestic has carpeted bedrooms with firm beds, TVs, and air-conditioning. The airy neoclassical lobby leads to an ornately plastered dining room reminiscent of Versailles; a Moorish reception room; and a verdant courtyard equipped with a pool and bar. ⌖ *Cra. 53 No. 54–41,* ☎ *58/512933,* FAX *58/413733. 46 rooms. Restaurant, bar, pool. AE, DC, MC, V.*

Santa Marta and the Sierra Nevada

Santa Marta, founded in 1525, lies at the foot of the snowcapped Sierra Nevada, the highest coastal range of mountains in the world. These nearby peaks are home to both the stunning Tayrona National Park and impressive pre-Columbian ruins known as La Ciudad Perdida.

Visitor Information

In Santa Marta, the **Oficina de Turismo** (Calle 10 No. 3–10, El Rodadero, ☏ 54/227291) provides maps and can recommend a guide; also try **Inderena** (Cra. 1 No. 22–79, ☏ 54/215367).

Arriving and Departing

By Plane

There are daily flights between Bogotá and Santa Marta's **Simón Bolívar airport** (☏ 54/218480), 20 kilometers (12 miles) and an $8 taxi ride from the city center. Carriers include **Avianca, Aces,** and **Intercontinental; American Airlines** offers less frequent international service to Santa Marta.

By Bus

Expresso Brasilia (Santa Marta, ☏ 54/208612) regularly connects Bogotá with Santa Marta (20 hours). During the day, **La Costeña** (Santa Marta, ☏ 54/234273) has departures every 20 minutes or so on the five-hour Cartagena–Santa Marta route.

Tour Operators

TMA (Calle 15, No. 2–60, Edif. Bolívar, ☏ 54/211257) offers a range of city tours plus treks to Pueblito, La Ciudad Perdida, and Parque Tayrona. A more informal and flexible option is **Ecotours** (☏ 54/201672), run by Eduardo Bustamante—look for him at the Frutera Tropical, next door to Santa Marta's Hostal PanAmerican Miramar.

Exploring

Santa Marta

Although Santa Marta is the oldest surviving Hispanic town in Colombia, modern industry and architecture largely obscure its colonial look. Today the city's 200,000 inhabitants rely heavily on the natural deepwater port where banana boats lie anchored in thick clusters. Most of the cargo, of course, is legitimate, but Santa Marta also handles more contraband than any other port in Colombia. In the 1970s, that meant mostly Sierra Nevada–cultivated marijuana; in the 1990s, U.S.-solicited cocaine reigns supreme. Santa Marta is mostly nonchalant and friendly, but don't go looking for trouble: There are those here who carry weapons as a matter of course.

The **Museo Arqueológico Tayrona,** housed in a handsome erstwhile customs house on the main square, has a small collection of Tayrona gold and pottery and a model of the Lost City (La Ciudad Perdida), well worth a look *before* you set out. *Calle 14 at Cra. 2., no ☏. ☛ Free. ⏲ Weekdays.*

On the seafront, flag down a taxi or any bus marked MAMATOCO and ask to be let off at the **Quinta de San Pedro Alejandrino,** 20 minutes away. This pleasant honey-color hacienda is where a sick Simón Bolívar died in 1830, ironically enough as a guest of a Spanish royalist. On the grounds are a huge gleaming monument to the liberator and a helpful pictorial history of his life. *Mamatoco.* ☛ *Entry fee.* ☉ *Wed.–Mon. 9:30–4:30.*

Again from Santa Marta's seafront, you can catch a taxi or colectivo to **Taganga,** a small fishing village nestled in the next bay north—an easy 15-minute drive over tawny, brush-covered hillside. From the beach in Taganga you can hire boats to take you to Playa Grande across the bay, or make the 20-minute walk to "Big Beach" along the marked coastal path.

Parque Tayrona

Thirty-eight kilometers (22 miles) east of Santa Marta is Parque Tayrona (Tayrona National Park; ☛ Entry fee), a tropical treasure trove of steep jungle-clad slopes, ancient ruins, deserted palm-fringed beaches, and coral reefs, all approached from the Santa Marta–Ríohacha highway. (A taxi from Santa Marta costs less than $20 round-trip.)

At **Arrecifes,** a 45-minute walk west of the parking lot along a slippery jungle trail, a cluster of simple bars and restaurants nourishes the hippies who inhabit the string of nearby beautiful beaches. Note that swimming here and at Cañaveral (*below*) is extremely dangerous due to riptides, and, yes, sharks. **Pueblito,** an ancient Tayrona village that's currently being excavated, is a two-hour uphill hike from Arrecifes; the path is lined with a few basic camping areas. From Pueblito on a clear day you can glimpse the snowbound Sierra Nevada in the distance.

The eastern sector of the park around **Cañaveral** is far more lush than the west, and the final few kilometers to the beach at Cañaveral weave through damp jungle before arriving at a parking lot and restaurant. Get your bearings from the spectacular mirador, a 10-minute walk east, then descend to the beach to inspect the giant sculptured monoliths, which lend something of a Planet-of-the-Apes look to the scenery.

Stay overnight in Parque Tayrona in either one of Cañaveral's "Eco-habs," circular thatched huts (less than $10 per person) with paneled interiors, firm beds, cotton sheets, and balconies with 360° views; or rent a hammock at Arrecifes for about $1 and pray you don't fall victim to a falling coconut. Eco-habs should be reserved in Santa Marta through Inderena (*see* Visitor Information, *above*).

La Ciudad Perdida

Stumbled upon by *guaqueros,* or treasure hunters, in 1975, **La Ciudad Perdida** (the Lost City) is one of the largest pre-Columbian citadels ever discovered in the Americas. Founded sometime between AD 500 and 700, it is anchored at an altitude of 1,200 meters (3,937 feet) on the rugged northern slopes of the Sierra Nevada and can only be reached by means of a six-day guided trek or a three-hour helicopter ride, both of which can be arranged from Santa Marta (*see* Tour Operators, *above*). The mortarless buildings and terraces linked by steep stairways are sacred to the Kogui Indians who still inhabit the region; not surprisingly, they take unkindly to loudmouthed, litter-spilling tourists. Still, despite the time and energy required, the trek to La Ciudad Perdida is unforgettable.

Shopping

In Santa Marta, **Almacenes Típicos El Tiburón** (Cra. 2A No. 18–05) and **Artesanias Park** (Cra. 1 No. 18–65) have wide selections of hats, leather, and handicrafts.

Sports and the Outdoors

Beaches

The beaches at Santa Marta and Taganga are dirty; but just south is **El Rodadero,** a white-sand beach with excellent lodging facilities (*see* Dining and Lodging, *below*). Farther north are the spectacular and deserted white-sand strands on the outskirts of Parque Tayrona. Swimming here is extremely dangerous, however, due to riptides and sharks. Drownings are *very* common.

Trekking

The Sierra Nevada has some outstanding hiking and climbing that includes Pueblito, La Ciudad Perdida, and the 18,930-foot-high summit of Picó Colón. The latter two require guides (*see* Visitor Information *and* Tour Operators, *above*).

Snorkeling and Diving

Parque Tayrona has various good snorkeling spots that can be explored with Ecotours (*see* Tour Operators, *above*). The western bays of **Concha** and **Negangue,** reached via paved but unsignposted roads, are both good snorkeling spots; at Negangue, have a boat take you for a dive in the coral, then dine at one of the beachfront restaurants.

Dining and Lodging

For price ranges, *see* Dining *and* Lodging *in* Colombia Essentials, *below.*

El Rodadero

DINING AND LODGING

$$$$ Irotama. This fully equipped resort several miles from Santa Marta features cabanas—some indigenous in design, others plain suburban, all air-conditioned and with bath—sprinkled among landscaped jungle that fronts a long stretch of secluded beach. ☎ *Via Cienaga at km 15,* ☎ *54/218021,* ☒ *54/218077. 155 cabins. 3 restaurants, 3 bars, pool, hot tub, massage, sauna, tennis court, exercise room, snorkeling, boating, fishing, dance club. AE, DC, MC, V.*

Santa Marta

LODGING

$ Hostal PanAmerican Miramar. Despite its concrete-block appearance, this friendly hotel offers efficient service and huge, bright, airy bedrooms with TVs and phones. Insist on a sea-facing room with a balcony; air-conditioning is available for a small charge but scarcely needed with the sea breeze. ☎ *Cra. 1a No. 18–23,* ☎ *54/214756. 43 rooms. AE, DC, MC, V.*

$ Sol Hotel Inn. Rooms here are slightly small and lack TVs, but most have sea-facing balconies, comfortable beds, and powerful fans. The hotel also offers inexpensive daily minibus service to Tayrona National Park. ☎ *Cra. 1 No. 20–23,* ☎ *54/211131. 32 rooms. DC, MC, V.*

San Andrés and Providencia Islands

On his fourth voyage to the New World, Christopher Columbus became the first European to set foot on San Andrés and Providencia islands, which lie 645 kilometers (400 miles) off Colombia's Caribbean coast. The uninhabited islands were later settled by English pilgrims (who landed in their vessel, the *Seaflower,* at the same time pilgrims landed at Plymouth Rock) and then by Jamaican cotton growers. Centuries of intermingling have produced a "native" population that speaks an English patois, although with the recent influx of mainlanders, Spanish is also prevalent.

Visitor Information

On San Andrés, there's the **Oficina de Turismo** (Sesquicentenario Airport, ☎ 811/6110; Av. Colombia, ☎ 811/4230) and **Islatur** (Hotel Cacique Toné, Av. Colombia, ☎ 811/24251).

Arriving and Departing

By Plane

San Andrés's **Sesquicentenario** airport (☎ 811/26110), a short taxi ride from the island village of El Centro, is regularly serviced by **Avianca, Aces, Intercontinental,** and **Sam.** The 90-minute flight from Bogotá costs $125 each way; the one-hour flight from Cartagena about $95 each way. Sam also links San Andrés with Providencia Island three times daily for less than $55 round-trip.

Exploring

San Andrés

The island's duty-free status is responsible for the cluster of bland boutiques and shops in the concrete jungle of **El Centro,** San Andrés's commercial center. Although the prices are not very attractive to U.S. and European visitors, the surrounding coral cays and reefs certainly are. Diving is a big draw on San Andrés, as is angling for sailfish, bonito, and marlin; you can organize a diving trip or rent snorkeling gear from **Aquamarina** (Av. Colombia, next to El Aquamarina hotel, ☎ 811/26649).

San Andrés is only 13 kilometers (8 miles) long, and the best way to see the island is to rent a bicycle or motor scooter from one of the many shops along Avenida Colombia in El Centro and complete a circuit of the coastal road. **Cueva Morgan,** a small beachfront settlement, is where the pirate Henry Morgan (who also, conveniently, was England's lieutenant governor of Jamaica) reputedly stashed his loot after pillaging coastal Cuba and Panama in the 1670s. Beach bums should head for **Johnny Cay** or **San Luis,** the island's two most popular strands.

Providencia

Volcanic in origin and ringed by coral cays, Providencia Island has rugged hills, abundant fresh water, and far less development than neighboring San Andrés, 90 kilometers (56 miles) southeast. The pace of life on Providencia is decidedly laid-back, even jolly; islanders gather on the beach at sunset to drink and chat, and most people are happily tucked into bed by 11 PM.

In **Aquadulce,** the island's largest town, you can hire bicycles and motor scooters, or join a boat tour of the surrounding islets. The best beaches are in Manzanillo and South West Bay; Crab Cay is best for snorkeling. Choose a clear day to hike up the 1,000-foot summit of **El Pico,** which gives superb views of the island's turquoise seashore and necklace of coral; it's a 90-minute trek each way from Casa Baja.

Dining and Lodging

Lacking rivers, San Andrés's big snag is the absence of fresh water; a desalination plant is planned but persistently postponed, and all but the most expensive hotels have saltwater showers. For price ranges, *see* Dining *and* Lodging *in* Colombia Essentials, *below.*

Providencia

$ **Cabañas El Paraiso.** On the beach in Aquadulce, these wooden cabins have clean and simple fan-ventilated rooms with ocean views and

freshwater showers. Adjoining the complex is a no-frills but dependable restaurant. Cabaña reservations are booked through Islatur on San
Andrés (*see* Visitor Information, *above*). 🏨 *Aguadulce, Apdo. 958,* ☎
811/48036. 15 rooms. Restaurant. No credit cards.

San Andrés

$$$$ **Maryland.** Somewhat overpriced but one of the few hotels at press
time (winter 1995) with fresh water, the Maryland has small chintzy
rooms that open onto a seafront balcony—the architectural norm
around here. The airport is nearby. 🏨 *Av. Colombia 9–38, Apdo. 1197,*
☎ *and* FAX *811/24825. 65 rooms. Restaurant, bar, pool, hot tub. AE,
DC, MC, V.*

$$$ **Nirvana Inn Palace.** Midway along the coast, this secluded series of
★ white villas has airy and eccentric rooms—saltwater sinks are perched
on coral pilings, and the wood ceilings have a definite slope. There's
no beach, but the surrounding garden is lush and the jagged shore ideal
for snorkeling; the hotel rents diving gear, as well as cars and motor
scooters. 🏨 *Km. 14, Apdo. 1290,* ☎ *811/27013,* FAX *811/27928. 22
rooms. Restaurant, bar, pool. AE, DC, MC, V.*

$$ **El Aquarium.** Large fan-ventilated suites occupy 13 diminutive islands
at the fringe of the sea; insist on a sea view. Freshwater showers are
planned for the near future. 🏨 *Av. Colombia 1–19, Punta Hansa,* ☎
811/23117, FAX *811/26174. 135 rooms. 3 restaurants, bar, saltwater
pool. AE, DC, MC, V.*

COLOMBIA ESSENTIALS

Customs and Duties

On arrival the duty-free allowance per person is 200 cigarettes, 50 cigars,
up to 250 grams of tobacco, and two bottles of either wine or spirits.
You can also bring into the country electronic equipment such as a video
camera as long as it bears clear signs of use. There is no limit on the
amount of money tourists can bring in and take out of the country.
On departure, gold and platinum articles and emeralds require proof
of purchase.

Dining

Specialties

Colombian cuisine is a fusion of Spanish, Indian, and African culinary
traditions. It is varied and regional by nature, but unfortunately the
same cannot be said of the standard *almuerzo,* or lunch, offered day
after day by a majority of restaurants throughout the country. It starts
with soup and is followed by a main dish, or *bandeja,* consisting of a
piece of chicken or fish garnished with fríjoles, vegetables, and rice.
The only good news is the price: $2–$4.

On the Caribbean Coast try *cazuela de mariscos,* a seafood soup traditionally made with shrimp, squid, crab, lobster, and red snapper. Also
popular is sancocho *de sábalo,* fresh fish prepared in coconut milk with
strips of potato, plantain banana, and yucca. On San Andrés and
Providencia islands, the local favorite is *rendón,* a fish-and-snail soup
slowly cooked in coconut milk with yucca, plantain, breadfruit, and
dumplings. In the Andes, and particularly in Bogotá, ajiaco—a thick
soup prepared from three types of potato, chicken, corn, capers, fresh
cream, and avocado—is among the most typical dishes. So, too, are
tamales, which consist of chicken, corn, and potatoes rolled in a maize
dough and wrapped in banana leaves.

Colombians are fond of bread, particularly dinner rolls and muffins: be sure to try *mogollas*, whole-wheat muffins with raisin-flavored centers; *roscones*, sugar-sprinkled buns filled with guava jelly; and *almojábanas*, corn muffins enriched with cottage cheese. Popular desserts include obleas, giant wafers spread with sugar and milk paste, and empanadas.

Colombians do not necessarily drink alcoholic beverages with dinner, although they are fond of imported Chilean wines and two reasonable national offerings: Santo Tomás, a full-bodied red wine, and the Chianti-like Vino Moriles.

Mealtimes

Restaurants serve lunch between 12:30 and 2:30. In the provinces people tend to have their evening meal just after sundown, but in Bogotá hours are much more Spanish: you may find yourself sitting down to an "early" dinner at 9.

Dress

The best restaurants in Bogotá and Medellín can certainly compete with those in Rio de Janeiro or Buenos Aires, and in such establishments a jacket and tie for men and smart dress for women is the norm; everywhere else informal dress is appropriate.

Ratings

Prices are per person and include an appetizer, main course, and dessert. Wine and gratuities are not included.

CATEGORY	COST
$$$$	over $30
$$$	$20–$30
$$	$10–$20
$	under $10

Embassies and Consulates

United States

Embassy: Calle 38 No. 8–61, Bogotá, ☎ 1/285–1300.

Canada

Embassy: Calle 76 No. 11–52, Bogotá, ☎ 1/217–5555.

United Kingdom

Embassy: Calle 98 No. 9–03, Bogotá, ☎ 1/218–5111.

Getting Around

By Plane

Faced with almost insurmountable natural barriers, Colombia has developed one of the best air-transportation systems in the world. Avianca, the oldest airline in the Americas and the second-oldest in the world, operates daily flights between Colombia's major cities. The airline also offers a Conozca Colombia ("Know Colombia") air pass that permits travel to as many as 10 cities in 30 days as long as you don't stop in the same city twice except for connections. The air pass, which can only be purchased outside Colombia, costs $250 if San Andrés Island and Leticia are not included, $365 if they are.

There are daily flights to Bogotá, Barranquilla, Medellín, and San Andrés Island with **Avianca** (Carrera 7 No. 16–36, Bogotá, ☎ 1/341–5497 or 1/282–2341; U.S. ☎ 800/284–2622). Other airlines offering domestic service are **SAM** (Carrera 13 No. 28–01, office 401, Bogotá, ☎ 1/266–9600), **Aces** (Carrera 10 No. 27–51, office 201, Bogotá, ☎ 1/341–8499 or 1/281–7800; U.S. ☎ 800/846–2237), **Intercontinen-**

tal de Aviación (Carrera 10 No. 28–31, Bogotá, ☎ 1/281–5152 or 1/283–3057), and **AIRES** (Av. 13 No. 79–56, Bogotá, ☎ 1/610–9653 or 1/257–3000).

By Car
Road Conditions

Driving in Colombia is recommended only for confident, experienced drivers. Roads are narrow, winding, not always signposted, and often in poor condition, with unpredictable surfaces. During the rainy season roads can turn to mud or wash out completely. Even in good weather, maniac truck and bus drivers—combined with the likelihood of encountering stray animals—make negotiating the highways extremely difficult. Nighttime driving is especially dangerous because many vehicles lack headlights. Tolls (up to $1.50, payable only in pesos) are common; motorcycles are usually exempt. In town leave your car in an attended parking lot, especially at night.

RULES OF THE ROAD

National driver's licenses are accepted but must be accompanied by an official translation—a lot of bureaucratic bother that can be avoided by getting an international license before you leave home. Police checkpoints are common and you should make sure your documents are always at hand. There is an automatic fine for running out of gasoline on the road.

RENTALS

Car rentals in Colombia cost $190–$215 per week including mileage. Even if you pay in pesos—dollars are not usually accepted—a credit card may be needed in addition to your passport or driver's license as proof of identity.

EMERGENCY ASSISTANCE

In an emergency contact the **Policía Vial** (☎ 1/247–1151), who have a mobile workshop for fixing breakdowns. Otherwise, when hiring a car it is a good idea to affiliate yourself with the **Automóvil Club de Colombia** (Diagonal 187 No. 41–85, Bogotá, ☎ 1/288–1313), who will tow your car to a mechanic if they cannot fix it themselves. American Automobile Association (AAA) members can contact the local representatives, Allen and Mary Lowrie, for maps and driving hints (Carrera 7 No. 19–29, 3rd Floor, Bogotá, ☎ 1/243–2546 or 1/243–2457).

GASOLINE

Gasoline comes in two grades: *premium* (95 octane), available only in large cities for about $1.25 per U.S. gallon; and *corriente* (84 octane), sometimes called "regular," which costs around $1 per U.S. gallon and is available throughout the country. Most towns hugging a highway tend to have at least one working pump, though the towns themselves are few and far between.

By Bus

Colombia has an extensive bus network that connects the major cities with even the smallest mountain villages. There are two classes to choose from: the very standard corriente, *sencillo,* or *ordinario* service; and a first-class service variously called *pullman, metropolitano, de lujo,* or *directo.* There are also deluxe air-conditioned buses known as *thermo* or *climatizado,* but these are common mainly on routes between Bogotá, Medellín, and the Caribbean Coast. Standard bus service costs $1.50–$2 per 100 kilometers (62 miles), and the ancient vehicles (which probably should have been scrapped decades ago) tend to be very crowded. First-class and deluxe coaches can be quite comfortable, with reclining seats and respectable toilets; the average cost is $2–$5 per 100 kilometers (62 miles). On longer journeys buses stop for meals, but not necessarily at mealtimes and not for very long.

Language

The official language is Spanish, though you will probably encounter more than one of the roughly 90 Indian languages spoken in Colombia. English is widely understood on San Andrés and Providencia islands and commonly spoken in resort hotels and restaurants in the major cities.

Lodging

Colombia's resort hotels are of a very high standard, though on the coast, in the capital, and particularly in Medellín, resorts are sometimes completely booked for conventions. Away from the resorts quality is more variable. Nevertheless, in most areas you'll find moderately priced pensions equipped with private bathrooms. (Hot water, however, may only be available at certain hours of the day.) The local tourist office can normally book visitors into the better hotels and provide recommendations regarding the rest.

Ratings

Prices are for two people in a double room, based on high-season rates but not including 15% tax.

CATEGORY	COST
$$$$	over $125
$$$	$80–$125
$$	$60–$80
$	under $60

Mail

All international airmail is handled by Avianca, Colombia's largest airline. Airmail post offices are normally next to the airline's offices and are open weekdays 7:30 AM–8 PM, Saturday 8–5. Airmail service costs less than 50¢ to the United States and is relatively reliable; most letters reach their intended international destination in 10–14 days.

Receiving Mail

Avianca holds letters for up to 30 days, and you will need your passport to reclaim them from the poste restante desk. Letters should be sent to Post Restante, Correo Aéreo Avianca, followed by the city and province name.

Money and Expenses

Currency

Colombia's monetary unit is the peso, which has lost so much value it is no longer divided into centavos. Peso bills are circulated in the following denominations: 100, 200, 500, 1,000, 5,000, and 10,000. Peso coins come in denominations of 5, 10, 20, 50, and 100. At press time (winter 1995) the official exchange rate was 850 pesos to the U.S. dollar and 1,600 pesos to the pound sterling.

Changing Money

U.S., British, and Canadian currency can be exchanged for a small fee in many hotels, banks, and travel agencies. To squeeze the most out of your dollars and pounds, use your credit card for cash advances whenever possible: In Colombia, credit cards give the most stable and highest rate of exchange. Either way, keep your exchange receipts. Upon departure you can convert unused pesos back into U.S. dollars (up to $60).

Forms of Payment

Credit cards and traveler's checks are accepted in resorts and in a large number of shops and restaurants in major cities.

Costs

Colombia is one of the few countries in South America where inflation remains relatively stable. Bogotá, Cali, Cartagena, and San Andrés are the most expensive destinations; but, even then, you can find first-class accommodations for less than $50 per night. The least-expensive areas are coastal and mountain villages, where you may have difficulty parting with more than $2 for a meal and $5 for accommodation.

TAXES

Throughout Colombia hotels add 15% to your bill, and there is a 14% value-added tax (IVA) on most anything you might want to buy.

SAMPLE PRICES

Cup of coffee, 25¢; bottle of beer, $1; bottle of wine in a restaurant, $15–$20; bottle of wine in store, $7–$10; 1-mile taxi ride, $2; city bus ride, 50¢; theater or cinema ticket, $2.

Opening and Closing Times

Banks

Standard hours at banks are weekdays 9–3 (until 3:30 on Friday), with several hours off for lunch. In Bogotá many banks are open weekdays 9–2 only. On the last working day of the month banks are open only in the early morning, though in Bogotá they stay open until noon.

Museums

Museums have similar hours to shops but tend to be closed on Monday rather than Sunday.

Shops

There are no standardized opening hours for shops and stores, though a majority close daily for lunch between 12:30 and 2 PM. Many are also closed on Sunday.

National Holidays

Circumcision of Our Lord (Jan. 1); Epiphany (Jan. 6), St. Joseph's Day (Mar. 21); Maundy Thursday and Good Friday (1996: Apr. 4–5; 1997: Mar. 27–28); Labor Day (May 1); Ascension Day (1996: May 16; 1997: May 8); Corpus Christi (1996: June 6; 1997: May 27); Sts. Peter and Paul's Day (July 4); Independence Day (July 20); Battle of Boyacá (Aug. 7); Assumption Day (Aug. 15); Discovery of America (Oct. 17); All Saints' Day (Nov. 1); Independence of Cartagena (Nov. 14); Immaculate Conception (Dec. 8); Christmas (Dec. 25).

Precautions

Although its reputation has been marred by the Medellín and Cartagena drug cartels, Colombia is hardly a war zone. To be sure, you will encounter machine-gun-toting soldiers in many cities and military checkpoints on otherwise peaceful mountain roads. But there is a fairly well-established "gringo trail," and thousands of people visit each year without mishap.

Health

Water in Bogotá and Medellín is heavily chlorinated and safe enough to drink, but rely on bottled or bagged water in other parts of the country. Also avoid eating unpeeled fruit, uncooked vegetables, salads, and ice cubes. You don't need to bring stacks of medical supplies with you: Colombia's pharmacies are well stocked. Some people experience dizziness and headaches upon arrival in Bogotá because of the thin mountain air. Take it easy and be careful with alcohol until you acclimatize.

Safety

Violence from the drug cartels and guerrilla groups are a fact of life in Colombia, but travelers who take the same precautions they would in, say, a big city back home are unlikely to run into problems. Certain land journeys are best not undertaken at night, or avoided altogether, because of the risk of ambush by guerrillas (the road from Bucaramanga to Santa Marta, for example, should be avoided). Have nothing to do with drug dealers, especially because many of them freelance as police informers. Possession of cocaine or marijuana can lead to a long jail sentence—not a pleasant thought in Colombia.

In many of the large cities, especially the downtown area of Bogotá, do not be taken in by plainclothes "policemen" demanding to register your money—they are almost certainly thieves. Nor should you change money on the black market or get involved in any dubious transactions aimed at getting a better rate of exchange. Don't accept gifts of food, drink, cigarettes, or chewing gum from strangers, especially on bus journeys; there have been reports of travelers being drugged and relieved of their valuables in this way.

Shopping

Colombia is a shopper's paradise, both for the high-quality locally manufactured clothes, and for the range of indigenous handicrafts. In all of the major cities there are good department stores and boutiques to tempt you. In rural areas, village markets and shops stock a full range of Colombian handicrafts. Among the best buys are natural wool ruanas woven by the Indians in the south, embroidered blouses from Cali, and replica pre-Columbian jewelry in Bogotá. Antiques are also sold in shops throughout Colombia. Colonial objects can be taken out of the country without hindrance, but exporting pre-Columbian artifacts is against the law.

Telephones

Local and Long-Distance Calls

Colombia's telephone service is reasonably efficient, though direct dialing is still not available from many places in the Andes and along the coast. Public telephones, which are common in large cities but scarce everywhere else, accept 5-, 10-, 20-, and 50-peso coins. For intercity calls use the blue-and-yellow or red long distance booths marked *larga distancia* (which only accept 20-peso coins). If you cannot find one, or if you do not have access to a private or hotel telephone, go to the local Telecom office—there is one in most towns. When dialing long distance from within Colombia, dial 9, the area code, and then the number.

International Calls

Direct-dial international calls are best made from a Telecom office, where you must leave a deposit of roughly $25; or from your hotel at a *substantially* higher rate (the average rate per minute to the United States is $6; from a hotel, about $10).

To make credit card and collect calls through an **AT&T** operator, dial 980–11–0010. For **MCI,** dial 980–16–0010. For **Sprint,** dial 980–13–0010.

Tipping

Taxi drivers do not expect tips. Porters at airports and hotels are usually given 300 pesos for each piece of luggage. In many restaurants, bars, and cafés, a 10% service charge is automatically added to the bill; if not, a 10% tip is common. Hotel maids or clerks are seldom tipped.

When to Go

December, January, and February are the best—in other words, the driest—months to visit Colombia. Yet, Colombians themselves tend to travel during these sometimes hot and humid months, when tourist prices peak and some nontourist businesses close. Visiting during one of the country's festivals adds an exciting cultural edge to your trip, but expect inflated prices and often overwhelming crowds.

Climate

Although Colombia is perceived as a steamy tropical country, climate is very much a matter of altitude. Temperatures range from an average of 82°F (28°C) along the Caribbean Coast to a chilly 54°F (12°C) in Bogotá, which, like Medellín, is perched in the Andes mountains.

Seasons as such do not exist in Colombia, but rainfall and brisk winterlike weather is common October–November and April–June. Rainfall is rarely excessive and only a problem if you plan to travel off the beaten track on Colombia's rough-paved mountain roads. The dry season usually runs December–March in mountainous areas, mid-December–April and July–September in low-lying coastal regions.

The following are the average monthly maximum and minimum temperatures for Bogotá.

Jan.	67F	19C	May	66F	19C	Sept.	66F	19C
	48	9		51	10		49	9
Feb.	68F	20C	June	65F	18C	Oct.	66F	19C
	49	9		51	10		50	10
Mar.	67F	19C	July	64F	18C	Nov.	66F	19C
	50	10		50	10		50	10
Apr.	67F	19C	Aug.	65F	18C	Dec.	66F	19C
	51	10		50	10		49	9

8   Ecuador

A patchwork of highland and jungle, this tiny nation claims colonial cities preserved from the days of the Conquistadores, impressive volcanoes quilted with green terraced plots, and stunning natural wonders that, at their most impressive, change the very way we see ourselves and the world.

By Jane Onstott

SANDWICHED BETWEEN Peru and Colombia, tiny mainland Ecuador could easily be overlooked, or worse, dismissed as a mere stepping stone to the more famous Galápagos Islands. But mainland Ecuador itself is an adventurer's paradise: The growing market for ecotourism and adventure travel means that visitors may now choose from a wide variety of stimulating activities—white-water rafting along wild rivers, trekking and mountaineering among some of the world's highest volcanic peaks, horseback riding and mountain biking through lush subtropical valleys. Dedicated birders will spot many of Ecuador's more than 1,500 indigenous and migratory species—from toucans and tanagers to macaws and parrots—in cloud forests, tropical dry forests, and of course, the rain forests of the Amazon Basin.

Traversing the entire country from north to south, the rugged Andes embrace a series of fertile, high-altitude valleys easily accessed from the Pan-American Highway. Culture vultures will devour the sights, sounds, and smells of market day, when highland Indians dressed in tiny felt fedoras and woolen ponchos or bright embroidered skirts sell miniature mountains of hand-wrought crafts, textiles, and locally grown produce. In Otavalo, one of Ecuador's largest and most prosperous market villages, you can barter for rugs, sweaters, and weavings; the locals favor squealing pigs, candied apples, and medicinal herbs.

Most travelers to Ecuador begin or end their trip in the highlands, with a visit to Quito, which, at 2,907 meters (9,530 feet) above sea level, is South America's second-highest capital city. Quito is a pleasant mixture of sights modern and colonial: You'll find art galleries and stylish cafés in the New City and a historic Old City with striking colonial architecture that's protected by UNESCO.

West of Quito towers the now-dormant Pichincha volcano, beyond which the Andes plunge toward the coast. Although tourist infrastructure along Ecuador's Pacific coast is spotty, Machalilla National Park is beginning to draw both development and adventurous tourists to the central coast. Guayaquil, South America's busiest port, attracts more foreign business than tourism; although it's noisy and neglected-looking, the city still has its share of excellent restaurants and first-class hotels.

More impressive is Ecuador's upper Amazon Basin, the *Oriente*, which while comprising one-third of the country's landmass has only about 4% of its population. Border wars with Peru, the most substantive in 1942, have reduced Ecuador's portion of the Oriente by half—a fact that Ecuadoran mapmakers have yet to accept. Despite this, tourists have little to fear in the Oriente. Rather, there are endless waterways large and small to explore, many species of wildlife to discover, and little-known Indian cultures to encounter deep within Ecuador's enigmatic rain forest.

Ecuador's most touristed treasure is the Galápagos Islands, separated from the mainland by 600 miles of Pacific Ocean. This barren, volcanic archipelago is inhabited not only by giant tortoises and spiny marine iguanas, but also by modern Robinson Crusoes who have traded creature comforts for an island existence in shorts and sandals. Tour the islands by boat, swimming with sea lions and snorkeling or diving in the warm waters rich with marine life, and you too may understand why locals willingly accept a lack of civilization in exchange for life in what's known as Darwin's "living laboratory of evolution."

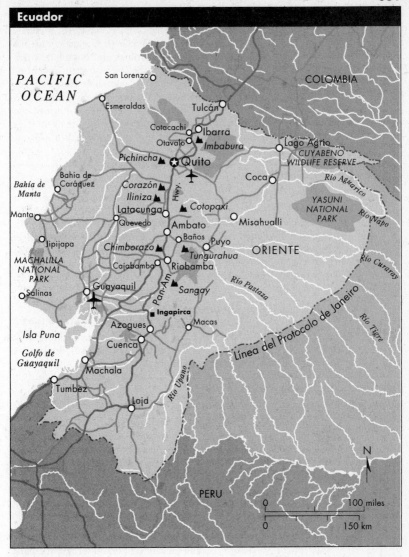

PACIFIC
OCEAN

San Lorenzo

COLOMBIA

Esmeraldas

Tulcán

Cotacachi · Ibarra
Otavalo · Imbabura

Lago Agrio
CUYABENO
WILDLIFE RESERVE
Río Aguarico

Pichincha · Quito

Coca

Bahía de
Manta

Bahía de
Caráquez

Corazón
Iliniza
Latacunga
Quevedo

Cotopaxi

YASUNI
NATIONAL
PARK

Río Napo

Manta

Ambato
Baños
Puyo

Misahualli

Jipijapa

Chimborazo

Tungurahua

ORIENTE

Río Curaray

MACHALILLA
NATIONAL
PARK

Cajabamba
Riobamba

Río Pastaza

Salinas

Guayaquil

Sangay

Isla Puna

Ingapirca

Macas

Golfo de
Guayaquil

Azogues

Cuenca

Línea del Protocolo de Janeiro

Río Tigre

Machala

Tumbez

Río Upano

Loja

N

PERU

0   100 miles

0   150 km

Pan-Am

Hwy.

QUITO

More than a simple stopping-off point on the way to the Galápagos
Islands, Quito is an engaging city and an excellent base for excursions
into the nearby Central Highland and Imbabura regions. Ecuador's capital is scenically situated in a long and narrow valley at the foot of the
slumbering Pichincha Volcano. Rugged, dark-green mountains surround
the city, providing the sort of photogenic backdrop you might not expect in a sprawling metropolis of 1.2 million people. Quito lies only
15 miles south of the equator, but because of its altitude it has a mild,
springlike climate all year. Quiteños are fond of saying that their city
gives you four seasons in one day—a statement supported by the cool
mornings, warm days, and often cold nights.

After the weather, Quito's other surprise is its Old City, a maze of colonial mansions, cathedrals, and crowded cobblestone streets, preserved and vibrant. UNESCO has declared the Old City a World Heritage Site, banning the destruction of colonial buildings and limiting the construction of new buildings and leaving the colonial sector one of the best preserved in South America. Recent relaxation of a law requiring that buildings be painted the traditional white with blue trim has led to applications of pastel paints, with pleasing results. Nonetheless, after a morning in the hectic Old City, the relative tranquility of the New City, with its outdoor cafés, galleries, and smart shops, is a welcome change of pace.

Visitor Information

CETUR (Av. Eloy Alfaro 1214 at Calle Carlos Tovar, ☎ 02/225190 or 02/225191) provides maps and brochures and is open weekdays 8:30–4:30. **LibriMundi** (Calle J. L. Mera 851, ☎ 02/234791) carries maps and tourism-related publications. For members, the **South American Explorers Club** (Calle Tolededo 1254 at Calle Cordero, ☎ 02/566076; U.S. ☎ 607/277–0488) has an information board and travel library; they can also put members in touch with reliable guides for a variety of activities.

The English-language newspaper *Inside Ecuador* has restaurant reviews and ads for sporting and cultural events; a free booklet titled "The Explorer" lists restaurants, bars, and shops, and gives general tourist information. Both publications can be found at newsstands, bookstores, and other locations throughout the city.

Arriving and Departing

By Plane

Quito's international **Aeropuerto Mariscal Sucre** (☎ 02/440083 or 02/440081), 6 miles north of the city center, is regularly served by **American Airlines, Continental,** and **Saeta.** Ecuador's major domestic carriers, **Saeta/SAN** and **TAME,** fly daily from Quito to Guayaquil (30 minutes) and Cuenca (40 minutes) for $30 or less one-way. Those flying Saeta internationally may book two internal flights at no extra charge—either on the continent or round-trip to San Cristóbal in the Galápagos Islands.

Taxis in Quito use meters, but those leaving the airport are exempt. Agree on a price before you enter a cab. Unless you seem particularly green, expect to pay about $5 to the Old City and $4 to the New City (a bit more during rush hour).

By Train

Service on the Quito–Riobamba line has resumed after years of neglect, but runs on Saturdays only, departing at 8 AM from the Quito **train station** (Av. Maldonado at Calle Sincholagua, Quito, ☎ 02/656144). Train fares for foreigners have recently risen appreciably, yet remain quite reasonable. The train has a Pullman coach and an open-sided car that's often crowded with farmers, their produce, and sometimes small farm animals.

Metropolitan Touring (*see* Tour Operators, *below*) operates the most dependable, albeit pricey, train service with a special car that they attach to the regular train. Their two- to four-day treks by train and *autoferro* (buses converted to ride the rails) join Quito with Riobamba and Cuenca and cost $288–$660 per person, including food, accom-

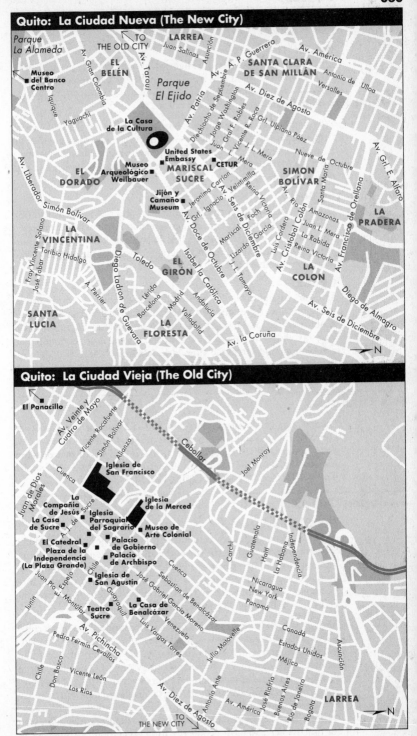

Quito: La Ciudad Nueva (The New City)

Parque La Alameda

TO THE OLD CITY

LARREA
Juan Salinas
Asunción

Av. Gran Colombia

Av. Taroui

Museo del Banco Centro

EL BELÉN

Parque El Ejido

SANTA CLARA DE SAN MILLÁN

Av. A. P. Guerrero

Av. América

Antonio de Ulloa

Versalles

Iquitae

Yaguachi

La Casa de la Cultura

Av. Patria

Dieciocho de Septiembre

Jorge Washington

Gral F. Robles

Grl. Ulpiano Páez

Av. Diez de Agosto

Av. Liberador

EL DORADO

Simón Bolívar

Museo Arqueológico Weilbauer

United States Embassy

MARISCAL SUCRE

CETUR

Juan L. Vicente R. Roca

J. L. Mera

Mera

Reina Victoria

Nueve de Octubre

SIMÓN BOLÍVAR

Santa María

Av. Grl. E. Alfaro

LA PRADERA

LA VINCENTINA

Simón Bolívar

Fray Vincente Solano

Toribio Hidalgo

José Tobar

A. Perrier

Diego Ladrón de Guevara

Toledo

Jijón y Camaño Museum

Jeronimo Carrión

Av. Grl. Ignacio

Av. Seis de Diciembre

Av. Doce de Octubre

Isabel la Católica

EL GIRÓN

Lérida

Barcelona

Madrid

Andalucía

Valladolid

Av. Veintimilla

Mariscal Foch

Lizardo García

J. L. Tamayo

Av. Cristóbal Colón

Amazonas

Juan L. Mera

La Rabida

Reina Victoria

Luis Cordero

LA COLON

Av. Francisco de Orellana

Diego de Almagro

SANTA LUCIA

LA FLORESTA

Av. la Coruña

Av. Seis de Diciembre

N

Quito: La Ciudad Vieja (The Old City)

El Panacillo

Av. Veinte y Cuatro de Mayo

Vicente Rocafuerte

Simón Bolívar

Alianzo

Ceballos

Joel Monroy

Cuenca

Juan de Dios Morales

Iglesia de San Francisco

La Compañía de Jesús

La Casa de Sucre

Av. J. de Sucre

El Catedral Plaza de la Independencia (La Plaza Grande)

Iglesia Parroquial del Sagrario

Iglesia de la Merced

Museo de Arte Colonial

Palacio de Gobierno

Palacio de Archbispo

Cuenca

Sebastián de Benalcázar

Carchi

Guatemala

Haití

La Habana

Independencia

Nicaragua

New York

Panamá

Juan Pío E. Espejo

E. Montúfar

Iglesia de San Agustín

José Gabriel García Moreno

Junín

Guayaquil

Teatro Sucre

La Casa de Benalcázar

Venezuela

Luis Vargas Torres

Canadá

Estados Unidos

Méjico

Ascunción

Av. Pichincha

Pedro Fermín Cevallos

Julio Matovelle

Chile

Don Bosco

Vicente León

Los Rios

Av. Diez de Agosto

Antonio Ante

Av. América

José Riofrio

Buenos Aires

Rio de Janeiro

Bogotá

LARREA

TO THE NEW CITY

N

modations, and tours. (Expect a 15% discount if you purchase your tour in Ecuador.)

By Car

Quito is on the Pan-American Highway, about a twisty, four-hour drive (269 kilometers/167 miles) from Tulcán, on the Colombian border.

Getting Around Quito

It's roughly 3 kilometers (2 miles) from the center of the Old City to the beginning of the New City at Avenida Amazonas. Sights in the Old City are relatively easy to explore on foot, but the New City—apart from the Mariscal, Colón, and La Floresta districts—is larger and best conquered by cab.

By Bus

Quito's buses are inexpensive (about 10¢) and run frequently during the day, but during the morning and afternoon rush, when commuters are packed in like sardines, it's best to walk or hail a taxi. The new *executivo* buses cost 20¢ and guarantee seating, making them the more comfortable option.

By Taxi

Taxis are ubiquitous and inexpensive, making them an ideal form of transportation. Agree on a price beforehand if the driver says his meter is not working. Standard crosstown fare is less than $5, much less if you stay within the Old or New City, and tipping is not common. Pay a maximum 50¢ surcharge after dark. **Tele Taxi** (☎ 02/250845), a reliable cab service, will send a taxi to your door for no extra charge; no English is spoken, however.

Tour Operators

Guided, English-language tours cost $10–$25 per person and cover Quito's principal sights in about three hours. Contact **Kleinturs** (Av. de los Shyris 1000 at Calle Holanda, ☎ 02/430345) or **Metropolitan Touring** (Av. República de El Salvador 970, Quito, ☎ 02/464780, FAX 02/464702; U.S. ☎ 800/527–2500, FAX 214/783–1286).

Exploring Quito

The Old City

The oldest part of Quito was founded in 1534 by the Spanish explorer Sebastian Benalcazar, on the site of the ancient Indian town of Shyris. The original colonial town was bordered by its four most important monasteries: San Francisco, La Merced, San Agustín, and Santo Domingo. Today, informal markets and street vendors still crowd the Old City's cobbled plazas and walkways.

At the southern foot of the Old City sits **El Panecillo,** "the bread roll," a rounded hill that affords a marvelous view of the city and surrounding countryside. At the top stands the monumental cast-aluminum statue of the city's protectress, the Virgin of Quito—a copy of Bernardo de Legarda's famous 18th-century sculpture *Virgin of the Apocalypse of the Immaculate Conception,* on display in the Church of San Francisco. A long flight of stairs at the foot of Calle García Moreno climbs to the top of El Panecillo; however, muggers often lie in wait for tourists here, so most people opt for a taxi (about $3 one-way, or $6.50 round-trip with a half-hour wait at the top).

Quito's main square, called **La Plaza Grande** or **Plaza de la Independencia,** is a charming plaza shaded by palms and pines, where tourists and locals alike enjoy the Andean sunshine, a shoe shine, and a bit of local color. The white neoclassical **Palacio de Gobierno** (Government Palace), built in the 19th century, occupies the west side of the plaza. Tiny porticoed shops line the sides of the plaza; hidden within their cool interiors are souvenir and sweet shops.

El Catedral (The Cathedral), flanking the square on the south, houses the tomb of Quito's liberator Field Marshal Antonio José de Sucre. The exceptional sculpting abilities of Manuel Chili Caspicara can be appreciated in the 18th-century tableau *The Holy Shroud,* which hangs behind the choir, and in the intricate designs of the rococo Chapel of St. Ann, in the right nave. *Plaza de la Independencia.* ☛ *Free.* ⊘ *Mon.–Sat. 8–10, 2–4.*

Adjoining the cathedral is the elegant **La Iglesia Parroquial del Sagrario** (Cathedral Chapel), noted for its beautiful facade in sculpted stone and the lovely 18th-century painting of eight archangels covering the cupola. *Main entrance at Calle García Moreno and Calle Espejo.* ☛ *Free.* ⊘ *Mon.–Sat. 8–11, 1–5.*

One block south, **La Compañía de Jesús** (Church of the Company of Jesus), with its magnificently sculpted stone facade, is considered one of the most beautiful religious structures in the Americas. The high central nave and the delicacy of its Arab-inspired, gilded plasterwork—undergoing extensive restoration at press time (winter 1995)—give the church a sumptuous, almost sinfully rich appearance. Indeed, almost 1½ tons of gold were poured into the ceilings, walls, pulpits, and altars during its 170 years of construction, between 1605 and 1775. At the center of the main altar is a statue of the Quiteña saint, Mariana de Jesús; her remains are entombed at the foot of the altar. *Calle García Moreno at Calle Sucre.* ☛ *Free.* ⊘ *Daily 9:30–11, 4–6.*

Established by Franciscan monks in 1536, **La Iglesia de San Francisco** (Church of St. Francis), Quito's largest colonial church, is named for the patron saint of the city. The twin towers, destroyed by an eruption of Pichincha Volcano in 1582, were rebuilt at half their original size, contributing to the facade's less than impressive appearance. The church's extraordinary interior, however, represents the first New World example of walls, columns, and ceilings entirely covered with sculpted, gilded, and painted wood—a style later copied not only in Quito but also throughout the continent. Stationed at the main altar is Bernardo de Legarda's famed 18th-century sculpture *Virgin of the Apocalypse of the Immaculate Conception.* The convent at the north end of the complex now houses an interesting museum. Although the museum is officially closed for renovations, the monks often give tours, including a visit to the church brewery, where homemade ale was made until the 1970s. *Plaza San Francisco,* ☎ *02/211124.* ☛ *Donation accepted at museum.* ⊘ *Weekdays 9–noon, 3–4:30.*

Recent restorations at **La Iglesia San Agustín** (Church of St. Augustine) highlight its stunning coffered ceilings, patterned in precise geometric and floral designs. Crowding the side naves are paintings of St. Augustine. The gilded, polychrome, wooden crucifix on the main altar is an impressive example of School of Quito art, a baroque style combining Spanish and Indian artistic themes. *Calle Chile at Calle Guayaquil.* ☛ *Free.* ⊘ *Daily 9–1, 3–5.*

A few blocks west, the rather sober Spanish baroque facade of **La Iglesia de la Mercéd** (Church of Mercy) belies an interior of surprising light and beauty. The polychrome image of the Virgin of Mercy, which occupies a central niche by the main altar, was sculpted to honor a virgin who supposedly intervened to save Quito from earthquakes and volcanic eruptions. The church's adjoining convent, shown by appointment only, houses a rich collection of colonial paintings and sculptures, and a vast library that includes *La Celda del Provincial* (the Provincial's Cell), whose walls are covered with exquisite paintings of the 12 apostles. *Calle Chile at Calle Cuenca.* ☛ *Free.* ⊙ *Mon.–Sat. 7:30–noon, 3–5.*

La Casa de Sucre, the home of Field Marshal Antonio José de Sucre, displays 19th-century furniture and clothing, as well as photographs, historical documents, and letters. The house, from the kitchen to the adjoining stables, has been entirely restored, and to many it may be more interesting than the hodgepodge of memorabilia within. *Calle Venezuela 573 at Calle Sucre,* ☎ *02/512860.* ☛ *Entry fee.* ⊙ *Tues.–Sat.*

The **Museo de Arte Colonial** (Museum of Colonial Art) is in a restored 17th-century colonial mansion; the collection includes colonial furniture and 16th- to 18th-century sculpture and paintings by Miguel de Santiago and various members of the School of Quito. The amusing *Vices and Virtues of the European Countries* is a series of 12 18th-century paintings by Colonial masters Samaniego and Rodríguez that depicts the supposed characters of various Western European countries. *Calle Cuenca at Calle Mejía,* ☎ *02/212297.* ☛ *Entry fee.* ⊙ *Tues.–Fri. 10–6, Sat. 10–3, Sun. 10–2.*

The New City

In the triangular **Parque La Alameda,** at the southern extreme of the New City, students and businessmen stroll in their free time, and lovers embrace under shady trees. A few blocks north, in the larger **Parque El Ejido,** Ecuadorans gather to play *ecuavoli* (three-man volleyball), and theater groups hold impromptu performances. On Saturday, in the morning and early afternoon, there are open-air art exhibitions.

On the east edge of Parque El Ejido, **La Casa de la Cultura** (House of Culture) is home to the **Museo del Banco Central** (Central Bank Museum). Ground-floor exhibits concentrate on pre-Columbian archaeology, while upstairs there's an excellent collection of colonial religious art and two additional floors of contemporary Ecuadoran works. *Av. Patria at Av. 6 de Diciembre,* ☎ *02/565808.* ☛ *Entry fee. Closed Mon.*

Also housed in La Casa de la Cultura, **El Museo de Arte Moderno** (Museum of Modern Art) exhibits contemporary Ecuadoran and indigenous art, as well as religious and children's art and an excellent collection of pre-Columbian and colonial musical instruments. ☎ *02/527440 (ext. 47).* ☛ *Entry fee.* ⊙ *Tues.–Sat.*

Across the street, the **Museo Arqueológico Weilbauer** (Weilbauer Archaeology Museum) offers free English-language tours of its extensive collection of pre-Columbian ceramics. *Av. Patria at Av. 12 de Octubre,* ☎ *02/230577.* ☛ *Free.* ⊙ *Weekdays 8–1.*

The nearby **Jijóny Caamaño Museum,** in the Catholic University, has a large collection of colonial art, with paintings and sculptures from some of the masters of the School of Quito. There also is a small collection of Ecuadoran and Peruvian archaeological finds. Well-informed docents lead free English-language tours. *Av. 12 de Octubre at Calle Roca,* ☎ *02/529250 or 02/529260.* ☛ *Entry fee.* ⊙ *Weekdays 9–4.*

El Museo Amazónico (Amazon Museum) houses an impressive collection of artifacts and utilitarian items from different Amazonian cultures, including cook pots and bowls, jewelry, hunting implements, and clothing. The bookstore on the first floor has a superb collection of books about Latin American culture and its indigenous peoples, although most are in Spanish. *Av. 12 de Octubre 1430,* ☎ *02/562633.* ☛ *Entry fee.* ⊘ *Weekdays 8:30–1, 2:30–6:30.*

Oswaldo Guayasamín, one of Ecuador's most famous living artists, has a **workshop** and **museum** in the residential neighborhood of Bellavista in the New City. On display are pre-Columbian ceramics and colonial sculptures and paintings, as well as a permanent exhibit of Guayasamín's paintings. T-shirts with Guayasamín's designs, as well as other handicrafts, are sold in the gift shop. *Calle José Bosmediano 543,* ☎ *02/242779 or 02/244373.* ☛ *Free. Closed Sun.*

Shopping

Quito's specialty and crafts stores are reasonably priced, and although they don't rival the outlying Indian markets for bargains, the quality of the merchandise is sometimes superior. Look for brightly painted balsa-wood birds made in the Amazon region and cedar statues from highland villages. Wool and cotton sweaters, shawls, and tapestries vary in quality and price, as do items made of leather. Stores throughout Quito are generally closed Saturday afternoon and Sunday.

Shopping District
In the New City's Mariscal district—between Avenidas Amazonas, 6 de Diciembre, Patria, and Colón—is a tightly packed collection of all sorts of boutiques and crafts stands.

Specialty Shops
Casa Indo Andina (Calle Roca 606, at J. L. Mera) sells top-of-the-line items, including original and reproduced religious art and silver- and bronze-gilded frames; there are alpaca wool sweaters from Peru, reproductions of pre-Columbian ceramic ware, and a showy collection of silver jewelry. **Centro Artesanal** (Calle J. L. Mera 804) specializes in hand-knit apparel. **Galería Latina** (Calle J. L. Mera 833) offers an enormous variety of sterling-silver jewelry, woven rugs, ceramic figures, and antiques. In addition to its regional handicrafts, **La Bodega** (Calle J. L. Mera 614) has an extensive collection of hand-knit wool and cotton sweaters. **Olga Fisch's Folklore** (Av. Colón 260) is one of Quito's more expensive boutiques, specializing in handwoven rugs and tapestries designed by the late owner and inspired by indigenous motifs.

Markets
You can lose yourself among the stalls at the **Santa Clara market,** in the New City at the corner of Calle Versalles and Calle Marchena. At this traditional neighborhood market, you'll find fruit piled high in pleasing geometrical arrangements, bundles of dried and fresh herbs, grains, and huge bunches of freshly cut flowers. You can listen to a musician play soulful accordion tunes, or light a candle at the neon shrine to the Virgin Mary tucked between the vendors' stalls.

In the Old Town, the streets around the Plaza Grande constitute a gigantic informal marketplace specializing in polyester pants, cheap watches, brooms, buckets—you name it! It's more a place to watch people, however, than to shop for handicrafts, and you'll want to keep careful watch on your pockets amid the crowds.

Shopping Centers
At the intersection of Avenidas Amazonas and Naciones Unidas there are three shopping centers: **El Caracol, CCI,** and **Unicornio.** The popular **Quicentro** is just a block away at Avenida Naciones Unidas and Avenida

República del Salvador. Possibly the best selection of shops and restaurants can be found at **El Bosque** (Av. Occidental at Calle Carvajal).

Sports

Bullfighting

The only regularly scheduled bullfights are held during the weeklong Fiestas de Quito, in early December. Hotels will sometimes purchase tickets for guests with room reservations. The bullring (☎ 02/246037 or 02/247850) is at Avenida Amazonas and Calle Ascaray.

Soccer

Games are held during the season (Mar.–Dec.) at around noon on Sunday, with an occasional Saturday game, at the **Estadio Olímpico "Atahualpa"** (☎ 02/247510), at Avenida 6 de Diciembre and Avenida Naciones Unidas. Tickets, which cost $2.50–$10, must be purchased at the stadium, though try asking your hotel concierge first.

Dining

Quito's better restaurants are in the New City. At even the most tony establishments, formal attire is more of a guideline than a requirement. Many restaurants close between 3 and 7 PM, plus all day on Sunday. For price ranges *see* Dining *in* Ecuador Essentials, *below.*

Eclectic

$ ★ **The Magic Bean.** It's not magic but the powerful spell cast by good food that draws travelers, expatriates, and locals to "the Bean" to socialize over healthy salads and do business over a cappuccino or cocktail. Blackberry pancakes light up the morning, while lunch and dinner menus emphasize salads, soups, personal-size pizzas, and pastas. ✗ *Calle Foch 681 (at Calle J. L. Mera),* ☎ *02/566181. AE, DC, MC, V.*

Ecuadoran

$$$$ ★ **La Querencia.** Appreciate the excellent views of Quito from the dining room, or dine in the serene outdoor garden, the perfect place to linger over a meal. La Querencia is best known for its superb Ecuadoran dishes; try the lamb stewed with fruit, or king prawns flambéed in cognac. ✗ *Av. Eloy Alfaro 2530 (at Calle Catalina Aldaz),* ☎ *02/461664. AE, DC, MC, V. No dinner Sun.*

$$ **La Ronda.** During the day businesspeople gather for traditional Ecuadoran meals such as seafood casserole or *mote pillo,* a traditional peasant dish of corn, cheese, avocado, and scrambled egg. Sunday brunch is extensive, inexpensive, and features live Ecuadoran music. ✗ *Calle Belo Horizonte 400 (at Calle Almagro),* ☎ *02/540459 or 02/545176. AE, DC, MC, V.*

$$ **Wonder Bar.** This restaurant, housed on the second floor of a 1930s-era movie house, is a welcome respite from the bustling crowds of the Old City. Stop in for an enormous serving of ceviche (seafood marinated in lime juice, onions, and cilantro), or try the filet mignon smothered in mushrooms or the empanadas *de morocho* (white corn turnovers filled with ground beef, rice, and peas). ✗ *Cine Bolívar, Calle Espejo (at Calle Flores),* ☎ *02/215778. DC, MC, V.* ☉ *Mon.–Sat. 10–4.*

$ **La Canoa Manabita.** Virtually unknown to tourists despite its location in the Mariscal district, this no-frills eatery serves exquisite renditions of coastal Ecuadoran dishes. Try the *viche,* a hearty fish soup with corn, peanuts, and bananas, or the fried fish served with rice, lentils, and *patacones* (fried green bananas). ✗ *Calle Calama 231 (at Calle Almagro),* ☎ *02/525353. DC. Closed Mon.*

Italian/Continental

$$$$ La Gritta. Reserved, tuxedoed waiters serve well-presented Italian and Continental dishes in this grotto popular with local artists as well as executives. The steak tartare is perfectly rendered, as are the homemade pastas—try the *paglia e gianni* (shrimp and pasta cooked in foil with olive oil and herbs). ✕ *Calle Santa María 246 (at Calle Rábida),* ☎ *02/567628. AE, DC, MC, V. Closed Sat. lunch, Sun.*

$$$ La Taberna Piedmonte. Locals and resident diplomats have been com-
★ ing to this superb Italian eatery for years. They indulge in *rosette de margro* (homemade spinach pasta baked with herbs) or *pizzaiola* (fillet of beef topped with cheese, vegetables, and fresh herbs). At night the view of Quito from the intimate dining room is breathtaking. ✕ *Calle C. J. Arosemena Tola 173 (at Av. Eloy Alfaro),* ☎ *02/433607 or 02/433608. Reservations advised. DC, MC, V. Closed Sun.*

Steak Houses

$$$ La Terraza del Tártaro. Situated in the heart of the New City, this long-time Quito favorite is known for its reliable service and its delicious yet simply prepared meats. The penthouse restaurant is cheered by a blazing fire at night, when low lighting draws attention to the brilliantly lit city below. ✕ *Calle Veintimilla 1106 (at Av. Amazonas),* ☎ *02/527987. DC, V.*

$$ Colombia Steakhouse. Both locations of this bustling, informal restaurant serve large portions of every type of meat—from steaks to kidneys—and many side salads, all on display for your inspection. Office workers crowd the booths and Formica tables during midweek lunches, and families take over on the weekends. ✕ *Av. Colón 1262 (at Av. Amazonas),* ☎ *02/551857; and Av. Tarqui 735 (at Av. 10 de Agosto),* ☎ *02/541920. AE, DC, MC, V.*

Lodging

Most hotel rooms in Quito have neither air-conditioning nor heating, nor are these ambience controls missed in Quito's moderate climate. For price ranges *see* Lodging *in* Ecuador Essentials, *below.*

$$$$ Hotel Colón Internacional. In the New City across from the Parque El Ejido, this large modern hotel has numerous shops and on-site services. The rooms, in which the color brown prevails, are functional but nondescript; the lower floors are noisy because of street traffic. ⊞ *Av. Amazonas (at Av. Patria),* ☎ *02/560666,* FAX *02/563903; U.S.* ☎ *800/224–5889. 415 rooms. 2 restaurants, 2 coffee shops, pool, barbershop, sauna, exercise room, bookstore, casino, travel services. AE, DC, MC, V.*

$$$$ Hotel Oro Verde. Quito's most luxurious and expensive high-rise hotel
★ is comfortable and welcoming despite its opulence. Rooms have sea-green carpets, floral spreads, and modern, attractive screen prints. ⊞ *Av. 12 de Octubre 1820 (at Calle Cordero),* ☎ *02/568079 or 02/569189,* FAX *02/569189; U.S.* ☎ *800/223–6800. 193 rooms, 48 suites. 4 restaurants, bar, indoor-outdoor pool, sauna, steam room, exercise room, racquetball, squash, casino, business services. AE, DC, MC, V.*

$$$ Hotel Quito. Only a 15-minute walk from the center of the New City, this high-rise hotel overlooks both the valley of Guápulo and Quito itself, with exceptional views around sunset; the rooftop bar and restaurant are prime viewing spots. Ask for one of the redecorated rooms on the upper floors, as some of the older ones are a bit shabby. ⊞ *Av. González Suárez 2500,* ☎ *02/543631 or 02/544600,* FAX *02/567284; U.S.* ☎ *800/528–1234. 230 rooms. Restaurant, bar, coffee shop, pool, sauna. AE, DC, MC, V.*

$$$ **Hotel Sebastián.** This attractive, new, eight-story hotel is ideally situ-
★   ated in the busy Mariscal district, near shops and restaurants. A taste-
ful color scheme of mauve and grey green prevails, with handsomely
framed watercolors as accent pieces. The comfortable suites cost only
a little more than the regular rooms. ☎ *Calle Almagro 822,* ☎ *02/222400
or 02/222300,* ℻ *02/222500. 49 rooms, 7 suites. 2 restaurants, bar,
convention center. AE, DC, MC, V.*

$$ **Apart-Hotel Antinea.** Once you check into one of the spacious apart-
★   ments in this charming inn, you may never want to check out. White-
washed brick walls and rough-hewn, exposed-wood beams show a
pleasing mixture of French and Flemish architecture, and each of the
simple yet elegant apartments has its own well-stocked kitchenette, wonderfully cozy beds, and plenty of space to work, read, or write. Amenities include on-site parking and direct-dial phones. ☎ *Calle Juan
Rodríguez 175 (at Calle Almagro),* ☎ *02/506839 or 02/506838,* ℻
*02/504404. 8 apartments. Cafeteria (breakfast only), laundry service.
AE, MC, V.*

$$ **Café Cultura.** Attention to detail makes this self-assured, anglophone
hotel—formerly the Center for Arts and Culture of the French Embassy—
stand out from the competition. A fire in the stone-trimmed hearth heats
the wood-paneled library-cum-sitting room, hammocks sway in the pri-
vate garden, and each small yet refined room has subtly unique decor.
☎ *Calle Robles (at Calle Reina Victoria),* ☎ *and* ℻ *02/224271. 16
rooms. Cafeteria. DC, V.*

$$ **Hostal Los Alpes.** This intimate colonial inn has been designated a World
Heritage Site by UNESCO. There are several cozy sitting rooms with
fireplaces, and a sunny, cactus-filled reading room on the second floor.
Creaky floors and the early-rising zealots at the nearby police academy
may pose a challenge for light sleepers. ☎ *Calle Tamayo 233 (at Calle
Jorge Washington),* ☎ *02/561110 or 02/561128. 25 rooms. Restaurant. AE, MC, V.*

$ **Hostal La Casona.** This is the most charming hotel in the Old City—a
★   lovely, restored colonial-style house near the Sucre theater. Decorative
touches include embossed white-plaster ceilings and floors of terra-cotta
tiles framed in cow vertebra. The rooms are small but have firm beds
and colonial furnishings. ☎ *Calle Manabí 255 (near Calle Flores),* ☎
02/514764, ℻ *02/563271. 23 rooms. Cafeteria. V.*

$ **Hotel Ambassador.** Centrally located in the New City, the Ambassador
is clean and cheerful, though somewhat anonymous. There are several
sitting rooms, one of which has a fireplace, and the rooms themselves
are comfortable, if a tiny bit threadbare. ☎ *Av. 9 de Octubre (at Av.
Colón),* ☎ *02/561777,* ℻ *02/503712. 60 rooms. Restaurant, bar. AE,
DC, MC, V.*

$ **La Posada del Maple.** It's the air of easy camaraderie (and not the plain
rooms) that lures everyone from seasoned travelers to Peace Corps vol-
unteers to this friendly, inexpensive bed-and-breakfast. The price includes a hearty American-style breakfast and kitchen privileges. ☎ *Calle
Juan Rodríguez 148 (near 6 de Diciembre),* ☎ *02/544507. 10 rooms.
Cafeteria. DC, V.*

The Arts

Quito's arts' scene has grown significantly in the last few years. Check
local papers *El Comercio* and *Hoy,* the free monthly cultural agenda
"La Gazette," and the English-language newspaper *Inside Ecuador* (sold
in bookstores and at newsstands) for information about theater, concerts, and art expositions.

Ballet

The **National Folkloric Ballet "Jacchigua"** performs Wednesday and Friday at 7:30 PM in the San Gabriel Theatre (Av. América at Calle Mariana de Jesús, ☎ 02/506650, ext. 131). Tickets cost $14–$20 and can be purchased in advance at the theater or through Metropolitan Touring (*see* Tour Operators, *above*).

Concerts

Classical and folkloric concerts sometimes are held at the **Corporación Financiera Nacional** (National Financial Corporation, Calle J. L. Mera, behind Hotel Colón, ☎ 02/561026) and also at other venues throughout the city. Check the sources listed above for information.

Film

Cinemas in Quito often show American films in English with Spanish subtitles; for strictly English-language or art films, try the cinema at **La Casa de la Cultura** (Av. Patria at Av. 12 de Octubre, ☎ 02/565808); **The British Council** (Av. Amazonas 1646, at Av. Orellana, ☎ 02/5082820); and **La Casa de al Lado** (Calle Valladolid 1018, at Calle Cordero, ☎ 02/226398).

Nightlife

As with cultural events, the number of bars and dance clubs has boomed in the past few years, and there are now plenty of *salsatecas* (for lovers of salsa music) and discotheques. At the *peñas*, you can hear traditional Ecuadoran music, and drink late into the night with locals. Bars usually open in the late afternoon, dance clubs and peñas around 10 PM. Cover charges for the latter two range from free to $10; many peñas are closed Sun.–Tues.

Bars and Cafés

El Vikingo (Calle Calama 247, at Calle Reina Victoria) is a cozy, one-room pub that serves hot mulled wine and great Hungarian goulash. At **Ghoz** (Calle La Niña 425, at Calle Reina Victoria, ☎ 02/239826) you can play darts, pool, or board games while listening to high-decibel rock and salsa music. **El Pobre Diablo** (Calle Santa María 338, at Calle J. L. Mera, ☎ 02/231982) is a gathering place for local artists and young intellectuals. The more tranquil **Bangalô Tea House and Bar** (Calle Carrión 185, at Calle Tamayo, ☎ 02/520499) features a blazing fireplace and nonstop Brazilian music; you can relax in the tea salon upstairs with coffee, imported teas, quiche, and Brazilian pastries.

Dance Clubs

Rock and salsa are featured at **Blues** (Calle La Granja 132, at Av. Amazonas), a popular and noisy, Western-style discotheque. Locals have been coming to **Salsateca Serseribó** (Calle Veintimilla 325, at Av. 12 de Octubre) for years to dance *cumbia, son,* salsa, and merengue.

PEÑAS

Established, not-too-rowdy peñas in the New City are **Ñuncanchi Peña** (Av. Universitaria 496, at Calle Armero, ☎ 02/540967) and **Nuestra América** (Calle Iñaquito 149, at Av. Amazonas, ☎ 02/444356). In the Old City, try **La Taberna Quito Colonial** (Calle Manabí at Calle Vargas, ☎ 02/213012).

Excursions from Quito

Equatorial Monument

La Mitad del Mundo (the middle of the world) monument marks the spot that the French Geodesic Mission determined to be the exact latitudinal center of the earth in 1736. Visitors today may have less scientific interest, but seem to enjoy themselves as they leap back and forth between the Northern and Southern hemispheres or have their photograph taken as they straddle the equatorial line (latitude 0° 00′ 00″).

The monument proper—a 33-foot-tall trapezoidal stone—is not particularly attractive, but it houses an informative ethnographic museum with displays on Ecuador's diverse cultural groups. Although the explanatory text is in Spanish only, the exhibits themselves prove interesting to most English speakers. ☛ *Entry fee.* ☉ *Tues.–Fri. 9–3, weekends 10–4.*

Getting There

Buses depart daily from the Old City at the intersection of Calle Mejía and Calle José López; the 60-minute ride costs about $1.50. A taxi will take up to four people for $20, including the wait while you visit the monument and museum. Most Quito-based tour operators offer half-day tours for $10–$20 per person.

Guápulo

The village of Guápulo, nestled in a secluded valley below the Hotel Quito, grew up around its impressive 17th-century church, **El Santuario de Guápulo** (Guápulo Sanctuary). The church contains pieces by some of Quito's most exceptional sculptors and painters: The paintings in the central nave are the work of Miguel de Santiago, while the side altar and pulpit—completed in 1716 and considered masterpieces of colonial art—were carved by Juan Bautista Menacho. ☛ *Free.* ☉ *Mon.–Sat. 8–11, 3–5.*

Guápulo itself, its narrow cobblestone lanes lined with traditional two-story white houses trimmed in blue, is a preserved pocket of colonial architecture only 10 minutes by foot from Quito's New City. If you visit in early September, you can help celebrate Guápulo's annual festival, with food and drink and marching bands.

Getting There

Walk downhill to Guápulo via the steep staircase directly behind the Hotel Quito; to return, make the uphill trek back the same way or take a taxi for about $1.

Mindo

Just 81 kilometers (50 miles) west of Quito lies the 47,000-acre **Mindo-Nambillo Protected Forest,** which extends from the small village of Mindo to the slopes of Pichincha. The forest is largely subtropical and ranges in altitude from 4,000 to 15,000 feet above sea level. The reserve harbors more than 300 species of birds, including the quetzal, cock-of-the-rock, numerous tanager and hummingbird species, falcons, woodpeckers, and toucans. Walking trails cut a rough course through thick, canopied vegetation, and dedicated hikers will be rewarded with good views of the park's many waterfalls.

Getting There

The gravel road to Mindo and the reserve is not a good one, and even in a four-wheel-drive vehicle it takes three hours in good weather (the road may be impassable during the rainy season). Consider booking through a Quito-based tour operator such as **Metropolitan Touring** (*see* Tour Operators, *above*) or **Amigos de la Naturaleza** (*see below*).

Dining and Lodging

Within the reserve there are two basic huts for overnight stays, one about a three-hour hike from Mindo, the other at the edge of town. Both facilities are administered by **Amigos de la Naturaleza** (no address, ☎ 02/455344), a local ecotourism group. Mindo itself is just beginning to be developed for tourism, and its services are still rudimentary. The new **Hostería El Carmelo de Mindo** (no address, ☎ 02/538756, FAX 02/408355; $), just outside Mindo, has a pool, restaurant, and rooms with or without private bath. An alternative is **Mindo Gardens** (Mindo, reservations ☎ 02/230463 or 02/564235, FAX 02/564235; $$), a rustic yet pleasant thatch-roof hotel and restaurant on a riverbank; all four double rooms have a private bath with hot water, but no electricity.

Papallacta Hot Springs

A stunning drive over the eastern range of the Andes brings you to the small village of **Papallacta**. A mile beyond town you'll find a pair of natural springs, one hot and one cold. It's a beautiful setting, and on a clear day you can see the snowcapped peak of Antisana. The site—which includes a café and changing facilities—is under new ownership and is undergoing extensive renovations.

Getting There

If you travel by bus to Papallacta, 60 kilometers (37 miles) southeast of Quito, you may have to pay the entire Quito–Tena fare, which is nonetheless under $5. For $35–$40 you can hire a taxi to take you to the springs, wait for an hour or two, and then return you to Quito.

Pasochoa

Pasochoa Protected Forest is administered by **Fundación Natura** (☎ 02/447341 or 02/246072), a private conservation organization dedicated to preserving the remaining 988 acres of high Andean forest that once covered the region. Nearly 100 species of birds have been identified here, including hummingbirds, honeycreepers, and tanagers. There are many walking trails, from short loops to all-day hikes; the trail to the summit (13,800 ft.) is popular but rigorous, and you should take drinking water and snacks. Guides can be hired through Fundación Natura. Camping is permitted within the park, and there are picnic areas with spigots and latrines. However, fires are not permitted, and you should bring all of your own supplies. The park fee is $7 for day use, $12 for a multiday camping permit.

Getting There

There are no direct buses to Pasochoa; in fact, the closest you can get by bus is about 7 kilometers (4½ miles) away. It's best to hire a taxi for the day—the going rate is around $30.

IMBABURA PROVINCE

When the Spaniards conquered the territory north of Quito—called Imbabura after the 15,190-foot volcano of the same name—they introduced sheep to the indigenous people of the region. Over time the mountain-dwelling Otavaleños became expert wool weavers and dyers; even today you may find craftspeople who painstakingly collect and prepare their own natural dyes, despite the increasing popularity of modern synthetic colors. Traditional dyeing methods may be declining, yet the Otavaleños themselves proudly retain many of the old customs, including their manner of dress. The women are striking in their embroidered white ruffle-and-lace blouses, straight blue wraparound skirts, black or blue head cloths, and row upon row of beaded gold necklaces. The men, extremely handsome with their beige felt hats and long braided hair, are most often seen in Western attire, although some of the older men still wear the traditional calf-length white pants, white shirt, and dark blue poncho.

Many small weaving villages dot the green and gold valleys of Imbabura, and artisans make the trek to Otavalo—the largest and most prosperous of these crafts towns—for its fabulously colorful market. Otavalo's *Plaza de Ponchos* (Poncho Plaza) fills up each Saturday with merchants selling weavings, rugs, ponchos, colorful cotton and wool sweaters, jewelry, and antiques. At a nearby street market, locals shop for *alpargates* (rope-soled sandals) and medicinal herbs; just outside town, livestock dealers do a brisk business in squealing pigs, cackling hens, and colossal guinea pigs. Such smaller villages as Cotacachi (famous for its leather) and San Antonio de Ibarra (known for its woodwork) host their own colorful markets, though none on such a grand scale as the Saturday market in Otavalo.

Visitor Information

There's a **CETUR** (Calle Colón 743, ☎ 06/955366, FAX 06/955711; closed weekends) office in Ibarra.

Arriving and Departing

By Car or Taxi

Otavalo is just off the Pan-American Highway, 113 kilometers (70 miles) north of Quito. For around $65, taxis that carry up to four passengers can be hired in Quito for a daylong trip to Otavalo and the surrounding countryside or other towns. A taxi ride between Otavalo and Ibarra costs about $6.

By Bus

From Quito's Terminal Terrestre, buses depart every 30 minutes for Ibarra (2½ hours) and Otavalo (2 hours); round-trip fare costs less than $5. **Transportes Otavalo** (☎ 02/570271) deposits passengers in Otavalo's center; **Flota Imbabura** (☎ 02/572657) has direct service to Ibarra, but for Otavalo they drop you a few blocks outside of town.

Tour Operators

Extensive and economical daylong treks depart from Otavalo. Two reliable operators are **Diceny Viajes** (Sucre 1014, Otavalo, ☎ or FAX 06/921217), which is owned and operated by indigenous people, and **Zulaytur** (Calle Sucre at Calle Colón, 2nd Floor, Otavalo, ☎ 06/921176, FAX 06/920461). In addition, most operators in Quito offer one- and two-day tours, which typically include visits to several weaving villages and sometimes overnights at *hosterías* (country inns). **Metropolitan Touring** (*see* Tour Operators *in* Quito, *above*) has daily departures; **Safari** (Calle Calama 380, at Calle J. L. Mera, Quito, ☎ 02/552505, FAX 02/220426) offers tailor-made excursions.

Exploring Imbabura Province

Otavalo

Otavalo is situated in the rugged lake district nearly 8,530 feet above sea level. Days in this high-altitude valley—a patchwork of small gardens, cerulean lakes, and plowed and fallow fields—are often sunny and warm. Over the picture-book landscape rise the craggy peaks of three now-extinct volcanoes—Imbabura, Cotacachi, and Cayambe, Ecuador's third-tallest mountain. Villagers trudge along the road carrying huge burdens or prodding their laden burros to do the same; come Thursday or Friday, there is a good chance they're headed for Otavalo's famous Saturday market, held at the **Plaza de Ponchos.** Although tourist-oriented, the market is still a remarkable event—beautiful and self-assured Otavaleñas crowd the stalls and stands surrounding the plaza, selling piles of woolen and cotton sweaters; traditional and modern ponchos; tapestries, rugs, and wall hangings; antiques; and sterling silver and *alpaca* (nickel silver) jewelry imbedded with Andean jade, lapis lazuli, and other semiprecious stones.

Near the corner of Calles Modesto Jaramillo and García Moreno locals shop for embroidered blouses, rope-soled sandals, and herbs for curing ailments and attracting lovers. The produce market held simultaneously on **Plaza 24 de Mayo** does an equally brisk business; so, too, does the animal market on **Plaza San Juan,** where people from both town and the surrounding countryside—many colorfully dressed in traditional clothing—bargain for cows, pigs, and other livestock. The animal market begins at 5:30 AM, and most sellers are packing to go by 11 AM. The Plaza de Ponchos market doesn't reach full swing until 7 or 8 AM and lasts all day; a secondary market is held on Wednesday, and some vendors appear every day of the week.

Lago San Pablo

Easily accessible from Otavalo is deep blue Lago San Pablo (San Pablo Lake), 8 kilometers (5 miles) southeast. From the lakeshore you have an unobstructed view of Imbabura Volcano (15,190 feet), which dominates the landscape. The lake can be reached via paths behind Otavalo's defunct train station, or you can take a taxi for around $5.

Cotacachi

Cotacachi, 15 kilometers (9 miles) north of Otavalo, is famous for leather, proffering jackets, skirts, shoes, purses, and luggage of respectable quality. Stores tend to offer identical designs at nearly identical prices, but dedicated shoppers may find bargains lurking in one of the many cramped shops along the main streets. Although most people pass quickly through Cotacachi, it is a pleasant, lived-in sort of town where children play and old men sit gossiping around the small main plaza.

Laguna de Cuicocha

Nearly 18 kilometers (11 miles) west is mile-wide Laguna de Cuicocha, a nearly circular lake cradled in a crater on the lower flanks of an extinct volcano. Marked hiking trails meander along the crater's rim, giving good views of the Imbabura and Cayambe volcanoes and Chile. There are also good views of Cuicocha's two vegetation-covered volcanic islands, which are part of an ecological reserve and closed to the public. Both the lakeshore **Restaurant Muelle Bar** (☎ 06/951965) and the cliff-hugging **Restaurant Mirador** (no ☎) have fantastic views of the lake. Motorboats moored by the former can be hired inexpensively for half-hour lake tours.

Ibarra

Ibarra, capital of Imbabura Province and roughly 25 kilometers (16 miles) north of Otavalo, is a pleasant colonial city, but most tourists stop first at **San Antonio de Ibarra,** on the Pan-American Highway a few miles before the capital. San Antonio is the "Cotacachi of wood carvings"— stores surrounding its central plaza sell variations on identical woodworking themes. Religious statuary of cedar or walnut—costing anywhere from a few dollars to several hundred dollars—is ubiquitous; also available are pieces with more bawdy or whimsical themes.

Sports and the Outdoors

Bicycling

Aventura Flying Dutchman (Calle La Pinta 146, at Calle Almagro, Quito, ☎ 02/449568) organizes day and overnight bicycle treks in the Imbabura region; all equipment is provided.

Boating

Motorboat tours are available inexpensively on Laguna de Cuicocha at the Restaurant Muelle Bar (☎ 06/951965). The Hostería Puerto Lago (*see* Dining and Lodging, *below*) rents paddleboats, rowboats, and motorboats on Lago San Pablo.

Horseback Riding

IntiExpress (Calle Sucre 1106, Otavalo, ☎ 06/921436, ⨳ 06/920737) arranges single and multiday horseback treks to local villages and to natural mineral springs. Horses can also be rented by the guests of Hostería La Mirage in Cotacachi and Hostería Cusín in Lago San Pablo.

Dining and Lodging

Lodging reservations are advised on weekend nights, when tourists fill the region's hotels and hosterías in anticipation of Otavalo's Saturday market. There are few dependably good restaurants in the area, but hosterías typically serve simple, wholesome meals; most serve nonguests, although some require advance reservations. For price ranges, *see* Dining *and* Lodging *in* Ecuador Essentials, *below*.

Cotacachi
DINING AND LODGING

$$$$ **Hostería La Mirage.** La Mirage, built specifically as a country inn, or
★ hostería, is elegant and sophisticated. An eclectic mix of local and European furnishings adds to the refined atmosphere, as do the many windows, which provide views across the formal gardens to the Imbabura volcano, beyond. The rooms and suites are tastefully decorated and equipped with comfortable four-poster beds. ⊡ *Av. 10 de Agosto,* ☎ *06/915237,* ⨳ *06/915065; U.S.* ☎ *800/327–3573. 22 rooms. Restaurant, bar, cafeteria, sauna, steam room, tennis court, horseback riding. DC, MC, V.*

Ibarra
DINING AND LODGING

$$ **Hostería Chorlaví.** Wide, shaded verandas, thick whitewashed walls,
★ and spacious antiques-furnished rooms make this inn a favorite weekend retreat for Ecuadorans and tourists alike. The restaurant emphasizes fresh fish and typical Andean dishes, all served on a flower-filled patio where folkloric groups serenade diners on weekend afternoons. ⊡ *Pan-American Highway S., 2 km (1¼ mi) south of Ibarra,* ☎ *06/ 955777 or 06/955775,* ⨳ *06/956311. 42 rooms. Restaurant, pool, hot tub, sauna, steam room, tennis court, basketball, squash, volleyball. DC, MC, V.*

Lago San Pablo

DINING AND LODGING

$$ Hostería Cusín. This quiet hacienda, draped in a thick carpet of flowers and foliage, was built in 1602 and continues to function as a working farm despite its status as an inn. You can rent a horse or mountain bike and, after a day of rambling through the farm-dotted countryside, mingle with fellow travelers in the congenial fireside bar. ⌘ *Lago San Pablo,* ☎ *06//918013,* ℻ *06/918003; U.S.* ☎ *212/988–4552,* ℻ *212/ 988–4935. 25 rooms. Restaurant, bar, horseback riding, mountain bikes. MC, V.*

$$ Hostería Puerto Lago. A panorama of volcanic peaks forms the backdrop for this lakeside country inn, just a few miles southeast of Otavalo. In the downstairs restaurant, women in traditional dress serve the locally famous and quite outstanding pan-fried trout, served head and all. Amenities include satellite TV and paddleboats and rowboats ⌘ *Pan-American Hwy. S., Km. 5½,* ☎ *06/920920,* ℻ *06/920900. 19 rooms. Restaurant, bar, cafeteria, boating. AE, V.*

Otavalo

DINING

$ SISA. The clean, bright downstairs cafeteria at this cultural complex serves fresh juices, pastries, and sandwiches, and a more intimate restaurant on the second floor has Ecuadoran and international cuisine. A coffee bar, with a different style of music presented each night, is in the works. There is also a gift shop and an extensive bookstore. ✗ *Abdón Calderón 409,* ☎ *06/920154. No credit cards.*

DINING AND LODGING

$ Ali Shungu. The American owners of this squeaky-clean hotel go out of their way to make guests feel at home. The terra-cotta–tile bedrooms are supremely comfortable, and there's plenty of steaming hot water for showers. Dinner selections include such wholesome international dishes as vegetarian lasagna or deep-dish chicken pie served with organically grown vegetables. ⌘ *Calle Quito (at Calle Miguel Egas),* ☎ *06/920750. 20 rooms. Restaurant. V.*

The Arts and Nightlife

Many of the hosterías (*see* Dining and Lodging, *above*) present local bands on Friday and Saturday nights and during Saturday lunch. The music is traditional Andean, the crowds a mix of Ecuadoran and foreign tourists. During the week things are very quiet in the Imbabura region (some would say downright dull). In Otavalo, SISA (*see* Dining and Lodging, *above*) presents occasional art exhibits, live music, dance, and films. Otavalo also has a reasonable selection of peñas—clubs where traditional Andean musicians perform in a less formal venue than that served up at the hosterías. One reliable peña is **Amauta** (Calle Morales at Calle Sucre, no ☎); it's open Friday and Saturday after 8 PM, and there is a small cover charge.

THE CENTRAL HIGHLANDS

South of Quito the Andes rise sharply on either side of the Pan-American Highway, creating a narrow corridor of fertile, high-elevation valleys that are home to nearly half of Ecuador's population. Along this 175-kilometer (109-mile) stretch between Quito and Riobamba are seven of Ecuador's 10 tallest volcanoes. Alexander von Humboldt, the German scientist who explored the area in 1802, was so impressed by the landscape that he coined a sobriquet still used today: the Avenue of the Volcanoes.

Latacunga, just a few hours south of Quito, is an excellent base for visiting the area's colorful market villages, including Saquisilí, Pujilí, and San Miguel de Salcedo. Among the Central Highlands' most attractive destinations is Baños, a sleepy tourist town surrounded by natural beauty. Die-hard cyclists should contemplate the 65-kilometer (40-mile) downhill trek from Baños to Puyo (you and your cycle can return to Baños by bus). Riobamba, the pleasant, unruffled capital of Chimborazo Province, makes a good ending point for a tour of the Central Highlands as it is connected by rail with Guayaquil (and, when trains are running, with Cuenca). Both rail routes pass through some of the country's most spectacular scenery, and both descend the infamous **Nariz del Diablo** (Devil's Nose)—a 305-meter (1,000-foot) drop that the narrow-gauge train negotiates via an ingenious system of hairpin turns, span bridges, and tunnels.

Visitor Information

Baños
There is no **CETUR** office in Baños, but an informative map, "Proyección Panorámica de Baños," provides useful information, especially for walks and hikes.

Riobamba
CETUR (Av. 10 de Agosto 2433, at Calle García Moreno, ☎ 03/941213; closed Sun.–Mon.).

Arriving and Departing

By Train
At press time (winter 1995), regular rail service between Quito and Riobamba ($8 one-way) existed only on Saturday mornings, and was still somewhat unreliable after years of disruption in service (*see* Arriving and Departing: By Train *in* Quito, *above*).

By Car
Latacunga lies just off the Pan-American Highway, 89 kilometers (55 miles) south of Quito. The nearby villages of Pujilí, San Miguel de Salcedo, and Saquisilí are accessed via unpaved but hard-packed roads. Baños is 40 kilometers (25 miles) east of Ambato on the road to Puyo. Riobamba is nestled along the Pan-American Highway 188 kilometers (117 miles) south of Quito.

By Bus
From Quito there are frequent buses to Latacunga (2 hours), Baños (3½ hours), and Riobamba (4 hours). All cost less than $5. Local buses connect Latacunga with Pujilí, Saquisilí, and San Miguel de Salcedo.

Tour Operators

Reliable tour operators that offer day and overnight excursions to the *ferias* (markets) in the Central Highlands include **Nuevo Mundo** (Av. Amazonas 2468, Quito, ☎ 02/552839, FAX 02/565261) and **Metropolitan Touring** (*see* Tour Operators *in* Quito, *above*). **Safari** (Calle Calama 380, at Calle J. L. Mera, Quito, ☎ 02/552505, FAX 02/220426) specializes in smaller, off-the-beaten-track markets and excursions, as well as hiking, climbing, and jungle trips.

Exploring the Central Highlands

Latacunga and the Market Villages

The capital of Cotopaxi Province, Latacunga has been rebuilt three times following massive eruptions of Cotopaxi, the volcano whose perfect snow-covered cone dominates the city. Latacunga's main plaza, **Parque Vicente León,** is dominated by juniper trees trimmed in an assortment of geometric shapes. At the Saturday market held on **Plaza San Sebastián,** most of the goods for sale are geared for locals—fruits and vegetables, plastic ware, and medicinal herbs. Still, you may find *shigras,* the colorful, handwoven hemp bags used by indigenous people. With its 40,000 inhabitants, Latacunga represents a slice of real Ecuadoran life. While this "Ecuadoran reality check" may or may not interest the typical tourist, Latacunga is an excellent base from which to explore some of the Central Highlands markets and mountaintops.

In the tiny mountain village of **Pujilí,** 10 kilometers (6 miles) west of Latacunga, colorful markets are held on Sunday and, with much less ado, on Wednesday. Few tourists find their way to Pujilí—so instead of sunburned gringos, you'll see locals in bright turquoise or carmine red ponchos and miniature fedoras buying and selling produce, pottery, and costume jewelry. In **Saquisilí,** 13 kilometers (8 miles) north, indigenous people in regional dress fill all eight of the village's dusty plazas during the Thursday market, where you can pick through piles of traditional wares—including grotesque, painted wooden masks of animals and devils. **San Miguel de Salcedo,** 14 kilometers (9 miles) south of Latacunga on the Pan-American Highway, is a third interesting and accessible market town. Although Salcedo's picturesque streets and plazas make it appealing on any day, it's most interesting to plan your visit around the Sunday market or the smaller one held on Thursday. Taxis between Latacunga and Pujilí, Saquisilí, and Salcedo cost less than $10 each way.

Baños

Forty kilometers (25 miles) east of Ambato on the road to Puyo is Baños—a tourist town, no doubt about it. Quiteños have been soaking in the curative thermal springs here for decades, if not centuries, and the locals are well used to outsiders. Despite the tourists, Baños retains its enormous appeal, largely because of its superb location by a river at the foot of Tungurahua Volcano. Many species of birds and butterflies inhabit this thickly vegetated subtropical valley, and there are hiking trails, waterfalls, and rivers. In town, the twin spires of **La Iglesia de la Virgen del Agua Santa** rise above the tree-lined plaza. The church, whose black-and-white facade is slightly startling, was built to honor Baños's miracle-working Virgin; the huge paintings inside are testimonials from her many exultant beneficiaries.

There are several thermal springs in town, but the best is a series of pools called **El Salado** (The Salty), 2 kilometers (1 mile) outside town on Vía al Salado, off the main road to Ambato. Its six man-made pools overflow with brownish mineral water of various temperatures and are adjoined by a refreshing, fast-moving stream. The pools are drained and refilled each morning at dawn. ☛ *Entry fee.* ☉ *Dawn–dusk.*

Riobamba

Three of Ecuador's most formidable peaks—Chimborazo, Altar, and Tungurahua—are visible from Riobamba, a pleasant high-altitude town with wide tree-lined streets and some well-preserved colonial architecture. There are good buys at the tourist-oriented Saturday market held in the **Parque de la Concepción** (Calle Orozco at Calle Colón);

look for embroidered belts, hand-knit sweaters and weavings, shigra bags, and locally produced clothing and jewelry.

Across the street from the market, the **Museo de Arte Religioso** (Museum of Religious Art), housed in the beautifully restored church **La Concepción,** has an impressive collection of colonial art. *Calle Argentinos,* ☎ *03/952212.* ☛ *Entry fee. Closed Sun.–Mon.*

Sports and the Outdoors

Bicycling

RENTALS

Mountain bikes can be rented inexpensively at **Expediciones Amazónicas** (Calle Oriente at Calle Halflans, Baños, ☎ 03/740506). Both 18- and 21-speed bikes are available (less than $5 and $7 per day, respectively), and can be reserved. A popular route is the five-hour, 65-kilometer (40-mile) downhill ride to Puyo, which winds its way through subtropical jungle and past thundering waterfalls. You can board a bus in Puyo, bike and all, for the return trip to Baños.

TOURS

Aventura Flying Dutchman (Calle La Pinta 146, at Calle Almagro, Quito, ☎ 02/449568) organizes overnight bike treks from Quito along the Avenue of the Volcanoes. Packages include transportation as well as helmets, knee and elbow pads, and of course, bicycles.

Horseback Riding

Many excellent day trips or overnight horseback excursions are accessible from Baños. **Caballos con José** (Calle Maldonado, near Calle Martinez, ☎ 03/740746) is a reliable operation, and probably the only one in Baños that will rent horses with or without a guide. Two excellent and personable guides are available for tours lasting from two hours to several nights. Hourly rates are $4 per person; overnight rates are equally reasonable.

Mountaineering

There are many exciting climbing possibilities along the Avenue of the Volcanoes, from technically difficult ascents to relatively straightforward (albeit arduous) hikes. Most accessible is Tungurahua Volcano (16,684 feet), Ecuador's 10th-highest peak. It is not a technically difficult mountain to climb, but hidden grottoes make it extremely dangerous without an experienced guide. **Cotopaxi National Park** (☛ Entry fee) is home to the world's highest active volcano, Cotopaxi, and there are day hikes with breathtaking views of the *páramos* (moors) on the volcano's lower flanks. Reliable guides for treks to both mountains, as well as to Chimborazo, can be arranged in Baños; contact **William Navarette** (*see* address for El Higuerón *in* Dining, *below*), **Francisco Alomoto** (☎ 03/740315), or **Expediciones Amazónicas** (*see* Bicycling: Rentals, *above*).

Dining and Lodging

The region has several hosterías with comfortable, homespun rooms. These former haciendas are, logically, found outside the cities and towns, so count on country solitude if you choose one. For price ranges, *see* Dining *and* Lodging *in* Ecuador Essentials, *below.*

Latacunga and the Market Villages

DINING AND LODGING

$$ **La Ciénega.** This hacienda turned country inn has been owned by the
★   descendants of the Marquis de Maenza since colonial days. The coun-

try-style furnishings in the main salon are elegant, though the room decorations are more functional than inspired. The lovely ornamental gardens behind the hotel give way to open fields; in the distance, the huge cone of Cotopaxi can be seen. The restaurant serves respectable Ecuadoran cuisine. 🖭 *Lasso, Km 72 Pan-American Hwy. S. (20 km/12 mi north of Latacunga),* ☎ *03/719093,* FAX *03/719182; reservations* ☎ *02/549126,* FAX *02/228820. 30 rooms. Restaurant, horseback riding. DC.*

$$ **Rumipamba de las Rosas.** The overdone ranchero decor of this hostería, 10 kilometers (6 miles) south of Latacunga, is pleasing despite all odds; there are cowhide rugs and lots of antique farm implements adorning lava-rock and whitewashed-brick walls. Sunday lunch includes barbecue-grilled meats and live folkloric music. 🖭 *Pan-American Hwy. S., Km. 100, San Miguel de Salcedo,* ☎ *03/726128,* FAX *03/727103; Quito* ☎ *02/507121. 30 rooms. Restaurant, bar, pool, tennis court, playground. DC.*

$ **Hotel Rodelu.** Not in the least charming, but clean and adequate, this four-story hotel represents the best lodging in the city of Latacunga. The restaurant serves a respectable pizza as well as baked chicken and other standard fare. 🖭 *Calle Quito 7331, Latacunga,* ☎ *03/800956 or 03/811264. 25 rooms. Restaurant. V.*

Baños

DINING

$$ **Le Petit Restaurant.** Reminiscent of a French country restaurant, Le Petit
★ features French, Ecuadoran, and international dishes. Baños's most sophisticated menu includes French champagne, crepes, and fondues of Gruyère and Camembert cheeses. Service may be slow, but the food is good, and the portions are enormous. ✕ *Calle Eloy Alfaro 246 (at Calle Martínez),* ☎ *03/740936. No credit cards.*

$ **El Higuerón.** Natural wood decor and plenty of windows overlooking jubilant flower gardens unite for a pleasant, peaceful dining atmosphere. Choose from well-prepared steaks, salads, and pastas, including vegetarian selections. ✕ *Calle 12 de Noviembre 270, no* ☎. *No credit cards. Closed Wed.*

DINING AND LODGING

$$ **Hotel Sangay.** Numerous recreational facilities compensate for the small, plain rooms that characterize this family-oriented hotel; ask for one of the 26 cabins, which are newer and more pleasant than the hotel accommodations. The Sangay's second-story bar has good views of the Waterfall of the Virgin, just across the road. Nonguests can use the sports facilities for $4. 🖭 *Plazoleta Ayora 101,* ☎ *03/740490,* FAX *03/740056. 51 rooms. Restaurant, bar, pool, 2 hot tubs, tennis court, squash. DC.*

LODGING

$ **Casa Nahuazo.** Near El Salado hot springs just outside town, this friendly
★ B&B has lots of special touches, such as small fruit baskets and mineral water in the rooms. There are lovely views of the surrounding mountains and many hiking trails. The English-speaking owners will book tours and make travel arrangements for guests. 🖭 *Vía al Salado, Casilla 18-02-1922,* ☎ *03/740315. 5 rooms. No credit cards.*

Riobamba

DINING AND LODGING

$$ **Hostería El Troje.** This is Riobamba's premier sleeping stopover despite a preponderance of purple and the odd interior design. Every room has a fireplace, and the staff is helpful and eager to please. 🖭 *Box 50, Ri-*

obamba, 4½ km southeast of town on minor road to Chambo, ☎ and
FAX *03/960826 or 03/964572. 33 rooms. Restaurant, bar, pool, tennis
court, basketball, playground. AE, DC, MC, V.*

$ **Hostal Montecarlo.** This charming, turn-of-the-century house, with its
fern-filled central courtyard, is conveniently located mid city. Its elegant
yet homelike restaurant, just around the corner from the hotel, is first
rate. ▥ *Av. 10 de Agosto 2541, ☎ 03/960557. 18 rooms. Restaurant,
cafeteria. No credit cards. Restaurant closed Mon.*

EL ORIENTE

The Ecuadoran Amazon, called El Oriente (literally, the east), accounts
for roughly one third of Ecuador's landmass but just 4% of its population. One of the world's biodiversity hot spots, it is home to hundreds of unique bird species, including massive macaws, toucans, and
the prehistoric-looking hoatzin. Jaguars, pumas, tapir, and peccaries
are present but elusive; however, pink river dolphins are frequently
sighted, as are quite a few species of monkey, including the howler,
woolly, squirrel, spider, and tarmarin. In addition to these larger mammals, an abundance of interesting insects thrive under the jungle
canopy, including workaholic leaf-cutter ants, society spiders, and
enormous, electric blue morphos butterflies. Myriad plant species co-
exist, and in some cases even cooperate, with the jungle animals. The
giant kapok tree, the Oriente's tallest species, soars to nearly 200 feet
above the jungle floor. Creeping vines cascade from strangler figs,
which in turn envelop other species.

In this exuberant world, eight different native peoples continue, to varying degrees, to live their traditional lifestyles. Indeed, one group still
lives a nomadic life and hostilely repels any attempts at rapprochement
by outsiders. Other indigenous peoples, however, including the Cofán
and the Siecoya of Cuyabeno Wildlife Reserve and the Huaorani who
live in and around Yasuni National Park, receive groups and share their
tremendous knowledge of plants and animals.

Arriving and Departing

By Plane
Coca, Lago Agrio (officially known as Nuevo Loja), and Macas are
just 40 minutes and $46 (one way) from Quito on TAME airlines. Coca
and Lago Agrio are served Monday–Saturday, Macas, three times a week.
There are also several small charter companies specializing in jungle
towns and other remote destinations.

By Car or Bus
The long land trip through lush cloud forests of giant tree ferns, orchids,
and bromeliads is a beautiful opportunity to see transitional zones between the Andes and the rain forest. The Quito–Lago Agrio trip takes
six hours in a private vehicle; Quito–Coca takes eight hours; both routes
are longer by bus. Misahuallí can be reached from Quito ($3) via Baeza
and Tena or via Baños ($4). Both journeys take five–six hours by car, a
bit longer by bus. At press time (winter 1995) detours on the road to
Macas make the long trips from Quito and Cuenca (about 14 and 10
hours, respectively) even longer, and it is advisable to fly from Quito.

Exploring El Oriente

Trips to El Oriente are best planned with a tour operator, who will usually arrange all details of transportation, lodging, and exploring. Tours

to both Cuyabeno and Yasuni, both of which are dominated by primary rain forest, offer the best possibilities for viewing wildlife.

Cuyabeno Wildlife Reserve, a 642,000-acre reserve with more than 500 bird species, can be reached via a short flight from Quito to Lago Agrio, on the headwaters of the Aguarico River. Worthwhile jungle expeditions in Cuyabeno include the Iripari and Flotel Orellana packages offered by **Metropolitan Touring** (*see* Tour Operators *in* Quito, *above*) and cultural trekking trips with the Huaorani arranged by **Safari** (Calle Calama 380, at Calle J. L. Mera, Quito, ☎ 02/552505, FAX 02/220426).

Yasuni National Park is most easily accessed by the frontier town of Coca (known officially as Francisco de Orellana); tours to this area are based on the Napo River and its tributaries. Ninety-six kilometers downstream from Coca is the entrance to Garzacocha and the very remote but effectively run **La Selva Lodge,** which is booked by a number of U.S.-based tour operators (*see* Amazon Jungle Camping and Lodges *in* Chapter 2, Adventure and Learning Vacations). **Tropic Ecological Adventures** (Calle Santa María 212, at Calle Reina Victoria, Quito, ☎ 02/225907 or 02/238324, FAX 02/225907) is committed to the rights of indigenous peoples and can arrange everything from rustic stays in and around Cofán villages to upper-end tour itineraries.

The jungle around the town of Misahuallí is popular, especially among backpackers, for its accessibility and economic tour prices, however heavy colonization in the area makes spotting wildlife difficult. **The Butterfly Lodge** (reservations: Av. Río Coca 1734, Quito, ☎ 02/253267, FAX 02/253266), formerly known as Cabañas Aliñahui, just downstream from Misahuallí on the shores of the Napo River, offers a taste of the Amazon for those who haven't time for a more extensive trek. The comfortable lodge is affiliated with **Jatun Sacha,** a biological research station dedicated to conservation, education, and study of the rain forest.

The pleasant town of Macas is the gateway to the southern Oriente, which is more heavily settled and has less primary rain forest than the northern sector. Nonetheless, there is still spectacular rain forest to be found. A trip with **Ecotrek** (Calle Larga 7–108, Cuenca, ☎ 07/842531, FAX 07/835387; for U.S. representative, Southwind Adventures, *see* Chapter 2, Adventure and Learning Vacations) will put you in dignified contact with the Shuar indigenous people around the missionary town of Miazal. Also out of Macas, **River Odysseys Worldwide** (also known as ROW) leads five-day white-water rafting trips on the scenic Upano River (*see* White-Water Rafting and Kayaking *in* Chapter 2, Adventure and Learning Vacations).

CUENCA

Cuenca is a walker's—and shopper's—paradise. Its bright, blustery blue skies and bold sun draw people out onto the cobblestone streets, where restored colonial- and republican-style mansions, their iron-grill balconies filled with potted plants, line the streets. Old men gossip in the many plazas, oblivious to the call of scruffy shoe shine boys, while cars and taxis trundle by in a relaxed manner unthinkable in Quito or Guayaquil. One of Ecuador's most visitor-friendly cities, Cuenca was isolated for centuries from the country's more cosmopolitan centers—paved roads were not laid from Cuenca to Guayaquil and Quito until the 1960s. It's not surprising that Cuencanos have, over the years, developed a stubborn pride in themselves and their workmanship, such that Cuenca is among Ecuador's leaders in cottage industries, producing fine ceramics, textiles, weavings, and Panama hats.

On market days—Thursday and Sunday—hundreds of townspeople and *indígenas* from surrounding towns throng Cuenca's open-air plazas to buy and sell handicrafts and household items. The *cholas cuencanas* dress for the day in their finest straw hats. These female descendants of mixed Spanish and Cañari couples, famed for their beauty, are striking in their colorful *polleras*—gathered wool skirts in violet, emerald green, rose red, or marigold—and satiny, peasant-style *polka* blouses.

Visitor Information

CETUR (Calle Hermano Miguel 686, at Calle Presidente Córdoba, ☎ 07/822058; closed weekends).

Arriving and Departing

By Plane

Cuenca's **Aeropuerto Mariscal Lamar** (Av. España, ☎ 07/862203) is 2 kilometers (1 mile) from the city center, just past the bus terminal. A cab from the airport to downtown costs around $3. **SAN/Saeta** (☎ 07/831850) and **TAME** (☎ 07/827609) fly twice daily between Quito and Cuenca; the 30-minute flights cost $28 each way. On weekdays only, TAME makes the 30-minute flight between Guayaquil and Cuenca ($24 each way).

By Train

At press time (winter 1995), regular train service between Alausí and Cuenca has been interrupted. The only reliable—albeit pricey—option is **Metropolitan Touring** (*see* Tour Operators *in* Quito, *above*), which joins Riobamba and Cuenca by autoferro. Two- to four-day treks cost from $288 to $660 per person and include accommodations, guide services, transportation, and meals.

By Car

Cuenca is 472 kilometers (293 miles) south of Quito via the Pan-American Highway. The drives from Quito (eight hours) and Guayaquil (four hours) both have fantastic scenery: The former takes you along the Avenue of the Volcanoes, while the latter climbs through subtropical lowlands before beginning a dizzying mountain ascent—8,300 feet in just over 240 kilometers (150 miles).

By Bus

From Cuenca's **Terminal Terrestre** (Av. España), 1½ kilometers (1 mile) from the town center, there are daily departures to Quito (10 hours) and Guayaquil (5–6 hours), both priced under $5.

Getting Around

Cuenca's center is small and extremely easy to negotiate on foot. Most of its churches, museums, and shops are within a six-block radius of the main plaza, Parque Calderón. Taxis do not use meters, so agree on a price beforehand.

Exploring Cuenca

In the heart of Cuenca's compact center lies pleasant, tree- and flower-filled **Parque Calderón,** where stocky, dignified matrons sell candies from ambulatory carts, and shoe shine boys ply their trade. The periwinkle blue domes of Cuenca's **Catedral de la Inmaculada,** also known as the New Cathedral, dominate the park below. Inside, what little light enters through the miniature stained-glass windows becomes diffused and

golden, casting a pale glow over thick walls of brick. The heavy atmosphere of the church, which was built in fits and starts between 1886
and 1967, is lightened somewhat by pillars of Ecuadoran marble and
Italian marble floors. ☛ *Free.* ☉ *Mon.–Sat. 6–7* AM *and 6–7* PM*, Sun.
10:30–11:30* AM *and 7–8* PM.

Opposite the New Cathedral sits the small, unimposing **El Sagrario**
(also called the Old Cathedral), begun in 1557, the year the city was
founded. At press time (winter 1995), the Old Cathedral was closed
to the public.

One block west of Parque Calderón are the twin-spire church and nun-
nery of **Carmen de la Asunción.** The stone carvings surrounding the
doorway are a good example of Spanish Baroque design, while the
church's interior is typically ostentatious—especially noteworthy is the
gold-covered pulpit encrusted with mirrors. The flower market held
on the square outside is in full blossom every day until sunset. *Calle
Mariscal Sucre (at Calle Padre Aguirre).* ☛ *Free.* ☉ *Mon.–Sat. 6–7* AM
and 6–7 PM*, Sun. 10:30–11:30* AM *and 7–8* PM.

One block south, vendors occupy a maze of stalls at **Plaza de San Francisco,** hawking a variety of shoes and sweaters, lipstick, shampoo, and
bric-a-brac. Under the northern colonnade, Otavalo Indians sell their
more attractive handmade wares, mainly colorful handwoven ponchos,
hand-knit sweaters, and woven wall hangings. Across the plaza is the
tan-and-white **Iglesia de San Francisco,** built in the 1920s and famous
for its intricately carved, gold-drenched main altar. Its hours are sporadic; try it at the same times the cathedral's open. Among Cuenca's
other attractive churches are the blue-spired **Iglesia San Alfonso** (Calle
Simón Bolívar at Calle Presidente Borrero) and the twin-towered **Iglesia de Santo Domingo** (Av. Gran Colombia at Calle Padre Aguirre).

In the 16th century one of Cuenca's leading citizens, doña Ordóñez,
donated her house (which filled an entire city block) to the Catholic
church, whereafter it became the cloistered convent of the Order of
the Immaculate Conception. Four centuries later, part of this spacious
and well-preserved edifice houses **El Museo de las Conceptas,** containing an impressive collection of religious art from the 16th to 19th
centuries. *Calle Hermano Miguel 6–33 (at Calle Presidente Córdova),*
☎ *07/830625.* ☛ *Entry fee. Closed Sun.*

The **Museum of Modern Art** always has several interesting, well-presented exhibitions of local artists, though its permanent collection
consists mainly of dark, bleak paintings by anonymous colonial masters. *Calle Mariscal Sucre (at Calle Coronel Talbot),* ☎ *07/831027.* ☛
Free. Closed Sun.

The concrete and glass **Central Bank Museum** houses an ethnographic
and archaeological museum, in addition to exhibits of colonial and republican-era art. Near the river behind the museum there is a small
archaeological site under excavation. *Calle Larga (at Av. Hauyna-
Capac,* ☎ *07/831255, ext. 234).* ☛ *Entry fee. Closed Sat. afternoon
and Sun.*

Shopping

Cuenca is among Ecuador's leaders in cottage industries, producing
fine ceramics, textiles, silver and gold jewelry, and leather. Among its
most important products is the Panama hat, whose name sticks in the
collective craw of proud Ecuadorans. (These finely made straw hats—

also known as *toquilla* hats—are named for the country to which they were first exported en masse, hence the Panama sobriquet.)

Specialty Stores

Artesa (Av. Gran Colombia at Calle Luis Cordero) is Cuenca's leading producer of utilitarian and decorative ceramics. **Concuero** (Calle Mariscal Lamar 1137) has good-quality leather jackets, shoes, wallets, and handbags. **Fundación Jorge Moscoso** (Calle Presidente Córdova 614) has a limited but precious collection of antiques, well-made modern regional indigenous clothing, and a small archaeological museum. **Kinara** (Calle Mariscal Sucre 770) stocks stylish gold and silver jewelry, women's hats, and jackets and shawls featuring traditional *ikat* textiles, where the threads are knotted and dyed prior to weaving. **Señor Ortega** (Calle Vega Muñoz at Calle Padre Aguirre) has a good selection of Panama hats; if you don't see what you want at the store, ask for a tour of the factory where the hats are made.

Dining

Cuenca suffers a dearth of restaurants and bars—Cuencanos are a stay-at-home lot and tourism is still relatively new. Most family-owned restaurants—but not necessarily hotel restaurants—are closed Sunday. For price categories, *see* Dining *in* Ecuador Essentials, *below.*

Ecuadoran

\$\$ Los Capulies. This blue and white, glass-domed restaurant is a good place to sample traditional Ecuadoran cuisine. The *plato típico,* a kind of sampler plate, consists of *llapingachos* (potato pancakes), grilled pork, mote pillo, blood sausage, and empanadas. A variety of live music is presented Thursday to Saturday after 8:30 PM. ✕ *Calle Borrero at Calle Córdova,* ☎ *07/831120. AE, DC, MC, V. Closed Sun.*

\$ Dos Chorreras. Located 14 miles outside Cuenca on the road to El Cajas, this is a great place to stop on the way to or from the recreational area. For about \$5 you get a welcome cocktail, *locro* (potato soup with avocado), fresh grilled trout, rice, fried yucca, coleslaw, dessert, and coffee. After lunch you can stroll around the grounds of this working trout farm. ✕ *14 mi from Cuenca on Ordóñez Lazo; reservations at Hotel Inca Real,* ☎ *07/825571. Lunch only (or group dinners by prior arrangement). V.*

\$ La Picantería 10 de Agosto. This is the place to experience honest-to-goodness, to-die-for Ecuadoran dishes. You can look into the giant pots of delicious goat stew, tripe, or *encebollado de pescado* (a succulent fish dish with pickled onions, yucca, cilantro, and lots of lime) and decide what you want. Absolutely no frills and no tourists. ✕ *Av. 10 de Agosto at Av. Solano, no* ☎. *No credit cards. Closed Tues.*

International

\$\$\$ Villa Rosa. Cuenca's newest international restaurant is perfectly ensconced
★ in a meticulously restored republican-era house, with massive white-washed walls and marble floors. Soft music floats through several tastefully decorated salons to the upper balcony, where an open fireplace blazes. Try the grilled trout with almonds and, for dessert, the fruit-and-chocolate fondue. ✕ *Av. Gran Colombia 1222,* ☎ *07/837944. Reservations advised. AE, DC, MC, V. Closed Sun.–Mon.*

Mexican

\$\$ El Pedregal Azteca. This savory Mexican food may prove a welcome change of cuisine, but beware the man-eating margaritas. Try the *chile relleno* (breaded, deep-fried chile pepper stuffed with cheese), or the specialty of the house, *carne asada a la tampiqueña* (beef grilled with salt and lemon). ✕ *Av. Gran Colombia 1033 (at Calle Padre Aguirre)*, ☎ *07/823652. No credit cards. Closed Sun.*

Lodging

Deluxe hotels are not the norm in Cuenca, though several moderately priced establishments offer friendly, reliable service in elegant surroundings. For price ranges, *see* Lodging *in* Ecuador Essentials, *below.*

$$$ **Hotel Oro Verde.** This classy, Swiss-run, three-story hotel caters mainly to international businesspeople and package-tour groups. The rooms shine, both with lots of dark polished wood and such special touches as extra-large closets. A 2-kilometer taxi ride away from the town center, the hotel overlooks the lagoon on the south side. The restaurant is famous for its trout—try the smoked trout appetizer in brandy. 🖬 *Av. Ordóñez Lazo,* ☎ *07/831200,* ℻ *07/832849; U.S.* ☎ *800/447–7462. 80 rooms, 2 suites. Restaurant, coffee shop, room service, pool, sauna, steam room, airport shuttle. AE, DC, MC, V.*

$$ **Hotel Crespo.** This intimate hotel overlooking the Tomebamba River
★ on the southeastern edge of town combines comfort with a friendly, unpretentious setting. About a third of the rooms and the restaurant have good views of the river. Numerous sitting and reading rooms give the Crespo a familiar, homey atmosphere. 🖬 *Calle Larga 973,* ☎ *07/834937,* ℻ *07/839473. 31 rooms. Restaurant, bar. AE, DC, MC, V.*

$$ **Hotel El Conquistador.** This five-story hotel has amenities not frequently found in Cuenca's other budget-friendly hotels, such as bathtubs, hair dryers, satellite TV, and panoramic views of the city. An enormous breakfast buffet is included in the price. 🖬 *Av. Gran Colombia 665 (at Calle Presidente Borrero),* ☎ *07/831788,* ℻ *07/831291. 44 rooms. Restaurant, bar, dance club, airport shuttle. AE, DC, MC, V.*

$$ **Hotel Inca Real.** Comfortable rooms and reasonably priced suites surround the three stately patios of this restored colonial home. Rooms off the back patio are less noisy in the morning. 🖬 *Calle General Torres 840,* ☎ *07/823636,* ℻ *07/840699. 30 rooms. Restaurant, bar, meeting room. AE, DC, MC, V.*

$ **Hostal Macondo.** This youth hostel affiliate, with blond hardwood floors
★ and bright turquoise trim, is unpretentious, comfortable, and conducive to meeting other travelers. The open, grassy courtyard has play equipment for kids. After breakfast has been served restaurant-style, guests are free to use all kitchen facilities. 🖬 *Calle Tarqui 1164 (at Calle Lamar),* ☎ *07/831198. 12 rooms. Cafeteria, playground. No credit cards.*

The Arts and Nightlife

Cuenca is not about nightlife. Locals usually stay home during the week and sally forth on Friday and Saturday nights to have dinner and drinks, or maybe to see a movie or a play.

The Arts

Theater is sometimes performed at **La Casa de la Cultura** (Calle Luis Cordero 750, ☎ 07/828175), and movies are shown most nights at 9. For information regarding other events, look in the daily newspaper, *El Mercurio,* or contact **La Fundación Paul Rivet** (Calle Luis Cordero 932, ☎ 07/835655), which distributes a monthly newsletter of cultural events.

Nightlife

La Cantina (Calle Presidente Borrero at Calle Córdova) is one of Cuenca's most attractive and lively bars and a popular local hangout on weekend nights. For dancing, check out the discos at **Hotel El Do-rado** (Av. Gran Colombia 787, ☎ 07/831390) or **El Conquistador** (*see* Lodging, *above*).

Excursions from Cuenca

Mirador de Turi

For a fantastic view of Cuenca by night or day, hike or take a taxi to the mirador at the tiny village of **Turi**, where there is also a photogenic mural-covered church. If you walk along Turi's main street you will soon find yourself in green, sometimes burnt-brown hills where stucco and adobe farmhouses punctuate cornfields and potato patches.

Getting There

Either hike south (and uphill) for several miles along Avenida Fray Vicente Solano, or take a taxi (less than $2). Since taxis can be few and far between in Turi, you may want to plan to walk back down or pay your driver to wait.

Ingapirca

Long before the Inca invasion of Ecuador in the latter half of the 15th century, the fierce and industrious Cañari people ruled Guapondélig ("Plain as Wide and Beautiful as the Sky"), their name for the fertile highlands surrounding Cuenca. Yet while **Ingapirca** was an important religious and political center to the Cañari, the site is better remembered for its Inca ruins; after the Inca king Tupac-Yupanqui conquered the Cañari, he added his own temples and monuments to the site. (Ingapirca literally means Wall of the Inca.) The mortarless stone-built structures are thought to be Cañari temples to the moon, while the elliptical building at the center is acknowledged to be the conquering Incas' vast temple to the sun. There is also a museum, and an excellent restaurant ½ kilometer away serves luscious local dishes. ☛ *Entry fee. Site ☉ daily; museum ☉ Tues.–Sat.*

Getting There

Guided tours can be arranged through most Cuenca-based operators for $30–$40 per person, including lunch. Try to book a tour that makes several stops along the way—in, for example, Azogues, the center of Ecuador's Panama hat industry and the site of a colorful Saturday market, or tiny Cañar, which has a small Sunday market.

El Cajas Recreational Area

Less than 20 miles west of Cuenca are the wild, cold, cloudy moors of El Cajas, where the average elevation is 10,500 feet. The rugged terrain is the legacy left by glaciers as they retreated some 5 million years ago. Today the nearly 70,000 acres of moors are home to Andean condors, hawks, and the elusive gray-breasted mountain toucan, as well as wolves, gazelle, and white-tailed deer. Fishers appreciate the abundant trout in many of the area's 230 lakes.

El Cajas is best explored with an accomplished guide, because visitors can easily become disoriented in the stark landscape. **Ecotrek** (Calle Larga 7–108, at Calle Cordero, ☎ 07/842531, FAX 07/835387), Cuenca's leading ecotourism operator, leads treks to the recreation area of up to four nights. An experienced guide will point out the unique páramo vegetation and set up camp each evening. If you don't want to take a tour, try to hike with a local who knows the area, or take your compass. In any case, go prepared for strong sun, cold wind, and the possibility of rain. Sunglasses and sunscreen are also recommended. There is a park station near the entrance where one can sometimes sleep for a small fee, although if the accommodations are full, you'll have to make other plans. Camping is permitted throughout the park—pay the nominal charge at the ranger station—but is advised only for well-equipped, experienced campers.

Getting There

You can reach the park by bus, which leaves between 6 and 6:30 AM only, from the Church at San Sebastián (corner of Calles Bolívar and Coronel Talbot). Be forewarned: Weekend trips can be crowded, the bus ride takes nearly two hours, and you may have to stand. The only bus back returns at *about* 3 PM; check with the driver, and whatever you do, don't miss it! An alternative is to take a taxi and arrange to be picked up later in the afternoon. Considering the difficulties involved, those truly interested in bird-watching and incredible, albeit stark, landscapes, should seriously consider a guided excursion.

Gualaceo and Chordeleg

East of Cuenca, along 23 miles of paved highway, lies the market and weaving town of Gualaceo, a picturesque hamlet that seems plucked from another time. It has many well-preserved, republican-era buildings, and throngs of well-dressed Cañari women in polleras and jaunty straw or felt hats gather around the main square, particularly on market day. At the Sunday market, locals buy and sell an assortment of plastics, costume jewelry, clothing, and other necessities of life, as well as a wide variety of produce and cooked foods, but the town is best known for producing the traditional Azuay shawl, the *macana*. The ikat weaving style is thought to have originated in Polynesia. Try to visit during one of Gualaceo's major festivals—in early March there's the annual Peach Festival, and the religious Festival of St. James is celebrated on June 25.

Just a few miles from Gualaceo is the silver- and gold-mining town of Chordeleg. Some complain that the quality of the gold and silver filigree jewelry has diminished, but it's still quite remarkable, and there are good bargains. Ikat weavings, embroidered clothing, pottery, and Panama hats—as well as mountains of jewelry—are sold in the little shops surrounding the tree-shaded plaza.

GETTING THERE

Buses from Cuenca's Terminal Terrestre leave throughout the day and cost less than $1. The trip, which normally takes 45 minutes, has been extended to almost two hours since a stretch of the road was washed out in early 1993.

GUAYAQUIL AND THE COAST

Guayaquil, the capital of Guayas Province, is South America's busiest Pacific port and Ecuador's largest city, with a population of nearly 2 million people. Although the people are friendly and hospitable, the city itself is unattractive and dirty. Still, if business takes you to Guayaquil, there are several first-rate museums and restaurants, and several pleasant parks that may lift your spirits.

The nearby Atlantic coast is something else entirely. During the hot and stifling rainy season, usually December to April, Guayaquil becomes particularly unbearable, and Guayaquileños head en masse for the beach city of Salinas, about 145 kilometers (90 miles) east. Here the blue waters of the Pacific Ocean teem with sailfish, albacore, wahoo, dolphin, and black, blue, and striped marlin, providing a year-round lure for sport fishermen. Some 100 kilometers (62 miles) north are Puerto López and Machalilla National Park. Ecuador's newest park is attracting more visitors than ever to appreciate the rare flora and fauna—and lounge on the beaches!—of the central coast.

Guayaquil

Visitor Information

CETUR (Calle Aguirre 104, at Calle Malecón, ☎ 04/325607; closed weekends).

Arriving and Departing

By Plane

Guayaquil's domestic and international airport, **Aeropuerto Simón Bolívar** (Av. de las Américas, ☎ 04/319958), is 6 kilometers (4 miles) north of the city center; taxis to downtown cost less than $4. From Guayaquil, **TAME** (☎ 04/562279 or 04/561751) and **SAN/Saeta** (☎ 04/303128 or 04/329855) fly daily to Quito ($30), and TAME has one flight each weekday to Cuenca ($25). For the Galápagos, SAN flies five times a week to San Cristóbal Island while TAME flies daily to Baltra, both for $320–$350 round-trip.

By Train

At press time (winter 1995), rail service joins Guayaquil's **Estación Durán** (☎ 04/800036), across the Guayas River in the suburb of Durán, with Alausí (4 hours, $10). From Alausí there are connections to Riobamba. Taxi fare from downtown to the station costs less than $2.

By Car

From Riobamba drive southwest through Cajabamba and El Truinfo. From Quito (416 kilometers/259 miles) drive west along a narrow paved road over the Cordillera mountains, descending through stunning subtropical landscapes to Santo Domingo de los Colorados on the way to Quevedo and Babahoyo.

By Bus

Guayaquil is eight–nine hours by bus from Quito, and around five hours from Cuenca. Both treks cost less than $5.

Getting Around

The most pleasant sector for strolling in Guayaquil is Urdesa; the adjacent neighborhoods of La Garzota and Nueva Kennedy also have numerous bars, cafés, and restaurants. El Parque Centenario lies at the heart of the city at Calle 6 de Marzo and Calle Velez, and Avenida 9 de Octubre—the main financial and shopping street—runs roughly west–east on either side. Taxis throughout the city are inexpensive, but most do not use meters; be prepared to haggle a bit.

Exploring

A walk along the **Malecón**, Guayaquil's waterfront promenade, is pleasant around sunset; small fishing trawlers and the occasional native dugout add a dash of life to this otherwise busy commercial waterway. Overlooking the river at the foot of Avenida 9 de Octubre, the impressive stone monument **La Rotunda** commemorates the historic meeting in 1822 between Ecuador's venerated liberator, Simón Bolívar, and Argentine general San Martín, who liberated Chile and Peru.

Both the **Nahim Isaias Museum** (Calle Clemente Ballén at Calle Pichincha, ☎ 04/329099; closed Sun.) and the **Archaeological Museum of the Banco del Pacífico** (Calle P. Ycaza 113, at Calle Pichincha, ☎ 04/566010 or 04/563744; ☉ Tues.–Fri. 10–6, weekends 11–1) are free and present rotating archaeological exhibits in addition to extensive displays of colonial and 19th-century South American art.

Dining

The majority of Guayaquil's nicer restaurants are clustered in the Urdesa, La Garzota, and Nueva Kennedy districts, north of downtown. Many close daily between 4:30 and 7:30, only to reopen for dinner. For price ranges, *see* Dining *in* Ecuador Essentials, *below.*

$$$ **Paper Moon.** This lilac and white restaurant is nestled in the rich hills of the Urdesa district. Thursday to Saturday the menu features traditional Ecuadoran dishes—mainly barbecued and grilled meats. At other times you can indulge in a wider range of dishes such as grilled suckling pig or trout with almonds. ✕ *Av. Séptima 302 (at Calle Las Lomas),* ☎ *04/386702. DC, MC, V.* ☉ *Sun. for lunch only.*

$$$ **Trattoria da Enrico.** Tiny shuttered windows set into thick whitewashed
★ walls, and a profusion of plants reflect this restaurant's Mediterranean influence. After a prosciutto and melon appetizer, try a fresh homemade pasta, or chicken with sour cream, vodka, and mushroom sauce. ✕ *Calle Bálsamos 504 (at Calle Ebanos),* ☎ *04/387079. DC, MC, V. Closed Tues.*

$$ **El Cangrejo Criollo.** The atmosphere is casual and maritime at this popular La Garzota district eatery. Waiters dress in swashbuckling attire and serve steaming plates of local crab, shrimp in coconut sauce, and other fresh-caught seafood. ✕ *Av. Principal, La Garzota,* ☎ *04/232018. DC, MC, V.*

$$ **La Parrillada del Ñato.** Local families and a sprinkling of tourists fill this enormous, pleasantly informal restaurant seven days a week. South American barbecue is the house specialty, from suckling pig and pork ribs to chicken and beef. Pizzas also appear on the menu. ✕ *Av. V. E. Estrada 1219 (at Calle Costanera),* ☎ *04/387098. AE, DC, MC, V.*

Lodging

For price ranges, *see* Lodging *in* Ecuador Essentials, *below.*

$$$$ **Gran Hotel Guayaquil.** Gray-green carpets contrast nicely with the sand-color walls in this modern, well-furnished high-rise. Suites contain a spacious sitting room, as well as a kitchenette stocked with all the necessary accoutrements. 🏨 *Calle Boyaca (at Av. 10 de Agosto),* ☎ *04/ 329690,* 🖷 *04/327251; U.S.* ☎ *800/334–3782. 160 rooms. 4 restaurants, pool, sauna, steam room, exercise room, car rental. AE, DC, MC, V.*

$$$ **Ramada Inn.** Businesspeople will appreciate not only the location, across from the Guayas River near the financial district, but also this hotel's secretarial and business services. Tourists will enjoy the river views and excellent on-site restaurants, which serve delicious *comida criolla,* traditional coastal dishes. 🏨 *Malecón Simón Bolívar, Box 10964,* ☎ *04/562475 or 04/565555,* 🖷 *04/563036. 2 restaurants, 2 bars, pool, sauna, steam room, casino, business services. AE, DC, MC, V.*

$$$ **Uni Hotel.** This clean and modern downtown high-rise features bathroom phones and fine views of the adjacent Parque Seminario. The build-

ing's first four floors house a shopping center. ⊡ *Calle Clemente Bal-lén 406,* ☏ *04/327100,* 匧 *04/328352, U.S.* ☏ *800/223–5652. 110 rooms, 36 suites. 2 restaurants, hot tub, sauna, exercise room, casino. AE, DC, MC, V.*

\$\$ **Hotel Del Rey.** This pleasant midsize hotel, a favorite of visiting soccer players, is about a 10-minute taxi ride from the financial district. The well-kept rooms are on the small side, but this is one of the few mod-erately priced hotels in town that has exercise facilities. Continental breakfast is included. ⊡ *Calle Aguirre (at Calle Andrés Marín),* ☏ *04/ 453037 or 04/452053,* 匧 *04/453351. 47 rooms. Restaurant, bar, sauna, exercise room. DC, MC, V.*

\$ **Hotel Velez.** The very plain but well-kept Velez has few amenities aside from rooms with firm beds and ceiling fans. The clientele largely con-sists of businessmen and budget-minded foreigners. ⊡ *Calle Velez 1021 (at Av. Quito),* ☏ *04/525430 or 04/526292. 30 rooms. Cafete-ria. No credit cards.*

Salinas

Guayaquileños flock to **Salinas's** long, if sometimes dirty, sand beach on holidays and during the hot and humid rainy season (during the off-season many restaurants and hotels close). For tourists, sea fish-ing is the main draw here. The continental shelf drops sharply to the ocean floor just 19 kilometers (12 miles) offshore, providing a fertile feeding ground for Pacific sailfish, swordfish, amberjack, tuna, sail-fish, grouper, and shark, as well as striped, blue, and black marlin. The biggest catches are made November through May, but fishing contin-ues year-round. **PescaTours** (Guayaquil, ☏ 04/443365, 匧 04/443142; Salinas, ☏ 04/772391) organizes daylong charters for two to six peo-ple for around \$250. Taxis will take you from Guayaquil to Salinas for less than \$10 each way.

Machalilla National Park and Environs

In the extreme southwest corner of the state of Manabí is the 136,850-acre Machalilla National Park, created in 1979 to halt the destruction of Ecuador's remaining tropical dry forests. Unlike the lush greenery associated with rain forests, typical dry-forest vegetation includes kapok (or silk-cotton) trees, prickly pear cactus, strangler fig, and lau-rel. The \$20 entrance fee is good for five days and includes access to the offshore **Isla de la Plata,** a 3,000-acre seabird sanctuary where red-footed, blue-footed, and masked boobies can be observed. Waters sur-rounding the island teem with flying fish, dolphins, and from July through October, whales. Both the park and the island are most accessible from the small town of Puerto López, which is home to both the **Na-tional Park visitor center** (diagonal from church, ☏ 05/604170, ⊘ Daily 7–5) and most of the area's visitor services.

Arriving and Departing

By Plane
You can fly from Quito to Manta or Puertoviejo (\$27 one way) and take a bus (less than \$4) or taxi (about \$50) through Jipijapa and on to the coast (*see* By Bus or Car, *below*).

By Bus or Car
To get to Machalilla and Puerto López from Guayaquil, take the bus from the Terminal Terrestre (main bus station) to Jipijapa and change buses at the CITM bus station (one block from main square, on Calle

Sucre). Catch a bus heading south toward La Libertad, and get off in Machalilla, Puerto López, Salango, or Ayambe (about 4 hours). You'll have to tell the driver where you want to get off as there are no scheduled stops. A longer route takes you along the coast from Guayaquil via La Libertad (5½ hours), passing the above-named towns in reverse order. Both journeys cost less than $5.

Tour Operators

Spanish-speaking guides can be hired at the park visitor center for less than $10 a day for up to 10 persons. Non-Spanish speakers may arrange English-language guided tours through **Manta Raya** (☎ 05/604167; Quito ☎ 02/467980, FAX 02/437645), on the *malcón*, the boardwalk running through the center of town.

Sports and the Outdoors

Fishing
Manta Raya (*see above*) arranges fishing charters ($570 per day for up to 20 passengers) with advance notification. Most experienced fishers will be happier if they bring their own gear; otherwise, gear of dubious quality can be rounded up by the agency.

Horseback Riding and Trekking
Trips to beautiful Los Frailes cove can be arranged through **Pacarina** (Puerto López, ☎ or FAX 05/604173) or at Alandaluz (*see* Dining and Lodging, *below*) for less than $5 for a half-day trip. Pacarina also arranges overnight camping trips within Machalilla National Park. An excursion popular with birders is the seven-hour hike from Agua Blanca to San Sebastián, which passes through dry forest to cloud forest to, finally, tropical rain forest—each climate with its own distinct species of flora and fauna. After a night camping outside San Sebastián, you can return to Agua Blanca on foot or by horse. The fee for horses (including guide service), for this or other excursions in the area, is less than $7 per day.

Dining and Lodging

Most of the hotels listed have beach access, but swimmers should be aware of the rip tide off Puerto López. Although the water is swimmable year round, it's warmest during the rainy summer months (Dec.–May). For price ranges, *see* Dining *and* Lodging *in* Ecuador Essentials, *below*.

Puerto López
DINING

$ **Carmita's Restaurant.** After 24 years in the business, doña Carmita and
★ her sister have the seafood business down pat. The signature dish at this simple beachfront eatery, *pescado al vapor con vegetales* (lemony fish soup with vegetables), is truly to die for. A wide variety of drinks, including German and Chilean wines and liqueurs, are available. ✗ *Malecón s/n, ☎ 05/604148 or 05/604149. V.*

DINING AND LODGING

$ **Hotel Pacífico.** There's nothing fancy about this three-story hotel one block from the beach and the boardwalk, but the fan-cooled rooms are clean and comfortable, the hot water is free-flowing, and the owners are friendly. At press time (winter 1995), a restaurant and swimming pool were in progress. ☎ *Puerto López, ☎ 05/604133 or 05/604147. Cafeteria. 24 rooms.*

Along the Coast

DINING

$ Delfín Mágico. This simple cabana in Salango, halfway between Puerto López and Atamari, is built in the traditional style of the area, with open sides and a thatch roof. It's the food (and not the sometimes slow service) that makes this restaurant magic. Try such regional favorites as pescado *en salsa de maní* (in peanut sauce) or shrimp in garlic butter. ✕ *Salango (no address or ☎). No credit cards.*

DINING AND LODGING

$$ Hotel Atamari. This isolated hotel is perched atop a rocky promontory 28 kilometers (17 miles) south of Puerto López, well away from civilization. Bright purple bougainvillea, papayas, and palms grow among the white A-frame, thatch-roof cottages, which have simple wooden interiors. The outdoor restaurant serves international cuisine, with an emphasis on seafood and German dishes. Although taxis are not unavailable here, it may be easier (albeit more expensive) to have the hotel arrange transportation. ☎ *Ayambe (no street address or ☎). Reservations: Box 17–12–91, Quito,* ☎ *02/227896 or 02/228470. 10 rooms. Restaurant, pool. DC, V.*

$ Alandaluz. The two- and three-story, split-bamboo, thatch-roof cabanas
★ at this laid-back hotel face several miles of blond sand beaches, which are frequented by fishers and Alandaluz' languid guests. About 15 minutes south of Puerto López, near the village of Puerto Rico, this relaxed hotel might as well be called Shangri-La. Many travelers come for a night and end up spending a week, lounging in hammocks and talking travel at the friendly open-air bar. The owners seem to practice true ecotourism; they conserve water by using biodegraders and inoffensive pit toilets and do all their construction with local split bamboo and straw. The open-air restaurant, which emphasizes vegetarian fare, is supplied with organic produce from their own orchards and gardens. In fact, if you get tired of sea and sun, you can take day or overnight trips to Alandaluz's working farm, where coffee, pineapple, cacao, bananas, and tagua nut are grown. ☎ *Reservations: Puerto López* ☎ *and* FAX *05/604173; Quito* ☎ *02/237583,* FAX *02/525671. 28 rooms. Restaurant, bar, travel agency.*

THE GALÁPAGOS ISLANDS

It is possible that indigenous coastal tribes were the first to discover the remote Galápagos Islands—the chain of rocky, highly active volcanic islands that lie roughly 1000 kilometers (620 miles) off the coast of Ecuador; at least some think this is the explanation for legends among Ecuador's coastal peoples referring to "a land of fire across the sea." Less dramatic, perhaps, and certainly better documented, was the arrival of Fray Tomás de Berlanga, the Bishop of Panama, in 1535. His ship was becalmed on a fact-finding mission to Peru and eventually drifted on strong currents to the Galápagos. Berlanga's dutiful report to the King of Spain may have put the Insulae de los Galopegos on the map, but seafaring men found the black volcanic islands inhospitable, lonesome, and lacking a regular source of fresh water. Centuries later, English pirates used the remote Galápagos as a place to rest and recoup after plundering the Ecuadoran and Peruvian coast. Many of the islands received their English names—some of which are still in use— during the patriotic tenure of these scurrilous buccaneers.

The Galápagos's most famous visitor was Charles Darwin, in 1835. A dropout theology student with no formal scientific training, Darwin nonetheless visited the islands in the capacity of resident naturalist aboard the sailing vessel HMS *Beagle* during its five-year, around-the-world scientific mission. Darwin stayed just five weeks and visited only a handful of islands, but his findings contributed enormously to his theories of evolution and adaptive radiation eventually published in 1859 in his revolutionary work, *On the Origin of Species by Means of Natural Selection.*

Despite the interest generated by Darwin's publication, the islands attracted mainly adventure seekers and recluses until well into the 20th century. Tourism began in a limited fashion after the Ecuadoran government declared the islands a national park in 1959. Nearly five decades later, the Galápagos must cope with more than 80,000 yearly visitors, and some ecologists are concerned that the steadily increasing numbers will prove destructive to this unique, irreplaceable environment.

Carried by winds and ocean currents, everything from seeds and plants to birds and reptiles miraculously have made their way to these remote volcanic islands. Over the course of thousands of years many have evolved in response to the Galápagos's harsh environment and are now classified as distinct species—an integral aspect of Darwin's theory of natural selection. Some species, including the flightless cormorant, the Galápagos mockingbird, and both marine and land iguanas, are found nowhere else on earth. In the sea, the confluence of cold Antarctic currents and warmer currents originating off the coast of Panama nurtures a rich variety of oceanic species: penguins, fur seals, and sea lions share the multicolor underwater world with green and hawksbill turtles, rays, sharks, dolphins, urchins, and countless other creatures.

Despite this diversity of life, reptiles are king in the Galápagos. (Both amphibians and native land mammals are noticeably absent on the islands; in fact, the latter, represented by only two species of rice rats, are now extinct. The most easily seen reptiles are the tiny lava lizards: males do push-ups both to intimidate would-be aggressors and impress females, who develop a bright red throat during mating season. Definitely the oddest looking are the marine iguanas, who lie in huge, friendly piles in the sun and resemble small dragons with their spiny crests, sharp front claws, and thick scaly hides. Undoubtedly the most famous are the giant Galápagos tortoises, which can weigh up to 550 pounds. To their disadvantage, these gentle giants are capable of surviving almost a year without food or water, providing 19th-century whalers with a delicious source of fresh food, and contributing to the species' extinction on three islands.

The best months to visit the Galápagos are generally May–June and November–December. Of the Galápagos's 13 principal islands, Santa Cruz and San Cristóbal are the most developed, each with a population of roughly 6,000 year-round residents. Of the two, Santa Cruz has more allure for visitors, with its dozen or so hotels and restaurants, boutiques, and even dance clubs. The archipelago's four populated islands can be visited on a limited basis without guides, but the uninhabited islands can be visited only with a guide licensed through the Galápagos National Park Service. Visitors commonly book their own airfare and prearrange a one- to two-week ship-based package that includes guided visits to islands such as Española and Isabela. Cruises of 10 days or longer generally are needed to reach the more remote northern islands or to climb either of Isabela's two accessible volcanic craters.

The Galápagos

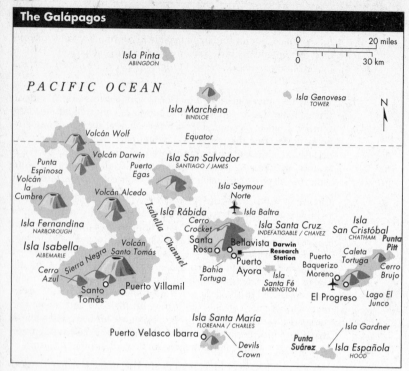

Visitor Information

Although telephone lines now connect the Galápagos with mainland Ecuador, phone service is poor, and tour reservations are typically booked through agencies in Quito, Guayaquil, or the United States. **CETUR** (Av. Charles Darwin, Santa Cruz Island, ☎ 05/526174) offers limited information about tours and guides.

Arriving and Departing

By Plane

SANTA CRUZ

TAME flies once daily between Quito, Guayaquil, and Baltra, a tiny island just north of Santa Cruz. The flight takes roughly three hours and costs $350–$400 round-trip. To reach Puerto Ayora, on Santa Cruz, follow the crowds to the ferry and, once across the channel, hop on any bus for the trek across the island.

SAN CRISTÓBAL

SAN/Saeta has one flight per day, five days a week, from Quito and Guayaquil to San Cristóbal Island. If you fly round-trip internationally with Saeta you can arrange a free stopover on San Cristóbal Island (30 days maximum).

Getting Around

Limited interisland transportation is available by boat with the municipal agency **INGALA** (no ☎), on Santa Cruz Island on the road to Bellavista. Currently there is one trip per week from Santa Cruz to Floreana and Isabela Islands, and there are two boats per week between Santa Cruz and San Cristóbal. Each trip costs approximately $20.

Tour Operators

Three classes of boat offer tours of the Galápagos: luxury, tourist, and economy. Economy vessels (often converted fishing trawlers) can be booked from the islands for day tours costing $35–$75 per person, but such boats are often poorly maintained and accompanied by auxiliary guides who need a refresher course in English. Luxury and tourist class vessels generally offer three-, four-, and seven-night tours for $100–$275 per day. You dine and sleep on board, and much of the sailing is done at night to maximize time spent touring the islands. Most of these vessels employ naturalist guides who are knowledgeable in biology and related sciences, and who speak at least two languages. At least once a day you will have an opportunity to swim or snorkel. (For more information, *see* Chapter 2, Adventure and Learning Vacations.)

Cruise Ships

There are three cruise ships currently operating in the Galápagos, all of which can be booked through **Metropolitan Touring** (*see* Tour Operators *in* Quito, *above*). The **Santa Cruz,** which departs from Baltra, and the **Galápagos Explorer,** which departs from San Cristóbal Island, each carries up to 90 passengers and has comfortable dining rooms and bars (the latter also has a swimming pool). The *Galápagos Explorer* has a reputation as the "party" boat and seems to attract more Ecuadoran nationals; the *Santa Cruz* has a slightly more academic bent. The most luxurious—and expensive—option is the 38-passenger **Isabela II** (also based in Baltra), equipped with a hot tub, sauna, and exercise room.

Yachts and Motor Sailers

Luxurious 6- to 40-person yachts can be booked FIT (for individual travelers) or as private charters. You may save money by booking directly with operators within Ecuador; contact **Angermeyer's Enchanted Excursions** (Calle Foch 769, at Av. Amazonas, Quito, ☎ 02/569960, FAX 02/569956) or **Quasar Naútica** (Av. Los Shyris y Gaspar de Villarroel, Edificio Autocom, 3rd Floor, Quito, ☎ 02/446996, FAX 02/446997; U.S. ☎ 800/247–2925, FAX 813/637–9876).

Land-Based Tours

Those who do not relish three to seven nights aboard a ship should consider Metropolitan Touring's land-and-sea Delfin package. The three-, four-, or seven-night itineraries combine lodging at the comfortable Hotel Delfin, on Santa Cruz, with daily island excursions on the newly refurbished, 36-passenger *Delfin II*. However, all but the most queasy landlubber should seriously consider a ship-based package, which allows you to see more of the islands and their wildlife.

Exploring the Galápagos Islands

Santa Cruz

Overlooking Academy Bay on the island's southern shore is **Puerto Ayora,** a relatively developed town with hotels, souvenir shops, restaurants, and even a few clubs. Follow the main road east to the **Charles Darwin Research Station** and its Van Straelen Visitor Center, which has an informative exhibit explaining the basics of Galápagos geology, weather patterns, volcanology, and ecology. Self-guided trails lead to the station's tortoise pens, where several different populations can be viewed. ☎ 05/526189. ☛ *Entry fee. Closed Sun.*

Tortuga Bay, 3 kilometers (2 miles) southwest of Puerto Ayora, has a long white-sand beach where marine iguanas sometimes strut along the water's edge. There are no facilities along the water, but if you walk from town (take the road to Bellavista and turn left just past the bank) you will pass a soda and beer stand at the top of a lava-rock staircase.

Near the small village of **Bellavista** you can explore amazing underground lava tubes. **Los túneles,** as they are known on the island, were created when flowing lava cooled more quickly on the surface, forming a crust that enclosed a labyrinth of tall, empty chambers. The underground tunnels are nearly a mile long, and you can easily walk upright as you grope through the caverns with the aid of a flashlight. To reach the tunnels from Puerto Ayora go north on the road to Bellavista; turn right (east) at the crossroad and walk about a mile until you find a farm with a sign announcing LOS TÚNELES. A small entrance fee is collected by the farm owners, who also provide flashlights.

The road to **Santa Rosa,** 13 kilometers (8 miles) beyond Bellavista, is lined with giant elephant grass, avocado and papaya trees, and boughs of yellow trumpet vines, all of which are in marked contrast to the dry, cactus-spotted lowlands. About 2 kilometers (1 mile) beyond Santa Rosa look for a pair of giant sinkholes called **Los Gemelos,** one on either side of the road.

The unattended **National Park Tortoise Reserve** is one of the few places in the archipelago where you can view giant Galápagos turtles in the wild. An unmarked track leads to the reserve from Santa Rosa. Along the way keep alert for Galápagos hawks, Darwin finches, and short-eared owls. In Santa Rosa, a small restaurant across from the church sometimes rents horses, which you are allowed to ride inside the tortoise reserve.

San Cristóbal

Puerto Baquerizo Moreno is the capital of Galápagos Province and the largest town on San Cristóbal, though with only a few hotels and restaurants it is less tourist-oriented than Puerto Ayora. Still, Puerto Moreno's harbor provides anchorage for numerous tour boats, and there is some good hiking in the area. Two kilometers (1 mile) east of the port is **Frigate-bird Hill,** where both great and magnificent frigate birds—two species of black seabirds famed for their courtship displays—make their nests. On a clear day there are sweeping views of Bahía Wreck Bay.

El Progreso, one of San Cristóbal's first colonies, is a small village about 8 kilometers (5 miles) east of Puerto Moreno at the end of one of the island's few roads (buses connect the two towns twice daily). You can rent a Jeep in town and explore the shores of **Laguna el Junco,** one of the archipelago's few permanent freshwater lakes, 10 kilometers (6 miles) east.

Punta Pitt, at the northeastern tip of the island, is the only place in the Galápagos where you can view three species of boobies—masked, blue-footed, and red-footed—nesting together, as well as frigate birds, storm petrels, and swallow-tailed gulls. The site is accessible by motor launch from Puerto Moreno; inquire at your hotel for details.

Isabela

Although **Isabela** is the largest island in the archipelago, no tour boats are based here and its infrastructure is extremely limited. Its few hotels are very basic, with intermittent hot water, and there are only two restaurants. Sleepy **Puerto Villamil,** founded in 1897 as a center for extracting lime, is the focus of the island's scant tourist trade. Nearby there are several lagoons where flamingos and migrant birds can be viewed up close, and sand-and-lava beaches with large populations of herons, egrets, and other birds.

Isabela's active volcano, **Sierra Niegra** (4,488 feet), can be climbed with local guides based in Puerto Villamil or Santo Tomás, a rural village 18 kilometers (11 miles) northwest. From Santo Tomás you can also hire horses for the 9-kilometer (5½-mile) trek to the volcano's rim. The view from here is awe-inspiring: The volcano's caldera—roughly 10 kilometers (6 miles) in diameter—is the largest in the Galápagos and the second-largest in the world. A more ambitious climb, requiring adequate planning and equipment, is **Volcán Alcedo** (3,600 feet). The site can only be reached by boat, after which a 10-kilometer (6-mile) trail climbs over rough terrain. Your rewards: stunning vistas and the opportunity to view the archipelago's largest population of Galápagos tortoises.

Dining and Lodging

Island restaurants and lodgings can be quite rustic. Many hotels have only cold running water, and rooms often lack electrical outlets; even if there is an outlet, electricity is shut off nightly between midnight and 7 AM. For price categories, *see* Dining *and* Lodging *in* Ecuador Essentials, *below.*

Santa Cruz

DINING

$$ **Four Lanterns.** The Italian proprietress of this popular restaurant takes
★ pride in her culinary creations—the lasagna, gnocchi, cannelloni, and pizza are all homemade and excellent. An accepted piece of local wisdom: Everyone eventually ends up at the Four Lanterns. ✗ *Av. Charles Darwin, Puerto Ayora, no* ☎. *No credit cards. No lunch.*

$$ **La Garrapata.** This popular restaurant, which is translated as "the tick," is run by the offspring of one of Galápagos's pioneer families. It attracts both tourists and locals who spy friends at the exclusively outdoor tables. The menu includes meats, seafood, and pasta, as well as beer, wine, and cocktails. Just next door is the popular discotheque, La Panga, where salsa and disco music are mixed until the lights shut down or the last patron leaves. ✗ *Av. Charles Darwin, Puerto Ayora, no* ☎. *No credit cards. Closed Sun.*

$$ **Narwahl.** Set in the lush highlands of Santa Cruz, with a gorgeous view of the island on a clear day, this hideaway eatery features set meals that include a welcome cocktail, soup or salad, and a dependably good entrée of chicken, fish, or beef (vegetarian entrées are available with advance notification). ✗ *Road to Santa Rosa, no* ☎. *Reservations required—reserve at CETUR (see Visitor Information, above). No credit cards.*

DINING AND LODGING

$$$$ **Hotel Galápagos.** This casual, comfortable hotel—drenched in bougainvillea and other flowering plants—is halfway between Puerto Ayora and the Darwin Research Station—a relatively short walk to either. The rustic rooms have cement floors covered by palm frond mats, and some have ocean views; the seaside lounge has hammocks, bookshelves, and a self-serve bar. The restaurant serves healthy but uninspired dishes; meals for nonguests are by previous arrangement only. ☎ *Av. Charles Darwin, Puerto Ayora, no* ☎ *(for reservations* ☎ *02/ 545777 or* FAX *02/502449). 18 rooms. Restaurant, bar. MC, V.*

$$ **Gran Hotel Fiesta.** This Mediterranean-style complex is administered by the former mayor of Santa Cruz. Each of the small, comfortable three-person cabins has a separate dining room and small refrigerator. Hot water is provided by electric showers. ☎ *Las Ninfas, Puerto*

Ayora, no ☎ *(for reservations* ☎ *02/530449). 6 cabins. Restaurant. No credit cards.*

San Cristóbal
DINING AND LODGING

$$$ **Gran Hotel San Cristóbal.** Although it is expensive and not particularly attractive, this is the best hotel in town. Air-conditioning and hot-water showers help to make up for the lack of charm. ☒ *Playa Man,* ☎ *179. 15 rooms. Restaurant.*

ECUADOR ESSENTIALS

Customs and Duties

On Arrival
You can import one liter of spirits, 300 cigarettes or 50 cigars, and reasonable amounts of perfumes, gifts, and personal effects. Do not bring firearms, ammunition, drugs, fresh or dried meats, or plants and vegetables into the country.

On Departure
There is a $25 airport departure tax, which can be paid in U.S. dollars or sucres.

Dining

In the major cities you can enjoy international and traditional Ecuadoran dishes at pleasingly low prices, although wines and most hard liquors are imported and can double the tab. The main meal of the day is lunch, *el almuerzo,* which typically features soup, a meat or fish plate accompanied by rice and fried potatoes, and a small salad. Time to relax or sleep after such a large meal is essential! Seafood is a mainstay on the coast, though even Quito menus feature fresh fish and seafood.

Specialties
For the adventurous carnivore, there are succulent suckling piglets and guinea pigs, often roasted—teeth, paws, and all—over a charcoal fire. *Seco de chivo* is a traditional goat stew. *Humitas* are sweet corn tamales eaten by tradition-minded Ecuadorans only in the late afternoon, with black coffee. Other Andean favorites include llapingachos, mashed cheese and potato pancakes; and *locro de queso,* a milk-based soup containing corn, potatoes, and a garnish of fresh avocado. An Ecuadoran favorite is ceviche, fish or seafood marinated in lime juice and seasoned with onion, tomato, chili peppers, and cilantro and often served with *cangil* (popcorn). Typical coastal cuisine is based around *arroz con menestra,* huge portions of white rice served with either beans or lentils, and patacones, green bananas fried in oil, smashed, and refried.

Mealtimes
Cafeterias and inexpensive restaurants often are open throughout the day. Better restaurants open for lunch between noon and 4 PM, and reopen for dinner at 7 PM. Many restaurants close early on Saturday and all day Sunday.

Dress
While most $$$$ and $$$ restaurants do not actually require a coat and tie, Ecuadorans spending that amount on dinner *do* dress up. You may feel uncomfortably shabby, or be spurned by your waiter, if you do not follow suit.

Ratings

CATEGORY	COST*
$$$$	over $20
$$$	$12–$20
$$	$5–$12
$	under $5

per person, excluding tax, alcohol, and service

Embassies and Consulates

United States
Embassy: Avenida 12 de Octubre at Avenida Patria, Quito, ☎ 02/562890.

Canada
Embassy: Avenida 6 de Diciembre 2816, at Calle J. Ortón, Quito, ☎ 02/543214.

United Kingdom
Embassy: Calle González Suárez 111, ☎ 02/560670 or 02/560669.

Getting Around

By Plane
Ecuador's principal domestic carriers are **Saeta/SAN** (Calle Santa María at Av. Amazonas, Quito, ☎ 02/502706 or 02/542148) and **TAME** (Av. Amazonas 1354 at Av. Colón, ☎ 02/509382). Both fly regularly between Quito and Guayaquil ($30), between Guayaquil and Cuenca ($24), and between Quito or Guayaquil and Baltra, in the Galápagos Islands ($330–$375).

Saeta flies internationally from Miami, Los Angeles, and New York to the Galápagos Islands and Quito's **Aeropuerto Mariscal Sucre** (☎ 02/440083 or 02/440081). With the purchase of a round-trip international flight, the airline offers a stop-over in the Galápagos (for up to 30 days) or two internal flights at no additional charge. Other carriers offering service from Quito include **American Airlines** (Av. Amazonas 353, at Calle Robles, Quito, ☎ 02/553464 or 02/540443) and **Continental** (Av. Amazonas at Av. Naciones Unidas, Quito, ☎ 02/461489).

By Train
Ecuador's railroad network presently operates in chunks and slices, and by no means services the entire country. Only three lines exist, and service is regularly disrupted due to flood damage and repairs. There is, in theory, daily rail service ($3 one-way) between Ibarra, capital of Imbabura, and San Lorenzo, on the northern coast, although disruptions are frequent. Service on the Quito–Riobamba line has resumed after years of neglect, but at press time (winter 1995), it runs on Saturdays only, departing at 8 AM from the Quito **train station** (Av. Maldonado at Calle Sincholagua, ☎ 02/656144). The most popular train runs most days from Riobamba to Durán, on the coast. Train fares for foreigners have recently jumped appreciably but remain quite bearable ($10, Quito–Riobamba). An alternative to the public rails is **Metropolitan Touring** (*see* Arriving and Departing: By Train *and* Tour Operators *in* Quito, *above*), which combines reliable train service with a variety of one- to three-night tours.

By Car
ROAD CONDITIONS
The Pan-American Highway runs the length of the country, entering from Colombia in the north, passing through Quito and the major cities of the Andes, and continuing south into Peru. The highway is usually

in fair condition except during the rainy season, when potholes form. The coast road is incomplete in some areas, requiring inland detours.

RULES OF THE ROAD

On the narrow mountain roads, bus drivers are notorious for passing on curves and for making other dangerous maneuvers. Road signage is poor, especially outside the major cities.

RENTALS

Car rental offices outside Quito, Guayaquil, and Cuenca are virtually nonexistent. In Quito, the most reliable agency is **Budget** (Av. Amazonas 1408, at Av. Colón, ☎ 02/237026; at the airport, ☎ 02/459052). Other Quito-based agencies include **Avis** (Av. Colón at Av. 10 de Agosto, ☎ 02/550238; at the airport, ☎ 02/440270) and **Hertz** (at the Hotel Oro Verde, Calle Cordero 433, at Av. 12 de Octubre, ☎ 02/569107). If you rent a car, make sure to check your headlight alignment, tires, spare tire, and jack, and inquire about deductibles for damage and theft, which can be quite high. The average rental rate per week is $175–$250, including mileage but excluding insurance and taxes.

EMERGENCY ASSISTANCE

No emergency roadside service exists, although passing motorists will frequently stop to help a disabled vehicle.

GASOLINE

Regular leaded gasoline is called "extra" and costs about $1.15 per U.S. gallon; higher-octane, unleaded "super" costs roughly $1.50 per U.S. gallon.

By Bus

Buses run frequently and are extremely cheap: the two-hour Quito–Otavalo bus ride costs $1, the 10-hour Quito–Guayaquil about $5. Sadly, pickpocketing and bag slashing are on the rise, so keep a close eye on your valuables. Private bus companies, such as **Reytur** (Calle Gangotena 158, Quito, ☎ 02/565299 or 02/546674) and **Expreso Internacional Ormeño** (Calle Shyris 1168, at Calle Portugal, ☎ 02/460024) travel within Ecuador and internationally, and usually are equipped with air-conditioning, toilets, and VCRs.

Language

Ecuador's two official languages are Spanish and Quechua, the language introduced by the Inca and still spoken by indigenous peoples in both the highlands and the Oriente. English is the lingua franca of tourism, and you will find many young Ecuadorans in travel-related fields who speak excellent English. In rural areas you may have to struggle along in Spanish.

Lodging

A wide variety of accommodation is available in Ecuador, and the most money does not always buy the most charm. The larger high-rise hotels offer services such as on-site restaurants and bars, saunas, gyms, and business centers, but the staffs can be impersonal and sometimes downright cold. For less money you can find restored colonial and republican-era homes furnished with antiques, with more ambience and more personalized service. In rural and jungle regions, accommodations range from rustic to *really* rustic: Expect cold-water showers and, occasionally, pit toilets. Basic accommodations are also the norm in the Galápagos Islands, although cruise ships and most first-class yachts are equipped with hot-water showers.

Ratings

Prices are for two people in a double room excluding 20% tax, based on high-season rates.

CATEGORY	COST
$$$$	over $120
$$$	$65–$120
$$	$27–$65
$	under $27

Mail

Post offices throughout the country keep fairly standard hours: weekdays 9–5. First-class mail costs about 30¢ to the United States, 40¢ to Europe. The casualty rate for letters and postcards is surprisingly low, and you can expect most to reach international destinations within two weeks.

Money and Expenses

Currency

Ecuador's currency, the sucre, is named for its revered liberator, Field Marshal Antonio José de Sucre. Thanks to inflation, bills under 100 sucres are rarely seen, with the usual denominations being 100, 500, 1,000, 5,000, and 10,000 sucres. Coins are rarely used, but you may receive a 10-, 20-, or 50-sucre coin in change from time to time. Prices, unless otherwise noted, are listed in U.S. dollars.

Changing Money

You can change money quickly at the many exchange houses in larger cities and get the same rate as at a bank. While U.S. dollars are accepted in payment at larger hotels and restaurants and by dollar-wise locals, you should carry sucres when traveling to smaller towns and the Galápagos Islands. At press time (winter 1995), the exchange rate was 2,240 sucres to the U.S. dollar and 2,900 sucres to the pound sterling.

Forms of Payment

Visa, Diners Club, MasterCard, and American Express cards are widely accepted (especially the first three). A few businesses add a surcharge of 3% to 10% on credit-card purchases.

What It Will Cost

Many items—from taxi fare and domestic air travel to ceramic tea sets— are extremely reasonable in price. You can gorge yourself at even the most elegant restaurants and still struggle to spend $20 for dinner. Accommodations ranging from simple and clean to downright charming cost $10–$30 per person, though international chain hotels charge $70–$200 per night for a comfortable yet generic double room. Tourist facilities are sometimes scarce outside the major cities, but when you do find them they will inevitably fall into the "bargain" category.

TAXES

Most hotels and restaurants add a 20% tax to your bill. Some include this government tax when quoting prices, others do not, so be sure to inquire.

SAMPLE PRICES

A 750-milliliter bottle of beer at a restaurant, $1; bottle of wine, $6; 1-mile taxi ride, 50¢; city bus ride, 20¢; a newspaper and shoe shine (including tip), 40¢.

Opening and Closing Times

Banks

Banks are open weekdays only 9–1:30; exchange houses, which are much more efficient and less crowded, often open in the afternoon as well, usually from 3 to 5:30.

Museums

Hours at Ecuador's museums vary. (Be aware that descriptions and printed materials are almost without exception in Spanish; some museums, however, have English-speaking docents.)

Shops

Traditional shop hours are 9–1 and 3 or 4 to 6. Tourist-related shops generally do not close for lunch, but many are closed Saturday afternoon and all day Sunday.

National Holidays

New Year's Day (Jan. 1); Easter (1996: Apr. 7; 1997: Mar. 30); Labor Day (May 1); Battle of Pichincha (May 24); Simón Bolívar's birthday (July 24); Independence Day (Aug. 10); Columbus Day (Oct. 12); All Souls' Day (Nov. 2); Christmas (Dec. 25).

Precautions

Health

Cholera and dysentery are not serious problems in Ecuador. Nevertheless, drink only bottled water to reduce the risk of contracting intestinal parasites, and avoid ice and uncooked or unpeeled vegetables and fruits that have been washed in tap water. Consider malaria pills if you're traveling to the rain forest or to the northern coast around Esmeraldas. In the Galápagos, the most serious threat you'll face is sunburn—do not underestimate the intensity of the equatorial sun. Those prone to seasickness should bring pills or patches if planning a ship-based tour of the archipelago.

Safety

Although political turmoil and violence are not a part of the Ecuadoran landscape, pickpockets and purse slashers are a growing problem. Leave your valuable jewelry at home, keep a good grip on cameras and day packs, and avoid displaying cash. Use extra caution in all crowded metropolitan areas. In Quito be especially wary in the Plaza San Francisco, where pickpockets lurk, and on the stairs and road leading to El Panecillo, where muggers lie in wait.

Shopping

Browsing and bartering at one of Ecuador's markets is a must for all but the most black-hearted shopping haters. Weekly markets are a tradition in the Andes region, where indigenous peoples wearing colorful regional dress arrive from the countryside on foot, horse, burro, llama, and in fancy new pickup trucks. Bargaining is an indispensable yet polite ritual. Mild curiosity, with a *slightly* shocked look when the price is offered, begins the process. A counteroffer of half the asking price is usual, and the norm is to agree on a price of about 75% of the original asking price.

Telephones

Local Calls

Coin-operated pay phones have become nearly obsolete. Those few in existence require a one-sucre coin or a token purchased at a newsstand or nearby shop. Some stores sell local calls just as they sell candy bars, at about 15¢ for a brief call; look for a sign in the window announcing TELÉFONO or LLAMADAS. Another alternative is **EMETEL,** Ecuador's communications agency, which now offers fax services as well. Offices are in every major and minor city and in many small towns, and most are open daily 8 AM–9:30 PM.

Long-Distance and International Calls

To make collect or credit-card calls through an English-speaking **AT&T** operator, dial 999–119. To reach an **MCI** operator, dial 999–170. To contact **Sprint,** dial 999–171. These calls are nominally free, but some hotels charge for the service. Calls made through hotels are subject to a 20% surcharge. You can also call direct or collect from any EMETEL office. Most hotels and tour operators now have faxes.

Tipping

A tip of 5%–10% is appropriate for waiters, although you are not expected to tip if the service is poor. (A 10% surcharge added to your bill is supposed to go toward service, although whether waiters actually receive this gratuity is questionable.) Taxi drivers are not tipped. Porters and bellhops receive the equivalent of 50¢ per bag. Naturalists and other expert guides expect $7–$10 per person per day, drivers about $2 per person per day.

When to Go

You may want to plan your trip around one of the country's many festivals or, if snorkeling or diving in the Galápagos is on your itinerary, during the hotter, albeit wetter, winter months. The high season revolves around holidays, especially Christmas, New Year's, Carnival, and Easter week. During these peak periods hotel rooms become scarce and prices jump noticeably.

Climate

Ecuador's climate is strongly influenced by ocean currents, trade winds, and altitude, which make generalization difficult. One constant is the rainy season, which lasts from December to May and occasionally precipitates landslides or power outages. On the coast, the rainy season is hot and muggy, especially in Guayaquil; the rest of the year the coast is much cooler and drier than might be expected on the equator. In the Galápagos, the weather is generally hot and humid from January through April, with frequent afternoon showers. Cooler temperatures prevail the rest of the year, creating *garua,* a fine, light mist. The seas are roughest in September and October, when many Galápagos tour boats head for dry dock.

The following are the average daily maximum and minimum temperatures for Quito.

Jan.	69F	20C	May	69F	20C	Sept.	72F	22C
	46	8		47	8		45	7
Feb.	69F	20C	June	70F	21C	Oct.	70F	21C
	47	81		46	8		46	8
Mar.	69F	20C	July	71F	22C	Nov.	70F	21C
	47	8		44	7		46	8
Apr.	69F	20C	Aug.	71F	22C	Dec.	70F	21C
	47	8		44	7		46	8

9 Paraguay

Visitors to this largely undiscovered and unspoiled land enter a world where time and tradition have stood still for generations. Although this means that Paraguay may be short on extravagant facilities, it is long on the charm and the authenticity that are missing in many other parts of South America.

By Richard
Jarvie

Updated by
Matthew
Doman

VIEWED BY EVEN SEASONED travelers as a curious footnote to South America's more glamorous regions, Paraguay remains a largely unknown quantity. Isolated by its landlocked position and by more than three decades of authoritarian rule under General Alfredo Stroessner, whose regime was toppled in a 1989 coup, the country was left behind while neighboring Brazil and Argentina made rapid economic progress. Institutions and services catering to tourists are still rare: Museums are run-down, maintained more by enthusiasm than government funds, the highway system is primitive, and good hotels are few and far between.

But the advantages to this less-than-perfect infrastructure are enormous. Paraguay has not entered the rat race, and many visitors comment on the easy pace of life and the charm of the people, with their Old World courtesies and generous hospitality. Crowds are never a problem, and both the wild countryside and places of historic interest—restored Jesuit missions and, in the capital, Asunción, fine examples of both Spanish colonial and 19th-century architecture—can be explored without the controls and restrictions common in Europe and North America. Visitors to a Jesuit ruin can find themselves totally alone and, without a hawker in sight, allow the overwhelming tranquillity of the site to transport them back to the time when missionaries worked the fields alongside their Guaraní Indian converts.

Nature lovers can explore the subtropical jungle of the northeast—home to parrots, macaws, and toucans as well as the fast-disappearing jaguar—or observe varied and abundant bird life in the swamps of the Paraná plateau. Rivers that teem with salmonlike *dorado* and giant *surubí* catfish offer some of the best fishing in the world. Anglers can test their skills as clouds of snowy egrets take flight and monkeys swing through riverside trees. Vultures, kites, and eagles soar over the sun-scorched plains of the Chaco, an arid scrubland that covers half of Paraguay and is one of the most sparsely populated spots on earth, with less than one inhabitant for each of its 250,000 square kilometers (97,500 square miles).

More than a quarter of Paraguay's 4.5 million people live in Asunción, and most of the rest live in or around the numerous small towns to the east. Spanish and Guaraní are the official languages, reflecting a society in which about 80% of the population is of mestizo—mixed Spanish and Indian—stock. (Some say that while Spanish is the language of business, the soft-toned Guaraní is the language of love.) Paraguay also has a fairly large and influential German community—one reason for the high quality of the local beer—while more recently many Korean immigrants have become shopkeepers in Asunción, Ciudad del Este, and Encarnación, where they sell a wide range of imported goods.

Agriculture, particularly cotton and soybeans, and cattle breeding are the driving forces of the Paraguayan economy. Since 1927, when the first Mennonite settlers arrived from Canada, 2.5 million acres of the Chaco's inhospitable scrub have been turned into fertile farmland, supplying more than half of Paraguay's dairy produce. Industry is still in its infancy. After an economic boom in the 1970s, fueled by the construction of the Itaipú Dam with Brazil, Paraguay's economic growth has slowed to a trickle, the most important factor being the success or failure of the cotton and soybean harvests.

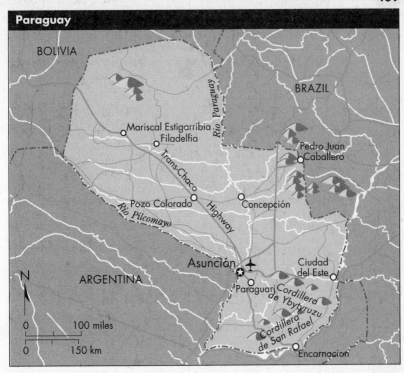

Paraguay is a partner with Brazil, Uruguay, and Argentina in the Mercosur Common Market, which came into full effect on January 1, 1995. Opinions as to the benefits are mixed. While the market's promoters say integration will give Paraguay access to new markets, enabling industry and agriculture to expand, opponents argue the local economy could drown in a flood of imports.

But Paraguay faces an even greater challenge. Although press and individual freedoms have been fully restored, and free elections have been held, vestiges of the past hold on. Widespread corruption and smuggling continue as beneficiaries of the old system refuse to yield to the new. It remains to be seen whether Paraguay's still fragile democracy can withstand and eventually destroy these forces.

ASUNCIÓN

Like most Latin American cities, Asunción suffers from haphazard development and an inadequate infrastructure. During office hours the city center is packed. Street vendors crowd sidewalks, and traffic hurtles by. Drivers play a dangerous game of chicken at every intersection. Crossing the street becomes a terrifying experience as buses bear down on pedestrians with seemingly murderous intent.

But take a step back, and you will see another side of the city that was once the colonial capital of southern South America. On the drive from the airport, the taxi whisks by remnants of Asunción's prosperous past, the magnificent mansions lining Avenida Mariscal López. A glimpse through a doorway reveals a peaceful patio reminiscent of those in southern Spain, and above the neon signs of a hamburger bar, the delicately decorated facade and balconies of a Belle Epoque building have sur-

vived the vagaries of fashion. Alongside the money changers and peddlers of fake Rolex watches, Indian women offer bundles of herbs and
roots—centuries-old remedies for every bodily ailment. Contrasting with
the hustle and bustle of the commercial center 100 yards away, the pristine columned Government and Legislative palaces overlook the Bay
of Asunción as cool river breezes rustle through jacaranda and flame
trees in the nearby park.

During the day rich and poor rub shoulders, air-conditioned limousines
jostling at crossroads with packed buses. At nighttime the wealthy drive
home to their elegant suburban mansions while street vendors lug their
unsold wares back to the reclaimed swampland of La Chacarita shantytown just below the Legislative Palace. Yet despite the chasm between
the classes, visitors need not be overly concerned with theft and violence.
Rich or poor, the Asunceño is invariably courteous and helpful.

Visitor Information

The helpful staff at the reception desk of **Direccion Nacional de Turismo** (Palma 468, Ground Floor, ☎ 021/491230) provides information and pamphlets about Paraguay weekdays 7 AM–7 PM and Saturday
8–11:30. More detailed information can be obtained from the offices
upstairs, open weekdays 7–1. **Lions Tour,** a travel agency (*see* Tour Operators, *below*) operates a desk at the airport that can help visitors with
transportation and hotel and tour bookings throughout the country.
The desk is open when international flights arrive. Most hotels provide pamphlets and maps, give advice, arrange tours, and hire cars.

Arriving and Departing

By Plane

Several international airlines, most of them South American (*see* Getting Around: By Plane *in* Paraguay Essentials, *below*), serve the **Silvio
Pettirossi International Airport,** which is 15 kilometers (9 miles) from
the city center. Taxis, the most practical means of getting into town,
charge a fixed rate to downtown, which at press time (winter 1995)
was about $16; for the current rate check at the transport information
desk. The desk can also arrange for an *omnibus special* whenever
there are six or more passengers. This bus costs $5 and will take pas-
sengers to any address in central Asunción. **Local Bus 30A**—which leaves
not from the airport grounds but from the tollbooths on the road into
the airport (about 200 yards from the terminal)—departs for downtown Asunción every 15 minutes; the fare is 25¢. Some hotels provide
minivan service for passengers with hotel reservations; the minivans
meet each international flight.

By Car

There are only three major entrances to Asunción. Access from the eastern cities of Encarnación or Ciudad del Este can either be through Luque,
feeding into the city center via Avenida Mariscal López or Aviadores del
Chaco (which branches off Mariscal López), or by a more direct route:
via Avenida Pettirossi. The former is recommended because Pettirossi,
which passes through suburban shopping areas, frequently becomes
jammed with heavy, chaotic traffic. The remaining access is from the Trans-
Chaco Highway (Route 9), which runs through Presidente Hayes, joins
with the road from the frontier post of Puerto Falcon (across from the
Argentine border town of Clorinda), and then crosses the Puente Remanso
bridge spanning the Paraguay River 20 kilometers (12 miles) from Asunción. Turning right, the route is still called the Trans-Chaco Highway
and runs into Avenida Primer Presidente. Turn right for a few hundred

yards and left onto General Artigas. The route is clearly signposted. Heading out of Asunción, you can take Avenida Pettirossi and then the left fork into Avenida Eusebio Ayala, which then becomes Route 1.

By Bus

All intercity services leave from **Terminal de Omnibus Asunción** (España and Fernando de la Mora, ☎ 021/551732). Many bus companies have information and ticket offices on Plaza Uruguaya, in the city center. The main companies are **Pluma** (☎ 021/445024) and **Rápido Yguazú** (☎ 021/551618).

Getting Around Asunción

All attractions in the center of Asunción can be seen on foot easily and safely; the city does not suffer from the violent street crime common in other South American capitals. Unless you plan to travel out of town, avoid renting a car—driving in Asunción can be nerve-racking.

By Bus or Tram

Local buses are crammed and uncomfortable. During business hours, old yellow **tramcars** trundle through downtown along Palma from the Plaza Uruguay to Colón, running approximately every half hour. The fare is about 10¢.

By Taxi

Taxis, all metered, are inexpensive and can range from a modern Mercedes to a rattly Volkswagen Beetle. They can be hailed in the street and found at the more than 70 taxi stands dotting the city. They also wait outside the main hotels. (Some hotels have their own limousine service.) Beware at night, when taxi drivers frequently do not put on their meters and then charge an outrageous fare at the end of the ride. Longer taxi rides that involve waiting time can be bargained. At night it can be difficult to find a taxi, so ask the hotel or restaurant to call a radio cab.

Tour Operators

Lions Tour (Alberdi 454, 1st Floor, ☎ 021/490278 or 021/490591), **VIP's Tour** (Mexico 782, ☎ 021/497117), and **Agen Par** (Montevideo 419, ☎ 021/497496 or 021/444539) can all arrange guided tours of the city's major sights and parks for between $10 and $25 a person, depending on the number of people.

Exploring Asunción

The city is built on a rise overlooking a large bay formed from the Paraguay River to the northeast. The downtown area runs southwest from the bay for about 10 blocks to Teniente Fariña and from Estados Unidos in the southeast for 17 blocks to Colón. Most hotels, restaurants, shops, and offices can be found in this rectangle. Asunción's streets follow a grid; downtown they are narrow and generally have one-way traffic. Three downtown squares—Plaza de los Héroes, Plaza Independencia, and Plaza Uruguaya—provide cool resting places in the shade of jacaranda trees.

Paraguayan addresses often are given not with street numbers but as the intersection of two streets, for example, "Ayolas y Brasil"; such addresses are listed below as "Ayolas and Brasil."

Around Plaza de los Héroes

Just about everything worth seeing in Asunción is in the city center, within a few blocks of the **Plaza de los Héroes,** the central square. The plaza is a fine place to rest in the shade and observe Paraguayan life. Indians wander by, selling feather headdresses and bows and arrows, artisans put their wares on display, and traveling salesmen hawk anything from patented cures to miracle knife sharpeners. You can also climb onto a high chair for a shoe shine, or have a photo taken by an old box camera. On public holidays the square is often the scene of live music and folk-dance performances.

In the corner of the square stands the pink-domed **Panteón Nacional de los Héroes.** Modeled after Les Invalides in Paris, this columned mausoleum bears homage to the heroes who died in Paraguay's major wars: the War of the Triple Alliance (1865–70) against Brazil, Uruguay, and Argentina, in which 80% of Paraguay's menfolk perished and half the country's territory was lost; and the Chaco War (1929–35) against Bolivia. The Panteón, guarded around the clock by two grenadiers, houses the remains of President Carlos Antonio López (who, during his administration, from 1841 until his death in 1862, was responsible for many of the public buildings in Asunción) and his son, Mariscal Francisco Solano López, the most venerated hero of the War of the Triple Alliance. Paraguay's commander in the Chaco War, José Felix Estigarribia, is also buried here, along with the remains of two unknown soldiers. *Plaza de los Héroes, no* 🕾. ☛ *Free.*

Two blocks to the east, off Palma, which runs along the north edge of the square, is the **Casa de la Independencia,** a late-18th-century house with typical whitewashed walls, brick floors, and a shady patio. Now a museum displaying colonial and 19th-century furniture and religious artifacts—some dating from the early 17th century—the building was the meeting place for revolutionaries plotting independence from Spain, which was declared in 1811. *14 de Mayo and Presidente Franco,* 🕾 *021/493918.* ☛ *Free.* ☽ *Tues.–Fri. 7–noon and 2:30–6:30, weekends 8–noon.*

One block farther north on 14 de Mayo, at the intersection with El Paraguayo Independiente, is **Casa de la Cultura.** Once the military college, this museum houses documents, artifacts, and trophies from the War of the Triple Alliance and the Chaco War. *14 de Mayo and El Paraguayo Independiente,* 🕾 *021/445212.* ☛ *Free.* ☽ *Weekdays 7:30–noon and 1:30–6, weekends 8–noon.*

Around Plaza Independencia

Across from the Casa de la Cultura is the Plaza Independencia. Most of Asunción's important public buildings can be seen around this square and along **El Paraguayo Independiente,** which runs east from the plaza's southeast corner. Chief among these structures is the neoclassical, horseshoe-shape **Palacio de Gobierno** (El Paraguayo Independiente and Ayolas), or Government Palace, an elegant building overlooking the bay, with verandas and wide spiral staircases. It is not open to the public. On the plaza proper is the **Palacio Legislativo** (Plaza Independencia, 🕾 021/441077 or 021/441078; ☛ Free; ☽ Weekday mornings only), where the National Congress meets. The upper floor was added in 1857, destroying the symmetry of the original single-story Jesuit building. Debates of both senators and deputies are open to the public. On the southeast corner of the square is the **Catedral Metropolitana** (Plaza Independencia, 🕾 021/449512; ☛ Free), which dates from 1687. Inside is an enormous gilded altar and many 18th- and 19th-century religious statues and paintings.

Behind the cathedral toward the river is **La Chacarita,** a shantytown that now has running water and its own school and is steadily establishing itself as a permanent community. It's well worth a visit for those whose only exposure to life in Asunción has been in luxury hotels and restaurants and gleaming high-rises. In the narrow, unpaved streets that wind between rickety tin, wood, and bare-brick huts, barefoot, near-naked children play while chickens peck amid the garbage. The area is slowly becoming urbanized with the installation of electricity and a sewage system.

Around Plaza Uruguaya

One block west and two blocks south of the cathedral, the **Museum of Fine Arts** (Mariscal Estigarribia and Iturbe, ☎ 021/447716; ☛ Free; ☾ Tues.–Fri. 7–7, weekends 8–noon) houses a collection of paintings and sculpture by both Paraguayan and foreign artists. Estigarribia runs west into the **Plaza Uruguaya,** a shady square where locals meet to share *tereré* tea. On one side is a covered book market and on the other the colonnaded **railway station,** built in 1861. In one corner of the terminal you can see a pristine old steam locomotive, the *Sapucaí,* no longer in use.

Other Attractions

A 15-minute taxi or bus ride from the center will take you to the **Parque y Museo de Historia Natural.** Although poorly maintained, these botanical gardens have an enormous array of plants and a small zoo. There is also an 18-hole golf course and campsite. The grounds and a fine example of a Paraguayan country house, typically surrounded by verandas, once belonged to President Francisco Solano López. The residence now houses the museum, which has exhibits of Paraguayan wildlife, ethnology, and history. *Gral Artigas and Primer Presidente,* ☎ 021/25680. ☛ *Free.* ☾ *Weekdays, except 11–2:30.*

Even if you don't stay or eat there, don't miss taking a peek inside the **Gran Hotel del Paraguay** (Calle de la Residenta 902, ☎ 021/200051), about 20 blocks from downtown. The former home of Madame Lynch, the Irish mistress of Solano López, the well-preserved mansion, surrounded by verandas, is set amid lush tropical gardens and has a fine collection of 19th-century furniture and paintings.

Mansions reflecting Paraguay's wealthy past can be seen along the tree-lined **Mariscal López** and **España** avenues, which lead into the city from the southeast.

Shopping

The best shopping in Asunción falls into two distinct and very different categories of objects: handicrafts and electronics. Prices for both are among the lowest in South America, and hard bargaining can make them even cheaper.

The best-known local craft is the delicate *ñandutí,* a type of spider-web lacework. Designs represent plants, animals, or scenes from local legends, and, although traditionally made with white silk or cotton thread, colored threads are now worked in. Both this and *ao p'oí,* a type of embroidery, are incorporated into tablecloths and place mats. Wood carvings, intricately decorated gourds, and figurines—including nativity figures—are all attractive and reasonably priced. Leather items, such as suitcases, tote bags, knapsacks, and briefcases, are more rustic than those sold in Argentina, but they are long-lasting and only a fraction of the price. Plain white or colorful woven hammocks are another good buy.

Shopping Districts

All of the above handicrafts are sold in the area bordered by Palma, Estrella, Colón, and the Plaza de los Héroes. Bargains can be found on the sidewalks, but for top-quality goods stick to the specialty stores. In the same area are hundreds of small stores selling imported watches, electronics, cameras, pens, and athletic shoes. Largely run by Koreans, many of these shops sell the same items, and competition is keen. Watch out for fake perfumes and whiskeys. The phony Rolex, Cartier, and Gucci watches are so obvious that even the vendors don't pretend they are genuine.

Paraguayan harps, guitars, and fine silver filigree jewelry can be bought in the town of **Luque,** a settlement of craftspeople near the international airport.

Specialty Shops

One of the best shops for lacework is **Ao P'oí Raity** (F. R. Moreno 155, ☎ 021/494457). **Overall** (Mariscal Estigarribia 399, ☎ 021/448657) also has excellent lace. **Arte Popular** (Ayolas 360, ☎ 021/492548) carries a wide selection of carved woodwork, as well as ceramics, filigree jewelry, and lacework. For leather goods try **Casa Vera** (Mariscal Estigarribia 470, ☎ 021/445868). **Constancio Sanabria** (Av. Aviadores del Chaco 2852, ☎ 021/662408 or 021/609657), in Luque, is highly recommended for musical instruments.

Market

The **Mercado 4,** on Avenida Pettirossi, is a throbbing, crowded street market that overflows onto several blocks, its stalls laden with produce, cheap clothing, hammocks, and live poultry. An early start is advised, not only because the market begins before dawn but also because the heat and crowds can be suffocating. The market is open all day, every day, except Sunday afternoons.

Sports

Soccer

Soccer is Paraguay's main sport. The most important teams are **Cerro Porteño** and **Olimpia.** Matches are played on Sunday throughout the year, with the best first-division games held at the **Defensores del Chaco** stadium in the suburb of **Sajonia.** Local newspapers publish the most current information on game schedules and how to get tickets.

Tennis

Tennis tournaments between different South American teams, including zone matches of the Davis Cup, are held at the **Yacht y Golf Club Paraguayo** (Av. del Yacht 11, Lambaré, ☎ 021/36117).

Dining

For its small size, Asunción offers a surprising variety of top-class restaurants serving international and Paraguayan cuisine. The more expensive dining spots tend to have international menus, some offering nouvelle cuisine. The ethnic cuisine available reflects the range of immigrant groups—including Korean, Japanese, and German—that have settled here. A number of economical lunchtime eateries scattered throughout the city center serve fast foods such as steaks, french fries, and some local specialties. Locals particularly favor **Bar Asunción** (Estrella and 14 de Mayo; *see below*), **Bar Carioca** (Independencia 1793), **Bar San Miguel** (Espana and Padre Cardoso), **Le Grand** (Oliva between Alberdi and 14 de Mayo; *see below*), and **San Roque** (Ayala and Tacuari). For price-category definitions, *see* Dining *in* Paraguay Essentials, *below.*

German

$$$ **La Hosteria del Caballito Blanco.** Wild boar and deer trophies, wooden
★ chairs with heart-shape backs, and red-checked tablecloths create a rus-
tic look at this traditional German restaurant, where the portions are
so huge that they almost beg to be shared. The extensive menu fea-
tures several types of sausage and plenty of pork, including *kassler*
(smoked chops) and *eisbein* (knuckles). ✗ *Alberdi 631,* ☎ *021/444560.
AE, DC, MC, V.*

International

$$$$ **La Cascada.** The sound of the waterfall that tumbles through the Hotel
Excelsior's foyer (*see* Lodging, *below*) into the luxurious, lower-level
dining room helps soothe nerves frayed by the patchy service. The food,
international dishes with an emphasis on local fish, is good—the su-
rubí in shrimp sauce is particularly tasty—but overpriced in compar-
ison to the many excellent alternatives in downtown Asunción. ✗
Chile 980, ☎ *021/495632. AE, DC, MC, V.*

$$$ **La Pérgola Jardin.** Smoky floor-to-ceiling mirrors, modern black lac-
quer furniture, lots of plants, and live sax and piano make this restau-
rant one of Asunción's most sophisticated dining spots. The service is
efficient and friendly, and the menu, which changes weekly, is international with nouvelle tendencies (warning—the hot *pan de queso*, small
cheese-flavored rolls that come in the bread basket, are irresistible). ✗
Peru 240, ☎ *021/210219, 021/214014, or 021/214015. Weekend
reservations advised. AE, DC, MC, V.*

$$$ **Talleyrand.** Downtown near the Hotel Cecilia, this recently renovated
★ restaurant serves up seasonal dishes that range from lamb with duck
pâté wrapped in pastry to venison, nutria, and alligator. Although
culinary director Georgy Sander, one of the new wave of talented Ar-
gentine chefs, succeeds in blending traditional French cuisine with a
touch of the latest European trends, the oversize, nouvelle-cuisine-style
china clashes somewhat with the soft green color scheme and hunting
prints that lend the dining rooms a refined Continental ambience. ✗
Estigarribia 932, ☎ *021/41163 or 021/445246. Reservations advised,
especially Fri. and Sat. AE, DC, MC, V. Closed Sun.*

$$ **Oliver's.** One block from the Plaza de los Héroes, this favorite executive lunchtime meeting place, decked out in fashionable pinks and
grays, has a buffet at midday and in the evening. Patrons can choose
from a range of all-you-can-eat hot dishes such as goulash, pasta with
mushrooms and cream sauce, and cold cuts, or they can order
chateaubriand Oliver and other Continental dishes from an à la carte
menu. ✗ *Azara 128,* ☎ *021/494931 or 021/494932. Reservations advised. AE, DC, MC, V.*

Italian

$$$ **Il Capo.** Just opposite La Pérgola Jardin (*see above*), this small, 15-table
eatery is simply decorated with whitewashed and brick walls, wooden
beams, and tile floors. The excellent main courses include the home-
made pasta, such as lasagna *con camarones* (with shrimp), and *melan-
zana alla parmegiana* (gratinéed eggplant with tomato and herb sauce);
the Italian wine list is reasonably priced. ✗ *Peru 291,* ☎ *021/213022.
Reservations advised. AE, DC, MC, V.*

Japanese

$$$$ **Akari.** The high percentage of Japanese diners among the clientele
★ vouchsafes the quality of the food at this restaurant in the Hotel Ce-
cilia (*see* Lodging, *below*). It has fewer than a dozen tables, but you
have the option of eating at the center-of-the-room sushi bar, where
you can observe the chef's skills at close range. ✗ *Estados Unidos 341,*

☎ *021/210365, 021/210366, 021/210367, 021/210033, or 021/210034. Reservations advised. AE, DC, MC, V. Closed Sun.*

Paraguayan

$$$ **La Preferida.** Rub shoulders with politicians and diplomats at this restaurant in the Hotel Cecilia (*see* Lodging, *below*), where the Austrian owners give off an air of friendly efficiency in the two dining areas (one no-smoking at peak hours), set with crisp, no-nonsense white linen tablecloths and classic silver and glassware. Among the specialties on the menu, which includes a variety of dorado and surubí dishes, are surubí *ahumado* (smoked) as a starter; the mild *curry de* surubí; and *lomo de cerdo a la pimienta* (peppered pork tenderloin)—ask for it if it's not on the menu. ✕ *25 de Mayo 1005,* ☎ *021/210365, 021/210366, 021/210367, 021/210033, or 021/210034. Reservations advised. AE, DC, MC, V. Closed Sun.*

$$ **Churrasquaria Acuarela.** A 10-minute taxi ride from the city center, ★ this enormous, 1,300-seat *rodizio*-style restaurant must be the best value in town, charging around $7 for all you can eat. The bill of fare consists of a variety of sausages, chicken, pork, and beef cut to order, all straight off the barbecue, with a buffet laden with salads, vegetables, and desserts. For something different, ask for *cupim,* a cut of meat taken from the hump of the Brahma-like cattle bred in Paraguay and Brazil. ✕ *Mariscal López and Teniente Zotti,* ☎ *021/601750. DC, MC, V.*

$$ **La Paraguayita.** At this, the best of a host of grills on Avenida Brasilia, ★ you'll sit out on the terrace beneath jacaranda trees while the waiters bring huge portions of perfectly done beef and pork cooked over white-hot coals and served with the wonderful Paraguayan corn breads, *sopa paraguaya* and *chipá-guazú*. The chorizo sausages make a good starter, especially when dunked in the *criollo* sauce of onion, tomato, garlic, pepper, and vinegar. ✕ *Brasilia and Siria,* ☎ *021/204497. DC, MC, V.*

$ **Bar Asunción.** Open 24 hours a day, this no-nonsense eatery with plastic tables and chairs is in the heart of the commercial center. Grilled steak and chicken, *milanesas* (fillets) of beef, chicken, and surubí, and the empanadas are recommended. ✕ *Estrella and 14 de Mayo,* ☎ *021/ 445411. No credit cards. Closed Sun. and bank holidays.*

$ **Le Grand.** In an old, high-ceilinged building, this favorite lunchtime ★ haunt of office workers, who come for specialties such as *puchero* and milanesa de surubí, is decorated with brightly colored tablecloths and wood chairs. In the evening diners are serenaded with live Latin popular music. ✕ *Oliva between Alberdi and 14 de Mayo, no* ☎. *No credit cards. Closed Sun.*

$ **Tio Lucas.** Glossy cream and black decor with matching Thonet bentwood chairs give this corner bar-restaurant a crisp, modern look. Here, the specialty is pizza. ✕ *25 de Mayo and Yegros, no* ☎. *No credit cards. Closed Sun. and bank holidays.*

Lodging

Accommodations in Asunción are limited to hotels, which vary from modest, no-nonsense establishments costing less than $15 a night to the luxury Yacht y Golf Club Paraguayo resort (*see below*), which charges about $200 a night. Most hotels are situated downtown, where only the most expensive have swimming pools. Air-conditioned rooms, generally available at all but the cheapest hotels, are recommended in summer, but ceiling fans are adequate in winter. For details and price-category definitions, *see* Lodging *in* Paraguay Essentials, *below*.

$$$$ **Hotel Casino Yacht y Golf Club Paraguayo.** Considered one of South ★ America's finest hotels, this resort 13 kilometers (8 miles) southeast of

Asunción is set on the riverbank in the midst of a 200-acre residential and leisure development. Your recreational options include water sports of all kinds, fishing, golf, tennis—10 of the nearly 20 courts are lighted—and squash on two courts. Some of the rooms, which are decorated with modern wood furniture, open onto verdant patios where hummingbirds nest in the foliage. ☎ *Av. del Yacht 11, Lambaré; mailing address: Casilla Correo 1795, Asunción;* ☎ *021/36117 or 021/36121,* FAX *021/36120 or 021/36133. 128 rooms, 5 suites. 3 restaurants, bar, pool, 18-hole golf course, 18 tennis courts, health club, squash, windsurfing, boating, jet skiing, casino, airport shuttle. AE, D, DC, MC, V.*

$$$$ Hotel Excelsior. Elegantly decorated with Regency-style striped wallpaper, antique and reproduction dark-wood furniture, and Oriental carpets, the Excelsior is the most luxurious hotel in downtown Asunción, despite the fact that some of the guest rooms are starting to show signs of wear and tear. It has a pleasant pool area with a grill and a snack bar, and a basement-level discotheque. ☎ *Chile 980,* ☎ *021/495632 through 021/495639, 021/496743, 021/496744, or 021/496745,* FAX *021/496748. 160 rooms. 2 restaurants, bar, pool, beauty salon, health club, dance club, airport shuttle. AE, D, DC, MC, V.*

$$$ Guaraní. Set right on the Plaza de los Héroes, the Guaraní underwent
★ a much-needed renovation in 1992. Guest rooms are now furnished with modern wood furniture and pastel carpets and curtains, and the reception and lounge areas are filled with modern black-leather seating. The service, fortunately, did not change—it's as friendly and efficient as ever. ☎ *Oliva and Independencia Nacional,* ☎ *021/491131. 168 rooms, 28 suites. 2 restaurants, bar, pool, health club, casino. AE, D, DC, MC, V.*

$$$ Hotel Cecilia. Priding itself on personalized attention, the Cecilia has established a devoted clientele. The double rooms are large though slightly austere, with nondescript modern decor; the single rooms are small and the air conditioners perilously close to the bed, blasting the sleeping guest with an icy wind. ☎ *Estados Unidos 341, 021/210365, 021/210366, 021/210367, 021/210033, or 021/210034,* FAX *021/441637. 2 restaurants, bar, pool. AE, D, DC, MC, V.*

$$ Chaco. This comfortable but rather unremarkably decorated hotel can be recommended for its large carpeted rooms, good breakfasts, and friendly service. There is a small rooftop swimming pool. ☎ *Caballero 285,* ☎ *021/492066. 73 rooms. Restaurant, bar, pool. AE, D, DC, MC, V.*

$$ Continental. Added in a recent renovation, lacquer furniture and abstract paintings give the former Husa Hotel a modern look. Some of the guest rooms have a view of the bay. ☎ *Estrella and 15 de Agosto,* ☎ *021/493760,* FAX *021/496176. 66 rooms, 12 suites. Restaurant, bar, pool, sauna, exercise room. AE, D, DC, MC, V.*

$$ Gran Hotel Armele. This hotel in the main shopping district reopened in 1995 after a complete refurbishment. All guest rooms have air-conditioning, some have bay views, and the management is friendly. ☎ *Colón and Palma,* ☎ *021/444455,* FAX *021/445903. 240 rooms. Restaurant. D, MC, V.*

$$ Internacional de Asunción. Built in 1987, this centrally located hotel has a pleasant reception area, with abundant plants and floral arrangements and a bar at the rear. Many of the rooms, which are redecorated every year, have views of the bay. ☎ *Ayolas 520,* ☎ *021/ 494114,* FAX *021/494383. 100 rooms. Pool, sauna, exercise room. AE, D, DC, MC, V.*

$$ Presidente. A total renovation plus efficient new management have won
★ high praise for this hotel a block from the Plaza de los Héroes. The reception and lounge areas are crammed with plants, a theme repeated

in the floral bedspreads and curtains; some of the rooms have bay views. ☎ *Azara 128, ☎ 021/494931 or 021/494932, ℻ 021/444057. 54 rooms, 5 suites. Restaurant. AE, D, DC, MC, V.*

$$ Renacimiento. Little remains of the original interior of this converted Belle Epoque building on the Plaza de los Héroes, and the heavy wooden furniture coupled with low ceilings make the rooms and hallways seem cramped. Still, the location is unbeatable, and guests get to use the pool and gardens of a mansion owned by the hotel just 2 kilometers (1 mile) away. ☎ *Chile 388, ☎ 021/445165, ℻ 021/496500. 48 rooms, 9 suites. AE, D, MC, V.*

$ Asunción Palace. Built 150 years ago as a private residence and now a national monument, this beaux-arts-style hotel is, for all its charm, noisy and rather shabby. However, all the sparsely furnished rooms have air-conditioning and private bathrooms, making it a good value. ☎ *Colón 415, ☎ 021/492152, ℻ 021/492153. 41 rooms. Restaurant. AE.*

$ Senorial del Paraguay. This hotel with Spanish colonial–style decor (whitewashed walls, heavy wood furniture, dark-wood window frames and doors) is an option for those who are willing to give up convenience— the property is a 10-minute bus ride (No. 12) from the city center—for a setting among the elegant mansions of Avenida Mariscal López. Amenities such as a swimming pool and lush gardens must be weighed against the rather offhand, sometimes uncooperative management. ☎ *Av. Mariscal López 474, ☎ 021/24304. 38 rooms. Pool. AE.*

$ Stella D'Italia. A bit run-down and austere but a good value, this hotel
★ conveniently situated in the heart of the city has a friendly staff and air-conditioning and showers in all the rooms. ☎ *Cerro Corá 933, ☎ 021/448731. 25 rooms. No credit cards.*

The Arts

Chief among Paraguay's outstanding contributions to the arts are its harp music—classical, contemporary classical, and Latin American popular—and folk dancing. Traditional dances include the polka, imported from northern Europe; the *chamamé*, danced with partners holding each other to the accompaniment of lively accordion music; and *la danza de las botellas*, literally "dance of the bottles," a mixture of grace and balance in which the female dancer moves in time to the music while stacking six empty wine bottles on top of her head. Both the harp music and dances can be enjoyed at the shows put on at the **Jardín de la Cerveza** (Mariscal Estigarribia 932, ☎ 021/600752) and **Ygazú** (Choferes del Chaco 1334, ☎ 021/601008). Although both clubs prefer that you dine as you watch the performance, buying a meal is not mandatory, and, given the mixed quality of the food, you might do better eating elsewhere.

The standards of local modern dance and theater groups and orchestras is not high. Visiting international performers usually can be seen at the **Teatro Municipal** (Presidente Franco and Chile, ☎ 021/445169).

Nightlife

Bars and Dance Clubs

Asunción does not have an exciting and varied nightlife. International disco music is featured at **Chaco's Pub** (Republica Argentina 1035, ☎ 021/660821) and **Thunder,** at the Hotel Excelsior (Chile 980, ☎ 021/ 495632). Dress at both is semicasual—tennis shoes, jeans, polo shirts, and T-shirts are not permitted. The bars at the Guaraní and Excelsior hotels are favorite preprandial watering holes.

Casinos

You can try your luck at roulette, baccarat, and blackjack at casinos in the **Hotel Casino Yacht y Golf Club Paraguayo** (Av. del Yacht 11, Lambaré, ☎ 021/36117 or 021/37161) and the **Guaraní Hotel** (Oliva and Independencia Nacional, ☎ 021/491131). The casinos are open to anyone over 21. Minimum stakes are around 20¢ in the Guaraní and 60¢ in the classier Yacht y Golf Club Paraguayo.

Excursion from Asunción: San Bernardino

A day trip to the popular holiday resort of San Bernardino, on the shores of **Lake Ypacaraí,** takes you through **Itaguá,** where ñandutí lacework (*see* Shopping, *above*) is made and a wide variety of handicrafts are sold. The town is also interesting for its large plaza skirted by dwellings with typical Jesuit-style layout.

December–March, this resort town is packed with middle- and upper-class weekenders and families who take up residence for the season. They come for the good restaurants; the clear, dark blue waters ringed in places by thick semitropical undergrowth; and the excellent watersports facilities—boats and Jet Ski and Windsurfer equipment can be rented at one of several clean, white-sand public beaches near the cloverleaf or the Condovac Hotel or the Hotel Casino San Bernardino (*see below*). The town of **Areguá,** also set on the lake, is a quieter alternative to San Bernardino.

Looping back toward Asunción, the road passes through the religious center of **Caacupé,** where every December 8 the Day of Our Lady of the Miracles is celebrated. The basilica there of the same name was consecrated by the Pope in 1988.

Getting There

This circuitous route is best done by car. A travel agency can provide a car and driver for between $35 and $50 per person, depending on the number of passengers. Leave the center of Asunción by Avenida Silvio Pettirossi and, where the road ends, take the left fork along Avenida Eusebio Ayala. This avenue becomes Route 1. Pass through San Lorenzo and follow the signs to Route 2, which should be followed to Ipacaraí, 35 kilometers (22 miles) from Asunción, where a turnoff to the left skirts the lake to San Bernardino.

Dining and Lodging

For price-category definitions, *see* Dining *and* Lodging *in* Paraguay Essentials, *below.*

$$ Hotel Casino San Bernardino. Great views and lush landscaping distinguish this large, comfortable lakefront hotel. Diners enjoy a spectacular view of the lake from the spacious, rather starkly decorated restaurant. Recommended are the *lomito bonne femme* (medallion of beef in a wine sauce) and surubí *a la Fiorentina* (in a white sauce served with *acelga,* Swiss-chard-like beet leaves). ☎ *Ruta General Morínigo, km 47,* ☎ *0512/2391. 100 rooms. Restaurant, bar, pool, sauna, 2 tennis courts, casino, dance club. AE, MC, V. Closed weekdays Apr.–Nov. except on holidays.*

$ Hotel del Lago. This low-key, Spanish-style hotel is on the lake; the charming, small restaurant is decorated with rustic colonial-style furniture and has a fine view of the water. The menu offers a wide range of pastas, but the forte is the roast meats, beef or pork, cooked in a wood-fired oven and served with sopa paraguaya. ☎ *Caballero and Teniente Weiler,* ☎ *0512/2201. 25 rooms. Restaurant, pool. DC, MC, V.*

SOUTHERN PARAGUAY AND THE JESUIT RUINS

The 405-kilometer (253-mile) drive from Asunción to Jesús takes in seven 17th-century Jesuit missions and affords the visitor glimpses of Paraguayan rural life amidst a variety of landscapes. The missions date from 1609, when the newly formed Society of Jesus was granted permission to organize the nomadic Guaraní Indians, threatened by slave traders from Brazil, into stable, self-sufficient communities based on agriculture and Christianity. Each mission, called a *reducción* (literally, "reduction") had a population of about 3,000 Guaraní under the charge of two or three priests who taught agricultural and other practical skills such as stone-masonry and metalwork. The reduction was based around a large, central plaza with a church, an adjacent bell tower, the priests' living quarters, and usually a school. The Guaraní's houses were built in rows spreading back from the central square. The main buildings were most often constructed of red sandstone blocks, with terra-cotta-tile, semi-circular cantilever roofs that formed wide verandas.

The Guaraní not only embraced Christianity but also proved to be sensitive artists and particularly fine musicians, performing mainly in church choirs and orchestras and able to adapt the complex European Baroque counterpoint to their own traditional musical styles. The Guaraní also excelled at wood carving and showed skill in pottery and calligraphy. The experiment, however, was so successful that the Spanish monarchs became jealous of the Jesuit's power and banned them from the South American continent in 1766. The 100,000 Guaraní soon returned to their old way of life and the missions fell into disrepair.

Visitor Information

Tourist information about southern Paraguay is available from the **Secretaría Regional de Turismo** (Monseñor Wiessen and Mariscal Estigarribia, Encarnación, ☎ 071/5326). The office is open weekdays 8–noon.

Arriving and Departing

By Car

Take Route 1 to Encarnación, a 370-kilometer (230-mile) drive from Asunción. From Encarnación Route 6 goes northeast to Ciudad del Este, 280 kilometers (175 miles) away, on the border with Brazil and Argentina near Iguazú Falls. All of the missions are on or just off Route 1 or Route 6. A bridge links Encarnación with the Argentine town of Posadas.

By Bus

There is frequent bus service between Asunción and Encarnación (Lomas Valentinas 1031). The five-hour trip costs $7.35. Bus companies operating this route are **Rapido Iguazú** (☎ 021/551601) and **La Encarnaceña** (☎ 071/3448). The latter runs local bus service to the ruins at Trinidad and Jesús. Travelers can get off the buses along Route 1 to visit the Jesuit missions and then flag down the next bus, which will stop as long as it is not filled. Both companies also have service between Encarnación and Ciudad del Este. The one-way fare for the three-hour trip is $7.35.

Exploring Southern Paraguay and the Jesuit Ruins

Although some Asunción tour operators offer a one-day marathon of the region, visitors starting from Asunción should allow nearly two days for the round-trip, staying overnight in either Villa Florida or Encar-

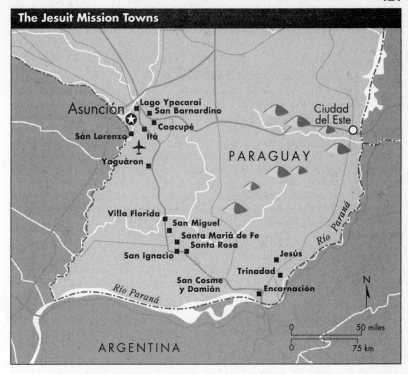

The Jesuit Mission Towns

nación. Travelers who have more time can continue on to Ciudad del Este and Iguazú Falls (*see* Chapter 3, Argentina), returning to Asunción via Route 2, a 327-kilometer (204-mile) journey. Restaurants and cafés in southern Paraguay are few and far between, but bottled drinks can be bought at the many *despensas,* small roadside general stores, found alongside the highway.

Heading South from Asunción

Leave Asunción from the southeastern part of the city on Route 1, going through San Lorenzo. The road then splits, one branch going east to Ciudad del Este (Route 2) and the falls, the other southeast to Encarnación. Continue on Route 1 heading southeast. As you approach the town of **Itá** there is a state-run handicraft exhibition on the right side of the road with local ceramics and hammocks for sale. After Itá the countryside opens up into fruit orchards, sugarcane fields, and maize plantations bordering the road. **Yaguarón,** 11 kilometers (7 miles) farther on, was the center of the Franciscan missions and has a fine church built between 1640 and 1720 and subsequently restored. The interior is notable for its brightly colored wood sculptures by Guaraní artists.

Villa Florida

Over the next 130 kilometers (80 miles) along Route 1 to Villa Florida, the geography changes as the fertile, hilly land becomes rolling grasslands dotted with white Brahma-like Nelore cattle. Cowboys wearing wide-brim hats sit astride sheepskin saddles and tend the herds, while sheep and goats graze outside tiny cottages with exuberant hibiscus- and bougainvillea-filled gardens. Villa Florida itself is a popular tourist spot on the **Tebicuary River,** once the western border of the Jesuit mission area and now an attraction for its many fine sandy beaches. Anglers know it as a prime spot for catching dorado and surubí (*see* Sports and the Outdoors, *below*). The town is not particularly pretty, but there are magnificent sunsets over the water and a complement of hotels and restaurants (*see* Dining and Lodging, *below*).

San Miguel and San Ignacio

Continuing on Route 1, you will pass through San Miguel, where handwoven woolen blankets, rugs, and ponchos for sale are hung outside the houses. A few miles farther on is the Jesuit town of San Juan Batista. The first mission, however, is found at San Ignacio, where the **Museo de San Ignacio** (no address or ☎; ☛ Free; closed daily noon–3) houses a fine collection of Guaraní wood carvings such as gilded pulpits, door panels, statues, and other period artifacts. A highlight is a statue of St. Paul signaling new lands to be evangelized; at his feet are carved a number of faces, most with Guaraní features. The building itself, with its thick adobe walls, is believed to be the oldest in Paraguay, dating from 1609.

Santa María de Fe

About 12 kilometers (8 miles) farther, take a left onto a dirt road leading to Santa María de Fe, where nearly 7,000 Guaraní lived during the early 18th century. The original church was destroyed by fire. In the museum are displayed some 70 Guaraní carvings and statues; the latter represent the life of Christ. The nativity scene is particularly fine. (To gain admission to the museum, find the priest or one of his helpers.) Some of the original houses in the compound have been restored.

Santa Rosa

Back on Route 1, the main attraction in Santa Rosa is the red sandstone bell tower, built in 1698 and still in use. Inside you can see frescoes, part of the old altar, and a group of carvings representing the Annunciation, considered to be among the finest of their kind.

San Cosme y Damián

The vegetation becomes denser as the road nears the Paraná Valley; just before Coronel Bogado, a 25-kilometer (15-mile) paved highway runs to the village of San Cosme y Damián, near the banks of the Paraná River. Follow the signs along a dirt track to the red sandstone mission buildings, still functioning as a school. The church was recently restored and many of the original Guaraní houses are still in use.

Encarnación and Trinidad

The main road continues to the border city of Encarnación, about an hour's drive away, which is of little interest to the visitor except as a place to eat and spend the night. Linked by bridge to the Argentine town of Posadas, its muddy streets are lined with shops selling cheap imported goods. Outside of the city, the **Tirol de Paraguay** (*see* Dining and Lodging, *below*) attracts guests for its spa waters.

The hotel is just 8 kilometers (5 miles) from Trinidad, reached by taking a well-marked turnoff from Route 6. Here are the biggest and most impressive Jesuit ruins, most of which have been, or are in the process of being, restored. The reduction stands on a slight rise in an open field, enabling its size to be appreciated. Built between 1712 and 1764 of red sandstone, much of it was destroyed by the official put in charge after the expulsion of the Jesuits. (He ripped out stones to build his own residence, causing the structure to collapse.) Although the church is open to the elements, many of its walls and arches are intact. Note the elaborately carved doors and wall friezes depicting angels playing the clavichord, harp, and other musical instruments. The pulpit is made from thousands of pieces of stone and depicts the Evangelists.

The only building with a roof is the sacristy, with intricate relief work above the main entrance. Also surviving are the school and cloister foundations as well as a sandstone tower.

Jesús

The Jesuits were expelled from South America before they could finish the church they were building on a hilltop at Jesús, 10 kilometers (6 miles) from Trinidad, which is reached by taking a turnoff from Route 6. The architecture is distinguished from that of the other missions by its Moorish-style arches.

Sports and the Outdoors

Fishing

Paraguayans claim to have some of the best fishing in the world. Anglers come chiefly to catch dorado, spectacular fighters that leap high into the air when hooked, and surubí, giant fast-water catfish that take off like an express train if caught. Dorado generally run between 4 and 12 kilos (9 and 27 lbs), although they have been known to weigh up to 18 kilos (40 lbs). Surubí that weigh as much as 20 kilos (44 lbs) are not uncommon, while monsters of more than 40 kilos (90 lbs) are occasionally caught.

The two best spots for anglers to test their skills against these fish are **Ayolas,** on the Paraná River, about 350 kilometers (220 miles) from Asunción, and **Villa Florida,** on the Tebicuary River. In Ayolas, the **Hotel Nacional de Turismo** (Av. Costanera, ☎ 072/2272 or 072/2273) can arrange for boat charters, guides, and bait. Anglers should take their own medium-weight rod, line, and lures suitable for trolling, spinning, and live baiting.

Similar arrangements can be made in Villa Florida, which is 160 kilometers (100 miles) from the capital, through the **Hotel Nacional de Turismo** (Rte. 1, km 161, ☎ 083/207) or **Hotel Centu Cué** (Rte. 1, km 163; Desví, km 7, ☎ 083/219). Seven kilometers (4 miles) from the highway, Centu Cué is smack-dab on top of one of the river's best fishing spots.

Dining and Lodging

Restaurants and hotels are few and far between in southern Paraguay, as many of the villages are just a few hundred yards long and consist of little more than a handful of houses, a couple of general stores, a bakery, and, sometimes, a gas station. For price-category definitions, *see* Dining *and* Lodging *in* Paraguay Essentials, *below.*

Encarnación

$$ **Cristal.** Situated downtown and four blocks from the bus terminal, this nine-story hotel built in 1988 has guest rooms furnished with modern wood furniture, green carpets and drapes, and abstract paintings. The restaurant, which has a busy lunchtime trade from local businesspeople, offers international cuisine and local fish specialties. 🕾 *Mariscal Estigarribia 1157,* ☎ *071/2371 or 071/2372. 75 rooms. Restaurant, pool. No credit cards.*

$$ **Novotel.** Located 3 kilometers (2 miles) from the town center, the hotel is set back from the main highway amid spacious gardens that include sports facilities. The decor throughout is modern, with beige and white the predominant shades. The restaurant's menu is divided between international cuisine and Paraguayan dishes such as local fish, milanesas, sopa paraguaya, and cassava. 🕾 *Rte. 1, km 361, Villa Quiteria,* ☎ *071/4131,* ⨳ *071/4224. 102 bedrooms, 4 suites. Restaurant, bar, pool, tennis court, soccer, volleyball. AE, DC, MC, V.*

$$ Tirol de Paraguay. With spectacular views of verdant, rolling coun-
tryside, the Tirol is built on a hillside 18 kilometers (11 miles) from
Encarnación, on Route 6 running to Trinidad and Ciudad del Este.
The guest rooms, which have either ceiling fans or air-conditioning,
are in single-story bungalows set around four swimming pools that
are fed by natural springs said to have therapeutic qualities. Rates in-
clude all meals. ▣ *Rte. 6, Capitán Miranda,* ☎ *071/2388,* ℻ *071/5555.*
56 rooms. 4 pools. V.

Villa Florida

$$ Centu Cué. A group of bungalows scattered along the banks of the
Tebicuary River comprise this isolated lodge frequented mainly by an-
glers and wildlife observers. Seven kilometers (4 miles) from the junction with Route 1, it is an ideal spot from which to fish or explore one
of South America's most beautiful rivers—or you could just lounge on
the private beach. At the simply furnished riverside restaurant, festooned
with mounted heads of enormous fish and photos of fishermen with
their catches, what else would one eat but dorado or surubí, grilled or
in a casserole, caught only a few yards from the table? ▣ *Rte. 1, km
163, Desvío, 7 km,* ☎ *083/219. 24 rooms. Restaurant, pool, horseback riding. No credit cards.*

$$ Hotel Nacional de Turismo. In this one-story building built around a cen-
tral courtyard, the rooms, sparsely decorated in Spanish colonial style
with heavy wood furniture, all open onto a shady veranda. The high-
ceilinged restaurant, which maintains the hotel's colonial style, offers a
wide variety of grilled meats and poultry, but a must is the milanesa made
with freshly caught surubí; the chef is highly obliging, and with reason-
able notice, will prepare special orders. ▣ *Rte. 1, km 161,* ☎ *083/207.
20 rooms, 1 suite. Restaurant, cafeteria, pool. AE, DC, MC, V.*

PARAGUAY ESSENTIALS

Customs and Duties

Visitors may bring into the country any items considered to be for per-
sonal use plus one liter of spirits or two bottles of wine, and 400
cigarettes. Pets must have a valid health certificate. If arriving from a
non-bordering country the certificate should be validated at a Paraguayan
consulate in the country of issue. Sums of more than $10,000 or its
equivalent per person may not be taken in to or out of Paraguay.

Dining

Asunción has plenty of excellent restaurants, bars, and cafés, but out-
side the capital and other major cities the choices drop dramatically.
Visitors traveling along the highways will find a few good roadside restau-
rants serving grilled meat, fish, and fast food. Paraguayan portions tend
to be generous; don't hesitate to ask to share a dish.

Specialties

The *parrillada,* or mixed grill—barbecued meats, assorted sausages in-
cluding blood sausages, and organ meats—served in large portions at
restaurants called *parrillas* (grills), is a staple of Paraguayan dining. Beef
is the mainstay, but pork, chicken, and fish are also common. The usual
accompaniments are salad (Paraguay's tomatoes are said to be the best
in the region) and boiled manioc, a white, fibrous root with a bland
taste. Hearts of palm are considered a delicacy and served with salad
at most good restaurants. *Sopa paraguaya,* a kind of cornbread made
with cornmeal, *queso fresco* (a type of cheese), eggs, and onions, or

chipá-guazú, similar but substituting roughly ground corn for corn-meal, may also accompany meat dishes. *Chipá,* a type of bread made from corn flour, ground manioc, and sometimes cheese, is sold in bakeries, on the street, and alongside roads, and is best eaten hot. *Puchero* is a meat, sausage, vegetable, and chick-pea stew, eaten in the cooler months. *Bori-bori* is a hearty soup with bits of meat, vegetables, and balls molded from cheese and corn.

Cafés and bars usually sell a limited menu of quickly prepared, mostly fried or grilled foods. Popular is milanesa, thin slices of beef, chicken breast, pork, or fish that are batter fried. Other favorite snacks are the empanada, an envelope of pastry filled with beef, pork, chicken, corn, or cheese; *croquetas,* minced meat or poultry fashioned into a sausage shape, rolled in bread crumbs, then deep fried; and the *mixto,* a sandwich of ham and cheese. Many cafés have a dish of the day—*plato del día*—on the menu. Pasta dishes are also common.

Paraguay's rivers abound with edible fish, the favorites being surubí, a giant fast-water catfish, and dorado, a ferocious, salmonlike predator. These are prepared in a variety of ways, but to appreciate the full flavor, try milanesa de surubí (battered and deep-fried fillets) and plain grilled dorado. The soup made from the fish's head and other leftovers is delicious.

Typical desserts include *dulce de leche,* a mixture of milk and sugar heated until it turns into a thick, light brown sauce; papaya preserved in syrup; and fresh fruit such as pineapple, banana, mango, and melon.

Few Paraguayans are seen without their *guampa,* a drinking vessel made of cow's horn, metal, or wood, from which they sip tereré, a cold infusion made from *yerba maté* tea. Maté is drunk hot throughout South America, but the cold version, often mixed with medicinal herbs, is more common in Paraguay. Paraguayan beers, which are pilsner in style, are good; the Baviera brand is especially recommended. Beer on tap is known as *chopp* (pronounced "shop"). The local wine is not recommended. Taking tea is a tradition among society women, who can be seen at the tables of the top hotels in Asunción. Baby showers and women's wedding-eve parties often take the form of teas. Espresso or, in cheaper bars and restaurants, filter coffee is served demitasse except at breakfast.

Mealtimes
Paraguayans start the day early, and mealtimes are correspondingly earlier than in many other parts of Latin America. Lunch can begin at 11:30, but 12:30 is more typical. Some restaurants stop serving lunch as early as 2. Dinner is often available at 7 PM, with restaurants staying open until 11; more sophisticated dining spots open at 8 PM and serve until shortly after midnight. On weekends and special occasions dinner hours are extended until much later. Café hours are generally 7 AM–10 PM.

Dress
Although jackets and ties are worn to business lunches, the general rule is smart casual attire in most restaurants. Some of the most deluxe establishments turn away people wearing jeans or running shoes.

Ratings
The 10% value-added tax (IVA) is included in the menu price. Make sure that you are not charged the tax when you are dining at a restaurant in your hotel and charge the meal to your room bill. Service charges are not added to the bill; leave a tip of 5%–10%, depending on the quality of the restaurant or bar and the level of service.

Prices below are per person and are for a three-course meal with coffee and 10% IVA, but not including alcoholic beverages or tip.

CATEGORY	COST
$$$$	over $30
$$$	$15–$30
$$	$10–$15
$	under $10

Embassies and Consulates

United States
Embassy: Av. Mariscal López 1776, Asunción, ☎ 021/213717; ⊘ 8–11:30 AM.

Canada
Consulate: Benjamin Constant and Colón, Asunción, ☎ 021/449505; ⊘ 8–11:30 AM.

United Kingdom
Embassy: Presidente Franco 706, Piso 4, Asunción, ☎ 021/444472; ⊘ 8 AM–1 PM.

Getting Around

However you get around, remember that in Paraguay the same street can be called a different name at different points along its course, frequently causing the street numbers to run out of sequence. Therefore, addresses often are given as the intersection of two streets, for example, "Ayolas y Brasil" or "Ayolas con Brasil" (*y* means "and" and *con* means "with"). In this guide, addresses of this sort are listed as "Ayolas and Brasil." The word *calle* (street) is almost never used before the name of a street.

By Plane
American Airlines, Aerolíneas Paraguayas (ARPA), Aerolíneas Agrentinas, Varig, Pluna, Ladeco, Iberia, and Lloyd Aéreo Boliviano (LAB) have flights to Asunción. **LATN** (Líneas Aéreas de Transporte Nacional, Brasil and Mariscal Estigarribia, ☎ 021/212277) and **TAM** (Transportes Aéreas Militares, Oliva 467, ☎ 021/447315), an airline run by the Paraguayan armed forces that civilians can use, provide almost daily service between Asunción and the major cities in the interior. Fares are reasonable. The one-hour flight to Ciudad del Este from Asunción costs $36, while the nearly two-hour flight to Pedro Juan Caballero, on the northeastern border with Brazil, costs $49. Visitors planning to go to the northeast jungle, including the Cerro Corá National Park, should consider going by plane, as the overland journey is arduous. Two air taxis operate out of Asunción: **Paraguayo SRL** (Próceres de Mayo 783, ☎ 021/206300) and **C Ruben Viveros** (Manuel Dominguez 2795, ☎ 021/23297).

By Car
Road maps can be obtained from the **Instituto Geográfico Militar** (Artigas and Perú, Asunción).

ROAD CONDITIONS
Paraguay has few paved roads and only a few, either in or on the approaches to the main cities, have more than one lane in each direction. Two main roads leave Asunción to the east, one cutting south to Encarnación and the other heading to Ciudad del Este and Iguazú Falls. To the northwest is the Trans-Chaco Highway, which when completed will link Paraguay with Bolivia. At press time (winter 1995) the road

was paved as far as Mariscal Estigarribia, some 600 kilometers (372 miles) from Asunción. The main highways and some bridges have tolls, approximately $1 per car.

The dirt roads that crisscross most of the country can be uncomfortable, dangerously riddled with potholes, ruts, and puddles, and liable to be closed because of flooding. Beware of wild animals, cattle, and horses that wander onto the highways, particularly at night. On weekends and around public holidays, access roads in and out of the capital can be blocked as the city's residents spend their leisure time in the countryside.

RULES OF THE ROAD

Visitors' home driver's licenses are accepted by the local authorities. The speed limit throughout the country outside the cities is 80 kph (50 mph), although this is widely disregarded in isolated areas. The speed limit in urban areas is 40 kph (25 mph). Paraguayans drive on the right, and seat belts are not obligatory. Care should be taken at intersections in Asunción, as drivers rarely offer to give way.

RENTALS

You can rent cars in Asunción. Contact **Budget** (Av. Mariscal López 2801, ☎ 021/661200), **Hertz** (airport: ☎ 021/206196 or 021/206199; downtown: Av. Eusebio Ayala, km 4.5, ☎ 021/605708 or 021/503921), **National** (Yegros 501, ☎ 021/491848, 021/492157, or 021/491379), or **Touring Cars** (airport: ☎ 021/206195, ext. 24; downtown: Iturbe 682, ☎ 021/447945).

GASOLINE

Distances between gas stations can be long, so drivers should top off their tanks regularly. Stations are normally open until midnight. Two grades of gasoline, sold by the liter, are available: normal and super. Fuel costs about $1 a gallon.

By Bus

Paraguay has an extensive privately owned bus network, which serves as the basic form of transport for most of the population. Buses are inexpensive, fast, and reliable. Long-distance buses, some air-conditioned and with reclining seats (and some showing videos!), race between the major centers, while bone-shaking local buses, known as *colectivos,* rattle between villages and along city streets. The 370-kilometer (230-mile) journey from Asunción to Encarnación takes about five hours by bus and costs $8; the 330-kilometer (205-mile) trip from Asunción to Ciudad del Este also takes five hours and costs $7.35. For the names and telephone numbers of the companies serving each route, call Asunción's main bus terminal (☎ 021/551732).

By Boat

Passenger boats run up the Paraguay River to northern ports. The scenery along the river is interesting for its bird life and the possibility of sighting monkeys, *carpinchos,* tapirs, and alligators. Some of the ships go as far as the Brazilian state of Mato Grosso where you'll find the Pantanal wetlands, one of the world's greatest nature reserves, teeming with bird life, alligators, jaguars, and piranhas. Air-conditioned cabins with full board are available at a reasonable price. For schedules and reservations contact the travel agency **Chacotur** (Montevideo 1447, ☎ 021/440448). **Flota Mercantil del Estado** (☎ 021/490086), the state-owned shipping fleet, has a boat leaving every Tuesday for Concepción. The boat also makes a weekly three-day trip to Corumbá in Brazil. Tickets are available at the line's booking office at Estrella 672 in Asunción.

Language

In the more expensive hotels the reception staff speaks English. Few restaurant staffers speak English, although many menus are in several languages. Outside the main cities it is unusual to find anyone who speaks anything but Spanish or the native Guaraní language. There are some immigrant communities where German is spoken; some Mennonites speak Platdeutsche, a German dialect.

Lodging

Aside from the first-class hotels in Asunción, Encarnación, and Ciudad del Este, the visitor to Paraguay must be content with basic, although generally clean, accommodations—and even in the best places service can be sloppy. Whenever possible, try to plan overnight stays where there are recommended hotels, as many towns offer only primitive lodgings, most frequently with shared bathrooms. With the exception of San Bernardino and other resorts around Lake Ypacaraí, where many Asunceños spend the summer and weekends, rates do not vary according to season. Room rates usually include breakfast, which most often consists of a buffet of juice, fresh fruit, breads and croissants, ham, and cheese. You will generally be charged extra for eggs. In some budget hotels, showers are heated by electric heaters incorporated into the shower head. On no account should the apparatus be touched if it is not working; the wiring could be live and highly dangerous, especially if the floor is wet.

Hotels
For a list of all hotels operating in Paraguay, including rates, contact the **Dirección Nacional de Turismo** (Palma 468, ☎ 021/441530), the government tourist department.

Camping
There are a number of campsites along the highways running from Asunción to Ciudad del Este and Encarnación, around the shores of Lake Ypacaraí, and in national parks. Facilities range from bathrooms to swimming pools and electrical hookups. For locations of campsites contact the Dirección Nacional de Turismo (*see above*). In Asunción, camping is permitted in the Botanical Gardens. In isolated areas campers should take precautions against poisonous snakes: zipping up flaps when the tent is left unattended, checking out the tent before entering, and shaking out sleeping bags, blankets, and other bedding. Never put on clothes or shoes without first inspecting them.

Ratings
Prices below are for two people in a double room with breakfast and excluding 10% IVA.

CATEGORY	COST
$$$$	over $125
$$$	$75–$125
$$	$40–$75
$	under $40

Mail

Postal Rates
Airmail letters and postcards to North America and Europe cost about 25¢ and take about a week to arrive. Hotels generally sell stamps. Documents and anything else of value (or valuable-looking) should be sent by courier service provided by **DHL International** (Haedo 105, Asun-

ción, ☏ 021/496683) or **World Courier** (Haedo 179, 14th Floor, Asunción, ☏ 021/448683).

Receiving Mail

Travelers who want to receive mail but don't know where they will be staying can have it sent to Dirección Nacional de Correo, Poste Restante, Alberdi 130, Asunción, where it will be held for collection on production of identity. **American Express** (Yegros 690, Asunción, ☏ 021/490111) will hold members' mail for free at their office in the Inter-Express building. There are no postal codes in Paraguay.

Money and Expenses

Currency

The unit of currency in Paraguay is the guaraní (G). There are bills of 500, 1,000, 5,000, 10,000, and 50,000 guaraníes, with coins in units of 10, 50, and 100 guaraníes. At press time (winter 1995) the exchange rate was around 1,900 guaraníes to the U.S. dollar and 3,000 guaraníes to the pound sterling. The value of the guaraní against the U.S. dollar falls at a rate that roughly offsets inflation, meaning that prices remain constant in dollar terms.

Changing Money

It is most convenient to change money either at the *casas de cambio* (exchange houses) or at major hotels, which offer a slightly lower rate than casas de cambio. Banks have longer procedures, probably more forms to fill out, and more lines in which to wait. Their tourist exchange rates are normally less competitive than the casas de cambio. (The bank at the Asunción airport, however, changes money at competitive rates.) There are several casas de cambio along Calle Palma and around the main square in Asunción that accept both cash and traveler's checks; no commission is charged. Visitors should shop around for the most competitive rates. U.S. dollars are easiest to change. Rates for other currencies might not reflect their true international value. Money changers also operate in the streets, but because their rates are generally no better than in the casas de cambio, it is probably not worth the risk of counting and showing money in public.

As it is virtually impossible to change guaraníes outside the country, visitors should exchange them before leaving Paraguay. The constant devaluation of the currency means it is not worth saving for a future visit.

Forms of Payment

Most hotels and restaurants in the main cities accept credit cards. American Express, MasterCard, and Visa are the most widely accepted, although the majority of more expensive establishments also take Diners Club. Some department stores accept the major cards, but smaller shops generally expect payment in cash. Small stores selling electronics and other imported items sometimes impose a surcharge on credit card sales, or will limit the degree to which you can bargain. These stores also accept payment in U.S. dollars. Outside major cities businesses rarely accept payment by credit card or in U.S. dollars, so be prepared to pay for everything in guaraníes.

What It Will Cost

Unlike neighboring Brazil and Argentina, Paraguay has not experienced hyperinflation. Although prices rise faster than in Europe and the United States, the constant devaluation of the guaraní means that the costs for foreign visitors remain relatively constant—and quite reasonable. Prices run as low as $15 for a non-air-conditioned double room in a budget hotel and up to $200 or more in a luxury establishment. In between there are numerous options, but high-quality accommodations in a well-situated hotel with private bathroom and air-conditioning can easily be found in the $60–$120 per night range for two people, including breakfast. Gourmet meals with imported wines can be enjoyed at very reasonable prices—$40 per person, including tip—while a three-course meal without alcoholic beverages in a good restaurant runs around $12 a head. Long-distance buses and internal flights are inexpensive, and cab fares are much cheaper than in the United States or Europe. Gasoline is around $1 a gallon. Most museums are free, but contributions are welcome, especially in churches. The budget-conscious traveler touring South America might consider taking care of shoe and luggage repairs, laundry, and dry cleaning while in Paraguay, where such services cost only a fraction of what they do in, for example, Argentina.

TAXES

A 10% value-added tax, known as IVA, was introduced in 1992, and is charged on all goods and services. Although it is incorporated into most prices, including restaurant and bar bills, it is added to hotel bills. Guests checking out of hotels should ensure that the tax has been charged only on accommodation and services such as laundry; it should not be added to restaurant and bar bills charged to the room.

SAMPLE PRICES

In Asunción, a cup of espresso coffee costs around 60¢; a pint of beer in a bar, $1.20; hamburger and french fries, $2; ham and cheese sandwich, $1.20; ice-cream cone, 35¢; local bus ride, 15¢; and 1-mile taxi ride, 80¢.

Opening and Closing Times

Siestas, generally between noon and 3:30, are taken to beat the heat. Everything except restaurants, cafés, and some supermarkets and department stores closes during this period.

Banks

Banks are open weekdays 9:30–12:30. The bank at the Asunción airport is open daily 9–6. Casas de cambio are open weekdays 8–12:30 and 3:30–7.

Museums

Opening times vary, but most are open weekdays 8–noon and 4–6 and Saturday morning.

Offices

Public offices operate weekdays 7 AM–1 PM (post offices are open 7–noon and 2:30–7:30), while private businesses start between 7:30 and 8, work until midday, and reopen from 3 to 6.

Shops

Most stores open weekdays at around 7:30 AM, close for the siesta between 12:30 and 3:30, and then reopen until around 8. Butcher shops, grocery stores, bakeries, and other food shops open between 7 and 8, closing at noon and reopening from around 3 until between 7 and 8 PM. Department stores are open weekdays 8–7:30.

National Holidays

New Year's Day (Jan. 1); Day of San Blas, Patron Saint of Paraguay (Feb. 3); Heroes Day (Mar. 1); Maundy Thursday (1996: Apr. 4; 1997: Mar. 27); Good Friday (1996: Apr. 5; 1997: Mar. 28); Easter (1996: Apr. 7; 1997: Mar. 30); Labor Day (May 1); Independence Day (May 15);

Armistice of Chaco War (June 12); Founding of Asunción (Aug. 15); Day of the Immaculate Conception (Dec. 8); Christmas (Dec. 25).

Precautions

Health

Although tap water is safe to drink in Asunción, it's advisable to drink bottled water everywhere. *Agua con gas* and *agua sin gas* are the respective terms for water with and without carbonation.

Shopping

International visitors cannot get refunds on the IVA. Prices in department stores, general stores, and supermarkets are fixed, but in handicrafts stores and stalls and stores selling electronic goods, watches, and other luxury goods, substantial reductions can be won by hard bargaining. Always shop around. Try offering street vendors approximately half the asking price and others around two-thirds. You know that your final offer is too low if the seller lets you walk away.

Telephones

Phone service, run by ANTEL, is improving rapidly, with direct dialing to most main cities in and outside Paraguay. The peak period is weekdays 8–5 except national holidays. Hotels normally add a surcharge to telephone calls made from guest rooms.

Local Calls

Pay phones are few and far between, taking tokens called *fichas* (approximately 10¢), which can be purchased at tobacco kiosks, bars, and post offices. The cost of a three-minute local call is 9¢. For operator assistance for local calls, dial 010; for information dial 12.

Long-Distance and International Calls

Long-distance and international calls cannot be made from public phones other than those in ANTEL telephone offices or in some roadside service stations that have operators in attendance. International calls can be made directly by dialing 002 followed by the country code and local number; calls to the United States cost $2.85 per minute during peak hours, $2.53 off-peak. Lines can become congested at peak hours. For international operator assistance dial 0010. To reach an **AT&T** operator, dial 008–1–800. To reach **MCI,** dial 008–11–800. To reach **Sprint,** dial 008–12–800; this may connect you to a Spanish-speaking operator, who will be able to transfer you to an English-speaking colleague.

Tipping

Service charges are not added to restaurant bills; an appropriate tip is 5%–10% of the bill, more if the service is exceptionally good. The same rule applies to the smarter bars, but in cheaper, less fashionable places, round up the bill to the nearest thousand guaraníes. Taxi fares are rounded up to the nearest 500 G. Hotel and airport porters should receive around 50¢ per bag; a doorman should get the same for hailing a taxi. Leave the chambermaid $1.50 per day and $5–$10 after a week's stay. Shoe-shine boys are paid 30¢–50¢, but they will try to charge you extra. Gas-station attendants are tipped up to 30¢ for filling the tank, cleaning the windshield, and checking tires and oil. Cinema and theater ushers are given about 10¢. Checkroom and rest-room attendants should be given 10¢–30¢. Give hairdressers and barbers around 10% of the bill.

When to Go

Although Paraguay has no high or low tourist seasons, visitors should make advance reservations for accommodations in Asunción, where space in high-quality hotels is limited. Since the opening up of both the country and the economy in 1989, the stream of businesspeople looking for opportunities in Paraguay has increased dramatically. This, coupled with frequent conferences and congresses linked to the country's move from isolation to integration, means that rooms in all price categories can be scarce.

Climate

Rain falls throughout the year in Asunción and the southeast, frequently in the form of torrential cloudbursts that can turn streets into torrents of muddy red water, bringing traffic to a standstill. The wettest months are December through April, the driest June, July, and August. Temperatures are high most of the year, and visitors should make sure that guest rooms have air-conditioning or fans. In the summer months (Nov.–Mar.), the heat is usually so intense that it is advisable not to plan activities between midday and 4 PM. Remember, the siesta is a national institution in Paraguay!

The following are the average daily maximum and minimum temperatures for Asunción.

Jan.	93F	34C	May	77F	25C	Sept.	80F	27C
	72	22		55	14		60	16
Feb.	93F	34C	June	72F	22C	Oct.	84F	29C
	72	22		55	13		62	17
Mar.	91F	33C	July	75F	24C	Nov.	88F	31C
	70	21		57	14		66	19
Apr.	82F	28C	Aug.	77F	25C	Dec.	91F	33C
	64	18		57	14		70	21

10 Peru

Nowhere else in South America is there such a wealth of history—famed Machu Picchu, the lost city of the Incas, is only the greatest of innumerable pre-Columbian sites, and Peru's capital, Lima, once enjoyed power and prestige such as no other city in the colonial Americas.

By Corinne
Schmidt-Lynch
and Nicolás
Lynch

Updated by
Peter Hudson

THE **"LAND OF THE INCAS,"** Peru is a nation of extraordinary beauty and myriad attractions, both geographic and archaeological. Although the majestic Andes mountain chain is perhaps the best known of these, Peru's sights are scattered among markedly different regions, each with its own character.

Although Peru is considered an Andean nation, it is in fact 57% jungle. Its vast and still largely pristine Amazon Basin rain forests end only 250 kilometers (155 miles) from the coast. From there, the Andes pierce the heavens, forming an impenetrable barrier of snowcapped peaks, high plateaus, and intermontane valleys. Beyond them to the west, an utterly barren strip of coastal desert stretches north–south for 2,000 kilometers (1,240 miles), broken by dozens of fertile but narrow river valleys.

The Costa, the arid desert coast, is the setting for the Nazca lines, a mystery etched in the sand centuries before the Inca civilization appeared. North of Lima, ruins of vast ancient cities and adobe pyramids linger like echoes of the sophisticated Moche and Chimú societies that thrived in the desert oases as early as 200 BC. In the Sierra is the monumental city of Cuzco, once the capital of the Tawantinsuyo (the name of the Inca empire in the native tongue, Quechua), later a Spanish colonial city, and today a mestizo (mixed-blood) city where Spanish and Indian heritages jostle for space. Spanish culture maintains a tighter hold in the colonial city of Arequipa, while the nearby Colca Valley, the deepest canyon on earth, is crisscrossed with Inca and pre-Inca agricultural terraces.

In Peru's Amazon Basin, known as the Selva (jungle), lies the tropical rain forest and the gateway city of Iquitos. The region's marvels include the Canopy Walkway in the northeast, which takes the visitor among the treetops of one of the world's last frontiers. Farther south are the jungles of the department of Madre de Dios (aptly named Mother of God): remote, nearly untouched, but accessible to the adventurous. In the highland jungles, which Peruvians call the Ceja de Selva (eyebrow of the jungle), is the famous "lost city of the Incas," Machu Picchu. Its vertiginous setting and stunning architecture make it a centerpiece of humanity's archaeological record and one of the true wonders of the world.

As a nation and a people, Peru has a strong character, not unlike the national drink, *pisco,* a heady grape brandy distilled in the coastal valleys south of Lima. As pronounced as it is, however, the Peruvian personality is heterogeneous, perhaps the product of such markedly different terrains and climates. The people of the Andes, often called Serranos, tend to be introverted, especially in dealings with outsiders, with a sharp sense of identity and a melancholic side best expressed in their haunting music. Quite the opposite are the friendly and more light-hearted inhabitants of the Costa and Selva. The Costeño is quick with a joke but, like his beloved cuisine, *comida criolla* (literally, Creole food), has is a piquant, teasing side to his nature that sometimes stings. Perhaps the most easygoing people in Peru are those of the jungle; their friendliness is matched only by the fabulous richness of their natural surroundings.

Since before recorded history, Peru's inhabitants have shown a fierce determination to tame their environment. The results of their efforts

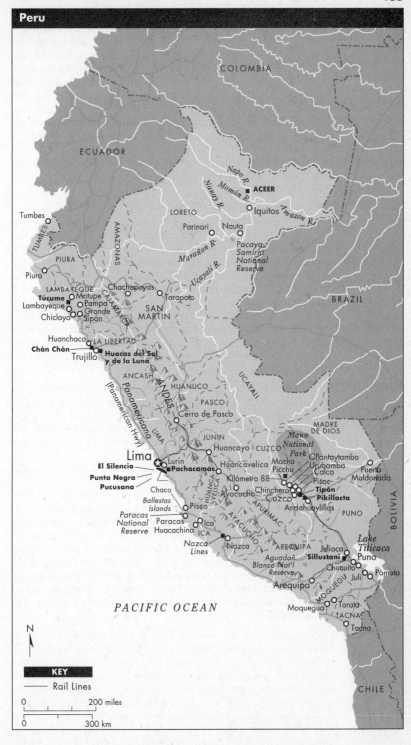

Peru

COLOMBIA

ECUADOR

Tumbes

TUMBES

PIURA

Piura

LAMBAYEQUE
Túcume
Lambayeque
Chiclayo

Motupe
Pampa
Grande
Sipán

CAJAMARCA

Chachapoyas

Tarapoto

SAN
MARTIN

AMAZONAS

LORETO

Parinari

Nauta

Iquitos

ACEER

Napo R.

Nanay R.

Momón R.

Amazon R.

Marañón R.

Ucayali R.

Pacaya-
Samiria
National
Reserve

BRAZIL

Huanchaco
Chán Chán
Trujillo

LA LIBERTAD
**Huacas del Sol
y de la Luna**

ANCASH

ANDES

HUANUCO

PASCO
Cerro de Pasco

UCAYALI

MADRE
DE DIOS

(Panamericana

Panamerican Hwy)

LIMA

JUNIN
Huancayo

Lima
Lurín
Pachacamac

El Silencio
Punta Negra
Pucusana

Chaco

*Ballestas
Islands*

Pisco

Paracas
National
Reserve

Paracas
Huacachina

ICA
Ica

*Nazca
Lines*

Nazca

Huancavelica

HUANCAVELICA

Ayacucho

AYACUCHO

APURIMAC

CUZCO

*Manu
National
Park*

Machu
Picchu
Kilómetro 88
Chinchero
Cuzco

Ollantaytambo
Urubamba
Calca
Pisac
Tipón
Pikillacta
Andahuaylillas

Puerto
Maldonado

PUNO

BOLIVIA

*Aguada
Blanca Nat'l
Reserve*

AREQUIPA

Sillustani

*Lake
Titicaca*

Juliaca
Puno
Chucuito
Juli
Pomata

Arequipa

MOQUEGUA

Moquegua

Torata

TACNA
Tacna

PACIFIC OCEAN

N

KEY
Rail Lines

0   200 miles
0   300 km

CHILE

can be seen in the agricultural terraces that still lace the highlands and in the elaborate irrigation systems that watered the desert a thousand years ago. Today, this nation of 22 million has had to focus that determination on a fight for survival. For the past three generations, millions of *campesinos* (peasants) have left the countryside for the cities, principally on the coast, in the hope of building a better life. Their faces are the new landscape of cities such as Lima, Trujillo, Cuzco, and Arequipa. In an unfamiliar urban environment, the campesinos transform rocky hillsides and sand dunes into neighborhoods; there they build their homes and struggle to make a place for themselves, working in small factories and workshops and as street vendors. Through this struggle, the majority of Peruvians—long without a political, social, and economic voice in society—are recovering their rights and becoming citizens of a new Peru.

Unfortunately, Peru has not enjoyed the vigorous industrialization process that would have rewarded its migrating campesinos with the jobs and comforts associated with modern urban life. The resulting deep economic crisis, poverty, and frustration of expectations is an explosive mix that has erupted into political violence over the past 14 years, most intensely at the end of the 1980s and the beginning of the 1990s. Particularly brutal among the rebel groups is the Shining Path, a Marxist-Leninist-Maoist political party that launched its "people's war" in 1980, practicing violence against anyone who questions their authority; more than 27,000 people have been killed since the group took up arms. Following captures in 1992 and 1994 of the organization's top leadership, the situation has become more tranquil and terrorism has begun to subside.

With the decline of terrorism, the major problem facing the country is its endemic poverty. The economy has stabilized under a free-market model that is apparently accepted by most of the political players, and it enjoyed one of the highest growth rates in the world in 1994, but there are few signs that the benefits have begun to trickle down to those most in need.

LIMA

Lima, Peru's "City of Kings," provokes very different, and often extreme, responses from visitors. With nearly 6.5 million people, more than a quarter of the nation's population, it is a city to love or hate, a microcosm of all of Peru's ills and much of its appeal in a few square miles of seaside desert. Founded in 1535 by Francisco Pizarro on the site of a small native city, Lima was for 300 years the capital of Spain's South American empire. Its vice-regal history lingers on in its sophistication, the decaying beauty of its boulevards, and the liveliness of its intellectual life.

Over the past 30 years, however, Lima has lost its elite character as Peru's rural population, recognizing that the bulk of the country's resources is concentrated in the capital, has migrated here in hopes of finding jobs, homes, and education. Today Lima's streets are packed with immigrants, most of them wretchedly poor. Some are beggars, often refugees from the political violence in the highlands and recognizable by their native dress: a felt hat and broad, petticoated skirt called a *pollera*. Others are reduced to trying to sell something—anything—to anyone who will buy. The press of *ambulantes* (street vendors) vigorously hawking their wares can be overwhelming.

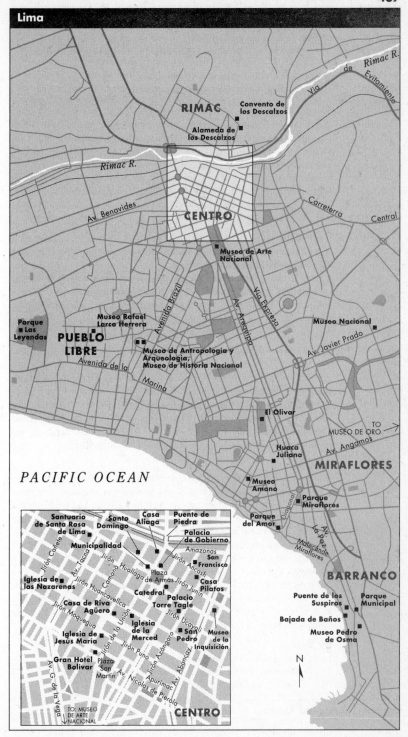

Lima

RIMAC

Convento de los Descalzos

Alameda de los Descalzos

Rimac R.

Rimac R.

Via de Rimac R.

Evitamiente

Av. Benavides

CENTRO

Carreterra

Central

Museo de Arte Nacional

Avenida Brazil

Av. Arequipa

Via Expresa

Museo Rafael Larca Herrera

Museo Nacional

Parque Las Leyendas

PUEBLO LIBRE

Museo de Antropología y Arqueología, Museo de Historia Nacional

Av. Javier Prado

Avenida de la

Marina

El Olivar

TO MUSEO DE ORO →

Huaca Juliana

Av. Angamos

MIRAFLORES

PACIFIC OCEAN

Museo Amano

Av. Diagonal

Parque Miraflores

Parque del Amor

Av. La Paz

Malecende Miraflores

BARRANCO

Puente de los Suspiros

Parque Municipal

Bajada de Baños

Museo Pedro de Osma

Santuario de Santa Rosa de Lima

Santo Domingo

Casa Aliaga

Puente de Piedra

Palacio de Gobierno

Municipalidad

Jirón Cañete

Av. Tacna

Jirón Huancavelica

Comana

Jirón Huallaga

Plaza de Armas

Amazonas

San Francisco

Jirón Ancash

Iglesia de las Nazarenas

Casa de Riva Agüero

Jirón Moquegua

Catedral

Jirón Junín

Casa Pilatos

Jirón de la Unión

Iglesia de la Merced

Palacio Torre Tagle

Jirón Ucayali

San Pedro

Museo de la Inquisición

Iglesia de Jesús María

Gran Hotel Bolívar

Av. G. de la Vega

Plaza San Martín

Jirón Puno

Jirón Azángaro

Av. Abancay

Av. Nicolas de Piérola

Apurímac

N

CENTRO

TO: MUSEO DE ARTE NACIONAL

TO: MUSEO DE ARTE NACIONAL

Visitor Information

Oficina de Información Turística (Jirón de Unión 1066, ☎ 01/432–3559; ⊙ Weekdays 8–7). **Miraflores Municipal Tourist Office** (San Martín 537, Miraflores, ☎ 01/447–9539 or 01/444–3915; ⊙ Weekdays 8:30–5). **American-Peruvian Chamber of Commerce** (Ricardo Palma 836, Miraflores, ☎ 01/447–9349, FAX 01/447–9352).

The daily newspaper *El Comercio* carries the most complete listing of activities in Lima. An English-language monthly, the *Lima Times*, is available at kiosks and at the publication's office (Pasaje Los Pinos 156, Office B–6, Miraflores, ☎ 01/445–3761 or 01/446–9120, FAX 01/446–7888; ⊙ Weekdays 9–5), which also sells a selection of English-language books on Peru. *The Peru Guide*, an advertising monthly with tourist information, is available free at most major hotels.

Arriving and Departing

By Plane

Such international carriers as **AeroPerú, American,** and **Faucett** serve **Jorge Chavez International Airport** (☎ 01/452–3135). Peruvian domestic airlines include **Aero Continente, Americana, Expresso Aereo, Imperial Air,** and regional airlines like **Aerocondor** and **Aerotransporte S.A.** AeroPerú and Faucett also provide domestic service.

The airport is 10 kilometers (6 miles) and a 30-minute ride from downtown Lima or the residential and hotel district of Miraflores. Cab fare to either area should be approximately $15, although hard bargaining can bring it down to $10. Sharing a taxi is common and will lower the fare. There are no meters, so make sure you fix the price before you get in. **Transhotel** (Ricardo Palma 280, ☎ 01/446–9872) operates a shuttle to and from the airport, charging $10 for the first passenger and $2 for each additional passenger. The shuttle's hours of operation vary, and it is most dependable as a means of transportation from town to the airport, especially to catch an early morning flight.

By Car

Lima is on the transcontinental Carreterra Panamericana (Pan-American Highway). Panamericana Norte (north) becomes the ring road known as the Via de Evitamiento, which hits a large and well-marked cloverleaf at Avenida Javier Prado. Javier Prado leading west will take you into San Isidro; from there it is easy and safe to get to Miraflores, where visitors are more likely to be staying. From Panamericana Sur (south), you can get off onto Avenida Benavides heading east, which takes you directly to Miraflores, or again, onto Javier Prado. If you are mad enough to drive into the center of Lima, go past the Javier Prado cloverleaf to Evitamiento. Once you cross the Rimac River, you will be north of the center, and there are several bridges (Ricardo Palma, Santa Rosa) crossing back down into the center.

By Bus

Lima's bus stations include **Cruz del Sur** (Jirón Quilca 531, ☎ 01/427–1311), **Ormeño** (Javier Prado Este 1059 or Av. Carlos Zavala 177, ☎ 01/427–3650), and **Tepsa** (Paseo de la República 129, ☎ 01/427–6271).

Getting Around Lima

Lima is divided into neighborhoods, each with its own distinct flavor. The most important for visitors are **Lima** (also known as **Centro**), **Miraflores,** and **Barranco.** Walking is your best bet within a neighborhood, but you will need to take a taxi or bus between neighborhoods.

By Car

Avoid driving in Lima if you can. Many roads are in pitiful condition, while drivers are rude, reckless, and anarchic. If you must drive, park in a lot to protect the car against theft, or hire a child offering *"cuidar su carro"* (to look after your car). Pay him S/0.50–S/1 when you return and find your car intact.

RENTALS

In Lima, rental-car agencies include **Avis** (Sheraton Hotel, Paseo de la República 170, ☎ 01/433–5959; airport, ☎ 01/452–4774), **Budget** (La Paz 522, Miraflores, ☎ 01/444–0760; airport, ☎ 01/452–8706), **First Rent A Car** (La Paz 745, Miraflores, ☎ 01/446–2100), **Hertz** (Rivera Navarrete 550, San Isidro, ☎ 01/442–4475; airport, ☎ 01/451–8189), and **National** (Diez Canseco 319, Miraflores, ☎ 01/444–2333; airport, ☎ 01/452–3426).

By Bus

Regular buses, the school-bus-size *micros,* and the van-size *combis* offer frequent service, are inexpensive (S/0.40 or S/0.50; no free transfers), and stop at almost every corner. You must flag them down, but it is often difficult to know where they are going. If you're not sure, ask before you board. Be warned: Combi drivers are notorious for their lack of driving skills, and their vehicles are usually uncomfortable and accident-prone.

By Taxi

Cabs are plentiful and cheap. You will find taxi stands with big black *remisse* taxis beside most of the luxury hotels; these are the most expensive because they are generally larger and well cared for. On the street, cabs come in all makes, models, and stages of decay. To recognize them, look for a plastic TAXI sign on the windshield. If the car looks decrepit, don't get in; another is sure to come by soon. There are no meters, so always ask the fare before you get in, and offer 10%–25% less. Some local radio cab companies are **Taxi Fono** (☎ 01/422–6565 and 01/440–0714), **Taxi Metro** (☎ 01/437–3689), and **Taxi Seguro** (☎ 01/448–7226 or 01/448–3446); radio taxi fares are not negotiable.

Tour Operators

Lima Tours arranges bus tours that include access to some of Lima's finest colonial mansions. It also has information about—and branch offices in—destinations around Peru. *Belén 1040 (mailing: Box 4340, Lima 1, Peru),* ☎ *01/427–6720 or 01/427–6624,* ℻ *01/426–9878 or 01/426–2010.*

The **Miraflores Municipal Tourist Office** organizes one- and two-day trips in and around Lima; these excursions depart from the town hall on the district's central park. *San Martín 537, Miraflores,* ☎ *01/447–9539 or 01/444–3915.*

Exploring Lima

Old and new blend and sometimes clash in Lima. Gracious but occasionally run-down colonial and republican-era streets, mansions, and churches are concentrated in the chaotic downtown area, the Centro, where you'll also see skyscrapers and dreadful government buildings from the 1960s and 1970s. The Centro is clogged with hundreds of thousands of street vendors and unmanageable traffic. Other neighborhoods, like Miraflores, offer shopping, good eating, and a chance to relax and people-watch. Here, luxury high rises and fancy stores filled with glittering imported items contrast with the grimy street children begging for tips and tidbits at the sidewalk cafés. Museums exploring the country's long history are scattered throughout metropolitan Lima.

From downtown, the main roads lead like spokes of a wheel to Lima's most important districts, through working-class neighborhoods like Breña, Rimac, and La Victoria to the huge shantytowns ringing the city and to upscale seafront residential neighborhoods like Miraflores and San Isidro. There are also posh neighborhoods like La Molina in the foothills of the Andes, where Lima's wealthiest live among watered lawns behind guarded gates and high walls. From central Lima west to the sea, the city is flat, but the Peruvian coast is so narrow that the barren Andean piedmont juts spiky hills into the sky just 10 minutes east of the city center. Most parks begin on downtown's western fringe, becoming more frequent as you near the sea.

Visitors should plan on spending a day or two seeing the Centro, with an additional one or two days devoted to whichever of the other museums—on archaeology, textiles, gold, and so on—are of interest. Take time to wander through Barranco, once a seaside vacation spot for people who lived in downtown Lima. The café scene is lively here, attracting artists and intellectuals.

Centro

Many of Lima's most interesting historical sites are contained in the Centro, within walking distance of the **Plaza de Armas.** Around the broad, open plaza are the buildings that formed the nucleus of power in Spanish colonial Peru. The imposing **Palacio de Gobierno**—the official residence of the president, which also houses his offices and those of his staff—was completed in 1938. On the north side of the square, it was built on the site of Francisco Pizarro's palace, where he was murdered in 1541. An equestrian statue of the conquistador watches over the palace from across the street. The changing of the palace guard takes place daily at noon. Free tours are available by pre-arrangement (☎ 01/428–7444).

On the east side of the plaza stands the **cathedral** (☎ 01/431–7056; ☛ Entry fee), completed in the 17th century and rebuilt after the 1746 earthquake nearly destroyed it. In addition to impressive Baroque decoration, especially the intricately carved choir stalls, the cathedral houses a museum of religious art and artifacts, whose highlight is a coffin said to hold the remains of Pizarro. Across the plaza is the 20th-century neocolonial **Municipalidad** (City Hall; ☎ 01/427–6080; ☛ Free). Beside it, one block off the plaza, the late-16th-century church of **Santo Domingo** (first block of Jirón Camaná, ☎ 01/427–6793; ☛ Entry fee) holds the tombs of two venerated Peruvian saints, Rosa de Lima and the black Martín de Porres.

One block west is the **Casa Aliaga,** which can be seen by appointment through the administration or travel agencies. Said to be the oldest colonial mansion in South America, the house has been owned and occupied by the Aliaga family since Pizarro granted the land to Jerónimo de Aliaga in 1535. Its elaborate rooms are decorated with colonial furnishings. *Jirón de la Unión 224, ☎ 01/427–7736. ☛ Entry fee.*

Behind the palace is one of Lima's most interesting churches, **San Francisco,** completed in 1674. Note the beautiful *mudejar* decoration (a hybrid of Moorish and Spanish styles) on its vaulting and columns, Seville tiles, and paneled ceilings. The adjoining monastery's immense library contains thousands of antique texts, some dating back to the 17th century. You can visit the church's vast catacombs, with the remains of some 70,000 dead, discovered only in 1951. The monastery can be seen only on a guided tour, which takes place daily at 12:45 and 5:45. *Ancash 471, ☎ 01/427–1381.* ☛ *Entry fee.*

Just across the street is a beautifully restored colonial mansion, **Casa Pilatos.** It now houses the National Cultural Institute, which sponsors exhibitions on Peruvian culture both ancient and modern. *Ancash 390, ☎ 01/428–7990.* ☛ *Free.* ☉ *Weekdays.*

One of the more gruesome aspects of Peru's history is explored in the **Museo de la Inquisición,** three blocks away in the building that was the Spanish Inquisition's headquarters in South America from 1570 to 1820. You can visit the original dungeons and torture chambers. Stomach-churning, life-size exhibits illustrate methods of extracting information from the accused. *Junín 548, ☎ 01/428–7980.* ☛ *Free.* ☉ *Mon.–Sat.*

Nearby is Lima's most splendid colonial mansion: the **Palacio Torre Tagle,** built in 1735. Because the Foreign Ministry has offices here, visits by the public are limited to the patio and courtyard, but even that peek reveals tiled ceilings, carved columns, and a 16th-century carriage complete with portable commode. *Ucayali 363, ☎ 01/427–4722 or 01/427–6064.* ☛ *Free.* ☉ *Weekdays.*

Across from the ministry is one of the finest examples of early colonial religious architecture in Peru: **San Pedro,** a Jesuit church built in 1638. The interior is richly appointed with gilded altars, Moorish-style wood carvings in the choir and vestry, and glazed, decorated tiles throughout. *Corner of Ucayali and Azángaro, ☎ 01/428–3010.* ☛ *Free.*

Once the most fashionable boulevard in Lima and now for pedestrians only, **Jirón de la Unión** runs between the Plaza de Armas and the more modern **Plaza San Martín.** Persistent vendors and pickpockets (skilled but not violent) abound here; still, the walk affords a colorful foray into modern Lima. Halfway between the two plazas is the **Iglesia de la Merced** (corner of Unión and Miro Quesada, ☎ 01/427–8199; ☛ Free), a church with colonial facade and peaceful cloisters that was begun by Hernando Pizarro, Francisco's brother, in 1535. Facing the bustling Plaza San Martín are elegant buildings such as the **Gran Hotel Bolívar,** a pleasant place to stop for tea or a sandwich, and the exclusive **Club Nacional,** both dating from the 1920s. The plaza itself is a stage for a wild variety of street performers, from magicians and comedians to hawkers of modern-day snake medicine.

West of Jirón de la Unión is the **Iglesia de Jesús María** (corner of Camaná and Moquegua, ☎ 01/427–6809; ☛ Free), a simple church dating to 1659 that became a Capuchin monastery in the 18th century. The nearby **Casa de Riva Agüero** (Camaná 459, ☎ 01/427–7678; ☛ Free; ☉ By appointment weekdays) is a typical colonial mansion with ornately carved wooden terraces overlooking courtyards; balconies with *celosías* (intricate wood screens through which ladies could watch passersby unobserved); and an interesting museum of folk art on the patio. Within the small, simple 17th-century **Santuario de Santa Rosa de Lima** (first block of Av. Tacna, ☎ 01/428–7725; ☛ Free), the tiny adobe cell that was Santa Rosa's hermitage keeps alive the memory of the first saint in the Western Hemisphere. The church also houses the **Museo Etnográfico,** with ethnographic exhibits detailing the lives of Peru's jungle peoples.

Three blocks away, the **Iglesia de las Nazarenas** is an 18th-century church that has become the repository of the icon of the **Señor de los Milagros,** the patron of Lima's most passionate and important religious festival. In the mid-1600s, a black freeman living on this site painted a mural of Christ on the wall of his hut. When an earthquake destroyed most of the surrounding shantytown in 1655, the wall with the mural remained standing, and the miraculous mural became the patron icon of Lima. Every year on October 18, 19, and 28 and November 1, purple-robed devotees carry an oil copy of the mural, resplendent in a gold frame atop a silver litter, through the streets of Lima. *Corner of Tacna and Huancavelica, no ☎. ☛ Free.*

Near the "entrance" to the Centro, where the expressway to Miraflores and Barranco begins, the **Museo de Arte Nacional** chronicles four centuries of Peruvian art and design. Highlights are 2,000-year-old weavings from Paracas and paintings from the Cuzco School. *Colón 125, ☎ 01/423–4732. ☛ Entry fee. Closed daily 1–2 and Mon.*

Rimac

An extension of the colonial center, the district of Rimac has declined into a somewhat rough neighborhood, especially at night. Just across the often arid Rimac River from the Palacio de Gobierno, Rimac is linked to the center by the 17th-century **Puente de Piedra,** whose builders strengthened their mortar with thousands of egg whites. A few blocks from the bridge, the **Alameda de los Descalzos,** a tree-lined courtship walk, is graced by 12 marble statues representing the signs of the zodiac.

This sadly deteriorated lovers' lane ends at the **Convento de los Descalzos,** a 16th-century Franciscan monastery with four main cloisters and two lavish chapels. In one chapel a Baroque altar gleams with gold leaf. The kitchen still contains antique wine-making equipment, and there's a fine collection of colonial paintings. *Alameda de los Descalzos, Rimac, ☎ 01/481–0441. ☛ Entry fee. Closed Tues.*

Miraflores

An upscale residential district, the seaside suburb of Miraflores is an attractive place for strolling and window shopping among chic fashion boutiques, art galleries, and crafts shops. Some of Lima's swankiest hotels and restaurants are here. Oddly enough, this posh neighborhood is also the setting for an enormous pre-Inca *huaca* (ruin of a religious site), the **Huaca Juliana.** *Corner of Larco Herrera and Elías Aguirre, Miraflores. ☛ Entry fee. Closed Mon.*

The **Museo Amano,** seven blocks away, displays a very fine private collection of pre-Columbian ceramics and weavings by the Chancay culture, a small, central-coastal state around present-day Lima dating from AD 1000–1500. You must call ahead to arrange a tour. *Retiro 160, ☎ 01/441–2909. ☛ Free. Closed weekends.*

The heart of Miraflores is a roughly triangular area around the **Parque Miraflores,** which lies between Larco and Diagonal avenues. The park is the site of a daily arts and crafts fair; there are also frequent open-air concerts. If you continue down either Larco or Diagonal, you will come to the **Malecón,** a cliff-top road that looks out over the Pacific. Turning left or right, you'll pass small parks and the houses and apartments of the well-to-do. It's especially lovely during a summer sunset. Also along this street is the offbeat **Parque del Amor,** which celebrates the time-honored Peruvian tradition of courting in parks with a huge statue of two lovers in the grass.

Barranco

A sort of artists' quarter, with galleries, cafés, and lots of nightclubs, this funky seafront district has a charming *malecón* (coastal road) and winding, tree-lined streets. Above the Bajada de Baños, a cobblestone street lined with wonderful old houses that leads down to the ocean, is Lima's own Bridge of Sighs, the **Puente de los Suspiros.** The **Museo Pedro de Osma,** a few blocks south along the seafront, has a fine collection of colonial paintings, sculpture, and silver. *Malecón Pedro de Osma 501,* ☎ *01/467–0141.* ☛ *Entry fee.* ☽ *By appointment only.*

The **Parque Municipal,** one block from the Puente de los Suspiros, is one of the best places in Lima to just sit and watch Peruvians at their best—relaxing with friends, their children playing about them. Surrounding the park and on Barranco's lanes are several trendy bars and cafés (*see* Nightlife, *below*).

Museums Around Town

The **Museo Nacional de Antropología y Arqueología,** in the district of Pueblo Libre (about 8 kilometers/5 miles northwest of Miraflores), houses the nation's most extensive collection of pre-Columbian artifacts, intelligently labeled and arranged around two colonial-style courtyards. Beginning with 8,000-year-old stone tools, Peru's precolonial history comes to life through such highlights as the granite obelisks of the Chavín culture, the weavings of Paracas, and the ceramics of civilizations such as the Nazca, Moche, Chimú, and Inca. Next door is the Museo de Historia Nacional, a collection of period clothing, furniture, and other items dating mainly from the War of Independence. *Plaza Bolívar, Pueblo Libre,* ☎ *01/463–5070.* ☛ *Entry fee.*

Another museum in Pueblo Libre, the **Museo Rafael Larco Herrera,** has an enormous collection of ceramics, including the largest gathering of erotic pre-Columbian ceramics in Peru. Peru's ancient artists were surprisingly explicit and uninhibited. *Bolívar 1515, Pueblo Libre,* ☎ *01/461–1312 or 01/461–1835.* ☛ *Entry fee. Closed Sun.*

Although hit by economic hard times, the **Museo de la Nación,** in San Borja, 6 kilometers (4 miles) northeast of Miraflores, still provides an impressive exploration of Peru's many civilizations through special exhibitions and scale and life-size models and diagrams. *Av. Javier Prado Este 2466, San Borja,* ☎ *01/476–9875 or 01/476–9880.* ☛ *Entry fee.*

Far out of downtown Lima, in a basement vault, the **Museo de Oro** (Gold Museum) possesses an excellent collection of pre-Columbian gold jewelry and artifacts. There are other fascinating items as well, including a child's Nazca poncho of yellow feathers, a skull with a full set of pink quartz teeth, and an extensive array of military artifacts, uniforms, and weapons from around the world. *Alonso de Molina 1100, Monterrico,* ☎ *01/435–2917.* ☛ *Entry fee.*

Parks and Gardens

Lima sits in a desert where it never rains, so its many parks tend to look a bit wilted. The most interesting one is also a zoo, the **Parque Las Leyendas.** Although the administration eventually caved in to popular demand and bought an elephant and other non-indigenous animals, the zoo was designed to present the wildlife of Peru's three great regions: the Costa (coast), Sierra (highlands), and Selva (jungle). Don't expect a first-world zoo with animal-friendly enclosures. *Av. La Marina, block 24,* ☎ *01/452–6913.* ☛ *Entry fee. Closed Mon.*

One of Lima's prettiest public parks is the ancient olive grove **El Olívar** in San Isidro, adjacent to Miraflores. Now sprinkled with houses, the park has brick pathways and park benches among the nobly gnarled old olive trees.

Shopping

Shopping Districts

On **Avenida La Paz** in **Miraflores,** crafts, jewelry, and antiques stores abound. Also on La Paz are two small shopping arcades with a wide variety of sweaters and handicrafts: **El Alamo** (5th block, no ☎) and **El Suche** (6th block, no ☎). A similar arcade in downtown Lima is called **1900** (Belén 1030, no ☎).

Several large markets known collectively as the **Mercado Indio** are between the 6th and 10th blocks of Avenida La Marina, running from Lima to the airport. All sell only crafts: woolen and alpaca clothing, carved-wood objects, tooled-leather cushions and stools, and silver jewelry and curios. Shop carefully—plan on spending a few hours rooting around—and don't be afraid to bargain. Similar, though more expensive, crafts are sold at another, smaller **Mercado Indio** in Miraflores, in the 52nd block of Avenida Petit Thouars.

Specialty Shops

CLOTHING

Most handicraft stores sell alpaca-wool clothes. **Alpaca 111** (Camino Real Shopping Center, Camino Real, level C, shop 36, San Isidro, ☎ 01/441–9294) and **La Casa de la Alpaca** (La Paz 679, Miraflores, ☎ 01/444–2656) specialize in them.

FABRIC

Silvania Prints (Diez Canseco 376, no ☎; Conquistadores 905, San Isidro, ☎ 01/422–6440) sells colorful, original Peruvian designs printed by hand on pima cotton. You can buy fabric by the meter, along with clothing, scarves, purses, and other accessories.

HANDICRAFTS

Some of the better shops for traditional Peruvian arts and crafts are **Antisuyo** (Tacna 460, Miraflores, ☎ 01/447–2557), **Artesanías del Perú** (Av. Jorge Basadre 610, San Isidro, ☎ 01/440–1925), **Kuntur Huasi** (Ocharán 182, below 2nd block of Benavides, Miraflores, ☎ 01/444–0557), and **Las Pallas** (Cajamarca 212, parallel to 6th block of Av. Grau, Barranco, ☎ 01/477–4629).

JEWELRY

In Lima the three branches of the Brazilian firm **H. Stern Jewelers** (Lima Sheraton Hotel, Paseo de la República 170, ☎ 01/433–3320; Miraflores César's Hotel, corner of La Paz and Diez Canseco, ☎ 01/444–1212; Museo de Oro, Alonso de Molina 1100, Monterrico, ☎ 01/437–7691) specialize in gold and silver jewelry with Peruvian designs. **Joyería y Bisutería** (Centro Comercial Pharmax, Salaverry, 31st block, San Isidro, ☎ 01/461–9987; El Suche, Av. La Paz 646, store 21, no ☎) sells silver jewelry in colonial-inspired designs at its two locations.

Sports and the Outdoors

Beaches

Whatever you do, and no matter how many local people you see doing it, *do not* swim at the beaches in Lima itself. The Peruvian Ministry of Health and the municipality of Lima regularly warn people that the beaches are highly contaminated. The beaches south of the city, however, are not polluted (*see* Excursions from Lima, *below*).

Bullfighting

Bullfighting in Peru is Spanish style (that is, the bull is killed) and is quite popular. The season is in late October and November, and the spectacle takes place at the **Plaza de Acho** in **Rimac** (Cajamarca, block 5, Rimac, ☎ 01/482–3360).

Soccer

Peru's leading teams are **Alianza, Universitario, Sport Boys,** and **Cristal.** Their most important games are played at the **Estadio Nacional** (Paseo de la República, Lima, ☎ 01/433–4192), pretty much year-round.

Dining

Lima's glory days live on in its extraordinary cuisine, as well as in the cosmopolitan breadth of its restaurants. Whether you want comida criolla (heavily spiced meat, fish, or poultry dishes, often with onions and prepared fried, as stews, or simmered with rice), the fresh bounty of the Pacific Ocean, or something more ethnic—*chifa*, or Chinese, is a favorite here—Lima won't disappoint you. For the freshest and least expensive seafood, look for *cebicherías*. These informal eateries, which usually serve only lunch, have, in addition to *cebiche* (seviche), fish prepared in a variety of ways: *a lo macho* (in a spicy seafood sauce), *a la chorillana* (fried with hot peppers, tomatoes, and onions), *al vapor* (steamed), or *sudado* (in a stew). You'll also find seafood such as octopus or squid deep fried. Typical snacks include empanadas and *papas rellenas* (mashed potatoes rolled into a ball and filled with a spicy mixture of ground beef, onions, and raisins). For dessert or after-dinner coffee, visit one of Lima's cafés. These gathering spots play an important role in the city's social and intellectual life, especially among the middle-class 30s–50s set. The biggest café action is between 5 and 7 PM and after 10. For price-category definitions, *see* Dining *in* Peru Essentials, *below.*

Cafés

$ **Haiti.** This landmark sidewalk café is a favorite hangout for Lima's aging artists and intellectuals. Stick to the sandwiches, coffee, and beer. ✕ *Diagonal 160, Miraflores,* ☎ *01/447–5052. AE, DC, MC, V.*

$ **Las Mesitas.** An old-fashioned Limeño café with tables of wrought-iron
★ and marble, this romantic spot a half-block north of the Parque Municipal in Barranco is a magnet for fans of traditional sweets. The *mazamorra morada,* a sweet pudding of cornmeal and candied fruit, is heavenly. ✕ *Av. Grau 323, Barranco,* ☎ *01/477–4199. V.*

$ **La Tiendecita Blanca.** Excellent pastries, a baby grand piano for ambience, and shelves chock full of delicacies and confections attract foreigners as well as locals to this European-style café. ✕ *Larco 111, Miraflores,* ☎ *01/445–9797. AE, DC, MC, V.*

Chinese

$$$ **Lung Fung.** About 8 kilometers (5 miles) from downtown is a spectacular
★ chifa, with interior Chinese gardens complete with tiny bridges and ponds. Try the *kam-lu wantan* (fried wontons with shrimp and sweet-and-sour sauce). ✕ *Av. República de Panamá 3165, San Isidro,* ☎ *01/ 441–8817. AE, DC, MC, V.*

$$ **Pun Kay.** The decor is comfortable and refreshingly simple in this ex-
★ cellent restaurant, with none of the cheap paper lanterns or reproduction prints of Chinese scenery that normally characterize the genre. For an appetizer, choose from the delicious selection of dumplings. ✕ *Av. Benavides 1949, Miraflores,* ☎ *01/438–7445. DC, MC, V.*

$$ **Shanghai.** Big and breezy, decorated with plants and a fish tank, the Shanghai offers both typical Peruvian Chinese cuisine and spicy Szechuan dishes, served by an efficient staff. ✕ *Av. San Luis 1988, San Borja,* ☎ *01/435–9132. DC, MC.*

$ Chifa Kun Fa. Serving excellent Chinese-Peruvian food in intimate private rooms separated by Chinese screens, this chifa is popular with locals and also up to foreign standards of cleanliness. ✕ *San Martín 459, Miraflores, no ☎. No credit cards.*

Creole

$$$ Crillón Sky Room. At this penthouse restaurant in the Hotel Crillón downtown, dine on a varied menu of criollo and international dishes while taking in the panoramic view, accompanied by live music (no performances Tues., Wed., or Sun.). Peruvians and tourists alike come here to enjoy such favorites as *tacu tacu* (fried rice and beans), and grilled fish and meat. ✕ *Hotel Crillón, Colmena 589, ☎ 01/428–3290. AE, DC, MC, V.*

$$$ El Otro Sitio. Part folk-music bar, part restaurant, this establishment with stucco walls and exposed wooden beams just off Barranco's Bridge of Sighs features live-music evenings and a criollo buffet, in addition to the à la carte menu. Buffet dishes might include *carapulcra* (a stew of dried potatoes), *arroz con pollo* (rice with chicken), and cebiche. ✕ *Sucre 317, Barranco, ☎ 01/477–2413. AE, DC, MC, V.*

$$$ Las Brujas de Cachiche. This upscale spot is in a pleasant location overlooking a secluded park on a Miraflores back street. ✕ *Av. Bolognesi 460, Miraflores, ☎ 01/447–1883. AE, DC, MC, V.*

International

$$$ El Minotaurio. Lavishly decorated, with striking cast-iron chairs and cut-glass chandeliers, this restaurant's specialty is duck, whether raw, in the form of carpaccio, or cooked, as *magret de pato* (in a creamy pepper sauce). The menu also includes many Peruvian dishes. ✕ *Av. Grau 498, Miraflores, ☎ 01/447–4838. AE, DC, V.*

$$$ La Gloria. Catalan cooking meets nouvelle cuisine here, with great suc-
★ cess. Although reluctant to recommend any of his dishes above any other, the owner is most proud of his *suquet de peix*, steamed fish with herbs. ✕ *Atahualpa 201, Miraflores, ☎ 01/446–6504. AE, DC, MC, V.*

$$ L'Eau Vive. Dine in an old downtown colonial mansion on international dishes cooked by friendly French nuns. ✕ *Ucayali 370, ☎ 01/427–5612. V.*

Seafood

$$$$ La Costa Verde. One of several luxurious seafront restaurants in Lima, the Costa Verde has a rustic-chic dining room with polished-wood columns, opening onto a glassed-in terrace with bamboo furniture and palm-leaf umbrellas. ✕ *Barranquito Beach, Barranco, ☎ 01/477–2424. AE, DC, MC, V.*

$$$$ La Rosa Nautica. Lima's loveliest restaurant is set in a Victorian-style pink-and-green rotunda at the end of a pier, perched over the Pacific Ocean. Dishes include scallops grilled with Parmesan cheese, and corvina or *lenguado* (flounder) fish with seafood sauce. For dessert, try the crepes Suchard, wrapped around ice cream and topped with hot fudge sauce. ✕ *Espigón 4, Costa Verde, Miraflores, ☎ 01/447–0057. AE, DC, MC, V.*

$$ Alfresco. Excellent cebiches are the draw at this chain of light and airy
★ fish restaurants. ✕ *Miraflores: Malecón Balta 790, ☎ 01/444–7962. San Isidro: Santa Luisa 295, ☎ 01/422–8915 or 01/440–5099. AE, DC, MC, V.*

$$ El Suizo. A popular lunch spot, this casual beachfront restaurant with
★ patio tables serves fish and seafood, including tasty cebiche. ✕ *La Herradura, Chorrillos, no ☎. DC, MC, V. Lunch only.*

$ Canta Rana. This modest restaurant alongside Barranco's municipal mar-
★ ket is decorated with a diverse collection of posters of soccer teams, both

local and international. The decor might be simple, but the service is good and the food is excellent. Try any of a range of cebiches or suda-dos. ✕ *Genova 111, Barranco,* ☎ *01/447–5066. AE, DC, MC, V.*

Steak House

$$$ **El Rincón Gaucho.** Nestled on a hillside above the ocean, in a rustic setting of rough-hewn wood ceilings, cowhides hanging on the walls, and other such touches, is this steak house serving tender Argentine beef. The best bet is the *parillada,* a mixed grill of steaks, beef-heart kebabs, kidney, liver, pork chops, chicken legs, and blood pudding; the order for two will feed three or four people. ✕ *Parque Salazar, Miraflores,* ☎ *01/447–4778. AE, DC, MC, V.*

Vegetarian

$ **Bircher-Benner.** In a colonial-style house amid gardens on a quiet street in Miraflores, choose from a wide variety of meatless international and Creole dishes. The salads are excellent, as is the soy-protein *cau-cau.* ✕ *Schell 598,* ☎ *01/444–4250. AE, V.*

Lodging

Hotels are concentrated in downtown Lima and in Miraflores (on avenidas La Paz and Alcanfores). There are a variety of price ranges in each area. Hotels through the $$ price range are probably comparable with those in the rest of South America. The cheap ones are awfully basic. Prices do not tend to vary by season, but it is useful to make reservations for the smaller hotels. People who want to concentrate on the Centro can stay there, although even in Miraflores you're within easy reach (10–20 minutes by cab when it's not rush hour). Miraflores has lots of shops and eateries, and you can stroll there at night with little fear of being mugged. Don't attempt to bargain hotel rates, except in some of the older downtown hotels. Most Lima hotels do not include breakfast in their rates; those that do serve a Continental breakfast. For price-category definitions, *see* Lodging *in* Peru Essentials, *below.*

$$$$ **Hotel El Condado.** The most aggressively neocolonial of Lima's luxury hotels is on a pedestrian-only, cobblestone shopping street. Rooms have full-size colonial-style mirrors and paintings, and some have private saunas and whirlpool tubs. 🏨 *Alcanfores 465, Miraflores,* ☎ *01/444–3614. 50 rooms. Restaurant, bar, coffee shop, sauna. AE, DC, MC, V.*

$$$$ **Hotel Las Américas.** Lima's newest deluxe hotel has a rather impersonal
★ lobby and a shopping arcade up a long, curving ramp. Rooms have modern furniture and paintings and miniature cactus gardens. 🏨 *Benavides 415, Miraflores,* ☎ *01/445–9494 or 01/444–7272,* FAX *01/444–1137. 151 rooms. Restaurant, bar, coffee shop, pool, hot tub. AE, DC, MC, V.*

$$$$ **Hotel Sheraton.** At the edge of downtown Lima is this big and somewhat cold luxury hotel; its guest rooms could be in a Sheraton anywhere in the world. The staff is attentive, but sometimes communication snags between departments can slow down the service. 🏨 *Paseo de la República 170, Lima,* ☎ *01/433–3320. 490 rooms. Restaurant, bar, coffee shop, sauna. AE, DC, MC, V.*

$$$$ **Miraflores César's Hotel.** Neocolonial elegance is the watchword here,
★ with such touches as carved headboards, exposed beams, and highland handicrafts. The bar is decorated as a railroad car, complete with a minilocomotive. 🏨 *La Paz and Diez Canseco, Miraflores,* ☎ *01/444–1212,* FAX *01/444–4440. 150 rooms. 2 restaurants, bar, coffee shop, indoor pool, sauna, health club. AE, DC, MC, V.*

$$$ **Hotel El Olívar.** Amid the greenery of San Isidro's olive grove—a great
★ place for a morning jog—this new hotel has a glistening lobby full of
plants and deep-green tile floors. Rooms in pastel mauves have pais-
ley spreads and wood accents; some have their own saunas and
whirlpool tubs. ☎ *Pancho Fierro 194, El Olívar, San Isidro,* ☎ *01/441–
1454,* FAX *01/441–1388. 67 rooms. Restaurant, bar, coffee shop, pool.
AE, DC, MC, V.*

$$$ **Hotel María Angola.** Smallish and friendly, this modern hotel has a for-
★ mal, colonial-style lobby that contrasts with comfortable, modern rooms
done in stucco with bedspreads of swirling earth tones. Some rooms have
whirlpool baths and saunas. The rooftop pool is closed April–November. ☎ *La Paz 610, Miraflores,* ☎ *01/444–1280,* FAX *01/446–2860. 54
rooms. Restaurant, bar, pool, casino. AE, DC, MC, V.*

$$ **Gran Hotel Bolívar.** This decades-old institution on the Plaza San
Martín has declined somewhat in terms of service, and its rooms are
a little worn. The public rooms, however, retain their grandeur, and
the stained-glass dome over the rotunda lobby is magnificent. ☎ *Plaza
San Martín,* ☎ *01/427–2305,* FAX *01/428–7674. 290 rooms. Restau-
rant, bar. AE, DC, MC, V.*

$$ **Hostal La Castellana.** A favorite with foreign visitors, this neocolonial
hotel is built around a sunlit courtyard. Rooms have whitewashed walls,
wood-shuttered windows, and industrial carpeting. Reservations should
be made at least a month in advance. ☎ *Grimaldo del Solar 222, Miraflores,* ☎ *01/444–4662,* FAX *01/446–8030. 29 rooms. Restaurant.
AE, DC, MC, V.*

$$ **Hostal Miramar Ischia.** Set on a quiet street on a cliff above the ocean,
★ this discreet hotel offers stunning views, floors of Spanish tile and par-
quet, and meals cooked by the Italian-Peruvian couple who own the
establishment. Reserve a month in advance. ☎ *Malecón Cisneros
1244, Miraflores,* ☎ *01/446–6969,* FAX *01/445–0851. 17 rooms.
Restaurant, bar. AE, DC, MC, V.*

$$ **Hotel José Antonio.** Modest rates don't mean modest comfort in this business hotel in Miraflores. The bright rooms, some with ocean views and
whirlpool tubs, are decorated with Peruvian weavings and plush carpets,
while the restaurant and bar, blending latticework and leather seating,
are elegant but cozy. ☎ *28 de Julio 398, Miraflores,* ☎ *01/445–6870,*
FAX *01/446–8295. 83 rooms. Restaurant, bar. AE, DC, MC, V.*

$ **Hostal El Patio.** This family-oriented, rather ramshackle home (no sign
outside), popular among foreigners in town to adopt Peruvian children,
allows guests to use a common kitchen. Rooms have beamed ceilings,
colonial mirrors, and bare tile floors. ☎ *Diez Canseco 341A, Miraflores,* ☎ *01/444–2107. 11 rooms. No credit cards.*

$ **Hostal Señorial.** A former home on a quiet street near downtown Mi-
raflores, this hotel is family run and has an informal atmosphere, colonial paintings, and tile floors. Rooms have French doors leading to a
dove-filled garden. ☎ *José González 567, Miraflores,* ☎ *01/445–
9724. 30 rooms. Bar. AE, DC, MC, V.*

$ **Hostal Torreblanca.** Indoor-outdoor carpeting and bamboo headboards
decorate guest rooms at this homey but slightly run-down hotel set above
a park near the sea, 15 blocks from downtown Miraflores. ☎ *Av. Pardo
1453, Miraflores,* ☎ *01/447–9998,* FAX *01/447–3363. 19 rooms.
Restaurant, bar. AE, DC, MC, V.*

The Arts

Galleries

Miraflores is full of art galleries showing the work of Peruvian and occasionally foreign artists. The **Miraflores Municipal Gallery** (corner of

Av. Larco and Diez Canseco, Miraflores, ☎ 01/444–0540, ext. 16) sponsors a wide variety of exhibitions featuring sculpture, photography, and
paintings, as does the **Alliance Française** (Av. Arequipa 4595, Miraflores, ☎ 01/445–0436 or 01/446–0481). Two private galleries
with works for sale are **Formas** (Av. Larco 743, Office 605, Miraflores, ☎ 01/444–0770) and **Trapecio** (Av. Larco 743, Mezzanine 2, Miraflores, ☎ 01/444–0842).

Music and Theater

Lima does not often attract the top-notch musicians and theatrical performances that, say, Buenos Aires or Mexico City can garner. There
are, however, a number of venues where you can catch performances
of classical and popular (including Latin American) music. The **Centro Cultural Juan Parra del Riego** (Av. Pedro de Osma 135, Barranco,
☎ 01/477–4506) features Peruvian and Latin American music. The
Santa Ursula Auditorium (Av. Santo Toribio, San Isidro, ☎ 01/440–
7474 or 01/440–4582) often hosts classical music concerts by international performers; the shows are usually sponsored by the **Sociedad
Filarmónica** (Porta 170, Office 301, Miraflores, ☎ 01/445–7395).
The **Instituto Cultural Peruano Norteamericano** (corner of Av. Angamos
and Av. Arequipa, Miraflores, ☎ 01/446–6315) offers a range of cultural events, including theater, jazz, classical, and folk music.

Nightlife

The most popular nightlife in Lima is at *peñas,* bars offering creole music
(romantic ballads and waltzes that combine native Peruvian, black, and
Spanish influences) or folk music, and occasionally jazz. This scene centers on Barranco, especially around the municipal square. Most peñas
exact a cover charge and are open from around 9 or 10 PM until the
wee hours of the morning.

Criollo Peñas

Los Balcones (Av. Grau, in front of the Parque Municipal, Barranco,
no ☎) specializes in *música negra,* the black variant of *música criolla.*

Manos Morenos (Av. Pedro de Osma 409, Barranco, ☎ 01/467–0421
or 01/467–4902) is probably the most upmarket of the peñas, with a
$15 cover charge and a menu featuring typical Peruvian dishes (ex-
pensive). The atmosphere tends to be rather staid, however, in comparison with other peñas.

Sachún (Av. del Ejército 657, Miraflores, ☎ 01/441–0123) is one of
middle-class Lima's favorite spots for dancing and drinking.

Folk-Music Peñas

At **Hatuchay** (Trujillo 228, Rimac, ☎ 01/427–2827; closed Sun.–Wed.)
the patrons often dance with the performers. Call a cab to get back to
your hotel, because the neighborhood is a bit rough.

La Estación de Barranco (Pedro de Osma 112, Barranco, ☎ 01/467–
8804), in an old train station, is frequented by locals and tourists.

Bars

The recently opened **Amnesia** (Bul. Sánchez Carrión 153, ☎ 01/477–
9577), where there is sometimes an entry charge, is the trendiest of the
bars lining Sánchez Carrión Boulevard, a pedestrian street off one corner of Barranco's municipal square.

El Ekeko (Av. Grau 266, ☎ 01/477–5823), another artsy bar, has a
bookshop attached. It stages poetry readings and literary events on

Mondays and Tuesdays and has traditional or rock concerts the rest of the week.

At the far end of Sánchez Carrión Boulevard is **La Noche** (Bolognesi 307, Barranco, ☎ 01/477–4154), the quintessential Barranco bar, offering videos and artistic events from time to time, and a youthful, noisy atmosphere all the time.

Excursions from Lima

Beaches

The coast south of Lima is strung with beaches—a bit arid by foreign standards but often backed with massive, glistening sand dunes. The ocean is rough and cold; lifeguards, as well as such amenities as bathrooms and changing rooms, are nonexistent. At most beaches, however, you will find kiosks serving cold drinks and fresh seafood. Two of the most popular beaches are **El Silencio,** 42 kilometers (26 miles) from Lima, and **Punta Negra,** 50 kilometers (31 miles) away. Continuing south, you'll come upon **Pucusana,** a charming cliff-top fishing village 60 kilometers (37 miles) from Lima.

Getting There
The beaches are all off the Pan-American Highway leading out of Lima; exits are well marked.

Pachacamac

Thirty-one kilometers (19 miles) south of Lima, in the Lurín Valley, the imposing ruins of **Pachacamac** are all that remain of this ancient center of a powerful religious order linked to the Chincha culture. Though it was conquered by the Incas, Pachacamac's mystique was so great that it continued to draw pilgrims throughout the Inca rule. The Spaniards were less broad-minded; they sacked the Temple of Virgins in 1533 (it has been rebuilt).

Getting There
Take the Lurín exit off the Pan-American Highway heading south out of Lima.

THE NORTH COAST

Long before the Inca empire raised its stone marvels in the southern Andes, civilizations flourished in the fertile river valleys striping the deserts of Peru's northern coast. A thousand years ago, the Moche, Lambayeque (Sicán), and Chimú societies built their cities and pyramids of adobe brick, leaving behind the massive and enigmatic ruins that today dot the northern deserts. Their sophisticated canal and aqueduct systems irrigated more land than is cultivated even today. The Spaniards who settled these lands built their own cities—Trujillo, Chiclayo, and Lambayeque, among others—neglecting the spectacular agricultural and architectural achievements of earlier days. Although voracious looters, or *huaqueros,* have stolen many of the gold, silver, and ceramic treasures left in the ruins, modern archaeologists sifting through the sand still occasionally make miraculous finds. The tomb of the Lord of Sipán, discovered intact in 1987, is the most famous example.

Arriving and Departing

By Plane
AeroPerú, Americana, and **Faucett** have flights from Lima to both the Trujillo (☎ 04/423–2301) and the Chiclayo (☎ 07/422–9059) airport.

By Car
The major highway serving the north coast—and the only route from Lima—is the Pan-American Highway.

By Bus
Cruz del Sur (Jirón Quilca 531, ☎ 01/427–1311), **Ormeño** (Javier Prado Este 1059 or Av. Carlos Zavala 177, Lima, ☎ 01/427–5679), and **Tepsa** (Paseo de la República 129, Lima, ☎ 01/432–1233) have bus service from Lima to Trujillo and Chiclayo. **Expreso de Chiclayo** (Av. Grau 653, Lima, ☎ 01/428–9273) has service from Lima to Chiclayo. **Emtrafesa** (Calle Miraflores 127, Trujillo, ☎ 04/424–3981; corner of Colón and Bolognesi, Chiclayo, ☎ 07/423–4291) plies between Trujillo and Chiclayo, a three- to four-hour trip.

Trujillo

A lively metropolis that vies with Arequipa for the title of Peru's Second City, Trujillo was founded in 1534 by the Spaniards, who named it in honor of conquistador Francisco Pizarro. Most visitors who come to this splendid Spanish colonial city, however, come to marvel not at the works of Spain but at those built nearby by the Moche and Chimú—gigantic temple pyramids and a sprawling city made solely of mud.

Visitor Information

Touring and Automobile Club (Av. Argentina 258, Urbanización El Recreo, ☎ 04/423–2635; ⊘ Daily 8:30–12:30 and 3–6). **Tourist police** (Municipalidad, Plaza de Armas, ☎ 04/424–1936; ⊘ Daily 8–1 and 3–6).

Getting Around

Hiring a driver and guide through a reputable travel agency such as **Trujillo Tours** (Diego de Almagro 301, Trujillo, ☎ 04/423–3091) is the best way to see the ruins outside the city; some of the sites are isolated, and one can easily get lost on the unnamed little back roads leading to them. Taxis can be hired for about $6 per hour.

Exploring

Trujillo
Trujillo still maintains much of its colonial charm. A piece of the 30-foot-high city wall, dating from 1685–87, remains standing, at the corner of Estete and España. The heart of the city is the broad **Plaza de Armas,** fronted by the 17th-century cathedral and surrounded by the *casonas* (colonial mansions) that are Trujillo's architectural glory.

Like most of the restored casonas in Trujillo, **Casa Urquiaga** was saved by a bank whose offices now occupy part of the building. You can visit this early 19th-century mansion on the Plaza de Armas, with its baroque patio and fine collection of furniture, mirrors, paintings, and pre-Columbian ceramics. *Pizarro 446, ☎ 04/425–6517. ☛ Free. Closed weekends.*

A block away is the **Casa del Mayorazgo de Facala,** built in 1709. Constructed of thick adobe and covered with white stucco, this is a clas-

sic example of Trujillo colonial architecture. The open courtyard is surrounded by cedar columns and houses a colonial carriage. Notable features inside the house are the Moorish-style carved-wood ceiling and
the upstairs balcony, with its celosías (wooden screens). *Pizarro 314
Banco Wiese,* ☎ *04/425–6600.* ☛ *Free. Closed Sun.*

Trujillo declared its independence from Spain on December 29, 1820,
in the nearby **Casa de la Emancipación,** which has an interesting scale
model of colonial, walled Trujillo. *Pizarro 610,* ☎ *04/424–6061.* ☛
Free. Closed weekends.

Moche Ruins

Although monument-building city-states existed in the environs of
present-day Trujillo more than a thousand years before Christ, the first
such city-state to spread its influence over much of the north coast was
Moche, between AD 100 and 700. The Moche, sometimes referred to
as the Mochica, built their capital city and two enormous adobe pyramids, both constructed around AD 100, about 10 kilometers (6 miles)
southeast of modern Trujillo. To get there, head south from Trujillo
on the Pan-American Highway; the ruins are across the Moche River
in the Campiña de Moche (no ☎; ☛ Free).

The **Huaca del Sol** (Pyramid of the Sun) stands over 130 feet high and
measures 1,105 by 520 feet—and is only half as big as it once was. At
least 140 million bricks went into building this, the largest extant
adobe-brick structure in the New World. Scattered around the pyramid's base are examples of "signature bricks," with distinctive hand,
finger, and foot marks that identify the community whose tribute labor
produced the bricks for their Moche lords. Archaeologists believe that
the pyramid served as an imperial palace and mausoleum, a center of
political and religious power. Once a stronghold of untold treasures,
it has been stripped clean over the centuries by huaqueros. So great
were its riches that in 1610 the Spaniards diverted the Moche River
to wash away the pyramid's base and lay bare the bounty within.

Southward across a plain 1,625 feet wide that once held a bustling royal
city stands the smaller **Huaca de la Luna** (Pyramid of the Moon),
painted with anthropomorphic and zoomorphic reliefs. If you visit on
a weekday with a guide, you may be allowed to observe archaeologists at work preserving one of the faded but still colorful reliefs.

Chimú Ruins

Three hundred years after the Moche civilization faded, a new empire,
the Chimú, arose in its place. Although much less famous than the Inca
empire, which in 1470 conquered it, the Chimú empire, called Chimor,
was the second largest in pre-Columbian South American history. It
stretched along 1,000 kilometers (620 miles) of Pacific coastline, from
Chillón, just north of present-day Lima, to Tumbes, on the border with
Ecuador.

Chimor's capital, **Chán Chán,** a huge adobe-brick city whose ruins lie
5 kilometers (3 miles) west of Trujillo, has been called the largest mud
city in the world. It once held boulevards, aqueducts, gardens, palaces,
and some 10,000 dwellings. Within the city were nine royal com-
pounds, one of which, the Tschudi (named for a 19th-century Swiss
explorer of the ruins), has been partially restored and opened to the
public. Each compound was built by a Chimú ruler, who upon his death
was buried in the compound, which his family and retainers maintained.
Although wind, huaqueros, and the occasional rain storm have damaged the city, its size—20 square kilometers (8 square miles)—still im-
presses, and the walls are studded with adobe friezes. If you have not

come with a guide, it's best to hire one at the entrance to the site for a few dollars; the ruins are largely unlabeled, and tourists accompanied by a guide are less likely to be victims of crime. The ticket for Chán Chán covers the entrance fees for the Huaca El Dragón and Huaca Esmeralda (*see below*). *Carretera Huanchaco, no* ☏. ☞ *Entry fee.*

Two kilometers (1¼ miles) west of Trujillo is the Chimú **Huaca Esmeralda.** Like other pyramids on the north coast, this ancient temple mound served as a religious ceremonial center and burial site for the priest-kings. The highlights of the ruins are the two stepped platforms and unrestored friezes of the fish, seabirds, waves, and fishing nets that were central to the life of the Chimú. *Av. Mansiche exit, Pan-American Hwy. N, no* ☏. ☞ *Entry fee.*

Jarringly out of place in an urban setting north of Trujillo's center is the restored—some say overrestored—**Huaca El Dragón** (Temple of the Dragon), also known as the Huaca Arco Iris (Rainbow Temple). This early Chimú walled temple pyramid is decorated with the repeating figure of a mythical creature that looks like a cross between a giant serpent or dragon and a rainbow. After the National Cultural Institute restored the ruin in 1962, only half of the original huaca remained, and the contrast between the fresh-looking but crudely reconstructed friezes and the eroded but delicately intricate originals, some bearing traces of the original yellow paint, is glaring. *Pan-American Hwy. N, La Esperanza district, no* ☏. ☞ *Entry fee.*

About an hour north of Trujillo, near the village of **Magdalena de Cao,** archaeologists are at work on one of the latest Chimú sites to be discovered, the **El Brujo** complex. They have already unearthed some striking raised murals. Trujillo Tours (*see* Getting Around, *above*) can organize visits.

Moche and Chimú Artifacts

In the northern sector of the city, the privately owned **Museo Cassinelli** is in, of all places, the basement of a gas station. Among the most spectacular objects in the 2,800-piece collection, which covers pre-Columbian ceramics dating from 1200 BC through the Inca period, are realistic Moche portrait vases, with surprisingly sensitive renderings of individuals. The Moche ceramics also show a degree of humor, as in the charming *Potato Face,* which gives human features to the Andean tuber. The Moche and other ancient Peruvian ceramicists were famous for their erotic art, which the museum keeps in closed cabinets that the staff opens for adults. Although the collection is overcrowded on wooden shelves and interpretive materials are practically nonexistent, the museum's informality does give the visitor the opportunity to handle the objects. *Nicolás de Piérola 601,* ☏ *04/423–2312.* ☞ *Entry fee. Closed weekends.*

Shopping

Throughout Trujillo you may be approached by vendors offering *huacos,* usually hollow ceramic figurines, vases, or bowls. It is illegal to export genuine pre-Columbian artifacts, but anything offered you is probably not authentic. Stands at the Huaca El Dragón and Chán Chán offer imitations; for these and handicrafts, try the **Liga de Artesanos** (Artisans' League) store at Colón 423 (no ☏).

Beaches

Although there are two popular swimming beaches near Trujillo, the water is cold year-round. **Huanchaco,** 11 kilometers (7 miles) northwest of Trujillo via the Carretera Huanchaco, is a fishing village with a long beach lined with seafood kiosks (we recommend you don't partake). The fishermen here still fish aboard *caballitos de totora* (little reed horses); for a few soles, they will take you out to ride the waves on one of these arc-shape rafts, whose earliest representations appear on Moche and Chimú ceramics.

Dining

Trujillanos are big on fish dishes, like their compatriots to the south. Cebiches of fish or shellfish are extremely popular, as is *causa*, a cold casserole of mashed potatoes molded around a filling of fish, *ají* (hot peppers), and onions and topped with olives and slices of hard-boiled egg. *Cabrito al horno* and *seco de cabrito* (roast and stewed kid) and *shámbar,* a bean stew, are two other local specialties. Restaurants in Trujillo tend to be casual and unpretentious, making up for their lack of decorative pizazz with outstanding seafood and comida criolla. Many also make a fair stab at Italian recipes. Bringing picnic food bought in Trujillo for trips to isolated sites like Chán Chán is a good idea. Buy fresh food in the market in the sixth block of Gamarra; other foodstuffs are available in the many *bodegas* (the word here means a mom-and-pop grocery, not a wine cellar) in downtown Trujillo. For price-category definitions, *see* Dining *in* Peru Essentials, *below.*

$$$ ★ **Las Bóvedas.** This quiet, elegant restaurant in the Hotel Libertador (*see* Lodging, *below*) has a vaulted brick ceiling—a *bóveda* is a vaulted chamber—and arched, plant-filled wall niches. The house specialty is the local delicacy shámbar, a thick soup made with beans, split peas, wheat grains, bacon, and pork and garnished with *canchita* (semipopped corn) and ground hot-pepper sauce. ✕ *Independencia 485,* ☎ *04/423–2741. AE, DC, MC, V.*

$$ ★ **De Marco.** Right on the street, this noisy but cheery spot, popular with locals and tourists for its excellent comida criolla, has paneled walls decorated with original local art. Try the tacu tacu, a typical coastal dish of rice and beans, with the seco de cabrito. ✕ *Pizarro 725,* ☎ *04/423–4251. MC, V.*

$$ **El Mochica.** Set in an old casona, in a long, open hall with white-washed walls and chandeliers, this seafood restaurant has a down-at-the-heels flair. A typical meal starts with an industrial-size portion of spicy, fresh cebiche de lenguado, followed by a *picante* (seafood sauce served over rice) of *camarones* (shrimp) or other *mariscos* (shellfish). ✕ *Bolívar 462,* ☎ *04/425–2457. No credit cards. Lunch only.*

$$ **Romano.** This small street-side restaurant has a café atmosphere, serves good Italian classics such as spaghetti Bolognese and fettuccine Alfredo, and is justly famed for its cakes and pies. The mouthwatering desserts may include lemon meringue pie, chirimoya meringue pie topped with chocolate shavings, or a thick, almost fudgy chocolate cake. ✕ *Pizarro 747,* ☎ *04/425–2251. MC, V.*

Lodging

If you are planning to visit Trujillo in January and October during the local festivals (*see* The Arts, *below*), be sure to make hotel reservations at least a month in advance. For price-category definitions, *see* Lodging *in* Peru Essentials, *below.*

$$$ ★ **Hotel Libertador.** The former Hotel de Turistas on the Plaza de Armas has been splendidly renovated to blend modern comfort and colonial elegance. The patio pool, surrounded by a hummingbird-filled garden, is especially delightful. Rooms, some with celosías, are decorated with modern paintings interpreting pre-Columbian designs, locally tooled leather and wood, and wrought-iron wall lamps. ⊞ *Independencia 485,* ☎ *04/423–2741,* F̄A̅X̄ *04/423–5641. 75 rooms. Restaurant, bar, café, pool, sauna. AE, DC, MC, V.*

$$ Hotel Los Jardines. About 10 minutes by taxi from the Plaza de Armas, this "garden hotel" in the northern district of Los Jardines lives up to its name: Each room is a simple, uncarpeted bungalow with a big picture window looking out on gardens and trees. ⊞ *Av. América Norte 1245,* ☎ *04/424–5337,* F̄A̅X̄ *04/425–4721. 60 rooms. Restaurant, bar, pool, tennis court. AE, DC, V.*

$ Hotel Continental. The rooms are simple and clean at this hotel above a shopping arcade 1½ blocks from the Plaza de Armas and across the street from the Central Market. The rooms on the seventh floor have a good view of the city. ⊞ *Gamarra 663,* ☎ *04/424–1607,* F̄A̅X̄ *04/424– 9881. 51 rooms. AE, DC, MC, V.*

$ Hotel Opt-Gar. Vinyl and Formica meet Moche at this safe, conveniently located downtown hotel, where huacos are scattered like knickknacks throughout the lobby and other public spaces. The rooms are clean and wallpapered. ⊞ *Grau 595,* ☎ *04/424–2192; Lima* ☎ *01/449–8717. 66 rooms. Restaurant. DC, MC, V.*

The Arts

Trujillo has two important festivals. January's four-day **National Marinera Competition** (contact the Club Libertad, San Martín 299, Trujillo, ☎ 04/424–4941, 04/424–5131, or 04/425–6982) celebrates a romantic local dance performed to the accompaniment of guitars and the *cajón*, a boxlike wood percussion instrument. The 10-day **Festival de la Primavera** (Spring Festival) in October includes dance performances, art shows, and much more (contact the Club de Leones, Estete 411, Trujillo, ☎ 04/423–4501 or 04/425–2835).

Local newspapers, such as *La Industria*, have listings of cultural events at venues like the **Instituto Cultural Peruano Norteamericano** (corner of Húsares de Junín and Venezuela, ☎ 04/423–2512) and the **Alianza Francesa** (San Martín 858, ☎ 04/423–2012).

Nightlife

The **Pussy Cat**, also known as Billy Bob's (Piérola 716, ☎ 04/423–3592), is a friendly cocktail lounge with a disco. The area around the Central Market, on the sixth block of Gamarra, is full of movie theaters.

Chiclayo

A lively commercial center, Chiclayo is both prosperous and easygoing, two qualities not often found in combination. It is not as big as Trujillo, 219 kilometers (131 miles) to the south, nor does it have as much preserved colonial architecture. However, the discovery in 1987 of the unlooted tomb of the Lord of Sipán set off a minor tourism boom. Chiclayo now provides a comfortable base from which to visit the tomb and other archaeological sites, as well as the famed Brüning Museum, all of which are in such nearby towns as Sipán and Lambayeque.

Visitor Information

Tourist police (Saenz Peña 836, ☎ 07/423–8112; ◷ Mon.–Sat. 8–6). **Touring and Automobile Club** (Calle Marte 120, Urbanización Santa Elena, ☎ 07/423–1821; ◷ Weekdays 9–5, Sat. 8–1).

Tour Operator

Indiana Tours (Colón 556, Chiclayo, ☎ 07/424–0833) can provide private guides for the ruins outside the city.

Exploring

The Moche and Chimú both had major administrative and religious centers in the area around Chiclayo, as did a third culture, the Lambayeque (Sicán), which flourished from about AD 700 until Chimor conquered it, around 1370.

The Moche **tomb of the Lord of Sipán**—saved from huaqueros in 1987 by renowned Peruvian archaeologist Walter Alva in a dramatic last-minute rescue—stands in the Huaca Rajada, a pyramid near the town of Sipán, about 35 kilometers (21 miles) south of Chiclayo. The trip out takes you through the fertile valley of Chancay, past sugar plantations, to a huge, fissured mud hill that is actually the Huaca Rajada. The smaller hill beside it is part of the pyramid, once connected to the bigger one by a platform. The three major tombs found in the smaller mound date from about AD 290 and earlier, and together form one of the most complete archaeological finds in the Western Hemisphere.

The most extravagant funerary objects were found in the tomb of the so-called Lord of Sipán, now filled with replicas placed exactly where the original objects were discovered; the originals, normally on view in the Museo Brüning in Lambayeque (*see below*), were touring the United States at press time (winter 1995) but should return by 1996. Among the highlights are exquisitely worked gold and silver necklaces, masks, nose ornaments, pectorals, armor, and other objects. A small museum next to the tomb has excellent interpretive displays that describe in Spanish the discovery of the complex and the Moche culture. The dig at the complex is ongoing, and other tombs continue to be excavated. *No* ☎. ☛ *Entry fee.*

About 15 minutes' drive east from Sipán is the 8th-century Moche capital, **Pampa Grande**, a 6-square-kilometer (2.3-square-mile) archaeological complex that contains one of the largest pyramids ever built in the Andes, the 178-foot-high **Huaca Fortaleza.** Pampa Grande marked the final years of the Moche empire, and for unknown reasons, the city was put to the torch and abandoned near the beginning of the 9th century. *No* ☎. ☛ *Free.*

With the decline of the Moche civilization, legend has it that a lord called Naymlap arrived in the Lambayeque Valley, accompanied by his wife and retinue and a fleet of balsa boats. Naymlap and his 12 sons founded the Lambayeque dynasty, whose cities included the immense pyramid complex of **Túcume,** some 35 kilometers (21 miles) northwest of Chiclayo. Here, from the heights of the natural rock hill **El Purgatorio,** you can see 26 giant adobe pyramids and dozens of smaller ones spread across a desert sprinkled with hardy little algarobo trees. Norwegian explorer Thor Heyerdahl, of *Kon-Tiki* fame, has built a home here and is directing excavations of the pyramids. *No* ☎. ☛ *Entry fee.*

These and other pre-Inca cultures, including the Cupisnique, Chavín, Moche, Chimú, and Sicán, are explored at the **Museo Brüning** in Lambayeque, 12 kilometers (7 miles) north of Chiclayo. Directed by archaeologist Walter Alva, it is one of the finest archaeological collections in Peru. Among the highlights are the Sipán treasures; a group of ceramic frogs dating from 1200 BC; a small gold statue of a woman known as the *Venus de Frías,* 100 BC–AD 300; and Moche and Sicán ceramics. The museum has excellent interpretive displays, but since the legends are in Spanish, you may wish to go with a guide. *Av. Huamachuco s/n,* ☎ *07/428–2110.* ☛ *Entry fee. Closed weekend and holiday afternoons.*

Shopping

Chiclayo's market, on Avenida Balta, is justly famed for its colorful mix of fresh food and live animals, handicrafts such as ceramics and weavings, and herbalists' stalls selling a wide variety of herbs and charms from local *curanderos* (folk healers). If the subject interests you, ask at one of the stalls for an evening session with a local shaman.

Dining

Chiclayo is most famous for a pastry called the "king kong" (sometimes bastardized into *kinkón*), a large, round, crumbly cookie with *manjar blanco*—a very sweet filling made of sweetened or condensed milk and cinnamon boiled down until it is very thick and caramel colored—in the center. Another local specialty is *pescado seco* (dried fish, often a ray), used in stews or fried. For price-category definitions, *see* Dining *in* Peru Essentials, *below.*

$$$ Restaurante Típico Fiestas. The decor is rather garish at this restaurant in the Tres de Octubre district, but the main attraction is the chef, whose showcases of *comida norteña* (typical food of northern Peru) in Lima have earned him kudos. Everything served is outstanding, especially the shellfish, cebiche, and tacu tacu. ✗ *Salaverry 1820,* ☎ *07/422– 8441. V. Lunch only.*

$$ Las Tinajas. A woven-cane roof, wicker chairs, and ceiling fans give this simple restaurant a tropical flair. The seafood is top-notch. ✗ *Elías Aguirre 952, no* ☎. *No credit cards. Lunch only.*

$$ La Terraza. Chiclayo's version of penthouse dining, this fourth-floor restaurant has plush blue velour and steel chairs and a panoramic view of the city. The food is regional, with an emphasis on seafood and co-mida criolla. ✗ *Elías Aguirre 635, no* ☎. *AE, DC, MC, V.*

Lodging

For price-category definitions, *see* Lodging *in* Peru Essentials, *below.*

$$ Garza Hotel. A pleasant poolside patio and bar, cable TV in each room—
★ a rarity in Peru—and very friendly staff make this modern, centrally located establishment the nicest in Chiclayo. The restaurant, with attractive stucco walls, a fireplace, and brass chandelier, serves excellent regional cuisine. ⊡ *Bolognesi 756,* ☎ *07/422–8171. 71 rooms. Restaurant, pool. AE, DC, MC, V.*

$$ Hotel de Turistas. Chiclayo's biggest hotel is a bit run-down and quite noisy, thanks to traffic nearby. Some rooms, decorated in a mélange of dark wood and green vinyl, have a balcony overlooking the pool. ⊡ *Federico Villareal 135,* ☎ *07/423–4911. 128 rooms. Restaurant, bar, pool, dance club. AE, DC, MC, V.*

$ Inca Hotel. Although the hallways look somewhat grimy, the rooms are clean, with indoor-outdoor carpeting and ceiling fans. Rooms not facing the street have less light but are quieter. ⊡ *Luis Gonzales 622,* ☎ *07/423–5931,* ⅢX *07/422–7651. 69 rooms. Restaurant. AE, DC, MC, V.*

The Arts

Festivals

The little town of **Monsefu,** 12 kilometers (7 miles) south of Chiclayo on the Pan-American Highway, has an annual crafts fair July 27–29 known as the **FEXTICUM.** Among the wares are woven textiles (especially in cotton), ponchos, and blankets, woven straw objects, and ceramics. You can join in the general merriment fueled by *chicha* (maize beer) and see marinera performances as well as prancing *caballo de paso* horses. On August 5, a festival known as **Cruz de Chalpón,** or **Cruz de Motupe,** takes place in the town of **Motupe,** some 80 kilometers (48 miles) northwest of Chiclayo on the Pan-American, drawing thousands of religious pilgrims. For more information about both events, contact the Oficina Regional de Turismo (Elías Aguirre 830, Office 202, Chiclayo, ☎ 07/422–7776).

Nightlife

There are a few peñas in town where you can listen to criollo ballads. These simple but friendly bars include **Brisas del Mar** (Elías Aguirre, no ☎) and **Los Hermanos Balcázar** (Lora y Cordero 1150, no ☎).

THE SOUTH

More Spanish than other regions in the country, southern Peru is a dry land of dusty coast and rocky hills garlanded with unexpectedly verdant oases. Although earlier civilizations have left such traces as the mysterious Nazca lines, European culture is firmly entrenched in the plazas and convents of Arequipa and other cities and in the vineyards of Ica. The animals common to all of Peru's desert coast are concentrated and protected in the Paracas National Reserve, Peru's mainland version of the Galápagos Islands.

Arriving and Departing

Peru's coastal south can be explored by land or by air, but combining both means of transportation is the most efficient way to see the region.

By Plane

Aero Continente, AeroPerú, Americana, Faucett, and **Imperial Air** fly daily from Lima and, three or four times a week, from Juliaca, near Puno, to the Arequipa airport, **Rodríguez Ballón,** which is 7 kilometers (4 miles) from town. They also have direct service from Cuzco.

Aerocondor offers flights in smaller passenger planes from Lima to Ica and Nazca, as well as between both. The airline also conducts overflights of the Nazca lines, with planes departing from and returning to Lima, Ica, or Nazca itself.

By Train

Twice a week, **ENAFER** runs a night train (10 hours) between Arequipa (corner Tacna and Huáscar, ☎ 05/421–5350) and Puno. Be sure to request the safer, more comfortable Pullman class, which costs about $20. For current schedule information call ENAFER in Lima (☎ 01/428–9440 or 01/427–1824).

By Car

Depending on your appreciation of desert scenery, the trip south from Lima via the Pan-American Highway may strike you as starkly beautiful or grimly monotonous. Either way, the government has invested heavily in road repairs, and at least for now the highway is in mainly good condition.

By Bus

Cruz del Sur (Jirón Quilca 531, Lima, ☎ 01/427–1311), **Ormeño** (Javier Prado Este 1059, Lima, or Av. Carlos Zavala 177, Lima, ☎ 01/427–3650), and **Tepsa** (Paseo de la República 129, Lima, ☎ 01/432–1233) all have daily service from Lima to Pisco, Ica, Nazca, and Arequipa.

Tour Operators

Most Lima travel agencies offer three- to seven-day minivan tours of Paracas, Ica, and Nazca. Some include Arequipa on the overland tour, but ask carefully about the condition of the Pan-American Highway before going. Operators offering overland trips from Lima to southern Peru include **Explorandes** (Tudela y Varela 450, San Isidro, ☎ 01/442–1738 or 01/445–0532, FAX 01/445–4686), **Hirca Travel** (Bellavista 518, Miraflores, ☎ and FAX 01/447–3807), and **Lima Tours** (Box 4340, Lima, ☎ 01/427–6720 or 01/427–6624, FAX 01/426–9878 or 01/426–2010).

Pisco and the Paracas National Reserve

Pisco, a run-down port town, is mainly interesting as a jumping-off point for the Paracas National Reserve, 15 kilometers (10 miles) down the coast. The reserve lies on a desolate, sand-swept peninsula and includes a cluster of offshore islands. As inhospitable as the landscape looks—a hybrid of Saudi Arabia and the moon—it includes stunning beaches and is home to lizards, sea lions, flamingos, pelicans, and other sea birds (the reserve has one of the highest concentrations of marine birds in the world), as well as the occasional condor.

Visitor Information

One of the better tourist agencies in Pisco that offer advice, guided tours of the reserve and the area, and trips to the Ballestas Islands (*see* Exploring, *below*) is **Ballestas Travel Service** (San Francisco 249, ☎ 03/453–3095; in Lima ☎ 01/476–4115 or 01/476–5861). For information on the reserve, contact the Dirección de Areas Protegidas y Fauna Silvestre, **INRENA** (Petirrojos 355, Urb. El Palomar, San Isidro, Lima, ☎ 01/441–0425, FAX 01/441–4606).

Exploring

Pisco has little of special interest to the visitor and seems to lie under a permanent fishy miasma caused by the nearby fish-meal factories. There is a typical Peruvian main square, with some interesting colonial buildings, a bustling market, and many hotels, restaurants, and travel agencies. Buses and taxis shuttle back and forth from the market to the reserve office and to Chaco, the starting point for boat trips to the Ballestas Islands.

Besides wildlife areas and stunning beaches, the **Paracas National Reserve** (no ☎; ☛ Entry fee) encompasses two fishing villages and a small port, Puerto General San Martín. You can explore the peninsular section of the reserve in a day, but if you want to see the islands and spend some time on the beach, allot two days.

At the park office, you will find maps and a museum (no ☎) devoted to natural history and archaeology. Humans have lived in the area for thousands of years, and the Paracas culture, which produced some of the most exquisite woven textiles in pre-Columbian America, thrived here from about 500 BC to AD 200. (The finest examples of Paracas textiles are in the Museo Histórico Regional in Ica and the Museo de Arqueología y Antropología in Lima.) You can hike the 12 kilometers (9 miles) from the museum to the **Mirador de Lobos,** a cliff overlooking a raucous sea lion colony. Just before the cliff are beaches that can be reached on foot, but don't swim alone—there are no lifeguards on duty. It's an easier walk to the flamingo colonies (best seen in June and July) on the north side of the peninsula. Be aware that although many visitors walk and bicycle alone on the peninsula, there have been reports of assaults on lone hikers.

Just offshore lie the **Ballestas Islands,** also part of the reserve. Here seals and sea lions stake a noisy claim to the beaches below rocky outcrops white with the guano (droppings) of thousands of sea birds. Pelicans, boobies, terns, cormorants, and even the small Peruvian penguin vie for nesting space on the rocks in a flapping, rowdy mass of feathers. A boat tour will take five hours in a *lancha* (a large launch) or two hours in a smaller *deslizador* speedboat. The slower launch takes slightly longer to round the islands, but most of the extra time is spent on a much less exciting haul between the mainland and the islands, so the speedboat is recommended for all but the most dedicated. Most hotels in Pisco or Paracas will arrange the trip for you, including transport from the hotel, or you can book it in Pisco at a travel agency or a kiosk on the Plaza de Armas. The **Hotel Paracas** (*see* Lodging, *below*) runs its own 3½-hour cruise. To be safe, take a cruise leaving before 9:30 AM; as the day wears on, the winds get high and the sea very choppy.

Shopping

It is illegal to export whole Paracas weavings. While you can purchase small boxes with lids covered in squares of ancient textiles, you should be aware that by buying these trinkets, you are encouraging the destruction of the weavings. Turtle shells also abound, but since the animal is in danger of extinction, much the same principle applies.

Sports and the Outdoors

Beaches

The Paracas National Reserve has lovely, if isolated, beaches. None have lifeguards, and only strong swimmers should swim outside the sheltered bays. There are jellyfish in these waters. The beaches are often deserted but are becoming popular with Limeños on weekends, especially in summer. Try not to go alone, and be warned that there are very few amenities. Get a map from the park office before you try **La Mina** or **Yumaque** beaches, or the longer, straighter beach at **Arquillo.**

Bicycling

Although some of the roads are in poor shape, they are largely free of traffic, making the reserve one of the few spots along the Peruvian coast that are suitable for bike riding. A map of the reserve is available in the park office. The prevailing northerly winds can make the outward trip tough going but the return a breeze. The **Viento Sur** agency at the Hotel Paracas (Los Libertadores 173, Chaco, ☎ 03/422–1736) rents mountain bikes.

Fishing

The **Hotel Paracas** (*see* Lodging, *below*) can arrange for fishing trips in Paracas Bay, where mackerel is the most likely catch. The hotel will provide transportation and will lend you a hook and a roll of fishing line (no rentals of more sophisticated tackle). No fishing license is required.

Dining

At Chaco, just before the national park and the starting point for most cruises to the Ballestas Islands, the seafront is lined with simple fish restaurants. The floors of these eateries usually consist of undecorated cement, and the furnishings and service are rustic, but the food is excellent, prices are cheap, and portions are enormous. For those whose tastes include hastening the demise of endangered species, *tortuga*, or turtle, is available. More conscientious diners will stick with flounder, sea bass, mackerel, shellfish, or the omnipresent cebiche. The only thing resembling fine dining is in Pisco (*see below*). For price-category definitions, *see* Dining *in* Peru Essentials, *below*.

$$ **As de Oro's.** Always crowded with locals and recently installed in new premises, this is one of Pisco's finest restaurants. The pink walls and the curved bar, all mirrors and black steel, seem to be an attempt at upscale decor and may not be to everyone's taste, but the food will be: Try the miraculously greaseless *pejerrey*, boneless strips of mackerel dipped in batter and fried. ✕ *Av. San Martín 472,* ☎ *03/453–2010 or 03/453–2258. AE, V. Closed Mon.*

Lodging

The Hotel Paracas is really your best bet, but if you choose to spend the night in Pisco, you can pick one of two equally featureless hotels within a couple of blocks of each other, both of which were built within the last five years. For price-category definitions, *see* Lodging *in* Peru Essentials, *below*.

$$$ **Hotel Paracas.** This popular resort near the entrance to the Paracas National Reserve has flower-bedecked bungalows with terraces overlooking the bay. Its only drawbacks are a sporadic odor from a nearby fish-meal factory and reports of occasional thefts from the rooms. The restaurant is excellent but expensive. 🏨 *Los Libertadores 173, Chaco,* ☎ *03/422–1736,* FAX *03/422–5379; Lima* ☎ *01/446–5079 or 01/446–5138,* FAX *01/447–6548. 105 rooms. Restaurant, bar, pool, miniature golf, tennis court, boating, travel services. AE, DC, MC, V.*

$$ **El Candelabro.** International decor, minibars, and TVs in all the rooms—plus dust behind most of the doors—are among the few salient points of this hotel. 🏨 *Jirón Callao 198, Pisco,* ☎ *03/453–2620 or 03/453–3045; Lima* ☎ *01/435–2156. 24 rooms. Bar, cafeteria. No credit cards.*

$$ **Embassy Suite Hotel.** This is marginally the best equipped of Pisco's accommodations and is therefore slightly more expensive. Rooms are functional rather than extravagant, although they all have satellite TV. 🏨 *Av. San Martín 202, Pisco,* ☎ *03/453–2040; Lima* ☎ *01/472–3525. 56 rooms. Restaurant, bar, conference room. No credit cards.*

$$ **Hostal El Mirador.** Cement walls and linoleum floors give this place little charm, but the owner is helpful, the rooms are fairly clean, and the setting overlooking the Bay of Paracas is lovely. 🏨 *Ribera del Mar, Entrada a Chaco,* ☎ *03/422–0212; Lima* ☎ *01/432–5757,* FAX *01/432–0109. 35 rooms. Restaurant, bar, pool under construction at press time (winter 1995). V.*

Ica

Ica, a colonial town 93 kilometers (56 miles) south of Pisco, has one of the most pleasant climates in Peru—hot, dry days and cool nights. It is in the heart of Peruvian wine country and is the center of pisco production. A visit to the region's bodegas (wineries) provides a glimpse of old Peru, when the area was famous for its gracious lifestyle amid the desert and for its high-stepping caballo de paso horses.

Visitor Information

Oficina Regional de Turismo (Av. Grau 150, ☎ and ℻ 03/423–3416; ⊙ Weekdays 7:30 AM–1:15 PM). **Touring and Automobile Club of Peru** (Av. J. M. Manzanilla 523, ☎ 03/423–5061 or 03/422–1434; ⊙ 24 hours).

Tour Operators

Costa Linda (Prolongación Ayabaca 509, ☎ and ℻ 03/423–4251; Lima ☎ and ℻ 01/451–1733) and **Pelican Travel Service** (Independencia 156, Oficina E, ☎ 03/422–5211 or 03/423–4046, ℻ 03/423–4688) offer tours of the city and can arrange trips to Paracas and to the Nazca lines (although, at around $110, flying over the lines from Ica is roughly twice as expensive as flying from Nazca).

Exploring

Chilean and Argentine wines generally outstrip Peruvian wines in quality and price; but some of the finer Peruvian labels hold their own in competition, and Peruvians disparage Chile's attempts at producing pisco. The winery most convenient to visit is the Bodega Vista Alegre (La Tinguiña, km 2, ☎ 03/423-1432), about 3 kilometers (2 miles) outside of town. Eight kilometers (5 miles) beyond it is the Bodega Tacama (La Tinguiña, km 10, ☎ 03/423–1422; closed Sat. PM and Sun.), which produces some of Peru's finest wines; try the Blanco de Blancos. About 24 kilometers (15 miles) south of Ica, the Bodega Ocucaje (Pan-American Hwy. S, km 336, ☎ 03/422-0215; Lima ☎ 01/440-7977, ℻ 01/428-7145) is attached to a tourist center, principally comprising a hotel and restaurant. At all three bodegas, you can see wine presses and cellars and taste samples.

Ica's **Museo Regional** is a little dingy and has sparse explanatory notes in Spanish only, yet this small museum covering a thousand years of pre-Columbian history possesses some splendid Paracas textiles, still colorful despite the passage of centuries. From the Nazca culture, which flourished in the Nazca, Pisco, and Ica valleys around AD 500, a remarkable ceramic sculpture shows a pregnant princess pointing at her belly—and in profile shows the fetus in her womb. Many ancient Peruvian civilizations carried out cosmetic cranial deformations, the products of which are on display; perhaps the resulting headaches were what led the Paracas and other ancient societies to practice skull trepanations and simple brain surgery. Examples of that medical handiwork are also on display. Behind the museum, a 1:500 scale model of the Nazca lines, complete with viewing platform, offers a substitute for visitors whose stomachs or budgets can't support the flight over the real thing. *Av. Ayabaca s/n,* ☎ *03/423–4383.* ☛ *Entry fee. Closed Sun.* PM.

A 10-minute drive southwest from downtown Ica will take you to the oasis of **Huacachina,** a green gem nestled amid towering sand dunes. In the 1920s, wealthy Peruvians flocked to this resort beneath the palm trees crowding the shores of a lagoon. After decades of decline, the resort is on the upswing. The lagoon's soft, sandy bottom reportedly makes swimming hazardous, although that does not deter the locals who come regularly for a dip on weekends.

Shopping

For wines or pisco, buy either in the bodegas themselves, where the wines are slightly discounted, or in the liquor stores clustered around the Plaza de Armas. Look for Tacama's Blanco de Blancos and Occucaje's rich red Fond du Cave.

Dining

Ica is an important pecan-growing region, and pecans are reasonably priced in the stores around the Plaza de Armas, the town's main square. Dried fruits and nuts in a sugary-sweet coating, called *tejas,* are another favorite local snack available in many shops around town, although **Delicias Ica** (Salaverry 220, ☎ 03/423–4127) has a particularly good selection. Besides the options below, some of the best dining in Ica is at the **Las Dunas** and **Mossone** hotels (*see* Lodging, *below*). For price-category definitions, *see* Dining *in* Peru Essentials, *below.*

$$ **El Otro Peñoncito.** This friendly, relaxed restaurant serves Peruvian and international cuisine. The fettucini *con ajo,* with a spicy sauce similar to that used in the traditional *papa a la huancaina* (potatoes in a spicy cheese sauce), is intriguing. ✕ *Bolívar 255,* ☎ *03/423–3921. DC, MC, V.*

$$ **Pizzería Venezia.** There's a lot more than just pizza here, served by a friendly staff. The spaghetti Bolognese and grilled steak are recommended. ✕ *Bolívar 440,* ☎ *03/423–2241. V. Closed Mon.*

Lodging

If you are planning to visit Ica during the Vendimia, the wine harvest festival in March, be sure to reserve a hotel room at least a month in advance. One treat available only during the festival is *cachina,* a partially fermented wine. For price-category definitions, *see* Lodging *in* Peru Essentials, *below.*

$$$$ **Hotel Las Dunas.** A resort hidden amid sand dunes, this colonial-style
★ complex is a favorite getaway for Lima families. It is one of the few resorts in Peru that has special activities for children, including a skateboard rink and rentals and sandboarding equipment; baby-sitters and cradles are available for hire. Spacious rooms with balconies are set in clusters of whitewashed buildings among palm-lined canals and lush lawns. At the restaurant, you can dine poolside or in a gazebo-like structure on such dishes as flounder with seafood sauce and a spicy *lomo saltado* of steak, tomatoes, potatoes, and onions. Flights over the Nazca lines leave from the hotel's airstrip. ☎ *Av. La Angostura 400,* ☎ *03/423–1031,* FAX *03/423–1007; Lima* ☎ *01/442–3090,* FAX *01/442–4180. 109 rooms. Restaurant ($$$), bar, cafeteria, 2 pools, sauna, 9-hole golf course, tennis court, exercise room, horseback riding, dance club. AE, DC, MC, V.*

$$$ **Hotel de Turistas.** The decor and design at this hotel just on the edge of town, half-way to Huacachina, appear to have been preserved without change since the 1960s; however, this former state hotel was privatized in 1995 and was undergoing modernization at press time (winter 1995). In any case, the rooms are light, airy, and comfortable. The restaurant serves traditional dishes from the area and has a reasonable $10 set lunch. ☎ *Av. Los Maestros s/n,* ☎ *03/423–3330,* FAX *03/423–3320. 60 rooms. Restaurant ($$), bar, cafeteria, pool, dance club. AE, DC, MC, V.*

$$$ **Hotel Mossone.** Set in a century-old mansion that was a plush resort
★ hotel in the 1920s, the Mossone, fully restored in 1989, is a soothing trip back in time. The rooms, with parquet floors and bright floral cot-

ton upholstery and bedspreads, are built around an interior garden patio. Dining is on a veranda overlooking the Huacachina lagoon. Come for lunch or dinner if you can't spend the night; the comida criolla is excellent, especially the papa a la huancaina. ⊞ *Balneario de Huacachina,* ☎ *03/423–1651 or 03/423–6136,* FAX *03/423–6137. 53 rooms. Restaurant ($$), bar, pool. AE, DC, MC, V.*

$$ **Hostal El Carmelo.** At this colonial-style, slate-roof hotel 5 kilometers (3 miles) from downtown Ica, rooms are in several buildings around a flower-filled courtyard. An inviting garden house has wicker furniture and a 19th-century wine press. ⊞ *Pan-American Hwy., km 301,* ☎ *03/423–2191,* FAX *03/423–2191. 40 rooms. Restaurant, bar, pool. DC, V.*

$$ **Hostal Silmar.** This budget hotel a block from the Plaza de Armas has clean, comfortable, and carpeted rooms. All have TVs and phones— quite posh for the money. ⊞ *Castrovirreyna 110,* ☎ *03/423–5089. 17 rooms. No credit cards.*

The Arts

Festivals

The **Vendimia,** or wine festival, is a series of celebrations in early March that include wine tastings, displays of the high-stepping caballo de paso horses, and a fair in the city stadium. Torchlit all-night processions highlight the **festivals of the Señor de Luren** (Holy Week and the third Monday of October).

Nazca

Nazca, 141 kilometers (85 miles) south of Ica, is the site of one of the world's great archaeological mysteries: the geoglyphs known as the Nazca lines, drawn on the rock-strewn Pampa de San José, 20 kilometers (12 miles) north of the city. Ranging from straight lines to geometric forms to stylized human and animal shapes, these giant markings—the straight lines vary in length from ½ to 8 kilometers (0.3 to 5 miles)—have stirred the popular imagination for decades.

Visitor Information

Information and tours of the pre-Columbian ruins in the area are available from **Alegría Tours** (Lima 168, Nazca, ☎ and FAX 03/452–2444).

Exploring

Although theories about the origin of the Nazca lines include extraterrestrial intervention, two main schools of thought prevail in the archaeological community. One—propounded by German mathematician Maria Reiche, who has dedicated her life to studying and preserving the lines—suggests that they were part of an immense astronomical calendar noting the rainy season in the highlands (where Nazca's water supply originates) and seasonal changes in the region's climate. The other theory suggests that the lines were physically and ritually related to the flow of water from the mountains to and across the Nazca plain. What is clear is that between 1900 BC and AD 660, the Nazca people etched the lines through the desert's dark surface layer into underlying, lighter-color soil and then outlined them with stones. The most famous drawings are in the shapes of animals, such as the 150-foot-long spider and the 300-foot-long monkey.

The best way to see the lines is from the air, in one of the many small planes that offer overflights. The trip is not recommended for anyone prone to airsickness; others are advised to fly early in the morning, when there is less turbulence (and don't eat just before). **Aero Ica** (Hotel La Maison Suisse, ☎ 03/452–2434; Lima ☎ and FAX 01/440–1030) and **Aero Nasca** (Ignacio Morsesky 120, ☎ 03/452–2297) offer 45-minute overflights from the Nazca airport for $55 per person. The former also offers flights in a light aircraft from Lima, for one or two days, taking in the lines and Paracas. You can also charter a plane at the Hotel Las Dunas in Ica (*see* Lodging *in* Ica, *above*) for $140.

Dining

For price-category definitions, *see* Dining *in* Peru Essentials, *below.*

$ **La Taberna.** With a ceiling fan over the bar and live music most Saturdays, this popular criollo restaurant is so laid-back that many guests sign their names on the walls. ✗ *Lima 321*, ☎ *03/452–3322. V.*

Lodging

For price-category definitions, *see* Lodging *in* Peru Essentials, *below.*

$$$ **Hotel de la Borda.** Surrounded by cotton fields in an 80-year-old hacienda, this somewhat isolated, old-fashioned hotel 1½ kilometers (1 mile) from Nazca airport offers a taste of coastal farm life. Rooms are set around a huge garden. Recreational options include horseback riding and excursions in a jeep or by mountain bike. ⌸ *Pan-American Hwy. S, km 447*, ☎ *03/452–2576. 39 rooms. Restaurant, pool. DC, MC, V.*

$$$ **Hotel de Turistas.** Guest rooms are laid out around a courtyard oasis
★ and decorated with wrought-iron headboards and charcoal drawings; many rooms have a sun porch beside a sunken garden. Meals are served on a tiled walkway beside the courtyard. An occasional treat is the evening lectures that Nazca expert Maria Reiche's sister, Renata, sometimes gives here. ⌸ *Jirón Bolognesi*, ☎ *03/452–2293. 34 rooms. Restaurant, bar, pool, tennis court. AE, DC, MC, V.*

$$$ **Maison Suisse.** Conveniently located by the airport, this hotel has gardens and comfortable, if somewhat graceless, rooms with old-fashioned wood furniture. The suites have hot tubs. ⌸ *Pan-American Hwy. S, km 445*, ☎ *03/452–2434. 32 rooms, 6 suites. Restaurant, pool. AE, DC, MC, V.*

Arequipa

Perhaps the proudest and most Spanish of Peruvian cities, the "city of the volcanoes" is in the department of the same name, which has been dubbed the Independent Republic of Arequipa. Arequipeños love their city and are highly resentful of the notion that Peruvian life begins and ends in Lima.

Founded in 1540 by the Spaniards in the shadow of the snowcapped El Misti volcano, Arequipa is today a thriving city of 1 million that has somehow managed to preserve the best of its traditions, embodied by its broad, colonial Plaza de Armas. Situated at 7,500 feet above sea level, Arequipa enjoys constant sunshine, warm days (averaging 23°C, or 73°F), and comfortable nights (14°C, or 57°F).

Visitor Information

Oficina de Información Turística (Portal de la Municipalidad 110, Plaza de Armas, ☎ 05/421–1021; closed afternoons and weekends). **Touring and Automobile Club of Peru** (Goyeneche 313, ☎ 05/421–5640). **Tourism Police** (Jerusalén 317, ☎ 05/25–4000 ext. 272).

Tour Operators

A list of the members of the **Asociación de Guías de Turismo,** a local organization of professional guides, is available from member Melchor Delgado (☎ 05/425–2589). **Lima Tours Arequipa** (Santa Catalina 120, ☎ 05/424–2271 or 05/424–2293, FAX 05/424–1654) offers an excellent orientation tour of the city, as well as other services.

Exploring

Arequipeños call their home "the white city" because of the grayish-white local volcanic rock, *sillar,* used to build most of its colonial buildings and churches. The city's architectural crowning glory is the **Santa Catalina Convent,** a miniature walled town founded in 1579 a few blocks from what is now downtown's Plaza de Armas. Twenty nuns and three novices live there today; at the Dominican convent's height, there were 400 women residents—nuns, slaves, and servants. Once inside its high walls, the nuns never again left the five-acre convent, which had its own cemetery. This city of women was a faithful reflection of the highly stratified Peruvian society of the time: Novices had to pay to join the convent, and nuns were separated according to how much they had paid—the higher the "contribution," the more luxurious the cell. Nuns (or their slaves) prepared their own food in the tiny kitchens each cell included. The convent's residents took up communal life in 1871. It's a good idea to hire a guide at the entrance (tip about $2.50), but leave some time to wander the twisting streets on your own. *Corner Santa Catalina and Ugarte, no ☎.* ☞ *Entry fee.*

The colonial aristocracy left its mark in the fine mansions of downtown Arequipa, many of which you may enter through high, arched portals. Tall gateways were a 17th-century status symbol, designed to allow the passage of an armored knight on horseback bearing an upright lance. Two particularly striking mansions are open to the public. A block from the Plaza de Armas is **Casa Ricketts** (Calle San Francisco 108, ☎ 05/421–5060; ☞ Free; closed weekends), once the archbishop's palace. Today it houses a small museum displaying colonial paintings, books, costumes, and furniture. **Casa del Moral** (corner of Moral and Bolívar, ☎ 05/421–3171; ☞ Free; closed weekends), a block from Santa Catalina, has a stunning sillar portal carved in a mestizo design (or Baroque mestizo, a style blending indigenous and Spanish motifs) that combines puma heads with snakes emerging from their mouths and a Spanish coat of arms.

Just off the Plaza de Armas, **La Compañía church** consists of a fine series of buildings in traditional Arequipa style. The 1525 church is well worth seeing, and once inside, you should also visit the **St. Ignatius chapel,** the former church sacristy, covered from floor to dome with 17th-century paintings from the Cuzco school. The former cloisters, now converted into shops, contain two fine courtyards with carved-stone pillars. They may be entered from General Morán or Palacio Viejo. *Corner of General Morán and Alvarez Thomas, no ☎.* ☞ *Entry fee (chapel). May close Sun.*

Another religious center well worth visiting is **La Recoleta Monastery,** just across the Chili River from the city's colonial center. Founded in 1648, the Franciscan monastery comprises a huge ancient library, a museum of the Amazon, a colonial-art collection, and, of course, cloisters and cells. Hire a guide to make sure you don't miss the library (tip about $2). *Calle Recoleta, ☎ 05/422–3058.* ☞ *Entry fee. Officially closed Sun., although if you ask nicely, you may be given a tour anyway.*

From Recoleta, you can take a pleasant stroll through two charming colonial suburbs. **Yanahuara,** within walking distance of the city center and home to many *picantería* restaurants (*see* Dining, *below*), has an overlook with a stunning view of the city and El Misti. Uphill from Yanahuara is **Cayma,** whose 16th-century church is an outstanding example of local colonial architecture. Built of sillar and decorated with mestizo ornamentation, the church, like most of those in Arequipa, avoids the cluttered ostentation typical of colonial churches in other Peruvian cities.

Shopping

The Plaza San Francisco is the site of a year-round **handicrafts fair,** open daily until about 7 PM. Jewelry and knickknacks made of Arequipa agate, as well as local handicrafts (Arequipa is known for its leather work and alpaca textiles), are sold at boutiques behind the cathedral, on the narrow, pedestrians-only **Pasaje Catedral.** The Ibérica brand of chocolates and sweets, made and widely available locally, are among the best in Peru.

Dining

Arequipa's cuisine is something special among the comida criolla. Perhaps the most famous dish is *rocoto relleno*—a very hot pepper, large and red, stuffed with a mixture of meat, onions, and raisins and then baked. The dish may bring tears to your eyes. Comida Arequipeña, however, is not always spicy. There are also rich, succulent stews, like *adobo,* a beef stew that is particularly popular as a cure for hangovers! Try to at least sample the *cuy* (guinea pig), an Andean staple. You'll find comida Arequipeña served at picanterías, casual restaurants open only for lunch. For price-category definitions, *see* Dining *in* Peru Essentials, *below*.

$$$ **La Posada del Puente.** Leather-shaded hanging lamps and ocher walls,
★ daytime views of the Chili River and the volcano, and evening dining by candlelight make this Arequipa's most delightful restaurant. Pastas, including that old standby fettucine Alfredo, are excellent, and the wine list has a fine selection of Peruvian and Chilean wines. ✕ *Av. Bolognesi 101,* ☎ *05/425–3132. AE, DC, MC, V.*

$$$ **Sambambaias.** In a leafy suburb a 10-minute walk from the center of
★ town, this restaurant has pink decor, mirrors, and a pianist that may all strike you as charming or horribly kitsch, depending on your tastes. The food is almost certain to please, however, and (unusual for Peru) there is service to match. The place is run by a Brazilian, and the food is basically international—and splendidly presented. ✕ *Luna Pizarro 304, Vallecito,* ☎ *05/422–3657. AE, DC, MC, V.*

$$–$$$ **Tradición Arequipeña.** Just outside town, in the Paucarpata district, this restaurant offers the same traditional dishes and music as the picanterías, served in more comfortable surroundings. ✕ *Av. Dolores 111,* ☎ *05/424–2385. AE, DC, MC, V. Lunch only.*

$$ **El Café.** This clean, well-lit eatery with mirrored walls is extremely popular. Try the sandwiches and lomo saltado; the fresh fruit juices are also especially good. ✕ *San Francisco 125, no* ☎. *AE, DC, V.*

$$ **El Papayal.** Although its immediate neighbor, Tradición Arequipeña, is longer-established and probably a shade better in quality, this Paucarpata eatery wins on surroundings: It is set in a papaya orchard, from which it takes its name. ✕ *Av. Dolores 119,* ☎ *05/423–2968. MC, V. Lunch only.*

$$ **Pizzería San Antonio.** A curving white bar, white barstools, and bright yellow walls give this attractive little pizza-only restaurant a quirky flair. ✗ *Jerusalén 222,* ☎ *05/421–3950. MC, V.*

Lodging

For price-category definitions, *see* Lodging *in* Peru Essentials, *below.*

$$$ **Hotel Portal.** The location of this friendly hotel, next to the cathedral on the Plaza de Armas, couldn't be better. The guest rooms have whitewashed brick walls and colonial-style furniture, and the bar's terrace overlooks the square. ☎ *Portal de Flores 116,* ☎ *05/421–5530,* FAX *05/423–4374. 58 rooms. Restaurant, bar, indoor pool. AE, DC, MC, V.*

$$$ **La Posada del Puente.** Set amid gardens and patios, this charming hotel
★ is about 10 minutes from the Plaza de Armas. The whitewashed rooms, decorated in pastel colors, have small terraces with wicker furniture overlooking the river. ☎ *Av. Bolognesi 101,* ☎ *05/425–3132,* FAX *05/ 425–3576. 22 rooms. Restaurant, bar. AE, DC, MC, V.*

$$ **El Conquistador.** Housed in a restored colonial mansion with sillar walls and a cobblestone courtyard, this hotel also has a modern section with rooms overlooking a garden. All the rooms have modern furniture and brown-striped bedspreads. ☎ *Calle Mercaderes 409,* ☎ *05/421–2916,* FAX *05/421–8987. 27 rooms. Cafeteria. AE, DC, MC, V.*

$$ **Hotel Maisón Plaza.** At this small hostelry in a colonial building on the Plaza de Armas, the parquet-floor rooms are clean but somewhat dark. The obvious lure is a super location at budget prices. ☎ *Portal San Agustín,* ☎ *05/421–8931. 18 rooms. AE, V.*

$ **La Casa de Mi Abuela.** A ramshackle complex of houses turned into a hotel, "my grandmother's house" has lovely gardens and homey, wood-paneled rooms with worn easy chairs. Some even have a small kitchen. Popular with the younger crowd, the hotel is six blocks from the Plaza de Armas. ☎ *Jerusalén 606,* ☎ *05/424–1206,* FAX *05/424–2761. 32 rooms. Cafeteria, playground. No credit cards.*

The Arts and Nightlife

The **Instituto Cultural Peruano Norteamericano** (Melgar 109, ☎ 05/424–2493) often hosts evening concerts of traditional and classical music. **El Sillar** (Santa Catalina 215, no ☎) is a peña bar offering traditional Andean music from 8 PM nightly. The **Bar Romie** (Plaza San Francisco, ☎ 05/423–4465 or 05/423–5306; closed Sun. and Mon.) is a peña with a more eclectic selection that also embraces popular music; it opens around 10 PM.

Colca Canyon

Said to be the deepest canyon in the world, twice as deep as the Grand Canyon, the Colca Canyon is a rare blend of natural and man-made beauty. Surrounded by snowcapped mountains and home to immense Andean condors, the Colca is also the site of a vast pre-Columbian agricultural terracing network.

Visitor Information

There is no tourist office for the canyon. For information on the **Reserva Nacional de Aguada Blanca,** contact the Dirección de Areas Protegidas, INRENA, in Lima (Petirrojos 355, Urbanización El Palomar, San Isidro, ☎ 01/441–0425, FAX 01/441–4606).

Arriving and Departing

It's possible to take a guided day trip to the canyon from Arequipa. However, it involves about 10 grueling hours on the road and allows only two in the canyon itself, which, with all there is to see, seems almost criminal. (In fact, the Ministry of Industry and Tourism has tried to ban day trips to the Colca.) **Transcontinental Tours** (Puente Bolognesi 132, Arequipa, ☎ 05/421–3843, FAX 05/421–8608) conducts overnight trips and will arrange lodging; if you insist, other agencies will do the same. Don't let them convince you, as they often try, that "a day trip is more than enough." It's not—not if you travel overland. An alternative is to charter a flight from the airport at Arequipa through **AQP** (☎ 05/424–2030, FAX 05/425–6068), a local charter airline. The flight lasts about a half hour, and the cost varies according to the number of passengers on board.

Exploring

About 150 kilometers (93 miles) of rough driving from Arequipa brings you to the magnificent Colca Canyon, slicing a green and fertile trough through rocky, barren mountains. The road takes you through the **Reserva Nacional de Aguada Blanca,** where herds of graceful, long-necked vicuñas graze. Once you arrive at the canyon, be on the lookout for Andean condors; the best place to spot them is from the **Cruz del Condor** overlook in mid-canyon. Colca's complex of agricultural terraces is, in its way, as impressive as Machu Picchu—especially since, 450 years after the Spanish conquest, they are still in use (the crops are corn and the indigenous, high-protein grains *quinoa* and *kiwicha*). In the canyon's unspoiled Andean villages, people of the Collaguas and Cabana tribes still wear their traditional costumes and embroidered hats.

Sports and the Outdoors

Trekking

The Colca Valley offers spectacular scenery for hiking, especially around **Misma Mountain,** the source of the Amazon. **Transcontinental Tours** (Puente Bolognesi 132, Arequipa, ☎ 05/421–3843, FAX 05/421–8608) can arrange treks on foot or horseback; or contact Alejandro Rebaza at **TMR** (Coop. Lambramani C-4, Arequipa, ☎ 05/424–1498) for guided hikes and trail riding.

White-Water Rafting

The **Majes River,** which runs through the Colca Valley, is too rough for rafting in the central part of the valley. Between January and March, however, the river above Chivay offers excellent conditions. **Transcontinental Tours** (*see* Trekking, *above*) can outfit these trips. Below the Colca Canyon, toward Camaná, the conditions are once again superb for rafting. **Majes Tours** (Villa Flórida B-7, Cerro Colorado, Arequipa, ☎ 05/425–5819) outfits trips down this part of the river and offers accommodations at a rustic lodge on the river in Ongoro.

Dining and Lodging

For price-category definitions, *see* Dining *and* Lodging *in* Peru Essentials, *below.*

$ **La Posada del Inca.** This new budget hotel in Chivay is simple but homey. The rooms are airy, some with views of the mountains and the valley. ▣ *Chivay, Colca Valley, no* ☎. *24 rooms. Restaurant. No credit cards.*

PUNO AND LAKE TITICACA

Legend has it that Manco Capac and Mama Ocllo, founders of the Inca empire, emerged from the waters of Lake Titicaca. Indeed, as one watches the mysterious play of light on the water, and the shadows on the mountains here on the rooftop of the world, the myths seem tangible. This is the altiplano of Peru, the high plains, where the earth has been raised so close to the sky that the atmosphere takes on a luminous quality.

Divided by the border between Peru and Bolivia, Lake Titicaca draws visitors both for its magnificent scenery and for the vivid Quechua and Aymara native cultures that still thrive on its shores. Surrounded by high, barren mountains, the lake is truly an inland sea, whose opposite shores are often beyond view. Some 12,500 feet above sea level, Lake Titicaca is the largest lake in South America (8,288 square kilometers/3,200 square miles and 900 feet deep) and the highest navigable lake in the world. The Bay of Puno, separated from the lake proper by the two jutting peninsulas of Capaschica and Chucuito, is home to both the floating Uros Islands and to surface plants that blossom thanks to water pollution; the lakeshores are lush with totora reeds, valuable as building materials, cattle fodder, and even, in times of famine, food for humans.

Puno, the capital of the department of the same name, is a drab and unpretentious little town. In February and November, however, it is dressed with colorful and timeless pageantry as Inca legends live on in the phantasmagorical masks and dances of the town festivals. Because it is one of Peru's poorest departments, Puno has long drawn the attention of the Shining Path. But thanks largely to the democratizing influence of peasant unions, progressive Catholic priests, and political parties, the terrorists were never able to make Puno a stronghold. With the government's successes against them, even the department's highlands above Titicaca are becoming safe again; nevertheless, we recommend that you consult a reputable travel agent before straying too far from the town and the "low-lying" areas (in relative terms!) that hug the shores of Lake Titicaca, where terrorist activity has long been almost nonexistent. Don't forget, too, that at 12,500 feet above sea level, Puno will be a challenge to your cardiorespiratory system, so take it easy your first full day there (*see* Precautions *in* Peru Essentials, *below*).

Visitor Information

Touring and Automobile Club of Peru (Arequipa 457, Puno, ☎ 05/435–1544).

Arriving and Departing

By Plane

Americana flies three times a day from Lima (with stops at Cuzco or Arequipa) to the **Aeropuerto Manco Capac** (☎ 05/432–2905) at Juliaca, a commercial and industrial center 50 kilometers (31 miles) north of Puno. **Aero Continente, AeroPerú,** and **Faucett** also have daily flights. If your trip has been arranged through a travel agency (a good one is **Turpuno,** Lambayeque 175, Puno, ☎ 05/435–2001), you will be met at the airport. Alternatively, you can take a taxi to Puno, which costs about $20, or share a minibus, which leaves only when it is full, for $2.

By Train

An **ENAFER** train runs directly between Arequipa and Puno (Av. La Torre 224, ☎ 05/435–1233) four times a week; the trip takes up to 12 hours. The train between Puno and Cuzco also runs four times a week; it takes 12 hours or more and requires a change of trains in Juliaca, where you must wait for two hours. (Watch your belongings carefully during the layover—Juliaca's train station is notorious for its thieves.) Never travel in first or second class, as thievery in both is rampant. On the Arequipa train, travel Pullman, and on the Cuzco train take the *coche de turismo*. Both classes use locked and guarded cars. Food is available on board but is expensive. Be sure to bring bottled water.

By Boat

There is no direct service across Lake Titicaca between Bolivia and Puno. You can, however, go by bus and catamaran or by bus and hydrofoil from Puno to La Paz, Bolivia. Both trips from Puno start with a three-hour bus ride to Copacabana, where passengers have lunch. The hovercraft takes 2½ hours to cross the lake to Huatajata, Bolivia; the catamaran takes six hours to Huatajata. Passengers continue by bus to La Paz. You can buy combined tickets for the bus/catamaran trip from **Transturin** (in Puno, Jirón Libertad 176, ☎ 05/435–2771; in Cuzco, Portal de Panes 109, Office 1, Plaza de Armas, ☎ 08/422–2332) or from a travel agency. **Crillón Tours,** based in La Paz, runs the bus/hydrofoil trip; although the company does not have an office in Puno, it does have a representative there, Señor Zárate (☎ 05/435–3850). Arrangements in La Paz for both the bus/catamaran and bus/hydrofoil trips to Puno can be made through **Diana Tours** (Calle Saranaga 328, ☎ 02/340356).

Exploring Lake Titicaca

There is little to see in Puno itself, and for most mainland excursions you will need a car (you can get around Puno by bicycle-powered taxi; the average fare is about 25¢). You can sign on for a tour with a travel agency, or hire a car and driver on your own from travel agencies for about $35 a day. You can also hire a guide directly. One who is multilingual and highly recommended is **Alcides Huanca** (Jirón Lambayeque 175, Puno, ☎ 05/435–3272).

The Lakeshore
SILLUSTANI
High on a hauntingly beautiful peninsula in Lake Umayo, about 30 kilometers (19 miles) northwest of Puno, is the necropolis of Sillustani (no ☎; ☛ Entry fee). Twenty-eight stone burial towers represent a city of the dead that predated and coincided with the Inca empire. The proper name for the tower is an *ayawasi* (home of the dead), but they are generally referred to as *chullpas,* which are actually the shrouds used to cover the mummies that were deposited inside. This was the land of the Aymara-speaking Colla people, and the precision of their masonry rivals that of the Incas. Most of the chullpas date from the 14th and 15th centuries, but some were erected as early as AD 900. The tallest chullpa, known as the Lizard because of a carving on one of its massive stones, has a circumference of 28 feet and is 39 feet high.

Sillustani's mystique is heightened by the view it affords over Lake Umayo and its mesa-shape island, El Sombrero, and by the utter silence that prevails, broken only by the wind over the water and the cries of lake birds. On your way back to Puno, keep an eye out for shepherds watching over their sheep and alpacas. If you look closely at their fields, you will see that the earth is often wrinkled in *waru warus,* rows of raised beds of earth interspersed with small canals, a pre-Columbian system used to irrigate and protect crops from the altiplano's frequent frosts.

CHUCUITO, JULI, AND POMATA

Strung like a necklace along Titicaca's shore southeast of Puno are three fascinating towns. **Chucuito,** 20 kilometers (12 miles) from Puno, is surrounded by hillsides crisscrossed with agricultural terraces. Be sure to take a look at the stone sundial gracing its main plaza, as well as at the local lakefront cottage industry: making reed boats for use on Titicaca.

Sixty kilometers (37 miles) farther down the highway is the town of **Juli,** considered a sort of altiplano Rome because of its disproportionate number of churches. The village, which may have been an important Aymara religious center (whose hold over popular devotion the Spanish Jesuits wanted to transfer to Catholicism), became a Jesuit base in the altiplano. Four churches dominate: **San Juan de Letran,** now a museum that displays 17th-century paintings chronicling the lives of John the Baptist and St. Teresa, among other artworks; **La Asunción** (apply to guard at San Juan for entry), which has lovely murals and a large courtyard; **San Pedro,** still a functioning parish church, with gilded-wood screens; and **Santa Cruz,** in sad disrepair and at press time (winter 1995) closed to the public. None of the churches has a phone, and only San Juan charges admission. While they are generally closed in the afternoon, hours are irregular; there seems to be more chance of gaining access on the weekend.

Continuing on for 20 kilometers (12 miles), you'll come to **Pomata.** The mestizo baroque carvings and alabaster windows of the church of **Santiago Apostle** (no ☎; ☛ Free; irregular hours) are spectacular.

Lake Titicaca

THE FLOATING ISLANDS

The most famous excursion from Puno is a trip to the Uros "floating islands," 8–24 kilometers (5–15 miles) offshore. These man-made islands of woven totora reed afford a fascinating look at a form of human habitation evolved over centuries. At the same time, the visit is a bit sad, with lots of runny-nosed children begging for a handout (if you don't want to give money, bring fresh fruit or candy) and adults trying to sell you miniature reed boats. You can walk around the springy, moist islands, hire an islander to take you for a ride in one of their reed boats, see the islanders—Uro Indians who have intermarried with the Aymara—weaving and drying fish in the sun, and marvel at the microwave telephone stations on the islands of Torani Pata and Balsero. The excursion, which lasts three to four hours, can be arranged through **Candelaria Tours** (Teodoro Valcarcel 147, ☎ 05/435–1581 or 05/435–3051, FAX 05/435–1111), **Feiser** (Teodoro Valcarcel 155, ☎ 05/435–3112), **Turpuno** (Lambayeque 175, ☎ 05/435–2001), and other travel agencies in Puno; buying a boat ticket yourself at the Puno dock is slightly cheaper.

TAQUILE AND AMANTANI

The agencies all run one- or two-day trips to two natural islands in the lake, Taquile and Amantani, around an hour by launch from Puno. Unlike the floating islands, which are in the Bay of Puno, Taquile and Amantani are in Lake Titicaca proper, and are surrounded by a vast, oceanlike panorama. The proud, Quechua-speaking people of **Taquile,** whose hills are topped with Inca and Tiahuanaco ruins, weave some of Peru's loveliest textiles, which are difficult to find anywhere else. They still wear traditional dress and have successfully maintained the strong community ties and cooperative lifestyle of their ancestors, though there are signs that the island may be losing its unspoiled character under the weight of tourism. **Amantani,** also with pre-Columbian ruins, was discovered by tourists more recently. It has a larger, mainly agricultural population, whose traditional way of life has therefore stood up better to outside pressure.

For a day visit to the islands, it is probably best to go with one of the agency tours, which leave at around 7:30 AM and include a visit to one of the floating islands on the way. If you want to make an overnight stay on Taquile or Amantani (which is recommended), travel instead on the slower local ferry, since there are sometimes problems with the agency services if you try to break your trip and continue the next day. The overnight stay costs about $4, and you stay in rooms in the local people's homes. Nights can be cold and the blankets inadequate, so you may wish to bring a sleeping bag. You should bring your own water or water-purification tablets.

Shopping

Model reed boats, small stone carvings, and sheep, llama, and alpaca wool articles are among the local crafts sold at the **public market** in Puno, near the train station on Calle Cahuide. A small shop in the **Hostal Los Uros** (Jirón Teodoro Valcarcel 135, Puno, ☎ 05/435–2141) offers fine-quality handmade alpaca sweaters. Just down the road, at No. 164, **Aresanías Puno** (☎ 05/435–1291 or 05/435–1801) sells woolen items. On the island of Taquile, a **cooperative store** on the main square sells weavings and the elegantly embroidered clothing the islanders wear. Near Sillustani, the village of Atuncolla has a regular Thursday-morning **country fair** where the campesinos of the district gather to buy and barter animals, food, and manufactured goods.

Sports and the Outdoors

Fishing

Lake Titicaca has been stocked with trout and has such native fish as pejerrey. There are no tackle shops in Puno, but if you've brought your own fishing gear, you might consider hiring a boatman at the Puno dock. **Candelaria Tours** (Teodoro Valcarcel 147, ☎ 05/435–1581 or 05/435–3051) will organize trips on request.

Trekking

Due to the recent history of terrorist attacks, consult with informed locals before hiking on the mainland, but there is no risk of attack in the interesting hikes to hilltop Inca and pre-Inca Tiahuanaco ruins on the island of Taquile. The island people can give you directions. Another hike out of Puno is up the road to Juliaca (the continuation of Avenida La Torre). After about 2 kilometers (1 mile) a dirt road leading to the right is marked with a sign to Huerta Huaraya, a peasant community on the lakefront. The walk there is an easy and beautiful one that takes about an hour.

Dining

Dining choices in Puno are fairly limited, with a lot of modest restaurants in town and more elegant, more expensive dining in the Hotel Isla Esteves (*see* Lodging, *below*). There's not much variety—mostly Peruvian cuisine, grilled chicken or meats, and the one true local specialty, fish from the lake. The two favorites are *trucha* (trout) and pejerrey. Both are delicious and usually grilled or fried. For price-category definitions, *see* Dining *in* Peru Essentials, *below*.

$$ **Pizzería Europa.** The decor is simple, the clay ovens are right in front of your table, and the pizza is surprisingly good. The more exotic toppings include *aceitunas* (olives) and *a la Hawaiana* (Hawaiian style, with ham and pineapple). The restaurant is on the ground floor of the Hotel Colon Inn (*see* Lodging, *below*). ✕ *Tacna 280, ☎ and FAX 05/435–1432. MC.*

$ **Don Piero.** This offbeat, slightly seedy spot has parquet floors, hunting trophies on the walls, plastic tablecloths, and a life-size cutout of Marilyn Monroe to welcome guests at the door. The fresh fish—try the pejerrey—is a house specialty. ✕ *Lima 364, ☎ 05/435–1766. V.*

Lodging

It is not advisable to stay in a hotel in one of the small towns outside Puno, more because they are generally run-down and unpleasant than for security reasons. The high season, when prices can rise as much as 30%, is during local festivals, in February and November. It's a good idea to reserve at least a month in advance if you're visiting then. Puno's hotels are not adequately heated, so be sure to ask for an electric space heater when you register. For price-category definitions, *see* Lodging *in* Peru Essentials, *below.*

$$$$ **Hotel Isla Esteves.** One of the jewels in the government's Hotel de Turistas chain, this massive hotel set on an island connected to Puno by a
★ causeway is decorated with local masks and weavings; the excellent restaurant has a view directly out over the lake. Guest rooms have modern Formica-top dressers and metal wall lamps, but if your room looks out on the lake, the hypnotizing view will make you forget the undistinguished furnishings. ⌸ *Isla Esteves, 5 km (3 mi) from Puno, ☎ 05/435–2271, FAX 05/435–3860. 126 rooms. Restaurant, bar, dance club. AE, DC, MC, V.*

$$ **Hotel Colon Inn.** This pleasantly simple hotel has whitewashed walls
★ and wooden floors. ⌸ *Tacna 280, ☎ and FAX 05/435–1432. 19 rooms. Restaurant, bar. MC.*

$$ **Hotel Sillustani.** On a quiet street downtown, this hotel looks out over rooftops and hillsides. The rooms, set around an interior courtyard with a three-story-high cathedral ceiling, have cable TV and are decorated with orange bedspreads, flowered wallpaper, and stiff leather chairs. ⌸ *Lambayeque 175, ☎ 05/435–2641 or 05/435–1881, FAX 05/435–2641. 22 rooms. Restaurant, bar. V.*

$ **Hostal Italia.** This hotel with an interior garden and rooftop sun terrace has a restaurant that's considered one of the best in Puno. The rooms are simple but comfortable, with parquet floors and wood furniture; those on the fourth floor have a view of the lake. ⌸ *Teodoro Valcarcel 122, ☎ 05/435–2521, FAX 05/435–2131. 30 rooms. Restaurant (\$\$). V.*

The Arts and Nightlife

Folk music and dancing are popular in Puno, especially at festival time (*see* When to Go *in* Peru Essentials, *below*). The hotel reception staff will know of any concerts. Performances are often held at the **Club Samana** (Jirón Puno 334, ☎ 05/435–2110), which has a rustic thatched roof and wooden benches. The **Hotel Isla Esteves** (☎ 05/435–2271) has a disco, open to the public, with pop, salsa, and folk music.

CUZCO, MACHU PICCHU, AND ENVIRONS

Cuzco is a grandiose city, not so much for its size or population but for the monumental character of which its people are so proud. A cultural melting pot, the city has existed for nine centuries: first as the capital of the Inca empire, then as a city conquered by the colonial Spanish, and finally as home to the mestizo culture of today. The signs of these successive groups are evident at every step, in nearly every building of Cuzco's historic center.

The presence not far from Cuzco of Pikillacta, a pre-Inca city of the Wari culture, which existed AD 600–1000, is an indication that this territory, like most of Peru, was the site of sophisticated civilizations long before the Incas appeared on the scene—an event, according to Inca lore, which occurred around AD 1100. While the name Inca originally applied only to the royal family, in particular the emperors (e.g., Inca Pachacuti), today it is used to describe the people as a whole. The language of the Incas was Quechua, and their name for their empire was the Tawantinsuyo.

Cuzco is also a gateway to other historical areas and monuments, such as Machu Picchu, the famed Inca city and a UNESCO World Heritage site; the fortress at Sacsayhuaman, on a hill overlooking Cuzco; the Inca Trail, connecting Cuzco with Machu Picchu; and the Sacred Valley of Urubamba, an Inca breadbasket for centuries, still marked with the footprints of its imperial past. The Incas called Cuzco "the navel of the world," and the city and its surroundings certainly remain the focus of tourism in Peru. A visit is almost obligatory, and we highly recommend that you resist travel agents who will try to sell you a two- or three-day package to the area. You should plan on staying a minimum of five days.

Visitor Information

The **Oficina de Información Turística** (☎ 08/422–2159) at the airport and the **Asociación de Agencias de Turismo** (Av. Sol, Pasaje Grace, Edificio San Jorge, Oficina 2, ☎ 08/422–3761) offer information about the city and surrounding attractions.

To better understand and appreciate Cuzco, two books are indispensable: Peter Frost's *Exploring Cusco* and John Hemming's *The Conquest of the Incas*. Both are available at bookstores in town.

Arriving and Departing

By Plane

Aero Continente, AeroPerú, Americana, Faucett, and **Imperial Air** have flights to Cuzco's **Aeropuerto Velasco Astete** (☎ 08/422–2611) from Lima, Arequipa, Tacna, Puerto Maldonado, Juliaca, and other major cities and towns in Peru. Faucett offers direct service from Cuzco to Iquitos, whence there are direct flights to Miami. The airport is 3 kilometers (2 miles) from the city.

By Train

There are four trains a week between Cuzco and Puno, with connections to Arequipa. Always travel in Turismo, or Pullman, class, rather than first or second class, where thieves abound. The Puno train arrives and departs from the Wanchaq station on Pachacutec (☎ 08/422–2441).

By Car

Although one can drive from Lima to Cuzco, poor road conditions and security problems make it highly inadvisable (*see* Precautions *in* Peru Essentials, *below*).

By Bus

The bus trip from Lima to Cuzco via Arequipa can take up to two days. Do not travel by bus via Apurímac and Ayacucho, as the route is dangerous. Cuzco's **Cruz del Sur** (Av. Pachacutec 510, ☎ 08/422–1909) and **Ormeño** (Plaza Tupac Amaru 114B, ☎ 08/422–8712) have bus service to Lima via Arequipa.

Getting Around Cuzco

For information on getting between Machu Pichu and Cuzco, *see* Machu Picchu *under* Excursions from Cuzco, *below*.

By Car or Taxi

To visit areas such as Pikillacta, Chinchero, or the Sacred Valley, you must go by car. For about $50 a day, you can hire a taxi, either on the street or by phone (try **Radio Car Alpha,** ☎ 08/422–2222).

By Foot

In compact downtown Cuzco, the best way to get around is on foot. If you are in good health, you may want to make the ½-hour hike to Sacsayhuaman, on the northern outskirts of Cuzco. Remember, though, that at 11,000 feet above sea level, Cuzco will be almost as much a challenge to your cardiorespiratory system as Puno, so you should take it just as gently your first full day in town (*see* Precautions *in* Peru Essentials, *below*).

Tour Operators

Recommended travel agencies that offer tours of Cuzco and the surrounding area are **Lima Tours** (Portal de Harinas 177, Plaza de Armas, ☎ 08/422–8431, FAX 08/422–1266) and **Milla Turismo** (Av. Pardo 675, ☎ 08/423–1710, FAX 08/423–1388).

Some recommended tour operators in Cuzco offering guided treks along the Inca Trail are **Explorandes** (Jirón Sucre J8, Urbanización Huancaro, ☎ 08/423–8380, FAX 08/423–3784; in Lima, Tudela y Varela 450, San Isidro, ☎ 01/442–1738 or 01/445–0532, FAX 01/445–4686), **Hirca Travel** (Retiro 128, Oficina 100, ☎ 08/422–5384, FAX 08/423–4147; in Lima, Bellavista 518, ☎ and FAX 01/447–3807), and **Peruvian Andean Treks** (Av. Pardo 705, ☎ 08/422–5701, FAX 08/423–8911). The last offers probably the most complete range of expeditions in the area around Cuzco, including hikes of four to 20 days in the **Vilcabamba, Urubamba,** and **Vilcanota** ranges, splendid areas for hiking because of their cultural and geographical diversity.

Exploring

To visit the region's most important historical sites (not including Machu Picchu), you must purchase a *boleto turístico* ($10, $5 for students with an international student ID), a combined ticket available at each of the 14 sites. The **Oficina del Boleto Turístico** (Av. Sol 103, Office 102, ☎ 08/422–6919) also sells the ticket, good for five days' unlimited use, as do the **Coricancha, Santa Catalina,** and the **cathedral,** which offer a 10-day version for the same price.

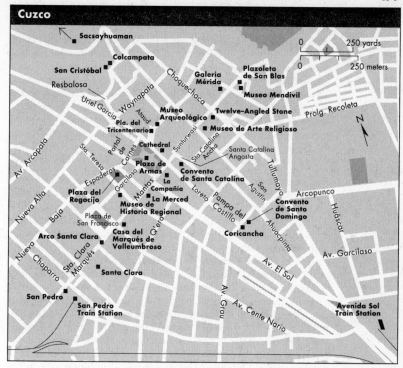

Cuzco

Sacsayhuaman
Colcampata
San Cristóbal
Resbalosa
Choquechaca
Galeria Mérida
Plazoleta de San Blas
Museo Mendívil
Uriel Garcia · Waynapata
Museo Arqueológico
Twelve-Angled Stone
Prolg. Recoleta
Pla. del Tricentenario
Museo de Arte Religioso
Cathedral
Santa Catalina Angosta
Plaza de Armas
Convento de Santa Catalina
Plaza del Regocijo
La Compañia
La Merced
Arcopunco
Convento de Santo Domingo
Museo de Historia Regional
Plaza de San Francisco
Coricancha
Arco Santa Clara
Casa del Marqués de Valleumbroso
Av. Garcilaso
Santa Clara
Av. El Sol
San Pedro
San Pedro Train Station
Av. Grau
Av. Cente Nario
Avenida Sol Train Station

0 — 250 yards
0 — 250 meters

Cuzco's Historic Center

Most of Cuzco's main attractions lie within its historic center, whose heart is the **Plaza de Armas.** The imposing plaza is a direct descendant of imperial Cuzco's central square, which the Incas called the Huacaypata and which extended beyond the area covered by the present-day square to as far as the Plaza del Regocijo. In the eastern corner of the Plaza de Armas, you can still see remnants of an Inca wall, part of the **Acllahuasi,** or House of the Chosen Women. The palace of the great Inca (Emperor) Pachacuti, who turned the Inca kingdom into an empire, once stood on what is now the western corner of the plaza. The **cathedral** (no ☎; ☛ Entry fee; closed daily noon–3) sits on the northeast side, where the palace of the Inca Wirachocha is believed to have been located. The Baroque church, whose construction began in 1550 and ended a century later, is considered one of the most splendid Spanish colonial churches in the Americas. Within its high walls are some of the best examples of the Cuzco school of painting (which added Andean motifs to its basically European style), including one of the Last Supper with a local specialty, cuy, as the main dish. Other highlights include a massive, solid silver altar and the enormous 1659 Maria Angola bell, the largest bell in South America, which hangs in one of the towers. The cedar choir has carved rows of saints, popes, and bishops, all in stunning detail down to their delicately articulated hands.

Nearly rivaling the cathedral in stature is the church of **La Compañía** (no ☎; ☛ Free; closed daily noon–2:30), on the corner diagonally across the plaza. Named for the Company of Jesus, the powerful Jesuit order that built it, the church was finished in the late 17th century. Note the outstanding carved facade and, inside, the Cuzco school paintings of the life of St. Ignatius of Loyola.

As you face the cathedral, you will see to the right a steep, narrow street, Triunfo, now rebaptized with its original Quechua name of Suntur-wasi. One block up on the right, where the street name changes to Hatun-rumiyoc, stands what is believed to have been the **Palace of the Inca Roca,** who lived in the 13th or 14th century. Halfway along the palace's side wall, nestled amid other stones in perfect harmony, is the famous **12-angled stone,** an example of the Incas' masterful masonry. Today, the colonial building that rests on the Inca foundations is home to the **Museo de Arte Religioso** (Museum of Religious Art). A highlight of the collection is a 17th-century series of paintings depicting the city's Corpus Christi procession. *Corner of Hatunrumiyoc and Herejes, ☎ 08/422–2781. ☛ Entry fee. Closed Mon.–Sat. 11:30 AM–3, all day Sun.*

The street continues up a steep, cobblestone hill known as the Cuesta de San Blas, the entry into the traditional artists' quarter of **San Blas.** Recently restored, this area of whitewashed adobe homes with bright blue doors shines anew. The Cuesta de San Blas is sprinkled with galleries selling paintings done in the religious Cuzco school style of the 16th through 18th centuries. Continue on the same street for one block to reach the **Plazoleta de San Blas,** with a simple adobe church (no ☎; ☛ Entry fee; closed daily until 2) that houses one of the jewels of colonial art in the Americas—the **Pulpit of San Blas,** an intricately carved 17th-century wooden pulpit dominated by the figure of Christ triumphant. Also on the square, the **Museo Mendívil** (☎ 08/422–6506; ☛ Free), set in the home of a famous 20th-century Peruvian religious artist, Hilario Mendívil, displays the sculptures of the Virgin, with the elongated necks that are the artist's trademark. The work of contemporary ceramicist Edilberto Mérida is shown a few blocks away at the **Galería Mérida** (Carmen Alto 133, ☎ 08/422–1714; ☛ Free), which is also the artist's home; if the gallery is closed, you'll find his works at a shop on the square (Plazoleta San Blas 120, no ☎).

Starting again from the Plaza de Armas, left of the cathedral, the street named Cuesta del Almirante will take you to a beautiful colonial mansion, the **Palacio del Almirante,** which today houses Cuzco's **Museo Arqueológico.** Among the displays of pre-Inca and Inca objects is a collection of Wari, turquoise figures from Pikillata. *Corner of Ataud and Córdoba de Tucumán, ☎ 08/422–3245. ☛ Entry fee. Closed weekdays noon–3 and weekends.*

To the left of the modern fountain in the **Plazuela del Tricentenario,** in front of the mansion, is a walkway 656 feet long with a fine view of the Plaza de Armas and central Cuzco.

Once again starting from the Plaza de Armas, follow Santa Catalina Angosta street along the Inca wall of the Acllahuasi to the **Convento de Santa Catalina.** Still an active convent, Santa Catalina has a church with high and low choirs and a museum displaying religious art. *Santa Catalina Angosta, no ☎. Museum: ☛ Entry fee. Closed Mon.–Sat. noon–3 and Sun.*

A few blocks away is one of the most splendid examples of Inca architecture, the Temple of the Sun, with a colonial church superimposed on it. Called **Coricancha,** the temple was built to honor the Tawantin-suyos' most important divinity and served as the central seat of government and the repository of the realm's gold treasure. Terraces facing it were once filled with life-size gold and silver statues of plants and animals. In the 16th century, above its looted ruins, the Spanish constructed the **convent of Santo Domingo,** using stones from the temple. An ingenious restoration to recover both buildings after the 1953 earthquake allows visitors the chance to see how the convent was built on and around the walls and chambers of the temple. In the Inca structures left exposed, one can admire the mortarless masonry, earthquake-proof trapezoidal doorways, curved retaining wall, and exquisite carving that exemplify the Incas' artistic and engineering skills. *Pampa del Castillo and Santo Domingo, no ☎. ☛ Entry fee. Closed daily noon–3.*

West of the Plaza de Armas, along the Calle del Medio, is the Plaza Kusipata, still commonly referred to by its former name, Plaza Regocijo. Beyond it is the **Casa de Garcilaso,** the colonial childhood home of Inca Garcilaso de la Vega, the famous chronicler of the Conquest who was the illegitimate son of one of Pizarro's captains and an Inca princess. The mansion, with its cobblestone courtyard, now houses the **Museo de Historia Regional,** which displays a collection of Cuzco school paintings and Inca mummies, ceramics, metal objects, and other artifacts. *Corner of Heladeros and Garcilaso, ☎ 08/422–3245. ☛ Entry fee. Closed Mon.–Sat. noon–3, Sun. until 3.*

Walk down Heladeros to calle Mantas to reach the church and monastery of **La Merced,** rebuilt in the 17th century. The monastery's cloister, surrounded by two stories of portals and graced with a colonial fountain, gardens, and benches, is decorated with a spectacular series of murals depicting the life of the founder of the Mercedarian order, St. Peter of Nolasco. A small but impressive museum of the convent's treasures displays, among other objects, the **Custodia,** a solid gold monstrance encrusted with hundreds of precious stones. *Calle Mantas. ☛ Entry fee. Church ⊙ Daily 7–8 AM and 6–8 PM. Museum closed Mon.–Sat. noon–2, Sun.*

Follow calle Mantas to the **plaza and church of San Francisco** (no ☎). The plaza, though unimpressive, has an intriguing garden of native plants; at press time (winter 1995), the church—which has two sepulchers with arrangements of bones and skulls, some pinned to the wall to spell out morbid sayings—was closed for restoration. From here, through the attractive **Arco Santa Clara,** a colonial archway, Cuzco's public market area begins. Ahead are the churches of **Santa Clara** (calle Santa Clara, no ☎; ☛ Free), the oldest cloistered convent in Peru, whose altar is decorated with thousands of mirrors, and **San Pedro** (corner of Santa Clara and Chaparro, no ☎; ☛ Free; closed Mon.–Sat. noon–2 and Sun.), built with stones from Inca ruins. The market, though colorful, is rife with thieves and muggers, and particularly dangerous for tourists.

For the energetic, the 15-minute walk to Colcampata offers a tour through colonial neighborhoods to the heights above the city. Following Procuradores from the Plaza de Armas to Waynapata and then Resbalosa, you will come to a steep cobblestone staircase with a wonderful view of La Compañía. Continuing to climb, you will come upon the church of **San Cristóbal,** which is of little intrinsic interest but affords another magnificent panorama of the city. The church stands atop **Colcampata,** believed to have been the palace of the first Inca, Manco Capac. The Inca wall to the right of the church has 11 niches in which soldiers may once have stood guard. Farther up the road, the lane on the left leads to a post-Conquest Inca gateway beside a magnificent Spanish mansion.

Northern Outskirts

Dominating a hilltop 2 kilometers (1 mile) north of the city is the massive complex of **Sacsayhuaman,** perhaps the most important Inca monument after Machu Picchu. Built of stones of astonishing size and weight—the largest is 361 tons—the center seems to have served both religious and military ends, with zigzag walls and cross-fire parapets that allowed defenders to rain destruction down on attackers from two sides. Today only ruins remain of the original fortress city, which the Spaniards tore down after crushing Manco Inca's rebellion in 1536 and then ransacked for years as a source of construction materials for the new Spanish city at Cuzco. Sacsayhuaman is a half hour's walk past Colcampata toward the right. *No* ☎. ☛ *Entry fee.*

Smaller archaeological sites around Sacsayhuaman include **Qenco** (no ☎; ☛ Entry fee), 2 kilometers (1 mile) away, a huaca with a small amphitheater where the mummies of nobles and priests were kept and brought out on sunny days for ritualistic worship. Continue 6 kilometers (4 miles) to reach **Puka Pukara** (no ☎; ☛ Entry fee), which some archaeologists believe was a fort and others claim was an inn and storage place used by the Inca nobility. Nearby **Tambomachay** (no ☎; ☛ Entry fee) is a huaca built on a natural spring. Perhaps a place where water, which the Incas considered a source of life, was worshipped, the huaca is almost certain to have been the scene of sacred ablutions and purifying ceremonies.

Valley of Cuzco

Along the highway running southeast of Cuzco to Sicuani are a number of lesser-known pre-Columbian sites. Despite the fact that they are easy to visit in one day by car, you may find that you have these magnificent ruins all to yourself, for they are off the traditional two-day Cuzco–Machu Picchu tourist circuit.

Tipón (no ☎; ☛ Free), 23 kilometers (14 miles) southeast of Cuzco, is one of the best surviving examples of Inca land and water management. It consists of a series of finely constructed terraces crisscrossed by aqueducts and irrigation channels edging up a narrow pass in the mountains. One theory is that the Incas used Tipón as a kind of agricultural station for developing special crop strains. Unfortunately, the rough dirt track leading to the complex is in wretched condition. If you visit, either walk up (about two hours each way) or go in a four-wheel-drive vehicle (about 45 minutes to the site and 30 minutes back). **Peruvian Andean Treks** (Av. Pardo 705, Cuzco, ☎ 08/422–5701, ℻ 08/423–8911) conducts four-wheel-drive tours of the area out of Cuzco.

Nine kilometers (5 miles) down the highway from the Tipón turnoff stand the haunting ruins of **Pikillacta** (no ☎; ☛ Entry fee), a vast city from the pre-Inca Wari culture, which existed between AD 600 and 1000. Like other Andean cultures, the Wari empire (which at its height stretched from near Cajamarca to the border of the Tiahuanaco empire based around Lake Titicaca) had a genius for farming in a harsh environment and built sophisticated urban centers such as Pikillacta. Wari's capital was at Ayacucho, but little is known about the empire. The rough ruins, once enclosed by a defensive wall whose remains are still evident, confirm the Incas' superiority in architecture and masonry. They are spread over several acres and include many two-story buildings. At the thatch-roofed excavation sites you can see uncovered walls that show that the city's stones were once covered with plaster and whitewashed. Across the road lies a beautiful lagoon, **Lago de Lucre.**

Continuing 8 kilometers (5 miles) along the same highway, you'll come to the small town of **Andahuaylillas,** whose main attraction is a small 16th-century church (☛ Entry fee) on the plaza. The contrast between the simple exterior and the rich, expressive colonial Baroque art inside is notable. The gilt that once covered the church walls is still evident.

Shopping

Cuzco is full of opportunities to shop for both traditional crafts and artwork and more modern handmade items, especially clothing made of alpaca, llama, or sheep wool. Vendors will approach you relentlessly on the **Plaza de Armas,** and if you keep your eyes open and bargain hard, you may find attractive sweaters. Better bets, with less of a hard sell, are three enclosed handicraft markets: the **Feria Inca** (corner of San Andres and Q'era); a fair at Loreto 208, on the passage beside La Compañía; and **Yachay Wasi** (Triunfo 376).

Triunfo is lined with crafts shops as far as San Blas. One of the best, **Taller Maxi** (Triunfo 393, no ☎), sells dolls in historical and local costumes (you can also have them custom made), *retablos* (dioramas) showing Cuzco's most popular sites, and alpaca jackets decorated with local weavings. At No. 387, a nonprofit cooperative store, **Antisuyo** (☎ 08/422–7778), sells high-quality handicrafts from all over Peru. Religious art, including icons and elaborately costumed statues of the Virgin Mary, by a famous family of local artists is sold at the shop at the **Museo Mendívil** (Plazoleta San Blas, ☎ 08/422–6506). Also in San Blas, the **Galería Mérida** (Carmen Alto 133, ☎ 08/422–1714) sells the much imitated ceramics of Edilberto Mérida.

Sports and the Outdoors

Fishing

The rainbow trout in the Vilcanota and Urubamba rivers make the towns of **Urubamba** and **Yucay** popular fishing spots. There are no tackle shops; most locals just use hand lines—very successfully!

Trekking

The stunning Inca Trail runs from outside Cuzco to Machu Picchu; for more information, *see* By Foot: The Inca Trail *in* Excursions from Cuzco, Machu Picchu, *below.*

White-Water Rafting

The Cuzco region offers some of the best rafting in Peru, east of the highlands where the rivers rapidly drop toward the Amazon Basin. Many adventure travel agencies (*see* Tour Operators, *above*) in Cuzco offer rafting trips on the Vilcanota River, known as the Urubamba River after it passes Huambutío.

Dining

Cuzco has an enormous variety of restaurants fit for every taste and price range. There are excellent places with international menus, especially Italian, while other eateries serve local delicacies that include cuy (guinea pig), often served in a hot sauce, and *chicharrón,* fried pork or chicken. Accommodations are just as varied, and bargaining is expected. For price-category definitions, *see* Dining *in* Peru Essentials, *below.*

$$$ **El Paititi.** Set on the Plaza de Armas, this tourist-oriented restaurant has good fish, especially the grilled or fried trout, and local food—try the spicy *aji de gallina* (chicken), served over rice. Additional lures are live folk-music shows nightly and a free pisco (grape brandy) sour for all diners. ✗ *Portal de Carrizos 270,* ☎ *08/422–6992. AE, MC, V.*

$$$ **El Truco.** Big and a bit cold-looking—and cold!—with colonial paintings and high ceilings, this spot a block from the Plaza de Armas offers local specialties such as chicharrón. There's a $3 cover charge for

the nightly show of folk music and dancing. ✕ *Plaza Regocijo 261,* ☎ *08/423–5295. AE, DC, MC, V.*

$$$ La Retama. Exposed Inca stone walls, a cartwheel chandelier, and a
★ nightly folk music show make for a charming ambience. The local dishes
and the international fare are both outstanding; try the trout in fennel
cream sauce. ✕ *Pampa del Castillo 315,* ☎ *and* FAX *08/422–5911. AE,*
DC, MC, V.

$$$ Mesón de Espaderos. You'll be drinking in history as you dine on a
rustic, second-floor terrace above the Plaza de Armas. The steaks and
parilladas (mixed grill) are the best in Cuzco; the parillada for one person is more than enough for two. ✕ *Espaderos 105,* ☎ *08/423–5307.*
AE, MC, V.

$$ El Arriero. This is another tourist-oriented restaurant, but its specialty
is steak cooked before your eyes on the grill. Folk-music shows start
at 8 PM, and diners receive a free pisco sour. ✕ *Portal de Harinas 195,*
Plaza de Armas, ☎ *08/425–2533 or 08/425–2160. AE, DC, MC, V.*

$$ Tratorria Adriano. Solid and unexciting Italian fare, relying on pasta
with the traditional red and white sauces, is served at this cozy eatery
with a carved-wood ceiling. It's a great spot for people-watching while
dining next to the big picture windows but don't try the coffee—it is
vile. ✕ *Mantas 105,* ☎ *08/423–3965. AE, DC, MC, V.*

$ Café Varayoc. Perfect for a midday snack, this café with exposed
wooden beams and whitewashed walls serves good pastries and huge
glass mugs of *mate de coca* (coca tea) with fresh leaves floating in them.
A popular place with arty types. ✕ *Corner of Espaderos and Plaza Re-*
gocijos, ☎ *08/423–2404. No credit cards.*

$ Chez Maggy. If you're cold and tired, you can warm up in front of the
★ open brick ovens that produce the café's great pizzas and calzones. The
atmosphere is casual and friendly; everyone shares two long wooden
tables. ✕ *Procuradores 365,* ☎ *08/423–4861. AE, V.*

$ El Ayllu. This café on the Plaza de Armas serves hearty breakfasts ac-
companied by a big glass mug of *cafe con leche* (steamed milk with
coffee), and mouthwatering pastries, including a scrumptious apple
strudel. ✕ *Portal de Carnes 208, Plaza de Armas,* ☎ *08/423–2357.*
No credit cards.

$ Govinda. This vegetarian restaurant run by Peruvian Hare Krishnas
has appropriately austere benches and Hindu decoration and background
music. The breakfast of juice, yogurt, fresh fruit, and granola is especially good. ✕ *Espaderos between the Plazas de Armas and Regocijo,*
no ☎. *No credit cards.*

$ Quinta Eulalia. Set on the patio and courtyard terrace of a somewhat
decrepit mansion, this is where Cusqueños go for local cooking. Seco
de cabrito (goat stew), pork chicharrón, and *choclo* (an ear of corn
served with fresh, salty cheese) are some of the dishes of choice. ✕
Choquechaca 384, ☎ *08/422–4951. No credit cards. Lunch only.*

Lodging

Although Cuzco is cold, most hotels provide enough extra blankets,
and the most expensive hotels have central heating. If you visit during
June, the time of the Corpus Christi and Inti Raymi festivals, it's a good
idea to reserve a hotel room at least a month in advance; prices are
likely to be higher then as well. For price-category definitions, *see* Lodging *in* Peru Essentials, *below.*

$$$$ Hotel El Dorado. The El Dorado has successfully avoided the white-
★ washed neocolonial style that makes most of Peru's hotels look alike.
Rooms have vaulted brick ceilings, curving walls, alpaca-skin bedcovers,

and gas lanterns remade into lamps. ☎ *Av. Sol 395,* ☎ *08/423–1232,* FAX *08/424–0993. 63 rooms. Restaurant, bar, indoor pool, sauna. AE, DC, MC, V.*

$$$$ **Hotel Libertador.** Guests are greeted with a coca tea by the fireplace before going to their rooms, which have whitewashed walls, colonial decorations, and views of patio gardens. A welcome—and unusual—amenity is the central heating. ☎ *San Agustín 400,* ☎ *08/423–1961,* FAX *08/423–3152. 130 rooms. Restaurant, bar, café. AE, DC, MC, V.*

$$$ **Hotel Pichoaga.** The front half of this excellent mid-range hotel con-
★ sists of a colonial building, with rooms ranged around an attractive courtyard. Behind it is a modern wing, with a restaurant that overlooks the Plaza de Armas. ☎ *Santa Teresa 344,* ☎ *08/422–7691 or 08/425–2330,* FAX *08/422–1246. 70 rooms. Restaurant, bar, casino. AE, DC, MC, V.*

$$$ **Hotel Royal Inka I.** Guests at this older sister of the Inka II (*see below*) can use all the facilities of the newer hotel, one block away. The style here is colonial, with rooms centered on a flagstone patio. ☎ *Plaza Regocijo 229,* ☎ *08/422–2284,* FAX *08/423–1067. 36 rooms. AE, DC, MC, V.*

$$$ **Hotel Royal Inka II.** The guest rooms at this modern hotel are clean and spacious, each with its own heater and attractive wood-frame windows. ☎ *Santa Teresa 335,* ☎ *08/422–2284,* FAX *08/423–4221. 45 rooms. Restaurant, bar, hot tub, sauna. AE, DC, MC, V.*

$$$ **Hotel Savoy.** About 10 blocks from Cuzco's colonial center, this is a large hotel with shops on the first floor and richly carved wood appointments in the rooms. ☎ *Av. Sol 567,* ☎ *08/422–4322,* FAX *08/422–1100. 139 rooms. Restaurant, bar. AE, DC, MC, V.*

$$ **Hostal Colonial Palace.** Built inside the 17th-century Santa Teresa con-
★ vent, about a block from the Casa del Marqués de Valleumbroso, this hotel has simply furnished rooms, with either French doors or picture windows, laid out around a lovely brownstone patio. Space heaters are available. ☎ *Q'era 270,* ☎ *08/423–2151. 38 rooms, 32 with bath. Restaurant. AE, V.*

$$ **Hostal Residencial Corihuasi.** Up a long, steep cobblestone street from the Plaza de Armas, the Corihuasi occupies a ramshackle 17th-century mansion. Rooms have a rustic look, with wood floors and sloping ceilings; some overlook the city, and others are grouped around a flower-filled courtyard. ☎ *Uriel Garcia (Suecia) 561,* ☎ *08/423–2233. 15 rooms. AE, V.*

$ **Hostal Loreto.** In a colonial building with an attractive sunlit courtyard,
★ this tiny hostel's glory is four rooms with an original Inca wall. ☎ *Loreto 115,* ☎ *08/422–6352. 9 rooms. No credit cards.*

Nightlife

Cuzco is full of bars and discos where you can listen to live folk music or recorded pop dance tunes. **El Muki** (Santa Catalina Angosta 114, no ☎) is like a crowded little cave, popular with the younger crowd. A favorite gringo bar, **Kamikaze** (above the Café Varayoc, Plaza Regocijo, ☎ 08/423–3865), plays disco and has live folk music. Several restaurants have shows featuring local folk dancing and music (*see* Dining, *above*). For a beer and a game of darts, try **Cross Keys** (Portal de Confiturías 233, Plaza de Armas, 2nd Floor, no ☎), a British-style pub.

Excursions from Cuzco

Sacred Valley of the Incas

In the time of the Tawantinsuyo, this area's pleasant climate, fertile soil, and proximity to Cuzco made it a favorite with the Inca nobles, many of whom are believed to have had private country homes here. Today Inca remains dot the length of the valley, which is filled with Inca agricultural terraces and dominated by the archaeological remains of Pisac and Ollantaytambo.

Getting There

Many travel agencies offer one-day tours of the valley, but a two- or three-day trip is recommended. This will give you time not only to see the archaeological sites but to enjoy the relaxation for which the valley has been famous since Inca times. Perhaps the best center of operations for a visit of this kind is Urubamba or neighboring Yucay, home to the magnificent Alhambra III hotel (*see* Dining and Lodging, *below*). Both towns are at mid-valley and have unparalleled views.

Exploring

The Sacred Valley of the Incas, along the Urubamba River, is traditionally held to begin at Pisac, about 30 kilometers (18 miles) northeast of Cuzco. The valley "ends" 60 kilometers (36 miles) northwest of Pisac at Ollantaytambo, where the cliffs flanking the river grow closer together, the valley narrows, and the agriculturally rich floodplain thins to a gorge as the Urubamba begins its abrupt descent toward the Amazon Basin. (Machu Picchu is farther downriver, among the cloud forests on the Andean slopes above the Amazon jungle.)

At the valley's southern extreme, set amid rugged sandstone cliffs, is **Huambutio,** a launching point for raft trips (*see* Sports and the Outdoors *in* Cuzco, *above*). The road from Cuzco meets the valley at a better-known point, **Pisac.** Pisac has two parts: the colonial town, which holds a popular Sunday market (*see* Shopping, *below*), and the Inca ruins up on a hill. From the market area, you can rent a horse to ride up to the ruins, or you can drive up the winding but well-maintained road. Archaeologists think there was a fortress here to defend the empire from the fierce Antis (jungle peoples). The terraces and irrigation systems also support the theory that it was a refuge in times of siege. The fortress is a masterpiece of Inca engineering, with narrow trails winding tortuously among and through solid rock. Another Sunday attraction takes place in Pisac's simple **stone church** (no ☎; ☛ Free), where a Quechua mass is held, with the local Indian *varayocs* (mayors) attending in full ceremonial regalia.

From Pisac, the valley road passes through the quiet colonial towns of **Calca, Yucay,** and **Urubamba** and, 60 kilometers (37 miles) from Pisac, ends at **Ollantaytambo** (no ☎; ☛ Entry fee), a well-preserved Inca site. The fortress of Ollantaytambo, a formidable stone structure climbing massive terraces to the top of a peak, was the valley's main defense against the Antis and was the site of the Incas' greatest victory against the Spanish during the wars of Conquest. Below the fortress lies a complete Inca town, also called Ollantaytambo, still inhabited and with its original architecture and layout preserved.

To return to Cuzco, take the road from Urubamba climbing the valley wall to the town of **Chinchero.** Apparently one of the valley's major Inca cities, Chinchero has a colonial church that was built on top of the remains of an Inca palace (☞ Entry fee), as well as immense agricultural terraces. A colorful Sunday market is frequented by tourists and locals.

Shopping

Both Pisac and Chinchero hold Sunday **markets** that sell, in addition to foodstuffs and household goods, a wide variety of handicrafts, including woolens, weavings, ceramics, and painted leather masks, mostly of feline demons and worn to scare away other evil spirits. Pisac has a smaller market on Tuesdays and Thursdays.

Dining and Lodging

For price-category definitions, *see* Dining *and* Lodging *in* Peru Essentials, *below.*

$$$ **Hostal Turquesa.** This country house 21 kilometers (13 miles) from Ollantaytambo has verdant gardens and comfortable rooms. Under new management since 1993, the hotel now caters heavily to the tourist market, with a self-service restaurant much frequented by tour groups. ▨ *Via Cuzco, km 69, Urubamba,* ☎ *08/422–1174 (central booking office in Cuzco). 42 rooms. Restaurant, pool. AE, DC, MC, V.*

$$ **Hotel Alhambra III.** In the heart of the Sacred Valley, this 300-year-old
★ former convent features gardens, cobblestone walkways, a church, and a public museum with extensive holdings of pre-Inca and Inca ceramics. The colonial-style guest rooms, with brick-tile floors, unstained wood ceilings, and carved-wood headboards, have balconies overlooking the gardens or the terraced hillsides. The food in the restaurant, unfortunately, does not live up to the rest of the hotel. ▨ *Plaza Manco II, Yucay,* ☎ *and* ▨ *(in Cuzco) 08/420–1107. 65 rooms. Restaurant, bar. AE, V.*

Machu Picchu

This mystical city, a three-hour train ride from Cuzco, is the most important archaeological site in South America, and its beauty is so spectacular that the disappointed visitor is rare indeed. Its attraction lies in the exquisite architecture and the formidable scenery that surrounds it, in the synergism between the Incas' massive stone structures, the steep sugarloaf hills around them, and the winding Urubamba River far below.

Ever since American explorer Hiram Bingham "discovered" the city in 1911, debates over Machu Picchu's original function have raged. What *is* clear is that it was an Inca religious center and small city of some 200 homes and 1,000 residents, with agricultural terraces to supply the population's needs and a strategic setting that overlooked but could not be seen from the valley floor. Exactly when Machu Picchu was built is not known, but one theory suggests that it was a country estate of Inca Pachacuti, which means its golden age was in the mid-15th century. The site's belated discovery has led some academics to conclude that the Incas abandoned Machu Picchu before the Spanish Conquest. Whatever the reason, this "lost city of the Incas" was missed by the ravaging conquistadors and survived untouched until the beginning of this century.

Machu Picchu deserves a two-day visit. There are two trains back to Cuzco every afternoon, but even taking the second train, a day-tripper will have to leave the ruins no later than 5:30 PM, allowing little time to linger and absorb the mysterious, time-laden atmosphere. On the other hand, if you stay overnight, you'll not only be able to wander the ruins after most tourists have gone; you'll also have time for a soak in the thermal baths in the village of Aguas Calientes—1½ kilometers (1 mile) from the Puente Ruinas train station, where you catch a bus to take you on the 30-minute zigzag climb to the ruins. The baths, which come as a welcome relief after a day of hard climbing or scrambling around the ruins, are 10–15 minutes from Aguas Calientes on the path that leads out of the main square.

Getting There
BY TRAIN

The most popular way to get from Cuzco to Machu Picchu is the tourist train, known as the *autovagón*. It leaves Cuzco daily at 6 AM. The first part of the trip, as far as the station of Poroy, 15 kilometers (9 miles) outside Cuzco, is actually made by bus; on the return leg you may have to transfer to a bus in Ollantaytambo, 92 kilometers (55 miles) from Cuzco.

The train arrives at Machu Picchu at 9:30 AM. The first stop in the area, which has signs that say MACHU PICCHU, is actually Aguas Calientes, the small town at the foot of the mountain. *Don't get off here!* A few minutes later, the train stops at a station labeled PUENTE RUINAS; disembark there and get in line for the buses to the ruins. The autovagón is comfortable and reliable, with few breakdowns and accidents; tickets ($63 round-trip) may be bought from the station or a travel agent.

Local trains to Quillabamba, which stop at Machu Picchu, leave twice daily from San Pedro station (☎ 08/423–5201) in front of the main city market, where you should take great care because of the many thieves. Although they cost considerably less than the tourist train, local trains take longer and the risk of theft is much greater. They do, however, stop at Kilómetro 88, where Inca Trail (*see below*) hikers begin their trek; the tourist train does not.

BY FOOT: THE INCA TRAIL

The Incas traveled their empire via a system of carefully built and well-maintained paths. The **Inca Trail,** a 50-kilometer-long (31-mile-long) section of the road that probably went from Cuzco to Machu Picchu, connects the Sacred Valley and Machu Picchu. Hiram Bingham "rediscovered" the trail in 1915, although research has shown that parts of it were used during the colonial and early republican eras and that it was, of course, well-known to the people of the area all along. Now a famous hiking route, the trail begins three hours by train from Cuzco on the line to Machu Picchu and Quillabamba, close to the **Corihuayrachina** station at a place known as **Kilómetro 88** (where you sign in and pay a fee of around $15, which includes one day in Machu Picchu), and ends at the fabled ruins themselves. Still largely paved with stones, the Inca Trail is the toughest but most beautiful way to get to Machu Picchu. Unique in the world, the walk takes visitors past a series of ruins and through stunning scenery that starts in the thin air of the highlands and ends in Machu Picchu's cloud forests.

The hike usually takes three to five days. The best months in terms of weather are May–September (July is coldest), with chances of rain increasing in April and October and becoming a certainty the rest of the year. Since this is the principal hiking destination in South America, conservation is becoming a real problem, and careless hikers are causing irreparable damage to the ruins along the route. At press time (winter 1995) the local authorities were considering demanding permits to walk the trail, so check before you set out.

Should you choose to make the trek without a guide (*see* Tour Operators *in* Cuzco, *above*), do not go with fewer than four people; there have been armed thefts on the trail, although they are not common. Even if you intend to hire porters, you need to be in decent shape, since the trail is often steep and climbs to over 13,775 feet; you must be in excellent shape if you will be carrying your own pack. If you've never backpacked, get professional advice, or first try a short trip near home. Also, the trail is occasionally narrow and hair-raising, so go only if you have a cool head for heights. If you decide you hate backpacking in the middle of your Inca Trail trip, there's no solution except to continue or hike back the way you came.

Make sure you bring a waterproof tent with fly, a sleeping bag, rain gear, and clothing necessary to confront cold, rainy weather. You should wear sturdy hiking boots and bring mosquito repellent, sunblock, a hat, a gas stove, all the food you need, water and water purification tablets, matches, a flashlight, a towel, and plastic bags.

You should carry all your garbage off the trail with you and avoid lighting fires, camping in the ruins, or cutting flowers and vegetation. By all means carry toilet paper, as this is a rustic trail with few comfort stations, but go off the trail and bury your waste. There are seven well-spaced, designated campsites along the trail, and you should camp only there. A bed for the night can be found at a badly maintained hotel at Wiñay-Wayna, 7 kilometers (4 miles) from Machu Picchu.

A sine qua non companion for the trip is Peter Frost's book *Exploring Cusco,* which includes maps, detailed descriptions, and heartening comments for those long, steep hauls. The best source for other maps is the **South American Explorers Club** (*see* Precautions *in* Peru Essentials, *below*).

BY HELICOPTER

Helicuzco (Portal de Comercio 195, Plaza de Armas, Cuzco, ☎ 08/423–4181 or 08/422–7283) has daily flights to Machu Picchu. The flights take about 20 minutes, leave at 10 AM and return at 3:30 PM, and cost $130 round-trip and $65 one-way. The company also organizes charter flights to destinations like the Sacred Valley on request.

Exploring

After you enter the ruins through the terraces at the agricultural sector, you come to a series of 16 small ritual baths linked to the Inca worship of water. Beyond them is the round **Temple of the Sun,** apparently an astronomical observatory; the straight edge of the rock in its center is aligned with the window to point to the rising sun on the morning of the summer solstice. Ancient stone staircases slice through the ruins, leading to places like the ridge on which sits the **Temple of the Three Windows.** There are few better examples of the Inca love affair with stone—one entire wall is built from a single massive rock with trapezoidal windows cut into it. Beside this temple is the **Principal Temple,** so dubbed because its masonry is among Machu Picchu's best. Past the temple is a hillock leading to the famous **Intihuatana,** the **Hitching Post of the Sun.** Every important Inca center had one of these vertical stone columns (called gnomons), but their function is a mystery. Across and around a grassy plaza are many more buildings and huts. ☛ *Entry fee (reduction on 2nd-day ticket with 1st-day stub).* ☉ *Daily 7:30–5; for permission to enter the ruins after hours, go to the Instituto Nacional de Cultura (Colegio San Bernardo s/n, ☎ 08/422–3831) in Cuzco, or ask at the front gate during the day.*

Several trails lead from the site to surrounding ruins. A 45-minute walk southeast of the main complex is **Intipunku,** the Sun Gate, a small ruin in a pass through which you can see the sun rise at different times of the year. It is also the gateway to the Inca Trail (*see above*). A two- or three-hour hike beyond it along the Inca Trail will bring you to the ruins of **Huiñay Huayna,** a complex that climbs a steep mountain slope and includes an interesting set of ritual baths.

From the cemetery at Machu Picchu, a 30-minute walk along a narrow path leads to yet another example of the Incas' ingenuity and engineering skills: the **Inca Bridge,** built rock by rock up a hair-raising stone escarpment. A trail up the sugarloaf hill in front of Machu Picchu, **Huayna Picchu,** offers another exhilarating, if challenging, hike. The climb, much of it straight up, follows an ancient Inca path that is still in good condition. At the top and scattered along the way are Inca ruins. The walk up and back takes at least two hours—more if you stay on the summit to enjoy the sun and drink in the marvelous view of Machu Picchu. You will have to sign in at a park kiosk before beginning the climb. Use insect repellent; the gnats can be ferocious.

Dining and Lodging

For price-category definitions, *see* Dining *and* Lodging *in* Peru Essentials, *below.*

$$$$ **Hotel de Turistas de Machu Picchu.** The decoration of the neocolonial rooms—earth-tone carpets and bedspreads—is beside the point. The charm here is sleeping at the foot of the ruins, then waking up and seeing the sun rise over Machu Picchu. As a bonus, you'll have the run of the ruins when the busloads of tourists have gone. The restaurant makes an attempt at elegance with candlelight and white linens and has an international menu featuring such standbys as pepper steak with a creamy black pepper sauce, and grilled chicken. The hotel was privatized in early 1995 and the new owners plan to upgrade it, so expect improvements. Confirm a reservation through a travel agent before leaving for Machu Picchu, as you may not be able to obtain a room otherwise. 🖾 *Machu Picchu,* ☎ *08/421–1038 or 08/421–1039. 32 rooms. Restaurant ($$$), bar. AE, DC, MC, V.*

$$$$ **Machu Picchu Pueblo Hotel.** In this semitropical garden paradise near
★   Aguas Caliente, the stone bungalows have cathedral ceilings, exposed beams, flagstone floors, and cartwheel headboards, creating an atmosphere of rustic elegance. The dining is first rate (try the *crema de choclo,* corn chowder) and the staff friendly. An 8% surcharge is added to your room rate when you pay by credit card. 🖾 *Aguas Calientes,* ☎ *08/421–1032. For reservations in Cuzco, Procuradores 48,* ☎ *08/423– 2161,* 🅵🅰🆇 *08/422–3769; in Lima, Andalucía 174, Miraflores,* ☎ *01/446– 7775,* 🅵🅰🆇 *01/445–5598. 26 rooms. Restaurant ($$$), bar. AE (accepted at hotel and in Cuzco); MC, V (Cuzco only).*

MADRE DE DIOS

The department of Madre de Dios is like nowhere else in Peru—a seemingly paradisiacal appendage that has somehow been spared many of the country's most tragic ills. Its national parks, reserves, and other undeveloped areas are among the most biologically diverse in the world—sheltering some 15,000 plant, 1,000 bird, and 200 mammal species—and offer a rare opportunity to see large mammals, such as tapirs and jaguars, as well as birds. Small wonder that Madre de Dios has garnered the attention of conservationists around the world. Groups such as the Nature Conservancy and Conservation International view the department as one of the world's arks, a place where the rain forest has a chance for survival.

Two areas of Madre de Dios are of special interest to visitors. One is around the city of Puerto Maldonado, including the Tambopata–Candamo Reserve; easily accessible, it offers lodges amid primary (unlogged) rain forest and excellent birding. Manu National Park, though more difficult to reach, provides unparalleled occasions for observing wildlife in one of the largest virgin rain forests in the New World. Both areas are best visited between May and October, the dry months; the lodges, however, are open year-round.

During the dry season, especially July, sudden *friajes* (cold fronts) bring rain and cold weather to Madre de Dios, so be prepared for the worst. Temperatures can drop from 32°C (90°F) to 10°C (50°F) overnight, so bring at least one jacket or warm sweater. No matter when you travel, bring a rain jacket or poncho and perhaps rain pants, since rain may come at any time, with or without friajes.

For more information about Madre de Dios and the southern Peruvian rain forest, contact the Conservation Association of the Southern Rain Forest (Asociación para la Conservación de la Selva Sur, Attn: Daniel Blanco, Portal los Panes 123, Oficina 305, Plaza de Armas, Cuzco, Apartado 1002, ☎ and FAX 08/424–0911; E-mail, postmaster£acss.org.pe).

Puerto Maldonado

Arriving and Departing

A long, rough jungle road leads to Puerto Maldonado from Cuzco, but it is a grueling two- to three-day truck ride. The most sensible way to reach the area is by plane. Starting in Lima and stopping in Cuzco, **Aero Continente, AeroPerú, Americana, Faucett,** and **Imperial Air** fly several times a week to **Aeropuerto Padre Aldamiz** (☎ 08/457–5133), 5 kilometers (3 miles) from Puerto Maldonado.

Exploring

Puerto Maldonado lies at the meeting point of the Madre de Dios and Tambopata rivers. It is a rough-and-tumble town whose main attraction is the **municipal market,** where you can buy freshly harvested *castañas* (Brazil nuts) very cheaply. (Buying them also gives the local people an economic incentive to protect the rain forest and the majestic castaña trees.) Maldonado is a convenient jumping-off point for visiting the rain forest, which you can do in one of two ways. The safest and most comfortable way is to spend a few days in one of the area's jungle lodges (*see* Dining and Lodging, *below*). More adventurous travelers may choose to hire a private guide in Puerto Maldonado, who generally provides camping equipment and handles details like stocking up on food and hiring a boat. One guide is particularly recommended: Orlando Carlton James (Cambridge Language Center, Calle Loreto 658, ☎ 08/457–1857; in Cuzco, ☎ 08/422–6671).

Up the Tambopata River from Maldonado is the **Tambopata–Candamo Reserve,** a 3.8-million-acre "reserved zone" in which only environment-friendly activities—such as ecotourism, rubber cultivation, and Brazil-nut harvesting—are permitted. The area holds world records in the number of bird and butterfly species recorded by scientists, and is the site of a *colpa* (clay lick) visited daily by hundreds of parrots and macaws.

Dining and Lodging

The listings below are all jungle lodges, which provide rustic but more than adequate accommodations in wooden huts raised on stilts, with mosquito netting in the windows and no electricity. Price ratings are based on package rates, which include transportation and meals. For price-category definitions, *see* Dining *and* Lodging *in* Peru Essentials, *below.*

$$$–$$$$ **Cuzco Amazónico.** A 45-minute boat ride downriver from Puerto Maldonado on the Madre de Dios River, this is the most accessible of the jungle lodges. Each of its private bungalows, set amid trees beside the river, has a flush toilet, a shower, and a porch hammock. Because the lodge is relatively close to Puerto Maldonado, large mammals are rare, but visitors often see smaller ones, such as anteaters and agoutis. Opportunities for wildlife viewing include a day trip to Lago Sandoval, where birds abound and, on very rare occasions, the giant Amazon river otter may be seen. The typical jungle dinner—fried bananas, *pacamoto* (fish or chicken cooked inside bamboo over coals), and fresh papaya for dessert—is very good. ☎ *Reservations: Andalucía 174, Miraflores, Lima,* ☎ *01/446–2775,* FAX *01/445–5598; Procuradores 48, Cuzco,* ☎ *08/423–2161. 48 bungalows. AE, MC, V.*

$$$–$$$$ **Explorer's Inn.** At this lodge about three hours up the Tambopata River from Puerto Maldonado, you may see monkeys in the surrounding forest. In addition to four-bedroom bungalows, each with private flush toilet and shower, it has a small library, a specimen collection, and interpretive displays about the rain forest. Foreign and Peruvian researchers are always on hand to serve as guides for the nature walks. The lodge and its grounds (including a soccer pitch!) are immaculately groomed, and it probably has the largest number of surrounding trails of any of the lodges. Wildlife viewing includes a night trip on the Tambopata River, with a chance to see small caimans (the big ones flee deeper into the forest, away from contact with humans). If you are planning to stay at the inn during the rainy season, coordinate your visit well in advance; boats will not make the run to the inn for just one passenger. ☎ *Reservations through Peruvian Safaris: Garcilaso de la Vega 1334, Lima,* ☎ *01/431–6330,* FAX *01/432–8866; Plateros 329, Cuzco,* ☎ *08/423–6919. 30 rooms. AE, MC, V.*

$$$ **Tambopata Jungle Lodge.** A little farther up the river from the Explorer's
★ Inn (*see above*), a 3½-hour boat ride from Puerto Maldonado, this lodge offers a chance for observing birds, butterflies, and some mammals on two- to five-night excursions that include visits to colpa and oxbow lakes. Four bungalows have two double rooms each, and two bungalows have two quad rooms each; every room has a private bathroom. ☎ *Reservations: Peruvian Andean Treks, Av. Pardo 705, Cuzco,* ☎ *08/422–5701,* FAX *08/423–8911. 44 beds. AE, MC, V.*

$$$ **Tambopata Research Center.** Four hours upriver from the Tambopata
★ Jungle Lodge (*see above*), this lodge has the most pristine setting of any in the area and thus offers the best chance to see wildlife, including monkeys and the hundreds of macaws and parrots that put on a colorful show each morning at the nearby clay lick. It is, however, the most primitive of the lodges, consisting of a raised, roofed platform divided into cubicles where guests sleep on netting-enclosed mattresses; an open dining area; and latrines and showers. A unique on-site research project on macaws allows visitors to interact with wild but hand-reared macaws. A four- or five-day package combining this with the Tambopata Jungle Lodge (*see above*) is available. ☎ *Reservations: Rainforest Expeditions, Calle Galeón 120, Chacarilla del Estanque, San Borja, Lima,* ☎ *01/435–3510,* FAX *01/447–2497; in the U.S., Wildland Adventures, 3516 N.E. 155th St., Seattle, WA 98155,* ☎ *206/365–0686 or 800/345–4453,* FAX *206/363–6615. MC, V.*

Manu National Park

Arriving and Departing

The overland trip from Cuzco to Mano, 12 hours over rugged terrain, is via a road called the Carreterra a Shintuya, which plunges spectacularly from the *páramo* (highlands) down into the cloud forests at Atalaya. Here or at Shintuya, farther downriver, you take a boat along the Alto Madre de Dios River deep into the rain forest and Manu National Park. A more expensive alternative is to charter a plane from Cuzco on **Aerosur** (☏ 08/422–4638) to the gravel airstrip at Boca Manu, the visitors' entrance to the park. From here you must travel by boat into the park—and be sure to hire one with a 55-horsepower outboard motor, not the much slower *peke-peke* boat. Also *see* Exploring, *below,* for tour operators that arrange all transport.

Exploring

This national park the size of Massachusetts encompasses more than 4.5 million acres of pristine wilderness, ranging in altitude from almost 12,000 feet down through cloud forest and into a seemingly endless lowland tropical rain forest at less than 1,000 feet. Not surprisingly, this geographical variety shelters a stunning biodiversity, and the park's untouched state has left its animal inhabitants remarkably unafraid of human beings. Most visitors see myriad bird species (amazingly, there are more in this park than in the entire United States and Canada combined), including macaws, toucans, roseate spoonbills, and 5-foot-tall wood storks. The park's 13 monkey species observe visitors with curiosity. White caimans sun themselves lazily on sandy riverbanks while the larger black ones lurk in the *cocha* (oxbow) lakes. Giant river otters and elusive big cats, such as jaguars and ocelots, sometimes make fleeting appearances.

To enter the park, you need permission from park authorities. Entry costs $25. We recommend that you travel with a reputable tour operator or guide (*see* Dining and Lodging, *below*), who will take care of getting the proper authorization. Beware of freelance guides for hire in Cuzco and Boca Manu; although most offer relatively cheap rates and are familiar with the area, their respect for its wildlife may be questionable. For instance, although it is forbidden to camp on beaches where birds and turtles nest, let alone raid the nests, travelers with freelance guides have returned with tales of scrambled turtle eggs for breakfast.

Manu Nature Tours, which owns the park's only lodge (*see* Dining and Lodging, *below*), offers two basic programs. The eight-day program takes guests into the park by land and river and out by river and charter plane. Mountain biking and white-water rafting on the Quosñipata River, in the park's highland region, is an option. The more expensive four-day program uses charter flights to enter and leave the park.

If you wish to travel alone, you must send a written request to the Dirección de Areas Protegidas y Fauna Silvestre, INRENA (Petirrojos 355, Urb. El Palomar, San Isidro, Lima, ☏ 01/441–0425, FAX 01/441–4606; Urbanización Mariscal Gamarra 4-C, Apartado 1057, Cuzco, ☏ 08/422–3633). These offices also can supply information about the park.

Dining and Lodging

For price-category definitions, *see* Dining *and* Lodging *in* Peru Essentials, *below*.

Jungle Lodge

$ **Manu Lodge.** Set deep in the park, on a 2-kilometer-long (1-mile-long) oxbow lake called Cocha Juarez, is its only lodge, a rustic building with a two-story dining area. Guests have access to three habitats: the cochas, the river, and a trail network spanning 10 square kilometers (4 square miles) of rain forest. The lodge also has tree-climbing equipment to lift visitors up onto canopy platforms for viewing denizens of the treetops. ☎ *Reservations: Av. Sol 582, Cuzco,* ☎ *08/422–4384,* FAX *08/423–4793; Centro Comercial Plaza Conquistadores, Av. Conquistadores 396, San Isidro, Lima,* ☎ *and* FAX *01/442–8980; E-mail, postmaster£mnt.com.pe. In the U.S., Wildland Adventures, 3516 N.E. 155th St., Seattle, WA 98155,* ☎ *206/365–0686 or 800/345–4453,* FAX *206/363–6615. MC, V.*

Camping

Those who wish to combine a lodge visit with some camping might contact one of the agencies that conduct camping trips in the park. They usually provide all equipment (unless you specifically request a very low-budget version of the trek) and food, but you must bring your own sleeping bag. One of the most experienced guide services, the Cuzco-based **Manu Expeditions** (Procuradores 50, ☎ 08/422–6671, FAX 08/423–6706), offers park camping trips lasting five to nine days. Another reliable agency, **Hirca** (Bellavista 518, Miraflores, ☎ and FAX 01/447–3807; Retiro 128, Oficina 100, Cuzco, ☎ 08/422–5384, FAX 08/423–4147), operates five- and nine-day full-service treks into Manu.

IQUITOS AND ENVIRONS

Iquitos is on the Amazon River at the center of Peru's northwestern jungle, one of the most biologically diverse rain forests in the world. Although the friendly and relaxed jungle port town itself has little in the way of tourist attractions, a walk along the river promenade can be pleasant. The main reason to visit is to explore the surrounding rain forest.

Visitor Information

Oficina de Información Turística (Jirón Napa 177, ☎ 09/423–4081; closed afternoons and weekends).

Arriving and Departing

By Plane

The easiest, if not the only, way to reach Iquitos is by plane. The most convenient route from the States is **Faucett's** weekly direct flight from Miami. There are daily flights from Lima to Iquitos airport (☎ 09/423–2401) on **Aero Continente, AeroPerú, Americana,** and **Faucett.** The Brazilian carrier **Cruzeiro do Sul** (*see* Chapter 5, Brazil) serves Iquitos from Manaus.

Exploring

Iquitos enjoyed its greatest importance as a port around the turn of the century, during the rubber boom. Some of the wealth of that time can still be detected in the attractive imported tiles that face many buildings along the riverbank, notably the former **Palace Hotel** (Putumayo and Malecón Tarapacá), now converted into an army barracks and looking a little worn around the edges. A smaller oil boom during the 1970s gave the city a burst of modern growth. Today, with a population of roughly 280,000, it is still the biggest city in the Peruvian jungle, and though mainly a local port, it is navigable for oceangoing ships coming from the Atlantic Ocean.

About 50 kilometers (31 miles) from Iquitos, the jungle can more precisely be called primary rain forest, where there has been no regular logging or farming, only hunting and gathering. Sadly, even this light touch of man's hand has had an effect, and hunting has all but eliminated large animals from accessible areas around Iquitos. However, visitors are likely to see birds, all kinds of insects, the occasional monkey, the lovely little freshwater dolphins of the Amazon, and, very rarely, caimans. There are three possible ways to visit the rain forest: a river cruise along the Amazon River (which usually includes guided overland hikes), an inland tour with a strong ecological component, or a stay at a relaxing resort lodge. Rates for jungle cruises usually include meals; meals and river transportation at lodges are generally included in the lodge rates.

River Cruises

While cruising the Amazon, you may see freshwater dolphins, wildfowl, parrots, and, very rarely, small monkeys. **Amazon Camp Tourist Services** (Requena 336, Iquitos, ☎ 09/423–3931, FAX 09/423–1265; in the U.S., 8700 W. Flagler St., Suite 190, Miami, FL 33174, ☎ 305/227–2266 or 800/423–2791, FAX 305/227–1880) deals exclusively in river cruises ($$$$), using boats of 8, 10, 16, or 21 cabins. The longest and most comprehensive cruise is a six-day round-trip run on the Amazon River between Iquitos and Leticia, Colombia. Trips depart weekly on comfortable riverboats with private cabins, some air-conditioned. Rooms have private or shared bathrooms and may be furnished with Amazon mahogany. The boats stop at various points for guided nature tours. The agency also arranges shorter cruises on smaller boats that are usually group chartered. These travel upriver to Nauta, where the Ucayali and Marañon rivers join to form the Amazon, and where some of the most beautiful women in Peru are said to live. Each boat has a restaurant, a bar, and a sun deck. **Explorama Tours** (Av. de la Marina 350, Box 446, Iquitos, ☎ 09/423–5471, FAX 09/423–4968; in the U.S., ☎ 800/633–4734) offers a weeklong cruise ($$$$)— timed to connect with Faucett's weekly flight from Miami—on *La Esmeralda*, a graceful Brazilian-built ship with 16 berths. The boat sails up the Tapiche River, a tributary of the Amazon, with frequent stops along the way to explore the surrounding jungle.

Environmental Tours and Lodges

Perhaps the best tour operator in Iquitos is **Explorama Tours** (*see* River Cruises, *above*), which owns four lodges and is one of the sponsors of the spectacular Canopy Walkway (*see below*). All arrangements for stays at the lodges—which are in the $$$$ price category (for price-category definitions, *see* Lodging *in* Peru Essentials, *below*)—must be made through the office in Iquitos.

Explorama Inn is the firm's facility closest to the city, only 40 kilometers (24 miles) away. The most resortlike of the company's properties, with palm-thatch cottages that have private bathrooms, fans, running water, and electricity, it offers guided tours around the area. **Explorama Lodge,** 80 kilometers (50 miles) and a three-hour cruise down the Amazon from Iquitos in an area called Yanamono, is built jungle style. Its palm-thatch buildings have private rooms and shared toilet and shower facilities, a dining area, and a bar, but no electricity or running water. Tours on foot and by boat of the nearby primary rain forest, with more than 2,000 plant species and hundreds of species of birds and insects, are offered.

Deeper into the rain forest—70 kilometers (43 miles) up the Napo River, 3½ hours by boat, from the Yanamono area—is the **Explornapo Camp.** Set in the middle of a reserve run by Explorama, this is literally a camp where you sleep on a mattress on a roofed platform. Guided nature walks in the forest are offered. A half-hour walk from the camp is **ACEER,** the Amazon Center for Environmental Education and Research, an education-and-research post open to scientists and visitors. With basic facilities similar to those of the Explorama Lodge (arrangements to stay at the center are made through Explorama Tours), ACEER features the most important attraction in the Iquitos region: the **Canopy Walkway,** the only such facility in the Americas. Imagine a suspended bridge strung between immense primeval trees. Imagine being eye to eye with tropical woodpeckers. Imagine wandering along a walkway 110 feet above the ground with the jungle at your feet, and you have imagined the Canopy Walkway.

Other facilities include the **Anaconda Lara Lodge** ($$$), open only by advance reservation. West of Iquitos, up the Amazon River on the Momón River tributary, it has a 2,000-acre reserve but not much primary rain forest. The operator is **Anaconda Lara** (Pevas 210, Iquitos, ☎ 09/423–9147, 𝔽𝔸𝕏 09/423–2978), which also organizes camping expeditions to the **Pacaya-Samiria National Reserve,** 150 kilometers (93 miles) up the Amazon from Iquitos, between the Marañon and Ucayali rivers, and to other places in the Amazon rain forest. **Paseos Amazónicos** (Pevas 246, Iquitos, ☎ 09/423–3110; in Lima, ☎ 01/446–3838, 𝔽𝔸𝕏 01/446–7946) runs the **Sinchicuy Lodge** ($$$), 26 kilometers (16 miles) down the Amazon on Sinchicuy Creek. The lodge has little primary rain forest to boast of but organizes butterfly- and orchid-watching expeditions.

Shopping

The tourist industry is not as well-developed in Iquitos as in Cuzco and, thus, there are not as many crafts or souvenir shops. Two **Amazon Arts and Crafts** shops (Napo 149, ☎ 09/423–4263, 𝔽𝔸𝕏 09/423–4968), across from each other just off the main square, contain handicrafts typical to the region, such as brightly painted balsa-wood parrots and potions brewed from local herbs that are said to make one irresistible to members of the opposite sex. At the **Mercado Artesanal,** a crafts market on the road to the airport, a number of stalls sell the ubiquitous parrots and mounted insects.

Dining

For price-category definitions, *see* Dining *in* Peru Essentials, *below.*

$$ ★ **La Casa de Jaime.** The service is slow at this simple, neon-lit restaurant (nicer if the power fails and the staff light the candles), but the food is worth the wait. Try the mouthwatering *lanza de pescado* (catfish kebabs), and be sure to ask the English-speaking owner to put melted water-buffalo-milk mozzarella on top to make them doubly wonderful. ✗ *Malecón Tarapacá 246,* ☎ *09/423–9456. DC, V.*

Lodging

Besides the jungle lodges (*see* Environmental Tours and Lodges, *above*), there are a number of more conventional lodging options in and around Iquitos. For price-category definitions, *see* Lodging *in* Peru Essentials, *below.*

Hotels

$$$ **El Dorado Hostal.** Similar in style to the Acosta II (*see below*), this hotel is a little plusher and slightly more expensive. The rooms are comfy, with wood ceilings and fittings, but the staff are a bit heavy-handed with the air freshener. ⊞ *Napo 362,* ☎ *09/423–7326 or 09/423–1742,* ℻ *09/423–2203. 52 rooms. Restaurant, bar, air-conditioning, pool, hot tubs. AE, DC, MC, V.*

$$$ **Hostal Acosta II.** The better of the two Acosta hotels in town, this is a
★ modern, airy building, with rooms around a courtyard containing a small swimming pool. ⊞ *Ricardo Palma 252,* ☎ *09/423–1983 or 09/423–2904,* ℻ *09/423–2499. 42 rooms. Restaurant, bar, air-conditioning, pool. AE, DC, V.*

Resort

$$$ **Las Colinas de Zungarococha Lodge.** Part of the Acosta hotel chain, the lodge is on the Zungarococha Lake along the Nanay River, 1½ hours upriver from Iquitos and 45 minutes away by car. This comfortable resort has almost all the facilities of a city hotel, including private, motel-like rooms with bathrooms in palm-thatch bungalows, as well as a small zoo and a lake. Although the restaurant serves local specialties, such as *paiche* fish and hearts of palm, the focus is on international cuisine. ⊞ *Reservations: Hostal Acosta, Próspero 652, Iquitos,* ☎ *09/423–2131,* ℻ *09/423–2499; Ricardo Rivera Navarrete 645–E, Lima,* ☎ *01/442–4515. 24 rooms. Restaurant, bar. AE, DC, V.*

PERU ESSENTIALS

Customs and Duties

You may bring duty-free into Peru $1,000 worth of personal goods and gifts; everything thereafter is taxed at a flat rate of 25%. You may also bring a total of three liters of liquor; jewelry or perfume worth less than $300; and 20 packs of cigarettes or 50 cigars. If after arrival you pass through the "nothing to declare" line and a red light flashes, your baggage will be examined and any taxable items you failed to declare will be confiscated.

Dining

The cost and quality of dining out in Peru can vary widely, but a modest restaurant that looks clean may serve as splendid a meal as one with snazzier decor. Most smaller restaurants offer a lunchtime *menú,* a prix-fixe meal ($2–$5) that consists of an appetizer, a main dish, dessert, and a beverage. Peru is also full of cafés, many with a selection of delicious pastries. Food at bars is usually limited to snacks and sandwiches.

Specialties

Breakfast for the urban Peruvian usually is Continental but sometimes includes eggs or oatmeal with cinnamon, along with fruit and juice. Highlanders might have soup or stew for breakfast; in the jungle, it might consist of fried manioc or bananas.

On the coast, fresh seafood is reasonably priced and prepared in a hundred ways. The most famous is cebiche, a cold stew of raw fish or seafood marinated in lemon juice and smothered with onions and hot peppers. Other favorite fish preparations are *a la chorillana* (fried with tomatoes and onions) and *a lo macho* (drenched in a spicy seafood sauce). The delicately flavored corvina is the most highly prized deep-sea fish in Peru; other excellent seafood includes *cojinova* (a white fish that is somewhat fishier-tasting than corvina), lenguado (flounder), *pulpo* (octopus), *conchitas* (scallops), and *calamares* (squid).

Chicken is a staple, and you can find anything from simple chicken *a la brasa* (grilled) to *ají de gallina,* shredded chicken cooked in a creamy piquant sauce. In the Sierra, try cuy (guinea pig). Typical meat dishes include *anticuchos* (kebabs of marinated beef heart) and lomo saltado, a Chinese-Peruvian hybrid of stir-fried beef, onions, tomatoes, hot peppers, and potatoes served over rice. The best ethnic cooking in Peru is Chinese, known as chifa.

Comida criolla (Creole cooking) is the favored fare along the coast. It is generally heavily spiced with hot peppers, usually includes onions, and may use fish, chicken, or meat. It is often fried, although *arroz con pollo, arroz con pato* (stews and rice simmered with chicken or duck) are also staples.

Peru gave the world the potato, and hundreds of varieties are grown here. Among the tastier potato recipes are papa a la huancaina (in spicy cheese sauce), *ocopa* (in spicy peanut sauce), and *carapulcra* (a stew of dried potatoes served over rice). Peru has wonderful fruit, such as *chirimoya* (custard apple) and *tuna* (cactus fruit).

Do try Peru's national drink, the pisco sour, made from distilled grape liquor. Don't let its icy sweetness deceive you—it packs quite a kick. Peruvian beers are not bad, and each region boasts its own. In Lima, the market leaders are Cristal and the slightly more upscale Pilsen Callao, both produced by the same brewing group. In the south, another brewer produces two lagers—Arequipeña, from Arequipa, and Cusqueña, from Cuzco—that are making inroads in the Lima market and are now preferred by connoisseurs. Peruvian wines, such as Oc-cucaje or Tacama, are quite good; Tacama's Blanco de Blancos is considered the country's best.

Mealtimes

Top-notch restaurants offer lunch and dinner, but most Peruvians think of lunch as the main meal of the day, and many restaurants open only for lunch. Served between 1 and 3, lunch is traditionally followed by a siesta, though the custom has largely died out. Dinner can be anything from a light snack to another full meal. Peruvians tend to dine late, between 7 and 11 PM. Cafés are open from 10 AM to 10 PM or later; bars open at around 6 PM but become lively at 10 or 11.

Dress

Peruvians dress quite informally when they dine out, and often a sport jacket is sufficient for men even at very expensive restaurants. A smart pair of slacks or a skirt is always appropriate for women. Shorts are frowned upon everywhere except at the beach, and T-shirts should be worn only in very modest restaurants.

Ratings

Meals are subject to an 18% sales tax, which should be included in the bill. Better restaurants also include a 10% service charge. Prices below are per person and include appetizer, main course, and dessert but exclude alcoholic beverages, tax, service charge, and tip.

CATEGORY	LIMA	OTHER AREAS
$$$$	over $35	over $20
$$$	$15–$35	$10–$20
$$	$6–$15	$5–$10
$	under $6	under $5

Embassies and Consulates

United States
Embassy: Garcilaso de la Vega 1400, Lima, ☎ 01/433–8000. Consulate: Grimaldo del Solar 346, Miraflores, Lima, ☎ 01/444–3621.

Canada
Embassy and consulate: Libertad 130, Miraflores, Lima, ☎ 01/444–4015.

United Kingdom
Embassy and consulate: Edificio El Pacifico, Avenida Arequipa (5th block), Plaza Washington, Lima, ☎ 01/433–4738 or 01/433–4839.

Getting Around

By Plane
Flying is the easiest, fastest, and safest way to get around Peru. **Americana** (☎ 01/444–0202 or 01/447–1919; in the U.S., contact Andina Tour and Travel, ☎ 206/820–9966) offers a "Discover Peru" pass, valid for 30 days' unlimited use, which costs $250. Other airlines have similar deals. **AeroPerú** (☎ 01/447–8900) and **Faucett** (☎ 01/464–3322; in the U.S., ☎ 800/334–3356) also have regularly scheduled flights to major cities and towns in Peru. **Aero Continente** (☎ 01/442–7829), **Air Imperial** (☎ 01/476–4542 or 01/476–0775), and **Expresso Aereo** (☎ 01/445–2545 or 01/445–2745) are new airlines that fly to the major cities but offer less regular and less reliable services. **Aerotransporte S.A.,** or ATSA (☎ 01/452–9161 or 01/452–9230, ⊠ 01/451–5712) provides charters to most of the country.

A number of smaller regional airlines, such as **Aerocondor** (☎ 01/440–1754), offer "taxi" service and some regular flights to smaller cities, especially in the jungle. Airplane taxis, small planes that depart when there are sufficient numbers of passengers, include **Aerotaxis Carlos Palacin** (☎ 01/451–9623) and **Taxi Aereo Selva** (☎ 01/452–6217), both of which fly throughout the jungle.

By Train
Train travel in Peru is limited to six lines, operated by **ENAFER** (☎ 01/427–6620 or 01/428–9440), the government-owned railway company. For reasons of safety, only two routes are recommended: Arequipa–Juliaca–Puno–Juliaca–Cuzco and Cuzco–Machu Picchu–Quillabamba. Tickets can be purchased either at train stations or through travel agencies; top-class tickets should be bought in advance.

Except on the Cuzco–Machu Picchu tourist train, railway travel in Peru tends to be somewhat slow, and theft is very common. Food and drinks are often not available on board, and although vendors clamber aboard at every stop or will sell you food from the station platform, you are advised to bring food and bottled water with you. If you are traveling via Puno or La Oroya, bring a blanket, a sleeping bag, or very warm clothes, as it can get very cold at high altitudes.

By Car
Since taxis and public transportation are inexpensive, driving is not recommended. If you do drive, remember that most Peruvians see traffic laws as suggestions rather than commands. Outside cities, drive only during daylight hours, fill your gas tank whenever possible, make sure your spare tire is in good repair, and carry planks to help you out of soft spots on or off the road.

The major highways in Peru are the Panamericana (Pan-American Highway), which runs along the entire coast of Peru, and the Carretera

Central, which runs from Lima to Huancayo and from there to the central jungle. Most highways have no names or numbers; they are referred to by destination, e.g., "the highway to Arequipa." You can purchase good maps from the **Touring and Automobile Club of Peru** (Av. César Vallejo 699, Lince, ☎ 01/440–3270). Members of the American Automobile Association and affiliates can get these maps at members' prices.

ROAD CONDITIONS

Highway conditions have improved markedly on the Pan-American and the Carretera Central due to a multimillion-dollar government road-improvement drive. Elsewhere, including all of Lima, roads tend to be littered with potholes, and farther afield conditions degenerate rapidly. Security on some highways is also a serious problem (*see* Precautions, *below*). Signs outside Lima are relatively rare, except at major turnoffs, and lighting is nonexistent. In Lima, vehicular chaos quite literally rules, while traffic in other major cities is only slightly better.

RULES OF THE ROAD

You can drive in Peru with a foreign license for up to six months, after which time you will need an international driver's license. Driving is on the right, passing on the left. Speed limits are 25–35 kph (15–20 mph) in residential areas, 85–100 kph (50–60 mph) on highways. Traffic tickets range from a minimum of $4 to a maximum of $40. The police and military routinely do vehicle spot checks, sometimes for reasons of security, and drivers with their documents in order (driver's license, car registration, and for foreigners, valid passport) are waved on. If, however, the officer wants a bribe, he will look for the slightest violation, and you should be prepared either to argue hard or to come up with $3 or so. Peruvian law makes it a crime to drive while intoxicated, although many Peruvians ignore that prohibition. If you are caught driving while under the influence, you will either pay a hefty bribe or spend the night in jail.

EMERGENCY ASSISTANCE

The **Touring and Automobile Club of Peru** (emergency ☎ 01/440–3270 or 01/422–5957) will provide emergency road service for members of AAA and affiliates on presentation of their membership cards.

GASOLINE

Gas costs around $2. Gas stations on the highway are widely spaced, and most close at 11 PM.

PARKING

Parking lots charging about a dollar an hour are common and provide the best security. Parking on the street costs between 30¢ and 50¢; you should tip someone to watch over your car.

By Bus

The intercity bus system in Peru is extensive, and fares are usually very cheap. Beware, however, of the informal, "pirate" bus lines, whose safety records are abysmal. Some of the better lines are **Cruz del Sur** (☎ 01/427–1311), **Ormeño** (☎ 01/427–5679), and **Tepsa** (☎ 01/432–1233). All three offer regular and first-class service. The regular second-class buses (*servicio normal*) tend to be overcrowded and uncomfortable, while the more expensive first-class service is safer, more comfortable, and much more likely to arrive on schedule.

An alternative form of public transportation is the *colectivos,* small vans or large cars that cover the same routes as the buses. They charge about twice as much but are usually much faster. The catch is that they don't leave until they fill up. Colectivos are organized by *comités* (a group of drivers who cover a given route) and usually cover specific regions. You will find them listed in the yellow pages of the telephone directory under "Transportes Terrestres," or ask at your hotel desk for a comité that will take you where you want to go.

For longer bus trips, you may wish to bring bottled water, snacks, and toilet paper. If you are traveling into the Sierra, take warm clothing or a blanket. You can buy bus tickets through a travel agent. Whenever possible, travel and arrive at your destination during daytime. For caveats on where not to travel by bus, *see* Precautions, *below.*

By Boat

Passenger boats are the most important means of transportation in the jungle. If you visit a jungle lodge, your hosts will probably pick you up in an outboard-powered canoe. Larger boats make 4- to 10-day cruises on the Amazon from Iquitos. In smaller towns throughout the jungle, you can arrange private river excursions by hiring a *peke-peke,* a wood longboat that has a small motor, may or may not have a roof, and is slower and cheaper than a boat with an outboard motor. On Lake Titicaca, small boats offer taxi service to the Uros floating islands and the larger island of Taquile.

Language

Spanish is Peru's national language, and native languages also enjoy official status. Many Peruvians speak Quechua, the language of the Incas, as their native tongue, but most speak Spanish as well. Other native languages include the Tiahuanaco language, Aymara, which is spoken around Lake Titicaca, and several linguistic groups in the jungle. Wealthier Peruvians and those working with tourists often speak English, but they are the exception. If you speak any Spanish at all, by all means use it. Your hosts will appreciate the effort, and any laughter that greets your words will be good-natured rather than mocking.

A word on spelling: Since the Incas had no writing system, Quechua developed as an oral language. With European colonization, words and place names were transcribed to conform to Spanish pronunciations. Eventually, the whole language was transcribed, and in many cases words lost their correct pronunciations. During the past 30 years, however, national pride and a new sensitivity to the country's indigenous roots have led Peruvians to try to recover consistent, linguistically correct transcriptions of Quechua words. As you travel, you may come across different spellings and pronunciations of the same name. An example is the city non–Latin Americans know as Cuzco. The city government uses "Qosqo" as the official spelling, though most Peruvians still use the "Cusco" spelling. To avoid confusion, the "Cuzco" spelling is used throughout this chapter. Note, however, that Peruvians may prefer the Quechuan pronunciations and linguistically correct transcriptions.

Lodging

Accommodations in Peru range from bare-bones rooms with shared bathrooms to luxury hotels. They come with names such as *hostal, pensión, residencial,* and *hotel,* and though the implication is that the last is more upscale, this is not always the case. Televisions in rooms are becoming more common but are usual only in the best hotels—and not always there. Moderate and more expensive hotels tend to have telephones in guest rooms, but ask to be sure. Tourism is taking off again in Peru, making it difficult at times to find good hotel accommodations, especially in Lima. If you're planning on visiting during a festival, it's best to reserve in advance.

Camping in Peru is limited to some beaches (where Peruvians camp in large groups for protection) and as part of mountain and jungle treks. The only legal campsites are in some national parks, such as Manu National Park (*see* Madre de Dios, *above*). Camping is pretty much required for those hiking the Inca Trail.

Ratings

Hotels usually charge an 18% tax and occasionally service charges of up to 13%. Prices below are for a double room and include tax and service charge. A Continental breakfast is often but not always included in the room rate; the most expensive hotels are least likely to include breakfast.

CATEGORY	LIMA	OTHER AREAS
$$$$	over $120	over $70
$$$	$70–$120	$45–$70
$$	$35–$70	$20–$45
$	under $35	under $20

Mail

Note that, except in Lima, Peru does not have postal codes.

Postal Rates

Airmail letters and postcards sent within the Americas cost 89¢ for less than 20 grams; outside the hemisphere, they cost 80¢. Airmail packages sent within the Americas cost $47 for up to 3 kilograms, $63 elsewhere. Packages sent second class cost one-third to one-half less. Bring packages to the post office unsealed, and be prepared to wrap them in white burlap and sew them shut after showing the contents to postal workers. Mail theft is occasionally a problem.

Receiving Mail

If you don't know where you will be staying in advance, you can have mail sent to you (mark the letters POSTE RESTANTE) at the following addresses: A/C Correo Central, Pasaje Piura, Lima 1; Correo de Miraflores, Avenida Petit Thouars 5201, Lima 18. If you or the sender are an American Express cardholder, you can receive mail at AmEx offices at Belén 1040, Lima. Thomas Cook (Comandante Espinar 331, Miraflores) will also hold mail.

Money and Expenses

Currency

Peru's national currency is the nuevo sol (S/), or new sun, divided into 100 céntimos. Bills are issued in denominations of 5, 10, 20, 50, and 100 soles. Coins are 1, 5, 10, 20, and 50 céntimos, and 1, 2, and 5 soles. Be careful not to confuse the 1-sol coin with the older and now worthless 1-inti coin. The recently introduced 2- and 5-sol coins are also confusingly similar.

At press time (winter 1995), the exchange rate was S/2.25 to the U.S. dollar and S/3.60 to the pound sterling. The Peruvian currency is volatile, however, and the economy is dollarized—that is, when the number of soles per dollar increases, so do the prices in soles (though prices in dollars may remain unchanged). Therefore, all prices in this chapter are given in dollars, a more stable indicator.

Changing Money

Although the *cambistas* (freelance money changers) waving pocket calculators on city streets may offer a slightly better exchange rate than the banks, they sometimes stiff clients. If you do change on the street, look for the identity badges that indicate licensed money changers, who tend to be more reliable. Tricks used by the less scrupulous include tampering with their calculators to come up with less than they should (work out the sum for yourself if your math is up to it), or "realizing" halfway through a transaction that they don't have enough local currency to change your bill and then giving you back a counterfeit note instead of your good one (hold onto your money until you are satisfied that the cambista has handed over the right sum).

Exchanging money at your hotel may be safer and more convenient, but the rates can be as much as 5% below that offered at banks. The exchange rate at the different banks is the same, so there is no advantage to shopping around. Money can also be changed at *casas de cambio* (exchange houses). Neither banks nor casas de cambio charge commissions.

Forms of Payment

Traveler's checks are accepted at casas de cambio, banks, and big hotels. The rate is usually the same as for cash, but many banks have a ceiling on how much they will exchange at one time. Stores, smaller hotels, and restaurants rarely accept traveler's checks. Major credit cards, especially Visa, are accepted in most tourist-oriented hotels, restaurants, and shops.

Costs

Peru's economy has stabilized after the chaos of the eighties and early nineties, but although the basics are reasonably cheap, anything that might loosely be called a luxury tends to be moderately expensive in South American terms. Monthly inflation has dropped to around 1%, and the dollar is undervalued but slowly rising. An 18% sales tax, known as *impuesto general a las ventas,* or IGV, is levied on everything except items bought at open-air markets and from street vendors. It is usually included in the advertised price of merchandise and should be with food and drink.

Restaurants have been ordered to publish their prices, including taxes and a 10% service charge that is sometimes added on, but they do not always do so. They are also prone to levy a cover charge for anything from live entertainment to serving you a roll with your meal. It is best to check before ordering. Small restaurants tend to be the least expensive; eateries serving French, Italian, Japanese, or Argentine food are apt to be pricey. Hotel bills may also have taxes and a 10% service charge added on. If you avoid topflight tourist hotels and restaurants, you will find food and lodging in Peru to be reasonably priced. Restaurants and hotels outside the capital are likely to be less expensive, except in Cuzco, where prices are comparable to those in Lima. In the jungle, food is only slightly less expensive than in Lima, but accommodations are generally moderate.

The cost of transportation is high; at press time (winter 1995) gasoline cost around $2 per gallon. Airport taxes are approximately $18 for international and $4 for domestic flights. State-owned attractions usually charge only a nominal entrance fee, except in Cuzco and environs, where admission prices are quite hefty by Peruvian standards.

SAMPLE PRICES
In Lima: cup of coffee, $1; bottle of beer, $2; pisco sour, $2–$5; glass of wine, $2; soft drink, 90¢; chicken-and-avocado sandwich, $3; 1-mile taxi ride, $1.35.

Opening and Closing Times

Banks

Opening hours vary from bank to bank and season to season, with most of the larger ones closing for a couple of hours at lunchtime and reopening until as late as 6 PM. Some banks are open on Saturday morning.

Museums and Churches

Most museums are open Monday–Saturday 9–6. Some close at lunch, usually between 1 and 3 or 4 PM. Church hours are more irregular. Some are open to visitors only in the early morning, while others have hours similar to those of museums, except that they are also open Sunday.

Shops

Stores are generally open Monday–Saturday 10–8. Many smaller stores close for two hours at lunchtime and on Saturday are open in the morning only.

National Holidays

New Year's Day (Jan. 1); Easter holiday, which begins midday on Maundy Thursday and continues through Easter Monday (1996: Apr. 4–8; 1997: Mar. 27–31); Labor Day (May 1); St. Peter and St. Paul Day (June 29); Independence Day (July 28); St. Rosa of Lima Day (Aug. 30); Battle of Angamos Day, commemorating a battle with Chile in the War of the Pacific, 1879–81 (Oct. 8); All Saints' Day (Nov. 1); Immaculate Conception (Dec. 8); Christmas (Dec. 25).

Precautions

Health

VACCINATIONS

Before coming to Peru, all travelers should receive a typhoid vaccination, which consists of two injections given four weeks apart. The injections can be painful and cause a fever, so don't leave them until the last minute. Also make sure that as an adult you have had a polio booster, and that you have had a tetanus-diphtheria booster within the past 10 years. Hepatitis A is common in Peru; immune serum globulin is usually recommended. Although hepatitis B is found both in Lima and in the jungle, it is considerably rarer than hepatitis A. Travelers who visit only Lima and vicinity, the coastal area south of Lima, or Lake Titicaca, Cuzco, or Machu Picchu are not at risk of contracting yellow fever. If you intend to travel in the jungle, however, you do need a yellow fever vaccination. Another threat in the jungle is malaria, for which you should take antimalarial tablets starting two weeks before and continuing six weeks after your visit.

ALTITUDE SICKNESS

Soroche (altitude sickness) hits most visitors to sky-high cities such as Cuzco and Puno, but with care its symptoms remain mild. Headache, shortness of breath, and insomnia are common. When visiting areas at least 10,000 feet above sea level, always rest a few hours before going out to explore, and take it easy on your first day. Avoid heavy foods, alcohol, and cigarettes, and drink plenty of liquids. To fight soroche, Peruvians swear by mate de coca, a tea made of coca leaf.

FOOD AND DRINK

In 1991, an epidemic of cholera, a potentially deadly illness causing severe diarrhea and vomiting, swept Peru. The number of cases reported in subsequent years has dropped dramatically, but you should still take care. Tap water may be risky, so stick to bottled water and beverages. Anything raw merits caution, including cebiche (*see* Dining, *above*) sold on the street or at piers, although in a good restaurant cebiche should be safe. Cebiche made from deep-sea fish such as corvina, cojinova, or lenguado is unlikely to have cholera. In restaurants, avoid salads and fruits that you can't peel. In Lima you can buy solutions, such as Zonalin, for disinfecting fresh fruit and vegetables. Remember also that it is just as important to watch where you eat as what you eat. Food from street stalls, for instance, is notorious for causing stomach problems, while a clean, well-kept restaurant is much safer.

Safety

All the areas covered in this chapter are basically safe for tourists. Although fragments of the Shining Path terrorist organization are still active, the current wisdom is that there is little chance of attack in the main tourist areas. Nonetheless, some areas remain dangerous, whether because of guerrillas, bandits, drug runners, petty thieves, or simply the state of the roads.

Don't let this litany of doom make you paranoid, however—most visitors enjoy their time in Peru without major mishaps. By staying alert and using your common sense, you should be able to avoid problems. Wherever you travel in Peru, your best safeguard is to use a reputable travel agency. Their knowledge and experience should keep you out of unsafe areas and can also help you avoid some of the headaches of traveling in a country where underdevelopment still means too much bureaucracy and too little logical organization. Some Lima-based agencies, such as **Lima Tours** (Belén 1040, Box 4340, Lima 1, ☎ 01/427–6720 or 01/427–6624, ☎ 01/426–9878 or 01/426–2010), have offices throughout the country.

CRIME

Crime is common throughout Peru. Urban bus and train stations, some train routes, and markets are sometimes the scenes of purse and camera snatching and backpack slashing. Tourists have been mugged at knifepoint in Cuzco at night. In addition, buses traveling by night are occasionally stopped by armed bandits in some areas.

You can protect yourself by traveling by day, not wearing flashy jewelry or watches, avoiding dark and empty streets, leaving your valuables in a safe deposit box at your hotel, and keeping a firm grip on your belongings. It is reported that a diversionary tactic used by thieves is to squirt you with liquid and then offer to help you clean up, so don't be fooled into loosening your hold.

TERRORISM

Although guerrilla violence has plagued Peru, the two major terrorist groups, the Sendero Luminoso (Shining Path) and the Tupac Amaru Revolutionary Movement (MRTA)—while no friends to foreigners—have not targeted foreign tourists, and attacks on them are extremely rare. Both have also suffered serious defeats in the last two or three years, and the guerrillas that remain have fallen back to areas largely removed from those visited by tourists. Political violence in Peru, in any case, has not taken the form of a conventional war and tends to be quite localized. Being in the wrong place at the wrong time can be dangerous, as it can be in New York or Los Angeles, but skipping Manu

National Park because of reports of violence some 200 miles away in Ayacucho is like avoiding the Delaware Water Gap because of muggings in the South Bronx.

In general, air travel is safe everywhere, while long-distance overland travel can be dangerous in places, especially at night. Some jungle areas and much of the central and south-central highlands can be dangerous. You should still not travel overland from Cuzco to Lima via Nazca, partly because the trip takes you through Apurímac and Ayacucho, two departments where Shining Path attacks are still possible, but mainly because the road is in poor shape and frequented by bandits. The Shining Path has been known to stop buses traveling that route and has killed foreign tourists it has found on board.

You should certainly avoid the following departments: Apurímac, Huancavelica, Pasco, Ucayali, Huánuco, and San Martín. In the last two departments, *under no circumstances* should you visit the drug-ridden Huallaga Valley.

For more specific information about terrorist activity in Peru, or if you want to travel to areas of Peru not covered in this chapter, contact the **South American Explorers Club** (in the U.S., 126 Indian Creek Rd., Ithaca, NY 14850, ☎ 800/274–0568; in Peru, República de Portugal 146, Breña, Lima, ☎ 01/431–4480). This member-supported, nonprofit organization offers guidebooks, maps, and constantly updated tips on how and where to travel. Although some of its services are available to the general public, it offers special privileges to members. For additional updates, contact the **Peruvian Consulate** (215 Lexington Ave., New York, NY 10016, ☎ 212/481–7410) or the **Peruvian Embassy** (1700 Massachusetts Ave., Washington, DC 20036, ☎ 202/833–9860). The **Citizens' Emergency Center** (☎ 202/647–5225) at the U.S. State Department Bureau of Consular Affairs publishes travel advisories available by fax (*see* U.S. Government Travel Briefings *under* Important Contacts A to Z *in* The Gold Guide).

Shopping

Most visitors will be interested in Peru's handicrafts. Textiles are often in the form of handwoven wall hangings in earth tones of Andean genre scenes, or brightly colored folk designs in geometric shapes or of stylized animals or other pre-Columbian motifs. You can also buy vests, tote bags, and camera straps in similar designs. Clothes made of alpaca and sheep wool, usually sweaters, are attractive, as are carved gourds, silver and gold jewelry and other items (especially in pre-Columbian motifs), and ceramics.

Large stores have fixed prices, but those devoted mostly to the tourist trade are willing to bargain. In markets and crafts stores and with street vendors, bargaining is expected.

Telephones

Local and Long-Distance Calls

Peru does not have a "telephone culture," and many attractions, especially churches, either do not have telephones or their staffs are not accustomed to answering tourists' questions on the phone. Thus, if you call a church, for example, you may get a quizzical or rude response. **Telefónica del Peru,** the newly privatized and merged telephone company, has promised a $2 billion investment splurge on Peru's phone system by 1998, and there are signs that things may be improving. New "intelligent" pay phones are a start, although you may still run across older models, for which you need a token called a *RIN* or *ficha*. They are available from candy sellers and newspaper kiosks for 20¢. Local calls cost about 20¢ for the first three minutes. To call another area in Peru, first dial 0 and then the area code.

International Calls

International calls are easy to make from Lima and the coast, at times difficult in the highlands, and sometimes impossible in the jungle. Hotels add hefty surcharges to international calls made from guest rooms, so you may want to call from the telephone company's calling centers or try to find a newer pay phone from which you can make international calls. Calls to the United States cost $1.50 per minute.

To dial direct, dial 00, then 1 for the United States and Canada, 44 for the United Kingdom. To make an operator-assisted international call, dial 108. For information inside Peru, dial 103. To reach an **AT&T** operator, dial 191. For **MCI,** dial 190. For **Sprint,** dial 176.

Tipping

If a 13% service charge has been included, only a nominal tip is expected (2%–5% of the pre-tax bill); otherwise 5%–10% is sufficient in most restaurants. Porters in hotels and airports expect 50¢–$1 per bag. There is no need to tip taxi drivers. At bars, tip 20–50 céntimos for a beer, more for a mixed drink. Bathroom attendants get 20 céntimos, gas station attendants 50 céntimos for extra services such as adding air to your tires or oil. Tour guides and tour bus drivers should get 5–10 soles each per day.

When to Go

The tourist season in Peru runs from May through September, corresponding to the dry season in the Sierra (highlands) and Selva (jungle). The best time to visit is May through July, when the cool, misty weather is just beginning on the Costa (coast), and the highlands are dressed in bright green and topped with crystalline blue skies. June brings major festivals, such as Inti Raymi (the Inca festival of the sun) and Corpus Christi, to Cuzco. Other important festival months are February, which means Carnival throughout Peru and the Virgen de la Candelaria (Candlemas) celebrations in Puno, and October, when chanting, purple-clad devotees of the Lord of the Miracles fill the streets of Lima.

Climate

When it's dry in the Sierra and the Selva, it's wet on the Costa, and vice versa. The Selva is hot and humid year-round, with endless rain between January and April. Friajes (cold fronts) from Patagonia occasionally sweep through the southern rain forests of Madre de Dios, but the average daily minimum and maximum temperatures in the Selva are 20°C (69°F) and 32°C (90°F).

In the Sierra, expect rain between October and April, and especially January through March. The rest of the year, the weather is dry and the temperatures fickle. The sun can be hot, but in the shade it's refreshingly cool. Nights are chilly, and temperature may drop to freezing. Temperatures during Cuzco's dry months average 0°C (32°F)–22°C (71°F).

It never rains in the coastal desert, but a dank, heavy fog called the *garua* coats Lima June through December. Outside Lima, coastal weather is clearer and warm.

The following are average daily maximum and minimum temperatures for Lima.

Jan.	27C	81F	**May**	25C	77F	**Sept.**	19C	66F
	21	70		19	66		15	59
Feb.	28C	82F	**June**	23C	73F	**Oct.**	21C	70F
	21	70		17	63		16	61
Mar.	29C	84F	**July**	18C	64F	**Nov.**	23C	73F
	23	73		15	59		17	63
Apr.	27C	81F	**Aug.**	18C	64F	**Dec.**	24C	75F
	22	72		15	59	18		64

11 Uruguay

Aside from the sparkling resorts along its coast, gently rolling hills and grasslands are the hallmarks of Uruguay, but its people—well-educated yet unpretentious, industrious yet relaxed—are the most remarkable aspect of the country for many travelers.

By Parker
Pascua

Updated by
Lyndell
Brookhouse-Gil

ONE OF THE SMALLEST COUNTRIES in South America, Uruguay might be described as a lonely city buffeted by the sea, surrounded by vast amounts of farmland and gently rolling hills (nothing in the country is over 2,000 feet tall). In sparsely developed Uruguay, all roads lead to the capital, Montevideo, which has the country's largest university, half the newspapers (with 90% of the circulation), half the doctors, and almost half the population. Montevideo's only cosmopolitan rival is Punta del Este, one of a handful of Atlantic Ocean resorts popular with well-heeled Brazilians and Argentines who can afford the region's high-priced variety of fun (mornings and afternoons at Gucci, evenings at heady bars and discos).

Uruguay has long been considered the most European of South American countries. Its population is almost all of European descent—largely Spanish, Portuguese, and Italian—and the influence of these cultures is readily apparent in Uruguay's architecture and outlook. Even the country's "traditional cuisine" brings to mind pasta, paella, and slabs of succulent steak.

Uruguay's original inhabitants, the seminomadic Charrúas Indians, were driven out first by the Portuguese, who settled the town of Colonia in 1680, and by the Spanish, who in 1726 established a fortress at Montevideo. In 1811, José Gervasio Artigas, captain of the Spanish forces in Uruguay, mobilized Creoles and natives to fight against the heavy-handed influence of Buenos Aires. Though Artigas's bid for Uruguayan independence was unsuccessful, Uruguay finally became an autonomous state in 1825. On July 18, 1830—a date that gives the name to many a street in Uruguay—the country's first constitution was framed.

Following a period of civil war, José Batlle y Ordóñez was elected president in 1903. Under his guidance, Uruguay became the first Latin American country to grant voting rights to women and the first country to sever relations between church and state—a striking maneuver considering the Catholic Church's strong influence on the continent. Since then, except for a brief period from 1973 (when the military staged a coup) until 1985 (when free elections were once again held), Uruguay has been one of the strongest democracies in South America.

With the continent's highest literacy rate (94%), Uruguay rightfully takes pride in its great number of outstanding artists. Local theaters and galleries are full of works by masters such as José Belloni (1880–1965), the internationally famed sculptor; Joaquín Torres-García (1874–1949), the founder of Uruguay's Constructivist movement; and Pedro Figari (1861–1938) and Pedro Blanes Viale (1879–1926), both of whom influenced a generation of Uruguayan painters. As in Argentina, the legendary gaucho is Uruguay's most potent cultural fixture, and it is difficult to pass a day without some reference to these cowboys who once roamed the country singing their melancholy ballads. (Remnants of the gaucho lifestyle may still be seen on active ranches, or *estancias*, throughout the country.)

Uruguay attracts internationally known artists who perform during the Montevideo opera season or cavort in the resort city of Punta del Este during the Southern Hemisphere summer. Montevideo's lively *Carnaval*, the annual celebration that marks the beginning of Lent, attracts its fair share of celebrants and performers from across the continent, though you will probably want to plan your trip around the weeklong

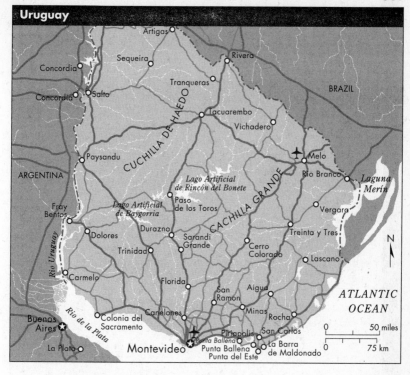

festival if large crowds, strained facilities, and high prices are not on your itinerary.

MONTEVIDEO

Montevideo, Uruguay's capital and only major city, has its share of glitzy shopping avenues and modern mid-rise office buildings. But few visitors come here specifically in search of big city pleasures; Buenos Aires, after all, is where Montevideans themselves go when they need a dose of urban stimulation. Montevideo, a city of 1.5 million, can be underwhelming if you let it, so turn your attention to the simpler things: walking down a quiet lane under a canopy of lavender-flower jacaranda trees, or wandering through a warren of vendors hawking crafts and caramelized peanuts. In Montevideo, your best memories are apt to be the result of serendipity.

Legend has it that Montevideo gained its name when a Portuguese explorer first laid eyes on the 435-foot-tall El Cerro hill at the mouth of the harbor and uttered the words *"monte video"* (I see a hill). Built along the eastern bank of the Río de la Plata (Plate River), Montevideo takes full advantage of its scenic locale. When the weather is good, La Rambla, a waterfront avenue that links Ciudad Vieja (Old City) with the eastern suburbs, is packed with fishermen, ice cream vendors, sun worshipers, and fashionably dressed grandmothers. Around sunset, volleyball and soccer matches smooth the way for hand-in-hand strolls and music—perhaps from a street musician playing tangos on his accordion.

Montevideo

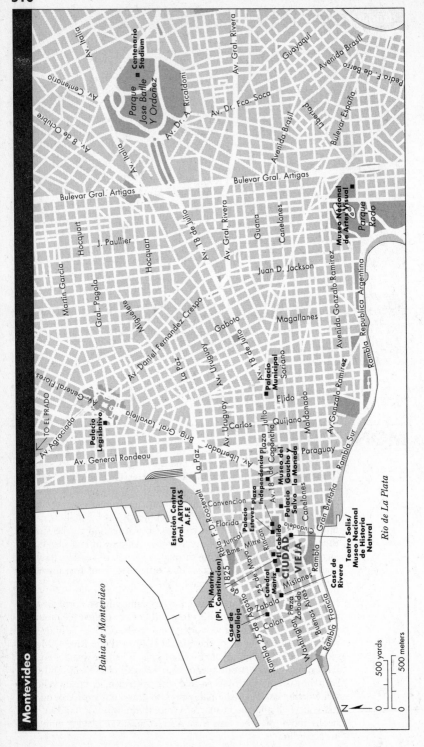

Bahia de Montevideo

Río de La Plata

Parque Jose Battle Y Ordoñez

Centenario Stadium

Av. Centenario

Av. 8 de Octubre

Av. Jalal

Av. Gral. Rivera

Guayaquí

Avenida Brasil

Pedro F. de Barro

Av. Dr. A. Ricaldoni

Av. Dr. Fco. Soca

Bulevar Gral. Artigas

Bulevar España

Libertad

Paralel

Av. Jalal

Av. 18 de Julio

Bulevar Gral. Artigas

Av. Gral. Rivera

Museo Nacional de Artes Visual

Parque Rodo

Bulevar Gral. Artigas

Hocquart

J. Paullier

Martin Garcia

Gral. Pagola

Hocquart

Miguelete

Av. Daniel Fernandez Crespo

Av. Gral. Rivera

Guana

Canelones

Juan D. Jackson

Av. 18 de Julio

Gaboto

Magallanes

Avenida Gonzalo Ramirez

Rambla Republica Argentina

La paz

Av. Uruguay

Av. 18 de Julio

Soriano

Palacio Municipal

Ejido

Rambla Sur

Av. General Flores

TO EL PRADO

Palacio Legislativo

Av. Agraciada

Brig. Gral. Lavalleja

La Paz

Av. Libertador

Av. Uruguay

Carlos

Quijano

Julio

Maldonado

Paraguay

Av. Gonzalo Ramirez

Av. General Rondeau

Estación Central Gral. ARTIGAS A.F.E

Convencion

Pza. F. D. Roosevelt

Florida

Juncal

Bme. Mitre

Av. 18 de

Independencia Plaza

Cagancha

Esteves Plaza

Museo del Gaucho Y la Moneda

Palacio Salvo

Canelones

Ciudadela

Gran Bretaña

Rambla Sur

Pl. Matriz (Pl. Constitucion)

Palacio Estevez

Rincon

25 de

El Cabildo

CIUDAD VIEJA

Teatro Solis/ Museo Nacional de Historia Natural

Casa de Rivera

Casa de Lavalleja

Rambla 25 de Agosto

Zabala

Colon

Washington Zabola

Catedral Matriz

Misiones

Plaza

Buenos Aires

Rambla Francia

500 yards

500 meters

N

Río de La Plata

Visitor Information

Ministerio de Turismo (Av. Libertador 1409, 4th Floor, ☎ 2/901078 or 2/914340, FAX 2/916907), with additional offices at Carrasco Airport and Plaza Cagancha, has city maps and other basic information. **Cecilia Regules Viajes** (Bacacay 1313, Montevideo, ☎ 02/963011 or 02/957308, FAX 2/963012), a travel agency with English-speaking agents, can arrange everything from city tours and excursions to the country to departing flights; one division of the agency, Estancias Gauchas, books popular packages at working ranches in the countryside (*see* Estancias in the Uruguayan Countryside *in* Excursions from Montevideo, *below*).

Arriving and Departing

By Plane

Uruguay's principal airport, **Carrasco International Airport** (☎ 2/611991), is 24 kilometers (15 miles) east of Montevideo and regularly served by **PLUNA** (Calle Colonia 1021, Montevideo, ☎ 2/920273 or 2/921414) and **United Airlines** (Calle Colonia 981, 15th Floor, ☎ 2/924630). Getting from the airport to your hotel is as easy as hailing a cab ($20 to downtown).

By Car

Coming from Brazil take Route 1 west, which eventually becomes La Rambla, Montevideo's riverside thoroughfare; turn north on Calle Ciudadela to reach Plaza Independencia. Route 1 also connects Montevideo with Colonia.

By Bus

Montevideo's new centrally located, state-of-the-art bus terminal—called **Tres Cruces** (Bul. Gral. Artigas and Calle Galicia, ☎ 2/418998)—makes taking the bus an easy option. Carriers offering frequent bus service to and from Montevideo include **CITA** (Plaza Independencia 826, ☎ 2/912021), **COIT** (Calle Paraguay 1473, ☎ 2/908906), **COT** (Tres Cruces, ☎ 2/494949), **Rutas** (Tres Cruces, ☎ 2/425451), and **TTL** (Tres Cruces, ☎ 2/915482).

By Ferry

Buquebus (Calle Rio Negro 1400, ☎ 2/920670 or 2/920671, FAX 2/912555) recently began hydrofoil service between Montevideo and Buenos Aires. Fares are reasonable (from $75 round-trip), and the trip, including boarding and customs at either end, takes roughly 3½ hours.

Getting Around Montevideo

A revitalization of the Old City has made it safer to walk at night, but as in any large city, you should always be extra cautious after dark. Most of Montevideo's residents stay up quite late, so the streets are usually full of people until 1 AM.

By Bus

Montevideo's public buses crisscross the entire city during daylight hours and offer a great alternative to the often difficult task of obtaining a taxi during peak hours, but they are only for the adventurous. It takes some extra effort on your part to find out exactly where buses stop and where to get off, but you don't need exact change, and the price is only N$2.80, or about 50¢.

By Taxi

All cabs have meters and the initial fare is roughly 65¢ at flag fall and 40¢ per ⅓ kilometer. You can hail taxis on the street; or, to practice your Spanish, call **Radio Taxi La Española** (☎ 2/499744), **Radio Taxi Carrasco** (☎ 2/600416), or **TeleTaxi** (☎ 2/812931 or 2/474238).

Tour Operators

Bus Tours

Viajes Buemes (Av. A. Arocena 1596, ☎ 2/606047 or 2/607594) organizes half-day, English-language bus tours. Passengers are collected from the major hotels starting at 9 AM. On Friday and Saturday nights the "Montevideo by Night" tour includes an abbreviated city tour, dinner and a tango show at the Columbia Palace hotel, and a casino visit.

Walking Tours

Contact **Cecilia Regules Viajes** (*see* Visitor Information, *above*) or **Free Way** (Colonia 994, ☎ 2/908931 or 2/908933), both of whom organize city tours and other excursions.

Exploring Montevideo

Modern Montevideo expanded outward from the peninsular Ciudad Vieja which is still noted for its narrow streets and elegant colonial architecture. The El Prado district, an exclusive enclave a few miles north of the city center, also retains the look and attitude of colonial Montevideo with its lavish mansions and grand parks. Bear in mind that these magnificent mansions were once summer homes for aristocratic Uruguayans who spent most of the year elsewhere, and you'll get some idea of the wealth this small country once enjoyed.

Ciudad Vieja

Plaza Independencia marks the eastern border of the Old City and is where modern mid-rises begin to outnumber the city's colonial and republican artifacts. Portions of the plaza were once occupied by the Cuidadela (Citadel), a military fortification built originally by the Spanish but deemed militarily useless and destroyed in 1833. In the center of the square stands a 30-ton statue of General Gervasio Artigas, the "father" of Uruguay and the founder of its 19th-century independence movement. At the base of the monument, two flights of polished granite stairs lead to the tomb where Artigas's remains are interred; a spotlight at night ensures that the general's urn is never in the dark.

When it was built in 1927, the 26-story **Palacio Salvo,** on the east side of Plaza Independencia, was the tallest building in South America; today this commercial office block is still the tallest building in Montevideo. The **Palacio Estevez,** on the south side of the plaza, was acquired by the government in 1878 and used by the president on occasion for ceremonial purposes.

The **Teatro Solís,** a short walk east, was completed in 1856 and named in honor of the discoverer of the Río de la Plata, Juan B. Solís. Famed for its acoustics, it is still the most important theater in Montevideo and the site of numerous national and international cultural events. Sharing the building is the **Museo Nacional de Historia Natural** (National Museum of Natural History), with rotating history exhibits in addition to a few antiques and republican-era paintings. *Calle Buenos Aires 652,* ☎ *2/960908.* ☛ *Free. Call for hours.*

A few blocks west in the center of the Old City is **Plaza Matriz** (officially Plaza Constitución, but nobody calls it that). The cantilever fountain in the center of the square was installed in 1871 to commemorate the inauguration of the city's water system. Facing the plaza is the modest **El Cabildo,** the old city hall where the Uruguayan constitution was signed in 1830. This two-story colonial edifice now houses an impressive collection of paintings, antique furnishings, and costumes, plus rotating history exhibits. English-speaking guides are available. *Calle Juan Carlos Gómez at Calle Sarandí, no ☏.* ☛ *Free.* ☉ *Tues.–Sun.*

On the opposite side of the square sits the oldest public building in Montevideo, **Catedral Matriz,** its distinctive pair of dome-capped bell towers guarding the plaza like sentinels. Except for small touches in its stained glass and domed sanctuary, the cathedral is most notable as the final resting place of Uruguay's most important political and military figures. *Calle Sarandí at Calle Ituzaingó.* ☛ *Free.*

Calle Rincón marks the commercial and financial heart of the Old City; banks with names both familiar and obscure are cheek by jowl with art galleries and antiques dealers. At the corner of Calles Rincón and Misiones looms the **Casa de Rivera,** once the home of General Fructuoso Rivera, Uruguay's first president. Acquired by the government in 1942, it currently houses a branch of the National History Museum. Exhibits inside document the development of Uruguay from the colonial period through the 1930s. *Calle Rincón 437, ☏ 2/951051.* ☛ *Free. Call for hours.*

Casa de Lavalleja was built during the early 18th century and later became the home of General Juan A. Lavalleja, who distinguished himself in Uruguay's war for independence from Brazil (1825–28). Donated to the state in 1940 and incorporated into the National History Museum system, this pristine colonial home now displays period manuscripts and historical memorabilia. *Calle Zabala 1469, no ☏.* ☛ *Free.* ☉ *Tues.–Sun.*

The **Palacio Taranco,** built in 1908 atop the rubble of Uruguay's first theater, is representative of the French-inspired architectural styles favored in turn-of-the-century Montevideo. Today it has been converted into a cultural center filled with period furniture, statuary, draperies, clocks, and portrait paintings. *Calle 25 de Mayo 376; call tourist office (☏ 2/901078) for hours.*

Avenida 18 de Julio

Montevideo's main street has a little of everything—shops and museums, cafés and plazas, bustling markets, and chrome-and-steel financial towers. Avenida 18 de Julio runs east from Plaza Independencia, away from the Old City. In a lush 19th-century rococo mansion near Calle Julio Herrera y Obes, four blocks east of the plaza, is the **Museo del Gaucho y la Moneda** (Gaucho and Coin Museum). Fascinating articles from everyday life, from traditional gaucho garb to the detailed silver work on the cups used for maté (an indigenous herb from which tea is brewed), make this the city's best museum. Displays of ancient South American and European coins are on the first floor, and other floors house paraphernalia associated with Uruguay's cowboys. English tours are available with two-day notice. *Av. 18 de Julio 998, ☏ 2/908764.* ☛ *Free.* ☉ *Tues.–Sun.*

In its basement, the **Palacio Municipal** (City Hall) houses the **Biblioteca de Historia del Arte** (Library of Art History) and the **Museo de Historia del Arte** (Museum of Art History). Bypass the library's large academic holding and spend some time browsing the museum's small collection of pre-Columbian and colonial artifacts. At the Calle Soriano entrance you can take an elevator to the building's 26th-floor observation deck for a panoramic view of the city. *Calle Ejido 1326, ☎ 2/989252, ext. 500. ☛ Free. ☉ Weekdays.*

El Prado

The El Prado district lies roughly 6 kilometers (4 miles) north of Plaza Independencia and the Old City; you could make the very long uphill walk along **Avenida Agraciada**—a busy commercial street loaded with every sort of shop—but most prefer to take a taxi straight to the diminutive **Sagrada Familia** (Sacred Family) chapel. Too tiny to need flying buttresses, this ornate gothic gem is complete in all other respects; a troop of gargoyles peers down at you, and the finely wrought stained-glass windows become radiant when backlit by the sun. Like many churches in secular Uruguay, Sagrada Familia is open only on Saturday afternoons and Sunday mornings; the grounds, however, are always open. *Calle Luis Alberto de Herrera 4246, ☎ 2/236824. ☛ Free.*

Calle Luis Alberto de Herrera cuts to the heart of the district, past numerous 18th- and 19th-century mansions. In many instances, estate grounds have been sold off and used for the later—and frankly bland—constructions that now occupy portions of this stretch. Breaking the tedium is the **Museo de Bellas Artes** (Museum of Fine Arts, known locally as the Blanes Museum), which is housed in an elegant colonial mansion that once belonged to Uruguay's foremost 19th-century painter, Juan Manuel Blanes. Although he was entirely self-taught and did not begin painting until he was in his fifties, his realistic portrayals of gauchos and the Uruguayan countryside compose the core of the museum's otherwise bland collection. *Av. Millán 4015, ☎ 2/362248. ☛ Free. ☉ Tues.–Sun.*

Enter the vast **Parque El Prado,** the district's namesake, at Rambla Costanera and work your way toward Avenida Buschantal. This street meanders past the park's famous rose garden and into a neighborhood of imposing colonial mansions. Near the intersection of Calle Ruiz and Avenida 19 de Abril, look for some of El Prado's most splendid colonial homes; many have been immaculately restored, and several house private international foundations. Avenida 19 de Abril eventually leads to Avenida Agraciada and the **Palacio Suarez** (Av. Agraciada 3423), the president of Uruguay's official residence. The magnificent complex is closed to the public but can still be appreciated from the street.

Other Attractions

Almost 50 different types of native marble were used in the construction of the **Palacio Legislativo** (Legislative Palace), the seat of Uruguay's bicameral legislature. Free Spanish-language tours are available when the congress is in session; passes are available inside at the information desk. *Av. Agraciada at Av. Flores, ☎ 2/201334. ☛ Free. ☉ Weekdays.*

Parque Rodo has a little something for everyone—two amusement parks, a number of decent eateries, and the **Museo Nacional de Artes Visuales** (National Museum of Visual Arts), which recently hosted exhibits from as far afield as China and Poland. Between December 5 and January 6, Parque Rodo is also the site of Montevideo's best *feria artesanal* (crafts fair). *Av. T. Giribaldi and Av. J. Herrera y Reisig, ☎ 2/716124. ☛ Free. ☉ Wed.–Sun. 4–8.*

Shopping

Specialty Shops

In Montevideo shops are generally open weekdays 9–6 and Saturday 9–noon.

ANTIQUES

Due to Montevideo's wealthy past, antiques are plentiful. Calle Tristan Narvaja north of Avenida 18 de Julio is packed with shops; **El Rincón** (Calle Tristan Narvaja 1747, ☎ 2/402283) is one of the area's best antiques dealers. In the Old City, Calle Bartolomé Mitre and Calle Rincón are also lined with antiques stores. You can get good deals from the vendors on the streets surrounding the Tristan Narvaja Market on Sundays.

GEMSTONES AND JEWELRY

Gemas de America (Av. 18 de Julio 948, ☎ 2/922572) carries amethyst and topaz jewelry, agate slices, and elaborate objects made of gemstones. **Cuarzos Del Uruguay** (Calle P. Sarandí 604, ☎ 2/959210) also specializes in agates, as well as amethyst, topaz, and other gemstone jewelry. **La Limeña** (Calle Buenos Aires 542, no ☎) has good prices on unset stones.

HANDICRAFTS

Manos de Uruguay (Calle Reconquista 602; Calle San José 111; Montevideo Shopping Center, Av. Luis Alberto de Herrera and Calle Gral. Galarza; no ☎) has three locations with a wide selection of woolen wear and locally produced ceramics. **Ema Camuso** (Av. 8 de Octubre 2574, no ☎) offers a sophisticated line of hand-knit sweaters popular with style-conscious Montevideans. The **Louvre** (Calle Sarandí 652, no ☎), an antiques store, is the only source for handmade and painted trinket boxes—the perfect *recuerdos* (souvenir).

LEATHER

Shops near Plaza Independencia specialize in hand-tailored nutria coats and jackets. **Peleteria Holandesa** (Calle Colonia 894, ☎ 2/915438) carries a wide array of leather clothing. **Pendola** (Calle San José 1087, ☎ 2/901524) also has a particularly good selection of different leather apparel. Also try **Casa Mario** (Calle Piedras 639, ☎ 2/962356). Custom-made boots are available from **Damino Botas** (Calle Rivera 2747, no ☎).

Shopping Centers

There are three major shopping centers in Montevideo, offering everything from imported designer-label clothing to gourmet foods to art supplies: the original, called **Montevideo Shopping Center** (Av. Luis Alberto de Herrera and Calle Gral. Galarza), near Parque Rodo; **Portones de Carrasco** (Avs. Bolivia and Italia), in the suburb of Carrasco; and **Punta Carretas Shopping Center** (Calles Ellauri and Solano). The latter is especially interesting because it is housed in a former prison, of which a portion is preserved and open to the public.

Markets

Weekend *ferias* (open-air markets) are probably the best forum for leisurely browsing among a warren of crafts stalls. Government regulations dictate that all ferias must close in the early afternoon, so plan to begin your visit around 10 AM. **Feria Tristan Narvaja** was started more than 50 years ago by Italian immigrants and nowadays is Montevideo's premier Sunday attraction. It not only spreads across both sides and down the middle of Calle Tristan Narvaja but also over most cross streets. The Saturday morning feria at **Plaza Biarritz** in Pocitos, a nearby suburb, features foodstuffs, *artesania* (crafts), and some antiques. At **Plaza Cagancha,** between Avenida 18 de Julio and Calle Rondeau, there is a daily crafts market—a good place to find offbeat souvenirs. In 1996 this fair becomes part of a larger artisan market at Calle San José and Yaguaron.

Dining

Menus do not vary all that much in Montevideo—meat is king—so the food may not provide a distraction from the blinding light: Even the toniest restaurant in Montevideo is brightly lit; you may dine by candlelight while all the house lights blaze. For a light meal try one of the city's ubiquitous *parrilladas,* informal and often family-operated steak houses. For price ranges, *see* Dining *in* Uruguay Essentials, *below.*

Chinese

$$$ **Shang Hai.** Popular with Montevideo's growing Asian community, this informal Chinese restaurant is an unexpected find close to the business district. Recommended are the hot and garlicky *kung pao* dishes and the steamed dumplings. Uruguayans appear allergic to spicy foods—just say *"bien picante"* for extra oomph. ✕ *Calle San José 1216,* ☎ *2/900232. AE, MC, V.*

French

$$$$ **Doña Flor.** Housed in a renovated turn-of-the-century home in Punta Carretas, a nearby suburb of Montevideo (take a cab for less than $8), this quiet, elegant restaurant offers a diverse menu heavily indebted to the French (the pâté is rich as butter and twice as smooth). The house specialty is green lasagna with salmon. ✕ *Bul. Artigas 1034, Punta Carretas,* ☎ *2/785751. Lunch reservations required. AE, D, MC, V. Closed Dec. 20–Easter.*

$$$$ **Olivier.** Stone walls and cozy French provincial decor set the mood in
  ★ the intimate split-level dining room of one of Montevideo's finest restaurants, which occupies a renovated colonial home in the Old City. French chef Olivier Horion prepares an exquisite pâté de foie gras, and you shouldn't pass up his rabbit marinated in white wine and served with olives and salted potatoes. The desserts are delicately decorated and superb. The restaurant is always open for lunch, and special dinners are held on various days throughout the month. ✕ *Calle Juan Carlos Gómez 1420,* ☎ *2/950617. Reservations advised. AE, D, MC, V. Lunch daily; call about dinner.*

$$$ **L'Hippocampe.** This casually sophisticated, art deco restaurant overlooks the river from the Rambla and serves good French cuisine. Any of the fresh fish dishes are recommended, as is the pork in plum sauce. It is also impossible not to be tempted by the decadent dessert table. ✕ *Rambla O'Higgins 5303,* ☎ *2/697767. Reservations advised. MC, V. Closed Sun.*

Swiss

$$$$ **Bungalo Suizo.** This small restaurant makes you feel as though you are dining at the informal but refined home of a good friend. The split-level dining area is subdued and intimate, with private tables tucked into quiet corners. Fondue is the specialty of the house, supplemented by various cuts of beef. ✕ *Calle Sol 150,* ☎ *2/611073. Reservations advised. MC, V. Dinner only; closed Sun. and Dec.–Apr.*

Uruguayan

$$$ **Meson Viejo Sancho.** What draws the post-theater crowds to this friendly but essentially nondescript downtown restaurant are gargantuan portions of smoked pork chops and *papas Suez* (fried potatoes). ✕ *Calle San José 1229,* ☎ *2/904063. Reservations advised. No credit cards. Closed Sun.*

$$ **El Buzon.** This unassuming restaurant-cum-bar serves excellent pastas and *parrilla* (grilled beef). For dessert try the *massini* (whipped cream sandwiched between extra-thin slices of caramelized sponge cake). ✕ *Calle Hocquard 1801,* ☎ *2/297643. MC, V. Closed Sun. dinner.*

$$ **La Proa.** In front of the Mercado del Puerto, the Old City's best food
★ plaza, this restaurant offers excellent dining in a lively outdoor atmo-
sphere. The proprietor, Darwin, loves to talk about the artistry of re-
fined cooking—he recommends his beef in prune sauce, "like Chaplin
ate"—but most Montevideans come to La Proa because it's the best
parrillada in the city. ✕ *Calle Pérez Castellano and Calle Yacaré,* ☎
2/962575. Weekend reservations advised. AE, MC, V.

$ **La Pasiva.** This popular *chopperia* (beer house) has three locations in
the Old City. None of them accept credit cards, but all stay open late
and serve ice-cold beer and uncomplicated bar food; try the *chivitos*
(sandwiches). ✕ *Calle Sarandí at Calle J.C. Gomez; Calle Rinconada
de Plaza Independencia; Av. 18 de Julio at Calle Ejido; no ☎s. No credit
cards.*

$ **Río Alegre.** Carmen, the proprietor of this intimate but lively restau-
rant, will stuff you full of homemade chorizo sausage and grilled pro-
volone sprinkled with oregano. For a main course, *asado de tira* (short
ribs) or *filete a la pimienta* (pepper steak) are good choices. ✕ *Calle
Pérez Castellano and Calle Yacaré, in the Mercado del Puerto,* locale
(stand) 033, ☎ *2/956504. No credit cards. Closed Sun.*

Lodging

Many downtown hotels are grouped around Plaza Bolívar and Plaza
Libertad. In the weeks before and after Carnival in February, hotel rooms
become scarce; be sure to book well in advance and be prepared to
pay handsomely for even low-end rooms. The **Victoria Plaza,** once Mon-
tevideo's finest accommodation, is being turned into Montevideo's first
five-star hotel, due to be finished in mid-1996. For price ranges, *see*
Lodging *in* Uruguay Essentials, *below.*

$$$$ **Hosteria del Lago.** Set among 10,000 square meters of parkland in Car-
★ rasco, 12 kilometers (7 miles) from downtown, this white, stucco, Span-
ish-colonial hotel offers a relaxed atmosphere, a private lakefront beach,
and a friendly multilingual staff. The suite-size rooms are split-level and
fully carpeted; all have views of the lake. ⌑ *Av. Arizona 9637, Carrasco,*
☎ *2/612210. 70 rooms. Restaurant, room service, pool, tennis court,
horseback riding, playground, airport shuttle. AE, D, MC, V.*

$$$$ **Plaza Fuerte Hotel.** This renovated turn-of-the-century hotel is in the
★ heart of the Old City. While the rooms tend to be very small, they're
quite stylish and immaculate. Each has a distinct look—themes range
from "Zen" and "Pompeii" to an updated colonial style in the Del Vir-
rey Room—rendered by a different interior designer. Wrought iron, flow-
ing draperies, glass walls, and french windows are common touches.
Most rooms are bi-level to accommodate complete baths, and some
have hot tubs. Landmark-preservation laws forbid changes to the
hotel's public areas, so the lobby is virtually nonexistent—as it was in
1913—but abundant art, the original elevator, and elegant common
sitting areas convey fin de siècle luxury. ⌑ *Bartolomé Mitre 1361, at
Calle Sarandí,* ☎ *2/959563,* FAX *2/959569. 22 rooms. Restaurant, pub,
tea shop, room service, sauna, exercise room. AE, D, MC, V.*

$$$$ **Victoria Plaza.** The venerable grande dame of Montevideo's accom-
modations is undergoing major renovations but remains open for busi-
ness. Although the Vic was once the poshest hotel in Uruguay—and
still dominates the rococo kitsch of Plaza Independencia—its Belle
Epoque splendor is all but disguised by neglect and construction de-
bris from the work site next door. The new wing—ostensibly opening
by mid-1996—will be a luxurious glass-and-brick contemporary struc-
ture that's slated to be Uruguay's only internationally recognized five-
star hotel. Until the "new" Vic opens, however, expect plaster dust in

the lobby, temperamental plumbing, and a host of other problems at this grand old hotel. ☎ *Plaza Independencia 759,* ☎ *2/920237,* ℻ *2/921628. 642 rooms. 2 restaurants, bar, coffee shop, room service, pool, exercise room, squash, airport shuttle. AE, D, MC, V.*

$$$ **Balmoral.** Despite ongoing renovations noticeable only from the back of the hotel, the lobby and accommodations here are a pleasant surprise—contemporary, bright, large, and quiet (double-pane windows nearly eliminate city noise). A gracious multilingual staff and convenient downtown location make the Balmoral a favorite with business travelers. ☎ *Plaza Libertad 1126,* ☎ *2/922393,* ℻ *2/922288. 75 rooms. Restaurant, 2 bars, room service, sauna. AE, D, MC, V.*

$$ **Ermitage.** This unprepossessing, sandstone-fronted building overlooks
★ Plaza Tomas Gomensoro and the beach. The Ermitage has developed a loyal core of long-term residential guests, giving it a pleasant homey feeling; patrons visit over a drink or sit and play cards in the huge wood-paneled lobby. Rooms are furnished with 1920s furniture and light fixtures, reminiscent of kinder and gentler times. ☎ *Calle Juan Benito Blanco 783,* ☎ *2/704021 or 2/717447,* ℻ *2/704312. 90 rooms. Restaurant. AE, D, MC, V.*

$$ **Oxford.** Glass walls, broad windows, and mirrors that date from a recent renovation give the small lobby an open but intimate feel, much like the hotel itself. The rooms are immaculately clean, the staff friendly and heroically helpful. Despite its downtown location, street noise is not a problem. ☎ *Calle Paraguay 1286,* ☎ *2/920046,* ℻ *2/923792. 66 rooms. Bar. AE, D, MC, V.*

$ **El Palacio.** El Palacio is a no-frills sort of place, yet it is also comfortable, and extremely well located. The rooms are all furnished with antiques, and each has its own balcony overlooking the Old City. ☎ *Calle Bartolomé Mitre 1364,* ☎ *2/963612. 14 rooms. No credit cards.*

$ **Lancaster.** Hidden away in a corner of Plaza Cagancha, near the bus terminal, the Lancaster might be past its glory days, but no one has told either the staff or loyal patrons. The rooms are sunny and large, with full-length French doors that open over the plaza. ☎ *Plaza Cagancha 1334,* ☎ *2/920029 or 2/921054,* ℻ *2/981117. 78 rooms. Bar, cafeteria. AE, D, MC, V.*

The Arts

Both **Teatro Solís** (Calle Buenos Aires 678, ☎ 2/959770) and **SODRE,** the Servicio Oficial de Difusió Radio Elétrica (Av. 18 de Julio 930, ☎ 2/912850) host symphonies, ballet, and opera between May and November. A number of binational centers such as the **Alliance Française** (Calle Soriano 1176, ☎ 2/908084), the **Instituto Goethe** (Goethe Institute, Calle Canellones 1524, ☎ 2/493499), and the U.S.-sponsored **Alianza Artigas-Washington** (Calle Paraguay 1217, ☎ 2/902721) host plays and concerts by foreign talent.

Nightlife

Montevideo has all kinds of nightlife if you know where to find it. There are quiet late-night bars as well as hip-hopping clubs and folk music shows. The entertainment and cultural pages of local papers are the best sources of information; particularly useful is the *Guía del Ocio,* a magazine inserted into the Friday edition of *El Pais.* With few exceptions bars and clubs come to life around 1 AM and do not close until it is time for breakfast.

Dance Clubs

You can dance to Top 40 music at **Clave de Fu** (Av. 26 Marzo 1125). **Otro Planeta** (Calle Jackson and Calle Durazno) is popular with the MTV generation. **New York** (Calle Mar Artico 1227) draws an older crowd. The retro set flocks to **Aquellos Años** (Calle Beyrouth 1405), which features music from the '50s and '60s.

Pubs

Amarcor (Calle Julio Herrera y Obes 1231, ☎ 2/901207) is popular with young Montevidean artists, actors, and intellectuals. Also try **Peroidos en la noche** (Calle Yaguarón 1099, ☎ 2/926733). **Riff Gallery Pub** (Bul. España 2511) is the only bar in the city devoted to jazz, with live shows on Thursday and Saturday.

Tango Shows

Although you need reservations for most tango shows, they are not blatantly geared for tourists. The weekend shows at **La Vieja Cumparista** (Calle Carlos Gardel 1181, ☎ 2/916245) feature a tango and *candombe*—dance and music associated with Carnival. **Tanguieria del 40** (Hotel Columbia, Rambla República de Francia 473, ☎ 2/955451) has dinner tango shows Monday–Saturday.

Excursions from Montevideo

Colonia del Sacramento

Originally a Portuguese settlement founded during the 17th century, Colonia del Sacramento is the small but lovely *barrio historico* (historic district) of greater Colonia. The city's tourist office (Av. General Flores 499) stocks maps, but everything here is within walking distance. Start at the municipal museum, housed in the two-story **Casa de Brown** (Calle San Francisco), with a collection of colonial artifacts and documents. The city's oldest church, **La Vieja Iglesia** (Calle 18 de Julio), dates from 1680. The impressive **Callejon de Susperos** (Street of Sighs) is lined with single-story colonial homes over which bougainvillea grows with abandon.

Getting There

Colonia is 242 kilometers (150 miles) west of Montevideo and serviced daily by bus from Montevideo; contact **COT** (Tres Cruces bus terminal, Montevideo, ☎ 2/494949). The three-hour ride costs less than $15.

Tour Operators

Full-day tours with an English-speaking guide are offered by **J. P. Santos Travel Agency** (Calle Colonia 951, Montevideo, ☎ 2/920397).

Lodging

$$$ **The Hotel Plaza Mayor.** This renovated hotel in the historic district is an experience in colonial lodging. The simple, clean rooms, many with high ceilings and bevelled-glass doors, overlook a peaceful garden. ⊡ *Calle Del Comercio 111, ☎ 522/3193. AE, D, MC, V.*

Estancias in the Uruguayan Countryside

One of the nicest ways to experience Uruguay's vast unspoiled countryside is to stay at an estancia. These large ranches usually raise cattle or sheep for the country's most-prized export goods—wool, beef, and leather. Although some now exist solely to host tourists, most are fully working ranches that cultivate nearly all the food consumed by visitors— from milk and honey to vegetables and the obvious meat. Guests may meet the *estancieros* (ranchers) and stay in quarters that date from the

colonial period. For most visitors, however, the highlight of their visit
is accompanying the gauchos, Uruguay's cowboys, while they herd cattle, shear sheep, tend farm animals, assist at calvings, or simply sit
around a fire roasting up some farm-fresh sausages for lunch.

Accommodations range from the comfortable to the most luxurious,
and meals are generally included. Some estancias have built swimming
pools and tennis courts; most offer guests a chance to roam their vast
estates on horseback and to fish, boat, and swim in local rivers, lakes,
or swimming holes. Still, the most important thing to do when visiting an estancia is to relax, eat well, and breathe the fresh air of the
open Uruguayan range.

Visitor Information

Estancias Gauchas/Cecilia Regules Viajes. English-speaking staffers at
this travel agency can provide information on more than 100 estancias;
they also book estancia packages which include your stay in Montevideo. *Calle Bacacay 1313, Montevideo,* ☎ *2/963011 or 2/757308,*
☎ *2/963012.* ✆ *Weekdays 9:30–7.*

Estancias

$$ **Estancia Caorsi.** Personalized service from owners Helena and Julio Caorsi
and an authentic estancia experience are the trademarks here. From
the delicious Uruguayan provincial style pâté to the fresh honey, ev-
erything you eat is cultivated and prepared at the ranch. The main house
has comfortable rooms adorned with fine antiques, and most rooms
overlook either a beautiful garden or the vast countryside. True seren-
ity is available at the guest house—El Olivo—which sits on the banks
of the Río Negro, 135 kilometers (84 miles) from the main house, with
nothing but hills, cows, horses, and river for miles around. If you stay
at the guest house, the Caorsis will provide ample supplies, but you're
on your own as far as cooking goes. ☎ *15 km (9 mi) from Durazno,*
☎ *362/3762. 5 rooms at main house, 3 at El Olivo. Pool, horseback
riding, boating, camping, fishing. No credit cards.*

$$ **Estancia La Calera.** This ranch, established in 1887, combines the true
feeling of an old estancia with all the comforts of the modern world.
Arched walkways surround a lush garden, and a fireplace makes the
salon feel cozy. La Calera offers walks in the country, rodeos, and a chance
to see other gaucho activities. ☎ *Book through Estancias Gauchas (see
above). 20 rooms. Pool, meeting rooms. AE, D, MC, V.*

$$ **La Sirena Estancia.** Checked tile floors, white stucco, and old stone walls
create a sense of history at this estancia near the Río de la Plata. Be-
sides traditional gaucho activities, guests can also partake of a wide
variety of sports and recreational facilities—everything from yachting
and polo to fishing and tennis. ☎ *Colón 274, Mercedes,* ☎ *532/2218,*
☎ *532/4193. 7 rooms. Pool, tennis court, boating, fishing, recreation
room. AE, D, MC, V.*

PUNTA DEL ESTE

Despite being a mere two hours down the pike from Montevideo,
Uruguay's highly touted Punta del Este is definitely a world apart. Punta
del Este (shortened to "Punta" by locals) and the handful of sur-
rounding beachfront communities are famous as jet-set resorts and sites
of countless international festivals and conferences—the sort of places
where lounging on white sand and browsing designer boutiques con-
stitute the day's most demanding activities.

Punta is not for everyone: The resort's colonial architecture has been
largely replaced with high-rise hotels and apartments, and those strik-

ing mansions you see hidden among tall pines on the beach house well-to-do Argentines, Brazilians, and Europeans, not museums. Still, Punta is justly revered for its long stretches of white-sand beach and elegant shopping avenues. For thousands of younger South Americans it is also *the* place (excluding Rio, of course) to let your hair down and watch the sunrise from the balcony of an all-night disco.

Punta is underwhelming in the low season—the buildings are shuttered against the elements, their tenants gone elsewhere. On January 1 the city comes alive, lured out of dormancy by the smell of tourist dollars. Plan on a visit in either December or March (except during Holy Week, when prices skyrocket). During these two months the weather is superb, with an average daily temperature of 75°F, and the beaches are not unbearably crowded.

Visitor Information

Liga de Fomento (Calle Gorlero and Calle 25, ☎ 42/44069; or Plaza Artigas, ☎ 42/40512, 42/46510, or 42/46511). Travel agencies on Calle Gorlero can assist with hotel bookings, onward travel plans, and excursions.

Arriving and Departing

Consider a package tour from Montevideo regardless of the length of your stay. There is much to see and do in nearby Punta Ballena and La Barra, and travel plans will be more difficult, not to mention costly, to arrange once you're in Punta. In Montevideo contact **Cecilia Regules Viajes** (Calle Bacacay 1313, Montevideo, ☎ 2/963011 or 2/957308, FAX 2/963012).

By Plane

There is no air service between Montevideo and Punta. However, **PLUNA** (☎ 42/41840) and **Aerolineas Argentinas** (☎ 42/43802) fly regularly between Buenos Aires and the **Aeropuerto de Punta del Este** (Camino del Placer, ☎ 42/81808), on the northern edge of the city. The flight takes 30 minutes and costs about $60 each way.

By Bus

Many bus lines travel daily between Montevideo and Piriápolis, with ongoing service to Punta del Este's **Terminal Playa Brava** (Rambla Artigas and Calle Inzaurraga). It is best to check with Montevideo's Tres Cruces bus terminal about departure times (*see* Arriving and Departing: By Bus *in* Montevideo, *above*), or in Punta del Este, call **Buquebus** (☎ 42/84995) or **COT** (☎ 42/86810).

By Car

From Montevideo follow Interbalnearia (Rte. 1) east to the Route 93 turnoff. The road is well maintained and marked, and the trip takes about 1½ hours.

Exploring Punta del Este

Piriápolis

First established as a private residence by an Argentine developer more than a century ago, nowadays Piriápolis is a laid-back beachfront enclave that lacks the sophistication—and the extortionate prices—of nearby Punta del Este. Piriápolis has plenty of stores and restaurants, a casino, and the grand Hotel Argentino, built in the old European tradition with spas and thermal pools (and an ice-skating rink!). **Punta Fría** and **Playa Grande** are the town's best beaches, with white sand

and large summertime crowds. The tourist office (Rambla de los Argentinos 1348) can provide you with hotel listings and maps.

Punta Ballena

About 25 kilometers (15 miles) east of Piriápolis and 10 kilometers (6 miles) west of Punta del Este is Punta Ballena. Built on a bluff overlooking the ocean, it's almost impossible to see from the main road—no cause for complaint for the resort's wealthy patrons. The main draw here is **Casa Ballena,** an exclusive artists' community perched at the tip of a rocky point with tremendous views of the Atlantic. Casa Ballena is a showpiece that fits no known architectural definition: Entirely of white stucco and adorned with strange projections and even stranger appurtenances, it can best be described as Dali meets Disney. Inside is an art gallery with a warren of rooms showcasing Picasso-derivative art, a restaurant, and an aloof hotel.

Inland, the **Arboretum Lussich** is a huge parkland that perfumes the air with the scent of eucalyptus. Farther up the same road is the **Country Cook,** an expanding American-owned shopping and amusement center with an Old West theme. The small main street, complete with raised wooden sidewalks, is lined with shops selling dried flowers and homemade breads and jams. *Camino Lussich and La Pataia,* ☎ 42/22973. ⊙ *Christmas–1st wk in Mar., daily 1* PM*–3* AM.

Punta del Este

The resort town of Punta del Este, which also lends its name to the broader region encompassing Punta Ballena and La Barra de Maldonado, has long been a favorite spot for sunseekers escaping the Northern Hemisphere winter. In Punta proper—the peninsular resort bounded by Playa Mansa (Mansa Beach) and Playa Brava (Brava Beach)—beach bumming is the prime activity. In fact, if you are not into eating, drinking, and worshiping the sun, about the only other attractions are the gypsies hustling tourists on Calle Gorlero, and the artisans' feria at Plaza Artigas. This colorful crafts market is held at the intersection of El Ramanso and El Corral and is open weekends 5 PM–midnight; between Christmas and Holy Week, it's open daily 6 PM–1 AM.

Punta is circumnavigated by **Rambla Artigas,** the main coastal road that leads past residential neighborhoods and pristine stretches of beach. **Calle Gorlero,** Punta's main commercial strip, runs north–south through the heart of the peninsula and is fronted with cafés, restaurants, and elegant shopping boutiques bearing names such as Yves St. Laurent and Gucci.

La Barra de Maldonado

Gaily painted buildings give La Barra (as locals call it) a carnival-like atmosphere, but this small resort less than 5 kilometers (3 miles) east of Punta del Este also has some of the area's cleanest and finest beaches. From Punta you can walk along the beach and cross over to La Barra on a cement camelback bridge. Just before you reach La Barra, at Parada (bus stop) 17, is Playa Verde, one such beach. In town, you'll find a handful of antiques dealers, surf shops, and pubs that are offer an afternoon's diversion—it's also where Punta's young people come to do their eating, dancing, and drinking. Once you move off Calle No. 7 (also called Del Encuentro), La Barra's principal thoroughfare, there's nothing notable except the ocean.

Sports and the Outdoors

Equipment rental, especially for water sports, is not an idea whose time has come in Punta del Este, despite the many surf shops that have sprung up over the last few years.

Golf

Two golf clubs are ostensibly open one day per week to nonmembers. Greens fees average $70 for 18 holes. Contact Punta's **Club de Golf** (☎ 42/82127) or Punta Ballena's **Club de Lago** (☎ 42/78423).

Horseback Riding

Mosey over to **Country Cook** (*see above*), the Old West theme park on the distant outskirts of Punta, for an afternoon of trail riding.

Dining

Restaurants come and go with seasonal regularity in Punta del Este. The better restaurants reopen from year to year, often transferring their operations to Montevideo during the low season and returning to Punta around Christmastime. Year-round options—none of them spectacular—are generally located along Punta's Calle Gorlero; they tend to be moderately priced and serve meat rather than seafood. For price ranges, *see* Dining *in* Uruguay Essentials, *below.*

Punta del Este

$$$$ **La Bourgogne.** A shaded terra-cotta terrace gives way to an arch-win-
★ dowed breezeway, while the intimate reception area opens onto a large split-level dining room where antique sideboards serve as "stations." The food, served by impeccably clad waiters who go about their business with cordial authority, is prepared with only the finest and freshest of ingredients; the breads are baked on the premises (an adjoining bakery sells them by the loaf), and the herbs and berries are grown in the backyard garden. Start your meal with the gourmet salad, then try the plaice with pink peppercorns. The desserts are sublime, and the sampler is a good way to try them all. ✕ *Av. del Mar and Calle P. Sierra,* ☎ *42/82007,* 𝖥𝖠𝖷 *42/87873. Reservations required. No credit cards. Christmas–Holy Week only.*

$$$ **Andrés.** Operated by a father and son, both of whom answer to Andrés, this unassuming restaurant on the Rambla offers fine French dining at reasonable prices. Most of the tables are outdoors under a canopy, so you can appreciate the excellent service while also enjoying the sea breeze. The fish Andrés (seasonally available fish in a white wine and tomato sauce), spinach soufflé, and grilled meats are recommended. ✕ *Parada 1, Edificio Vaguardia,* ☎ *42/81804. Reservations advised. AE, D, MC, V.*

$$ **Yacht Club Uruguayo.** Long a favorite with locals, this small eatery has a great view of the Isla de Lobos across the water. The menu includes a bit of everything, but the specialty of the house is seafood; perennial favorites are *brotola a la Roquefort* (baked hake) and *pulpo* Provençal, likely the most tender octopus you have ever eaten. ✕ *Rambla Artigas (between Calles 6 and 8),* ☎ *42/41056. No reservations. AE, D, MC, V.*

$ **Restaurante Ciclista.** This no-frills restaurant serves perhaps the best inexpensive meals in Punta. The *tortilla de papas* (potato pancake) is extremely hearty, as are the pastas. The homemade soups are another popular lure. ✕ *Calle 20, at Calle 27,* ☎ *42/40007. AE, D, MC, V.*

Lodging

There are more hotels in and around Punta del Este than you can possibly imagine, running the architectural gamut from wonderfully modern to bland ho-hum. Except during the high season many rooms are empty and often stay that way for months at a time; but during January and February, Punta teems with sunbathers and pleasure seekers, and rooms are extremely difficult to come by, so book well in advance. For price ranges, *see* Lodging *in* Uruguay Essentials, *below.*

La Barra de Maldonado

$$$$ La Posta del Cangrejo. From its stylish lobby to its relaxed lounge and
★   restaurant, this hotel takes an informal approach to luxury. The Mediterranean styling—red tile floors and white stucco walls—complements the impeccably decorated guest rooms; each is furnished with hand-stenciled antiques and canopied beds and has views of either the beach or the small country garden. The staff is warm, accommodating, and inordinately fond of their hotel. The adjoining seafood restaurant is equally outstanding. ☎ *La Barra de Maldonado,* ☎ *42/70021 or 42/70271,* FAX *42/70173. 29 rooms. Restaurant, bar, pool. AE, D, MC, V.*

Punta del Este

$$$$ L'Auberge. The small lobby of this hotel is bursting with antiques and cozy sofas, and there's an 18th-century crenellated water tower—which contains guest rooms—rising from its double-winged chalet. Rooms vary in age but all are tastefully adorned with beautiful antiques; some even have working fireplaces. The property is beautifully landscaped, with a rolling lawn and a lovely terraced flower garden; some of Punta del Este's finest beaches are just a few blocks away, but the secluded grounds create a world apart from the busy and often crowded beach. ☎ *Barrio Parque del Golf,* ☎ *42/82601,* FAX *42/83408. 40 rooms. Restaurant, bar, pool, hot tub. AE, D, MC, V.*

$$ Palace Hotel. The Palace occupies a central position on the Gorlero
★   shopping avenue inside one of Punta's oldest structures—a three-story Spanish colonial masterpiece complete with an airy interior courtyard. The restaurant has one of the largest wine cellars in the country. ☎ *Calle Gorlero, at Calle 11,* ☎ *42/41919 or 42/41418,* FAX *42/44695. 44 rooms. Restaurant, bar. AE, D, MC, V.*

$ Hotel Salzberg. This charming hotel occupies a white stucco, three-story chalet, with polished slate floors and exposed beams. Its rooms are blessed with ceiling fans, modern bathrooms, and fine views framed by flower-filled window boxes. ☎ *Calle Pedragosa Sierra and El Havre,* ☎ *42/88851. 14 rooms. Bar, cafeteria. No credit cards.*

Nightlife

The very name Punta del Este is synonymous with high-paced evenings in bars and nightclubs that start as late as 1 AM and only reach a fever pitch around sunrise. Nine out of 10 are open during the high season only, and nearly the same proportion have a cover charge—sometimes as much as $30 per person.

Dance Clubs

Hop in a cab and head for **Las Grutas** (Rambla Artigas), near Punta Ballena. This disco cannot be seen from the road, but most cab drivers know the route across the dunes to the entrance. The club itself is inside a grotto and has a clear acrylic floor under which the tide rolls in and out. In La Barra, **Space** occupies an enormous warehouse bursting with five different bars. It does not have an address, but, once again, your cabbie will undoubtedly know where to go.

URUGUAY ESSENTIALS

Customs and Duties

You may bring up to 400 cigarettes, 50 cigars or 500 grams of loose tobacco, 2 liters of alcoholic beverages. Live animals, vegetable products, and products that originate from plant or animal products are not allowed into Uruguay. There is no limit on the amount of currency you can bring into the country.

Dining

Specialties

Except in coastal fishing villages, beef is the staple of the Uruguayan diet. It is cheap, abundant, and often grilled in a style known as parrilla, descended directly from the gauchos (a meal in a parrillada, a Uruguayan steak house, is not to be missed). Beef is also made into sausages such as chorizo and *salchica*, or it's combined with ham, cheese, and peppers to make *matambre*. Seafood can be delicious but expensive; popular among Uruguayans are *raya a la manteca negra* (ray in blackened butter), *lenguado* (flounder), *merluza* (hake), and *calamare* (squid). If you are not up to a full meal, try Uruguay's national sandwich, the chivito, a steak sandwich smothered with all varieties of sauces and condiments; a popular version is *a la Canadiensa* (with cheese and Canadian bacon). Uruguayan wines under the Santa Rosa and Calvinor labels, a step up from table wine, are available in most restaurants.

Mealtimes

Lunch is served between noon and 3; restaurants begin to fill around 12:30 and are packed by 1:30. Dinner is served late: Many restaurants do not even open until 8 PM and are rarely crowded before 10 PM. Most pubs and *confiterías* (cafés) are open all day.

Dress

Formal dress is rarely, if ever, required. Smart sportswear is accepted at even the nicest establishments.

Ratings

Prices are per person during high season for a 3-course meal, excluding alcohol, tip, cover charge, and 12% IVA tax. All eateries, from the humblest to the most elegant, will bill you for the *cubierto* (cover charge), even if you have nothing more than a cup of coffee. The cubierto may be as little as $1 or as much as $4 or more per person.

CATEGORY	MONTEVIDEO	PUNTA DEL ESTE
$$$$	over $45	over $65
$$$	$30–$45	$45–$65
$$	$15–$30	$30–$45
$	under $15	under $30

Embassies and Consulates

United States

Embassy: Lauro Müller, No. 1776 (on the Rambla), Montevideo, ☎ 2/236061, FAX 2/487777; ⊘ Weekdays 9–1, 2–5.

Canada

The nearest Canadian embassy is in Buenos Aires.

United Kingdom

Embassy: Marco Bruto, No. 1073, ☎ 2/623650, ℻ 2/627815; ⊘ Weekdays 9–1, 2–5:15.

Getting Around

By Plane

All international commercial flights land at Montevideo's **Carrasco International Airport,** about 24 kilometers (15 miles) east of downtown. Uruguay's national airline, **PLUNA** (Calle Colonia 1021, Montevideo, ☎ 2/920273 or 2/921414), flies daily to Uruguay from major cities throughout South America. A small airport in Punta del Este is used for commuter flights to and from Buenos Aires.

By Train

Passenger train service was discontinued in 1988. Limited service between Montevideo and Cannelones is scheduled to resume by 1996, but few are placing hefty bets on it.

By Car

ROAD CONDITIONS

Roads between Montevideo and Punta del Este are quite good, as are the handful of main highways. Deeper into the Uruguayan countryside, roads are usually surfaced with gravel. If you want to drive to areas off the main highways, it's best to plan for extra travel time; if possible, speak with locals about current road conditions before setting off. On the up side, country roads have very little traffic and, in some places, spectacular scenery and a chance to see traditional Uruguayan gauchos.

RULES OF THE ROAD

Uruguayans tend to drive carefully, but visitors from Argentina have the reputation of driving with wild abandon. Since almost all roads have only two lanes, keep a close eye out for passing vehicles.

RENTALS

Special rates or package deals are virtually nonexistent in Uruguay, and rental rates are higher than in the United States because of the value-added tax (IVA). For an economy-size car, expect to pay around $45 per day, plus 22¢ per kilometer; upwards of $385 per week with unlimited mileage. In Montevideo, contact **Avis** (Rambla República de México 6333, ☎ 2/927579; Carrasco Airport, ☎ 2/617005); **Budget** (Calle Mercedes 935, ☎ 2/916363); or **Class** (Hotel Victoria Plaza, Room 105, Plaza Independencia 759, ☎ 2/920237, ℻ 2/921628).

EMERGENCY ASSISTANCE

For roadside assistance, contact the **Autómovil Club Uruguayo** (Montevideo, Libertador 1532, ☎ 2/919020; Punta del Este, 3 de Febrero y Roosevelt, ☎ 42/20156). They will help even if you are not a member, but expect to pay $25 to enroll on the spot.

GASOLINE

Shell, Esso, Texaco, and ANCAP (the national petroleum company) service stations throughout Uruguay are open Monday–Saturday until 9 PM or so. The ANCAP station at Carrasco Airport is open daily 6 AM–11 PM.

By Bus

You can go almost anywhere in Uruguay by bus. Some buses border on the luxurious, with air-conditioning, video players, rest rooms, and snack service. Departures are frequent and fares low—Montevideo to Punta del Este, for example, costs $12 round-trip. Most bus companies are based in Montevideo and depart from its new state-of-the-art Tres Cruces bus terminal. Dependable carriers include **COT, TTL,** and **Rutas** (*see* Arriving and Departing: By Bus *in* Montevideo, *above*).

Language

Spanish is the official language of Uruguay, though some descendants of early Italian and British settlers speak the language of their forefathers. Many Uruguayans speak at least a little English.

Lodging

Hotels and Resorts

Uruguay has no five-star hotels as of yet, but the Victoria Plaza in Montevideo and the Condrad in Punta del Este are under construction and due to be completed in early 1996. Uruguayan resorts are generally clean, comfortable, and well equipped to deal with foreign travelers. Many quote rates that include one or two meals a day, so be sure to ask when making a reservation. Summer in Uruguay can be onerous without air-conditioning, and many hotels are not yet equipped with that luxury; be sure to inquire. You can save up to 30% in the same hotel by requesting a *habitacion turística,* usually a bit plainer, smaller, and without a view, but with the same standards of cleanliness and service.

Estancias

Estancias are becoming a very popular tourist experience and offer a superb opportunity to see Uruguay as it once was. Many of these working country ranches have added horseback riding, nature tours (Uruguay is in the migration path of four major bird groups), and other delights to their overnight packages. Because of the range of activities, accommodations, and pricing, estancia visits are best booked in advance and through an agency that specializes in estancias. For more information *see* Estancias in the Uruguayan Countryside *in* Excursions from Montevideo, *above.*

Hosterias

Hosterias are country inns that not only offer modest rooms, but are open for tea and dinner as well. Menus tend to be limited, though the food served is unfailingly hearty. Outside the cities hosterias are likely to be charming, but rustic.

Ratings

All prices are for two people in a double room based on high season rates and including breakfast and 12% IVA.

CATEGORY	MONTEVIDEO	PUNTA DEL ESTE
$$$$	over $100	over $225
$$$	$80–$100	$150–$225
$$	$50–$80	$90–$150
$	under $50	under $90

Mail

Because of frequent strikes by Uruguayan postal workers, it is best to check with locals as to whether the postal system is running efficiently at the time of your visit. If the postal service is working, be prepared to pay for the privilege—it costs nearly $1.80 to send a standard-size piece of international mail. Anything sensitive should be sent via **Federal Express** (Calle Juncal 1351, Montevideo, ☎ 2/956627) or **DHL** (Calle Zabala 1377, Montevideo, ☎ 2/960217).

Money and Expenses

Currency

On March 1, 1993, the Uruguayan government changed the monetary system from Pesos Nuevos (N$) to Pesos Uruguayos. The latter is officially designated UYP$, but more often you will see prices listed with a simple dollar sign ($). For the moment, Peso Nuevo coins and bills are still in use and are convertible to Pesos Uruguayos by dropping the last three zeros on a given bill (N$l,000 = UYP$1). Prices everywhere are quoted in Pesos Uruguayos even though you pay with Pesos Nuevos. Currently the only Pesos Uruguayos currency being issued is a $1 coin; new bills will eventually be issued in denominations of $1, $5, $10, $20, $50, $100, and $200, but it's anyone's guess when those bills will be printed.

At press time (winter 1995), the exchange rate was 7.14 Pesos Uruguayos to the U.S. dollar and 11.4 to the pound sterling. Both rates escalate almost daily to keep pace with Uruguay's inflation. In this chapter all prices are listed in U.S. dollars unless otherwise noted.

Changing Money

All banks and exchange houses, which are plentiful in Montevideo, will change traveler's checks and/or cash. Most banks will also process cash advances from major credit cards. It is quite common for most establishments, including banks, to put a 5%–10% surcharge on all credit-card charges.

Costs

Once one of the best bargain spots in the Southern Hemisphere, Uruguay can no longer boast about its low prices. The inflation rate rises daily; many services, especially those catering to tourists, now quote prices exclusively in U.S. dollars. Although you will need to keep some pesos for taxis and small purchases, it is best to convert dollars to pesos only as needed. You can also save a substantial amount by visiting in the low season: Prices on everything from hotels to meals can literally double during January and February, particularly in Punta del Este. Throughout the country a value-added tax (called IVA) of 12% is added to hotel and restaurant bills. Almost all other goods and services carry a 22% IVA charge.

SAMPLE PRICES

Cup of coffee, $1.80; bottle of beer, $3; bottle of wine, $5; bus ride, considered an adventure by some, 50¢; cross-town taxi ride, $5.

Opening and Closing Times

Banks

In Montevideo, banks are open weekdays 1–5 PM. In outlying areas banks are usually open during the morning only.

Casas de Cambio

Money changers are open during regular business hours (9–5:30). Some are open later and on Saturdays and Sunday mornings.

Shops

Many shops stay open throughout the day (9–6), especially in Montevideo and Punta del Este, where they may also remain open until late in the evening. In smaller cities, it is common for shops to close at midday for an hour or two.

National Holidays

New Year's Day (Jan. 1); Three Kings' Day (Jan. 6); Maundy Thursday (1996: Apr. 4; 1997: Mar. 27); Good Friday (1996: Apr. 5; 1997: Mar. 28); Disembarkation of the 33 Exiles (Apr. 19); Labor Day (May 1); Battle of Las Piedras (May 18); Artigas's Birthday (June 19); Constitution Day (July 18); Independence Day (Aug. 25); Columbus Day (Oct. 12); All Souls' Day (Nov. 2); Christmas (Dec. 25).

Precautions

Health

Cholera is almost unheard of in Uruguay, so you can eat fresh fruit and salads with cautious abandon. You should avoid tap water, however, because many pipes in older buildings are made of lead. Almost everyone drinks locally bottled *agua mineral* (mineral water), which is available with or without carbonation (*con gas* or *sin gas,* respectively). Until you become accustomed to Uruguayan food and drinking water, La Tourista is likely to cause problems for your digestive system.

Safety

Pickpockets rather than guerrillas are your biggest threat in the larger cities in Uruguay. Street crime has risen dramatically in recent years, particularly in Montevideo, so keep a vigilant eye on your purse or wallet. Crime at the swank Punta del Este resorts is not a serious problem and in the countryside it is practically nonexistent.

Telephones

Local Calls

Public telephones in downtown Montevideo are usually not in working order, yet in better-kept areas they usually do work. To place a call you need either a token, called a *ficha,* or a magnetic phone card. These are used in place of coins and entitle you to three minutes of conversation, or more in the case of a phone card. One peso buys one ficha, and phone cards vary according to how many minutes you wish to purchase. Both can be purchased at kiosks and small stores near public phones. As if to make up for the frustration of not finding a working phone in downtown Montevideo, most establishments will allow the use of their phone for local calls, either for a small charge or at no charge at all.

Long-Distance and International Calls

To contact an English-speaking AT&T operator directly from Uruguay, dial 000410. You'll need one ficha if you are dialing from a pay phone. International calls can also be made—for a much higher price—through **ANTEL,** the national telecommunications company, which offers direct-dial services. In Montevideo there are ANTEL *telecentro* offices at Calle Fernández Crespo 1534 (9 AM–11 PM), Calle San José 1102 (24 hrs), and Calle Rincón 501 (9 AM–5 PM).

Tipping

In restaurants a flat 10% tip is considered adequate. For any other services, a tip of UYP$2 is the norm. For taxis, round off the fare to the next highest peso.

When to Go

The finest weather falls between mid-October and late-March, when the temperature is pleasantly warm, the whole country is in bloom, and prices will not yet have inflated with the annual influx of Argentines and jet-setters. However, unless you are prepared to tangle with the tsunami of tourists that overwhelms Punta del Este in January and February, late spring (Oct.–Dec.) is the most appealing season to lounge on the beach in Punta.

Climate

Uruguay's climate has four distinct but mild seasons. Summer (Jan.–Mar.) can be hot and humid, with temperatures as high as 90°F. Fall (Apr.–June) is marked by warm days and evenings cool enough for a light sweater. Winter (July–Sept.) is cold and rainy with average temperatures generally below 50°F. Although it seldom reaches the freezing point here, the wind off the water can provide a chill factor that feels like Chicago in late November. Spring (Oct.–Dec.) is much like the fall, except that the trees will be sprouting, rather than dropping, their leaves.

The following are average daily maximum and minimum temperatures for Montevideo.

Jan.	83F	28C	May	64F	18C	Sept.	63F	17C
	62	17		48	9		46	8
Feb.	82F	28C	June	59F	15C	Oct.	68F	20C
	61	16		43	6		49	10
Mar.	78F	25C	July	58F	14C	Nov.	74F	23C
	59	15		43	6		54	12
Apr.	71F	22C	Aug.	59F	15C	Dec.	79F	21C
	53	12		43	6		59	15

12 Venezuela

Venezuela is all flash and sparkle, but with a secret heart. Sophisticated Caracas reminds many of Los Angeles—terrible traffic jams but world-class restaurants, art galleries, and nightlife—and the Caribbean coast boasts such resort playgrounds as Margarita Island. Hidden inland are subtler pleasures—Mérida, a picturesque colonial city of tiled roofs, and Angel Falls, the world's highest waterfall, unknown for centuries in the remote highlands of the Gran Sabana.

By George
Soules

Updated by
Tony Bianchi

ALTHOUGH VENEZUELA IS TOUTED as a tropical paradise, that description actually sells the country's rich array of natural resources short. Besides the more than 2,750 kilometers (1,700 miles) of Caribbean coastline—think white-sand beaches and sparkling blue water—there are broad sweeping plains, tropical rain forests, Andean peaks, and an Amazon region that includes the world's tallest waterfall. With 42 national parks covering more than 15% of the country's landmass, it's not difficult to find your way into the Venezuelan outback, far off the beaten track: Venezuela's second-largest park, Canaima, is bigger than Belgium and encompasses hundreds of square miles of unexplored, pristine jungle. In both the Amazon and the Llanos, a vast grassy plain in southwestern Venezuela, the vegetation is exuberant and the landscape is impeccably wild, inspirational, and anything but trammeled.

In Caracas, the stylish, very cosmopolitan, always ebullient capital, things are a bit different. Taxis cut corners as if there were no mañana. At a sidewalk *arepera,* where Caraqueños gather for thick black coffee and the latest gossip, a Portuguese proprietor may serve Italian espresso to Argentinean businessmen and visiting French students. The red-tile roofs of colonial Caracas have all but disappeared in the march of apartment blocks and office towers, but modern Caracas still dazzles with its shopping avenues and neon-lit dance clubs. In this bustling city of 4 million, the pulse of Latin rhythms, salsa and merengue, fuel a society caught up in the endless search for the good life.

Just beyond Caracas, along the seacoast, traveling east or west, the lifestyle and the tempo is more unhurried than hectic, more Caribbean than South American. To the east, at the end of the 564-kilometer (350-mile) Route of the Sun—the road that joins Caracas with Cumaná, soon to become a modern four-lane highway—the Andes plunge sharply into the sea, leaving behind a series of half-moon coves and cliffs. Heading west, past the city of Valencia, 600 kilometers (375 miles) of sandy beaches stretch all the way to the Peninsula de Paraguaná; along the way is the remarkable Morrocoy National Park, a reserve of mangroves and a dozen small keys with extraordinary white sand and transparent blue waters. The coast's year-round mild climate attracts campers, fishermen, scuba divers, and simple sun worshipers who mix sporting activities with waterfront partying to the captivating beat of merengue and salsa music. Just offshore is Margarita Island, Venezuela's most prized Caribbean resort, an island paradise comprising shady beaches, mangrove-lined lagoons, and some of the country's most high-style (and duty-free) shopping streets.

In the southwest, where subtropical jungle gives way to rugged mountain slopes carpeted with coffee and wheat, the Andes rise sharply heading towards Colombia. On the barren, treeless *páramo,* the high-altitude plain perched between two arms of the Andes, weather-beaten Indians wrest a hard living from the stone-pocked land, plowing hillsides where even oxen walk precariously. In markets throughout the region, women weave sweaters, woolen blankets, and *ruanas* (ponchos); along the roadside, red-cheeked children hold up flowers and chubby puppies for sale. In Mérida, the capital of Mérida State and only a few hours' drive from the Colombian frontier, the world's longest and highest cable car makes scaling the Andes swift and unforgettable.

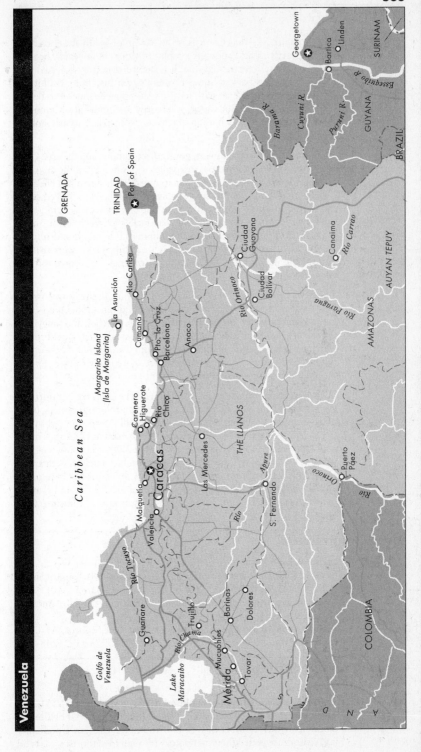

Venezuela

Caribbean Sea

GRENADA

TRINIDAD
✪ Port of Spain

Margarita Island
(Isla de Margarita)

○ La Asunción

○ Río Caribe
○ Cumaná
○ Pto. la Cruz
○ Barcelona
○ Anaco

Carenero
○ Higuerote
○ Río Chico

Maiquetía
✪ Caracas

○ Valencia

○ Las Mercedes

THE LLANOS

Río Tocuyo

○ Guanare

○ Trujillo

○ Barinas
○ Dolores

Río Chama

Mucuchíes
○
Mérida
○ Tovar

*Golfo de
Venezuela*

*Lake
Maracaibo*

COLOMBIA

A N D E S

Río

S. Fernando ○

Apure

Río Orinoco

○ Ciudad
Guayana
○ Ciudad
Bolívar

○ Canaima
Río Carrao

Río Paragua

AMAZONAS

AUYAN TEPUY

Río (Orinoco)

○ Puerto
Páez

Georgetown
✪
○ Bartica
○ Linden

SURINAM

Barama R.
Cuyuni R.
Puruni R.

GUYANA

Essequibo R.

BRAZIL

CARACAS

When pundits say that Caracas is the Miami of South America, they are only partly right. Venezuela's capital city does have nearby beaches and a generally frenetic nightlife. It is indeed served by a network of modern freeways packed bumper to bumper at rush hour. And it certainly caters to the jet set with its glitzy shopping avenues and beachfront country clubs. But Caracas is hardly a second-rate Miami—in this fast-paced city of 4 million, the feeling is tropical, stylish, and altogether more exotic.

The hub of Venezuelan business, government, culture, and the arts, Caracas spills out over a long, narrow valley separated from the coastline by majestic Mt. Avila. The city was founded by the Spaniard Diego de Losada in AD 1567, but today you have to look hard to find traces of the red-tile colonial homes that were once its trademark. Influenced by styles and tastes imported during Venezuela's 1970s "oil rush," modern Caracas is as swank and cosmopolitan as it is rough-and-tumble: an unwieldy hodgepodge in which high-rise financial towers seem as natural and inevitable as the shantylike dwellings that crowd the hills above downtown.

The city's bustling commercial life is ubiquitous. In the downtown El Centro district, street vendors with wares laid out on blankets compete with ambulatory salespeople pitching pens, watches, and sunglasses. On the other side of town, in the posh El Rosal district, stockbrokers clutching cellular phones pause to flirt with Caraqueñas on their way to lunch. At nighttime, these same denizens are likely to meet up in a fashionable discotheque or pub and dance until 4 AM.

Caracas is a sprawling metropolis, but it can be explored comfortably in the space of a few days. Worldly museums and cultural centers, lively bars, and refined dining establishments are all interconnected by the city's clean, efficient subway system, which opened in 1983 after much ado. The weather, too, facilitates exploring: at 3,000 feet above sea level, Caracas has one of the world's most comfortable climates, with an average daily temperature of 75°F. However, Caracas, is not immune to crime: visitors should not go out unescorted after 9 PM, and remember that taxis are recommended as the safest means of transportation after dark.

Visitor Information

Corporturismo has two offices: at Parque Central (Torre Oeste, 36th Floor, ☎ 02/507–8829 or 02/507–8612, FAX 02/574–8810) and at Simón Bolívar International Airport (☎ 031/551111 or 031/551410).
American Express (Torre Consolidado, Av. Blandín, Edificio "Anexo," ☎ 02/260–2451).
Thomas Cook Travel Agency (Edificio Adriático de Seguros, Av. Francisco de Miranda, Piso 6, Oficina 62, ☎ 02/313577 or 02/324846).

Arriving and Departing

By Plane

The **Simón Bolívar International Airport** (☎ 031/551111 or 031/551410), near Caracas in the coastal suburb of Maiquetía, is served by domestic carriers and a number of well-known foreign carriers. Upon landing, visitors are issued their mandatory (though free) tourist visa, valid for a stay of up to three months. Cab fare for the 30- to 45-minute

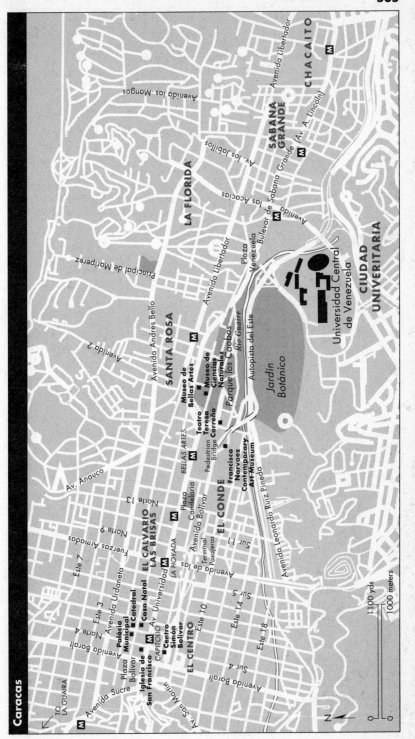

Caracas

TO
LA GUAIRA

Avenida Sucre

Av. San Martín

Avenida Baralt

Plaza
Bolívar

Avenida Urdaneta

Palácio
Municipal

Iglesia de
San Francisco

Catedral

Casa Natal

Av. Universidad

CAPITOLIO

Centro
Simón
Bolívar

EL CENTRO

Norte 4

Este 3

Este 7

Fuerzas Armadas

EL CALVARIO
LAS BRISAS

LA HOYADA

Norte 9

Norte 13

Av. Anauco

Avenida Andrés Bello

SANTA ROSA

Avenida 2

Principal de Maripérez

Avenida los Mangos

LA FLORIDA

Avenida Libertador

Plaza
Candelaria

Avenida Bolívar

Terminal
de los
Pasajeras

BELLAS ARTES

Teatro
Teresa
Carreño

Museo de
Bellas Artes

Museo de
Ciencias
Naturales

Pedestrian
Bridge

Parque los Caobos

Río Guaire

Plaza
Venezuela

Plaza
Venezuela

Bulevar de Sabana Grande

Av. los Jabillos

Avenida de las Acacias

SABANA
GRANDE

Av. A. Lincoln)

Avenida Libertador

CHACAITO

EL CONDE

Francisco
Narváez
Contemporary
Art Museum

Sur 11

Avenida Leonardo Ruiz Pineda

Autopista del Este

Jardín
Botánico

Universidad Central
de Venezuela

CIUDAD
UNIVERITARIA

Este 10

Sur 4

Este 14

Sur 5

Este 18

Avenida Baralt

N

0

0

100 yds

1000 meters

trip to downtown Caracas costs about $18; pay in advance inside the airport at the window marked TICKET DE TAXI, then present the receipt to any of the drivers outside. Otherwise, climb aboard any public bus parked directly outside the domestic terminal; for $2 these shuttle passengers to various downtown destinations, including the Gato Negro metro stop, with a final stop at Parque Central near the Caracas Hilton and Bellas Artes Metro stop.

By Bus

Most public and private buses depart from the hectic **Nuevo Circo** terminal (☎ 02/545–2060 or 02/545–2356) near the La Hoyada Metro stop. It is crowded and difficult to negotiate, but until the new stations are completed, Nuevo Circo offers the only means, besides flying, of moving onward from Caracas. Dependable bus carriers with agents at Nuevo Circo include **Expresos del Oriente** (☎ 02/462–5371), **Expresos de la Costa** (☎ 02/545–3835), and **Expresos Alianza** (☎ 02/620546).

Getting Around Caracas

Downtown Caracas covers a large area, but with a sturdy pair of shoes it can be explored reasonably well on foot. For outlying sights take a taxi or the subway. It is not recommended to venture too far by foot after nightfall.

By Car

Considering Caracas's heavy traffic and lack of parking—as well as the city's somewhat confusing layout—it is not recommended that visitors drive.

By Bus

Public buses connect all parts of the city and cost less than 50¢; they are also unbelievably crowded, slow, and sweaty. *Por puesto* buses run throughout the night but are best avoided after 9 PM or so. The main terminal is at Nuevo Circo, near the La Hoyada Metro stop.

By Metro

Caracas's excellent and very safe metro system traverses the city from east (Propatria) to west (Palo Verde) with a connecting north–south line from El Capitolio to Zoológico and the recently opened north–south line from Plaza Venezuela. The most important downtown stops are Bellas Artes, La Hoyada, and El Capitolio. Metro fares are Bs 30 (for rides of three stops or fewer). Tickets can be purchased in all stations; the orange-color *multiabono* card is valid for 10 rides, as is the *multiintegrado* card, which also allows you to ride city buses for free. The metro operates daily 5 AM–11 PM.

By Taxi

Crowded taxis cut corners and seemingly defy the laws of physics as they maneuver through downtown traffic. Legitimate taxis have secured signs on the roof; *pirata* (pirate) versions have portable signs. Negotiate the price with the driver before you get in, as meters are often ignored or simply "broken." Fares jump as much as 50% at night and on weekends.

Tour Operators

Larger hotels either organize guided tours of the city or have an office of a local tour operator near the lobby area; contact the concierge or a travel agency.

Exploring Caracas

Caracas can be divided into four principal areas: the downtown El Centro district and its monument-packed Plaza Bolívar; Parque Central and the surrounding Bellas Artes cultural district; Las Mercedes and the Bulevar Sabana Grande, with its sundry boutiques and restaurants; and the residential, very wealthy suburbs of Altamira and La Castellana. These far-flung districts are all connected with El Centro by subway. Taxis, too, are extremely cheap and convenient. Few museums, cathedrals, and government buildings in Caracas charge admission fees, but many houses of worship only admit visitors who are modestly dressed.

El Centro

Take the metro to El Capitolio to reach the historic heart of Caracas, **El Centro,** founded in 1567 by Diego de Losada (who named the original settlement Santiago de León de Caracas). From street level it's a short walk to **Plaza Bolívar,** a pleasant shady square with wooden benches, flocks of pigeons, and an imposing equestrian statue of the plaza's namesake, Simón Bolívar, dubbed "El Libertador" in 1813 for his leadership in the struggle against Spanish rule in South America.

Facing the plaza, the former **Corte Suprema** (Supreme Court) now houses government offices. Next door and sharing the same stately neo-Gothic facade is the **Palacio de las Academias** (Palace of the Academies), home of the academies of history, language, and science. Excepting a pair of flower-filled central courtyards that date from the colonial era, there is little to see inside.

The adjoining, attention-grabbing **Panteón Nacional** (National Cemetery) is the city's most striking monument, with its tall, slender twin towers and pale pink-and-green color scheme. Inside are the remains of 138 Venezuelan political and historical figures, including those of Simón Bolívar. ☛ *Free.* ☉ *Tues.–Fri. 9–noon, 2:30–5; weekends 10–noon, 3–5.*

The handsome **Catedral Metropolitana de Caracas** (Metropolitan Cathedral of Caracas), completed in 1674, is the only church in Caracas to retain unaltered its original colonial facade, which is characterized by graceful scroll designs. The highlight inside is the main altar, a magnificent Baroque creation gilded with more than 300 pounds of gold leaf. *Plaza Bolívar,* ☎ *02/862–1518.* ☛ *Free.* ☉ *Tues.–Sun. 8–1, 3–6.*

The adjacent art deco–style **Gobernación** (Government Palace), built in 1935, houses political offices and a ground-floor salon with rotating exhibits of international and Venezuelan art. ☎ *02/811111.* ☛ *Free.* ☉ *Tues.–Sat.*

The **Palácio Municipal** (City Hall), on the south side of Plaza Bolívar, is considered the cradle of Venezuelan nationhood: on July 5, 1811, the National Congress met inside and approved the Declaration of Independence. Nowadays, the City Hall hosts the **Museo de Caracas,** which exhibits a permanent collection of works by noted Venezuelan painter Emilio Boggio (1857–1920); scale-model miniatures by Raúl Santana, depicting every imaginable aspect of Venezuela's early culture; and Ruth Neumann's scale models of Plaza Bolívar at different points in its history. *Plaza Bolívar,* ☎ *02/545–6706.* ☛ *Free.* ☉ *Tues.–Fri. 9–11, 2:30–4:30; Sat. 10:30–4.*

The original plans for **Iglesia de San Francisco** (St. Francis Church) were drawn up in 1593, but the present church owes a heavy debt to President Guzmán Blanco, who ordered extensive renovations in 1887. According to Blanco's wishes, the church now meshes with the baroque flair of the capitol. Inside, 10 dazzling gilded altars vie with colonial icons and statuary for the attention of serious supplicants. *Av. Bolsa at Av. San Francisco,* ☎ *02/415707.* ☛ *Free.* ☉ *Daily 7–noon, 3–6.*

Venezuela's congress is housed in **El Capitolio Nacional** (National Capitol), formerly the site of the 17th-century convent of the Sisters of the Conception. In 1874, President Guzmán Blanco ordered the disbanding of all convents, razed the building, and began constructing the Federal and Legislative palaces. The latter, home to the Senate and Chamber of Deputies, was completed in just 114 days. Sessions of congress can be observed Tuesday–Thursday between 10 and noon (men must wear jacket and tie). The adjacent Federal Palace contains the **Salón Eliptico** (Elliptical Meeting Hall), divided into three sections—the Yellow, Blue, and Red Rooms—in honor of the Venezuelan flag. The massive dome capping the Blue Room contains a mural of the 1821 Battle of Carabobo (the decisive battle in Venezuela's War of Independence against Spain) painted by Martín Tovar y Tovar. Also on display is the chest that holds Venezuela's Declaration of Independence. *Av. Bolsa at Av. San Francisco,* ☎ *02/483–3644.* ☛ *Free.* ☉ *Tues.–Sun. 9–noon, 3–5.*

South of tree-lined Plaza Venezolano, where ice cream vendors and singing evangelists compete for the attention of passersby, the **Museo Bolívar** features documents and historical paraphernalia related to Simón Bolívar and Venezuela's War of Independence against Spain. *Av. San Jacinto at Av. Norte,* ☎ *02/459828.* ☛ *Entry fee.* ☉ *Tues.–Fri. 9–noon, 2:30–5; weekends 10–1, 2:30–5.*

Joined to the museum but with a different stone-carved facade, **Casa Natal** is the birthplace of Simón Bolívar, born July 24,1783. Although this 17th-century colonial mansion contains a number of artifacts from the Bolívar family, more attention is given to the monumental paintings of Tito Salas, with themes focusing on various aspects of Bolívar's early life (including his trip to Paris in 1804, where he witnessed the coronation of Napoléon). ☎ *02/541–2563.* ☛ *Entry fee.* ☉ *Tues.–Fri. 9–noon, 2:30–5; weekends 10–1, 2:30–5.*

To the south, it is hard to miss the twin-towered **Centro Simón Bolívar,** sometimes referred to as Torres de el Silencio, comprising office buildings, apartments, a mammoth shopping center, and two 30-floor towers—the tallest structures in South America when they were built in 1958.

Bellas Artes

Take the metro to the Bellas Artes stop; impossible to miss from street level are the twin 56-story towers that anchor the sprawling **Parque Central,** a complex designed to house 10,000 people within its two towers and seven condominium buildings. Besides shops and restaurants, there are schools, a swimming pool, the Anauco Hilton, the Sofía Imber Contemporary Art Museum, and a tourist office.

East of the Anauco Hilton, look for the outstanding **Museo de Arte Contemporaneo de Sofía Imber** (Sofía Imber Contemporary Art Museum), built in the 1970s on the heels of Venezuela's "oil rush." Displays include sculpture by Fernando Botero and Henry Moore, as well as a permanent Pablo Picasso exhibition. *Parque Central,* ☎ *02/573–7289 or 02/573–8289.* ☛ *Entry fee. Closed Sun.–Mon. 11–6.*

Just eastward, a pedestrian bridge spans a perpetually congested highway and leads to the impressive **Teresa Carreño Complejo Cultural** (Teresa Carreño Cultural Complex), where world-class ballet, opera, and classical concerts are regularly presented at the **Teatro Teresa Car-**

reño (Plaza Los Cabos, ☎ 02/574–9122). Hanging from the theater roof is the kinetic sculpture, *Yellow Pendants,* by Venezuelan artist Jesús Soto. Adjacent to the Teresa Carreño complex is the **Teatro Ateneo,** home of a popular movie theater, a bookstore, and the biannual International Theater Festival.

A short stroll north brings you through an open-air market filled with artisans and food stalls, part of **Plaza Morelos** and the main entrance to **Parque Los Caobos,** a lazy and tree-lined swath of green. One side of the plaza is taken up by the **Museo de Ciencias Naturales** (Museum of Natural Sciences), with displays of stuffed wildlife, insects, minerals, and pre-Columbian ceramics. *Museum: Plaza Morelos, ☎ 02/571–0464. ☛ Free. ☉ Tues.–Sun. 10–5.*

The **Museo de Bellas Artes,** on the opposite side of Plaza Morelos, harbors two exceptional museums: the National Art Gallery, which provides a forum for renowned Venezuelan artists such as Armando Reveron and Alejandro Otero, and the newer Fine Arts Museum, with a hodgepodge but excellent collection that includes Goya etchings, Chinese ceramics, and diverse Egyptian pieces, plus rotating exhibitions of modern international works. *Plaza Morelos, ☎ 02/571–3697. ☛ Entry fee. ☉ Tues.–Fri. 9–noon, 3–5; weekends 10–3.*

At the eastern end of Parque Los Caobos lies the circular **Plaza Venezuela,** with its great fountain and blazon of lights. It is a popular spot for throngs of students from the adjacent 60,000-student **Universidad Central de Venezuela,** designed by architect Carlos Raúl Villanueva. Campus hallmarks include stained-glass windows by Ferdinand Léger, murals by Léger and Mateo Manaure, and sculptures by Jean Arp, Henry Laurens, and Alexander Calder.

Sabana Grande and Las Mercedes

The **Bulevar de Sabana Grande** (sometimes called Avenida Abraham Lincoln) is a festive promenade where visitors and Caraqueños converge on weekends to sip a *marrón grande* (double espresso) at the famous Gran Café, to browse among the troop of street vendors, or to take in the fleeting panorama of street musicians, mime groups, comics, and flame swallowers performing for rapt crowds. Sabana Grande is flanked by two important avenues—Avenida Casanova and Avenida Francisco Solano—both lined with numerous restaurants and affordable hotels.

The far eastern end of Bulevar Sabana Grande is anchored by the **Central Comercial Chacaíto,** a large shopping complex that looms impressively over the lively Chacaíto district. The nearby Chacaíto metro stop opens onto a relaxed square, Plaza Chacaíto, fronted by fast-food eateries and cafés; most days an inexpensive clothing bazaar is held on the southern corner.

East of Chacaíto is the lively **El Rosal** district, noted for its covey of nightspots along Avenida Tamanaco. From here hop in a cab for **Las Mercedes,** considered one of Caracas's chicest districts, with discotheques, boutiques and art galleries, auto dealerships, and innumerable restaurants strewn throughout the side streets. The main strip, Avenida Principal de las Mercedes, is worth experiencing simply to marvel at—or decry—the extent to which U.S. mass-merchandising has infiltrated Venezuelan culture. Appropriately, at the end of the avenue is the large Paseo de las Mercedes shopping mall.

Altamira and La Castellana

These very safe and decidedly upscale neighborhoods cater to young and style-conscious Caraqueños and to the city's upper classes. The districts can be reached by subway (Altamira stop), or you can walk from Chacaíto along Avenida Francisco Miranda.

Elegant restaurants line La Castellana's main thoroughfare, Avenida Principal de la Castellana, which eventually funnels onto the district's main square, Plaza La Castellana. Here you will find the headquarters of Banco Consolidado and the **Centro Cultural del Banco Consolidado,** which houses a visual arts museum with rotating displays of international art as well as a small collection of precious gems, jewels, and medals that belonged to Simon Bolívar. *Av. Urdaneta,* ☎ *02/829821.* ☛ *Free.* ⊙ *Weekdays.*

Shopping

Thanks to shopping habits developed during the oil-bonanza years, as well as to European and U.S. influence, Caraqueños are a style-conscious breed. Western-style clothing, appliances, and gadgets are much sought after by this consumer culture, which explains the city's numerous modern shopping centers. In Caracas, leather goods, shoes, handbags, and luggage are the best bargains, as is, sometimes, jewelry. Browsing is a permissible pleasure, because Venezuelans typically scorn the high-pressure sale. Although a fading art, bartering is still acceptable, especially in smaller establishments and on the street.

Shopping Districts

In the downtown area, next to **Avenida Urdaneta,** you can find excellent shoe and leather shops owned by artisans who manufacture their own products. Two-mile-long **Bulevar Sabana Grande** is totally closed to traffic and has more than 300 shops. The **Las Mercedes** sector, the former American residential area turned into a 10-block cluster of fancy shops and fashionable restaurants, is another good bet, even though its main strip, Avenida Principal de las Mercedes, has an overwhelming but essentially bland collection of chintzy clothing stores and neon-lit trinket shops.

Specialty Shops

GEMS AND GOLD

Inside the CCCT shopping center (*see below*) in Chuao is **Muzo Gemologists** (3rd Floor, ☎ 02/261–4017), which has displays of gemstones, crystals, and rough stones. Another reputable gem dealer in the CCCT is **Diamoro** (3rd Floor, ☎ 02/955–0988). **H. Stern,** one of South America's largest gem dealers, sells all grades of gems at outlets in the Hotel Tamanaco (☎ 02/927313) and the Hilton (☎ 02/571–0520).

HANDICRAFTS AND TAPESTRIES

Handwoven baskets, pottery, wooden objects, carved icons and statuary, hand-crafted jewelry, and other crafts can be found in **Artesanía Amazonas** (Calle Paris at Calle New York), just off the Paseo Las Mercedes. Also in Las Mercedes, **Pablo's** (Av. Rio de Janeiro at Calle Londres) is the place to come for hammocks and handwoven ponchos. **Artesanía Venezuela** (Bul. de Sabana Grande at Gran Avenida) has a large selection of jewelry, ponchos, and textiles.

But for the best selection of crafts—and the kind of exquisite souvenirs you simply must take back home—take a taxi to **El Hatillo,** a restored colonial village on the southern outskirts of town. Its finely preserved streets and quaint 17th-century buildings house dozens of tiny handicraft shops, boutiques, and fancy restaurants, and are well worth the 30-minute trip and a couple of rolls of film.

Markets

The most popular open markets are the **Mercadito de Chacao,** held one block from Avenida Francisco de Miranda in the Chacao district, and **Mercado Guacaipuro,** three blocks from the Caracas Hilton on the corner of Avenidas Andrés Bello and Libertador. The best bargains for trinkets and artwork are had on the streets, in Sabana Grande, at Plaza Morelos, and Plaza Las Americas (a little off the beaten track in El Cafetal district—take a taxi.)

Shopping Centers

The **Central Comercial Ciudad Tamanaco or CCCT** (Chacaíto, ☎ 02/717435), east of Las Mercedes in the suburb of Chuao, packs in thousands of shoppers each day with its upstairs cinemas, fast-food restaurants, and swank boutiques. Nearby is the popular multistory mall **Central Comercial Chacaíto** (Chacaíto metro stop, Av. Francisco de Miranda, ☎ 02/959–2169). Las Mercedes has its own shopping complex, **Paseo de las Mercedes** (near Hotel Tamanaco Inter-Continental, ☎ 02/917242).

Sports

Soccer is the traditional favorite, but basketball and baseball are the current rage in Venezuela. (Baseball has been popular ever since Johnny Bench, Pete Rose, and, later, Daryl Strawberry played during the off-season in Venezuela's winter league.) The **Universidad Central** stadium (Ciudad Universitaria, ☎ 02/572–2211) is the most accessible venue for either baseball or soccer, depending on the season.

Boxing

Professional pugilism is big in Venezuela, with regularly scheduled fights held most Sundays (Nov.–Apr.) at the **Parque Miranda** stadium (metro stop: Parque del Este, ☎ 02/989–1127).

Bullfighting

It is more popular by far in Mexico City and Colombia, but bullfighting has its devoted adherents in Caracas; during the season (Nov.–Apr.) bullfights are held at the **Nuevo Circo** arena (☎ 02/915–2213).

Horse Racing

This sport's popularity is evidenced by the number of betting booths in Caracas, as well as all the radios and televisions tuned in to the beautiful **La Rinconada** racetrack (☎ 02/606–6111), in the suburb of El Valle. To participate in the fun and the wagers, take a taxi ($5 from downtown) any Saturday or Sunday between noon and 6 PM; admission fees to the track are less than $1, and there are betting windows manned by English-speaking staffers.

Dining

Eating out and eating well is considered a must in Caracas, a means for Caraqueños to both satisfy their sophisticated palates and prepare for a night on the town. Considering that many of the city's residents go out *every* night—with the exception of Mondays and a few religious holidays—it should come as no surprise that Caracas has one of the busiest and most varied restaurant scenes in Latin America. The capital's surprisingly diverse mix includes typical Venezuelan, Spanish, French, Italian, Asian, American, meat, and fish restaurants that range from the swank to quite affordable. Though you'll often feel comfortable in dressy sportswear, the dining dress code in Caracas is generally formal—make sure to inquire if a coat and tie are necessary when you make reservations, which are a must at most $$$$ and $$$ restaurants. For price ranges, *see* Dining *in* Venezuela Essentials, *below.*

Arab

$$ La Layalina. There are two fine Arab restaurants next door to each other in the El Bosque district, though La Layalina has the better menu and service. In addition to such traditional Middle Eastern dishes as shish kebab, it's is noted for its tomato-and-beet *fatouch* salad, not to mention its regular belly-dancing performances. ✗ *Av. Principal del Bosque at Av. Santa Clara,* ☎ *02/731–1651. AE, D, MC, V.*

Chinese

$$ Ho Kow. In the heart of the lively Las Mercedes district, this restaurant offers an assortment of Cantonese and Szechuan specialties, including excellent sweet-and-sour jumbo shrimp, a delightful house rice—with shrimp, diced chicken and pork, and vegetables—and the always acclaimed Peking duck. The decor is modern and service is good and fast. ✗ *Plaza Las Mercedes at Calle Orinoco,* ☎ *02/928880. AE, MC, V.*

French

$$$$ Lasserre. For more than 30 years Venezuelans have enjoyed the finest in classical French food at Lasserre. Though the antiques-filled dining room may at first look a bit too stuffy or conservative, owner Tito (he goes only by his first name—like Cher) quickly dispels that impression when he offers his "talking menu" and rolls out the superb game, fish, poultry, and meat entrées. House specialties include the hard-to-find *lapa,* a small tropical boar cooked to perfection in a rich red-wine sauce, and *pabon,* an exquisite freshwater peacock bass prepared in various ways. The Grand Marnier soufflé, which must be ordered in advance, is a great finishing touch, and the wine cellar is top of the class. ✗ *Av. Tercera at Cuarta Transversal, Los Palos Grandes,* ☎ *02/283–4558. Reservations advised. AE, D, MC, V. Closed Sun.*

$$$ Le Gourmet. Hotel restaurants are usually regarded a couple of notches below par; the exception in Caracas is Le Gourmet, the Tamanaco Inter-Continental's elegant and reserved eating place, a home of truly superb French cooking. Try *coquilles St-Jacques* (scallops with white wine and herbs), roast duckling in orange sauce, grilled salmon fillet, and the selection of cheeses. Challenge the sommelier to produce the best French, Spanish, and Italian wines. ✗ *Av. Principal de las Mercedes,* ☎ *02/208–7121. Reservations required. AE, D, MC, V.*

Italian

$$$$ Il Cielo. This new establishment has won the praise of connoisseurs and
★ been rated the best Italian restaurant in town. The constantly changing menu uses traditional Mediterranean ingredients but enlivens the Italian specialties by making extensive use of a wood-burning oven and carbon grill. Don't miss the antipastos. The wine cellar not only houses a fine collection but also does double duty as a dining room for small groups and private parties; reserve ahead. ✗ *Calle Paris at Av. Rio de Janeiro, Las Mercedes,* ☎ *02/293–1411. Reservations advised. AE, MC, V.*

$$ Vía Emilia. Only a couple of blocks from the Tamanaco Inter-Continental hotel, Vía Emilia is one of the capital's favorite Italian eateries. A pleasant modern setting and lively jazz trio add a great touch to the nouvelle cuisine of chef Tonino Frescobaldi, whose portly figure lends an additional guarantee of his kitchen's quality. Try black (squid ink) spaghetti in lemon and cream sauce or salmon and asparagus-tip rigatoni; follow that up with one of the many veal specialties, and bring your meal to a close with a delicious mocha *semifreddo* (ice cream molded in a cara biscuit). ✗ *Av. Orinoco at Calle Paris, Las Mercedes,* ☎ *02/ 926904. AE, MC, V. Closed Sun.*

Japanese

$$$$ Hatsuhana. This neat, modern, multifloor establishment in the posh Altamira area is the finest of a new wave of Japanese restaurants that have become fashionable in Caracas. The menu includes teppanyaki, sukiyaki, and teriyaki specialties in addition to sushi, sashimi, and a full range of other traditional Japanese dishes. The fish tempura is particularly good. ✗ *Av. San Juan Bosco at Av. Sexta de Altamira, Altamira,* ☎ *02/264–1819 or 02/265–9246. Reservations required. AE, MC, V. Closed Mon.*

Japanese/Peruvian

$$$$ Tambo. If you want to rub elbows with the Caracas jet set, this is the place to go. Sample fine Japanese food (served at the sushi bar or your table) or try the exquisite Peruvian specialties, including an excellent ceviche, all in an elegant setting with always lively company. Even if you don't want to eat, the bar is worth a visit. ✗ *Av. Francisco de Miranda at Calle Chacaíto,* ☎ *02/266–7216. Reservations advised. AE, MC, V. Closed Mon.*

Mexican

$ El Tizón. The most popular Mexican restaurant in Caracas is in the basement of the Centro Comercial Bello Campo. Besides tasty Mexican dishes, the menu also features a range of Peruvian specialties, such as *chupes de camarones* (shrimp soup). Margaritas and pisco sours seem to placate the sometimes large crowds. ✗ *Centro Comercial Bello Campo (on Av. Avila 1 block from Av. Francisco de Miranda), Bello Campo,* ☎ *02/ 316715. Reservations advised. AE, D, MC, V. Closed Sun.*

Spanish

$$$ Muñeiras. In the select east side of Caracas, a craving for Spanish food can only be satisfied at Muñeiras. This cozy provincial restaurant dishes out some of the best seafood in the capital, as well as such specialties as empanadas *gallegas* (Galician-style meat pies) and paella *Valenciana* (with saffron, shellfish, and chicken), in an elegant and yet not oversophisticated atmosphere. There's also a good wine list and a mega-caloric dessert cart that, despite the dangers, should not be overlooked. ✗ *Av. San Felipe near Av. El Bosque, La Castellana,* ☎ *02/261– 4461. AE, MC, V. Closed Sun.*

$$ Tasca Segoviana. In the downtown sector of La Candelaria, which many refer to as Little Spain, selecting which is the fairest of all Spanish restaurants can lead to endless arguments—they're all good. As of late, however, the aficionados have leaned towards Tasca Segoviana, where the grilled fish, shellfish, and paellas are always superb. This or other typical Spanish *tascas* (taverns) in this rowdy sector of the city are well worth a visit. ✗ *Calle Cruz de Candelaria at Calle Ferrenquín,* ☎ *02/ 572–6732. AE, MC, V. Closed Sun.*

Thai

$$$$ Samui. The very chic Samui in the La Floresta district is one of the only authentic Thai restaurants in South America. After all, the owners do grow their own vegetables, and they spice the varied dishes to perfection. Coveted entrées include *pra lad prik* (red snapper basted in garlic), and the dessert menu, weighted heavily with crème brûlée and chocolate mousse, is outstanding. ✗ *Av. Andrés Bello at Av. Francisco Miranda la Transversal,* ☎ *02/285–4600 or 02/283–4146. Reservations advised. MC, V. Closed Sun.*

Venezuelan

$$$ La Estancia. In this traditional Spanish-style restaurant, black-and-white photographs of famous bullfighters don't seem too out of place. Despite the obvious Spanish influences, *criollo* cuisine—a Venezuelan melding of Spanish and Caribbean flavors—is actually the house specialty. Start with the lobster bisque and move on to the *parrillas* (criollo-style grill) or to the rabbit or chicken basted in orange sauce. ✕ *Av. Principal 46, at Calle Urdaneta, La Castellana,* ☎ *02/261–2363. Reservations advised. AE, MC, V.*

$$$ Lee Hamilton Steak House. At this Caracas institution, the T-bone, *bife chorrizo* (heart filet), and mixed grill from the famous cattle of the town of Santa Barbara are said to be the best south of the Rio Grande and north of the Río de la Plata. Dinners are served with a typically Venezuelan side dish—fried yucca, the tuber from which cassava bread is made. ✕ *Av. San Felipe at Av. El Bosque, La Castellana, 02/261–0511. AE, MC, V. Closed Mon.*

$ Tarzilandia. Lush tropical vegetation, parrots and other birds, and small and large turtles crawling around in the garden are all part of the experience. The unique menu features such exotic Venezuelan dishes as *pabellón criollo* (mashed beef with black beans, rice, and plantain), turtle pie, and shrimp mixed with tropical fruit. As a closer, diners often indulge in mango flambée à la mode. ✕ *Av. San Juan de Bosco at Decima Transversal de Altamira,* ☎ *02/261–8419. AE, MC, V. Closed Mon.*

$ El Tinajero de los Helechos. This well-priced restaurant offers local spe-
★ cialties and meat grilled beside your table. Try *arepitas* (white-corn patties) with *natilla* (fresh whipped butter) and *queso guayanés* (a local white cheese) to start, and follow with a *parrilla mixta* (mixed grill) accompanied by watercress, palmetto, and avocado salad. ✕ *Av. Rio de Janeiro at Plaza La Trinidad, Las Mercedes,* ☎ *02/916502. AE, MC, V.*

Lodging

Many of Caracas's best hotels are a few kilometers north of downtown in the refined Bellas Artes and Altamira districts—a short but inevitable taxi ride away from Caracas's restaurants and nightclubs. Although security-minded visitors may feel more comfortable in established hotels such as the Hilton, Caracas does offer a variety of alternative lodging options that are easier on the budget and often more interesting in terms of that amorphous quality called character. The Sabana Grande district is considered especially desirable for more adventurous travelers; you can pick and choose from the many budget-price pensions crowding the lively Avenida Casanova and Avenida Francisco Solano. For price ranges, *see* Lodging *in* Venezuela Essentials, *below.*

$$$$ Caracas Hilton International. In the high-cultured Bellas Artes district, this mammoth complex has long been the primary destination of international businesspeople. While rooms suffer from a bland "international style" of decoration, the hotel is conveniently located and has such a wide array of facilities that it seems like a small city unto itself. ▥ *Av. Libertador at Calle Sur 25, near Bellas Artes metro stop,* ☎ *02/503–5000,* ℻ *02/503–5003; U.S.* ☎ *800/221–2424. 822 rooms, 27 suites. 2 restaurants, bar, room service, 2 pools, beauty salon, massage, sauna, 2 tennis courts, health club, concierge floors, business services. AE, D, MC, V.*

$$$$ Eurobuilding. Business travelers are especially fond of this modern high-rise hotel in the Chuao business district near the large CCCT shopping center. Glass-enclosed elevators carry you from the lobby, the site of numerous concerts and nightlife activities, up to spacious double rooms and suites, many with good views of Mt. Avila. The Eurobuilding's restaurant, Cassandra, is regarded as one of the best hotel eateries in Caracas. ☎ *Av. de la Guairita, Chuao,* ☎ *02/959–1133,* FAX *02/922069; U.S.* ☎ *800/325–3876. 450 rooms, 180 suites. Restaurant, bar, pool, sauna, exercise room. AE, D, MC, V.*

$$$$ **Tamanaco Inter-Continental**. The oldest and most traditional of the city's top hotels sits on a hill in the south-central part of the city. Both the old and newer wing offer good-size rooms, many with a clear view of Mt. Avila. Facilities include satellite TV, an on-site bank, a gigantic swimming pool, a great health club, tennis courts, and yes, the best bar in town, called El Punto. ☎ *Av. Principal de las Mercedes,* ☎ *02/208–7111,* FAX *02/208–7116; U.S.* ☎ *800/327–0200. 580 rooms, 23 suites. 3 restaurants, 3 bars, minibars, pool, 3 tennis courts, health club, jogging, travel services. AE, D, MC, V.*

$$$ **Continental Altamira.** Within walking distance from the Plaza Altamira metro station, Centro Plaza shopping center, and the Altamira restaurant sector, this modern hotel is a favorite of those who, while on a slightly tighter budget, demand good service and a great location. Rooms are amply sized, and the majority have balconies with views of tree-lined Avenida San Juan Bosco and Mt. Avila. ☎ *Av. San Juan Bosco, Altamira,* ☎ *02/262–0243,* FAX *02/261–0131 or 02/261–9091. 180 rooms, 2 suites. Pool. AE, D, MC, V.*

$$$ **Residencias Anauco Hilton.** This kin of the Caracas Hilton is just across the street from big brother in the Bellas Artes cultural sector, a block from the subway station of the same name. Accommodations range from studio suites to two- and three-bedroom apartments, many with kitchenettes. On-site sports, entertainment, and business facilities are limited, but guests have access to all the amenities at the Caracas Hilton. ☎ *Av. Lecuna at Parque Central, near Bellas Artes metro stop,* ☎ *02/ 573–4111,* FAX *02/573–7724; U.S.* ☎ *800/221–2424. 335 suites. Restaurant, bar. AE, D, MC, V.*

$$ **El Conde.** Despite its age, this newly remodeled 1950s mid-rise matches a convenient downtown location—near Plaza Bolívar and El Capitolio metro stop—with comfortable rooms and good facilities, including the Italian restaurant Il Coratino and an all-hours tasca. ☎ *Esquina El Conde,* ☎ *02/811171,* FAX *02/862–0928. 133 rooms, most with bath. 2 restaurants, bar, exercise room, meeting rooms. AE, D, MC, V.*

$$ **Lincoln Suites.** The well-appointed Lincoln Suites straddles the busy Bulevar de Sabana Grande, Caracas's principal pedestrian and commercial artery. The bright and comfortable rooms, mostly suites and spacious doubles, come equipped with minibars and televisions, but you'll probably spend more time in the popular watering hole Michael's Bar, which is in the lobby. ☎ *Av. Francisco Solano López at Av. Los Jabillos,* ☎ *02/762–8575 or 02/762–8578,* FAX *02/762–8579. 100 rooms (most with bath), 28 suites. Restaurant, bar, minibars. AE, D, MC, V.*

$ **Hotel Luna.** This modest hotel in the Sabana Grande district has compact, clean rooms and a friendly, multilingual staff. The two luxurious suites have a living room, refrigerator, and television. ☎ *Av. Casanova at Calle El Colegio,* ☎ *02/762–5851,* FAX *02/762–5850. 63 rooms, 2 suites. Restaurant, bar. AE, D, MC, V.*

$ **Savoy.** At this Sabana Grande budget hotel, service and style are not sacrificed for price. After tackling the nearby restaurants, bars, and shops, you can relax in the Savoy's small patio restaurant or retire to your comfortable, quiet room. ☎ *Av. Francisco Solano López (near Chacaito metro stop),* ☎ *02/762–1971 or 02/762–1979,* FAX *02/762–2792. 95 rooms. Restaurant. AE, D, MC, V.*

The Arts

Professional theater, as well as classical and popular music concerts, are popular nighttime diversions. For current listings, pick up a copy of the English-language newspaper *Daily Journal,* available at most newsstands.

MUSIC

The Venezuelan Symphony Orchestra regularly plays at the **Teatro Teresa Carreño** (opposite Caracas Hilton, ☎ 02/574–9122). The adjacent **Teatro Ateneo** (Plaza Morelos, ☎ 02/573–4622) hosts chamber music and operatic concerts between September and April. On the campus of Universidad Central, **Aula Magna** (☎ 02/619811, ext. 2505) features Sunday concerts at 11 AM by the Venezuelan Symphony Orchestra (except Aug. and Sept.) and acoustic "clouds" by Alexander Calder, who helped design the Aula Magna.

THEATER

The **Teatro Municipal** (Esquina Municipal, ☎ 02/415385) and **Teatro Nacional** (Av. Lacuna, ☎ 02/482–5424) feature active programs of dance, music, and cultural events. Traveling by taxi is a good idea because neither theater is in the best neighborhood.

Nightlife

Caracas sleeps only on Monday nights; beginning on Tuesday the intensity of the capital's partying gradually increases, peaking on Saturday, when the whole population seems to be out on the town with buckets of red paint. **Las Mercedes,** reminiscent of Mexico City's Zona Rosa, is packed with street cafés, fast-food outlets, restaurants, and dance clubs; the district gets quite rowdy (though in a friendly way) on Fridays and Saturdays. Although Caracas is a casual sort of town, jackets are typically required of men at dance and private clubs; ties, however, are optional.

BARS

In Las Mercedes, **Weekends** (Av. San Juan Bosco at La Segunda Transversal, ☎ 02/261–3839) is a popular sports bar that has live music and Tex-Mex food. In the El Rosal district, **Juan Sebastian Bar** (Av. Venezuela, ☎ 02/951–0595) is a distinguished yet swinging hangout that features live jazz most nights.

DANCE CLUBS

Mention a night on the town to a local and the first suggestion will probably be dancing. Unlike their North American counterparts, Caraqueños start dancing the salsa and merengue at a tender age. The proliferation of dance clubs and music venues testifies to this abiding passion. **Palladium** (Centro Comercial Ciudad Tamanaco, or CCCT, ☎ 02/931664) is where local John Travoltas show off their latest spectacular steps of merengue dirty dancing. **El Sarao** (Centro Comercial Bello Campo, ☎ 02/312503) features live merengue, salsa, and *tambores* (drum) bands nightly. In the Las Mercedes district, there's dancing on two levels at **Hollywood Dance Bar & Grill** (Calle Madrid at Calle Veracruz, ☎ 02/913257), where couples rather than singles are the preferred clientele. For salsa in Sabana Grande, **El Maní Es Así** (Calle El Christo at Av. Francisco Solano López, ☎ 02/617078) is a must; on weekends the dance floor is packed with celebrants of all ages, though during the week you're more likely to see a Brando or Bogart film playing on the club's large-screen televisions. The most popular Brazilian nightclub in Caracas is **Aquarela Brasilera** (Calle Humboldt, La Chaguarmos, ☎ 02/661–5897), which features live Brazilian music nightly and occasional belly dancing.

Excursions from Caracas

La Guaira and Macuto

These lively beach resorts are a good bet for visitors who need an escape from urban Caracas without the hassle and expense of renting a car. Both are in the El Litoral district, a 30- to 45-minute trek by subway and bus from downtown Caracas, and both offer sunbathing and the opportunity to indulge in fresh fish at any of a dozen oceanfront restaurants. The beach next to the Macuto Sheraton hotel is particularly popular.

Getting There

Take the subway to Gato Negro, and at street level climb aboard any of the vans or buses marked LA GUAIRA or MACUTO. By car, follow signs to the airport and La Guaira and then continue east along the same highway.

Lodging

$$$$ **Sheraton Macuto Resort.** If you actually check in to one of the attractive rooms here, you can take advantage of a wide range of sports facilities. Rental equipment is available for, among others, waterskiing, sailing, surfing, windsurfing, and some of the finest deep-sea fishing in the Caribbean. ☎ *Box 65, La Guaira,* ☎ *031/944300,* FAX *031/944317; U.S.* ☎ *800/325–3535. 493 rooms. 3 restaurants, 2 bars, room service, 2 pools, sauna, 2 tennis courts, bowling, health club, jogging, volleyball, business services, meeting rooms. AE, D, MC, V.*

Colonia Tovar

Colonia Tovar, roughly 65 kilometers (40 miles) from Caracas, was colonized by German immigrants in 1843 and today remains as authentically German as anything you'll find in the Black Forest. Some of the townsfolk are naturally blond, and given the cooler climate and chalet accommodations, one quickly forgets that this high-altitude (5,860-feet) and sometimes breezy mountain retreat is in a steamy tropical country. The real joy is to hike in the hills surrounding Tovar, or to spend an evening in one of the village's jovial chalets, chomping on sausage and other hearty German foods.

Getting There

Check with your hotel or the tourist office for information about frequent full-day tours to Colonia Tovar. There is no direct public transportation to the village, though you can take a public bus as far as Junquito and then hire a cab for the remaining 40-minute drive ($20).

Choroní

Choroní is a quiet and undisturbed coastal town, a veritable beach bum's paradise with freshwater bathing, nearby camping, and lots of friendly foreign slackers who gratefully have managed to "misplace" their airplane ticket home. At night, the fun switches to the adjoining village of Puerto Colombia and its central square. This is where the tambores takes place, in the form of heavy African percussion that inspires both locals and tourists to enter into small circles and gyrate wildly, all with the help of a potent local libation. Drum music and dancing take place most weekends, though the Feast of San Juan Bautista (June 23) draws the largest crowds. You could visit Choroní and Puerto Colombia in one very tiring day, but if you're intrigued by the tambores, it may be best to stay the night.

Getting There

Choroní is in Pittier National Park, and whether you go by car or bus, the drive from Caracas is a hair-raising experience. By car follow the main highway out of Caracas west to Maracay, then take the *carretera* (secondary road) from Maracay to Choroní. Buses leave regularly from Caracas's Nuevo Circo terminal for Maracay, where you can then find a bus to Choroní.

Lodging

You can stay at the relaxed **La Parchita Hotel** (El Malecón, ☎ 043/ 832560; $), which has an adjoining vegetarian restaurant, or get slightly more pampering at **Cotoperix** (El Malecón, ☎ 02/951–6226, FAX 02/951–7741; $$). If you want something more luxurious, stay at **La Posada de Humboldt** (Av. Principal, near the traffic police check point, no ☎; $$), a fine colonial inn only a mile up the road, and enjoy great rooms and healthy, savory meals; the inn can also arrange various excursions, including a visit to one of the local cocoa plantations, where Chuao, regarded as the best cocoa in the world, is cultivated.

THE CARIBBEAN COAST AND MARGARITA ISLAND

The Route of the Sun is what Venezuelans call the 563-kilometer (350-mile) stretch of highway that parallels the coast from Caracas to Puerto La Cruz and Cumaná. Fueled by a surge of tourism in the 1980s, major resorts and condominiums have blossomed along the sweeping sandy shores of Higuerote and Puerto La Cruz, contributing to weekend bottlenecks along the arterial Autopista del Oriente (Eastern Highway, also known as Hwy. 9). Still, the coast comprises unspoiled lagoons and rugged peninsulas, as well as many isolated beaches scarcely touched by tourism.

Though you may not realize it yet, your ultimate destination may be Margarita Island, reached by plane from Caracas or by ferry from Puerto La Cruz or Cumaná. Margarita is Venezuela's legendary island paradise, prized for its untamed beaches and relaxed, picturesque towns. However, Margarita is no quaint little island, nor is it especially inexpensive; a recent building boom has produced plenty of high-rise hotels and upscale shopping centers. (That this boom is being funded by a mushrooming number of bingo houses and casinos is a fact quietly ignored by the federal government, which officially does not allow gambling.) Still, the island has many charms, and chief among them, are the palm-lined beaches and friendly locals who don't seem too impressed by tourists—which is probably for the best.

Arriving and Departing

By Plane

Viasa flies directly from New York and Miami to Margarita Island. **Avensa, Aserca,** and **Laser** fly daily from Simón Bolívar International Airport in the Caracas suburb of Maiquetía to the coastal town of Barcelona. Most major domestic carriers also have daily service from Maiquetía, Cumaná, Valencia, and Maracaibo to Margarita Island's **Aeropuerto Internacional del Caribe** (☎ 095/691438), 29 kilometers (18 miles) south of Porlamar. No matter where you're flying from, a one-way domestic ticket costs less than $70.

By Car or Taxi

The often congested Autopista del Oriente (Hwy. 9) joins Caracas with Barcelona, Puerto La Cruz, and Cumaná; the highway has all road-side services because it is the major artery for coastal cities. Taxis are scarce at the Barcelona and Margarita airports, but most hotels are happy to book taxi transportation with 24 hours' notice. Also, inside the ter-minals are dozens of car rental agencies. Rates are high (an economy car rents for as much as $70 per day) but you can always count, how-ever, on cheap gas—it costs less than $4 for a fill-up.

By Bus and Por Puesto

There are daily buses—some with air-conditioning and snack service—from the Nuevo Circo terminal in Caracas to Barcelona, Puerto La Cruz, and Cumaná; one-way fare for each is less than $10. Advance reser-vations are a must and should be made as soon as possible; contact **Expresos CaMarGui** (Nuevo Circo, ☎ 02/541–0364) or **Unión Con-ductores de Margarita** (Nuevo Circo, ☎ 02/541–0035), both of which also offer bus-ferry packages to Margarita Island, a 12-hour trip that costs less than $12.

Another option is por puesto taxis, buses, and limousines. These carry three to 15 people and travel set routes between the Nuevo Circo ter-minal and the Caribbean Coast. Drivers shout the names of cities they serve and leave the terminal when their vehicles are full. Por puestos do not accept reservations, and the rates are fixed; expect to pay $20 between Caracas and Puerto La Cruz.

By Ferry

Conferry (Av. La Acacias at Av. Casanova, Caracas, ☎ 02/781–9711 or 02/782–8544) shuttles passengers and up to 150 cars six times daily from Puerto La Cruz (Terminal Los Cocos, ☎ 081/677847) to Punta de Piedras, 25 kilometers (16 miles) west of Porlamar on Margarita Island. It also offers twice-daily service from Cumaná (Terminal Puerto Sucre, ☎ 093/311462). **Naviarca** (☎ 093/26230) carries up to 60 cars on its daily ferry from Cumaná to Punta de Piedras.

Purchase tickets at least two hours in advance for all ferries, particu-larly on weekends and holidays. The crossings take from two to four hours and cost about $25 per car and $10 per passenger.

The Caribbean Coast

Visitor Information

Barcelona
CORANZTUR, Calle Freites 2–45, ☎ 081/777110.

Cumaná
Información Turístico, Calle Sucre, ☎ 093/24449.

Puerto La Cruz
CORANZTUR, Paseo Colón at Calle Maneiro, ☎ 081/688170.

Exploring

Higuerote and Nearby

A haggard-looking town perched on the coast 130 kilometers (80 miles) from Caracas, Higuerote is jammed with sun worshipers on week-ends—mainly Caraqueños who reserved space months ago in one of the sleek resorts that line the long stretch of beach. The silt-filled wa-ters offshore manage to attract thousands of swimmers and *guacucos,* a type of clam that locals gather and cook right on the beach—the genesis of the huge mounds of shells you'll see piled up on the sand.

Carenero, 8 kilometers (4 miles) north of Higuerote, is where more affluent Venezuelans go for their holidays. This small resort town does not have a swimmable beach, but from Carenero's Embarcadero Nena Mar, found at the end of a kilometer-long, marked dirt road, there are daily ferries ($3 per person) to **Buche Island** and its tidy beach. **Chirimena,** 4 kilometers (2½ miles) beyond Carenero, has the best beach around—a wide swath of white sand tucked into a crescent-shape cove. There is a paved parking lot here, plus stands offering light snacks and refreshments.

Río Chico

Thirty-seven kilometers (23 miles) southeast of Higuerote, Río Chico shares that town's dog-eared appearance, so head straight for **Playa Colada,** Río Chico's well-kept beach, lined with palm-thatched restaurants, lively bars, and umbrella-shaded tables. Join the hoard of sunbathers here, or follow the signs to **Parque Nacional Laguna de Tacarigua,** about 18 kilometers (11 miles) northeast. At the park's entrance is a fishing dock with an open-sided, very rustic bar where you can drink and dance with local beachgoers. In the late afternoon, the surrounding mangrove forest comes alive as thousands of white herons and scarlet ibis return home and settle down for the night.

Puerto Píritu

From Río Chico rejoin Highway 9 at El Guapo and continue past Clarines to Puerto Píritu, a sleepy village at the edge of the sea. The streets here are lined with preserved colonial mansions fronting wooden grills, carved eaves, and somber color schemes. The highlight, though, is Píritu's beach: For nearly 2 kilometers (1 mile), the bright blue Caribbean laps a wide ribbon of clean white sand. Restaurants, bars, and hotels are clustered at regular intervals along Píritu's shoreline drive, Boulevard Fernández Padilla.

Barcelona

The capital of Anzótegui State is 41 kilometers (25 miles) east of Puerto Píritu and the site of the region's largest airport. On the corner of Plaza Boyacá, the city's tree-lined main square, it's hard to miss **Iglesia de San Cristóbal,** a stunning two-story church built in 1748.

Even more impressive is the adjacent **Palacio del Gobierno** (Palace of the Government), built in 1671 and home today to the **Museo de la Tradición,** which has rotating exhibits of colonial and religious art. *Plaza Boyacá,* ☎ *081/773481.* ✆ *Free.* ☉ *Daily.*

Puerto La Cruz

Puerto La Cruz, the region's main tourist hub, is heavily industrialized, but its expanding marinas and canals are being transformed into attractive Venetian-style waterways lined with town houses and expensive villas. Visitors flock to the maze of shops on the waterfront **Paseo Colón,** a busy thoroughfare that links downtown with a sandy public beach—a seashell hunter's delight. During the day, the beach and its casual restaurants and bars are packed; at night, the crowds move to the bars and dance clubs in town. The ferry terminal for Margarita Island is at the western end of Paseo Colón; at the eastern end you'll find boats that shuttle beachgoers between Puerto La Cruz and many of the small islands visible in the bay. Expect to pay $6–$8 for round-trip service.

En Route to Cumaná

From Puerto La Cruz, follow signs for Guanta and Cumaná; along the way, in the tiny village of Chorrerón, you'll see a sign for **Parque La Sirena** (the entrance is 3 kilometers [2 miles] off the main highway), a small national park nestled in a valley and divided by a slow-moving river. La Sirena doesn't fall into the wildly stunning category, but there are two photogenic waterfalls, popular swimming holes, and a few marked hiking trails in addition to picnic tables, changing rooms, and a snack bar. ☎ *081/674432.* ☛ *Entry fee.* ⊙ *Tues.–Sun.*

Beyond Guanta, Highway 9 curves and climbs high above Santa Fe Bay, giving good views of the palm-lined coast. As you make your descent, signs direct you to two popular beaches: **Playa Arapito** and **Playa Colorada,** both of which have smooth sand, paved parking lots, and refreshment stands.

Seven kilometers (4 miles) beyond Santa Fe is the turnoff for **Mochima,** the launching point for boat trips to the tranquil beaches of **Parque Mochima,** which encompasses hundreds of small islands and sand spits just offshore. Contract a *peñero* (boatman) to bring you to any of the nearby beaches, where you can spend a relaxing morning or afternoon bathing and eating fresh fish. The going round-trip rate is $7–$10 per person.

Cumaná

The capital of Sucre State is the oldest European settlement in Venezuela, dating from 1521. Most of Cumaná's colonial mansions and buildings are within walking distance of the central Plaza Bolívar. One block south, the **Ateneo de Cumaná** (Calle Antonio, ☎ 093/311284) hosts dance and opera evenings in addition to periodic exhibits of contemporary and colonial art. **Casa Natal Blanco** (Calle Sucre; ☛ Entry fee), the birthplace of one of Venezuela's greatest literary figures, André Eloy Blanco (1896–1955), displays personal paraphernalia and some of the author's first edition works. Overlooking Cumaná from its hilltop perch, **Castillo de San Antonio de la Eminencia** (☛ Free; ⊙ Daily) is one of two forts commissioned in the 1680s to protect what was at the time the world's largest salt deposit. The four-point fort was built entirely of coral and outfitted with 16 guns, much like its companion, **Castillo de Santiago de Araya** (☛ Free; ⊙ Daily), on the rugged, treeless Araya Peninsula. Car and passenger ferries leave daily from Cumaná's harbor for the Araya Peninsula; the crossing takes 90 minutes.

It's estimated that **Cueva del Guácharo,** Venezuela's largest cave, has at least 10,204 meters (33,456 feet) of subterranean passageways. At the cave's entrance there's an information center—with a snack bar and rest rooms—where you can ponder a handful of displays and charts before plunging into the dank, eerie caverns. You are led in groups of 10 by a guide who totes a kerosene lantern so as not to upset the light-sensitive guácharos—nocturnal, fruit-eating birds that nest inside the cave. Visitors are not allowed to bring anything inside—no purses, flashlights, food, cameras, and the like. To reach the cave from Cumaná, take Highway 9 south toward Caripe for about 65 kilometers (40 miles) and follow the signs. *Parque Nacional El Guácharo,* ☎ *081/784445.* ☛ *Entry fee.* ⊙ *Daily.*

Shopping

In **Puerto La Cruz,** shops along **Paseo Colón** cater to tourists with trinket and crafts stands, as do the street sellers hawking jewelry and beach items—sandals, glasses, and sunscreen—at reasonable prices.

Sports and the Outdoors

For a small fee, resort hotels sometimes allow nonguests to use tennis courts, weight rooms, and spa facilities.

Fishing

Boat owners throughout the region will take you surf or lagoon fishing in their small, wooden, open-top peñeros. The price you pay will reflect your ability to bargain; the going rate is about $5 per person, including basic equipment, for a half-day excursion. **Amerinda Tours** (*see below*) charters deep-sea boats for serious anglers. **Cuante Agencia de Viaje y Turismo** (☎ 081/776–3304) charges $100 per person per day to fish and camp overnight on an island; the price includes boat transfers, all meals and accommodations, and fishing gear.

Snorkeling, Diving, and Sailing

The **Tecnisub Diving Center** (at the marina, ☎ 081/669081) in Puerto La Cruz offers diving and snorkeling lessons in addition to organized ocean dives for experienced—and certified—divers.

In El Morro, near Puerto La Cruz, **Odisea** (Hotel Doral Beach, ☎ 081/812222) rents sailboats, Windsurfers, and pedal boats. In Puerto La Cruz proper, you can rent sailboats from **Amerinda Tours** (Hotel Caribbean Inn, ☎ 081/670693).

Dining and Lodging

Hotels on the Caribbean Coast will add a 10% surcharge to your bill unless you have a Venezuelan passport. Reservations are a must on holidays and summer weekends. For price categories, *see* Dining *and* Lodging *in* Venezuela Essentials, *below*.

Cumaná

DINING AND LODGING

$$$ ★ **Hotel Los Bordones.** Cumaná's best address is this fairly modern four-star hotel, on the outskirts of town, with two restaurants, a vast swimming pool, and—best of all—access to a nearly secluded beach just a pebble's throw away. An on-site travel office can arrange snorkeling and windsurfing jaunts. **Polinesa**, the popular on-site restaurant, is considered the best in town for fresh seafood. 🖃 *Av. Universidad,* ☎ *093/653783 or 093/653644. 114 rooms, 3 suites. 2 restaurants, pool, 2 tennis courts. AE, D, MC, V.*

$$ **Gran Hotel.** This plain and functional hotel is in the center of town, opposite the entrance to the Universidad del Oriente. Most rooms are equipped with private bathrooms, air-conditioning, and televisions. The hotel restaurant is quite respectable. 🖃 *Av. Universidad,* ☎ *093/653711 or 093/653811. 50 rooms. Restaurant. AE, D, MC, V.*

Puerto La Cruz

DINING

$$ ★ **Casa Pueblo.** At this authentic colonial hacienda, the comfortable, romantic dining area is superbly complemented by a mile-long menu, printed in English, German, and Spanish. The house specialty is grilled fish, prepared with whatever is fresh. If you're an early riser, don't miss the hearty steak-and egg breakfasts starting at 7 AM. ✕ *Calle Carabobo (between Paseo Colón and Calle Bolívar),* ☎ *081/22018. AE, D, MC, V.*

$$ **Porto Vecchio.** This Italian restaurant is regarded as the best in eastern Venezuela. A lively clientele drops in from the paseo walk for delicious veal and the excellent house-specialty pastas with fish and shellfish. ✕ *Paseo Colón 117, at Calle Boyacá,* ☎ *081/21694. Weekend reservations advised. AE, D, MC, V.*

LODGING

$$$ **Hotel Punta Palma.** Built at the end of the long curve of the bay of Puerto La Cruz, this hotel has an enviable view of the city and the port from its idyllic El Morro location. Most of its pastel rooms face the sea and overlook the fine swimming pool, small beach, and marina. Service is impeccable, and the European chef deals handily with any appetite you've developed by making use of the many water-sports facilities. ⊞ *Prolongación el Morro,* ☎ *081/811211,* FAX *081/818277. 180 rooms. Restaurant, pool, dock, meeting rooms. AE, D, MC, V.*

$$$ **Hotel Rasil.** This high-rise at the end of Paseo Colón combines the amenities of a chain hotel—including shops and a pool with an overlooking bar—with the informal charm of a small pension. Most rooms have ocean views, whirlpool bathtubs, and cable TV. ⊞ *Paseo Colón at Calle Monagas,* ☎ *081/672422,* FAX *081/673121. 350 rooms, 34 suites. Restaurant, bar, pool, dance club. AE, D, MC, V.*

$$–$$$ **Hotel Caribe Mar.** Tucked behind the Hotel Rasil, this relatively new property offers comfortable, air-conditioned singles and suites—most with sea views—at lower-than-average rates. ⊞ *Calle Ricaurte No. 14,* ☎ *081/673291 or 081/674973,* FAX *081/672096. 74 rooms, 16 suites. Restaurant, bar. AE, D, MC, V.*

$$ **Hotel Gaeta.** A prime reason to stay here is location, on the Paseo Colón a short walk from Puerto La Cruz's restaurants and shops. Most of the Gaeta's simple, clean, air-conditioned rooms have balconies, and the beach is only a stone's throw away. If the main hotel is full, try the affiliated Hotel Gaeta City, only five blocks farther along Calle Maneiro. ⊞ *Paseo Colón at Calle Maneiro,* ☎ *081/691616. 50 rooms. Restaurant, bar. AE, MC, V.*

Nightlife

You won't have to look far to find bars and dance clubs in Puerto La Cruz: All of them are on either Paseo Colón or on adjacent side streets. A new and popular addition to the nightlife scene is **Harry's Pub** (Calle Bolívar No. 53, ☎ 081/613524), a dark but friendly watering hole with an interesting mix of young locals and seasoned wayfarers.

Margarita Island

Visitor Information

DTNA, Aeropuerto del Caribe, ☎ 095/691438; Av. Santiago Mariño, Edificio Don Ramón, Porlamar, ☎ 095/613065, FAX 095/011954.

Exploring

Isla de Margarita, along with the smaller islands of Cubagua and Coche and the 50 or so islets of Los Roques Archipelago, have long been favorite sea-and-sun playgrounds for Venezuelans. Margarita Island, in particular, has become the focus of vigorous hotel and resort development to accommodate the growing number of international tourists. Margarita is divided into two sections that are connected by a narrow spit of sand; the bulk of its 200,000 residents live on the more developed eastern half. Cars are the most convenient way of getting around and can be rented at the airport; however, taxis and por puesto buses connect Margarita's larger towns with one another and with the beach.

Porlamar

Founded in 1536, Porlamar is the commercial heart of Margarita Island; its streets have been packed with shops and hotels ever since the area was granted free-port status by the government in 1973. (In fact, moonlighting Caraqueños sometimes come to Margarita looking for clothes and gadgets to sell back on the mainland.) There are relatively few historic sights in Porlamar—perhaps the reason why the most popular pastimes here are shopping, sunbathing, and eating. For the first, try the maze of shops huddled between the pedestrian-only Bulevar Guevara and Bulevar Gómez, or try the local market near Plaza Bolívar.

A few blocks east of shady Plaza Bolívar is the **Museo de Arte Contemporáneo Francisco Narváez,** named after the native Margariteño sculptor whose works also can be viewed on the grounds of the Hotel Bella Vista (*see* Lodging, *below*). In the museum you'll find a permanent collection of Narváez's works, plus a rotating exhibit of national and international art. *Calle Igualdad at Calle Fraternidad,* ☎ *095/ 618668.* ☞ *Free.* ☺ *Tues.–Sun.*

El Valle

From Porlamar follow the road 2.5 kilometers (1½ miles) north to El Valle, Margarita's first capital, founded in 1529. Today it is a center for souvenirs and crafts, from hammocks to rag dolls. A point of pilgrimage for islanders—especially on September 8, the Virgin of El Valle's feast day—is the **Santuario de la Virgin del Valle,** a pink twin-towered edifice on El Valle's main plaza. Adjacent to the church, a small **museum** (☞ Entry fee; closed Mon.) contains the thousands of tokens, jewelry, and holy medals left by supplicants.

La Asunción

North of El Valle lies mountainous **El Copey National Park,** which gives striking views of the island (provided the national guard lets you in). The mountain road slowly descends to La Asunción, the modern capital of Margarita Island. Built in 1580, the **Catedral Nuestra Señora** (Church of Our Lady) stands prominently on La Asunción's main plaza and is one of the earliest examples of colonial architecture in Venezuela. Of particular note is its square, three-tier tower—the country's only surviving example of a colonial church tower. Adjacent to the church, the **Museo Nueva Cádiz** (☎ 095/41980; ☞ Entry fee; closed Mon.) contains a hodgepodge collection of wooden model ships, religious statuary, and seashells. Overlooking the main square, the **Castillo de Santa Rosa** (☞ Free; ☺ Daily) is a handsomely restored fort originally built in 1681. Those who make the short but arduous uphill trek (there's a path visible from the main square) will be rewarded with panoramic views of the island.

Pampatar

The coastal village of Pampatar, 10 kilometers (6 miles) north of Porlamar, is a popular anchoring spot for yachts. Strategically placed above the harbor is the impressive **Castillo de San Carlos de Borromeo,** a brawny fort built wholly of coral rock between 1664 and 1684. It's undergoing renovations and is closed indefinitely, but the adjacent 17th-century church, **Iglesia Santísimo Cristo,** is worth the short trek from town. Its most notable feature is a flat-faced bell tower accessed by an outside staircase—a feature found throughout Margarita Island but rarely elsewhere in Venezuela. In Pampatar proper, take a quick peek at the replica of Christopher Columbus's ship, the *Santa Ana,* before trying your best to feel like a kid again at the waterfront **Magic Isle** amusement park, somewhat downtrodden in appearance but popular for its Ferris wheel and rather tame roller coaster.

Elsewhere

If you rent a car you can circle Margarita Island, making side trips to beaches at **Guacuco** and **El Tirano.** Near Margarita's northern tip, **Playa El Agua** is rightly famous for its fine sand, coconut palms, and quiet restaurants.

Parque Nacional Laguna de la Restinga is a mangrove-lined nature reserve that's 36 kilometers (22 miles) west of Porlamar and reached via the road to Boca del Río. For $4–$8 per person, boatmen will give you a tour of the park's lagoons or bring you straight to a 23-kilometer- (14-mile-) long, shadeless beach, where you'll find palm-thatched restaurants and a few crafts stands. Boatmen leave from the El Indio dock behind the park information center. ☎ 095/42995. ☛ *Free.* ☉ *Daily.*

Shopping

Foreigners may not find the selection or prices very enticing on Margarita Island, but **Porlamar,** in particular, offers a good selection of local crafts, designer clothing, and electronic goods. Shops are concentrated around Porlamar's Plaza Bolívar, east along Calle Igualdad to the intersection of Avenida Santiago Marino, and up to Avenida 4 de Mayo, where serious, expensive shopping begins.

Dining

With the expansion of tourist facilities at least 12 new good restaurants have sprouted in Margarita during the past two years, turning the island into a dining delight. Whether on the beach of El Agua, where there are at least six moderately priced fish eateries, or in the Porlamar area, where restaurants offer more sophisticated dishes, the food is good and the dress code is always casual. Thanks to Margarita's freeport status wine is quite inexpensive. For price categories, *see* Dining *in* Venezuela Essentials, *below.*

$$–$$$ **Cocody.** A pleasing mixture of international and French dishes has made this one of the most select eateries on the island. Particularly tasty is the excellent local seafood, often served with savory sauces—try the bisque or the grilled fish platter with a selection from the thoughtful wine list. ✕ *Av. Raúl Leoni, on road to El Morro beach, Porlamar,* ☎ *095/618431. AE, MC, V.*

$$–$$$ **Martín Pescador.** This casual but busy restaurant is as popular with foreigners as it is with local families. Besides a good selection of Italian wine, the menu features Italian standards supplemented with fresh fish entrées (mostly red snapper or sea bass). For dessert, try the *Marquesa de Chocolate,* a decadent chocolate-mousse layer cake. ✕ *Av. 4 de Mayo, Porlamar,* ☎ *095/616697. AE, V.*

$$ ★   **Bahia.** The elegant dining area with large bay windows affords a striking view of the beach—part of the reason for Bahia's genuine popularity among locals. The international-style cuisine has a decidedly Spanish flavor. Wade into an appetizer of octopus before moving on to the jumbo shrimp bathed in cream and topped with cheese; in season, try the fresh lobster. ✕ *Av. Raúl Leoni, on road to El Morro beach, Porlamar,* ☎ *095/614156. AE, MC, V.*

$$ **Lucky.** Tired of fish? Try this lovely Chinese restaurant featuring Cantonese specialties, many vegetable dishes, and a savory Peking duck. ✕ *Av. Santiago Mariño, Porlamar,* ☎ *095/631345. AE, MC, V.*

$$ **Sevillana's.** This pleasant Spanish restaurant specializes in local fish and shellfish dishes—the paella is particularly good. The colonial-style decor—all leather and bulky wood furnishings—is oddly complemented by the ever-present sound of flamenco music from the owner's large taped collection. *Av. Bolívar, Bella Vista district, Porlamar,* ☎ *095/ 638258. AE, MC, V.*

Lodging

As on the Caribbean Coast, hotels add a 10% surcharge to your bill unless you have a Venezuelan passport. Reserve ahead during peak seasons. For price categories, *see* Lodging *in* Venezuela Essentials, *below.*

\$\$\$ **Bella Vista.** Despite obvious signs of wear and tear, the waterfront Bella Vista remains one of Porlamar's major landmarks. It's also in the heart of the downtown shopping district. The lobby restaurant has a solid reputation for its fresh seafood and good selection of imported wines. ⌘ *Calle Igualdad, Porlamar,* ☎ *095/617222 or 095/614157 for reservations,* FAX *095/612557. 231 rooms. Restaurant, pool, 2 tennis courts. AE, MC, V.*

\$\$\$ **Festival Flamingo Beach Hotel.** This first-class six-story complex a few
★   hundred yards north of Pampatar is one of the island's major lodging institutions. A glass elevator climbs to stylish rooms that have views over the sea and, in many instances, the island itself. Sumptuous breakfast and dinner buffets are served on a deck overlooking the nearby beach and tennis courts. ⌘ *Calle El Cristo, Sector La Caranta, Pampatar,* ☎ *095/624822,* FAX *095/622672; U.S.* ☎ *800/221–5333,* FAX *305/ 599–1946. 160 rooms. Restaurant, bar, pool, tennis courts, snorkeling, windsurfing, boating. MC, V.*

\$\$\$ **Margarita Hilton International.** Close to the beach and only 10 minutes from the city of Porlamar, the Hilton offers an enviable location as well as attractive amenities. Upper-floor rooms have balconies and all have satellite TV, but you may spend most of your time lying by the lovely pool or taking advantage of the lighted tennis courts and the water-sports facilities. ⌘ *Calle Los Uveros, Costa Azul,* ☎ *095/623333,* FAX *095/ 620810; U.S.* ☎ *800/221–2424. 269 rooms, 11 suites. 3 restaurants, lobby lounge, room service, pool, barbershop, beauty salon, massage, sauna, 2 tennis courts, health club, snorkeling, boating, jet skiing, parasailing, waterskiing, dance club, baby-sitting, business services, meeting rooms, airport shuttle, car rental. AE, D, MC, V.*

\$\$\$ **Margarita Laguna Mar.** This sprawling hotel with several wings, a waterskiing lagoon, several swimming pools—including a water slide and fun pool for the young (or young at heart)—and a beach, offers all you could ask for as far as water facilities are concerned. Rooms are large, and dining options range from a poolside cafeteria to a fine formal restaurant. ⌘ *Vía Agua de Vaca, Pampatar,* ☎ *095/620711,* FAX *095/621045; U.S.* ☎ *800/343–7821. 400 rooms. Restaurant, bar, cafeteria, 5 pools, 3 tennis courts, water slide, windsurfing, waterskiing, convention center, airport shuttle. AE, MC, V.*

\$\$ **Playa el Agua Beach Resort.** Just across the street from Margarita's favorite beach, this hotel offers a casual atmosphere and great service. Features include a pool, tennis courts, and a concierge who can arrange fishing and other water-sports options. Rooms are done in pastel colors and enjoy views of the 4-mile-long beach from which the hotel takes its name. ⌘ *Bul. Playa el Agua,* ☎ *095/48559 or 095/48601,* FAX *095/ 48565. 80 rooms. Restaurant, bar, pool, 2 tennis courts, surfing, windsurfing, boating, fishing. MC, V.*

\$ **Hotel Colibrí.** This is a safe, centrally located budget option where bland motel-style rooms are softened by the pleasant lobby restaurant—a good spot for breakfast before trekking to the beaches. A new pool and poolside bar were completed in mid 1995. ⌘ *Av. Santiago Mariño, Porla-*

mar, ☎ *095/616346 or 095/612195,* FAX *095/612195. 70 rooms. Restaurant. No credit cards.*

Nightlife

Nightspots are tucked behind Avenida Santiago Mariño in Porlamar. Don't miss the sophisticated **Mosquito Coast Bar & Grill** (Paseo Guaranguao, ☎ 095/613524), a moderately priced bar and dance club that offers good Tex-Mex food, great atmosphere, and rowdy fun. Behind the Bella Vista hotel, the Mosquito is extremely popular with the Venezuelan young and beautiful set. With its low lights and sultry looks, **Piano Blanco** (Calle Jesús María Patiño, ☎ 095/616902), also in Porlamar, is popular for tranquil jazz and unhurried drinking, ideal after a good dinner.

MÉRIDA AND THE ANDES

As you leave behind the subtropical lowlands and begin your ascent of the Andes, the changes are swift and unmistakable. Whether you approach the mountain range from the plain of Barinas on the east side, the hills of Trujillo State from the north, or via south of Lake Maracaibo on the west, obvious signs of climatic change begin to appear. In the foothills, thatched farms give way to tile-roof hamlets clinging to hillsides; at 10,000 feet, the rugged mountain landscape includes stone-strewn fields sprouting wheat and coffee. Colder and higher still, the spectacular **Transandina** (Trans-Andes) road winds its way through Timotes, looping in hairpin bends and finally climbing to the fogbound Paso del Aguila, a forbidding mountain pass at an altitude of 13,146 feet; it then descends to the capital city of Mérida and eventually winds back down to the foot of the range just south of San Cristóbal, to join the Pan-American Highway on its long trek through Colombia.

Mérida lies in the heart of the Andes. Sprawling in a high-altitude valley that's embraced by two arms of the mountain chain, Mérida's striking skyline is unequivocally defined by the peaks of the Five White Eagles (as Merideños call them)—La Caron, La Concha, La Columna, El Toro, and El León, each encrusted with glaciers and towering more than 15,000 feet above the distant sea. Given its proximity to these eminently climbable peaks, Mérida is a mecca for Andes-bound travelers.

Visitor Information

Mérida
Corporación Merideña de Turismo (Cormetur), Av. 1 at Av. 2, ☎ 074/529566 or 074/526972, FAX 074/523067.

Arriving and Departing

By Plane
Mérida's **Carnavali Airport** (☎ 074/636163), five minutes by taxi from the city center, is served twice daily by **Avensa.** One-way tickets from Caracas cost less than $30.

By Car
From Caracas take Highway 51 west to Valencia. From here, the road to Barinas keeps to low-lying valleys and the plains; from Barinas, you begin your ascent over the Andes via Barinitas and the Transandina Highway. Another option from Valencia is the highway via Barquisimeto, Carora, and Sabana de Mendoza. Either way, the journey takes about 12 hours.

By Bus

There are morning and evening departures to Mérida's **Antonio Paredes** bus terminal (☏ 074/661193) from Caracas's Nuevo Circo terminal. The 10- to 13-hour trip costs less than $15. Purchase your ticket at least a day in advance at Nuevo Circo terminal from one of the following operators: **Expreso Alianza** (☏ 02/541–1975) or **Expreso Mérida** (☏ 02/541–1975).

Exploring Mérida and the Andes

Mérida

Founded in 1558, Mérida has grown up around the **Plaza Bolívar,** a pleasant and popular open-air venue for the troupe of Indian artisans who regularly sell handmade crafts here. Fronting the plaza is Mérida's **Catedral Metropolitana** (Metropolitan Cathedral), considered one of the most striking in Venezuela. Begun in 1787 by Fray Juan Manuel António Ramos, the soberly colored Metropolitan bares its embellished baroque facade, carved with intricate zoomorphic and geometric designs, to the amber hills surrounding Mérida. *Plaza Bolívar.* ☛ *Free.*

At the opposite end of the square, the **Casa de Cultura Juan Felix Sánchez** hosts dynamic exhibitions of paintings, sculpture, ceramics, and woodwork by regional artists. Nearby is the Bulevar Paseo Libertador, where local painters sometimes gather to work and compare notes. *Plaza Bolívar,* ☏ *074/526101.* ☛ *Free.* ☉ *Tues.–Sun.*

Mérida's **Museo de Arte Colonial** (Colonial Art Museum) has a valuable collection of artifacts culled from the 16th to 19th centuries. *Av. 4, between Calles 18 and 19,* ☏ *074/527860.* ☛ *Free. Closed Sat.–Mon.*

Nearby, the **Museo Arqueológico** (Archaeological Museum) displays pre-Columbian art and ceramics. Opened in 1976, the museum has the region's finest collection of anthropomorphic figurines, ceramics, and tools from the pre-Hispanic cultures that once dominated the Andes. *Av. 3, Edificio Rectorado,* ☏ *074/402344.* ☛ *Entry fee.* ☉ *Tues.–Sun.*

Los Chorros de Milla, one of Mérida's 20-some parks, features indigenous Venezuelan fauna as well as tigers and other animals kept on display in cages. Yet the real attraction are the **Andean Falls,** a pleasant set of falls that make the steep walk through the park more worthwhile. *Av. Chorros de Milla.* ☛ *Entry fee.* ☉ *Tues.–Sun.*

On **Parque Reloj de Beethoven,** there's a well-known clock that ushers in the hour with music from the great German composer. More intriguing is the adjacent **Museo de Arte Moderno** (Modern Art Museum), with an excellent permanent collection of works by some of Venezuela's most heralded contemporary painters. *Parque Reloj de Beethoven,* ☏ *074/440819.* ☛ *Free.* ☉ *Tues.–Sun.*

Plaza Las Heroínas is where children gather in the late afternoon, and, as evening falls and the fog rolls in, where young lovers huddle together on benches. On Sunday it hosts an informal crafts market. More to the point, the plaza contains the substation of Mérida's **Teleférico,** the longest mountain cable car in the world and one of the town's most popular attractions. Built in the 1960s by French engineers, the Teleférico ascends in four breathtaking stages to Pico Espejo (15,633 feet), which is nearly 900 feet taller than Switzerland's Matterhorn. Unfortunately, this incredibly unique cable car ride is not always in operation because of an ongoing general overhaul. When it is working, the first car heads up around 7 AM, the last around 3 PM. It is best to take an early morning trip, because going in the afternoon only makes it harder to find a seat at the crowded mountaintop cantina. Purchase tickets early for the 90-minute trip from the Teleférico office on Calle 25. ☎ *074/525080.* ☛ *Entry fee.* ⊙ *Tues.–Sun.*

From Lomas Redonda station, currently the highest point served by the Teleférico, you can hire guides, mules, and horses for the four- to five-hour descent to **Los Nevados,** a secluded mountain village that was once a garrison for Spanish conquistadors. The first leg of the journey involves a sharp ascent through the Bosque de los Coloraditos, named for the flowering coloradito tree—one of the few species hearty enough to survive at this altitude. Soon you begin the descent to Los Nevados, along a boulder-strewn path best negotiated on donkey or mule rather than on foot. Bone-weary and winded, you finally come upon the red-tile outline of Los Nevados, where you can find unpretentious accommodations in local *posadas* (pensions) with open-air courtyards surrounded by small but functional rooms.

The Northern Andes

From Mérida, take the Vía al Paramo 14 kilometers (9 miles) north-east to **Tabay,** where Alexis Montilla has created the unique, 18-acre **Los Aleros,** a detailed miniature village-cum-museum peopled with Andeans in colonial dress. Montilla takes sightseers on an ancient bus through his make-believe town, while locals dressed as farmers, high-waymen, or herb collectors re-create a typical colonial scene. ☎ *074/440430 for information.* ☛ *Entry fee.*

East of Mérida and Tabay, the highland road brings you to the Mu-cuchíes region, the "land of water" in Indian dialect, where the starkly beautiful landscape—scrub-filled fields and barren hillsides—includes half a dozen lakes. **San Rafael de Mucuchíes,** 52 kilometers (30 miles) east of Mérida and at an altitude of 16,962 feet, is where Simón Bolí-var persuaded his ragtag army to begin their ascent of the Andes and initiate the liberation of Colombia. To appreciate how daunting a proposition this must have been to Bolívar's poorly clothed, barely fed troops, spend an afternoon walking the switchback trails in the hills encircling San Rafael, which give good views over the severe moun-tainous landscape. From San Rafael you can rent horses and mules for the one- to two-hour trek to Lagunas Say-Say and Montón, two iso-lated but locally popular trout-stocked lagoons.

The road north to **Apartaderos** passes through more barren, austere mountain terrain; this is the Andean páramo, or steppe, an arid region above the timberline where only moss and shrublike *frailejones* grow. At the junction of the Apartaderos and Santo Domingo roads, you can rent horses or mules and trek to some of the nearby trout lagoons—Laguna de los Patos, Laguna Negra, and La Canoa, among them. Catches in these lakes have been reported at more than 15 pounds. Local guides can be found in **Santo Domingo** and **Los Frailes,** or contact **Mon-taña Tours** (*see* Fishing *in* Sports and the Outdoors, *below*).

Those headed to Trujillo State by car should not miss the **Pico Aguila,** a 14,000-foot-high pass that connects Apartaderos with Jají and Valera. Venezuela's highest roadway, Pico Aguila also marks the spot where Bolívar and his army actually crossed the Andes in 1813 on their way to fight the Spanish in Colombia. The crossing, commanding a dizzy-ing view over the mountains, is commemorated by a statue, the *El Aguila Desplegada,* depicting a condor clutching between its beak and talons a medallion engraved with Bolívar's image. On cold and bracing days, a small stand sells hot chocolate and coffee near the statue overlook.

The Southern Andes

Jají, 35 kilometers (22 miles) west of Mérida on the Azulita Road, sparkles with whitewash, fountains, and flowers. Founded in the late 16th century, Jají and its colonial buildings have been restored by the government as a tourist attraction. The highlights consist of the town's church, the main square, and a few surrounding homes. If you're in the area in late September, Jají celebrates the **Feast of St. Michael Archangel** on the 24th with music, dance, and much fanfare.

Bailadores, 92 kilometers (54 miles) south from Mérida, boasts the **Parque de la India Curú,** named for the Indian princess Curú, wife of chief Toquizán, who ruled these parts prior to Columbus's arrival. The park has a large waterfall and several scenic, undemanding walking trails. ☞ *Entry fee.* ☉ *Tues.–Sun.*

Three kilometers (2 miles) east of Bailadores, **Parque Paez** (sometimes called Parque La Cascada) has picnic areas and pools as well as small falls that can be viewed up close with complete safety. ☞ *Free.*

Six hours and 300 kilometers (176 miles) beyond Bailadores lies **San Cristóbal,** capital of Táchira State and only 43 kilometers (27 miles) from the Colombian border. Every January its San Sebastián Fair draws thousands of cattle sellers, horse racers, and bullfight fans. The rest of the year, its old city provides only a minimal level of excitement. Yet even if you do not make it all the way to San Cristóbal, the mountain views from the highway are dazzling: lovely **La Negra Paramo,** a wild and desolate region where the Mocoties River has its source, may alone be worth the trip.

Shopping

On Sunday **Mérida's** Plaza Las Heroínas overflows with handmade crafts and locally produced weavings. Farther south, along Avenida Las Americas, is a smaller market with produce, housewares, and a handful of crafts stalls. In **Jají, Complejo Turístico de Antier** is a co-op selling high-quality arts and crafts from around Venezuela. Some 30 kilometers (19 miles) beyond Jají, in **Azulita,** painters and artisans sell their exquisitely crafted wares along the roadside.

Sports and the Outdoors

Bicycling

Montaña Tours (Apartado Postal 645, ☎ and FAX 074/661448) arranges multiday treks to El Tisure, the secluded village of Los Nevados, and along Pico Aguila, Venezuela's highest roadway. Bilingual guides, food, and bicycling equipment are provided. Montaña Tours' U.S. representative, Lost World Adventures (☎ 404/971–8586, FAX 404/977–3095), can book hiking treks throughout the region.

Fishing

Around Mérida, the Andes Mountains are liberally sprinkled with small lakes and lagoons regularly stocked with rainbow and brown trout. In remote reaches, hooking a 15-pound trout is not unheard of. Jeeps, horses, and mules can be rented for the sometimes arduous trek into the heart of the mountains; in Mérida, **Montaña Tours** (*see above*) offers guided fishing trips in season (March 30–September 30).

Trekking

Mérida is the base for three- to seven-day treks (Grade 1–4) in the Andes. Operators typically provide bilingual guides and all necessary equipment, as well as transportation to and from the sights, and food and accommodations along the way. Contact **Alpi Tour** (Av. Sucre, Centro Parque Boyaca, piso 1, Oficina 2, Caracas, ☎ 02/284–1433, FAX 02/285–6067), **Montaña Tours** (*see above*), or **Paramo Tours** (Calle 23, Edificio EDC, piso 2, Local 2–1, ☎ 074/525279 or 074/521370, FAX 074/525258).

Dining and Lodging

Although lodging is difficult to find in Mérida during the high season (book in advance whenever possible), room rates are generally reasonable. In the Andes you can expect simple, unpretentious *hosterías* offering clean rooms and attached restaurants. Outside Mérida, hosterías are often the best (and only) dining option. For price categories, *see* Dining *and* Lodging *in* Venezuela Essentials, *below*.

Mérida

DINING

$$–$$$ **Mira Me Lindo.** This relaxed, intimate restaurant inside the Chama Hotel is noted for its succulent Basque cuisine: specialties include peppers stuffed with fish, *pargo a la champagne* (snapper in champagne), and *muslo de pollo al ron* (chicken drumstick in rum). ✕ *Calle 29 at Av. 4,* ☎ *074/521011. AE, D, MC, V.*

$ **Marisquería Tu y Yo.** This colorful bar and restaurant is a fine place to swill beer and enjoy plates of fresh fish while conversing with locals. At "You and I," informal is the key word. ✕ *Av. 4 Bolívar 28–70,* ☎ *074/529138. AE, D, MC, V.*

$ **Tasca y Marisquería Vargas.** Mérida's best fish eatery is popular with local families who don't mind the modern, rather dull setting. The fresh fish specialties, particularly the trout, are excellent: try *trucha al ajillo* (trout with garlic) or *a la plancha* (grilled with butter). There's also a good wine list. ✕ *Av. Don Tulio Febres 30–71, at Calle 31,* ☎ *074/522769. AE, D, MC, V.*

LODGING

$$$ **El Tisure.** Mérida's newest hotel is only a five-minute walk north of Plaza Bolívar and features well-equipped, very neat and clean rooms overlooking a quiet square. This is the only hotel in town that has central air-conditioning, and all rooms have TVs. ▥ *Av. 4 Bolívar 17–47,* ☎ *074/520744 or 074/521744, FAX 074/520827. 33 rooms. Restaurant, bar. AE, D, MC, V.*

$$$ **Hotel Belensate.** The Belensate is in La Punta, a quiet residential quar★ ter on the western outskirts of Mérida (but still only a short walk from Plaza Bolívar). Its somewhat out-of-the-way location complements its mountain chalet flavor: spacious rooms and private cabins are well equipped and overlook a lush garden. La Nonna, the on-site restaurant, is a local favorite. ▥ *Urbanización La Hacienda,* ☎ *074/663722, FAX 074/661255 or 074/662823. 56 rooms, 7 cabins. Restaurant, bar. AE, D, MC, V.*

$$ **Caribay.** The centrally located Caribay features a helpful bilingual staff and modern, functional rooms. An on-site travel agency can help arrange tours in the Andes. ▥ *Av. 2,* ☎ *074/636451, FAX 074/637141. 80 rooms. Restaurant, bar, dance club, travel services. AE, D, MC, V.*

$ **Hotel Teleférico.** This popular but basic budget option is housed in a blandly modern, four-story block near the cable car station. Stay here if price counts more than comfort. ▥ *Plaza de las Heroínas,* ☎ *074/527370. 18 rooms. Restaurant. AE, D, MC, V.*

Northern Andes

DINING AND LODGING

$$$ **Los Frailes.** The "Friars" inn occupies a 17th-century monastery on the
★ road between Apartaderos and Santo Domingo. From the top of the
adjoining bell tower, once the monks' cells, you can see the rugged out-
line of Pico Agilar in the distance. On chilly nights, warm yourself by
the fire in the rumpus room, or retire to the comfort of your heated
bedroom with private bath. The staff can arrange fishing or horseback
trips to nearby lakes and lagoons. 🖾 70 km (44 mi) south from Mérida
on road to Varina, ☎ 074/637737; for reservations ☎ 02/564-0098,
FAX 02/564-7936. 48 rooms. Restaurant, bar. AE, D, MC, V.

$ **Los Andes.** This central town house in San Rafael Mucuchíes has been
attractively converted into a five-room inn with two shared bath-
rooms. The rooms have few amenities but are otherwise clean and cozy.
The adjacent restaurant is a local favorite. 🖾 Calle Independencia 42,
San Rafael Mucuchíes, ☎ 074/81151. 5 rooms. Restaurant. No credit
cards.

Southern Andes

DINING AND LODGING

$$ **El Tamá.** The 10-story El Tamá, situated in the residential Los Pirineos
district of San Cristóbal, is a typically characterless but well-equipped
resort. After trekking through the rugged Andes, however, you will think
it quite luxurious. 🖾 Calle 23, San Cristóbal, ☎ 076/554335. 112 rooms.
Restaurant, bar, pool, car rental. MC, V.

$ **Posada de Jají.** This is the most comfortable and intimate of the hand-
ful of inns that crowd Jají's main square. The attached restaurant features Andean cuisine and occasional folk music. 🖾 Plaza Bolívar, Jají,
no ☎. 4 rooms. Restaurant. No credit cards.

The Arts and Nightlife

The Arts

Toward the end of January, **La Feria de San Sebastián** (Festival of San
Sebastian) is a four-day explosion of bullfights, song and music processions, and markets in San Cristóbal. In February, Mérida celebrates
its **Feria del Sol** (Festival of the Sun) with bullfights and open-air salsa
and merengue performances.

Nightlife

In the Andes, hotels and inns are often the only choice for after-dark
excitement; many have informal bars and regularly host live folkloric
bands, particularly on weekends. In Mérida, the dance club **Birosca Tasca**
(Calle 24 at Av. 2) swings into the wee hours with live salsa, rock, and
Brazilian music.

ELSEWHERE IN VENEZUELA

The Llanos

Besides the Andes, Venezuela's most noticeable physical feature are the
Llanos, a 600-mile stretch of grassy plains, endlessly crisscrossed by
streambeds and riverbeds, that extends from the Orinoco River delta
westward into Colombia. The Llanos constitute almost a third of
Venezuela's landmass but less than 9% of its population, partly because
the plains are mercilessly sunbaked during summer and flooded by
rain-swollen rivers from June to September. Despite these climatic extremes, the Llanos nurture one of the most diverse groupings of wildlife
in the Western Hemisphere. Between December and April, as rivers dry

to a trickle, cows and other animals die of thirst while millions of wading birds compete for the fish trapped in shrinking ponds. When thunderclaps announce the first rains, green grass carpets the plains, and hungry animals return to the task of grazing. One of the many *hatos* (ranches) in the region, Hato Piñero (which banned hunting in 1950), has catalogued no fewer than 300 species of birds, 20 of reptiles, and 50 of mammals (including the ubiquitous capybara, the world's largest rodent). In the region's nature reserves and national parks, look forward to up-close encounters with otters and ocelots, jaguars, monkeys, crocodiles, and *caribes* (piranhas), not to mention pink flamingos, crakes, trogons, harpy eagles, and most any exotic bird you can imagine.

Arriving and Departing

Avensa flies daily to San Fernando de Apure, Barinas, Guanare, and Acarigua. Round-trip tickets cost roughly $120. Many ranches arrange transportation for guests.

Dining and Lodging

During the dry season the Llanos flatlands become a natural destination for birders and nature enthusiasts. More and more ranches, however, are remodeling and upgrading their facilities to attract visitors with broader interests—be it horseback riding, Jeep treks through the plains, or evenings of local *joropo* music. Ranch accommodations typically consist of small, private lodges equipped with televisions, and sometimes with air-conditioning, swimming pools, and recreation facilities. Lodges are often grouped around communal dining areas, where guests and *llanero* ranchers share meals. Three- to seven-day packages cost upward of $170 per person per day, which includes transfers to and from the airport, three meals a day, and daytime treks with experienced guides.

The best-known ranches are Hato Piñero, Hato El Frío, and Hato El Cedral. All three can be booked through **Alpi Tours** (☎ 02/284–1433, FAX 02/285–6067), **Lost World Adventures** (U.S. ☎ 404/971–8586 or 800/999–0558, FAX 404/977–3095), and **Turven Tour Express** (☎ 02/951–1787, FAX 02/951–1176).

Angel Falls

The Guayana Highlands in Bolívar State overwhelm mere mortals with their intense, dizzying beauty. At sunrise, fog and clouds rise from the grassy savanna and wrap around the flat mesas, or *tepuis*, that tower over the surrounding troop of waterfalls and lagoons. The area is known as **La Gran Sabana** (Great Savanna), and much of it forms **Canaima National Park,** the world's third largest, with more than 11,500 square miles of undisturbed—and in some cases, largely unexplored—mountain-bound grassland.

The highlight in Canaima is undoubtedly **Angel Falls,** the world's tallest waterfall. The drop from Auyán-tepuí's (Devil's Mountain) to the turgid lagoon below is 3,212 feet—more than twice the height of the Empire State Building. The falls were discovered in 1937 by a U.S. pilot, Jimmy Angel, who landed on Auyán-tepuí's vast mesa top in search of gold. After abandoning his wounded plane, Angel braved the rough terrain and eventually came across the falls later named in his honor.

Arriving and Departing

Avensa and **Aereotuy** regularly fly to Canaima from Ciudad Bolívar ($90 each way) and from the Caracas suburb of Maiquetía ($180 each way). Weather permitting, all flights to Canaima include a flyover of Angel Falls. The airlines each also arrange daylong hikes to Angel Falls and the tamer Kavac Falls for $120–$180 per person; two- to three-night treks cost $220–$350.

Dining and Lodging

The airline Avensa manages the popular **Canaima Camp** (☎ 02/562–3022, FAX 02/562–3475; U.S. ☎ 800/428–3672), perched on a lagoon at the base of Salto Hacha (Hacha Falls). The 160-person facility is often booked on weekends and holidays, and ticketed Avensa passengers have preference for overnight stays. Aereotuy operates a smaller overnight camp at **Kavac Falls,** while the family of "Jungle Rudy" Truffino maintains the intimate **Ucaima Camp** (☎ 02/693–0618, FAX 02/693–0835) upriver from Hacha Falls. The price for overnight accommodations at each camp is roughly the same: $90–$100 per person, per night.

Amazonas Territory

Although the Amazon is normally associated with the wilds of Brazil, Venezuela's vastly exotic Amazonas region has recently become the target of trekkers in pursuit of serious adventure. Venezuela's Amazonas basin includes the headwaters of the Orinoco River, not to mention a seemingly endless carpet of thick jungle and more than 2,000 largely unexplored river tributaries. A dozen different Indian tribes, each with its own language and culture, make the forests and rivers their home. You may not come into direct contact with a tribe like the Makiritare (masters of river navigation and the art of hollowing dugout canoes from tree trunks) or the Yanomami (who live in the deepest depths of the jungle), but their presence adds a sort of *Heart of Darkness* edge to your journey—whether you trek through the jungle by Jeep or ply the Orinoco in a thatched riverboat.

The Amazonas occupies one-fifth of Venezuela's landmass but has scarcely 85,000 inhabitants and less than 220 miles of roads. Needless to say, the Amazonas region is still little known away from the rivers that afford access to it. For this reason, most tours begin and end in Puerto Ayacucho, a small outpost perched on the banks of the Orinoco only a few miles from the Colombian frontier. From the docks in Puerto Ayacucho, launches cross over to Colombia and return again for less than $8, affording the opportunity to experience Amazonas river trekking in a single day. **Selva Tours** (☎ 048/22122) arranges one-to four-day river treks as well as overnight stays at jungle lodges near San Juan de Manapiare. **Expediciones Aguas Bravas** (☎ 02/284–7735) offers a thrilling river raft and rapid-shooting trek on the Orinoco, while **Alechiven** (☎ 041/211828) runs river tours from Puerto Ayacucho to San Simón de Cucuy.

Arriving and Departing

Avensa flies daily from Caracas's Simón Bolívar International Airport (San Fernando de Apure) to Puerto Ayacucho ($80–$100 one-way), the region's main and only tourist hub. **Aereotuy** flies once weekly to Puerto Ayacucho from Ciudad Bolívar (Ciacara). From Ciudad Bolívar, Ciudad Guayana, and Cabruta, ferries transport cars ($60–$75) and passengers ($15–$18) up the Orinoco River to Puerto Ayacucho; the uneventful trek can take up to three days when the river swells, and meals are not provided.

Dining and Lodging

Yutajé Camp in the Manapiare Valley, just east of Puerto Ayacucho, appeals to families who prefer beds, baths, cabins, and sit-down meals. Built and run year-round by José Raggi, the camp has a 5,000-foot airstrip and accommodations for about 30. During the day you'll probably find yourself trekking through the jungle in search of howler monkeys, or floating down a river in search of waterfalls and swimmable lagoons. **Alpi Tours** (☎ 02/283–1433, ℻ 02/285–6067) flies groups from Caracas to Yutajé for about $450 per person; the price includes three days, two nights, and full meals.

VENEZUELA ESSENTIALS

Customs and Duties

Persons entering Venezuela may bring in duty-free up to 400 cigarettes and 50 cigars, 2 liters of liquor, and new goods such as video cameras and electronics up to $1,500 in value if declared and accompanied by receipts. Plants, fresh fruit, and pork are prohibited.

Dining

In larger cities you will find a wide range of international cuisine that includes Italian, French, Spanish, Arab, and Chinese, and Venezuela's own criollo, which combines Spanish and Caribbean influences with the local favorites—plates of meat, chicken, and fish sided with rice. *Parrilleras*, restaurants that specialize in criollo or Argentine-style grilled meats, offer the chance to watch your meal cooked on a tableside charcoal grill. Menus in tascas—Spanish-style restaurants with bars—tend to offer some variation on hearty *hervidos* (soups) and pabellón, a popular bean, rice, and grilled meat platter.

Some restaurants offer a prix-fixe meal at lunchtime known as the *menu ejecutivo*. This includes a *primero* (appetizer of soup or salad); a *segundo*, the main course; and *postre* (dessert). Espresso or *guayoyo*, a lighter, American-style coffee, is included.

Throughout Venezuela, restaurants typically add a 10% surcharge to your bill.

Specialties

Fish and excellent shellfish dominate in the coastal areas and on Margarita Island; grouper, snapper, mackerel, tuna, and swordfish are available, as are lobster, crab, shrimp, and clams. In the Andean regions, ask for rainbow trout. Caracas and Maracaibo have fine red meats, the best being the *churrasco de Santa Barbara*, named after a southern Lake Maracaibo cattle town. In the city of Barquisimeto, in the southeastern Guayana region, and in the plains ask for the local white cheeses—*palmizulia*, guayanés, and *queso de mano*, respectively—which are some of the best low-fat dairy products in Latin America. If you visit during the Christmas season, try the holiday specialty called *hallaca*, a tamalelike combination of chicken, corn, olives, and pork, all wrapped in aromatic banana leaves.

Four typical desserts stand out—*bien me sabe* (a coconut cake), *torta de guanábana* (soursop cake), *merengón de nispero* (medlar meringue cake), and the always popular *cascos de guayaba*, (guava shells served with white cheese). Beer, whiskey, and rum are the favored libations among locals. French wines tend to be expensive, and old vintages suffer because of the preservatives used to withstand the tropics. More moderately priced are the light Italian reds Valpolicella or Bardolino, the Italian whites Pinot Grigio or Verdicchio, and Chile's Santa Carolina and Cousinho Macul, both white and red.

Mealtimes

Lunch, the main meal of the day, begins at noon and lasts until about 3. Dinner is taken between 7 and 10 PM; don't count on being served much past 10:30 PM, except in the Las Mercedes district of Caracas, where restaurants remain open until midnight.

Dress

The dress code in Venezuelan restaurants is generally quite casual. Formal dinners in all elegant Caraas establishments, however, call for a coat and tie for gentlemen and for ladies to show off their cocktail outfits.

Ratings

Prices are per person for a three-course meal, excluding alcohol, tax, and tip.

CATEGORY	CARACAS AND MARGARITA ISLAND	OTHER AREAS
$$$$	over $30	over $25
$$$	$25–$30	$15–$25
$$	$15–$25	$8–$15
$	under $15	under $8

Embassies and Consulates

United States

Embassy: Av. Francisco de Miranda at Calle La Foresta, Altamira district (near Altamira metro), Caracas, ☎ 02/285–0111.

Canada

Embassy: Torre Europa, 7th Floor, Av. Francisco de Miranda at Calle Chacaíto, Caracas, ☎ 02/951–6166.

United Kingdom

Embassy: Edificio Las Mercedes, Avenida La Estancia, Chuao, Caracas, ☎ 02/751–1022.

Getting Around

By Plane

Venezuela is served by its own international carriers—**Avensa** (Torre El Chorro, Floor 12, Caracas, ☎ 02/561–3366; U.S. ☎ 800/428–3672) and **Viasa** (Torre Viasa, Los Cabos, Plaza Morelos, ☎ 02/572–9522; U.S. ☎ 800/327–5454)—as well as by a number of strictly domestic regional carriers, including **Aereotuy** (Av. Abraham Lincoln, Bulevar de Sabana Grande 174, Ed. Gran Sabana, ☎ 02/717375 or 02/716397), **Air Valencia** (J. D. Valencia, ☎ 041/320705), **Laser** (Av. Principal La Castellana at Primera Transversal, La Castellana, Caracas, ☎ 02/263–4227 and 02/263–4047), and **Zuliana** (KLM building, Av. Romulo Gallegos, Caracas, ☎ 02/993–8507). Domestic plane service is good, and locals generally prefer it to traveling by bus or car. This popularity, however, means long lines during peak holiday periods. Despite inflation, prices are still moderate: a round-trip ticket between Caracas and Margarita Island, for example, costs $70.

By Train

Ferrocarriles de Venezuela, the national rail company, operates the one and only passenger line in Venezuela: between Puerto Cabello and Barquisimeto, in the northern foothills of the Andes, a trip that costs less than $7.

By Car

ROAD CONDITIONS

Although the Venezuelan highway system cannot be compared to those of developed nations—toll roads and freeways extend only 200 kilometers (125 miles) to the east and west from Caracas—over 80% of the country's roads are paved and provide easy access to the most popular tourist attractions.

RULES OF THE ROAD

Travel by day whenever possible; driving at night can be hazardous because of poor lighting and the sometimes erratic behavior of truck and bus drivers. Do not stop in the middle of nowhere at night—it is not safe. City traffic is aggressive: Watch out for impatient drivers who disregard red lights and other traffic signs.

RENTALS

The major rental companies are well represented in Venezuela, as are a few local, lesser-known agencies. Fees are rising swiftly with inflation; at the moment, the cheapest rental costs $50 per day including 150 free kilometers (93 free miles); dole out an additional 35¢ per kilometer after that. Your best bet is to arrange for unlimited mileage. It's a good idea to obtain liability and collision insurance, and make sure to get an air-conditioned vehicle, particularly if you'll be visiting the coast or Margarita Island.

In Caracas, contact **Budget** (☎ 02/283–4333, FAX 02/283–7504), **Hertz** (☎ 02/952–5511, FAX 02/952–1846), or **National Rent-A-Car** (☎ 02/239–3645, FAX 02/239–4119). On Margarita Island, contact **Budget** (☎ 095/691047, FAX 095/614298), **Hertz** (☎ 095/697237), or **National Rent-A-Car** (☎ 095/691171).

EMERGENCY ASSISTANCE

The major rental agencies will tow your car in an emergency, and along the main highways you will find tow trucks and *auxilios viales,* roadside service phones, at regular intervals. Towing services can be found under *grúas* in the phone book.

GASOLINE

At 10¢ per liter of 95-octane gas (or about 45¢ a gallon), leaded-gas prices are among the cheapest in the world, and will remain so even with a planned, controversial increase; unleaded gas is not available in Venezuela. Corpoven, an affiliate of the national oil company, Petroleos de Venezuela (PDVSA), operates some 24-hour stations on main highways, some of which have credit-card pumps.

By Bus

Almost all of Venezuela can be traversed by bus, the least expensive and often most agreeable way of seeing the country. Some lines now offer *servicio especial* (special service) buses—equipped with air-conditioning and videotape players—from the border town of San Cristóbal to Caracas, and from the capital to Mérida, Valencia, Puerto La Cruz, Puerto Ordaz, and Maracaibo.

Making sense of Caracas's busy **Nuevo Circo** bus terminal is not easy; public buses crowd under signs marked with the city of destination, leaving the station in a plume of fumes as soon as they are filled. A better bet are the private carriers, usually referred to as *rápidos* (expresses), which in Caracas also depart from the Nuevo Circo terminal. Private companies typically accept advance reservations and offer creature comforts such as numbered seats, air-conditioning, toilets, and on-board attendants. Two dependable carriers are **Rodovías de Venezuela** (Nuevo Circo, ☎ 02/572–3746) and **Rápido Guyana** (Nuevo Circo, ☎ 02/541–4894).

Language

Spanish is the official language in Venezuela. The Guajiro Indians in the Amazonas speak a dialect of their own, but you are unlikely to meet a local who does not speak at least some Spanish. In hotels, restaurants, and resort areas you will find a considerable number of people who speak English, but not so in outlying areas, where very few Venezuelans are proficient in English. Some European immigrants still speak their native Italian and Portuguese.

Lodging

Luxury hotels, common in large cities and resort areas, are rated within Venezuela on a scale of one to five stars; a five-star rating, however, is not always indicative of superior quality. Still, most five-star hotels are reasonably modern and feature such facilities as car rental offices, swimming pools and tennis courts, souvenir shops, clothing and jewelry boutiques, restaurants, bars, and dance clubs. Three- and four-star hotels usually offer a smattering of these. Water shortages and cutoffs are common even in the big cities, though resort hotels often have their own auxiliary supplies and thus are immune to the problem.

Beach resorts commonly have apartments for rent on a short-term basis; check listings in the classified sections of the English-language *Daily Journal* or the Spanish-language *Universal* and *Nacional* newspapers. Most rents are listed in U.S. dollars but are not particularly cheap. In fact, budget accommodation is difficult to come by except in smaller towns and villages, where local inquiries must be made. When available, a private room in a house will cost upward of $10 per night.

Posadas, the local version of pensions, are found mostly in beach areas and the Andes and typically offer accommodation plus meals. Luxury hotels rarely include breakfast—or any meal for that matter—when quoting room rates. Also note: room prices jump 10%–20% during holiday periods, particularly during Christmas and Carnival.

For a $2 fee, prepaid reservations for more than 300 hotels in Venezuela can be booked through **Fairmont Reserv-Hotel** (☎ 02/782–8433, FAX 02/782–4407).

Ratings

Prices are for two people in a double room, based on high-season rates and excluding tax.

CATEGORY	CARACAS AND MARGARITA ISLAND	OTHER AREAS
$$$$	over $150	over $100
$$$	$75–$150	$50–$100
$$	$25–$75	$20–$50
$	under $25	under $20

Mail

The state-owned postal service, **Ipostel**, is slow and not very reliable. It costs Bs 30 to send a letter domestically and Bs 100 internationally. One of the main Ipostel offices in Caracas is in the Edificio Sur Centro Simón Bolívar, near the Capitolio metro stop; it's open weekdays 8–6, Saturday 8–2.

Money and Expenses

Blessed with vast reserves of oil, Venezuela rode a tidal wave of prosperity in the 1970s, but dramatic devaluations of the bolivar in 1983 and 1994 have led to massive inflation and unemployment. Still, Venezuela's standard of living is one of the highest in South America, and while the country's reputation continues to suffer from bad press—concerning everything from widespread corruption to a high crime rate to money laundering—Caracas maintains one of the busiest international airports on the continent. Two coup attempts in 1992 marred Venezuela's reputation as South America's most enduring democratic state, but the 1993 free elections restored political stability and the new government is dedicated to improving economic conditions for Venezuela's inhabitants.

Currency
The bolívar is the official unit of currency. Bolívars (Bs) come in bills of Bs 5, Bs 10, Bs 20, Bs 50, Bs 100, Bs 500, and Bs 1,000. Coins include the Bs 1, Bs 2, and Bs 5, as well as smaller denominations, which are about to vanish. At press time (winter 1995), the government was continuing to mandate a fixed exchange rate of Bs 170 to the U.S. dollar.

Changing Money
Dollars are easily exchanged everywhere but it is best to use exchange houses and banks, which offer better rates and also accept Canadian dollars, British pounds, and most European currencies. Repurchasing dollars and other currencies is a complicated process; visitors are advised to change into bolívars only what is strictly necessary and use a credit card for purchases, in restaurants, and to pay their hotel bills.

Forms of Payment
Credit cards, like traveler's checks, are generally accepted in hotels, restaurants, and some shops in major cities and resorts, though much less often in outlying areas.

What It Will Cost
Travelers holding U.S. and strong West European currencies should find hotels and transportation relatively inexpensive, although plane fares have risen dramatically in recent years. The best hotels cost up to $150 per double, the less accommodating and spartan as little as $15. Going to the theater can cost from $4 to $60 for special shows or featured artists. Movies are still a bargain at $2.50. Nightlife ranges greatly in price; some of the best clubs charge upward of $5 for a hard-liquor drink. You will find the best prices and bargains outside the major cities and resorts.

TAXES
At hotels, foreigners must pay a 10% "tourist tax" that is soon expected to be increased to 15%. Venezuela has a 10% sales tax, which is added to the price of all articles except basic foodstuffs and medicine. Restaurants inevitably add 10% to the bill for service; you are expected to tip another 10%.

SAMPLE PRICES
Cup of coffee, 25¢–$1.80; soft drink, 25¢–40¢; bottle of beer, 50¢–$2; bottle of wine, $4 at a liquor store; crosstown taxi ride, $4.

Opening and Closing Times

Banks
Banks are open weekdays 8:30–11:30 and 2–4:30. Watch for special bank holidays—which are numerous—when all branches are closed.

Museums
Most museums are open 9–noon and 2–5.

Shops
Stores are open weekdays 9–1 and 3–7:30; on Saturday, they tend to stay open all day, from 9 to 7. On Sunday, most shops are closed.

National Holidays
New Year's Day (Jan. 1); Carnival, the week before Ash Wednesday (week preceding Feb. 21, 1996 or Feb. 12, 1997); Easter Thursday and Good Friday (Apr. 4–5, 1996 or Mar. 27–28, 1997); Proclamation of Independence Day (Apr. 19); Labor Day (May 1); Battle of Carabobo (June 24); Independence Day (July 5); Simón Bolívar's birthday (July 24); death of Simón Bolívar (Dec. 17); Christmas Eve and Day (December 24–25).

Precautions

Health
Fresh fruit and salads do not pose health risks in Caracas, nor do other dishes at any respectable restaurant; it is not advisable, however, to buy food from street vendors. In the interior, avoid washed fruits and vegetables, raw fish, and tap water because of cholera epidemics in Brazil and traces of cholera in Venezuela. Throughout Venezuela, bottled water is cheap and readily available. Bottled beer and soft drinks are equally safe.

Safety
Unsavory shantytowns—which should always be avoided—encircle modern Caracas, and even downtown you should avoid wearing expensive jewelry and wandering aimlessly after 9 PM. If you're planning a late dinner or an evening at a dance club, take a taxi, preferably one from the hotel taxi line. Petty theft and pickpocketing are on the rise; you're most vulnerable in busy marketplaces and in crowded subway and bus stations.

Shopping

Caracas is known for its selection of inexpensive and well-made clothing, shoes, and other leather goods. Maracaibo is famous for hand-woven tapestries and rugs, mostly of local design, made by the Guajiro people and by the tapestry school of Luis Montiel. The Mérida region offers folkloric items, particularly pottery, heavy wool sweaters, and wood carvings. Margarita Island is a duty-free haven that offers inexpensive European clothing and leather goods, liquor, tobacco, and perfume. Other favorite Margarita purchases are hammocks, known for their immense size—often they're as big as a king-size bed—and for their fine handicraft work. Bargaining is not common in city stores or shops, although it is acceptable at outdoor markets and sometimes in smaller towns and villages.

Telephones

The national phone company, CANTV, was recently purchased by a U.S.-led consortium and improvements are under way; in the meantime, expect raspy connections, crossed lines, and excessive busy signals.

Local Calls

Local calls cost Bs 3.50 per minute. Public pay phones accept coins, but phone cards, available at kiosks marked TARJETA INTELLIGENTE (smart card) in denominations of Bs 250, Bs 500, Bs 1,000, and Bs 2,000, are more convenient. To speak with a directory operator, dial 103.

Long-Distance and International Calls

International calls are extremely expensive: The average international rate per minute is $2.50 to the United States and $10 to Europe. Hotels typically add 40% to the CANTV rate, so avoid calling from your room; call from a CANTV office, where you can pay with a credit card. You can reach an English-speaking operator by dialing 122.

You can also use your AT&T, MCI, or Sprint calling card to dial direct to a U.S. operator; if you speak for more than six minutes, you'll get cheaper rates than those available from CANTV. To reach **AT&T**, dial 800–11–120. To reach **MCI**, dial 800–11–140. To reach **Sprint**, dial 800–11–110.

Tipping

It is customary to tip hotel porters, hairdressers, and guides from Bs 200 up to 10%. Taxi drivers do not expect a tip unless they carry suitcases. At restaurants, a 10% gratuity (in addition to the 10% surcharge) is generally expected.

When to Go

The most popular time to visit is between December and April, during Venezuela's dry season. During peak holiday periods, such as Christmas, Carnival in February, and Easter, an influx of tourists pushes prices higher and makes it more difficult to find accommodations. During the rainy season that runs from May to October—when there is still plenty of good weather—crowds are rare and hotel prices drop significantly.

Climate

Venezuela's weather is prized for its year-round mildness; temperatures range between 65°F and 75°F during the day and rarely drop below 55°F at night except in the Andean regions. Some coastal areas are hotter and more humid, but you can usually depend on a cool breeze to be blowing off the ocean. This is a country where you can leave your sweaters behind.

The following are the daily maximum and minimum temperatures for Caracas.

Jan.	79F	26C	May	81F	27C	Sept.	82F	28C
	60	16		66	19		64	18
Feb.	80F	27C	June	80F	27C	Oct.	81F	27C
	62	17		65	18		64	18
Mar.	81F	27C	July	80F	27C	Nov.	82F	28C
	62	17		65	18		62	17
Apr.	80F	27C	Aug.	84F	29C	Dec.	80F	27C
	64	18		65	18		61	16

PORTUGUESE VOCABULARY

Words and Phrases

English	Portuguese	Pronunciation

Basics

English	Portuguese	Pronunciation
Yes/no	Sim/Não	**see**ing/nown
Please	Por favor	pohr fah-**vohr**
May I?	Posso?	**poh**-sso
Thank you (very much)	(Muito) obrigado	(**moo**yn-too) o-bree **gah**-doh
You're welcome	De nada	day **nah**-dah
Excuse me	Com licença	con lee-**ssehn**-ssah
Pardon me/what did you say?	Desculpe/O que disse?	des-**kool**-peh/o.k. **dih**-say?
Could you tell me?	Poderia me dizer?	po-day-**ree**-ah mee dee-**zehrr**?
I'm sorry	Sinto muito	**seen**-too **moo**yn-too
Good morning!	Bom dia!	bohn **dee**-ah
Good afternoon!	Boa tarde!	**boh**-ah **tahr**-dee
Good evening!	Boa noite!	**boh**-ah **noh**ee-tee
Goodbye!	Adeus!/Até logo!	ah-**deh**oos/ah-**teh loh**-go
Mr./Mrs.	Senhor/Senhora	sen-**yor**/sen-**yohr**-ah
Miss	Senhorita	sen-yo-**ri**-tah
Pleased to meet you	Muito prazer	**moo**yn-too prah-**zehr**
How are you?	Como vai?	**koh**-mo **vah**-ee
Very well, thank you	Muito bem, obrigado	**moo**yn-too **beh**-in o-bree-**gah**-doh
And you?	E o(a) Senhor(a)?	eh oh sen-**yor**(**yohr**-ah)
Hello (on the telephone)	Alô	ah-**low**

Numbers

1	um/uma	oom/**oom**-ah
2	dois	**doh**ees
3	três	**treh**ys
4	quatro	**kwa**-troh
5	cinco	**seen**-koh
6	seis	**seh**ys
7	sete	**seh**-tee
8	oito	**oh**ee-too
9	nove	**noh**-vee
10	dez	**deh**-ees
11	onze	**ohn**-zee
12	doze	**doh**-zee
13	treze	**treh**-zee

14	quatorze	kwa-**tohr**-zee
15	quinze	**keen**-zee
16	dezesseis	deh-zeh-**seh**ys
17	dezessete	deh-zeh-**seh**-tee
18	dezoito	deh-**zoh**ee-toh
19	dezenove	deh-zeh-**noh**-vee
20	vinte	**veen**-tee
21	vinte e um	**veen**-tee eh **oom**
30	trinta	**treen**-tah
32	trinta e dois	**treen**-ta eh **doh**ees
40	quarenta	kwa-**rehn**-ta
43	quarenta e três	kwa-**rehn**-ta e **treh**ys
50	cinquenta	seen-**kwehn**-tah
54	cinquenta e quatro	seen-**kwehn**-tah e **kwa**-troh
60	sessenta	seh-**sehn**-tah
65	sessenta e cinco	seh-**sehn**-tah e **seen**-ko
70	setenta	seh-**tehn**-tah
76	setenta e seis	seh-**tehn**-ta e **seh**ys
80	oitenta	ohee-**tehn**-ta
87	oitenta e sete	ohee-**tehn**-ta e **seh**-tee
90	noventa	noh-**vehn**-ta
98	noventa e oito	noh-**vehn**-ta e **oh**ee-too
100	cem	**seh**-ing
101	cento e um	**sehn**-too e **oom**
200	duzentos	doo-**zehn**-tohss
500	quinhentos	key-**nyehn**-tohss
700	setecentos	seh-teh-**sehn**-tohss
900	novecentos	noh-veh-**sehn**-tohss
1,000	mil	meel
2,000	dois mil	**doh**ees meel
1,000,000	um milhão	oom mee-lee-**ahon**

Colors

black	preto	**preh**-toh
blue	azul	a-**zool**
brown	marrom	mah-**hohm**
green	verde	**vehr**-deh
pink	rosa	**roh**-zah
purple	roxo	**roh**-choh
orange	laranja	lah-**rahn**-jah
red	vermelho	vehr-**meh**-lyoh
white	branco	**brahn**-coh
yellow	amarelo	ah-mah-**reh**-loh

Days of the Week

Sunday	Domingo	doh-**meehn**-goh
Monday	Segunda-feira	seh-**goon**-dah **fey**-rah
Tuesday	Terça-feira	**tehr**-sah **fey**-rah
Wednesday	Quarta-feira	**kwahr**-tah **fey**-rah

Thursday	Quinta-feira	**keen**-tah **fey**-rah
Friday	Sexta-feira	**sehss**-tah **fey**-rah
Saturday	Sábado	**sah**-bah-doh

Months

January	Janeiro	jah-**ney**-roh
February	Fevereiro	feh-veh-**rey**-roh
March	Março	**mahr**-soh
April	Abril	ah-**breel**
May	Maio	**my**-oh
June	Junho	gy**oo**-nyoh
July	Julho	gy**oo**-lyoh
August	Agosto	ah-**ghost**-toh
September	Setembro	seh-**tehm**-broh
October	Outubro	owe-**too**-broh
November	Novembro	noh-**vehm**-broh
December	Dezembro	deh-**zehm**-broh

Useful Phrases

Do you speak English?	O Senhor fala inglês?	oh sen-**yor fah**-lah een-**glehs**?
I don't speak Portuguese.	Não falo português.	nown **fah**-loh pohr-too-**ghehs**
I don't understand (you)	Não lhe entendo	nown ly**eh** ehn-**tehn**-doh
I understand (you)	Eu entendo	**eh**-oo ehn-**tehn**-doh
I don't know	Não sei	nown say
I am American/ British	Sou americano/ inglês	sow a-meh-ree-**cah**-noh/een-**glehs**
What's your name?	Como se chama?	**koh**-moh seh **shah**-mah
My name is . . .	Meu nome é . .	mehw **noh**-meh eh
What time is it?	Que horas são?	keh **oh**-rahss **sa**-ohn
It is one, two, three . . . o'clock	São uma, duas, tres . . . . horas	**sa**-ohn **oo**mah, **doo**-ahss, **treh**ys **oh**-rahss
Yes, please/No, thank you	Sim por favor/ Não obrigado	seing pohr fah-**vohr**/ nown o-bree-**gah**-doh
How?	Como?	**koh**-moh
When?	Quando?	**kwahn**-doh
This/Next week	Esta/Próxima semana	**ehss**-tah/**proh**-see-mah seh-**mah**-nah
This/Next month	Este/Próximo mes	**ehss**-teh/**proh**-see-moh mehz
This/Next year	Este/Próximo ano	**ehss**-teh/**proh**-see-moh **ah**-noh
Yesterday/today tomorrow	Ontem/hoje amanhã	**ohn**-tehn/**oh**-jeh/ ah-mah-**nyan**
This morning/ afternoon	Esta manhã/ tarde	**ehss**-tah mah-**nyan** / **tahr**-deh
Tonight	Hoje a noite	**oh**-jeh ah **noh**ee-tee

What?	O que?	oh **keh**
What is it?	O que é isso?	oh **keh** eh **ee**-soh
Why?	Por que?	pohr-**keh**
Who?	Quem?	**keh**-in
Where is . . . ?	Onde é . . .?	**ohn**-deh eh
the train station?	a estação de trem?	ah es-tah-**sah**-on deh train
the subway station?	a estação de metrô?	ah es-tah-**sah**-on deh meh-**tro**
the bus stop?	a parada do ônibus?	ah pah-**rah**-dah doh **oh**-nee-boos
the post office?	o correio?	oh coh-**hay**-yoh
the bank?	o banco?	oh **bahn**-koh
the . . . . hotel?	o hotel . . . . .?	oh oh-**tell**
the cashier?	o caixa?	oh **kahy**-shah
the . . . .museum?	o museo . . . .?	oh moo-**zeh**-oh
the hospital?	o hospital?	oh ohss-pee-**tal**
the elevator?	o elevador?	oh eh-leh-vah-**dohr**
the bathroom?	o banheiro?	oh bahn-**yey**-roh
. . beach?	a praia de . . . .?	ah **prah**y-yah deh
Here/there	Aqui/ali	ah-**kee**/ah-**lee**
Open/closed	Aberto/fechado	ah-**behr**-toh/feh-**shah**-doh
Left/right	Esquerda/direita	ehs-**kehr**-dah/dee-**ray**-tah
Straight ahead	Em frente	ehyn **frehn**-teh
Is it near/far?	É perto/longe?	eh **pehr**-toh/**lohn**-jeh
I'd like to buy. . .	Gostaria de comprar . . .	gohs-tah-**ree**-ah deh cohm-**prahr** . . . .
a bathing suit	um maiô	oom mahy-**owe**
a dictionary	um dicionário	oom dee-seeoh-**nah**-reeoh
a hat	um chapéu	oom shah-**peh**oo
a magazine	uma revista	**oo**mah heh-**vees**-tah
a map	um mapa	oom **mah**-pah
a postcard	cartão postal	kahr-**town** pohs-**tahl**
sunglasses	óculos escuros	**ah**-koo-loss ehs-**koo**-rohs
suntan lotion	um óleo de bronzear	oom **oh**-lyoh deh brohn-zeh-**ahr**
a ticket	um bilhete	oom bee-ly**eh**-teh
cigarettes	cigarros	see-**gah**-hose
envelopes	envelopes	eyn-veh-**loh**-pehs
matches	fósforos	**fohs**-foh-rohss
paper	papel	pah-**pehl**
sandals	sandália	sahn-**dah**-leeah
soap	sabonete	sah-bow-**neh**-teh
How much is it?	Quanto custa?	**kwahn**-too **koos**-tah
It's expensive/cheap	Está caro/barato	ehss-**tah kah**-roh / bah-**rah**-toh

A little/a lot	Um pouco/muito	oom **pohw**-koh/ **mooy**n-too
More/less	Mais/menos	**mah**-ees /**meh**-nohss
Enough/too much/too little	Suficiente/ demais/ muito pouco	soo-fee-see-**ehn**-teh/ deh-**mah**-ees/ **mooy**n-toh **pohw**-koh
Telephone	Telefone	teh-leh-**foh**-neh
Telegram	Telegrama	teh-leh-**grah**-mah
I am ill.	Estou doente.	ehss-**tow** doh-**ehn**-teh
Please call a doctor.	Por favor chame um médico.	pohr fah-**vohr shah**-meh oom **meh**-dee-koh
Help!	Socorro!	soh-**koh**-ho
Help me!	Me ajude!	mee ah-**jyew**-deh
Fire!	Incêndio!	een-**sehn**-deeoh
Caution!/Look out!/ Be careful!	Cuidado!	kooy-**dah**-doh

On the Road

Avenue	Avenida	ah-veh-**nee**-dah
Highway	Estrada	ehss-**trah**-dah
Port	Porto	**pohr**-toh
Service station	Posto de gasolina	**pohs**-toh deh gah-zoh-**lee**-nah
Street	Rua	**who**-ah
Toll	Pedagio	peh-**dah**-jyoh
Waterfront promenade	Beiramar/ orla	behy-rah-**mahrr**/ **ohr**-lah
Wharf	Cais	**kah**-ees

In Town

Block	Quarteirão	kwahr-tehy-**rah**-on
Cathedral	Catedral	kah-teh-**drahl**
Church/temple	Igreja	ee-**greh**-jyah
City hall	Prefeitura	preh-fehy-**too**-rah
Door/gate	Porta/portão	**pohr**-tah/porh-**tah**-on
Entrance/exit	Entrada/ saída	ehn-**trah**-dah/ sah-**ee**-dah
Market	Mercado/feira	mehr-**kah**-doh/ **fey**-rah
Neighborhood	Bairro	**buy**-ho
Rustic bar	Lanchonete	lahn-shoh-**neh**-teh
Shop	Loja	**loh**-jyah
Square	Praça	**prah**-ssah

Dining Out

A bottle of. . .	Uma garrafa de. . .	**oo**mah gah-**hah**-fah deh
A cup of. . .	Uma xícara de. . .	**oo**mah **shee**-kah-rah deh
A glass of. . .	Um copo de. . .	oom **koh**-poh deh
Ashtray	Um cinzeiro	oom seen-**zeh**y-roh
Bill/check	A conta	ah **kohn**-tah
Bread	Pão	**pah**-on
Breakfast	Café da manhã	**kah**-feh dah mah-**nyan**
Butter	A manteiga	ah mahn-**tehy**-gah
Cheers!	Saúde!	sah-**oo**-deh
Cocktail	Um aperitivo	oom ah-peh-ree-**tee**-voh
Dinner	O jantar	oh **jyahn**-tahr
Dish	Um prato	oom **prah**-toh
Enjoy!	Bom apetite!	bohm ah-peh-**tee**-teh
Fork	Garfo	**gahr**-foh
Fruit	Fruta	**froo**-tah
Is the tip included?	A gorjeta esta incluída?	ah gohr-**jyeh**-tah ehss-**tah** een-clue-**ee**-dah
Juice	Um suco	oom **soo**-koh
Knife	Uma faca	**oo**mah **fah**-kah
Lunch	O almoço	oh ahl-**moh**-ssoh
Menu	Menu/ cardápio	me-**noo** / kahr-**dah**-peeoh
Mineral water	Água mineral	**ah**-gooah mee-neh-**rahl**
Napkin	Guardanapo	gooahr-dah-**nah**-poh
No smoking	Não fumante	nown foo-**mahn**-teh
Pepper	Pimenta	pee-**mehn**-tah
Please give me	Por favor me dê	pohr fah-**vohr** mee **deh**
Salt	Sal	sahl
Smoking	Fumante	foo-**mahn**-teh
Spoon	Uma colher	**oo**mah koh-ly**ehr**
Sugar	Açúcar	ah-**soo**-kahr
Waiter!	Garçon!	gahr-**sohn**
Water	Água	**ah**-gooah
Wine	Vinho	**vee**-nyoh

SPANISH VOCABULARY

Words and Phrases

English	Spanish	Pronunciation
	English	*Spanish*	*Pronunciation*

Basics

English	Spanish	Pronunciation
Yes/no	Sí/no	see/no
Please	Por favor	pore fah-**vore**
May I?	¿Me permite?	may pair-**mee**-tay
Thank you (very much)	(Muchas) gracias	(**moo**-chas) **grah**-see-as
You're welcome	De nada	day **nah**-dah
Excuse me	Con permiso	con pair-**mee**-so
Pardon me	¿Perdón?	pair-**dohn**
Could you tell me?	¿Podría decirme?	po-dree-ah deh-**seer**-meh
I'm sorry	Lo siento	lo see-**en**-to
Good morning!	¡Buenos días!	**bway**-nohs **dee**-ahs
Good afternoon!	¡Buenas tardes!	**bway**-nahs **tar**-dess
Good evening!	¡Buenas noches!	**bway**-nahs **no**-chess
Goodbye!	¡Adiós!/¡Hasta luego!	ah-dee-**ohss/ah**-stah-**lwe**-go
Mr./Mrs.	Señor/Señora	sen-**yor**/sen-**yohr**-ah
Miss	Señorita	sen-yo-**ree**-tah
Pleased to meet you	Mucho gusto	**moo**-cho **goose**-to
How are you?	¿Cómo está usted?	**ko**-mo es-**tah** oo-**sted**
Very well, thank you.	Muy bien, gracias.	**moo**-ee bee-**en**, **grah**-see-as
And you?	¿Y usted?	ee oos-**ted**
Hello (on the telephone)	Diga	**dee**-gah

Numbers

1	un, uno	oon, **oo**-no
2	dos	dos
3	tres	tress
4	cuatro	**kwah**-tro
5	cinco	**sink**-oh
6	seis	saice
7	siete	see-**et**-eh
8	ocho	**o**-cho
9	nueve	new-**eh**-vey
10	diez	dee-**es**
11	once	**ohn**-seh
12	doce	**doh**-seh
13	trece	**treh**-seh
14	catorce	ka-**tohr**-seh

15	quince	**keen**-seh
16	dieciséis	dee-**es**-ee-**saice**
17	diecisiete	dee-**es**-ee-see-**et**-eh
18	dieciocho	dee-**es**-ee-**o**-cho
19	diecinueve	**dee-es**-ee-new-**ev**-ah
20	veinte	**vain**-teh
21	veinte y uno/veintiuno	**vain**-te-**oo**-noh
30	treinta	**train**-tah
32	treinta y dos	train-tay-**dohs**
40	cuarenta	kwah-**ren**-tah
43	cuarenta y tres	kwah-**ren**-tay-**tress**
50	cincuenta	seen-**kwen**-tah
54	cincuenta y cuatro	seen-**kwen**-tay **kwah**-tro
60	sesenta	sess-**en**-tah
65	sesenta y cinco	sess-**en**-tay **seen**-ko
70	setenta	set-**en**-tah
76	setenta y seis	set-**en**-tay **saice**
80	ochenta	oh-**chen**-tah
87	ochenta y siete	oh-**chen**-tay see-**yet**-eh
90	noventa	no-**ven**-tah
98	noventa y ocho	no-**ven**-tah-**o**-choh
100	cien	see-**en**
101	ciento uno	see-**en**-toh **oo**-noh
200	doscientos	doh-see-**en**-tohss
500	quinientos	keen-**yen**-tohss
700	setecientos	set-eh-see-**en**-tohss
900	novecientos	no-veh-see-**en**-tohss
1,000	mil	meel
2,000	dos mil	dohs meel
1,000,000	un millón	oon meel-**yohn**

Colors

black	negro	**neh**-groh
blue	azul	ah-**sool**
brown	café	kah-**feh**
green	verde	**ver**-deh
pink	rosa	**ro**-sah
purple	morado	mo-**rah**-doh
orange	naranja	na-**rahn**-hah
red	rojo	**roh**-hoh
white	blanco	**blahn**-koh
yellow	amarillo	ah-mah-**ree**-yoh

Days of the Week

Sunday	domingo	doe-**meen**-goh
Monday	lunes	**loo**-ness
Tuesday	martes	**mahr**-tess
Wednesday	miércoles	me-**air**-koh-less
Thursday	jueves	hoo-**ev**-ess

Friday	viernes	vee-**air**-ness
Saturday	sábado	**sah**-bah-doh

Months

January	enero	eh-**neh**-roh
February	febrero	feh-**breh**-roh
March	marzo	**mahr**-soh
April	abril	ah-**breel**
May	mayo	**my**-oh
June	junio	**hoo**-nee-oh
July	julio	**hoo**-lee-yoh
August	agosto	ah-**ghost**-toh
September	septiembre	sep-tee-**em**-breh
October	octubre	oak-**too**-breh
November	noviembre	no-vee-**em**-breh
December	diciembre	dee-see-**em**-breh

Useful phrases

Do you speak English?	¿Habla usted inglés?	**ah**-blah oos-**ted** in-**glehs**
I don't speak Spanish	No hablo español	no **ah**-bloh es-pahn-**yol**
I don't understand (you)	No entiendo	no en-tee-**en**-doh
I understand (you)	Entiendo	en-tee-**en**-doh
I don't know	No sé	no seh
I am American/British	Soy americano (americana)/ inglés(a)	soy ah-meh-ree-**kah**-no (ah-meh-ree-**kah**-nah)/ in-**glehs** (**ah**)
What's your name?	¿Cómo se llama usted?	koh-mo seh **yah**-mah oos-**ted**?
My name is . . .	Me llamo . . .	may **yah**-moh
What time is it?	¿Qué hora es?	keh **o**-rah es?
It is one, two, three . . . o'clock.	Es la una. . . . Son las dos, tres	es la **oo**-nah/sohn lahs dohs, tress
Yes, please/No, thank you	Sí, por favor/No, gracias	**see** pohr fah-**vor**/no **grah**-see-us
How?	¿Cómo?	**koh**-mo?
When?	¿Cuándo?	**kwahn**-doh?
This/Next week	Esta semana/ la semana que entra	**es**-teh seh-**mah**-nah/lah seh-**mah**-nah keh **en**-trah
This/Next month	Este mes/el próximo mes	**es**-teh mehs/el **proke**-see-mo mehs
This/Next year	Este año/el año que viene	**es**-teh **ahn**-yo/el **ahn**-yo keh vee-**yen**-ay
Yesterday/today/tomorrow	Ayer/hoy/mañana	ah-**yehr**/oy/mahn-**yah**-nah
This morning/afternoon	Esta mañana/ tarde	**es**-tah mahn-**yah**-nah/**tar**-deh

Tonight	Esta noche	es-tah no-cheh
What?	¿Qué?	keh?
What is it?	¿Qué es esto?	keh es es-toh
Why?	¿Por qué?	pore keh
Who?	¿Quién?	kee-yen
Where is . . . ?	¿Dónde está . . . ?	dohn-deh es-tah
the train station?	la estación del tren?	la es-tah-see-on del train
the subway station?	la estación del Tren subterráneo?	la es-ta-see-on del trehn soob-tair-ron-a-o
the bus stop?	la parada del autobus?	la pah-rah-dah del oh-toh-boos
the post office?	la oficina de correos?	la oh-fee-see-nah deh koh-reh-os
the bank?	el banco?	el bahn-koh
the . . . hotel?	el hotel . . . ?	el oh-tel
the store?	la tienda . . . ?	la tee-en-dah
the cashier?	la caja?	la kah-hah
the . . . museum?	el museo . . . ?	el moo-seh-oh
the hospital?	el hospital?	el ohss-pee-tal
the elevator?	el ascensor?	el ah-sen-sohr
the bathroom?	el baño?	el bahn-yoh
Here/there	Aquí/allá	ah-key/ah-yah
Open/closed	Abierto/cerrado	ah-bee-er-toh/ ser-ah-doh
Left/right	Izquierda/derecha	iss-key-er-dah/ dare-eh-chah
Straight ahead	Derecho	dare-eh-choh
Is it near/far?	¿Está cerca/lejos?	es-tah sehr-kah/ leh-hoss
I'd like . . . a room	Quisiera . . . un cuarto/una habitación	kee-see-ehr-ah oon kwahr-toh/ oo-nah ah-bee-tah-see-on
the key	la llave	lah yah-veh
a newspaper	un periódico	oon pehr-ee-oh-dee-koh
a stamp	un sello de correo	oon seh-yo deh koh-reh-oh
I'd like to buy . . .	Quisiera comprar . . .	kee-see-ehr-ah kohm-prahr
cigarette	cigarrillo	ce-ga-ree-yoh
matches	cerillos	ser-ee-ohs
a dictionary	un diccionario	oon deek-see-oh-nah-ree-oh
soap	jabón	hah-bohn
sunglasses	gafas de sol	ga-fahs deh sohl
suntan lotion	loción bronceadora	loh-see-ohn brohn-seh-ah-do-rah
a map	un mapa	oon mah-pah
a magazine	una revista	oon-ah reh-veess-tah

paper	papel	pah-**pel**
envelopes	sobres	**so**-brehs
a postcard	una tarjeta postal	**oon**-ah tar-**het**-ah post-**ahl**
How much is it?	¿Cuánto cuesta?	**kwahn**-toh **kwes**-tah
It's expensive/ cheap	Está caro/barato	es-**tah kah**-roh/ bah-**rah**-toh
A little/a lot	Un poquito/ mucho	oon poh-**kee**-toh/ **moo**-choh
More/less	Más/menos	mahss/**men**-ohss
Enough/too much/too little	Suficiente/ demasiado/ muy poco	soo-fee-see-**en**-teh/ deh-mah-see-**ah**-doh/**moo**-ee **poh**-koh
Telephone	Teléfono	tel-**ef**-oh-no
Telegram	Telegrama	teh-leh-**grah**-mah
I am ill	Estoy enfermo(a)	es-**toy** en-**fehr**-moh(mah)
Please call a doctor	Por favor llame a un medico	pohr fah-**vor ya**-meh ah oon **med**-ee-koh
Help!	¡Auxilio! ¡Ayuda! ¡Socorro!	owk-**see**-lee-oh/ ah-**yoo**-dah/ soh-**kohr**-roh
Fire!	¡Incendio!	en-**sen**-dee-oo
Caution!/Look out!	¡Cuidado!	kwee-**dah**-doh

On the Road

Avenue	Avenida	ah-ven-**ee**-dah
Broad, tree-lined boulevard	Bulevar	boo-leh-**var**
Fertile plain	Vega	**veh**-gah
Highway	Carretera	car-reh-**ter**-ah
Mountain pass, Street	Puerto Calle	poo-**ehr**-toh **cah**-yeh
Waterfront promenade	Rambla	**rahm**-blah
Wharf	Embarcadero	em-bar-cah-**deh**-ro

In Town

Cathedral	Catedral	cah-teh-**dral**
Church	Templo/Iglesia	**tem**-plo/ee-**glehs**-see-ah
City hall	Casa de gobierno	kah-sah deh go-bee-**ehr**-no
Door, gate	Puerta portón	poo-**ehr**-tah por-**ton**
Entrance/exit	Entrada/salida	en-**trah**-dah/sah-**lee**-dah
Inn, rustic bar, or restaurant	Taverna	tah-**vehr**-nah
Main square	Plaza principal	plah-thah prin-see-**pahl**

Market	Mercado	mer-**kah**-doh
Neighborhood	Barrio	**bahr**-ree-o
Traffic circle	Glorieta	glor-ee-**eh**-tah
Wine cellar, wine bar, or wine shop	Bodega	boh-**deh**-gah

Dining Out

A bottle of . . .	Una botella de . . .	**oo**-nah bo-**teh**-yah deh
A cup of . . .	Una taza de . . .	**oo**-nah **tah**-thah deh
A glass of . . .	Un vaso de . . .	oon **vah**-so deh
Ashtray	Un cenicero	oon sen-ee-**seh**-roh
Bill/check	La cuenta	lah **kwen**-tah
Bread	El pan	el pahn
Breakfast	El desayuno	el deh-sah-**yoon**-oh
Butter	La mantequilla	lah man-teh-**key**-yah
Cheers!	¡Salud!	sah-**lood**
Cocktail	Un aperitivo	oon ah-pehr-ee-**tee**-voh
Dinner	La cena	lah **seh**-nah
Dish	Un plato	oon **plah**-toh
Menu of the day	Menú del día	meh-**noo** del **dee**-ah
Enjoy!	¡Buen provecho!	bwehn pro-**veh**-cho
Fixed-price menu	Menú fijo o turistico	meh-**noo** **fee**-hoh oh too-**ree**-stee-coh
Fork	El tenedor	el ten-eh-**dor**
Is the tip included?	¿Está incluida la propina?	es-**tah** in-cloo-**ee**-dah lah pro-**pee**-nah
Knife	El cuchillo	el koo-**chee**-yo
Large portion of savory snacks	Raciónes	rah-see-**oh**-nehs
Lunch	La comida	lah koh-**mee**-dah
Menu	La carta, el menú	lah **cart**-ah, el meh-**noo**
Napkin	La servilleta	lah sehr-vee-**yet**-ah
Pepper	La pimienta	lah pee-me-**en**-tah
Please give me	Por favor déme	pore fah-**vor** **deh**-meh
Salt	La sal	lah sahl
Savory snacks	Tapas	**tah**-pahs
Spoon	Una cuchara	**oo**-nah koo-**chah**-rah
Sugar	El azúcar	el ah-**thu**-kar
Waiter!/Waitress!	¡Por favor Señor/Señorita!	pohr fah-**vor** sen-**yor**/sen-yor-ee-tah

INDEX

NOTES

NOTES